Twentieth-Century Literary Criticism

Guide to Gale Literary Criticism Series

When you need to review criticism of literary works, these are the Gale series to use:

If the author's death date is:

You should turn to:

After Dec. 31, 1959
(or author is still living)

CONTEMPORARY LITERARY CRITICISM

for example: Jorge Luis Borges, Anthony Burgess,
William Faulkner, Mary Gordon,
Ernest Hemingway, Iris Murdoch

1900 through 1959

TWENTIETH-CENTURY LITERARY CRITICISM

for example: Willa Cather, F. Scott Fitzgerald,
Henry James, Mark Twain, Virginia Woolf

1800 through 1899

NINETEENTH-CENTURY LITERATURE CRITICISM

for example: Fedor Dostoevski, Nathaniel Hawthorne,
George Sand, William Wordsworth

1400 through 1799

LITERATURE CRITICISM FROM 1400 TO 1800
(excluding Shakespeare)

for example: Anne Bradstreet, Daniel Defoe,
Alexander Pope, François Rabelais,
Jonathan Swift, Phillis Wheatley

SHAKESPEAREAN CRITICISM

Shakespeare's plays and poetry

Antiquity through 1399

CLASSICAL AND MEDIEVAL LITERATURE CRITICISM

for example: Dante, Homer, Plato, Sophocles, Vergil,
the Beowulf poet

(Volume 1 forthcoming)

Gale also publishes related criticism series:

CHILDREN'S LITERATURE REVIEW

This ongoing series covers authors of all eras.
Presents criticism on authors and author/illustrators
who write for the preschool to junior-high audience.

CONTEMPORARY ISSUES CRITICISM

This two volume set presents criticism on
contemporary authors writing on current issues.
Topics covered include the social sciences,
philosophy, economics, natural science, law, and
related areas.

ISSN 0276-8178

Volume 23

Twentieth-Century Literary Criticism

**Excerpts from Criticism of the
Works of Novelists, Poets, Playwrights,
Short Story Writers, and Other Creative Writers
Who Died between 1900 and 1960,
from the First Published Critical Appraisals
to Current Evaluations**

Dennis Poupard
Editor

Marie Lazzari
Thomas Ligotti
Associate Editors

Gale Research Company
Book Tower
Detroit, Michigan 48226

STAFF

Dennis Poupard, *Editor*

Marie Lazzari, Thomas Ligotti, *Associate Editors*

Paula Kepos, Serita Lanette Lockard, *Senior Assistant Editors*

Sandra Liddell, Joann Prosyniuk, Keith E. Schooley,
Laurie A. Sherman, *Assistant Editors*

Sharon R. Gunton, *Contributing Editor*
Robin DuBlanc, Melissa Reiff Hug, *Contributing Assistant Editors*

Jeanne A. Gough, *Permissions & Production Manager*
Lizbeth A. Purdy, *Production Supervisor*
Denise Michlewicz Broderick, *Production Coordinator*
Kathleen M. Cook, Maureen Duffy, Suzanne Powers, Jani Prescott, *Editorial Assistants*

Victoria B. Cariappa, *Research Coordinator*
Maureen R. Richards, *Assistant Research Coordinator*
Daniel Kurt Gilbert, Kent Graham, Michele R. O'Connell, Filomena Sgambati,
Vincenza G. Tranchida, Mary D. Wise, *Research Assistants*

Linda M. Pugliese, *Manuscript Coordinator*
Donna Craft, *Assistant Manuscript Coordinator*
Jennifer E. Gale, Maureen A. Puhl, Rosetta Irene Simms, *Manuscript Assistants*

Janice M. Mach, *Permissions Coordinator, Text*
Patricia A. Seefelt, *Permissions Coordinator, Illustrations*
Susan D. Battista, Margaret A. Chamberlain, Sandra C. Davis,
Kathy Grell, *Assistant Permissions Coordinators*
Mabel E. Gurney, Josephine M. Keene, Mary M. Matuz, *Senior Permissions Assistants*
Margaret Carson, H. Diane Cooper, Colleen M. Crane, *Permissions Assistants*
Eileen Baehr, Kimberly Smilay, Anita Williams, *Permissions Clerks*

Frederick G. Ruffner, *Publisher*
Dedria Bryfonski, *Editorial Director*
Ellen T. Crowley, *Associate Editorial Director*
Laurie Lanzen Harris, *Director, Literary Criticism Division*
Dennis Poupard, *Senior Editor, Literary Criticism Series*

Library of Congress Catalog Card Number 76-46132
ISBN 0-8103-2405-9
ISSN 0276-8178

Computerized photocomposition by
Typographics, Incorporated
Kansas City, Missouri

Printed in the United States

Contents

Preface

It is impossible to overvalue the importance of literature in the intellectual, emotional, and spiritual evolution of humanity. Literature is that which both lifts us out of everyday life and helps us to better understand it. Through the fictive lives of such characters as Anna Karenina, Jay Gatsby, or Leopold Bloom, our perceptions of the human condition are enlarged, and we are enriched.

Literary criticism can also give us insight into the human condition, as well as into the specific moral and intellectual atmosphere of an era, for the criteria by which a work of art is judged reflects contemporary philosophical and social attitudes. Literary criticism takes many forms: the traditional essay, the book or play review, even the parodic poem. Criticism can also be of several types: normative, descriptive, interpretive, textual, appreciative, generic. Collectively, the range of critical response helps us to understand a work of art, an author, an era.

Scope of the Series

Twentieth-Century Literary Criticism (TCLC) is designed to serve as an introduction for the student of twentieth-century literature to the authors of the period 1900 to 1960 and to the most significant commentators on these authors. The great poets, novelists, short story writers, playwrights, and philosophers of this period are by far the most popular writers for study in high school and college literature courses. Since a vast amount of relevant critical material confronts the student, *TCLC* presents significant passages from the most important published criticism to aid students in the location and selection of commentaries on authors who died between 1900 and 1960.

The need for *TCLC* was suggested by the usefulness of the Gale series *Contemporary Literary Criticism (CLC),* which excerpts criticism on current writing. Because of the difference in time span under consideration *(CLC* considers authors who were still living after 1959), there is no duplication of material between *CLC* and *TCLC.* For further information about *CLC* and Gale's other criticism series, users should consult the Guide to Gale Literary Criticism Series preceding the title page in this volume.

Each volume of *TCLC* is carefully compiled to include authors who represent a variety of genres and nationalities and who are currently regarded as the most important writers of this era. In addition to major authors, *TCLC* also presents criticism on lesser-known writers whose significant contributions to literary history are important to the study of twentieth-century literature.

Each author entry in *TCLC* is intended to provide an overview of major criticism on an author. Therefore, the editors include fifteen to twenty authors in each 600-page volume (compared with approximately fifty authors in a *CLC* volume of similar size) so that more attention may be given to an author. Each author entry represents a historical survey of the critical response to that author's work: some early criticism is presented to indicate initial reactions, later criticism is selected to represent any rise or decline in the author's reputation, and current retrospective analyses provide students with a modern view. The length of an author entry is intended to reflect the amount of critical attention the author has received from critics writing in English, and from foreign criticism in translation. Critical articles and books that have not been translated into English are excluded. Every attempt has been made to identify and include excerpts from the seminal essays on each author's work.

An author may appear more than once in the series because of the great quantity of critical material available, or because of a resurgence of criticism generated by events such as an author's centennial or anniversary celebration, the republication or posthumous publication of an author's works, or the publication of a newly translated work. Generally, a few author entries in each volume of *TCLC* feature criticism on single works by major authors who have appeared previously in the series. Only those individual works that have been the subjects of vast amounts of criticism and are widely studied in literature classes are selected for this in-depth treatment. Sinclair Lewis's *Main Street* and Oscar Wilde's *The Importance of Being Earnest* are examples of such entries in *TCLC,* Volume 23.

Organization of the Book

An author entry consists of the following elements: author heading, biographical and critical introduction, principal works, excerpts of criticism (each followed by a bibliographical citation), and an additional bibliography for further reading.

- The *author heading* consists of the author's full name, followed by birth and death dates. The unbracketed portion of the name denotes the form under which the author most commonly wrote. If an author wrote consistently under a pseudonym, the pseudonym will be listed in the author heading and the real name given in parentheses on the first line of the biographical and critical introduction. Also located at the beginning of the introduction to the author entry are any name variations under which an author wrote, including transliterated forms for authors whose languages use nonroman alphabets. Uncertainty as to a birth or death date is indicated by a question mark.

- The *biographical and critical introduction* contains background information designed to introduce the reader to an author and to the critical debate surrounding his or her work. Parenthetical material following many of the introductions provides references to biographical and critical reference series published by Gale, including *Children's Literature Review, Contemporary Authors, Dictionary of Literary Biography, Something about the Author,* and past volumes of *TCLC.*

- Most *TCLC* entries include *portraits* of the author. Many entries also contain illustrations of materials pertinent to an author's career, including holographs of manuscript pages, title pages, dust jackets, letters, or representations of important people, places, and events in an author's life.

- The *list of principal works* is chronological by date of first book publication and identifies the genre of each work. In the case of foreign authors where there are both foreign language publications and English translations, the title and date of the first English-language edition are given in brackets. Unless otherwise indicated, dramas are dated by first performance, not first publication.

- *Criticism* is arranged chronologically in each author entry to provide a useful perspective on changes in critical evaluation over the years. All titles by the author featured in the critical entry are printed in boldface type to enable the user to ascertain without difficulty the works being discussed. Also for purposes of easier identification, the critic's name and the publication date of the essay are given at the beginning of each piece of criticism. Unsigned criticism is preceded by the title of the journal in which it appeared. When an anonymous essay is later attributed to a critic, the critic's name appears in brackets at the beginning of the excerpt and in the bibliographical citation. Many critical entries in *TCLC* also contain translated material to aid users. Unless otherwise noted, translations within brackets are by the editors; translations within parentheses are by the author of the excerpt.

- Critical essays are prefaced by *explanatory notes* as an additional aid to students using *TCLC.* The explanatory notes provide several types of useful information, including: the reputation of a critic; the importance of a work of criticism; the specific type of criticism (biographical, psychoanalytic, structuralist, etc.); a synopsis of the criticism; and the growth of critical controversy or changes in critical trends regarding an author's work. In many cases, these notes cross-reference the work of critics who agree or disagree with each other. Dates in parentheses within the explanatory notes refer to a book publication date when they follow a book title and to an essay date when they follow a critic's name.

- A complete *bibliographical citation* designed to facilitate location of the original essay or book by the interested reader follows each piece of criticism.

- The *additional bibliography* appearing at the end of each author entry suggests further reading on the author. In some cases it includes essays for which the editors could not obtain reprint rights.

An appendix lists the sources from which material in each volume has been reprinted. It does not, however, list every book or periodical consulted in the preparation of the volume.

Cumulative Indexes

Each volume of *TCLC* includes a cumulative index to authors listing all the authors who have appeared in *Contemporary Literary Criticism, Twentieth-Century Literary Criticism, Nineteenth-Century Literature Criticism,* and *Literature Criticism from 1400 to 1800,* along with cross-references to the Gale series *Children's Literature Review, Authors in the News, Contemporary Authors, Contemporary Authors Autobiography Series, Dictionary of Literary Biography, Something about the Author, Something about the Author Autobiography Series,* and *Yesterday's Authors of Books for Children.* Users will welcome this cumulated author index as a useful tool for locating an author within the various series. The index, which lists birth and death dates when available, will be particularly valuable for those authors who are identified with a certain period but whose death date causes them to be placed in another, or for those authors whose careers span two periods. For example, F. Scott Fitzgerald is found in *TCLC,* yet a writer often associated with him, Ernest Hemingway, is found in *CLC.*

Each volume of *TCLC* also includes a cumulative nationality index. Author names are arranged alphabetically under their respective nationalities and followed by the volume numbers in which they appear.

A cumulative index to critics is another useful feature in *TCLC.* Under each critic's name are listed the authors on whom the critic has written and the volume and page where the criticism may be found.

Acknowledgments

No work of this scope can be accomplished without the cooperation of many people. The editors especially wish to thank the copyright holders of the excerpted criticism included in this volume, the permissions managers of many book and magazine publishing companies for assisting us in securing reprint rights, and Anthony Bogucki for assistance with copyright research. We are also grateful to the staffs of the Detroit Public Library, the Library of Congress, University of Detroit Library, University of Michigan Library, and Wayne State University Library for making their resources available to us.

Suggestions Are Welcome

In response to various suggestions, several features have been added to *TCLC* since the series began, including: explanatory notes to excerpted criticism that provide important information regarding critics and their work; a cumulative author index listing authors in all Gale literary criticism series; entries devoted to criticism on a single work by a major author; and more extensive illustrations.

Readers who wish to suggest authors to appear in future volumes, or who have other suggestions, are cordially invited to write the editors.

Authors to Be Featured in *TCLC*, Volumes 24 and 25

Sherwood Anderson (American short story writer and novelist)—Among the most original and influential writers in early twentieth-century American literature, Anderson is the author of brooding, introspective works that explore the effects of the unconscious upon human life. Anderson's "hunger to see beneath the surface of lives" was best expressed in the short stories comprising *Winesburg, Ohio: A Group of Tales of Ohio Small Town Life*. *TCLC* will devote an entire entry to critical discussion of this work.

Max Beerbohm (English essayist and caricaturist)—Among the most prominent figures of the fin de siècle period in English literature, Beerbohm was the author of fiction, dramas, and criticism characterized by witty sophistication and mannered elegance. "Entertaining" in the most complimentary sense of the word, Beerbohm's criticism for the *Saturday Review*—where he was a longtime drama critic—exhibits his scrupulously developed taste and unpretentious, fair-minded responses to literature.

Henri Bergson (French philosopher)—One of the most influential philosophers of the twentieth century, Bergson is renowned for his opposition to the dominant materialist thought of his time and for his creation of theories that emphasize the supremacy and independence of suprarational consciousness.

Chaim Bialik (Hebrew poet)—The most important Hebrew poet of the twentieth century, Bialik is often called "the national poet of Israel." His works—which reflect the personal sufferings of his childhood as well as the sufferings of the Diaspora—are considered instrumental in the twentieth-century renaissance of Hebrew literature and the modernization of the Hebrew language.

R. D. Blackmore (English novelist)—A minor historical novelist of the Victorian era, Blackmore is remembered as the author of *Lorna Doone*. This classic of historical fiction is often praised for its vivid evocation of the past and its entertaining melodrama.

Edgar Rice Burroughs (American novelist)—Burroughs was a science fiction writer who is best known as the creator of Tarzan. His *Tarzan of the Apes* and its numerous sequels have sold over thirty-five million copies in fifty-six languages, making Burroughs one of the most popular authors in the world.

Joseph Conrad (Polish-born English novelist)—Considered an innovator of novel structure as well as one of the finest stylists of modern English literature, Conrad is the author of complex novels that examine the ambiguity of good and evil. *TCLC* will devote an entry to critical discussion of his *Nostromo*, a novel exploring Conrad's conviction that failure is a fact of human existence and that every ideal contains the possibilities for its own corruption.

Francois Coppée (French poet and dramatist)—A popular French poet during the latter part of the nineteenth century, Coppée earned a reputation as the "poete des humbles" for his verses devoted to the lives of humble people whose colorless exteriors often concealed great happiness or misery.

Euclides da Cunha (Brazilian historian)—Cunha is the author of *Os sertoes (Rebellion in the Backlands)*, considered by many critics to be one of the greatest works in Brazilian literature. A factual account of the Canudos rebellion in Brazil in 1896 and 1897, the work exhibits a deep concern with Brazilian national identity and has exerted a strong influence on twentieth-century Brazilian fiction.

John Davidson (Scottish poet)—Davidson is remembered primarily as the author of poems that reflect the changing social and philosophical attitudes of the late Victorian era, and his works have been recognized as instrumental in effecting the transition from nineteenth- to twentieth-century themes in English poetry.

Charles Doughty (English travel writer and poet)—Doughty is best remembered as the author of *Travels in Arabia Deserta*, one of the classics in the literature of travel and a celebrated model of epic prose.

Joseph Furphy (Australian novelist)—Furphy's most famous work, *Such Is Life*, is a complex comic novel combining sketches, tales, literary parody, and philosophical speculation in the guise of a realistic chronicle by its fictional narrator, Tom Collins.

George Gissing (English novelist)—Gissing was the author of novels portraying in meticulous detail the lives of the English lower classes. His works combine Victorian melodrama with concern for the individual's alienation from society and are considered notable examples of the literature of transition between the Victorian and modern novel.

Edmund Gosse (English novelist and critic)—A prolific man of letters in late nineteenth-century England, Gosse is of primary importance for his autobiographical novel *Father and Son*, which is considered a seminal work for gaining insight into the major issues of the Victorian age, especially the conflict between science and religion inspired by Darwin's *Origin of the Species*. Gosse is also important for his introduction of Henrik Ibsen's "new drama" to English audiences and for his numerous critical studies of English and foreign authors.

Frank Harris (Welsh editor, critic, and biographer)—Prominent in English literary circles at the turn of the century, Harris was a flamboyant man of letters described by one critic as "seemingly offensive on principle." His greatest accomplishments—which were achieved as editor of the

Fortnightly Review, the *Evening News,* and the *Saturday Review*—have been overshadowed by his scandalous life, his sensational biographical portraits of such contemporaries as Oscar Wilde and Bernard Shaw, and his massive autobiography, which portrays Edwardian life primarily as a background for Harris's near-Olympian sexual adventures.

Bret Harte (American short story writer and journalist)—Harte rose to fame in the latter half of the nineteenth century as the first local colorist of the American West. His most successful stories, including "The Luck of Roaring Camp" and "The Outcasts of Poker Flat," constitute a blend of humor and sentiment, and are often praised for their uncluttered style and fidelity to realistic detail.

Muhammad Iqbal (Indian poet and philosopher)—Considered one of the leading Muslim intellectual figures of the twentieth century, Iqbal was a political activist and the author of poetry calling for social and religious reform.

Henry James (American novelist)—James is considered one of the most important novelists of the English language and his work is universally acclaimed for its stylistic distinction, complex psychological portraits, and originality of theme and technique. *TCLC* will devote an entire entry to critical discussion of his novella *The Turn of the Screw,* which is considered one of the most interesting and complex short novels in world literature.

Henry Lawson (Australian short story writer and poet)—Lawson's stories in such collections as *While the Billy Boils* and *Joe Wilson and His Mates* chronicle the hard lives of working people in the backcountry of Australia and are considered characteristic of Australian writing of the late nineteenth and early twentieth centuries.

Edgar Lee Masters (American poet, novelist, and biographer)—Masters was a prolific writer who is remembered primarily for his *Spoon River Anthology,* a collection of epitaphs spoken by the dead in the Spoon River Cemetery. Controversial upon its publication for its free verse form, jaundiced view of small town life, and explicitly sexual considerations, the *Anthology* is considered important as one of the first works to view traditional small town America from an unsentimental perspective.

Dmitri Merezhkovsky (Russian novelist, philosopher, poet, and critic)—Although his poetry and criticism are credited with initiating the Symbolist movement in Russian literature, Merezhkovsky is best known as a religious philosopher who sought in numerous essays and historical novels to reconcile the values of pagan religions with the teachings of Christ.

John Muir (American naturalist, essayist, and autobiographer)—In such works as *A Thousand Mile Walk to the Gulf* and

The Mountains of California, Muir celebrated the North American wilderness. He was also a prominent conservationist who was instrumental in establishing the system of national parks in the United States.

Frank Norris (American novelist)—Norris is recognized as one of the first Naturalist writers in American literature. His most important novel, *The Octopus,* was the first volume in an unfinished trilogy concerning the production and distribution of wheat that Norris envisioned as an American counterpart to Emile Zola's *Germinal,* an epic portrayal of the effects of deterministic forces on laborers.

Eugene O'Neill (American dramatist)—Generally considered America's foremost dramatist, O'Neill is the author of works examining the implacability of an indifferent universe, the materialistic greed of humanity, and the problems of individual identity. *TCLC* will devote an entry to O'Neill's *Long Day's Journey into Night,* a portrait of a tormented, self-destructive family that has been called one of the most powerful dramas in American theater.

Wilfred Owen (English poet)—Inspired by his experiences in World War I, Owne's poetry exposed the grim realities of war and its effect on the human spirit.

Benito Peréz Galdós (Spanish novelist and dramatist)—Considered the greatest Spanish novelist since Cervantes, Peréz Galdós is known for two vast cycles of novels: the *Episodios nacionales,* a forty-six volume portrayal of nineteenth-century Spanish history; and the *Novelas españolas contemporáneas,* explorations of social and ethical problems in contemporary Spain which have been favorably compared to the works of Charles Dickens and Honoré de Balzac.

Oswald Spengler (German philosopher)—Spengler rose to international celebrity in the 1920s on the basis of *The Decline of the West,* a controversial examination of the cyclical nature of history. Although frequently deprecated by professional historians, *The Decline of the West* became one of the most influential philosophical works of the twentieth century.

Edith Wharton (American novelist and short story writer)—Wharton is best known as a novelist of manners whose fiction exposed the cruel excesses of aristocratic society at the turn of the century. Her subject matter, tone, and style have often been compared with those of her friend and mentor Henry James.

Thomas Wolfe (American novelist)—Wolfe is considered one of the foremost American novelists of the twentieth century. His most important works present intense and lyrical portraits of life in both rural and urban America while portraying the struggle of the lonely, sensitive, and artistic individual to find spiritual fulfillment.

Additional Authors to Appear in Future Volumes

Abbey, Henry 1842-1911
Abercrombie, Lascelles 1881-1938
Adamic, Louis 1898-1951
Ade, George 1866-1944
Agustini, Delmira 1886-1914
Akers, Elizabeth Chase 1832-1911
Akiko, Yosano 1878-1942
Aldrich, Thomas Bailey 1836-1907
Aliyu, Dan Sidi 1902-1920
Allen, Hervey 1889-1949
Archer, William 1856-1924
Arlen, Michael 1895-1956
Arlt, Roberto 1900-1942
Austin, Alfred 1835-1913
Austin, Mary Hunter 1868-1934
Bacovia, George 1881-1957
Bahr, Hermann 1863-1934
Bailey, Philip James 1816-1902
Barbour, Ralph Henry 1870-1944
Benét, William Rose 1886-1950
Benjamin, Walter 1892-1940
Bennett, James Gordon, Jr. 1841-1918
Benson, E(dward) F(rederic) 1867-1940
Berdyaev, Nikolai Aleksandrovich 1874-1948
Beresford, J(ohn) D(avys) 1873-1947
Bialik, Chaim 1873-1934
Binyon, Laurence 1869-1943
Bishop, John Peale 1892-1944
Blackmore, R(ichard) D(oddridge) 1825-1900
Blake, Lillie Devereux 1835-1913
Blest Gana, Alberto 1830-1920
Blum, Leon 1872-1950
Bodenheim, Maxwell 1892-1954
Bowen, Marjorie 1886-1952
Byrne, Donn 1889-1928
Caine, Hall 1853-1931
Cannan, Gilbert 1884-1955
Carducci, Glosue 1835-1907
Carswell, Catherine 1879-1946
Casely-Hayford, E. 1866-1930
Churchill, Winston 1871-1947
Coppée, Francois 1842-1908
Corelli, Marie 1855-1924
Cotter, Joseph Seamon 1861-1949
Croce, Benedetto 1866-1952
Crofts, Freeman Wills 1879-1957
Cruze, James (Jens Cruz Bosen) 1884-1942
Cummings, Bruce 1889-1919
Curros, Enriquez Manuel 1851-1908
Dall, Caroline Wells (Healy) 1822-1912
Daudet, Leon 1867-1942
Davis, Richard Harding 1864-1916

Day, Clarence 1874-1935
Delafield, E.M. (Edme Elizabeth Monica de la Pasture) 1890-1943
Deneson, Jacob 1836-1919
DeVoto, Bernard 1897-1955
Doughty, C(harles) M(ontague) 1843-1926
Douglas, (George) Norman 1868-1952
Douglas, Lloyd C(assel) 1877-1951
Dovzhenko, Alexander 1894-1956
Drinkwater, John 1882-1937
Drummond, W.H. 1854-1907
Durkheim, Emile 1858-1917
Duun, Olav 1876-1939
Eaton, Walter Prichard 1878-1957
Eggleston, Edward 1837-1902
Erskine, John 1879-1951
Fadeyev, Alexander 1901-1956
Ferland, Albert 1872-1943
Field, Rachel 1894-1924
Flecker, James Elroy 1884-1915
Fletcher, John Gould 1886-1950
Fogazzaro, Antonio 1842-1911
Francos, Karl Emil 1848-1904
Frank, Bruno 1886-1945
Frazer, (Sir) George 1854-1941
Freud, Sigmund 1853-1939
Froding, Gustaf 1860-1911
Fuller, Henry Blake 1857-1929
Futabatei, Shimei 1864-1909
Gladkov, Fyodor Vasilyevich 1883-1958
Glaspell, Susan 1876-1948
Glyn, Elinor 1864-1943
Golding, Louis 1895-1958
Gould, Gerald 1885-1936
Guest, Edgar 1881-1959
Gumilyov, Nikolay 1886-1921
Gyulai, Pal 1826-1909
Hale, Edward Everett 1822-1909
Hawthorne, Julian 1846-1934
Heijermans, Herman 1864-1924
Hernandez, Miguel 1910-1942
Hewlett, Maurice 1861-1923
Heyward, DuBose 1885-1940
Hope, Anthony 1863-1933
Hostos, Eugenio Maria de 1839-1903
Hudson, W(illiam) H(enry) 1841-1922
Huidobro, Vincente 1893-1948
Ilyas, Abu Shabaka 1903-1947
Imbs, Bravig 1904-1946
Ivanov, Vyacheslav Ivanovich 1866-1949
James, Will 1892-1942
Jammes, Francis 1868-1938
Johnson, Fenton 1888-1958

Johnston, Mary 1870-1936
Jorgensen, Johannes 1866-1956
King, Grace 1851-1932
Kirby, William 1817-1906
Kline, Otis Albert 1891-1946
Kohut, Adolph 1848-1916
Kreve, Bincas 1882-1954
Kuzmin, Mikhail Alexseyevich 1875-1936
Lamm, Martin 1880-1950
Lawson, Henry 1867-1922
Leino, Eino 1878-1926
Leipoldt, C. Louis 1880-1947
Leroux, Gaston 1868-1927
Lima, Jorge De 1895-1953
Locke, Alain 1886-1954
Long, Frank Belknap 1903-1959
Lopez Portillo y Rojas, Jose 1850-1903
Louys, Pierre 1870-1925
Lucas, E(dward) V(errall) 1868-1938
Lyall, Edna 1857-1903
Maghar, Josef Suatopluk 1864-1945
Manning, Frederic 1887-1935
Maragall, Joan 1860-1911
Marais, Eugene 1871-1936
Martin du Gard, Roger 1881-1958
Masaryk, Tomas 1850-1939
Mayor, Flora Macdonald 1872-1932
McClellan, George Marion 1860-1934
McCoy, Horace 1897-1955
Mirbeau, Octave 1850-1917
Mistral, Frederic 1830-1914
Monro, Harold 1879-1932
Moore, Thomas Sturge 1870-1944
Morley, Christopher 1890-1957
Morley, S. Griswold 1883-1948
Mqhayi, S.E.K. 1875-1945
Murray, (George) Gilbert 1866-1957
Nansen, Peter 1861-1918
Nobre, Antonio 1867-1900
O'Dowd, Bernard 1866-1959
Ophuls, Max 1902-1957
Orczy, Baroness 1865-1947
Owen, Seaman 1861-1936
Page, Thomas Nelson 1853-1922
Parrington, Vernon L. 1871-1929
Peck, George W. 1840-1916
Pessao, Fernando 1887-1930
Phillips, Ulrich B. 1877-1934
Pinero, Arthur Wing 1855-1934
Pontoppidan, Henrik 1857-1943
Powys, T. F. 1875-1953
Prevost, Marcel 1862-1941
Quiller-Couch, Arthur 1863-1944
Randall, James G. 1881-1953

Rappoport, Solomon 1863-1944
Read, Opie 1852-1939
Redcam, Tom 1870-1933
Reisen (Reizen), Abraham 1875-1953
Remington, Frederic 1861-1909
Riley, James Whitcomb 1849-1916
Rinehart, Mary Roberts 1876-1958
Ring, Max 1817-1901
Rohmer, Sax 1883-1959
Rozanov, Vasily Vasilyevich 1856-1919
Rutherford, Mark 1851-1913
Saar, Ferdinand von 1833-1906
Sabatini, Rafael 1875-1950
Saintsbury, George 1845-1933
Sakutaro, Hagiwara 1886-1942
Sanborn, Franklin Benjamin 1831-1917
Santayana, George 1863-1952
Sardou, Victorien 1831-1908
Schickele, Rene 1885-1940
Seabrook, William 1886-1945
Seton, Ernest Thompson 1860-1946

Shestov, Lev 1866-1938
Shiels, George 1886-1949
Skram, Bertha Amalie 1847-1905
Smith, Pauline 1883-1959
Sodergran, Edith Irene 1892-1923
Solovyov, Vladimir 1853-1900
Sorel, Georges 1847-1922
Spector, Mordechai 1859-1922
Squire, J(ohn) C(ollings) 1884-1958
Stavenhagen, Fritz 1876-1906
Stockton, Frank R. 1834-1902
Su, Hsuan-ying 1884-1919
Subrahmanya Bharati, C. 1882-1921
Sully-Prudhomme, Rene 1839-1907
Sylva, Carmen 1843-1916
Thoma, Ludwig 1867-1927
Tomlinson, Henry Major 1873-1958
Totovents, Vahan 1889-1937
Tuchmann, Jules 1830-1901
Turner, W(alter) J(ames) R(edfern) 1889-1946

Upward, Allen 1863-1926
Vachell, Horace Annesley 1861-1955
Van Dyke, Henry 1852-1933
Vazov, Ivan Minchov 1850-1921
Veblen, Thorstein 1857-1929
Villaespesa, Francisco 1877-1936
Wallace, Edgar 1874-1932
Wallace, Lewis 1827-1905
Walsh, Ernest 1895-1926
Webb, Mary 1881-1927
Webster, Jean 1876-1916
Whitlock, Brand 1869-1927
Wilson, Harry Leon 1867-1939
Wolf, Emma 1865-1932
Wood, Clement 1888-1950
Wren, P(ercival) C(hristopher) 1885-1941
Yonge, Charlotte Mary 1823-1901
Zecca, Ferdinand 1864-1947
Zeromski, Stefan 1864-1925

Readers are cordially invited to suggest additional authors to the editors.

Mark (Aleksandrovich) Aldanov

1888?-1957

(Pseudonym of Mark Aleksandrovich Landau, also transliterated as Aleksandrovič and Alexandrovič; also wrote under pseudonym of M. A. Landau-Aldanov.) Russian novelist, short story writer, critic, biographer, and essayist.

An émigré who left Russia after the Bolshevik Revolution, Aldanov is best known for his historical novels, many of which in some way elucidate the causes of the Revolution. His work, which is often compared to that of his literary model, Leo Tolstoy, is noted for its striking portrayals of historical figures. While some critics accuse Aldanov of an inability to create well developed fictional characters and disapprove of his extreme cynicism, his novels are praised for their direct style, intelligent assessment of historical events, scholarly accuracy, and insight into human nature.

The son of a prominent industrialist and his wife, Aldanov was born in Kiev and grew up speaking both Russian and Ukrainian. He demonstrated linguistic promise quite early, becoming proficient in French, German, English, and Italian as a boy, and learning Greek and Latin in secondary school. Aldanov later studied law and the natural sciences at the university of Kiev. Upon receiving his degree, he left the Ukraine for St. Petersburg, where he wrote several scientific and legal articles, took an interest in literature, history, and politics, and, in 1915, wrote an essay on Tolstoy, the writer who would become a primary influence on his work. Despite his moderately socialist politics, Aldanov viewed the February Revolution of 1917 with ambivalence and decisively condemned the violence of the October Revolution. The Bolsheviks returned Aldanov's scorn by persecuting him until he was forced to flee to the independent government of the Ukraine, which was at that time protected by German armed forces. When the Germans left and Aldanov's native Kiev was threatened, he emigrated first to Germany and then to France, where he began his historical novels, which were based upon months of research in the archives of numerous universities. One of the first books he published was a biography of Lenin, in which Aldanov described himself as a moderate socialist but also a counter-revolutionist and an anti-militarist.

During the years 1923 to 1927, Aldanov published the four volumes of his tetralogy *Myslitel (The Thinker)*, the work for which he remains best known. The four volumes, *Devjatoe termidora (The Ninth Thermidor)*, *Čortov most (The Devil's Bridge)*, *Zagovor*, and *Svjataja Elena: Malen'kij ostrov (Saint Helena: Little Island)*, dramatize the history of the French Revolution, and most critics agree that Aldanov used numerous allusions, especially in *The Ninth Thermidor*, to equate the French Revolution with the Russian. During the same period he published *Zagadka Tolstogo (The Enigma of Tolstoy)*, a critical assessment of Tolstoy's work. Following the *Thinker* series, Aldanov published a trilogy, this time explicitly concerning the Russian Revolution: *Ključ (The Key)*, *Begstvo (The Escape)*, and *Peščera*. He published two other novels as well: *Desjataja simfonija (The Tenth Symphony)*, which contrasts the life of Ludwig von Beethoven with that of the happier but less talented Jean Isabey, and *Mogila voina (For Thee the Best)*, a fictional account of Lord Byron's death while fighting for Greek independence from Turkey. In 1941, when France was occupied by German military forces, Aldanov moved to the United States. Cut off by the war from much of his income from royalties, he arrived in New York almost destitute. Soon afterward, however, Aldanov achieved commercial success with the publication in English translation of *Načalo konca (The Fifth Seal)*, a bitterly anti-Soviet novel which asserted that the idealistic aims of the Russian Revolution had been infected by the "moral syphilis" of the Bolsheviks' personal corruption. Profits from the work supported Aldanov and his wife until the end of the war, when they returned to France, where Aldanov lived for the rest of his life. During this period, Aldanov's income was once again diminished due to world events as he lost royalties from Eastern European countries that were absorbed into the Soviet bloc. To continue to support himself in a suitable manner, he had to produce novels more quickly, which some critics contend lessened the power of his work. Nevertheless, some of his most acclaimed fiction was written during this period, including *Istoki (Before the Deluge)*, which records the events leading to the assassination of Czar Alexander only two hours after he had emancipated the serfs, and *Živi kak choče š (To Live as We Wish)*, a novel which portrays how several Europeans who are sympathetic to the Marxist ideal must nevertheless come to America in search of personal freedom. Aldanov died suddenly at the age of seventy in Nice.

Throughout his career, Aldanov was compared to Anatole France for his pessimistic irony and to Leo Tolstoy for his historical subjects and narrative technique. Like Tolstoy, Aldanov belonged to the nineteenth-century realistic tradition: he wrote novels encompassing several generations of characters, depicted many different levels of society for the purpose of commenting on various aspects of human experience, and rendered an abundance of narrative detail in a straightforward prose style. But although he was a literary disciple of Tolstoy and had great respect for him, Aldanov did not follow Tolstoy's religious philosophy. He was a thorough agnostic as well as a skeptic concerning the possibilities of human progress, and it is this deeply felt cynicism that is reminiscent of France. Aldanov believed that even those who had idealistic aspirations were ultimately corrupted by their own emotions, a conviction which colored his opinion of the Soviet Union. Aldanov concluded that the vision of a socialist utopia inspired by the Russian Revolution was being undermined by self-serving leaders, and he gave these opinions voice through his major characters, who for the most part are of his own social group, the upper-middle class urban intelligentsia. Throughout his career, Aldanov also conveyed his strong belief that political and military leaders were not the makers of history, but were rather the pawns of haphazard impulses and events, a view which caused him to portray the Russian Revolution as a product of blind, ironic chance, not an inevitable development. For example, Aldanov suggests in *Before the Deluge* that if Czar Alexander had not been killed, he would have begun reforming Russia's autocratic political system. Although Aldanov has been widely criticized for creating insufficiently developed characters, he has also been praised for his adept portrayals of famous historical figures. These figures are presented as subject to considerable human weakness, undercutting, in the manner of Anatole France, idealized popular conceptions of "great" leaders. In this respect, Aldanov's work contrasts markedly with that of Tolstoy, whose fictitious characters in *War and Peace* are fully developed but whose portrayal of Napoleon is not. Critics conclude that while Aldanov lacked Tolstoy's immense artistic power, he surpassed Tolstoy in devotion to accurate historical detail.

Aldanov's ability to evoke the characteristics of a historical period and the people who were shaped by it gave life to his intense struggle to explore the causes of the Russian Revolution. Aldanov's achievement lies in his ability to transform the history of that conflict into a convincing novelistic form, speculating on the nature of historical events while remaining faithful to the historical record. Among a generation of Russian émigré writers, Aldanov stands as one of the foremost interpreters of the Russian Revolution.

(See also *Contemporary Authors*, Vol. 118.)

PRINCIPAL WORKS

*Lénine [as M. A. Landau-Aldanov]   (biography)   1919
   [*Lenin*, 1922]
**Devjatoe termidora   (novel)   1923
   [*The Ninth Thermidor*, 1926]
**Svjataja Elena: Malen'kij ostrov   (novel)   1923
   [*Saint Helena: Little Island*, 1924]
Zagadka Tolstogo   (criticism)   1923
   [*The Enigma of Tolstoy* (partial translation) published in
      Twentieth-Century Russian Literary Criticism, 1975]
**Čortov most   (novel)   1925
   [*The Devil's Bridge*, 1928]
**Zagovor   (novel)   1927
Sovremeniki   (essays)   1928
Junost' Pavla Stroganova   (essays)   1929
Ključ   (novel)   1930
   [*The Key*, 1931]
Desjataja simfonija   (novel)   1931
   [*The Tenth Symphony*, 1948]
Portrety   (essays)   1931
Begstvo   (novel)   1932
   [*The Escape*, 1950]
Zemli, ljudi   (essays)   1932
Peščera   (novel)   1936
Mogila voina   (novel)   1939
   [*For Thee the Best*, 1945]
Načalo konca   (novel)   1939
   [*The Fifth Seal*, 1943]
Punševaja vodka   (novel)   1939
Istoki   (novel)   1948
   [*Before the Deluge*, 1947]
A Night at the Airport   (short stories)   1949
Živi kak chočeš   (novel)   1952
   [*To Live as We Wish*, 1952]
Bred   (novel)   1954; published in journal *Novyj zurnal*
   [*Nightmare and Dawn*, 1957]
Samoubijstvo   (novel)   1958

*This work was originally written and published in French.

**These novels are collectively referred to as *Myslitel* [*The Thinker*].

HERBERT S. GORMAN   (essay date 1924)

[*Gorman was an American biographer, novelist, and critic. In the following excerpt, Gorman reviews* St. Helena, *Aldonov's first novel to appear in English translation.*]

In M. A. Aldanov's *St. Helena*, a meticulous study of Napoleon's last days on his isle of exile, the real hero is destiny. . . .

[*St. Helena*] is mainly a careful assimilation of documentary evidence. There is not a situation, hardly a speech by the Emperor, that is not to be found in extant annals, and yet the book is more than a slice of history, for it takes on the aspect of a rounded whole. Part of the Emperor's life is observed through the eyes of those personages living on the island with him, Susie Johnson, step-daughter of Sir Hudson Lowe, who married Count de Balmain; Las Cases, General Bertrand, Mentholon, and, best of all, little Betsy Balcombe, the fourteen-year-old child whose friendship with the Emperor is one of the most delightful things in history as well as in the novel. Aldanov creates his milieu in the first few chapters of his novel and he does this through the courtship of Count de Balmain and Susie Johnson. Then he turns to the Emperor, and those last months when the former Man of Destiny is awaiting his release by death are set down in a vivid and yet sententious manner. No one can doubt but that this is Napoleon as he really was in those last troubled years.

It is true that portions of the book read like direct transcripts of history, but yet there is a curious overtone of elemental powers which colors the material to more than historical description. Napoleon, one immediately understands, is in the clutches of that destiny which had observed him from a distance for so many years. There is a taut atmosphere of terror about this man who has circumvented time for so long and whose prodigious vision carried him so far from the artillery officer's pallet before Toulon. All of this is implied in prose that is never symbolic and which never attempts to grow mystical. This is mainly due to the fine juxtaposition of scenes, the vivid portraiture of the Emperor, in whose side the razor of death is slowly pressing, and in the reactions of those about him. Aldanov has constructed a powerful book here and he has done it within two hundred pages.

> *Herbert S. Gorman, in a review of "Saint Helena: Little Island," in* The New York Times Book Review, *February 24, 1924, p. 7.*

LAWRENCE S. MORRIS   (essay date 1926)

[*In the following excerpt, Morris reviews* The Ninth Thermidor.]

The Ninth Thermidor is the first volume of a trilogy dealing with the French Revolution and the period immediately after it. The concluding section, entitled *Saint Helena*, which is in reality an epilogue, has already been published in English. The second and central volume, which Mr. Aldanov tells us will be "the real picture of the revolutionary epoch" has not yet appeared, and the author begs us not to judge *The Ninth Thermidor* until we have read this second part, as many of the "chapters, episodes, and characters" in the first book will seem "unnecessary and useless" until we know the plan of the whole. While making reservations on this subject of the plan, it is still possible to form from *The Ninth Thermidor* an estimate of the spirit and method of the trilogy.

Mr. Aldanov has experienced one revolution personally. He was in Russia during the world war and the Russian revolution. In 1919 he left because of lack of sympathy with the Bolshevik régime, and returned to France where he had lived as a student. He does not, however, write of revolution as a counter-revolutionary—nor as a revolutionary. Perhaps it was this disinterestedness which made him uncomfortable in Russia. Reformers with programs to impose have never had much patience with the sceptic intelligence of artists and philosophers. Mr. Aldanov finds the contradictions of men more important than their doctrines. He broods over the profound discrepancy between their avowed principles and the unavowed needs out of which they act. In this first volume of his work he is absorbed by the problem of a reign of terror conducted in the name of liberty, *The Ninth Thermidor* culminates with the overthrow of Robespierre and the end of the Terror. "The unhappy enslaved country," says Mr. Aldanov, France, "was saved from fanatics by scoundrels." In short, he develops Anatole France's theme—though with less insight than the author of *Les Dieux Ont Soif*—that the passion, stupidities, and ambitions of the actors determined the crises of those heroic days as inevitably as they ensnare the most obscure and least conscious of our lives.

> It is easy to justify and more easy to incriminate whomsoever you choose (he makes Talleyrand say). Nobody is right. All are to blame. And it really would be better if the historians did not try to find a meaning—it is immaterial if it is positive or negative—in the terrible facts of the French Revolution. No sort of lesson can be drawn from the alterations of the elemental objectless acts generated by unbridled passions.

This spirit in which Mr. Aldanov approaches the "terrible facts" is important, since his book is essentially a series of historical portraits rather than a novel. By its fictional disguise and its panoramic scope it invites comparison with *War and Peace*. The comparison also reveals the difference. Tolstoy realized, even more profoundly than Mr. Aldanov, the puppetry of those who appeared to be directing great events. He, too, wished to reëstimate the characters of those sensational puppets from a historical point of view. But Tolstoy's work, despite its vast digressions, remains a single breathing novel. His historical and non-historical personages mingle, with the exception of Napoleon, with equal validity, and in a glowing passionate sense of life. They are people modelled in the round. Mr. Aldanov takes a figurehead for his nominal hero: a colorless young Russian adventurer named Staal, who appears at the court of Catherine the Great. This gives the author a chance to forget Staal for a few chapters, and sketch the life and character of Catherine. Staal is then remembered and sent to London, stopping on the way in Königsberg where he meets Immanuel Kant in a public garden. The philosopher has grown garrulous in his decline, and delivers a monologue which occupies one chapter. In London Staal is invited to a gathering at which Burke, Pitt, and Talleyrand are all present, and all talk for posterity. From London he goes to Paris, where he is completely forgotten—except for a perfunctory *liaison* which the author allows him. After all, isn't he is Paris?—for the exciting subject of Robespierre and his fate. Whereas Tolstoy chose the novel by genius, Mr. Aldanov writes fiction by an unfortunate accident. His essential *flair* is for dramatic historical portraits. His people are not in the round. Mr. Aldanov has dramatized, in strong colors but with a somewhat heavy hand, a few of the cross-currents of personal conflict and in-

trigue, to which the older historians were blinded by the spectacle of events.

> Lawrence S. Morris, "Giants in Undress," in The Saturday Review of Literature, *Vol. III, No. 10, October 2, 1926, p. 153.*

CLIFTON P. FADIMAN (essay date 1929)

[*Fadiman became one of the most prominent American literary critics during the 1930s with his insightful and often caustic book reviews for the* Nation *and the* New Yorker *magazines. In the following excerpt, Fadiman reviews* The Devil's Bridge.]

Aldanov does not write like a Russian at all. He organizes his historical episodes with a neatness and balanced precision that are more French than anything else; and, instead of falling in love with his main character, . . . he views Staal, his Byronic and rather disagreeable young hero, with an irony that, were it not deficient in depth and humanity, would recall Anatole France. *The Devil's Bridge* is the second volume of a historical trilogy of which *The Ninth Thermidor* was the first. It is concerned with the adventures and impressions of a young officer in Suvarov's army, in 1799 engaged in repelling the Napoleonic advance over the Alps. Its curious astringent tone and its bitterly realistic portrait of the old Russian general make it just worth reading; but one hardly feels that Aldanov is actually interested in or moved by the artistic possibilities of his subject. Rather, this seems to be the manufacture of a frigid and clever dilettante. It is more comprehensible to the American reader than was *The Ninth Thermidor,* which contained innumerable veiled allusions to the Russian Revolution; yet, if carefully examined, this sequel will reveal the same anti-Soviet bias that was so obtrusive in the first volume of Aldanov's Napoleonic trilogy. (pp. 588-89)

> Clifton P. Fadiman, "Immigrants among the Novels," in The Bookman, *New York, Vol. LXVIII, No. 5, January, 1929, pp. 588-90.*

MALCOLM COWLEY (essay date 1943)

[*Cowley has made several valuable contributions to contemporary letters with his editions of important American authors (Nathaniel Hawthorne, Walt Whitman, Ernest Hemingway, William Faulkner, F. Scott Fitzgerald), his writings as a literary critic for the* New Republic, *and, above all, with his chronicles and criticism of modern American literature. Cowley's literary criticism does not attempt a systematic philosophical view of life and art, nor is it representative of a neatly defined school of critical thought. Rather, Cowley focuses on works that he considers worthy of public appreciation and that he believes personal experience has qualified him to explicate, such as the works of the "lost generation" writers whom he knew. The critical approach Cowley follows is undogmatic and is characterized by a willingness to view a work from whatever perspective—social, historical, aesthetic—that the work itself seems to demand for its illumination. In the following excerpt, Cowley finds* The Fifth Seal *to be an anti-Soviet novel.*]

Mark Aldanov's novel, *The Fifth Seal,* deals with the great theme of revolutionary disillusionment. Its prophetic title is taken from the sixth chapter of Revelation: "And when he had opened the fifth seal, I saw under the altar the souls of them that were slain for the word of God and for the testimony which they held." But there are no real martyrs in the novel, only squirming victims, and there is nobody who suffers for the word of God. Its moral atmosphere was summed up for me by a sentence describing the household of Vermandois, a famous French writer who is almost but not quite its hero. "An old, querulous *femme de ménage*," Aldanov says, "performed an indifferent, listless task of cooking for him." The book also is old, querulous and embittered. . . .

Of the six principal characters in the novel, four are old men of a peculiarly unhappy type. Instead of transferring their interests to something or someone destined to survive themselves—a principle, an institution or simply their own children—they have become more and more self-centered. Three of them used to believe in communism and the future, but now they believe in nothing except indigestion and high blood pressure. They hope for nothing except to survive a few more years, in spite of Stalin and the doctors—the two enemies who stalk though their uneasy sleep. They have no friends. Kangarov, the Soviet Ambassador, always smiled when he spoke—"But his brown eyes never smiled, instead they were filled with constant uneasiness; at times they turned a bright yellow and became angry and mean." Wislicenus, the old revolutionist, had come to hate the whole world and himself—"Luxury irritated him; so did almost everything else." Vermandois, the Communist sympathizer, was "one of the five or six men whom any educated Frenchman was certain to mention in enumerating the great living writers of France." But there is nothing in the text to indicate that he was distinguished for anything more than his facility in using words and juggling ideas; his emotions are those of a peevish invalid. Only one of the old men is presented as a sympathetic character. He is a former Tsarist general who is now serving the Soviets, partly through Russian patriotism, but also—and this is a point that Aldanov is careful to explain—as a result of his incurable moral cowardice.

There are two young people who intrude into this home for the aged. One of them is Nadia, the Ambassador's secretary, with whom most of the old men are in love. It seems that the author intended her to be charming, but either he failed or else her charm was Russian and untranslatable. The other is Alvera, a congenital syphilitic, who dies on the guillotine for killing and robbing one of his employers. It is hard to say why he was introduced into the story, unless the author was trying to draw a parallel between his congenital syphilis and the moral syphilis which—Aldanov says—afflicts all the Russian leaders. (p. 641)

[It] seems to me that Aldanov's principal purpose in writing this book was to denounce, expose and deride the Russian revolution and all its fruits—political, social and merely human. Old Wislicenus says, at a moment when it clearly seems that he is speaking for the author:

> A human soul cannot exist under the terrific pressure to which we exposed it. Under such pressure, people turn to slime. We were depraving them in the name of a socialist ideal, but they became depraved without any aim or objective. . . . Then something happened that even the most practical among us could not foresee. . . . As soon as the governed ceased to resist, we also turned to slime. We had contaminated them with a form of moral syphilis, but they in turn contaminated us, and we became depraved, crippled human derelicts. . . . For their privations, for their hunger, for their enslavement and debasement, for the crippling of their souls, for their own cowardliness, for

their inability to resist, they pay us back with a savage, brutal hatred.

That is not unpolitical writing, and neither is it an isolated passage in Aldanov's work. It is true that this disillusionment of an old revolutionist is a theme that might have been treated in a powerful novel. There is, however, one condition that Aldanov or anybody else would have to meet in writing it. After attacking the Communists for sacrificing human lives to abstract social principles—and that has indeed been their gravest fault—he would have to show by example that human lives are valuable in themselves. He would have to present characters of whom we felt that it was shameful and criminal to see them sacrificed, and this is something he completely fails to do. The people he describes are not the martyrs who, in that sixth chapter of Revelation, "cried with a loud voice, saying, How long, O Lord, holy and true, dost thou not judge and avenge our blood on them that dwell on the earth." They are cold, scheming and pitiful creatures whose misfortunes, under a dictatorship, were exactly what they had coming to them. (pp. 641-42)

> *Malcolm Cowley, "Thunder over Aldanov," in* The New Republic, *Vol. 108, No. 19, May 10, 1943, pp. 641-42.*

JAMES GRAY (essay date 1946)

[*Gray is an American journalist, novelist, and critic. In the following excerpt, he discusses Aldanov's political skepticism as evidenced by* For Thee the Best.]

Completely and unapologetically a doubter is Mark Aldanov. His cultivated and sophisticated mind has dealt with the problem of man's ability to plan a better destiny and has come calmly to the conclusion that there is little health in the race's collective mind, little hope for its great plans. In *For Thee the Best* he pretends to be considering matters that agitated human society long ago, but actually he is considering the crisis of our own time.

On the surface this brilliant little novel appears to be the story of Lord Byron's last days, describing dramatically how he became bored with his talent for poetry and went to help the Greeks fight for their independence from the Turks. But I believe Mark Aldanov has slyly tucked another significance into this book. Out of the profound skepticism of his own highly sophisticated intelligence, he has brought the warning that when the great powers of the earth get together in international congresses, their leaders come equipped with weapons to sabotage the high-sounding intentions which the session has supposedly been called to further. (pp. 240-41)

The gist of [Aldanov's] philosophy, as it gets itself expressed between the lines of his new book, would seem to be that even the shrewdest, most discerning of men are too easily seduced by personal desire, too subject to boredom, too readily deflected by their emotional vagaries, to be capable of planning a livable human society.

He writes in this new book about the great figures of the early years of the nineteenth century who met, in an atmosphere of weariness and cynicism after the Napoleonic struggle, pretending that the Congress of Verona was designed to "defend . . . the eternal principles of virtue and of truth." Into the mouth of the Emperor Alexander of Russia he puts these words: "An independent English, Russian or French policy is no longer possible. There must be a coordinated policy that has the good of all nations as its aim.'' But even while he utters these words, the disillusioned liberal is deliberately destroying that dream and leaving all nations free to follow the policies that seem to serve their own myopic and greedy programs.

Over the shoulders of Alexander and Wellington and Castlereagh and Metternich, beyond the gates of Verona and the limits of the century, Aldanov is looking at the men of our own time, met in San Francisco or in London. Their curiously similar expressions of lofty ideals, he seems to warn us, may have similarly ironic overtones that are inaudible to the general public but quite clear to the masters of statecraft who know where to look for double meanings.

If one reads *For Thee the Best* in the dismal belief that it is meant to offer a parallel to the problems of our day and a translation of the terms of the present debate on international affairs, it is a profoundly depressing book. . . .

Idealism is short-lived even in the warmest heart; behind their masks of dignity and thoughtfulness, superior men hide their collections of wounds and vanities, pettiness, malice, boredom, indifference. And these explosives are enough to blow up any plan for an ordered society.

Aldanov is a disturbing writer because he makes this bleak prospect seem plausible. It is impossible to make the angry retorts one would like to make to his genial and impersonal analysis of the smallness of the human mind. . . . It is impossible not to admire his book and equally impossible not to resent it.

It should be read as a footnote to one of the tragedies of the past, in the hope that we shall learn how to demand better of our leaders and not allow another opportunity to be thrown away as was the world's opportunity at the Congress of Verona. (pp. 241-42)

> James Gray, "We Walk in Anguish," in his On Second Thought, *University of Minnesota Press, 1946, pp. 222-45.*

LEON I. TWAROG   (essay date 1949)

[*In the following excerpt, Twarog discusses Aldanov's tetralogy* The Thinker *and the differing critical reactions to several aspects of this work.*]

Although [*The Ninth Thermidor, Devil's Bridge, Conspiracy,* and *St. Helena: Little Island*] are primarily centered on the same basic themes, nevertheless they differ greatly with respect to individual features, one of the most obvious of which is plot structure. *Conspiracy* is the only novel which utilizes the conventional plot structure in which almost all incidents lead to and culminate in a single climax. This is probably due to the fact that the book deals almost entirely with Russia. On the other hand, *The Ninth Thermidor* has merely a semblance of a plot. It is in fact rather a series of dramatic portraits set into the proper historical and intellectual background and tied together though the experiences of a stock character, Staal, who travels to Germany, England, Belgium, and France and manages to meet through a remarkable series of coincidences many of the celebrities of the time. The extensive use of flashbacks, however, does not make for complete unity. *St. Helena,* too, is without conventional plot or form, but an extreme degree of unity is achieved through the simplicity and mellow timbre of the story. *Devil's Bridge* is virtually without any plot. Once again the important thing for Aldanov is not a neatly arranged plot, but rather a series of flashes and dramatic portraits taking in the episodes in Russia, France, and Italy. Only the battle at Devil's Bridge could be called a climax, yet it is a climax to only one of the many themes in the novel. It seems as if the author were attempting to cram into one book all of the major European developments of that period.

But whatever the type of plot, in all of his novels Aldanov sends a character traveling so that he may use him as a camera, or as an all-seeing eye. Aldanov's camera is always focused upon the very events any historian would have liked to observe in person. In the first three novels, Staal serves this purpose, and in the concluding book, De Balmain is used, although he really has almost no active part in the story. In all four novels, Aldanov has used dramatic portraits of historical personages predominantly to illustrate his themes.

It is in these character studies that the real strength of Aldanov's work is to be found. There is a richness and a wholeness about his brilliant dramatic portraits of historical personalities. One of Aldanov's favorite procedures is to make his characters say the most trite things and do things stripped of all importance, thus destroying the illusions most of us have kept since early schooldays of the mighty and of the great. Catherine the Great, Robespierre, Talleyrand, and Count Vorontsov, the Russian Ambassador to the Court of St. James, are all treated in this manner. In *Devil's Bridge,* Suvorov is not pictured as popular myth would depict him, but is shown as an ordinary little old man, hardened physically, but not mentally through the vicissitudes of his difficult life, but still possessed of the same frivolous thoughts, passions, and desires that other men have. It is almost sacrilege to show the great hero playfully dripping hot wax onto the nose of his servant in order to awaken him, but this shows him to be a human being and not a military robot. The description of Lord Nelson, Sir William and Lady Hamilton could well stand on its own merits, and is indeed a story all by itself, so graphically does Aldanov picture this relationship stripped of all its usual glamour. Perhaps in none of his character studies has Aldanov been so successful as in depicting the personality of Napoleon in *St. Helena.* The power which made him the greatest man in the world for a period of time still flows out to his followers, and leaves all of them in awe of his genius. Yet it is not the warrior Napoleon that the author shows in his book, but a little fat man, both good and bad-tempered, who is guarded by scores of soldiers so that he won't be able to get away. His tender side is shown in his relations with the little girl Betsy Balcombe, but some of his less admirable traits are also aired in these descriptions. The portrayal of Napoleon stands out particularly because Aldanov has not cluttered *St. Helena* with other equally interesting and important characters, as he has done in *The Ninth Thermidor* and *Devil's Bridge.*

It is constantly being brought to mind by Soviet, American, and British critics that Aldanov's *The Ninth Thermidor* was a novel about the French Revolution in terms of the Bolshevik Revolution of November, 1917, and that Aldanov was trying to prophesy future events as they were to take shape in the Soviet Union. On the other hand, there are some critics who disagree with this statement. In his introduction to *Devil's Bridge,* Aldanov vigorously denies that he attempted to draw any parallels between the two revolutions. He complains, moreover, about the fact that some of the critics have even picked out the contemporary Soviet citizens from whom Aldanov has drawn his characterizations of Talleyrand, Pitt, Robespierre, etc. Aldanov staunchly maintains that this was not the case, and that

Talleyrand and his other historical personages are drawn on the basis of studies he has made of these characters.

The Soviet critic, S. Monosov, is particularly bitter with respect to Aldanov's ideas. He insists that Aldanov is venting his own spite on the Soviets, that Talleyrand is Aldanov himself, and that like Talleyrand, Aldanov is awaiting the fall of the Soviet régime so that he may come back to help save his country. In addition to all of this, Monosov maintains that the reason for the inclusion of the Devil-Thinker is that Aldanov was trying to convince the world that the revolution was the work of the devil. He writes:

> In short, the emigré white guard element apparently has only one consolation these days; that is to hope for historical analogies. The French Revolution concluded with the Bonapartist coup d'état—says Aldanov with every line of his novel—wait and hope! It is with just such a coup d'état that the Russian Revolution too will end.

Of course, actually many things might be construed as being said in criticism of the Soviet Union, whether they are uttered by Talleyrand, Vorontsov, or Pierre Lamort who carries most of the philosophical ideas in the novel. But in fairness to Aldanov it should be pointed out that he showed also the other side of the revolution, the enthusiastic side of it. Beauregard who was awaiting death in prison together with Lamort and who was executed on the evening of the ninth of Thermidor, kept faith in the principles of the revolution in spite of the fact that he, an ardent supporter of the revolution, was scheduled to go to guillotine. In his conversation with Pierre Lamort, he says: "The path to good is through evil. Yes, the Revolution sends me to the scaffold, and on the scaffold I will shout, 'Long live the Revolution.'"

That there had to be some similarities between the French and Russian revolutions should have been taken into consideration by critics, for the Bolshevik leaders had studied the techniques of the French Revolution and had utilized these same techniques with some modifications. In a sense, Lenin and Robespierre, and later Stalin and Napoleon can be compared since their rôles had something in common. The end of the period of War Communism in the Soviet Union could be construed as the Russian Thermidor if one wanted to carry out this analogy. Perhaps it was because the Soviet critics did see the similarities that they attacked the book so bitterly on ideological grounds, for one often hates a replica of oneself much more than one would hate something completely different. (pp. 235-38)

Soviet critics attacked *Devil's Bridge* on much the same grounds as they used against *The Ninth Thermidor*. D. Gorbov claimed that Aldanov was flaunting the power of the British fleet and that behind all of this lay the hope that perhaps the British fleet would attack the Soviet Union. Gorbov also took offense at the fact that Cardinal Ruffo had made an agreement with the Republicans when he should simply have annihilated the group. According to Gorbov, Aldanov went to great pains to bring out this factor because he wanted to show that Christians could be expected to show mercy even though mercy at such a time was not in keeping with the usual methods employed in war.

Those who wish can find in *Conspiracy* the material which could be interpreted as being anti-Soviet propaganda. Pierre Lamort, in a talk before the Masons at the home of Talyzin, tells how Napoleon has given the people of France economic freedom, but has taken away from them the other freedoms,

such as the freedom of speech and of universal suffrage. Pierre goes on to say how all of these losses will be replaced by such things as medals, orders, ranks, and citations, that is, by anything that will bolster a man's vanity. The people at the meeting object violently to this sort of thing and express the opinion that such measures, if they were practiced in Russia, would be disastrous to the country. Whether or not Aldanov meant by these remarks to scourge the Soviet government is impossible to ascertain because the characters acted in their rôles just as one would expect the Russian noblemen of the time to do when confronted with such statements.

In view of these facts, it seems unwise to condemn Aldanov for the political message which the reader might find in his novels, even though Aldanov may have been somewhat prejudiced and may have injected his prejudice unconsciously into his works. After all, the artist is not a robot that sorts out facts, but rather an integrating agent who digests facts and brings them to the reader in some meaningful form. It may be that Aldanov wrote with the idea of understanding the present through a study of the past, whether he himself was aware of it or not. . . . In any case, Aldanov cannot be accused of distorting historical facts. He is sincere and truthful in what he has to say.

In their attempts to disqualify Aldanov, the Soviet critics missed completely the real theme of the book. Like Merezhkovsky, Aldanov wanted to teach something through his works, something deep, true and universal, and it was for this reason that he incorporated into his novels the pessimistic philosophy of history which overshadows everything. (pp. 239-40)

Sooner or later every Russian historical novelist is fated to be compared with Tolstoy and his *War and Peace*. Of the three great literary figures of the nineteenth century, Tolstoy stands much closer to Aldanov than do either Turgenev or Dostoevsky. Vladimir Pozner thinks that Aldanov constructs his historical novels in much the same way as did Tolstoy, that Aldanov discovers in past epochs and in the lives of historical personages those traits which connect them with all epochs, and especially with ours. Lawrence S. Morris finds some similarities [see excerpt dated 1926], but decides that Tolstoy's characters, both historical and fictional, are people "in the round" with the exception of Napoleon who is a bit artificial. On the other hand, he feels that Aldanov's characters do not mingle, that they are really not lifelike.

The Russian historian A. Kizevetter, however, claims that any similarity there may be in the works of Aldanov and of Tolstoy is purely superficial, for each author approaches the historical novel in a different way. Tolstoy is not very much concerned with historical accuracy whether in the depiction of separate historical figures or in the depiction of the general trend of historical events. Kizevetter feels that Tolstoy's descriptions of the epoch of 1812 are not in keeping with actuality because for Tolstoy the picture of the patriotic life was necessary only to illustrate the basic theme of the novel, namely, the naturalness of the process of life. Such characters as Speransky and Kutuzov, according to Kizevetter, were not fairly presented by Tolstoy, and if the reader today accepts this version as the real one, then this is merely a sign of Tolstoy's great artistic genius. However, he goes on to say that all of this does not mean that Tolstoy did not remain true to historical fact because of his inability to do so but rather, that he did not want to adhere to historical truth since it would not fit in with his general plan.

On the other hand, Aldanov's general trend of presentation of history, his characters, and every last detail are true, claims the critic. Of course, to further his artistic aims the author had to make a selection, but all of the selected episodes are pictured most accurately. Kizevetter maintains that all of Aldanov's facts were derived from careful study of historical documents which entailed extensive critical research. But Aldanov does not merely wish to portray history; he utilizes historical material as an artistic medium which is closely tied up with his philosophy of history.

Kizevetter has neglected to mention the fact that a large portion of Tolstoy's *War and Peace* was devoted to Tolstoy's philosophy of history, and it is here, in the realm of ideas that the great similarity exists between Tolstoy and Aldanov. Aldanov's views on war and revolution closely correspond to Tolstoy's version. In his style, Aldanov does utilize a wide scope, and he does write about war, but whereas Tolstoy's characters are primarily fictional, Aldanov's characters are primarily historical figures whose lives and actions can be checked by historical documents. One is inclined to agree with Kizevetter that Aldanov, as a historical novelist, outdoes Tolstoy, but must give way on the score of artistic genius.

Aldanov wrote his novels on the basis of most extensive critical research. The sources for the historical and social parts of *The Thinker* (according to Aldanov's own statements in his introduction to *The Ninth Thermidor*) were taken from material found in state libraries in France, and from many private collections. The most minute details are based on fact. For example, in the description of the battle on Devil's Bridge, the fact that Prince Meschhersky was the first to get across an improvised bridge and the fact that the soldier who followed him slipped and fell into the gorge are recorded just as they are given in well documented biographies of Suvorov.

Even when Aldanov invents a situation, it may very well be based on some historical fact. Although it may seem fantastic to us that Staal was chosen by Zorich as a candidate for the position of official lover at the court, there is a record of the fact that Gregory Orlov had tried to maneuver the seventeen-year-old son of Princess Dashkov into this very position.

When Aldanov is not completely sure of facts, he exercises extreme restraint. For example, instead of presenting the reader with either one or the other version of the shooting of Robespierre, the author presents us with the accomplished fact, and then has various theories propounded by outsiders in a discussion amongst themselves. This restraint is perhaps demonstrated even better with respect to the actual murder of Emperor Paul I. All historians agree that Paul was strangled with a scarf, but there is some question as to whose scarf it was. Leonid I. Strakhovsky maintains that the scarf belonged to Paul, K. Waliszewski writes that the scarf belonged either to Paul or to one of the conspirators, George Fowler claims that Nikolay Zubov used his own sash, whereas Waclaw Gasiorowski claims that Platon and Valerian Zubov tied their scarves together and did the job. Considerable discrepancy is also to be noted with respect to the actual person or persons who killed Paul. In the face of this conflicting evidence, Aldanov chose only those details which are accepted by all. Later in the story, he has a character, Ivanchuk, mention the fact that rumor has it that Nikolay Zubov and Skaryatin had strangled Paul with Skaryatin's scarf.

The inclusion of current discussions of the times is just the thing necessary to help the reader peg down certain phases of history in his mind and to orient himself with respect to world history. For example, in *The Ninth Thermidor,* Radishchev and his famous book, *A Journey from St. Petersburg to Moscow,* Fyodor Vasilevich Rostopchin, Prince Prozorovsky, the poet Derzhavin, and the free mason Novikov are brought into the background to indicate the cultural and intellectual milieu of the time. In England the reader is allowed to hear such leading political figures as William Pitt, Edmund Burke, and J. B. Priestly. The entire book is, however, overshadowed by the discussion of Rousseau, his theory of sovereignty and of the social contract. Against this theoretical background, the actual developments are shown by contrast.

Only one historical inaccuracy was noted and that was of a minor character. In *St. Helena,* Aldanov has made the mistake of marrying off De Balmain to Susana Johnson when, according to the island records, he had married Susana's sister.

Vladimir Pozner rightly remarks that Aldanov in his best moments comes close to giving a living synthesis of history and fiction. Another writer says that Aldanov is the master of the contemporary Russian historical novel and that his works surpass those of Merezhkovsky. D. S. Mirsky is of the same opinion, for he prefers the simplicity and lucidity of Aldanov to the overpretentious erudition of Merezhkovsky [see Additional Bibliography].

To conclude, Aldanov's novels have the quality of being both readable fiction and an accurate guide to history. The reader who is unaware of the fact that the characters of the books are historical personages can, nevertheless, enjoy the breadth and scope of Aldanov's work and can absorb the universal truths that Aldanov so ably demonstrates. The person who has delved into European history will find in Aldanov's novels a lucid and dramatic portrayal of historical events and persons. Contrary to the tenet that people who want to study history should not read novels to do so, Aldanov's tetralogy, *The Thinker,* presents the opportunity to acquire quite painlessly a detailed and accurate account of European history from 1793 to 1821. (pp. 241-44)

> *Leon I. Twarog, ''Aldanov as an Historical Novelist,'' in* The Russian Review, *Vol. 8, No. 3, July, 1949, pp. 234-44.*

GLEB STRUVE (essay date 1954)

[*A Russian-born educator, Struve is internationally known for his critical studies of Slavic literature. In the following excerpt, he briefly surveys Aldanov's novels and discusses general characteristics of his writing.*]

Mark Aldanov . . . , who was almost unknown on the eve of the Revolution, became in the late Twenties an *émigré* best seller and acquired an international reputation. His historical novels parelleled to some extent the vogue for the genre in the U.S.S.R., though they were differently conceived. He began with a series of closely interrelated novels about the period of the French Revolution and the First Empire. They combined great erudition and careful documentation with an interesting narrative and a general intellectual skepticism *à la* Anatole France, and a Tolstoyan attitude to history with a tendency to philosophize about human life and history and to suggest parallels between the past and the present. Many readers went to them for entertainment, but it was a highbrow, intellectual entertainment. The French Revolution series was followed in the late Twenties and early Thirties by a series about Russian life on the eve of and during the Revolution. These read more like modern psychological novels, even with some element of detective mystery loosely thrown in. But to some readers the main interest lay again in Aldanov's intellectualizings about the Russian Revolution. In *The Beginning of the End* (*The Fifth Seal* in English version) Aldanov switched his attention to contemporary history, to Soviet relations with the West and the Civil War in Spain. Since the war he has been equally prolific. *The Sources* (*Before the Deluge* in English)—one of Aldanov's best novels—was centered in the assassination of Alexander II and had among its many characters such international celebrities as Bakunin, Karl Marx, and Gladstone. In *Live as Thou Wilt* . . . Aldanov tackled a contemporary theme. Its action is set mostly in post-World War Two Paris and it has a witty description of a United Nations meeting. The novel is unwieldy, its philosophy obscure, its chief protagonists uninteresting. Even Aldanov's wit and intellectual brilliance and some well-drawn minor characters cannot save it from being a "flop." The inclusion of two full-length mediocre plays attributed to one of the characters—which might have been an interesting device aimed at obliterating the borderline between literary genres and revealing the different possibilities of different media—merely makes the novel still more heavy-footed. Aldanov's main failing is his inability to create three-dimensional fictional characters (his women are particularly unsatisfactory). His historical figures are more interesting and so are his comments on history through the mouths of various characters: They combine a great historical sense with an equally acute sense of the vanity of all things historical. It is significant that Aldanov's best work to date is a short *conte philosophique,* quite unique in Russian literature, entitled *The Tenth Symphony* . . . which is almost free from the usual fictional garb (one of its principal characters is Beethoven). And yet Aldanov's historical novels are superior, in their sophistication and their freedom of approach, to the majority of their Soviet counterparts. It is also interesting to note that his novels about the French Revolution, those about the Russian Revolution, and those about contemporary history are all subtly interrelated and designed to form a complex pattern of the spiritual history of modern man. They must therefore, in all fairness, be judged as a whole. (pp. 401-02)

> Gleb Struve, "The Double Life of Russian Literature," in Books Abroad, Vol. 28, No. 4, Autumn, 1954, pp. 389-406.

C. NICHOLAS LEE (essay date 1969)

[*Lee is the author of* The Novels of Mark Aleksandrovic Aldanov, *the most extensive study in English of Aldanov's work. In the following excerpt from that study, Lee discusses Aldanov's philosophical outlook as presented in his novels, contrasting it with that of Leo Tolstoy. Unattributed quotes throughout this excerpt are from D. S. Mirsky's* History of Russian Literature *(1927).*]

Any attempt to insist on Aldanov's place among the Russian classics must of necessity consider his ideas as a measure of his originality, profundity and permanency, quite apart from his ability to make a story compelling by superb construction and masterly narration. What answers does the whole body of Aldanov's fiction give to those who insist he merely apes Tolstoj, offers nothing to interest the modern reader, and regards humanity with an unpleasantly facile, hopeless skepticism?

In the following attempt to assess the enormously complex relationship between Aldanov and the man he recognized as his literary master, all remarks about Tolstoj have been taken from the comprehensive and thoughtful analysis of his work given in Prince Mirsky's *History of Russian Literature.* Both Tolstoj and Aldanov belong to the tradition of the nineteenth-century realistic novel, with its idealistic and civic character; its equal, level, sympathetic treatment of all humanity; its attention to emotionally significant "superfluous" detail; a satirical attitude to the negative aspects of life; a concentration on character and introspection; and simplicity of style. Both men concentrate their analysis on the infinitessimals of human experience, using the technique of "making it strange" to express especially satirical attitudes toward stereotyped interpretations of basic human situations. Aldanov, just as much as Tolstoj or Stendhal, "is particularly interested in discovering the semiconscious suppressed motives of his actions, in exposing the insincerity of the superficial, as it were, official, ego." . . . With Aldanov, as with Tolstoj, psychological analysis "is not the spontaneous revelation of the subconscious but the conquest of the subconscious by lucid understanding." Hence the view expressed by some critics that Aldanov characters are deduced analytically rather than created intuitively, parallel to the opinion of Gide, among others, that Tolstoj concentrates on typical, rather than exceptional, human types. Mirsky emphasizes in Tolstoj's "deliberately prosaic" style a "purity . . . of all extra-representational elements . . . purged of all 'poetry' and rhetoric . . . at its best . . . beautifully adequate and transparent." Sabaneev contends that Aldanov's prose lacks "the slightest hint of poeticality" and suggests that of all Russian writers he has the least phantasy and the most scientific mode of thinking. His style is more disciplined and varied than Tolstoj's, displaying frequent flashes of conscious virtuosity through special stylizations. From the outset Aldanov shows complete mastery of form, a tendency to the aphoristic and epigrammatic, a laconic terseness, a simplicity of syntax very different from the early Tolstoj and closer to the "adamantine phrase" of Anatole France. Slipping from the fictional to the historical plane, Aldanov reports incisively rather than engaging in the passionate polemics which fill so many pages of *War and Peace.* It is only in introspective monologues, the "long and dull spots" objected to by Struve and others, that important extra-narrative elements are introduced, and it may be argued persuasively that they, just like the theoretical chapters of *War and Peace,* were certainly at least intended to "add a perspective and an intellectual atmosphere one cannot wish away." They also stand out in especially high relief since Aldanov's novels are more consciously "constructed" than Tolstoj's, using significant detail not merely for characterization but also for increasing plot cohesiveness.

The "historicality" of both Tolstoj's and Aldanov's prose needs careful qualification. *War and Peace,* insists Aldanov along with other critics, was written too soon after the events it treats to be considered a genuine historical novel. At the same time, Tolstoj produced a magnificent novel of contemporary life in *Anna Karenina,* yet failed in his attempts to reproduce the era of Peter the Great. Conversely, yet with the same logic, Aldanov reconstructs periods prior to his birth with much greater precision and vividness than those following the October Revolution. Tolstoj cannot delve into the remote past because the present absorbs all his intellectual and psychic energies and confirms the optimistic philosophy of *War and Peace,* while Aldanov fails to assimilate a modern world which seems to have rejected all the values he holds dear. Both men succeed best in presenting not only the cultural climate most congenial to them, but also their own class, Tolstoj the established gentry, Aldanov the prosperous urban intelligentsia. Thus Mirsky sees that in the older man an "inclination towards the idyllic was from first to last an ever present possibility,'' and in the younger a tendency to the elegiac is just as inevitable. Tolstoj's attitude proceeds from "a sense of unity with his class, with the happy and prosperous *byt* of the Russian nobility,'' Aldanov's results from the cultural isolation of an émigré. . . . Aldanov, cut off not only materially, from class privileges, but also geographically, from his homeland itself, can only wistfully long for the stability of the hereditary aristocrats he portrays in his writings. This estrangement accounts for differences not just in philosophy, but also in literary temperament between the two writers, expressed in their fictional personages. Tolstoj's characters exude an almost superhuman self-confidence and corporeality, while Aldanov's people are more cautious and cerebral, thinkers incessantly trying to make some sense of life. The great moral crisis of Tolstoj's later years finds nothing like complete expression in *War and Peace*, whereas the major psychic trauma of Aldanov's existence, the October Revolution, preceded his entry into literature, so that the two men universalize their historical observations in opposite directions. Tolstoj glorifies what Aldanov calls the triumph of the *status quo* as the victory of the spontaneous life force in its endless continuity and renewal; the upheaval which precipitated Aldanov's spiritual crisis he attributes to the malevolence of chance acting through the pernicious vanity of Hegel's "world-historic individuals." Tolstoj's fictional creatures rise above history; Aldanov's must succumb to it.

Any attempt to explain Aldanov's reading of history as a mere justification of the intelligentsia against the Bolsheviks is a gross oversimplification. In this connection his thinking has been called anachronistic, but it is no less so than Tolstoj's. Nobody disputes the fact that the older writer "culturally had his roots in the old French and eighteenth-century civilization of the Russian gentry.'' The younger man feels the same attraction for the same century, but while Tolstoj follows Rousseau in his contempt for the unnecessary sophistications of civilization, Aldanov expresses an entirely different, scientific and cultural orientation through his admiration for Voltaire and the other rationalists of the Enlightenment. But this allegiance to the eighteenth century involves Aldanov primarily on the esthetic and intellectual plane, not psychologically, as it did Tolstoj. In the depths of his soul, Aldanov belongs instead to the late nineteenth-century intelligentsia, which Sabaneev characterizes by "great moral purity, an absence of asceticism, and complete religious and political unbelief'' and Mirsky by "social idealism'' and "the passion for improving the world.'' These attitudes determine his reaction to the October Revolution and the whole tonality of his writings. A careful reading between the lines, authorized by Aldanov's pet axiom, "Bene vixit bene qui latuit'' ["Well has he lived who has lived in obscurity''], permits the following reconstruction of his philosophical point of departure at the beginning of his literary career.

The triumph of the Bolsheviks doubtless convinced him that, Tolstoj notwithstanding, the goodness of things was not be trusted to any more than the perfectibility of the world which his generation had believed in, and that the "ambitious smallness'' of political and military leaders so denigrated in *War and Peace* did in fact have an enormous destructive effect in history. It also either produced or aggravated an all-pervasive misanthropy in him: Lenin's success in carrying out an inhuman social experiment by unleashing forces of hate and violence proved that man was governed not by reason, but by emotions, most of them negative. What was perhaps worst of all, Aldanov discerned in himself germs of the same criminal instincts he

saw running riot around him. It would seem that, faced with the necessity of rebuilding his standard of values from scratch, he determined to find a new truth free from any illusions which could once more betray him. As a product of nineteenth-century positivism, naturally devoid of any mystical leanings, he refuses to accept a God whose existence can not be rationally proven, and he has lost all faith in man. Trying to find an explanation for the Bolshevik victory, he rejects all deterministic hypotheses and fails to find any basic flaw in the idealism of his class and generation adequate to explain its humiliating defeat. Finally he reaches a conclusion from which he never wavers, that the October Revolution need never have happened had not His Majesty Chance worked in favor of forces which toppled a venerable and magnificent civilization. Politically, this view leads him to a conviction that any order is better than revolutionary disorder, a militant conservatism diametrically opposed to the anarchism inherent in some of Tolstoj's teaching. Philosophically, it provides him with a point of departure which can be extended to cover all revolutions throughout history, and in the *Thinker* cycle he cannily sets out to prove his point by applying it to a period and country other than his own. Doubtless from his intuition as well as his research, he chooses as a corollary to his basic theme, the irony of fate, the refrain from Ecclesiastes, "Vanity of vanities, all is vanity.'' To integrate fictional and historical elements and produce something like a rebuttal to the novel he holds to be the greatest in world literature, he applies his two fundamental concepts to people and events, great and small. The irony of fate he dramatizes beyond Potugin's simple assertion in *Smoke* that "Chance is all-powerful'': this bitter fact assumes such a tragic aspect because Aldanov's people, rather than renouncing happiness with Turgenevan resignation, pursue their goals with a determination eternally oblivious to the possibility that chance may cancel all their efforts or produce results quite different from their hopes. On the personal plane he devotes great attention to sickness, aging and death, refusing to build himself an illusory happiness by ignoring these ineluctable realities.

Given these metaphysical conditions, Aldanov's characters may go on living only from inertia, morbid curiosity, or refusal to face facts. However impressive such pure pessimism may be, he soon realizes its ultimate sterility and passes beyond it. Even in *The Ninth Thermidor* and *The Devil's Bridge* Lamort defends cultural values, while in *Conspiracy,* still maintaining that man "is bad enough,'' he insists "he can be improved, if he is worked on soon enough.'' Braun, for all his universal unbelief, admires the "honest, simple, courageous ideas'' Lamort mocked. *The Tenth Symphony* introduces the doctrine of indulgence for human weakness, extensively amplified in *To Live as We Wish* and implicit in the novels that follow it. Vermandois, for all his nihilism, offers some positive life maxims in *The Fifth Seal. Before the Deluge* affirms the beauty of life lived simply, despite the pernicious "people of the triple salto mortale.'' Only in *Punch Vodka* and *For Thee the Best* does the old undiluted pessimism return. In Tamarin Aldanov creates for the first time a character of religious temperament, and introduces personages with similar instincts in *A Story About Death* and *Suicide.* At the same time, skeptics occupy gradually less and less space in the novels of the late forties and the fifties. With the concluding remarks on Balzac in *A Story About Death* Aldanov justifies his early attitudes and explains the changes in his thinking: "Perhaps he no longer liked the general title of his principal books, which had given him such joy at one time. People do not always play a comedy, and is so much in their life so ridiculous and disgusting? . . . he had served art, even with mistakes, faithfully and truly—he had portrayed life as he saw it.'' In the same novel he propounds ''private'' human love as an ''eternal'' value, and from Lejden's tentative formulation of an immortality of the soul limited in time, Aldanov passes to a more positive affirmation in the suicide of the Lastočkins.

It is interesting to note that while Aldanov's spiritual evolution leads him away from his insistence on ''vanity of vanities,'' he never abandons his doctrine of chance. Lastočkin in *Suicide* repeats in identical terms the remark made in the preface to *The Key:* ''Our generation was *only* unfortunate.'' The fact that *Suicide* alone overlaps the author's other novels in the period it treats indicates once again the central role the Bolshevik Revolution plays in Aldanov's thinking. It may also be argued that the books built around this historical cataclysm, *Suicide, Before the Deluge,* an the *Key-Escape-Cave* cycle, constitute the most significant and permanent part of his entire literary output. Whether the reader agrees with the doctrine of chance or not, it offers Aldanov much greater artistic latitude than the determinist philosophy of Tolstoj. Despite some ''old-fashioned'' traits, the avoidance of stylistic innovation or fragmentation of consciousness in the presentation of reality, the problematics of Aldanov's work retains its relevance in a world where civil unrest remains a constant menace, and his agnostic approach to life certainly parallels a considerable segment of modern thinking. Moreover, his assessments of the impact the years 1914-1918 produced on a world which had not yet lost its innocence gain a new validity and current interest as historians intensify their efforts to put this period in proper perspective half a century after the fact. V. S. Pritchett's judgment of the Viennese novelist, Robert Musil, may be equally well applied to Aldanov: ''In only one sense (is he) out of date: he can conceive of a future; of civilized consciousness flowing on and not turning back, sick and doomed, upon itself.''

Sabaneev states, ''I personally think that precisely on the plane of abstract thought Aldanov could have created something more grandiose than he succeeded in doing; the 'literary plane' was too narrow for him and by no means absorbed him entirely.'' Since he considers Aldanov extraordinarily ''morally gifted,'' like Tolstoj, Sabaneev regrets that he gave no more attention to moral questions. Temperamentally Aldanov was more scholar than teacher or preacher, too much the skeptical scientist to promulgate any moral ''law,'' and his treatment of Tolstojism in *Zagadka Tolstogo* indicates how keenly he recognized the pitfalls of setting out to save souls. All the same, the morality inherent in his writings approaches or touches Tolstoj's on several points. Tolstoj bases his ethics on the moral teachings of the Gospels, in his own interpretation, and although Aldanov rejects Tolstoj's puritanism and the doctrine of resistance to evil, he also implicitly adopts a Biblical moral standard, that of the Ten Commandments. Both men reject the immortality of the soul and establish the human conscience as the final moral authority. But Aldanov goes a step further, in trying to strip the conscience of any irrational or mystical attributes by adapting it to Cartesian principles: searching methodical doubt, a boundless belief in reason, a negation of all ''mysterious properties,'' and the necessity to verify every statement. If Tolstoj ''boldly identifies absolute good with absolute knowledge,'' Aldanov's exegesis of the Platonic *Kaloskagathos* doctrine declares that what is perfectly rational is not only good but also beautiful, and worthy of man's best and most sustained efforts. His Cartesian ''metaesthetics'' in the moral sphere boils down to a ''live and let live'' attitude adopted to achieve the peace and freedom which constitute his *summum bonum.* While it presupposes indulgence for human failings, it lacks

the deep human sympathy of Dostoevskij's teaching, and it rejects the eudemonism of dogmatic Tolstojism: the Aldanovian saint must ''be good for goodness's sake,'' since happiness is impossible as long as sickness and death exist. For all the theoretical indifference it permits in application, Aldanov's Cartesian allegiance to the idea of Beauty-Good is basic to the positively humanitarian affirmations of his last books. Even when simply bewailing a world ''steeped in evil,'' he implies some standard of good. . . . Thus it may be argued that despite differences in character and temperament between the two men, not only Tolstoj the doubter, but to a significant degree Tolstoj the affirmer also strongly influenced Aldanov.

In Aldanov's metaphysics uneasily coexist an optimist and a pessimist, each partaking of elements in the thought of both Tolstoj and Dostoevskij. Aldanov the pessimist agrees with Tolstoj that ''the relative is in itself evil,'' but is too much a realist ever to consider the possibility of replacing it by any absolute: man is weak, stupid and evil, so there is no use trying to make him over into anything else. In the same hopeless vein he shares Tolstoj's ''contempt for the meaningless diversity of history'': how can any progress be discerned in the historical process if vanity rules man's nature and chance his destiny, in all ages past, present and future? Yet for Aldanov the optimist, as for Dostoevskij, ''all relative values were related to absolute values and received their significance, positive or negative, from the way they reflected higher values.'' Hence the conscious, occasionally operatic and overdrawn, symbolism characteristic of all Aldanov's writings, as of Dostoevskij's world view. The cautiously optimistic Aldanov adopts Dostoevskij's ''historical mode of thinking,'' on the one hand viewing history with alarm as an apocalyptic struggle between good and evil, which several of his characters identify with the devil, yet on the other hand setting out to win this struggle by reducing the power of ineluctable fate and increasing the areas of change over which man has some control. This determination to struggle with chance constitutes the most positive element in Aldanov's philosophy and the strongest affirmation of his faith in humanity: his later books clearly express his conviction that evil is not inherent in man, but forced on him by circumstances. Given the opportunity to lead a peaceful, free existence, provided he serves the Beauty-Good principle in some way, he will be good of his own accord.

Sabaneev remarks, ''In my opinion Aldanov's literary creation is made of more durable stuff than much that is recognized as more 'contemporary' in our days.'' Struve recognizes that ''of all the émigré writers of the older generation, Aldanov remained most faithful of all to the tradition of the novel, least guilty of its lyrical deformation.'' Taking the historical novel form from his idol Tolstoj, Aldanov infuses it with ''something of his own'' which makes him, for all his literary conservatism, a significant and original writer. Enriching the Russian realistic novel by giving it a skeptical orientation and a tight narrative structure reminiscent of Anatole France and other Western European writers, he takes a new direction in subject matter by concentrating his attention on politics, virtually *terra incognita* in literature earlier. At the same time his rare combination of objectivity and intuition enables him to raise the historical novel to a point of refinement never achieved before or since. Adding to the scientific accuracy of a historical scholar the penetrating observation and dramatic flair of a true artist, he reproduces the life of past and present, at the same time lingering over the eternal dilemmas of man's fate with the lucid rationalism, psychological penetration and deep moral concern of a Tolstoj. (pp. 369-78)

C. Nicholas Lee, in his The Novels of Mark Aleksandrovič Aldanov, *Mouton, 1969, 386 p.*

C. NICHOLAS LEE   (essay date 1971)

[*In the following excerpt, Lee discusses two of Aldanov's philosophical tales:* The Tenth Symphony *and* Punch Vodka.]

Both the life and work of M. A. Aldanov abound in so many paradoxes that it is no simple matter to make a definitive assessment of his place in the development of twentieth-century Russian literature. Simultaneously artist and scientist, writer and thinker, archaist and innovator, he uses all the resources of both intellect and intuition in an effort to extract some meaning from the confusing, contradictory experiences of his own generation. Searching for a rule of conduct which will enable secularly oriented modern man to face the terrifying anomalies of his existence without fear or illusions, Aldanov works not just as a writer of fiction, but also as journalist, historian, and philosopher. He first examines contemporary people and events in their own context. Then he relates them to similar personalities and situations in the past. Finally, he sets out to synthesize the conclusions from all these observations in accordance with transcendent philosophical principles integrating past and present to provide guidance for the future.

Aldanov's wide-ranging intellectual concerns doubtless affected his decision to cultivate three literary genres where formal rules were virtually lacking: the panoramic historical novel, the journalistic sketch, and the philosophical tale. And yet— one more paradox of his literary career—he introduces significant innovations in these genres precisely because of the discipline he imposes on them. The waywardness permissible in these loose literary and semi-literary forms permits him to combine notation and interpretation of data in any way he wishes. But he possesses such an ordered intellect that even when he sets out to show the irreducible dilemmas of life, he organizes his thinking methodically and thoroughly. In his fiction he frequently tries to integrate philosophy and psychology by assigning important ideas to invented personages. Yet despite this approach to the particular versus the general, many of his historical novels show the same demarcation between expounded thoughts and observed life which characterizes *War and Peace*. It is doubtless the obtrusiveness of the philosophical message in the novels which leads Gleb Struve among other critics to suggest that Aldanov is more successful in his journalistic sketches and philosophical tales, literary forms with a specific and restricted focus, than in his longer works [see excerpt dated 1954]. Questions of literary merit aside, Aldanov's philosophical tales resurrect a neglected minor genre and infuse it with a number of new attributes. (pp. 273-74)

Aldanov's eighteenth-century intellectual and aesthetic orientation doubtless partly determined his decision to experiment in this genre, which in its most brilliant previous, Voltairean, manifestation amounted to literary polemical journalism, built on elaborately implausible action, often set in deliberately fantastical times and places, where character development is reduced to the minimum necessary for illustrating a dominant philosophical idea or complex of ideas.

Of all Aldanov's philosophical tales *The Tenth Symphony* remains the most elusive and complex, despite, or perhaps because of, the preface in which he "explains" his intentions. The author's foreword begins with a poetic evocation of the room in the Louvre where the works of the French miniaturist Isabey are displayed, and continues with the following cryptic statements:

> These exquisite miniatures, in my opinion, have not yet been appreciated at their proper value. Nothing, it seems, connects them with each other, yet they contain a whole historical period: a real treasure for the historian and the novelist. They give us what the enormous canvases of Gros and David cannot give us.
>
> Isabey in his youth knew people who remembered Louis XIV. The author of these pages once in his life saw Empress Eugénie, who knew Isabey personally. The stirring bond of time in its entirety is incomprehensible—perhaps an argument in favor of fragmentary, miniature art.
>
> *The Tenth Symphony,* of course, is in no sense a historical novel, or even a novel at all. The author intends it to be close to what was called in the eighteenth century a philosophical tale, and what would be more correctly called a symbolical tale. The basic symbol is clear enough: "And there stands a ladder on the earth, and its top touches the sky." I am afraid that the basic symbol has been stated too crudely and the others too unobstrusively. But this is for the reader to judge. In any case, everything in this little book is connected in idea; the disparity of its two parts is due to the fact that I felt myself incapable of writing about Azef in a fictional form. . . .
>
> (pp. 275-76)

These remarks by Aldanov are cited here almost *in toto* for the various clues they give to the author's intentions and the peculiarities of the philosophical tale as modified by the addition of a new symbolical dimension. Aldanov shows his consummate virtuosity of style and composition more bafflingly here, perhaps, than in any other of his works. True to the implications of his introductory remarks, he presents each of his eighteen chapters as an exquisite miniature, complete with its own title, an epigraph which complements or ironically comments on the story action. Thanks to the transparently elegant expositional style, each chapter is a rounded, complete work of art in itself. Six chapters take place at the Vienna Congress of 1815; the Vienna premiere of Beethoven's Ninth Symphony on 7 May 1824 provides the focus for six more chapters; and the last six chapters show Isabey in Paris, enjoying a typically uneventful day in 1854. Yet despite this formal compositional balance, the parts add up to an ambiguous whole. There is no single character who unifies the three timed frames of the action. The Vienna Congress chapters introduce the three protagonists of the story, Isabey, Beethoven, and Count Andrej Kirillovič Razumovskij, but Isabey is absent from the second part of the story, while the deceased Razumovskij and Beethoven reappear only in Isabey's recollections at the end. And there is no obvious connection between the interpretive monograph on the notorious Imperial Russian *agent-provocateur* Azef and the subtle cameos from the nineteenth century to which it is appended.

The Tenth Symphony seems at first glance ambiguous because of several properties which radically differentiate it from the *conte philosophique* of Voltaire: a specified time and place with no intentional distortions, in a framework of scrupulous denotative realism; dialogue and inner monologue for portraying character *in extenso,* if not for developing it; and finally the absence of external action. While Voltaire exposes his cardboard characters to a frantic succession of implausible vicissitudes in order to sharpen the reader's awareness of their ethical dilemmas, the philosophical message of *The Tenth Symphony* can be extracted only by reading between the lines. The wicked in Voltaire subject the virtuous to schematic, easily recognizable evil. In contrast, life flows by the characters in *The Tenth Symphony* so unobtrusively that neither they nor the reader can discern its movement except in retrospect. There is reason to assume that Aldanov deliberately uses a "fragmentary, miniature" presentation of events as most suitable for evoking the "stirring bond of time" mentioned in his foreword. This theme, which Struve sees as the basis of all his fiction, gives pervasive unity to the rambling plot. Nothing seems to connect the chapters in this story any more than the miniatures of Isabey. Yet in both a whole historical period is reflected. The stirring bond of time finds its most complete fictional embodiment in Isabey, the benevolent spirit hovering over the action, either as a protagonist or as an acquaintance of other protagonists. In the final section of the story, when he is nearly ninety, he is portrayed in terms of the inner peace resulting from his extensive experience of life. However, his conversation, full of allusions to historical figures of his acquaintance long dead, produces in others a vague dread akin to the fear of mortality itself. In him, then, Aldanov combines all the contradictions inherent in the stirring bond of time, which teaches acceptance and love of life even as it leads inexorably to death.

Not only must the characters in *The Tenth Symphony* die, they must live. They are acutely aware of their subjection not only to time, but also to fate. The critic A. Kizevetter notes of Aldanov: "the central theme of all his historical narratives . . . is . . . the fatal subservience of man to the irony of fate. . . . The great and the petty are equally victims of this same fate, allotting obscurity to some and fame to others, and levelling them all in their common end: death and annihilation." This constant links the implied symbolism of the title *The Tenth Symphony* with the symbol stated as basic to the story: "And there stands a ladder on earth, and its top touches the sky." *The Tenth Symphony* represents the fulfillment denied to all men by the irony of fate. Just before the premiere of the Ninth Symphony, Beethoven's devoted friend Schindler listens as the deaf musical genius improvises at the piano: "His fantasia had nothing in common with the themes of the symphony which was to be performed today at the theater. Schindler knew that it no longer interested the old man, and guessed that he was playing something from the new tenth symphony he was composing." . . . Again in the last section, during ostensibly the idle conversation at a dinner party, the theme of the tenth symphony recurs, with a new ironical twist, as an insincere platitude uttered by one of the guests, an unusually successful public official:

> The music teacher mentioned that in the last years of his life Beethoven had been preparing a new work, in comparison with which all his others would have paled. It was to have been called the tenth symphony. Into it Beethoven wished to put his whole soul. But he never succeeded in writing the tenth symphony, he merely dreamed of it, and he died with his dream unfulfilled.

> "Really?" asked M. Isabey, this time with genuine interest. He sighed and grew thoughtful. "Everyone has his tenth symphony," he said.

> "That is true," agreed . . . Fuld. . . . "When it comes down to it, we are really all failures."

> The guests all laughed, so unexpected were these words in the mouth of a man who had succeeded in absolutely everything in life.

> (pp. 276-78)

Other peripheral details suggest the tragedy of frustrated aspirations and the irony of fate. The single most important device for accumulating these details is the disconnected discussion of the dinner scene in the last section. Various random conversational allusions permit Aldanov to insert material which unifies disparate elements introduced earlier in the action and which further illuminates the cryptic statements of the foreword. One snatch of dialogue even motivates the seemingly arbitrary attachment of the Azef monograph to the philosophical tale. One of the guests at the party, a young authoress, gives the group a reading of her latest story, a medieval Italian *novella* featuring "a complete villain, a man without any moral principles." . . . Afterwards someone attempts to prove that a pure villain is a thing of the past such as will never be seen again. "The ladies regretfully agreed." To allay all regrets, Aldanov complements the symbolical tale with the monograph on Azef, which had originally appeared serially in the Parisian émigré newspaper *Poslednie novosti* (*Les dernières nouvelles*). In a foreword to the newspaper serialization of the biographical study, omitted in the book version, Aldanov connects the notorious *agent-provocateur* with the basic ladder symbol of the philosophical tale by stating that Azef stood at the bottom of the human moral evolutionary scale.

The theme of human vanity runs throughout the polyphonic presentation of the irony of fate in the story. The fictional center for observing the futility of all human behavior, petty and self-seeking as well as altruistic and noble, is Count Andrej Kirillovič Razumovskij. He serves Aldanov in three ways: as a critical observer of the arrogance and aimlessness in Austrian high court society; as a medium for analyzing the anomalies of life without any optimistic "illusions"; and finally as a passionate amateur of painting and music, an ideal fictional polemicist in aesthetic questions concerning Beethoven and Isabey. Razumovskij's *tedium vitae* proceeds from advancing age, financial difficulties, and failing health, while his intimacy with Viennese high society results from his special status as a typical late eighteenth-century Russian magnate-diplomat with discriminating aesthetic tastes. His glittering life presents itself to him from its negative side: "Gossip, calumny, malice, envy, voilà le revers d'une médiocre médaille . . ." . . . . He falls victim to the irony of fate in its most savage form when his magnificent palace burns down from a defect in the ultramodern French heating system which, from motives of vanity, had been installed in it. The newfangled hook and ladder apparatus which the firemen use in their efforts to save the palace provides a concrete ironical variation of the ladder as a philosophical symbol.

The tale gains in complexity, richness, and ambiguity by the fact that not only Razumovskij but also Beethoven and Isabey react to the irony of fate and vanity of vanities, each in his own way. Aldanov does not contrast a right approach and a wrong approach to life, like Voltaire, but simply juxtaposes three human resolutions to the problem of fate. Beethoven is observed from without, fugitively by the kind-hearted Isabey, who pities the mental agony reflected in his interesting face, and in greater detail by Razumovskij, who is enraptured by the power of the Ninth Symphony:

> "... he is the greatest artist of all times, the king of that art which is more intelligent than all the sages and philosophers in the world. . . . And his pessimism is not from consciousness, not from the misfortunes of his life, not even from his deafness. Beethoven is possessed. He himself creates around him an atmosphere of torment and then consoles himself as best he can. . . . At the extreme heights of art voluntary martyrs are necessary: can anyone in a normal state create such a work of art?" . . .

Beethoven thus by implication takes his place at the top of Aldanov's moral ladder, albeit at tremendous cost to himself and others. Razumovskij himself occupies a neutral, middle, everyman status in the philosophical scheme of the story, despite the *grand seigneur* side of his life and habits. He experiences the universal joys and sorrows, lives out his allotted span of years, and then dies. The symbol of fire, a roaring conflagration in the chapters describing the destruction of his palace, reappears as a dying flame in the last pages of the story. (pp. 278-79)

The Tenth Symphony expands the form of the philosophical tale in several different directions. Since the main philosophical idea is the elusiveness of life and art itself, the action lacks an easily recognizable point of departure. Most of what happens occurs within the characters themselves, who are extensively developed through dialogue and inner monologue. The action, complex and ambiguous, internal more than external, has more affinities with a full-fledged novel than with the streamlined, stylized reality of the Voltairean philosophical tale. The clear-cut polemical orientation of Voltaire, where right is always distinguishable from wrong, is diametrically opposed to the muted chiaroscuro with which Aldanov represents severally equally convincing solutions to the same problem. Hence perhaps the absence of a subtitle giving the story an ideological focus, a feature which characterizes several Voltairean philosophical tales. The cast of characters includes almost exclusively people who actually lived, presented by the author as examples of human psychological types rather than as emanations of abstract philosophical essences.

Punch Vodka differs from *The Tenth Symphony* almost as much as from the Voltairean philosophical tale. Its ironically vague subtitle, "a tale (*skazka*) of all the five happinesses," recalls Voltaire's *Candide, ou l'optimisme* and *Zadig, ou la destinée.* But it again features actual historical personages: the eighteenth-century statesman Count Burckhardt von Münnich, Lomonosov, and Jakob Stählin, a German professor of eloquence at the Academy and the Russian imperial librarian. These people authentically reflect their time and place, Russia in 1762; they do not move in a fantastic world like the people of Voltaire's tales. But in the peasant diplomatic courier Mixajlov, young Valja, her lover Volodja, and her family, they are counterbalanced by fictional personages, who occupy only a peripheral place in the action of *The Tenth Symphony*. Vienna and Paris serve as the setting for *The Tenth Symphony,* but part of *Punch Vodka* follows Mixajlov from Petersburg to the Siberian village of Pelym, 2000 miles away, while the rest of the story takes place principally in the imperial capital. Although Aldanov

once more juxtaposes attitudes rather than illustrate one principle, this time he states a clearly defined central theme.

The narrative has two centers of focus, a historical catastrophe and a fictional peripatetic: the murder of Tsar Peter III affects the lives of all the characters, while Mixajlov in his travels provides the direct or oblique motivation for all the various combinations of fictional and actual personages in the story. While Mixajlov serves as a mechanical unifying device, he still belongs to realistic rather than fantastic literature, and he is an engaging personality in his own right. He also has a twofold philosophical significance; on the one hand he embodies the robust common sense Aldanov considers more genuinely Russian than Dostoevskian mysticism; and on the other hand he provides a splendidly ambiguous example of the moral and mental attributes most conducive to happiness. In his role as plot unifier he sets the action in motion: just before leaving on his Siberian assignment, he stops in at his favorite tavern for a drink of his favorite punch vodka and notices among the guards officers drinking there one with an unusually sinister face. Only after he has gone a long way on his journey does Mixajlov learn that he is bearing a pardon from Peter III to Münnich, who had been condemned to perpetual exile following Elizaveta Petrovna's overthrow of his patroness, Anna Leopol'dovna. The German general assigned to guard Münnich in Siberia fears a pardon from the tsar will prompt the older courtier to take revenge on everyone involved in his banishment. The general's pretty young daughter Valja, however, is more worried about whether her father will give her money to buy scarlet satin for her costume as the heroine in Lomonosov's *Tamira and Selim,* which is soon to be performed by the young people of the town. Back in Petersburg, Münnich quickly realizes that a coup involving Catherine and the guards officer Aleksej Orlov is brewing against Peter III, and ponders the course of action he must take. In the meantime Lomonosov and Stählin discuss the court ceremonials attending the imminent coronation of the tsar.

Having introduced his major characters and connected their destinies with the fate of Peter III, Aldanov proceeds to show how regicide affects what each of them regards as happiness. For Münnich happiness means power, for Lomonosov knowledge, for Stählin security, for Valja love, and for Mixajlov—punch vodka. In juxtaposing these attitudes to happiness, the author assigns a set of symbols to each, and has each character formulate his views to himself in inner monologue, Münnich presents the most complex psychology of all. Power for him involves self-denial and self-mastery as well as self-expression and self-aggrandizement. Passing by the spot where many years before he had been saved from execution at the last minute, he reflects: "I experienced the highest happiness in life on a mountain of corpses on the day of the Stavučan battle, and again on the night of the coup which I won by intrigue, and then on that day, when they were supposed to quarter me. . . . Because they didn't quarter me? Because of triumph and agitation." . . . Elsewhere Aldanov writes: "He thought that in every statesman's life there was, or could be—or had to be?—a catastrophe: ruin, prison, execution—it doesn't matter what kind: even quartering could be of different kinds, with horses and without—and there was perhaps a certain amount of justice to this." . . . Quartering is not the only symbolical force which frustrates Münnich's ambitions. Several impressive evocations of the wild, cold, empty Siberian vastness in which he spends his exile suggest not only that side of Russia indifferent to his strivings for enlightened political reform, but also those areas of human experience inaccessible to the dictates of reason. The fatality which results from Münnich's concept of happiness finds its expression in the card symbolism Aldanov frequently uses in describing political gamblers: "Sometimes . . . Münnich thought . . . that twenty years before he had bet on the wrong card." . . . His decision to support the incompetent tsar prompts Lomonosov to think: "If you are going to play political faro, at least bet on the right card . . . Count Münnich is by nature a *faro player:* all he wants is to play a game of chance, and he only plays *paroli,* always doubling the stake on the card. Such gamblers often end up losing everything." . . . The complexity of Münnich's character enriches the irony of his final fate. His highest happiness brings his doom, not merely because of his gambling instincts and greed for strong sensations, but also on account of the honor implicit in his support of the tsar who freed him from banishment: had he betrayed the man who returned him from exile, he would have benefited from that man's murder.

Stählin's ideal of happiness stands at the opposite pole from Münnich's. Frightened at portents of impending catastrophe which could affect even him in his comfortable position as a court functionary, he assesses his own attitude to life:

> . . . and he examined himself: What did he want? He wanted health and happiness for his wife, his son, himself. . . . He wanted financial security . . . to assure his family a comfortable, peaceful, dignified existence. . . . All that was necessary was to get along with people without involving oneself especially with anyone, keep away from insane affairs, not anger others, not forget oneself. . . . There could be no objection whatever to this, and this was the way the overwhelming majority of people behaved in every age, including respectable and celebrated people. You live your life honestly, without blood and without dirt. . . . This was the secret of happiness on earth. . . .

This proponent of a philosophy resembling in some respects Candide's decision to "cultiver notre jardin" derives no more satisfaction from his ideal of happiness than Münnich. The stateman falls victim to the irony of fate at its most sinister, while the mildmannered philistine suffers the indignities of destiny at their most ludicrous and pathetic. (pp. 281-84)

The man who has discovered the highest happiness, the author suggests, is the courier Mixajlov. The story is so constructed that he goes away on another assignment and returns just before the assassination of Peter III, when he discovers Münnich has left 200 rubles as a bonus for his services. After long deliberation, he decides to buy himself some new clothes and spend the rest of the money on an extended spree, just like a proper gentleman. An obliging prostitute named Maška helps him carry out his plans at his favorite public house. During one brief interval of sobriety he has another glimpse of the sinister looking guards officer who so struck him before he left for Pelym, and shortly afterwards learns that this man was responsible for the sudden death of Peter III from "colic." His last rubles go for drink:

> Then there was a drunken brawl with the clerk. Then they made up, he ordered another bottle, after it another. Mixajlov drank and thought blissfully that nothing was as bad as it seemed or worth getting upset about, that Maška was

lying—it wasn't just a matter of money—that there was happiness in the world, even though it gave you a headache, and that this happiness was punch vodka. . . .

In order to strengthen his ironical accusation of life, Aldanov has made his toper as sympathetic as possible. Mixajlov is a "strong, broad-shouldered, bald man of about forty, with an intelligent, sly, expressive face." . . . After a night of drinking he reports to work promptly, performs his duties impeccably, and enjoys the most cordial relations with his superiors. He is a robust, down-to-earth epicurean completely at peace with his conscience. Maška liked the courier: "Even though he was a peasant, in his soul he was purer than a fine gentleman." . . . At the end of the story, drink helps him forget the moral question he cannot resolve: why should Aleksej Orlov win wealth and power for murdering his sovereign? Mixajlov's happiness not only results in nothing worse than a hangover, it reconciles him to the horror of life.

Punch Vodka stylizes reality in order to prove a philosophical point, but in a very different way from the Voltairean philosophical tale. The device of the fictional peripatetic compresses action diffuse in time and place into a short narrative frame where every detail serves the central artistic purpose. Incident and attitudes are chosen arbitrarily in order to illustrate a governing philosophical idea: Münnich's defeat attracts more attention than Orlov's victory, and Aldanov chooses to endorse drink from a philosophic standpoint, as an escape from the anomalies of existence, rather than to present it as a psychological problem. Yet the story takes place at a specific time, marked with authentic linguistic and cultural peculiarities, and events are interlinked by plausible causal transitions. As in *The Tenth Symphony,* events and characters are complemented by a fully developed system of symbols. The most important difference between this philosophical tale and those that preceded it is that the story includes dialogues and inner monologues which not only portray character in depth, but show its development under crisis. (pp. 285-86)

In his full-length historical novels Aldanov offers his corrective to the optimistic determinism of *War and Peace.* In the symbolical tales he polemicizes with Voltaire's confidence in progress. In both genres he makes an original contribution not merely in terms of philosophical perspectives, but also in matters of construction and psychology. The preference of some critics for the miniature works of Aldanov may well result from the exquisite balance, lightness, harmony, and precision of the short pieces. In the symbolical tales the author's basic philosophical concerns make no pretense of hiding behind a comprehensive neutral portrayal of a broad realistic background. Yet the same economy and artistic discipline which enables Aldanov to distill several philosophical essences in a restricted narrative frame also permits him to impart an extraordinary richness and variety to the texture of the story. Thanks to his skill as a historian and an artist, he enriches the restricted genre of the philosophical tale by the addition of a symbolical dimension and by several devices of the realistic novel, including an authentic setting in time and place, extensive exposition of character by means of dialogue or inner monologue, and dynamic psychological development motivated by dramatic action. (p. 290)

C. Nicholas Lee, "The Philosophical Tales of M. A. Aldanov," in Slavic and East-European Journal, *n.s. Vol. 15, No. 3, September, 1971, pp. 273-92.*

ADDITIONAL BIBLIOGRAPHY

Colin, Andrew Guershoon. ''Mark Aldanov: An Appreciation and a Memory.'' *Slavonic and East European Review* XXXVI, No. 86 (December 1957): 37-57.
   A laudatory biographical discussion of Aldanov and his work.

Lee, Charles. ''Curtain-Raiser for Revolution.'' *The New York Times Book Review* (5 October 1947): 1.
   A review and plot summary of *Before the Deluge*.

Mirsky, Prince D. S. ''The New Prose.'' From his *Contemporary Russian Literature: 1881-1925*, pp. 281-315. New York: Alfred A. Knopf, 1926.
   A short assessment by a contemporary of Aldanov. Mirsky states, ''His historical novels are not an escape from the present. On the contrary, he studies the past to understand the present.''

Morris, Alice S. ''Aldanov's Pomps and Circumstances.'' *The New York Times Book Review* (24 October 1948): 34.
   A review of *The Tenth Symphony*.

Winner, Thomas G. Introduction to *Zagadka Tolstogo*, by Mark Aldanov, pp. vii-ix. Providence, R. I.: Brown University Press, 1969.
   Discusses Aldanov's treatment of Tolstoy in *Zagadka Tolstogo*.

Grazia (Cosima) Deledda

1875-1936

Italian novelist, short story writer, poet, dramatist, and auto-biographer.

Deledda's novels and short stories won her the distinction of becoming the only Italian woman to receive the Nobel Prize for literature. Although the greater portion of her works are set in her native Sardinia, most critics agree that her fiction transcends regionalism through its discussion of universal di-lemmas, most notably the tension between the desire for love and the demands of social respectability. Her attention to such themes, as well as her vivid prose style, made her one of the most popular Italian romance writers of the early twentieth century.

Deledda was born to a middle-class family in the village of Nuoro, on the island of Sardinia. Ninety-five percent of Sar-dinia's population, including Deledda's mother, were illiterate, but Deledda was fortunate enough to receive four years of formal education, and she grew up with a love of reading. Her father was mayor of Nuoro for a time, and she became sensitive to human suffering through hearing the stories of people who came to him for help. She secretly began to write when she was thirteen years old, and by the age of fourteen had published several short stories, first in magazines and later that same year in a short collection.

However, she endured public censure in Nuoro because she was Sardinia's first woman writer and because she used actual people and events as models for characters and incidents in her stories. The disapproval did not deter her writing, and by the time she married in 1900 she had already published two novels and another collection of short stories. She and her husband moved to Rome after they married, and Deledda lived there for the rest of her life. Writing on a schedule of two hours per day during the following thirty-six years, she produced one novel or collection of short stories every year. In 1926 she won the Nobel Prize for literature, the second woman, as well as the second Italian, to have done so. Her literary output con-tinued steadily until her death in 1936 from breast cancer; during her illness she wrote an autobiographical novel, *Cosima,* which treats the subject of breast cancer.

Deledda is not known for any single work, but rather for a characteristic type of story, set in her native Sardinia, that explores local customs and passions. Praised for her descrip-tions of primitive and exotic Sardinia, Deledda interwove por-trayals of native customs with the plot; in fact, these customs often produce the central conflict of the narrative. She also portrayed the deeply religious nature of Sardinian life, which combined a strong Catholicism with superstitions that had ex-isted on the island before its people had been introduced to Christianity. While Deledda's descriptions of Sardinia and its people have been widely admired, her primary strength, ac-cording to critics, lies in her ability to evoke the passions and personalities of her characters, particularly as they react to the pressures of love, duty, guilt, suffering, and tragedy. While Deledda's characters all exhibit a common Sardinian spirit, each one remains unique, rather than becoming merely a rep-resentative of a type.

One central conflict is consistent throughout most of Deledda's stories: the problem of love that is frustrated and unfulfilled because of social conventions or religious dogmas. Whether Deledda's lovers try to repress their feelings and remain so-cially respectable or attempt to defy the conventions that sep-arate them, the result is always pain and anguish. In many of her stories and novels, Deledda followed a consistent pattern of development: after establishing the love relationship of two characters, she portrays a period of denial of emotion and submission to social expectations that soon becomes untenable and is followed by a progression of sin, suffering, and expia-tion. An early novel, *Elias Portolu,* aptly illustrates this pat-tern: Elias Portolu, jailed for a crime of which he is innocent, returns home to Sardinia upon his release. He falls in love with his brother Pietro's fiancée, Maddalena Scale, who returns his love, but social customs prohibit the two from marrying. Pietro and Maddalena marry, but Elias remains near, and ultimately he and Maddalena commit adultery. Overcome with guilt, Elias enters a seminary in preparation for the priesthood. Before he is ordained, however, his brother unexpectedly dies; according to Sardinian tradition Elias can now marry Maddalena to pro-vide for her and her child, Berte, who is in fact Elias's own. Elias rejects this course, fearing public disapproval if he aban-dons his plans for the priesthood. Eventually Maddalena re-marries, and Berte dies in infancy; as Elias prepares the child's body for burial, he realizes he was wrong to relinquish his chance to marry. His life now determined by his vows, he has no choice but to accept his lot. Thus, Deledda most often portrayed expiation as coming in the form of stoic acceptance, and in her works the struggle between passion and duty is always won by duty.

Deledda consistently used this tension between traditional morality and individual passion to create her stories of tragic love against the backdrop of Sardinian life. Though some critics dismiss her as a regionalist or a formula writer, she has ardent defenders who praise the beauty and emotionally evocative quality of her work, particularly the realistic detail and sensitive portrayals of her characters. Today Deledda remains one of the most popular novelists in Italian literature.

PRINCIPAL WORKS

Nell' azzurro! . . . (short stories) 1890
Fior di Sardegna (novel) 1891
Racconti sardi (short stories) 1894
Anime oneste (novel) 1895
Il vecchio della montagna (novel) 1900
Dopo il divorzio (novel) 1902
   [*After the Divorce*, 1905]
Elias Portolu (novel) 1903
Cenere (novel) 1904
   [*Ashes*, 1908]
Nostalgie (novel) 1905
   [*Nostalgia*, 1905]
La via del male (novel) 1906
L'edera (novel) 1908
Il nostro padrone (novel) 1910
Sino al confine (novel) 1910
Colombi e sparvieri (novel) 1912
Canne al vento (novel) 1913
Le colpe altrui (novel) 1914
Marianna Sirca (novel) 1915
L'incendio nell' oliveto (novel) 1918
La madre (novel) 1920
   [*The Woman and the Priest*, 1922; also published as *The
    Mother*, 1923]
Il secreto dell'uomo solitario (novel) 1921
Il Dio dei viventi (novel) 1922
La fuga in Egitto (novel) 1925
Annalena Bilsini (novel) 1928
Il vecchio e i fanciulli (novel) 1929
Cosima (novel) 1937
Tutte le Opere. 4 vols. (novels and short stories) 1941-55

MAY BATEMAN (essay date 1904)

[*In the following excerpt, Bateman discusses Deledda's early work.*]

Grazia Deledda was the first, the only woman writer in an island whose primitive and simple habits made its inhabitants look upon the least deviation from accustomed courses with suspicion.

It has been said of Grazia Deledda that she shows but one side of her people—that another and an equally faithful Sardinian writer might depict the island from a different aspect, and never touch upon her themes. Yet the sincerity of her work is the

first quality which strikes us—therein lies her strength, her vigour in portraiture. Holding a mirror towards certain scenes, she shows their surroundings and their human interest. She turns the mirror towards them and away from herself, and so escapes the least reflection of her own image. . . . The leading actors in la Deledda's dramas are men and women of the people—a reason why she has been compared to Maxim Gorky. They are seldom, if ever, off the stage—other personages are purely subsidiary though characteristic. No side issues are allowed for a moment to lessen the value of the main theme. This may be consummate art; or, again, the purest simplicity. A Sardinian of Sardinia, Mme. Deledda is the voice of a people primitive and sincere even in their sins; her methods are consequently direct. She does not seek her stories—they seek her. Truth is to them what steam is to an engine—without it, they would not move. The reader never stops to ask himself why this is, or why that—granted the cause, the effects are inexorable. Each story is a circle: it comes back to the point from which it started, and joins neatly. (p. 616)

Grazia Deledda is barely thirty, and already famous. She has been widely translated and widely acclaimed. Her work appears serially not only in the leading reviews of Italy, but of France. Even our colder northern nation feels her power.

What of her future? Will her quick fame content her or will she rise even to better things? Some say that no great book was ever written, nor any great work done, by any but the truly great "mighty in mind, mighty in heart," as Ruskin has it. The writer needs a firmer faith in "the good, the beautiful, the true" than his fellow-men, since upon his own bruised wings he has to lift so many crippled beings to the skies. But the foremost Italian critic, Ruggero Bonghi, divined in Grazia Deledda this immortal power, and wrote thus to the young author, who was known to him only by her work:—

"You believe in this trinity, and you must continue to believe in it, unless you would have life bare and void of significance and aim, of harmony and hope. . . . The souls you paint are tender and honest, because of the tenderness and honesty of your own soul."

In her success we feel that Mme. Deledda must often turn to a letter, which takes an added pathos because it was the last that the dying critic ever wrote:—

"Farewell, dear child, and while you live remember the words of a tired old man, for whom twilight smiles while the dawn smiles for you." (p. 622)

        *May Bateman, "Grazia Deledda and 'Cenere'," in
        The Fortnightly Review, n.s. Vol. LXXVI, No. CDLIV,
        October 1, 1904, pp. 615-22.*

THE NATION (essay date 1908)

[*In the following excerpt, the critic reviews* Ashes.]

Sardinia is the scene of *Ashes (Cenere)*, the latest of Grazia Deledda's novels to be translated into English; and in it she paints the beauties and desolations of that island, and the characteristics of its primitive people with her usual vivid touch. It is in these things rather than in the conduct of her narrative that Grazia Deledda's power lies, and most readers will feel that the story wanders through its fascinating setting too slowly, with too many dreamy pauses and backward looks.

We start life with the hero at his birth, and in spite of the disproportionate minuteness with which certain stages of his development are traced, he holds our interest and sympathy throughout the story. Of peasant origin, and a foundling, he grows up ardent, ambitious, and idealistic, the two great aims of his life being to win a position which shall enable him to marry his patron's daughter, and to find and reclaim the mother who had deserted him in his childhood. The conflict of these aims makes up the drama of *Ashes*. The interest of the love-story is decidedly subordinate to that of Anania's relation to his mother, both before and after their tragic meeting in the mountain hut. This meeting is the great scene of the story—a scene of much dramatic power and truth, with touches of high imagination. The characters immediately surrounding Anania are, with the exception of the girl he loves, well-drawn and vital, but there is an outer circle of shadowy peasants whose talk is so lacking in the pith and humor of Hardy's rustics and of our own rural types that we can but feel it as a tiresome interruption. (pp. 579-80)

A review of "Ashes," in The Nation, *Vol. LXXXVI, No. 2243, June 25, 1908, pp. 579-80.*

THE NEW YORK TIMES BOOK REVIEW (essay date 1923)

[*In the following excerpt, the critic reviews* The Mother.]

It is seldom that a novelist achieves a satisfactory analysis of character coupled with a detailed study of emotional experience without hindering, or at times actually halting, the onward sweep of the essential narrative. Yet such a rare feat seems to have been accomplished by one of Italy's popular present-day writers, Grazia Deledda. Her simple yet powerfully written story, *The Mother,* . . . might profitably be used by the goodly swarm of analytical novelists as something in the line of a copy-book example. For Mme. Deledda never for a moment forgets that she is a storyteller; never forgets that her characters can best explain themselves by their own acts rather than by paragraph after paragraph of interpolated mental stage directions. As a result *The Mother* stands out as a swiftly moving and compelling tale. The story stands out also as a study, but a study far and away removed from the necessity of including page after page of transcribed notes of a college extension course in psychology.

Mme. Deledda places the scene of her story in a tiny Sardinian village similar to that in which she spent her girlhood. Her peasants live in a quiet backwater, as it were, and the great stream of civilization flows by without disturbing them by more than an occasional ripple. The result is that their faith has come to consist of a strange compound of traditional piety coupled with a deep-seated belief in devil-craft, witchcraft and allied superstitions. The story concerns itself chiefly with the young priest of this community, who, coming from the humbler ranks of life and with but a most meagre education, has made his vows while still too young and too unsophisticated to know what he was professing or renouncing. At the age of 28 he feels the stirring of an almost irresistible human passion and falls in love with Agnes, the only gentlewoman among his parishioners. His mother, Maria Madalena, who has slaved for him all his life, and worked as a servant in order that he might achieve the peasant's ambition of becoming a priest, discovers the untoward romance. Mme. Deledda tells the story, as her title, *The Mother,* would imply, chiefly in terms of this poor creature's emotional reactions to the situation. One may say at once that nothing in the book can be construed as offensive to any creed or form of Church government. The author has simply presented an intensely human problem, and has striven

to picture the distress of primitive piety and primitive passion in conflict with man-made laws.

The novel's main characters appear clear cut and well defined. Paul, the young priest, caught in a conflict between duty and desire, strikes one as a singularly appealing figure. But it is to the mother that the reader's sympathies are chiefly drawn. The poor woman finds herself pulled in diverse directions. Her mother's heart yearns for the mental peace and happiness of her son; her pious peasant soul fears in that son, as priest, the slightest transgression of the Church's laws. As a touch of brightness to relieve the shadows covering most of her canvas, the author gives us a wholly charming boy character in the person of Antiochus, the young sacristan. The depicting of this lad, at once the mischievous boy and sub-ecclesiastic—full of the devilment of his rambunctious youth and also of the elevation of his high office as assistant at the sanctuary—remains in the memory as a thoroughly sound study of boy psychology. The delineating of the lad's shy hero worship for the young priest is most deftly accomplished.

But all this insight and interpretation have been worked so skillfully into the actual narrative that the unfolding of the little drama moves on with an unchecked precision. By exquisite workmanship and a fine clarity of purpose Mme. Deledda has given to *The Mother* an almost epic air of inevitability.

A review of "The Mother," in The New York Times Book Review, *December 2, 1923, p. 8.*

D. H. LAWRENCE (essay date 1928)

[*Lawrence was an English novelist, poet, and essayist who is noted for his introduction of the themes of modern psychology to English fiction. In his lifetime he was a controversial figure, both for the explicit sexuality he portrayed in his novels and for his unconventional personal life. Much of the criticism of Lawrence's work concerns his highly individualistic moral system, which was based on absolute freedom of expression, particularly sexual expression. Human sexuality was for Lawrence a symbol of the Life Force, and is frequently pitted against modern industrial society, which he believed was dehumanizing. His most famous novel,* Lady Chatterley's Lover *(1928), was the subject of a landmark obscenity trial in Great Britain in 1960, which turned largely on the legitimacy of Lawrence's inclusion of hitherto forbidden sexual terms. In the following excerpt, Lawrence discusses the theme of frustrated human instinct in* The Mother.]

[Although Deledda] is not a first-class genius, she belongs to more than just her own day. She does more than reproduce the temporary psychological condition of her period. She has a background, and she deals with something more fundamental than sophisticated feeling. She does not penetrate, as a great genius does, the very sources of human passion and motive. She stays far short of that. But what she does do is to create the passionate complex of a primitive populace.

To do this, one must have an isolated populace: just as Thomas Hardy isolates Wessex. Grazia Deledda has an island to herself, her own island of Sardinia, that she loves so deeply: especially the more northerly, mountainous part of Sardinia.

Still Sardinia is one of the wildest, remotest parts of Europe, with a strange people and a mysterious past of its own. There is still an old mystery in the air, over the forest slopes of Mount Gennargentu, as there is over some old Druid places, the mystery of an unevolved people. The war, of course, partly gutted Sardinia, as it gutted everywhere. But the island is still a good deal off the map, on the face of the earth.

An island of rigid conventions, the rigid conventions of bar-barism, and at the same time the fierce violence of the instinctive passions. A savage tradition of chastity, with a savage lust of the flesh. A barbaric overlordship of the gentry, with a fierce indomitableness of the servile classes. A lack of public opinion, a lack of belonging to any other part of the world, a lack of mental awakening, which makes inland Sardinia almost as savage as Benin, and makes Sardinian singing as wonderful and almost as wild as any on earth. It is the human instinct still uncontaminated. The money-sway still did not govern central Sardinia, in the days of Grazia Deledda's books, twenty, a dozen years ago, before the war. Instead, there was a savage kind of aristocracy and feudalism, and a rule of ancient instinct, instinct with the definite but indescribable tang of the aboriginal people of the island, not absorbed into the world: instinct often at war with the Italian Government; a determined, savage individualism often breaking with the law, or driven into brigandage: but human, of the great human mystery.

It is this old Sardinia, at last being brought to heel, which is the real theme of Grazia Deledda's books. She is fascinated by her island and its folks, more than by the problems of the human psyche. And therefore this book, *The Mother,* is perhaps one of the least typical of her novels, one of the most "Continental." Because here, she has a definite universal theme: the consecrated priest and the woman. But she keeps on forgetting her theme. She becomes more interested in the death of the old hunter, in the doings of the boy Antiochus, in the exorcising of the spirit from the little girl possessed. She is herself somewhat bored by the priest's hesitations; she shows herself suddenly impatient, a pagan sceptical of the virtues of chastity, even in consecrated priests; she is touched, yet annoyed, by the pathetic, tiresome old mother who made her son a priest out of ambition, and who simply expires in the terror of a public exposure: and, in short, she makes a bit of a mess of the book, because she started a problem she didn't quite dare to solve. She shirks the issue atrociously. But neither will the modern spirit solve the problem by killing off the fierce instincts that made the problem. As for Grazia Deledda, first she started by sympathising with the mother, and then must sympathise savagely with the young woman, and then can't make up her mind. She kills off the old mother in disgust at the old woman's triumph, so leaving the priest and the young woman hanging in space. As a sort of problem-story, it is disappointing. No doubt, if the priest had gone off with the woman, as he first intended, then all the authoress's sympathy would have fallen to the old abandoned mother. As it is, the sympathy falls between two stools, and the title *La Madre* is not really justified. The mother turns out not to be the heroine.

But the interest of the book lies, not in plot or characterisation, but in the presentation of sheer instinctive life. The love of the priest for the woman is sheer instinctive passion, pure and undefiled by sentiment. As such it is worthy of respect, for in other books on this theme the instinct is swamped and extinguished in sentiment. Here, however, the instinct of direct sex is so strong and so vivid, that only the other blind instinct of mother-obedience, the child-instinct, can overcome it. All the priest's education and Christianity are really mere snuff of the candle. The old, wild instinct of a mother's ambition for her son defeats the other wild instinct of sexual mating. An old woman who has never had any sex-life—and it is astonishing, in barbaric half-civilisation, how many people are denied a sex-life—she succeeds, by her old barbaric maternal power over her son, in finally killing his sex-life too. It is the suicide

of semi-barbaric natures under the sway of a dimly comprehended Christianity, and falsely conceived ambition.

The old, blind life of instinct, and chiefly frustrated instinct and the rage thereof, as it is seen in the Sardinian hinterland, this is Grazia Deledda's absorption. The desire of the boy Antiochus to be a priest is an instinct: perhaps an instinctive recoil from his mother's grim priapism. The dying man escapes from the village, back to the rocks, instinctively needing to die in the wilds. The feeling of Agnes, the woman who loves the priest, is sheer female instinctive passion, something as in Emily Brontë. It too has the ferocity of frustrated instinct, and is bare and stark, lacking any of the graces of sentiment. This saves it from "dating" as d'Annunzio's passions date. Sardinia is by no means a land for Romeos and Juliets, nor even Virgins of the Rocks. It is rather the land of *Wuthering Heights*.

The book, of course, loses a good deal in translation, as is inevitable. In the mouths of the simple people, Italian is a purely instinctive language, with the rhythm of instinctive rather than mental processes. There are also many instinct-words with meanings never clearly mentally defined. In fact, nothing is brought to real mental clearness, everything goes by in a stream of more or less vague, more or less realised, feeling, with a natural mist or glow of sensation over everything, that counts more than the actual words said; and which, alas, it is almost impossible to reproduce in the more cut-and-dried northern languages, where every word has its fixed value and meaning, like so much coinage. A language can be killed by over-precision, killed especially as an effective medium for the conveyance of instinctive passion and instinctive emotion. One feels this, reading a translation from the Italian. And though Grazia Deledda is not masterly as Giovanni Verga is, yet, in Italian at least, she can put us into the mood and rhythm of Sardinia, like a true artist, an artist whose work is sound and enduring. (pp. 292-95)

> *D. H. Lawrence, "Preface to 'The Mother' (De-ledda)," in his* Selected Literary Criticism, *edited by Anthony Beal, The Viking Press, 1956, pp. 291-95.*

JOHN MIFSUD (essay date 1928)

[In the following excerpt, Mifsud discusses Ashes *and* L'edera.]

Grazia Deledda is to-day an author of many years' standing. She was acclaimed in Italy as a novelist of distinction more than twenty-five years ago; her output has been large, and last year was published *La Fuga in Egitto.* Many people in this country and in France have more than a nodding acquaintance with her work, either through reading it in the original or through the medium of translations. She is a writer of considerable dramatic power, exact and logical in the delineation of her characters; and along with these qualities there is a third—a remarkable power of description. People, places and scenes are drawn with great clarity and skill. For many of her novels she has chosen as a setting the wooded island of her birth. This is the case with *Cenere* (of which there is an excellent translation under the title, *Ashes*) and *L'edera.*

It is, I think, when she is writing of Sardinia and its people—who are hers—that she is at her best. And her best is a fine thing; her prose, which has many graces, has at times a poetic ring. The Sardinian scenes are so well depicted, so faithful, that the reader is projected into the daily lives of those who dwell in one or other of the smaller towns or villages. It is, of course, life under the patriarchal system with that strange intimacy of soul between members of the household, so alien to our own, that is lived there, or was lived there, not so long since. And one may suppose that in Sardinia customs change slowly and that to-day life does not differ greatly from that of one or two decades ago. And it is a life of primitive simplicity in which the very soil seems alive and imbued with a personality for good or evil.

Again and again Grazia Deledda has received unstinted praise for her skilful delineation of character and for the idealism which informs all her work. But it is seldom that she lets her "fancies run in soft luxuriant flow," and wit and humour are not generally to be sought for.

Cenere is a tragic and terrible story, the central idea in which is the search by an illegitimate son for a mother who has abandoned him in order to lead her own life which is not of the best. The story opens with the seduction of Oli, the mother, by a young workman. "Oli at this time is fifteen, with very large, very bright, feline eyes of greenish grey, and a sensuous mouth of which the cleft lower lip suggested two ripe cherries." The two young people meet in the country for their love-making; nor could they have met in a place more suited to their purpose. "The mountains were grey as if dried by the sun, the dark woods flecked with light. The sun had warmed the grass and waked sparkles in the streamlets; a little bird cried in the silence of the hour and place." Small wonder that they were romantic and filled with pretty superstitions.

He: "I've got to pick the pennyroyal to-night; have you forgotten it's midsummer eve? If you strew leaves of laurel here and there round the wall of a vineyard or a sheepfold, no wild animal can get in to gnaw the grapes or to carry off the lambs."

"Not till autumn did Micheli perceive that his daughter had gone wrong." When he does, he thrusts her out bag and baggage. She disappears from the scene, leads a nomadic life with a blind singer, and is seen at country festas. As for the love-child, her son, he is mothered by a bandit's widow, "who hushes him to sleep with the melancholy wail of strange dirges telling the heroic deeds of her bandit." This was the bandit who, if I remember rightly, had a silver nose as the result of a contact with the authorities. The boy grows up, falls in love with Margherita, and is frequently invited to the padrone's to dinner, but in the kitchen with the servants and the cats. In a home such as this: "they took their supper seated on the floor with meat and cakes in a basket before them. The kitchen was poor and dark but very clean. The walls were adorned with trenchers and hunting spears, with great baskets and other utensils for sifting flour." ... "A baby pig tied to the elder tree in the courtyard grunted gently, puffed and sighed. A red cat quietly placed himself by the little table and yawned, raising great yellow eyes to Anania."

The youth goes to the village school, distinguishes himself; the padrone watches his progress with approval; Margherita shall be his one day. And then—driven by the irresistible urge, not of love, but of duty, the young man begins the search for Oli, his mother. "You want to sacrifice yourself and ruin me, only for the glory of saying I've done my duty," Margherita says to her lover, and there is the final breach between them. At long last, Anania discovers his mother; the meeting between the two is an unforgettable scene which is really splendid in its horror:

> It was really she; this pale and emaciated creature, half seen through the dark window of the brothel. Her face was ashen grey, the great

luminous eyes, blue from weakness and fear, seemed like those of a sickly wild cat.

There is conflict in the son's mind; his wish to be rid of this woman and to return to his love, while Oli herself urges him to let her go. "You are going to marry a girl who is beautiful and who is rich, and if she knows you haven't cast me off you'll lose her," she tells him. He lets her leave him, and then, when it is too late, he hastens after her. The last scene, which depicts the suicide of Oli, is more terrible than the death of Emma Bovary:

> Upon the bed where he himself had slept, the outline of her body showed under the sheet which covered it. The bandage around her neck stained with dark blood, which passed under her chin and over ears was knotted against the thick black hair of the dead woman.

But the son still has youth before him and the tragic story ends on a note of hope.

Nostalgia and *The Woman and the Priest*—there are English translations of these books—make rather tedious reading.

Nostalgia mainly because it is the study of the modern woman of 1904; *The Woman and the Priest* because I happened to be re-reading *La Faute de l'Abbé Mouret* and the former will not stand the test of comparison. And perhaps it is unfair to make it at all. *L'edera,* however, is another matter. This book is fine drama; it was adapted for the stage and produced at the Teatro Argentini, Rome, in 1909. The action takes place in Sardinia. One would much like to see this three-act drama presented on the English stage. The central figure in the story which deals with the life of the Decherchis, a noble Sardinian family, is Annesa, the maid, who has been adopted as a child of three years old. She was found by the side of an old blind beggar, who has died on the roadside. After seeing Annesa for the first time one may predicate many things about her. The Decherchi household, which has fallen on evil days, consists of Don Simone, the head of the family; Ziu Cosimu, his brother, Donna Rachele, daughter of Ziu Cosimu, a widow, with a son, Don Paulu; Gantine, an illegitimate son of Rachele's dead husband, and Annesa, the maid. Owing to the extravagance of Don Paulu (a widower who has a sickly daughter, Rosa) the family are so poor that they take to live with them an old, miserly relation, Zio Zua (who keeps his money beneath his pillow), with the idea that he shall leave his money to Rosa when he dies. The old man, a tiresome and garrulous creature who has lost a leg in the Crimean War, is always bemoaning his fate, and infuriating Annesa with his attacks on Don Paulu, who is her lover. Shortly after becoming a member of the household, Zio Zua has a stroke and becomes paralysed and bedridden. And as he is asthmatical as well, someone, usually Annesa, sleeps on the sofa in his room. At this time she is young, impetuous, passionate, and engaged to Gantine whom she does not love; she is persistently pestered with his attentions.

The characters of the three old men, Don Simone, Don Cosimu, and Zio Zua—they are known as the three Magi with the five legs—are skilfully drawn, and the description of the old house and life within its walls is admirable.

The Decheichis have from time to time sold nearly all their land to pay the debts of Don Paulu. The only way in which affairs can be straightened out is by raising money from moneylenders, or by the death of Zio Zua.

Don Paulu, from time to time, makes journeys for the purpose of borrowing the money. During his absence Annesa is left in charge of the old invalid.

Outside the thunder peals, vivid flashes of lightning pierce the darkness of the room, lit only by a flickering candle. Annesa is reading a letter from her lover: "I don't know when I shall be able to return." She sits with her head between her hands. Suddenly the querulous voice of the old man breaks in upon her thoughts at the moment when she hears horse's hoofs.

> ZIO ZUA. Get me some water.
> (*Can it be Paulu? No, the sound is dying away.*)
> ZIO ZUA. It isn't he: useless to expect him, my pretty one, your gay fellow isn't coming back to you.
> ANNESA. (*In a fury*) What's that you say?
> ZIO ZUA. I tell you it's better not to think of him, he's not thinking of you.
> ANNESA. (*Threateningly*) Keep quiet, you old villain. (*She runs towards the bed as she speaks.*)
> ZIO ZUA. Help! Help!

Annesa, frightened, makes signs to silence him, but he continues shouting. Mad with fright she seizes the coverlet, and running towards the bed presses it down on the old man's face. "Keep quiet, for ever."

There is a brief convulsion beneath the coverlet, then all is still. . . .

At this moment, when Annesa is looking beneath the pillow for the money, a step is heard outside the door. Paulu has returned, tired from his journey, but in the best of spirits. There, with the victim lying on the bed in the next room, Paulu, unconscious of what has happened, presses his love, tells Annesa that he has obtained the money to set right the family fortunes. He has work and begs her to go with him. She refuses, flees the house and hides in a grotto with an old shepherd. The police arrive, arrest the members of the household; an enquiry is held and the doctor certifies that the old man died from an attack of asthma.

Meanwhile Annesa is away. A priest has found her work in another family. The master tries to seduce her, the mistress treats her cruelly. The years roll on. The old men are long since dead, the young have grown old. Rosa the invalid lingers on; Donna Rachele continues to spend most of her time at her prayers. One day at a festa, the mistress sees her old servant and asks her to return. And Annesa—the ivy—it is she who gives the title to the story, comes once again to the old house and marries Paulu. But what a dolorous affair it is; their emotions are dried up, the zest for life has gone.

> To-morrow Annesa will have a name. She will be called Annesa Decherchi. Everything is ready for the humble and melancholy wedding. Annesa has prepared all; and now sits weary, on the door-step. She is thinking—or perhaps not thinking but feeling, that her real penance, her real work of charity has at last begun. To-morrow, she will be called Annesa Decherchi; the ivy will once again cling to the tree, and cover it mercifully with its leaves; mercifully, because now the old trunk is dead.

To the novels must be added various short stories which are not lacking in charm, such as **"Il Nonno,"** "Solitudine" and **"Il Ritorno del Figlio."**

One may hazard the prediction that many of these novels will live as faithful pictures of Sardinian life as it was, perhaps indeed as it is to-day. (pp. 623-24)

John Mifsud, "The Latest Nobel Prize Winner," in New Statesman, *Vol. XXX, No. 774, February 25, 1928, pp. 623-24.*

L. COLLISON-MORLEY (essay date 1928)

[*In the following excerpt, Collison-Morley discusses prominent characteristics of Deledda's fiction.*]

The award of the Nobel Prize for literature to Grazia Deledda, the only Italian to receive it except Carducci, makes the present a fitting moment for reviewing her work. As she already has some thirty volumes to her credit it is unlikely that anything she may do in the future will materially alter her position. . . . [To] quote an Italian proverb, she came like the cheese on the macaroni. The regional, realistic movement, which looked to the Sicilians, Verga and Capuana, as its founders, was well under weigh. Sardinia, at that time probably the least known part of Italy, lacked its novelist, and this young writer brought to her task talents of no mean order.

First and foremost she could tell a story, a gift which is not especially common among Italians, to whom the *novella* seems a more natural means of expression than the novel. She is a novelist, a story-teller before all things, and her short stories, such as the **Conti Sardi,** are distinctly inferior to her novels. As a writer of *novelle* she cannot compare with Verga or even with Pirandello or Matilde Serao. Here again she would seem to be a daughter of her own island, where the art of the *cantastorie* held its own as a profession, as it did also in Sicily, till it was killed by the spread of education and the growth of the habit of reading. Her own father had a considerable reputation as a poet in the dialect.

Grazia Deledda was born just when the old medieval life, which lasted to within living memory in the remoter districts of Italy, was breaking down before the advance of the modern world, much as the forests were vanishing from the mountains before the "speculatore" and his charcoal-burners, so well described in **Il Nostro Padrone.** In this transition period she passed her impressionable young days. The discussion in **Sino al Confine,** as to whether Gavina on leaving school is to dress in national costume, must have taken place in the families of many of her friends. And something of the atmosphere of the popular story-teller seems to pervade her novels with their pictures of the life of a primitive people, whose passions are violent and elemental, their virtues and vices almost those of patriarchal days. Blood feuds between families have lasted for generations, as we learn from **Colombi e Sparvieri.**

She has made this primitive world so completely her own, it is so much a part of herself, that for her it becomes genuine tragedy. Only in an occasional tendency to twist her stories into happy endings does she seem to make concessions to popular taste. Of this world the brigand is the most striking figure. In the story of the widow of a bandit who perished in a raid, Deledda explains the popular attitude:—

> Then you think brigands are bad men? You are wrong, *sorella mia.* They are men who feel the need of displaying their prowess, that is all. My husband used to say, "Once upon a time men went to war. Now there are no more wars, but men must still fight, so they organize raids

and *bardane,* not with the intention of doing harm, but merely to show their strength and their pluck."

(pp. 353-54)

The old servant, Zia Fidè, tells the story of a bandit raid on a wealthy couple when the cruelty of the brigands so terrified her that from that day she ceased to be a woman from shock, a climax which always sent her young mistress into fits of laughter.

This rough, racy peasant humour, which Grazia Deledda has obviously caught from the life around her, is the only relief of the kind she allows herself in some of the best of her novels. The suddenness with which it flashes out is almost disconcerting in its effect. We have heard young Italians speak with dislike of the gloomy, Nordic character of her books, and she has been compared to the Russians. There is little of the brightness of the south about them. Fate seems to brood over them as does the mountain Orthobene over Nuoro. Nature too is no mere setting, but in close relation with man and his moods, as for instance in *Il Vecchio della Montagna;* and her leading characters are haunted by a dream world, which is as real to them as the world in which they live, and seems to deepen the mystery of existence.

Nor is it possible to escape the consequences of sin. Predu Maria in *Il Nostro Padrone* is convinced that in being forced into marrying the pretty, frivolous Sebastiana instead of Marielena, to whom he had been engaged, he is being punished for murdering his stepfather. Annessa feels during the beautiful scene in the tiny mountain chapel in *L'Edera,* where the sacristan has to ring the bell right through Mass to drive off the mice of which the old priest is so afraid, that the decision of the doctors that Zio Zuà died a natural death is a proof that her murder had been forgiven. But she must expiate her crime, as well as her guilty love for Paolo, by the terrible years she will spend with him and his degenerate daughter, when his dissipated life has produced the inevitable consequences; for drink plays havoc among these idle young land-owners. (pp. 355-56)

The subject of an old and respected family on the verge of ruin is a favourite one with Grazia Deledda. In *L'Edera* we find Don Paola is desperate straits to save his family which has been brought to the verge of ruin by his extravagance. His riding round the fairs, as he had been wont to do in his youth for pleasure, staying at the houses of friends (for the rite of hospitality is sacred in the island) gives opportunity for some admirable pictures of the life of these Sardinian land-owners, and we see the quantities of meat and bread prepared for a shepherd's feast. At home, Zia Rachele joyously and conscientiously prepares the dinner for the poor, who must be served on silver by herself, in accordance with a duty laid on the succession of the estate, the very day before the crash. Annessa's love for Paolo is as passionate as that of Marianna. It drives her to strangle the rich uncle who alone could save the family just when he had been induced by the priest to buy the house and pay the creditors. Clearly Annessa, "pilu brundu," as her lover calls her in the dialect, is a favourite with her creator. The portrait displays Deledda's powers of detailed observation, which adds so much to the vividness of her work.

> She was small and slender: she looked like a child. The lamplight threw a tint of gilded bronze on to her round, olive-coloured face, while the dimple on the chin increased its almost babyish

grace. But the mouth, a little large, with its brilliantly white, close, even teeth, wore a slightly mocking, cruel expression. The blue eyes, on the contrary, under the great dark eyebrows were gentle and sad. There was something contemptuous and soft, too; the smile of an evil old woman and the glance of a sad child were in the face of this silent and delicate servant, whose head bent backwards, as if drawn by the weight of an enormous plait of bright, fair hair twisted on her neck. The long neck, less dark than the face, stood out bare from the collarless blouse: the bodice of the country shut in a tiny breast; and the whole was graceful, active, youthful, bewitching; the long, skinny hands alone betrayed her mature age.

Thoroughly real though Deledda's characters are, one feels sometimes that these books are rather portions of a great popular frieze or even film of Sardinia, of which they give so varied a picture, than individual works of art. She is drawing on the vast store of her impressions and emotions which flow naturally into the mould of a novel.

Imprisonment is regarded as little more than a piece of bad luck in this Sardinian world. Elias, in *Elias Portolu,* is welcomed home by his family and friends after a term as a convict, much as he might be after a long illness, with the wish that a similar "disgrazia" may befall him a hundred years hence. His stories of prison life are listened to with the profoundest interest, for in a community where the bandit is the hero a great criminal also has his halo. The book contains a delightful picture of a pilgrimage to the church of S. Francesco, high up in the mountains, where all the families of the "tribe" of the founder have their own places and hearthstones in the great barn, as they have had since the days of its institution. The story is again one of temptation, of Elias' love for his brother's betrothed—temptation which, as a wise old man puts it, may let you go as a cat does a mouse, but catches you surely in the end; and to escape it Elias becomes a priest.

Naturally pictures of Sardinian scenery abound, usually tinged with Grazia Deledda's own melancholy. They are generally night scenes. Here is a view from the window of the cottage at the sheepfold in *Marianna Sirca.* There is a touch of D'Annunzio about it, as there is in other descriptions in this book.

> She saw the tree in the middle of the clearing and the dogs asleep in the shade: and beyond the two wings of the wood—that of the ilexes bright, that of the corks dark; and between the two wings the vastness of the distance lit up by the rising moon, while the mountains began to appear in outline as if advancing across a quivering veil of light.
>
> First was the mountain of Oliena, white, made of air; then the mountains of Dorgali to the right and those of Nuoro on the left, blue and black; and suddenly the whole horizon appeared to blossom with golden clouds. It was the moon rising. Suddenly over the veil of gold that stretched from the mountains to the Sarsa there seemed to spread a second veil, a net of pearls that shimmered over all things and made them more lovely, more alive in the dream. The forest laughed in the night, yet the leaves that fell

from the ilexes were like tears. It was the night-ingales that were singing.

Grazia Deledda's first successful novel was *Anime Oneste,* written when she was twenty. Round it clings a youthful fresh-ness and directness that distinguishes it from all her others. There is not a trace of the later melancholy. The life of this gay family of young people is drawn with a firmness and a sureness that leave no doubt as to the gifts of the writer, and the book displays the simplicity and sincerity that characterize all her work. We have the clever son, who squanders large sums in playing the fool while working to get a degree in law and is glad in the end to take a small mastership, contrasted with his brother, Sebastiano, who carries on his father's farm and even develops an uncultivated *tanca,* one of the open pastures which figure so largely in these Sardinian tales. The girls are all busy husband-hunting. Obviously she is describing her own young life in Nuoro. The picnic celebrating the cutting of the oakwood of little cousin Anna, whom Sebastiano mar-ries, must surely be a personal reminiscence.

Though Grazia Deledda sympathizes with Sebastiano, she her-self married into the intelligentsia and went to settle in Rome. It was here, in exile, that her most important work was done. The homesickness which the best Italians seem to feel for their own provinces comes out in such a passage as this:—

> Oh, the pale nights in the lonely solitudes of Sardinia! The quivering hoot of the owl, the wild fragrance of the thyme, the pungent odour of the lentisc, the distant moaning of the lonely woods unite in a harmony monotonous and mel-ancholy, as a feeling of awed sadness steals over the soul, a longing for things long past and pure.

Cenere is, on the whole, the best of the early novels. Nowhere does she give a better picture of Nuoro and its inhabitants than in this story of the growing to manhood of the son of the beggar woman, Olì, and his friends. It has much of the brightness of *Anime Oneste,* but is overshadowed by Anania's search for his mother and the tragedy and disillusion that follow the finding of her. This is symbolized by the little bag she hung round his neck, when she ran away from the brigand's widow at Fonni, which proves to contain nothing but ashes. The district soon becomes familiar to the reader, especially the road up the valley from Nuoro to Fonni by Mamojada. Mamojada appears

> . . . coming out from among the green of the gardens and the walnuts, with the bright church tower silhouetted against the soft blue of the sky; at a distance the picture had the delicate tints of a water-colour, but as soon as the post went on its way up the dusty road, the profile of the village took on gloomy hues, even stron-ger than those of the landscape. Outside the black houses built on the rock were grouped typical figures of peasants; graceful women with their glossy hair twisted round their ears, bare-footed, seated on the ground, were sewing, or suckling their babies, or embroidering. A cou-ple of *carabinieri,* a student, an old noble who was also a peasant, were gossiping in front of a carpenter's shop, round the door of which hung a number of sacred pictures painted in brilliant colours.

Whatever the cause, the war marked a sudden and notable advance in Grazia Deledda's art. *Marianna Sirca* was the first book to show the change; but in *L'Incendio nell' Oliveto* there is an intensity, a profound and all-pervading sense of tragedy, a sternness that is almost puritanical, as in the figure of the aged grandmother who dominates her family from her chair. The story stands by itself as a distinct whole; it is not a part of a picture of Sardinian life. Above all there is a deepening of the religious feeling which becomes more spiritual in char-acter.

But it is in *La Madre* that Deledda reaches her high watermark as an artist. Here for once all her qualities are successfully blended. The scene is laid in a remote Sardinian village, where Paolo has come to succeed a wicked old priest who lived a roystering life with the worst of his parishioners. But the story transcends all local colour and stands out as a real human tragedy, though the pictures of local life, as in the old dying hunter with his tame eagle hovering over him, are as good as any she has done. The action takes but a couple of days. The English translator calls the book *The Woman and the Priest,* but this gets the focus wrong. It is a struggle between the mother and the pretty, wealthy widow, Annessa, for the young priest whom she has infatuated, while through it runs an eerie feeling that the spirit of Paolo's predecessor is striving to drive the mother and the son from the village in order to recover his power. Annessa declares she will denounce Paolo from the altar unless he flies with her that night. He refuses, and the mother triumphs, but at the cost of her life, for, just as Annessa is advancing to fulfil her purpose something overwhelms her and she sinks in prayer, only to find as she leaves the church her lover's mother dead in her seat. (pp. 356-60)

> L. Collison-Morley, "The Novels of Grazia De-ledda," *in* The Edinburgh Review, *Vol. CCXLVII, No. DIV, April, 1928, pp. 353-60.*

DOMENICO VITTORINI (essay date 1930)

[*In the following excerpt, Vittorini discusses Deledda's literary development, the theme of love in her work, and her place among the Italian Naturalist writers.*]

Grazia Deledda is one of the outstanding writers of today. She made her entrance into the world of letters in the early Nineties, at a time when Giovanni Verga had raised the provincial novel to the height of great art. She took Verga's theme—the study of Sicily's country life—and transported it to Sardinia, her native island. Deledda loves the austere beauty of the rocky landscape, its silent and passionate inhabitants, its deeply rooted family traditions and ties, its picturesque customs that throw vivid spots of color in her novels. Sardinia forms, in fact, the background of almost all of Deledda's production. The fore-ground is occupied by the creations of her fancy, modeled after the people of the rocky island. Her characters are passionate, just as Verga's are born to toil in silence and to suffer in sacrifice. They carry in their hearts the precious burden of love, and in it they find the sum of their whole life.

Love is, in fact, the main theme in her work. In *Anime Oneste* (*Honest People*) . . . , her first novel, love appears suffused with an idyllic light, but, soon after, it assumes a new direction, as it is always directed toward a person who, because of social conditions, cannot satisfy it. Drama and tragedy derive from this situation, but they are not determined by the moralizing assumption that punishment follows a misplaced love. Love is, on the contrary, a redemption for these men and women of the solitary plains of Sardinia, as Deledda contends that they are blessed with life because they rely on instinct. In an interview with Alfredo Panzini, the gentle, grey-haired Deledda asked, "Why don't we entrust ourselves to instinct?" The sophisticated Panzini evaded the question.

The fact is that Deledda has remained magnificently naturalistic. She still has a profound faith in the forces of nature and a glowing enthusiasm for the richness and beauty of the earth. The different forces of life live in her spirit in a harmony that is never disturbed by ascetic aspirations or spiritual problems. She considers these aspirations and problems intellectual and arbitrary creations of man. Life, in its fatal unity, does not know how to separate nor isolate. Religious feeling and spirituality, however, live closely interwoven with human passions and they, too, are reduced to a form of instinct. Love, too, assumes in her a cosmic character, as the individual lives in the flux of nature; he is part of it, although rebellious to society and to any external force that may stand between him and nature.

This cosmic unity constitutes the raw material out of which Deledda fashions her novels. She sketches with a hand that is moved by the same passion for life that creates the hunger and thirst of the creatures of her fancy. But little psychological analysis accompanies the actions of her characters, yet we know them like familiar persons. They have passed before Deledda laden with the weight of life, precious and painful, and they now live in the immortality of her art.

Grazia Deledda's production is a perfect sublimation and projection of her own inner life. She has lived exclusively for her art, embodying in it her innermost thoughts, her dreams and moods. We can follow in her novels her growth from a young girl who dreamed life idyllic and pure to a woman who came to know the world and discovered in it the flame that burns in the heart of man.

Grazia Deledda attracted the attention of the literary public with the publication of *Anime Oneste* in 1896. It was a great honor for her to have Ruggero Bonghi, an illustrious scholar, write the preface to her novel. The book reconciled the old dean of Italian letters to modern literature, to which he was very hostile, having denounced it for its superficiality and even emptiness. Bonghi, who, perhaps, had not read Verga, stated that *Anime Oneste* was different from any other novel of the time. It is, on the contrary, a humble and somewhat uncertain continuation of Verga's novels. It has the background of Sardinia, and life is here rendered as it appeared to Deledda at the age of twenty-one, when she looked at the world through serene and limpid eyes, and saw in it only honest people. (pp. 57-9)

[Beauty] and art appeared in the dreams of young Deledda. Only from time to time a strange murmur and a chill wind pass over this idyl. Cesario Velena and his friend, Gonario Rosa, who are studying law in Rome, bring from the continent a disturbing element to humble and honest Sardinia. There follows a struggle, but the theme of the happiness enjoyed by honest people resumes and happily concludes the novel.

After four years, Deledda published *Il vecchio della montagna* (*The Old Man of the Mountain*). . . . One feels that a gust of pessimism has passed over Deledda's spirit. She confesses in this book that "the soul of a woman is a pool in the depth of which slumber monsters that the slightest noise can awaken." The ominous monster is the passion that burns in the heart of the shepherd, Melchiorre, and of his servant, Basilio, for the beautiful and wanton Paska.

The novel contains many references to criminology, a scientific element introduced by both Capuana and Verga as a basis for art. The characters are shepherds and country folk with their picturesque customs. The young artist lingers over the slightest detail and etches out the figures of Paska, Melchiorre, of his blind father, Zio Pietro, and of young Basilio. Naturalistic is also the study of the rudimentary inner life of these characters that is narrowed down to blind passions and to elementary instincts.

The lyric temperament of Deledda, however, was not made for the objectiveness of Naturalism, and this creates a contrast between the primitive characters that she portrays and the poetical feelings that she attributes to them. Basilio, the young servant, becomes at times grotesquely poetical. "He was seized by a violent desire to ride furiously through the plains, sending mad cries to the boundless distances of the horizon tinged with spring hues."

Deledda's return to Naturalism was not in vain. Through it, she learned how to give to her characters a greater concreteness than that possessed by the characters in *Anime Oneste*.

A noteworthy progress in the development of her art was realized in *Dopo il divorzio* (*After the Divorce*). . . . The disturbing contrast between her lyric temperament and the primitiveness of the content is wiped out by the poignant grief of the innocent Costantino Ledda, who is sentenced to twenty-seven years' imprisonment for homicide. His tragedy transforms the passion of the preceding novel into a drama—a drama written with the drops of blood that fall from the heart of the innocent victim, who has the soul of a child, of a poet, and of a mystic.

In no novel has Deledda poured out her sympathy over the sufferings of a character as she had done here. Dealing with Melchiorre Carta, she seemed disturbed by the presence of his passion. It was, in fact, passion for itself. But here, passion becomes pure love surrounded by a halo of unspeakable sorrow. "The more time passed, the more he felt he loved her [his wife, Giovanna]. She was his distant village, his family, his liberty, his life. Everything centered in her: hope, faith, strength, serenity, the joy of living, his very soul." Thus Costantino loved while pining away in the grim prison of Naples.

Costantino Ledda is the most lyric and sublime of Deledda's characters. He is a dreamer who loses everything: his love, his child, his liberty, but never loses faith. His faith is like the motif of a song in this novel. He has against him the inflexible law of necessity. Giovanna is young and beautiful and may marry again. Yet he continues to hope and, though his body is emaciated and weak, his soul is made strong by his faith. When, after many years, he goes home and finds Giovanna married to a rich shepherd, he acts like an automaton in obeying the bidding of nature and in embracing her. The novel is like a great voice that proclaims the irresistible power of nature.

Nature is a part of the drama of these human beings that struggle, suffer, hate, and love. The same mysterious urge that dulls Giovanna's love, kills her child, and drowns the moans of poor Costantino, makes the seasons revolve blindly year after year. The same sun warms the poor, quivering body of Costantino in the courtyard of the prison and fills the universe with a new life reminding Giovanna of her youth. The earth spreads its perfumes, its beauty, its light; it wounds the mountains with its storms while men plod along the endless path of life. Deledda has a sort of awe before its power and only notices the sorrow and joy, the destruction and the beauty that it spreads in the lives of men, in the mountains and plains.

This objectiveness which permeates the pages of *Dopo il divorzio* was determined by Deledda's attitude toward life. She was both struck and charmed by the unfeeling and passive character of nature. Costantino and Giovanna reflect in their lives the drama of Deledda, who had not yet found a solution for the conflicting thoughts that surged in her.

In *Cenere* (*Ashes*) . . . , a passionate cry rises: What is life? Deledda is on an ardent quest, and the query rises like a lonely voice above the sufferings of the characters. The answer is a tragic one: Life is but ashes. It is precisely what young Anania discovers before the body of his suicide mother.

Most of the characters crowded in this novel bear the stigmata of Deledda's mood, as they, too, are bent on a quest of their own. Olì and Anania meet in the silence of the fields and fall in love, bringing into the world a child that, with the name, inherits the dreamy temperament of his father and the impetuous character of his mother. Anania, the father, has the imagination of a poet. He is tall and handsome and in his eyes there flickers the shadowy light of the dreams that bewitched Olì. Love is a part of the quest of life for them. (pp. 60-3)

[In *Sino al confine*] we find two distinct groups of characters representing two conceptions of life—one based on repression, the other on freedom; the one plunging the soul of man into gloom, the other filling it with joyousness and spontaneity. Individuals with such contrasting points of view are to be found in every walk of life. A priest, Felix, is presented with a saintly and placid face, while another, Bellia, "dark and sad, with down-cast eyes, seemed a specter." Gavina is always sad and tormented; Francesco is always happy and joyous. "Ultimately he was a primitive. He did not lose himself in vain questions, and he loved life with joyousness, merely because it was life." The same happiness we find in Zio Soringhe, an extemporaneous poet, poor and old, whose wrinkled face wore a perpetual smile because he accepted life with the philosophy of the people.

Surrounded by these persons, Gavina is unable to understand herself, and she tortures herself with ascetic visions. Deledda, who appears to play the rôle of a mentor to her, seems to warn: Do not be afraid; it is Life; follow it with sincerity and candor. We notice, in fact, that Gavina is constantly placed in a situation in which she passes by happiness, but is unable to seize it because of her fears and scruples. One day, Gavina and Francesco are sitting side by side in the solitude of the fields. Francesco takes her hand and kisses it. "The sky was of an intense azure and the air was transparent as in a spring afternoon. By closing their eyes, the two young people could have believed themselves to be at the shore of the sea and could have passed a happy hour. But Gavina thought of something else and withdrew her hand." (pp. 64-5)

It is a long struggle for Gavina to conquer the influences that have separated her from life. Before the cold face of death, she realizes the joy of being alive, and wrests herself from fear and unhappiness. "Little by little, terror and anguish of death were followed by a sentiment that was unknown to her: the joy of living. Alive! Alive! She was alive!"

This is the final statement of Deledda's underlying philosophy. From the publication of *Sino al confine* her work has mainly expressed her faith in the unity and unerring character of instincts. In this novel she shows the process through which she

reaches that faith. In her later stories she further elaborates this thought by showing the tragic effects of thwarting instinct. From this subsequent mood is derived *Marianna Sirca.* . . . Deledda's art has here become more conscious of itself, and, therefore, more concentrated and restrained. Her characters move in the hieratic fashion of the Sardinian people, solemn and silent. They have the concreteness of statuary and not the elusiveness of a colorful shadow. Here is a servant of Marianna Sirca: "They all looked outside towards the gigantic and dark figure of the servant that advanced rigidly as if made of wood." The servant asks Marianna to put salt on the blood-pudding that he has cut. "It seemed that they were performing a rite, the servant rigid, with his black, square beard like that of an Egyptian priest, she pale and exquisite in her bodice red like the flower of the pomegranate." Her figures afford in this novel a stupendous example of a prose that approaches sculpture as far as words can replace the solidity of marble or bronze.

No longer are delicate colors diffused in her scenes of nature; no longer are poetic images evoked by a cloud or by snow; nature is now rendered in all its concreteness. We read: "Large drops of rain, hard and brilliant like pearls, began to fall with violence." And again: "The rain finally broke forth, raised by the wind like a veil woven with threads of steel. It writhed, falling furiously on the trees and on the underbrush which, in turn, writhed with anguish."

Likewise, she strikes a deeper vein in the humanity of her characters and she gains in depth what she loses in color. (pp. 66-7)

In *La Madre* (*The Mother*) . . . , we are no longer confronted by the primitive people of the preceding novels. We meet Paulo, a young priest who has lived for seven years in the silence of a small mountain village attending to his parish. Paulo, however, is not considered in any of his intellectual attributes. Deledda digs into this character till she finds the primitive being that is dormant in him. "The first year of their residence in the town, he spoke of going away, of returning to the world. Then, he had fallen into a kind of slumber, in the shadow of the cliffs, in the rustle of the leaves." He . . . was waiting to be awakened. He had kept in subjection the strong passionate nature of his ancestors, people of the soil, but that subjection was an offense against life. "He was a man of strong instincts, like his forefathers, and he suffered because he could not abandon himself to instincts." For him, too, as for the characters of this period, the shackles were broken by his meeting Agnese, a young woman who lived in the solitude of her ancestral home. Indeed, his love for Agnese gave him a glimpse of the infinite. "No, it was not his flesh that cried out for life; it was his soul that was imprisoned in the flesh and wanted to be freed." In no novel is the feeling of the oneness of love and life more evident than in *La Madre*. Although mainly an instinctive being, Paulo affords a more complex psychology than other characters of the preceding novels. He tries to stifle his love, but he discovers that all his arguments are empty sophisms. The drama of the young priest is not presented in an abstract analysis but is diffused in every act, in every word, in every posture of Paulo. A tragic struggle is depicted as he debates whether to flee with the girl or to remain chained to his duty. (pp. 68-9)

Deledda received the Nobel prize for this novel. In fact, it marks the highest point of development in the production of the Sardinian writer. She has reduced the number of her characters to three: the mother, Paulo, and Agnese, and all the light is focused on them. The language partakes of the artist's passion and it glows with her inward flame, having lost the diffused, but external character of the prose of the early novels.

Deledda later published *Il secreto dell'uomo solitario* (*The Secret of the Solitary Man*) . . . , and *Il Dio dei viventi* (*The God of the Living*). . . . In the former Deledda has felt the introspective tendency of the writers of the younger generation and this has determined a return to the lyricism of the early years of her career. The novel presents Cristiano living in a lonely plain and guarding a secret that is revealed in the last pages of the book. He falls in love with Savina, a young and beautiful woman who is married to a demented man. Cristiano's secret, his marriage to a wealthy woman older than he, stands between him and Savina. It is one of the few novels by her that do not deal with Sardinia. The characters are lacking in solidity just as their emotions do not possess the vehemence that leads to drama.

A deeply moral tone permeates the pages of *Il Dio dei viventi*, but without creating the magnificent figures we have admired in other novels. The characters that are crowded in this work, from the unscrupulous Zebedeo to his visionary wife, are without that inward force that has given life to Deledda's other characters. It is nothing but cold moralizing, enlivened here and there by a touch of humor. In fact, *Il Dio dei viventi* is a kind of parable that shows how Zebedeo, who has destroyed his brother's will so that his own son, Bellia, may inherit the money, is punished until he makes amends for his dishonesty.

Continuing to write with an amazing fervor, Deledda has published a novel in 1928, *Annalena Bilsini,* and another in 1929, *Il vecchio e i fanciulli* (*Old Age and Youth*). *Annalena Bilsini* has many points of similarity with Verga's *I Malavoglia*. The central figure of the book, Annalena Bilsini, has taken the place of Paron Ntoni, to be sure, but they both are given the task of toiling hard in order to keep their families united and to give them wealth and strength. In Deledda's work there also appears the black sheep of the family who, like Verga's young Ntoni, goes to take his military service and brings back the restlessness of the continent. Both Annalena Bilsini and old Paron Ntoni, after many hardships, succeed in realizing their modest dream.

The dramatization of their success, however, gives us the measure of the temperament of the master, Verga, and of his disciple, Deledda. To Verga (and in this he is a true naturalist) life offers so much pathos that it needs no embellishment. He presents Paron Ntoni with a directness and with such subdued tones as to make one feel that he has been bodily transported from life into art. His attributes are close to those of the average man in an amazing degree and his drama is the drama of the average individual. Deledda, on the contrary, brings out the emotional life of Annalena Bilsini, a true daughter of the Sardinian Mountains. She is a beautiful and still young widow who finds in her youth and beauty a hindrance to her task of bringing success to her family. For Deledda, the drama of success is of secondary importance compared with the dramatization of the emotional life of the heroine and of all her characters.

Verga and Deledda, representing two generations, have a different approach to life. We point out this fact merely to show that the severe, restrained, unimpassioned Naturalism of Verga has given place, with Grazia Deledda, to a new type of art, warm, passionate, full of poetry and imagination.

Annalena Bilsini stands next to Marianna Sirca in the glow with which the writer has enveloped her. However, in this new novel, Deledda has lost that supreme faith in instinct that made her create the passionate and love-sick Marianna Sirca. In Annalena Bilsini, the love motif has a great part but all her characters are conscious of its evil nature. "Love, yes," sighed Isabella, "it is a beautiful trap, all gold outside, with Death within." It seems that Deledda's Naturalism has been disturbed by religious feelings which, although they circulate in the book, do not succeed in asserting themselves. As it is, *Annalena Bilsini* is a great novel and has marvelous pages in which Deledda describes nature or presents picturesque and human figures. Uncle Dionisio is one of these. He is an old man the description of whose death from a paralytic stroke allows us to admire Deledda's art at its best.

In *Il vecchio e i fanciulli,* love is still the fundamental theme, but it is a more disturbing and tragic factor than in the preceding book. Deledda embodies her changed outlook on instinct and love in an overgrown boy, Luca, who runs away from home and goes to the fold of an old and well-to-do shepherd, Ulpiano Melis. From the time of Luca's arrival, everything seems to become disorderly both in the fold and at the home of old Ulpiano. The latter has a granddaughter, Francesca, who "seemed truly born to be a male; with a large head, a deep voice, hair on her upper lip; her body was strong although she was of small stature, slightly bow-legged through horseback riding." There arise between Francesca and Luca, the servant, feelings which are a strange mixture of hostility, hatred, and morbid interest in each other. The climax is reached when the two yield to their love, and tragedy darkens the hitherto peaceful life of Ulpiano Melis.

The tone of the novel is somewhat strained. It reminds one of the too lyrical feelings that young Deledda attributed, a quarter of a century ago, to Basilio in *Il Vecchio della montagna*. One remembers here the appearance of the characters rather than their drama.

Nevertheless, Deledda is a great literary figure and she has contributed an original, colorful, and deeply human chapter to contemporary Italian fiction. (pp. 70-3)

Domenico Vittorini, "A New Episode in Italian Naturalism," in his The Modern Italian Novel, *University of Pennsylvania Press, 1930, pp. 56-78.*

OLGA RAGUSA   (essay date 1966)

[*In the following excerpt, Ragusa discusses descriptive language in Deledda's writing.*]

The citation which in 1927 accompanied the award of the Nobel Prize to Grazia Deledda—"for her exalted idealistic writings in which she has so plastically described life on her native island, and dealt with warmth and depth of feelings with general human problems"—has the familiar ring of what René Wellek calls impressionistic appreciation. Yet this judgement probably accurately reflects the reasons for Deledda's popular success (she began publishing on the "continent," outside her native Sardinia, in 1888, at the age of seventeen, but had written for local papers even earlier), a success attested to by the many translations of her work, especially in the Scandinavian countries, in Germany and in France, which appeared even before the Prize bestowed international fame on her.

But exoticism of subject matter—the Sardinia of the days before air transportation was a land as mythical as Selma Lagerlöf's Värmland or Sigrid Undset's medieval Norway,—and understanding and sympathy for mankind are by themselves alone not sufficient to ensure for a writer a permanent place in the literary Pantheon. The question that should be considered here, therefore, is whether Deledda's work offers anything else; whether it is irremediably linked to the cultural conditions, the intellectual and artistic tenets, the canons of taste from which it sprang; or whether, as all great art, it soars beyond its time and place, and is capable of continuing to evoke a response, much as van Eyck's *Adoration of the Lamb* continues to draw the fascinated and awed gaze of a viewer who may no longer share the religious belief which the painting mirrors.

The reference to the Ghent altarpiece is not as gratuitous as it might seem. The *Adoration of the Lamb* is the first of the paintings used by Sir Kenneth Clark in his *Landscape into Art* to illustrate the chapter entitled "The Landscape of Fact." This chapter is placed between two parallel chapters, "The Landscape of Symbols" and "The Landscape of Fantasy," three felicitous formulas by which Sir Kenneth characterizes moments in the evolution of landscape painting prior to its final triumph as a self-contained and independent genre in the nineteenth century.

Deledda has always been recognized as a superb "paysagiste." Even those critics who by emphasizing the setting of her stories tried most insistently to reduce her art to folklore, and those others who even more insidiously read her work in the key of womanish sentimentalism and conformist morality, paid tribute to her gift for description. And indeed from the early Sardinian stories to the late continental ones, Deledda's work abounds in magnificent passages. Here is one, for instance, taken from **"Nel regno della pietra,"** a short story written in 1899 and set in a sheepfold at the foot of "a chain of monstrous granite rocks":

> The view was grandiose. This was the realm of stone, intersected here and there by sparse groves of holm-oaks and by slopes that in the springtime spread over with asphodels. One could see half of Sardinia, down to the gulfs, sky-blue on fair autumn mornings, down to the misty horizons, enclosed by great mountain walls that dawn and sunset turned red. When the wind was still, an indescribable silence reigned under the monstrous rocks, standing one next to the other, gray and enigmatic.

But to quote excerpts—and turn them into limping English—is to destroy the effect almost completely. For Deledda's descriptions are not incidental, they are not documentary; nor are they decorative, marking a pause and a change of tone and perspective in the narrative. In Deledda's most successful works, such as the 1912 novel *Canne al vento (Reeds in the Wind)*, her favorite, or the earlier *La via del male (The Way of Evil)* and *L'edera (The Clinging Ivy)*, there is complete fusion between setting and theme, between landscape and feeling. The destinies of man—of the old servant Efix and of his three impoverished mistresses—are as unsteady as blades of grass in the wind; the passion that unites the servant Pietro and the daughter of his wealthy master seems at first a caprice that can be curbed at will, but turns out to be the indissoluble link that binds together once and for all those who travel the road of evil-doing side by side; the clinging ivy—the orphan girl befriended by a family of landowners whose holdings disappear one by one through maladministration—is in the end stronger and more resourceful than the broad trunk about which it winds. In each instance, and the examples could be multiplied, Deledda conceives her story directly in metaphorical terms. And

yet her landscapes are not landscapes of symbols, they are landscapes of facts. The objects of nature are first and foremost themselves: clouds sweeping across distant skies, dark forests swaying in the wind, night following day, season hastening upon season, men growing bent and old, shepherds tending their flocks on lonely plains, and over and over again men and women walking along unending roads, as though Sardinia were not a rock-bound island but an infinite world. For, of course, the objects of nature also have hidden and mysterious meanings, but in Deledda they are meanings that are revealed to eyes that look at objects long and lovingly, not meanings that lie beyond and are discovered by eyes that look through objects, for whom objects do not exist.

"Facts become art through love," Sir Kenneth writes, "which unifies them and lifts them to a higher plane of reality; and in landscape this all embracing love is expressed by light." There might be some difficulty in agreeing on what exactly may be said to correspond to light in literary landscapes. But I suspect that it may be the metaphor. And just as there is no end to the visual pleasure that derives from the play of light and shadow, so there is no end to the intellectual and emotional pleasure derived from the play of logical and metaphorical meaning. Deledda's work, so much closer to symbolist poetry than to the narrative of naturalism, affords this pleasure, and I believe that it is this, rather than its moral and humanitarian ideals, that stamps it as art. (pp. 26-7)

> Olga Ragusa, "Grazia Deledda—Nobel Prize, 1927," in Cesare Barbieri Courier, *Vol. VIII, No. 1, Spring, 1966, pp. 26-7.*

SERGIO PACIFICI (essay date 1973)

[Pacifici is an American educator, translator, and critic specializing in Italian literature. In the following excerpt, he discusses the moral and philosophical basis for Deledda's work.]

Grazia Deledda's literary production has conveniently been divided into two distinct periods. Arnaldo Bocelli, in a perceptive essay written upon her death, identified them by pointing out how the vision of life is transcendental in the first phase and immanent in the second. In her early novels (1896-1920), God is presented as a kind of implacable, biblical dispenser of justice, "in that we are all sinners and there is no salvation either here or beyond."

The notable novels of the first creative "moment" are [*Elias Portulu, Cenere (Ashes), L'edera (Ivy), Colombi e sparvieri (Doves and sparrowhawks),* and *Canne al vento (Reeds to the wind)*]. The second period opens in 1920 with *La madre* and *Il secreto dell'uomo solitario (The secret of the solitary man)* . . . , both of which remain the finest work of Deledda's later years. In the novels brought out between 1921 and 1936 the role of property and the obsession with material things, key elements of the work of the *veristi* which had been Deledda's models, undergo considerable deemphasis. Love is no longer the sensual and potentially destructive force that it was, but is a restrained, almost religious feeling, a bond between one person and another. Through compassion, one attains a finer understanding of human sorrows, and such a different concept of love brings about notable changes in Deledda's narrative. The themes of her later books receive a more consciously intellectual treatment; the settings, so vividly depicted in the earlier novels, suddenly become secondary. We begin moving in a more abstract land, outside geography and time. However much such novels strive to broaden their meaning and application, they are unquestionably less effective and powerful than the early ones. Deledda herself must have perceived where her real strength as a novelist was, for she soon returned to the fatalism and the haunting pessimism of her "regional," veristic period.

Deledda's early novels as *Le colpe altrui (Someone else's faults)* . . . , *L'incendio nell'oliveto (Fire in the olive grove)* . . . , and even *La madre* . . . may be seen, after Eurialo De Michelis's suggestion, as extreme efforts "to grasp once more in rigorously moral terms a drama, which is still [the same as] that of Elias Portulu, between love and duty. . . ." In point of fact, love is very much at the center of most of Deledda's novels, a love presented as a source of conflict, now love-fatalism, now love-remorse, now love-guilt—an experience, in short, that brings about a profound sense of shame and which, for mysterious reasons, is never allowed to be assuaged except by repentance and expiation. Deeply and irretrievably caught in the web of their passions, Deledda's characters sense that fate prevents them from fulfilling even their most modest dream. In turn, their disappointment becomes a kind of pervasive disenchantment with their lot. Suppressing their feelings, on the other hand, even when by prevailing standards they may be considered amoral or immoral, is hardly a satisfactory solution, for much wretchedness ensues. There is neither an end nor a final answer to such an unbearable, vicious cycle. (pp. 89-91)

La via del male and *Elias Portulu* give an intimation of Deledda's view of life. Man's lot is far from being a happy one. Much like the events of a fable narrated by a servant to the writer in her girlhood, they form sad segments of a journey when the questions are many and the answers are few. The fable, as Deledda relates in the autobiographical book *Cosima*, made "a profound, almost physical impression; the mystery of the fable, the final silence, the eternal story of [man's] error, punishment, sorrow." "[Human] destiny, death, man" who is himself nothing but ashes (and *Ashes* is the apt title of another of her novels); "fate is like the wind," she remarks in *Canne al vento*. What does man understand of the reasons for living, suffering, dying? Is he not doomed to eternal ignorance, a slave of an unknown Master, always buffeted by his many tormenting passions only to be haunted by spiritual remorse?

These are the chief questions posed, but never directly answered, in the narrative of Grazia Deledda. The Sardinian prefers to present her heroes and heroines suffering, pursued by temptations, thrown into perplexing situations, groping in their quest for the answer to their dilemmas. Perhaps such is man's greatest punishment.

The story of man's original sin, of God's subsequent wrath, and of man's sense of loss in a universe that makes little sense to him is repeated again and again by Deledda's characters. They are frequently easy preys of their sensual instincts, persecuted by conventions they cannot overcome. Even an honest repentance proves to be insufficient to restore their peace of mind. It is difficult, however, to resist temptations, for man is by nature weak and his flesh is willing. Traditions, social customs, nature itself seem almost to become enjoined in a conspiracy to make the human dream of happiness on earth but a dim mirage. Life is toil, deprivation, sorrow, restlessness. (pp. 92-3)

Deledda's heroes are perennially under the spell of destiny. If they are uneducated this should not be construed to mean that they are insensitive. It does mean that ultimately they are able to view their predicament only emotionally. They can neither

intellectualize their experience nor draw from it significant norms of conduct. It has been said that their crises take place in their conscience: in the dramatic confrontation between good and evil that forms the very core of their drama, they find themselves at once unwilling participants and spectators, suspecting but never certain that their dilemma has neither an end, except in death, nor a solution, except in resignation. Whatever happens to them seems preordained by a superior force, and there is little indeed they can do to change what seems an inevitable course of events. They sense the presence of the demon in the air about themselves, but are unable to detect it clearly. "What is the demon?" asks Uncle Martinu in *Elias Portulu*. The cryptic answer has a Sartrian flavor: "The demon is ourselves."

It is an unavoidable factor of man's condition that he is condemned to experience pain. There cannot be real joy in life for him, unless he has first undergone the trial of suffering: man can hardly be ready for salvation unless he first experiences evil and learns to reject it. We know but little about life and ourselves, Martinu points out in *Elias Portulu,* until we have felt the touch of pain, the anguish of having to break a rule or a law, or to hate, betray, until we know what it is to persecute or to be persecuted. Evil, in one form or another, is ever-present in life: in the world of Deledda, man is engaged in a fierce battle to combat it, for it must be destroyed not just once but every single day of our lives.

Evil is indeed the element most directly responsible for the predicament in which Deledda's heroes find themselves. If this is an obvious fact to the attentive reader, it is less easy to define just what is the nature of such evil. An exhaustive reading of Deledda's novels sheds precious little light upon this question. In fact, rather than expanding her original definition of evil as something inherent to man, Deledda contents herself with pointing out its variety and complexity. To be sure, there is a definite Verghian coloring to the substance of her tales. Unlike Verga, whose characters are doomed to be vanquished despite the small victories they secure in their struggle "to improve their economic lot," Deledda is more intent in showing us the human incapacity of understanding life, the futility of combating the rigid social and religious structure in which her characters live. At times, evil springs unexpectedly from an act certainly not intended to break an existing order. In *Canne al vento,* for example, the tragedy that soon overtakes many lives is directly traceable to Efix's bold glances at his mistress Lia, who eventually abandons her native town in Sardinia for the mainland, where she hopes to find love and happiness. Both characters have broken an established order; and both will pay the consequences of their act. Similarly, Elias Portulu violates God's law by wanting his brother's betrothed, then simply aggravates the situation by deciding not to marry the girl, even though circumstances have changed and his brother's death makes their union possible. After having failed to seize his last opportunity to be happy, he lives the balance of his life regretting his decision.

For Deledda, life is a source of continuous temptations that are hard to avoid. Only an iron will or total resignation to a feudal condition succeeds in resisting the opportunities life holds out to man. In *La via del male (The path of evil)*, . . . for a long time the protagonist Maria avoids a direct involvement with her servant Pietro Benu, who loves her deeply and, despite his inferior social condition, hopes that his love will be returned. The power of conventions is too strong, and Maria marries a moderately wealthy landowner, Francesco Rosana, while Pietro, unjustly accused of participating in the theft of some sheep, is jailed. When he is released several weeks later he decides to revenge himself, becomes a professional thief and amasses a small fortune in a short time. One day, Francesco is found murdered; five years later Maria accepts Pietro's request to marry him. A few days later, she receives a letter from Sabina, a woman obviously in love with Pietro. The letter reveals that Francesco was actually murdered by Maria's second husband. The two are now condemned to a special kind of punishment, for they will live together as man and wife with a haunting awareness of the individual role thay have played in a crime that has killed a man and ruined another. Thus, Deledda's characters live perennially torn between resigning themselves to a condition that will not bring them happiness, or violating certain social codes, in full knowledge that their actions will inevitably disturb the precarious balance of an order presumably capable of bringing about both peace and happiness.

It would be futile, in the last analysis, to insist on demanding of Deledda a coherent, rationally expressed vision of life, a statement that through images and events might explain the human condition. As some critics have perceived, her fiction exists not to expound a well-defined social or moral ideology, but in order to re-create a mood, a feeling, an atmosphere. In the vagueness of her tales resides much of her charm as well as her limitations as a writer; in the indefiniteness of the psychology of her characters is their authenticity as people. Deledda's heroes do what they do—love, suffer, resign themselves to stifling conventions, commit acts of violence, and live a life haunted by tragic memories—simply because this is the lot of a human being's conscience to bear. Perhaps the answer to why life must be so is to be found in the final pages of Deledda's early novel, *La via del male*. Maria has just learned that her husband is the killer of her first mate. Whereupon the author comments: ''She was born to fight, to struggle, to stab people in their back. She has always betrayed. She betrayed Pietro, her relatives, Sabina. She has betrayed even Francesco by not confessing the truth to him. Perhaps he would not have died had she spoken. But the world is full of betrayals and deceits: man must fight against man so as to have his share of sun and earth.'' (pp. 94-7)

> *Sergio Pacifici, 'Voices from the Provinces: Grazia Deledda and Marino Moretti,'' in his* The Modern Italian Novel: From Capuana to Tozzi, *Southern Illinois University Press, 1973, pp. 86-107.*

SHEILA MᴀᴄLEOD   (essay date 1985)

[The following excerpt is from MacLeod's introduction to a recent edition of After the Divorce.*]*

D. H. Lawrence, who was one of Deledda's admirers, described [the remote and mountainous region of the Barbagia around Nuoro in·Sardinia] in 1928 as a place

> of rigid conventions, the rigid conventions of barbarism, and at the same time the fierce violence of the instinctive passions. A savage tradition of chastity, with a savage lust of the flesh. A barbaric overlordship of the gentry, with a fierce indomitableness of the servile classes. A lack of public opinion, a lack of

belonging to any other part of the world, which makes inland Sardinia almost as savage as Benin [see excerpt dated 1928]. . . .

But it is also a landscape of wild and wonderful beauty, a backdrop more suitable to *Wuthering Heights* than to the sentiments of mainstream Italian literature.

After the Divorce is Grazia Deledda's eighth novel, first published in 1902 and subsequently appearing in 1920 with a different title. It is set around the turn of the century. The cruel and miserly Basile Ledda has been murdered and his nephew Costantino arrested, tried, then sent across the sea to prison for twenty-seven years. His young and pretty wife, Giovanna, is left to cope as best she can for their baby son and her ageing mother Bachisia. The future looks bleak and beggarly for the two women, poorest of peasants as they are, without a man to support them and with few opportunities for work of their own in a land devoid alike of rich soil and rich employers. But a new divorce law is about to come into operation, a law which allows for the wives of convicts to divorce their husbands and so, perhaps, remarry. Is there, then, some hope, some way out, for Giovanna and her son? And should there be? This is the moral dilemma of *After the Divorce,* and the consequences of Giovanna's decision to divorce carry the novel through to a conclusion as inevitable as that of any Greek tragedy.

At first the action alternates between Giovanna's village of Orlei and the mainland prison in which Costantino has been wrongfully incarcerated. We see Giovanna missing Costantino, ground down by deprivation, and worn down by her mother's urging her to marry her former suitor, Brontu, the shepherd son of a rich but mean neighbouring widow, Martina Dejas. We see Costantino desperately missing his wife and son and bewildered by the harsh new world of strangers and immediately arbitrary authority. He composes a hymn on behalf of all convicts to his namesake, San Costantino, the patron saint of Orlei, a hymn which he has to write with his own blood and have smuggled out of prison. Neither he nor Giovanna curses God or their fate: scarcely do they even ask why this terrible thing has happened to them. Much less are they motivated towards finding the real murderer, the possibility of whose existence is only glancingly considered. They cannot believe in their own innocence because they do not believe in themselves as people possessing universally recognizable human rights. And yet they are innocent.

In the absence of what Lawrence defines as public opinion, their only moral referents are those of the village community or tribe; the Church with its pale priesthood which has never quite been able to conquer the local pre-Christian rituals and beliefs; and the Law, which is laid down and administered by foreigners on the other side of the sea. Sometimes those forces mesh into something approaching a coherent whole, but more often they are in conflict, and most of the characters are capable of invoking any one of the three to suit themselves—or in sheer desperation. Lawrence found ''the human instinct still uncontaminated'' in Deledda's work, but it seems to me that her characters are forever seeking to justify their instinctive passions in the name of one authority or another. ''Unevolved'' (Lawrence's word again) they may be in all sorts of ways, but they are in a state of evolution: the human consciousness struggling towards conscience in an environment which often seems fitter for conscienceless beasts.

Both Giovanna and Costantino believe that they are being punished for having contracted a civil marriage rather than having waited until such time as they could have afforded the more expensive church ceremony. Their marriage was in accordance with Law, if not with the Church. And so the Church is prepared to condone the divorce and Giovanna's subsequent remarriage to Brontu. But Giovanna's decision is by no means wholly that of a devout Catholic: her son has died of malnutrition and, according to the mores of the tribe which places a high value on paternity and its proof, there need now be no shame accruing to Brontu in the raising of another man's child. Similarly, the child will not have to undergo the ignominy of knowing his mother, as she is known to her neighbours, as "the woman with two husbands." When the child of the new union is born "green and sickly" and fails to thrive, no one is surprised: after all, his parents are living in mortal sin. But they have also contravened the mores of the tribe: if Giovanna and Brontu had simply lived together, no one would have blamed them overly: the flesh is weak, life is hard, and saintly beggarliness not natural to the young and attractive. It is the fact that they have invoked the higher authorities of the Law and (to a lesser extent) the Church to justify their behaviour which arouses moral indignation.

In flouting the unwritten mores of the tribe, Giovanna and Brontu have, as it were, brought unconscious material (the manner in which ordinary people live their unsanctioned but all too human lives) into consciousness. Because both Law and Church have recognized and condoned their conduct, it can no longer be regarded as part of the submerged behaviour of the tribe, the sort of behaviour by which it has managed to preserve its independence of either authority. Thus the cohesiveness of the tribe itself is threatened. Its members must now attempt some form of reconciliation among the three conflicting loyalties.

Some condemn the Law which can allow remarriage without widowhood, rejecting it as the immune system rejects a foreign body. According to this view, the Church has to pay lip-service to the Law, but has shown its disapproval in Father Elias's refusal to attend the new baby's baptismal feast. Others condemn the Church, castigating Father Elias and his colleagues as vacillating and cowardly. Their confidence, which was never particularly strong in the first place (apart from personal allegiances to San Costantino and the Virgin) has now been shattered. When one of the villagers is bitten by a tarantula, the neighbours enact a pagan rite to cure him, and a procession of seven widows, seven married women and seven virgins, dances and sings its mournful way through the streets. Order—the fragile order which depends on the tension among split allegiances—has been disrupted.

There are many who can condemn both Giovanna and Brontu as individuals, citing lust and greed, but there are few prepared to condemn the tribe—and those only in part. One such is the fisherman and leech-gatherer, Isidoro Pane, who alone of the congregation actually listens to Father Elias's sermons and can find compassion in his heart for the wretched Giovanna and Costantino as well as the yet more wretched real murderer. Curiously enough, Isidoro is a figure reminiscent of Wordsworth's leech-gatherer, a lonely self-sufficient man, a bit of an outcast, and a character in whom the reader is expected to find some unspecified embodiment of wisdom. Like others of Deledda's characters he could well belong in the *Lyrical Ballads* beside Simon Lee or the Mad Mother: all have the same understated but monumental quality of standing stones whose endurance speaks of a mysterious "resolution and independence" beyond the exigencies of circumstance.

But Grazia Deledda is as far from drawing Wordsworth's moral conclusions (although I suspect she may share some of them) as she is from making a virtue out of simplicity. Indeed she is one of the least sentimental writers I have ever come across and knows all too well that simplicity is a necessity which, on rare occasions, can be converted to a virtue but is more likely to be synonymous with ignorance and hence perhaps meanness, jealousy, greed and spite. The characters in *After the Divorce* are not divided into good and bad, or even into sympathetic and unsympathetic. Each has his/her moments of strength and weakness, doubt and faith, purity and corruption. It is the shared circumstance of deprivation which arouses sympathy, and the surging, faltering struggle towards a greater humanity which engages and compels.

To judge by the translation, Grazia Deledda is no great stylist and her prose, though capable of lyricism, is without tricks or flourishes. Italian critics have found it difficult to "place" her in their own literature, and one (Paolo Milano in a 1982 Radio Three programme, "The Cactus and the Rope") has gone so far as to claim that she was awarded the Nobel "because she was so Scandinavian." Far-fetched though this may seem, I think there may be a grain of truth in the claim. There is something Northern and Protestant rather than Southern and Catholic in Deledda's perceptions, thought and overall thrust. Although the milieu she describes is very different from that of Ibsen or Strindberg, there is, as Paolo Milano hints, a similar emphasis on guilt and the possibility (which is often to say, the impossibility) of absolution. I myself was often reminded of the Walter Scott couplet:

> O Caledonia stern and wild,
> Meet nurse for a poetic child.

As often with Scandinavian or Scottish writers, Deledda's Sardinian landscape and her unadorned prose are all of a piece: the sparseness and the apparent harshness have a beauty of their own which often verges on the poetic.

And yet . . . I find that Paolo Milano's comments, perceptive as they are, also fail to "place" Grazia Deledda. It seems to me that there is no absolution in *After the Divorce* because there was never any real guilt. It is not the Protestant we are dealing with but the Pagan. If the outcome of the novel seems pessimistic, it is not because human sin lacks divine redemption but because human existence at its most existential and threadbare gives little cause for optimism. Any struggle towards self-awareness, whether individual or collective, must be a poignant one, and yet it is in the struggle itself that the cause for optimism lies. The individual may be defeated by circumstances—the Law, the Church, the tribe or, even more surely, poverty—but the fact that she/he has seen fit to fight and question, however misplaced the target, is in itself a sign of victory.

If this were not so, Grazia Deledda's writing would be unrelievedly gloomy, unreadable. But *After the Divorce*, although sombre indeed at times, is not a depressing novel and seems not to have been written out of despair. On the contrary, it shines and sometimes burns with love and compassion for Sardinia and its people, a love and compassion which never amount to conflagration but maintain a pure and steady flame. (pp. v-x)

Sheila MacLeod, in an introduction to After the Divorce *by Grazia Deledda, translated by Susan Ashe, Quartet Books, 1985, pp. v-x.*

ADDITIONAL BIBLIOGRAPHY

Balducci, Carolyn. *A Self-Made Woman: Biography of Nobel-Prize-Winner Grazia Deledda*. Boston: Houghton Mifflin Co., 1975, 200 p.
  An account of Deledda's childhood and young adulthood in Sardinia.

Fraser, Mary. "Grazia Deledda." *The Bookman*, London LXXXII, No. 491 (August 1932): 239-40.
  Biographical sketch.

Gregor, D. B. "Polychrome in Grazia Deledda." *Modern Languages* LI, No. 4 (December 1970): 160-66.
  Discusses Deledda's symbolic use of color.

Gunzberg, Lynn M. "Ruralism, Folklore, and Grazia Deledda's Novels." *Modern Language Studies* XIII, No. 3 (Summer 1983): 112-22.
  A sociopolitical study of Deledda's fiction. Gunzberg discusses possible reasons why Deledda obtained such popular acclaim and won the Nobel Prize for literature when the majority of European critics disliked her work.

Kennard, Joseph Spencer. "Grazia Deledda." In his *Italian Romance Writers*, pp. 351-67. New York: Brentano's, 1906.
  An examination by a contemporary of Deledda's early novels.

Marble, Annie Russell. "Grazia Deledda and Her Stories of Sardinia." In her *The Nobel Prize Winners in Literature*, pp. 296-312. New York: D. Appleton and Co., 1932.
  A general discussion of Deledda, her work, and reactions to her work.

McCormick, E. Allen. "Grazia Deledda's *La madre* and the Problem of Tragedy." Symposium XXII, No. 1 (Spring 1968): 62-71.
  Discusses the moral struggle presented in *La madre*. McCormick posits the question of whether or not the novel can be considered a true tragedy.

O'Brien, Justin. "Grazia Deledda's Debut." *Italica* IX, No. 1 (March 1932): 10-12.
  Announces the discovery of an early collection of previously unknown short stories by Deledda.

Vittorini, Domenico. "Grazia Deledda and Her Early Literary Contacts." In his *High Points in the History of Italian Literature*, pp. 247-53. New York: David McKay Co., 1958.
  Discusses the influence of Enrico Costa on Deledda's writing.

Laxmiprasad Devkota

1909-1959

(Also transliterated as Laxmi Prasad, Lakshmi Prasad, Laksh-mīprasādā; also Deokota, Devakotāko) Nepali poet, short story writer, essayist, and dramatist.

Devkota is regarded as modern Nepal's greatest poet. By combining the themes and techniques of classical Sanskrit literature with elements derived from modern Nepali culture and from the European Romantic movement in literature, Devkota created unique narrative and lyric poetry which is both thoroughly infused with a regional character and totally modern. Political and economic factors, however, prevented the publication of much of Devkota's work during his lifetime, and, as a result, the full extent of his contribution to Nepali and world literature is still being assessed.

The son of an impoverished Hindu priest, Devkota was born in Katmandu. Hoping to improve the family's fortunes, the young poet studied those subjects which seemed to offer the best opportunities for earning a good living—English, science, and law. He was, however, forced by his adverse financial circumstances to leave school before completing his education, and he began to write poetry as a means of earning money. In 1934, three of Devkota's poems were published in the Nepali literary journal *Shāradā*, bringing the poet national attention and unanimous approval from critics. Two years later, with the publication of his first volume of poetry, *Munā Madan*, Devkota established himself as one of Nepal's foremost poets. During his lifetime, Devkota produced a prodigious amount of poetry, some of which was censored by the repressive Rana regime because of its populist tone. In addition, he participated in several organizations formed for the purpose of promoting native Nepali literature, taught English and poetry at the University of Patna, and served as an official in his country's cultural ministry after the 1951 overthrow of the Ranas. Devkota's activities, however, brought him surprisingly little monetary recompense, and he lived in a continual state of poverty. As a result, when he developed cancer in the early 1950s, he was unable to afford adequate medical treatment, and the disease continued unchecked until it took his life in 1959.

David Rubin has said that with the work of Devkota "modern Nepali poetry reaches full maturity with a kind of explosion." His statement refers in part to the sheer volume of the poet's works, written speedily, continuously, and with almost no revisions, and in part to the variety and originality of Devkota's poetic techniques. The poet's early works were strongly influenced by his studies of Wordsworth, often extolling the virtues of poor, simple people and asserting the importance of close contact with the natural world. As Devkota matured, however, his search for a more personal artistic expression led him to experiment with a combination of Indic and Western themes and techniques. Although he preferred to use the traditional narrative forms of ancient Sanskrit poetry, he consistently introduced contemporary Nepali linguistic and cultural elements; for example, he wrote one of his most popular works, *Munā Madan*, in a Nepali folk-song meter called *jhyāure*, which, Rubin noted, "had been neglected by poets previously as vulgar and unfit for serious poetry." Devkota also based several narratives upon Western stories which lent themselves to the ex-

ploration of conventional Sanskrit conflicts such as the separation of lovers and courageous endurance of adversity, as in *Pramithas,* based on the myth of Prometheus. While Devkota wrote innumerable short lyric poems in various forms, all of which are highly regarded, the longer narratives, best exemplified in *Nepālī sākuntala* and *Sulocanā,* are considered his finest achievements.

Devkota's renown within his native country remains undiminished, due in part to the fact that his work inspired the creation of other uniquely Nepali works. In addition, the continuing discovery and release of hitherto unpublished works maintains a high level of critical interest in his poetry. Until recently, however, this interest was necessarily confined to Nepali-speaking regions. Currently, with the release of English translations of his works, Devkota's name is becoming more familiar to non-Nepali readers.

PRINCIPAL WORKS

Munā Madan (poetry) 1936
Sāvitrī-Satyavān (drama) 1940
Gāine gīt (poetry) 1943?
Kunjinī (poetry) 1945
Nepālī sākuntala (poetry) 1945
Rāvan-Jatāyu-yuddha (poetry) 1946

Sulocanā (poetry) 1946
Putalī (poetry) 1952
Sundarī Projerpina (poetry) 1952
Bhikhārī (poetry) 1953
Mhendu (poetry) 1958
Kṛṣi-bālā (drama) 1964
Cillā pātharū (poetry) 1966
Lūnī (poetry) 1967
Mahārāna Pratāp (poetry) 1967
Manoranjan (poetry) 1967
Māyāvinī Sarsī (poetry) 1967
Ākāś bolcha (poetry) 1968
Navaras (poetry) 1968
Van Kusum (poetry) 1968
Chāngāsanga kurā (poetry) 1969
Katak (poetry) 1969
Bhikārī (poetry) 1970; revised edition, 1974
Pramithas (poetry) 1971
Campā (unfinished novel) 1972
Lakṣmī katha sangrah (short stories) 1975
Lakṣmī kavita sangrah (poetry) 1976
Nepali Visions, Nepali Dreams (poetry and essay) 1980

Selections of Devkota's poetry also appear in the collection *Modern Nepali Poems (1972)*.

LAXMIPRASAD DEVKOTA (essay date 1953)

[*In the following excerpt from an essay written in the third person, Devkota discusses his poetry.*]

[In] Devkota the reflection of English Romantic style is very evident. Many of his poems are filled with exuberant feeling, the worship of beauty, and love of nature. . . . Devkota, instead of giving advice, is impelled toward an art that touches the heart.

He believes that the nature of true art is to touch the heart, and through the heart to fully involve the intellect. In Balkrishna Sama-ji the poetry comes forth with an effort—the flowers are embroidered with much of the skill of a painter or fine artificer. Devkota's poetry comes flowing forth of itself, without effort . . . the poet like a springtime bird pours out his heart's joy. He does not have to fashion a meter or count syllables or stop often in his writing. In his style are dash, speed, and power. One is often afraid that, like a rivulet, in the rain it may overflow the banks with an excess of power and break the dikes. And one also fears that such a flood, becoming murky, will turn into mud and dirt and tiny bits of gold.

Devkota does not pause to edit, refine or go over a second time, and occasionally the poetry is marked by lack of clarity, confused grammatical structure, and obscurity *(aspaṣṭatā, duranvaya, durbodhatā)*. He sees the form of the external world as the reflection of his own inner activity.

Or he sees his own profound inner truths shining in the portrayal of nature. . . . [For] Laxmiprasad Devkota nature is seen as a living companion or a mine of beauty. In this tendency we find the influence of Wordsworth or Shelley or Keats in him. The flavor of English literature, particularly Romantic literature, makes a profound and colorful impression in this poet who sucks the juice of English literature. In Devkota there is the quality of theism. . . . He sees a supreme deity as monarch of the world and the soul as monarch of the body. In a word, his flight has always been toward immortality. In **"The Beggar,"** in the form of the man who comes into the courtyard begging, it is as though a god were standing there, who keeps on calling with the human speech of pain to awaken the soul of man, but this god is not found on the road of blind ritual, the tradition of credulity. (pp. 161-62)

There is no lesson of inactivity in Devkota's dharma. He insists most particularly on service to man: "to the city of the heart I bring a message of service."

Also in Devkota, as in the English poets, particularly Wordsworth, one finds the tendency to idealize childhood. He sees in the child the pure and divine imagination and the life of feeling which it is not possible for man to receive in the grief-shrouded state of adulthood. . . . The portrayal of the greatness of the common man, which is a Romantic quality, is also present in Devkota, as in the description of the greatness of the joyful life in the poem called **"The Peasant."** Devkota's worship of beauty shines in such poems as **"Cāru," "Spring," "Evening,"** and **"The Grasscutter."**

He is an enemy of blind tradition, as in **"Pilgrim."** . . . The duty of his life he understands to be to make the world shine with the outpouring of inner strength. And similarly, he wishes to persuade others of this duty. Devkota's heart is deeply touched by this feeling of service to man. The holy feeling of the grasscutter lighting a lamp in the heart of the poet Bhanubhakta and illuminating the development of Nepali literature—(Devkota) wishes that there shall be more just such grasscutters and poets filled with the sentiment of divine service to Nepal. (pp. 162-63)

Laxmiprasad Devkota, "Devkota on Devkota," in his Nepali Visions, Nepali Dreams: The Poetry of Laxmiprasad Devkota, *edited and translated by David Rubin, Columbia University Press, 1980, pp. 161-64.*

PRABHAKAR MACHWE (essay date 1978)

[*In the following excerpt, Machwe praises Devkota's poetry.*]

In the First Asian Writers' Conference in New Delhi in 1956, I had the pleasure of seeing [Laxmiprasad Devkota] in person, talking with him in the receptions at Royal Nepalese Embassy and at Soviet Embassy, listening to his inspired oration at the Conference. All this left an impression on my mind that he was a genius, an erratic and irrepressible artist, one who belonged to the galaxy of Baudelaire and Mayakovsky, Michael Madhusudan Datta and Kazi Nazrul Islam, Nirala and Muktibodh, Mardhekar and Amar Shekh and so many others who I had read and re-read. I had the honour of seeing Nirala and Muktibodh, Mardhekar and Amar Shekh, even having the *darshan* of Kazi Nazrul Islam in 1973, in Dacca. I have deliberately chosen these names as many of them had what the Sanskrit poetics, long ago, enumerated as the qualities of genius or *Pratibha:*

> Beyond the dictates and rules of destiny, having the power of creating an unprecedented reality, ever giving newer stimulations.

Nietzsche called such people with *Wille zur macht* ("Will to Power") as "Beyond Good and Evil." Probably such persons cannot be judged by mundane norms of morality. They are a law unto themselves.

Ghalib, the Urdu poet died in penury. Excessive drinking took the lives of Dylan Thomas, "Majaz," Shiva Kumar Batalvi and many other poets at a young age. There may be so many others. Devkota was also fond of good things of life. This monograph mentions chain-smoking and gluttony. But all these weaknesses pale into insignificance when one looks at their gorgeous contribution to the poetry of their own languages. Devkota's life was cut short by deprivation, destitution, dissipation and disease. Is not all great poetry some kind of frenzy, ecstasy or what Shakespeare called as "lunacy"? Ezra Pound and Heine, even nearer home, Nirala and Nazrul Islam were not quite normal when they died an untimely death. Muktibodh had [undiagnosed] illness, Mardhekar died of jaundice, Dhumil had brain tumour and Rajkamal Chaudhury so many complicated diseases. Devkota fell a victim to so many persecutions—social, mental, economic, political, literary and so on. So our sympathies go to this group of poets. Allen Ginsberg asked this question in *Howl*—why so many young geniuses die of madness, excessive anxiety, unbalance, want of basic sympathy. Subramanya Bharati, Balkan Thombre, Jibananda Das died young of accidents. Others' lives were cut short by a cruel and apathetic system. Essenin or Tingling, Sukanta Bhattacharya or Phanishwarnath "Renu"... the list is really very long.

Devkota's life is an elegy. His poetry has an undercurrent of pathos which is beyond words. Hence he chooses such themes and characters, who silently suffer. They end in either suicide or are victims of the supreme capricious "dreadful figure of Death" (Letter to Hari Shrestha). They end in "cosmic conflagration" as Devkota spoke to Dom Moreas. There is some Promethean "angst" about such people. I hold Devkota in awe and respect, for all such attempts at going beyond one's material self. But how few amongst us, though so many who practise versification or woo the Muse to grant them a Pegasus, really feel this anguish so strongly, and who are prepared to undergo this extreme sacrifice?

Devkota's poetry has another charm. He is linked with the classical—not only with *Shakuntala* or *Mahabharata* or *Ravana-Jatayu-Yuddha* of *Ramayana* and Circe and Prometheus of Greek Mythology; but also in using the strict and rigid Sanskrit prosodaic forms and in adopting a self-imposed discipline as Michael did with sonnets or Srikrishna Puvale did with *Rubais*. Language in the hands of such exceptional poets, assures a pliant pattern. It borrows freely from technique of folk-songs, their elusive simplicity, their improvisation, their lyrical crystal clarity, their deep and passionate love for nature, their humour based on common sense, their sure feel for the taste of the common man and masses. Here is an interesting combination of the classical grand design of sublimity and grandeur with the utter unsophisticated directness and spontaneity of a folk-song. The spoken word, unadorned and unhewn, fresh from the oven, taken the task of interpreting the most profound truths of life and even beyond, Devkota succeeded in this "dual vision." Hence he is aptly regarded as *Mahakavi* ["great poet"]. (pp. ix-xi)

Prabhakar Machwe, "Introduction B," in Mahakavi Laxmi Prasad Deokota *by Paras Mani Pradhan, Bhagya Laxmi Prakashan, 1978, pp. ix-xi.*

DAVID RUBIN (essay date 1980)

[*Rubin is the editor and translator of the only volume of Devkota's poetry published in English. In the following excerpt from his biographical and critical introduction to that book, Rubin discusses the poet's major works.*]

Devkota's creative life can be roughly divided into three major periods. The first, extending through the thirties, includes the sentimental genre poems of *Bhikhārī* (*The Beggar,* published as a collection for the first time in 1953); the verse drama *Sāvitrī-Satyavān* ...; and *Munā Madan* ..., the first of many narrative poems. The second period, the mid-forties, saw the great flowering of Devkota's inspiration in the series of extended narrative poems, among them such works as *Nepālī Śākuntala* ..., *Sulocanā* ..., and *Rāvan-Jatāyu-Yuddha* (*The Battle of Ravana and Jatayu* ...). The final period begins with the revolutionary poems written in exile in Banaras, reaches its height with the epic *Prometheus* (*Pramithas* ...), and includes a vast number of short lyrics, children's poems, and long poems such as "**Pāgal**" ("**Crazy**" ...), "**Ek Sundarī Veśyāprati**" ("**To a Beautiful Prostitute**" ...), and the various deathbed poems—the poems from inside the cage. (p. 27)

[The] precise dating of many of Devkota's poems, including major works like *Prometheus,* is difficult because of the great gap between the time of composition and the actual date of publication. But the main outline is clear enough, with the peak of the poet's accomplishment represented by the great narrative poems of the mid-forties. The best work of the fifties shows a decline not so much in quality as in sheer scope, although in fact it is my belief that Devkota's imagination and technique both became most original and most expressive in the unrestricted expanse of the narrative poem.

Devkota's first published poem appeared in a 1934 winter issue of the *Gorkhāpatra* under the title "**Pūrnimāko Jaladhi**"—"**Ocean of the Full Moon**." It is rhapsodic and depends very much on alliteration, internal rhymes, and repetitions, along with sanskritized diction and an occasional Hindi word. It is not a good poem, but it is interesting because it stands in such sharp contrast to most of the work that was to follow.

> In the beauty of the full moon
> wildly wildly breaking the depths
> the waves surge, on the shores a language
> clashing clashing,
> the singing of the deep resounds;
> my soul in the wind,
> cresting emotions rise
> in wave after wave,
> the rays the rays
> draw high up the inner torrents,
> shedding the gorgeous foam of bliss,
> tossing tossing
> hurling the ocean over all,
> driving every atom of the water,
> washing and rinsing the darkness in moonlight,
> grand hurly-burly,
> uproar and tumult of the waves,
> in the tumult in the breast
> the singing of the deep resounds
> voicing the unbroken song.

This kind of ecstatic (and in the original mostly unpunctuated) outburst reappears occasionally later, though with somewhat more coherence, as in "**Saghan Tamisrāprati**" ("**To a Dark Cloudy Night**"). In sharp contrast is "**Garīb**" ("**Pauper**"), which appeared only four months later in the spring of 1935 in the first issue of *Sāradā*. This poem also is not distinguished in itself when compared to what was soon to follow, but it is interesting for the simplicity of its language and syntax. This is not to say that here Devkota has actually begun to write in colloquial Nepali—there is a generous sprinkling of Sanskrit nouns, though in this respect too it is far more down to earth than **"Ocean of the Full Moon."** In thirteen four-line stanzas Devkota presents a sentimentalized portrait of the pauper and his life in the form of a monologue. The following stanzas are typical.

1. Poor you say? But you'll find no one
    anywhere in the world as rich as I.
    I am no slave to the yearning for luxury,
    my pleasant labor is sweet to me.

3. My forehead is beaded with sweat—
    they're pearls of a price beyond reckoning.
    A fine lamp of peace is in my house;
    in every mouthful I eat is the taste of nectar.

9. My hut is a happy dwelling.
    You reach it by climbing a stony peak.
    The winds play unobstructed all about,
    with the endless blue sky overhead.

And with his imagination—"the fine vehicle of the mind"—he can cruise the earth, moon, and stars. (pp. 27-9)

But in **"Yātrī"** (**"Pilgrim"**) and **"Bhikhārī"** (**"The Beggar"**), both written about 1940 . . . , the tone is different, harsher and more realistic. The beggar's misery is graphically portrayed—in his look is the "silent light of misery"—while in **"Pilgrim"** the poet satirizes conventional religious ideas. In *Munā Madan* the view of poverty is much less idealized, though the poem contains what is probably Devkota's most famous tribute to the simple life, lines which are known by heart by Nepalis of every station:

> Dirty hands and golden plates—
> what can you do with wealth?
> Better to eat greens and nettles
> with a happy heart.

The emphasis in *Munā Madan* is on the conflict of love and money, with real love—charity—usually found in the poorest and humblest.

Devkota's fascination with Wordsworth during this decade is apparent not only in his descriptions of the poor, particularly in terms of the harmony of their lives with nature, but in poems that bear titles like **"Samjhanā"** (**"Memory"**) . . . , and **"Bālakkāl"** (**"Childhood"**) . . . ; and, as mentioned earlier, there are long Nepalized versions of "The Solitary Reaper" (**"Tinko Ghānsiyā Gīt,"** i.e., her grass-cutting song) . . . , and "Lucy Gray" (**"Cāru"**). . . .

Devkota's first published book . . . , and still his most popular, was *Munā Madan.* The indebtedness of this romance to Tennyson's *Enoch Arden* has been exaggerated. For all the similarity of the basic plot structure, *Munā Madan* has little in common with Tennyson's once popular narrative, which today seems so insipid and rhetorically inflated. The theme of the separation of lovers, *viraha,* as was pointed out before, is the fundamental stuff of a vast number of Indian literary works of all ages and held for Devkota a special appeal. (pp. 29-30)

Munā Madan is written in a popular folk-song meter called *jhyāure,* which had been neglected by poets previously as vulgar and unfit for serious poetry. Devkota begins the poem with an address to the readers.

How beautiful and sweet our Nepali songs in *jhyāure*!
this sprout planted unseen in our fields.
May it bloom and wither, as God wills,
but grant me this, brother! don't trample it underfoot—
let it flower and bear fruit! Invite the spring,
and scorn not the *jhyāure,* dear sir! . . .
Napali seed and Nepali grain, the sweet juicy song
watered with the flavor [*ras*] of Nepal—
What Nepali would close his eyes to it?
If the fountain springs from the spirit
what heart will it not touch?

No doubt it was the combination of the singable (and sometimes singsong) *jhyāure,* the appeal to national feeling, and the attention to local detail, along with the many charming descriptions of Himalayan landscapes, that made *Munā Madan* so popular. In its way it was an epoch-making achievement, a break with the literary past that added a new dimension to Nepali poetry. The simplicity of its emotions and ideals is utterly genuine, though scarcely possible to convey through translation, since it inevitably resides in the poet's diction and the relationship this diction bears to his own earlier poetry as well as contemporaneous literature. *Munā Madan* is only the first of Devkota's many ambitious narrative poems and his first major treatment of *viraha.* The subsequent works are infinitely more complex and subtle, but at their best, as in *Sulocanā,* they recapture the early simplicity, and while they express it with far greater poetic resourcefulness and refinement, they still manage to convey the spring-like naiveté that constitutes the special charm of the earlier work. Not long before he died Devkota is supposed to have said, "It would be right to burn all my works except for *Munā Madan.*"

Other important works of this first period are the *Gāine Gīt* . . . ; songs in the manner of a now dwindling community of wandering minstrels, and a verse play, *Sāvitrī-Satyavān* . . . , based on the well-known story in the *Mahābhārata* of a wife who, through her devotion to truth, obliges Death to restore her husband to life. The drama is overextended, but certainly there is eloquence enough in Savitri's dialogues with Death. As so often in the narrative poems the most successful moments are those of the greatest restraint and simplicity of diction, e.g., as when Satyavan, returning to life and unaware of what has happened, says to Savitri:

> I thought I dreamt they carried me to heaven
> and I would not stay
> because I could not find you there.

(pp. 32-4)

The other major works of the early forties are four somewhat more ambitious narrative poems, three of them with contemporary settings and one, *Van Kusum (Forest Flower* not published until 1968), set in a mythical country that seems modeled on Nepal under the Ranas in the nineteenth century. *Van Kusum* has been criticized on many counts—incorrect Sanskrit usage, too many borrowings from Hindi and even "Hinglish" (*powervālā!*), distortion of Nepali for metrical purposes, inconsistency in the names of some of the chief characters, and grammatical solecisms. Its plot is complicated and is probably Devkota's most operatic invention, with suicides, disguises, palace conspiracies, and magical drugs that can even bring the dead back to life. All this notwithstanding, the poem makes its satirical point against the Rana oligarchy's oppression and licentiousness. Even more significant is the fact that at the end the hero marries a peasant girl (the Van Kusum of the title), so that intercaste marriage is implicitly sanctioned. The little epic is important as an anticipation of the *Nepālī Śākuntala,* with a brief invocation to Sarasvati, extensive use of diverse classical meters, and a more elaborately developed metaphorical style with a consistent use of color symbolism and imagery derived from water and birds.

By way of contrast, *Mhendu . . . , Lūnī . . . ,* and *Kunjinī . . . ,* all written at about the same time as *Van Kusum,* are purely pastoral, the first two celebrating the life of the hill people who are variously referred to as Tamang, Sherpa, and Bhote. Of *Mhendu* Devkota writes, ''In it is the twilit blue enchantment which flowers on the misty slopes up toward Gosainthan . . . a Nepal here sweetly blending Mongol and Aryan civilizations in an imaginary love story, which . . . I hope may be heard speaking in the sounds of wild birds and waterfalls.'' The same might be said of *Lūnī* and *Kunjinī.* (pp. 35-6)

Most astonishing is the fact that these numerous varied works of the forties were no more than incidental music, as it were, for the creation of the poet's masterpieces, *Nepālī Śākuntala* and *Sulocanā,* a staggering instance of prolificness and unflagging inspiration.

Nepalis tend to rank *Nepālī Śākuntala* as Devkota's greatest accomplishment. It is without doubt a remarkable work, a masterpiece of a particular kind, harmonizing various elements of a classical tradition with a modern point of view, a pastoral with a cosmic allegory, Kalidasa's romantic comedy of earthly love with a symbolic structure that points to redemption through the coinciding of sensual and sacred love. (p. 40)

[*Nepālī Śākuntala*] may be seen as a pastoral, an evocation of the Golden Age. Significantly set in legendary times, it is one of Devkota's few narratives with a happy ending. (Happy endings apparently struck the poet as incongruous in the age of the Ranas, as *Sulocanā* was soon to demonstrate.) The view of the peasant's life is shown idyllically, again a view very different from the harsh one to be found in *Sulocanā.* The pastoral world is exalted, the court criticized.

> All insipid is the palace, the realms of the crafty,
>   the colors clashing, the city ways cheap.
> Shallow all the glitter, hollow the youthful days there,
>   and our tender flowers twisted on their stems.

As in Kalidasa (and like Shakespeare's Touchstone), the *vidūṣaka,* the Brahman jester, makes a good case against country life in his satirical outbursts. Just as in *As You Like It* there is a double irony, for the Arcadian world, despite all its charms, cannot suffice in itself; ultimately, the Golden Age ceases to be a matter of geography. But when the *vidūṣaka* criticizes the forest girls Dushyanta corrects him: ''These flowers are wild ones, natural, blooming with the beauty of vines, and free of city fickleness.'' And Shakuntala's innocence, like Miranda's in *The Tempest,* is so complete that when she first sees Dushyanta she asks, ''Is he a man or a *kinnar,* a deity or Māra [Kāma]?''

As in Shakespearean romance, reconciliation is the goal. Even the two hostile goddesses of art and wealth are finally at peace with one another: ''Lakshmi dwelt now in harmony with Sarasvati.'' Other opposites are fused together in Shakuntala herself:

> She, part celestial nymph and part royal,
>   wanders taking earth and heaven together;
> scorning the bliss of sages' austerities,
>   like bliss incarnate she takes new heaven.
>
>   (pp. 42-3)

Nepali critics, while heaping praises on Devkota's *Śākuntala,* have nevertheless pointed to shortcomings which have come to be regarded as typical of his work and which he himself cites: obscurity, faults in the classical meters, solecisms and stylistic oddities, and over-sanskritization. But there is no doubt that the quality of the poem is sustained prodigiously and, despite the rapidity of its composition, technique and melodic charm falter but rarely. The *Nepālī Śākuntala* represents a kind of apotheosis of Devkota's love for the classical Indian tradition. From this point on in his career his attention was to be almost entirely given to the present-day world. The one notable exception, *Prometheus,* is a timeless allegory as well as a baleful prognostication of its author's own destiny.

Sulocanā at first glance seems much like the earlier romances, except for its great length (15 cantos, 312 pages). But even a casual perusal reveals that it is of quite a different order.

The whole first canto is devoted to an elaborate invocation to various divinities, and the second to the somewhat fanciful genealogy of Sulocana's family before it settled in Kathmandu. In a vague place and time, the founder of the family, a Kshatriya, repenting his killing of a deer (a conscious echo of the Sanskrit epics), builds a temple and founds a petty kingdom on the banks of the Ganges. His descendants, like Devkota's ancestors, move their residence to Devkut in Western Nepal (occasion for a splendid descriptive hymn of praise for the beauty of the country) and a generation later move on to Kathmandu where Sulocana and her brothers, Chand Mardan and Timir Mardan, are born, the children of Shatru Mardan Singh, a World War I hero, and his wife, Makhna.

But from the end of the second canto on it is clear that this is not a conventional romance when a classical Sanskrit meter is used to inform the reader that Shatru Mardan has lost an eye in the war, or to convey such facts as:

> The two brothers eagerly studied English together
> and they got their B.A. Pass in the year '95 [1938].

In his introduction Devkota writes that the work might be a *mahākāvya,* an epic, in name only. ''In this work I may be a poetic dramatist or a novelist in verse.'' The poem is built of ''common social novelistic materials.'' And indeed it is filled with minute observation of contemporary upper-middle-class Kathmandu society. The poet had written a fragment of a ''social novel,'' as he called it, *Campā,* in the early forties, and many of the realistic short stories belong to this period, as well as the humorous and genre-description essays (**''Gambling,'' ''Moustaches,'' ''The Bengali Doctor's Skinny Jackass''**). But characteristically only in verse was he able to give full expression to that domain which provides other writers with the material for the naturalistic novel. The formal meters—*anuṣṭubh, śārdūlavikrīḍita* etc.—are made to convey minutiae of dress, furniture, and eating as naturally as for other poets they served their more conventional function of expressing every sort of emotional and esthetic refinement.

This is not to say that the Romantic elements disappear, for they continue to abound—the praise of love, ideal devotion, complete self-sacrifice; but for the most part they are treated with greater success than in the earlier poems and harmonized with the realistic setting. (pp. 45-7)

Sulocanā stands apart from [Devkota's earlier romances] not only by virtue of its much greater scope and the dense accumulation of social and political details, but also by reason of its generally tight organization and the sharp psychological analysis that supports the characters' motivations. If at moments the melodramatic climaxes, so typical of the earlier poems, seem to clash with the naturalistic and psychological tone, it should be remembered that Devkota is not part of a Western tradition (no matter how important the influence of the West on his work may be), nor, for that matter, is there any clear Indic tradition behind his work in this form. In the narrative poems he is authentically *sui generis*, creating quite new vehicles for the expression of his thought. The moments of high melodrama sweep one along by their eloquence and conviction, so that one is quite willing to suspend disbelief for the moment, just as in certain nineteenth-century operas one is moved by the power of the music and the fundamental truth of the universal emotions to accept—or not even to notice—the extravagant theatricality of the dramatic action. And as has been noted before, both the unexpectedly violent act and the public (and lengthy) outpouring of intense emotion are far from strange to everyday life in the Kathmandu Valley.

Also analogous to romantic operatic convention is the use of the set piece, the elaborately developed *scena*, as it were, in thr form of aria or ensemble. In *Sulocanā* Nepalis respond with particular warmth to the long lyric set pieces on love or *viyoga*, religious fervor, denunciation, or justification.

There is a vague underlying allegorical structure in *Sulocanā*. The significance of some of the characters' names bears this out. Sulocana herself (''the girl with the beautiful eyes'') is a personification of ideal innocence and beauty destroyed by hypocritical social convention and ossified traditions. Her father is paradoxically named Shatru—enemy—and her lover Anang—''bodiless,'' an epithet of Kāma, the Hindu Eros, but here ironically also indicative of Anang's ultimate ineffectuality and his passive capacity to suffer (like Madan, another epithet of Kāma, in *Munā Madan*). Vilas, ''luxury'' or ''philandering,'' and Bijuli, lightning,'' are obvious enough, and it is Bijuli who humanizes the rather drily intellectual Timir, ''darkness.''

From the beginning of the work it is emphasized that Shatru Mardan's ancestors were petty rajas far to the South in India, and that today the family's pride is excessive, incommensurate, certainly, with its relative unimportance in the twentieth century. Apart from lineage and wealth these people have no claim to distinction, either in the esthetic or in the moral sphere, as they demonstrate with their brutal treatment of Sulocana, she being in effect the human sacrifice they insist on making to their own absurd notion of themselves. Their hostility to Anang's family stems from much more than the gambling dispute. Anang is a *khatrī*, born of a Brahman father and a Kshatriya mother. The abuse Shatru and Anang's father hurl at one another is mostly along caste lines, untranslatable in large part because Nepali is rich in abusive epithets referring to caste and meaningless to those outside the system. And just as Shatru Mardan represents a self-important and obsolescent autocracy (the Ranas), so Anang's father stands for the hypocritical and parasitical community of those Brahmans who wield a power far out of proportion to either their intelligence or their moral integrity. Both classes are the enemies of love, spontaneous and honest feeling, general human decency, and even common sense. Their power is destructive where it should be sustaining, according to both natural familial bonds and the religious precepts they proclaim. Sulocana and Anang are far too fragile to persevere against them, but Bijuli and Timir Mardan are not: by falling in love in the unacceptable modern way and then by living together they affront the tradition of marriage and, worse,

that of the suppressed, near-invisible role a widow is expected to play.

In the tradition of Sanskrit literature there is theoretically no room for tragic endings, and in practice they scarcely ever occur. If *viyoga* is an almost inevitable element of the dramatic substance of both drama and classical *kāvya*, it is also true that such separation is expected just as inevitably to conclude with the reunion of the parted lovers. The drama and *kāvya* constantly allegorize the cyclical nature of human experience, the renewal of the seasons and of time itself, and the potential (and ultimate) harmony of all the workings of the universe. By dealing in his romances with *viyoga* as a situation tragic because it is, as it were, irreversible, Devkota departs strikingly from the tradition with which he was so imbued. The characteristically modern note of tragic irreconcilability, not surprising in itself, is startling in the traditional Indian contexts Devkota provides for it. In his work *Sulocanā* is the apotheosis of the tale saturated in *viyoga* led to a desperately pessimistic conclusion.

Sulocanā makes an interesting companion piece for the *Nepālī Śākuntala,* the latter celebrating a traditional glory and the former castigating the decadence and cruelty of a modern Hindu kingdom. Both dramatize the cause of the wronged woman and her vindication, one as an epic set in legendary times, the other set among tragic realities of the present day. Each is remarkable for its conviction and intensity, and together they may be said to represent the height of Devkota's poetic achievement.

While in exile in Banaras Devkota apparently became fascinated with Greek mythology. Of the five narrative poems of this period, two—*Vasantī* and *Mainā,* short song-narratives in *jhyāure,* both published in 1952—have Nepali subjects. The others are *Māyāvinī Sarsī (Circe the Enchantress . . .), Sundarī Projerpinā (The Fair Prosperina . . .)* and *Pramithus (Prometheus . . .).*

Whether or not this interest in the Hellenic tradition sprang from Devkota's quest to find new analogues to express his criticism of the Rana regime, the scope of the poems is much broader than the nationalistic fervor which informed *Mahārāṇā Pratāp,* to say nothing of the revolutionary poems of the same period of exile, occasional pieces marked by propagandistic sermonizing and slogan-making. *Prometheus,* Devkota's final experiment with epic poetry, is particularly significant as a synthesis of the poet's democratic humanism with the esthetic moralism that so strongly characterized his sense of the poet's vocation; both these elements are electrified by his own intense experience of personal suffering.

Prometheus, though it ends at approximately the same point as Aeschylus' drama, is closer in spirit to Shelley. There is, for instance, no suggestion (as in the Greek work) that for all his heroic opposition to Zeus and his immense benefaction of humankind, Prometheus is nevertheless guilty of hubris. The action of the poem spans the whole story of Gaea and her children, the Titanomachy, Prometheus's civilizing mission to the world of men, and his punishment by Zeus, and ends with Hermes' unsuccessful attempt to reconcile Prometheus with Zeus, with the ensuing rending of the earth

> as though the cosmic panther,
> shaped of blackness, to swallow up all earth
> gaped with the bestial mouth of the vast.

As in the case of the *Nepālī Śākuntala*, Devkota makes only minor changes from the traditional story. Io is omitted, while the Daughters of Okeanos, as consoling as those in Aeschylus, also summon a group of goddesses—Freedom, Hope, Beauty, the Arts, and Love—to comment and prophesy, with Beauty recounting the future wars provoked by Helen in the West and Sita in the East. Devkota emphasizes the altruism and heroism of Prometheus, his compassion for mankind, and his stoic willingness to bear an all-too-human suffering. "Promethean pain I bear," Devkota was to begin his final poem in English a few days before his death, continuing, "Yet a song of joy must I raise," while Prometheus, bearing human pain, after his first night of torment on the rock in the Caucasus, greets the dawn with a magnificent hymn of praise to Apollo. Devkota also speaks of the oppressive regime in Nepal in the course of the work and raises a cry for revolutionary change, but it seems fanciful to cite such lines as the following, as some critics have done, as Marxist:

> Rise armed against the darkness, O man,
> Die deriding the darkness in the red or white heat,
> Take on the awareness of immortality, rise up against
>   heaven.

As in the other narrative poems, there are set pieces, invocations, arguments, and hymns of praise, such as the one to Apollo mentioned above and one to fire, which has an almost Vedic ring to it:

> Hail! Thou art the god of fire,
> O giver of universal life, creator of the jungle,
> destruction of the forest, shaper and dissolver thou!
> thou nourishment of all the world.

There are also occasional echoes of Murray's translation of *Prometheus Unbound*, as [Napali critic Kumarbahadur] Joshi has pointed out, and possibly of Shelley and Wordsworth as well. All in all, the sense of Nepalization is much less apparent than in the *Śākuntala*, and one wonders if Devkota was consciously aiming at a more universal poetry in which the two great traditions that he knew could be synthesized harmoniously. Certainly, no other writer of the subcontinent has dealt with Western classical material with such ambition and such conviction.

The poems that follow *Prometheus* tend to be more intimate and subjective, even before the lyrics that relate specifically to the writer's final illness. Although the obscurities continue, there is less sanskritization, and the material relates more immediately to the poet's experience and to the contemporary life of Nepal without benefit of allegory or transmutation through myth or tradition. Some of the best of these poems appeared in the six issues of *Indrenī* (1956), which was edited by Devkota—poems like **"Pāgal"** (**"Crazy"**), **"Dāl-Bhāt-Ḍukū"** (**"Beans and Rice and Mustard Greens"**) and **"Bhūtlāī Jhaṭāro"** (**"Beat the Ghost"**). This is also the time of the children's poems of *Sunko Bihāna* (*Golden Morning*), published in 1953, and the 1958 collection of humorous verse entitled *Manoranjan* (*Entertainments*), not published until 1967. Even in this essentially light verse the dark note rings unexpectedly, as in the poem called **"Palṭan"** (**"The Battalion"**), a conventional patriotic poem:

> Clay is this body,
>   it flies up and turns to wind.

Or later in the same poem:

> The body becomes dust and goes,
>   only the soul will bloom.

The final poems in Nepali from the last weeks at Shanta Bhavan give every evidence of a trend toward more personal speech, intense and even stark:

> Like sand in a vast desert I am hot,
> I burn, dying without hope, dumb,
> I am empty as a dried-up tree. . . .

This represents the final purgation of the long-lived Romantic spirit in Devkota's works. These last poems suggest strongly that the poet had not ceased growing and had begun to move toward a radically new phase in his development. What precisely it would have been we can only speculate upon, but to judge from the poems of September 1959, the darkening of the spirit would have shone forth with an ever surer clarity of utterance. (pp. 49-55)

> *David Rubin, "Introduction: Laxmiprasad Devkota, His Life and Work and His Place in Nepali Literature," in* Nepali Visions, Nepali Dreams: The Poetry of Laxmiprasad Devkota by Laxmiprasad Devkota, *edited and translated by David Rubin, Columbia University Press, 1980, pp. 1-62.*

ADDITIONAL BIBLIOGRAPHY

Crown, Bonnie R. Review of *Nepali Visions, Nepali Dreams*, by Laxmiprasad Devkota. *World Literature Today* 55, No. 1 (Winter 1981): 182.
  Brief review of *Nepali Visions, Nepali Dreams* which characterizes Devkota as "a writer who is on the periphery of the periphery of world literature" yet is "one of the contemporary poets of the world."

Moreas, Dom. "Dying Poet." In his *Gone Away: An Indian Journal*, pp. 135-50. London: Heinemann, 1960.
  An account of Moreas's meeting with Devkota on the day of the poet's death.

Nathan, Leonard. Review of *Nepali Visions, Nepali Dreams*, by Laxmiprasad Devkota. *The Journal of Asian Studies* XL, No. 4 (August 1981): 838-39.
  Review of *Nepali Visions, Nepali Dreams* in which Nathan points out that Devkota drew upon both Sanskrit and English Romantic traditions and that "these two modes work together smoothly to exaggerate certain characteristics they share, for example, a tendency to emotional grandiosity and a continual dependence on pathetic allegory."

Pradhan, Paras Mani. *Mahakavi Laxmi Prasad Deokota*. Kalimpong, India: Bhagya Laxmi Prakashan, 1978, 84 p.
  Study of the poet's life and works.

Shrestha, Chandra Bahadur. *My Reminiscence of the Great Poet Laxmi Prasad Devkota*. Katmandu: Royal Nepal Academy, 1981, 116 p.
  Reminiscences of Devkota's early years written by a close friend.

James Norman Hall

1887-1951

Charles (Bernard) Nordhoff

1887-1947

American novelists, short story writers, essayists, and historians. Hall was also an autobiographer and poet and wrote under the pseudonym of Fern Gravel.

Nordhoff and Hall collaborated on the three novels of the *Bounty* trilogy—*Mutiny on the Bounty, Men Against the Sea,* and *Pitcairn's Island*—books that remain among the most famous sea adventure stories of all time. Both writers brought to their work a deep familiarity with life in the South Seas, and their meticulous research of the historical events upon which they based their works revealed to them a story that contained, as Robert Roulston noted, "all the elements with which they were most comfortable: a South Sea setting, a clash between freedom and authority, an interplay between primitive and civilized peoples, and a multiplicity of exciting incidents." Although in recent years Nordhoff and Hall have received some criticism for misrepresenting historical fact to suit the purposes of an enthralling narrative, for hundreds of thousands of readers the events of the *Bounty* mutiny are best put forth in their trilogy, and the collaborators have been almost universally praised for their

ability to infuse history with the color, drama, and art of skillfully contrived fiction.

Hall, the elder member of the collaborating team by some two months, was born and raised in Iowa, graduating from Grinnell College in 1910. Afterward, he worked as a social worker in Boston and began publishing poetry and essays in magazines. At this time he met *Atlantic Monthly* editor Ellery Sedgwick, who encouraged his early literary efforts and remained a prominent influence on his life and career. Hall was on a bicycle tour of England when World War I began; lying about his citizenship, he promptly joined the British Army and then the French Flying Service, distinguishing himself as an air ace in the Lafayette Flying Corps. Later, as a flight commander with the United States Air Service, Hall led a fighter squadron that included Lieutenant Eddie Rickenbacker. During the war, Hall published essays about his experiences in the armed forces of three different nations, and his first book, *Kitchener's Mob: The Adventures of an American in Kitchener's Army,* is about his life as an American in the British Army. In 1918 Hall's

53

plane was shot down behind German lines, and he spent the war's last months in a prisoner-of-war camp.

Nordhoff, born in London to American parents, was raised in California and Mexico, where his family owned extensive ranchlands. After graduating from Harvard in 1909, he returned to the American West until enlisting in the French Ambulance Corps during the war. Later, Nordhoff also joined the Lafayette Flying Corps. His letters home, filled with vivid descriptions of his days as an ambulance driver and of aerial battles as a fighter pilot, were sent by his mother to Sedgwick at the *Atlantic Monthly,* where they appeared as true-life war stories, often concurrently with Hall's latest wartime essay. At the war's end Nordhoff and Hall, both decorated pilots and published writers, were asked to write an official history of the Lafayette Flying Corps. The men later recalled that their initial meeting was uncongenial, promising nothing of the close friendship that was to follow.

After overcoming their early dislike of each other, Nordhoff and Hall found that in fact they had a great deal in common, sharing in particular a profound dissatisfaction with the rapid pace of life in postwar Europe and the United States. Deciding that a South Sea island would better suit their temperaments, they obtained a cash advance from *Harper's* magazine for a proposed series of articles about island life and sailed for Papeete, Tahiti, where they lived most of the rest of their lives. After the appearance of the essay collection *Faery Lands of the South Seas,* drawn from their magazine articles, both men continued to write and publish individually. Nordhoff wrote several novels, including *The Fledgling, Pícaro, The Pearl Lagoon,* and *The Derelict,* while Hall published *High Adventure: A Narrative of Air Fighting in France* and *Flying with Chaucer,* volumes of essays based on his wartime flying experiences, as well as two collections of philosophical and travel essays, *On the Stream of Travel* and *Mid-Pacific.*

Acting on a suggestion from Nordhoff's publisher to write a sequel to his popular juvenile adventure novel *The Pearl Lagoon,* Nordhoff and Hall collaborated again, on *Falcons of France: A Tale of Youth and the Air,* in which the now-grown hero of the earlier novel becomes a pilot in the Lafayette Air Corps. The brisk sales of this work, and the pleasure they derived from working together again, led Nordhoff and Hall to look for another theme on which they might collaborate. Both men were familiar with the basic historical facts of the 1789 mutiny aboard the British ship H.M.S. *Bounty*—in fact, Hall lived within sight of the bay where the *Bounty* first anchored, and stories about the mutiny abounded on the island. Their research into the incident revealed that only two earlier books—Sir John Barrow's factual 1831 account and a fictionalized 1845 children's book about Pitcairn's Island—had been written about this famous episode in British naval history. Excited by the prospects of the romantic narrative, the authors began to read through the mass of information available about the mutiny. With the help of a retired British naval officer who combed Admiralty records for them, Nordhoff and Hall obtained thousands of pages of material, including mutineers' diaries, Bligh's account of the event, interviews with the only surviving mutineer found on Pitcairn's Island eighteen years after the mutiny, and transcripts of the trials of those crewmen who were captured on Tahiti and returned to England for court-martial and, in some cases, execution. It was soon apparent to Nordhoff and Hall that the events surrounding the *Bounty* mutiny fell naturally into the three parts of a trilogy: one volume to cover the mutiny itself and the fates of the mutineers and

crewmen left on Tahiti; a second volume chronicling Bligh's incredible feat of navigating the ship's small, overloaded launch across more than three thousand miles of open sea; and finally, a third volume to piece together the turbulent history of the mutineers who went with Fletcher Christian to Pitcairn's Island and who—all but one—died violently there within a few years.

Nordhoff and Hall divided the writing of *Mutiny on the Bounty* about equally, with Nordhoff planning to write the first eight chapters, introducing the main characters, establishing the conflicts between them, and detailing the dramatic difference between the harsh life aboard the ship and the idyllic period spent on Tahiti. Hall took over the story at the outbreak of the mutiny and, after Nordhoff contributed a couple of chapters treating the lives of the men who remained on Tahiti, Hall continued with the account of the arrest of these men, their return to England, and their trial. Nordhoff then wrote an epilogue. The chapter divisions, however, did not remain distinct: the collaborators passed newly completed chapters back and forth between them, reading, commenting on, and often revising one another's work, so that gradually the lines of demarcation between each man's writing became difficult to distinguish. The resulting novel is generally regarded as one of the most finely integrated collaborative efforts in literature.

While three years were devoted to the research and writing of *Mutiny on the Bounty,* the remaining two novels of the trilogy were largely researched and plotted during the work on the first book. Nordhoff and Hall began writing *Pitcairn's Island,* concerning the fate of the mutineers who followed Christian, after completing *Mutiny,* but encountered many difficulties in framing the story, chief among them being the contradictory nature of later reports about the mutineers' lives on the island, and a basic difference in the way they wanted to relate the events. Nordhoff wanted to tell the island's sordid history "in a robust, bloody, and slightly pornographic Elizabethan fashion," while Hall preferred to utilize the history of Pitcairn to expound on his characteristic themes, which have been enumerated by his biographer Robert Roulston as "solitude, Polynesian tranquility menaced by the white man's greed, and the ultimate goodness of mankind." Unable to reconcile their divergent approaches, they sought the advice of editor Edward Weeks, who suggested using as a first-person narrator Alexander Smith, the only Englishman to survive on Pitcairn's Island. Since Smith was wounded and in hiding during the massacre that wiped out every other adult male on the island, his first-person narrative had to be abandoned partway through the book for an omniscient narrator. It is generally agreed that the shift in narrative point of view and the lack of a strong central character (Fletcher Christian is killed about halfway through the story) make *Pitcairn's Island,* despite the obvious drama inherent in the story, the weakest volume of the trilogy.

Originally planned as the final novel of the *Bounty* saga, *Men Against the Sea* was written in about two months after the collaborators temporarily set aside *Pitcairn's Island.* It proved to be the least demanding of the three *Bounty* books. Nordhoff and Hall chose to rely heavily on Bligh's published account of the mutiny and his log of the voyage that he and eighteen loyal crewmen made to Timor in the Dutch East Indies after being cast adrift following the mutiny. Oliver LaFarge, an early reviewer, praised the characterization of Bligh that emerges from the first-person narrative of acting ship's surgeon Thomas Ledward. Roulston differed, calling Ledward "in effect a ventriloquist's dummy for Bligh's self-serving version of the voyage" and maintaining that "Ledward's unvarying idealization'' of the captain contradicted the earlier depiction of Bligh as a tyrant. Nevertheless, Roulston, like all reviewers of the *Bounty* trilogy, acknowledges the gripping excitement of this skillfully told adventure story.

Nordhoff and Hall went on to collaborate on six more novels, three of which—*The Hurricane, The Dark River,* and *No More Gas*—utilize the South Sea island settings that the authors had employed with such facility in the past in both their fiction and nonfiction. *Botany Bay* is a historical novel about the British colonization of Australia, while *Men without Country* and *The High Barbaree* are war stories—the former chiefly memorable for its adaptation as the Humphrey Bogart movie *Passage to Marseilles.* These later collaborations sold fairly well, primarily on the strength of the authors' reputations for crafting exciting adventure novels. However, critical reception was increasingly unenthusiastic. R. L. Duffus, for example, in a review of *The Dark River,* complained of the predictable nature of the plot, though commending those elements of the novel that were characteristic of all of Nordhoff and Hall's fiction: their intimacy with the Polynesian setting and their skill in evoking ''the land, the people, the weather, the language'' of the South Seas.

Although they were ostensibly collaborating on the same footing as always, in fact Hall did more and more of the work on each volume after *Pitcairn's Island.* Personal problems, including the dissolution of his marriage and the exacerbation of his alcoholism, increasingly occupied Nordhoff to the detriment of his writing. Near the end of his life he moved to California with two of his legitimate children and remarried, leaving Hall to oversee his Tahitian property and his other children by his first wife and a mistress. After ten years of ill-health, Nordhoff died of a heart attack in 1947. Hall continued to write essays, short stories, and a novel on his own, and in the 1940s he attained some critical recognition as an essayist, dealing as usual with themes of the beauty of the South Seas and the tendency of white men to despoil the natural rhythms of life on the islands. Hall was at work upon his autobiography, *My Island Home,* when he died four years after Nordhoff.

Nordhoff and Hall's novels received attention primarily in the review columns of the periodical press. From the first reviews of *Mutiny on the Bounty,* their best-known work, critics were enthusiastic in praising the accuracy of detail they brought to their work, as well as the enthralling nature of the adventure stories they chose to relate. David W. Bone, an early reviewer of *Mutiny on the Bounty,* noted that the collaborators infused the historical tale with ''the very breath of life, color, vigor,'' and similarly, Fred T. Marsh, in a review of *Botany Bay,* approved of ''the historical romanticist's approach'' that enabled Nordhoff and Hall to turn history into an adventure story. Although their work has received little retrospective critical commentary, their novels, particularly the three volumes of the *Bounty* trilogy, remain popular with readers and retain a place among the most highly regarded historical novels about the sea.

(See also the Hall entry in *Something about the Author,* Vol. 21; see also the Nordhoff entries in *Contemporary Authors,* Vol. 108, *Dictionary of Literary Biography,* Vol. 9, and *Something about the Author,* Vol. 23.)

PRINCIPAL WORKS

BY CHARLES NORDHOFF AND JAMES NORMAN HALL:

The Lafayette Flying Corps. 2 vols. (military history) 1920

Faery Lands of the South Seas (essays) 1921
Falcons of France: A Tale of Youth and the Air (novel) 1929
Mutiny on the Bounty (novel) 1932
Men Against the Sea (novel) 1934
Pitcairn's Island (novel) 1934
The Hurricane (novel) 1936
The Dark River (novel) 1938
No More Gas (novel) 1940
Botany Bay (novel) 1941
Men without Country (novel) 1942
The High Barbaree (novel) 1945

BY JAMES NORMAN HALL:

Kitchener's Mob: The Adventures of an American in Kitchener's Army (autobiographical essays) 1916
High Adventure: A Narrative of Air Fighting in France (essays) 1918
On the Stream of Travel (essays) 1926
Mid-Pacific (essays) 1928
Flying with Chaucer (autobiographical essays) 1930
The Tale of a Shipwreck (nonfiction) 1934
The Friends (poetry) 1939
Dr. Dogbody's Leg (novel) 1940
Oh, Millersville! [as Fern Gravel] (poetry) 1940
Under a Thatched Roof (essays) 1942
Lost Island (novel) 1944
A Word for His Sponsor (poetry) 1949
Far Lands (novel) 1950
The Forgotten One and Other True Tales of the South Seas (essays) 1952
My Island Home (unfinished autobiography) 1952

BY CHARLES NORDHOFF:

The Fledgling (novel) 1919
Pícaro (novel) 1921
The Pearl Lagoon (novel) 1924
The Derelict (novel) 1928

THE NATION (essay date 1916)

[*The following excerpt is a favorable review of Hall's first book,* Kitchener's Mob.]

James Norman Hall, in **Kitchener's Mob,** . . . takes us over some of the same ground that was covered by Ian Hay's *The First Hundred Thousand.* The title, ''Kitchener's Mob,'' which was applied to the early thousands of the new armies and has stuck to them now that they are counted by millions, is by no means a sobriquet of contempt; it is the name the men chose for themselves, and the fact that they did so is perhaps as good an answer as could be found to the fear that England herself may be subdued to the militaristic spirit which she is fighting. One cannot imagine a body of Prussian troops alluding irreverently to itself as ''Hindenburg's Mob.'' The author is a young American who happened to be in England when war broke out and over whom, in his own words, "the mob spirit gained its mastery" in August, 1914. . . . Mr. Hall's story is of the Fusiliers, Cockneys most of them, but with a sprinkling of men from all parts of the kingdom. The nine months of training—a weary ordeal—is described vividly and picturesquely in the first few chapters. The rest of the book has to do with the battalion's experiences at the front, culminating in the bloody part which it bore in the Battle of Loos. As an American of good breeding and education sharing as a private the fortunes of his British companions in arms, Mr. Hall writes from an interesting point of view. His comrades were principally of the "lower middle class," innocent of much culture or education. Says Mr. Hall, summarizing at the end Thomas Atkins as he found him: "In England, before I knew him for the man he is, I said, 'How am I to endure living with him?' And now I am thinking, how am I to endure living without him; without the inspiration of his splendid courage; without the visible example of his unselfish devotion to his fellows?" The book is full of high tributes to the qualities, moral and physical, of the men of these new armies. . . . Naturally, Mr. Hall's narrative covers much ground that is now more or less familiar, but his style is lively and vigorous and his observation keen. Some things in the book are particularly well done, notably the very interesting and detailed description of the trench-system.

A review of "Kitchener's Mob," in The Nation, *Vol. CII, No. 2658, June 8, 1916, p. 626.*

THE NATION   (essay date 1919)

[*The following excerpt is a review of Nordhoff's first book,* The Fledgling.]

The literature which deals with that once undiscovered country, the sky, is still, in its non-technical aspect, entirely composed of war reminiscences. It is not surprising that it should emphasize the flyer rather than the region in which he flies. Nevertheless the point to which this emphasis is carried is at times irritating. Readers who open a volume with some hope for a taste of the superb panorama and strange exhilaration which flight must give are buried under a trivial narrative of the squadron mess, of night scrambles from the bombs of "Boches," or, at best, descriptions of aerial combats in terms of the number of yards at which the aviator began firing, the jammings of a machine-gun, and the escape of one or the other of the combatants by certain acrobatic manoeuvres. Too rarely does the scenic or dramatic word break this technical recitative. One cause for this is fairly obvious. "You don't get time to think," says Mr. Boyd Cable for the flyer. "If you stop to think, you're dead." The intense absorption of the aerial fighter in the business of fighting doubtless accounts for the frequent flatness of his narrative. (p. 251)

It is the peculiar merit of Mr. Nordhoff's *The Fledgling* that it [escapes from chronology into the glow of art]. The two hundred pages of the little volume are an artistic unit. Trivialities of flying school and squadron mess, scanted as they deserve, become golden. Combat in the skies has all the vividness a poet could "wish upon" it. The air is "rocked and torn with the passage of projectiles" beneath. The woods are alive with the "winking flash of batteries." The foe ("dark ugly brutes with broad, short wings and pointed snouts"), the combat with its "luminous streams of bullets," "incandescent sparks," "stutter of guns," the escape from danger in a "furious rush of air"—all are embedded in a simple but eloquent

art which proves the writer's ability to recount as well as he can fight. No more vividly colored and artistic picture of the fighting flyer has been drawn, though many have essayed the portrait with a richer palette at hand.

Mr. Nordhoff does more than paint the flyer. Although personality dominates his record, the sky has a real place in it, too. Like one of the forty-niners who could hunt for gold and wonder at Yosemite at the same time, Mr. Nordhoff, even if busy with "stick" or gun, observes "a world of utter celestial loneliness—dazzling pure sun, air like the water of coral atoll, . . . cloudy prairies, great fantastic mountains . . . foothills and long divides, vast snowy peaks, impalpable sisters of Orizaba or Chimborazo, and deep gorges, ever narrowing, widening, or deepening, across whose shadowy depths drove ribbons of thin gray mist." No wonder that for him, twenty thousand feet above earth, "there are moments when infinite things are very close." (p. 252)

"War and the Air," in The Nation, *Vol. CIX, No. 2825, August 23, 1919, pp. 251-52.*

FREDERICK O'BRIEN   (essay date 1921)

[*O'Brien was an American journalist and travel writer whose books* White Shadows in the South Seas *(1919),* Mystic Isles of the South Seas *(1921), and* Atolls of the Sun *(1922) are credited with arousing interest in the South Seas and helping lead to a revival of interest in the works of Herman Melville. In the following excerpt, O'Brien praises Nordhoff and Hall's first collaborative effort,* Faery Lands of the South Seas.]

About two years ago, two young American men, who had fought as aviators throughout the great war, sought aloofness from the people and scenes of the civilization which had caused the conflict in Europe. They set out for the South Seas to find a quieter adventure and a different humanity. *Faery Lands of the South Seas* is the result of their quest, and is a beautiful and true portrayal of life in their new environment, the atolls of the Pacific Ocean, which lie far below the Line, and which are the most fantastic and amazing spawn of the pregnant, tropic main.

I met Hall and Nordhoff in Tahiti after they had been a few months there; and I marked the manner of their life, their honest, inquiring attitude towards the native and his customs, their simple way of moving about. I felt then, though I had read nothing by them, that if they could use words skilfully they were sure to write challenging and factual stories of the people and islands of those latitudes.

They have exceeded my hopes, and in their book, *Faery Lands*, they present a little world of salt water and coral strand, of ships and seamen, chiefs and castaways, passionate brown women and more wilful white men, that is as a lovely orchid among the many weedy volumes upon the South Seas lately sprung from a gainful desire.

They write in an undertone, carefully, restrainedly, but with an appreciation of the values of the romance and the bizarre atmosphere of their activities that is found in few recent books upon a theme dear to the reading public, who also have their dream of perfection. They are young Americans who have come through a fiery ordeal, who have sailed through more terrible airs than the languorous ones of the tropics, and whose spirits, though neither tamed nor blunted by their constant tourney with death in the most desperate lists of all time, have been attuned to a hatred of the shams in our deadening civilization. (p. 226)

[The] plain relation of their daily hazards, their voyages on tiny schooners, their tossings in whale-boats and canoes, their contacts with strange and interesting men and women, their casual unfoldment of the tragedies and comedies of the lives of these people of the Dangerous Archipelago, have an epic quality, a poetic relation to the soul of mankind everywhere throughout the ages, that is thought stirring and of solid fibre.

Hall and Nordhoff are self-effacing men who keep as much as possible in the background of their chapters, but whose sympathetic personalities, however hidden by their modesty, shine through their interest in the waifs of the atolls, and the brown indigenes among whom they have cast their lot. There is naught of the wretched air of superiority so common among British and American writers, the contempt of the legend and mystery of native life, or the feeble burlesque and ridicule so often heaped upon the white men who have chosen a surrounding so simple as to be unsupportable by the victims of the psychoses of cities.

The joint authors of *Faery Lands* write alternate chapters, and their wanderings are not together, yet there is a cohesion and continuity to the book which makes the appearance of flowing narrative. There are many delineations of the character of aborigines and whites, vivid sketches of picturesque and puzzling beachcombers and students, men who have stowed themselves away in this bight of the loneliest sea of all the world's waters, and whose fleeing from their fellows is often unsolved in these pages.

The wondrous skill of diver and fisher, the pantomimic dances, the ancient games, the savage songs, and the ways of love upon these low and treacherous coral reefs are told with a fidelity and a charm commensurate with the square purpose and fine instinct of these former fliers in the face of the sun. It must be considered that they are not worn-out products of our industrial machine, but courageous, tremendously alive youths, strong in body, proven of soul, educated, and sophisticated. In the last paragraph, when Hall had finished his tale of a narrow escape from death in shipwreck, and Nordhoff asked him: "What are your plans? Our year in the South Seas is up. Where are you going now?" the answer was, "I have no plans except that I doubt if I shall ever go north again. I may be wrong, but I believe I've had enough of civilization to last me the rest of my life. We are happy here. Why should we leave the islands?"

They are there now, Hall and Nordhoff, two among the few men I know who are fitted by what they have been and are to live happily in the South Seas, to bring happiness to the gentlest and most admirable of uncultured peoples, and to write about them in an informing, sympathetic, and realistic manner. (pp. 226-27)

Frederick O'Brien, "Salt Water and Coral Strand,"
in The Literary Review, *December 3, 1921, pp. 226-27.*

THE NEW YORK TIMES BOOK REVIEW (essay date 1924)

[*In the following excerpt, the anonymous reviewer discusses Nordhoff's novel* Pícaro.]

It has always seemed that there was much to be said for the elder brother in the parable of the prodigal son—his fit of the sulks, as the lovable wastrel feasts on the fatted calf, finds its universal parallel in the despairing envy of the sober dependables as they witness the triumphs of the less worthy but far more charming irresponsible playboys over their own more staid but more enduring virtues. Mr. Nordhoff in *Picaro* supplies a modern twist to the beautiful contrast in temperaments of the biblical anecdote.

The two brothers in Mr. Nordhoff's novel, Enrique, or "Picaro," and Blaise, are derived from a union of two vanished cultures; their father is an irreconcilable of the defeated Confederate Army, while the mother is a descendant of proud old Spanish grandees. The California ranch which is their home is a last refuge of the punctilios and customs of the old South and the Latin West. Mr. Nordhoff tells the story of the two boys in a vein of finely sustained romantic irony. It is Picaro, whose nickname belies his nature, who glories in the abstract side of the mechanical progress of his age, yet its speed and recklessness are mirrored in the younger brother. Picaro, creator, inventor, constructor of new values of the machine, is willing to leave to Blaise the allurements of the city for the unreal serenity and loveliness of the ranch. Blaise, the profligate, is no less able a horseman than a motorist, and he takes the good things of country and town without giving a fragment of himself. It is, then, Blaise who is to carry on the family name and tradition on the ranch, while Picaro goes to the city to make his own way.

Picaro's renunication of the domain and the girl he loves to Blaise, who receives both with indifference, is accomplished with a deft quirk of antithesis. The two brothers are again brought into one arena in Paris, where Picaro has gone to learn the trade of airplane motors and to perfect his own invention. Picaro and Blaise are thrown into high relief by the coming of the war; Picaro's company makes the motors which propel Blaise's airplane. Mr. Nordhoff gives a lively sense of the romance of the air. Blaise in the clouds, bored at having no Germans to kill, and Picaro in the foundry, luminous with the visions of power coming to form under his hands, are again the man of action and the man of reflection. Blaise sees nothing of the magic and marvel of unfolding panoramas beneath him; Picaro's drawing-board is transparent to his vision of future developments of motor science.

After the war the return of the two brothers to the California ranch is an inevitable projection of their divergences. Blaise brings back a broken body and a discontented spirit, Picaro a small fortune and a ripened philosophy. Picaro restores the hereditary patrimony, while Blaise scours the countryside in his automobile, racing at eighty miles an hour. The girl, standing between the two of them, turns at length to Picaro. The misfit, who was a hero in the air and wholly fulfilled in war, eliminates himself from the more intricate and pedestrian exactions of peace.

Picaro, both the character and the novel, show minor defects of execution. The author is, almost, at too much pains to balance each brother within himself and one against the other. At times it is perilously close to formula and again the sharp design is lost in a maze of extraneous details. Accident is, perhaps, too kind to Picaro. The ranch and Paris and a multitude of colorful personalities are not only vividly visualized, but are an authentic enrichment of Mr. Nordhoff's intention. It is an able first novel.

"Two Brothers," in The New York Times Book Review, *December 21, 1924, p. 16.*

Hall's family picnicking on a hill overlooking the bay where the Bounty *first anchored off Tahiti.*
Reproduced by permission of Little, Brown & Company.

ELLERY SEDGWICK   (essay date 1932)

[*Sedgwick was the editor of the* Youth's Companion, Leslie's
Monthly Magazine, *the* American Magazine, *and, from 1909 until
1938, of the* Atlantic Monthly. *Sedgwick was a friend and mentor
of both Nordhoff and Hall, and in the following excerpt from an
introduction to* Mutiny on the Bounty, *he briefly explains how
the two came to collaborate on the novel.*]

They began it as buddies. Nordhoff was a graduate of the
Ambulance Service. Norman Hall was a veteran of Kitchener's
Army. Just by chance he was in London during the first August
days of 1914, and when the mob which went swirling round
Nelson's Column to the lilt of ''Good-bye, Leicester Square''
was hammered into the kernel of an army, he was part of it.
Honorably discharged, he reenlisted, this time in the French
aviation service, and found the berth he had been fashioned
for in the Escadrille Lafayette. Flying was the thing for Charles
Nordhoff, too, and when he joined the squadron two contributors to the *Atlantic Monthly* met each other for the first time,
and interchanged compliments gracefully given and received.
This chance friendship, springing from a common love for
letters, was riveted by the comradeship of high adventure. Each
found in the other a man whose silence and whose speech
delighted and refreshed him. From that day to this, they have
shared a common destiny as brothers. (p. vii)

When both men were mustered from the service I saw them
again on a memorable occasion. Each wrote to me without the
other's knowledge, asking for advice. Both had lived with

intensity lives high above the conflict, and to both the stridency
and (as they felt) the vulgarity of post-war civilization was past
endurance. Each had ambitions, talents, and memories of great
price. To transmute these intangibles into three meals *per diem*
was the prosaic problem put up to me. How well I remember
the day they came to Boston. Reticent and illusive, there was
something in each of them that in its pure essence I have not
known elsewhere. Conrad called it Romance. When Romance
and Chivalry come to refresh my cumbered mind, I see those
two young men just as I saw them then.

We talked and we talked, and then we adjourned for counsel
to a little Italian restaurant. . . .

We planned with the resolution of genius. Then and there Hall
and Nordhoff drew up the rough outline of a miraculous work
on the South Seas. . . . (p. viii)

Historically, the first work of [Hall and Nordhoff] was the
official history of the Lafayette Flying Corps. Then came, I
believe, the work on the South Seas which, as I have said, I
had the honor to sell. Nordhoff wrote by himself a capital boy's
story, ***The Pearl Lagoon,*** based on his own early life in Lower
California. Hall meantime turned out some admirably individual essays, stories, and poems, but the firm added enormously to its reputation when the story of the Escadrille was brilliantly
retold as fiction under the title, ***Falcons of France.*** Of all aerial
narratives, this, in my judgment, takes the first place both in
its thrilling realism and in that delicate understanding of the

coordination of mind, body, and spirit which is at once a flyer's inheritance and his salvation.

A play followed—*The Empty Chair*—accepted for production on the screen. Of this I know only at secondhand, and will not speak, though I cannot but remark how strange is that conjunction of the planets under whose influence Hall and Nordhoff are reborn in Hollywood.

Now comes the firm's latest and best bid for fame and fortune. Reader, have you ever heard of the strange history of His Majesty's Ship *Bounty*? If ever the sea cast up a saltier story, I should like to know it. A chronicle of its events, clumsy enough in the telling, appeared—Lord, how long since: *The Pitcairn Islanders*, I think was the name of this particular volume. Anyway, it was bound in green and stamped in gold, and for all its heavy-footed style, a boy curled up on a sofa fifty years ago wore the pages through. There was mutiny on the good ship, as the world remembers. Lieutenant Bligh, the Commander, was lowered into his long boat to drift, God knows where, and the mutineers cracked on sail for Tahiti and Fate. At any rate, that story is of the primeval stuff Romance is made of, and if Captain Hall and Lieutenant Nordhoff are not the men to write it, then, thought I, Providence has been clean wrong in all the games she has played on them from the very beginning. I broached the idea to Hall, or perhaps he mentioned it first to me. Anyway, we both knew this was not a chance to be missed, though one thing we were certain of— that a story so perfect must be told with perfect accuracy. A whole literature has been burgeoning about it for a century, and if the ultimate account is to go into a novel, nothing of the truth must be sacrificed. For Romance is not capricious, it is an attitude of Fate, and Fate, my friends, is greatly to be respected. So on a visit to London in the Spring of 1931 I sought the assistance of Dr. Leslie Hotson, who knows the British Museum as if it were the lining of his trousers pocket. We hit on the perfect record worker, and in due time this lady and I laid hands on every scrap of pertinent evidence. We had photostatic copies of every page of the reports of the court martial of the mutineers, hand written in beautiful copper plate. We assaulted the Admiralty, to which our bountiful thanks are due, for within its sacred precincts Captain Tufuell of His Majesty's Navy made copies of the deck and rigging plans of the *Bounty*, and in his goodness even made an admirably detailed model of the ship. Meanwhile, booksellers, the mouldier the better, were put on the trail for volumes of the British Navy of the period. Engravers' collections were searched for illustrations of Captain Bligh and of the rascals he set sail with. Item by item, a library unique in the annals of collecting was built, boxed, and shipped to Tahiti. The firm of Hall and Nordhoff hired by way of inspiration the first room that ever they lived in on the Islands. They pinned maps to the walls, stuck up deck and rigging plans, propped photographs of the model on the table in front of them, and, wonder of wonders, in spite of the fascination of their collection, in the face of the perfume blowing in at their windows, in defiance of the Heaven that Idleness is in the tropics, they fell to work!

[*Mutiny on the Bounty*] is the book they have written. Read it, and you, too, will know that Romance has come into her own. (pp. ix-x)

Ellery Sedgwick, in a foreword to Mutiny on the Bounty *by Charles Nordhoff and James Norman Hall, Little, Brown, and Company, 1932, pp. vii-x.*

DAVID W. BONE (essay date 1932)

[*Bone was a Scottish naval officer and a historian, novelist, and short story writer whose works invariably deal with nautical themes.*

In the following excerpt, he praises the verisimilitude and enthralling nature of Mutiny on the Bounty.]

Quite frequently the annals of sea tragedy and disaster have been enlisted by the romantic novelist to provide structure for a plot, but it is not often that one finds a noteworthy case brought up and paraphrased with such understanding and sympathy and such fidelity to the truth of it as in the instance of [*Mutiny on the Bounty*]. The general practice is to graft the pet and particular subject vogue of the day of writing on to the gnarled trunk of a bygone period, with results that are rarely other than a distorted growth. South Sea Island nonsense is largely the vogue of today: there is not a "sea ghost" but is busy (a weather eye on Hollywood) on a script in which the pelvic wrigglings of a movie *tapu* are given the first consideration. In this book the authors make no effort to plunge into the tide that flows towards the silver screen although they could—with ample warrant—have out-Horned any vivid imaginer in detail of a South Sea idyll. They maintain the spirit and, indeed, the language, of 1787 and present the full and thrilling tale as Roger Byam, once midshipman in the *Bounty*, would recall it—after many years—in the quiet of his West Country home.

Superficially, one might be inclined to consider that the authors had the book already written for them, but that is very far from the case. Into the old formal tale they have succeeded in putting the very breath of life, color, vigor, and all with admirable restraint. Under their hands Roger Byam becomes a living character and his tale reveals the genesis of mutiny at sea, the dilemma of conflicting loyalties and likings, duress, trial by court-martial, and the final whiplash of authority that left three dark figures to dangle from the yard-arm of the *Brunswick* in full view of a sullen Fleet.

The art of the book is well nigh perfect. In all my acquaintance with the literature of the sea I can recall no more believable and arresting figure than the Roger Byam whom the authors have created, largely—or so I surmise—from the detailed account of the court-martial held in the *Iron Duke*, September '17 . . . and from the known fact that, after being condemned to death and later exonerated from the charge of complicity, Byam attained to the rank of Captain in the Royal Navy. The character, kindly and serious minded, of the youthful midshipman (as evinced in that dark trial) is developed in the aged narrator who "in the evening, when the unimportant duties of an old man's day are done," conjures up the ghosts of bygone shipmates in the *Bounty* and gives to each, loyalist and mutineer alike, his due. The reader is engaged by this kindly attitude at the very first opening of the volume. All passion dissolved in retrospect, the narrator displays no rancor at the folly of his commander and his shipmates that brought him to the prisoner's bar. There is no embittered apportionment of blame, no fierce revolt at the naval system of his day that encouraged mutiny from such trifles as a theft of cocoanuts. As something inevitable, he traces the source of the disaster: petty tyrannies, stifled murmurings, meanness in the establishment of rations, inconsiderate reprimand in full hearing of the ratings of the crew (that fashioned the leader of the revolt from among the commissioned ranks), it is all credible, all too true.

Altogether, an unusual and completely satisfying book that the reader of this review is entreated to consider antidote to so much of the spectacular and specious poison that passes for "sea" literature today. (pp. 141, 144)

David W. Bone, "The Captain's Cocoanuts," in The Saturday Review of Literature, *Vol. IX, No. 11, October 1, 1932, pp. 141, 144.*

OLIVER LA FARGE (essay date 1934)

[*In the following excerpt from a review of* Men Against the Sea, *La Farge commends Nordhoff and Hall's accomplishment in writing a "sea story" without falling into the use of specialized terminology incomprehensible to nonseafaring readers. The critic also notes the novel's skilled characterizations and the quiet restraint that typifies the authors' prose style.*]

Some men reach their full stature only in times of crisis and disaster; when things go normally, they may abuse power if they have it, be overbearing, exercise an excessive force and even cruelty, or, if they be of another type or in different circumstances, show themselves careless, incompetent, thoughtless until a situation arises which really calls upon them to show their mettle. Captain Bligh of H. M. Armed Transport *Bounty* was a man of the former class. Cold history, and the splendid reinterpretation of it by these same authors in *Mutiny on the Bounty,* have amply set forth the man's violence and heartlessness when none but the relatively routine difficulties of his task confronted him. What happened to his character when his violent nature was counterbalanced by conditions of continuous and imminent, deadly danger, when daily and hourly his own life and those of eighteen men depended upon his firmness and self-control, forms the fascinating major theme of [*Men Against the Sea*].

The story of the *Bounty* is well known. The strange phenomenon of Pitcairn Island, continuing to this day, has intrigued many writers, though perhaps none so felicitous as Messrs. Nordhoff and Hall. Much less attention has been given to the story of the loyal group which followed Captain Bligh overside into the *Bounty*'s launch to sail more than three thousand miles in an open boat too small for the load, on starvation rations, in every kind of weather.

The sheer feat of seamanship and the plain endurance recorded is amazing; perhaps without parallel in the annals of the sea. To lovers of salt water, a mere log of the cruise would perhaps be sufficiently interesting reading, but this book offers more varied fare. True, one sails the whole distance as one reads; there is no sparing of storm, starvation, sickness, and narrowly averted disaster. But neither is this a "sea story" in the sense that the reader must know about, and care for, nautical matters to find interest in it. Without skimping or omitting, the writers have succeeded in giving full value to the performance of the launch and the men who sailed her, and yet there is scarcely a phrase in the whole book not comprehensible to any landsman. And better still, all of this serves as the means through which the characters of Captain Bligh and his eighteen men are revealed—the craven Lamb; Nelson, the sensitive, gallant scientist; the surgeon, Ledward, through whom the tale is told; men of all ranks and ratings, the character of each developing under successive trials, and over all the dominant figure of Bligh.

The story is the captain's. . . . The portrayal of his character, its complexities and its consistency despite apparent inconsistencies is in itself enough to make the book worthwhile.

There must have been many temptations for the authors to overwrite their story. The dramatic dangers, the pathetic revelations of human nature, and such situations as the starving crew, weak and sick from lack of food, water, and rest, coasting along fertile, lovely islands on which they dared not land for fear of the savage inhabitants, would have lured many writers into purple passages. But the whole book is written with a steady, quiet factualness which does not grow stale, and which in the end creates cumulatively more dramatic effect than any amount of fervid writing could have done. Of course, it also serves excellently the purpose of the authors, which is to give the impression, not of a partly fictitious reconstruction, but of a true first-hand account.

A few of the characters, particularly the midshipmen, go unrealized. . . .

Whatever the unevennesses may be, this is a story of a great feat upon salt water, told with unflagging interest; it is also a fine delineation of character, a thorough study of men under stress. That would seem to be a sufficiency of perfections in one book.

Oliver La Farge, "Bligh of the 'Bounty' Becomes a Hero," in The Saturday Review of Literature, *Vol. X, No. 25, January 6, 1934, p. 393.*

LINCOLN COLCORD (essay date 1934)

[*In the following excerpt, Colcord discusses Nordhoff and Hall's necessarily fictionalized account of what happened to the* Bounty *mutineers on Pitcairn's Island.*]

Several years ago Charles Nordhoff and James Norman Hall set themselves the task of reviving in narrative form and full romantic detail the famous old story of the mutiny on board H.M.S. Bounty in the South Seas in 1789. Readers are familiar with the two previous volumes, *Mutiny on the Bounty* and *Men Against the Sea,* in which the authors so vividly and authentically recount for a modern era this imperishable drama of the Pacific, the former being the story of the mutiny itself, the latter the tale of Captain Bligh's remarkable 3,000-mile trip in an open boat after he and eighteen others had been set adrift by the mutineers.

Now comes the third volume in the trilogy, *Pitcairn's Island,* which aims to tell what happened to Fletcher Christian and his mutineers, with their women folk from Tahiti, after they had rid themselves of Captain Bligh and the others, and found an uninhabited refuge in the midst of the vast ocean, and burned the *Bounty* to the water's edge and settled down to live out their lives beyond the world's horizon. I say "aims to tell what happened" because here for the first time in their work the authors must necessarily fall back on their imaginations and weave not only the setting but also the plot of the tale. No dependable record exists for this most romantic consummation of an utterly romantic episode in history.

Pitcairn's Island was re-discovered to the world in 1808 by the American sealing vessel Topaz, commanded by Captain Mayhew Folger, eighteen years after the Bounty refugees had established their colony there. At that time only one of the mutineers, Alexander Smith, was alive; all the others, with one exception, had met violent deaths. Stark tragedy had lived on this lonely island during the intervening period, with only Smith to tell the tale. He never wrote down the facts. From 1808 to 1829 Smith related his story to half a dozen different explorers who called at the island; it is from their half-dozen different second-hand accounts that we have all we know of the terrible early years of the Pitcairn colony. Thus the true explanation of events and motives is anyone's choice, subject to certain broad facts like the massacre by the natives, the distilling of

Scene from the 1964 film Mutiny on the Bounty. *The Granger Collection, New York.*

liquor by McCoy, and the final revolt of the women against the besotted remnant of the Bounty's company after Christian had been killed.

This part of the *Bounty* story has always appealed most fascinatingly to the public eye; generations of British and American families lavished their sympathies on it in the forgotten days when sea life touched the northern home lands in an active way. . . . The patriarch Alexander Smith, the head of the colony and the only white survivor, had "found religion" at last; he had taught the half-breed children their catechism, and they had come off to the first ships singing veritable English hymns and saying "sir" to the officers. Everything about it was perfect from a sentimental standpoint.

Yet eighteen years previously the ill-starred Bounty had landed on this island nine white mutineers, six native men and twelve native women, of whom some seventeen or eighteen persons had died violently in the interval. Lust and drunkenness had reigned for years; the island had run blood. No one could say precisely who the fathers of these fabulous children were. What had happened? Who had killed whom and why? Was Smith telling the truth, or was he covering up a part of the past? Which of the varying accounts of what Smith said was to be believed? How could such beauty and truth have sprung from such vile beginnings? In short, what was the real story?

No one could ever answer that question, of course; and there lies the chief fascination. . . .

By its very straightforwardness and simplicity, and by its fidelity to the scene, everything that Nordhoff and Hall have written about the South Seas bears a special stamp of worth and charm. The story they have outlined as an explanation of the dark and mysterious Pitcairn years is certainly the most acceptable I have ever read—a genuine and thrilling tale. My own suspicion has always been that the real truth of Pitcairn, if it could be run down in detail, would be too grim and sordid to read about at all or make into a proper story. The scene has to be glossed over with romance or it cannot be borne.

It must be confessed, though, that one feels the artificiality of the present effort too keenly at times; *Pitcairn's Island* is not a book to stand with *Men Against the Sea.* One wonders, for instance, over the reason for the native massacre. Christian knew there was talk of dividing the land and leaving the natives out of the division; why didn't he do something about it? He was not a man to sit idle and let a crisis burst over his head. The plot here seems arranged for purposes of tragedy.

And there is something in the characterization of both Alexander Smith and Edward Young that seems fundamentally inconsistent. These men sink too willingly into the debaucheries of the period induced by McCoy's manufacture of liquor.

But regardless of these points, pretty thin when the tale itself goes so bravely, *Pitcairn's Island* serves with power and insight to bring out once again the classic outlines of the old *Bounty* drama, that incredibly perfect tragedy, full in every detail, that actually happened in the world of men some hundred and fifty years ago. Young people who have never heard of the *Bounty* may think of this book as a romance and nothing more; but it is from the standpoint of history that it really should be considered.

> Lincoln Colcord, ''The Mystery of the 'Bounty' Mutineers,'' in New York Herald Tribune Books, *November 4, 1934, p. 4.*

PERCY HUTCHISON   (essay date 1936)

[*In the following excerpt from a review of* The Hurricane, *Hutchison notes the authors' facility and familiarity with South Sea settings.*]

With that instinct for picking up in document and tradition the material for a rousing yarn which they showed in their trilogy based on the Bounty mutiny, Charles Nordhoff and James Norman Hall in *Hurricane* have turned out a romance of South Sea island folk that many will find affecting, and all will vote exciting. Messrs. Nordhoff and Hall know their atolls and their coral reefs. They have for some years lived in Tahiti; they have sailed all the nearby seas. They are discriminatingly aware of cultural variations. When these two novelists write of Polynesia and the Polynesians, they write of realities with which they have lived in close touch. In its essentials *Hurricane* is as soundly based as any of the Malaysian tales of Joseph Conrad. It has not the same depth as *Almayer's Folly* or *An Outcast of the Islands*. But perhaps the Malay has more intelligence, certainly a deeper wiliness, than the Polynesian, who appears to exhibit the sensitiveness of the deer rather than the cunning of the fox or the ferocity of the tiger.

Inevitably the title suggests the sea. As a matter of fact, the story is primarily of the land, of an atoll, an island in the broad expanse of sea which lay in the hurricane's path. For plausibility's sake, the tale is told from the point of view of one familiar with the series of events, in this case the French physician of the islands. . . .

The authors have done a fine job of cumulative narrative description. . . . In the dropping of the glass, the increasing velocity of the wind, the steady heightening of the sea, the reader feels, with all its sinister cumulation of terrific impact, the hurricane creep up on him. . . .

The tale closes on a romantic note.

Hurricane is a grand yarn. It is full of action from the first page to the last. Its successive climaxes arouse the reader as successive reports from a gun might do. Only by attenuating the definition to the utmost may the book be called a novel. The psychology is too direct and simple even to suggest that there is any combat of psychological forces. Nevertheless, *Hurricane* remains a tale that stirs one's deeper feelings. And the story is told with unaffected beauty. Also, there is originality, both of plot and scene. Messrs. Nordhoff and Hall have again struck a fresh note.

> Percy Hutchison, ''A South Sea Island Story by Nordhoff and Hall,'' in The New York Times Book Review, *February 9, 1936, p. 4.*

CHRISTOPHER MORLEY   (essay date 1936)

[*Morley was a popular American novelist, journalist, and literary critic. Throughout his long career he worked on the editorial staffs of several newspapers and magazines, including the New York* Evening Post, Ladies' Home Journal *and for nearly twenty years, the* Saturday Review of Literature. *In the following excerpt, Morley favorably reviews* The Hurricane.]

Nordhoff and Hall have made the South Pacific real to many, from Pitcairn Island to the Great Barrier Reef. They now follow their great saga of the *Bounty* and her men with [*The Hurricane*], a story of today, cast as fiction but having all the force and terror of fact. It is told somewhat in the Conrad tradition, an all-night narrative by the grizzled Breton doctor who has been for fifteen years the medical officer of a group of coral islands. It will very likely send some of us back to reread *Typhoon*, but I hope I am not silly enough to suggest comparisons. This story does not percolate through such finely meshed commentary, ironic and philosophized, as was Conrad's habit. But its clear simplicity is its peculiar merit, and I rather think it takes its place alongside the great storm-pieces. There will hardly be a reader, if he should chance to encounter the book on a night of wind, who will not anxiously wish to consult a barometer. . . .

The story is wise and kind, witty in character-drawing, horrible in power, superbly told.

> Christopher Morley, ''All Night Narrative,'' in The Saturday Review of Literature, *Vol. XIII, No. 6, February 15, 1936, p. 7.*

R. L. DUFFUS   (essay date 1938)

[*In the following excerpt from a review of* The Dark River, *Duffus suggests that the authors have lost their usual aggressiveness and originality and have instead told a predictably plotted story.*]

Readers of *Mutiny on the Bounty* and *Men Against the Sea* may be surprised when they have penetrated a little way into this novel of ill-fated young love, of a baby changed in the cradle, and, in fact, of almost all the romantic trappings except the strawberry mark on the left shoulder. There is no character in this book who would eat nails, except General Hardie, who would eat them if he thought his duty as a true-born Englishman and his allegiance to the lighter-colored races of mankind required it. The two veterans of the Lafayette Esquadrille have not exactly gone soft, but it does seem as though they had been reading Pierre Loti or somebody. They have told a story which has its moments of poignancy and beauty, but which just hasn't any bite in it. It may have a motion picture in it, but not until Hollywood has given it a shot in the arm. (p. 2)

[*The Dark River*] is the sort of story that one begins eagerly and reads with great expectations. Naturally no one can tell Messrs. Nordhoff and Hall anything about Tahiti. They have lived there since 1920, which is different from stopping off between ships. They are sensitive to its loveliness and its melancholy, and they were plainly willing to bust their buttons getting a new story out of it. The story is of young love, which is tremendously interesting to young lovers, but needs spice if it is to hold the interest of middle-aged persons or of persons who do not at the moment happen to be what is called in love—all told, quite a sizable fraction of the book-buying public. The standard South Sea romance must necessarily be inter-racial—and in a way this one is, even though the lovely Naia is really as free from the Polynesian bar sinister as the general himself.

A plot demands obstacles, and this one has them. . . . A South Sea romance should have some superstition in it—if you shout from the echo rock you will never go away from Tahiti; the dead may still have desires and influence the living—and this romance has it. There must be physical adventure—and we have that, and it is good.

But on the whole the authors have not been successful in their inventions. What is good in the book, and what will help carry it with numerous readers who wish them well, is their knowledge of the South Seas, their feeling for atmosphere, and two or three characters perhaps not drawn too remotely from life. Nothing can wash these assets away. The authors know the land, the people, the weather, the language. . . .

What they wanted to give us, no doubt, was the undertones of Taiarapu, the southeastern peninsula of Tahiti—what one hears beyond the voices of surf, waterfalls and wind in the *mapé* trees. In a way they do this, when they step out of their narrative. . . . (p. 2)

But what of the framework of narrative? (pp. 2, 4)

One goes slipping along from page to page, as with the drift of a gentle river, never with the rush of tides or sweep of tropical winds. There isn't propelling force enough in the narrative to carry one any faster. The best one can say is that Messrs. Nordhoff and Hall are never completely negligible. One can afford to read this book for what it tells of the way things are in Polynesia. But without their distinguished names this book would never set the Hudson or the Mississippi River on fire, and probably won't, in any case. All things considered it must be said, and with real regret, that the old comrades of the Lafayette Escadrille need a change of scene or something. Maybe they ought to go on a diet of raw meat for a while before they write their next book. (p. 4)

> R. L. Duffus, " 'The Dark River' Is a Standard South Sea Romance," in The New York Times Book Review, July 3, 1938, pp. 2, 4.

FRED T. MARSH (essay date 1941)

[*In the following review of* Botany Bay, *Marsh applauds "the historical romanticist's approach" that Nordhoff and Hall took in telling the story of Australia's first colonists.*]

[**Botany Bay**] is, in the authors' own description in the dedicatory letter to the Australian scholar, Dr. George Mackaness, "a romance of the First Fleet, in which, for dramatic effect, we have been obliged to take certain liberties . . . but our purpose throughout has been to keep close to fact." . . . Grant them the historical romanticist's approach, after a great tradition, and that would appear to be exactly what they have done, and in the same manner, with respect to the use of historical material, as in their justly celebrated *Bounty* trilogy. The team of Nordhoff and Hall is scrupulous as well as brilliant.

How much of this story as narrated by Hugh Tallant looking back on his youth is based on an actual life I do not know; but certainly some of these characters who play the leading roles in the tale have their historical prototypes. . . .

There are the sad, and in some cases tragic and in others bawdy and rowdy, scenes of embarkation; there is the endless voyage, the fleet of six ships, as in the case of a convoy, forced to regulate its speed by the slowest. There are the landing, the shift to Sydney (Botany Bay is now a suburb of the city of Sydney), the storied incidents out of early Australian history,

the terrible and true description of the arrival of the second fleet. There is the story of the slow emergence of the colony under a great Governor, Commodore Arthur Phillip, who had a tough job on his hands, was unsupported at home, but whose humanity and firmness, in equal proportions, made the experiment a go. Few Americans know this story; they should; it is the story of a plain naval officer doing a thankless job ably and honorably. All this, of course, is the background for the story which is about Hugh Tallant and his friends among the eight hundred.

They are not all pretty characters; the convict fleets served as a clearing house for the overcrowded British jails. But there was good stuff among them. Everybody's favorite, as obviously the authors', will be Nellie Garth, a heroic female of sound parts, fierce in wrath but, in the old phrase, gentle as a woman, as indeed she was, and a great one in time of trouble. . . . There are certain Hogarthian scenes among the others, and a lass of the underworld named Moll Cudlip, worthy of the pencil of Hogarth or the pen of Defoe, proves herself to be the best Christian of them all—even though she does run away with a heathen savage afterward. Then there is the political exile, more respectfully treated than the criminal element, whose daughter, Sally, turns out to be the heroine, a very nice but somewhat pale heroine in the light of circumstances. I would take Nellie Garth, likewise no criminal, although wittingly and legally an accessory.

The crisis of the novel comes with the escape in an open boat of Hugh and Tom and Nellie and others . . . , a tale reminiscent of **Men Against the Sea,** of the *Bounty* trilogy, but with a very different flavor. This is considerable of a story. But for the events leading up to the crisis, the rescue by a Dutch merchantman, the return to England, the climax and the aftermath you will have to read the book. . . .

For a critical appraisal, I think it is sufficient to say that the authors of **Mutiny on the Bounty** have repeated.

> Fred T. Marsh, "A Romance of the Bad Times That Settled Botany Bay," in The New York Times Book Review, November 9, 1941, p. 4.

KATHERINE WOODS (essay date 1942)

[*In the following essay, Woods praises the witty and introspective nature of the essays collected in Hall's* Under a Thatched Roof.]

James Norman Hall, as a writer, is not merely one-half of the combination which produced such favorite reading as the *Bounty* trilogy. He is an essayist in his own sole habit as well. From time to time, and from place to place, he produces delightful individual pieces of reflection, of reminiscence, of protest, of whim. Over a period of fifteen years, and in happy variety of subject, twenty of these have been gathered together [in **Under a Thatched Roof**].

It is a book which is marked by both variety and urbanity; and for that reason its title is not wholly fortunate. Mr. Hall lives, as is well known, in Tahiti. Some of the most pleasing papers in this volume have grown, so to speak, from roots in his home there. But others range far afield, to Europe and America, to cities, to New England meadows and Midwestern towns. And all, again, are the unlabored expression of an urbanity of mind and spirit for which the "thatched roof" certainly offers no connotation. One of Mr. Hall's most charming and allusive essays makes a far pilgrimage among the books of his Tahiti library—Ben Jonson, Coleridge, Conrad, Thoreau. But a "thatched roof" as such holds out no such promise to a prospective reader! Whereas the primitive escape to which it might be construed as beckoning simply does not exist.

Exception to Mr. Hall's title is taken, however, merely by way of pointing to the real riches of Mr. Hall's book. He takes up the cudgels bravely and wittily for the essayist on his first page; and there is substance as well as wit in his plea for urbanity and proportion—the essayist's most important contribution—even in our desperately turbulent time. Later he pleads, too, for leisure: not too much of it, but the ability to enjoy and make good use of what we have or can get. And if his outcry against modern mechanization is "dated" (it literally is: New York, 1928), it is well balanced in point of time by a 1941 essay which praises the gallant serenity of Logan Pearsall Smith in wartime England and calls attention to the need for such spirits in the building of any brave new world.

The paper on the **"Spirit of Place"** is one of the most charming, of course. Essays on the *genius loci* are almost sure to be charming, because only charming and sensitive individual minds even know that there is such a thing. But Mr. Hall's treatment is peculiarly fetching, as he recalls his meeting with "an exiled spirit of place" in the Marquesas, and the reminder of New England thus insinuated into that South Pacific scene; on another tropical island he had a curious encounter with a native spirit of place, too. And in another, very different, chapter, spirit of place and spirit of time come together in engaging boyhood reminiscence under the suggestive title of **"Trains."**

In regard to time, James Norman Hall is a man who frankly loves the past. He has an outspoken essay on that subject. Several of the most enjoyable of the papers linger among books and authors, with the same authors—notably Thoreau and Conrad—happily appearing more than once. And in one called **"The Scribbling Mania"** there are some pungent meditations on the difficulties of writing on the one hand and on the other the indubitable fact that too many people follow the writer's trade. A broad jump to specific narrative is offered in the recollection of a companion's escape from a German prison train in 1918. And humor plays merrily with the author's vain efforts to master Icelandic conjugations, and ends (as do several other chapters) in verse.

Four satiric fables on not-too-remote themes comprise one of the most entertaining of all twenty chapters. They are set down with suggestive economy of punctuation (not only colons and semincolons but commas also are disdained), and they attack (in a quite literal sense) various aspects of modern progress. Under their collective title of **"Happy Endings,"** these tales are very funny, and very good.

The whole book is good. There are times, even now, when we may sit still, and read, and remember, and think. That is the example James Norman Hall gives us, under his thatched roof or anywhere.

*Katherine Woods, "James Norman Hall's Essays,"
in* The New York Times Book Review, *November
8, 1942, p. 14.*

JAMES NORMAN HALL (essay date 1952)

[*In the following excerpt from his autobiography, Hall outlines
the circumstances of his first literary collaboration with Nordhoff
after the two arrived in Tahiti, followed with some discussion of
their collaborative work on the* Bounty *trilogy.*]

*Hall in his library at Papeete. Collection of Igor Allen,
Tahiti.*

Tahiti thirty years ago—to say nothing of other remote islands, both east and west in the Pacific—was a far different place from what it is today. Only the tips of the octopuslike tentacles of Western civilization, as we know it now, had reached this far into the Pacific, and the effect of them was scarcely felt. The character of the life was very much what it had been in the seventies and the eighties of the last century. There were, to be sure, a few motorcars, but not so many but what I could pretend not to see them.

Nordhoff and I could not, of course, begin writing our book for Harper's immediately. We had to know something about the islands and the life of their people before setting pens to paper; and so followed a period of loafing and observing that was entirely to my taste. Nordhoff loved fishing and made trips out to sea with the native boys who fished for the Papeete market. I made excursions into the valleys and up the mountains, where no one lives, and at times prowled the streets of Papeete by day and by night. Having been inland born, with dreams of islands running through my head since boyhood days, I found that Tahiti surpassed by most hopeful expectations. Even with my feet on solid earth I could scarcely believe in the reality of the place. I liked being abroad at the time of the midday siesta when I had the streets almost to myself, and my first writing was a sketch in which I tried to put into words my feeling about that particular time of day. (pp. 248-49)

Nordhoff had a practical, matter-of-fact mind, while I had—and still have to this day—that of a woodshed poet. (p. 250)

I was in a world wholly unlike anything I had known in the past, and new impressions came flooding in upon me so fast that I scarcely had time to make note of them. I tried to concentrate upon the travel book, but it was useless. At last I told Nordhoff that I would have to get this sketch-writing frenzy out of my system somehow. I proposed making a bicycle trip around the island for the purpose. Nordhoff didn't want to come with me. He liked Papeete and his offshore fishing excursions. Furthermore, the Bougainville Club was the rendezvous for schooner captains, pearl buyers, traders and the like, and their company was well worth cultivating. So it was decided that, while he remained in town, I would take my bicycle trip around the island, hobnobbing with the country people. I had seen enough of the islanders to be certain that a more friendly, hospitable people could not be found anywhere, and that I would have no difficulty in finding places to put up for the night. (p. 251)

I spent ten days making my first tour of the island, the main part of which is eighty-five miles around. But I was not pressed for time and loitered on the way, halting for a day or night whenever inclination prompted me. This was a happy experience, and I returned to Papeete with a whole sheaf of sketches and impressions which I read to Nordhoff who listened to them with no great amount of enthusiasm. (pp. 254-55)

Upon returning to Papeete, Nordhoff and I began discussing ways and means of working on our Harper's book which was to be called *Faery Lands of the South Seas.* We finally decided upon the following plan: we would separate, Nordhoff going to the Cook Islands, and I was to voyage among the lagoon islands of the Low Archipelago. I was to begin the story of our wanderings and to carry the thread of it throughout. Nordhoff's contributions were to be in the form of letters to me. A more clumsy device could scarcely have been hit upon, but it was the only one we could think of at that time, having had so little practice in collaboration. I will say no more of *Faery Lands* except that the book, when published, stayed in print, greatly to our surprise, for a good ten years; we more than canceled our debt to Harper's. Having completed that task, it did not occur to us, strangely enough, to continue writing together nor did we collaborate again until 1927 when we joined forces in writing our book for boys, *Falcons of France.* Nordhoff wanted to write a novel, so I continued voyaging throughout the years 1920 and '21, on copra schooners, Low Island cutters and other small craft. I wandered widely throughout eastern Polynesia, halting at various islands for a few days or weeks. . . . (pp. 256-57)

After our first joint venture in Tahiti we had gone our separate ways and by the year 1929 Nordhoff and I knew that we were not making much progress toward our hoped-for literary careers. We had collaborated in writing *Faery Lands of the South Seas*. . . . Then Nordhoff wrote a novel, *Picaro,* also for Harper's, which was stillborn, like two volumes of essays and sketches that Houghton Mifflin Company had published for me. I have Ferris Greenslet to thank for the fact that they, at least, saw the light of print, but I doubt whether either of them paid the cost of publication. Then, at Ellery Sedgwick's suggestion, Nordhoff wrote two boys' books, *The Pearl Lagoon* and *The Derelict*—published by the Atlantic Monthly Press—which sold well and are still in print. In the meantime, the Atlantic Monthly Press had amalgamated with Little, Brown and Company.

Nordhoff and I had done no collaborating since the *Faery Lands* volume. But, after the publication of his two boys' books, he

wanted to carry his young hero, Charles Selden, of those tales, through another series of adventures during World War I. He wanted to make him a pilot in the Lafayette Flying Corps, and he asked if I would collaborate with him on this tale. I was glad to do it, and so we wrote *Falcons of France.* . . . (p. 311)

To proceed: after we had written *Falcons of France,* Nordhoff said: "Why don't we go on writing together? Two heads are better than one, and neither of us seems to be making much progress writing alone." I was more than willing, so we began searching around for a story that both of us would be interested in. Nordhoff suggested that we might continue his boy, Charles Selden: bring him back to the South Seas, after the war, and put him through another series of adventures, concerning a hurricane, perhaps. But I was not greatly interested in boys' books, although publishers had told us that a good boys' book was like an investment in government bonds, bringing in small but steady returns, sometimes over a period of many years.

One day I said to Nordhoff: "Have you ever heard of the *Bounty* mutiny?"

"Of course," he replied. "Who hasn't, who knows anything about the South Seas?"

"Well, what about that for a story?"

Nordhoff shook his head. "Someone must have written it long since."

"I doubt it," I replied. "The only book I have seen is Sir John Barrow's factual account of the mutiny. Barrow was Secretary of the British Admiralty at that time. His book was published in 1831."

I saw in my friend's eyes a Nordhoffian glow and sparkle which meant that his interest was being aroused. "By the Lord, Hall!" he said. "Maybe we've got somthing there! I wish we could get hold of a copy of Barrow's book."

"I have it," I replied. "I bought it in Paris during the war."

The result was that Nordhoff took the book home to read and the next day he was back, and he was in what I can only call a "dither" of excitement. "Hall, what a story! What a story!" he said, as he walked up and down my veranda.

"It's three stories," I replied. "First, the tale of the mutiny; then Bligh's open-boat voyage, and the third, the adventures of Fletcher Christian and the mutineers who went with him to Pitcairn Island, together with the Tahitian men and women who accompanied them. It's a natural for historical fiction. Who could, possibly, invent a better story? And it has the merit of being true."

"You're right, it *is* a natural," said Nordhoff, "but . . ." he shook his head, glumly. "It must have been written long since. It's incredible that such a tale should have been waiting a century and a half for someone to see its possibilities."

Nevertheless, after having made the widest inquiries and the most painstaking researches, the only book we discovered concerned with the *Bounty* mutiny—outside of Bligh's own narrative, Sir John Barrow's account, and others written by British seamen such as Captain Staines and Pipon who had written of Pitcairn after the discovery of Christian's refuge by Captain Folger, in 1808—was a tale called *Aleck, the Last of the Mutineers, or, The History of Pitcairn Island,* published anonymously by J. S. & C. Adams, at Amherst, Massachussetts, in 1845. This book was designed for young readers, and was made up of a compilation, culled from other books, of the facts then known about the *Bounty* mutiny.

I will not go into a detailed account of our collection of source material, although it was a matter that interested us tremendously, and that interest was fully shared by Ellery Sedgwick, of the *Atlantic*. Mr. Sedgwick again proved himself the staunch friend he has always been to the pair of us. He found for us in London a retired British naval officer, Captain Truefell, whose help was beyond price. Captain Truefell had an exact model made of the *Bounty,* and he sent us, via Mr. Sedgwick, blueprints of her deckplans, her sail-and-rigging plans, so that we became thoroughly familiar with the ship. Not only this: we received photostat copies of all the old Admiralty records concerning the *Bounty* and her voyage, and of the court-martial proceedings which, at that time, had never been printed, although they were, later. We had boxes and bales of the old records, and the interest and pleasure with which we sorted and read them can easily be imagined.

Although we saw, from the beginning, what a superb trilogy the *Bounty* story would make, we could not assume that the general public would take the interest in it that we did; so our plan was, first, to write a tale concerned with Bligh's voyage to Tahiti, the collection there of the breadfruit trees, and the mutiny that followed on the homeward voyage, with just enough about Bligh's open-boat voyage and the later experiences of Christian and his men on Pitcairn to make an intelligible story of the whole *Bounty* affair, in case only one book was called for. But we hoped, of course, that there would be enough public interest in the story to warrant our going on with the two additional books we had planned: *Men Against the Sea* and *Pitcairn's Island.*

I well remember the day when, after months of preparation— reading and rereading our source material, endless discussions, the laying out of chapters, and the like—we were ready to begin the actual writing at the Aina Paré.

The *Mutiny* met with a surprising response and we went on to complete the trilogy. (pp. 312-14)

> *James Norman Hall, in his* My Island Home: An Autobiography, *Little, Brown and Company, 1952, 374 p.*

JAMES MICHENER   (essay date 1952)

[*Michener is a popular American novelist and nonfiction writer whose lengthy narratives often combine fictional stories with meticulous histories of distinct geographical areas. His first book, following a social studies text coauthored with Harold M. Long, was the loosely connected series of short stories* Tales of the South Pacific *(1947). This immediate bestseller won the Pulitzer Prize in fiction in 1948, and was adapted by Richard Rodgers and Oscar Hammerstein III into the enormously popular and long-running stage musical* South Pacific. *Royalties from the musical and later the movie version of* South Pacific *enabled Michener to work exclusively as a writer thereafter, giving him the means to travel and exhaustively research the regions in which he later set books. He is perhaps best known for his "family sagas," in which the history of hundreds of years may be contained in the accounts of many generations of several prominent, interconnected families. In the following excerpt from a review of Hall's uncompleted autobiography, Michener praises Hall's facility with the essay form.*]

Hall may one day be remembered as the last of the great essayists, for he published several books like *Faery Lands of*

the South Seas . . . , which contained highly polished examples of this now-outmoded form. More likely his reputation will rest on his tales of tropical adventure, but his position among his peers is yet to be decided. Stevenson commanded a more gracile pen, Rupert Brooke was a greater poet, Maugham a finer master of plot, Pierre Loti a lusher romanticist, Louis Becke knew far more about the Pacific, Conrad had a deeper sense of the mysterious, and Melville a greater sense of the tragedy of the sea.

Yet Hall accomplished something that none of his distinguished predecessors attained. He wrote, or helped to write, those fortunate masterpieces which epitomize the tropics. I know of no more skillful Pacific romance than *The Hurricane.* None of Jack London's South Sea stories equal Hall's cruel and bitter *The Forgotten One.* Surely nothing Stevenson accomplished in Samoa approaches the *Bounty* series. And I know an occasional poem, or part of a poem, in which Hall equals Brooke's best Pacific lyrics. Not the greatest man to have written about the Pacific, he nevertheless wrote some of the greatest books.

His last work was [*My Island Home*]. It is a curious book and he would be amazed to know that it can be read as tragedy. That was not his intention, for he devotes a major portion to the golden days he spent in Iowa. . . .

He recalls his experiences while waiting table in a house of prostitution, acting as social worker in the slums of Boston, serving as a volunteer with the British Expeditionary Force in France, and flying with Eddie Rickenbacker over Germany. He became an ace, knocking down five German planes, and he met with his future collaborator, Charles Nordhoff. . . .

Finally, on Page 301, he settles down in Tahiti (1923) and the reader takes a deep breath, prepared to discover what it was in the tropics that captivated men like Hall and Conrad or how two such dissimilar writers as he and Nordhoff happened to become collaborators.

The tragedy is that when he reached the important days in Tahiti time was running out for Jimmy Hall. He lived to complete only two chapters, an inconclusive one on a famous hotel and haunting verbatim conversation with Nordhoff. The mysteries of the South Seas he does not touch upon and we are deprived of the understanding we sought. "All of my roots are still in America, in the prairie country of the Middle West. I realize now that it is useless trying to grub them up to transplant on this little island. They won't come up."

Hall can be understood only as an eighteenth-century English gentleman. Spiritually he was close to that perfect man, Capt. James Cook; artistically he held much in common with Goldsmith and Addison. He cultivated innumerable eighteenth-century reticences. (p. 1)

Hall's truncated biography is good reading. It tells of a distinguished gentleman lost in a modern world, of an Iowa boy who perpetually longed to return home. . . . (p. 42)

> *James Michener, "A Gentleman Lost in a Modern World," in* The New York Times Book Review, *October 19, 1952, pp. 1, 42.*

ROBERT ROULSTON   (essay date 1978)

[*Roulston is an American educator and critic. In the following excerpt from his critical biography of Hall, he discusses in detail the three novels of the* Bounty *trilogy.*]

It is unlikely that many people who have read it would deny that *Mutiny on the Bounty* is one of the best books of its kind ever written. But what kind of book is it? Cultivated readers would probably characterize it as melodrama. And in numerous respects they would be correct. Nordhoff and Hall's novel shares with the Western, the crime thriller, and the soap opera such features as a stark contrast between good and evil, sudden reversals, a portentous tone, and a dire sequence of events moving logically toward disaster only to swerve at the very end toward a happy resolution. Some of these features it also shares with Goethe's *Faust,* Dostoevski's novels, *Wuthering Heights,* and even *War and Peace.* It would be absurd, of course, to equate *Mutiny on the Bounty* with *Faust* or *War and Peace.* But a careful reading of Nordhoff and Hall's book reveals that a finely wrought popular work with melodramatic elements can have its subtleties, complexities, and can even produce something akin to catharsis.

Especially admirable is the use to which Nordhoff and Hall put their extensive research. For the purposes of plot or even of characterization they need not have looked beyond Sir John Barrow's marvelous book. In slightly more than three hundred pages, Barrow covered not merely the major events surrounding the *Bounty*'s voyage, the mutiny, the court-martial, and the Pitcairn Island story, but he also presented his facts with a justice to all, particularly admirable in view of his position as Secretary of the British Admiralty.... Barrow even provided Nordhoff and Hall with their narrator, because he gave an extended and sympathetic account of Peter Heywood, the midshipman who served as a model for Roger Byam.

But what Barrow alone could not have given them was that feeling for specifics which permeates *Mutiny on the Bounty*—specifics about how the *Bounty* looked, about its layout, what the men ate, drank, and wore; specifics about English ports, prisons, and laws. Such accuracy of detail often imparts a sense of reality to incidents which, however historical, sometimes border on the incredible. Yet much of the effectiveness of the book is due to the selectivity with which Nordhoff and Hall employed those details. There are no lengthy descriptions and no digressions crammed with data. Specifics are injected sparingly—frequently enough to heighten verisimilitude but never intrusively enough to impede the narrative flow. (pp. 67-8)

[Byam] is not simply the narrator. In fact, it is around him that the plot pivots. Bligh vanishes in Chapter Nine to reappear only briefly in the epilogue. Christian makes his exit in Chapter Eleven, less than halfway to the end of this twenty-seven-chapter work, and is not seen again. Thereafter the focus of interest is on Byam's arrest, trial, and acquittal. Even the events leading up to the mutiny serve, in purely structural terms, as a preparation for Byam's decision not to support it despite his sympathy for Bligh's victims and his detestation of Bligh's harshness. *Mutiny on the Bounty* is thus the story of a young conservative who decides that, although all is not well with his world, order must be preserved. After being condemned to death by his superiors, he is pardoned at the last moment. He thereupon returns to the navy, serves with distinction, and finally becomes a captain.

The foregoing is essentially what happened to Byam's historical prototype, Peter Heywood. Now, of course, by choosing Heywood as the model for their protagonist, Nordhoff and Hall in a sense converted events which were tragic for most of the participants into a success story. Of the eight men who sailed off with Christian on the *Bounty,* only Alexander Smith survived the bloody events on Pitcairn Island. Of the sixteen who

remained on Tahiti, two died there, four perished in the wreck of the *Pandora,* three were later hanged, and seven were either acquitted or pardoned. Of those who escaped the hangman's rope, Heywood alone went on to live a long and prosperous life. (p. 69)

Yet, although their decision to concentrate on Heywood was to opt for melodrama over tragedy, Nordhoff and Hall's approach to the story was probably the wisest they could have chosen given their talents, their experience, their method of composition, and their philosophies. Both authors, to begin with, were most comfortable with first-person narration, having used it extensively in the works they had produced individually as well as in *Falcons of France.* They had also demonstrated a partiality to the initiation-story pattern in which a young man from the provinces would come to maturity after a set of new and trying experiences. Heywood was, in many respects, a real-life, eighteenth-century counterpart of Charles Selden, the hero of Nordhoff and Hall's earlier book—a bright young man who enlisted in a military organization in search of adventure. He offered the further advantage of having been in a position to observe a wider range of events than any other man aboard the *Bounty.* He was also callow enough for both of the two highly individual mature writers to identify with him as they could never have done with more complex, more idiosyncratic figures like Bligh and Christian. Yet he was reflective and literate enough for Nordhoff and Hall to use him on occasion as a mouthpiece for some of their own ideas about authority, revolution, and the South Seas.

After stating in the opening chapters his Tory predilections as well as, somewhat incongruously, his fondness for books depicting the South Pacific as a new Eden, Byam becomes throughout the next seven chapters principally a set of eyes and ears. No sooner is he in uniform than he witnesses a sailor being flogged to death. Afterward, at dinner the high-ranking officers, while savoring their victuals, express approval of such severities, and none approves more heartily than Captain Bligh.

Thereafter, through the next six chapters, Bligh demonstrates that he is a man who practices his principles. The *Bounty*'s voyage becomes a nightmare of beatings, imprisonments in the hold, and assorted harangues and harassments relieved only by an idyllic interlude in Tahiti while the ship is being loaded with saplings of breadfruit trees. (pp. 69-70)

Byam's narration in these chapters ... makes the mutiny seem both inevitable and justified. His frequent tendency to refrain from commenting on events merely damns Bligh all the more because the reported incidents, which invariably put the captain in the worst possible light, are thus presented with a semblance of objectivity. When Byam does have a good word to say for his commander, the compliment promptly turns into denigration: "Had his character in other respects been equal to his courage, his energy, and his understanding Bligh would today have a niche in history among the greatest seamen of England." ... (p. 71)

But, although the first eight chapters lucidly and briskly prepare for the uprising, they do little to foreshadow Byam's instant and unequivocal refusal to support the mutineers led by his good friend Christian. At least Peter Heywood, according to Barrow's account of the court-martial, was confused during the turmoil on deck.... But Byam, Heywood's fictional counterpart, not only unhesitatingly resolves to resist but plans to recapture the ship and is finally prevented from accompanying Bligh by sheer bad luck.

This dearth of foreshadowing, however, is not a blunder on the part of Nordhoff and Hall. On the contrary, it is the master stroke of the novel. The remainder of the book becomes, in effect, a vindication of Byam's seemingly perverse decision. No sooner are the mutineers in control of the *Bounty* than they begin quarreling among themselves. And, even though Christian is a natural leader, he is no longer a legitimate one; consequently, his authority shows signs of eroding from the start, thus portending the anarchy that will destroy all but one of the men who go with him to Pitcairn's Island. Conversely, the legitimate commander, Bligh, transformed into a superb leader by dire circumstances, safely conducts his launch across the Pacific in one of the greatest feats in maritime history. So remarkable is his achievement that Byam, under the threat of death because of Bligh's accusations against him, concedes that Bligh alone could have performed such a deed. As for Byam's faith in British justice, it is ultimately vindicated when the innocent men are either acquitted or, like himself and Morrison, pardoned as Heywood was.

Just as events from Chapter Nine to the end of the book justify Byam's decision, the portrait of him in those pages explains it. In fact, long before the epilogue, his refusal to support the mutineers has come to seem in retrospect as inevitable as the first eight chapters had made the mutiny appear. As the novel progresses, it becomes increasingly clear that Byam could not have supported any massive assault on authority and order because he is what today might be called a "square." He has the square virtues of a sense of duty, devotion to work, and loyalty to country, family, and friends (in just about that order). He also has the square vices of stolidness and primness. Byam, however, is a square who instinctively hates bullies and who sympathizes with their victims. He is, in addition, one who sometimes seems to yearn to become an eighteenth-century prototype of the South Sea beachcomber.

Because Byam is most dominant in Hall's chapters, it is tempting to regard him as Hall's persona. But the temptation should be resisted. To be sure, Byam's antipathy toward change, his retrospective cast of mind, his attachment to his rural birthplace, and his optimism make his attitudes, although hardly his chilly personality, seem like Hall's. Furthermore, some of Byam's remarks about the South Seas duplicate ones Hall was to attribute to himself in *Under a Thatched Roof* in a record of a conversation with Nordhoff—remarks with which Nordhoff took issue. In essence Hall there defended South Sea lotus-eating, rambling, and reverie. Nordhoff denounced all three and praised a more active kind of life. At the same time his tone was pessimistic and even cynical, whereas Hall's was sanguine. (pp. 71-2)

Byam's words and deeds were determined largely by his functions in a story line that the two writers had hammered out together. In order to participate in such a wide spectrum of incidents and be credible in his account of them, he has to be adventurous enough to set off for the South Seas but cautious enough and patriotic enough not to join the mutiny; educated enough to be writing the book and sufficiently well born to have friends powerful enough to obtain his pardon, but ignorant enough of the navy to be shocked by its code; fond enough of Polynesian life to get involved with it but not so fond that he would succumb to an urge to return to Tahiti after his pardon rather than reenlist in the navy—and so on. It is astounding that a character who is so obviously a device coheres at all, let alone emerges in this collaborative work with some kind of identity.

No less remarkable is it that Nordhoff and Hall were able to achieve a stylistic homogeneity while avoiding a jarring sense of anachronism. Although no reader familiar with eighteenth-century literature is likely to be under the impression that he is reading an authentic manuscript of the period, neither is he apt to be painfully aware that he is *not* reading one. There is also none of that disconcerting clash between narrative prose and dialogue that often mars historical fiction, a fact all the more extraordinary when one recalls that statements made by characters in *Mutiny on the Bounty* were sometimes taken verbatim from contemporary records.

The question remains to be answered: what kind of work is *Mutiny on the Bounty*? Of its melodramatic elements we have already spoken. But melodrama is more a mode of development than a genre. "Historical novel" seems an apt designation. Yet, for all its historicity and verisimilitude, the book possesses a quality normally lacking in realistic fiction, historical or otherwise. Years ago in his doctoral dissertation the author of this study referred somewhat disdainfully to the novel as a fairy tale. Having reexamined it with more mature and less patronizing eyes, he is now convinced that the essentially childlike view of the *Bounty*'s tragic story is a major source of the work's strength. This is no *Terry and the Pirates,* though, conjuring up silly escapist fantasies. What the book does, rather, is to take some of the most elemental fears and wishes many and perhaps most of us bear from our childhood years and project them upon a vast historical canvas without doing radical violence to history itself. Thus *Mutiny on the Bounty* is a hybrid which fuses fact and myth, realism and fantasy.

On the fantasy level Bligh is every bullying authority figure who has ever terrified a child—the sarcastic teacher, the officious principal, and—yes—the wicked stepfather. Christian is the good-natured, reckless older brother or stronger friend who we keep hoping will thrash the bully. At the same time, we realize that the brother-friend will suffer retribution if he actually strikes the tyrant because behind this odious authority figure stands the awesome, omnipotent structure of all authority everywhere. Thus Byam—not so much Everyman as Everyboy—cannot admit to having wished this punishment to befall his friend or brother. Yet the fact remains that Byam has hated Bligh and has certainly not wished him well. Indeed, his entire account of Bligh is a portrait of a man who deserves a sock on the jaw or a kick on the shins. And so, when the revolt comes, Byam must be punished because his heart has been full of disrespect for an authority figure. But he must ultimately be rescued because he is innocent of any word or deed that could even remotely be construed as rebellious. (pp. 73-4)

Now there is some historical basis for much of this. Peter Heywood was convicted and then pardoned. Heywood's reprieve, however, came much earlier in his progression toward the gallows. . . . Furthermore, Heywood's case did not depend, as Byam's does, on incidents which could have been verified only by three missing persons, two of whom were dead. The court, having heard all the evidence including Heywood's own lengthy and eloquent testimony, concluded that he was guilty in only the most technical sense, and, while deciding against him, recommended mercy.

Byam, however, is both more guilty than Heywood and more innocent—more involved, that is, through friendship and sympathy with the mutineers but less hesitant in his rejection of them when the mutiny transpires. He is also punished more terribly, coming closer to being hanged, than Heywood ever came. What is more, Byam, like Bligh but unlike Heywood,

Engraving of Pitcairn's Island (1867). The Granger Collection, New York.

is a protégé of Banks, the prime mover of the voyage; consequently, Byam stands closer to the center of the story than Heywood stood.

What these shifts in emphasis accomplish is to make the mutiny and its aftermath the story of Byam's fears, sympathies, antipathies, sufferings, and final vindication. And, because he has some of that blankness which characterizes mythic heroes, he often functions less as a mask for Nordhoff and Hall than as a stand-in for readers youthful enough in spirit to identify with him. *Mutiny on the Bounty* thus provides such readers with the thrill of vicariously smashing all authority; then it first punishes and finally exculpates them for that thrill.

The view toward rebellion which pervades the book, therefore, is a conservative one. The novel suggests, in effect, that even though a tyrannical individual may deserve to be removed from power, a precipitous and illegal assault on constituted authority will cause more suffering than do the abuses which the assault was meant to eliminate. Certainly the mere facts of the *Bounty*'s voyage support such a view. . . . (pp. 74-5)

A final observation needs to be made about *Mutiny on the Bounty*. It would be unjust to Nordhoff and Hall to leave someone who has not read the book with the impression that they cheapen the terrible events surrounding the *Bounty*'s voyage by having their hero at the end sail off into the sunrise ready to fight for king and country, his heart athrob with forgiveness. In the epilogue, Byam returns many years later to Tahiti. En route, while in Australia, he briefly encounters Bligh who, as governor of New South Wales, has become the central figure of another uprising. Byam discovers that the old man, as irascible and overbearing as ever, has learned nothing from his experiences. Moreover, Byam's return to Tahiti is a melancholy experience. The place soon becomes for him a "graveyard of memories." Worse, it has become a literal graveyard

where, because of pestilence, four-fifths of the population has perished in the valley in which he and Tehani had their idyll twenty years earlier. To be sure, life goes on. Although Tehani is dead, Byam's daughter by her survives, as does a granddaughter. But, as he leaves the island, he reflects: "suddenly the place was full of ghosts—shadows of men alive and dead—my own among them." . . . (pp. 75-6)

The book thus concludes on an appropriately disquieting note. The incidents depicted in *Mutiny on the Bounty* have not suggested that all is right with the world but that rebellions make bad conditions worse and that, in a free society like England's, justice will prevail although perhaps only after long and painful delays. The epilogue, moreover, indicates that Byam finally learns that, however things turn out, the essential sadness of life remains: youth perishes, lovely primitive cultures vanish or become tainted, delights of the past slip away—hardly childish lessons. (p. 76)

Although Nordhoff and Hall had done most of their work on *Pitcairn's Island* before starting *Men Against the Sea,* the latter book was published earlier because extensive revising delayed the appearance of *Pitcairn's Island*. This reversal in the originally planned sequence was fortunate. The events in *Men Against the Sea* are more integrally related to those in the first volume of the trilogy, *Mutiny on the Bounty,* than the incidents in *Pitcairn's Island* are. Nordhoff and Hall had recounted the main details of the story of Bligh's 3,618 mile open-boat voyage across the Pacific in *Mutiny on the Bounty* probably because its outcome had had such an impact on the fate of its protagonist, Roger Byam. On the other hand, they said nothing in the earlier book about the occurrences on Pitcairn Island because those events had no effect on Byam. The proper place of *Men Against the Sea,* therefore, is between its two companion works.

In *Men Against the Sea* Bligh, the harsh master of the *Bounty,* becomes a heroic figure when confronted with responsibility for the lives of the nineteen men crammed into the small ill-supplied launch. Thus, whatever he might have done before or whatever he was to do later, he vindicates in this book the favorable opinion held of his abilities by Sir Joseph Banks, Captain Cook, and the British Naval High Command. A simple sense of justice may have prompted the authors to create such a laudatory portrait. Except for a few sentences of praise, Nordhoff and Hall had presented a relentlessly unfavorable picture of him in *Mutiny on the Bounty.* Yet Bligh's record was mixed. If his irascibility provoked mutiny, his courage, self-discipline, and indomitable will made him as effective a commander in combat during the Napoleonic wars as they made him during the voyage of the crowded launch across thousands of miles of treacherous water strewn with islands inhabited by fierce cannibals.

In rectifying their harsh picture of Bligh in *Mutiny on the Bounty,* Nordhoff and Hall went even further in praising him in *Men Against the Sea* than they had gone in vilifying him in the earlier novel. In fact, in *Men Against the Sea* the erstwhile quarter-deck tyrant is so wise and humane that the mutiny seems in retrospect incomprehensible. No crew would ever have risen up against such a benevolent commander—and no crew would have dared depose such a firm and resourceful one. Now, of course, the facts themselves suggest that the Bligh who provoked the mutiny was not altogether the same man as the one who took the launch and its starving crew safely to the Dutch East Indies. But altered circumstances could not have transformed him beyond recognition. Yet, whereas nothing in the earlier book had implied that Bligh lacked courage, determination, and competence, everything in *Men Against the Sea* makes it inconceivable that he could ever have resorted to the petty thievery or the gratuitous harassment of officers Nordhoff and Hall attribute to him in *Mutiny on the Bounty.*

These discrepancies, however, may have been less a result of the authors' desire to be fair to Bligh than of a reluctance to stray from contemporary accounts of the launch's voyage. In writing about the mutiny, they could choose between divergent versions—Bligh's on the one hand and on the other Morrison's journal, Heywood's letters, and records of the testimony of some of the mutineers. Of the incidents in the *Bounty*'s launch, their only detailed sources were Bligh's published volume about the mutiny and his private journal. Both, needless to say, presented the commander of the *Bounty* in a favorable light. Evidently Nordhoff and Hall were unwilling to fabricate details that went counter to Bligh's account. Moreover, the collaborative nature of their project as well as the dictates of popular adventure fiction precluded a sustained and subtle internal portrait of the captain.

Having decided once more to write a first-person narrative, they chose the point of view of Thomas Ledward, the acting surgeon, who becomes in effect a ventriloquist's dummy for Bligh's self-serving version of the voyage. But, whereas Bligh's own book recounts the story with at least a pretense of modesty and objectivity, Nordhoff and Hall's Ledward is so adulatory that he often sounds downright sycophantic. (pp. 78-9)

As the voyage proceeds, Ledward proffers a veritable litany of the captain's merits. Bravery and self-assurance we had been prepared to accept. His unwillingness to resort to guile to pacify a native chief comes as no great surprise. But, when we find him described as "cheerful, kindly, and considerate," we remain astonished even when Ledward assures that he would not have forseen the emergence of these traits to such a degree before the mutiny. . . . (pp. 79-80)

Nordhoff and Hall, of course, could have reconciled their accounts of Bligh's tyranny aboard the *Bounty* with their portrait of his benignity in the launch by giving *Men Against the Sea* a narrator who is initially hostile to the captain but who gradually recognizes Bligh's merits. But this sort of slowly evolving change of perspective would probably have been unattainable by a team of writers working away at separate portions of the tale, regardless of how often they conferred with each other. And, had they used an omniscient narrator, they undoubtedly would have exposed the book to the disjointing shifts of tone that almost confounded their attempt to write *Pitcairn's Island,* where initially they did employ such a point of view. In subordinating their individual perceptions of Bligh to Ledward's unvarying idealization of him, Nordhoff and Hall were able to unify their efforts. They achieved this unity, however, at the expense of subtlety and sometimes, at least for the reader familiar with *Mutiny on the Bounty,* at the expense of credibility.

Yet, if read without reference to its predecessor, *Men Against the Sea* is a thoroughly satisfying adventure story. It moves along briskly. It depicts actions, people, and places vividly and economically. Since the only sustained conflict is the one indicated in the title—the clash between nature and the men in the launch—the book is inevitably more episodic than *Mutiny on the Bounty,* but the fact in no way abates the forward thrust of the work. The individual episodes are engrossing enough to pull the reader along. In them Bligh and his subordinates are menaced by storms and doldrums, hostile savages, and the selfishness of some of the men in the boat. Yet always they survive, sometimes by apparent good luck, as when a tern alights on the bow to provide them with sorely needed sustenance. More often, however, Bligh is responsible for saving them. In every crisis he has the proper response: firmness when firmness is appropriate, gentleness when the men need to be comforted. Sometimes readers who pause to reflect may wish that Bligh would be human enough to make an error or two in judgment. Aboard the *Bounty* he was, at least in that regard, very human indeed.

Men Against the Sea gave its authors so little difficulty that they completed it in about two months. Writing *Pitcairn's Island,* however, proved such an ordeal that, after grinding out thirteen chapters, they sent off their abortive manuscript to [their editor] Edward Weeks, who returned it with some advice that finally enabled them to finish the novel.

At first it appears surprising that *Pitcairn's Island* should have caused Nordhoff and Hall such acute birth pains. The actual Pitcairn story contained every element essential to either high tragedy or thrilling melodrama. It offered a gentleman officer who had become a renegade; a seized ship manned by cutthroat mutineers like Quintal, McCoy, and Williams; and a remote, deserted, all-but-unknown island where the fugitives sought refuge with their Polynesian wives. There they turned a paradise into a veritable hell. Men stole each other's wives and drank themselves into stupors; they killed themselves and murdered each other until only one mutineer remained alive. Finally, there was redemption: the sole surviving mutineer renounced drink, turned to the Bible, and taught the gospel to his own children and those of his dead companions. Here, in short, was a hero worthy of Conrad, an orgy of violence worthy of an Elizabethan dramatist, and a moral tale worthy of Tolstoy. Now, of course, Nordhoff and Hall would never have attempted to rival Conrad, Shakespeare, or Tolstoy. But this rich, varied, thrilling material contained elements perfectly suited to the interests of both of the partners. Surely even Nordhoff could not have wished for more action, villainy, or heroism. As for Hall, here he had an opportunity to exploit the themes most dear to him—solitude, Polynesian tranquility menaced by the white man's greed, and the ultimate goodness of mankind.

Perhaps their difficulty grew out of the fact that, while the Pitcairn material could readily be used to express the outlook of either Nordhoff or Hall, it could not be made to reflect the viewpoint of both men without distorting it considerably. One problem that plagued them was finding a narrative center. At first they attempted to relate the story from an omniscient point of view. But, as their book came to seem increasingly like a catalogue of horrors, they gave up and sent their fragmentary manuscript to Edward Weeks. Weeks proposed that they have Alexander Smith, the sole surviving mutineer on Pitcairn, tell parts of the story to the crew of the *Topaz*, the American ship which happened upon the island in 1808. Weeks suggested that Smith tell only of those events he observed before his wounding and argued that Smith's narration, having been softened "by time and loyalty" to his dead comrades, would not unduly stress the more sordid aspects of the story. This advice helped Nordhoff and Hall to complete the novel, but it did not altogether resolve the problem of unifying the work. The shifts in point of view tended to fragment the book rather than to give it a Conradian complexity. A strong central character might have bound everything together the way Jim makes *Lord Jim* cohere. But Christian, who dominates the first part of *Pitcairn's Island*, dies halfway through the story. As for Smith, who narrates much of the concluding part, he tends to get lost among the horrendous incidents he relates.

Another problem, as Weeks's comments cited above indicate, was the plethora of violence. Weeks reports that Nordhoff, who disagreed with Hall about the matter, wanted to maximize the bloodshed and even went so far as to suggest in a letter that the story "*should* be told . . . in a robust, bloody, and slightly pornographic Elizabethan fashion" [see Weeks entry in Additional Bibliography].

The disagreement here between the partners represented, one suspects, more than a quibble over literary strategy. The sort of book Nordhoff envisioned might have been a better one. But Hall could not have contributed to it without having done considerable violence to many of his most firmly rooted convictions. The novel they actually wrote, therefore, may not be so much the result of a compromise with the tastes of female readers (as Nordhoff misogynistically implied) as of an imperfect compromise between the two authors—a compromise in which Hall got more than he gave but in which he did not get enough to make the work a completely satisfactory vehicle for his ideas.

Some of those ideas are difficult to reconcile with the events that actually transpired on Pitcairn. No talented writer determined to refute primitivism and to depict man as innately depraved would have had much trouble accommodating himself to those events. Hall, however, was anything but an antiprimitivist, and to the end of his life he insisted upon the essential goodness of man. Thus, whereas a Joseph Conrad or a William Golding might have emphasized the viciousness of all concerned, Polynesians as well as white men, Hall and his collaborator placed the onus on the English mutineers. This is not to say that the natives in *Pitcairn's Island* do not at times behave with savage ferocity. Such ferocity, however, is invariably provoked by the misdeeds of the white man. (pp. 80-3)

But, although white aggressiveness provokes the Polynesians in *Pitcairn's Island* to go on a savage rampage, paradise is not lost but only temporarily misplaced. After the carnage, Alexander Smith, the native women, and the children of mixed parentage rediscover it. But what a fragile little paradise it is! An isolated kindergarten presided over by a Bible-reading patriarch, it is an Eden without adult males except for the virtuous and elderly Smith and, hence, an Eden without sex. When a ship from the outside world finally intrudes, Smith says: "I do believe ye might search the world around without finding children more truly innocent and pure-minded than these." . . . The epilogue, however, implies that their innocence will not last long. Having learned of the civilized world through contact with the *Topaz*, one of the boys tells Smith: "But we want to know. All of us do! Why have you never told us of the other lands?" . . . Once more Hall and his collaborator are blaming Western civilization for the demise of a South Sea paradise. Yet surely the intrusion of an American vessel was not needed to bring tribulations to those children: puberty alone would have sufficed. But to make such an admission is to precede the possibility of paradise, white or Polynesian, Christian or pagan—in a world of adults. Rather than wrestle with such a dilemma, Hall and Nordhoff simply evade the problem.

The evasion, like similar ones throughout *Pitcairn's Island*, prevents the book from being told in the "robust, bloody, and slightly pornographic Elizabethan fashion" Nordhoff thought appropriate for the material. Perhaps his realization that the 1930s public would have rejected such a book made him consign to his partner the most violent scenes, the killing and drinking episodes, which the manuscript in the Grinnell College Library reveals to be Hall's work. But, even if such pressure had not existed, it is unlikely that Nordhoff, the author of such lightweight fare as *The Pearl Lagoon* and *The Fledgling,* working alone could have produced a successful novel of the kind he envisioned. And it is inconceivable that Hall, given his temperament and values, could have contributed to the writing of it. In fact, in view of their divergent attitudes toward their inharmonious subject matter, *Pitcairn's Island* is probably the best work they could have contrived about the terrible events on Pitcairn. No one, after all, could reasonably expect that almost perfect fusion of talents which had made *Mutiny on the Bounty* so extraordinary to have occurred often. The remarkable thing is that it occurred even a few times. In writing *Pitcairn's Island,* Nordhoff and Hall came close enough to achieving it to produce an engrossing novel but not close enough to contain completely the centrifugal forces that beset the unity of the book. (pp. 85-6)

> *Robert Roulston, in his* James Norman Hall, *Twayne Publishers, 1978, 167 p.*

ALFRED FRIENDLY (essay date 1982)

[*Friendly was an American journalist and nonfiction writer whose works include a biography of Sir Francis Beaufort, a contemporary and occasional sailing companion of William Bligh. In the following excerpt, Friendly disparages what he considers the historical inaccuracies and outright falsehoods in Nordhoff and Hall's portrayal of Bligh, regretting that a reissue of "that wonderfully narrated, riveting concoction," as he acknowledges the* Bounty *trilogy to be, is likely to perpetuate the misconception of Bligh as a tyrant.*]

Although my lifetime consumption of junk historical fiction is considerable, it is insufficient to let me state categorically that the famous collaboration of Charles Nordhoff and James Norman Hall wins the All-American cup for traducing the truth, but I am nevertheless confident that it is among the top contenders.

Granted, it was the movie (with Charles Laughton as the despicable monster, Captain Bligh, Clark Gable as Fletcher Christian, the noble and self-sacrificing leader of the mutineers, and Franchot Tone as the winsome innocent caught up in near-tragedy) that disseminated the phony message even more widely and convincingly than the book. But the movie was faithful to the book, whereas the book was faithful only to the author's dream version of the mutiny on His Majesty's frigate *Bounty* and, no doubt, to their shrewd calculation of what would make a best-seller.

If that notorious of all mutinies at sea (in 1798, some 400 miles southeast of the Fiji Islands), lies almost two centuries in the past, its documentation remains abundant and quite adequate for determining the essential truth. Dozens of historians and biographers have bent themselves to the task. . . .

From the research there emerges not "the Bounty Bastard" of earlier British navy tradition, not the tyrant, brute and sadist against whom any mutinous act could be forgiven, but a more complex and therefore more believable all-too-human figure.

A magnificent seaman and navigator, Bligh was almost obsessively protective of his crew when the going was tough, but was singularly inept and unappealing in trouble-free times and placid seas. His achievement in bringing 17 loyal members of the Bounty's crew set adrift with him, in an open boat on a 3,900-mile voyage, safely to Timor in the dutch East Indies remains unrivalled in maritime history.

Portrait of William Bligh by George Dance (1794). The Granger Collection, New York.

He endeared himself to Nelson for his skill and bravery as a captain in the Napoleonic Wars. But his raging, intolerable and sometimes close to irrational outbursts of temper flawed the character of a man of integrity and intense loyalty to king and country. . . .

To be sure, in *Pitcairn's Island,* the third volume of the trilogy, Nordhoff and Hall tell of the mayhem and tragic end of the mutineers on their hoped for (and subsequently much romanticized) Shangri-La. What they do not make clear is that Christian's and his fellow mutineers' behaviour there was of unmatched brutality, bloodiness and insanity. They, not Bligh, were murderers and the villains of the story.

Between the work of Christian's family in England and the deft sea-lawyers among those mutineers who were captured and brought home for trial, Bligh's name was marvelously blackened. It is likely to remain black as doddering fools of my antiquity remain who have seen that gripping film and who have read that wonderfully narrated, riveting concoction of Nordhoff, and Hall. One could have hoped, however, that when that deluded generation dies off, as must happen relatively soon, perspective would be regained.

But now the book is to be reissued and another generation or two seduced into the Land of Hokum. For, with the publicity that may be expected, the new edition will doubtlessly sell as abundantly (and make as much money) as the original. Ah well, *mundus vult decipi* ["the world wants to be deceived"].

> *Alfred Friendly, "The Truth about Captain Bligh,"*
> in Manchester Guardian Weekly, September 12, 1982,
> *p. 18.*

ADDITIONAL BIBLIOGRAPHY

Binns, Archie. "The Odyssey of the *Bounty* Mutineers." *The Saturday Review of Literature* XI, No. 16 (3 November 1934): 257.
    Review of *Pitcairn's Island* that draws parallels between the story of the marooned mutineers and Homer's *Odyssey.*

Briand, Paul. *In Search of Paradise: The Nordhoff-Hall Story.* New York: Duell, Sloan & Pearce, 1966, 395 p.
    Detailed biography of both men.

Colcord, Lincoln. "A Story Destined to Become a Sea Classic." *New York Herald Tribune Books* 10, No. 18 (7 January 1934): 1-2.
    Enthusiastic and highly favorable review of *Men Against the Sea* that also praises the first volume of the *Bounty* trilogy. The critic later reviewed *Pitcairn's Island* (see entry dated 1934).

Hutchison, Percy. "A Stirring Sequel to the *Bounty* Mutiny." *The New York Times Book Review* (7 January 1934): 9.
    Briefly recapitulates the plot of *Mutiny on the Bounty* and favorably reviews *Men Against the Sea,* praising the "more than ordinary literary talent" of the two collaborators as well as the extensive knowledge of their subject that lends verisimilitude to their works.

Marsh, Fred T. "A Tale of Men and Ships." *New York Herald Tribune Books* 9, No. 5 (9 October 1932): 1, 4.
    Review of *Mutiny on the Bounty* that notes the "soundness and authenticity" of the narrative and the authors' skilled use of historical fact in the construction of a thrilling story.

"A Vivid Tale of Maritime Adventure." *The New York Times Book Review* (16 October 1932): 7.
    Review of *Mutiny on the Bounty* that briefly recounts the historical background of the incident and concludes that "the book is a

superb achievement in its genre'' and is ''what the historical novel should be—a bit of history brought to life in a book.''

Sedgwick, Ellery. ''Men of the Species.'' In his *The Happy Profession*, pp. 216-28. Boston: Little, Brown, and Co., 1946.
    Discusses Nordhoff and Hall's long friendship and career as collaborators.

———. ''James Norman Hall: 1887-1951.'' *The Atlantic* 188, No. 3 (September 1951): 19-21.
    Obituary tribute to Hall's life and works by his longtime editor.

''An American in the British Army.'' *The Spectator* 117, No. 4595 (22 July 1916): 103-04.
    Account of Hall's experiences in the British Army as told in his *Kitchener's Mob*.

Trilling, Diana. ''Fiction in Review: *Lost Island*.'' *The Nation* 158, No. 26 (24 June 1944): 742.
    In a review of Hall's *Lost Island*, a fictionalized account of a tiny South Sea island taken over as a Pacific air base during World War II, Trilling discusses the tragedy implicit in the destruction of one civilization for the preservation of another.

Weeks, Edward. ''Charles Nordhoff and James Norman Hall.'' In his *In Friendly Candor*, pp. 65-83. Boston: Little, Brown, and Co., 1946.
    Biographical account of Nordhoff and Hall's career as collaborators by their editor at the *Atlantic*.

Welch, Murray D. ''James Norman Hall: Poet and Philosopher.'' *The South Atlantic Quarterly* XXXIX, No. 2 (April 1940): 140-50.
    Approbatory discussion of Hall's little-known poetry and essays.

Jerome K(lapka) Jerome

1859-1927

English novelist, dramatist, essayist, short story writer, and editor.

Jerome is best known as the author of *Three Men in a Boat (To Say Nothing of the Dog)*, a humor classic that has been in print for nearly a century. Despite his involvement in many areas of late nineteenth and early twentieth-century London literary life—especially as the author of many successful comic plays, and as the editor of two prominent humor periodicals—Jerome's place in world literature was earned for him by that rarest of achievements, a work of topical humor that has appealed to millions of readers in dozens of countries from the time of its appearance to the present.

Jerome was born in Walsall, Staffordshire, to a Nonconformist minister and his wife. His father's various business dealings failed at about the time of Jerome's birth, and he and two older sisters were raised in a shabby dockside area of London's East End. Jerome's father died when he was twelve; two years later his formal schooling ended when, after his mother's death, one sister's marriage and the other's distant employment left him on his own. Jerome held a number of clerical jobs, eventually finding work as an extra with a touring theatrical company, in whose production of *Hamlet*, he later claimed, he had played every part but that of Ophelia. When the company disbanded Jerome lived a hand-to-mouth existence on the streets of London for several months before turning his writing and shorthand skills toward journalistic, and then secretarial work. During this time he was writing humorous and autobiographically-based stories and sketches about life as a traveling player; in the early 1880s these articles began to appear in theatrical and humor magazines. Although it is common to maintain, with Arthur Conan Doyle, that Jerome "shot into fame with his spendidly humorous *Three Men in a Boat*," in fact Jerome was an established humorist by the time the first installments of his most successful work were appearing serially in *Home Chimes* magazine. Some of his early sketches were collected and published as *On the Stage—and Off: The Brief Career of a Would-Be Actor*. The book was a popular success, and Jerome followed it with two others culled from his periodical contributions: *Stage-Land: Curious Habits and Customs of its Inhabitants* and *The Idle Thoughts of an Idle Fellow*, both of which were brisk sellers despite their earlier serialization. These early books, however, gained Jerome a primarily local London readership. It was with *Three Men in a Boat* that he achieved truly phenomenal success, and the book remains an all-time best seller in both England and the United States. The book's American sales were always a sore point with Jerome: pirated before international copyright laws would have protected his interests, he received nothing from the approximately one million copies sold in the United States during his lifetime. Although he remained somewhat bitter about this loss of revenue, Jerome's attitude toward the United States softened sufficiently after the turn of the century for him to travel there on three occasions to oversee productions of his plays, several of which enjoyed successful runs in American theaters. He combined these visits with lecture tours of the country, and some of his

later books of comic sketches contain humorous essays on the various deficiencies he found in American life and culture.

At the beginning of World War I, Jerome—despite being aged fifty-six—attempted to enlist in the British armed forces. Rejected, he joined the French Ambulance Corps, and in his autobiography wrote movingly and with little of his characteristic humor about the hardships of living in the trenches near the actual fighting; driving the unreliable ambulances, often in total darkness; and witnessing various large and small acts of heroism, which reinforced his always steadfast faith in humanity. After his term of service ended, Jerome lived quietly. He continued writing, but in his later years turned from the comic writing that had gained him his greatest fame, to polemical novels that examined more serious topics, and to composing his autobiography, *My Life and Times*. He died of natural causes in 1927.

Three Men in a Boat (To Say Nothing of the Dog) has enjoyed—or endured—a fate similar to that of many other such light works of entertainment: an immediate favorite with readers, the book was regarded askance when noted at all by critics, until its enormous popularity necessitated some disparaging explanation of its appeal. It was typically dismissed as a leading example of "new humor," a derogatory term applied to the works of light sentimental comic fiction that appealed to a new class of British reader characterized by Barbara J. Dunlap as the "literate but not literary . . . educationally enfranchised millions" who "turned to journalism for amusement and information" during the Victorian and Edwardian eras, "in which general education and leisure became widely available to more Britons than ever before." Termed "common" and "vulgar" by the literary establishment, "lowbrow" and "Philistine" by the fin de siècle Decadents, "the new humor" bore the further onus of deriving from (or, according to some critics, merely copying) the thoroughly American comic writing of such working-class authors as Mark Twain and Artemus Ward.

Typical of the initial critical reception afforded *Three Men in a Boat* is that given by an anonymous critic in the *Saturday Review,* who found that "the life it describes and the humor that it records are poor and limited, and decidedly vulgar," leaving the reviewer to "sigh . . . at the narrowness and poverty of the life it only too faithfully represents." However, unlike most humorous books, which tend to be highly topical and therefore transitory in their appeal, *Three Men in a Boat* has remained popular with readers. It has been translated into twenty-three languages, filmed at least three times, and is both the only one of Jerome's books to remain consistently in print and one of the very few humor books from his era to do so. While most humor "seldom outlasts the vagaries of fashion and temperament it reflects," according to Peter De Vries, "the universal appeal of the book must lie, partly at least, in the universality of the subject matter." Edmund Pearson noted that "the things that happened in it had happened to all of us on holidays or at picnics, but [in *Three Men*] they were related by a man with the gift of humor which is possessed by one man in a billion."

Three Men in a Boat is episodic in structure. While this format was largely dictated, or at least suggested, by its initial appearance as a periodical serial, it was also the ideal means of telling this particular comic tale of three young city men out for a week's holiday boating on the Thames. According to Jerome, "the book was to have been 'The Story of the Thames,' its scenery and history," intermingling guidebook-style travelogue with lighthearted accounts of the various mishaps commonly experienced by river travelers, introduced for "humorous relief." But, in Jerome's phrase, the book "seemed to be all 'humorous relief' "; furthermore, the magazine editor who was running *Three Men* serially deleted the "slabs of history" that Jerome wrote with "grim determination" and worked into each chapter. Jerome himself recognised the universal and timeless appeal of his account of a boating trip, writing that it seemed likely enough that "some troop of ancient Britons . . . listened amused while one among them told of the adventures of himself and twain companions in a coracle"; similarly, he expected that in 30,000 A.D.—"if Earth's rivers still run"—the experiment would be repeated. *Three Men on the Bummel,* a sort of sequel to *Three Men in a Boat* that traced the adventures of the same three men on a bicycle trip through Germany, was moderately successful but never met with the same enthusiasm as *Three Men in a Boat.*

After the great popularity of *Three Men in a Boat,* Jerome turned his attention primarily to play writing. For more than fifty years following the 1888 appearance of his first dramatic works and stage adaptations of the works of others, Jerome's plays appeared regularly and with some success on London and American stages. For the most part he wrote formula comedies, which was ironic, since his *Stage-Land* contained amusing and sometimes very perceptive satires of stock character types and cliched dramatic situations. Although critics agree that Jerome rarely strayed from the commercially successful but artistically uninspired dramatic conventions of his time, his comedies were at least noted for skilled, believable dialogue. Jerome's reputation as a comic writer was so secure in the public mind that he had difficulty in interesting a producer in his idea for a stage version of his short story "The Passing of the Third Floor Back." In the story the presence of a mysterious, Christlike roomer at a shabby boardinghouse leads the other boarders to examine and reform their lives. When the drama was eventually produced, audiences attending "a new play by the author of *Three Men in a Boat*" were unsure of how to react to the modern morality play. At least one prominent theater critic, Max Beerbohm, savagely denounced the play as "twaddle and vulgarity," concluding with the suggestion that the play was blasphemous. *The Passing of the Third Floor Back* never became very popular, but it is the only one of Jerome's plays that has been occasionally revived. It is also the only one of his plays to have attracted any sustained critical comment. Jerome critic and biographer Ruth Marie Faurot succinctly described Jerome's dramatic output when she wrote "Jerome's plays served their purpose in providing good theater for the audiences of their time, but they were not intended to be considered as literature."

Although best known as a comic writer, Jerome was widely involved in other aspects of the literary life of his era. He edited two popular humor periodicals: the *Idler,* the editorship of which he assumed in 1892, and *To-day,* which he founded in 1893. The court costs from a libel suit in 1897 necessitated the selling of both papers, but in the intervening years Jerome's two journals had presented the works of Mark Twain, Bret Harte, Arthur Conan Doyle, Israel Zangwill, Marie Corelli, Robert Louis Stevenson, and W. W. Jacobs, among many others, to London readers. Late in his career Jerome turned to more serious subjects in his novels, producing the critically well-regarded autobiographical novel *Paul Kelver* and the polemical novels *All Roads Lead to Calvary* and *Anthony John.* In these works Jerome was primarily concerned with exploring the problems of good and evil, idealism, the impact of poverty on individuals, and the nature of religious belief. Most of Jerome's novels, serious and humorous alike, drew upon some part of his own background, so that episodes from his childhood, his early theater and newspaper work, and later success as a dramatist, all figure in one or more of the longer fictional works.

Despite his contributions to many other areas of literature, it is as a humorist that Jerome was most popular and is best remembered. Jerome succeeded as a humorist because of his mastery of basic comic writing techniques: summarized by Faurot as the "ability to make a good story out of the most trivial of incidents. . . . The laugh comes either because he turns the joke on himself—his embarrassments, his mistakes, even his conceit—or because he gives an unexpected twist to the climax of an incident or even a sentence." Like most successful humorists, Jerome employed both exaggeration and understatement to good effect. Pearson noted that most "light humorists get too much pleasure out of educated periphrasis and self-congratulatory club wit. . . . [Jerome] escaped the danger. His prose is clear and simple. . . . In anecdote, he is a master of leading the reader on quietly and then of rushing in a line that suddenly makes the joke take to the air and go mad." But many commentators have warned of the danger of overanalyzing humor, and for millions of readers it remains sufficient that nearly a century ago, Jerome, with *Three Men in a Boat,* wrote a comic classic that remains fresh and funny today.

(See also *Contemporary Authors,* Vol. 119; *Dictionary of Literary Biography,* Vol. 10: *Modern British Dramatists;* and Vol. 34: *British Novelists, 1890-1929: Traditionalists.*)

PRINCIPAL WORKS

On the Stage—and Off: The Brief Career of a Would-Be Actor (essays and sketches) 1885
Barbara (drama) 1886
The Idle Thoughts of an Idle Fellow (essays, sketches, and short stories) 1886
Fennel (drama) 1888
Woodbarrow Farm (drama) 1888
Stage-Land: Curious Habits and Customs of its Inhabitants (essays and sketches) 1889
Three Men in a Boat (To Say Nothing of the Dog) (novel) 1889
The Diary of a Pilgrimage (essays and sketches) 1891
Told after Supper (short stories) 1891
Novel Notes (essays and short stories) 1893
John Ingerfield and Other Stories (short stories) 1894
The Prude's Progress [with Eden Philpotts] (drama) 1895; produced in the United States as *The Councillor's Wife,* 1892
The MacHaggis [with Eden Philpotts] (drama) 1897
The Second Thoughts of an Idle Fellow (essays, sketches, and short stories) 1898
Miss Hobbs (drama) 1899
Three Men on the Bummel (novel) 1900; also published as *Three Men on Wheels,* 1900
Paul Kelver (novel) 1902
Tommy and Co. (novel) 1904
The Passing of the Third Floor Back, and Other Stories (short stories) 1907
The Angel and the Author and Others (essays) 1908
Fanny and the Servant Problem (drama) 1908; produced in the United States as *The New Lady Bantock,* 1909
The Passing of the Third Floor Back (drama) 1908
They and I (novel) 1909
All Roads Lead to Calvary (novel) 1919
Anthony John (novel) 1923
A Miscellany of Sense and Nonsense: From the Writings of Jerome K. Jerome, Selected by the Author with Many Apologies (essays, sketches, and excerpts from short stories and novels) 1923
My Life and Times (autobiography) 1926
The Other Jerome K. Jerome (essays, sketches, and excerpts from short stories and novels) 1984

THE SATURDAY REVIEW OF LITERATURE, LONDON **(essay date 1889)**

[*In the following excerpt from an early review of* Three Men in a Boat, *the anonymous critic decries the colloquial narrative style and expresses doubt that the book was worth writing.*]

To tell the truth, we hardly know what to make of *Three Men in a Boat,* of which we have no desire to make much, either good or ill. It is not a piece of fiction, as might be supposed,

since the author goes out of his way to say in a preface that "its pages form a record of events that really happened." Again, "George and Harris and Montmorency"—that is the dog, a fox terrier—"are not poetic ideals, but things of flesh and blood." There can be no meaning in these words unless we are intended to understand that the book is a more or less realistic account of what it professes to describe—a week's trip, in early summer, on the Thames. The events are, obviously, exaggerated for purposes of humour, but they seem to be real events. "Other works," says Mr. Jerome, "may excel this in depth of thought and knowledge of human nature; other books may rival it in originality and size; but for hopeless and incurable veracity nothing yet discovered can surpass it." On the whole, after reading *Three Men in a Boat,* we come to the conclusion that this is not intended for irony. These are what French novelists call "documents"; this is the genuine relation of a passage in the lives of actual people. (p. 387)

The whole chronicle is an account of how the author and two young friends went up the Thames from Kingston to Oxford, and back so far as Pangbourne, in a double-sculling skiff. It reproduces all the minute adventures of such a summer outing, mildly describes, for the thousandth time, but in a novel spirit, the objects on the shore, and is written entirely in colloquial clerk's English of the year 1889, of which this is an example taken at random:—

> She was nuts on public-houses, was England's Virgin Queen. There's scarcely a pub of any attractions within ten miles of London that she does not seem to have looked in at, or stopped at, or slept at, some time or other. I wonder now, supposing Harris, say, turned over a new leaf, and became a great and good man, and got to be Prime Minister, and died, if they would put signs over the public-houses that he had patronized. "Harris had a glass of bitter in this house"; "Harris had two of Scotch cold here in the summer of '88"; "Harris was chucked from here in December 1886."

This is not funny, of course; to do Mr. Jerome justice it is not intended to be particularly funny; but it is intensely colloquial, and, as an attempt to reproduce, without any kind of literary admixture, the ordinary talk of ordinary young people of to-day, it seems to us remarkable, especially as the whole book is kept at the same simple and yet abnormal level of style. It will be observed that in this short passage just quoted there are no less than six phrases which would be wholly unintelligible to a foreigner thoroughly conversant with the English of books, and yet not one of the six is in the least strained, or, though vulgar, would offer the least difficulty to a Londoner. For the future student of late Victorian slang, *Three Men in a Boat* will be invaluable, if he is able to understand it, and if, by the time he flourishes, the world of idle youth has not entirely forgotten what a "bally tent" and "sunday-school slops" and "a man of about number one size" are. In some of the sporting news-papers slang of this kind, and indeed of a much worse kind, may be discovered, but we do not recollect to have met any other book entirely written in it. In a sense, too, *Three Men in a Boat* is a much truer specimen of lower middle-class English than are the paragraphs in the coloured newspapers, because they are exaggerated and non-natural, while Mr. Jerome is amazingly real. That it was worth doing, we do not say; indeed, we have a very decided opinion that it was not. But the book's only serious fault is that the life it describes and the humour that it records are poor and limited, and decidedly vulgar. It is strange that a book like *Three Men in a Boat,* which is a *tour de force* in fun of a certain kind, should leave us with a sigh on our lips at the narrowness and poverty of the life it only too faithfully reflects. (pp. 387-88)

> A review of "Three Men in a Boat," in The Saturday Review, *London, Vol. 68, No. 1771, October 5, 1889, pp. 387-88.*

THE NATION   (essay date 1890)

[*In the following excerpt from a review of* Three Men in a Boat, *the critic disparages "new humor" and its practitioners.*]

Every man who writes a book assumes a certain responsibility, both direct and indirect. Not only is he directly responsible for the goodness or badness of his own book, and for its effect on the minds of readers, but, if his book is remarkable or successful, he is quite certain to cause others to seek success by following in his footsteps, and so he becomes indirectly responsible for all the wearisome failures that result from such attempts. In this sense Mr. Samuel L. Clemens may be said to be indirectly responsible for [*Three Men in a Boat*] and a number of other books published of late years by would-be English humorists. When *The Innocents Abroad* first appeared, several English critics, entirely unacquainted with its peculiar vein of humor, in good faith and with due solemnity pointed out its defects as an adequate and accurate record of places and people. Since that time, however, English readers have become familiar with the various forms of American humor as exemplified in Mr. Clemens, Bret Harte, Artemus Ward, and others, and one of the results of this familiarity is a crop of books—of which Mr. Jerome's are fair samples—which constantly recall the above-named humorists. But these imitations, while doubtless, as such, sincerely flattering to the originals, cannot truthfully be called successful. The flavor of American humor in them is unmistakable, but the solution or trituration thereof is of the weakest, and a large quantity of current English slang is therefore added to give strength and local color to the whole. . . . Mr. Jerome's *Three Men in a Boat* tells the tale of a week spent in going in a boat from Kingston to Oxford—not a strikingly original subject, by the way—and the author kindly varies the serious business of being humorous by poetic rhapsodies over the beauties of nature, and by a number of references to places of historic interest in the Thames valley. These latter passages smack somewhat of the guide-book, and recall the accounts of the Oxford colleges which a certain undergraduate, who disliked original composition, used to copy out and send in instalments to his venerable and confiding mother in lieu of a weekly letter.

So far, most of the humorists of this new school are adventurous people who like roughing it and camping out, and they evidently regard as irresistibly funny the difficulty of packing their provisions, the mixing of strawberry jam and meat pies, the upsetting of salt over everything, and so forth. It may be that such books will give pleasure to those who go down to the sea in ships, or up the river in boats, because as a rule they are very easily pleased; but the ordinary landsman will inevitably class them as "books one would rather have left unread."

In the same category must be placed Mr. Jerome's *Idle Thoughts of an Idle Fellow,* although for somewhat different reasons. A dozen essays on such well worn subjects as **"The Weather," "Shyness," "Babies,"** etc., etc., are here brought together, and, as they present but little claim to originality of ideas or style, it is difficult to see why they should have been inflicted on the community. Their humor has a strong resemblance to that of the previous volume, but it is somewhat less boisterous, and is, moreover, varied by occasional passages of pathos and cynicism. Sometimes, indeed, Mr. Jerome struggles with thoughts that seem almost poetic by comparison with the general dull level of the book; but on these occasions he comes dangerously near to burlesque. In the essay on **"Being in Love,"** for instance, the reader is informed that "love is too pure a light to burn long among the noisome gases that we breathe, but before it is choked out we may use it as a torch to ignite the cosey fire of affection." This is what Thackeray used to call "the hoighth of foine language entoirely," but why should it appear in book form instead of in the literary corner of a country newspaper? *That* is the true resting-place for such gems of thought, and the friends of Mr. Jerome who, according to his preface, induced him to print this book, would have exercised a wiser discretion if they had allowed matters to take their regular course.

> A review of "Three Men in a Boat—The Idle Thoughts of an Idle Fellow," in The Nation, *Vol. L, No. 1294, April 17, 1890, p. 321.*

BERNARD SHAW   (essay date 1895)

[*Shaw is generally considered the greatest and best-known dramatist to write in the English language since Shakespeare. During the late nineteenth century, he was also a prominent literary, art, and music critic. In 1895 he became the drama critic for the* Saturday Review, *and his reviews therein became known for their biting wit and brilliance. It was rare for Shaw to review a play in wholly genial and approbatory terms; however, in the following excerpt, originally published in* Saturday Review, June 1895, *he does this for Jerome's play* The Prude's Progress.]

[Mr. Jerome K. Jerome's] *Prude's Progress* is much better than its name. Happy is the nation that has no history, and happy the play that has no criticism in this column. **The Prude's Progress** is a shrewd, goodnatured, clever cockney play (Mr. Jerome will not think me foolish enough to use cockney as a term of disparagement), interesting and amusing all through, with pleasantly credible characters and pleasantly incredible incidents, ending happily but not fatuously; so that there is no sense of facts shirked on the one hand nor of problems stage-solved on the other. The play, from which, thanks to its unattractive name, not much was expected, won its way and was very favorably received. (pp. 139-40)

> Bernard Shaw, "Sardoodledom," in his Our Theatres in the Nineties, *Vol. I, Constable and Company Limited, 1932, pp. 133-40.*

THE TIMES LITERARY SUPPLEMENT   (essay date 1902)

[*In the following favorable review of Jerome's semi-autobiographical novel* Paul Kelver, *the anonymous critic finds the depiction of the protagonist's childhood especially well done.*]

No contemporary writer has been more persistently underrated by the critics than Mr. Jerome K. Jerome. The authorship of **Three Men in a Boat** has been a millstone round his neck; and he has been alternatively derided for grinning through a horse-collar, and censured for not confining himself to that humble branch of the literary art. He has been labelled "new humorist" by superior persons who forgot that novelty is no disadvantage to a joke, and would not see that the merits of **Three Men in** *a Boat* resided not merely in its rollicking fun, but also in its shrewd observation of a certain habit of mind and type of character; while his serious work has generally been received with rather supercilious prejudice. He had, therefore, undeniably, a reputation to live down, and in literature, in these days, it is much more difficult to live down a reputation than to make one. Let us hasten to add that, so far as that reputation was a bad one, *Paul Kelver* . . . ought to kill it at a blow. *Paul Kelver* is autobiographical in form, purporting to give the writer's recollections of his childhood and early manhood. To what extent Mr. Jerome has drawn upon personal experience for the scenes and circumstances of his story, it is, of course, no part of our business to conjecture. Their actual truth would neither add to nor detract from their artistic truth; they have the true ring, and that suffices. The psychology, on the other hand, is quite obviously not invented but remembered, as the psychology of child-life always must be when it is done convincingly and well. For children could not confess their secrets if they would, and would not if they could, so that those who cannot read them in their own hearts have no chance to find them out. Mr. Jerome has remembered childhood, and has recorded his memories with the touch of the true artist. He looks back as it were through a veil which blurs the outlines; but what he sees is not a blur but a picture. The child at one puzzled and hurt by its environment has not been better rendered in any recent work of fiction. So far as our recollection goes, the only recent novels which challenge comparison with it in this regard are *The Beth Book* and *The Story of an African Farm;* and it seems to us less morbid and more human than either of them. Indeed, for a comparison that could be sustained one must, in our opinion, convoke the masterpieces—it recalls, though it does not rank with, the books which chronicle the childhood of David Copperfield and Paul Dombey. The latter chapters which tell of Paul Kelver's early struggles as an actor and a journalist are not perhaps quite as good. But it is this part of the book which proves that Mr. Jerome has lost none of his old power of compelling laughter, though he exercises it with more moderation and restraint than heretofore. The misadventures of the hero, when, through circumstances out of his control, he found himself engaged to be married to a barmaid, and was taken by her to be introduced to her family, constitute a comedy which occasionally crosses the border line of farce. This interlude, however, is only what the dramatists call "comic relief." Humour throughout the book is kept subordinate to sentiment, and the sentiment is never overstrained or maudlin. The book is a remarkably good book—a book which places its author in a rank far above the many popular entertainers of literature.

A review of "Paul Kelver," in The Times Literary Supplement, No. 36, September 19, 1902, p. 276.

MAX BEERBOHM (essay date 1908)

[*Although he lived until 1956, Beerbohm is chiefly associated with the fin de siècle period in English literature, more specifically with its lighter phases of witty sophistication and mannered elegance. His temperament was urbane and satirical, and he excelled in both literary and artistic caricatures of his contemporaries. "Entertaining" in the most complimentary sense of the word, Beerbohm's criticism for the* Saturday Review—*where he was a long-time drama critic—everywhere indicates his scrupulously developed taste and unpretentious, fair-minded response to literature. He was, however, capable of virulent attacks upon writers and works that he thought warranted scorn: throughout Jerome's career he deplored the success and popularity of Jer-*ome's works and reserved especial invective for his review of The Passing of the Third Floor Back, *originally published in the* Saturday Review *in 1908 and here excerpted.*]

How can Mr. Forbes-Robertson expect me to be polite about his production [of *The Passing of the Third Floor Back*] at the St. James'? In the provinces, recently, he produced a play by Mr. Henry James—a play that was reported to be a great success. It would be a privilege to produce a play by Mr. Henry James, even though the play failed utterly. In its failure, it would be more interesting, and would bring higher esteem to its producer, than any number of successful plays by second-rate men. Having produced Mr. James' play with success, what does Mr. Forbes-Robertson do so soon as he comes to London? Apparently in doubt whether Mr. James be good enough for the metropolis, he gives us Mr. Jerome Klapka Jerome. This tenth-rate writer has been, for many years, prolific of his tenth-rate stuff. But I do not recall, in such stuff of his as I have happened to sample, anything quite so vilely stupid as *The Passing of the Third Floor Back.* I do not for a moment suppose that Mr. Forbes-Robertson likes it one whit more than I do. And I wish his pusillanimity in prostituting his great gifts to it were going to be duly punished. The most depressing aspect of the whole matter is that the play is so evidently a great success. The enthusiasm of a first-night audience is no sure gauge of success. Nor is the proverbial apathy of a second-night audience a sure gauge of failure. It was on the second night that I saw *The Passing of the Third Floor Back;* and greater enthusiasm have I seldom seen in a theatre. And thus I am brought sharply up against that doubt which so often confronts me: what can be hoped of an art which must necessarily depend on the favour of the public—of such a public, at least, as ours? Good work may, does sometimes, succeed. But never with the degree of success that befalls twaddle and vulgarity unrelieved. Twaddle and vulgarity will have always the upper hand.

The reformation of a bad person by a supernatural visitor is a theme that has often been used. Mr. Jerome, remembering the converted miser in *A Christmas Carol,* and the converted egoist in *A Message from Mars,* and many a similar convert, was struck by the bright idea that the effect would be just a dozen times as great if there were a dozen converts. So he has turned a supernatural visitor loose in a boarding-house inhabited by a round dozen of variously bad people—"A Satyr," "A Snob," "A Shrew," "A Painted Lady," "A Cheat," and so on. Now, supposing that these characters were life-like, or were amusing figments of the brain, and supposing that we saw them falling, little by little, under the visitor's spell, till gradually we were aware that they had been changed for the better, the play might be quite a passable affair. But to compass that effect is very far beyond Mr. Jerome's power. He has neither the natural talent nor the technical skill that the task requires. There is not a spark of verisimilitude in the whole dozen of characters. One and all, they are unreal. Mr. Jerome shows no sign of having ever observed a fellow-creature. His characters seem to be the result solely of a study of novelettes in the penny weekly papers, supplemented by a study of the works of Mr. Jerome K. Jerome. Take Major Tompkins, and his wife and daughter, for example. Could anything be more trite and crude than their presentment? Major and Mrs. Tompkins are anxious to sell their daughter for gold to an elderly man. "His very touch," says the daughter, according to custom, "is loathsome." The Major persists and says—what else could a stage-major say?—"Damn your infernal impudence!" The unnatural mother tries to persuade the unwilling daughter to wear a more décolleté dress. The daughter, of course, loves a young painter in a brown velveteen jacket; but she is weak and worldly, and she is like to yield to the importunities of the elderly man. The young painter—but no, I won't bore you by describing the other characters: suffice it that they are all ground out of the same old rusty machine that has served the *Family Herald* and similar publications for so many weary years. Mr. Jerome's humour, however, is his own, and he plasters it about with a liberal hand. What could be more screamingly funny than the doings at the outset? The landlady pours tea into the decanter which is supposed to hold whisky, on the chance that the drunken boarder won't notice the difference. Then she goes out, and the servant drinks milk out of the jug and replenishes the jug with water. Then *she* goes out, and the "Painted Lady" comes in and steals a couple of fresh candles from the sconces on the piano and substitutes a couple of candle ends. Then *she* goes out, and the Major comes in and grabs the biscuits off the plate and drops them into his hat. The *he* goes out, and the "Cad" and the "Rogue" come in and unlock the spirit-case with an illicit key and help themselves to what they presently find is tea. He's inexhaustibly fertile in such sequences is Mr. Jerome K. Jerome. When the "Passer-by" knocks at the front-door, and is admitted with a limelight full on his (alas, Mr. Forbes-Robertson's) classic countenance, the sequences set in with an awful severity. The beneficent stranger has one method for all evildoers, and he works it on every one in turn, with precisely the same result. He praises the landlady for her honesty; then the landlady is ashamed of her dishonesty and becomes honest. He praises the Major for his sweet temper; then the Major is ashamed of his bad temper, and becomes sweet-tempered. He praises the "Painted Lady" for her modesty in not thinking herself beautiful without paint; then the "Painted Lady" is ashamed of her paint, and reappears paintless. He praises—but again I won't bore you further. You have found the monotony of the foregoing sentences oppressive enough. Picture to yourselves the monotony of what they describe! For a period of time that seemed like eternity, I had to sit knowing exactly what was about to happen, and how it was about to happen, and knowing that as soon as it had happened it would happen again. The art of dramaturgy, some one has said, is the art of preparation. In that case Klapka is assuredly the greatest dramatist the world has ever known. It is hard to reconcile this conclusion with the patent fact that he hasn't yet mastered the rudiments of his craft.

The third and last act of the play, like the second, consists of a sequence of interviews—next man, please!—between the visitor and the other (now wholly reformed) persons of the play. Steadily, he works through the list, distributing full measure of devastating platitudes, all the way. The last person on the list, the Major's daughter, says suddenly "Who are you?" The visitor spreads his arms, in the attitude of "The Light of the World." The Major's daughter falls on her knees in awe. When the visitor passes out through the front-door, a supernatural radiance bursts through the fan-light, flooding the stage; and then the curtain comes slowly down. Well, I suppose blasphemy pays. (pp. 516-19)

Max Beerbohm, "A Deplorable Affair," in his Around Theatres, *revised edition, 1930. Reprint by Simon and Schuster, 1954, pp. 516-19.*

JEROME K. JEROME (essay date 1926)

[*In the following excerpt from his autobiography,* My Life and Times, *Jerome discusses the circumstances surrounding the writing of some of his major works.*]

My first book! He stands before me, bound in paper wrapper of a faint pink colour, as though blushing all over for his sins. *On the Stage—and Off.* By Jerome K. Jerome (the K very large, followed by a small j; so that by many the name of the author was taken to be Jerome Kjerome). The Brief Career of a would-be Actor. One shilling nett. Ye Leadenhall Press. London. 1885.

He was born in Whitfield Street, Tottenham Court Road, in a second floor back overlooking a burial ground. (p. 67)

By luck, my favorite poet, just then, was Longfellow. . . . Always when things were at their worst, or nearly so, I would go to him for comfort; and one evening, crouching over my small fire, I struck the poem beginning:

> By his evening fire the artist
> Pondered o'er his secret shame;

I had the feeling that Longfellow must have been thinking about me. And when I read the last two lines:

> That is best which lieth nearest;
> Shape from that thy work of art,

it came to me that Longfellow was telling me not to bother about other people's troubles—those of imaginary maidens turned into waterfalls, and such like—but to write about my own. I would tell the world the story of a hero called Jerome who had run away and gone upon the stage; and of all the strange and moving things that had happened to him there. I started on it that same evening, and in three months it was finished. (pp. 68-9)

For a workroom I often preferred the dark streets to my dismal bed-sitting-room. Portland Place was my favourite study. I liked its spacious dignity. With my note-book and a pencil in my hand, I would pause beneath each lamp-post and jot down the sentence I had just thought out. At first the police were suspicious. I had to explain to them. Later they got friendly; and often I would read to them some passage I thought interesting or amusing. There was an Inspector—a dry old Scotchman who always reached Langham church as the clock struck eleven: he was the most difficult. Whenever I made him laugh, I went home feeling I had done good work.

When finished, it went the round of many magazines. (pp. 70-1)

Eventually, despairing of the popular magazines, I sent it to a penny paper called the *Play,* which had just been started; and four days later came an answer. It ran:

"Dear Sir, I like your articles very much. Can you call on me to-morrow morning before twelve? Yours truly, W. Aylmer Gowing. Editor, the *Play.*"

I did not sleep that night.

Aylmer Gowing was a retired actor. . . . He was the first "editor" who up till then had seemed glad to see me when I entered the room. He held out both hands to me, and offered me a cigarette. It all seemed like a dream. He told me that what he liked about my story was that it was true. He had been through it all himself, forty years before. He asked me what I wanted for the serial rights. I was only too willing to let him have them for nothing, upon which he shook hands with me again, and gave me a five-pound note. It was the first time I had ever possessed a five-pound note. I could not bear the idea of spending it. I put it away at the bottom of an old tin box where I kept my few treasures: old photographs, letters, and a lock of hair. Later, when the luck began to turn, I fished it out, and with part of it, at a secondhand shop in Goodge Street, I purchased an old Georgian bureau which has been my desk ever since. (pp. 72-3)

All my new friends thought it would be easy to find a publisher for the book. They gave me letters of introduction. But publishers were just as dense as editors had been. From most of them I gathered that the making of books was a pernicious and unprofitable occupation for everybody concerned. Some thought the book might prove successful if I paid the expense of publication. But, upon my explaining my financial position, were less impressed with its merits. To come to the end, Tuer of the Leadenhall Press offered to publish it on terms of my making him a free gift of the copyright. The book sold fairly well, but the critics were shocked. The majority denounced it as rubbish and, three years later, on reviewing my next book, *The Idle Thoughts of an Idle Fellow,* regretted that an author who had written such an excellent first book should have followed it up by so unworthy a successor.

I think I may claim to have been, for the first twenty years of my career, the best abused author in England. *Punch* invariably referred to me as "'Arry K'Arry," and would then proceed to solemnly lecture me on the sin of mistaking vulgarity for humour and impertinence for wit. As for the *National Observer,* the Jackdaw of Rheims himself was not more cursed than was I, week in, week out, by W. S. Henley and his superior young men. I ought, of course, to have felt complimented; but at the time I took it all quite seriously, and it hurt. Max Beerbohm was always very angry with me. The *Standard* spoke of me as a menace to English letters; and the *Morning Post* as an example of the sad results to be expected from the over-education of the lower orders. (pp. 74-5)

I was still a literary man only in the evening. From ten to six I remained a clerk. . . . My chief recreation was theatre-going. I got the first-night habit. For great events, such as an Irving production at the Lyceum or a Gilbert and Sullivan opera, this meant a wait of many hours, ending in a glorious scrimmage, when at last the great doors creaked, and the word ran round "They're opening." First nights were generally on a Saturday. I would leave the office at two, and after a light lunch, take up my stand outside pit or gallery entrance, according to the state of the exchequer. With experience, some of us learned the trick of squirming our way past the crowd by keeping to the wall. The queue system had not yet been imported. It came from Paris. We despised the Frenchies for submitting to it. Often, arriving only a few minutes before opening time, have I gained a front seat. Looking behind me at poor simple folk who had been waiting all the afternoon, my conscience would prick me. But such is the way of the world, and who was I to criticise my teachers?

We regular "First Nighters" got to know one another. And to one among us, Heneage Mandell, occurred the idea of forming ourselves into a club where, somewhere out of the rain, we could discuss together things theatrical, and set the stage to rights.

That was the beginning of The Playgoers' Club, which gained much notoriety; and is still, I believe, going strong: though no longer the terror to hide-bound managers and unjust critics that it was in the days of its youth. (pp. 80-2)

I speak of the Playgoers' Club here because it led to my writing *Stageland.* Heneage Mandell, the founder of the club, was connected with a firm of printers, and persuaded his chief to start a paper called *The Playgoer.* Poor Heneage died not long afterwards, and the paper came to an end. I seem to have written the editorial notes—or some of them. I had forgotten this, until glancing through them the other day. I must have been a bit of a prig, I fear. I trust I have outgrown it, but one can never judge oneself. (p. 83)

It was in the *Playgoer* that *Stageland* first appeared. The sketches were unsigned, and journals that had been denouncing me and all my works as an insult to English literature hastened to crib them. Afterwards Bernard Partridge illustrated them, and we published them in partnership at our own risk. It proved to me that publishing is quite an easy business. If I had my time over again, I would always be my own publisher. (pp. 83-4)

The book was quite a success. (p. 84)

I see from old letters that I was studying at this period to become a solicitor. Not that I had any thought of giving up literature. I would combine the two. If barristers—take, for example, Gilbert and Grundy—wrote plays and books, why not solicitors? Besides, I had just married. A new sense of prudence had come to me: "Safety first," as we say now. I was with a Mr. Anderson Rose in Arundel Street, Strand. . . . He was a dear old gentleman. In the office, we all loved him. And so did his clients, until soon after his death, when their feelings towards him began to change. (pp. 84-5)

His death put an end to my dream of being a lawyer. He had been kindness itself to me in helping me, and had promised to put work in my way. I decided to burn my boats, and to devote all my time to writing. My wife encouraged me. She is half Irish, and has a strain of recklessness. (p. 85)

Three Men in a Boat (To Say Nothing of the Dog) I wrote at Chelsea Gardens, up ninety-seven stairs. But the view was worth it. We had a little circular drawing-room—I am speaking now as a married man—nearly all window, suggestive of a lighthouse, from which we looked down upon the river, and over Battersea Park to the Surrey hills beyond, with the garden of old Chelsea Hospital just opposite. (p. 106)

I did not intend to write a funny book, at first. I did not know I was a humorist. I never have been sure about it. In the Middle Ages, I should probably have gone about preaching and got myself burnt or hanged. There was to be "humorous relief"; but the book was to have been "The Story of the Thames," its scenery and history. Somehow it would not come. I was just back from my honeymoon, and had the feeling that all the world's troubles were over. About the "humorous relief" I had no difficulty. I decided to write the "humorous relief" first—get it off my chest, so to speak. After which, in sober frame of mind, I could tackle the scenery and history. I never got there. It seemed to be all "humorous relief." By grim determination I succeeded, before the end, in writing a dozen or so slabs of history and working them in, one to each chapter, and F. W. Robinson, who was publishing the book serially, in *Home Chimes,* promptly slung them out, the most of them. From the beginning he had objected to the title and had insisted upon my thinking of another. And half-way through I hit upon *Three Men in a Boat,* because nothing else seemed right.

There wasn't any dog. I did not possess a dog in those days. Neither did George. Nor did Harris. . . . Montmorency I evolved out of my inner consciousness. There is something of the dog, I take it, in most Englishmen. Dog friends that I came to know later have told me he was true to life.

An 1889 illustration by A. Frederics for Three Men in a Boat.

Indeed, now I come to think of it, the book really was a history. I did not have to imagine or invent. Boating up and down the Thames had been my favourite sport ever since I could afford it. I just put down the things that happened. (pp. 107-08)

From all of which it would appear that anyone, who had thought of it, could have written *Three Men in a Boat*. Likely enough, some troop of ancient Britons, camping where now the Mother of Parliaments looks down upon old Thames, listened amused while one among them told of the adventures of himself and twain companions in a coracle: to say nothing of the wolf. Allowing for variation in unimportant detail, much the same sort of things must have happened. And in 30,000 A.D.—if Earth's rivers still run—a boat-load of Shaw's "ancients" will, in all probability, be repeating the experiment with similar results, accompanied by a dog five thousand years old.

George and Harris were likewise founded on fact. (pp. 110-11)

We three would foregather on Sunday mornings, and take the train to Richmond. There were lovely stretches then between Richmond and Staines, meadowland and cornfields. At first, we used to have the river almost to ourselves; but year by year it got more crowded and Maidenhead became our starting-point. (p. 111)

Sometimes we would fix up a trip of three or four days or a week, doing the thing in style and camping out. Three, I have always found, make good company. Two grow monotonous, and four or over break up into groups. Later on we same three did a cycle tour through the Black Forest: out of which came *Three Men on the Bummel* (*Three Men on Wheels*, it was called in America). In Germany it was officially adopted as a school reading-book. Another year we tramped the valley of the Upper Danube. That would have made an interesting book, but I was occupied writing plays at the time. It lingers in my memory as the best walk of all. (p. 112)

Three Men in a Boat brought me fame, and had it been pub-lished a few years later would have brought me fortune also. As it was, the American pirate reaped a great reward. But I suppose God made him. Of course it was damned by the critics. One might have imagined—to read some of them—that the British Empire was in danger. One Church dignitary went about the country denouncing me. *Punch* was especially indignant, scenting an insidious attempt to introduce "new humour" into comic literature. For years, "New Humorist" was shouted after me wherever I wrote. Why in England, of all countries in the world, humour, even in new clothes, should be mistaken for a stranger to be greeted with brickbats, bewildered me. (p. 114)

Of all my books I liked writing *Paul Kelver* the best. Maybe because it was all about myself, and people I had known and loved.

It changed my luck, so far as the critics were concerned. (p. 130)

I ought, of course, to have gone on. I might have become an established novelist—even a best seller. Who knows? But hav-ing "got there," so to speak, my desire was to get away. I went back to the writing of plays. It was the same at the beginning of me. My history repeats itself. Having won success as a humorist I immediately became serious. I have a kink in my brain, I suppose I can't help it. (pp. 130-31)

A lady, on one occasion, asked me why I did not write a play.

"I am sure, Mr. Jerome," she continued with a bright en-couraging smile, "that you could write a play."

I told her I had written nine: that six of them had been produced, that three of them had been successful both in England and America, that one of them was still running at the Comedy Theatre and approaching its two hundredth night.

Her eyebrows went up in amazement.

"Dear me," she said, "you do surprise me." (p. 132)

Barbara was my first play. (p. 133)

Barbara ran, on and off, for years, and amateurs still play it. . . . Another one-act play, *Fennel,* I wrote for George Giddens, who had taken the Novelty, now the Kingsway—or rather adapted it from the French of François Coppée. Managers clamoured then for adaptations from the French. Sydney Grundy, one of the most successful authors on the English stage, never wrote an original play. He was quite frank about it. "Why should I cudgel my own brains," he would say, "when I can suck other men's?"

Fennel was chiefly remarkable for introducing Allan Aynesworth to the London stage. He played Sandro, the lover. I see that I describe him in the script as "a fine, dashing, good-looking young fellow." Aynesworth was all that right enough; but on the first night he got stage fright. I was watching from the wings. I could see him getting more and more nervous; and when he came to his big speech, his memory snapped. I had prided myself upon that speech. I had done my best to put Coppée's poetry into English blank verse. It was all about music and the sunrise, and Heaven and love: some two pages of it altogether. I could have forgiven him forgetting it, and drying up. But, to my horror, he went on. He had it fixed in his mind that until the old man returned home he had to stand in the centre of the stage and talk poetry. And he did it. Bits of it, here and there, were mine; most of it his own; a good deal of it verses and quotations that, I take it, he had learnt at his mother's knee. (pp. 136-37)

"Sorry I forgot the exact lines," he said to me, as he came off. "But I was determined not to let you down."

Woodbarrow Farm was my first full-sized play. Gertrude Kingston produced it at a *matinée,* playing herself the adventuress. The trial *matinée* was a useful institution. I think it is a pity it has dropped out. The manager would lend the theatre in return for an option on the play; and the leading parts could generally be arranged for on a like understanding. At the cost of about a hundred pounds, a play could be put before the public and judged: in the only way a play can be judged—through the test-like tube of an audience. (p. 137)

I wrote *The MacHaggis* in collaboration with Eden Phillpotts. . . . Our heroine shocked the critics. She rode a bicycle. It was unwomanly, then, to ride a bicycle. There were so many things, in those days, that were unwomanly to do. It must have been quite difficult to be a woman, and remain so day after day. She smoked a cigarette. The Devil must have been in us. Up till then, only the adventuress had ever smoked a cigarette. In the last act, she said "damn." She said it twice. Poor Clement Scott nearly fell out of the *Daily Telegraph.* (p. 146)

I wrote *The Passing of the Third Floor Back* for David Warfield. I worked it out first as a short story. It was John Murray, the publisher, who put the idea into my head of making it into a play. . . . I thought I could do it without giving offence. . . . It was not an easy play to write: one had to feel it rather than think it. I was living in a lonely part of the Chiltern hills with great open spaces all around me, and that helped; and at last it was finished. (pp. 161-62)

We produced the play at Harrowgate. The audience there mistook it for a farce. It was by the author of *Three Men in a Boat,* so they had been told. That evening the Robertsons and

myself partook of a melancholy supper. It was Blackpool that saved the play. Forbes wired me—

"It's all right. Blackpool understands it and loves it."

In London, on the first night, the curtain fell to dead silence which lasted so long that everybody thought the play must be a failure, and my wife began to cry. And then suddenly the cheering came, and my wife dried her eyes.

I was not present myself. I have shirked my own first nights ever since a play of mine that Willard produced at the Garrick. I thought the applause was unanimous, but was received with a burst of booing. The argument is that if an author is willing to be applauded, he must not object to being hissed. It may be logic, but it isn't sense: as well say that because a man does not mind being patted on the back, he ought not to object to being kicked. (pp. 164-65)

Jerome K. Jerome, in his My Life and Times, *Harper & Brothers Publishers, 1926, 318 p.*

EDMUND PEARSON   (essay date 1927)

[*Librarian, editor, and critic, Pearson edited the* Bulletin of the New York Public Library *from 1914 to 1927 and is widely regarded today as one of America's most authoritative writers on celebrated crimes. In the following excerpt, he briefly surveys Jerome's career, noting his great popular appeal.*]

Jerome K. Jerome's *Three Men in a Boat* brought him instant fame. It appeared in 1889, and has been reprinted in tens of thousands of copies, read all over the earth, and translated into foreign languages. A simple and unpretentious account of a trip on the most thoroughly tamed and domesticated of all rivers, its humor appealed to nine readers out of ten. The things that happened in it had happened to all of us on holidays or at picnics, but they were related by a man with the gift of humor which is possessed by about one man in a billion.

The time was opportune. Such other humorists as there were in England were members of the perfectly well-bred, teacup-and-saucer school of village-curate humor. In America, Mark Twain's best books were written, and the finest of them had appeared five years earlier. Artemus Ward and the Civil War humorists were partly forgotten, except by older people. It is no wonder that the adventures of George and Harris and Montmorency went around the world and furnished allusions and anecdotes for thousands. (p. 288)

The conservative writers of England and the editorial staff of *Punch* disapproved of Mr. Jerome. They thought him a cockney, like Dickens. Moreover, he had the grievous handicap, from the view-point of Oxford and Cambridge, of being a humorist who made his readers laugh out loud. The academic mind hates a writer who can provoke anything more than a faint smile, unless that writer is named Rabelais and is sanctified by centuries of tradition. But nearly all others took the Three Men into their hearts. Their chronicler could diverge into bypaths, and still be hilariously readable. (pp. 288-89)

The Three Men wandered about the Thames and never got anywhere in particular. It has been divulged recently, in the author's autobiography [see excerpt dated 1926], that the book was planned for a serious history of the river, just as Pickwick was planned to be the text to accompany some sporting prints. Harris and George and the narrator are human and recognizable, and attract other familiar persons wherever they go. Harris is the experienced traveler, or man-full-of-useful-information, who can act as a guide-book at any time. He volunteers to guide some people through the maze at Hampton Court and is blessed by them as an angel, until he lands them all in more of a mess than they were at first. He sings comic songs and spoils the evening for every one but himself. No one who has been boating or camping can fail to enjoy the incident when George's shirt fell overboard, or when all three tried to open the can of pineapple.

Mr. Jerome wrote a number of humorous books and some serious ones after *Three Men in a Boat,* but he never surpassed it in merit or in popularity. It was his third or fourth book, and it is possible that he had written a briefer but more perfect example of humor when the *Three Men* came out. This is *Stage-Land: Curious Habits and Customs of Its Inhabitants.* . . . Its humor is of that very high form which combines with amusement acute observation and criticism. I doubt whether from Aristotle to Alexander Woollcott there have been uttered any more discerning comments upon the drama. It was, of course, the old-fashioned melodrama which was satirized, but the characters of hero, heroine, and villain are eternal, and eternally true are these studies of them. We see their peculiarities, as Mr. Jerome described them, if not on the stage, then on the moving-picture screen, and if I taught a class of students in play-writing I would make them read this book word for word. (pp. 289-90)

For a while after his early success Mr. Jerome wrote humorous books. His *Told After Supper* is one of the few tolerable examples of the comic ghost story, and contains the delicious anecdote of the curate who tried to exhibit his skill in playing three-card monte. *The Diary of a Pilgrimage* took its author to Oberammergau and other parts of Germany, a country which he always regarded with affection, due to his early residence there. He tried the dangerous experiment of sending the youthful heroes of his boating trip years later on a bicycle tour, and made a readable book of it. Like Mr. W. W. Jacobs, he could write a good horror story, as he showed in parts of his *Novel Notes* and in the tale called "The Woman of the Saeter." Like America's greatest humorist, he grew increasingly serious as he grew older, and, like him, his heart was torn by the sorrows and suffering which men inflict on their fellow-men. Probably his most successful novel was *Paul Kelver,* and certainly his most popular play was *The Passing of the Third Floor Back.* . . . This play was expanded from a delicately beautiful short story, and its theme, the appearance of a personage like Christ in modern life, is widely known. The only production of it which I have ever seen, by highly competent amateurs, gave me the impression of a rather cloying sweetness. Mr. Jerome had been an actor, and of his many other plays, before and after the *Third Floor Back,* the one best known in this country was probably *Miss Hobbs.* . . . Mr. Jerome made extensive lecture tours in America. His recent autobiography, *My Life and Times,* reveals a humorist, a passionate reformer, and a man of deeply religious nature. (p. 290)

Edmund Pearson, "Jerome K. Jerome," in The Outlook, *Vol. 146, No. 9, June 29, 1927, pp. 288-90.*

V. S. PRITCHETT (essay date 1957)

[*Pritchett is a highly esteemed English novelist, short story writer, and critic. Considered one of the modern masters of the short story, he is also one of the world's most respected and well-read literary critics. Pritchett writes in the conversational tone of the familiar essay, a method by which he approaches literature from the viewpoint of a lettered but not overly scholarly reader. A twentieth-century successor to such early nineteenth-century essayist-critics as William Hazlitt and Charles Lamb, Pritchett employs much the same critical method: his own experience, judgment, and sense of literary art are emphasized, rather than a codified critical doctrine derived from a school of psychological or philosophical speculation. His criticism is often described as fair, reliable, and insightful. The following excerpt is taken from a review originally published in the* New Statesman and Nation, *June 15, 1957. Pritchett discusses Jerome's* Three Men in a Boat *as a superlative example of English light humor of the Victorian period.*]

One of the nice things about foreigners is their faithful regard for English light humor. When we disclaim it, when we snobbishly indicate that this fanciful persiflage goes out of date very quickly, they reproach us. If we explain that the speciality had become sententious at the turn of the century and was in decline after 1914, when wit, impatience, cruelty and vivid scorn returned to our comic writing, the foreign reader persists that our gracious light humor was civilization itself. Victorian civilization, we may reply; but millions have read a book like Jerome K. Jerome's *Three Men in a Boat* and in all the languages of Europe and Asia. One would hardly have thought that this modest little tale of the misadventures of three can-opening suburban clerks on the Thames would stand up to American connoisseurs of Mark Twain's Mississippi, but it did. Pirated at once, the book conquered America as it amused the students of Bombay, Peking and Valparaiso. (p. 238)

The American response to Jerome arose possibly because he had the episodic digressing, garrulous quality of their vernacular writers. He is close to the Twain of *The Jumping Frog.* But Jerome, like the authors of *The Diary of a Nobody,* and like W. W. Jacobs, belongs to a secure, small Arcadia where the comic disasters of life are the neater for being low. Jerome's humor is a response of the emerging lower middle class to the inconvenience of their situation. Their dreams have left a legacy of small comic defeat. Overworked, they regard idleness as a joke. They have to do everything in penn'orths and ha'porths. Genteel, they have to repress their hilarious envy-disapproval of any burst of bad language on the part of the undeserving poor. The humor of life's little troubles was called the "too real," the joke lying in deadly and misleading accounts of humiliating trivia. One might take Jerome as the signal that, in 1889, holidays for this overworked and masochistic class became possible. It is "too real" that the tin-opener (new emancipating gadget of democracy) has been forgotten. It is "too real" that George and Harris have to share the same bed; that the bed is two foot six wide and that they have to tie themselves together with the sheets in order to keep themselves from falling out. It is "too real," *i.e.,* only too likely, that the dog will bring a rat to drop into the terrible stew they are making. . . . The packing, the rain, the clubbing together to hire a cab, the mockery of small boys, the troubles with towropes, laundry, butter, the belief that the banjo is a lovely instrument and that *Two Lovely Black Eyes* is a beautiful song are the vulgarities of life. There is nothing surreal about the "too real"; it is the chronic. We know little about the inner lives of Jerome's characters. It is true that Harris has a comic nightmare, but this is merely the traditional joke about strong drink. The odd thing is that the "too real" could be appreciated in Bombay. Is the tale of Uncle Podger a universal domestic myth? Would Arabs laugh at it? The appeal of Jerome lies in his gentleness and irony, in his habit of digression, his gift of capping his comic moments with a final extravagant act that outbids life altogether. Above all, his book is an idyll. Jerome himself, astonished by the book's success, guilefully argues that it could not be due to its vulgarity alone. The absence of women gives us a clue—there is one, but she is a mere body that floats by, drowned; *Three Men in a Boat* has the absurdity of a male pipe dream. *Huckleberry Finn* is basically this also; but the tobacco is stronger and indeed, generally, chewed.

The idyll is of the stream on which the loud, bickering, banjo-playing boatload floats lightly along. Not lightly, of course; sculling blisters and half kills them. The joke lies in the modesty of the incident; bumping the bank, getting someone else's shirt wet, eating the horrible camping food, annoying fishermen and motor launches, singing with self-confidence and out of tune, drifting unawares toward the weir, getting the tent up for the night. A lot of it is stock comedy. We know the tent will fall down; the question that awakens the ingenuity of the masters is, how will it fall down? At Cookham these suburbans will imagine themselves in the "wild heart of nature." They are not mugs; they have to match their bounce against the primeval cunning of landladies and the pensive malice of innkeepers, anglers and boatmen. Skillfully Jerome plays everything down. He relies on misleading moral commentary and on that understatement which runs like a rheumatism through English humor. Certain jokes date. Bad language is no longer a joke since swearing came in after the first World War. Idleness is no longer a joke—we have moved into an age that says it believes in leisure. And we find nothing piquant in the silliness of girls. The silly girl in light humor was soon replaced by Wodehouse's pretty power stations. (The light humorists of Jerome's period were obliged to avoid sex; they became experts in femininity.) But the dating of a joke does not matter; the laughter in Jerome is caused less by any fact than by the false conclusions drawn from it. He will mildly note that bargees are sometimes "rude" to one another and use language "which, no doubt, in their calmer moments, they regret." Again the work joke has the intricacy of a conceit in Jerome's skillful hands. (pp. 238-41)

The light humorists get too much pleasure out of educated periphrasis and self-congratulatory club wit. These lead inevitably to heavy prose. Jerome, like W. W. Jacobs, escaped the danger. His prose is clear and simple. It muses on like some quiet, ironical tune played on a malicious whistle. He is free from the journalistic vice of exhibitionism and frantic juggling with bright ideas. He sits by himself on the river bank and drifts on from tune to tune, happily and regardless. He is a very economical writer. In anecdote, he is a master of leading the reader on quietly and then of rushing in a line that suddenly makes the joke take to the air and go mad. The tale of Uncle Podger hanging the picture is a notable piece of technical virtuosity. The packing of the trunk begins as a joke but ends in the complexity of French farce or Restoration comedy. The good light humorist is not a careless fellow with one or two brainwaves and surprises only; he is a deedy lover of the detail that delays the action until the pressure has reached the proper bursting point. There are some conventional phrases in Jerome's famous account of opening the can of pineapple, but it is a model. They had tried the penknife, a pair of scissors and a hitcher: the tin merely rolled over, broke a tea cup and fell into the river. George and Harris were no more than a little cut about the face:

> Then we all got mad. We took that tin out on the bank and Harris went up into a field and got a big sharp stone and I went back into the boat and brought out the mast, and George held the tin and Harris held the sharp end of his

stone against the top of it and I took the mast and poised it high in the air and gathered all my strength and brought it down.

> It was George's straw hat that saved his life that day . . . Harris got off with a flesh wound.

> After that I took the tin off myself and hammered at it with the mast till I was worn out and sick at heart whereupon Harris took it in hand.

> We beat it out flat; we beat it back square; we battered it into every form known to geometry. Then George went at it and knocked it into a shape so strange, so weird, so unearthly in its wild hideousness that he got frightened and threw away the mast. Then we all three sat down on the grass and looked at it.

> There was one great dent across the top that had the appearance of a mocking grin and it drove us furious, so that Harris rushed at the thing and caught it up and flung it into the middle of the river, and as it sank we hurled our curses at it and we got into the boat and rowed away from the spot and never paused until we reached Maidenhead.

This is pure music hall, of course; much of Jerome is quiet comic patter. He was, in fact, something of an actor. But the idyll frames it all. And peacefully transforms it. A collection of light sketches becomes a complete mirage. A world is never created on any level without the secret structure of conflict. Jerome's case was like that of Dickens in the *Pickwick Papers*. He was commissioned to write an historical guide to the Thames and bits of that survive in the book. He was also a meditative man with a religious background. One or two little sermons are embedded in the text. To us they are incongruous, but late-Victorian farce was not hostile to sentiment. These pieties give an engaging wash of pure sentimental purple to Jerome's water color. He was always saved by his lightness of touch. He succeeds less with history. Jokes about Queen Elizabeth and Magna Carta are heavy going. It takes a schoolmaster or a Mark Twain to get the best out of them. Nonconformists like Jerome are apt to be too fervently conventional about history. As for the landscape, it is agreeably kept in its place. The glitter of the main stream, the rankness of the shadows, the gushing of the locks and the streaming of the weirs at night are done with a pleasant subdued versifying. These sights do not overwhelm his true business—that row of elderly anglers (for example) sitting on their chairs in a punt, who are suddenly knocked off, fall into the bottom of the boat and are left—in sublime phrase—"picking fish off each other." (pp. 241-43)

> *V. S. Pritchett, "The Trippers," in his* The Living Novel & Later Appreciations, *revised edition, Random House, 1964, pp. 238-44.*

PETER De VRIES (essay date 1964)

[De Vries is an American author of humorous novels that have attained great popularity in the United States and England. In his fiction he is primarily concerned with demonstrating, through puns and aphorisms, the inadequacy of language as a means of expressing reality. In the following excerpt de Vries notes that the ephemeral nature of humor writing makes the universal and

timeless appeal of Jerome's Three Men in a Boat *even more remarkable.*]

It was Stendhal who said that "wit lasts no more than two centuries." Humor has an even shorter life span, as any practitioner of that precarious trade knows, often from personal experience. In fact, the statistical chances of his outliving his own stuff are good—hardly a consoling thought. (p. xv)

An average early mortality is, of course, true of any creative work (think of all those runaway bestsellers galloping steadily into oblivion), but it is truer of comedy than of any other kind. Humor is a highly perishable product that seldom outlasts the vagaries of fashion and temperament it reflects; in its acutely topical form, it can begin to rot on the way to the market. All humorists know this, and that is why they constitute a special order of wretches at once brooding and frenetic. They know the score. They are always playing against time. Today a head of bright green lettuce; tomorrow leaf mold.

What puts a given work into that small company of exceptions that age cannot wither nor custom stale is, therefore, a mystery as well as a tantalizing challenge to speculation. Perhaps the author's own mind and spirit are the preservative, eluding definition and mocking analysis but securing immortality, or at least a few generations of grace. Maybe his own sense of humor was not all that contemporary but consisted rather of a simple and universal grasp of the absurd which centuries and peoples other than his own can relish—a humor, that is, not subject to the fluctuations of style even though a particular style may be what his comedy consummately catches.

Something like that may account for the fact that *Three Men in a Boat* has since it was first published in 1889 sold by the millions in more languages than even the Berlitz people know about. The universal appeal of the book must lie, partly at least, in the universality of the subject matter. Who has not gone on a boating or camping trip, or both, with the stated intention of roughing it for a bit? The river on which the three companions take off in this hardy perennial is the Thames, but it stands for any body of water anybody ever essayed by sail, oar or pole. Not even the regular digressions into such chapters of English history as the changing scenes inspire can diminish the universality of that appeal. Humor is oftener than not hardship recollected in tranquillity, or at least in dry clothes. Nor need one endure the rigors of Mark Twain's Mississippi. A simple dunking in the Thames will do.

Someone has remarked that anybody who doesn't like Schubert doesn't like music. It might similarly be said that anyone who doesn't like Jerome K. Jerome (at his best, of course) doesn't like humor. Jerome seems to meet the twofold test that any reader may legitimately apply to a humorist, and that any humorist worth his salt must willingly submit to. He must, first, afford a continual amusement that, second, erupts at intervals into outright mirth. Nobody can be reasonably expected to keep you in stitches from beginning to end; a pleasurable smiling, or even unsmiling, amusement is enough. But he must, at some point, break you up. He has got to serve you, here and there, an episode that sets the springs to rocking in the chair you're sitting in or the bed you're lying on. If you're riding on a train or subway, you must be mortified by the glances of your fellow passengers as, seizing a handkerchief, you pretend to a coughing fit. What passages in *Three Men in a Boat* can be adduced as Jerome's credentials to the title of humorist from this standpoint?

Well, for one, I think, the section in which the narrator recalls how he carted a couple of ripe cheeses from Liverpool to London for a friend. For another, the sequence which relates the attempts of our voyagers to open a tin of pineapple without a can opener. These moments bear comparison with, say, "The Night the Bed Fell" in James Thurber's *My Life and Hard Times*, the fracturing page or two in which Robert Benchley describes the men in a Turkish bath and those in which Evelyn Waugh introduces the Welsh band in *Decline and Fall* . . . , and the section in *Huckleberry Finn* in which Jim must be rescued according to the rules of romantic fiction from a shack of which it would have been a simple matter merely to break the padlock. (pp. xv-xviii)

Looking back on this rather random but, I think, impressive little catalogue, I see that the entries have little in common save the definitive hysterics above mentioned. They make you put the book down until you have recovered. Everyone carries in his head a list of such favorites for ready conversational nomination as candidates for Great Comic Moments. You may or may not add the cheese-toting or can-opening episode to yours; if not, I think you will find others in the book worthy of consideration—perhaps the visit to the maze at Hampton Court. If the spectacle of the crowd of sightseers confidently tramping in the wake of a man as lost as they are, till the keepers have to go in and rescue them all from the labyrinth they have paid twopence for the fun of traversing—if that doesn't slay you, then I would like to have a look at your list to see what I am missing.

You may have noticed that only one of my three nominations, the murder of the can of pineapple, actually has to do with camping or boating. The other two illustrate the sightseeing stopovers, incidental musings and personal reminiscences with which the author continually interrupts his account of the voyage. The digressions are among the most appealing parts of the book, ironically reversing the author's original intention, which was to write a historical and topographical account of the river. The humorist and casual philosopher took over every time, with such happy results that the editor of the magazine in which the book was serialized cut out great chunks of the documentary stuff in favor of the tangents—fortunately for his readers, and for us.

Besides its merits as pure amusement, *Three Men in a Boat* offers us, in both the main thread and its detours, a sharply focused and charmingly authentic glimpse of a time gone by, a particular variant of the continuing human adventure stated in a minor key. I have no doubt that in the next century or so there will be a series of sketches portraying the inconveniences of space travel or that they will be as engaging as these relating a holiday on the Thames in an age we have also just missed. And therein lies, one likes sentimentally to think, something of that unifying and cherishable bond that we have come to call the Human Condition. We are all, after all, in the same boat, as we shall discover afresh when tomorrow's rockets shall have made today's jets obsolete. (pp. xviii-xix)

Peter De Vries, in an introduction to Three Men in a Boat: To Say Nothing of the Dog *by Jerome K. Jerome, Time Incorporated, 1964, pp. xv-xix.*

RUTH MARIE FAUROT (essay date 1974)

[*Faurot is an American critic and educator who specializes in the field of Victorian literature. She has devoted considerable study to the "new humourists" of the 1890s, of whom Jerome was held to be a prime example. In the following excerpt from her study of Jerome's life and career, Faurot discusses his major works.]*

Jerome's first book, *On the Stage—and Off* . . . , in some respects, is not surpassed by his later, better-known works. The book is short, 170 pages; and the humor is not belabored. He writes with a happy mixture of brashness and pity combined with honest observation.

In *My Life and Times* he records the provenience of *On the Stage—And Off*. He had been writing romantic stories of medieval knights and fairies, and not selling them. "It came to me . . . not to bother about other people's trouble . . . but to write about my own. I would tell the world the story of a hero called Jerome who had run away and gone upon the stage; and of all the strange and moving things that happened to him there." . . . Indeed, Jerome does capture the "sense of strange and moving things." . . . Jerome, excited about the book, finished it after working-hours in three months. The freshness comes through to the reader.

The interest of the book is twofold. First, the narrative of a young man making his entry into the working world appeals. Second, the world of the theater is perennially interesting, and that of traveling troupes even more so. To Jerome's public was added a sense of nostalgia for the theater many had known, the theater of the 1870's in the provinces and in the suburbs. Jerome's experiences cover three or four types of companies— the popular theater in London, those numerous houses that played to the middle and lower classes in the suburbs and London's East End; the touring and provincial stock companies; and the "Fitup," which Jerome calls "only one grade higher than a booth."

Not only did the book provide contemporaries with an inside look at the popular theater, but it provides today a treasury of information on the working-class drama for the enthusiast trying to clear the muddy picture of nineteenth-century drama between Sheridan and Shaw. (pp. 36-7)

The book contains a wealth of information seen through the eyes of an eager young man. He is at first curious and excited over what is backstage, learning how scenery is painted, how props are made, what the procedures are—what the layman does not know. Gradually, his disillusionment sets in as he discovers no dress rehearsals, no Green Room, often no dressing room, and sometimes no pay. But the tone is never bitter, never unkind.

The humor turns mostly on the knack of deflating himself . . . ; upon making a situation ridiculous by exaggeration . . . ; or, the feature he was to develop in his *Idle Thoughts,* the shared exasperation—for example, "They charged me extra for the basket on the Great Eastern Line, and I have hated that company ever since." . . .

Jerome's narrative style is that of the familiar essay, even the familiar letter, colloquial and friendly. He relates conversation in standard English or in Cockney with good effect and with ease. The structure is loose. . . .

The book is not a novel, and no characters other than the narrator are given more than temporary attention. By the end of the book the narrator has achieved a clear personality. Others are briefly but clearly sketched, and they are in some ways better than the characters from this same theatrical experience that Jerome uses in his autobiographical novel *Paul Kelver.* . . . (p. 38)

In summary, *On the Stage—and Off* provides good humorous reading and authentic information for an increasingly interesting phase of the nineteenth-century drama.

Stage-Land, Curious Habits and Customs of its Inhabitants, described by Jerome K. Jerome and illustrated by Bernard Partridge, is Jerome's second humorous book on the theater. . . . While the book stems from Jerome's personal experience in the theatrical world, the approach differs from *On the Stage—and Off. Stage-Land* comprises fourteen short chapters about the stereotypes of melodrama. Jerome's own summary from *My Life and Times* best condenses the book:

> The Stage Hero, his chief aim in life to get himself accused of crimes he had never committed; the Villain, the only man in the play possessed of a dress suit; the Heroine, always in trouble; the Stage Lawyer, very old and very long and very thin; the Adventuress, with a habit of mislaying her husbands; the Stage Irishman, who always paid his rent and was devoted to his landlord; the Stage Sailor, whose trousers never fitted him—they were well-known characters. All now are gone. If Partridge and myself helped to hasten their end, I am sorry. They were better—more human, more understandable—than many of the new puppets that have taken their place. . . .

The tone of the entire book is tongue-in-cheek satire—the innocent refusal to divorce stage life from reality. (p. 39)

The essays, set pieces, are amusing when not carried on too long. The later ones on minor characters are shorter and relatively better. (p. 41)

The most popular of Jerome's work, *Three Men in a Boat— To Say Nothing of the Dog,* began as a serious travel book— descriptions of the Thames with bits of history and humorous relief. He succeeded in writing the "slabs of history"; but F. W. Robinson, who was publishing the book serially in *Home Chimes,* rejected them. Halfway through, Jerome changed the idea and the title and quickly finished the book. (pp. 41-2)

Almost any page would yield anecdote, homely reflection, young man-about-town slang, and innocent ragging.

It is a sobering process to analyze humor; and, on the whole, criticism must give way to simple appreciation. Jerome was always quick to recognize that what seems funny depends often upon time and the mood. (p. 45)

Jerome's humor in *Three Men in a Boat* consists first of all in the basic ability to make a good story out of the most trivial of incidents. He is a raconteur who can tell funny stories. The laugh comes either because he turns the joke on himself—his embarrassments, his mistakes, even his conceit—or because he gives an unexpected twist to the climax of an incident or even a sentence. V. S. Pritchett . . . says that the laughter in Jerome is caused less by any fact than by the false conclusions drawn from it [see excerpt dated 1957]. . . . To Pritchett, "Skilfully Jerome plays everything down. He relies on misleading moral commentary and on that understatement which runs like a rheumatism through English humor."

Like most humorists, Jerome depends on exaggeration and understatement. He may make the reality absurd or, inversely, treat absurdity with gravity. There is nothing new about these characteristics, but what succeeded at the time as something fresh with a large public was just that touch of brashness in treating ordinary subjects. (p. 46)

In England, in America, where pirated copies ran to the millions, and in dozens of translations *Three Men in a Boat* has become a classic of humor. Of all Jerome's books it is the most easily available and perhaps the most appreciated. (pp. 46-7)

Idle Thoughts of an Idle Fellow collects fourteen essays on miscellaneous subjects which Jerome first wrote for monthly serialization. . . . (pp. 49-50)

The humor of *Idle Thoughts of an Idle Fellow* is not the boisterous fun of the young men, nor the laughter of release. It is rather thoughtful laughter, based on common sense and observation; and it frequently gives rise to sober reflection by both author and reader. The subject matter roams the field of everyday experiences: "**On Being Hard Up,**" "**On Being in the Blues,**" "**On Vanity and Vanities,**" "**On Getting on in the World,**" "**On Being Idle,**" "**On Being in Love,**" "**On the Weather,**" "**On Cats and Dogs,**" "**On Being Shy,**" "**On Babies,**" "**On Eating and Drinking,**" "**On Furnished Apartments,**" "**On Dress and Deportment,**" "**On Memory.**"

After a dedication to his pipe, a mocking preface introduces the essays, claiming a public demand for them—that is, by his relatives, but disclaiming any elevated thought: "All I can suggest is, that when you get tired of reading 'the best hundred books,' you may take this up for half an hour. It will be a change." (p. 50)

Sentiment and laughter continually contrast and converge in the essays, for Jerome believed that the two moods were the stuff of human life. His cynicism is light, very light—more a lament that the glow of idealism dims than a feeling of bitterness or scorn toward life's ironies. Only when he reflects on the poor, the really destitute, does he become severe. The subjects of his essays are not controversial; continuing in the tradition of [Charles Lamb's] "Elia," they comment genially on familiar universals.

His style is casual. He makes no pretense to Augustan polish. Characteristic, in fact, of the new humor is the conversational style of the ordinary person. Jerome uses contractions plentifully and an occasional "he don't." Part of the pleasure lies in the occasional ambiguity of colloquial speech—for example, "I had a nephew who was once the amateur long-distance bicycle champion. I have him still—", or "Our next door neighbour comes out in the back garden every now and then, and says it's doing the country a world of good—not his coming out into the back garden, but the weather." Some of the metaphors are fresh—for example, the cat swears "like a medical student." Slang, dialect, homely phrasing, such as "the curtains want washing," abound. He spares us the pun, that foundation of so much of *Punch* humor. The essays read easily and sound like the conversation of a good talker. Anecdotes remain brief, and each of the essays is short.

Critics of his time labeled Jerome's style vulgar, and the writing ungrammatical; but the public liked it. Today, the style seems journalistic, familiar in the way of current newspaper columns. Underlying his subject matter and style is what George Meredith in his *The Idea of Comedy* stated in 1877 to be the truest test of comedy—that it should awaken thoughtful laughter and that the foundation of its appreciation should be common sense. *Idle Thoughts of an Idle Fellow* meets the test.

Jerome in middle age. © Strand Magazine.

In *Idle Thoughts of an Idle Fellow* Jerome established himself firmly with a mass audience. (pp. 56-7)

If the modern reader does not know Jerome K. Jerome as the author of *Idle Thoughts of an Idle Fellow* or as the humorist of the best-seller *Three Men in a Boat,* he may have heard of *The Passing of the Third Floor Back* . . . ; for his play had sensational runs in both England and America and became one of the most popular plays in the first quarter of the twentieth century, and is still revived from time to time. The theater had opened the literary world to Jerome K. Jerome; indeed, activity and interest in drama run through his professional career. From clerking in the Euston railroad station, Jerome's first show of independence was to join a traveling troupe. Playing every part from low-comedy roles to the First Walking Gent. at thirty-five shillings a week, he covered the touring circuit of Great Britain, including the East End and Surrey-side theaters of London. In *On the Stage—and Off* . . . , written after time had distanced by a few years his immediate disillusionment, Jerome records his observations of stage life and theater roles in a book which entertained his contemporaries and provides now an authentic stage history. His second book about the theater, *Stage-Land* . . . , also provides a valuable account of that period before Ibsen, Shaw, and Wilde when nothing good seemed forthcoming from the English theater world. (p. 100)

Jerome had closed the door on acting as a profession after three youthful years on the stage; but he turned, naturally enough, to the writing of plays while he was making his way into the field of journalism. (pp. 100-01)

The Passing of the Third Floor Back . . . , dramatized from Jerome's own short story, marked the peak of Jerome's dramatic fame. . . .

Everyone talked about the play: ministers quoted from it, clubs discussed it, and sophisticated critics deplored it. (p. 106)

In October, 1908, the same year of *The Passing of the Third Floor Back,* Jerome satisfied his audiences who wanted humor with *Fanny and the Servant Problem,* a pleasant comedy about an aristocrat who marries a show-girl on the continent. When she proves to be related to his entire staff of servants, complications arise. (p. 107)

Class problems and hypocrisy in religion are humorously touched upon in *Fanny and the Servant Problem. The Master of Mrs. Chilvers* . . . , which Jerome labels "An Improbable Comedy," deals seriously with the question of women's rights and presents the new woman quite attractively and quite fairly. The nearest of Jerome's plays to a problem play, it makes a creditable plea for woman's independence; however, the solution involves Mrs. Chilvers's capitulation to her husband's point of view. (p. 108)

Today, with the exception of *The Passing of the Third Floor Back,* Jerome's plays are little known and virtually unobtainable. . . . About twelve were published as reading editions, but even they are scarce. Jerome's plays served their purpose in providing good theater for the audiences of their time, but they were not intended to be considered as literature. (pp. 108-09)

The Passing of the Third Floor Back derives from a double source: Jerome's preoccupation with the dual nature of man, and his memory of a mysterious figure. (p. 126)

Jerome recounts how the idea of the Stranger of *The Passing of the Third Floor Back* came to him:

> I followed a stooping figure passing down a foggy street, pausing every now and then to glance up at a door. I did not see his face. It was his clothes that worried me. There was nothing out of the way about them. I could not make out why it was they seemed remarkable. I lost him at the corner, where the fog hung thick, and found myself wondering what he would have looked like if he had turned round and I had seen his face. I could not get him out of my mind, wandering about the winter streets; and gradually he grew out of those curious clothes of his.

From Jerome's mysterious stranger, along with the conviction of the struggle between a person's evil and better self, *The Passing of the Third Floor Back* was born, first as a short story, then as a play. It was not an easy play to write. "One had to feel it rather than think it" [Jerome wrote later]. (p. 127)

The subtitle of *The Passing of the Third Floor Back—, An Idle Fancy. In a Prologue, A Play, and an Epilogue*—indicates the three-act structure and hints at an imaginative interpretation. The cast of characters, like the cast of a modern morality play, in the Prologue appear solely as types: a Satyr, a Coward, a Bully, a Shrew, a Hussy, a Rogue, a Cat, a Cad, a Snob, a Cheat, a Passer-by. No such abstractions appear, however, in the realistic boardinghouse action of the Prologue. Instead, the reader (or playgoer) matches the type names to shrewish Mrs. Sharpe, the landlady; Stasia, the sluttish "slavey"; Joey Wright, the lecherous, retired bookmaker; Major Tompkins, retired and

a cad; Mrs. Percival de Hooley, a snob—all of whom appear in action in the Prologue. Personal names are listed only before Part II, "The Play." At the beginning of "The Epilogue," personal names and types have been replaced by a new listing; and the type and specific names bcome general nomenclature: "The Lady of the House," "An Old Bachelor," "A Husband and Wife," "A Rich Aunt." Only the Stranger remains nameless; he appears first as "A Passerby," then specifically as "The Third Floor Back," and finally as "A Friend." (p. 128)

The boardinghouse guests, with each encounter with the Stranger, find themselves looking into their own hearts and not liking the traits found there—lust, petty vengeance, and belittling each other. (p. 129)

Each boarder finds himself searching for his better self and condemning his own malice as he comes face to face with the Stranger. Moreover, each also has a vague recollection of having known the Stranger before.

The Epilogue opens on the same boardinghouse scene, but the place has now become pleasant and homelike. *"Good taste, among other things, would seem to have entered into the house since last we saw it,"* read the stage directions. When a Friday afternoon open-house brings all boarders except the Stranger into the drawing room as guests, each character shows that he has been transformed. Each now lives his better self as the result of the brief encounter with "the third-floor back." Consideration for one another, honesty, and pride in their efforts to overcome weaknesses mark their behavior. The Stranger appears—at first only as a voice or as music heard; but he appears to Stasia and to Mrs. Sharpe in actuality, not as the Wanderer or Stranger, but as "A Friend." As each guest leaves, he too recognizes the Stranger and tells him of the reform in his own life. The Stranger then takes leave of Mrs. Sharpe, who promises always to have room for him. (p. 130)

The idea of the mysterious supernatural visitor who effects changes in the lives of those he contacts appears a fairly constant theme in literature. The Stranger in this play, never identified as Christ, nevertheless makes his entry accompanied by increasing sunlight, the sound of music, or overtones of the Bible. Because of the subtitle *An Idle Fancy,* the play can be interpreted as the answer to the question, "What would happen if Christ were here?" That the Stranger appears to the shoddy, the foolish, and the fallen reinforces the message that Christ came to save not the righteous but the sinner. The power of Jerome's Stranger, however, operates solely as a catalyst, not a miracle; for the reformation of each character is accomplished by himself. Basically, each character proves to be good, and the faith which the Stranger has in each person's innate nobility serves to make each one determine to live his nobler self.

The pattern, in fact, of recognition, rejection, and the positive thrust forward establishes the structure of the play. Each character . . . recognizes the ugly nature that he has grown into. He becomes angry, not at the Stranger who persists in seeing the good in him, but at himself for what he now is. The former innocent, idealist, artist, kind woman, loving wife, or whatever turns on his or her base behavior, renounces it, and recaptures his earlier good self. Triggered by the Stranger's reaction to him, his direction in life changes. (p. 131)

As a morality play, *The Passing of the Third Floor Back* makes an appeal to the consciences of the audience. Its appearance was in tune with a generation that found satisfaction in Jerome's message, even as today's audiences react to themes of psychoanalysis and social violence. The Stranger, a most difficult part, had to be kept from being maudlin or saccharine. Jerome in the short story wishes to show the Stranger at times as burdened and old with cares of the world, but at other times as vigorous and full of young manhood. On the stage this portrayal is a matter for the actor. Jerome could depict the "beggar-saint" better in the short story and in the similar characters he uses in the novels. For example, the minister in *All Roads Lead to Calvary* is the old man with the haunting eyes; but he becomes a young peasant in the war trenches at the end of the novel. In *Anthony John,* he is the legendary figure, "Wandering Peter," whom the poor folk know. In these works Jerome makes a convincing mystic character. In the play, the dialogue carries the burden; and Jerome is dependent entirely upon the actor.

As in most of Jerome's plays, the dialogue of *The Passing of the Third Floor Back* surprisingly does not have the sparkle of Jerome's dialogue in humorous essays, the "Idler" type of humor. In the play, it is often disappointingly commonplace. We can only surmise that Jerome's experience on the stage convinced him how much the performers contribute, and assume from the actual success of his plays on stage that the actors and audience do find the lines adequate in performance. (pp. 132-33)

Jerome K. Jerome began writing novels only after he had won acclaim as a humorist, an editor, and a playwright. (p. 134)

Of all his books, Jerome liked writing *Paul Kelver* . . . the best, "Maybe because it was all about myself, and people I had known and loved." It changed his luck with the critics; for after Francis Gribble had praised it, other critics did so. Though *Paul Kelver* received praise and its success surprised Jerome, he turned back to playwriting. Then, in 1904, he wrote another novel, *Tommy and Co.,* a loosely tied-together story in which Jerome records half-seriously and half-comically the newspaper world he knew so well. *They and I,* a novel published in 1909, humorously bridges the generation gap in its theme.

With the tremendous popularity of his moral drama *The Passing of the Third Floor Back* and the critical acclaim of *Paul Kelver,* Jerome felt secure in the knowledge that he could write seriously. No longer accepted only as a humorist, he could now turn to "the world's cry of pain." *All Roads Lead to Calvary* . . . , written at the end of World War I, more than any other work of Jerome's, confronts the problems of a protagonist and her problem as an independent woman, her personal idealism, her dream of society. *Anthony John,* the last of Jerome's four novels, returns to the Midlands of his birth and again, with autobiographical overtones, deals with wealth, poverty, and evil. It also becomes a vehicle for Jerome's religious idealism.

The novel form was congenial to Jerome. Jerome had skill in the dramatic arts, and he had ability to write good humor; but the novel, with its opportunity for character analysis through the author's comments, provides Jerome an ideal medium. In *Paul Kelver,* in *All Roads Lead to Calvary,* in *Anthony John,* and, to a lesser extent, in *Tommy and Co.,* Jerome could build from his own experiences a portrait of the young individual who struggles to establish his identity. (pp. 134-35)

Paul Kelver is autobiographical, . . . it is the best of his novels, and . . . it treats the themes that recur in Jerome's work. Though autobiographical, *Paul Kelver* covers the years of the protagonist from early memories only to young success and prospective marriage. The formative period of life in the pattern of *David Copperfield* structures the novel. (p. 143)

Jerome has divided *Paul Kelver* into two parts and a prologue, and the first book ends with the death of Paul's mother. This first part as autobiography differs in minor details from Jerome's own life, but the changes simplify and focus attention upon relationships, influences, the formation of the protagonist's character. . . .

Part two takes Paul at the age of fourteen, orphaned, without money, into the working world of London, where, like Jerome himself, he works at meanly paid clerkships, battles loneliness and hunger, but fortifies himself with a Carlylean respect for work and duty. Like Jerome, Paul tries the theater and then moves into journalism. (p. 144)

Part two of *Paul Kelver* may have appeared as a *roman à clef* to readers at the turn of the century. Whether or not the characters are identifiable, they convince by their similarity to the accounts given in memoirs and other reports of the period. Certain of the humorous bits are close to Jerome's journalistic reportage and sketching in other works. (pp. 144-45)

Jerome has a strong sense of place; for like the reader of a Dickens' novel, we can go from section to section of the London mentioned in *Paul Kelver,* sure that the streets are accurately named and placed in the fiction. But any writer putting his own life into his novel has the advantage of a schizophrenia that permits truthfulness when useful—and artistic license when needed.

Paul Kelver comes to the reader as a novel, and it must be judged as such. What remains poignant about the association between Jerome's life and that of his protagonist is the idealization, for example, in the novel of the family scene at the theater. (p. 145)

The novel, however, by itself merits attention for its story and for the skill with which it unfolds. Although the story progresses chronologically and divides into two parts, the novel has another structural framework that gives artistry to the work. Chapter headings form a continuous "Paul's Progress" in language that echoes the allegory of John Bunyan's *Pilgrim's Progress.* (p. 146)

The novel, in addition to the themes of love and religion, deals with poverty—as Paul faces it genteelly in his own family . . . , and as Paul encounters it in the world of London clerks. (p. 151)

Paul Kelver is by no means all seriousness or pathos. There is an irrepressible sense of humor all the way through, particularly in Part II. The companions of the second part of the book form two groups, the London journalists and the boardinghouse company that is primarily connected with the theater. (pp. 151-52)

Paul Kelver remains a fine novel, universal enough to survive the times. Like Samuel Butler's posthumous *The Way of All Flesh* (which appeared in 1903, a year later than Jerome's novel) and Edmond Gosse's autobiography, *Father and Son* (1907), *Paul Kelver* gives a picture of a young man reared in a strict Evangelical home. Unlike these two bitter accounts of Victorian piety, Jerome's hero is tolerant, non-vindictive. *Paul Kelver* engrosses the reader. (pp. 153-54)

In concluding a study of Jerome K. Jerome, three aspects should be considered; the complete Jerome; his place in his time; and his position today. Humorist, editor, playwright, novelist, lecturer, and emissary for war and peace—the scope of Jerome's work seems broad; but fragmented it is not. From the humor of young men boating to the sermonizing of a mysterious stranger, Jerome's characters comprise a picture in which there is no discrepancy between the laughter on the one hand and the moralizing on the other. The binding thread is Jerome's attitude. "Pity is akin to love" is a phrase that recurs in Jerome. Its obvious application occurs in incident after incident in Jerome's fiction and plays, but the laughter, too, becomes a part of it, not only for what his humor is but for what it is not. The jesting never mocks, for Jerome is not bitter. When he tells of cats or dogs, errand boys, or boating young men, the laughter is good-natured, tempered with tolerance. (p. 177)

In some of Jerome's works he is all humor, as in *Three Men in a Boat* and *Stage-Land;* in some he is all serious, as in *All Roads Lead to Calvary;* but he is best, perhaps, where the mixture prevails, as in *Paul Kelver, On the Stage—And Off, Tommy and Co.,* or most of *The Idler* collections. Perhaps the charm of these works comes from the overlay of nostalgia which can be tender about yesterday's mistakes and smile.

On reform, Jerome is also both serious and humorous. The battle of the sexes he can treat as standard comic material, but he is never brutal. His major reform efforts in the plays and in one or two novels concern the position of woman, and he works for the dignity of her life. (pp. 177-78)

Jerome's idealism becomes a pressing message in his later works. The Stranger in *The Passing of the Third Floor Back* sees good in every man, and a redeeming quality when man chooses to allow his good to prevail. (p. 178)

Jerome, despite touches of fancy—sometimes absurd romanticism—has a sense of the real that can depict not only the grim but the evil. But this same common sense can look at the literature of Realism and deflate it; for literature itself, he recognizes, is not life. The world of the theater, for all his participation in it, he sometimes sees as pitiful pretense. . . . Jerome's voice at the turn of the century came as near as anyone's to a non-distorted echo of the lives of masses who read him. He spoke for the genial, middle way. (p. 179)

In the field of drama, Jerome was prolific. That he was successful is confirmed by his stellar casts, record runs, and the frequency with which his plays traveled to America or were translated for Continental performances. The subjects concerned current problems of caste, the vote, the new woman, or the plays provided situation comedy. *The Passing of the Third Floor Back* alone could have made him famous. Its worth, however, was debated immediately; reviewers like Max Beerbohm thought it tawdry; others reverenced the work as a moving, modern morality. But reviewers had little to do with audiences, and audiences loved it.

In the field of the novel, Jerome scarcely established himself. His autobiographical *Paul Kelver,* published in mid-life, perhaps excels as literature anything he wrote. The novels that followed it are either light entertainment, like *Tommy and Co.* or *They and I,* or lopsidedly didactic as in *All Roads Lead to Calvary* and *Anthony John.* Unlike Tolstoy, Jerome could not balance his ideology with his art, nor did he keep pace with the changes in the novel being initiated by the new school of James Joyce.

When we examine the magazines *The Idler* and *To-day,* we are impressed with the wealth of good writing and reputable authors in their pages. But the life of periodicals is ephemeral; perhaps the best of it reappears in books. From the first, Jerome's journalistic contributions reached book form, and his *On the Stage—And Off, Three Men in a Boat, Idle Thoughts of an Idle Fellow,* and a few other collections became familiar

in the households on both sides of the Atlantic. Their fame, however, is fast fading. *Three Men in a Boat* remains popular. An occasional reader, picking up the *Idle Thoughts,* is surprised at how pertinent the ideas are. "A collection of light articles becomes a complete mirage," as V. S. Pritchett says. As a humorist, Jerome will probably last, for he is as much recognized outside England as in. As for his plays, they remain period pieces or comedy to be brought up to date by amateur players. Even *The Passing of the Third Floor Back* asks for a proper mood and time, or it is likely to be misplayed as melodrama. Jerome's novel *Paul Kelver* not only records a period, a temperament, and an individual, but it is a well-written novel, deserving of more fame than it has.

The twentieth century, looking back with more interest, to the literature of transition between mid-Victorianism and the Post-World-War-I movements, may well decide that Jerome K. Jerome crystallizes a large segment of the thought at the turn of the century. He stays, a humorist for all time—a "fortress of laughter." (pp. 180-81)

Ruth Marie Faurot, in her Jerome K. Jerome, *Twayne Publishers, Inc., 1974, 200 p.*

JOSEPH CONNOLLY   (essay date 1982)

[*Connolly's biography of Jerome is the most comprehensive to date, for he was granted access to previously unpublished letters, diaries, and memoirs during its composition. In the following excerpt from his concluding chapter, Connolly summarizes Jerome's lasting place in literature as "the author of a deathless humor book."*]

[Jerome] was never one to claim greatness, but he did wonder, as authors do, whether after his death he would be remembered, and whether he would be read. Within the realms of English Literature, Jerome was never sure of his standing, and even now it is hard to clarify. He was no Dickens, but he shared his campaigning spirit. In his later work, he strove to draw attention to the evils of the world, though he recognized that his effect upon them was non-existent. Jerome had a voice—indeed, this was one of the major reasons why he continued to write—but it was not the voice of a lion. His philosophies were wise, but they remained parochial; they appealed to the sort of person who had already half-formulated his own, but was too inarticulate or inconclusive to express them as Jerome had done. And yet, no one of conscience could disagree with any of his nobler apsirations. Jerome remains known today only for *Three Men in a Boat;* even *The Third Floor Back* has passed. But he is remembered as one of a rare breed: the author of a deathless humorous book. This knowledge pleased him, as it would any writer, but there remains little doubt that he would instantly have traded this accolade for that of having written a book that had changed men's thinking. He did not write for money, and rarely from artistic compulsion; after his initial popular successes, Jerome wrote because he wanted "to *say* something." As has been seen, he spoke out on many occasions, but as the years advanced, he perceived that people were not listening with adequate attention; or maybe he was just not speaking loudly enough. Greatness, then—by his own definition—had eluded him.

His youthful ambitions, however, were amply realized. He had become in turn a successful novelist, editor, and dramatist, and . . . he might well have become a Member of Parliament, had he so chosen. His influence upon modern lighter writing may now be seen to be greater than previously supposed, for although it would be presumptuous to suggest that Jerome had been Wodehouse's guiding spirit, many of Wodehouse's beloved devices may be traced back directly to the mannerisms of the "new humour." Certainly Jerome's influence upon popular journalism was profound, and the deliberately idle and casual approach has persisted to this day. Nonetheless it is true that during his lifetime, Jerome looked with hope to the higher reception of his work in Europe. Although he recorded the ambition glibly in his memoirs, he really did hope to become "quite a swell dead author."

The name Jerome K. Jerome is a famous one, and *Three Men in a Boat* approaches its centenary; in this sense, Jerome may be said to have reached his goal. "Dickens" warned Paul Kelver never to attempt "somebody else's best," and Jerome was never guilty of it: his achievements were all his own, and ultimately, this knowledge would have satisfied him.

"God will find work for us," he said, "according to our strength." (pp. 197-98)

> *Joseph Connolly, in his* Jerome K. Jerome: A Critical Biography, *Orbis Publishing, 1982, 208 p.*

ADDITIONAL BIBLIOGRAPHY

Adcock, St. John. "Jerome K. Jerome." In his *The Glory that Was Grub Street: Impressions of Contemporary Authors*, pp. 158-68. Toronto: Musson Book Co., Ltd., 1928.
  Biographical and critical essay outlining Jerome's life and career.

Beauchamp, Gorman. "The Proto-Dystopia of Jerome K. Jerome." *Extrapolation* 24, No. 2 (Summer 1983): 170-81.
  Extensive examination of Jerome's "The New Utopia," variously classified as an essay, short story, or comic fantasy, in which Jerome prefigured many of the common motifs of late nineteenth- and early twentieth-century utopian and dystopian fiction.

Book-Worm, Baron de. "Our Booking-Office." *Punch* 98, No. 2534 (1 February 1890): 57.
  Satirical dismissal of *Three Men in a Boat* as unfunny.

———. "Our Booking-Office." *Punch* C, No. 2582 (3 January 1891): 4.
  Finds Jerome's *Told after Supper* "occasionally very amusing" but in need of judicious editing.

———. "Our Booking-Office." *Punch* C, No. 2601 (16 May 1891): 239.
  Disparaging review of *The Diary of a Pilgrimage*, finding it "occasionally rather amusing," but noting that "only a little of it goes a great way."

Chesterton, G. K. "The Divine Detective." In his *A Miscellany of Men*, pp. 277-83. New York: Dodd, Mead, 1912.
  Briefly mentions *The Passing of the Third Floor Back*, in a discussion of literary works with religious themes, as "a humane and reverent experiment" with some artistic and moral flaws.

Doyle, [Sir] Arthur Conan. "Norwood and Switzerland." In his *Memories and Adventures*, pp. 111-120. Boston: Little, Brown, 1924.
  Reminiscence mentioning Jerome, who occasionally accompanied Doyle on European hiking and camping trips. Doyle praises Jerome's "splendidly humorous *Three Men in a Boat*" as having "all the exuberance and joy of life which youth brings with it."

Dunlap, Barbara J. "The Idler." In *British Literary Magazines: The Victorian and Edwardian Age, 1837-1913*, edited by Alvin Sullivan, pp. 177-82. Westport: Greenwood Press, 1984.
  Essay detailing Jerome's editorship of the *Idler*, calling the periodical's "most enduring contribution to literary journalism" the number of new authors whom Jerome selected for publication, including Arthur Conan Doyle, Eden Philpotts, Israel Zangwill, Barry Pain, Marie Corelli, Anthony Hope, Robert Louis Stevenson, and W. W. Jacobs. The essay is followed by a bibliography of source information about the *Idler* and a brief publication history.

Hamilton, Clayton. Review of *The Passing of the Third Floor Back*. *The Forum* XLII (November 1909): 440-41.
  Approbatory review, calling Jerome's *The Passing of the Third Floor Back* "not, in any technical sense, a play: but . . . it is a parable that is sweetly intentioned and sincerely written." The dialogue is praised as realistic, and the critic discusses at length a stratagem of stage direction, conceived by Jerome, that placed the actors at the front and center of the stage for crucial scenes.

Moss, Alfred. *Jerome K. Jerome: His Life and Work*. London: Selwyn & Blount, 1928, 255 p.
  Noncritical biography in the form of a reminiscence by a friend of Jerome.

Nathan, George Jean. "On Jerome K. Jerome." In his *Another Book on the Theatre*, pp. 138-41. New York: B. W. Huebsch, 1915.
  Rambling essay in a musing tone, noting that the unforced, spontaneous comic quality of Jerome's prose is lacking in his writing for the stage.

"The Elder Novelists." *The Nation* CIX, No. 2842 (20 December 1919): 801-02.
  Reviews new works by three established authors, including Jerome's penultimate novel, *All Roads Lead to Calvary*. The critic notes a great change in Jerome's writing, from the "early humorous novels and sketches" to his recent emergence as "a more sensitive artist, a more careful thinker, and a friend of mankind."

Orcutt, William Dana. "Untaxable Literary Returns." In his *Celebrities Off Parade*, pp. 133-91. Chicago: Willett, Clark, 1935.
  Personal reminiscence of literary London including anecdotes about Jerome.

Shaw, Bernard. "More Masterpieces." In his *Dramatic Opinions and Essays*, Vol. One, pp. 213-19. New York: Brentano's, 1907.
  Review of a 19 October 1895 production of Jerome's *The Rise of Dick Halward*. Shaw deplores Jerome's "maudlin" brand of pessimism as evinced in the play, which assumes and accepts human perfidy.

Walkley, A. B. Review of *New Lamps for Old*. In his *Playhouse Impressions*, pp. 163-67. London: T. Fisher Unwin, 1891.
  Suggests that Jerome's farce *New Lamps for Old*, subtitled "A (Comparatively Speaking) New and Original Play," closely resembles theatrical works by Marivaux and Meilhac.

Watkins, Charlotte C. "To-day." In *British Literary Magazines: The Victorian and Edwardian Age, 1837-1913*, edited by Alvin Sullivan, pp. 416-22. Westport: Greenwood Press, 1984.
  Essay tracing the history of the humor periodical *To-day*, which Jerome founded in 1893 as "a new weekly paper that should be a combination of magazine and journal." The essay is followed by a bibliography of source information about *To-day* and a brief publication history.

Weales, Gerald. "Sentimental Supernaturalism." In his *Religion in Modern English Drama*, pp. 38-50. Philadelphia: University of Pennsylvania Press, 1961.
  Discusses Jerome's *The Passing of the Third Floor Back* as the archetype of a specific kind of play: one in which a supernatural character or concept is introduced for sentimental or comic effect.

Alfred Kubin

1877-1959

Austrian artist, novelist, short story writer, autobiographer, poet, and essayist.

Kubin was a graphic artist and the author of the fantastic novel *Die andere Seite (The Other Side)*. Like his drawings and engravings, which reflect Kubin's peculiar vision of the world in their idiosyncratic depiction of the grotesque and horrific, his novel portrays life in a "dream kingdom" where the material and spiritual worlds freely intermingle. *The Other Side* has been cited as an influence on Franz Kafka's *Das Schloss (The Castle)* and as a precursor of Expressionism, Surrealism, and the Theater of the Absurd.

Kubin was born in Leitmeritz, Bohemia, and raised in northern Austria. His father was a civil servant and former officer in the Austro-Hungarian army, his mother a talented pianist who died when Kubin was ten years old. Kubin was deeply affected by her death, as well as by his father's grief, which was compounded two years later by the death of his second wife in childbirth. Soon afterward Kubin was expelled from secondary school for failing Latin and mathematics. He wrote in his memoirs that he returned home in disgrace, experiencing "for the first time a period of real hell" as his grieving father banished Kubin from his presence and beat him for laughing or showing other signs of happiness. According to Kubin, this period of isolation and abuse fostered his already active and morbid imagination (as a child, he recalled, he "covered countless sheets of paper with pencil sketchings and paintings" of "magicians, comic and terrifying cattle," and "landscapes consisting entirely of fire," and took "acute pleasure" in "staging ingenious scenes of torture with any wretched creatures" he found in the family garden). As an adolescent, his fascinations included fights, arrests, military campaigns, and especially the bodies of drowning victims dragged from the lake near his home. Following two years of relative inactivity he was sent to trade school, and later was apprenticed to a photographer, a relative of his father's third wife. However, after four years of performing only menial tasks—which he detested and which exacerbated his natural tendency toward nervous instability—Kubin attempted suicide, and was subsequently dismissed from his position. He then enlisted in the army; here he delighted in his duties but was released from service as the result of a prolonged bout of delirium.

Kubin finally found his calling in 1902 when a family friend who had seen and admired his drawings suggested that he be sent to art school in Munich. There Kubin was exposed for the first time to, and was deeply impressed by, works of the great masters. He wrote of his first visit to Munich's Alte Pinakothek: "It was a turning point in my life. I felt as though dissolved in delight and amazement, and ventured on tiptoe from hall to hall. I was completely overcome by such an immense accomplishment and such a radiant outburst of the human spirit." A second turning point came with Kubin's discovery of the works of German artist Max Klinger, whose engravings demonstrated an affinity to Kubin's drawings in their narrative quality and their fantastic and symbolic elements. Under the influence of Klinger's etching cycle "The Found Glove," Kubin experienced what he called a "psychological event" that decisively

affected his art. He wrote: "All at once, in the faces of those sitting around me, I saw something strangely mixed, part animal, part human. . . . I was suddenly inundated with visions of pictures in black and white. . . . I wandered aimlessly . . . , ravished by a dark power that conjured up before my mind strange creatures, houses, landscapes, grotesque and frightful situtations." In the wake of this experience Kubin drew prolifically and soon gained the attention of the artistic community. His first exhibition, at the prestigious Cassirer Gallery in Berlin in 1902, was denounced by one critic as a "chamber of horrors," but also received many favorable reviews, and the following year Kubin published a portfolio of fifteen drawings to critical acclaim.

In the years after 1904 Kubin abandoned drawing to experiment with various styles of painting, but achieved only moderate success in establishing himself as a painter. In 1908 he suffered an emotional crisis that one commentator has attributed to the sudden deaths of Kubin's fiancée and father, with whom he had recently reconciled. Finding himself unable to draw or paint, Kubin turned to fiction and within twelve weeks had completed *The Other Side*. Described by its author as an "adventure tale," the novel depicts a Central Asian kingdom inhabited by individuals who are physically or psychologically abnormal. The realm is under the mysterious psychic control of its ruler, Claus Patera, and is eventually destroyed by psychic forces released by the arrival of a challenger to Patera's authority. According to Wieland Schmied, Kubin's book "displays the same merits and weaknesses as his drawings: the psychological characterization of the protagonists remains pale if compared with the unbelievable atmospheric density, and, like the drawings, it is an obvious projection of psychic moods and conditions." Robin Magowan offers a similar assessment of the novel's characterization in more negative terms, describing the protagonists as "a few battered types evoked in hardly a page and allowed to reappear whenever the rest of the landscape apparatus won't any longer do." Magowan adds that the narrator, the "only character of any sort" in the novel, is more clearly depicted in the autobiographical essay appended to several editions of *The Other Side,* including the English translation. The novel's evocation of psychic moods, however, has been highly praised, as has its representation of an unseen reality beyond the surface of the material world. Critics have noted that the relationship between the narrator and Patera is symbolically similar to that of Kubin to his father, and this, combined with the book's pervasive dream imagery, has led to at least one Freudian reading of *The Other Side.* Other critics have seen the novel as a prescient allegorical representation of the decay and ultimate collapse of the Austro-Hungarian Empire.

The book, which has been praised by Jane Kallir for its "apotheosis of the mundane," was pivotal in both Kubin's aesthetic and philosophical development. He stated: "during its composition I achieved the mature realization that it is not only in the bizarre, exalted, or comic moments of our existence that the highest values lie, but that the incidental-commonplace contain these same mysteries." As a result, Kubin abandoned the more prestigious career of a painter to return to that of a draftsman. He similarly altered his subject matter, eschewing the bizarre in favor of depictions of everyday life. Kallir notes, however, that although Kubin's early works contain "reflections of the artist's personal turmoil" and his later works comprise "relatively 'ordinary' images," "it is the latter, with their layers of meaning and hidden insights, that are actually more complex." *The Other Side,* containing drawings by the author, also established Kubin as an illustrator, and he subsequently gained fame as the illustrator of works by Edgar Allan Poe, Gerard de Nerval, E.T.A. Hoffman, and Fedor Dostoevsky. After 1909 he lived an increasingly quiet, reclusive life, drawing and illustrating at his country home in Zwickledt, Austria, until his death in 1959.

PRINCIPAL WORKS

Die andere Seite (novel) 1909
  [*The Other Side,* 1967]
Der Guckkasten (short stories) 1925
Dämonen und Nachtgesichte (autobiography) 1926
Vom Schreibtisch eines Zeichners (essays) 1939
Nüchterne Balladen (poetry) 1949
Abendrot (drawings and autobiography) 1950
Alfred Kubin: Book Illustrator (drawings and essays) 1950
Briefe an eine Freundin (letters) 1965

WIELAND SCHMIED (essay date 1967)

[*In the following excerpt, Schmied examines Kubin's vision of the world as expressed in* The Other Side. *This essay was originally published in Germany as* Der Zeichner Alfred Kubin *(1967).*]

In many respects, Alfred Kubin belonged to that group of highly talented, hypersensitive, clear-sighted, afflicted, conflict-torn, and tragic characters, so much part of the *fin de siècle* Austria, who fought against themselves, and whose thoughts and work ultimately questioned the positions they had won and tended to destroy all they had achieved and built. So many died young: Weininger committed suicide; Gerstl and Trakl took the same way out; and Schiele and Kafka also died young. Only Kafka lived to be more than thirty years old! Kubin, as threatened as they in his early years, and often closer to suicide than to a secure existence, survived—but at the price of a radical retreat from his time into the stillness of a rural hermitage. When Klee said that Kubin fled this world because physically he could no longer "make it," he touched the core of the problem. Withdrawal to Zwickledt was a vital necessity for Kubin. The small country estate was in fact the "ark" in which he could sail across the eddying fears of his early night visions to the dusky world of his later drawings, to the wisdom, the detached world view, and resigned humor of his old age.

That is how Kubin saw himself. His wishful dreams of an artist's life were probably not unlike those he wrote about in *The Other Side.* A mere three days after the narrator in the novel arrives in Perle, the capital of his dream world, where he has found a room on the third floor of a bay-windowed house in the Lange Gasse, he hears a knock on the door, and in comes the editor and publisher of the *Dream Mirror,* an illustrated journal, to offer him a job as an artist at a monthly salary of 400 guilders. A monthly salary all year, regardless of whether he would do many, few, or no illustrations—that was something! "Of course I immediately put my name there," he writes, and the contract with the *Dream Mirror* is signed. "And please bring me very gaudy and eerie things! I want to increase the circulation," the editor gaily tells him in parting.

That is the vision of a life that, in its mixture of scurrility and self-directed irony, in its juxtaposition of cozy security and stimulating horror, strikes one as uniquely Austrian: the salaried seeker after the demonic, the visionary in house slippers sitting next to the stove, with a monthly paycheck and pension rights, who, from time to time, sends his soul on flights over the abyss of the metaphysical into the realm of the shades, to Nirvana or Nifelheim, to Hades or Hell, to adventures with a round-trip ticket, to the great dream with the possibility of escape by waking up in time. That is the wishful thinking of a man who did not want to pay again the price of trafficking with the forces of psychic darkness that early in life had driven him to feverish illness and semiconsciousness, to wishful thinking, which he quickly sees through and disavows. He tells us how the plot develops and how the hopes of the artist collapse in themselves: the salaried position in Perle turns out not to be a lasting one—as nothing in the world of dreams lasts—and the artist is happy to escape with his life from the horrors and the decay of the city, horrors far greater than his gaudy and eerie pictures for the *Dream Mirror.*

But *The Other Side* is an autobiography of Kubin's psyche in a far broader sense, just as the world of dreams combines significant parts of his view of the world and of life. This dream world is, all in all, our world as Kubin saw it, exaggerating its characteristics into the grotesque, raising them to higher levels of consistency and inconsistency. The logic according to which the dreamers—or dreamlings—act and according to which everything in the dream world functions (and at times fails to function) resembles that of a work of art: it is not the rational logic of everyday life and science but an irrational and seemingly arbitrary one, an inner, emotionally conditioned, leitmotif-like sequence of ideas, people, and situations. The laws of imagination rather than those of reality have validity here; imagination becomes reality, and thus *The Other Side* must be seen as a broad allegory and apotheosis of the life of the artist, in which life becomes a dream and the world a dream world. The book is replete with symbols. It contains various levels of partially unconscious historical and cultural allusions and parallels; perhaps the author never became consciously aware of all of them. Literary historians have called the country of *The Other Side,* located somewhere in the heartland of Asia, a twenty-four-hours' journey from Samarkand, the legendary realm of Marco Polo's *Old Man of the Mountain,* presumably historically rooted in the medieval Ismaili state. But, in my opinion, the book is more a parable of the old Austria and premonition of its decline. Ernst Jünger saw in it the end of the bourgeois age, and Hellmuth Petriconi described it as the "paradise of decline."

The dream city Perle could be any former imperial provincial city in the Balkans or in Galicia. In fact, the narrator, whom the mysterious Mr. Patera remembers from their youth in Salzburg, comes to the Lange Gasse for the first time and says, "That's how it looks at home in every miserable village." None of the houses in Perle were built after 1870; most are older. They come from various European cities, were bought by Patera, taken down, and rebuilt there in their original forms. They are buildings with a history, bloodstained and haunted, in which evil things have happened. The shops contain no merchandise or equipment more recent than the buildings, and all stores, except the food stores, are antique shops. Nobody is given what he asks for, but each must take what a hidden authority considers suitable for him.

The civil service hierarchy might be called Kafkaesque were it not Kubinesque, if Kubin had not in delicate thoroughness and detailed topography anticipated Kafka's description of the village and the unreachable castle of Count Westwest. Kubin's dream world is governed from a vast archive, a long, dull building, yellowish-gray, dusty, and sleepy, with offices, corridors, and halls filled with files, in which every entry is hopelessly and forever lost. In its incidental, more attractive and eerie, more harmless and exasperating traits, Kubin's world offers the reader a breath of the old Hapsburg Empire, which already then seemed to Kubin like the air of a remote past, wafting across to him like a "certain indefinable aroma" from yellowed books, music boxes, clothes, furniture, buildings, from all corners of the city, inhabited by demons fashioned of plush and dust.

All signs point to the end of this empire, to the end of an era. Foundations collapse and turn out to have been built on swampy soil; walls become brittle, and sand seeps through the cracks— a superb image of the passage of time. But the dreamers either do not notice or have become accustomed to it; they go to the cafés, they play chess, they collect insects, they live childlessly for themselves, and then become disturbed only when strange animals begin to run through the streets, and rats come out of the cellars. Only when a natural catastrophe breaks out, when the river runs over its shores, and when the collapse of the dream city takes on apocalyptic dimensions does a lust for life

stir in the dreamers; and just as in Hieronymus Bosch the tortures of hell spill over into the garden of lust, the death of the dreamers is accompanied by the sort of unbridled passions described with such naïve dismay in medieval town chronicles of the days of the plague.

What interests us above all in this connection is the attitude of the narrator toward the events described. It will seem surprising only at first glance. He sides with nature whose scheme of creation provides for death and decline. He is a fatalist. Hercules Bell, the Philadelphia millionaire and Patera's counterfoil, represents the power of America; he is the symbol of life who wants to open up the dream empire to the world, to bring in business, work, and life in general. He himself has satanic traits—the vertical lines on his forehead evoke an association with Satan's horn—and the organization he founds is named "Lucifer." The dying Patera, on the other hand, who has walled himself off from the world, who wants to put a stop to time, and who personifies the communion with dream, death, and collapse, is reminiscent of a "Greek god" and resembles the "picture of an ancient god," and to him, beyond all momentary doubts, belongs the affection of the author.

The Other Side, written in just a few weeks in 1908, represents, as Kubin writes in his autobiography, the "turning point of a

Illustration from The Other Side, *by Alfred Kubin. English translation © 1967 by Crown Publishers, Inc. Used by permission of Crown Publishers, Inc.*

psychic development,'' which, in turn, dominates his work. *The Other Side* launched him, at the age of thirty, on his career as an illustrator and, forty-four years later, when he duplicated the illustrations for a new editon, also closed his career. The novel ranks with Kubin's most powerful drawings and furnishes even greater insight into his person and view of the world; the title itself, *The Other Side,* is characteristic of his body of work, as are the titles of his later published writings: *At the Edge of Life, My Dream World, Demons and Night Visions,* and *Secret World.* His prose displays the same merits and weaknesses as his drawings: the psychological characterization of the protagonists remains pale if compared with the unbelievable atmospheric density, and, like the drawings, it is an obvious projection of psychic moods and conditions. In his old age, he called the book ''a series of personal experiences and a *Weltanschauung.* . . . In one sense I never went beyond it pictorially—it is simply fate, and the years I lived after finishing the book brought clarification in a sense, but no total revision. Intellectually seen therefore, my pictorial work is in accord with the visions of this peculiar book.'' (pp. 22-5)

> *Wieland Schmied, in his* Alfred Kubin, *translated by Jean Steinberg, Pall Mall Press, 1969, 445 p.*

ROBIN MAGOWAN   (essay date 1969)

[*Magowan is an American poet, translator, travel writer, and critic. In the following excerpt, he discusses what he considers the artistic and moral inadequacies of* The Other Side.]

A book spatters its rain all over us. If it is good we are enlarged. If it is bad we just feel dirty.

Alfred Kubin's *The Other Side* . . . is a book which somehow does both. Inscribed a ''fantastic novel'' and long acclaimed as a surrealistic classic, it is hardly—or only infuriatingly—a novel. Its voyage framework, to a mid-Asia kingdom called quite simply Dreamland, is such an obvious put-on that the reader has all he can do to last out the first 35 pages. And once there what does he find? A few battered types evoked in hardly a page and allowed to reappear whenever the rest of the landscape apparatus won't any longer do. The only character of any sort is the narrator, and this grim-jawed, totally colorless fellow is better represented in the 78 page memoir that the translator . . . has tacked on as a kind of afterword.

But then must a book written by a thirty year old Austrian painter-engraver, a man who had never before in his life written a poem, be a novel? In his memoir Kubin tells us that at a certain point of his life he found himself stuck. His father had died, and for a year he had been unable to work. When once again he wanted to he had too many ideas on his hands:

> I returned home full of impatience and eagerness. But then when I tried to start a drawing I could not do it. I was not capable of putting down coherent lines. It was as though I were a four-year-old child trying for the first time to counterfeit nature. This new phenomenon filled me with alarm, for, I repeat, I was inwardly bursting with the need to work.

And rather than wreck canvas after canvas he hit upon the expedient of a novel:

> In order to do something, no matter what, to unburden myself, I now began to compose and write down an adventure story. The ideas came

flooding into my mind in super-abundance; they forced me to work day and night, so that in twelve weeks' time my fantastic novel *Die andere Seite (The Other Side)* was finished.

The justification for all this was speed. As Kubin later put it:

> The fact that I wrote instead of drawing lay in the nature of the problem; this happened to be the right means to discharge my thronging ideas more rapidly than would otherwise have been possible.

The record for mind-races is still Stendhal's *Chartreuse,* and from this angle it doesn't look as if Kubin has threatened its 52-day standard.

What one gets right off is a distinct lack of love for the medium; a sort of bad grace that expresses itself in short clipped sentences, in a tone that waxes ever grimmer, more sardonic as the novel draws towards its close. True ideas swirl—but how different are they from the ideas that possess any insomniac, and at which one looks next morning in despair! Those orange swans. Towing a bug-bright boat. Waiting for a horse to come up who will probably say in that horse voice of his, ''Howdy.'' All this may sound bad but *The Other Side* is, perhaps because of its inadequacies, like a jerky hand-held camera, compelling. You do read on, and at the end of all that reading you are not the same man that you were when you first took it up.

In most novels things change. In this nothing does. The one narrative principle is somehow to survive, outlast the various forces that are trying to put each other to sleep. In the first part the game as such is a dead loss, and it is only the reader who feels himself succumbing (but beware putting yourself to the test after 11 P.M.!). Once at Dreamland the characters come into something—their second wind—and you can be sure they make the most of it. It is here at any rate in this landscape of greens and browns and beclouded skies that the Kubins are fitted out in their dream shoes and told to go-walk. ''How?'' Mrs. K. asks. And the answer comes back, ''O.K., sit then—it's only a word.'' While they are quibbling sleep raised to the second power comes and kills poor Mrs. K. Does Kubin feel remorse? No. He just vows himself to a more complete passivity.

The aim of the novel is to keep itself from action. Everything is engaged in this behalf: the Dreamland landscape with its muffled fogs and uncertain twilight; the currency which has no more reality than any other dream action (a punch on your sister's face). And it is true that those whose dreams are an important part of their lives don't want to possess but be possessed. Their writings are few largely because it is their passivity that has to well into a poem (think of Redon). For the dreamer joy, exhilaration, comes to the extent that the passivity allows a greater acceleration to what surrounds you. When it has accelerated enough it will blow itself up and release you (if when awake you choose to get back on the dream ferris wheel, well, that's your business).

You might think it easy to write a novel and have yourself survive. Not true, if you are Kubin (just try to list the artists who have not been tempted by suicide!). You are weak, faceless, a pimp in all but name. You would like to be calm, totally passive, but there are things in the way, things like a wife, a job, a bourgeois apartment. Imagine the horror of such a man when he struggles out from behind his shutters and gets on the bus marked Dreamland and arrives to find not a baseball game going on but a bunch of exhibitionists in old fashiond clothes playing that down-in-the-swamp older woman sex game that he, Kubin, had first known as an eleven year old (see the memoir). This movement with its urge to participate, to link hands, is cut short with the death of Kubin's wife—a death which in the narrative is tellingly juxtaposed with two pages describing the Don Juanism of his best friend. And through that death (which is obviously the death of a great deal of himself) Kubin does achieve a measure of calmness. But the total moral disinvolvement of the book's last pages is reached only after a prolonged struggle. The crux comes in the third section with the re-emergence of the abhorrent active principle in the person of the tall pipe-smoking whip-handling American, Hercules Bell. As such he is the antithesis of Kubin's friend, Patera, the inventor of the death directed Dream Kingdom. With his coming the capital of Dreamland, Perle, divides. So many parts flame, so many parts horse manure. And as it divides, everything starts speeding up. Finally the miracle happens. It is not Kubin but the landscape that changes! It erupts, it slides, monsters appear on the goo of its surface, and as a carnival-like plague mentality develops Kubin finds himself watching with a more and more beautiful imperturbability. That getting rid of things—fast—which is the point of the book has begun to happen. And faster and faster until out of the din and the tired erasers a great cathartic ending takes place in which the novel and its characters all go woosh, and there is only Kubin and some blue eyed monks left.

But does Kubin want enlightenment? Does he join the blue eyed ones? No, he goes back to Germany—and when we next see him (in that memoir of his) he is holding up his bloody, baffled hands and in a voice secretly proud saying, "Look, Ma, what I've done!" And you look—a whole dream-reality eclipsed in horror—and at the end of it what do you say, "Great work, kid—and may I please see some more of your art marvels?" We have all seen self-destroying kinetic sculpture. . . . But to have written fifty years ago a self-destroying novel is no mean achievement, given the special conditions that surrounded the composition.

The reality of dream is obviously not that of waking life. If sleep is, as Kubin believes, death, we can only admire the courage with which on page afer page he has confronted that death, that moral horror which, because of its attendant passivity, lies at the heart of his own creative act. Sometimes the fact of his courage makes him tip his hand a little. Then it looks as if the horror itself, rather than withstanding it, is what counts. In a mandala only so much is demons. Too often Kubin mistakes his artist's preoccupation, that corner of reality to which he has given his working life, with truth. Sleep isn't death (or death is only one of the possibilities of sleep). To equate the two as Kubin does is to exploit the dream medium for sadistic effect. And this we have—as would-be dream-writers ourselves—to buck. (pp. 91-4)

> Robin Magowan, " 'The Other Side': A Fantastic
> Novel," in Chicago Review, *Vols. 20 & 21, Nos. 4
> & 1, May, 1969, pp. 91-4.*

EDOUARD RODITI   (essay date 1969)

[*Roditi is a French-born poet, short story writer, biographer, translator, and critic whose works include studies of such diverse topics and figures as art history, literary Surrealism, Oscar Wilde, and Ferdinand Magellan. In the following excerpt, he examines themes and techniques in* The Other Side *and discusses the novel's place in literary history.*]

Illustration from The Other Side, *by Alfred Kubin. English translation © 1967 by Crown Publishers, Inc. Used by permission of Crown Publishers, Inc.*

The American publication of a long overdue but very capable translation of the Austrian artist Alfred Kubin's strange novel *Die Andere Seite,* which the author also illustrated, may inspire discussion at several levels of our intellectual community. Firstly, *The Other Side* will now acquaint the increasingly numerous English-speaking Kafka-commentators who do not read German with an important source that can serve as a key to their interpretations of some of the ambiguities of Kafka's allegorical genre and of his evolution as a writer. As early as 1913, Kafka indeed noted in his diaries that the had met Kubin in Prague. Though he discusses this only briefly, Kafka expressed enough interest in the author of *Die Andere Seite* to lead us to believe that he subsequently made a point of reading it if he was not already familiar with it. Kafka's evolution as a writer of allegorical fiction is less puzzling if we consider it in the light of his probable previous knowledge of the writings of Alfred Kubin and of another odd-ball, the Swiss novelist Robert Walser, authors who had both produced and published allegorical novels of the same general kind as *The Castle, The Trial,* and *America* some years before Kafka began to write his own major works. In *America,* in particular, Kafka seems to be consciously improving on the less broadly meaningful kind of dream-world allegory that he could find in the works of both Walser and Kubin.

Secondly, *The Other Side* might provoke some comment in a very different area of scholarship, among students of the English novel of the latter part of the Nineteenth century. Kubin's only novel indeed fills a gap between two types of novels that now appear to be much more closely related than one might at first suspect, between Samuel Butler's *Erewhon,* on the one hand, and, on the other hand, Rider Haggard's *She* or John Buchan's *Prester John.*

The dividing line between adventurous archaeological or exploratory "science fiction" set in the mysterious heart of some exotic continent and a more philosophical or satirical kind of utopian or allegorical fiction has never been very clear; and few critics have yet dared to tread the cloudy no-man's-land that spreads between these two areas of fantasy. The opening chapters of *Erewhon* and of *She* have nevertheless much in common, progressing only gradually from realistic descriptions of the known or relativity familiar to equally realistic descriptions of the utterly alien. In this respect, both Butler and Rider Haggard have chosen to borrow stylistic devices from the published accounts of the travels of such contemporary explorers as Richard Burton and Mungo Park. Kubin, however, takes for granted that his readers can no longer be fooled as easily. Instead of abolishing any stylistic distinction between the real and the unreal by describing both the known and the unknown with equally plausible precision, his hero disposes of his journey from Munich, through Russian Central Asia, to his Dream Kingdom set in the Chinese Turkestan, in the most banal terms: "What an Oriental city looks like is, I assume, known to everyone. It is exactly the same as one of our cities, only Oriental." After that, Kubin's autobiographical hero plunges us in *medias res,* to flounder with him and his wife, as soon as we reach its grimly fortified frontier, among the disturbing absurdities of the Dream Kingdom to which one obtains admission only by a special invitation from its founder and ruler, the mysterious and fabulously wealthy and powerful Claus Patera, a long-lost schoolfriend of Kubin's hero. (pp. 237-38)

In a purely autobiographical narrative . . . , Kubin offers us discreetly what may well be the key to the mystery of his weirdly visionary drawings and writings. Again and again, he refers to his recurring fits of depression or melancholia and even to seizures; more rarely, he also appears to have experienced the epileptoid phenomena of Kalopsy or of Kakopsy, in which his world appeared to him more beautiful or more repulsive than usual. All this might also explain why Kubin's writings and his art rely to such an extent on equally contradictory and epileptoid impressions of both *déjà-vu* and self-alienation. Nor would it then be by mere chance that Kubin chose, quite clearly in his career as book-illustrator, to provide drawings for a magnificent German edition of *Aurélia,* the French poet Gérard de Nerval's autobiographical account of his own insanity. (p. 238)

Yet we can discover, in much of this literature that ranges from Nerval and Kubin to Samuel Butler and even Rider Haggard, a certain number of constant themes or of Jungian archetypes that tend to suggest how little freedom human madness, hallucination and fantasy really enjoy. To list them all systematically would unfortunately lead us very far. For instance, unlike Butler's Erewhon, Kubin's Dream Kingdom is not only "cut off from the surrounding world" by the natural barriers of its geographical remoteness or inaccessibility, but is also jealously enclosed within monumental walls and fortifications that its founder, Claus Patera, has had built, like the Great Wall of China that also fired Kafka's imagination. Patera's

Kingdom is moreover intended to be "a place of asylum for those who are disgusted with modern culture;" all its institutions and invited inhabitants, with the exception of a small and mysterious aboriginal tribe of blue-eyed Mongolians, are housed in ancient or merely dilapidated buildings which have been purchased at great expense in distant Europe, to be transported and reassembled here with as much care as William Randolph Hearst once devoted to adorning San Simeon with architectural masterpieces of the past. But Patera, like the more sociologically-minded curators of some Scandinavian open-air museums of architecture of the past, has also been careful to endow his Dream Kingdom with a suitable number of tumbledown old tenements and other architectural eyesores, so that his capital has a realistically nightmare quality of *déjà-vu* that precludes its ever appearing truly Utopian. As for the city's imported inhabitants who have been mysteriously selected, invited and brought here to live as in a Nazi concentration-camp from which there can be no escape except in death, they all wear . . . the cast-off finery of the past. As in *Erewhon,* the Dream Kingdom's ruler "cherishes a profound aversion for all forms of progress." In real life, Kubin expressed moreover an analogous distaste for novelty: nearly all his original drawings are executed on old or antique papers that he took great trouble to collect in second-hand bookstores and from dealers in waste paper.

Kubin's Dream Kingdom gradually turns out to be, as we slowly explore it with his hero, an even more ambivalent Utopia than Butler's Erewhon, in fact as disturbing a Dystopia as Kafka's world or as the mythical primitive empire ruled by Rider Haggard's She-who-must-be-obeyed. Kubin's hero finally escapes from Patera's dictatorial realm only after an apocalyptic collapse of the whole Dream Kingdom; its disintegration culminates in a supernatural scene when Patera dies or merely disappears in an underground temple lit only by a strange naphta altar-flame, indeed in circumstances very similar to those in which Rider Haggard's She is released from the curse of her eternal youth.

As one reads *The Other Side,* one becomes increasingly aware of the disturbed and disturbing quality of Kubin's imagination and style of writing. Like Kafka, he writes a matter-of-fact style, but with the visionary urgency of a prophet of doom. On the one hand, he presents us a nightmare version of the real-life stagnancy and decay of the institutions of the crumbling and creaking Austro-Hungarian Empire, threatened at its core both by Socialism and by Pan-Germanism, and on all its marches by the national liberation movements of its many subject peoples. On the other, Kubin already seems to visualize, as if in a clairvoyant's crystal ball, the macabre parodies of a kind of old-world Germanic Disneyland that some half-mad Kommandants of Nazi extermination-camps later forced their victims to build hurriedly as a facade to deceive squeamish higher-echelon visitors. But Kafka's allegorical visions are more mild and masochistic, those of a resigned victim, whereas Kubin's often suggest a streak of mischievous and infantile sadism; in his descriptions of the strife, the orgies and the catastrophes that finally exterminate almost all the inhabitants of the Dream Kingdom, Kubin vies with Lautréamont's rhapsodic *Chants de Maldoror* rather than with any of Kafka's allegorical fiction. Patera's Dream Kingdom thus falls apart in a welter of absurd but apocalyptic disasters that all appear to have been directly or indirectly caused by his own double and rival, a mysterious American who has appeared in the Dream Kindgom's captial to spread "progressive" or subversive ideas in order to save its citizens from themselves or from Patera's dictatorship; but the American then destroys them while seeking to save them. . . . (pp. 238-39)

The Other Side is the only full-length novel of an Austrian painter and writer who also deserves to be better known in America as one of the more prominent artists of the famous Munich *Blue Rider* group. Though Kubin's fantastic or satirical drawings never influenced Kandinsky or Jawlensky, one can detect his characteristic fusion of humor and horror in some of the earlier and more fantastically caricatural work of Klee and of Feininger. As a writer, Kubin remains moreover, even more strikingly than Robert Walser, the prototype of a whole school of later German allegorical writers among whom one can now include, in addition to Kafka and Elias Canetti, such varied types as Fritz von Herzmanovsky-Orlando, Hermann Kasack, Ernst Jünger, Werner Kraus, Ernst Kreuder, Joachim Karsch and, beyond the linguistic frontiers of German literature, the Polish writers Bruno Schulz and Witold Gombrowicz. (pp. 239-41)

Edouard Roditi, "Allegory and Alienation," in Arts in Society, *Vol. 6, No. 2, Summer-Fall, 1969, pp. 237-42.*

STUART HOOD (essay date 1969)

[*In the following excerpt, Hood finds that the value of* The Other Side *lies in the author's treatment of dreams.*]

The Other Side . . . might be described as an anti-Utopian vision. It concerns the city of Pearl . . . , which has been founded by Claus Patera, a boyhood friend of the narrator. Lured there together with his wife, the narrator finds that it lies in the heart of Central Asia, protected by the barriers of geography and a great surrounding wall. The town is composed of old houses, transported there from all over the world and filled with old furniture, the bric-à-brac of bourgeois culture; it is inhabited by men and women dressed in the clothes of a previous generation, who have been summoned there because of some psychological quirk—a mania for gambling, hyper-religiosity or hysteria—or else some physical peculiarity such as a goitre, a hunchback or an enlarged nose.

In this grey dream city where there is no sun but only a filtered twilight, the narrator finds employment as illustrator to a newspaper, contracted to provide drawings that are both sensational and horrifying. With his old friend, Patera, he has no contact; the ruler of Pearl lurks in his residence like the lord of the castle in Kafka, protected by an impenetrable bureaucracy, entrenched behind mazes of dusty files. His power is challenged by a newcomer, an American millionaire of immense energy, Hercules Bell. The city is riven by factions and in their struggle the whole structure goes down in blood and nightmare, from which the narrator, whose wife has died miserably, barely escapes.

It would be easy to dismiss *The Other Side* as a period piece, an example of *fin de siècle* macabre, to feel that—like much of Kubin's art—it is somehow peripheral to the mainstream of European culture, the product of that decay which some of his contemporaries felt to be spreading through the Austro-Hungarian empire. If it is not possible to do so, their reason is to be sought in what Kubin has to say about dreams. "The scraps of memory—that is all they are—that stay with us after a dream seem illogical only to superficial observers, on whom the splendid power and beauty of this kingdom are lost." Like Freud he made a systematic study of dreams. It is, I believe, because

of the precise use of dream symbols and dream situations that Kubin can still excite, move and frighten us. The blind mare galloping along a tunnel in the dark is indeed a nightmare. His vision of dirt, filth, entrails and carcasses of beasts and men pouring down like a river of lava with dislocated arms and legs, spraddled fingers and clenched fists is one we have seen become real in our own times. (p. 412)

Stuart Hood, "Dream City," in The Spectator, *Vol. 223, No. 7370, September 27, 1969, pp. 410, 412.*

VERNA SCHUETZ (essay date 1974)

[*Schuetz is an American educator. The following excerpt, in which she discusses the principal themes and techniques of* The Other Side, *is taken from a doctoral dissertation examining the fantastic fiction of Kubin, Gustav Meyrink, Hanns Heinz Ewers, and Karl Hans Strobl.*]

Alfred Kubin . . . appropriates motifs from the Apocalypse to portray the collapse of a society in *Die andere Seite.* . . . An artist, the first-person narrator of the novel, is invited to emigrate to a dream realm created by a boyhood friend, Patera, in a remote area of the Orient. The action of the novel covers the narrator's trip to the dream city Perle, his experiences there, and the collapse of the realm. As part of the prelude to the

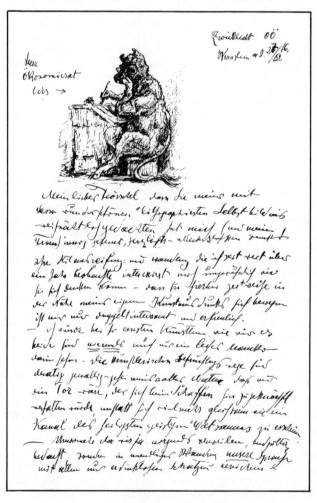

Holograph copy of a 1916 letter from Kubin to Rolf Von Hoershelmann.

ultimate disintegration of Perle, Kubin has the afflictions of the four horsemen of the Apocalypse descend on the city's inhabitants. Sickness, primarily nervous disorder, spreads through the population; the people split into warring factions. Famine sets in, and death stalks the streets in many forms. Also from Revelations is the plague of animals. All animals and insects in the dream realm begin to reproduce at a rapid rate. They take over the streets and buildings and devour the food supplies. Drunkenness and murder are common; buildings crack and cave in. Sexuality also becomes uncontrollable among the humans and leads to a monstrous sexual orgy in which every inhabitant of Perle except the narrator participates. Toward the end of the city's dissolution, blood flows in the streets. However, unlike Revelations where destruction is followed by a new heaven and a new earth, . . . *Die andere Seite* ends with Perle nothing but a heap of rubble.

The Apocalypse was apparently not Kubin's only literary source for his portrayal of the decay and disintegration of Patera's realm. The visions the narrator has following the actual physical collapse of Perle are for the most part paraphrases of an Indian legend.

The inhabitants of Perle . . . represent a cross section of human society. However, the dreamers do not represent a typical cross section, for each one has some peculiar quirk of personality. This is one of the criteria for being invited to emigrate to the dream empire. These people have been selected by and have come together at the personal invitation of Patera, and as soon as they enter his realm, they come under his mysterious, subliminal control. Whenever any newcomer resists too strongly the order of life in the dream land, the whole community is frightened back into submissiveness by some terrifying occurrence such as the appearance of a phantom white horse, also a motif from the Apocalypse. Assembled by Patera and subject to his control, the residents of Perle are, as the narrator comes to realize, marionettes in Patera's hands. They are aware that a certain destiny is being carried out on them, and they accept that destiny as inevitable until Herkules Bell arrives in Perle and leads a revolt.

As the result of a mysterious inner compulsion somehow linked to Patera's control of them, Patera's subjects daily pay homage to the lord Patera in a strange ritual that borders on worship. However, . . . the people of Perle do not turn in religious fervor to their deity when their world begins to disintegrate. Instead, under Bell's defiant leadership they become apostates and liberate themselves from Patera's puppetlike control. However, they thereby only propel themselves unsuspectingly into fulfillment of the ultimate fate for which they and the entire dream world have been destined: death and destruction.

Of all Perle's residents, only the contemplative, blue-eyed aborigines lead a life independent of Patera's control. They inhabited this region before Patera came, and they survive both him and his creation. Considerably before the fall of the dream realm, the narrator begins adopting the contemplative ways of the natives. By the time the end finally comes, he has attained a certain spiritual equanimity, and he, like the aborigines, escapes the fate of his fellow immigrants. (pp. 188-91)

The events in *Die andere Seite* take place in the first decade of the twentieth century, but Kubin, or more specifically Patera, banishes the twentieth century from Perle. Immigrants to the dream realm must relinquish all objects and clothing that postdate the 1860's before they can enter Perle's restrictive walls. One Freudian critic [Hanns Sachs], possessed of the

knowledge that Kubin's parents married in the 1860's, has interpreted Kubin's using the 1860's as the cut-off date for the origin of articles allowed in Perle as an expression of Kubin's Oedipus complex. Other aspects of the novel, particularly the father-son polarity in Patera's relationship to the narrator, seem to justify a psychoanalytical reading of *Die andere Seite*. However, the novel is not primarily the story of the relationship between Patera and the narrator but rather the story of the dream realm and its collapse. The destruction of Patera's empire results not from conflict between Patera and the narrator but from conflict between Patera and Bell. And it is in the context of the Patera-Bell confrontation that the arrestment of time in Patera's domain has its greatest significance.

Bell represents the modern industrialized world with its committment to materialism, progress, and the future. As an American, he possesses wealth, novelty, and boldness of endeavor. Bell, the product of a land of universal political participation, awakens the dream-land dwellers to political life and tries to make them aware of their subservience to Patera by telling them that they are being controlled through mass hypnosis.

Patera's world is that of Europe in the 1860's. It is a world in which industrialization, modern inventions, and progress have not yet permeated the fabric of everyday life. Politically, the inhabitants resemble the masses of the Germans and Austro-Hungarians of the 1860's. Until Bell arrives, they are apolitical and content to live under Patera's benevolent paternalism. Although Bell is an American, the conflict is not between Europe and America, but rather between the contemporary world and that of fifty years previous. The old world is clearly doomed even before Bell's arrival. The houses are rickety, the population is not reproducing, and uncanny events make every inhabitant aware of the precariousness of his own existence.

Bell symbolizes what has already replaced this dying world beyond its limited borders. However, his efforts to introduce a new order into the dream realm result in anything but a desirable alternative to the dependency, sterility, and dilapidation characteristic of the old order. Once Bell arouses their interest in political life, the residents of Perle immediately splinter into numerous factions, each with its own different and contradictory wishes. Money becomes an idol and leads to greed, envy, and murder. Sterility is replaced by uncontrollable reproduction among the animals which then devour the food supply and cover the city with filth. Bell's introduction of modernity into Perle's dated world brings not progress but final disintegration.

The narrator in *Die andere Seite*, although he clearly discerns the weaknesses of the old order and personally suffers under many of its unpleasant features, does not embrace Bell's new order as salvation. In fact, he is more sympathetic toward Patera than toward Herkules Bell. Even so, he withdraws from the conflict between the two orders and becomes a spectator, a stance not dissimilar to Kubin's own toward the real world. Sequestered within his protecting ark at Zwickledt, Kubin sat back and treasured the past more highly than the "poesielose" ["unpoetic"] present that was changing the world around him. (pp. 194-96)

In *Die andere Seite*, all mysterious events as well as the entire uncanny atmosphere of the dream land can be traced back to Patera. He controls forces not limited by the normal restrictions of the material world. He can alter material substance such as his own appearance, and he can even control something as immaterial as the wills of the dream-realm inhabitants. For

Illustration from The Other Side, *by Alfred Kubin. English translation © 1967 by Crown Publishers, Inc. Used by permission of Crown Publishers, Inc.*

Kubin, there are inexplicable, non-material forces behind the strictly material surface of the world, but . . . he ascribes neither religious nor moral value to these forces. He depicts their effects through uncanny events in *Die andere Seite* just as he often depicted a second, mysterious level of reality lurking behind the simple concrete reality of the material world in his drawings. In both his novel and his drawings, the uncanny is as much a part of the real world as physical reality itself. (pp. 200-01)

The world of *Die andere Seite* has been brought into being by a single person who possesses absolute control over it, including the ability to destroy it. Patera created Perle, and he destroys it. The dream realm experiences spasms of mysterious horrors long before the events leading to its final collapse and even long before Bell's arrival. Several critics have pointed out that this empire is dedicated to decay and collapse. (pp. 201-02)

The adversary who precipitates the fall of both Patera and his realm is Herkules Bell. But Bell and Patera are identical inasmuch as they are both expressions of the same archpower, albeit polar expressions. Patera is both creator and destroyer. He is imagination incarnate and imagination's counterpole: nothingness. In the narrator's first interview with him, Patera

shows himself as the creative imagination, in the second as the destroyer. In each interview, Patera goes through a number of transformations before the artist's eyes, and at the end of the second interview, he appears as Bell.

On January 30, 1944, Kubin wrote: "*Die andere Seite* ist eine Erlebnisreihe und eine Weltanschauung. . . . Im gewissen Sinn bin ich anschaulich auch niemals darüber hinausgekommen—es ist eben Schicksal; und die Jahrzehnte, welche nach Abschluss des Bandes für mich noch kamen, brachten in einigen Beziehungen Klärung, in keiner Totalberichtigung. Deshalb deckt sich auch meine bildkünstlerische Arbeit, geistig aufgefasst, mit den Visionen dieses sonderbaren Buches" ["*Die andere Seite* is a series of personal experiences and a *Weltanschauung*. . . . In one sense I never went beyond it pictorially—it is simply fate, and the years I lived after finishing the book brought clarification in a sense, but no total revision. Intellectually seen therefore, my pictorial work is in accord with the visions of this peculiar book"—translation by Jean Steinberg].

In light of these comments, the critic Robert Mühler seems justified in interpreting *Die andere Seite* (1909) in connection with Kubin's later essay *Fragment eines Weltbildes*. . . . In that philosophical fragment, Kubin stated that man consists of chaos and the self. Out of chaos, the self—or imagination—forms life, but life is an irreality and is eaten away again by chaos. The narrator in *Die andere Seite* ascribes a similar philosophy to the aborigines. Connecting the novel with the *Fragment,* Mühler writes: "So stellt denn der Gehalt der *Anderen Seite* in seinem ersten Teil das unfassbare Wesen der Einbildungskraft dar, während die zweite Hälfte den Einbruch des Nichts, des Chaos und Abgrundes schildert, der die von der Einbildungskraft geschaffene Welt wieder zur Auflösung bringt" ["The first part of *The Other Side* thus depicts the incomprehensible essence of the power of the imagination, while the second half portrays the irruption of nothingness, of chaos and abyss, returning the world created by the power of the imagination to dissolution"]. Mühler's overall reading of the novel supports the interpretation that the dream realm's destruction is inherent in its being from the beginning and that Bell and Patera are polar expressions of one and the same being.

Since Patera and Bell are one being, and since the dream land was conceived as a realm doomed to destruction, its collapse is not a failure of Patera's plan, and Patera is not a victim of his own failure. Perle simply fulfills its destiny, and Patera, the lord of a dying realm, relinquishes visible dominion to his counterpart Bell, the representative of life. (pp. 202-04)

> *Verna Schuetz, "Three Fantastic Novels," in her* The Bizarre Literature of Hanns Heinz Ewers, Alfred Kubin, Gustav Meyrink, and Karl Hans Strobl, *The University of Wisconsin, 1974, pp. 178-207.*

PHILIP H. RHEIN (essay date 1977)

[*In the following excerpt, Rhein examines ideological and technical similarities between Franz Kafka's story* The Metamorphosis *and Kubin's drawing "The Painter."*]

The association of Franz Kafka and Alfred Kubin took place in the real world of Prague in the early years of the twentieth century. Kafka's diaries frequently mention his encounters with Kubin, and it is a known fact that Kubin was sufficiently fascinated by the Kafka vision of the world that he illustrated Kafka's short story, *The Country Doctor*. Yet, as intriguing as the meetings of the two men in the world of reality may be, it is their ideological and technical association in the world of illusion and fantasy that is particularly interesting to analyze and compare.

Now no one doubts the contrasting impact of verbal and visual images. Ever since Lessing's critical proclamation on the division of arts, it has been generally accepted that the dynamics of prose depend primarily upon the extended experience of events in a linear fashion, whereas painting, because of its fixed, spatial orientation, produces a simultaneity of experience. Although this is an acceptable and logical division of the arts, many contemporary writers, aware of the impossibility of denying the time duration demanded by narration, have nonetheless attempted to manipulate language and verbal images in such a way that succession of moments, experienced in a temporal sequence, becomes fused into a single perceived image within the mind of the reader. Just as the painter uses perspective in order to extend and manipulate the space into which the picture plane locks him, the contemporary writer applies a variety of technical maneuvers in an attempt to overcome the temporal sequence to which language confines him. The techniques vary from artist to artist and depend upon the unique way a particular writer perceives the world and seeks to effect his vision upon his reader.

It is with these comments in mind that one can begin to approach a comparison of Kafka and Kubin from the ideological and technical points of view. For the purpose of comparison, the following comments are specifically directed to Kafka's *The Metamorphosis* and Kubin's *The Painter*. Ideologically, these two men belonged to that generation of artists who at the beginning of the twentieth century had to build anew the essential framework of the world. It is specifically in this building of framework, or of providing a form for the chaotic world of this time, that their art meets and that the point of comparison is established. Unwilling to accept the role delegated to man by the new world of technology, Kafka and Kubin sought to break through the heaviness and the limitations of this world into a world that did not follow the rational logic of everyday life and science. To them, the irrational and often arbitrary world of the emotionally experienced inner sequences of ideas, people, and situations was the real world which mirrored the anxieties and beauties of life. Imagination, and not hard-core observation, became the means of perceiving reality for Kafka and Kubin; and it is from this point of view that their works must be critically analyzed. Blurring the edges of the seen world by reference to other worlds, these artists moved from the nineteenth-century preoccupation with natural appearances to an analysis of the subjective world; and, as paradoxical as it may seem, this subjective, visionary world expresses an order as real, if not as tangible, as any physical phenomena could ever be.

Everyone is familiar enough with the uniqueness of the Kafka and Kubin world, a world from which the reader or viewer is often alienated by fantastic objects and events. Logic as we ordinarily speak of it has no meaning in this world that lies beyond the limits of man's workaday experience, if not beyond man's understanding. It is not a fairy-tale world of dreams, but a world of dreams in which enough reality is retained that the reader or viewer is forced to acknowledge its familiarity. Gregor in Kafka's *The Metamorphosis* (1915) or Death in Kubin's *The Painter* (1918) are obviously unreal figures in the ordinary world; yet both are treated in terms of the clearest, most concise logic. They *are*. The logical treatment of the unreal, so obvious in these instances, is true for all of Kafka's

writings and Kubin's drawings. Once the original situation is accepted, the dénouement follows in the most logical manner.

The world as revealed by Kafka and Kubin is a product of their personal, inner experience; and because of their persistent preoccupation with the details and clutter of the real world, we are forced to be concerned with the living, the human, and the real in an apparently unreal situation. This emphasis upon detail is most significant when we are aware of the economy of expression employed by both artists. Nowhere are we bogged down under a torrent of needless verbal or visual description. The minutiae of the real world are retained as a point of contact between our reality and the suprareality of the art products and as an environmental backdrop to unreal or strange characters who are misfits in an otherwise fluid situation. The reader or viewer is constantly tossed between the extremes of reality and unreality which are on the point of meeting but never meet.

One one level, Kafka's and Kubin's works express keen psychological observation and social criticism; but beneath this surface level, they seek to shape a metaphysical experience through which a man may find his freedom from time and actuality. They do not pretend that modern life is beautiful and humane; their intent is quite different. They do not seek to resolve man's social problems but rather to release man from them so that he can attain a level of understanding that transcends the imposed limits of time and space.

This world that they create is an abstract world: not abstract in the way that science is abstract, but abstract in that it deals only with the essential. Here the personal problem no longer

Kubin's drawing "The Painter." Serge Sabarsky Gallery, Inc.

exists, and that which seems still personal, is the very moment it is uttered, dissolved into the realm of myth. Kafka and Kubin succeed in projecting the personal problems of the individuals into the realm of the universal problems of men. In a work by either of the men, the initially private problem of the piece is extended and modified until it no longer exists on the purely personal level. By means of the artist's selection and manipulation of material, the personal evolves into the suprapersonal, and the problems of the individual are superseded by the problems of man. Camus, in writing about Kafka, stated that, "His work is universal to the extent to which it represents the emotionally moving face of man fleeing humanity, deriving from his contradictions reasons for believing, reasons for hoping from his fecund despair and calling life his terrifying apprenticeship in death." Camus' statement is equally applicable to the art of Kubin.

As we move from the ideological world that frames the works of Kafka and Kubin into the particular world that is locked within that frame, we enter a world of language and line that is systematically ordered and controlled with absolute precision. In *The Metamorphosis* by Kafka and *The Painter* by Kubin, the ideological similarities of the two artists are underscored by the selection and arrangement of details that serve to guide the reader or viewer of these works. To begin at the beginning, the titles themselves invite speculation. Just as the transformation of the commercial traveler Gregor Samsa is completed in the first sentence of the Kafka story, so too is the death of the painter an obvious and immediately conveyed visual fact of Kubin's pencil drawing. Gregor's metamorphosis and the painter's death are the unquestionable givens of the two art products, and these facts are never doubted by the reader or viewer. Unlike the pattern of traditional analytic tragedy in which the questions of guilt and innocence are raised and resolved, these questions are never addressed by either Kafka or Kubin. Paradoxically, however, these same questions become the central concern of the reader or viewer as he seeks to untangle the meaning of the presented details. The initial problem is further complicated by an additional given fact. The ambiguity of the titles emphasizes the impossibility of any facile interpretation of either the story or the drawing. Obviously, the metamorphosis of Gregor and the death of the painter are accomplished acts; however, the title of the Kafka story might apply to Gregor's sister, Grete, with more justification than to Gregor himself, for it is, after all, her metamorphosis that is revealed in the unfolding of the narrative. The title of the Kubin drawing is equally ambiguous. On first glance the painter of the title seemingly refers to the lifeless human form that lies before the canvas; yet the linear arrangement of details within the drawing quickly moves the viewer's eyes to the central figure of death, here portrayed with an artist's palette in his hand, completing the as yet unfinished canvas. Death is the focal point of the drawing; and he, like Grete in *The Metamorphosis*, is the figure we witness acting out the drama of the composition.

The movement inherent within the two art works is also comparable. The Kafka or Kubin character is brought into the conflict between the world of everyday life and the world of supernatural anxiety. As he moves more deeply into this conflict, no problem is resolved; everything begins over and over again. He attempts to capture meaning through what negates that meaning, but he is constantly thrown back upon himself, upon the one thing that has no definition. He is caught in the circular movement of a whirlpool that inevitably sucks him under. This circular movement is emphasized in *The Meta-*

morphosis by Gregor's perpetual motion that never budges him from the spot. The circle that forms the frame of the story by enclosing the action between two metamorphoses is repeated internally in several ways. In the first part of *The Metamorphosis*, the constant ticking of the alarm clock symbolically reflects the irrevocable circle of Gregor's past life as a traveling salesman, locked into the world of clock time. Later in the story, when specific time no longer has any meaning in Gregor's world, the alarm clock disappears and is replaced by Gregor's own ceaseless, atemporal, circular movement that binds him within a world that is no longer understood or measured realistically. Finally, Gregor's aimless circular wanderings are halted by the round apples that are embedded in his hard shell. Through Gregor's death, temporal order is restored, the shapeless vagueness that permeates the story is eradicated and the circle of the metamorphoses is completed.

The movement in Kubin's drawing, like that within *The Metamorphosis,* is circular. The horizontal line of the diagonally stretched out body of the painter leads us visually into the drawing, past the vertical lines of the mounted canvas and finally to the figure of Death in front of it. This movement carries us rapidly from the world of reality to the world of the fantastic, from a dead human form to the symbol of death, from the temporal to the atemporal world. The central figure of Death is psychologically so overwhelming that it momentarily freezes visual movement. In much the same way that the rapid flow of time in the first part of *The Metamorphosis* is stopped in the second part in order to fix the reader's attention upon the meaning of the tale, here visual movement is halted so that the viewer will confront Death and accept his position as central to the artistic and the life processes. However, in order to return the viewer to the temporal, real world, Kubin carried the viewer's gaze away from the figure of Death to the easel behind him. This visual movement is accomplished by the repetition of line. Behind the easel, an outline of a stove is sketched, and the curved pipe of this stove repeats the composition on the canvas and the bent posture of Death. The visual movement consequently proceeds from the dead painter to the figure of Death to the canvas to the stove and once again back to the canvas, to Death, and finally to the dead figure. To express the same idea another way, the movement flows from the temporal to the atemporal to the temporal. This circular movement is reinforced by the circular shape of the stove cover, Death's hat, the palette he holds, the electric light above him, and finally in the curved arm of the dead painter. Each of these details powerfully contributes to the excitement and vibrancy of the drawing, and each of them visually repeats the movement of the entire composition. As we experience the drawing, we move from the specific, corporal world—conveyed by the body of the artist, the stove, the electric light—into the realm of the enigmatic, unreal world conveyed by the figure of Death. Just as the two worlds are joined in the third part of *The Metamorphosis* to convey the essentiality of each to meaningful, human existence, these same two worlds are visually combined in the drawing to portray the one world of man. The impact of both is that of a never-ending circle, of an unresolved questioning.

Perhaps questioning is the point. Kafka and Kubin were both absorbed in the realm of ideas, and the ideas that they sought to convey were given verbal and graphic form in such a way that the details the art products contain repeat the rhythm of a world in which good and evil, beauty and ugliness, life and death, the real and the unreal not only depend upon one another for meaning, but are ultimately perceived as inseparably fused.

Their art seeks to capture the indivisible essence of reality; and for them, evil, decay, and death are never "the other side" of a divisible world, but are individual parts of a world that must be accepted in its totality. (pp. 61-5)

Philip H. Rhein, "Two Fantastic Visions: Franz Kafka and Alfred Kubin," in South Atlantic Bulletin, *Vol. XLII, No. 2, May, 1977, pp. 61-6.*

JANE KALLIR (essay date 1983)

[*Kallir is an American art critic. Her works include studies of Austrian Expressionism, Gustav Klimt, and Egon Schiele. In the following excerpt, she discusses biographical and social background to* The Other Side.]

Die andere Seite was a result of the artist's attempt to come to terms with his father's death. Not with exaggeration he called it "a turning point in my spiritual development." Quite clearly, the plot of the novel parallels the emotional crisis taking place in Kubin's life at the time he wrote it. The book tells the story of a "Dream Kingdom" and its eventual destruction by the forces of reality. This conclusion, however, does not necessarily entail victory for one side and defeat for the other, but rather the resolution of the two into a coherent whole.

Most of the novel takes place on "the other side," in a fantasy world where dreams are real. This idea, of course, was not entirely original with Kubin. Freud's *Interpretation of Dreams* had been published in 1899, and Kubin by his own admission was an avid connoisseur of dream literature. The netherworld of the unconscious was a rich source of artistic images that he never gave up trying to mine. Some ten years after finishing *Die andere Seite,* he wrote: "The scraps of memory—that is all they are—that stay with us after a dream seem illogical only to superficial observers, on whom the splendid power and beauty of this kingdom are lost." If the fragments of dream that remain in the waking mind could somehow be reassembled, if the dream world could be reconstituted in the conscious world, one might capture not only the secret of art, but of life itself.

At the beginning of *Die andere Seite,* the reader is told that the "Dream Kingdom" is the deliberate creation of a wealthy eccentric by the name of Patera (note the allusion to the Latin word for father), who has "a profound aversion to all forms of progress." A "place of asylum for those who are disgusted with modern culture," the Kingdom is located in the "mountains of heaven" in Chinese central Asia. Patera first visits this area in order to hunt a rare Persian tiger. After the beast turns on its attacker and wounds him, Patera is forced to prolong his stay in China while he recuperates. During this period, he becomes acquainted with the leader of a strange, blue-eyed tribe, under whose auspices (so to speak) the Dream Kingdom is eventually constructed.

The appeal of exotic locations, like the appeal of dreams, was very much present in the cultural climate of Kubin's time. It was, if anything, a relic of his father's generation. Nineteenth-century taste had been colored by tales of travel and adventure. Scenic views of faraway places became popular during the Biedermeier period at the beginning of the century. Later on, Hans Makart, the most popular artist of the *Ringstrasse* era, initiated a fad for peacock feathers and more sumptuous Orientalia.

Kubin's first exposure to distant lands came in the photographer's studio where he apprenticed as an adolescent. His employer sent back plates from Italy and the Orient that had to be developed in the shop. It is not difficult to imagine the daydreams these images must have provoked in the unhappy boy. The mystery of unexplored territory—whether psychic or geographic—had an undeniable allure. "We are all wanderers, without exception, all of us," he wrote. "As long as there have been human beings, it has been so, and so it will be forever."

The narrator of *Die andere Seite,* sharing Kubin's wanderlust as he shares so many of the author's other traits, is about to depart for India when the book begins. It is therefore not difficult for Patera to convince him to change his destination and head for the Dream Kingdom instead. After a journey of many days, he and his wife finally arrive in Perle, the Kingdom's capital. Their first impressions are less than favorable.

Contrary to what the narrator (whose expectations certainly mirror those held by most readers of the novel) has anticipated, the Dream Kingdom is surprisingly dreary. "Why, this is the way it looks in our worst slums!" he exclaims in dismay. Indeed, Patera has assembled decrepit buildings from all over Europe and transported them to the Kingdom. In keeping with his avowed aversion to progress, everything in his domain is old, and much of it in a state of disrepair. Visitors are searched at the border; any new or unused possessions are confiscated.

The inhabitants of Perle are a motley crew. Their clothing, like the dilapidated architecture of the city, is "completely out of fashion." "These people wear the clothes of their parents and grandparents," the narrator remarks to his wife. Moreover, he tells us, the citizens have "been selected with an eye to abnormal or one-sided development" and include "splendid specimens of drunkards, wretches dissatisfied with themselves and the world, hypochondriacs, spiritualists, daredevil ruffians, blasé characters seeking adventure and old adventurers seeking peace, legerdemain artists, acrobats, political fugitives, murderers wanted abroad, counterfeiters, thieves and others of that ilk."

Selected aspects of the real world are magnified in the Dream Kingdom; everything seems strangely out of proportion. The Kingdom is actually humorous, a caricature of reality. To be specific, it is a caricature of Kubin's reality. The exaggerated personalities of its inhabitants represent the types who inhabit his drawings. Or rather they represent the types that he, with something akin to X-ray vision, unmasks beneath the most unprepossessing exteriors. Similarly, Patera's world of old houses, seemingly mired in the past, is actually not so different from the world Kubin chose to live in. He found his own "dream kingdom"—a real-life retreat from modern civilization—in Zwickledt, a small, secluded estate near the Inn River at the northwestern border of Austria that he bought in 1906.

In a larger sense, Patera's Dream Kingdom may be interpreted as representing the entire Austro-Hungarian Empire in its waning days. Quite clearly, this is to some extent what Patera intends; why he has taken special pains to import buildings of European origin. And, after all, these efforts have been largely successful. "In the most general terms, the country seemed like central Europe," the narrator reports. "By far the majority of the Dreamers were German by birth. . . . Other nationalities hardly counted." So the Kingdom exists, an oasis of German civilization in the Orient, much as Austria herself exists at the frontier of Eastern Europe. The old houses, the old-fashioned clothing, reflect the characteristic dowdiness of Austrian society—a little behind the times, a little frumpy, but charming, endearing. The importance of the military and the civil service—of rank and title—in the Austrian social hierarchy suggests another parallel between the real and fictive lands. As the narrator remarks in one of his more sarcastic moments, "That's what was most important in this country—to represent something, anything at all."

Commentators tend to stress the fantastic element in *Die andere Seite*. Of equal importance, however, are the realistic aspects of the novel: those that limn, with the gentle lines of caricature and compassion, the foibles of the artist's compatriots. The triumph of Kubin's novel, and of his art, is the apotheosis of the mundane, the merging of the worldly with the spiritual. By writing the book, he "achieved the mature realization that it is not only in the bizarre, exalted or comic moments of our existence that the highest values lie, but that the painful, the indifferent, and the incidental-commonplace contain these same mysteries." (pp. 20, 22, 26, 28, 30, 34)

Jane Kallir, in her Alfred Kubin: Visions from the Other Side, *Galerie St. Etienne, 1983, 46 p.*

ADDITIONAL BIBLIOGRAPHY

Adams, Brooks. "Decadence and Beyond." *Art in America* 71, No. 11 (December 1983): 125-26.
 Reviews an exhibition of Kubin's graphic art at the Galerie St. Etienne in New York, noting a development in his art from "the young Kubin's seemingly inconquerable phobias and fixations" to "the ostensibly contained yet ineffably pungent observations of a country recluse."

Horodisch, Abraham. Introduction to *Alfred Kubin: Book Illustrator*, by Alfred Kubin, pp. 11-16. New York: Aldus Book Co., 1950.
 Discusses Kubin's most important and representative illustrations.

Huneker, James. "Kubin, Munch, and Gauguin: Masters of Hallucination." In his *Ivory Apes and Peacocks*, pp. 222-39. New York: Charles Scribner's Sons, 1922.
 Discusses dominant characteristics of Kubin's art, stressing his preoccupation with the bizarre and the hideous.

Mitgang, Herbert. "Fantasy and Art in the Novel." *The New York Times* (3 January 1968): 45.
 Review of the first translated edition of *The Other Side*. The critic concludes that "*The Other Side* is signficant European fiction, but hardly as universal a novel as *The Trial* or other Kafka masterworks."

Prawer, S. S. "The Horror and the Idyll." *The Times Literary Supplement*, No. 3935 (12 August 1977): 974-75.
 Reviews four recent German-language publications of works by and about Kubin.

Schroeder, Richard. "From *Traumreich* to *Surréalité:* Surrealism and Alfred Kubin's *Die andere Seite*." *Symposium* XXX, No. 3 (Fall 1976): 213-35.
 Maintains that *The Other Side* "reads like a creative manifesto" of Surrealism, in that Kubin's "quest for the imagination began with a fictional excursion to the realm of sleep and led to a new knowledge of the true nature of the fantastic and the real. In doing so, it prefigured and paralleled the road that the Surrealist movement was to take more than a decade later."

Sebba, Gregor. Introduction to *Kubin's "Dance of Death," and Other Drawings*, by Alfred Kubin, pp. v-x. New York: Dover Publications, 1973.
 Discusses Kubin's life and his literary and graphic art.

Francis Ledwidge

1887-1917

Irish poet.

Often called "the Burns of Ireland," Ledwidge is considered one of the most talented traditional poets to rise out of the Irish peasantry in the twentieth century. His intimate association with the countryside of County Meath as a farm laborer and road worker provided him with the material for the pastoral, romantic verses that prompted Lord Dunsany to proclaim him "the poet of the blackbird." Although Ledwidge produced only a small body of work before he was killed in World War I, his verses have received consistent critical praise for their simplicity, spontaneity, and original phrasing.

Ledwidge was the seventh of eight children born to a farm laborer and his wife. When Ledwidge was four years old his father died, leaving his mother to support her children single-handedly. Neighbors suggested that the widow put some of her children in a state home or send them to work, but, determined to keep her family together and resolved that her children should be educated, Ledwidge's mother resisted and herself assumed several local farming jobs. Described as an "erratic genius" by his schoolmaster, Ledwidge was a bright, interested student who acquired the nickname "The Boy Who Knew Too Much." His early interest in writing verse was sharpened by his membership in a newspaper-sponsored junior literary society. He entered and won prizes in the club's competitions and was at the top of his class when he left school at age thirteen in the spring of 1901. Upon leaving school, he worked as a farm laborer for landowners in the neighborhood and, over the next several years, held a number of positions, including domestic servant, shop assistant, road worker, and copper miner. Popular, talkative, and entertaining, he often recited humorous or impromptu verses to his amused coworkers. While working at the mine he once read his "Song of Spring" as an encouragement to the winter-weary miners, and one of his coworkers was so stirred by the verse that he sent it, without Ledwidge's knowledge, to the *Drogheda Independent;* it was published in the next issue, and Ledwidge soon became a frequent contributor to the newspaper. In 1912, emboldened by his success with the *Independent,* Ledwidge sent a copybook of poems to Lord Dunsany, a widely known Irish dramatist and poet. Dunsany responded to the verses enthusiastically and initiated a bond of friendship and patronage. The younger man frequently cycled to Dunsany Castle, where Lord Dunsany allowed him the use of the library and tutored him in poetics. Acting on behalf of Ledwidge, Dunsany sent several of Ledwidge's verses to notable periodicals for publication. The first to respond affirmatively was the *Saturday Review,* which published "Behind the Closed Eye" in September 1912. Through Dunsany, Ledwidge also met other Irish writers, including A. E., Thomas MacDonagh, and Katherine Tynan, and he became increasingly conscious of the heritage he shared with them, both literary and political. An ardent nationalist, Ledwidge became involved in local politics and was a member of the Irish Volunteers.

When Britain declared war on Germany in August 1914, Ledwidge enlisted in the Royal Inniskilling Fusiliers, a predominantly Irish regiment of the British Army in which Dunsany had received a commission. In July 1915, Ledwidge's division

was ordered to Gallipoli, and in October the Fusiliers were sent to battle the Bulgars in Serbia, where Ledwidge received a copy of his first published volume, *Songs of the Fields.* As he had done since the beginning of his service, he continued to send new poems to Dunsany, who was then training recruits in Ireland. According to Ledwidge: "I scribble [poems] off in odd moments, and, if I do not give them to someone, they become part of the dust of the earth and little things stuck on the ends of hedges when the wind has done with them." He collapsed due to exhaustion and cholecystitis on the retreat march through Macedonia and was taken to a hospital in Egypt. He recovered slowly and was consequently shipped to Manchester on medical leave in April 1916. He arrived in England in time to hear the first reports of the Easter Rebellion in Dublin. His initial satisfaction was replaced by sorrow, however, as he mourned those who were executed by the British after the uprising. Among those executed was his friend and fellow-poet, Thomas MacDonagh.

After a lengthy recuperation, Ledwidge was assigned to the Western Front. Writing to Katherine Tynan in Januray 1917, he explained: "I am a unit in the Great War, doing and suffering, admiring great endeavour and condemning great dishonour. I may be dead before this reaches you, but I will have done my part. Death is as interesting to me as life. I have seen so much of it from Suvla to Serbia and now in France. I am always homesick. I hear the roads calling, and the hills, and the rivers wondering where I am. It is terrible to be always homesick.'' Six months later he was killed when a shell exploded near him during the Third Battle of Ypres. Ledwidge was buried near Boesinghe, Belgium.

The verses comprising Ledwidge's first volume of poetry, *Songs of the Fields,* were collected by Lord Dunsany in 1914, but publication was delayed for two years due to the uncertainty of wartime conditions. According to most critics, Ledwidge's first volume contains the best of his verse written before the war. Reflecting his abiding love for and fascination with the Meath countryside, Ledwidge's poetry is romantic in mood and traditional in form. According to a contemporary critic writing in the *Saturday Review,* these pastoral verses exhibit an ''especial grace to be even, to flow without harsh pauses or sudden arresting of the ear. They are not deep or grasping. They are slender and fluent, without dropping into commonplace.'' Ledwidge's second volume, *Songs of Peace,* was also highly praised by contemporary reviewers. Critics have observed in Ledwidge's verses an unaffected spontaneity and original and beautiful phrasing reminiscent of John Keats. Although all of the poems collected in *Songs of Peace* were written by a soldier—in the barracks, at the front, in the hospital, or on leave—none takes war as its subject. Indeed, some critics have proposed that Ledwidge does not belong to the group of soldier-poets, among whom he is often placed, because he never wrote conventional war poetry. While Ledwidge did continue to write of the woods and rivers, he did so not with the optimism and artlessness of *Songs of the Fields,* but with nostalgia. Critic A. C. Ward has suggested that ''Ledwidge, though his poems are quiet in mood, seemed to induce calm within his soul by deliberately turning his eyes and thoughts from the actualities of war; turning to Nature as an antidote for the poison of conflict.'' Included in *Songs of Peace* are two poems inspired by the Easter Rebellion, an event which aroused new feelings of national pride in Ledwidge. The more successful of the two poems, ''Thomas MacDonagh,'' which is patriotic as well as personal in subject, is often cited by critics as one of Ledwidge's finest achievements.

Last Songs, Ledwidge's third and generally considered best collection, was posthumously compiled from the manuscripts he had sent Dunsany while on medical leave and at the Western Front. Yet, as John Drinkwater has noted, even *Last Songs* ''has little of the war in it, and only once, in the charming 'Soliloquy' is there a martial note.'' Composed of the same subjects as his earlier volumes, and demonstrating an increasing mastery of form, the verses in *Last Songs* again nostalgically recall the Meath countryside. And, according to Ledwidge's biographer Alice Curtayne: ''The notable point about these songs is that they are not visual but remembered descriptions, drawn with the same fidelity of detail as if he wrote within sight of the hills and the river.''

In Ledwidge's own opinion, his brief career ended before he had written to his full potential. He wrote: ''I feel something great struggling in my soul but it can't come until I return; if I don't return it will never come.'' Many critics agree that he might have become a major poet if he had lived, and none dismiss the success that he did achieve. According to Padraic Colum, Ledwidge ''wrote about simple and appealing things, and he wrote about them in a way that may leave his poetry more cherished than the poetry of any of the young men who have been lost to us in the disaster of the war.'' Curtayne has

concluded that ''hundreds of poets have gone down into the Limbo of the forgotten during the past fifty years, but Ledwidge's poetry lives on. It is no small triumph that it has survived the death of the Romantic School and the final fading of the Celtic Twilight.''

(See also *Dictionary of Literary Biography,* Vol. 20: *British Poets, 1914-1945.*)

PRINCIPAL WORKS

Songs of the Fields   (poetry)   1916
Songs of Peace   (poetry)   1917
Last Songs   (poetry)   1918
The Complete Poems of Francis Ledwidge   (poetry)   1919; also published in an enlarged edition in 1974

LORD DUNSANY   (essay date 1914)

[*An Irish dramatist, fiction writer, poet, and critic, Dunsany is viewed as a significant force in modern fantasy literature for his novels and stories based on an invented mythology of gods and demons. He is also considered instrumental in the development of a national dramatic literature for Ireland. He wrote his first drama,* The Glittering Gate *(1909), for Dublin's Abbey Theatre at the request of William Butler Yeats. Dunsany's dramas, often set in exotic or imagined locations, depict reckless men whose greed and pride result in their undoing. Poetic in style, his works reflect his interest in the romantic and the mystic, as well as his preference for well-made plots and surprising conclusions. In the following excerpt from his introduction to* Songs of the Fields, *which was written before the outbreak of World War I in Europe, but not published until 1916, Dunsany characterizes Ledwidge's poetry and assesses its virtues.*]

If one who looked from a tower for a new star, watching for years the same part of the sky, suddenly saw it (quite by chance while thinking of other things), and knew it for the star for which he had hoped, how many millions of men would never care?

And the star might blaze over deserts and forests and seas, cheering lost wanderers in desolate lands, or guiding dangerous quests; millions would never know it.

And a poet is no more than a star.

If one has arisen where I have so long looked for one, amongst the Irish peasants, it can be little more than a secret that I shall share with those who read this book because they care for poetry.

I have looked for a poet amongst the Irish peasants because it seemed to me that almost only amongst them there was in daily use a diction worthy of poetry, as well as an imagination capable of dealing with the great and simple things that are a poet's wares. Their thoughts are in the spring-time, and all their metaphors fresh: in London no one makes metaphors any more, but daily speech is strewn thickly with dead ones that their users should write upon paper and give to their gardeners to burn.

In this same London, two years ago, where I was wasting June, I received a letter one day from Mr. Ledwidge and a very old copy-book. The letter asked whether there was any good in the verses that filled the copy-book, the produce apparently of

Lord Dunsany in August 1914. By permission of Martin Brian & O'Keeffe Ltd.

four or five years. It began with a play in verse that no manager would dream of, there were mistakes in grammar, in spelling of course, and worse—there were such phrases as "'thwart the rolling foam," "waiting for my true love on the lea," etc., which are vulgarly considered to be the appurtenances of poetry; but out of these and many similar errors there arose continually, like a mountain sheer out of marshes, that easy fluency of shapely lines which is now so noticeable in all that he writes; that and sudden glimpses of the fields that he seems at times to bring so near to one that one exclaims, "Why, that is how Meath looks," or "It is just like that along the Boyne in April," quite taken by surprise by familiar things: for none of us knows, till the poets point them out, how many beautiful things are close about us.

Of pure poetry there are two kinds, that which mirrors the beauty of the world in which our bodies are, and that which builds the more mysterious kingdoms where geography ends and fairyland begins, with gods and heroes at war, and the sirens singing still, and Alph going down to the darkness from Xanadu. Mr. Ledwidge gives us the first kind. When they have read through the profounder poets, and seen the problem plays, and studied all the perplexities that puzzle man in the cities, the small circle of readers that I predict for him will turn to Ledwidge as to a mirror reflecting beautiful fields, as to a very still lake rather on a very cloudless evening.

There is scarcely a smile of Spring or a sigh of Autumn that is not reflected here, scarcely a phase of the large benedictions

of Summer; even of Winter he gives us clear glimpses sometimes, albeit mournfully, remembering Spring.

> In the red west the twisted moon is low,
> And on the bubbles there are half-lit stars:
> Music and twilight: and the deep blue flow
> Of water: and the watching fire of Mars.
> The deep fish slipping through the moonlit bars
> Make death a thing of sweet dreams,—

What a Summer's evening is here.

And this is a Summer's night in a much longer poem that I have not included in this selection, a summer's night seen by two lovers:

> The large moon rose up queenly as a flower
> Charmed by some Indian pipes. A hare went by,
> A snipe above them circled in the sky.

And elsewhere he writes, giving us the mood and picture of Autumn in a single line:

> And somewhere all the wandering birds have flown.

With such simple scenes as this the book is full, giving nothing at all to those that look for a "message," but bringing a feeling of quiet from gleaming Irish evenings, a book to read between the Strand and Piccadilly Circus amidst the thunder and hootings.

To every poet is given the revelation of some living thing so intimate that he speaks, when he speaks of it, as an ambassador speaking for his sovereign; with Homer it was the heroes, with Ledwidge it is the small birds that sing, but in particular especially the blackbird, whose cause he champions against all other birds almost with a vehemence such as that with which men discuss whether Mr.——, M.P., or his friend the Right Honourable——is really the greater ruffian. (pp. 7-11)

Let us not call him the Burns of Ireland, you who may like this book, nor even the Irish John Clare, though he is more like him, for poets are all incomparable (it is only the versifiers that resemble the great ones), but let us know him by his own individual song: he is the poet of the blackbird.

I hope that not too many will be attracted to this book on account of the author being a peasant, lest he come to be praised by the how-interesting! school; for know that neither in any class, nor in any country, nor in any age, shall you predict the footfall of Pegasus, who touches the earth where he pleaseth and is bridled by whom he will. (pp. 11-12)

> *Lord Dunsany, in an introduction to* Songs of the Fields *by Francis Ledwidge, Herbert Jenkins Limited, 1916, pp. 7-12.*

THE SATURDAY REVIEW, LONDON   (essay date 1915)

[*In the following excerpt, the critic offers an enthusiastic review of* Songs of the Fields, *portions of which appeared in the* Saturday Review *prior to their publication in book form.*]

The appeal of these songs . . . is sharpened to-day as the appeal of the remoter countryside is sharpened, or of any far corner of life untroubled by the war. In reading them we are released from the present and again secluded among the late incredible years of peace. All that belongs to the past years has now a quality of reminiscence. The river or beach where once we were able to refresh ourselves we cannot now enjoy as a contemporary thing. "This," we say to ourselves, "is the place we used to frequent in that former life." We see it as we saw it in the past, not as we see it to-day. So with these songs; we seem to be listening less to the songs themselves than to the echo of a song whose charm to-day is chiefly that yesterday, when all was quite different, it chimed with an irrevocable mood.

Mr. Ledwidge is now a corporal in the 5th Battalion of the Royal Inniskilling Fusiliers; but all these songs were composed before the war, and all are songs of the country. It was their rare merit to be really simple—simple in a natural and unstudied fashion—at a time when simplicity was desperately sought after, very closely studied, and very rarely natural. The simplicity of Mr. Ledwidge is not the false simplicity of neo-primitives—a mannered aping of the tramp and vagabond, which caused fresh young men from Oxford to tie up their boots with string and suspect the good faith of any author who wore a hard hat. His simple verses are the spontaneous expression of his simple love of the Irish fields, and the feeling of these songs is sincere enough to take us back from the present fields of war. They distil for us the peace we have almost forgotten, before the blackbird's song was heard against the bugles. Mr. Ledwidge was really happy in the fields, not with the happiness of an escaped townsman, but with the happiness of one who has never known or been broken to the town.

Mr. Ledwidge plays upon a boxwood flute. It is an instrument he should covet; for an English poet has already given it to the blackbird, who is the most constant presence in these Irish songs. To spend elaborate criticism upon his verses would be out of keeping with their quality. It is their especial grace to be even, to flow without harsh pauses or sudden arresting of the ear. They are not deep or grasping. They are slender and fluent, without dropping into commonplace. To insist upon this verse or that, to point to any especial image or thought in them, would be an injustice to the essential roundness of their accomplishment. Mr. Ledwidge does not strike out single lines which insist upon the ear. He begins and finishes his song in the same key; and his songs must be quoted whole or not at all. This is a book upon which new readers must have the personal assurance of those who have already read. Neither quotation nor comparison will serve. Quotation is rarely just, and comparison is invariably foolish. Is Keats a greater poet than Shelley? Is Wordsworth or Milton the better man? These are questions which no wise person asks; and not the wisest person can satisfactorily answer. We shall not compare Mr. Ledwidge with his contemporaries, but say merely that we like his verses and look to him to fulfil their promise in happier years than this.

> *"A Boxwood Flute,"* in The Saturday Review, London, Vol. 120, No. 3129, October 16, 1915, p. vi.

THE NEW YORK TIMES BOOK REVIEW (essay date 1916)

[*In the following excerpt, the reviewer favorably assesses* Songs of the Fields.]

When one opens a new book of verses and finds that the first line of the first poem is "I love the wet-lipped wind that stirs the hedge," reads a few pages further that "dykes are spitting violets to the breeze," and that on a rainy day in April "the meek daisy holds aloft her pail"—then one is glad that he has opened the book! For such engagingly fresh phrasing as this promises well for the general excellence of the collection in which it is found.

And this promise is most abundantly fulfilled. Francis Ledwidge's *Songs of the Fields* is a delight—it is the work of a man who, in addition to being an original and accomplished maker of lovely phrases, is that much rarer thing, a poet. The reader of his accurately beautiful studies of the Irish countryside ceases to marvel at his verbal dexterity, so compelling is the spirit behind his work, so apparent is that indefinable quality which is the sure evidence of what we call poetic inspiration.

Francis Ledwidge is a soldier—he is a Lance Corporal in the Fifth Battalion of the Royal Inniskilling Fusiliers. But his work has no resemblance to that of the suddenly famous soldier-poet, the late Rupert Brooke. Ledwidge is not, as was Brooke, an eager experimenter in poetic forms, nor is he an interested student of his own emotions. His best verse is objective, and his lyrics are as simple in scheme as they are direct in thought.

Few contemporary literary biographies are more picturesque than that of this new-found Irish singer. He is a peasant, and began in his boyhood to work on a farm. This labor, arduous as it may have been, is a thing for which the world may well be grateful, for it stamped upon his brain and heart impressions of meadows and gardens which the town-bred poet, however great his love of nature, must regard with admiration and envy. . . .

Ledwidge's poetry cannot be accurately described or symbolized. The originality of his metaphor suggests some of the Elizabethans—Ben Jonson would not have disdained that "Bee-sucked bough of woodbine." But the Elizabethans were usually conscious of the beauty of their own conceits; their most striking phrases were deliberately original, the result of ingenuity and effort, while Ledwidge is original chiefly because he is spontaneous. He is not a poet trying to share a peasant's experiences; he is a peasant with a poet's gift of utterance. His soul has been thrilled with the blackbird's melody, and he knows the grateful freshness that comes over his whole body when, after a sunny afternoon's labor in the hayfield, he thrusts his dry mouth into the great barrel that stands hospitably open to the skies down by the East Gate. And so he says that the blackbird's flute is sweet as rainwater—when a poet less gifted would say "sweet as honey."

There is something about Ledwidge's work which suggests W. H. Davies. Davies, too, is a genuine lover of nature, and, like Ledwidge, he has been obliged by circumstances to live more intimately with nature than do poets with comfortable incomes. But Davies is more whimsical than his Irish brother poet; he is more given to portraying the ideas which a meadow or a forest give him than in portraying the meadow or the forest. Also he has—or had in his earlier work—certain bad habits, such as trying to rhyme words that no one could make rhyme, and padding out his meter with "do's" and "did's." These faults Ledwidge avoids, perhaps on the advice of Lord Dunsany, who taught the poet, he tells us [see excerpt dated 1914], to give over the use of such phrases as "'thwart the rolling foam" and "waiting for my true love on the lea." His rhymes are accurate, his rhythms musical, and there is a grateful absence of "poetic" turns of speech and other affectations. . . .

There is one poem in this book, (it bears the typically Celtic title **"Behind the Closed Eye,"**) which Ledwidge wrote when he was only 16 years old. He was working in a grocer's shop in Dublin, and among the sacks of potatoes, barrels of flour and festoons of bacon, he dreamed of Slane, where he was born. And the thing that called him most strongly was not the church-spire "toned smoothly down as the holy minds within," nor the poppies "weeping the dew," nor the dawn cobweb "like an apron full of jewels"—it was not any of these lost delights that tugged most strongly at his heartstrings, it was the blackbird, "wondrous, impudently sweet," calling down the lane "like the piper of Hamelin." . . .

It is the blackbird that gives Ledwidge a theme for some of his loveliest songs. But he has also an appreciative ear for "the dropping words of larks," and all the sweet gossip of "the roadside birds upon the tops of dusty hedges in a world of Spring." He has not been left untouched by the renascence of ancient Irish lore, in which Lord Dunsany has played so important a part, and his **"The Sorrow of Findebar"** and **"Before the War of Cooley"** are strikingly vivid reconstructions of heroic legend. But even more genuinely Irish is the feeling of that brief and melancholy poem called **"Waiting"**—a poem of which the very indefiniteness has a haunting magic power.

It is unfair to represent a poet by quoting unconnected stanzas. Nor can any one poem give an adequate idea of the richness and strength of this most unusual volume. But the first poem in this book is a typical Ledwidge poem—it shows his brave simplicity, his power to make out of words things lovely in color and sound, and, (in the last three lines,) his kinship with William Blake. So it is quoted here, merely as a sample, and with the candid declaration that, good as it is, it is not the best poem in the book. It is called **"To My Best Friend."**

> I love the wet-lipped wind that stirs the hedge
>   And kisses the bent flowers that drooped for rain,
> That stirs the poppy on the sun-burned ledge,
>   And like a swan dies singing, without pain.
> The golden bees go buzzing down to stain
> The lilies' frills, and the blue harebell rings,
> And the sweet blackbird in the meadow sings.
>
> Deep in the meadows I would sing a song,
>   The shallow brook my tuning fork, the birds
> My masters; and the boughs they hop along
>   Shall mark my time; but there shall be no words
>   For lurking Echo's mock; an angel herds
> Words that I may not know, within, for you,
> Words for the faithful meet, the good and true.

"A Peasant-Soldier's Gift of Poetry," in The New York Times Book Review, *January 23, 1916, p. 25.*

THE TIMES LITERARY SUPPLEMENT (essay date 1917)

[*In the following excerpt from an obituary tribute to Ledwidge, the critic reviews* Songs of Peace.]

Last week brought the news that the author of these *Songs of Peace* has been killed. We have to sacrifice our young poets, like our other youth, even though all poets are born for a life of peace. But we feel the loss of this one peculiarly, not only because of his promise, but because in all his work he is a poet of peace. Even when a soldier he could not write of war. He did his duty; but he was homesick for peace all the while, and in this book he expresses his longing, not in any weak complaints, but in the memory and evocation of peaceful images.

No one can say what he would have been if he had lived. One cannot be confident about the promise of the queer tender beauty in these poems. He reminds us of Keats in his love of beautiful phrases, phrases that he makes himself, that are his own answer to the beauty of the earth, not merely phrases that

he remembers. But we are sure about the lost future of Keats, because of an intellectual power which does not seem to be implied in these poems. There is a beautiful nature, a beautiful answer to the beauty of the earth and of humanity; but it seems to be strangely passive, and where there is need, as there is in all art, of a little will power, a little conscious contrivance, he fails utterly to supply it. Often at his very best he spoils it with a piece of feeble versifying. It is not like the worst of Keats, which is perversity and misdirected cleverness. Rather it is sheer impotence, which is far more difficult to overcome than perversity. But we say this only because it must be said; and the moment we have said it we remember a hundred beauties and confess our own ingratitude. We have not read the first poem, **"A Dream of Artemis,"** often enough yet to be sure of it. We do not know whether it has cumulative power or whether it is merely a succession of beauties, not invented, but uttered in that strange passivity which seems to us to have been both the gift and the danger of Ledwidge. But of the beauties there can be no doubt. . . . One thing is certain; he did not write about Artemis because it is proper for poets to write about classical Goddesses. He wrote about her because there was for him a Goddess of the woods; she meant that which he had never seen in the woods yet knew to be there; the personal beauty which the impersonal beauty of nature tells us of; the Goddess who is like a woman yet wild, and who might be tender if she found her Endymion. And the poet always dreams of himself as her Endymion, of the reconciliation between nature and man in love, the love of the divine and the human for each other. It is Pagan in beauty, Christian in suffering, but it is always the same story; and the poet is apt to make it rather Pagan than Christian.

So when Ledwidge writes of Greece he gives us no stale classical fancies. It is an eternal Greece to him not the Greece of a literary past;—

> Before the early stars are bright
> Cormorants and sea-gulls call,
> And the moon comes large and white
> Filling with a lovely light
> The ferny curtained waterfall.
> Then sleep wraps every bell up tight
> And the climbing moon grows small.

He might be writing of his own Ireland; all countries under the moon are the same country to him.

There is a poem called **"My Mother,"** written in hospital in Egypt, where the mother is an imagined spirit that the poet has inherited:—

> She came unto the hills and saw the change
> That brings the swallow and the geese in turns.
> But there was not a grief she deemed strange,
> For there is that in her which always mourns.
>
> Kind heart she has for all on hill or wave
> Whose hopes grew wings like ants to fly away.
> I bless the God Who such a mother gave
> This poor bird-hearted singer of a day.

He was, indeed, born out of his due time, to quote the poet whom he echoes so beautifully; and he has been sacrificed to the needs of his time:—

> My song forsakes me like the birds
> That leave the rain and grey,
> I hear the music of the words
> My lute can never say.

That is the last verse of the book. And we, too, seem to hear a promised music as we read it. Whether a finer music we cannot tell. We only know that, like so many other beautiful things, it has been lost to this troubled earth.

"Lost Music," in The Times Literary Supplement, *No. 813, August 16, 1917, p. 391.*

JOHN DRINKWATER   (essay date 1918)

[*An English dramatist, poet, biographer, and critic, Drinkwater also directed and performed in numerous stage productions while serving as general manager of the Birmingham Repertory Theatre. He wrote his most notable play, the historical drama* Abraham Lincoln, *for that company in 1918. In works such as* Lincoln *and the verse drama* X = o: A Night of the Trojan War *(1917), Drinkwater espoused his fervent antiwar sentiment and "lifelong intolerance of intolerance." While these plays brought him popular renown on both sides of the Atlantic, critics were generally more enthusiastic in their reception of his light comedy* Bird in Hand *(1927), which has been cited as a well-crafted departure from his didactic historical dramas. In the following excerpt, Drinkwater surveys prominent characteristics of Ledwidge's works.*]

To [*Songs of the Fields, Songs of Peace,* and *Last Songs*] Lord Dunsany has contributed intimate little prefatory notes, full of generous delight in a new poet's work.... He says, in introducing the poet's first book [see excerpt dated 1914]:

> I have looked for a poet amongst the Irish peasants because it seemed to me that almost only among them was in daily use a diction worthy of poetry, as well as an imagination capable of dealing with the great and simple things that are a poet's wares. Their thoughts are in the spring-time, and all their metaphors fresh....

Ledwidge, he concludes, is the poet for whom he has been looking. We believe that underlying this passage is a misconception in general æsthetics, and that the definition arising from it demonstrably fails to fit the particular case of Ledwidge. In its profounder issues poetry depends little enough on the artificial—but not therefore negligible or worthless—culture that a man absorbs from the prosperous condition of his descent and his own early advantages of society and education. In the process, however, by which a poet comes to the final realization of his faculty such things are of considerable moment, and the nature of their influence is not such as is commonly supposed. Every poet, if he is to do work of any consequence at all, has to find himself through tradition; that is an unescapable condition of his function. Native wood-notes wild are no more of the most natural lyrist's untutored sounding than is the bird's ecstasy unaware of the generations, and almost invariably the personal ease of the young poet's song depends upon the degree of intimacy with the poetic resources of his tongue that he has acquired unconsciously by natural inheritance and early association. The most mannered early verse, after the merely imitative period, is nearly always the work of poets with no assimilated knowledge of literature in their blood who have suddenly become conscious of examples that others have never lacked. One cannot help contrasting with Ledwidge the case of poets such as Mr. Robert Graves and Mr. Siegfried Sassoon, who set out upon their poetic careers at twenty, having already made in the progress of boyhood the sound adjustment to tradition, the necessity of which some of us had to waste several precious years of early manhood in laboriously perceiving and meeting. It is they, and not Ledwidge, who fetch their first proper tunes to their own easy impulses, assured of a technical

Ledwidge in Mudros (after Gallipoli), November 1915. By permission of Martin Brian & O'Keeffe Ltd.

behaviour that they need not strain at. There are, no doubt, earlier poems by Ledwidge than any that Lord Dunsany has published, but we may take it that in *Songs of the Fields* we have the first work of any personal character. And from this through the three volumes nothing is more notable in the poet's external habit than his certain progress from a manner heavy with self-conscious discovery of English poetry, through which his genius struggles often but brokenly to its own gesture, to clear deliverance from this tardy constraint, when he writes of his own simple and lovely world with no touch of untutored circumstance, but in the sweetest and most delicate tradition of English song.

Whether these poems are printed in chronological order we are not told, though the dates given in the last volume suggest that they are, and they are certainly so arranged as to show direct continuity of development. From the beginning there are signs of imaginative waywardness and of the suddenness of inspired thought that are unmistakable in their meaning. On the first page we find, "And the sweet blackbird in the rainbow sings"; and the presence of poetry is clear. But for long the smallest flight is marred by the mannered or insincere turn. The wind "like a swan dies singing," the dusk is velvet, the moon is a pilgrim, the harebells ring. Not yet, either, can he use such a word as "sublime" in "Ah! then the poet's dreams are most sublime," with any of the sureness that belongs to mastery.

In his anxiety to do well by the demands of poetry for significant figures, moreover, he falls at first often into triviality and sometimes into real gaucherie. The "woodbine *lassoing* the thorn" is as unimpressive as the crane watching the troutlets' circles grow "as a smoker does his rings," and there is the same kind of poverty in "Autumn's crayon." Worse than these, as indicating some deeper defect of judgment, from which, however, he wholly recovered, are such phrases as "fog of blossom," and "facefuls of your smiles." Another uncertainty in his earliest work comes from the occasional confusion—by no means unknown in poets of far greater experience and power—of scientific knowledge with vision. It would be interesting to know something of Ledwidge's adventures in learning; one imagines that his eager mind, something after boyhood, went through a phase of delight in mere contact with formal instruction, and that for a little while to know a fact was as exciting as to realize a thing. Out of such a mood surely comes the little town's "*octagon* spire toned smoothly down," which is strangely what poetry is not; and yet he could turn his learning sometimes in his verse to right account, as in, "When will was all the Delphi I would heed."

These are indications in particular of the general directions in which the first book is weak. Against them, even among the poems that fail in any complete effect are to be set many tender and exact felicities, such as:

> And like an apron full of jewels
>   The dewy cobweb swings . . .

Or again:

> And in dark furrows of the night there tills
>   A jewelled plough . . .

Or, speaking of a poet,

> And round his verse the hungry lapwing grieves.
>   (pp. 180-83)

It is interesting to note that of the half-dozen or so poems in *Songs of the Fields* that have a legendary or historical source, all but one have little to distinguish them from the exercises of a true poet, while that one is, unexpectedly, the most completely successful poem in the volume. The explanation is, probably, that the set subject-matter at once subdued the natural play of his genius, and, by keeping him intent on an external responsibility, held him from the excesses to which he was yet liable in his freer meditation. And so, when with such a theme his faculty did for once break through restraint and soar above the occasion, as it did in **"The Wife of Llew,"** he wrote what seems to me, if the arrangement of the book is significant, to be his first delicate masterpiece:

> They took the violet and the meadow-sweet
> To form her pretty face, and for her feet
> They built a mound of daisies on a wing,
> And for her voice they made a linnet sing
> In the wide poppy blowing for her mouth.
> And over all they chanted twenty hours.
> And Llew came singing from the azure south
> And bore away his wife of birds and flowers.

It is fragile, a thing partly of the fancy; it has not the vivid and intimate contact with reality that was to make some of the later songs of such fine bearing in their little compass, but it is a lovely device, surely made. There are three other poems in this first volume that may be chosen for their rounded achievement as distinct from occasional excellence: **"The**

Coming Poet"** (though the first stanza is hardly good enough for the second), **"Evening in February,"** and **"Growing Old,"** with its perfect conclusion:

> Across a bed of bells the river flows,
>   And roses dawn, but not for us; we want
> The new thing as ever as the old thing grows
>   Spectral and weary on the hills we haunt.
> And that is why we feast, and that is why
> We're growing odd and old, my heart and I.

Songs of the Fields is a book full of expectancy. The reader leaves it in the assurance of an impulse that will overcome all its difficulties, and break presently from hesitant and alloyed grace into sure and bright authority. The development came, beautifully, and, in a few happy moments of complete liberation, to the height of promise, but it was won with tragic difficulty in the preoccupation into which the poet was called, and in which he was finally to perish. *Songs of Peace,* issued after an interval of a year, and presumably containing work most of which was written in that time, opens with Ledwidge's longest poem, **"A Dream of Artemis."** Here and there are slack lines, as, "Such music fills me with a joy half pain," and the poem generally, although it has dignity, and although its "Hymn to Zeus," has lovely touches in it, is unimportant in the body of the poet's work. From a word in Lord Dunsany's preface, however, we gather it to be of earlier composition than the rest of the book. The short lyric, **"A Little Boy in the Morning,"** has a first verse of lucky gaiety that is hardly maintained in the second. Then follows a series of poems under divisional headings, "In Barracks," "In Camp," "At Sea," "In Serbia," and so on, in which for many pages disappointment seems to be the destined end of our hopes. Still we have the frequent witness that here is a poet of the true endowment:

> The skylark in the rosebush of the dawn,

a beautiful image that he uses twice, by the way—or the right sort of particularity in:

> Dew water on the grass,
>   A fox upon the stile . . .

but still the full and easy realization of the manifest gift is deferred. The earlier blemishes are seldom present—it is but once and again we come across words of such relaxed imagination as "filigree," and yet the positive advance in creation waits. Then, towards the end of the book, we come to a poem headed, **"Thomas McDonagh,"** of which Lord Dunsany says, "Rather than attribute curious sympathies to this brave young Irish soldier, I would ask his readers to consider the irresistible attraction that a lost cause has for almost any Irishman." The political equation in the matter does not concern us here, nor does it concern anybody in the presence of what happens to be Ledwidge's first encompassing of profound lyric mastery. Its occasion was, certainly enough, an accident; we know that these enfranchisements of the spirit are dependent upon no outward circumstance. Here is the poem:

> He shall not hear the bittern cry
>   In the wild sky, where he is lain,
> Nor voices of the sweeter birds
>   Above the wailing of the rain.
>
> Nor shall he know when loud March blows
>   Thro' slanting snows her fanfare shrill,
> Blowing to flame the golden cup
>   Of many an upset daffodil.

But when the Dark Cow leaves the moor,
    And pastures poor with greedy weeds,
Perhaps he'll hear her low at morn
    Lifting her horn in pleasant meads.

The first stanza seems to me to be flawless, the second to have one slightly insensitive phrase—fanfare shrill—and an epithet in the last line that, while it is exactly appropriate, is somehow not perfectly used, while in the last stanza the precisely significant "greedy weeds" falls doubtfully on the ear. For the rest, it is a poem of that limpid austerity that comes only from minds slowly but irresistibly disciplined to truth. Its inspiration is a quality that, while it is immeasurably precious to those who can perceive it, escapes the sense of many altogether. It has mystery, but it is the mystery of clear modulation and simple confidence, not that other mystery of half-whispered reticence and the veiled image; it is at once lucid and subtle, and it has the repose of vision, not of fortunate dream; it is of the noon, not of the dusk. Preferences in these matters are temperamental; there will always be many more to divine the spirit of wonder in the depths and distances of a Corot than in the flat perspicuousness of a Cotman, but for some the very ecstasy of revelation is touched by the Norwich drawing-master. So it is with poetry; the shy song, the shadow-haunted, with its ghostly quavers and little reluctances, makes its own gentle and enchanted appeal, but for some of us it often leaves half-created what in intention was but to be half-said. For us, the power of presenting, in hard and definite outline, experience perfectly adjusted by the imagination to figures of reality, with imagery that never denies its relation to some intellectual concept and design by claiming sufficiency for itself, is the most hardly won and richest gift of poetry. It was to this power that Ledwidge's development moved, in the poem just quoted, where he comes first to its unquestionable exercise. Like all fine verse, it needs to be read not in silence only, but also aloud.

From this point in *Songs of Peace* we have two other poems, **"The Wedding Morning"** and **"September,"** of perhaps, as rare a quality, and two others, **"Thro' Bogac Ban"** and **"The Blackbirds,"** of almost equal attainment, and in *Last Songs* at least half the poems are written with assured lyric maturity and lightness. **"Autumn," "Pan," "To One Who Comes Now and Then,"** and **"Had I a Golden Pound,"** are, it may be, the most striking of them. This is the last-named:

Had I a golden pound to spend,
    My love should mend and sew no more.
And I would buy her a little quern
    Easy to turn on the kitchen floor.

And for her windows curtains white,
    With birds in flight and flowers in bloom,
To face with pride the road to town,
    And mellow down her sunlit room.

And with the silver change we'd prove
    The truth of Love to life's own end,
With hearts the years could but embolden,
    Had I a golden pound to spend.

The book, which, as a whole, is decidedly the poet's best, has little of the war in it, and only once, in the charming **"Soliloquy,"** is there a martial note, and there it is sounded in a slightly conventional contrast with a gayer mood. His songs, here as in the beginning, are almost always of the quiet fields of Ireland or the quiet fields of the mind, and his tenderness for this tranquil and fertile world was not, as it has so often

and less significantly been, the fruit of reaction against the squalor and confusion of war. He went to France bearing it in his heart, and there it prospered, in witness of his natural vocation, until he was killed.

Such a gift as that of a few lovely lyrics was at no time greatly esteemed by the world, and in these days, although love of beauty is by no means rare, indifference often smoulders into open hostility. And yet the world's esteem is so little a thing, and beauty so durable, asking but a little companionship. Ledwidge's poems gain nothing from that other gift that he so devotedly gave, that we so forlornly receive. That the world should spend a poet so may be the tragic necessity of the time's folly, and the poet himself least of all would make dispute about it. But nothing justifies the world's pitiable pretence that in making the supreme sacrifice the poet exalts and sanctifies his art; nothing is meaner than the appropriation to our own hearts of the glory of the soldier's death—a glory which is his alone. . . . And it is well for us to keep our minds fixed on this plain fact, that when he died a poet was not transfigured, but killed, and his poetry not magnified, but blasted in its first flowering. People, says Lord Dunsany in a letter, "seemed to think that one poet dead more or less didn't much matter." So many people, indeed, find in a poet's untimely death an emotional excitement, which if they were honest with themselves they would have to confess was far from being wholly unhappy, that is more vivid than anything else that they ever get from poetry at all, and if the untimely death is also a noble one, yet more punctual is this facile compassion for the arts. But to those who know what poetry is, the untimely death of a man like Ledwidge is nothing but calamity. There are indeed poets who, dying young with what seems measureless promise unrealized, we may yet feel to have so far outrun the processes of nature in early achievement that the vital spirit could no longer support the strain. Keats was such a one; the constructional perfection of the odes alone bears witness to an intellectual disciplining of genius so far beyond the normal reach of what was but boyhood, that nature had to sink exhausted under the pressure, and there was, perhaps, little of unhappy incident in the stroke that was but an inevitable squaring of the account. In other words, I cannot but think, however profitless such surmise may be, that if Keats had lived to mature manhood, the poetry of his first youth would have been of far less grandeur than it is. But nothing of this can be said of Ledwidge. His development was slow, and, while it was certain enough, it moved with no remarkable concentration nor to fierce purposes. He was cultivating his glowing lyrical gift with tranquil deliberation to exquisite ends, and nothing is clearer than that when he died he had but begun to do his work. His future was plainly marked. Already he had come through the distractions of imitation to a style at once delightedly personal and in the deepest and richest traditions of English lyric poetry. It is, perhaps, strange that his Irish nature should have sung its homeland in a manner that is, it seems to me, not Irish at all, but so it is. He was coming, in a few songs had come, to mastery in the succession of Wyatt and Herrick and Marvell and the lyrical Wordsworth and Matthew Arnold, and such later poets as Mr. Davies and Mr. Hodgson. And across his gentle maturing, with no providence of beauty won beyond the common achievement of poets thus young, death came violently, with no healing, against nature. (pp. 183-89)

John Drinkwater, "The Poetry of Francis Ledwidge," in The Edinburgh Review, *Vol. CCXXVIII, No. CDLXV, July, 1918, pp. 180-89.*

T. STURGE MOORE   (essay date 1919)

[Moore was an English poet, verse dramatist, artist, and critic. A "poet's poet," he was greatly admired by his contemporaries, most notably by William Butler Yeats, Ezra Pound, and Yvor Winters. Moore created verses recognized for their moral force and aesthetic beauty which combined both romantic and classical qualities, and, although he infused his verses with modern themes, many of his subjects were borrowed from early Greek and Christian writings. Composed in a heightened, archaic diction, his verses never found a popular audience equal to the unstinted critical praise they received. In the following excerpt, he appraises Ledwidge's verse, briefly comparing it with that of John Clare and the soldier-poet Charles Hamilton Sorley.]

Francis Ledwidge, as a poet, is the complement of Sorley; each brings us what the other lacks. Ledwidge has no constructive power, and the impetus of his cadences rarely carries him satisfactorily through even a short poem, whereas Sorley's rode on unchecked by weak lines and poor phrasing. Our new poet's language is, on the other hand, often over-poetical, and his images sometimes fantastically dazzling—an excess of the quality which critics perceive most easily and welcome most widely! And a vivid coloured flash on its surface is an important element in great verse. (p. 69)

[Lord Dunsany's preface (see excerpt dated 1914)] likens him to John Clare, our English pauper poet, of one hundred years ago, whose life among a nation of shopkeepers is the saddest idyll; and even to-day I fancy that Ledwidge might have been congratulated on his birth the other side of St. George's Channel, among people more patient with and more appreciative of poets. John Clare's poems were a series of delights over detail, grouped more or less as in nature by locality and season, yet rarely, if ever, shaped into a poetic whole. Ledwidge's verse stores details too, but they are less varied and less realistic, though better transmuted by his moods, for he is moved even more by the image that caps the perception than by the thing perceived. As a poet, at least, he too lived in a dream not yet articulated by reason and purpose. And one is tempted, though one has no right, to suppose that his life also may have had something of the ineffectual simplicity of John Clare's. His rhymes are related to those of Mr. Yeats and the minor Irish poets of to-day, as Clare's were to Keats', Wordsworth's and Cowper's, and I think this is all that can be really meant when he has been praised for style. Irish work may often seem to have more style than English, even when it is far weaker in the fundamental qualities of great literature. Dominant moods give it a singleness and independence of outlook which condones the absence of complexity in emotion and of balance in intellectual grasp.

> I saw the little quiet town,
> And the whitewashed gables on the hill,
> And laughing children coming down
> The laneway to the mill.
>
> Wind-blushes up their faces glowed,
> And they were happy as could be,
> The wobbling water never flowed
> So merry and so free.
>
> One little maid withdrew aside
> To pick a pebble from the sands.
> Her golden hair was long and wide,
> And there were dimples on her hands.

> And when I saw her large blue eyes,
> What was the pain that went through me?
> Why did I think on Southern skies
> And ships upon the sea?

I think this is as near as Ledwidge ever comes to organic perfection, though two freaks of phrasing fleck its very real beauty and success.

> And Gwydion said to Math, when it was Spring:
> "Come now and let us make a wife for Llew."
> And so they broke broad boughs yet moist with dew
> And in a shadow made a perfect ring:
> They took the violet and the meadow-sweet
> To form her pretty face, and for her feet
> They built a mound of daisies on a wing,
> And for her voice they made a linnet sing
> In the wide poppy blowing for her mouth.
> And over all they chanted twenty hours.
> And Llew came singing from the azure south
> And bore away his wife of birds and flowers.

If the success of this is smoother, there is to my mind a suspicion of the happy moment of a professor of poetry in its well-worn theme and the refurbished stock images of the Celtic Muse. **"The Death of Aillil,"** the most successful of his attempts at narrative, fails for me in the same way. *Songs of the Fields,* his first volume, rewards the reader far better than *Songs of Peace,* in good part written since the war began. (pp. 69-71)

The trouble produced by a soldier's life in such a mind accounts for the comparative poverty of the second book, rather than any failure of impulse or resource. Neither book is so much a collection of poems as a store-house of lines, phrases and images, with here a cadence caught and lost, there a striking thought—choice things, but rarely mounted to advantage, rather, to use his own words, like

> . . . an apron full of jewels
> The dewy cobweb swings.
>
> (p. 72)

> Day hangs its light between two dusks, my heart,
> Always beyond the dark there is the blue.
> Some time we'll leave the dark, myself and you,
> And revel in the light for evermore.
>
> But in the dark your beauty shall be strong.
>
> Pigeons are home. Day droops—the fields are cold.
> Now a slow wind comes labouring up the sky
> With a small cloud long steeped in sunset gold,
> Like Jason with the precious fleece anigh
> The harbour of Iolcos. Day's bright eye
> Is filmed with the twilight, and the rill
> Shines like a scimitar upon the hill.

These things are strung together with little apparent connection except the rhymes, each poem's structure being the pattern that these make. However, you could glean felicities in such quantities from no other of these Soldier Poets, not even from Brooke; and note that this underlines Brooke's superiority; his reflective and organic power makes more of fewer treasures. The best effect of reading Ledwidge is that which he describes in a poem dedicated to M. McG. ("Who came one day when we were all gloomy and cheered us with sad music").

> Old memories knocking at each heart
> Troubled us with the world's great lie:
> You sat a little way apart
> And made a fiddle cry.

And rivers full of little lights
Came down the fields of waving green:
Our immemorial delights
Stole in on us unseen.

The delight with which a child first perceives beauty, though it be forgotten, must never be barred and shuttered from return into the mind by coarsening habit or humbling care. If this happens, the enchantment of poetry is powerless. And as Antaeus' strength was increased whenever his feet touched the earth, aesthetic power revives when these primordial joys return into the lofty buildings of a master mind; and should these smiling visitors desert it finally, however noble the building, its charm grows cold; so important is this love of particular things and particular aspect of things to the mind. This tenderness over detail means more to poetry and painting than the theorist easily allows. Though perceived as a flash on the surface, this is a pulse of health that, having made youth perfect, can recreate maturity and old age. Everything that exists is holy, or at least demonic, when seen as a new and solitary portent; thus it appears first to the child, and must reappear to inspire the artist.

In these small books, those whom the war has hurried too much and too long, and those whom it has deafened and sickened with evil sounds and evil sights, may find a well of refreshment suitable to a convalescent mood that has not the energy to appreciate more elegant, noble or massive creations. Had he lived Ledwidge might very well have shown more constructive power than I seem to allow. He was still quite young when he was killed in Flanders; and those finer things that his genius would have created when it was fully organised were lost for ever. The choice and subtle images which crown his perceptions so frequently are in themselves structures, just as the cells of the body are living organisms. (pp. 73-5)

> *T. Sturge Moore, "Francis Ledwidge," in his* Some Soldier Poets, *Grant Richards Ltd., 1919, pp. 69-76.*

CONRAD AIKEN   (essay date 1920)

[*An American man of letters best known for his poetry, Aiken was deeply influenced by the psychological and literary theories of Sigmund Freud, Havelock Ellis, Edgar Allan Poe, and Henri Bergson, among others, and is considered a master of literary stream of consciousness. In reviews noted for their perceptiveness and barbed wit, Aiken exercised his theory that "criticism is really a branch of psychology." His critical position, according to Rufus A. Blanshard, "insists that the traditional notions of 'beauty' stand corrected by what we now know about the psychology of creation and consumption. Since a work of art is rooted in the personality, conscious and unconscious, of its creator, criticism should deal as much with those roots as with the finished flower." In the following excerpt, Aiken characterizes Ledwidge as an "idiosyncratic" poet who refines an aspect of well-explored poetic subject matter.*]

In a preface written in 1914 [for **Songs of the Fields** by Francis Ledwidge], Dunsany remarks that he has always looked for a poet to arise from among the Irish peasantry, because there "there was a diction worthy of poetry," and the "metaphors fresh: in London no one makes metaphors any more, but daily speech is strewn thickly with dead ones . . ." [see excerpt dated 1914]. In this, perhaps, Dunsany is mistaken. The Irish peasant diction is charming, fresh, but only from our point of view, being really static: it is not in the provinces that language is re-created, but in the clash of the metropolis. The Irish "peasant" diction, in so far as Ledwidge used it, has already been

thoroughly traditionalized—Yeats, Synge, Joseph Campbell, O'Shaughnessy, Lady Gregory, "A.E.," and a hundred lesser poets in Ireland, in England, and in America, have worn it out to the last thread. And it is fortunate for us, as for Ledwidge, that Dunsany has very greatly exaggerated the extent to which Ledwidge adopted this tradition.

That he did adopt it somewhat, of course, there can be no question. The Irish legendary heroes are here, the Irish tradition of oppression, the epithets of endearment which are becoming as commonplacently sentimental as rhymes in "June . . . moon." But these, as a matter of fact, are not "peasant" properties, and for any peculiarly "peasant" diction or sharpness of metaphor we search here for the most part in vain. Ledwidge has not at all for us the charm of the poetic *ingénu:* he is quite clearly a poet of the literary species. And, oddly enough, it is not the usual Irish tradition with which he had most to struggle for emancipation, but the English tradition, and in particular that strain of it which has come down to us by way of Spenser and Keats.

And it is above all as an "emerging" traditionalist in this line that we must see Ledwidge: he is a nature poet, melancholy, much given to the crepuscular mood, richly sensuous, but for the most part seeing the Irish landscape rather too much as Keats might have seen it, giving it rich phrase and full-vowelled rhythm rather too much as Keats might have given it. Let us grant that his temper, his sensibility, was very like that of Keats, that to see and phrase his landscape in this way would have been natural for him even had he not known the odes and sonnets: the fact remains that as Keats did precede him, it would have been vital for Ledwidge to have found, in the long run, some way of escape. There is little in the slight evidence before us to indicate that he would have made his place by sheer power: his success, had he lived, and had he obtained it, would have been of the idiosyncratic sort. And success of this sort he would, I think, no doubt have obtained. For through all his work runs a strain of lyric magic, now of tone, now of phrase; and if this is sometimes a little precious, or sentimental, or, in the literary sense, abraded, it is nevertheless, also, often sharp and sweet. The general average is extraordinarily high. And there are at least a dozen lyrics, and one or two very short narrative episodes, which represent in the best way what we call the "refinement" on the traditional—the traditional plus the singular, idiosyncratic bitterness or sweetness. These things have great beauty, are in a small way perfect. And they raise further the tantalizing problem of the extent to which Ledwidge would have freed this note from among notes less his own, or even, perhaps, discovered in himself yet others. (pp. 379-80)

> *Conrad Aiken, "Idiosyncrasy and Tradition," in* The Dial, *Vol. 69, March, 1920, pp. 376-80.*

LOUIS C. ZUCKER   (essay date 1922)

[*In the following excerpt, Zucker compares facets of Ledwidge's poetry with the works of William Butler Yeats, John Keats, and Robert Herrick, among others.*]

No other poet so often rises out of Ledwidge's poems as Yeats; and first knowledge will see Ledwidge germane to Keats; an ardent brightness of line, in later poems, trails the flame of Herrick. Yet, above all, he is unlike these others—Yeats takes the charms of open nature as material for a beauty of his own ideal, and for symbolic beauty—he transmutes his first vision of the earth, keeping only a few actual traditional things for permanent symbols; Keats and Herrick are Hellenes, to whom nature comes in flame, and for whom her overflowing sensuousness is a stir to the voluptuousness of the rose-sandalled philosophers; but Ledwidge holds to his immediate absolutely natural vision, as a naïve nature—voluptuary, and so he remains.

Slane is his universe—likely, it is the ordinary ancient Irish village, as fertile and quiet as the old places in Andalusia—as beautiful, in season, as the constellated skies, and as unexciting to the sane. But for this Irish peasant, the skies and flowers and birds, with all their soul-influencing galaxies, are his vital being. With his clear, knowing eye and love of the place of the old race, and his abnormal fervor, he perceives the growing, moving things, flora or fauna—hardly any unfamiliar thing— and puts into his book, not merely their color and sound, but the grace, élan, mood, seemingly human purposefulness, nervous temper, of their motion or stillness—actual or divined. In the wake of the stirred silences of the early evening, he feels far splendors flicker (**"In the Mediterranean"**). He knows the life that is acting out in the hollows; he finds the glittering pleasure hidden by other admired things. And this whole virile play of the élan vital, in all its gradations, almost imperceptible reverberations, vividly discerned and heightened, set in native spaces and artless infinitudes of pure blue or flaming-white, lives upon his saint-white soul, communicating to him immediately its feelings, so that his poems give the life, in all fulness of beauty, in its air, its own feeling, the poet's feel of the whole, the disturbance in his heart—as has been said, in a naïve, sturdy simplicity, with a ripening sense of the pathos of it all.

Such is his world—without the witching persons and communal play of Herrick, without the pervasive concern with vivid human semblances of Keats or Rossetti; the personages he alludes to are, almost all, shadowy and have the same part in his settings as human figures do in post-impressionist landscapes. And his apperception admits only the Slane which the lone tiller in the fields, in the lines of a time-old knowledge, can know. More explicitly he sings:

> The silence of maternal hills
> Is round me in my evening dreams;
> And round me music-making bills
> And mingling waves of pastoral streams.
>
> Whatever way I turn I find
> The path is old unto me still.
> The hills of home are in my mind,
> And there I wander as I will.
>   February 3rd, 1917.

When the pangs of disappointment, of bitter wisdom, get barnacled in his soul, he still perceives them lyrically, as peculiar arrangements of his cosmos, turning his heart asmoulder, the while, perhaps, certain persons are before his vision; and when he is moved to analysis of emotion in a person, where he speaks out of his primordial mind, the outward signs and changes take him always to his skies, fields, and loves there habitationed,— beautiful for their own gorgeous lyric sake first.

> You looked as sad as an eclipsèd moon
> Above the sheaves of harvest, and there lay
> A light lisp on your tongue, and very soon
> The petals of your deep blush fell away;
> White smiles that come with an uneasy grace
> From inner sorrow crossed your forehead fair,
> When the wind passing took your scattered hair
> And flung it like a brown shower in my face.
>   (**"Before the Tears"**)

In his seclusive way, he approaches the heart of mankind—of plain, rural, perhaps untutored mankind,—by way of solitary things once used, now cast-off: old far-wandered boots,—by way of lonely places, marked with the vicissitudes or anodynes of men—"the battered bin that heard the ragman's story," "blackened places where . . . circuses made din"—by way of solitary or thronging somber places, deeming it

> "Noble love
> To sing of live or dead things in distress
> And wake memorial memories above."

Such is for Ledwidge the greater workaday world—storied driftings along his unchanging lanes. Yet, beloved and natural as his world is to him, certain of the ardently imaginative modern poets have turned his undertow of slight, unapparent wearying to a fitful hankering after fiery, mysteriously sensuous places—after Babylon [A.E.?] (**"After My last Song"**).

Ledwidge feels his world with an earnest, divining, tender immediacy, a lyric rapture or lift of swelling heart; at times, with a hastening of rapturous beat, as in certain wild passages of Keats and Yeats, mingling appeals to our associations of tender, majestic, voluptuous, sweet-tuned, fantastic, imaginative beauty or, with the same artistic power, to our moods of tragic strangeness, forlornness, perpetual defeat, interblent always with splendid nature-sensuousness. (pp. 259-62)

When sundered from Slane, there rises in him a pounding, paining, yearning back to the luxuriance, gorgeous vitality, and peace; he has rapturous, burning vision of each particular space there, living in its own peculiar splendor; a break springs in his heart, and, out of it, a hot high-maned surge, aglitter with many-colored fragments of dear, futile memories, with all his vain longings and burdens, all mingled in the one passionate, hopeless sorrow. It is the consuming cry of the bird carried afar from its nest.

> On the heights of Crocknaharna,
> (Oh, thy sorrow Crocknaharna)
> On an evening dim and misty
> Of a cold November day,
> There I heard a woman weeping
> In the brown rocks and the grey.
> Oh, the pearl of Crocknaharna
> (Crocknaharna, Crocknaharna),
> Black with grief is Crocknaharna
> Twenty hundred miles away.
>   (**"Crocknaharna"**)
>   (p. 262)

A naïve nature-worshipper, his being, at first, mainly in the world outside him, caressing of the gentle and the frail, kindled with the bright and the dynamic, with a deep racial feeling for the legendary, a son of the golden naked light, he was early fain of the majestic halo of more somber elements. The defeats which come perpetually to men of feeling were bound to visit and deepen him also—the Great War would surely have done enough, unaided. But, being purely a personality of feeling— never as mature intellectually as Keats—he was easily affected by subtle emotional tendencies peculiar to such a personality, and by convergent influences from greater poetic minds. From reading, he early became anxious for profound-seeming motifs, and allowed himself to drift, under the influence, as I surmise, of Morris, Swinburne, Rossetti, Keats, Yeats, A. E. perhaps, and, it may be also, of certain modern Donnians—into a consciousness of weariness with Time's changes, a darkness of amorous passion as idle as Petrarch's, a submission to vague sorrow. Ledwidge's one absolutely personal plaint was his passionate pleasure in and longing for Slane—the earth-child's love of place.

> I'd make my heart a harp to play for you
> Love songs within the evening dim of day,
> Were it not dumb with ache and with mildew
> Of sorrow withered like a flower away.
> It hears so many calls from homeland places,
> So many sighs from all it will remember,
> From the pale roads and woodlands where your face is
> Like laughing sunlight running thro' December.
>
> ("**To Eilish of the Fair Hair**")

Wherefore his devotion to the blackbird, as time out of mind associated in his soul with his home-fields, and also as symbol of Ireland as was the blackbird of Daricarn. He shares with impassioned sympathy the same emotion in Brooke.

> A little flock of clouds go down to rest
> In some blue corner off the moon's highway,
> With shepherd winds that shook them in the West
> To borrowed shapes of earth, in bright array,
> Perhaps to weave a rainbow's gay festoons
> Around the lonesome isle which Brooke has made
> A little England full of lovely noons,
> Or dot it with his country's mountain shade.
>
> ("**Evening Clouds**")

When life's moves and war took him from Slane—I repeat it here for the sake of continuity—his lyric was more and more of his inmost being, so that now the passion inspired by the out-of-doors there, and his own one deep yearning, were interfused, with a perfected lyric and artistic power, in poems like "**The Homecoming of the Sheep**," "**To One Dead**," "**Home**," "**The Lure**." (pp. 263-64)

And with changes which for him were harsh, aided by his reading, fell on him the three-fold burden of time, bereavement, being. Naturally an undesponding soul, he was by the shadow of uncertain doom, and by the deprivation of his loves, made melancholy unto death with a fatalistic languishment. (p. 264)

He came to utter himself, in moments, with the melancholy, passion-weary gesture, the bitter swelling of heart, of Dowson ("**The Lost Ones**"). It was tragic for Ledwidge to have come to this pass—he died before he was killed.

A few poems go in the high-pitched chant of Yeats; "**Thomas McDonagh**," among others, is even of Yeatsian imagery, while moving to the anguish of Chopin's *Marche*.

> He shall not hear the bittern cry
> In the wild sky, where he is lain,
> Nor voices of the sweeter birds
> Above the wailing of the rain.
>
> ("**Thomas McDonagh**")

In the later poems Yeats comes out, time and again—those being of a more voluptuous ardor of tone, more given to trouvère's language ("**Youth**"), of a different clarity, beat, and grace, though not an unnatural:

> And for her windows curtains white,
> With birds in flight and flowers in bloom,
> To face with pride the road to town,
> And mellow down her sunlit room.
>
> ("**Had I a Golden Pound**")

And other poems are interblent with Yeat's timeless pathos and seer's glow, and full-hearted, captivated beat ("**The Find**")—brightly or silvery sweet, or dimmed sad-hearted. There are, too, incursions of Yeats' fantastic mythic lore: "**Fate**" is a masterly instance. And at least one poem ("**After My Last Song**") is adorned with a Yeatsian motif ("When I am old and grey and full of sleep"). In the Irish poems ("**Before the War of Cooley**," etc.), William Morris seems to be the influence—Ledwidge, with his clear, earthly eye, could not follow where Oisin wandered. For discerning the subtler changes of mood as seen in a person's face, he has found, quite suddenly, a finesse and finality, a dramatic, unsymbolic mysticism, a naked eloquence of poignancy which, I feel, verge toward Rossetti's, without the Dantesque pomp, and with the plainer fervor of a simpler race. And strange to say, I have heard, now here, now there, the ecstatic wailing cadence of Wilde. In other words, Ledwidge is a soul of rapture for the beauty of the fields, of simple things, simple feelings—with a clear eye, with voice glowing into molten gold or silver, a heart growing into poignant discontent, a mind wishing for the subtelty and elegiac grandeur it was denied—therefore yielding to the influence of the Pre-Raphaelite and neo-Celtic poets—influences which, therefore, kindled higher his own psyche, heightened his art, his beauty.

We have looked at Ledwidge's world and the consciousness in which he approached it—what of his imagination? Its terms are from the minds of the Slane people, and the life out-of-doors there, with a few from the sea, the Bible, and romance. What the eye has seen and the ear heard, the imagination sees and hears with exceeding vividness:

> And he remembered me as something far
> In old imaginations, something weak
> With distance, like a little sparking star
> Drowned in the lavender of evening sea.
>
> ("**God's Remembrance**")
> (pp. 264-66)

It discerns imperceptible though haunting shades of hue and sound,

> Lovely wings of gold and green
> Flit about the sounds I hear,
> On my windows when I lean
> To the shadows cool and clear.
>
> ("**In the Mediterranean**")

Likewise it catches the dynamic in psychic silences,

> Yet something calls me with no voice
> And wakes sweet echoes in my mind.
>
> ("**The Lure**")

It makes deeper use of the mere lovely things of nature ("**In the Shadows**"). It imbues such a natural fact with immense human values. . . . (p. 266)

It opens out spacious and emotional infinitudes. Its stranger workings are motions under the influences already spoken of. It was, *au fond*, an imagination mirroring his immediately actualizing perceptive consciousness.

Now in singing his cosmos, it is immediately actualized with words, each of which is immediately complete, full of the color, movement, vitality, sound, air, feel, and emotional value, of the thing or motion—with gentle words, delicate-sweet words, words aglow, words of sharp dynamic leap, gorgeous words, glamorously complete elementary color-words, words disclosing life ("finny quiets," "ferny turnings") or naming it ("And when the sunny rain drips from the edge of the midday wind")—with most brief, swift strokes—the whole, musically modulated in mellifluously filed phrase, and set in a plasticity of flow, an amplitude of limpid clarity:

> . . . the twisted moon is low,
> And on the bubbles there are half-lit stars:
> Music and twilight: and the deep blue flow
> Of water: and the watching fire of Mars:
> The deep fish slipping thro' the moonlit bars
> Make Death a thing of sweet dreams . . .
>
> ("**Music on Water**")

There are single lines as magical as those in Keats' nature poems, "And silent changes color up the hedge."

Where the poet's idea was larger than the simple phrase, it will be discernible even there,

> She leans across an orchard gate somewhere
> Bending from out the shadows to the light.
>
> ("**May**")

More and more the absolutely natural medium acquired silver-stringed overtones, and sensuous glamor and hauntings, and the tones of an older ardor.

To complete the picture of Ledwidge as poet, the Irish poems should be painted in, before proceeding to the close of the paper. They are of a nakedly simple, brief, half-hushful, half-elegiac beauty, verging toward the majesty of certain Biblical passages. A certain gleam suffuses them which is rare in the other poems. They, too, are full of words touchingly, fascinatingly immediate in their setting down an actual world, with persons and moods actual in their way. They are full of an impersonal pathos, and reverence of return to the ancient of the race. The dramatic element, important part as it is of the beauty, is embraced in a subduedly-ardent lyrical beat. It may be taken as symbolical of eternal human motives, but it is not mystical;—simple as Rossetti's "Staff and Scrip," it is without the glowing flame and intense gorgeousness. A pattern of reverberating, if slender dramatic power, and of subtle thrill and lyric grace, "**Before the War of Cooley**" has not the high import of Antony's dying scene in Shakespeare's play, but I feel it is as fine in mere beauty—and here, as in the other narrative poems, are effortless, astonishing Wordsworthian wonders of portrayal ("And his grey head came shouting to the ground"). How majestic in almost shadowy sounds is the close of "**The Passing of Caoilte.**"

> And Caoilte, the thin man, was weary now,
> And nodding in short sleeps of half a dream:
> There came a golden barge down middle stream,
> And a tall maiden colored like a bird
> Pulled noiseless oars, but not a word she said.

While written with absolute artistic earnest and racial feeling, I yet feel that, in the main, it all came—not the matter only, but also the imagery and air—from Ledwidge's reading of the modernly popularized sources, and the new poets—chiefest of whom was Yeats. See "**Thomas McDonagh**," "**The Wedding Morning**," "**The Death of Leag, Cuchulain's Charioteer.**" Dr. Douglas Hyde's works were also of fertile use to our poet.

By way of final argument, let me include an analysis of the appeal of "**The Homecoming of the Sheep**":

Naïve largeness, delicately gorgeous simplicity.

Ledwidge's natural pagan-worship, of pure loveliness for itself—ardor in finding it, ardor of poignant surprise, with hauntings of pangs of yearning, and pangs for the strange fragility of it all.

The caressing closeness of Pre-Raphaelite vision.

Wondrously immediate actualization of certain place, movement, and mood, in all their color,—psychic, emotional, vital, motor fullness, touching the heart as with the side of a blade, shaking the blood with a ringing flower-strewn, fire-strewn waterfall. The lyric art is in a sort of magic mantle.

The delicately modulated peace and sounds and hues—the absolute virtue pervading.

A dominant, sensuously grateful atmosphere.

Withal here is a poet—his soul not only in the line of an ancient race, but unswerved from it—his eye for the kind of actuality always charming with its voluptuously grateful sights and sounds, crystal clear—his peasant love of place inextinguishable, yea, ever a poignant cry;—surely these appeal to our racial memory. Combined with these, are a fervor of gold and mellifluence of silver, both in a medium giving the life which his eye, ear, and heart were fashioned for, wholly and immediately, and in a pervasive halo of virtue, of universal spontaneous sympathy, and utter unfamiliarity with intentional pain,—appealing to fundamental ecstasies, to deep-seated adoration of the creative intellect, to instinctive ultimate preference for Nirvana or Arcady. And all these fascinations have been heightened with influx from the magic of Yeats, Rossetti, Morris, and other poets of like tone and vision. (pp. 267-69)

> *Louis C. Zucker, "The Art of a Minor Poet," in*
> South Atlantic Quarterly, *Vol. XXI, No. 3, July, 1922,*
> *pp. 259-69.*

PADRAIC COLUM   (essay date 1926)

[*An Irish-born American dramatist, poet, novelist, biographer, children's writer, and critic, Colum was a central figure in the Irish Literary Renaissance. He first gained recognition in 1902 as one of the founders of the Irish National Theatre, later known as the Abbey Theatre. Unlike William Butler Yeats and Lady Gregory, who were also cofounders of the Abbey, Colum rejected intellectual treatment of Irish issues and believed that Ireland would be most accurately represented by the dialect and lifestyle of its peasantry. Colum and John M. Synge are regarded by many critics as the company's most important nationalistic dramatists because of their emphasis on the speech and the attitudes of the common Irishman. Throughout his works, Colum sought to expand international recognition and appreciation of Irish literature, and his stories and tales are rich in mythology and Irish folklore. In the following excerpt, he favorably assesses Ledwidge's pastoral poetry.*]

Francis Ledwidge's is the poetry of the plain—specifically of the demesne land that is the County Meath. The land is beautiful under the light that gives its fields the greenness of jade, but it has scant variety of interest: fields, hedgerows and streams; larks, blackbirds and pigeons, with a castle or an ancient ruin amongst ivy-enwreathed trees, are what the eye of a poet would mostly note there. There are villages and people, of course, but the poet I have just been rereading might not approach the people unless they grouped themselves as people in an idyll.

He has been compared to Robert Burns, because his poetry came out of country life as seen through the eyes of a young man of the soil. But Francis Ledwidge saw country people and saw the country not at all in the way that Burns saw them. Indeed, his genius was at the other side of Burns'—it was idyllic where Burns' was dramatic; Francis Ledwidge responded not to the tumult but to the charm of life; it was his triumph that he made us know the creatures of his world as things freshly seen, surprisingly discovered. The first poem in his first volume let us know the blackbird's secret.—

> And wondrous impudently sweet,
> Half of him passion, half conceit,
> The blackbird whistles down the street.

He finishes the stanza with the line "like the piper of Hamelin," and spoils it with a literary allusion. Too often, indeed, he gives us the hieroglyphics of literary tradition. It was the fault of a young country poet who had something of the hedge-school in his culture, but it was a fault that he would, most likely, have got away from—"When will was all the Delphi I would heed," "Aeolus whispers to the shadows," "Like Jason with his precious fleece anigh the harbour of Iolcos." He discovered for us the blackbird's secret and he showed us the mystery that is in the slow-winged flight of the herons.—

> As I was climbing Ardan Mor
>   From the shore of Sheelan lake,
> I met the herons coming down
>   Before the water's wake.
>
> And they were talking in their flight
>   Of dreamy ways the herons go
> When all the hills are withered up
>   Nor any waters flow.

He did not attempt to conquer new forms, but he restored their graces to old ones. In **"To a Linnet in a Cage," "The Home-coming of the Sheep," "A Little Boy in the Morning,"** and **"The Herons"** he has left us lovely poems.

I have said that his genius was at the other side of Burns'. It was idyllic and akin to the genius of Theocritus. Indeed Francis Ledwidge was the Sicilian singer of our day, and it is probable that he would have made the discovery that Theocritus was his master. (pp. 244-46)

What the world now has of him is but his first song-offerings; the whole of his personality had not come under his control, and his verse-technique was not yet perfected. Let us be critical and say that he was unvarying and that he was immature. But we will have to say, too, that in everything he wrote there was the shapely and the imaginative phrase. He wrote about simple and appealing things and he wrote about them in a way that leaves them for us as glimpses of beauty—"Haw-blossoms and the roses of the lane" . . . "Spring with a cuckoo upon either shoulder" . . . "maids with angel mien, bright eyes and twilight hair" . . . "the bloom unfolded on the whins like fire." He knew the fields and hedgerows and he knew their haunters. Has anyone told us more about the blackbird, the magpie, the robin, or the jaythrush?

> And wondrous impudently sweet,
> Half of him passion, half conceit,
> The blackbird whistles down the street.
>
>   (p. 249)

His is hardly personal poetry. As we read it we feel that we might have dreamt the phrases he uses in his verses, or that

we might have heard them spoken by someone we met upon a road. How easily natural images arise in his poetry.—

> She came unto the hills and saw the change
> That brings the swallow and the geese in turn.

What he saw in the far places that war brought him to were things that reminded him of this Meath scene—the sheep coming home in Greece, and the rose torn from its briar in Serbia. The poems that he entitled **"In Barracks"** and **"In Camp"** are mostly made of memories of places and people at home.—

> And when the war is over I shall take
> My lute a-down to it and sing again
> Songs of the whispering things amongst the brake.

And he remembered.—

> White clouds that change and pass,
> And stars that shine awhile,
> Dew water on the grass,
> A fox upon a stile.
>
> A river broad and deep,
> A slow boat on the waves,
> My sad thoughts on the sleep
> That hollows out the graves.
>
>   (pp. 250-51)

Padraic Colum, "Louth, Meath and the County Dublin," in his The Road Round Ireland, *The Macmillan Company Publishers, 1926, pp. 219-59.*

LYLE DONAGHY (essay date 1931)

[In the following excerpt, Donaghy examines significant characteristics of Ledwidge's poetry and challenges Lord Dunsany's original definition of Ledwidge's poetic genius.]

It happened that while Ireland was remembering Padraic Pearse, and England was remembering Rupert Brooke, Francis Ledwidge was forgotten. One voice was raised in protest. In a Dublin newspaper run by Paddy Little there appeared a sonnet to Lord Dunsany, who had written prefaces for the successive editions of Ledwidge's poetry. The sonnet, signed "Fiat Justitia," included the lines:

> How could you think, a moment, it were not
> Better that England sink, than Ledwidge die.

In England the 'Last Poems' of Francis Ledwidge were reviewed in the *Times Literary Supplement* and I remember well my impression when I had finished reading that review. It was an impression of a slight volume of verse, the chief merit of which was its freedom from pretension, of a poet who rose now and again into gentle lyricism, but who could never really have been anything but very minor, who, indeed, had left nothing written of much meaning or importance. The best of him was represented by the quotation:

> I took a reed and blew a tune,
>   And sweet it was and very clear,
> To be about a little thing
>   That only few hold dear.

And what of this poetry? However much Lord Dunsany appreciated Ledwidge's genius, and I believe that he appreciated it more than any critic in Ireland, "Fiat Justitia" excepted, he was still far from appreciating it justly. What is to be thought of the critic who, quoting these verses:

Above me smokes the little town
   With its whitewashed walls and roofs of brown,
And its octagon spire toned smoothly down
   As the holy minds within.

And wondrous impudently sweet,
   Half of him passion, half conceit,
The blackbird calls adown the street
   Like the piper of Hamelin.

jams the two together, thwarting the cadences which close each; denying us two unities and producing a whole without centre of gravity, in which the parts have lost their true relationship—incidentally bringing the last line into too dignified a frame? Already weak, as he had observed, this was only tolerable while it closed a ballad-like four-line verse. The misquotation recurred in the collected edition.

It is true that Lord Dunsany deserves our gratitude for his part in bringing about the publication of Ledwidge's poetry; it is possible, also, that Ledwidge was in debt to him for a far more important service, for invaluable hints, advice, assistance; but in this article I bring a charge against him as a critic. The gravest part of this charge is concerned with his description of

Ledwidge's grave in Boesinghe, Belgium. By permission of Martin Brian & O'Keeffe Ltd.

Ledwidge's genius. Rightly pleading that Ledwidge shall not be dubbed "The Burns of Ireland" or spoken of in terms of John Clare, he proceeds, himself, to label him as the poet of the blackbird, at least to leave such an impression in the mind of the reader. If he had stopped there, little harm would be done; but in another preface he refers explicitly to Ledwidge's "rustic" muse, which seems to limit the possible range and power of the poet it is applied to—perhaps because it directly qualifies the genius rather than the materials through which a particular genius expresses itself. This is the heaviest footprint Lord Dunsany has left, for he reimpresses it again and again in the prefaces. But Ledwidge was only the poet of the blackbird because he was the poet of fields and hedgerows, of fields and hedgerows because of the flat land of Meath, of these because of nature, of nature because of life. He was simply a poet, singing a very clear song—for the rest, he used the colour to his hand. As to his muse being rustic, Dunsany only forgets this on one occasion, and that is where he remarks, in passing, on Ledwidge's not very frequent use of poetic diction, and instances his use of the word "lea." But surely for a word to be poetic diction it must be a transfer from poetry to life, and is it quite certain that such was the source of the word in Ledwidge's poetry? "Lea" is used by the country people in Ireland, north and south, to distinguish between the uncultivated and the cultivated. It is by no means in the same class with words like "kirtle," "steed," etc., and I think the distinction achieved, partly by its use, in one verse of Ledwidge's argues against its being poetic diction with him:

While the wild poppy lights upon the lea
   And blazes 'mid the corn.

To pass to the poetry itself, if Ledwidge's has any affinities in poetry, they are with Keats and Shakespeare, all of whose spontaneity he possesses, though he lacks much of their firmness and variety of rhythm, with other of their more splendid imaginative qualities. Again, if the type of his poetry could be aptly expressed by any phrase, more particularly than by the word "lyrical," I believe it would be expressed by saying that he is a "Golden Age Poet," for this quality is inseparable from the spirit of all his finest work, and is almost explicit in **"An Old Pain,"** where he seems to sing above peasanthood, culture, mythology, and yet in touch with all, listening how "old querns turn round within the brain," and crying:

I hold the mind is the imprisoned soul,
   And all our aspirations are its own
Struggles and strivings for a golden goal,
   That wears us out like snowmen at the thaw,
And we shall make our heaven, where we have sown
   Our purple longings.

Ledwidge is a "Golden Age Poet" by virtue of his own purple longings, and by means of the magic of his words. I will give one example of this latter from **"Before Tears"**:

Tear-fringed winds that fill the heart's low sighs
   And never break upon the bosom's pain,
But blow unto the windows of the eyes
   Their misty promises of silver rain.

It might be said that Ledwidge's strength is in the description of nature; but this would be far from adequate. To some extent it is true of him that he had no need to think philosophy—he saw it. His best lyrics are themselves symbols universally true; for so great telling always becomes great making. In many of the poems images are, as it were, supercharged with meaning:

And here the robin with a heart replete
   Has all in one short plagiarised rhyme.

Like steeping stones within a swollen river
The hidden words are sounding in my brain
Too wild for taming. . . .

Occasionally he is more directly philosophical, as in **"In the Dusk"**:

how could you wend
The songless way contentment fleetly wings?

Ledwidge's technique calls for more remark. He uses words as a master. Indeed, he was one of the earliest of modern poets whom all words served: the humblest are gold in his verse. I remember:

And like an apron full of jewels
The dewy cobweb swings.

And chrism droppeth on the world.

And breezes honed on icebergs hurry past.

. . . Bound to the mast of song.

Even when he is just half successful, as with:

You brought me facefuls of your smiles to share.

And dykes are spitting violets to the breeze.

we still have a feeling of complete sincerity about the attempt, and guess, moreover, that though it eludes us still, the vision was caught truly for the poet. (pp. 823-24)

In **"Thoughts at the Trysting Stile"** he sings of the orchard maid:

Inly I feel that she will come in blue,
With yellow on her hair, and two curls strayed
Out of her comb's loose stocks.

This is sophisticated, but Ledwidge could be more sophisticated still, and, be it remarked, more beautiful:

And her peal
Of laughter will ring far, and as she tries
For freedom I will call her names of flowers
That climb up walls.

Sadder, and yet more beautiful, it is this same sophisticated tone we catch in **"The Lost Ones,"** the one poem of Ledwidge which may be said to be well known, since it has found its way into more than one anthology; and yet one of the most surprising things about him is the bulk of his work which is good. **"Behind the Closed Eyes,"** **"The Linnet in a Cage,"** **"The Broken Tryst,"** **"The Lost Ones,"** **"The Herons"** are all beautiful lyrics; but, indeed, the lyric note is pure in almost everything he wrote, so that, as I have just suggested, his good work is remarkable were it from the point of view of bulk alone.

To conclude, I forbear all speculation as to the poet he might have become had he lived. Enough to be grateful for the poet he was. Especially in Ireland we should prize him; but we in Ireland are unhappily more concerned, at present, to build against a possible Upas than to make much of our garden, where the poetry of Francis Ledwidge is like apple blossom that shall not now come to fruit. (p. 824)

Lyle Donaghy, "Francis Ledwidge," in The Saturday Review, *London, Vol. 151, No. 3945, June 6, 1931, pp. 823-24.*

CORNELIUS WEYGANDT (essay date 1937)

[*A historian and critic, Weygandt was one of the first American scholars to examine contemporary Irish drama, introducing its major practitioners to American readers in his* Irish Plays and Playwrights *(1913). In the following excerpt, he emphasizes Ledwidge's reputation as "the poet of the blackbird."*]

You come to a rereading of Francis Ledwidge . . . with a quiet happiness. You sit and think of him with the book unopened in your hands. You remember certain lyrics very clearly, **"Behind the Closed Eye"** first, with its pictures of his birthplace, Slane, in that English-looking county of Meath. You remember **"The Homecoming of the Sheep,"** the background of which is Greece. You remember **"A Little Boy in the Morning,"** and you are in Ireland again. Then you find you can recall no other lyric by name. It is difficult, too, to recall any lines save:

The sheep are coming home in Greece,
Hark the bells on every hill!

You find that you have not all the lines even of this one poem in your memory. You cannot go on from the opening, but you recall lines toward the close of the poem:

And the moon comes large and white
Filling with a lovely light
The ferny curtained waterfall.

You thought you would never forget this poem, so way-off and sleepy it was, so intimately of the evening, so soft with moonlight. Yet you have forgotten most of it. You have had in your mind, from the moment that thought of Ledwidge rose there, that he was killed in Flanders. You are thinking now of what might have been, of what he might have written had he lived. You remember that Dunsany called him "the poet of the blackbird." You try to call up a line in which he praises the bird, or a line in which he catches its song. "The mellow ouzel fluted in the elm" of Tennyson comes to you, and "the boxwood flute" that Henley said the blackbird blew, but not what Ledwidge heard him whistle. You were too old, perhaps, when you first read Ledwidge to have lines stick in your memory as they did in the twenties. Or is there a lack of incisiveness, a lack of emphasis, in the phrasing of this peasant Keats? Is it that you delight in the soft rhythms as you read, but that the images are not hard enough to cut into what of you remembers and remain clear and sharp against the effacing years?

You remember what pleasure you had in reading Ledwidge, how many "purple patches" there were, and you open the book, thinking you will hunt for them first. You find yourself, however, turning the pages, looking for **"Behind the Closed Eye."** You find it is the second poem of your book. This book is *The Complete Poems of Francis Ledwidge.* . . . It comprises *Songs of the Fields* . . . [*Songs of Peace,* and *Last Songs*]. You thought **"The Homecoming of the Sheep"** came next of your favorites, but it does not. **"A Little Boy in the Morning"** came next. These two are from *Songs of Peace,* and as you read through the three collections you find this second collection contains most of his best poems. They were written, no doubt, after he was a soldier, but before he had a good deal of his vitality sapped by his service in the East. The verses written in Londonderry in 1916 and in France and Belgium in 1917 have a tired air.

You marked, of course, the lines you liked on your first reading, and you found others, on your second reading, that you had missed on your first. Now, on what is perhaps your seventh reading, you are finding others, as is always your experience in reading poetry that really counts. Dunsany, in his preface to *Songs of the Fields*, had called your attention to the first lines you marked. They are the lines in which Ledwidge praises his beloved blackbird:

> And wondrous, impudently sweet,
>   Half of him passion, half conceit,
> The blackbird calls adown the street
>   Like the piper of Hamelin.

Turning back to the "Contents" for the "B's" you wrote in for reference to the blackbird, you find there are sixteen poems so marked. As there are one hundred and twenty-two poems altogether in *The Complete Poems* there can be no doubt at all of how large was his concern for this bird. The blackbird is, indeed, to the British child what our robin is the the American child. Both are yellow-billed, and thrushes, and the friendliest of birds. They are both our familiars of lawn and garden, and they are both thieves of strawberries and cherries. Both run on the ground and listen for earthworms with heads cocked to one side. Both are cheery singers, the blackbird perhaps something more. The blackbird has been praised time and again by the poets. He is:

> The ousel-cock, so black of hue,
>   With orange-tawny bill

that Shakespeare sings. He is sung at length by Richard Jago, Cornishman and friend of Shenstone, in that mid-eighteenth century, which no matter how formal its poetry and its gardens, still felt neither complete without the presence of "feathered songsters." William Barnes and Thomas Hardy, Dorset men both, said their say about the blackbird in verses that all who read poetry have nearly by heart. (pp. 229-32)

How do the lines of Ledwidge in praise of the blackbird stand comparison with those of other poets, of old time and of to-day? The lines I quoted above give the fullest description we have of the song in all English poetry. I was tempted to say the most exact, too, but the songs of birds of the same species differ a good deal, and not only in quality and pitch and tone, but even in the phrasing. Hardy has told us that the blackbird whistles "pret-ty de-urr" in Wessex, and "purrity dare" in Ireland, a difference of phrasing as well as of tone.

In the first poem of *Songs of the Fields* is the first reference of Ledwidge to his bird of birds:

> And the sweet blackbird in the rainbow sings.

In **"A Rainy Day in April"** we find:

> And sweet the little breeze of melody,
> The blackbird puffs upon the budding tree.

In May, "only in spasms now the blackbird sings," but that song is so clear in his memory that he can hear it when he will. He can make it sound again in his ears. He hears it in "river voices," which are "sweet as rainwater in the blackbird's flute." Walking the paved streets of Manchester he thinks of Meath, "where Peace shuts the blackbird's wings." He notes with joy the singing of the bird after its first singing season is over:

> I heard a blackbird whistle half his lay
> Among the spinning leaves that slanted down.

He carries with him memories of blackbirds seen against backgrounds that made little wonders of composition:

> The blackbird in a thorn of waving white
> Sang bouquets of small tunes.

At war, Ledwidge longs for peace and Ireland, and the chance to be writing once more down by the Boyne:

> And when the war is over I shall take
> My lute a-down to it and sing again
> Songs of the whispering things among the brake,
> And those I love shall know them by their strain,
> Their airs shall be the blackbird's twilight song,
> Their words shall be all flowers with fresh dews
>   hoar.—
> But it is lonely now in winter long,
> And, God! to hear the blackbird sing once more.

It is curious how fully symbolical the song of the blackbird is of the verse of Ledwidge. It is not one of the rare songs, it is not one of the complicated songs, there is no bravura in it, no coloratura. It is a simple song, a homely song, but sweet and rich and clear. Every second poet speaks of its flute-notes, and rightly, but it is a very simple flute it suggests, a flute that is cousin to a penny whistle, that is not far from the old straight flute of village bands,—in short, a peasant flute. And all this that I have said of the blackbird's song might be said of the verse of Ledwidge. The imperfections of his verse are the imperfections of the blackbird's song. Says John Burroughs, describing the song as he heard it in England: "It was the most leisurely strain I heard. Amid the loud, vivacious, work-a-day chorus it had an easeful *dolce far niente* effect. . . . It constantly seemed to me as if the bird was a learner, and had not mastered his art. The tone is fine, but the execution is labored; the musician does not handle his instrument with deftness and confidence." With the exception of the "labored," this description of the song of the blackbird fits admirably, as I have said, the verse of Ledwidge. And so, too, does the comment of W. H. Hudson, who after quoting the above words of Burroughs, goes on to say: "Perhaps it may be said that, of all the most famed bird-songs, that of the blackbird is the least perfect and the most delightful." (pp. 232-34)

Ledwidge is more than just the poet of the blackbird, though to be that in itself would be a good thing. He is the poet of other birds, over thirty of them, "this poor bird-hearted singer of a day." . . . He knows the birds, his "masters in song," as few poets know them. A Hodgson or a Frost is as exact, but not many others. When he is not sure of a bird, as in **"Evening in England,"** he calls it "a marsh bird," and when he cannot recognize a song, as in **"Autumn Evening in Serbia"** or **"The Lure"** he refers to its singer as "a strange bird . . . singing Sweet notes of the sun," or to the song as "music of a foreign bird." So it is that when I read of "a brown rail" in his verses in one place and of a "corncrake" in another I put them down as different birds, as water-rail and land-rail; and when I read of a "thrush" and a "throstle" I believe him to be distinguishing between a stormcock and a song thrush.

He knows skylark and robin, linnet and sparrow, goldfinch and yellowhammer, owl and cuckoo, swallow and martin, swift and nightjar, kingfisher and woodpecker, crow and magpie, wood-pigeon and stock-dove, quail and curlew, lapwing and bittern, heron and swan, wild geese and duck, cormorant and seagull. Only in his reference to these last four is there question as to the variety mentioned. He is just as exact, too, in his reference to flowers. The birds have few poems to themselves, but they come in, as do the flowers, to add the beauty of little things known and loved to poems intimately human in feeling and conception.

Ledwidge writes about his home places in the countryside of the Boyne, Crewbawn, Crocknaharna, Currabwee and Faughan. He writes about his art of poetry; and love; and Celtic legend; and city scenes; and death; and vision; and country customs. **"All Hallow's Eve"** is a glimpse of what store of folklore he had, folklore as much English as Irish. His poems on Celtic legend are none too good. His poetry, like his name, is English. His place-names are Irish, but the poems in which we meet Faughan and Crocknaharna are English in quality. It is true not only that the Englishman's house is his castle, but that the village where he lives is holy ground, from which he can see now and then a vista of Paradise. So it is with Ledwidge. The light that never was on land or sea invests these little places by the Boyne. Places, indeed, as I once heard Masefield point out, have inspired almost as many English poems as love. (pp. 234-36)

It is the old, old stuff of English poetry that you find in Ledwidge, freshly felt and freshly phrased, and put in the old proved way that has come down to us from Spenser, and that has been followed by poet on poet who has held the old proyed beauty best. It is loveliness that Ledwidge is concerned with first and last, a kind of childlike loveliness, a loveliness of tender and gentle things; and there is no attempt made to avoid sentiment. He does not fall into sentimentality in what Dunsany has given us of his writing, but we, speaking of this kind of poetry, are in danger of so falling. It is moments of beauty that he writes about, moments of beauty awakened for him by nooks and corners that he loved, by flowers and bird voices, and by girls.

It is easy to cull good phrases from Ledwidge, good lines, "purple patches" that are gray and white and blue in their colors. "Bright eyes and twilight hair," "The blue distance is alive with song," "grey twilight hushed the fold," I find marked in the earlier poems. In **"Music on Water"** is a passage of which Keats would not have been ashamed:

> In the red West the twisted moon is low,
> And on the bubbles there are half-lit stars:
> Music and twilight: and the deep blue flow
> Of water: and the watching fire of Mars.

I marked a line in **"In the Dusk"** on an early reading of the poem, but it is only lately that it has begun to knell slowly in my ears whenever I think of its maker, "Always beyond the dark there is the blue." And here is a fellow to it which also, as Yeats puts it, "articulates sweet sounds together":

> And lifting slowly on the grey evetide
> A large and lovely star.

The loss of Ledwidge was, to my way of thinking, the greatest loss English poetry suffered through the World War. It must be remembered that he had had no trained criticism of his verse until he sent some of it, at twenty-one, to Dunsany in 1912. There was not much help from others until he came to be a little known in Ireland for his *Songs of the Fields. Songs of Peace* was an advance on the first collection. And if *Last Songs* merely marked time, that is easily understood. Poetry for all his love of it could not be first in his life while he was fighting. Nor can a man bled of strength by such experiences as were Ledwidge's in the East be at his best even in such moments of rest as he had in France and Belgium.

There are many kinds of attainment presaged in his early work. In **"A Dream of Artemis"** Ledwidge tells of some of the things

he loved, somewhat after the fashion of Rupert Brooke in "The Great Lover." Many of the things here listed he had still to write about. And, all the time, as the world opened before him, there were more and more things to write about. He liked the strange landscapes of Serbia and Greece, and they moved him to new effects in his poetry. At twenty-four he had felt:

> A hundred books are ready in my head,
> To open out where Beauty bent a leaf.

He was writing down to within a few days of his death, writing under the most forbidding conditions. There was never a young man with a greater impulse to create beauty. He who is a minor poet might well have been a major poet by now had the war spared him. (pp. 236-38)

Cornelius Weygandt, "William Butler Yeats and the Irish Literary Renaissance," in his The Time of Yeats: English Poetry of To-Day against an American Background, *1937. Reprint by Russell & Russell, 1969, pp. 167-251.*

ALICE CURTAYNE (essay date 1972)

[*Curtayne is an Irish novelist, historian, biographer, and critic whose numerous works combine her interests in Roman Catholicism and Irish history and culture. In the following excerpt from her biographical study of Ledwidge, she provides an overview of his poetry.*]

Ledwidge's poetry is of the Romantic School, which enjoyed great prestige in the Victorian era, but was rapidly losing favour in the second decade of the twentieth century. It was revived through the active, practical patronage of Edward Marsh whose volumes of *Georgian Poetry* and the interest aroused by the Poetry Bookshop infused new life into it. The influence of the Celtic Twilight, too, is on Ledwidge's poetry in its dreamy moods and dim landscapes.

Among the poets of the past on whom Ledwidge modelled his early work, Keats came first as is well known and has been too often said. (pp. 192-93)

The influence of Yeats's early poetry is also evident on Ledwidge's work: dwelling on unrequited love, repining for a lost Arcadia, recalling the heroic personages of the Celtic Sagas, being comforted by fairy visitants. But Ledwidge very soon learned to dominate the echoes of his contemporary and develop his own mature and distinctive mode of expression.

The best feature of his style is simplicity, not achieved without immense effort and for that reason deceptive to the uninitiated. People like Lady Dunsany and [Ledwidge's younger brother] Joseph Ledwidge, who had the opportunity of observing him at work, told me that he slaved at perfecting his verse. "You know how I love short words," he wrote in a letter to Dunsany. He preferred not only short words, but short lines, too, and short poems. This passion for terseness and economy sometimes led him into awkward constructions and flawed lines, but on the other hand its effect when completely successful was a dewy freshness, a delicate airy lightness as in that near perfect lyric **"A Little Boy in the Morning."**

He pursued intensity of expression not only in his choice of words and in the calculated length of lines and poems, but in his metre. Most of his first fifty poems are in lines of two-syllable feet, usually four or five iambs, varied with the trochee. But if the ground beat of his verse is simple, his rhyme patterns are attractively original. In his later period, Ledwidge becomes more adventurous, embarking on two long poems, **"A Dream of Artemis"** and **"The Lanawn Shee,"** and using a greater variety of two-syllable metre. But he never resorts to novel experimental verse merely to convey effect.

The notable development of his personal poetic genius was when he made his own of the Gaelic verse form of internal rhyme and assonance. The deep satisfaction of communicating with the past then thrilled through his poems. Notice the new assurance in the metre of his laments for Easter Week: **"The Blackbirds," "Thro' Bogac Ban," "The Dead Kings."** If the poet was snuffed out of life in his springtime, his genius had reached maturity in more than one enchanting lyric, such as:

> Had I a golden pound to spend,
> My love should mend and sew no more.
> And I would buy her a little quern,
> Easy to turn on the kitchen floor.
>
> And for her windows curtains white,
> With birds in flight and flowers in bloom,
> To face with pride the road to town,
> And mellow down her sunlit room.
>
> And with the silver change we'd prove
> The truth of love to life's own end,
> With hearts the years could but embolden,
> Had I a golden pound to spend.

"Let us not call him the Burns of Ireland, you who may like this book, nor even the Irish John Clare, though he is more like him, for poets are all incomparable," wrote Dunsany in his Introduction to **Songs of the Fields** [see excerpt dated 1914]. Since that time, however, Ledwidge has been likened with monotonous repetition to the Scottish national poet and to the English rural one. Burns, too, was born in poverty, lived in the country, made nature his inspiration, had to earn his living before he was fifteen, struggled for expression without benefit of formal education. But there the resemblance ends. Burns was a tedious moralist, Ledwidge was never didactic.

The nineteenth-century John Clare was also the son of a farm labourer, poor, uneducated, and would probably never have been heard of without the energetic help of a patron. Clare, too, had a deep appreciation of nature and of his homeland. He could conjure up rural scenes in vivid detail. But in a sense the comparison between Ledwidge and Clare is futile because the latter left a huge output, about 860 published poems.

Since the death of Patrick Kavanagh, Ledwidge's name has been evoked in his connection, too, because of the resemblance in their circumstances. Both were isolated phenomena in their native countries.

Ledwidge's first book went through three editions; his second two; and his **Complete Poems** followed his third book so quickly that it superseded the separate volumes. This final collection was reprinted three times, the last date being 1955. The book is still selling and the original publishers still hold the copyright. These hard facts prove that the poems acquired a vitality of their own. . . . Hundreds of poets have gone down into the Limbo of the forgotten during the past fifty years, but Ledwidge's poetry lives on. It is no small triumph that it has survived the death of the Romantic School and the final fading of the Celtic Twilight. His permanent place among the poets of the Irish Renaissance is secure. (pp. 193-95)

> *Alice Curtayne, in her* Francis Ledwidge: A Life of the Poet (1887-1917), *Martin Brian & O'Keeffe, 1972, 209 p.*

ADDITIONAL BIBLIOGRAPHY

Adcock, A. St. John. Chapter Three. In his *For Remembrance: Soldier Poets Who Have Fallen in the War*, 49-53. London: Hodder and Stoughton, n.d.

> Includes an appreciative essay on Ledwidge's poetry concluding: "There is enough, and more than enough, in his three volumes to indicate what our literature has lost by his early death and to justify Lord Dunsany, who discovered and fostered his genius."

Chase, Lewis. "Francis Ledwidge." *The Century* 95, No. 3 (January 1918): 386-91.

> Quotes a lengthy autobiographical letter to Chase from Ledwidge, who was writing from France in June, 1917. Ledwidge remarks: "My favourites amongst my own are always changing. Of those published I, perhaps, like 'Thomas MacDonagh' best."

Dudley, Dorothy. "Celtic Songs." *Poetry: A Magazine of Verse* IX, No. 4 (January 1917): 209-11.

> Review of *Songs of the Fields*. Dudley comments that "a sense of beautiful language and a deep sense of fields and woods and waters meet in [Mr. Ledwidge's] poems. Lord Dunsany, who introduces him, explains that he found him, where he has long looked for a poet, among the Irish peasants. The only pity is that Mr. Ledwidge has not looked much for himself there, but instead has too often sought expression in borrowed language."

Eagle, Solomon. "Current Literature: Books in General." *The New Statesman* IX, No. 227 (11 August 1917): 449.

> An obituary tribute and assessment of Ledwidge's *Songs of the Fields* and *Songs of Peace*. According to Eagle: "['Thomas MacDonagh'] will, both on its merits and because of its occasion and the circumstances of its authorship, appear, with a few others of the poet's, in the Irish anthologies of the future."

Farren, Robert. "Francis Ledwidge: Meathman." In his *The Course of Irish Verse in English*, 114-23. New York: Sheed and Ward, 1947.

> Places Ledwidge's verses in the context of Irish poetry. According to Farren, Ledwidge "wrote in verse of much beauty of the Easter Rising; it is through these poems he properly joins Irish literature."

Heaney, Seamus. "The Labourer and the Lord: Francis Ledwidge and Lord Dunsany." In his *Preoccupations: Selected Prose 1968-1978*, pp. 202-06. New York: Farrar, Straus, Giroux, 1980.

> A biographical account of the literary relationship that "developed between the cottage and the castle, the ganger of the roadworks team playing grateful poet to the noble lord's undoubtedly generous patronage."

Morton, David. "The Natural World and Its Creatures." In his *The Renaissance of Irish Poetry: 1880-1930*, pp. 55-123. New York: Ives Washburn, 1929.

> Praises Ledwidge's nature poetry. According to Morton: "Not many poets of our day, in Ireland or out of it, looked out on the world of nature with the intimacy of feeling and the minuteness of observation that are everywhere present in Ledwidge's verse. Belonging to a race of poets noted for these qualities, he stands out as one possessing them in an even more marked degree than his fellows."

O'Conor, Norreys Jephson. "Three Poems." *The Sewanee Review* XXIX, No. 2 (April 1921): 153-54.

> Includes the poem "For Francis Ledwidge (After reading his *Complete Poems*)."

Tynan, Katharine. "Francis Ledwidge." *The English Review* XXVI (February 1918): 127-37.

> Biography and tribute in which Tynan maintains: "They are wrong who call Francis Ledwidge a peasant poet. . . . There was nothing of him peasant—not his beautiful handwriting, his lovely and distinguished choice of words, his delicate colour-sense, his music, his mind, himself; they were all gentle."

Van Doren, Mark. "Aria and Recitative." *The Nation* CXI, No. 2884 (13 October 1920): 414-15.

Brief review of the *Complete Poems*. According to Van Doren: "Francis Ledwidge was an honest songster, a poet of the blackbird in a time of hawks and vultures, a peasant poet not afraid to be gentle and archaic—to write 'athwart' and 'adown' and 'anon'—when others beat on loud new gongs."

Ward, A. C. "Poetry." In his *Twentieth-Century Literature: The Age of Interrogation 1901-25*, pp. 104-62. Rev. ed. London: Methuen & Co., 1931.

Briefly compares Ledwidge's poetry with the work of soldier-poet Julian Grenfell. According to Ward: "Ledwidge, though his poems are quiet in mood, seemed to induce calm within his soul by deliberately turning his eyes and thoughts from the actualities of war; turning to Nature as an antidote for the poison of conflict."

(Harry) Sinclair Lewis

1885-1951

(Also wrote under pseudonym of Tom Graham) American novelist, short story writer, essayist, journalist, critic, dramatist, and poet.

The following entry presents criticism of Lewis's novel *Main Street,* published in 1920. For a complete discussion of Lewis's career, see *TCLC,* Volumes 4 and 13.

Main Street is regarded as one of the most effective satires in American literature. With its publication in 1920 Lewis assumed leadership in the literary movement known as "the revolt from the village," a tradition begun by Mark Twain and carried on in the works of Edgar Lee Masters, Sherwood Anderson, and others. In *Main Street* the town of Gopher Prairie, Minnesota, is depicted as a typically drab settlement populated by unimaginative, complacent philistines. Contemporaries considered the satire a vengeful attack on the smug provincialism of the American middle class; however, many modern commentators find the novel's perspective ambivalent, an opinion supported by Lewis's acknowledgment of his love/hate attitude toward small town America. Although *Main Street*'s technical and stylistic shortcomings preclude serious criticism of such elements, thematic analyses of the novel have yielded numerous political and sociological interpretations. A milestone in American literary history, *Main Street* helped deflate sentimental myths of the ideal American community and promoted realistic, self-critical American fiction.

Main Street was Lewis's first commercial success. Ironically, after years of writing potboilers to earn money, Lewis disregarded profits to write *Main Street,* telling a friend, "I have been whoring long enough. I'm going to write a book this time *for myself.*" The idea for the novel was conceived fifteen years earlier with the title "The Village Virus," signifying the dullness which infects progressive minds exposed to the type of pettiness and monotony Lewis observed in his hometown of Sauk Centre, Minnesota. Contrary to this long-germinating theme, however, Lewis's fiction before *Main Street* affirmed middle class values and presented a positive view of human nature. None of the numerous short stories that Lewis published in the *Saturday Evening Post* and other popular magazines, or his early novels anticipate the parody of narrow-minded hypocrisy found in *Main Street.* A critical and popular success, the novel sold over 390,000 copies in two years and became the impetus of a national controversy about the myths and realities of "Main Street, U.S.A.," the widely embraced slogan for stifling American provincialism.

Earlier works treating "the revolt from the village" theme had not generated the same interest that surrounded *Main Street.* Edgar Lee Masters's poetry collection *Spoon River Anthology* (1915), for example, was published when the image of the small town as friendly and wholesome was still accepted. Mark Schorer attributes the success of *Main Street* to its comic-satiric narrative tone, its conformity to the shifting mood of the nation, and to the publicity generated by the controversial nature of the work. Perceived as an indictment of traditional nineteenth century values which were no longer acceptable in the jaded, sophisticated Jazz Age, *Main Street* appealed to a generation

that had witnessed the mechanized mass slaughter of World War I and was ready for a literature that would reflect its rejection of genteel optimism, blind nationalism, and traditional religion. During the 1920s Lewis published other popular satires which attacked various aspects of American life, including *Babbitt, Arrowsmith, Elmer Gantry,* and *Dodsworth.* These works, with *Main Street,* comprise the major achievements of his career.

In *Main Street* and his later satires, Lewis created grotesque yet recognizable caricatures of middle-class Americans with a skill which has been likened to that of Charles Dickens. Unlike Dickens's characters, however, Lewis's characters rarely rise above the level of caricatures, and most critics have little positive comment on the artistic aspects of the work other than to praise Lewis's ability to capture the speech of his small town characters. For this reason there is also little character analysis in criticism of Lewis's novel; rather, the characters are generally examined as mere keys to an understanding of Lewis's political and sociological themes. Most critics agree that in *Main Street,* the character Carol Kennicott most closely articulates Lewis's attitudes, and Lewis confirmed this view, calling her a woman who was, like himself, "always groping for something, . . . intolerant of her surroundings and yet lacking any clearly defined vision of what she really wants." Throughout *Main Street,* Carol fights to express herself through the cultural, social and beautification projects she proposes for Gopher Prairie's improvement. By criticizing the dullness, meanness, and hypocrisy of the town, Carol unwittingly establishes an adversarial relationship with her new community which gradually affects her marriage as well. At the same time, Carol has also been viewed as a subject of satire, although critics debate whether Lewis intended her to be viewed as such. A self-styled sophisticate, Carol's tastes and opinions are often naive, provincial, and romantic, and they are as smugly held as the hypocritical values of the town she seeks to change.

While Carol serves as critic of the small town, her husband Will, Gopher Prairie's most respected doctor, represents the finest aspects of the community. An honest, practical man dedicated to his profession, his wife, and his hometown, Will Kennicott takes for granted the innate charm he perceives in Gopher Prairie's simple amusements and sees nothing wrong with the many practices his wife roundly condemns. While many minor characters appear in *Main Street* as reinforcers of the town's negative qualities, Will and Carol represent two divergent yet seemingly valid responses to small-town life. Schorer asserts that Will and Carol share equally in representing different aspects of Lewis's personality, stating that "just as in his life these two parts of himself struggled against each other, so at the end of the novel, the husband and wife are still 'enemies yoked'."

Main Street has been interpreted from a variety of standpoints. The Kennicott marriage, for example, has been the focus of discussions concerning modern marriage, feminism and the modern woman, and the importance of individual expression. Gopher Prairie, a town experiencing a postwar economic boom, retains social and economic policies established when the town was struggling to survive, and the depiction of the town's resistance to Carol's more reasonable social service proposals has been read as an attack on spiritual meanness arising from misplaced frugality and on the uncharitable attitude of the middle class toward the equal distribution of goods and services. America's melting pot myth is explored through the Swedish farmers who work the land surrounding Gopher Prairie and sacrifice their traditions to assimilate with a community that still looks down on them. An exception is the character Miles Bjornstram, who embodies the independent thinking and vigorous pioneer spirit traditionally admired in American folklore. A socialist and atheist, Bjornstram's attempt to establish his own independence from the values of the community leads to the death of his wife and child. A broken man, Bjornstram is reminded by a neighbor that, even in view of his tragedy, the town will neither forget nor forgive his defiant nonconformity. Because *Main Street* lends itself to so many interpretations of American life and is so artistically undistinguished, most critics concur with Floyd C. Watkins's evaluation of the novel as "more message than fiction."

Lewis's work is no longer the subject of extensive critical discussion, for many critics consider the themes and structures of his novel self-evident. He is most often discussed in a historic context, for in his time Lewis performed the important role of American gadfly, creating works which paved the way for much of the self-critical fiction of mid-twentieth-century American literature. *Main Street,* the work by which Lewis established himself as a national agitator, has been credited with giving Americans greater insights into the moral shortcomings of their nation and with defining "the victimization of the individual in a world of mass vulgarity."

(See also *Contemporary Authors,* Volume 104; *Dictionary of Literary Biography,* Volume 9: *American Novelists: 1910-1945;* and *Dictionary of Literary Biography Documentary Series,* Volume 1.)

THE NATION (essay date 1920)

[*In the following excerpt, the critic discusses dialogue, theme, and characterization in* Main Street.]

Dreiser alone and at his best remains superior to Sinclair Lewis. He has hours of a more rapt absorption, of a more visionary identification of himself with the objects he renders. Mr. Lewis, on the other hand, has a clearer and more orderly intelligence and a precise and cultivated style. Dreiser has the more brooding eye, Mr. Lewis the acuter and more sensitive ear. Thus while his narrative masses are less impressive, his dialogue, which he uses very freely, is brilliant. The exactness of this dialogue is a literary achievement of a very high order. Novelists and playwrights put us off with symbols and adumbrations. Mr. Lewis has given literary permanence to the speech of his time and section. But the dialogue in *Main Street* is anything but literature in the sense of Verlaine; it is living talk. When Dr. Kennicott declares (to take an inferior but brief and quotable example) that "Miss Sherwin in the high school is a regular wonder—reads Latin like I do English," we know where we are. We know that we have heard that very remark in Springfield or Peoria and have heard it from a physician. To produce such authenticity of speech once or twice would be merely clever; never to miss it in four hundred and fifty pages is magnificent.

In building his book Mr. Lewis has not permitted his larger purpose to crowd or distort the things that were actually to be communicated. His thesis is the standardization of the innumerable Main Streets of our small towns, the savorless flatness of that life, the complete substitution of the mechanical for the vital, the tawdry spiritual poverty of a people that "has lost the power of play as well as the power of impersonal thought," and the menacing extension, like a creeping paralysis, of this form or existence, so that the Minnesota Swedes exchange "their spiced puddings and red jackets for fried pork-chops and concealed white blouses," and trade "the ancient Christmas hymns of the fjords for 'She's my Jazzland Cutie.'" He has a stern enough sense of the danger of what Alice Meynell once called "decivilization" and of the incredible arrogance of the actors in that process. He has notes toward an "American Credo" . . . that should be inscribed on tables of brass as both record and warning. But he is never tempted into the didactic or prophetic. His business is with Gopher Prairie, Minnesota. He makes nothing symbolical; he lets it be so. He neither strays nor preaches. His method is undeviatingly creative; he is secure in the knowledge that to show things truly is to show them up.

His people are many and they have not only mobility, the appearance of gesture and speech that come from an inner impulse; they have the rarer quality of solidity; they detach themselves from the page and are in space, smelling of flesh and hair, cloth and leather. Carol Kennicott, through whose sensitive and feebly rebellious soul we see Gopher Prairie, is not the most exact or convincing. But Dr. Will and Sam Clark, Mrs. Bogart and her son Cy, Vida Sherwin and the "Red Swede," Professor Mott and the Rev. Zitterel—these are all triumphs. There are no minor characters. Some are more involved in poor Carol's adventures and some less. But we know the Harry Haydocks and the Jack Elders and even the Nels Erdstroms as well as we do Guy or Erik. It is a richly peopled world—a world that may become some day like the worlds of Fielding or Hauptmann. Mr. Lewis, unlike the masters with whose beginnings his present work may justly be compared, has done a good deal of shoddy work in his time. Was he not even responsible for a certain play called *Hobohemia*? He is making a full atonement. *Main Street* would add to the power and distinction of the contemporary literature of any country. He must not again forget the responsibility which his talent involves, nor his own sure knowledge that our literature and our civilization need just such books as this. (p. 536)

"The Epic of Dulness," in The Nation, *Vol. CXI, No. 2888, November 10, 1920, pp. 536-37.*

THE NEW YORK TIMES BOOK REVIEW   (essay date 1920)

[*In the following excerpt the critic gives* Main Street *a laudatory review, concentrating his discussion upon the characterization of Carol Kennicott.*]

[*Main Street*] is the portrait of a town—typical, one of thousands of common little American towns scattered all over the country, each with its own markings and idiosyncrasies, of course, but alike in essentials, alike as the average small town person, who is found quite as usually in the cities and the country as in the village or the towns, the common person, the common people, of whom there so many. . . .

A remarkable book is this latest by Sinclair Lewis. A novel, yes, but so unusual as not to fall easily into a class. There is practically no plot, yet the book is absorbing. It is so much like life itself, so extraordinarily real. These people are actual folk, and there was never better dialogue written than their revealing talk. The book might have been cut without harm, possibly, for there is an infinite amount of detail, yet this very detail has its power, exerts its magic. The latter half is the more forcefully, clearly written, moves more soundly. In fact, one cannot shake off the impression that this book was begun long ago, when Mr. Lewis was but recently out of college, laid aside, and taken up lately, to be rewritten and reconstructed and finished. There is the sharp reaction of youth to so much of it, a personal note in the hatred Carol has for the people, the ways, the thoughts and the place of Gopher Prairie, a reaction and a note that savor of the agony, undimmed by intervening years, of a sensitive young creature coming from the free outlook and tolerant sympathies of a broader environment into such a prison atmosphere as that of this small Minnesota town. This impression that the book is partly by a college boy and partly by a man with many contacts with life and the world will not down; there are some poorly written pages, some jejune bits that add to it. Yet one would not wish to eliminate this youthful stand in the book. It belongs there.

As we have said, the book is a portrait of a town. It is also an amazing study of the girl Carol, the foil and critic of that town.

Carol is an alien. She comes of New England parentage, of a home that had its tone and color, and reached back to rich things that were lost. She had had a college training of a sort, some experience of Chicago, and she had been a librarian in St. Paul. She had known hopes and visions, a desire to transform the dull and the ugly into charm and beauty, but she had fallen into the routine of work, and the dream to go forth and to improve had faded. . . .

She marries and she goes with her husband to the burg he loves and admires. From that moment she and Gopher Prairie are at grips.

First it is the hopeless ugliness of Main Street that strikes at her, then the deadliness of the social life of the creators of this street, the leading citizens of the town. There is genius in Mr. Lewis's description of the party given in honor of the homecoming of the bride and groom. The awful stiffness of human beings to whom the joys of social intercourse are not alone unknown but distrusted, whose sole notion of entertainment consists in the performance of stunts. "Let's have some stunts, folks," cries the host to the circle that has sat silent and watchful, or rattling personalities, or surreptitiously watching Carol. And they shriek assent. Upon which the few who can do stunts take their turn doing them. There is Dave—"Say, Dave, give us that stunt about the Norwegian catching a hen," and there is Ella Stowbody, spinster, with her recitation, "That Old Sweetheart of Mine." And there were four other stunts. They concluded the social part of the evening. What is more, they appeared at each and every party of the leading set of Gopher Prairie, and when they had been done the party sank back into coma until the coming of the refreshments, practically identical at each house. About then the party began to be natural. That is, the men got together and talked of their shops and their hunting, the women herded and discussed their servants and their children and their sicknesses.

And Carol, brave with youth's untriedness, foolish with that youth, not any too expert herself, starts to make Gopher Prairie beautiful and amusing, to give it some notion of the world outside its own limits, to bring in art and literature and landscape gardening.

And in the end she is allowed to plant a few geraniums in a vacant lot. But a great deal comes in between.

In the first place, she finds that the town doesn't want to be reformed; that the people in it resent the fact that she has seen and done more than they; that they are critical and sneering. . . .

And for a while Carol is terror-stricken. She cannot walk the streets without the feel of those eyes on her; she cannot talk naturally to any one, thinking of the gossip and the criticism that is being poured upon her; she dreads to go to the stores, where the merchants grin superciliously over her requests for something they don't keep—in Gopher Prairie it is a virtue not to keep things you haven't kept before.

But this does not last. Once again she decides that she will do what in her lies to prod the town. . . .

[She] finds that some of the people do like her. There is the pariah of the village, the Red Swede, the handy man of the town, who senses her difference from the villagers and who talks to her one day, laughs at the prejudices and the narrowness of the place, makes fun of its big men, gives the girl a realization that freedom does exist, after all. And here and there some one is kind, smiling, affectionate. She bucks up. She joins the Thanatopsis Club, which is engaged in culture, she stops being either scared or patronizing, and she dreams of tearing down the blank horror that does service for a City Hall and seeing in its place a Georgian structure of warm brick and white stone, &c.

Of course, it won't do. No individual could conquer a town like Gopher Prairie. No alien can bring sweetness and light where it is not wanted or missed. Carol is a silly girl. She does not know as much as she thinks she does, she misses doing what good she might because she cannot see the good there is. But she is sensitive, proud and keen. She is alive, and she moves in a different strata from the townspeople of the prairie town. She has no business there, and yet she is caught there, by the fact of her marriage, by the later fact of her child. She gives up, she sinks almost to coma—and then, for a while she awakened, yanked back to the feeling of her own individual existence and reality by falling rather feebly in love with the tailor, the one man who has some vision, some despair to match her own.

It doesn't last. But it leads to a wonderful interview between wife and husband, a few pages that are as good as anything can be. There are more such pages in this book than in any other book we have read this year, perhaps in several years, written by an American.

A review of "Main Street," in The New York Times Book Review, *November 14, 1920, p. 18.*

STUART P. SHERMAN   (essay date 1922)

[*For many years Sherman was considered one of America's most conservative literary critics. During the early twentieth century he was influenced by the New Humanism, a critical movement which subscribed to the belief that the aesthetic quality of any literary work must be subordinate to its support of traditional moral values. During ten years of service as a literary critic at the* Nation, *Sherman established himself as a champion of the Anglo-Saxon, genteel tradition in American letters and a bitter enemy of literary Naturalism and its proponents. Theodore Dreiser and his chief defender, H. L. Mencken (who also praised Lewis's works throughout the 1920s), were Sherman's special targets during the World War I era, as Sherman perceived the Naturalism they espoused to be a life-denying cultural product of America's enemy, Germany. During the 1920s Sherman became the editor of the* New York Herald Tribune *book review section, a move that coincided with a distinct liberalization of his hitherto staunch critical tastes; in the last years of his life, he even praised his old enemies Dreiser and Mencken. In the following excerpt from his* The Significance of Sinclair Lewis, *a work commissioned by Lewis's publishers, Sherman compares* Main Street *with Gustave Flaubert's* Madame Bovary (1857), *concentrating on the characterizations of the female protagonists and the representation of provincial bourgeois society in each work.*]

Mr. Lewis had been incubating [*Main Street*] for six or seven years, though I suspect that his critical faculties were edged for its final revision by his comparative study of American small towns, made on [an] excursion over the Lincoln Highway, which he so gaily chronicled in *Free Air.* A second novel as deeply rooted in his native soil and in his own past would be as difficult a feat for him as, for their respective authors, a second *Huckleberry Finn,* a second *David Copperfield,* a second *Mill on the Floss,* a second *Pendennis,* a second *Clayhanger.* Like these other five great novels, *Main Street* appears to be the harvest of the writer's best land, which is so often his native heath and the deep impressions of early life, ineffaceable by the lapse of years, and poignantly touching the heart through the revisiting eyes of age. In its exhibition of the interwoven lives of the community, it has the authority, the intimacy, the many-sided insights, the deep saturation of color, which no journalist can ever ''get up,'' which are possible only, one is tempted to say, to one who packs into his book

the most vital experience and observation of a lifetime. One must have *lived* that stuff in order to have reproduced it as living organism. And it is with some vague sense that a man can contain only one great autobiography that many readers of *Main Street* have prophesied against Mr. Lewis's future.

To those who wish to believe that they have found not merely a new novel but also a new novelist, capable of fresh flights for distance and altitude, certain reassuring considerations may be presented. *Main Street,* unlike three-fourths of the novels of the day, is not autobiographical. It is to an extraordinary degree an objective representation of contemporary society extended through a period of not more than half-a-dozen years. In this society Mr. Lewis himself has not a single ''personal representative.'' Neither Dr. Kennicot, nor Carol, nor Guy Pollock, nor Vida Sherwin, nor Sam Clark, nor Percy Breshnahan, nor Erik Valborg, nor Miles Bjornstam, nor Fern Mullins, nor Mrs. Bogart is his ''register.'' Each one of these persons is a perfectly distinct individual with firm centre and contours honestly constructed after innumerable observations and hard, earnest work of the realistic imagination. Mr. Lewis will not exhaust his material while he retains his present capacity for research. Deeply indebted as he may be to Mr. Wells for the illumination of his point of view as an observer of the human spectacle, he has studied the art of constructing the novel under other masters with far greater respect for their profession than that famous producer who semi-annually charges a new lay figure with the task of communicating to the world the latest state of his own consciousness. The contemporary English novelist whose best work is most nearly comparable with *Main Street* is Mr. Bennett in *The Old Wives' Tale* and *Clayhanger.* But the book from which, I should say, Mr. Lewis without losing a particle of his own idiom or the independence of his American vision, has learned his most valuable ''secrets'' is *Madame Bovary.*

Both *Main Street* and *Madame Bovary* are mordantly critical representations of contemporary civilization. In each case, the criticism is intensely focussed upon the bourgeois society of a representative provincial town. In each case, the ''hero'' is a country doctor, who is, thanks to an insensitive aesthetic organization, sufficiently content with his lot and in love with his young wife. In each case, the ''heroine'' has been touched by literature and contact with the city to revolt against the Philistinism of her husband and the restrictions of her life, in behalf of romantic ideals of which she is unable to find any worthy incarnations. In each case, the searching criticism which plays over the scene and the actors is delivered indirectly by an intricate system of contrasts and the cross-lighting and reflected lighting of subordinate characters. I will add an observation which many readers fail to make: Flaubert was in love with Emma and Mr. Lewis is in love with Carol; and both authors analyze and expose the object of their affection with a merciless rigor which no woman can either understand or pardon—she can understand the rigor but not the love which inflicts it and survives it. They treat their heroes with similar austerity—with the difference that Flaubert despises his, and the American author does not. To the student of Mr. Lewis's indirect analytical method, I commend his remorseless twenty-fourth chapter, beginning with the ''thesis'': ''All that midsummer month Carol was sensitive to Kennicot''; likewise his subtle record of Carol's reaction to Breshnahan in relation to her husband. So much for the parallelism between the French master and the American disciple.

As for the divergence, it is not all to the advantage of Flaubert. Mr. Lewis saw more types of people, more kinds of activity,

Lewis's boyhood home in Sauk Centre, Minnesota. Photography Collection, Harry Ransom Humanities Research Center, University of Texas at Austin.

more meshes of the social network in Gopher Prairie than Flaubert saw in Rouen. Without destroying their artistic subordination, he made more of his secondary personages. He increased greatly the significance and the tension of his novel by choosing, as the principal representatives of middle-class revolt and middle-class stability, characters with a far higher degree of general and professional intelligence than is possessed by the French protagonists. He faithfully presents the specific erotic passion as only occasionally or seasonally perturbing the average American temperament—not obsessing it, not hounding it. Flaubert sees this passion as the centre of his theme. Mr. Lewis does not. If our novelists generally were not dissuaded by the terrors of our censorship, if they dared to tell the truth, would they like many of their European colleagues and like one or two of their American confreres, would they represent the average middle-class American as living feverishly from one liaison to the next? Mr. Lewis does not appear to think so. Dr. Kennicot had, before his marriage, been around "with the boys" and perhaps he never became utterly incapable of a slip; but I doubt whether Mr. Lewis has been guilty of any important suppression of the truth in declaring that his mind was absorbed in his five hobbies: medicine, land-investment, Carol, motoring, and hunting. As for Carol—that well-turned, dynamic, rather intensely feminine, too taut a young woman whom I meet with greater frequency each year, flinging her coat into chairs and "exploding" into other living rooms than those of Gopher Prairie, to the disgust of the stodgy and to the delight and the refreshment of the others—; she might be more simply happy or more simply miserable if the sex instincts were stronger in her; if she could content herself with being either mother, wife or mistress; if she could repeat *ex animo* that sweet and wistfully cadenced Mid-Victorian line which, alas, I have forgotten, to the effect that love is only an incident in a man's life—"'tis a woman's whole existence"—something like that. (pp. 10-13)

Now so far as *Main Street* is "the story of Carol Kennicot," it shows an eager young creature beating her luminous wings

rather wildly, as young creatures do, yet not without some sense of the direction in which light and freedom are. A "backyard" affair with Erik Valborg—that for example, she discovers decisively, is not the way out. That might be an alleviant to the yearnings of Emma Bovary but it would not be even a temporary sop to her. With true insight into the significant aspect of the present unrest among young women, the revolt of Carol is shown to have very little relation with the much-advertised movement for "sexual freedom." Carol is, on the contrary, rebellious precisely at the fetters which accepting such things of sex as a "woman's whole existence" has imposed upon her. Her revolt is inspired by a general hunger of the heart for its own development through appropriate activities of hand and will and brain. In so far as this is true, I judge her revolt to be not only significant but beautiful and not altogether hopeless. . . . (pp. 14-15)

Stuart P. Sherman, in his The Significance of Sinclair Lewis, *Harcourt Brace Jovanovich, 1922, 28 p.*

C. E. BECHHOFER (essay date 1923)

[*Bechhofer was an English critic. In the following excerpt, he discusses* Main Street *as a distinctively American work which realistically analyzes the small midwestern American town.*]

The outstanding recent American literary success is Mr. Sinclair Lewis's *Main Street*. . . .

Main Street is essentially an American book, and a good American book. I do not know what its sales have been in England since its publication here, but, if one may judge from reviews, it is unlikely to be very popular. This is natural enough; for, though it is one of the most important American books that have appeared for a long time, it is one that the foreign reader cannot hope to appreciate without some explanation of its character. (p. 105)

The book has no ending, either happy or sad; for there is no easy solution to the problem of *Main Street*.

The story after all does not much matter; for the essential part of the book is its description of the clash between the culture of the more or less civilized Eastern American cities and the arid self-complacency of the Middle Western small towns, "as planless as a scattering of paper boxes on an attic floor."

The importance of *Main Street* lies in its merciless, sardonic study of Middle Western life. This, Mr. Lewis seems to say, this is the life that all good, patriotic Americans hold up to each other and to the world as the high-water mark of domestic civilization; these are the standards of taste and opinion that young America is urged to support and follow. The book, to any one who has a first-hand experience of American life, is a vivid social satire, the more persuasive in that its purpose is never underlined, never even stated. It is the book that Mark Twain ought to have written in his own style. After the first enormous vogue of *Main Street* one now hears many objections to it; it is said to be exaggerated, to be too severe. But it is difficult to see how these complaints can be sustained. In the first place, the chapters are as obvious as photographs. The cruelly nerve-racking adventures of Carol, the heroine, with the men and the women of Gopher Prairie, her vain attempts to educate the town, her disgust with the snobbishness of the people and the sordid atmosphere of their lives and upbringing, her delight at the colour that the non-English immigrants, a despised class, bring into the place—the last, the underlying idea, as we have seen, of so much of Miss Willa Cather's work—all this is too real to be dismissed, even partially, as malicious or exaggerated. Mr. Lewis is perfectly honest with his readers. . . . (pp. 106-08)

In fact, Main Street is present-day America at its most intolerable. (p. 109)

[If Mr. Lewis] occasionally uses, for purposes of his own, the dialect and emphases of Main Street, he is also capable of excellent descriptive writing. His picture of Mrs. Bogart, for example, "a widow, and a prominent Baptist, and a Good Influence," whose three sons have run amuck as the result of her careful training of them, and whose mind, with its amazing interest in vice and its suppression, is the foulest thing in the sordid atmosphere of Main Street, is an excellent piece of delineation. One is tempted to generalize about American characteristics on the basis of nearly every chapter of this book. It sums up brilliantly and mercilessly everything that the new generation in America detests. If *Main Street* is read with this in mind, the English reader should enjoy it, long as it is; but it is a great pity if the book is to be taken as just a novel, as any other novel might be, of small-town life in the Middle West. It is perhaps as good a sign of the American renaissance of to-day as anything could be that the public throughout the United States is buying and reading this book; without such willing self-analysis there would be little hope for the intellectual future of the country. (pp. 110-12)

> *C. E. Bechhofer, in a chapter in his* The Literary Renaissance in America, *William Heinemann Ltd., 1923, pp. 105-25.*

WALDO FRANK   (essay date 1924)

[*Frank was an American novelist and critic who was best known as an interpreter of contemporary civilization, particularly that of Latin America. A socialist and supporter of various radical groups in the United States, he was a founding editor of the* Seven Arts *(1916-1917), a leftist, avant-garde magazine of literature and opinion. One of Frank's most significant works of criticism,* Our America *(1919), derides the "genteel tradition" in American letters and is considered an influential work in its support of realism in the nation's literature. In the following excerpt, Frank offers an ambivalent review of* Main Street, *praising the detailed delineation of the town of Gopher Prairie but criticizing the unrealistic characterization.*]

I do not know if the shouts of the acclaim of *Main Street* have yet reached Paris. Mr. Lewis is an intelligent young writer who, in the grips of economic need, for some years made his way by writing sparkling and ephemeral stories for the magazines. The stories brought him very moderate funds and very little standing: also they brought him an accumulated sense of sin—all of which Mr. Lewis, being a gentleman, resented. So a year ago Mr. Lewis "let go." As he put it to a friend: "I have been whoring long enough. I am going to write a book this time *for myself.* And I don't give a damn if it sells or if it doesn't!" . . . Mr. Lewis, in a spirit of purity for once, writes a good book—it brings him the return which his bad tales never did. Mr. Lewis, in a fresh spirit of hatred for America, excoriates the life of the typical American man and woman—he becomes the season's idol of the American world!

Surely, this is a fascinating literary comedy and well worth noting. The book itself is distinguished by its fidelity to detail, its humble devotion to the clear portrayal of surface characters. "Main Street" is the name of the central thoroughfare of tens of thousands of American towns. Mr. Lewis has with the fervor

of rebellion etched its portrait. His heroine is our Emma Bovary—passionless, opinionative, prim. She perishes in the even insipidity, the complacent ugliness of her provincial world. But being American, she does not take to her lovers: she tries to reform the town. And in her failure she does not resort to poison: she falls away into a vague and sterile resignation. The artistic value of the book, one feels, is rather unconscious as regards its author. Mr. Lewis takes his heroine's revolts seriously: but her poignance lies really in the fact, splendidly portrayed, that she is very little wiser than the Town she would reform and that her ideals of "culture" are quite as absurd as those of her husband or the grocer. Mr. Lewis lavishes his attention on what he believes to be foreground characterization. And yet the book in its entirety gives the aesthetic form of a full and stifling background from which no human beings saliently emerge. This lack of foreground, of *personality*, is American, and Mr. Lewis has unconsciously recorded in it what is perhaps the outstanding feature of American life. The American novelist who stresses the dominant delineation of the person is unconsciously imitating Europe and is doomed to failure.

Now *Main Street,* which is compounded of the paprika of protest, has achieved the sort of popularity heretofore judged by the wise men of the world of books to be the privilege of the purveyors of undiluted saccharine—of the most supine flatterers of American complacence. The vogue of the unimaginative sycophants has, however, for many years been declining. Albeit the growing population of the country as a whole assured to these products a creditable sale, a new world has uprisen in America which detested these adulterated literary bon-bons and would have none of them; which longed for the zest of acute although not too searching criticism in the guise of comedy and satire. It has gone hungry. *Main Street* appears and it comes forth, hungry and avid and articulate at last. The long tottering edifice of infantile pioneer taste falls with a blow and the new structure is revealed—the taste for emotional bitters, for the stimulation of running down one's past. The taste that responds to Mr. Lewis is no longer childish, it is adolescent. (pp. 203-06)

> *Waldo Frank, "The American Year," in his* Salvos: An Informal Book about Books and Plays, *Boni and Liveright, Publishers, 1924, pp. 201-16.*

E. M. FORSTER   (essay date 1929)

[*Forster was a prominent English novelist, critic, and essayist whose works reflect his liberal humanism. His most celebrated novel,* Passage to India *(1924), is a complex examination of personal relationships amid the conflicts of the modern world. Although some of Forster's critical essays are considered naive in their literary assessments, his discussion of fictional techniques in* Aspects of the Novel *(1927) is regarded as a minor classic in literary criticism. In the following excerpt, originally published in 1929, Forster discusses the photographic vividness with which Gopher Prairie is described and the extent to which the narrator is involved with the town and people.*]

"I would like to see Gopher Prairie," says the heroine of Mr. Sinclair Lewis's *Main Street,* and her husband promptly replies: "Trust me. Here she is. Brought some snapshots down to show you." That, in substance, is what Mr. Lewis has done himself. He has brought down some snapshots to show us and posterity. The collection is as vivid and stimulating as any writer who adopts this particular method can offer. Let us examine it; let us consider the method in general. And let us at once dismiss the notion that any fool can use a camera. (p. 129)

I have never been to Gopher Prairie, Nautilus, Zenith, or any of their big brothers and sisters, and my exclamations throughout are those of a non-American, and worthless as a comment on the facts. Nevertheless, I persist in exclaiming, for what Mr. Lewis has done for myself and thousands of others is to lodge a piece of a continent in our imagination. America, for many of us, used to mean a very large apron, covered with a pattern of lozenges, edged by a frill, and chastely suspended by a boundary tape round the ample waist of Canada. The frill, like the tape, we visualized slightly.... And then Sinclair Lewis strode along, developed his films, and stopped our havering. The lozenges lived. We saw that they were composed of mud, dust, grass, crops, shops, clubs, hotels, railway stations, churches, universities, etc., which were sufficiently like their familiar counterparts to be real, and sufficiently unlike them to be extremely exciting. We saw men and women who were not quite ourselves, but ourselves modified by new surroundings, and we heard them talk a language which we could usually, but not always, understand. We enjoyed at once the thrills of intimacy and discovery, and for that and much else we are grateful, and posterity will echo our gratitude. Whether he has ''got'' the Middle West, only the Middle West can say, but he has made thousands of people all over the globe alive to its existence, and anxious for further news. (pp. 130-31)

For all his knowingness about life, and commercially-travelled airs, Mr. Lewis is a novelist of the instinctive sort, he goes to his point direct. There is detachment, but not of the panoramic type: we are never lifted above the lozenges, Thomas Hardy fashion, to see the townlets seething beneath, never even given as wide a view as Arnold Bennett accords us of his Five Towns. It is rather the detachment of the close observer, of the man who stands half a dozen yards off his subject, or at any rate within easy speaking distance of it, and the absence of superiority and swank (which so pleasantly characterizes the books) is connected with this. Always in the same house or street as his characters, eating their foodstuffs, breathing their air, Mr. Lewis claims no special advantages; though frequently annoyed with them, he is never contemptuous, and though he can be ironic and even denunciatory, he has nothing of the aseptic awfulness of the seer. Neither for good nor evil is he lifted above his theme; he is neither a poet nor a preacher, but a fellow with a camera a few yards away. (p. 132)

His likes and dislikes mean less to him than the quickness of his eye, and though he tends to snapshot muscular Christians when they are attacked with cramp, he would sooner snap them amid clouds of angels than not at all. His commentary on society is constant, coherent, sincere; yet the reader's eye follows the author's eye rather than his voice, and when Main Street is quitted it is not its narrowness, but its existence that remains as a permanent possession.

His method of book-building is unaffected and appropriate. In a sense (a very faint sense) his novels are tales of unrest. He takes a character who is not quite at ease in his or her surroundings, contrives episodes that urge this way or that, and a final issue of revolt or acquiescence. In his earlier work both character and episodes are clear-cut.... Carol Kennicott, the heroine of his first important book, is a perfect medium, and also a living being. Her walks down Main Street are overwhelming; we see the houses, we see her against them, and when the dinginess breaks and Erik Valborg arises with his gallant clothes and poet's face, we, too, are seduced, and feel that such a world might well be lost for love. Never again is Mr. Lewis to be so poignant or to arrange his simple impres-

sions so nearly in the order of high tragedy; ''I may not have fought the good fight, but I have kept the faith'' are Carol's final words, and how completely are they justified by all she has suffered and done! (p. 133)

E. M. Forster, ''Sinclair Lewis,'' in his Abinger Harvest, *Harcourt Brace Jovanovich, 1936, pp. 129-36.*

HARLAN HATCHER   (essay date 1935)

[*Hatcher, an American historian and novelist, has written extensively on the midwestern region and its history. In the following excerpt he compares* Main Street *with ''revolt from the village'' novels which preceded it, noting the importance of America's political and cultural climate to the success of Lewis's work.*]

During the first two decades of this century Theodore Dreiser was the greatest single force in the rise of the American novel and by all odds its most important liberator. Then came Sinclair Lewis, not to rival but to supplement and to popularize. Theodore Dreiser was neither a reformer nor a satirist, and he never wrote a caricature. Sinclair Lewis was a satirist and by implication therefore a reformer, and he did not hesitate to advance his thesis with caricature. Theodore Dreiser said: Here is the way men live in this incomprehensible world; it is a strange and pitiable spectacle. Sinclair Lewis said: Look at these stupid fools living in bondage to smugness and mass pressures when they might have gay and amusing lives; they're dumb and they're scared. The possibility for satirical treatment of life in American towns and villages seemed to be especially preserved against the emergence of the valuable genius of Sinclair Lewis. The time was so ripe for his work, and it was so inevitably the next and necessary step in creating the American novel, that the time made the man at least as much as the man made the time. (p. 109)

All that was needed was a vigorous writer who knew the cultural poverty of an American small town because he had lived there long enough to understand it thoroughly before he revolted against it. Then allow him to escape to the world centers where the currents of modernity were running fast and high, there let him become emancipated and veneered, and then watch him tear away the veil of pretense which had modestly concealed the tawdriness of life in Gopher Prairie. Sinclair Lewis, fortuitously conjoining with the drift of the time, precipitated a formless American mood into a smash satiric attitude which set the self-conscious country by the ears.

The country might have spared itself the shock if it had kept up with its better fiction. Chapter Twenty-one of Ed Howe's *The Story of a Country Town* contained much of **Main Street** forty years earlier. One could find no publisher, the other was a best seller and brought to an intersection the curves of popular sales and the new realistic novel. Ed Howe found the public in its customary mood of complacency. It would not listen when he described with graphic realism over a Victorian plot the petty quality of life in a Western village. (p. 111)

The country was quite unprepared for such indictments in the 1880's. It was accustomed to romance and the neighborly tradition. To go from *The Story of a Country Town* to Zona Gale's *Friendship Village* (1908) is like moving from Wuthering Heights to Sweet Auburn before it was deserted. Friendship Village is of course as true to life as Gopher Prairie. They represent the eternal duality of life. In Zona Gale's book we meet the gentle Calliope so full of benevolence and good will and wanting people to be happy. It contains heart-warming episodes which make human beings irresistibly interesting because of their humanity, as when Calliope compels Mrs. Postmaster Sykes to bring her guests to the poor old charwoman's début party. . . . (pp. 112-13)

Freud's theories had first come to these shores about the time *Friendship Village* appeared. No future study of village life could ever be quite the same because of Freud. His shadowy form lies dark across the *Spoon River Anthology* (1915) which anticipated Sherwood Anderson's *Winesburg, Ohio*. . . . In a series of dramatic monologues presenting a crucial episode in each life, Edgar Lee Masters analyzed, satirized, and exposed society, telling a story in flashes, and presenting "a working model of the big world." But this working model shocked even advanced spirits like Amy Lowell, who thought it consisted of "one long chronicle of rapes, seductions, liaisons, and perversions." . . . When the depositions are all taken, the village has been laid bare, the good in those whom the citizens condemned, the evil in the hearts of the righteous, and the final feeling is one of despair over a life so stale and so barren of joy or nobility, so pitifully mean and cruel. The outcry that went up in 1915 was a foreshadowing of that to come in the winter of 1920-1921 when the right satiric note was struck in a novel. And that was the mission of Sinclair Lewis.

As the whole world now knows, he was born in 1885 in the little town of Sauk Center, Minnesota. It is in the heart of the state and on the south edge of the lake he writes of with such poetic feeling. After a long period of hesitation and searching of heart, the village finally concluded that this was a great honor to it, and by 1931 was advertising itself with a banner across the street as the authorized and original Main Street. (pp. 113-14)

The assurance with which Sinclair Lewis draws his people is the product of the early years spent among them. He shares with every other exceptional boy in a small town the distinction of being considered queer by the more normal neighbors. (p. 114)

Main Street was published in October, 1920, when the citizens were so weary of idealism and world improvement that they were turning to a small town newspaper-man senator for their new leader. While the typesetters were putting the book into print, Senator Warren G. Harding was standing on his front porch assuring a people fatigued with internationalism that "there is more happiness in the American village than in any other place on the face of the earth." (p. 115)

In one form or another [Lewis's novels which preceded *Main Street*] contained nearly all the ingredients which were now expanded or rearranged into the pattern of that successful novel. But there is no getting away from the element of coincidence in the popularity of *Main Street* because, as any one who will trouble himself to read it along with its predecessors may now see, it is not as a novel enough better than *The Trail of the Hawk* or *The Job* to become of itself a phenomenon. But the country was finally ready for *Main Street* and *Babbitt,* and the discouraged Sinclair Lewis was prepared to write them and accept the sudden conspiracy of a capricious public to take him seriously.

The story of Carol Kennicott's plunge into Gopher Prairie and what she saw there is now known throughout the world. For the first time we paused in our hypocritical post-War narcissism and had a good look at ourselves in a mirror distorted just enough to focus attention upon our defects, and while the whole continent lifted up its voice in cries and curses and lamenta-

tions, the jealous and delighted European world which had been amazed at American efficiency in mechanics and engineering rejoiced in the picture of our cultural deficiencies, the students at the Sorbonne wrote essays on backward America as seen in the realism of *Main Street* and *Babbitt,* and the eminent committee at Stockholm presented the author with a purse and a crown. It is really more interesting as a social than as a literary event. (p. 118)

The novel was received as a satire, as a realistic report of small-town life, or as a protest against the absorbing poverty of American culture. It brought to the national attention the critical attitude of the young generation toward the hometown life. The cleavage which had developed between the way of life of the folks back home and this group of young Westerners who had escaped the West, received a college education, and adopted the cosmopolitan customs of the cities, was a shock to many people and added to the interest in this novel. For it was an examination of Gopher Prairie by one who was measuring it by a standard quite alien and unfamiliar to the natives of that village, and his heroine was a college-girl educated away from village life and panting for uplift. Both the author and the reader tacitly accept this inferred ideal when they walk down Main Street.

The protest was against the same contemptible qualities which infuriated the author of *The Story of a Country Town:* the smugness of the village mind lost in a rut without knowing it and venomously hostile to other values and to change, with no conversation except gossip and no social resources about Dave Dyer's stunt about the Norwegian catching a hen, secure in repeated platitudes about "the best people on earth here." The ugliness and absence of plan in the towns is especially depressing to Carol, and she analyzes this perfectly when she discerns that the symbol of beauty in these hideous places is old Rauskukle with his filth and his dollars and not beautiful streets and lovely buildings. She longs for some spark of gayety, charm and amusement to overcome the slow contagion of the village which infects and destroys the ambitious people who have looked upon the world where these graces are in favor and then have gone back to a profession in Gopher Prairie. Her two-year escape was futile. Gopher Prairie remained the same, and in the end, Carol too contracts the disease and looks after her baby, her conforming village-doctor husband, and her conventional house, a part of the "social appendix" still far from obsolescence. And while she rationalizes her failure with the spoken thought that she has kept the faith while losing the fight, Dr. Will is thinking about putting up the storm windows—if he can find the screwdriver.

Sinclair Lewis weakened the force of Carol by making her the mouthpiece for criticizing the small town and at the same time making her futile and a little ridiculous. She is often fantastic in her discontent; her idea of reforming this country town is to replace the Thanatopsis Club program of planting trees and establishing rest rooms for farmers' wives with Strindberg plays, classic dancers, and a black, Rabelaisian Frenchman to kiss her hand. She is a silly girl, dreamy, naïve, impractical, unsettled by her "culture" like hundreds of other co-eds of her day. It was right and proper for the natives to resent her puerile superiorities and to consider her flip and stuck-up and faintly scarlet when she spoke of legs, silk stockings, high wages for servants, and B.V.D.'s in mixed company. But the finer side of village life is carefully omitted in this satire, and the people are somewhat manhandled as a result.

The truth is that every single quality that is castigated in *Main Street* was and is as much a part of metropolitan life as of small-town life. Only it was easier to isolate it in Gopher Prairie. (pp. 119-20)

> Harlan Hatcher, "Sinclair Lewis," in his Creating the Modern American Novel, *Farrar & Rinehart, Incorporated, 1935, pp. 109-26.*

MARK SCHORER (essay date 1961)

[*Schorer is an American critic and the author of the definitive biography of Sinclair Lewis. In his often anthologized essay "Technique as Discovery" (1948), Schorer put forth the argument that fiction deserves the same close attention to diction and metaphor that the New Critics had been lavishing on poetry. He determined that fiction viewed only with respect to content was not art at all, but experience. Schorer also argued that the difference between content and art is technique and that the study of technique demonstrates how fictional form discovers and evaluates meaning, meaning that is often not intended by the author. In the following excerpt from his afterword to* Main Street, *Schorer discusses the novel as a history of the rise and fall of progressivism in the American small town.*]

Today, when the emancipation of women, for better or worse, is an accomplished fact, and when the sociological fate of the small town has largely been settled, we can, perhaps, read *Main Street* only as one reads a historical novel. The story opens in about 1906, with Carol Milford still a student in Blodgett College, but in quick summary it passes over her graduation and her year of study in Chicago and her three years as a librarian in St. Paul, and the story proper begins in about 1912, when she marries Dr. Will Kennicott and moves to Gopher Prairie, Minnesota. It ends in 1920, when, after her attempt to escape, she subsides into Gopher Prairie.

These dates, whether one stretches them from 1906 to 1920, or compresses them into the span from 1912 to 1920, in themselves mark off an era in American cultural history. It is the era, the manners of a closing stage of culture and (in the distant cities) the transition into another stage, that this novel memorializes, rather than any individual tragedy or comedy. It was a critical fashion at the time that *Main Street* was published to call it the American *Madame Bovary*, and Sinclair Lewis the American Flaubert. The comparison cannot be sustained today. *Madame Bovary* is more than a study of provincial manners in a certain time and place in France; that much is only the setting for a highly dramatic presentation of human catastrophe. But *Main Street* cannot be lifted out of its historic setting, which is, in effect, the whole of it.

It was a period that, in its earlier years, was imbued with a peculiar optimism about the potentialities of American life, a period, too, that engendered a native political progressivism that was intent on realizing those potentialities for as many people as possible and throughout society at large. America could be beautiful, because, in Van Wyck Brooks's phrase, America was at last "coming of age." The air was charged, in the early years of the second decade of this century, with the promise of a whole new upsurge in culture. Everyone was reading H. G. Wells. In the theater one saw the plays of Bernard Shaw and Henrik Ibsen, and the *cognoscenti* were talking about the discoveries of Sigmund Freud, which seemed to offer a whole new understanding of human nature. Every month, it seemed, a new "advanced" little magazine was being born. Post-impressionist painting broke on New York and then on the United States as a whole like a flood of light. All over

America, poets were "tuning their fiddles" in anticipation of a whole new era in American poetry, a poetry that would be daring, experimental, brilliant. It was the eve, in Ezra Pound's phrase, of the "American Risorgimento."

In 1912, when Carol Kennicott married Dr. Will, she had been exposed to something in every part of this ferment. . . . But when Carol moved from St. Paul, it was not on the wave of progress to New York, where she could have cultivated her interests, but on an ebb-flow into a backwash of American history, the dying American small town, Gopher Prairie, where her interests could only be crushed. (pp. 434-35)

When Carol came to Gopher Prairie, it was only fifty years old, bearing still the rough scars of its origin, such a short time before, as a crossing of frontier trails. Its growth, up to a certain point, had been rapid, and she finds that the villagers expect it to grow still, to become a city, even while they suffer from a kind of communal inferiority complex when they think about the cities. Carol, too, has hopes for it, and attempts to make real there ambitions she had acquired in the city: civic and social improvement, an experimental theater, exciting discussions of advanced ideas, the appreciation of fine poetry—the poetry of Yeats; but in every attempt she is rebuffed. And at last, like thousands of other young Americans, in precisely those years (and the novel itself comments on this shift in the population), she flees from the village to the city, where she is determined to find her career and herself. Abandoning her husband and trying to live an independent life with her young child, she is too late, and the village pulls her back. It is June in 1920.

Between the time of her first attempts to improve Gopher Prairie and the date of her submission to it, a world war had been fought and ended. With the advance of the war, the older American progressivist hopes had faded and by the time that it was over, much in American life seemed to many Americans themselves chauvinistic, hypocritical, unbearably provincial. For five years, the "revolt from the village" had been finding more and more voices in American literature, and in 1920, with the spread of a new attitude of post-war cynicism in American life, this particular dissatisfaction had reached its peak. With the failure of Carol Kennicott, Sinclair Lewis, his novel perfectly timed for the American audience, seized upon his first great triumph. It could hardly have been otherwise—this extraordinary phenomenon in American publishing and cultural history. Two years later Robert Littell said, "If *Main Street* lives, it will probably be not as a novel but as an incident in American life." It was "an incident in American life" because it put the seal on a period in American history. "She had fancied that all the world was changing." It had.

Main Street had certain other publishing advantages than its timing over its predecessors in the "revolt from the village." Most of the novels of "revolt" that came before it—books by writers like Sherwood Anderson, Zona Gale, Floyd Dell—were solemn about their subject when they were not lugubrious. Sinclair Lewis chose to write, in large part, satirically, and so even his vicious characters become figures in a kind of comedy. His satire is, of course, not evenly distributed. Carol, who seems naïve to us today when she does not seem downright silly, is spared all satire except for an occasional kindly prick. Will Kennicott is not satirized, nor is Guy Pollock nor Miles Bjornstam nor Fern Mullins and a number of others. The satire does not begin until Carol is looking into the window of Ludelmeyer's grocery store, and from then on it is directed only at the most complacent denizens of Gopher Prairie. Taken together, these provide a formidable collective picture of the trap into which Carol has fallen at the same time that they lighten the pathos of her dilemma.

Satire, which is essentially an art of over-simplification since it concentrates on a few if not only on a single characteristic, is inevitably in danger of overlooking the complexity of human nature. Thus, for example, the characterization of Juanita Haydock is as simple as a cartoon, and her husband, Harry, is not more than a shadow in a cartoon. Yet Lewis's gift extended to much more subtle satiric portraits. There is, for example, Vida Sherwin, the school teacher who had been in love with Kennicott before he knew Carol.

> She saw Carol during the first five minutes in Gopher Prairie. She stared at the passing motor, at Kennicott and the girl beside him. In that fog world of transference of emotion Vida had no normal jealousy but a conviction that, since through Carol she had received Kennicott's love, then Carol was a part of her, an astral self, a heightened and more beloved self. She was glad of the girl's charm, of the smooth black hair, the airy head and young shoulders. But she was suddenly angry. Carol glanced at her for a quarter-second, but looked past her, at an old roadside barn. If she had made the great sacrifice, at least she expected gratitude and recognition, Vida raged, while her conscious schoolroom mind fussily begged her to control this insanity.

In such curious touches as this, the Lewis satire takes on a deeper psychological realism than it has sometimes been credited with.

It was another kind of realism, however, that most compelled Lewis's early readers, and that was the realism of the scene, the persuasiveness of the physical details together with that of the midwestern vernacular that he so lovingly reported. Some early readers complained that the book was too unselective for art, but it was the very volume of packed detail that H. L. Mencken, for example, chose to praise in his review of the novel. It was, of course, the detail that Sinclair Lewis could bring out of the hoard of his experience as a boy and young man in Sauk Centre, Minnesota. . . . Lewis can go far beyond the simple catalogue . . . :

> Under the stilly boughs and the black gauze of dusk the street was meshed in silence. There was but the hum of motor tires crunching the road, the creak of a rocker on the Howlands' porch, the slap of a hand attacking a mosquito, a heat-weary conversation starting and dying, the precise rhythm of crickets, the thud of moths against the screen—sounds that were a distilled silence. It was a street beyond the end of the world, beyond the boundaries of hope. Though she should sit here forever, no brave procession, no one who was interesting, would be coming by. It was tediousness made tangible, a street builded of lassitude and of futility.

Here the catalogue of carefully observed details not only supports the generalizations but provides the drama itself. It is no individual but the entire environment that is Carol's antagonist. And sometimes the frustrating tension of the stalemate in which she finds herself forces the detail into a peculiar and rather alarming eloquence: ''. . . from the Chautauqua itself she got

nothing but wind and chaff and heavy laughter, the laughter of yokels at old jokes, a mirthless and primitive sound like the cries of beasts on a farm.''

The image of the American village that Lewis created through such details remains pretty much the image of the village that most of us still hold today, more than forty years later, and this in spite of the fact that today the novel, as a novel, reads in large part like a period piece. That scene he populated with a whole gallery of persons who are enduring memorials to familiar American types: the village atheist (Miles Bjornstam), the cruelly sanctimonius widow (Mrs. Bogart), the local ''queer'' (Erik Valborg), the town bully (Cy Bogart), the defeated liberal (Guy Pollock), and many another. In the midst of these he poses his two central characters, and they, too, are familiar American types—the complacent husband of common sense and the discontented wife with romantic dreams. (pp. 436-39)

At one point, away from Gopher Prairie, Carol decides to settle for ''the nobility of good sense,'' best represented by her husband, and in the end, she is forced to settle for it, although she cannot then and never will learn to believe in its ''nobility.'' Early in the novel, Will Kennicott had warned her:

> ''. . . I want—oh, my dear, do you know how much I want to like the people you like? I want to see people as they are.''

> ''Well, don't forget to see people as other folks see them as they are.''

At the end, having learned very little, she continues to see people only as she was in the first place prepared to see them.

Sinclair Lewis does not chide her. Generally speaking, he views the material of his novel as she views it, and all his life, a good half of his nature was given to the same kind of romantic reverie that motivates Carol. But the other half of his nature was Will Kennicott's—downright, realistic, sensible, crude. The two together make the author, and just as in his life these two parts of himself struggled against each other, so at the end of his novel, the husband and wife are still ''enemies, yoked.''

It is interesting to note, however, that in order to end his novel, one or the other of them must have the last word. Forced to choose, he gives it to Doctor Will.

> ''Well, good night. Sort of feels to me like it might snow tomorrow. Have to be thinking about putting up the storm-windows pretty soon. Say, did you notice whether the girl put that screwdriver back?''

Neither noble nor ignoble, good sense rules at last, and in no way whatever has life in Gopher Prairie become ''more conscious.'' This, the author seems to say in the end, is not only as things must be but even as things should be. This is the reality. (p. 439)

Mark Schorer, in an afterword to Main Street *by Sinclair Lewis, New American Library, 1961, pp. 433-39.*

DANIEL AARON   (essay date 1965)

[*Aaron is an American historian and literary critic. In the following excerpt, he assesses* Main Street's *literary and historical significance and counters critics who consider Lewis's satirical treatment of Gopher Prairie one-sided and abusive.*]

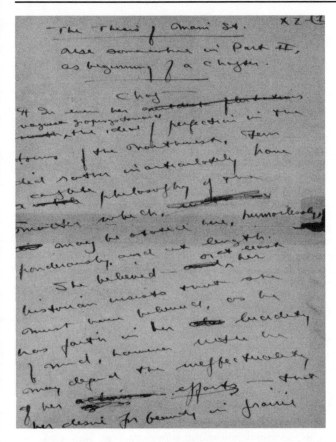

Lewis's early notes for the novel Main Street. *Harry Ransom Humanities Research Center, University of Texas at Austin.*

Main Street may or may not be Sinclair Lewis' best novel (many readers would rank it below *Babbitt*), but it is one of those symptomatic books that literary historians find so convenient as milestones or turning points. It belongs to the special category of book—there is no name for it—which is at once a valid literary work and an explosive cultural event. Greater novelists than Lewis have had to wait decades or longer for a responsive audience, but the publication of *Main Street* in October 1920 (I say this on the authority of Prof. Mark Schorer, Lewis' most searching biographer), turned out to be "the most sensational event in the twentieth-century American publishing history." (p. 166)

It may seem odd, in retrospect, that a novel without any strikingly original characters, without suspense, without any remarkable stylistic merits, should have aroused such a clamor. The plot is ambling and unspectacular. It is merely the story of a romantic half-educated Middle-Western girl, tinged with vague longings, who marries a small-town doctor, rebels against the monotony and drabness of her life, and grudgingly—after a brief flurry of nonconformity—accommodates herself to her husband and her destiny. And yet the day-to-day experiences of Lewis' heroine, Carol Kennicott, devoid of tragedy and often trivial, proved absorbing to hundreds of thousands of readers who vicariously shared them.

Some readers, it must be said, were shocked and angered. Lewis, they felt, had indulged in cheap fun at the expense of the American institutions and at men and women who had made the nation great. He had depicted the small town, that microcosm of Eden, without love or understanding. Sherwood

Anderson, for one, never forgave Lewis for reducing American small towns to hot dusty places peopled by boasters and liars, "never tender about anything or anybody, never human." But there were others who rejoiced in his iconoclasm. They saw him as the articulator of their own case against what was mean and dispiriting in North American life. (p. 167)

Lewis' portrait of the small town is not unrelievedly dismal nor are all of its inhabitants drooling Yahoos. Some have private heroisms. He had modeled Gopher Prairie on Sauk Center, Minnesota, where he was born and where he spent a not very enjoyable adolescence; his home town was not without the kind of brave beauty Carol conceded to Gopher Prairie. In moments of nostalgia, Lewis would recall the friendliness of Sauk Center, the swimming and the fishing, the ten-mile tramp with a shotgun in October,

> sliding on Hoboken Hill, stealing melons, or listening to the wonders of an elocutionist at the G.A.R. Hall. It was a good time, a good place, and a good preparation for life.

Such a confession would seem to moderate Sherwood Anderson's complaint that Lewis missed the poetry of rural life; still, such mellow evocations are not characteristic. If he sometimes remembered boyish pleasures, his biographer has shown us that Lewis was more deeply touched by his humiliations. One of the reasons he wrote *Main Street,* Lewis said later, was to puncture humbug notions about the alleged neighborliness of small towns; and he described how irritated he was, after returning from Yale University during the summer of his sophomore year, by the comments of his father's friends:

> Why don't Doc Lewis make Harry get a job on the farm instead of letting him sit around readin' a lot of fool histories and God know what all?

Some of these early frustrations undoubtedly went into the making of *Main Street,* but the novel must have owed a great deal to what Lewis once called his "extraordinarily discrepant" literary ancestors—Dickens, Swinburne, H. G. Wells, Housman, Hardy, Hamlin Garland, H. L. Mencken—as well as some unacknowledged ones.

On more than one occasion Lewis honored his debt to Mencken, a brilliant literary and social critic who had begun his derisive commentary on the American bourgeoisie (or "booboisie," to use his own coinage) long before *Main Street* was even an idea in Lewis' head. I have sometimes thought it was Mencken's jovial satire—especially as it applied to that area of the United States he called the "Bible Belt"—that prepared the way for his younger follower and partially accounted for the enthusiastic reception of his work. (pp. 168-70)

Another subversive voice echoing in *Main Street* belongs to Thorstein Veblen, an economist, sociologist, and critic of the business ethos who had become the darling of the literary radicals after the publication of *The Theory of the Leisure Class* in 1899. On the one occasion I met Lewis, he told me that he had never read Veblen. If so, it is still interesting that Miles Bjorstam, Gopher Prairie's handyman and radical, has a book of Veblen in his library; and it is certainly a coincidence, if nothing more, that the town's banker, merchants, real estate men, lawyers, and clergymen are very much as Veblen described them in 1915. Local patriotism and civic pride, Veblen observed at that time, provided the rationale for real estate speculators. (p. 170)

A third less obvious influence but the key to the blurred thesis of *Main Street* was another disturber of the peace, Henry David Thoreau. Lewis repeatedly named Thoreau as the pervasive influence on all of his work—a paradoxical admission considering Lewis' unwillingness or inability to lead the simple life. But the burden of Lewis' message to his fellow Americans was indeed Thoreauvian. Mark Schorer has rightly said that the basis of his plots was "the individual impulse to freedom and the social impulse to restrict it." *Main Street,* at bottom, is a variation on a theme of *Walden.*

The best way to illustrate this Thoreauvian link is to consider more closely Lewis' heroine, Carol Kennicott, that controversial figure maligned and betrayed by her creator. Many of the admirers of the novel—Mencken, to name only one—refused to take her seriously. She was a romantic ninny, after all, dreaming of medieval castles, bearded Frenchmen, nymphs and satyrs, jeweled elephants. Her vision of a remodeled Gopher Prairie as a New England village nestling in a Swinburnian landscape was as pathetic as it was ridiculous. And yet Lewis allows this same woman, whose artistic and literary notions were not so vastly superior to those of the bluestockings in the Gopher Prairie Thanatopsis Club, to preach his satirical sermon to his sheeplike contemporaries and to assail the institutions that enslaved them.

Apparently, in 1920 Lewis was as unabashed a romantic as Carol (in fact he never stopped hankering for a bookish fairyland inhabited by amorous sylphs) and he held his heroine in much higher esteem than did his more sophisticated and cynical friends. Even in the earlier versions of the novel, where she appeared as a character named Fern, Lewis had expressed a faith in her "lucidity of mind" if not in the effectiveness of her efforts, and there is little to indicate that he disagreed with her indictment of the "brisk, spectacled, motor-driving businessmen" of Main Street. To be sure, then and later, he never entirely approved of her nor did he minimize her deficiencies, but he certainly shared her distaste for Gopher Prairie's complacency and hypocrisy, and he encouraged her attempts to stave off what Lewis calls in *Main Street,* the "village virus."

The principal sufferer of that disease is the lawyer, Guy Pollock, a dim and appealing figure who in the early draft of the novel was probably intended to play a larger role than he does in the final version. As he explains it to Carol, the village virus is an infection to which ambitious people in small towns are peculiarly susceptible. Gradually, imperceptibly, it saps them of their hope and energy, narcotizes rebelliousness, reduces the victim to the same dead level of the lifeless majority residing in "a respectable form of hell." Carol finally discontinues her one-woman revolt (it is hard to say whether or not she actually contracts the disease), but she protests, with Lewis' approval, until the end.

In a retrospective look at *Main Street,* Lewis maintained that he was not indebted to Masters' *Spoon River Anthology* nor did he have in mind a corn-fed Emma Bovary, two assertions I accept unhesitatingly, but his claim that he had carefully implanted the idea that "Carol wasn't of as good stuff as her husband," although true enough, is still a little disingenuous. She lacked the stability and perseverance of Dr. Will Kennicott, perhaps even his humanity and quiet courage, but her crusade was Lewis' as well, and it was Carol who conveyed his subversive ideas, not her husband.

Dr. Will is a good physician and surgeon, but he is quite at home with the 100 per cent boosters. He laughs at their jokes. He believes in their primitive politics, and declares:

> Tell you, Carrie, there's just three classes of people: folks that haven't got any ideas at all; and cranks that kick about everything; and Regular Guys, the fellows with sticktuitiveness, that boost and get the world's work done.

Carol, who presumably fits into the second category, cannot swallow this nonsense, and although she loves her husband, she will not sacrifice her individuality to become like him, as he unconsciously desires her to. In one of her frank moments, she says she is a crank not because she is trying to "reform" the town but in order to save her own soul; and here is the real thesis of *Main Street.* The Carol who speaks in this vein is the daughter of Emerson and Thoreau and not the American sister of Emma Bovary.

Then why does Lewis turn against her and later side with her bumbling husband? Why did he write an article in 1924 (a visit by the author of *Main Street* to the office of Dr. Will Kennicott) the point of which is to debunk his former alter ego? (pp. 171-73)

Lewis, the apologist or celebrator of the middle class, is more assertive than the Lewis who assails it. He prefers the company of the doctor to that of his querulous wife with whom he had never openly identified himself. . . . Like Dr. Will, like Babbitt, he respected the men responsible for reliable automobiles and tiled bathrooms, as a glance at any of his novels will show. Among his portraits of business and professional men, Babbitt is presented sardonically but without rancor, Dodsworth almost reverently, Cass Timberlane romantically. One of the most admirable specimens (to Lewis, at any rate) was Fred Cornplow, an automobile salesman from Sachem, New York, and the hero of one of the weaker novels, *The Prodigal Parents.* . . . Lewis remained as loyally committed to the best representatives of the middle class as William Dean Howells, a writer he dismissed as a "pious old maid" but to whom he was more closely linked than he perhaps realized.

The panegyric to Fred Cornplow, published in the radical thirties, irritated a number of critics for whom "middle class" was almost a term of abuse. They contrasted the sharpness and pungency of *Main Street, Babbitt,* and *Elmer Gantry* with the increasingly mellow novels that ducked, they thought, the real issues of the day. Lewis, one of them complained, "drew a revolutionary picture of American middle-class life without coming to revolutionary conclusions about it."

Remarks of this sort betrayed an ignorance of Lewis and his position. He had always written as an "insider" even though he seemed to be peering at his society from without. If he rebuked the Babbitts and the whole "crowd" of Dr. Kennicott's friends with their "coarse voices, large damp hands, tooth-brush mustaches, bald spots, and Masonic watch-charms," it was for failing to measure up to their capacities, and the fault lay less with them than with their society. . . . The language of the people he admires hardly differs from the language of the people he debunks. Professional men, businessmen, social workers, teachers, laborers, technicians all "bumble" or "chirp" or "warble" or "boom" or "gurgle." His serious discussions on science or religion, as Rebecca West noted, were likely to sound like "Babbittry in reverse."

No reader of *Main Street* can forget the speech of the "Booster and Hustler," Jim Blausser, invited by the Commercial Club to inaugurate their campaign to bring industry to Gopher Prairie and incidentally boost real estate values. Jim Blausser talks in a subliterate, squalid Americanese as remote from standard English as Chinese. . . . (pp. 173-75)

[It] is pure parody. But it is parody, nonetheless, of deeply cherished beliefs. Constance Rourke, our wisest and most subtle student of American humour, has written that "American audiences enjoyed their own deflation," and Lewis (whose humour is very much in the American vein) knew his audience well. He shared their sentimentality, their cynicism, their Philistinism, their cheerful irreverence, their dislike of pomposity. Like Jim Blausser, he also exulted in the superiority of his countrymen and relished the pure *Homo americanibus* unspoiled by what he called "the hard, varnished, cosmopolitan cleverness." (p. 176)

Main Street is a work of historical importance, then, not merely as a reflection, partly unconscious, of popular American tastes and assumptions, but also because it helped Americans to understand themselves. T. K. Whipple, one of Lewis' best critics, once described him as a Red Indian "stalking through the land of his enemies." The metaphor is apt, suggesting as it does that Lewis was at once a part of his society and detached from it. On the other hand, is it quite precise? If Red Lewis stalked his enemies, was he not also prowling his tribal land? Were his enemies not fellow Indians who had abandoned the faith in their gods? He was too much a part of his nation, too deeply involved with its hopes, too impatient with its failures, to treat it simply in a tender or simply in a clinical way. Yet somehow, he managed to make his prosaic materials appear fabulous (for America, he said, was as strange to him as Russia and as complex as China) and in a few books to translate his commonplace boobs into archetypes. (p. 177)

> Daniel Aaron, "Sinclair Lewis, 'Main Street'," in The American Novel: From James Fenimore Cooper to William Faulkner, *edited by Wallace Stegner, Basic Books, Inc., Publishers, 1965, pp. 166-79.*

STEPHEN S. CONROY (essay date 1970)

[*In the following excerpt Conroy analyzes* Main Street *as a sociological novel which, like* Babbitt, *is concerned with a character's adjustment to the culture of a community.*]

Sinclair Lewis was a novelist blessed with what C. Wright Mills called "the sociological imagination," the capacity to see and be interested in the overriding dramatic quality of "the interplay of man and society, of biography and history, of self and world." Lewis was often accused of being a kind of social scientist, although usually the similarity noted was in investigative and preparatory techniques and not in quality of mind. . . . Lewis too recognized the assumptions which underlay most of his work; he certainly was aware that his habits of mind and method of composition resembled the habits and practices of the social scientist. Most writers, he tells us, when asked what form the first idea of a story takes, will reply that they think first of a plot, of a person, or even of a setting. But speaking of his own practice Lewis says, "Actually, these three are from the beginning mixed in your mind; you want to do a story about a person who, as he becomes real to you, dwells in a definite house, street, city, class of society." It is, of course, this view of the individual imbedded in a matrix of neighborhood, city, and class which constitutes the basis of the sociological imagination.

The power that this matrix has over the behavior of the individual is enormous. The universal recognition of this fact leads many to conclude that the human individual is completely bound up and hemmed in by his culture. Yet somehow the human remains intractably human and stubbornly individualistic. He believes that he has free will and he acts on that faith; he often rebels, questions, and struggles against any confining force. The individual who does this is capable of becoming, in his own eyes at least, a worthy opponent of the collective will of society. The "interplay" Mills speaks of then becomes a kind of combat, a drama whose resolution is not always tragic, even though the antagonists are grossly unequal. The observer with the sociological imagination is one who is aware that this drama is being played out around him and focuses on it. He may be either a social scientist or an artist; the important factor is his view of life, not his professional preoccupations. Without question, Sinclair Lewis's imaginative frame of reference was sociological.

Given the nature of the struggle occurring, the problem for Sinclair Lewis, as for any novelist of a similar bent, is to determine just what responses or alternative modes of behavior are available to the protagonist vis-à-vis his culture. It is to Lewis's credit that he anticipated the formulations of David Riesman and even went beyond them in at least one instance. Riesman too, of course, possesses the sociological imagination, with perhaps a more legitimate claim to it than Lewis. In *The Lonely Crowd* and other works Riesman theorized about the responses open to the individual and concluded that there were only three: adjustment, anomie, and autonomy. Adjustment means conformity to the universals of the culture and an acceptance of the narrow range of choice left to the individual. Anomie in an individual, on the other hand, is virtually synonymous with maladjustment. A characteristic of the anomic is that he is never able to conform or feel comfortable in the roles assigned to him by society since he rejects its traditional norms and values. The third possibility is autonomy. The autonomous person may or may not conform. He makes choices; he lives up to the culture's norms when it is advantageous for him to do so, and he transcends them when there are reasons to do so. Lewis depicts two kinds of autonomy, positive and negative. He realized that the man indifferent to the demands of his culture could use his freedom for either good or evil.

The major works of Sinclair Lewis's greatest decade may be shown to be the working out in dramatic form of these sociological insights. *Main Street* and *Babbitt* both show the sometimes painful process of adjustment. (pp. 348-50)

Carol Kennicott, the heroine of *Main Street,* is usually characterized as a brave young bride who struggles pridefully against the spiteful parochialism of a prairie village, but George F. Babbitt is generally thought of as a near-villain of urbanized conformity. Usually overlooked is their similarity of outlook and aspiration, and the parallelism of their fates. They are both unhappy and restless in the society in which they find themselves; they both rebel ineffectually, and they both finally become largely adjusted to their surroundings. There are differences, of course, but they are often overemphasized at the expense of more important similarities.

Carol goes through a definite three-stage process of rebellion, withdrawal from and reconciliation to Gopher Prairie. Her rebellion begins with her first tour of Main Street during which she is repelled by its ugly drabness. She also overreacts to the general blankness of the town society and to the dullness of her new companions. She then overcompensates with almost frenzied activity, gives silly but lively parties, and takes up and drops many useless projects. The village misunderstands her vitality and rebuffs her efforts. Carol feels, appropriately enough, that the townsfolk have rejected her, and she also suspects that they are scoffing at her. This reaction of the town has a double-edged effect on Carol. In one way it deepens her rebellion and causes her to involve herself in a situation even further outside the town's standard of acceptable behavior; it causes her flirtation with an ardent young apprentice tailor, which could have led to public scandal and disgrace. That it does not is due, paradoxically enough, to the town itself, for she rejects the young man's advances largely because she has grown to fear Gopher Prairie. She has made the first step in the process of adjustment when she cuts off a personal relationship for social reasons. Even if her action is largely motivated by terror, it constitutes a recognition on her part (and on Lewis's) of the power of the society to control behavior.

When rebellion within the confines of Gopher Prairie proves to be either impossible or too costly, Carol takes a step toward withdrawal. Her removal to Washington, D.C., like her earlier rebellion, is paradoxically but a step in her ultimate adjustment. Washington's sophistication and refinement prove not to be enough to replace the loss of family and status. She spends a good deal of time planning someday to take her son back to the open fields and friendly barns around Gopher Prairie. Also, in Washington she learns that there are Main Streets everywhere, and as Lewis tells us, in comparison to some Gopher Prairie's is a model of beauty and intelligence. In addition she begins to see that there is a thick streak of Main Street in Washington and doubtlessly in other large cities as well, a truism which George Babbitt is soon to learn in Zenith. Thus is the way paved for a reconciliation with her village; her sojourn in Washington has enabled her to come to terms with Gopher Prairie. "At last," she rejoiced, "I've come to a fairer attitude toward the town. I can love it now." Her view becomes more than fair, even hazily romantic: "She again saw Gopher Prairie as her home, waiting for her in the sunset, rimmed round with splendor. . . ."

At the end of *Main Street* Carol Kennicott is at home in Gopher Prairie in every sense of the word. She has not been beaten into submission; she has decided to adjust. Her return home is the result of three factors: her desire for her son to grow up in what she presumes to be the healthy environment of the prairie village, her love for her husband, and her newfound love for the town itself. Near the conclusion of the novel Carol voluntarily gets into the back seat of an automobile with a woman friend in order to let their "menfolk" sit together in the front. This symbolic act shows her to be, all unaware, finally a true citizen of Gopher Prairie. Originally Carol had too strongly insisted on her individuality against the pressure of her culture. She engaged in a battle which she could not win on her own terms; she did not have either the personal force or the social backing to change the ways of town significantly. She either had to continue fighting and paying the terrible personal costs involved, or she had to adjust. Adjustment of course spells defeat for her aspirations, but it is a peculiar kind of defeat, almost without sting. When Carol adjusts she is comfortable in her adjustment; only occasional, and mild, twinges remain, and only for a time.

Babbitt's struggle is very little different from Carol Kennicott's. He too squirms uneasily under the pressure of his society, rebels against it, and finally returns meekly to conformity to it. There is one important difference between Carol Kennicott and George F. Babbitt; Carol comes as an outsider into Gopher Prairie, but Babbitt is a longtime citizen of Zenith.

Carol reacts to the village as if it were an icy pool she had just been thrown into; her immediate and almost overwhelming desire is to get out. Babbitt, on the other hand, is immersed in his surroundings as in a warm bath. (pp. 350-52)

The emphasis in the beginning of the novel is on Babbitt as conformist, although he has already become aware of some disturbing impulses. He conforms outwardly but he is no longer completely adjusted; he has vague dissatisfactions and is full of veiled rebellions and escapist daydreams. What finally sets Babbitt loose, what causes such a conformist to go so far astray, are the shocking events surrounding Paul Reisling's attempted murder of his wife, his trial and imprisonment. After the sentencing, "Babbitt returned to his office to realize that he faced a world which, without Paul, was meaningless." And so his rebellion begins.

When a conformist becomes rebellious, when he is, as Lewis says of Babbitt, "determined to go astray," what can he do? He can stray sexually, or at least try to; Babbitt's attempts to seduce first a neighbor's coquettish wife and then a tough young manicurist meet with little success. These episodes are the somewhat more shabby equivalent of Carol Kennicott's flirtation with a tailor's apprentice, and are no more meaningful. There is also with Babbitt, as there was with Carol, a compulsion to make the rebellion known. . . . The first part of his rebellion consists of an entanglement with the bohemian element of the city, and continues with an adulterous affair with one of its leaders, Tanis Judique. The second part of his rebellion is political rather than sexual or social. He publicly avows some of the positions of the liberal minority, defends "radicals," and refuses to join an organization devoted to the repression of dissent. Although the first part of his rebellion is more colorful, the second part proves more dangerous to him. (pp. 352-53)

Carol never really feels the full weight of her society's displeasure; Babbitt, however, receives penalties ranging from loss of business through threats of ostracism and even violence. (p. 353)

Babbitt is a rather stubborn man, so that fearful as he is, he will not give in to these pressures. It would have been interesting to see how far society would have moved against him, and at what point he would have broken down. But Lewis is not yet willing to let the conflict between an individual and his culture work itself out. With perfect timing, Myra Babbitt is rushed off to the hospital for an emergency appendectomy. Her surgery and extended recovery give Babbitt and his clan a pretext for patching up their squabble. With his wife's illness, the hostility toward Babbitt seems to disappear. He is even given another chance to join the Good Citizen's League, and "within two weeks no one in the League was more violent regarding the wickedness of Seneca Doane, the crimes of labor unions, the perils of immigration, and the delights of gold, morality, and bank accounts than was George F. Babbitt."

Thus is Babbitt's conformist nature slendidly reestablished; once again he sinks into his culture "up to his chin and over." Yet, once again, like Carol Kennicott, he is not completely submerged. He is the adjusted man, but there is in him as in Carol a residue of dissatisfaction. In both cases it is displaced onto the next generation. Carol looks upon her daughter as the one who will win the struggle with the village culture, and Babbitt defends his son's life plan even though it is not very promising. Babbitt urges him to have courage and to do what he wishes to do with his life. To Babbitt as to Carol children represent the hope for a brighter future. This hope is, of course, the culturally approved way in which a defeated rebel may find solace. Lewis still saw this deferred and displaced gratification as the best solution to the problem facing the individualist in a culture demanding conformity. The bohemian response he had no taste for, and he still seems largely unaware of the possibility of real autonomy. There is in *Babbitt* no character with the requisite intelligence and force to make the autonomous response. All that is left is conformity, adjustment, and a vague hope for a freer future. (p. 354)

Stephen S. Conroy, "Sinclair Lewis's Sociological Imagination," in American Literature, Vol. XLII, No. 3, November, 1970, pp. 348-62.

GEORGE H. DOUGLAS   (essay date 1970-71)

[*Douglas is an American author and educator whose works include* H. L. Mencken: Critic of American Life *(1978). Primarily concerned with popular American culture, Douglas has stated that "I write both nostalgically and critically about the American past and its relation to the present." In the following excerpt, he finds that a retrospective reading of* Main Street *reveals a work of gentle, naive optimism rather than the biting satire usually associated with the novel.*]

Sinclair Lewis, we should all now know, was a man of vulgar tastes, who was nevertheless possessed of superficial but sometimes brilliant powers of observation; a writer with an incredibly poor sense of exposition and logical development whose characters seldom come to clarity and completeness even when they "drip with human juices," as H. L. Mencken once put it; and finally a man totally lacking in the tragic depth and understanding necessary to sustain the kind of artistic power he did possess. This latter characteristic, of course, more than anything else, separates him from more important writers such as Dreiser and O'Neill, who will surely outlive him in critical acclaim even though they began with artistic limitations nearly as great.

But what of *Main Street*? What is it like in the reading today? It is, of course, still considered to be one of Lewis's five or six most important novels (of the twenty-two novels he wrote in his lifetime only those written in the twenties and, in this writer's opinion, *Cass Timberlaine* from the forties, are still worth reading), although surely it is the poorest and least rewarding of these from an artistic point of view. It is a book that perhaps few would care to read if Sinclair Lewis had not written it and if it had not made the kind of social and literary history that it did.

Nevertheless, reading (or rereading) *Main Street* fifty years after its publication is a curiously rewarding experience because it is not at all the kind of experience that matches our working stereotypes. It is a gentle book, full of optimism and naiveté, and in its tone and mood there is little of the feverishness that one associates with Lewis; surprisingly not the kind of satiric bite one expects from the author of *Babbitt* and *Elmer Gantry*. There is strong justification for the remark of Grace Hegger Lewis, Lewis's first wife, that *Main Street* was not a satire until the critics discovered it as such.

Of course *Main Street* is not one thing only; like most of Lewis's novels it is peculiarly fragmented and leaves one with a series of impressions that are difficult to develop into a unified whole. Satire of small-town life is one of the persistent qualities of the novel, to be sure, but it does not dominate the novel in the way that one may expect. Satire here, as elsewhere in Lewis,

is a mood that comes and goes, not a consistently developed point of view of an all-pervasive attitude. The dominant attitude that does appear on reading the book today seems to be something quite different.

I have suggested that in the reading today *Main Street* reveals itself as a gentle book. This is so not merely because so many unsettling things have happened to the world since 1920, or because we have become so immunized against the brutal and the depraved around us that a dissection of small-town life and mores is naturally innocuous by comparison. Before 1920, after all, our literature had already seen everything it was necessary to see of the cruelty and squalor of American life on all its levels, and writers like Dreiser and Upton Sinclair were, from the beginning, much more unsettled by their experiences, and unsettling in their writings, than Lewis was or ever became. . . . Lewis instinctively wanted to believe in the goodness and healthiness of small-town life, and this instinct is manifest in *Main Street,* although doubtless it became nearly obscured in Lewis's other novels of the twenties.

In the reading today *Main Street* bears a curious relationship to the seldom-read novel *Free Air* which Lewis published immediately before *Main Street* and which he composed partly simultaneously with it (*Main Street* in fact seems in many ways more like Lewis's early novels than the celebrated novels of the twenties). Both novels have the feel of a journey into the vastness of the plains states, both exude a nostalgia for the simplicity of open country. In both, the depressing, boring, commonplace qualities of the midwest are brought into view only to be cleansed by the brisk morning air of the northern plains. Both novels remind one of the midwestern spring, particularly that of Minnesota, which invariably arrives just when one has come to believe that it doesn't exist. Both seem to be devoted to one thing above all others: the free air that is just around the next bend in the road to wash away all the staleness of the settlements. This "free air" of course was never seen by Lewis as being among the privileges of the Easterner or the European because of the bondages of their social lives, and above all their restrictions of geography, their lack of space and invigorating air.

What I am suggesting is that if the modern reader reads *Free Air* as an introduction and companion piece to *Main Street* he will be moved to an entirely different perspective on the tone and ultimate intention of *Main Street,* a novel which has become beclouded by our stereotypes of Lewis as heckler and village atheist. Something of a passion for "free air," something of a craving for openness, seems an essential part of *Main Street* and seems to be carried over from the earlier novel, in such a way that the two seem to enjoy a symbiotic relationship and unity. (pp. 339-41)

[*Main Street*] is a work of weak development and poor characterization which nevertheless exerts an inexplicable charm on its reader, the charm that belongs to journeys, to topography, to the pleasures of following a writer to places for which he has a fondness, nostalgia, and ultimately an uncritical affection. It is, much more than one would expect, a novel of unspoiled Minnesota; its dominant mood is not satire but motion, change, seasonableness, possibility. Satire there is, to be sure. Lewis's greatest gift, one which he was to exploit subsequently to great advantage, is his malevolent and uncharitable eye and ear; but *Main Street* seems to be the work of an agitated man seeking a peace, a quiet and openness, which he both hopes and believes to be somewhere along the road.

An epiphany that gives **Main Street** to us is the journey which brings Mr. and Mrs. Will Kennicott to Gopher Prairie from St. Paul. This journey sets the pace for all that is to come, gives us the cumulative feel of the novel. And the feel is one not of judgment and opprobrium but of watchful waiting.

> Under the rolling clouds of the prairie a moving mass of steel. An irritable clank and rattle beneath a prolonged roar. The sharp scent of oranges cutting the soggy smell of unbathed people and ancient baggage.
>
> Towns as planless as a scattering of pasteboard boxes on an attic floor. The stretch of faded gold stubble broken only by clumps of willows encircling white houses and red barns.
>
> No. 7, the way train, grumbling through Minnesota, imperceptibly climbing the giant tableland that slopes in a thousand-mile rise from hot Mississippi bottoms to the Rockies.
>
> It is September, hot, very dusty.
>
> There is no smug Pullman attached to the train, and the day coaches of the East are replaced by free chair cars, with each seat cut into two adjustable plush chairs, the head-rests covered with doubtful linen towels.... There is no porter; no pillows, no provision for beds, but all today and all tonight they will ride in this long steel box—farmers with perpetually tired wives and children who seem all to be of the same age; workmen going to new jobs; traveling salesmen with derbies and freshly shined shoes.
>
> They are parched and cramped, the lines of their hands filled with grime; they go to sleep curled in distorted attitudes, heads against the window-panes or propped on rolled coats on seat-arms, and legs thrust into the aisle. They do not read; apparently they do not think. They wait....
>
> (pp. 342-43)

For what do they wait? What hope can they have? What hope can Carol Kennicott have? At one glance nothing but more smoke, more stale air. Each small town beside the track seems more depressing than the next, each seems to add confirmation that nothing can breathe free here.... Even the prairie became frightening to Carol, ''the width and bigness of it which expanded her spirit an hour ago began to frighten her.'' It was too big and she could never know it. But in looking out the window again the scene changes as it always will here in this country. The stuffiness and feeling of hopelessness vanish into the air....

> All this working land was turned into exuberance by the light. The sunshine was dizzy on open stubble; shadows from immense cumulus clouds were forever sliding across low mounds; and the sky was wider and loftier and more resolutely blue than the sky of cities ... she declared.
>
> ''It's a glorious country; a land to be big in,'' she crooned....
>
> (pp. 343-44)

Later when the town of Gopher Prairie comes into view the dread and hopelessness creep back, for Gopher Prairie was not, as Will had promised, a more civilized and beautiful place than any she had seen along the way; ''it was merely an enlargement of all the hamlets which they had been passing. Only to the eyes of a Kennicott was it exceptional. . . . It was unprotected and unprotecting; there was no dignity in it or any hope of greatness. . . . It was not a place to live in, not possibly, not conceivably.'' . . . (pp. 344-45)

But as in **Free Air** the momentary dread is always to fade with the next shifting of the scene; there is always the possibility that the wind will blow something else along the tracks, always the possibility of another perspective to offer beauty and hope. This something else is not only nature, although there is plenty of nature and the outdoor life in **Main Street,** but motion and change itself. Lewis in later telling us that Kennicott's hobbies were medicine, land-investment, Carol, motoring, and hunting, suggests the predominance of motion, motion like that of the train which constantly brings something new into sight, some different scent in the air. And so much of what Lewis has to say about Gopher Prairie, not only here but throughout the book, is revealed in motion, revealed while the scene is changing as it does from the train window. Lewis himself was a curiously mobile man, a man of nervous and peripatetic ways who could never live in one place very long, whose mental health required frequent changes of environment, and **Main Street** best comes into view in walks outdoors, in automobile rides, yes in these even more memorably than in lampoons of village types.

Later in their marriage, for example, when Will is away with a surgical patient in Rochester, Carol takes a walk in a bleak February day, temperature thirty below zero. She is overcome by loneliness as her body shivers in the wind. ''She wondered why the good citizens insisted on adding the chill of prejudice, why they did not make the houses of their spirits more warm and frivolous like the wise chatterers of Stockholm and Moscow.''

This loneliness passes, however, not because Carol is with nature, not because it is washed away by the winter wind, but because the village itself has the antidote to loneliness. (p. 345)

It was not nature, vastness, openness alone which served as the antidote to gossip, stuffy rooms, and garish decor, but, strange as it may seem, the commonplaces of industry—the bank, the planing mill, the railroad. Carol, like Sinclair Lewis himself, despised the sameness and monotony of the small town's appearance nearly as much as the standardization of small town manners, but she had become infected, as she could hardly have realized consciously, by a need to have familiar things around her which in their very repetitiousness held all the hope and magic one needed in the world. There is much loving space, many thousands of words devoted in **Main Street** to the joys of the familiar and the commonplace, joys which perhaps are foreclosed to the more cosmopolitan citizens of Rome, Paris, Copenhagen, or New York, available though they be to all.

The railroad, for example. ''The East remembered generations when there had been no railroad, and had no awe of it; but here the railroads had been before time was.'' Railroads did something for the spirit of man in that their very obtrusiveness and commonplaceness could provide a measure of mystery, awe, magic, and melodrama. (p. 346)

To the small boys the railroad was a familiar playground. They climbed the iron ladders on the sides of the box-cars; built fires behind piles of old ties; waved to favorite brakemen. But to Carol it was magic.

She was motoring with Kennicott, the car lumping through darkness, the lights showing mud-puddles and ragged weeds by the road. A train coming! A rapid chuck-a-chuck, chuck-a-chuck, chuck-a-chuck. It was hurling past—the Pacific Flyer, an arrow of golden flame. Light from the fire-box splashed the underside of the trailing smoke. Instantly the vision was gone; Carol was back in the long darkness; and Kennicott was giving his version of that fire and wonder: ''No. 19. Must be 'bout ten minutes late.'' . . .

(p. 347)

So Carol and Will share this awe and wonder, each in a distinct sort of way. (People have often believed that Lewis sees Gopher Prairie through Carol's eyes, but it is obvious that just as often, if not more often, Lewis wants to accept this world categorically, to enjoy it uncritically and routinely, as Will is able to do.) Will has made a duality of wonder and the commonplace in a way that is never to be possible for Carol, although it is a way often dreamed upon by Lewis himself.

There is, then, in *Main Street,* so much childish wonder and awe, so much love of nature, glorification of motion, so much of hunting, of motoring, of the passing of trains, of the changing of seasons, that one cannot help but feel that here satire is something merely occasional and compulsive-like for Lewis, that the craft of the satirist is something done in passing, something done while waiting at the station, or perhaps something accompanying the momentary displeasure of waiting for one's car to be repaired at the local garage. So much in *Main Street* reaches out and yearns for the possibility that one will be able to park by the tracks in the darkness of a country lane as the train passes like a flame of light and exclaim only, ''No. 19. Must be 'bout ten minutes late.''

This is surely why *Main Street* today has the feel of a mild and easygoing book, why it is not essentially a disquieting and painful experience. In writing it Lewis must often have believed, as he did when writing *Free Air,* that he was writing in praise of ''the wholesome atmosphere of American life,'' and *Main Street,* when read today, has much more about it that is wholesome, light, and open-ended than we have come to expect.

As long as forty years ago E. M. Forster made the telling comparison of Lewis's art to that of the photographer. Lewis's great gift, he pointed out, was for a photography of words. ''Neither for good or evil is he lifted above his theme; he is neither a poet nor a preacher, but a fellow with a camera a few yards away'' [see excerpt dated 1929]. The comparison is a good one in that it helps us to see why *Main Street* is often such a disorganized book, why Carol Kennicott is such an ill-conceived character if not a downright incredible or ridiculous one—so many clickings of the shutter cannot be counted on to result in a rounded and unified point of view. But in describing Lewis as ''neither a poet nor a preacher, but a fellow with a camera few yards away,'' Forster is, while speaking quite accurately, not saying precisely what sort of fellow this is and what sort of pictures he likes to take. And in Lewis's

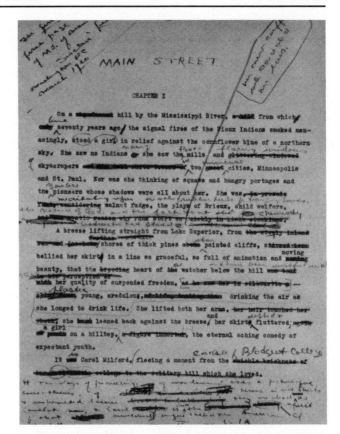

Lewis's revised typescript for Main Street. *Harry Ransom Humanities Research Center, University of Texas at Austin.*

case at least this is extremely important. In *Main Street,* as I have already suggested, there are so many different pictures, from so many different angles, that these questions are not easily answered. But of one thing we may be certain. The fellow with the camera loves and belongs to the land and the people he describes; he is not simply standing in intellectual judgment of them, but standing among them because he wants and needs to do so. Lewis was not, as many believe, the country boy who went to Yale, became a city slicker, and came back to torment the folk who had given him a lonely and introspective boyhood. His instinct to stalk his fellow countrymen in their uninspired moments was no greater than his poorly concealed desire to assimilate their world into his own. (pp. 347-48)

George H. Douglas, '' 'Main Street' after Fifty Years,'' in Prairie Schooner, *Vol. XLIV, No. 4, Winter, 1970-71, pp. 338-48.*

JAMES LUNDQUIST　(essay date 1973)

[*Lundquist is an American novelist and critic who has written extensively on Lewis in works which include* A Guide to Sinclair Lewis *(1970) and* A Sinclair Lewis Checklist *(1970). In the following excerpt from his biographical and critical study* Sinclair Lewis, *Lundquist discusses* Main Street *as a work which demonstrates the consequences of outmoded economic and moral principles in early twentieth-century American society.*]

The plot of *Main Street* is so unembellished that the setting, Gopher Prairie, a central Minnesota town of some two thousand inhabitants, becomes as important as what happens to the characters in the story. Carol Kennicott, the heroine, is a Saint Paul librarian who marries Gopher Prairie physician Will Kennicott. Lewis then proceeded to give a cross section of life in a midwestern small town as seen through Carol's eyes. In a series of encounters she becomes acquainted with almost everyone in Gopher Prairie: the Dave Dyers and the Sam Clarks of the business class; the Champ Perrys of the old pioneering class; Guy Pollock, the aging radical lawyer; Miles Bjornstam, the village atheist; Vida Sherwin, the schoolteacher, and many others. Carol is soon caught in a love-hate relationship with the town and its people. She is depressed to the point of a near breakdown by the dullness of provincial life; at the same time she is stirred by the beauty of the countryside and the solidity of her plain-spoken but sometimes heroic physician husband— a solidity she, for all her liberal sentiments, lacks. At last, distressed by her failure to reform Gopher Prairie through various schemes to intellectualize the ladies' literary society (the Thanatopsis Club), renovate the village architecture, increase the public library holdings, and sustain a little-theater group, she leaves with her small son, Hugh, for Washington, D.C. and work in the war effort. She finds, however, that the big city is nearly as dull as Gopher Prairie. She becomes homesick, and Dr. Kennicott wins her back. Carol returns home, but she makes it clear that her capitulation is not complete. She is still uncertain about the possibilities for happiness in middle America.

Contrary to what many critics have assumed, *Main Street* was not addressed to the spirit of youthful revolt that followed the Armistice of 1918. When the story of Carol Kennicott ends, she is middle-aged, middle-aged in 1920; and it is to Carol's generation, the generation in power, that *Main Street* and all of Lewis's 1920s novels are addressed. This at once sets Lewis off from the younger writers of the era such as Fitzgerald and Hemingway, and also explains much of their discontent with him. Lewis's heroes are people who grew up with progressivism, fed upon the liberalism of Upton Sinclair and the economics of Thorstein Veblen, and sat through World War I on the home front. "Life had begun with war" for Fitzgerald and Hemingway, "and would forever after be shadowed by violence and death." But life had begun for Lewis with the prewar optimism of the socialist vision, and he never lost his belief that the United States could become civilized through an awakening of the social conscience of the middle class. Socialism in America has historically differed from communism in directing its revolutionary efforts at the middle class instead of advocating destruction of that class in favor of the proletariat. This is why Lewis's novels are aimed at Matthew Arnold's philistines—the doctors' wives, the businessmen, the scientists, the preachers—in an attempt to explain to them, as Lewis wrote late in 1914, why "almost all of the people who do think are agreed that things are not as they should be; that education is either absurd or weightily inefficient; that under the present economic system—technically called 'capitalism'—products do not get distributed as they should."

Perhaps there was not enough national wealth prior to 1920 to provide the comforts of the modern society for everybody: some people had to be content to do without. When Carol proposes to Mrs. Champ Perry at a meeting of the Thanatopsis Club that they modernize the tawdry rest room Gopher Prairie provided for the farmers' wives, Mrs. Perry says: "When Champ and I came here we teamed-it with an ox-cart from Sauk Centre to Gopher Prairie, and there was nothing here then but a stockade and a few soldiers and some log cabins. When we wanted salt pork and gunpowder, we sent out a man on horseback,

and probably he was shot dead by the Injuns before he got back." She goes on to say that nobody—and she was a farm wife herself in those days—expected any restroom at all.

Again and again when Carol proposes reform in Gopher Prairie, whether the proposal is for more library books or a remodeling project for the buildings along Main Street, the answer she gets is much the same—compared to pioneer times, things are pretty good the way they are now; besides, improvement would be too expensive. Carol tries unsuccessfully to convince the ruling powers in Gopher Prairie that the economy has changed, that there is enough money to go around, that the old pioneer mentality and its obsession with scarcity is no longer essential, that it is no longer necessary to live like the old settlers who got through the winters by eating rutabagas "raw and boiled and baked and raw again." She suggests to her husband that the farmers ought to have a fairer share of the material benefits enjoyed by the townspeople, but such a notion is all but incomprehensible to him. "Where'd the farmers be without the town?" he asks. "Who lends them money? Who—why, we supply them with everything!" "Everything," of course, amounts to little more than the bare necessities of life on the frontier.

Lewis knew the strangeness the world of 1920 held for middle-aged people, people who had been born, after all, when the northern midwest was still largely wild and unsettled. . . . Like so many of the economic assumptions Lewis challenged, the economy of scarcity was attacked because with changing times it had become worse than outdated; it had become immoral.

The real shock value of *Main Street* thus lay not in its naturalistic exposé of life in a small town, but in its attempt to suggest how outmoded, how immoral, were some of the moral principles upon which the town and the nation itself had been founded and survived.

It was up to Carol's generation more than it had been to any other in American history to confront the inadequacy of the values and the solutions that were given to them as they grew up. *Main Street,* it must be remembered, is the history of a generation. The novel begins in 1906 when the "days of pioneering, of lassies in sunbonnets, and bears killed with axes in piney clearings, are deader now than camelot" and the American middlewest is a "bewildered empire." This bewilderment is reiterated throughout the novel, first in Carol who cannot make up her mind about what sort of work she should do, and later in Kennicott and other citizens of Gopher Prairie who are driven to reject, out of frustration, the one principle that came automatically to their lips whenever they thought of the glories of their homeland: freedom. As Kennicott says to Carol in the argument that leads to their separation, "There's too much free speech and free gas and free beer and free love and all the rest of your damned mouthy freedom, and if I had my way I'd make you folks live up to the established rules of decency even if I had to take you—"

Kennicott is echoing, in his own way, the same thing Walter Weyl expressed in his 1912 book, *The New Democracy:* "America is in a period of clamor, of bewilderment, of an almost tremulous unrest. We are hastily reviewing all our social conceptions. We are profoundly disenchanted." On one side was great economic growth, the gross national product rising from $30.4 billion in 1910 to $71.6 billion in 1920. But on the other side was the clamor of labor unrest (there were over 2,000 strikes during the first half of 1916), demonstrations for women's rights, racial equality, leftist agitation, and World

War I itself, the irony of which soon became apparent when the democratic principles the United States was fighting for—freedom of the press, free speech, and free thought—were curtailed at home in the name of patriotism.

A last-ditch effort was being made to buttress the old values inherent in the pioneer mentality, and the results were Prohibition, the witch-hunting conservatism that brought about the Big Red Scare (the night of 2 January 1920, when Attorney General A. Mitchell Palmer arrested some 5,000 alleged communists in simultaneous raids in cities across the country), a revived Ku Klux Klan and other fascist organizations, and the religious fundamentalism manifested in the 1925 Scopes Monkey Trial. But the inadequacy of the values that came out of the rural state of mind was soon apparent, as *Main Street* so timely testified. Sinclair Lewis knew what Carol's generation had been through because he was a member of it himself, and it was this quality of sympathy that made him so appealing to an audience made up largely of the same kind of people who appear in the novel—the Carols and Wills, the Dyers, the Sam Clarks, and even the Guy Pollocks—the solid, respectable, middle-class people who were running things. (pp. 35-40)

James Lundquist, in his Sinclair Lewis, *Frederick Ungar Publishing Co., 1973, 150 p.*

FLOYD C. WATKINS (essay date 1977)

[*Watkins is an American educator and the author of several works on Southern literature. In the following excerpt, he contends that* Main Street *is artistically weak but significant both as a representation of a segment of American life and as a publishing phenomenon. Watkins also notes Lewis's contradictory attitudes toward the fictional town of Gopher Prairie and Sauk Centre, Minnesota, his hometown.*]

Without subtle satire or ridiculous and exaggerated humor, it may be impossible to write a good book about a stereotyped and shallow society. It is possible to write a good historical or social essay about a bad book, but it may be impossible to write good literary criticism of a bad and shallow book. Sometimes, however, it is a task one must attempt: one must know the good from the bad; weak fiction reveals true history; and one must account for the enormous popularity of shallow fiction which the world buys and reads late into the night. The reader may wish to see himself or to see others like himself without real self-recognition; or the half-educated one indulges in a feeling of superiority induced by reading about those no better than he. *Main Street* is a cultural and historical and even a literary phenomenon. It is a dull book about dull people. Would that it were not so.

Whether it is possible to create great art in fiction when the characters carry on their lives in social and cultural situations first as illustrations of the condition and only then as people is a question usually answered by the taste of the reader. It is difficult to conceive of *Main Street* with a title like *The Tragedy of Carol Kennicott* or of a critical article about the book as an artistic study of the psychology of the heart of a hero or a heroine. Sinclair Lewis did not write it that way, and his critics have not taken it that way. Granted for the moment that *Main Street* may be a superbly accurate fictionalized representation of a large part of American life over a substantially long period of time, it still may not be meritorious as art. The heroine is shallow; the other characters, except for a few undeveloped walk-on parts, are shallow and two-dimensional. Given such premises, can *Main Street* be a good book? It can be significant

in history as a representation of a segment of American life, and it can be an important phenomenon in the study of American taste, what the people like to read. But it cannot be a great tragedy or a great novel, I believe, in any sense of the term. It follows, then, that there may be superb uses by scholars of *Main Street* for many purposes; it is a "document," but there may not be profound or probing criticism of the subtle art of the novel.

Like all Gaul, the reactions of Sinclair Lewis to Gopher Prairie as an assembly of people is divided into three parts, or three emotional responses. He hated it, he liked it, and he was just not quite sure what he felt about it. The assumptions of modern criticism have been that certain characteristics of a novel and the responses to it prove greatness: much ambivalence in reactions to characters, widespread interest in the book, much and widely varying disagreement among leading critics about what it is and what it means, and sometimes widely divergent, even contradictory statements about the book itself by the author after he has written it. Sometimes it seems that no work is worthy of notice unless there are more interpretations of the book than there are arts and meanings in it. One hardly expects the diversity of response to *Main Street* to resemble that to *Moby-Dick* or to *Absolom, Absalom!*, but there is not a great deal of difference. Certainly the criticism of *Main Street* is more various than the book itself.

Lewis's own reactions, I believe, his prevailing attitudes, were marked by rejection and sometimes strong dislike. One of the most well-known criticisms of *Main Street* has called Lewis's hatred "cordial and malignant." If as a native he had "the right," as he maintained in a speech at St. Cloud, "to criticize the things that I think are wrong in the small town," he sometimes attacked his home town in the mouth-twisted frenzy of those who espouse frantic causes, not in the tones of a gentle counselor. Given what Lewis was, his disposition, he would have been vehement in any time, but the particular phase of the town's history when he knew Sauk Centre or Gopher Prairie defined the nature of his animosities. His first wife, Grace Hegger, saw the problem as Lewis's hating his neighbors for claiming the virtues of the frontier and "the log-cabin tradition" while they enjoyed the ease of the age of automobiles. Basically, this response is a hatred of hypocrisy. He wanted the small town to know and to be what it was and not to try to be what it was not. If there was to be praise, it should come from without the town; self-praise is the boosterism of Babbitt, or "smugness," a term which Lewis hurled at Sauk Centre time after time.

The way the local citizenry spent their leisure time reflected their smug self-centeredness. A party given by young Mr. and Mrs. Lewis on Sunday morning offended delicate Puritan sensibilities. The town's own imagination provided only dullness, typical local small-town parties or idle hanging about the drugstore in one classical American pursuit. Lewis had a point of view with blinders. He "seemed never to have participated," Sherwood Anderson wrote in his *Memoirs,* "in the thrills and pleasures of the small town." The citizenry gossiped themselves, but they could not tolerate criticism; they preferred "orderly, thought-stifling, conventional living." The lack of depth enabled the Thanatopsis Club to cover "Scandinavian, Russian, and Polish literature, with remarks by Mrs. Leonard Warren on the sinful paganism of the Russian so-called Church." . . . Physically, the streets of the town were "a black swamp from curb to curb." . . . The architecture, which was as dull and false as the two-storied fronts on one-story buildings in the old West, made Carol in her usual foolish way think at least of rebuilding the town and at most of asking someone else to give it a start.... (pp. 200-02)

Carol Kennicott is an unusual perspective or point of view for an American author who writes autobiographical narrative about the country or the town of his origins. The tradition is that the author chooses a central character not unlike himself, especially in age and sex. Examples are numerous. Mark Twain was one of the best practitioners of the pattern in this phenomenon of literature in America. At least nine of Faulkner's novels (not counting the short stories) create the life of Yoknapatawpha County in a story that begins with the perspective of a boy growing up. Chick Mallison and Quentin Compson are more representative. Thomas Wolfe saw Altamont from the perspective of Eugene Gant and then Libya Hill from that of Monk Webber. The short stories of Sherwood Anderson and Ernest Hemingway tell of the movement from boyhood to maturity in Michigan and Ohio. Willa Cather's Ántonia moves from girlhood to a wise womanhood. Black authors such as Richard Wright and Ralph Ellison use narrators of the author's own sex and background. This kind of point of view provides a sensitive and usually a sympathetic outlook. (pp. 202-03)

Lewis's fictional study of a town breaks the pattern more completely perhaps than any other American book ever has. There are almost no children in Gopher Prairie. The characters are adults or babies, Carol's and Bea Bjornstam's. It is almost as if Lewis leaves a great generation gap in the town during the years of his own growing up. A few delinquents lurk around generally in undesirable hang-outs. Carol agonizes that "there was no youth in all the town ... they were born old, grim and spying and censorious." ... She might as well be speaking literally, because there is no teen-ager who is more than incidental in the book.

Lewis's onlooker is a woman, not a person of the author's own sex; she is not a native of the town but a stranger; nothing of the joys of childhood serves as a palliative in her acrimony; her attitude is overdelicately womanish, perhaps indicating something about the sensibilities of her creator; masculinity itself is thus one of the causes of the boorishness of her environment. She might endure the adventuresomeness of Ishmael, but Huck Finn or Ahab would be simply boors. Much of the character of Sinclair Lewis may be revealed by the choice of his heroine, but the effect on his fiction is the point at hand. A delicate and foreign female sensibility almost has to be an enemy to the ways of the town. Carol fancies herself in all sorts of roles, but she is no Margaret Mead, no Lily Pons, no Marilyn Monroe brought to perish in the boondocks. (pp. 203-04)

To Charles Breasted, Lewis asserted simply and with little amplification that "Carol is 'Red Lewis.'" Lewis's wife Gracie and critics Grebstein, Dooley, and Schorer agree that "Sinclair Lewis did not intend deliberately to satirize her." Although Heywood Broun sees Carol as "puerile," Lewis wrote that she was "sensitive and articulate," and Will and Carol were the "halves of his divided being." She looks different to our age: Schorer remarks that Lewis "by no means thought of 'her superior culture' as 'chiefly bogus.'" (pp. 205-206)

The novel itself provides no infallible statement or evidence that Carol is a heroine and a spokesman for her creator or that she is a fool and an intellectual blackguard. So instead of a mouthpiece, she is taken by many as Lewis's mouther of nonsense. Warren Beck ridicules her, especially in her "Winky Poo" dramatic appearance, but says that Lewis takes her se-

riously. Her plans are "formless," because of her naiveté, and no character in the book represents the author's point of view. Lewis is said even to sneer at her. To another detractor she is a "featherbrained romantic." Carol is an opportunity for many other critics to indulge in name-calling, enough to make her pitiable if not sympathetic. Thus some say that Lewis and Carol are not at all to be identified. Lewis satirized her as "a null," "a blank at the center of the book." Whether or not he changed his mind after he had considered all the reactions to his heroine and his book, he took elaborate pains to deny the identification of himself with his heroine. He said she was silly and had been at the time of her creation: "For example," Lewis explains his methods, "I deliberately had her decorate a room in bad taste. A couple of critics used that to show what a fool I was." The climactic view of Lewis's attitude toward his heroine, perhaps, is the contention that he created her as the mouthpiece of his protest, later recognized that she was too conventional and naive to be associated with himself, and then turned on his own intended heroine. Apparently an interpreter of *Main Street* can pay his money, but he had better not make his choice. The author (as well as his heroine) is "really not one person, but four or five people of various temperaments, all mixed together."

If Lewis and Carol together and apart form a gallery of so many possible portraits, what can be said of what they see— the town itself? *Main Street* is "an affectionate story," according to its own author, who said he loved the town and the "dull people" who lived in it. His friend William Rose Benét said he loved the "essential humanness of the people." Again, "In the Midwest lies the hope of Carol—and of Lewis—for a richer and fuller life than has ever before existed." It has been possible for one reader at least to wax poetic over the glories of Gopher Prairie and the small town as the gem of America if not the world. Lewis had dreamed that "small-town America was the place where democracy could thrive," and despite all the "distasteful culture" Lewis "instinctively wanted to believe in the goodness and healthiness of small-town life, and this instinct is manifest in *Main Street*." The novel has, indeed, a "feeling of wholesomeness." The book is a paean of praise for what so many have regarded as cheap and shallow. More realistically, Sherwood Anderson felt that "Lewis never laughs at all," that he could not love life about him, and that he was "blind to the minor beauties our lives hold." On the whole the criticism tends toward abuse of the town created in fiction, of all small towns, and of authors who condemn them in shallow books. If Lewis lacked, as Anthony Hilfer has said, "the subjective sensibility" to enable him to create the tensions of a character like Quentin Compson at the end of *Absalom, Absalom!* he also lacked even the lyrical vacillation to express the ambivalence of Wolfe's Eugene Gant. He did not have the negative capability of the disciplined artist or the emotional response to pour words into uneven tomes of ranting and lyricism.

When a town passes away in time and the place changes, it is perhaps the primary truism of all that nothing can bring it back—neither history, fiction, pageants, nor festivals. The return of Sauk Centre or Gopher Prairie in *Main Street* is partial, as it has to be; but it seems finally less complete than the portraits of most well-known towns in literature. One perspective, written before the fiction, gives a different account of the town. Carol presumably settled with her new husband, Will, in Gopher Prairie in 1912, and there is at least one way of seeing what was going on in Sauk Centre at the time—the newspaper. These two versions—one of fiction, one of journalism—differ, of course, in form, but the content is dissimilar as well as the method. (pp. 206-08)

The dismal and ugly little town which Carol saw when she came to Gopher Prairie was not to be seen in the Sauk Centre *Herald*. It proclaimed the glory, wealth, and beauty of the railroad, "the wonderful Park Region of Minnesota," ten-mile long Sauk Lake (there is "no finer Summer Resort on earth"), fifteen miles of sidewalk (Carol covered the paved walkways of Gopher Prairie in thirty-two minutes), at least twenty-six businesses and factories besides the stores, twenty-four-hour electric light service, sports (a ski tournament, basketball, fishing), and a school exhibit (which displayed the products of months of work of all the children). The celebration of the Fourth of July perhaps best symbolizes the vigorous activity of the little town. There were about thirty parades, games, contests, and concerts, dances which lasted from 9:00 in the morning until the last dance began at 9:30 in the evening. Of course, these were primitive events suitable for that time, not staged for later years. But, indeed, some modern festivities attempt to re-create them. At great modern celebrations and sports events the people watch and appreciate and exclaim and even cheer from the sidelines or on the living room sofa. In Gopher Prairie the people idled away their time and criticized the goings on of their neighbors; but in Sauk Centre, at least according to the newspaper account, the people themselves played, grunted and groaned in competition, and displayed their abilities and accomplishments. The comparison of hometown journalism and satirical fiction is unjust, but despite the accepted identification of Sauk Centre and Gopher Prairie, the novel creates a world vastly different from the life represented in the weekly paper.

Satire like that in *Main Street* can successfully ridicule examples of the foibles of the people of a town and place like Sauk Centre, but it cannot do so with the authenticity that has been ascribed to it by many critics. Lewis's method is too much like riding through a place on a train, looking out at only one side of the track, seeing only the face and the dress of people and the paint and structure of the houses. It is less than a "sociological caricature unmasking the small town." It mirrors "banalities," true, but the mirror includes only a little of the landscape, and far in the background significant aspects of the life of the town appear in miniature rather than in fullness. Lewis Mumford was carried away with the historical accuracy of Lewis's account. The people were "of flesh and blood," truly "stodgy, self-satisfied" like their prototypes, representative of American life "all over the country," and so on. But Lewis and Lewis Mumford created and criticized in half-truths, and their accounts ignore some of the actuality of life apparent in the walking flesh of the real prairie town and even in the reportage of the Sauk Centre *Herald*. Much of the inhumanity of Gopher Prairie derives from the eccentricities and fidgetings and boredom of its author. Culturally, agriculturally, socially, geographically, the potentialities for fullness of being were greater than those in Red Cloud, where Willa Cather saw people whole; and Sauk Centre provided a richness which its most famous son never saw. (pp. 210-11)

For what the vitriolic Lewis wished to write, Sauk Centre was a perfect subject matter. He yearned for the beauties and luxuries of pharaohs and kings, but he had to submit himself to a high school and the discipline of a stern and puritanical small-town physician father. Later he pursued a restless, wandering, and nervously dissipated life, but he had grown up reading a book as he mowed or was supposed to mow the lawn. The

civilization of Sauk Centre and Gopher Prairie looks forward to what America as well as the small town became later in the century. Lewis was born to complain, and his people provided the opportunity. Even after half a century *Main Street* may help us see ourselves as we can be if all of us wish to be dull and alike. It is not a good novel; it is not a book wholly true of its own world or its country; it is a work to read and say, "God help us. May we never be like that." It is more message than fiction. (p. 213)

> *Floyd C. Watkins, " 'Main Street': Culture through the Periscope of Ego," in his* In Time and Place: Some Origins of American Fiction, *The University of Georgia Press, 1977, pp. 193-213.*

MICHAEL SPINDLER (essay date 1983)

[*In the following excerpt, Spindler examines the protagonist Carol Kennicott in relation to the sociological and political themes in* Main Street.]

Few writers can have staked a claim for the national representativeness of their fiction so boldly, so arrogantly even, as did Sinclair Lewis in his short preface to *Main Street*. . . . *"This is America,"* he begins sweepingly, and claims that Gopher Prairie's Main Street is *"the continuation of Main Streets everywhere."* And in the novel he attributes to his protagonist, Carol Kennicott, a representativeness that is both regional—as "the spirit of that bewildered empire called the American Middlewest"—and broadly social—as "commonplaceness, the ordinary life of the age, made articulate and protesting." (p. 168)

Dreiser in *Sister Carrie* portrayed Carrie Meeber as a migrant from the small town to the big city, for that was the common social pattern as the urban-industrial centres expanded and sucked in labour from the surrounding hinterland. But in *Main Street* Lewis reverses the direction of migration as part of his strategy for exposing the shortcomings of the small town. In 1912 and 1913 the new waves of modernist thought and art from Europe were penetrating metropolitan America with remarkable speed, and the bohemias of Greenwich Village and Chicago, the locations of the new arts, were rapidly expanding. Carol's contact with bohemia in Chicago and her work in the library in St. Paul have given her an interest in, and acquaintance with, the current intellectual ferment. She is thus portrayed as having attained a certain taste and sophistication before arriving in Gopher Prairie, and her first reaction, extensively and sympathetically delineated by Lewis, is an aesthetic revulsion at the small town's bleakness and desolate sense of temporariness. To her critical, urban eyes it seemed "a frontier camp," and her revulsion gradually extends from the town's physical arrangement to encompass the thinness and narrowness of its social existence as she discovers with deepening dismay that it is a cultural backwater.

It is essential for Lewis's purpose, of course, that Carol be a sympathetic figure—cultured but not a snob, critical but not shrewish—and to this end he imbues her with a combination of optimism and altruism that at times leads to a loss of psychological credibility. Filled with missionary zeal, she attempts to introduce the community to aesthetic diversity and the latest developments by means of Japanese decor, modern poetry, experimental drama and schemes for civic improvements. But Gopher Prairie's stolid citizens rebuff each attempt, as Lewis builds up his portrait of a middle class that is Puritan and provincial, hostile to the arts, and devoted solely to material values, a portrait that was vigorously endorsed by H. L. Mencken in the pages of the *American Mercury*. Some of Carol's aesthetic ideas seem quite fatuous today. Her imagination, as conveyed by Lewis, is excessively literary and derivative in part of stale, late-Victorian romanticism. As she leaves for Washington with her son she tells him they are going to "find elephants with golden howdahs from which peep young maharanees with necklaces of rubies, and a dawn sea colored like the breast of a dove, and a white and green house filled with books and silver tea-sets." If Lewis had established a proper distance between himself and his protagonist, he could have subjected such immature whimsy to the irony it deserves, but by allowing Carol's flights of fancy to escape his satire and receive his endorsement he weakens the authority of his criticism of the town's jejune existence.

That aspect of Lewis's criticism which draws on Carol's metropolitan perspective may be compromised then, but there are other aspects which retain their trenchancy. These draw upon her regional representativeness and are historical and nativist in perspective. Carol, having failed to imbue the villagers with a taste for the beautiful and cosmopolitan, turns to the frontier tradition as an indigenous source of value for the town, deciding that "in the history of the pioneers was the panacea for Gopher Prairie." From the opening description of Carol standing "on a hill by the Mississippi where Chippewas camped two generations ago," the close historical presence of the pioneering period in the West is a reiterated theme and the frontier myth plays a central role in the novel. (pp. 169-71)

[The] promise of a new society that the West held preoccupies Carol as she journeys into Minnesota with her husband for the first time. The Northern Middle West is "the newest empire in the world," "a pioneer land," and what is to be its future, she wonders? "A future of cities and factory smut where now are loping empty fields? Homes universal and secure? Or placid chateaux ringed with sullen huts? . . . The ancient stale inequalities, or something different in history, unlike the tedious maturity of other empires?" There are echoes here of Jefferson's distaste for industrialism and of Crèvecoeur's praise of an American egalitarianism based on the freeholder in contrast to feudal Europe, as Carol invokes the early hope for agrarian democracy as a new type of social organisation. But 1920 was not 1780 nor indeed 1870, and although the frontier as an image of hope and renewal lived on in American myth well into the twentieth century, as a material fact it passed out of American history in 1890 when the Superintendent of the Census declared it officially closed. As Lewis emphatically expressed it at the beginning of *Main Street,* "The days of pioneering . . . are deader now than Camelot," and the impossibility of recovering the frontier spirit across half a century of social change exists in tension with its tantalising historical closeness. The Middle West, Lewis makes plain, no longer enjoys the fluidity or vitality of frontier social conditions and has already settled into "the tedious maturity of other empires."

Carol's resort to cultural nostalgia is, therefore, doomed to disillusioning failure. Just as she discovers that the town has lost whatever pioneer vigour it once enjoyed without attaining any compensatory refinement—that it is "neither the heroic old nor the sophisticated new"—so she discovers that it has betrayed its social and political promise too. In Lewis's jaundiced image of the American small town the native tradition of openness and democratic sentiments has completely faded away. In its stead there reign social inequalities and a status system based on middle-class income and the strength of one's claim to be of early white Anglo-Saxon American stock. The

only person in the town to exemplify the exuberance and independence of the pioneers, Miles Bjornstam, is ostracised by the members of the middle class because his contempt for convention and his socialist beliefs threaten their conservatism and business values.

Above all, Gopher Prairie, and by implication, America, has failed to fulfil the frontier promise of personal freedom and a higher, more satisfying type of life for all. Once the problems of production had been overcome and scarcity eradicated, then it seemed American life could begin to realise those possibilities for individual development which, unhampered by European traditions and inequalities, it had always held. As we have seen, however, the fruits of the New World's development were not shared among the many but concentrated in the hands of a few, so producing a stratified society just like that of Europe. Lewis brings together Carol's regional and social representativeness in the key political speech she makes to Guy Pollock:

> I believe all of us want the same things—we're all together, the industrial workers and the women and the farmers and the Negro race and the Asiatic colonies, and even a few of the Respectables. It's all the same revolt, in all the classes that have waited and taken advice. I think perhaps we want a more conscious life. We're tired of drudging and sleeping and dying. We're tired of seeing just a few people able to be individualists. We're tired of always deferring hope till the next generation. . . . We want our Utopia *now*—and we're going to try our hands at it. All we want is—everything for all of us!

Identifying herself with all those social groups which have been excluded from those opportunities which America, and the West in particular, promised, Carol generalises her youthful personal disaffection into a widespread upsurge of utopian expectations. Lewis thus temporarily introduces a tone of broad social protest into the novel. (pp. 171-73)

Progressive reformers were optimistic that social and political injustices could be solved by returning economic, political and social institutions to a larger degree of popular control, and this confidence in the imminence of reform is evident in Carol's attitude. As Lewis indicates, such hopeful anticipation of the fruition of the American social promise is frustrated by the political conservatism, the single-minded commercialism, the vested interests and class divisions of small towns like Gopher Prairie. The pioneers' idealistic hope that something fine and grand might come out of the Middle West once the crude work of settlement was completed has, according to Lewis's critical portrait, been overwhelmed by a barren combination of conservatism, materialism and philistinism, and in *Main Street* he thus voices a social and political, as well as aesthetic, disillusionment with the civilisation of abundance that has come to pass there.

Even the small town's economic function, which Carol eventually considers its only justification, is exposed as a hollow sham. Gopher Prairie makes its living by selling retail services to the agricultural producers in the surrounding countryside and Lewis several times reiterates his charge that the town's middle class is parasitic upon the farmers. The town is founded on exploitative commercialism, and both its social sterility and its physical ugliness proclaim the dispiriting triumph of business values. Economically unjustifiable, hostile to the arts, socially divided, bigoted and prurient, Gopher Prairie represents Lewis's damning indictment of the Middle West and the small-town mentality.

At long last, it seems, Carol escapes, fleeing like thousands of young Americans in those years from the village to the city in search of independence and broader horizons. . . . Once she has left the stifling atmosphere of Gopher Prairie, however, Carol's attitude shifts from critical rejection of the small town to affectionate idealisation. Not that Lewis's portrait of her life in the Middle West has been all negative; there have been positives such as the duck-shooting and fishing expeditions, and Kennicott, in Lewis's rather eulogistic account of the country-doctor's practice, has shown qualities of quiet heroism and pioneer self-reliance which Carol admired. In the last stages of the novel, then, Lewis relinquishes his satirical tone for a sentimental one, as from the perspective of the national capital in the East Carol "saw Main Street in the dusty prairie sunset, a line of frontier shanties with solemn lonely people waiting for her, solemn and lonely as an old man who has outlived his friends." Lewis thus begins to reclothe Gopher Prairie with the folksy hues of that jaded frontier tradition which he has so effectively demolished in the earlier stages of the novel. That Carol should finally return to the small town after experiencing independence and a career in Washington seems a violation of her characterisation and is an unconvincing plot development.

The novel's final effect, consequently, is an unsettling ambivalence of satire and sentiment in Lewis's view of the small town. Despite the keenness of his earlier criticisms of Gopher Prairie, he eventually seems to endorse its values against those of the sophisticated metropolitan centre, so, ultimately, helping to sustain that myth of the American small town which he set out to undermine. This ambivalence, according to his biographer, reflects the tensions within his temperament between convention and freedom, crudity and refinement, but perhaps it can also be related to a change in the political climate. By 1920 Progressivism had become a dead letter, as the urge for reform seemed to fade away with the coming of post-war prosperity and consumerism. . . . There is sociological appropriateness, therefore, in having Carol, the "spirit" of the Middle

West and representative of "the ordinary life of the age," abandon her hopes of a richer, more exciting life and settle, like the nation, for conformity and dull abundance. (pp. 173-75)

Michael Spindler, "Satire and Sentiment: Sinclair Lewis and the Middle Class," in his American Literature and Social Change: William Dean Howells to Arthur Miller, *Indiana University Press, 1983, pp. 168-82.*

JAMES MARSHALL   (essay date 1985)

[*In the following excerpt, Marshall examines* Main Street *as a political allegory in which the character Carol Kennicott serves as a representative of a modern pioneer spirit in which socialist and populist ideologies are synthesized.*]

"The days of pioneering, of lassies in sunbonnets, and bears killed with axes in piney clearings, are deader now than Camelot," Sinclair Lewis writes on the beginning page of his classic Revolt-from-the-Village. The sentence that follows suggests his intent to transform the cultural symbol of the pioneer into a satirist's political allegory of the frontier cultural promise, one that nevertheless remains a legacy of individual and communal independence. He visualizes the rebellious twentieth-century woman as a type whose revolt against the ugliness of village life will transvalue the pioneer symbol into her protest as the new "spirit of that bewildered empire called the American Middlewest." . . . At first Carol Kennicott, his heroine, is helplessly naive, but with the maturity of increasing restraint her articulate outcry against land speculation, one of the Populist Party's anathemas in the 1883 election to which the mortgaged frontier farm had contributed, invokes a cultural promise that the homestead West once represented—an opportunity for economic independence and resultant freedom on the land. Carol's rebellion—a concealed allegorical shadow play of twentieth-century pioneering, so to speak—occurs within Lewis' unrecognized political context that enables his brilliantly executed satirical vision of cultural sterility. Critics have neglected this rewarding aspect of *Main Street*.

Lewis' political vision originates in Hamlin Garland's *Main-Travelled Roads*. As Mark Schorer suggests, Garland's bleak lives with their anguished pioneer hope echo loudly against the rubble hills of failed cultural promise on his desolate farms and in his cruel villages. The mortgage-ridden farmers, the Haskins family in "Under the Lion's Paw" and the destitute Smiths of "The Return of a Private," for instance, suggest Garland's (and the Populist's) frontier heritage. . . . In addition, David D. Anderson has suggested that Lewis' major characters are driven by psychic wolves of fear, namely, fear of failure inherited from the terror and collapsing idealism of the prairie frontier; they dream big dreams, as Carol does in her town planning, but suffer the cost of their idealism, voicing needless self-justification. . . . Like Garland, although for different reasons, Carol is preoccupied with mortgage-owning land speculators: Rauskukle, Luke Dawson, "Honest Jim" Blausser, and Dr. Will Kennicott, her husband for whom land speculation is at first merely a hobby, an activity like hunting, golf, and, for the practical Will, his marriage as well. Appropriately, she becomes a friend of Miles Bjornstam, the "half-Yankee, half Swede," as he describes himself, Lewis' free spirit and sociologically fated pioneer redivivus. Carol's rebellion is intended to suggest Lewis' transformation of the mythic pioneer into his allegory of twentieth-century political and personal freedom from the tyranny of Main Street, a thematic transvaluation that Garland's stories suggested to him. If Carol generates no reform, she finds a renewal that implies Lewis' allegory of the modern independent spirit, or pioneer. In sum, this article will suggest that Carol's rebellion, which reaches fruition in Washington, D.C., during her separation from Will, activates Lewis' framework of political allegory, Jeffersonian in nature.

In addition, Lewis' framework of idealism was influenced by the aspirations of a rising new literary generation. Like his friends, Lewis explored the socialist ideologies of his generation as a source of political allegory. Its promise of intellectual renewal and equalitarian government obviously interested the satirist of *Main Street*. Lewis' letter in November, 1920, to Floyd Dell, author of *Moon-Calf,* another novel of revolt from the village published just months previous to *Main Street,* suggests his stance toward these significant issues. Bantering and fraternal yet withal serious, he admires with fond irony Dell and other broadly socialistic American writers. . . . Although a romantic impulse in his nature frequently sought the ideal, political and cultural, he was a satirist and a writer. Not until *Ann Vickers* . . . does he commit a protagonist to socialism, and then with an artist's objectivity. A neglected achievement in *Main Street* is, I think, Lewis' synthesis of Garland's Populist democracy and a theoretic socialism in his political satire of small town economics and culture. (pp. 529-32)

Dell's criticism in his review of *Main Street* underlies Lewis' comparison of his heroine with Dell's Felix Fay. Carol's final acceptance of the commercialism and conventions of a stale culture, Dell's review had stated, undermines the implied lyric idealism of her rebellion. Without acknowledging Dell's criticism, Lewis diplomatically comments:

> Don't you think that the difs [*sic*] between M = C [*Moon-Calf*] and M St [*Main Street*] are 2, both important. One, Felix is young, unbound, a male—*free to go;* while Carol is (since she thinks she is) not free [italics Lewis']. Second, your Davenport [Iowa; called Port Royal by Dell in *Moon-Calf*] is just enough bigger

than G.P. [Gopher Prairie]—to be worlds bigger! Give Carol just one Felix Fay (who isn't silly and you know it) & she would be contented enough to begin to create life about her. Aren't those rather than our personal opinions of the midwest the differences in the two?

Lewis hints that Carol must exist without the stimulus of a cultured (and politically astute) city ("your Davenport") or an intellectual (and socialist) husband to "create life," that is, to be the free spirit she could be. Lewis curiously omits reference to Carol's unfolding progress toward inner freedom and its expression under the benign influence of his cosmopolitan Washington, the place of a "sensuous education" (Henry James's term) in society and culture. Her renewal takes an explicitly political form before she returns to Gopher Prairie, although she does not again disturb the sleep of the village.

Lewis' focus on Carol's inward growth never relaxes scrutiny of her democratic (and articulate) "commonplaceness." In the concluding chapter of the novel, he writes, "She had fancied that her life might make a story. She knew there was nothing heroic or obviously dramatic in it, no magic of rare hours, nor valiant challenge, but it seemed to her that she was of some significance because she was commonplaceness, the ordinary life of the age made articulate and protesting." . . . For Lewis, she thus represents the ordinary person of the time, like Whitman's "divine average" of "Song of Myself," involved in Howellsian social and commonplace life; her character, her naive struggle against Gopher Prairie and eventually against Will himself are defined by these limits. (If Lewis disliked Howells, his gift for the middle-class detail furnishes this novel with its brilliant settings.) For this reason, Lewis holds the characterization of his protagonist to a secure level of plausibility, or realism; Dell and most critics have held another viewpoint. Yet framed by Lewis' pioneer allegory of the democratic average, Carol's limitations—that is, the political fact of her womanhood, her victory-in-defeat by the unformed culture of Gopher Prairie as well as her democratic protests—imply a Jeffersonian ideal: in a Main Street context, she thus offers a measure of the cultural myopia. Though trapped by the pioneer freedom she dreams but can never realize, she is enabled nevertheless to dissent from cruel village norms and oppose Will's blind practicality. Carol cannot change either; she can express her difference, however. Walking, usually alone, is a source of refreshment in the countryside beyond Main Street and thus seems an element of Lewis' allegory of recovering the pioneer spirit of freedom even though troubled by the echoing howls of Garland's frontier wolves, the land speculators. Appropriately, Carol meets Lewis' pioneer and immigrant Miles Bjornstam while walking the open land beyond Main Street. Both seek independence.

Yet, perversely it seems, Lewis undermines his conscious intent. Two later articles refute her significance; one, "Introduction to *Main Street,*" explicitly assures a growing popular readership "that Carol was not as good stuff as her husband. As I most painstakingly planned that she shouldn't be—that she be just bright enough to sniff a little [independence] but not bright enough to do anything about it" . . . ; and a second, "Main Street's Been Paved!," attempts lugubrious humor at the Kennicotts' pretensions to culture with the influx of wealth into Gopher Prairie after the war. . . . As a result, whatever Lewis' original intention, his novel has been consistently misread. . . . For most critics, Carol seems to have become reduced to a simplistic point of view, thus a mere foil to the writer's performing wit.

Let us then clarify Lewis' development of a protagonist whose image is the pioneer idealist, that is, the democratic voice of "commonplaceness," rising to become "articulate and protesting." Her rebellion (as pioneer "spirit of the bewildered empire," the Midwest) against Main Street begins with a reflection on Mr. Rauskukle, a land speculator whose wealth lofts him to the eminence of leading citizen of Schonstrom village. It occurs during her bridal journey to Gopher Prairie, her new home, while the train waits endlessly in the apparently deserted station. Rauskukle crosses the street. He seems to emerge from the tedious barren of stale myth, an existential desert, into an empty and equally desolate Main Street. With naive pride, Will Kennicott identifies Rauskukle as a person "worth three-hundred thousand" who "owns lots of mortgages." . . . For her husband, the true measure of human worth is money. The couple's first marital argument ensues. Carol asks with scarcely veiled irony why villagers and nearby farmers don't rise in anger to demand reparation for Rauskukle's usurious suppression of independent people who, as Garland and Lewis knew, had been the mythic promise of the homestead. Unsatisfied with Will's response, she suggests that the land speculator in his glorious person must be a wholly fulfilling source and "symbol of beauty." (Shekinah, thus encountered, is ostensibly all necessary enlightenment, present and future.) There seems little need for his contribution to the cultural relief of bitter village monotony, that is, for improved schools, libraries, theaters, social centers, government, and commerce. Lewis' acerbic satire of communal impotence is implied by his democratic and broadly socialistic idealism. Shocked by the incident into a bride's painful awareness of her new husband's limits, Carol eases herself over the submerged rock of reality with an optimistic meditation on the prairie landscape.

She begins to consider the Northwest affluent if gauche in its new wealth, therefore rich with potential for the success of democracy. She observes that its people are "pioneers, these sweaty wayfarers, for all their telephones and bank-accounts and automatic pianos and co-operative leagues. And for all its fat richness, theirs is a pioneer land." . . . She reflects that like herself, perhaps, the region may mature into a self-conscious culture, ordering its mean business practices and enlivening its flat, sometimes puritanical conventions. She continues her brooding on the passing fields, wondering with democratic passion and an eruptive idealism if this "pioneer land" could "achieve something different in history" and thus avoid "ancient stale inequalities" that mark "the tedious maturity of other empires." . . . The satirist's context of a domestic tiff and Carol's ensuing escape into an idealist's romance of the pioneer juxtaposes the cultural promise of the myth with the reality of the land speculator. Her awakening has thus begun. The method of a satirist's allegory seems obvious.

A second encounter with a land speculator occurs during her bridal year as Dr. Kennicott's still insecure wife. Luke Dawson, a wealthy land speculator, is Gopher Prairie's Rauskukle, a member of its ruling class. Dawson admits to Carol that he has assets worth more than three million dollars. . . . But when she proposes that he build a new community social center, he simply laughs, unable to recognize obligation. In constant use, largely by the Scandinavian farmers' wives, the present center is small, colorless, and poorly maintained. Although Lewis suggests that Carol is naive in her request, Dawson is shortsighted in his refusal to understand that democracy can be "good business," as it were. For Lewis, impoverished, cul-

turally and politically denied citizens (usually immigrant farmers) undermine the economic vitality of Main Street and erode the Western ideal of independence.

Carol's maturation and renewal originate in such disillusioning incidents. She finds that Dawson, among others, is but a Main Street "parasite," destroying its potential with his usury and noxious moral inertia. (pp. 532-36)

Lewis' allegory of pioneers and land speculators is demonstrated further by Carol's relationship with Miles Bjornstam, the natural freemason of the earth. Miles embodies the traditional ideal of the independent person, the Westerner. He characterizes himself, for example, as a democrat: "I am about the only man in Johnson County that remembers the joker in the Declaration of Independence about Americans being supposed to have the right to 'life, liberty, and the pursuit of happiness'." . . . He finds these values in the bachelor independence of a clean one-room shack in "Swede Hollow." Byron, Tennyson, Stevenson, and Thorstein Veblen on his bookshelf suggest his rebellious and active freedom of mind; his decision to work as the village handyman for whom and when he chooses illustrates his freedom of action. Miles's distance as "the Red Swede," as the town names him for his moustache and socialist politics, from a conservative Anglo-American Main Street liberates him from the middle-class anxieties that initially destroy Carol's freedom. But it is the freedom of an underclass, politically ineffectual if socially aware. Nevertheless, Miles's ability to command his own destiny until this reversal characterizes him as the true pioneer, the ideal West reborn. (p. 536)

Miles . . . reflects an earlier time, an agrarian past with its democratic ideals. Thus he survives in Gopher Prairie only through persistent resistance to its twentieth-century Babbittry. Although he has neither the education nor temperament to be the cultural architect whom the unfriendly village requires if it would change, his limits further define Lewis' political allegory of pioneer and land speculator. Miles meets and falls in love with Bea Swanson, a Swedish immigrant who is Carol's maid-of-all-work. In the tradition of the Jeffersonian homestead model, the couple marries and prospers as farmers; they are self-reliant, independent, and joyous in the promise of their beautiful child, Olaf. An active principle of "liberty and the pursuit of happiness" enables their contentment and encourages resistance to the tawdry in American society. . . . However, Miles's outspoken agnosticism and seemingly alien socialism offend both Swedish-American and Anglo-American sides of Main Street. Lewis implies the loss of pioneer ideals of religious and political tolerance and the isolation of a village intellectual. The cost of the Bjornstam family's obviously allegorical independence is isolation, a kind of exile, within the community.

A catastrophic reversal then isolates Miles in one of Lewis' several circles of hell, a uniquely American hell where the individual destroys all he has gained, built, or created in the confidence of a cultural promise that he seemed destined to fulfill. Feisty and antagonistic, a closet socialist among conservative neighbors, Miles takes issue with Oskar Eklund, a kind neighbor who has allowed him to use his well because Miles has not taken the time to dig his own. Baiting him, Oskar asks Miles if he believes all wells, like wealth, should be shared. Afraid he will strike his neighbor, Miles leaves and subsequently draws water from an unused well fouled with typhoid. Neither Will Kennicott's skill, which he gives freely, nor Carol and Miles's nursing save Bea and little Olaf; within two weeks they are dead. . . . Miles sells his dairy farm, comparable to a Garland homestead and its thematic loss of individual and political freedom, and leaves for Alberta "far off from folks as I can get." . . . As Miles boards the train, Chad Perry tells him that leaving on his own volition is preferable to an uncomfortable exit on a rail for being a socialist. Among the pioneers who settled the village, the aging, now self-righteous and intolerant Perry further illustrates the fading social vision that sends Bjornstam farther West. He never returns. For Lewis, Miles and Carol, both seeking freedom as individuals, are eloquent allegories of the pioneer in continued agonic struggle against cultural erosion. Significantly, the underclass Bjornstam is silenced; only Carol remains to voice protest against cultural erosion.

Will Kennicott, Carol's husband and the village's most respected doctor, is by nature a follower. Like his Main Street friends, he has an uncritical mind; his horizons, like theirs (and the prairie setting), seem unlimited but linear. Will's world is composed equally of "medicine, land investment, Carol, motoring, and hunting." . . . For him, life holds neither uncertainty nor discriminating choices. He thus lives with awesome complacency in the harsh, acquisitive culture of an early twentieth-century small town, assuming the unconscious and at times tyrannical ignorance of his peers as his reality. Will is naturally delighted with a return from land speculation during World War One that is twice that of his medical practice. Although heroic as a country doctor who braves prairie winters in a horse-drawn sleigh at all hours to care for the immigrant farm families, he is essentially an obtuse individual, practical but inarticulate. When a land boom occurs, his uncritical mind accepts blind fortune as personal destiny, unable in this respect to perceive a communal (or cultural) failure in his financial success. (pp. 537-39)

Land speculators in Gopher Prairie are individually weak, yet collectively they represent a force that contributes profoundly to the communal apathy Lewis calls "village virus." Individually they are not clever, merely shrewd, practical minds (the influential man of wealth; Luke Dawson, for example), or hollow like James Blausser. They undermine the democratic society of Gopher Prairie by usurping the authority of leadership. Thus, Blausser, "Honest Jim" as he likes to be called, arrives in Gopher Prairie with the wartime land boom in farms; he soon becomes promoter, public relations man, speculator, and a recognized leader in the community. His allegorical roots are suggested by his appearance; he reflects the gaudy world of Twain's speculator/confidence man. "He was a bulky, gauche, noisy, humorous man, with narrow eyes, a rustic complexion, large red hands." . . . However, Twain's frontier Satan wore the conventional business suit of the land speculator; Lewis' invention is a flabby devil, concealed by loud clothes and voice. Blausser is a crowd pleaser, a successful Colonel Sellers, nothing more. Like Babbitt, whom he anticipates, he wears a transparent coat of the land speculator's familiar rhetorical colors; an inverted Joseph, his ironic lack of prophecy is among the finer achievements of the book. . . . Another speculator is Ezra Stowbody, a type of Yankee peddler, who is Gopher Prairie's respected banker. He, of course, owns numerous farm mortgages. Like Blausser, his concern is money, although concealed by a defensive posture of false respectability. Ella, Ezra's spinster daughter, asserts that her father hated to foreclose on farm mortgages and did so only to make certain that the Scandinavian immigrant farmers of the area learned to respect the laws of their new country. . . . Stowbody's flaccid disguise is patriotic bunk: he conceals moral cowardice; he is an enemy of the people, as it were, posing as benefactor. Such land

speculators reveal the political evils of sham and greed that undermine the independence of the people by creating a destructive illusion of economic freedom. (pp. 539-40)

Lewis' heritage of political discontent has obviously entered into the context of Carol's opposition to a series of land speculators, historically the Populist farmer's demon of tyrannous economic power. The Midwestern novelists, Edward Eggleston, Joseph Kirland, and Ed Howe, like Garland and Twain, reflect this folk Satan of the prairie in their awareness of deception commonly practiced by land speculators such as the railroads, larger banks, and Eastern mortgage houses (Marshall, "Unheard Voice"). But Lewis' political evil is the collective force of "eminently safe" men who, like the narrator of "Bartleby," see all human values from the inhuman perspective of cold profit. Theirs is the allegory that represents the motive underlying Lewis' insidious cultural erosion.

Carol's temporary separation from her husband (as the rebel/pioneer) begins with domestic conflict that originates in her dislike of Will's land speculation. Will's reply, reflecting Lewis' small-town ruling class, is to label his wife and other critics of business as political subversives, thus suggesting the politically intolerant who dominate Gopher Prairie's communal perspective. Will cites vigilante justice in nearby Waukamin to illustrate how best to deal with such people, in this instance the Scandinavian immigrant farmers who were neutral toward American involvement in World War One. They had asked speakers from the Nonpartisan League to address their group, but, without knowledge of the content of the speeches, the sheriff and Waukamin businessmen rode the Nonpartisans out of town, Twain-style, on a rail. In rebellious anger, Carol asks, "Precisely how do you expect these aliens to obey your law if the officer of the law teaches them to break it?" . . . Will's reply thrusts marital conflict into the stark Twainian chiaroscuro of Lewis' political allegory. "I suppose you'll be yapping about free speech next. Free speech! There's too much free speech and free gas and free love and all the rest of your damn mouthy freedom!" . . . Lewis' invective exposes unlawful and undemocratic suppression of free speech and the right to assembly during a war fought to uphold such democratic principles. Garland's evasive Judge Balser, the land speculator in *Jason Edwards*, has the silent guile of the wealthy smiling villain. Like his **Main Street** friends, Will is tyrannical, dull, and—terrifyingly—in the inarticulate, comfortable majority. His allegory is that of middle-class political indifference and its fear of human differences. Lewis' socialism and democratic passion fuse in his political attack on the land speculator, representative of a Main Street oligarchy.

At this point in the argument Carol begins to gain the strength to oppose Will's domineering attitudes. The pioneer moves westward, so to speak, though she returns as liberated woman conscious of a political and cultural mission she can only symbolically fulfill. She gains courage and eventually the inward freedom needed to complete her education and enjoy a renewal of confident endeavor.

After two months of painful discussion, the Kennicotts agree to a temporary separation that will free Carol to work in Washington. She shares remembered isolation with other small-town emigres; friendships with men and women ripen in a healthy cultural climate. Although she discovers she has not wholly escaped Main Street—it remains in the fusty boarding houses and churches, in periodic visits from Will—she finds enlivening people. . . . Lewis captures the noisy bohemianism, sometimes idealistic socialism, of wartime cosmopolitan Washington. In this atmosphere she finds a woman whom she believes has the key to survival in Gopher Prairie. A leader of the suffragette movement, this person advises persistent democratic challenge to its stale usages and unchecked power.

> Your Middlewest is double-Puritan—prairie Puritan on top of New England Puritan; bluff frontiersman on the surface, but in its heart it still has the ideal of Plymouth Rock in a sleet storm. There's one attack . . . perhaps the only kind . . . : you can keep on looking at your . . . home and church and bank, and ask, why it is, and who first laid down the law that it had to be that way. . . .

The suffragette adds that Gopher Prairie might be civilized in twenty-thousand years instead of two hundred thousand if an "articulate and protesting" minority challenge authoritarian and mindless custom. She enables Carol to accept her entrapment in history as a woman and civilizer and to believe that—with this strategy—she may effectively return to Will and Main Street. As this essay indicates, her achievement is to become an average person in revolt, that is, an allegorical pioneeer whose protesting voice of "commonplaceness" articulates strong resistance to the encroachments of dishonest authority. Lewis' "apathy-osis," as it were, of village inanition invites Carol's necessary political challenge of custom and her enlivening courage. The theoretic socialism of Lewis and a rising generation of writers as well as Garland's weary farmers underlie Carol's strategic withdrawal into the pioneer stance of the lonely idealist of Gopher Prairie, voicing grievances against a soulless culture.

Carol's two-year separation in Washington becomes an allegory of liberating education. If she effects no social reforms in Gopher Prairie, she undergoes change into an individual confident of her ability to challenge the shibboleths of village conformity. Lewis suggests that she finds an equanimity that was "not information about office systems and labor unions but renewed courage, that amiable contempt called poise." . . . Her actual change, however, is modest but allegorically significant. She feels confident in facing Ezra Stowbody and others who rule Main Street with their collective myopia; she feels she might invite Miles Bjornstam to dinner without fear of the Haydocks' intolerant opinion. Thus, although she does not threaten the security of Main Street land speculators, she learns the principle of questioning shameless materialism. In this way, Lewis extends the immediate narrative into the allegory (or shadow play) of a twentieth-century dispossessed pioneer whose lonely outcry against greed evokes the American myth of the land and its nineteenth-century promise. (pp. 541-43)

Lewis renews a pioneer myth through a rebellious woman whose passion for nature allegorically links her to the agricultural roots of democratic promise and whose struggle for inward freedom and external beauty relate pioneer and socialist aspirations to a bewildered century. (p. 544)

James Marshall, "Pioneers of 'Main Street'," in Modern Fiction Studies, *Vol. 31, No. 3, Autumn, 1985, pp. 529-45.*

BEA KNODEL   (essay date 1985)

[*In the following excerpt, Knodel examines the literary treatment of married women in Lewis's novels of the 1920s.*]

Sinclair Lewis, in the novels of his most satisfactorily productive decade, the 1920s, looks critically but often with incisive clarity at American life. In portraying the vulgarity and stultifying narrowness of the small town as exemplified by Gopher Prairie, the essential emptiness of the life of George F. Babbitt, or the yearnings and self-searchings of Sam Dodsworth as he measures the American experience against the European, Lewis was also portraying marriages—occasionally happy marriages, many humdrum marriages, and some utterly wretched marriages—and in the process he made some telling comments about what marriage meant to American wives in the first quarter of the twentieth century.

If it is true, as Daniel Aaron has said, that *Main Street* is "a work of historical importance . . . not merely as a reflection partly unconscious, of American tastes and assumptions, but also because it helped Americans to understand themselves" [see excerpt dated 1965] . . . ; if *The New York Times* saw the central character in *Babbitt* as "real, alive and recognizable as a known, familiar, and abundant type" . . . ; and if in *Dodsworth* Lewis presented once again a representative type of American, "the American boy-man, the 'mythical' archetype" . . . ; it then seems fair to use these three novels as a means of seeing into a time now gone and of examining the lives of women in that vanished time. Happy wives are not much seen in *Main Street, Babbitt,* and *Dodsworth.* Occasionally, there are wives who at least appear to enjoy their lives and their marriages; and there are two, Vida Sherwin Witherspoon and Bea Sorenson Bjornstam (both in *Main Street*), who are most definitely, most radiantly married.

It may be, of course, that some of the wives who appear to be happy are simply not unhappy, an entirely different thing; but there is a quality of enjoyment of life in women such as Juanita Haydock (*Main Street*) and Matey Pearson (*Dodsworth*) that seems to argue that they find their days, their husbands, and their own roles satisfactory enough.

Juanita is described as "acidulous and shrewd and cackling." . . . Her home, carefully detailed by Lewis, is new, an overheated concrete bungalow furnished to a pitch of Gopher Prairie fashion, and she herself is "highly advanced in the matters of finger-bowls, doilies, and bath mats." . . . That she sees herself as having achieved distinction as the leading light of the Young Married Set, Lewis assures us; that she sees any reason to question the absolute significance of that achievement, we are nowhere led to believe. She accepts the limitations of Gopher Prairie because she does not recognize it as having limitations. She enjoys the summers at the lake, the squabbles with the grocer, and the social eminence of the Jolly Seventeen. She is, in short, satisfied.

Matey Pearson, the wife of Sam Dodsworth's longtime friend Tub, is, in almost every particular, vastly different from Juanita Haydock; but Matey, like Juanita, has apparently found happiness in an acceptance of things as they are. Fran Dodsworth may dismiss Matey as "dreadfully uninteresting. And fat!" . . . , but Matey plays "a rare shrewd game of poker" . . . , dances lightly, grows Zenith's most admirable dahlias, and shows herself cheerfully affectionate toward her husband, whom she says, with apparent truth, she adores. (pp. 555-56)

Lewis goes much further, however, in showing the possibilities for wives' finding happiness when, in *Main Street,* he describes the marriages of Vida Sherwin and Bea Sorenson. And because, Tolstoy's remark to the contrary, all happy families are *not* alike, it is worthwhile to explore in some detail the reasons why Vida and Bea are so happily married.

Vida is thirty-nine years old when she marries Raymie Wutherspoon, and she has behind her long years of struggling with sexual "fears, longing, and guilt" . . . , of knowing she is perceived as plain, the stereotypical old maid schoolteacher, of making her home in boarding houses. For Vida, then, marriage means, among other things, having what no "nice" single woman in a small town in 1915 could have—a sex life. And Lewis, though he is the least likely of authors to attempt to paint an explicit sexual scene, assures the reader that after her marriage Vida becomes "daily and visibly more plump" . . . , happier, more self-assured, while her husband, Raymie, glows and feels masculine as he thinks of "the tempestuous surprises of love revealed by Vida." . . . Further, Vida has her own home "after detached brown years in boarding houses" . . . , and she triumphs in her new life, her status.

Bea Sorenson, after her marriage to Miles Bjornstam, is even happier, if possible, than the married Vida Sherwin. Bea is happy first because she loves Miles. He has, after all, enough appeal to have been able to charm even the fastidious Carol Kennicott, and to Bea he is indeed a Swedish Othello with adventures to tell and with a wealth of devotion to give. Beyond that, Bea, unlike any of the other wives to be discussed, is by class and by upbringing content to do domestic work and positively delighted to do it in her own home instead of as a hired girl in someone else's. And finally—and this is significant—she finds excitement and creativity in each household task because she is "Miles's *full partner*" (italics mine). . . . Here is a key; it is because she is her husband's full partner that her work has significance and meaning to her.

In the less-than-happy marriages Lewis portrays in *Main Street, Babbitt,* and *Dodsworth,* it is commonplace that the wives, even when they are much loved, and some of them are, are in no real sense their husbands' partners. We see the woman who is deliberately humiliated, kept in her place, by her husband; the woman who has, in most respects, ceased to exist for her husband; and, often, the woman who has been effectively crippled by being permitted, or even required, to remain irresponsible, immature, and selfish. The relationships between men and women, husbands and wives, in the years about which Lewis is writing, the years from 1910 to 1925 or so, were obviously established by the attitudes of the time; and he is reporting what he has seen. But he does not let it go at that. He seeks reasons and explanations for the dissatisfaction of the women he portrays; and, with one notable exception, he is ready to offer some word of defense for even the silliest or most disagreeable unhappy wife. He is, in fact, essentially sympathetic.

He pictures with feeling the humiliation of the woman totally dependent on her husband for money. In a moving scene, one that many readers may still recognize, he shows Maud Dyer (*Main Street*) asking her husband in front of an appreciative male audience at the corner drugstore for ten dollars to buy underclothes for her (and his) children, only to have him ask, as both the listening Carol Kennicott and the reader know he will, "Where's that ten dollars I gave you last year?" . . . When Maud is shown later as a rather silly hypochondriac, interested in religious experiments and in the possibility of seducing Will Kennicott, Lewis has provided if not an excuse for her behavior at least a suggestion as to its possible causes.

And he is sympathetic to Edith Cortright (*Dodsworth*), who, describing her deceased husband, says he was

a dreadful liar; one of these hand-kissing, smiling, convincing liars. He was a secret drunkard. He humiliated me constantly as a backwoods American; used to apologize to people, oh, so prettily, when I said "I guess" instead of the equally silly "I fancy." . . .

Mrs. Cortright, because she is nearly perfect, needs no excuses, but she most decidedly has Lewis' compassion.

More in need of excuses is Louetta Swanson (*Babbitt*), whose snappishness and flirtations are the responses of a woman who is also publicly embarrassed by her husband and privately bored and dissatisfied. (pp. 557-58)

The disasters that may be caused by restricting women's independence, intellectual activity, and maturity are shown by Lewis to go beyond the nagging and casual flirting of Louetta Swanson or the inarticulate unhappiness of Myra Babbitt. They may, for one thing, lead to the total collapse of a marriage, a more dramatic event in 1920 than in 1985. In *Dodsworth* Lewis presents the one unhappy wife for whom he shows no sympathy—the beautiful, mercurial, absolute bitch Fran—and shows her as she destroys her marriage and to some extent herself.

Fran Dodsworth is the classic character that readers love to hate. She is, of course, patterned on Lewis' first wife, Grace Hegger; and Lewis was writing *Dodsworth* at the time his marriage had just broken up. Nonetheless he, inadvertently no doubt, introduces some elements into his writing about Fran that reveal her, her husband, and the era in which they live in such a way that a reader can feel, if not sympathy, at least a bit of understanding for Fran.

Like so many of the wives Lewis describes, but at a different social level, Fran Dodsworth has been effectively stunted by the attitudes of society and even of the man—and in this case he is a kind, intelligent man—who loves her. Sam, for all that he adores Fran, thinks of her as a child, "his child" . . . ; and it is not until he meets the woman for whom he will eventually leave Fran that "his child" becomes, less attractively, "childish." In response to his insistence that she is "so young," "a child," "a girl," it is no wonder that Fran, though she is in her forties, talks baby talk; lies, even to Sam, about her age; hides the fact that she is a grandmother. Sam comes gradually to see her as shallow, but he never acknowledges that the causes of her shallowness may lie outside her control; that his continually thinking of her as a child may have contributed to making her irresponsible; that with her life occupied by clubs that, in her own words, "don't mean anything" but are "just make believe" . . . , with no purpose other than keeping her occupied, she has had little incentive to grow; that if he finds himself uncertain of his identity when he is no longer recognized as an important figure in the auto industry, she, whom he has resolved to keep in a shrine, who has never had work for which she might be recognized, may well have little clear sense of herself as a person. (pp. 560-61)

Lewis is understanding, at least generally, of the woman trapped in a life without meaning. And his greatest sympathy he reserves for the "woman with a working brain and no work" . . . , most clearly exemplified by Carol Kennicott (*Main Street*). Lewis' treatment of Carol is different from his treatment of the other wives in his novels. . . . [Throughout] most of *Main Street* Lewis presents Carol's point of view, Carol's thoughts. Carol is different, also, from the other wives, except Vida Sherwin, in that she has gone to college; and if Blodgett College is not Dodsworth's Yale, nor even Babbitt's State U, still Carol has been exposed to higher education and has even independently earned her own living. Once married, however, Carol loses most of her independence. Although Kennicott is a loving husband and honestly means to be fair, he never manages to establish a household allowance for his wife, and Carol is often in the absolutely dependent position of having to ask for money. At the same time, she finds that she has little opportunity for productive use of her intelligence or her imaginative or creative powers. That she cannot, as the wife of a professional man, have a career of her own is understood; and although she makes repeated attempts to find fulfillment in her husband's work, to make a career of being the doctor's wife, she finds that unsatisfactory. She even seeks, ludicrously, to create meaning for herself by taking interest in her husband's hobbies, but she concludes finally that "It isn't enough, to stand by while he fills an automobile radiator and chucks me bits of information." . . . With no opportunity for meaningful work apart from her home and family or for the dignity of financial self-sufficiency, Carol is effectively trapped.

The fact that Lewis' vision of Carol's dilemma is clear is verified by the letters he received, "scores" according to his biographer Mark Schorer . . . from women who saw themselves as "Carol Kennicotts." And the dilemma remains unresolved at the end of the novel; perhaps it is incapable of resolution. Lewis sees the problem, analyzes it, and finally, as has been often noted, gives Will Kennicott, the practical voice, the husband's voice, the last word. (pp. 561-62)

> *Bea Knodel, "For Better or for Worse . . . ," in* Modern Fiction Studies, *Vol. 31, No. 3, Autumn, 1985, pp. 555-63.*

ADDITIONAL BIBLIOGRAPHY

Anderson, Margaret. "The Little Review." In her *My Thirty Years' War: An Autobiography*, pp. 35-102. New York: Covici, Friede, 1930.
    Reminiscence of meetings with Lewis. Anderson states that "we did our best to be friends. But we couldn't communicate across the chasms that separated us." On her reaction to *Main Street* Anderson comments: "Could this be the book that had caused an outcry in recognition of its art? There is not art in it."

Bogardus, Emory S. "Social Distance in Fiction." *Sociology and Social Research* 14, (November-December 1929): 174-80.
    Considers *Main Street* a novel which affords "students of sociology a vivid laboratory for the study of social distance," using as examples the personality and cultural differences between the characters Will and Carol Kennicott, "an impassable personal-group distance" between Carol and the people of Gopher Prairie, and the permanent "long-standing class and race differences" between the people of the town and the nearby Swedish farmers.

Bourjaily, Vance. "Red Lewis' Town Is Kinder to Him than He Was to It." *Smithsonian* 16, No. 9 (December 1985): 46-52, 54, 56.
    Observations and interviews with citizens of present-day Sauk Centre, Minnesota, the town upon which Lewis patterned Gopher Prairie in *Main Street*.

Coard, Robert L. "College and Schoolhouse in *Main Street*." *Sinclair Lewis Newsletter* 1, No. 1 (Spring 1969): 3-4.
    "A study of formal education and dreams about formal education in the seminal novel *Main Street*" that attempts to "show how central to Lewis's thought formal education was."

Dooley, D. J. "The Revolt against Main Street." In his *The Art of Sinclair Lewis*, pp. 57-95. Lincoln: University of Nebraska Press, 1967.

Examines both *Main Street* and incidents in Lewis's life in an attempt to determine Lewis's true feelings about the small town the novel depicts.

Farrar, John. "Sinclair Lewis." In his *The Literary Spotlight*, pp. 32-42. New York: George H. Doran Co., 1924.
    Discusses the evocative power of "*Main Street*" as a catch phrase for a particular American milieu. Farrar also discusses Lewis's reaction to the success of *Main Street*.

Flanagan, John T. "A Long Way to Gopher Prairie: Sinclair Lewis's Apprenticeship." *Southwest Review* XXXII, No. 4 (Autumn 1947): 403-13.
    Discusses aspects of Lewis's early work which prefigure the style and characterization in *Main Street*.

Gannett, Lewis, "Sinclair Lewis: *Main Street*." *Saturday Review of Literature* XXXII, No. 32 (6 August 1949): 31-2.
    Retrospective reading of *Main Street*. Stating that "it is obvious that it is an affectionate story," Gannett argues that in 1920 American's "were so smug that any criticism seemed a hostile act."

Goist, Park Dixon. "The Ideal Questioned But Not Abandoned: Sherwood Anderson, Sinclair Lewis, and Floyd Dell." In his *From Main Street to State Street: Town, City, and Community in America*, pp. 21-34. Port Washington, New York: Kennikat Press, 1977.
    Examines the novels *Main Street, Winesburg, Ohio, Poor White*, and *Moon-Calf* as the works of "gifted writers born in midwestern towns in the decades after the Civil War" who challenged the "myth of the town as ideal community." Goist argues that such challenges represent a search for group solidarity and community, rather than a harsh criticism of small town life.

Loggins, Vernon. "Iconoclasm: Sinclair Lewis." In his *I Hear America . . . : Literature in the United States since 1900*, pp. 239-47. New York: Thomas Y. Crowell Co., 1937.
    Contends that "in spite of the humor and picturesque detail" in *Main Street* and Lewis's other significant novels, "Lewis's America . . . is a sick America—an America suffering from provincialism, puritanism, sentimentality, childishness, and false standards in politics, religion, education, love, marriage, and sex."

Luccock, Halford E. "Post-War Realism." In his *Contemporary American Literature and Religion*, pp. 52-98. Chicago: Willett, Clark & Co., 1934.
    Considers *Main Street, Babbitt*, and other Lewis novels "significant both for" their "expression of common attitudes and moods," and "influence on the popular mind."

Maglin, Nan Bauer. "Women in Three Sinclair Lewis Novels." *The Massachusetts Review* XIV, No. 4 (Autumn 1973): 783-801.
    Examines the protagonists of *Main Street, The Job*, and *Ann Vickers*, concluding that Lewis was "consciously exploring through fiction the choices and pressures that women felt personally and socially during the first third of the twentieth century." Maglin finds that these explorations remain relevant "emotionally and politically."

Marshall, Archibald. "A Browse among the Best Sellers." *The Bookman*, New York LIV, No. 1 (September 1921): 8-12.
    Review of *Main Street* in which Marshall states: "If the aim is only, or chiefly, to portray the meanness of life in a particular kind of community, . . . I don't see how it could be much better. . . . But it is not enough, if nothing is to come of it but still more detail. . . ."

———. "Gopher Prairie." *North American Review* CCXV, No. 796 (March 1922): 394-402.
    Analysis of *Main Street* in which Marshall observes that "the impression it did leave upon me was one of squalor, and the little towns I have seen in the West are far from being squalid." Marshall believes that although Lewis's portrait of the small town is not entirely untrue, it is too negatively slanted.

Morris, Lloyd. "Seven Pillars of Wisdom." In his *Postscript to Yesterday: America, the Last Fifty Years,"* pp. 134-71. New York: Random House, 1947.
  Examines *Main Street* in relation to Lewis's idealistic liberalism and the political and literary climates in the United States after the First World War. Morris also discusses *Babbitt*, Sherwood Anderson's *Winesburg, Ohio*, and other works critical of towns and cities.

Nichols, Beverley. "*Main Street*." *The Saturday Review* 132, No. 3434 (20 August 1921): 230-31.
  Review of *Main Street* in which Nichols states: "To those who love America and the American people, this book will come as a very unpleasant shock.... *Main Street* is perhaps one of the most wonderful literary photographs that this generation has seen. And like most photographs, it is a libel."

Nicholson, Meredith. "Let Main Street Alone." In his *The Man in the Street: Papers on American Topics*, pp. 1-25. New York: Charles Scribner's Sons, 1921.
  Discussion of the American small town, using *Main Street* as a point of departure.

Petrullo, Helen B. "*Main Street, Cass Timberlane*, and Determinism." *South Dakota Review* 7, No. 4 (Winter 1969-70): 30-42.
  Compares the plots of two Lewis novels set in Minnesota, showing that, although written twenty-five years apart, both works have a "deterministic idea underlying" them. Petrullo argues that both Carol Kennicott and Cass Timberlane mature, learning that "institutions ... are the real enemies, not individuals."

Piacentino, Edward J. "The *Main Street* Mode in Selected Minor Southern Novels of the 1920s." *Sinclair Lewis Newsletter* VII and VIII (1975 and 1976): 18-22.
  Considers *Main Street* a significant influence on Southern novels of the 1920s and "instrumental in convincing Southern novelists that critical social realism was an apt mode for treating provincial life in the contemporary South." Particular attention is given to the T. S. Stribling novels *Birthright*, *Teeftallow*, and *Bright Metal*.

Quinn, Arthur Hobson. "Critics and Satirists—The Radicals." In his *American Fiction: An Historical and Critical Survey*, pp. 644-69. New York: Appleton-Century-Crofts, 1936.
  Discusses *Main Street* and other Lewis novels as well as realistic novels of social criticism by Theodore Dreiser, Sherwood Anderson, Upton Sinclair, and others. Quinn concludes that this school of writing fails to attain "greatness by the supreme test, that of the creation of character."

Seligmann, Herbert J. "The Tragi-Comedy of *Main Street*." *The Freeman* II, No. 36 (17 November 1920): 237.

Favorable review.

Suderman, Elmer, "*Main Street* Today." *South Dakota Review* 7, No. 4 (Winter 1969-70): 21-9.
  Considers *Main Street*'s depiction of small town America "startling and often wrong, or at least incomplete." Suderman nonetheless believes that the novel provides a useful "way of looking at ourselves, and Lewis undoubtedly did America a favor by replacing the old stereotypes with new ones."

Taylor, Walter Fuller. "Naturalism and the Cultural Battle: H. L. Mencken and Sinclair Lewis." In his *A History of American Letters*, pp. 380-90. Boston: American Book Co., 1936.
  Discusses *Main Street* in a section on Lewis's satires. Taylor considers the method used in the novel "that of the problem novelist inclined ... toward invective and ridicule rather than toward thoughtful discussion," and the characters mere vehicles to illustrate the various sides of a view point.

Tanselle, G. Thomas. "Sinclair Lewis and Floyd Dell: Two Views of the Midwest." *Twentieth Century Literature: A Scholarly and Critical Journal* 9, No. 4 (January 1964): 175-84.
  Compares treatments of the midwest in *Main Street* and Floyd Dell's *Moon-Calf*. Tanselle reprints excerpts from letters written by Lewis and Dell in which they discuss their contemporary, much compared novels.

Turim, Maureen. "I Married a Doctor: Main Street Meets Hollywood." In *The Classic American Novel and the Movies*, edited by Gerald Peary and Roger Shatzkin, pp. 206-17. New York: Frederick Ungar Publishing Co., 1977.
  Compares *Main Street* with the 1936 film based on it, noting that the film took a point of view "at odds with Lewis's perspective in *Main Street*," changing Carol Kennicott from a "device for social commentary" and a "serious thoughtful reformer" into a "vivacious charmer," so that "entertainment value *replaces* critical expression."

Van Doren, Carl. "Sinclair Lewis." In his *The American Novel: 1789-1939*, pp. 303-14. New York: Macmillan, 1940.
  Discussion of Lewis's career with a section on *Main Street*. Van Doren regards the novel as a panoramic caricature of a provincial town in which the characters "are not remembered as Gopher Prairie is."

Waldman, Milton. "Tendencies of the Modern Novel: America." *The Fortnightly Review* n. s. CXXXIV (December 1933): 717-25.
  Regards *Main Street* and other Lewis novels as superior to the works of other 1920s era novelists who shared a "tremendous earnestness, a passion for political and economic reform ... and a distaste for the canons of orthodox English prose."

(Afonso Henrique de) Lima Barreto

1881-1922

Brazilian novelist, journalist, essayist, and short story writer.

Lima Barreto is recognized as the first novelist to examine the problems of black and mulatto Brazilians. Deeply affected by discrimination and prejudice, which he observed as a social critic and experienced as a black mulatto, he wrote essays, articles, and fiction around themes of social and political injustice in early twentieth-century Brazilian society. The examination of these provocative themes in such novels as *Triste fim de Policarpo Quaresma (The Patriot)* and *Vida e morte de M. J. Gonzaga de Sá (The Life and Death of M. J. Gonzaga de Sá)* put him irreconcilably at odds with the literary elite of his country, a situation exacerbated by his tendency to place intellectual substance above literary style in an era when Brazilian writers were preoccupied with artistic form. During the last two decades, however, critics have come to regard Lima Barreto's use of simple language and experimentation with narrative viewpoint as significant formal innovations in modern Brazilian fiction.

Lima Barreto was born in Rio de Janeiro and raised in Ilha do Governador, where his father was in charge of a mental institution. After completing secondary school he attended college for three years but was forced to abandon his education in order to support himself and his father, who had become incurably insane. Lima Barreto found work as a civil servant in the Brazilian war ministry, which was his main source of income for the rest of his life, and also began writing book reviews for a number of small periodicals. It was during this early period that he attempted his first novel, which examined the sexual exploitation of lower-class women. The work was not completed, however, until shortly before his death and was published posthumously as *Clara dos Anjos*. Lima Barreto continued writing book reviews and articles, contributing at one point to nearly a dozen Brazilian journals; his own magazine, *Floreal*, ceased publication after its third number in 1907. While he maintained long associations with two Rio magazines, the popular *Careta* from 1915 until his death and the more conservative *ABC* from 1916 to 1919, his most revealing journalism appeared in a daily column in *O Correio da Noite* in 1914 and 1915; much of this work is collected in *Bagatelas*. Often confronting the same social and political issues that are central in Lima Barreto's fiction, these articles reveal his long-lived crusades against a variety of conditions accepted in Brazilian society, including the destruction of landscape in the name of modernization, the legal tolerance of uxoricide, and American imperialism and racism.

Despite his renown as a controversial journalist and literary critic, Lima Barreto remained alienated from the literary mainstream: he had difficulty getting his novels published and was twice denied membership into the Brazilian Academy of Letters. His only supporter, the São Paulo editor Monteiro Lobato, assisted him in getting some works published, including his two most important novels, *The Patriot* and *The Life and Death of M. J. Gonzaga de Sá*. Lobato, the author of the regional novel *Urupes*, was one of the few contemporaries whom Lima Barreto admired. Finding little reflection of his artistic and personal ideals in the works of other Brazilian authors, he

turned for models to the works of Guy de Maupassant, Charles Dickens, Jonathan Swift, and others who shared his own reformist aspirations. Despite his production of seventeen volumes of prose, Lima Barreto never achieved an extensive readership or critical popularity, and at age forty-one died alone and impoverished, ravaged by alcoholism and bouts of insanity.

Lima Barreto's fiction earned the admiration of many young Brazilian writers and the censure of a powerful, European-influenced literati. In repudiation of the contemporary tendency to emulate the French Parnassian poets, who valued formal aspects of literature to an extreme degree, Lima Barreto considered artistic form relatively unimportant, perceiving fiction as "heightened" reality in which facts are manipulated in order to elucidate social and moral problems. In the novels *Recordações do escrivão Isaías Caminha* and *The Life and Death of M. J. Gonzaga de Sá*, for example, Rio de Janeiro is depicted in historical detail that accurately recreates the topography and moral attitude of the capital city during the opening decades of the twentieth century. The evocation of the tropical landscape and of the language and customs of the people throw into sharp relief the negative aspects of modernization during a period of rapid social and cultural change. Throughout his career Lima Barreto also sought to correct inaccurate cultural stereotypes. For example, *Clara dos Anjos,* set in a lower middle-class suburb of Rio de Janeiro, attacks the myth of the promiscuous mulatto woman with its portrayal of a naively romantic girl's seduction and abandonment by a dim-witted young white man of a slightly higher social station. Some critics find that because Lima Barreto depicted sexual exploitation of all lower-class women, rather than exclusively mulatto women, he weakened the point of the novel. Maria Luisa Nunes, however, has argued that despite the fact that "race and class are inextricably bound up in this society, Barreto makes it clear that race is the critical factor." Lima Barreto was also a vociferous critic of zealous nationalism, as evidenced by *The Patriot* which is also considered one of his greatest works. Through the life of its well-meaning but misguided protagonist Policarpo Quaresma, the novel satirizes political greed, intellectual mediocrity, a glory-seeking war ministry, and petty bureaucracy, among other aspects of Brazilian society. Lima Barreto counterposes a chaotic reality with the idealized Brazil envisioned by Quaresma, whose disillusioning life has led critics to differing interpretations regarding the author's attitude toward his character. While many critics have viewed Quaresma simply as an object of ridicule, others find a more complex and sympathetic message in the example of his farcical life and "sad end."

Despite the reduction of many minor characters to propagandist caricatures, protagonists in Lima Barreto's novels are portrayed with a depth and sophistication which predates modernist concerns with character psychology. This is especially true of *Recordações do escrivão Isaías Caminha* and *The Life and Death of M. J. Gonzaga de Sá*, first person narratives by black mulatto writers painfully aware of their precarious position in a racially hierarchical society. Coping with a morally corrupt upper class, each engages in self-analysis that in the course of their stories defines their relationships to a society from which they are alienated. Racism, classism, European and North American influences, and the difficulties of literary expression are explored with confessional desperation, leading Robert Herron to compare the urgency for self-understanding displayed in the works to the author's personal concerns recorded in his *Diário íntimo*.

Noting his position as a transitional writer, Elizabeth Lowe states that while Lima Barreto's "prophetic and deterministic conception of the city ties him to the nineteenth century, his schematic isolation of his protagonists as 'outsiders' is a very modern feature." Approximately fifty years after Lima Barreto's death, his works underwent a reevaluation, and he is now considered one of the most influential Brazilian authors of the early twentieth century. In addition, translation into English and other languages has earned international recognition for his works, which are perhaps better appreciated in a modern era distinguished by its greater sensitivity to the value of divergent human experiences.

(See also *Contemporary Authors,* Vol. 117.)

PRINCIPAL WORKS

Recordações do escrivão Isaías Caminha   (novel)   1909
Numa e Ninfa   (novel)   1915
Triste fim de Policarpo Quaresma   (novel)   1915
   [*The Patriot*, 1978]
Vida e morte de M. J. Gonzaga de Sá   (novel and short
   stories)   1919
   [*The Life and Death of M. J. Gonzaga de Sá* published in
   Lima Barreto: Bibliography and Translations, 1979]

Histórias e sonhos   (short stories)   1920
Os Bruzundangas   (novel and short story)   1922
Bagatelas   (journalism)   1923
Clara dos Anjos   (novel and short stories)   1923; published
   in journal *Cruze e Sousa*
   [*Clara dos Anjos* published in *Lima Barreto: Bibliography
   and Translations,* 1979]
Margiália   (notes, chronicles, criticism, folklore, and short
   stories)   1952
Cemitério dos vivos   (unfinished novel)   1953
Coisas do reino de Jambon   (essays)   1953
Diário íntimo   (diary)   1953
Feiras e mafuás   (essays)   1953
Impressões de leitura   (criticism)   1953
Correspondência 2 vols.   (letters)   1956
Obras completas. 17 vols.   (novels, short stories,
   journalism, folklore, essays, criticism, letters, and
   diary)   1956

ROBERT HERRON   (essay date 1971)

[*In the following excerpt, Herron compares the first-person narratives of* Recordações do escrivão Isaías Caminha *to Lima Barreto's* Diário íntimo, *arguing that both the author and his narrator are obsessed with their place in society, which leads them to distorted or inconsistent perceptions of reality.*]

Lima Barreto is usually thought of as primarily a social novelist, and it is true that social questions play an important part in his works. I believe, however, that the most interesting aspect of his writing is not the society that appears there but the mental processes of his characters in relation to that society. Their psychology is largely a result of their obsession with the social world that surrounds them and an attempt to determine three things: 1) their individual place in the world; 2) how that world influences them; and 3) how they can influence that world.

To understand Lima Barreto's protagonists one must understand Lima Barreto, especially in the case of Isaías Caminha, the protagonist of *Recordações do Escrivão Isaías Caminha,* published in 1909. Like his creator, Isaías is a mulatto and an artist, a writer. Many of his internal anguishes which are revealed to us in the course of the narration are those characteristic of racial sensitivity and of an artist unsure of himself or in the pain of creation. (p. 26)

In Lima Barreto's works, there is a constant preoccupation with the sociological result of his work, and the author does not always discreetly hide his anguish and uncertainty about whether or not he is accomplishing the purpose he has set for himself. In the specific case of *Recordações,* the anxiety shows through and is openly confessed, though in the words and under the guise of the protagonist Isaías Caminha. Let us compare the words of Isaías Caminha and a statement made by Lima Barreto in his *Diário Íntimo* about the time he was in the middle of the composition of the novel. After several chapters of *Recordações,* Isaías, who is relating to us in first person from memory his life history, interrupts the time sequence of events to insert an outburst of creative doubt:

> Penso—não sei porque—que é êste meu livro
> que me está fazendo mal . . . Talvez mesmo
> seja angústia de escritor, porque vivo cheio de

dúvidas e hesito de dia para dia em continuar a escrevê-lo. Não é seu valor literário que me preocupa, é a sua utilidade para o fim que almejo. Quem sabe se êle me não vai saindo um puro falatório!?

The above passage reveals the same creative anxiety as the following statement made by Lima Barreto in his diary:

Tenho um livro (trezentas páginas manuscritas), de que falta escrever dous ou três capítulos. Não tenho ânimo de acabá-lo. Sinto-o bêsta, imbecil, fraco, hesito em publicá-lo, hesito em acabá-lo. É por isso que me dá gana de matar-me; mas me parece que é isso que me tem faltado sempre.

Isaías' and Lima Barreto's doubts and anguish are explained by an ideological conflict which is at the same time sociological, philosophical, and literary in nature in the mind of the author and the character. The narrator says, in the first quote above, that his work has a practical purpose which he does not know whether he is accomplishing. He adds that the literary quality of what he is writing does not worry him. The practical purpose to which he refers is his desire to indoctrinate his reading public. The logical objection to this is, if he wants to propagandize, why has he chosen the literary form of the novel? The two contradict each other. Lima Barreto seems to be unaware of one of the essential characteristics of the novel, that, in the words of Edwin Muir, "the laws of the novel, the laws of imaginative creation in prose, are not within his control." A preconceived idea by the author of what the novel is or what it should do is frequently destroyed in the process of the writing of the novel. According to E. M. Forster, "All that is prearranged is false." Lima Barreto's previous idea of the novel as pure propaganda is gradually revealed to him as erroneous at the time he is composing *Recordações,* and he realizes that what he is writing is something quite different from what he had originally planned. This is not the only painful discovery made by the author as his work progresses. He also becomes conscious, much to his sorrow, that the idea he earlier wanted to convey is a mistaken one, at least in part.

Let us examine the purpose, intention, or thesis of the novel as Lima Barreto originally conceived it, and see why it does not succeed and what psychological repercussions it has as a result in the narrator-protagonist. Isaías tells us in the preface that he was inspired to publish his memoirs in order to disprove a theory he had read in an article, which stated that people with Negro blood experience a sharp decline of intellectual capacity in their mature years. The protagonist agrees that such a phenomenon seemingly occurs, but disagrees with the tendency of the author to attribute the blame for the deterioration to inherent characteristics of the race. Having analyzed his own experiences, Isaías arrives at the conclusion that only society has been to blame for his own apparent intellectual decline and failures, because of its prejudices and hostility. If he can prove this, he will have disproved the theory of intellectual racial inferiority, at least as it applies in his own case.

The statement of purpose is loaded with potential dangers as far as literary execution is concerned. First of all is the problem of how representative Isaías is of all Negroes. To begin with, the position of the mulatto in Brazilian society is quite different from that of the Negro. A recent study of racial attitudes by Marvin Harris claims that there is more hostility felt towards the Negro than towards the mulatto. In the study of L. A. Costa

Pinto, *O Negro no Rio de Janeiro,* however, it is proved, based on statistical evidence, that the discriminatory attitudes of whites towards mulattos in that city are stronger than those towards Negroes. The important thing here is that there is obviously a difference of attitude toward the Negro and the mulatto. (pp. 27-8)

In the novel, Isaías may perhaps be considered a representative of the mulatto, but of the type unable, because of his darker color (he refers to the color of his skin as "pronunciadamente azeitonada" . . .), or unwilling, because of his pride, to pass himself off as white. It is difficult to think of him, however, as being typical of all Negroes, even though he frequently uses the pronoun *nós* in general statements and conclusions instead of referring exclusively to himself. . . . Yet in the novel Isaías is in reality not representative of Negroes nor mulattos but rather a lonely exception in the high position which he has temporarily gained for himself as confidant to the director of a newspaper, which has given him the chance to be on close terms with this man and to prove his true value and capacities. Moreover, there is also evidence to show how much he feels different and superior to other members of his race, especially because of what he considers an exceptional intelligence. (p. 29)

Lima Barreto in his diary reveals a similar separation from those of his race. His feeling of superiority is patent in the following quotation:

Eu tenho muita simpatia pela gente pobre do Brasil, especialmente pelos de côr, mas não me é possível transformar essa simpatia literária, artística, por assim dizer em vida commun com êles, pelo menos com os que vivo, que, sem reconhecerem a minha superioridade, absolutamente não têm por mim nenhum respeito e nenhum amor que lhes fizesse obedecer cegamente.

In other words, as an intellectual spokesman for Negroes and mulattos, the author is representative. In real life and as an individual, because he does consider himself so much above the others, he cannot associate with them. His mind and his sentiments directly oppose each other. This apparent contradiction in his own personality, not openly stated in the novel *Recordações,* though it is hinted at in some of Isaías' statements and in his relationships with and opinions of other characters, caused Lima Barreto great shame, and he only confessed it directly to himself and to his diary which he did not expect anyone ever to read. . . . The real tragedy of Lima Barreto's inner life, which he tries hard to keep out of *Recordações,* is that deep down inside he doubts the very thing upon which he bases his superiority; that is, his intelligence. . . . (pp. 29-30)

In the novel the sadness of claiming to be intelligent while at the same time fearing not to be so is almost completely hidden in Isaías. We only get a glimpse of it in the anguish and doubt which he demonstrates in revealing himself in the creative process.

To the extent that he shows to himself and to us that he is different from other members of his race, Isaías is in a way, consciously or unconsciously, accomplishing what he wants: to invalidate the theory that all Negroes are innately inferior. He does it, not by showing that society is the cause of his "apparent" intellectual decline, as he states in the preface, but by demonstrating that generalizations about races are necessarily false, because individuals of a race are always exceptions to any general rules. The broad concepts of race and racial hierarchies are mental abstractions which have no meaning in real life when applied to specific individuals.

Isaías and Lima Barreto are less successful when they attempt to fight invalid racial generalizations with invalid generalizations of their own, as in Isaías' statement which tries by the use of the pronoun *nós* to make us believe that his failure is typical of the pre-determined failure of all of his race: "Lembrava-me da vida de minha mãe, da sua miséria, da sua pobreza . . . parecia-me também condenado a acabar e *todos nós condenados a nunca ultrapassar*" . . . [underlining is mine]. Isaías' failure in the novel is caused by factors much more complex than his color or his poverty. His attempt to blame society as the only cause of his downfall is also an extremely dangerous generalization. To the degree he admits in the course of the novel that he himself is at fault, and not society, his original broadly stated principle is disproved and the novel becomes a better novel. He would have done well to omit the pronoun *nós* completely.

One reason Isaías' failure cannot be generalized to include all Negroes is that he has a very personal interpretation of the word "failure." Failure to him means only the lack of success in an intellectual sense, the inability to realize the original dream he had when he came from his home in a small town in Espírito Santo to Rio de Janeiro, that of studying to become a medical doctor. He did fail in this sense, but he does not convince us that society was to blame. He convinces us more of his own lack of determination and will power, of his laziness and inertia, of his willingness to give up easily in order not to have to struggle to make his place in life. The weak part of Isaías' argument is his effort to show that the force of prejudice, if it existed, presented an impossible obstacle to his acquiring protection or a job which would enable him to support himself while attending the university. He tries to show us how he first became aware of the existence of prejudice by the experience of being prejudiced against. (It does not seem logical that only at the age of attending the university would he first become aware of it, as happened to Isaías.) Then he tries to persuade us that the experiences he had were the cause for his abandoning his ideal because he saw that he would inevitably be rejected and repelled in everything he could do to advance himself. He justifies the decision he made not to struggle any more to attain his ambitions on three experiences, only one of which seems to have any validity as far as being an act of racial prejudice is concerned: on his way from Espírito Santo to Rio de Janeiro, he was refused service at a refreshment stand in favor of everyone else, even though he was the first to get off the train and arrive at the counter. Another instance, which he attempts to explain as an example of discrimination, was the refusal of a congressman, to whom he had a letter of introduction, to help him obtain employment. The only sign of displeasure which the congressman registered was a frown on his brow, which Isaías interpreted as racial intolerance. We would possibly explain the protagonist's reaction as hyper-sensitivity and imagination, unjustifiable on the basis of one previous experience. The congressman's rebuff could be accounted for in many other ways: his egoism and lack of concern for others, or merely obsessive preoccupation with his own matters at the time Isaías went to see him for example. But reflecting to himself, Isaías used these two incidents as a sure indication of his "irremediável derrota" . . . , as a justification for giving up his striving to realize his intellectual ideals and for indulging in inertia. He preferred to envelop himself in self-pity, blaming his cowardliness on forces outside himself. . . . Isaías did react psychologically to his pusillanimity, abandoning temporarily a

plan to return to his family home in an attitude of complete defeatism. It is here that the thesis begins to weaken considerably because Isaías for the first time admits to himself that his downfall was in part a result of his own weakness, not merely the imposition of society. As an act of psychological compensation he resolved to be more heroic and positive in his outlook and in his actions. . . . Such an attitude of resolution, however, turns out to be merely a pose, a dreamy idealistic desire which had little effect on his conduct. His efforts the next day seem weak. He went to only one place in search of a job, was turned down, and tried no more. Once again he suspected the rejection was due to race prejudice, but he could not be sure then, nor can he prove to us now, that such was the case. At any rate, the incident was enough to make him abandon a courageous position once and for all. From this point on he became almost completely passive, and returned to his earlier, more comfortable position of defeatism.

To base his intellectual failure entirely on acts of racial prejudice, which he cannot prove but only suspects, is impossible for Isaías, and he begins to realize it more and more as the novel progresses. To verify prejudice of attitude is one thing, but to prove that everyone will act in accordance with it is something completely different. Acts of racial prejudice in Brazil have never formed any definite pattern, they have never taken on a violent aspect, they have appeared very seldom, always in mild form in rare, isolated cases. Even Lima Barreto admits in his diary: "Demais, há e houve sempre entre nós um grande sentimento liberal, com certas restrições, em favor dos negros." Because of this, from this time on in the novel Isaías changes his tune and explains his inability to reach his goal in terms of both individual psychology and outside influences. . . . (pp. 30-2)

The problem is that, once Isaías has admitted his weakness and lack of will power, he can no longer convince his reading audience of any of his accusations against society. His harshness with the social world can still be understood as a psychological process of rationalization. It is natural for all human beings to want to blame something on someone else outside of themselves for their own insufficiencies and failure to succeed. If Isaías cannot blame society for everything that happened to him, now he will at least blame it partially. The sad thing is that society may be guilty of the things of which he accuses it, prejudice in a general sense, but only in certain isolated cases, and maybe not in his own case. Because he does not really persuade us that enough prejudice was exercised against him to make him fail in life, we as readers tend to attach little importance to the question of prejudice. We would even doubt that it exists at all, from Isaías arguments, if we did not have at hand some of the sociological studies mentioned earlier which verify the presence of attitudinal racial bias in Brazilian society. For that reason we are tempted to dismiss any sociological significance at all to the novel.

If Isaías cannot be a representative racial type he can be a convincing psychological type: a suspicious defeatist who was afraid to act from fear that he would be hurt or that he would have to bear the full responsibility for his acts. Long before he ever came to Rio de Janeiro he showed a morbid anticipation of his future in the big city and demonstrated no real confidence or determination to be victorious. . . . (p. 33)

In his portrayal of a defeatist, Lima Barreto has chosen a psychological type that might be found amongst all races, in any country or society. For that reason his character may be considered universal, even though someone like Professor Costa

Pinto . . . would undoubtedly explain the cause of Isaías' defeatism because of peculiar racial circumstances. The tragedy of race relations between black and white in Rio de Janeiro, according to him, are not permanent and frequent manifestations of racial violence, but occasional cases which create in the mind of some of the individual members of the group anxiety and defeatism which prevent them from acting and moving ahead to improve their lot. At any rate, whether Professor Costa Pinto's theory applies to Isaías or not the protagonist is not differentiated racially as a result; rather, he is shown as having something in common with all human beings who try to justify their disinclination to move or act by blaming forces outside of themselves for their defeats.

It is ironical in the novel that when Isaías became most defeatist and inactive he most "succeeded" in society. He did not succeed in his own sense of the word, but in the sense that the society around him defined success, in terms of more money and a higher position. The reader is not easily convinced by Isaías' actions at this point. If he really had a burning ambition to study to be a doctor, there would be nothing to prevent him at this moment, since he now was employed, from attempting to pursue his studies at the same time he was working for the newspaper. He allowed himself, however, to be easily satisfied with a poor job and completely abandoned without remorse his individual study habits. (pp. 33-4)

Isaías the narrator tells us that only later did he react with shame to the position in which he found himself. He returned to his original ideals in principle, though it was too late to go back and realize himself according to them. He admits his own fault to us now, as he admitted it to himself then; at the same time he partially blames society for his having strayed so far from the original course of action which he had traced for himself. . . . (p. 34)

In describing the period of Isaías' life which covers the time he worked for the newspaper, Isaías the narrator no longer uses racial prejudice as a reason to explain his own and the protagonist's past failure. In a sense, Isaías could fail no more in life because he had already failed, in his own meaning of the word, when he began his job and left behind his professional aspirations. Moreover, at that point in his re-creation by recollection of his past life, the narrator Isaías has already failed the stated purpose of his work with regard to race because he has been unable to demonstrate convincingly that prejudice was the only thing keeping him from attainment. From that moment Isaías began to work for *O Globo*, the narrator and the novel take an entirely different course. Society still is depicted as a harmful force on the individual, but with a much broader base than the limitations imposed by a strictly racial thesis. For us Isaías becomes a human being rather than a racial symbol. Now his lack of integration into society, or rather, his quasi-absorption into it, then a revolt and re-separation from it, are explained in terms of individual integrity and morality. The narrator Isaías tells us that his rise on the newspaper was not because of individual merit, as it should have been, but because he let himself be used, without resistance, by the strong will of another. He became completely dependent on the whims and desires of director Loberant, had no longer any individuality of his own. Although at first he apparently did not care or particularly notice, he gradually became aware that almost everyone around him was corrupt and immoral, motivated purely by self-interest, especially in the acquisition of money and higher positions. Through the newspaper office he was able to observe not only newspapermen, but also representatives of all

of the ruling classes of society: politicians, businessmen, and literary figures of great fame. The image of nobility of spirit and profound intelligence which he had thought earlier they should have and did have completely vanished. As a result, Isaías' consciousness of his own worth, which had been stifled by his earlier reverses and by certain pleasures of his new "success," experienced a rebirth. . . . (pp. 34-5)

It is ironical that as a narrator and a writer Isaías Caminha now has another reason for being and striving. He is fighting to succeed, whereas as a younger man he let himself graciously retire from the battle to win what he wanted. In this sense there is no conflict or contradiction between Isaías the narrator and Isaías the man whose life, or a part of whose life, is being narrated, because one could say that the older man learned from the younger man's experiences the value of will power translated into action. There are certain errors of perspective, however, that cause apparent psychological inconsistencies between the chronicler Isaías, who refers to his present self and beliefs in the present tense, and the character Isías in the past tense. The critic A. A. Mendilow has called attention to the different time levels present in an autobiographical novel of this sort: the time of the pseudo-author at the moment of composition and the time span of the character who is being told about; he has also put his finger on what it is that bothers us about this method of story-telling in *Recordações:* "There are bounds which the *I* of the autobiographical novel cannot, except by means of unlikely and artificial tricks, overstep. He cannot present his own character . . . convincingly, though in a story where the emphasis is on action and adventure, this may not be the drawback it is in the novel where the accent is placed on character and psychology."

There are two sets of psychological changes in Isaías, those of Isaías the narrator, in present time and those of Isaías, the character, in past time. It is almost as if they are two different people, because the narrator makes the character's attitude change in accordance with the transformation of his own psychology. For example, if we are to accept as sincere and as psychologically valid Isaías' belief (as a narrator) at the beginning that society has been the only cause of his mental decline and failure, and his change later on (still as a narrator) to the view that he too was to blame, we must assume that Isaías (as a character) did not analyze or was never aware (or at least never admitted, even to himself while he was actually going through the experiences) that personally, he was at fault. Yet this is not true, because we have already seen how he confessed to himself at the time that he was lacking in will power. Of course this inconsistency could be justified or explained away by supposing that, at the time Isaías starts writing his memoirs, he has temporarily forgotten exactly what he felt and thought at specific moments in his life. As the narration proceeds, the effort of recollection makes him remember certain things which force him to bare his soul, both to himself and to us, and confess that his original statement was mistaken or merely wishful thinking. He experiences great pain in the re-revealment to himself (since he had voluntarily or involuntarily forgotten) and in the discovering to us of the flaws of his inner being. He is ashamed, not only because he sees himself forced to "undress" before us, but also because he does not like to see himself "undressed." . . . (pp. 35-6)

Other psychological or ideological inconsistencies still in relationship to the statement of purpose and still because of the two characters (or one character and one pseudo-author) cannot be justified or explained away so easily, except as mental confusion. To state categorically that society and only society has caused an individual to be defeated is social determinism, which denies the ability of the will or the person to be effective in self-determination or in changing in any way the surrounding world. Yet in practically the same sentence Isaías says that he is going to prove something, that he is going to try to convince people to think the way he does, which is an assertion of the power of the individual will. It is true that Isaías does not know whether he will be able to influence his reading public or not, but it is certain that he would not be writing if he did not have at least a vague hope of doing so. At least in his work at writing Isaías is active and enthusiastic and thus to that degree has overcome his passivity and defeatism of earlier days. . . . (p. 37)

Because of the uncertainty he feels, however, about his possible future influence on the world, and because he is forced to deny the validity of his original deterministic thesis, we can conclude this study by saying that the novel is one individual's search (an unanswered search) for a meaning of life, within the framework of the individual-society relationship, the procurement of an explanation and strategy of living, a formula by which he might know the best way to face his existence and the proper way to act in order to obtain the maximum of satisfaction. The narrator's attempt to be sincere, active, and undiscouraged by the future in spite of its uncertainty seems to be part of the answer. It does not eliminate the anguish of uncertainty, however, and it is this existential anxiety within the mind of the protagonist-narrator which makes *Recordações* primarily a psychological novel and not a sociological novel which would follow slavishly some dogmatic thesis. Although before Lima Barreto wrote *Recordações* he considered social content important, perhaps more important than any penetration into the mind of his characters, his doubt regarding the meaning of society as an abstract entity and his relationship to it made the final product turn out to be something quite different, a work which possessed all the elements which he later criticized the novelist Teo Filho for not having in the work *Virgens Amorosas:* a disturbing personal dream; unhappiness caused by the lack of correspondence between the ideal and the real; and the charm of hesitation, of vagueness, of imprecision, and of the mystery of a mind which finds itself submerged in an undecipherable universe and which is tortured by uncertainty and by the inability to comprehend itself. (pp. 37-8)

> Robert Herron, "Lima Barreto's 'Isaias Caminha' as a Psychological Novel," in Luso-Brazilian Review, *Vol. VIII, No. 2, December, 1971, pp. 26-38.*

J. C. KINNEAR (essay date 1974)

[*In the following excerpt, Kinnear discusses the validity of critical contentions that Lima Barreto viewed the title character of* Triste fim de Policarpo Quaresma *as either a sympathetic martyr or a misdirected nationalist. Kinnear considers the nationalist aspects of the characterization a parody of the contemporary nationalist tract* Porque me ufano do meu país (1901) *by Afonso Celso.*]

What is the "triste fim" of Policarpo Quaresma? What is the author's attitude to his character? Most critics have tended to answer these questions by seeing Policarpo as a likeable, if misguided, character, for whom the novelist has great sympathy: he is the idealist brought down by a society which does not understand. . . . Olívio Montenegro sees him as a Don Quixote figure, the idealist battling against an unjust world, therefore earning the author's sympathy. . . . Oliveira Lima also views him as a Don Quixote, because they both want to cure human and social ills by applying justice: they are both

visionaries. Finally Astorjildo Pereira interprets the character as a kind of father-figure, since Barreto's father, like Policarpo, went mad; the novelist is seen as sympathetic to the character and regretting his end.

Critical interpretation of his nationalism has tended to suggest that the author sees Policarpo as the ideal "new" Brazilian, looking for the roots of his nation. A recent English history of Latin-American culture includes the novel in a group which is said to show the select minority turning from Europe and looking into their own America to find an identity, but still being frustrated and broken by their environment. Moisés Gicovate paints the book as the story of a tragic hero, who sacrifices all for the nation, but who is defeated by that nation. . . . (pp. 60-1)

A different view of the author's attitude is given by an American historian [see Burns entry in Additional Bibliography], who says "he even chose to look at the humorous side of nationalism. In his brilliant novel *Triste fim de Policarpo Quaresma* . . . he poked fun at the nationalists, through the meticulously drawn picture of his hero—or anti-hero—a devoted nationalist." In other words, the author's intention is to hold Policarpo up to ridicule, not to see him as an ideal or to sympathize with him.

The intention of this essay is to show that these contradictory attitudes are only half-truths and to suggest that the truth lies in between: Policarpo *is* a martyr to a misunderstanding society and does earn sympathy, but he is also ridiculed as a nationalist, for it is shown that, far from being a harmless fool, his outlook is positively destructive in its effect on the nation.

Policarpo is abused by the society in which he works and he suffers greatly. His idea that Tupi should become the national language may be unsound, but the reaction from society is quite out of keeping: not only laughter in Parliament, but extensive mockery in the press, which, always ready for a good "story," loses no time in discovering many details about him. The bureaucratic world reacts against him violently, not because he is wrong, but because he has shown initiative; they detest him because they are jealous. They attribute to him the pretension which is evident in their own hostility to him. All of which contrasts vividly with his own innocent motive. . . . He is "desinteressado de dinheiro, de glória e posição," . . . unlike his fellow bureaucrats. He is victimized by them a second time, when he unthinkingly submits a document in Tupi, which is carelessly approved by the director of his department and passed to the minister. The director does not notice the language; the higher civil servants cannot even identify it and spend much time on this and the sterile question of whether laws can be presented in foreign languages. Barreto makes great fun of them: Tupi is of course a "national" language— and it is the officials who are to blame for passing the document. However, pride and prestige hurt, the director turns on Policarpo in a violent tirade . . . and suspends him from his job. Policarpo is an innocent victim. The author's obvious sympathy for him in the madhouse . . . only highlights the injustice, for it is society which has put him there: it was the newspaper's mockery which made him study Tupi all the more, to show he knew it . . . and it was a colleague's jibe about his literary pretensions which made him inadvertently translate the document into Tupi. . . . (pp. 61-2)

When he moves from Rio to his "sítio" to cultivate the land, he falls innocent victim to local politics. He has no political views, but believes time and energy should be spent in tilling the soil. . . . Tenente Antonino Dutra approaches him for one party and is horrified that he should not be concerned with the local political squabbles which are considered so important. . . . Dutra's reaction to such honesty is to suspect it:

> Aquilo devia ser um ambicioso matreiro; era
> preciso cortar as asas daquêle "estrangeiro,"
> que vinha não se sabe donde! . . .

Policarpo cannot escape: one of his employees reports that the other side—that of Doutor Campos—is claiming his support. . . . Dutra's party publishes a cruel satirical poem against the "estrangeiro." . . . His protests of innocence are ignored and his charity to the poor is considered an attempt to find political support among the people for himself. . . . *Doutor* Campos, on the other hand, only has sympathy for the rich. Campos expects a reward for his friendship with Policarpo, in the form of electoral connivance. . . . When Policarpo refuses, on grounds of principle ("não iria afirmar uma cousa que êle não sabia se era mentira ou verdade" . . .), Campos uses his power to intimidate the major:

> era intimado, sob as penas das mesmas posturas
> e leis, a roçar e capinar as testadas do referido
> sítio que confrontavam com as visas públi-
> cas. . . .

Policarpo contrasts such pettiness with the poverty of the interior . . . and the great need to improve the life of the poor man there. Dutra too has his revenge, for as local tax official, he can fine Quaresma for sending products away without paying local "dues". . . . Even transporters and buyers exploit him to the end. His protests are obviously just, but he is the victim again. Against this background he remains true to his aims: to improve agriculture regardless of personal profits. (p. 62)

Idealism and altruism expose the hypocrisy of others. [Quaresma] is mocked by the *doutores* for his devotion to books . . . , although he, not they, is willing to fight for the *pátria*. He is scorned by Tenente Fontes . . . because he is not a real major; however he wants to do far more for his country than do the "real"—in the sense of officially promoted—General Albernaz and Admiral Caldas, who have never seen a day's fighting in all their careers. While they boast of campaigns in which they never took part, he sees the horror of war. . . . They see war as a way to further themselves; he alone longs for its end, for the sake of man, and hopes that it may bring some good to the republic. After we see Floriano tear up his proposals, as note paper . . . , and dismiss him as a "visionary" . . . , how just seem Quaresma's complaints, now that he no longer idolizes the Marechal:

> Era pois para sustentar tal homem que deixara
> o sossêgo da sua casa e se arriscava nas trinch-
> eiras? Era, pois, por êsse homem que tanta
> gente morria? . . .

The military misjudge him for one last time: after he protests at the indiscriminate killing of prisoners, he is seen as 'um traidor, um bandido' . . .—and he is killed.

Such is the unjust fate of the idealist in the cruel world. Or is it? Quaresma is a martyr, in that society misconstrues his aims, but is he a martyr whose ideas should be resurrected and followed? Does Barreto consider his end entirely unjust? Quaresma himself certainly considers that he has been a martyr to his patriotism, when he looks back over his life from the condemned cell. . . . But is it only society which is responsible or does he not contribute to his fate significantly himself? Barreto

suggests strongly that the very idealism which puts him above the rest of society is in fact a major factor in his downfall, not because of the environment, but because of the nature of the idealism. His nationalism is not a reasoned and sensible concern for the welfare of the people of the nation—such as we shall see later in the character of Olga, whom Barreto seems to offer as a comparison—but an irrational glorification of the concept of *pátria*, lacking any real basis. His attitude is one of *ufanismo* and it bears a remarkable similarity, so remarkable that one doubts if it is purely coincidental, to the outlook of Afonso Celso's *Porque me ufano do meu país*. It would seem reasonable to suggest that Barreto takes to task this *ufanismo*, in the very character who exhibits the ideals with which he shows so much sympathy.

Afonso Celso (1860-1938) was an ardent nationalist. His *Porque me ufano* . . . paints a stubbornly optimistic picture of Brazil, yesterday, today and always; the noun *ufanismo* derives from its title. Although discredited today, it enjoyed immense popularity; it is now in its fourteenth edition and between publication in 1901 and the appearance of **Policarpo Quaresma** in book form (1915) there were seven editions. (pp. 63-4)

The book is addressed to the children of the nation. . . . The teaching is, as in Policarpo's case, absolute devotion to the *pátria*, whose greatness Celso sees on all sides. His words are a mixture of the emotional and the hysterical. He uses statistics frequently, in a far from objective way. For example, in order to illustrate the size of Brazil, he compares it mathematically with a host of other countries—especially the great Imperial powers—in such a way that he suggests Brazil's stature, as well as size, is greater than all others. . . . (p. 65)

The size of Brazil—which is said to contain within its borders *every* manifestation of nature and of mankind, all living in perfect harmony—is the first of eleven factors which make up "a grandeza do Brasil." (p. 66)

Many of these attitudes can be found in the person of Policarpo Quaresma and in those characters who represent the State. They are mocked, firstly, by Barreto's distortion of them, and secondly by the course of events which he makes the novel follow.

When talking of the greatness of Brazil, Celso "proves" his points by profuse quotation from travellers who have written of the marvels they have seen. Policarpo too lives very much in a "literary" world, like Celso, gaining his certainty of Brazil's greatness from the books he reads. The first chapter of the novel stresses the size of his library ("as estantes pejadas de cima para baixo" . . .), the claustrophobic atmosphere of this room, detached from the outside world, and most of all the fact that all the books there are *national*. . . . Barreto exaggerates greatly, when we compare Quaresma's books to Celso's, for the fictional character has every author imaginable. Barreto humorously points out, in parenthesis, as if it were to be expected, that Quaresma has *all* the works of the most nationalistic writers. It is to be noted that Quaresma like Celso has a great predilection for the writings of those who have travelled around Brazil. Clearly, he chooses his books according to their patriotism: it is an ironic understatement when Barreto comments: "Policarpo era patriota." . . . His bookish knowledge excludes reality, as is shown when he tries to apply his ideas, and as is shown symbolically when his reading of a patriotic text is interrupted by a knock at the door. The very passage that he is reading . . . , from Rocha Pita's *História da América Portuguêsa* is quoted by Celso . . . , which explains Barreto's reference to it as "aquêle famoso período." His treatment of the passage, involving a move from its sublime hyperbole to the ultimate in the banal, gives his opinion of it:

> Quaresma estava lendo aquêle famoso período: "Em nenhuma outra região se mostra o céu mais sereno, nem madrugada mais bela a aurora; o sol em nenhum outro hemisfério tem os raios mais dourados . . ." mas não pôde ir ao fim. Batiam à porta. Foi abri-la em pessoa. . . .

His living of his life and of his experience of Brazil through books is mocked as Barreto takes a consciously "literary" metaphor, to describe part of his everyday routine:

> Tôdas as manhãs, antes que a "Aurora com seus dedos rosados abrisse caminho ao louro Febo," êle se encerrava até ao almôço com o Montoya, *Arte y diccionario de la lengua guaraní o más bien tupí* e estudava o jargão caboclo com afinco e paixão. . . .

In addition to such incidental mockery, we see the attitude subjected to a positive test: Quaresma cannot understand why the *povo* has lost its traditional songs so quickly. He is disappointed that a *preta velha* . . . cannot remember cradle songs. He goes to a *literato* and optimistically expects him to provide the material. Like Quaresma's, this man's room is full of books and papers from floor to ceiling. Barreto loses no chance to make fun of the man: he has, for example, just received a letter from . . . Urubu-de-Baixo, a name which can hardly have been chosen by accident; and he tells a folk-story which is part of the "ciclo do macaco"—surely, a parody of folk-cycles. He tells of a folk dance, the *tangolomango*, look ridiculous but which nearly suffocates him and causes him to faint. When Quaresma pursues the matter further, he discovers the legends are not even Brazilian.

As Celso talks over and over again of *as riquezas nacionais*, so does Quaresma. . . . Like Celso, he talks of "um conhecimento inteiro do Brasil," . . . of a belief in the goodness of *every* region: he mentions the same regions and the same reasons for greatness—the coffee of São Paulo, the diamonds of Minas Gerais, the beauty of Guanabara, and the Paulo Afonso. As Celso plays with statistics, so does Quaresma. . . . Barreto makes the use of figures less subtle, more crude, and brings in the verb "amputar" to excite our laughter, as he does with this comment: "Êle amava sobremodo os rios: as montanhas lhe eram indiferentes. Pequenas talvez . . .". Like Celos, he always springs to the defence of Brazil against Europe. . . . (pp. 66-8)

Part II of the novel concerns Quaresma's experience of nature. As Part I opened with *ufanista* statements about Brazil's greatness, so does Part II, with respect to the land. Quaresma says: "A nossa terra tem os terrenos mais férteis do mundo." . . . He is full of *ufanista* optimism . . . and, before even looking at the ground, is making his plan. He knows all will go well. . . . Like Celso, he sees exotic crops flourishing; like Celso, he catalogues them. . . . He totally rejects the experience of the locals, who tell him his efforts are unlikely to succeed. (p. 69)

When the ideas are put to the test, there is disaster. The scientific equipment is useless, the land is in a poor state, and Quaresma finds great difficulty even in using a hoe. . . . Although he maintains his faith, despite his experience and the words of others, he has to reinforce his stance by further doctrinaire reading. . . . Ironically, Barreto follows this with—an invasion of ants, bad weather, an awareness of the poverty of rural workers and of the stupidity of government policies, the discovery that transport costs deprive him of any profit, the destruction of his crops and a further invasion of ants in the orange-groves. . . . In the face of the failure, Barreto's continued use of *ufanista* phrases is a harsh irony. . . . (pp. 69-70)

Another of Celso's claims for Brazil was the excellence of the national type, which summed up all that men thought ideal. . . . The politicians who destroy Quaresma's project are the precise opposite of the tenth "predicado do caráter nacional." . . . (p. 70)

Similarly, the military personnel of the story hold Celso's view of the army's glory, although their own action—or rather, lack of it, exposes them for what they are. As Celso sees war as continuous glory for the nation—to him, the deaths of war are nothing compared to the "glory" of the Retirada da Laguna . . .—so we read of one of Barreto's creations:

> De resto, contadas pelo General Albernaz, que nunca tinha visto a guerra, a cousa ficava edulcorada, uma guerra *bibliothèque rose*, guerra de estampa popular, em que não aparecem a carniçaria, a brutalidade e a ferocidade normais. . . .

Again, when we compare Barreto's portrayal of *ufanismo* with the original, we see the author has simplified it, in order to highlight its absurdity. Later, though, we find Albernaz using Celso's exact words, lest we be in any doubt as to the butt of the laughter:

> Esta terra necessita de govêrno que se faça respeitar . . . É incrível! *Um país como êste, tão rico, talvez o mais rico do mundo*, é no entanto, pobre, deve a todo o mundo . . . Porquê? For causa dos governos que temos tido que não têm prestígio, fôrça . . . É por isso. (. . . my italics.)

The question "why is Brazil poor?" has another answer, which Albernaz gives unwittingly: because it is led by men who think only of themselves and simply mouth commonplaces, without thinking.

The military men are travesties of officers: Caldas is an admiral with no ship, who nevertheless repeatedly talks about his prowess in naval matters . . . and who regrets the ending of hostilities because it means the end of his chance for promotion. . . . Albernaz is a general who has never fought in any wars, because he always fell ill just before the campaign started . . . and who also looks to war for personal advance. . . . Bustamante openly equates the country's ruin with his own lack of promotion . . . ; he offers to sell Quaresma a rank . . . ; he never fights, because he is always too busy with the accounts. (pp. 70-1)

As in the other cases, it is in Quaresma that we see the ideas put to the test. He has an *ufanista* view of war: to begin with, that is. . . . He enters war, believing in technical instruments and in the value of his cause. Experience of battle changes that opinion and he writes to his sister Adelaide, telling of the horror of war and revealing disillusionment. . . . Again, events prove Celso to be wrong.

We see here clearly the irony of Quaresma's misplaced energies, as with the persecution he suffers as the result of his *tupinismo*. He undergoes much hardship, but for no purpose.

As the novel draws to its close, he reviews his life and sees his failures; he realizes that his concept of *pátria* was false, because it ignored reality. Significantly, he alludes to his library and its isolation from the world: "A pátria que quisera ter era um mito; era um fantasma criado por êle no silêncio do seu gabinete." . . . He sees the way the concept has been used—with his own unwitting connivance—to exploit, not to help, the nation: he has been used to further the ends of those who seek power. . . . (pp. 71-2)

The sad end of Policarpo Quaresma is not that his environment frustrates his idealism. It is that he is a man of superior intelligence who can see the wrongs of society, who unthinkingly sacrifices his life to a worthless and misguided cause. (p. 72)

So the central character is not Barreto's ideal: this rôle being left to Olga, who is a nationalist, but who retains a balanced and sensible view throughout. She seems very much the mouthpiece of the author, for in the same way that he laments the sad state of the interior . . . , so she is impressed most of all in the interior by "a pobreza das cousas." . . . As Barreto tells of the faults of a society where marriage is "expected"—a requirement which causes Ismênia to lose her sanity—, so Olga feels the social pressures which make her marry. Unlike Ismênia but like Barreto, she analyses these forces and comments on their folly . . . , for he too comments on this. . . . Thirdly, as he criticizes the almost religious awe in which the republican leaders are held, despite the republican concept . . . , so Olga complains of the

> tom divino com que os senhores falam da autoridade. Não se governa mais em nome de Deus, por que então êsse respeito, essa veneração de que querem cercar os governantes? . . .

She is a nationalist, but less extreme than Quaresma. She refuses to dismiss his Tupi project out of hand, but sees it is impracticable; she sees his good motive rather than his silly action . . . , as she does when he offers his help to the President of the Republic. . . . She sees the absurdity of a "nationalist" policy which gives assistance to immigrants, to encourage them to come to Brazil, but which does not help the poor who were born in Brazil. . . . She responds with the voice of reason to Quaresma's wild enthusiasm about the unrivalled fertility of the Brazilian soil: "—Em tôda a parte—não acha, meu padrinho?—há terras férteis?" . . . Her love for her country is not based on clichés; she feels a genuine grief when she witnesses poverty. She wants to act, to ask practical questions . . . , whereas the *ufanista* Quaresma never asks the questions, because he already knows the answers. Two arguments with her husband reveal the force of her patriotism. Firstly, she criticizes its use simply to deceive people, as an emotional battle-cry. . . . Secondly, she criticizes her husband, and other self-proclaimed patriots, when he is afraid she might compromise him by trying to save Quaresma from his death. . . . Like Quaresma, she will go against the tide, but her reactions are more measured.

So another aspect of the irony of the *sad end,* is that, while Policarpo was capable of rising above others but failed to do so, being deceived by the very nationalism he sought to promote, another person altogether exhibits a valid Brazilian nationalism—a girl who is of direct European descent, for her father Coleoni is Italian. Quaresma the *ufanista* so criticized a colleague for wanting to visit Europe . . . ; yet his ideal is embodied in a girl who, we are told, acquires her special qualities from precisely her European origin. (p. 73)

"Calvary without the Resurrection" sums up Barreto's ambivalent attitude to Policarpo: the martyr who is also a madman. The critics quoted earlier all made the mistake of adopting either one view or the other; in doing so, they reveal they are deceived by the author's irony. For, in a way so similar to Machado de Assis, Barreto makes us sympathize with the martyr, whom we accept without thinking, as kind and harmless when compared to the vicious society in which he lives, when in fact Policarpo is very unbalanced from the start. We assume, falsely, that because he lacks the vices of the others, he is virtuous; when, all the time, there is evidence of madness. (p. 74)

In the same way that the reader finds himself sympathizing with a foolish *tupinista,* so, at the end of the novel, he finds that he is laughing at a man who carries out the only good and humane act in the book: the protest at the massacre of political prisoners. The irony mocks Quaresma in that, having spent the whole of his life as a "nationalist" and achieving nothing, when he does one thing which is good for man and for the health of the republic, it leads directly to his own death—as a traitor. To mock both reader and character, the author deceives in order to enlighten; this, after all, is the essence of irony. (p. 75)

> J. C. Kinnear, "The 'Sad End' of Lima Barreto's Policarpo Quaresma," in Bulletin of Hispanic Studies, *Vol. LI, No. 1, January, 1974, pp. 60-75.*

ANTONIO OLINTO (essay date 1977)

[*The following is an excerpt from Olinto's introduction to the English translation of* Triste fim de Policarpo Quaresma.]

"A Brazilian Don Quixote": this was how, in 1916, the essayist and critic Oliveira Lima hailed the novel ***Triste Fim de Policarpo Quaresma (The Sad End of Policarpo Quaresma)*** now published in English under the title of ***The Patriot.*** Its author, Lima Barreto . . . , a Mulatto from Rio de Janeiro, belonged to the lower middle-class of the Brazilian Second Empire, being born seven years before the abolition of slavery in the country, and eight years before the Republic. (p. vii)

Lima Barreto's first novel, ***Recordações do Escrivão Isaias Caminha,*** was published in 1909. ***The Patriot*** was written two years later especially to be serialized in the Rio newspaper *O Jornal do Comercio* where it ran from 11 August to 19 October 1911. Published in book form in 1915, it was not unanimously well received as Oliveira Lima's comparison with Don Quixote seems to indicate. By the standards of previous Brazilian literature the book was written in such a new narrative language that to some critics it had no meaning. However, many of his fellow-writers saw immediately that that poor Negro, who was then also a civil servant at the Ministry of War, had something to add to the literature of his country.

By calling it ***The Patriot,*** the English translator of the novel, Mr Scott-Buccleuch, shows the heart of the matter. What Policarpo Quaresma insists on being—as well as what Lima Barreto himself was—can only be explained by this perhaps old-fashioned word "patriot." Policarpo sees his country as the best possible place in the world to live in, and the rivers of Brazil are the widest, the longest, the most beautiful of all rivers, and the land is the most fertile, and he tops his patriotic ideology by proclaiming that the Tupí language—the old *lingua franca* of the Brazilian Indians—should be officially adopted by the country to replace the colonial language, the European Portuguese.

My generation was deeply influenced by Lima Barreto's, or Policarpo's ideas. We were all very nationalistic. When I was writing my very first poems and short stories, I and a group of young men in Rio decided to learn Tupí and to write our poems and stories in Tupí. . . . This was at the end of the thirties. In the Second World War Brazil was the only Latin American country to send soldiers to fight, under a British commander in Italy, and my generation accepted, perhaps a little reluctantly, the idea of also being part of a European cultural heritage.

In the novel Policarpo is, as Lima Barreto himself might have been, appalled by the contrast between the country—or his ideas on the country—and the establishment, or the people who, being the Government, were the symbols of the establishment. The strong man of the Brazilian Republic, Marshall Floriano Peixoto, is still today a controversial character, and Lima Barreto sees and depicts him with all the ideas of the Brazilian liberals of the last decade of the nineteenth century. In so doing he writes a political novel, in a different way from how Stendhal understood the expression, and he shows the Brazilian scene in a period of turmoil and change. Mainly on account of *The Patriot* Lima Barreto must be seen not only as the novelist of his time in Brazil but also as its historian.

His style, in writing his stories, is different from that of another Brazilian writer, Machado de Assis (1839-1908), also a mulatto from Rio de Janeiro, held by many as the best stylist in Portuguese prose in the last two centuries. Machado had a kind of Lawrence Sterne style, with an irony that made him the possessor of a literary excellence rare in the Americas. Lima Barreto, on the other hand, was more serious-minded, saying exactly what he meant to say, but the irony is also there, perhaps a bitter irony in which the weaknesses and strengths of the middle class parade before you.

The Patriot is also a novel of Rio de Janeiro. It shows the then capital-city of Brazil in its moment of change, when it started to transform its old colonial aspect into a new New World city. The novelist lived in the suburbs of Rio, and these suburbs were a new facet of the city he knew so well. He spent his whole life in Rio de Janeiro or its surroundings, having very rarely been far from it. (pp. vii-ix)

As an artist he believed in literature as firmly as in a religion. He believed man can be saved by the strength and the power of a literary mysticism. In his own words: ". . . through Art man is not dependent on the biases and prejudices of his time, his birth, his country, his race: he goes beyond all that to reach the total life of the Universe . . .". (p. ix)

Antonio Olinto, "A Brazilian Don Quixote," in The Patriot *by Lima Barreto, translated by Robert Scott-Buccleuch, Rex Collings, 1978, pp. vii-ix.*

MARIA LUISA NUNES   (essay date 1979)

[*Nunes' Lima Barreto: Bibliography and Translations contains primary and secondary bibliographies of Barreto as well as translations of the novels* Clara dos Anjos *and* The Life and Death of M. J. Gonzaga de Sa. *In the following excerpt from the introduction to that collection, Nunes discusses the portrayal of Brazilian racial attitudes in* Clara dos Anjos.]

Clara dos Anjos is Lima Barreto's reaction to the Brazilian stereotype of the mixed-blooded woman as the sexually promiscuous, easy target of a "macho" dominated society. His heroine, Clara dos Anjos, is far from the mulatto temptress so often depicted in Brazilian culture—from its literature to its samba lyrics.

The first version of *Clara dos Anjos* appeared in 1904. The definitive version was published in 1923-1924 in sixteen issues of the *Revista Sousa Cruz*. The action of the narrative consists of the seduction and abandonment of a young mulatto girl by a dimwitted, more upper-class, white seducer. Contrary to the stereotypical *mulata*, Clara is an overprotected daydreamer who has a very sentimental and idealistic idea of love with no basis in reality.

The novel is set in one of the lower-middle-class suburbs of Rio de Janeiro where there is free intermingling of individuals of all races and racial mixtures. Throughout the work, there are autobiographical references to a fictional mulatto artist, Leonardo Flores, who has suffered greatly because of his artistic aspirations as a man of color in Brazilian society. Like the creator of *Clara dos Anjos,* Flores abuses the consumption of alcohol and is subject to bouts of insanity.

The narrator of *Clara dos Anjos* maintains that all girls of color and humble origin are condemned by society *a priori*. He focuses on Clara's tragedy in its racial overtones but the question of class is also present. In reviewing the affairs of the seducer, Cassi Jones, the narrator informs us that he always got off free because the girls he dishonored were of humble social status and of all colors. His choice was dictated by their lack of protection or influence that might vindicate them. His mother, with her aristocratic pretensions, did not wish to see her son married to a black servant, a mulatto seamstress, or a white but illiterate washerwoman. Race, however, was still the most important factor in social relations according to the narrator. In the poor but integrated society of the Rio de Janeiro suburbs, the accident of color was a reason to judge oneself superior to one's neighbor.

The portrayal of Clara dos Anjos reflects Brazilian shade consciousness as the narrator tells us that Clara was light-skinned like her father and had straight hair like her mother. The more important aspect of her characterization is her psychology, however. One of the few outside influences in her life is that of the *modinha*, a melody conveying a simple-minded amorous sentimentalism. On the basis of the *modinhas* she heard, Clara built up a theory of love believing that it conquers all. Because of it, there are no obstacles of race, fortune, or class. Her cloistering fosters a life of daydreams, reinforced by the *modinhas* she hears. Furthermore, her curiosity about the outside world increases as a result of her excessively sheltered existence. On the basis of her lack of experience, penchant for daydreaming and fantasy, and her taste for the *modinha*, Clara becomes an easy prey for Cassi's attentions. Although, inwardly, she questions the racial difference between them, she concludes that it does not matter. (pp. 6-7)

Cassi's character is more of a caricature than a characterization. His negative traits are drawn with such a heavy hand that he emerges as a somewhat comic figure and, to those of particularly warped sensibilities, as an anti-hero.

After she has become pregnant and Cassi has run away, Clara realizes that her innocence and lack of experience blinded her. Cassi chose her because she was poor and a *mulata*. She fears ostracism and scorn from her family and friends and further exploitation by others worse than Cassi. . . . In the company of a strong-willed neighbor, Dona Margarida, Clara goes to Cassi's family. To Clara's appeal to Cassi's mother that he marry her, the older woman responds: "What are you saying, you nigger?" Clara's initiation into life is tragic and her final words in the novel are:

—Mother, Mother!

—What is it my child?

—We're nothing in this life.

Interspersed throughout the story of Clara's seduction and abandonment are criticisms of women in Brazilian society. Not only are they kept from a real knowledge of the world, but they often forget their educations entirely once they are married, as was the case of Clara'a mother, Engracia. Furthermore, they have no desire to master any skill which might be useful to them and their families. They pass from the protection of father to that of husband and they have no aspirations for self-realization. The narrator's advice to Brazilian women is to train the character, acquire will, like Dona Margarida had, to be able to defend oneself against the likes of Cassi and fight against those who oppose one's social and moral elevation. Nothing made black Brazilian women inferior to the others except the general opinion and the cowardice with which they accepted it.

Barreto is reversing stereotypes and explaining the social conditions that give rise to the widely accepted image of the moral corruption of the mulatto woman. Because of his own marginality in the society, he is able to enter the psychology of the character with a great deal of sensitivity. We understand the victim's mentality and the social forces acting upon her. Although race and class are inextricably bound up in this society, Barreto makes it clear that race is the critical factor. (pp. 7-8)

> *Maria Luisa Nunes, in her* Lima Barreto: Bibliography and Translations, *G. K. Hall & Co., 1979, 227 p.*

MARIA LUISA NUNES (essay date 1981)

[*In the following excerpt, Nunes discusses Lima Barreto's sociological and aesthetic theories, his experimentation with narrative techniques, and his independent position in Brazilian letters.*]

Afonso Henriques de Lima Barreto . . . presents a singular challenge to the study of Brazilian literature. Although he left an extensive body of letters and essays outlining his esthetic program, he remains an enigma for one critic who asks: "Was he a great writer who has been denied recognition because of his refusal to conform to the current patterns of racial adaptability? Did he fail to become a great writer because of this? Was he a great intellectual, fully conscious of the socio-racial problems of Brazil, but not a great novelist due precisely to his acid lucidity?" Underlying these queries is another: Was Lima Barreto successful in transforming his personal experience into an art form? (p. 223)

Why is Lima Barreto a problem for the critic of Brazilian literature? Because in a country whose traditional image is one of racial democracy, Lima Barreto, a man of color, refused to conform to the patterns of racial accommodation that that image implied as well as exposing the real ideological underpinnings of official Brazilian culture. Thus, the entire question of the mainstream position of the non-white writer in Brazil is opened to debate by the works of Lima Barreto, the success and fame of such mulatto writers as Machado de Assis, Coelho Neto, and Mário de Andrade notwithstanding.

Lima Barreto was born seven years before the end of slavery in Brazil. He spent his childhood on the Ilha do Governador where his father was in charge of a mental institution. He completed his secondary education at the Colégio Pedro II and attended the Escola Politécnica for three years. Lima Barreto began his literary career as a journalist. He earned his living for the greater part of his life as a civil servant in the Ministério de Guerra. Burdened with the care of his father who had become incurably insane, Lima Barreto struggled in poverty. His non-conformance to the Brazilian racial hierarchy in which a poor, dark-skinned mulatto ranked low always caused him difficulties, such as automatic assumptions about his social status and restrictions on his ability to participate fully in the social life of the nation. In addition, the tedium of his civil service job combined with the mediocrity of Brazilian literary life drove him to a bohemian life style and the excesses of alcohol, which carried him to an early death at the age of forty-one. (pp. 223-24)

The guiding principle of Lima Barreto's esthetic program was simplicity, by which he hoped to reach the common people with his message. Among his mentors were the positivist philosopher Auguste Comte and the natural scientist Herbert Spencer. (p. 224)

In *Vida e Morte de M. J. Gonzaga de Sá,* the narrator, Augusto Machado, a young mulatto, attributes to European authors such as Taine, Renan, M. Barrès, France, Swift, and Flaubert the sacred wisdom of self-knowledge and the ability to observe the rare spectacle of his emotions and thoughts. As models, Barreto would accept Maupassant, Dickens, Swift, Balzac, Daudet, Turgenev, or Tolstoi but he emphatically rejected Machado de Assis. . . . The sum total of these influences would seem to indicate a commitment on the part of Barreto to the scientific method and a belief in progress and human evolution towards an ideal society.

From Taine, Guyau, and Brunetière, Barreto learned that through its power to move the emotions, art is a means of persuasion with the goal of revealing souls to others, and of establishing bonds between them, of showing each other mutual sorrows and joys that the simple disarticulated facts of life don't have the power to do. Art contributes in its action, statement, and convincing power to the ruling of our conduct and the enlightenment of our destiny. . . . From Taine, he took the concept of the beautiful: through artistic and literary elements, it is the manifestation of the essential character of an idea expressed more perfectly than it could be expressed by the facts. It does not reside solely in form, as the neo-Helenists much in vogue during Barreto's life time believed. It is not in the extrinsic but in the intrinsic, the substance rather than the appearance. . . . Like Taine, Barreto believed that art is a human creation strictly dependent on milieu, race, and moment. . . . (pp. 224-25)

Referring to Guyau, Barreto further elaborated his esthetic credo: art is the expression of a reflective and conscious life. It evokes in us a deeper consciousness of existence, the highest feelings, the most sublime thoughts. It raises man from his personal life to the universal, not only through his participation in general ideas and beliefs but also through the profoundly human feelings it expresses. . . . From Brunetière, Barreto adopted the goal of art: by virtue of its form, it must interest all that pertains to our common destiny; and human solidarity, more than anything else, is essential to human destiny. . . .

Lima Barreto's exclusive commitment was to art and the ideal it was to facilitate: fraternity, justice among men, and sincere mutual understanding. Love, solidarity, and happiness are the ultimate aims of literature. Thus, the artistic phenomenon is a social phenomenon and art is social if not sociological. . . . Man's domination over the other animals rests on his intelligence and his sociability. He has an almost perfect means of communication in language by which he can enhance his thought through time, and written and oral records. . . . The art he produces not only established bonds among souls but with trees, flowers, dogs, rivers, seas, and stars. It helps us to understand the Universe, the Earth, God and the Mystery around us to which it opens infinite perspectives of dreams and higher desires. . . .

As for the literary situation in Brazil, Barreto's theoretical attitude was very much of the New World. He believed that Portugal had a great past; Brazil had none, but it had a future:

> It is this future that our literature should treat, in a literary manner. We must establish bonds, understand each other, speak of our qualities in order to carry the burden of life and destiny. Instead of praising gentlemen of suspect lineage and ladies descended from an aristocracy of warehouses, because they live in Botofogo or Laranjeiras, we should show in our works how a Black man, an Indian, a Portuguese or an Italian can get along and love each other in our common interest. . . .

For Brazilian letters, Barreto projected a novel that would describe the life and works of Blacks on a plantation. It was to have been a Black *Germinal* with appropriate psychology and greater epic inspiration. Barreto hoped this book would be his masterpiece. He dreamed of fame in Europe and of performing an enormous service for his people and for one of the races to which he belonged. Although Barreto never realized this work, he believed that carrying it out would have brought him many tribulations. . . . (p. 225)

Barreto stated that viewing the Winged Victory of Samothrace would be a similar experience to viewing a Yoruba idol or a Tupi pot. His powers of analysis would recognize an ethnographic document that would lead him to divine, reconstruct, sense, and think of the inspiration and feeling that created it. . . . In addition to facilitating communication of the spirit through space and time, art represented liberation for Barreto. For example, by means of art, man can transcend the prejudices of his time, his birth, his country, his race; he can go beyond this, as far as possible, to reach the total life of the Universe and to incorporate his life in that of the World. (pp. 225-26)

Lima Barreto's theoretical premises indicate many things about the man. Although he was of partial African ancestry, like most Brazilians, he subscribed to European culture. The difference between Barreto and many of his countrymen is that he recognized the real contributions of Europe to civilization and viewed its rational processes as a point of departure for a more authentic American culture, based not on the prestige of European phenotypes but on Europe's spiritual potential and intellectual prowess. A faith in literature as a vehicle for communion and mutual understanding among human beings bor-

dered on a religious conviction for Lima Barreto. It would seem to have a prominent role in the evolutionary progress outlined by Barreto's European mentors. Indeed, it is a religion without metaphysics leading to a higher level of Brazilian culture than the colonial and neo-colonial stages.

Although Osman Lins pointed to the theme of incommunicability in *Recordações do Escrivão Isaías Caminha* . . . , it seems to me that its presence functions like satire in that novel. It is a means of communicating the society's foibles and impediments to man's full realization. Thus, the theme of incommunicability in the work is not contradictory to the goal of communion for mankind found in Barreto's theory of literature.

More important to Lima Barreto than "the pretty" was "the real" in opposition to the norms of the day. "The real" or "the authentic" had more to do with the contemporary sociological mixture of Brazil than with the glorious past of Portugal. In a future Brazil, new men of different races would forge a New World together. Barreto's immediate experience as a man of color inspired him to focus on the most oppressed segment of society, those who had toiled under slavery or their descendants. His theoretical convictions seem to indicate a utopian attitude toward society, an attitude implicit in his satirical works and explicit in *O Triste Fim de Policarpo Quaresma* . . . and *Vida e Morte de M. J. Gonzaga de Sá*. . . . Let us look now at some of Barreto's criticism of other writers, criticism that further reflects his own esthetic values.

Barreto's advice to an aspiring writer was "to write a great deal at all times, narrate your emotions, your thoughts, discover the souls of others, try to see things—the air, the trees and the sea—in a personal way; seek the invisible in the visible, bring every thing together in one thought." Here, we see the underlying evolutionary impulse expressed in literary terms that might have led Barreto, a Black, to accept those European influences leading to a more advanced stage of Brazilian society. Barreto subsequently comments on his own theatrical processes: "What I do is draw characters, paint passions, put them in conflict, observe customs, make people laugh, move people, all this in literary and appropriate language to the kind of play I wish to represent." . . . (p. 226)

From his criticism and letters, it is apparent that Barreto valued . . . [a] writer's power of observation of himself and others, appropriate literary language, originality, simplicity, and gentleness. He did not, however, find these elements among his Parnassian contemporaries and had a great deal to say about them.

Repeatedly, Lima Barreto attacked the modish reign of "Greek Art" in Brazil. He maintained that even if Greece had had plastic beauty as an exclusive ideal, which was not true, Brazil could not emulate it because of the ideas accumulated since the time of the ancient Greeks, because of modern discoveries that had broadened the world and man's consciousness, and other factors. Consequently, the destiny of literature was no longer only beauty or pleasure of the delighting of the senses; it was something very different. . . . To the norms of the time represented by Coelho Neto's precious verbalism and Raul Pompéia's affected impressionism, Lima Barreto opposed a literary militancy. (p. 227)

Barreto accused Coelho Neto of being the most ominous person in the nation's intellectual life. He had no vision of Brazilian life, no sympathy for it, no vigorous discipline, no sure philosophical or social criteria, and he transformed the art of writing into pure chinoiserie of style. . . . Coelho Neto's notion of

Greece was mistaken in his preference for "the pretty" over "the real." At a time when militant literature was full of the preoccupations of political, moral, and social problems, Coelho Neto's writing remained contemplative and stylized. A poetic art consecrated by the moneyed upper classes was the limit of his reflections.... In addition to rejecting Coelho Neto and the Greek cliché, Barreto was outspoken against the written style in use by medical doctors whom he satirized and commented on in *Bruzundangas* ..., and in his journalism. Barreto decried their imitation of sixteenth century Portuguese. He considered medical doctors to be the most affected segment of Brazilian intellectuals. What was the sense, he asked, of writing in this way and speaking colloquial Brazilian Portuguese? He lamented that the great drama of love in Brazilian letters was a trivial story of courtship, influence, and money. He asked when Brazil would see a Dostoevski, a George Eliot, a Tolstoi—giants whose strength of vision and limitlessness of creation are not precluded by sympathy for the humble, for the humiliated, and for the sorrow of those people....

If Lima Barreto was adverse to the sterile Parnassianism of his day, he did not welcome the "futurism" of Marinetti as incorporated by the Modernists of 1922 either. In fact, he declared a sincere antipathy for it although he excluded the Modernist magazine *Klaxon* from this judgment.... Nevertheless, he was a precursor to Modernism's polemics. He desired literary renovation. In this respect, he prefigured the famous letter the Macunaíma wrote to the Icamiabas.

Throughout Barreto's *Correspondência,* there are exchanges about his techniques. Monteiro Lobato wrote that it was no exaggeration to say that Lima Barreto launched a new kind of novel in Brazil, the novel of social criticism without dogmatic indoctrination. Barreto harmonized character drawing with the painting of the scenario.... He declared to Almeida Magalhães that he had turned toward literature, history, and social and economic questions since he had resolved to combat tenaciously the upper classes and their ally, the Church.... (p. 228)

In his letters, Barreto often commented on his own works. He wrote to Esmaragdo de Freitas that in *Recordações do Escrivão Isaías Caminha,* his aim was to show that a young man like Isaías could fail not because of his intrinsic qualities, but beaten, crushed, compressed by prejudice and its entourage; failure was outside of his control.... In a letter to João Ribeiro, he defended Edgardo, the Ninfa of *Numa e Ninfa* ...:

> I must ask permission to protest against the qualifier of dissolute you applied to my Edgarda. I didn't intend that for her. She is the victim of a number of social influences, of terrors in familial traditions, when she marries Numa. After all, we, given the weakness of our characters, can not have an Ibsen heroine, and if I made her so, I would have fled from what you praised in me: the sense of life and the reality around it. ...

Although some of Barreto's philosophical precepts were drawn from Positivism, his esthetic attitudes coincide less with that philosophy's literary exponent, Naturalism, than might be anticipated. The sense of reality to which he refers is not photographic, but reflects the author's desire to represent the truth of human emotions and spirituality.

Up until this point, I have observed the social or sociological implications of Barreto's theory of literature. It is important to remember, however, that the form chosen by an artist can also be effective in making sociological points. Therefore, a discussion of Barreto's experimentation with point of view is not an application of an unrelated technique of formalist criticism. In fact, by means of analysis from this perspective, Barreto's perception of the fundamental structure of Brazilian society comes into focus. Furthermore, through this experimental technique, he elucidated his esthetic theory. In the Foreword to *Vida e Morte de M. J. Gonzaga de Sá,* Lima Barreto's implied author addresses the reader directly to inform us that he is the publisher of a biography written by his friend Augusto Machado. Machado wished Barreto to make revisions, which the implied author considered unnecessary. Although he felt uncomfortable with the classification of biography that Machado had given his work, Barreto encouraged Augusto Machado's literary vocation. For Barreto, the classification of biography was not appropriate if it implied a rigorous exactitude for certain data and a minute explanation for certain parts of the main character's life with careful attention to dates. This would seem to underscore Barreto's emphasis on the spiritual over the empirical aspects of biography and re-echo his belief in "the seeking of the invisible in the visible" or the great evolutionary laws at work under the surface of daily phenomena. Machado often speaks more of himself than he does of Gonzaga de Sá, and this frequent appearance of the "author" disturbed Barreto. In reality, Lima Barreto's implied author of the Foreword is giving the reader a premonitory indication of his character's identity. Augusto Machado, the young mulatto writer of plebeian origin who rejects the gaudiness of the new upper classes to identify himself with the grandeur of Brazil's tropical nature and its history of four centuries of slavery in contrast to the imported intellectual and cultural legacy of Germans and Greeks, and Gonzaga de Sá, the elderly, white scion of an old noble family, a sceptic, privileged Voltairean whose characterization is a contrast to the venality of the new republican bourgeoisie, and to the dull bureaucracy at which he works, are one moral and spiritual entity. They enjoy perfect communication and are equivalent to what is good in Brazilian society—artistic ability, racial tolerance, intelligence, nobility of the spirit, critical wit and self-analysis, and originality in their vision of Brazil. Thus Lima Barreto created a perspective that combined the oldest and most traditional aspects of Brazilian society in a new literary technique.

As for themes, Lima Barreto was the greatest portraitist of Rio de Janeiro and its natural beauty. Largely within this setting, he treated of life and death, art and creativity, pattern of race relations, the corruption of the world of journalism, Republican society and its foibles, the real versus the ideal, the exploitation of non-white women, egotism, the plight of the intelligent nonconformist, United States exploitation of Latin America and its treatment of the black population at home, art versus nature and the price of an artist's unique identity among others. Similar themes receive journalistic commentaries with attention directed to the Russian Revolution of 1917, feminism, the Versailles Treaty and World War I, soccer, and maximalism or the goal of a maximum of reforms.

Barreto's iconoclasm in his use of language brought him a great deal of censure. He, however, continued to reject and criticize the pedantic grammarians of his day as well as the medical doctors' archaic written style and the Parnassians. (pp. 228-30)

Despite Barreto's detractors, a famous contemporary, Monteiro Lobato praised his style. Barreto possessed the secret of seeing and saying things without any of the ignoble preoccupations of grammatical hygiene that made half of Brazilian authors useless. . . . Critics of our own day have maintained that it would be deceptive to assume that Barreto's simplicity detracted from the formal aspects of story telling or even from grammatical correctness. . . . He was accused of incorrectness and bad taste in writing, but in reality, he knew and had mastered thoroughly the subject of grammar and style. His writing is rich in communication and expression. Throughout his works, the question of language is present. He was disdainful of the purists of grammar. He strove continuously for the greatest possible effectiveness. He did not accept the standard rules completely. With a combative attitude, he sought all means— diversity, variety, equivalencies, sincretisms—to show that the authoritarian fixedness of grammar was far from corresponding to the living reality of language in its infinite potentialities. He was well grounded in grammatical and philological authorities. His publishers, often of the second rank, were responsible for many of the errors of his texts as was his terrible handwriting.

Finally, Lima Barreto was a great satirist pointing the foibles of his society. In *Vida e Morte de M. J. Gonzaga de Sá, Triste Fim de Policarpo Quaresma, Numa e Ninfa,* and *Recordações do Escrivão Isaías Caminha,* Barreto left a devastating portrait of Republican society. In three of these novels and in *Clara dos Anjos* (1923-24) he incorporated Black consciousness, a unique stance in Brazilian letters up to that time and for many years to come. (p. 230)

A Black man under the dominant culture of Europe who still retained a raised Black consciousness, Barreto suffered the very same dilemma as many Blacks in the New World. What differentiates Barreto's position from that of contemporary attitudes is his acceptance of positivist beliefs about progress and an evolutionary movement towards an ideal society. What his iconoclasm and rejection of the *status quo* indicate, what his utilitarian but somewhat religious and moralistic conception of literature signify, what his Black consciousness means can all be summed up in his utopian ideal, also inspired by his European mentors. As a descendant of African slaves and Portuguese masters, he bore the onus of that guilt-ridden relationship. In an attempt toward liberation, an effort clearly reflected in his literary output, Barreto was caught in a paradox of history, between the past of slavery and a utopian future. This paradox in which it would be necessary to annihilate the past in order to go forward is an aporia of contemporary society. We cannot escape from history because it is inextricably bound up with what is modern. In the case of Lima Barreto, his impulse toward the future is a window to a utopia that he believed it would take many years to achieve. On the other hand, the symbolism of America as a land of opportunity and hope inspired him as a writer to aim at the goal of communion, fraternity, justice and love. His quest, that of a man of color in a Brazil where it took courage to assert that identity, was a pioneering act. His art, iconoclasm, and idealism can be viewed as a paradigm for the realization of a New World Culture in which the history of slavery finds retribution through the highest expression of man's spirit, and can be realized. (pp. 230-31)

> *Maria Luisa Nunes, "Lima Barreto's Theory of Literature," in* From Linguistics to Literature: Romance Studies Offered to Francis M. Rogers, *edited by Bernard H. Bichakjian, John Benjamins B.V., 1981, pp. 223-34.*

ELIZABETH LOWE   (essay date 1982)

[*In the following excerpt, Lowe discusses Lima Barreto's treatment of the city in relation to the characters in his work.*]

Lima Barreto . . . brought the proletarian writer back to Brazilian urban fiction, reviving a literary point of view that ceded to the "aristocratic stance" after Manuel Antônio de Almeida's *Memórias de um Sargento de Milícias.* Barreto's humble origins and his views on the social function of the writer led him to a unique relationship with the city that was a passionate tangle of love and hate, a diachronic and synchronic embrace of city life. The protagonists of Barreto's polemical novels are his dogmatic mouthpieces, and the city acts strongly on them. A character of *Gonzaga de Sá* confesses: "I became saturated with that tangible melancholy which is the primal sentiment of my city. I live in it and it lives in me!" (p. 90)

Barreto's concept of the social function of the writer was one of democratic rapprochement between writer, subject, and reader. He reduced as far as possible the distance between himself and the life of the streets, cultivating the habit of "perambulation" as did Henry James and Virginia Woolf. He reacted vigorously to the wanton decimation of Rio's historical and natural heritage being perpetrated by the euphoric urban planners of the Early Old Republic during the administrations of Rodrigues Alves (1902-6) and Epitácio Pessoa (1919-22). With exceptional foresight Barreto objected to the vanity of trying to reduce Rio de Janeiro into a tropical New York.

> The unique topographical conditions of New York forced the city to prop up those ungainly multistory scarecrows, but we, on the other hand, have no reason to blight Rio de Janeiro with construction abhorrent to its nature.

Indeed, Rio seemed increasingly "more foreign" to Barreto, and he railed bitterly against "tourists, foreigners, invaders, barbarian scavengers, both Brazilian and foreign-born."

Notwithstanding Barreto's intense involvement with the immediate problems of the city, his intention clearly was to transform social reality into art. He criticizes the superficiality of both the regionalist writers who dwell on the picturesque and the urban writers who harp on the tired, frivolous themes of Romantic bourgeois literature.

> Our literary sensibility is only attuned to popular types of the backlands because they are picturesque. We do not concern ourselves too much with their authenticity.

Barreto set out to "scandalize" and "displease," to dig beneath the surface of events. His biographer, Francisco de Assis Barbosa, quotes this letter to Gonzaga Duque dated February 7, 1909:

> And so you will notice that the canvas I have blotted intends, as our Taine recommends, to say what the simple facts do not, to better heighten them, to give them importance, the power of literary form, to agitate them, because they are important for our future.

The theme of the conquest of the city is central to Barreto's narratives, and conventionally, his protagonists are often defeated. His characters seek the safety of the deserted city, in the traditional approach and withdrawal pattern. *Isaías Caminha* ends on a note of *fugere urbem,* as the protagonist tries to find balm for his wounded pride in the country. Yet Barreto finds only mediocrity in the country and the suburbs. The country is not only transformed by the urbanite's jaded eye, but is invaded by the conflicts and attitudes of the city. Major Quaresma's country home is robbed of its tranquillity, for the protagonist's city problems pursue him here. Barreto's interest in the interdependence of city and country is also apparent in *Gonzaga de Sá,* when Machado reflects:

> Those animals had no inkling of their own strength; they didn't even suspect that an entire city was waiting for those useful or tasty things that only their patience and their strength could haul over those perilous roads. . . .

Barreto, in spite of his *épater le bourgeois* attitude, cannot resist the pull of the city as cultural center, and the victory of "civilization" over "barbarism." He points out, though, that while the city creates aspirations, it is reluctant to satisfy them. Barreto's characters become victims of the various institutions of the city, which conspire to their defeat. Isaías Caminha gains entry as an outsider to both the newspaper office and the police station, where he sees the hidden gears of the city at work, and is outraged.

The law turns into a mockery, while the newspaper office is a travesty of the high value placed on literacy and articulateness by the tradition in Brazilian culture that equates education and social poise. Barreto, scrupulous about intellectual honesty, systematically exposes intellectual mediocrity in his city fiction. Real intelligence (Gonzaga de Sá) is lost in the power struggle. The ironic premise of *Isaías Caminha* is that the protagonist is armed for survival in the city because of his good command of the Portuguese language.

Woman embodies that conflict between the protagonist's aspirations and his defeat by the city in Barreto's fiction. She is both booty and pirate. With a new twist to the theme of cultural colonialism, Barreto's protagonist Machado compares the prostitute to the fleets that invaded America for gold. Thus, when Barreto's protagonists sense failure, they feel "at sea" in the city. In *Isaías Caminha* the protagonist compares his struggle to survive in the city to swimming against a current. Yet at the same time his male characters thrill to the spectacle of the "sea" of women on the streets.

Barreto's mark on Modernist and post-Modernist city fiction is most evident in his attempt to demythologize the Brazilian urban experience by confronting aspiration with reality. Machado de Assis achieved this with subtle literary techniques. Barreto "agitated" the facts of city life, not so much with carefully conceived metaphor and image patterns as with a polemical-essay style of fiction writing that was punctuated with authorial intrusion and argumentative dialogue. While Barreto's prophetic and deterministic conception of the city ties him to the nineteenth century, his schematic isolation of his protagonists as "outsiders" is a very modern feature. The "outsider" in contemporary Brazilian fiction since Barreto faces the harsh challenge of coping with a rapidly changing society, frantic in its attempt to imitate the northern industrial giants. (pp. 92-3)

> *Elizabeth Lowe, "The Urban Tradition in Brazilian Literature," in her* The City in Brazilian Literature, *Fairleigh Dickinson University Press, 1982, pp. 70-102.*

R. J. OAKLEY (essay date 1983)

[*In the following excerpt, Oakley uses Lima Barreto's short story* "A nova Califórnia" *to illuminate his novel* Triste fim de Policarpo Quaresma.]

In a mildly intentionalist analysis of *Triste Fim de Policarpo Quaresma* [see excerpt dated 1974], J. C. Kinnear has stressed an ambivalence in the figure of the eponymous hero, Major Quaresma, a martyr who earns our sympathy through his innocence and his ideals, while at the same time being clearly ridiculed by the author for his exaggerated nationalism. Kinnear demonstrates convincingly the parallel between Quaresma's nationalism and that of Afonso Celso in his patriotic tract, *Porque me ufano do meu país,* first published in 1901. This article endeavours to show that there is far more to this juxtaposition of two naive nationalists. *Triste Fim de Policarpo Quaresma* is much more than a fictional reflection of Afonso Celso's paradigmatic nationalism that created the term *ufanismo* (inspired by the title of Celso's book). Celso's brand of nationalism was just one of several preoccupations in the novel *Triste Fim* and other writings of the middle period in Lima Barreto's brief career. (p. 838)

In the course of this article, I hope to endorse further Kinnear's demonstration of the presence of the *ufanista* factor in Lima Barreto's *Triste Fim de Policarpo Quaresma.* More importantly, I hope to provide for readers of this novel a broader view of the way in which *ufanismo* and other factors manipulate the text, shaping it into the powerful, Realist novel it is.

Triste Fim is today the most universally admired of Lima Barreto's longer fictions. It is vitally relevant to note that his most highly-regarded short story, **"A Nova Califórnia,"** was written and published in 1910, a matter of months before the appearance in serial form of *Triste Fim.* A textual comparison of these two works not only sheds light on the genesis of *Triste Fim* but also helps us move towards a richer understanding and appreciation of the structure of the novel. First, it is necessary to summarize **"A Nova Califórnia."**

A mysterious stranger, Raimundo Flamel, comes to live in the small town of Tubiacanga, where he settles down to the life of a recluse. Some say he is a forger and others that he is in league with the devil, because of the oven installed in his dining-room and an array of scientific equipment. But gradually the locals are won over by his civility, his kindness to children, and his charity, which eventually earns him the epithet "pai da pobreza." Moreover, he earns their respect, since the correspondence and magazines he receives from abroad in several languages appear to indicate a learned and internationally famous scientist. Finally Bastos, the local pharmacist, comes across a reference to Flamel as a distinguished chemist in a magazine. One day Flamel enters Bastos's shop, requesting a private conversation. Flamel informs him that he has discovered how to make gold, and invites Bastos and any other two educated men of the town to witness his experiment, an essential ingredient for which is human bones. The day of the experiment is set for the following Sunday. It duly takes place, and a few days later Flamel disappears without trace or explanation. Not long afterwards, the sexton of the town's only cemetery announces that graves have been violated and human remains stolen. A guard is mounted by night and two men are shot in the act of violation. They turn out to be the additional witnesses, provided by Bastos, to Flamel's experiment. One of them, still alive, says that their accomplice, who has escaped, is the pharmacist, Bastos, and that they took the bones to make gold. The whole town now converges on Bastos's shop. Frightened that he may be lynched for body-snatching, the apothecary stands on a chair, brandishing a small gold bar, and promises to print the recipe for distribution the following day if they will spare his life. The mob agrees; but that same night, the whole populace rushes to the graveyard, gripped by the lust for gold. A pitched battle ensues as they dispute the remaining bones. There are not enough to go round and the violence increases. . . . Only one man takes no part in the sack of the graveyard. Belmiro, an alcoholic student drop-out, takes advantage of an unattended shop to steal a bottle of sugar-cane brandy. . . . (pp. 839-40)

A careful reading of this nightmarish tale reveals a text as ambiguous and mysterious as its central protagonist. There is no information about Flamel beyond the single reference in the magazine (indicating him to be a great chemist); his origins and destination are unknown. The same applies to his motives for his actions. His misanthropy might at first turn the reader against him, while, on the other hand, his compassion for the poor children of Tubiacanga presents him in the unexpected light of a sympathetic figure. Most important of all, his scientific experiment is ultimately impenetrable. We never know if his discovery is genuine or if Bastos's gold bar is part of some elaborate hoax. If the former, the story is of course transformed into fantasy, since the Philosopher's Stone is unattainable. The only clue is the clear indication that Flamel is an authentic scientist. Caught in the tissue of ambiguities that comprise the narrative, the reader is left at the end to make sense of the horrific denouement, a murderous struggle in a graveyard.

At this juncture, Arnoni Prado's view of the story may be helpful. Prado's book [*Lima Barreto: O crítico e a crise*] is an attempt to trace the fortunes of the author's stance as a socially and politically committed writer through a diachronic and synchronic juxtaposition of the ideology of official literature and that of Lima Barreto. Prado follows the brief essays of M. Cavalcanti Proença and Antônio Houaiss in examining Lima Barreto's extraordinary awareness, in the Brazil of the *Belle époque*, of the relationship between language and ideology: that in certain circumstances language itself can serve as a clear measure of progressive or reactionary attitudes. In an overtly Marxist analysis, Prado finds **"A Nova Califórnia"** the most eloquent of Lima Barreto's short stories in this respect. To this end, he examines the relationship between the mysterious inventor, Raimundo Flamel, and Capitão Pelino, the schoolmaster and editor of the local newspaper. Pelino is the only person to remain hostile to Flamel, despite his evident kindness, gentleness, and charity. Given that Pelino enjoys prestige in Tubiacanga as a man of learning, a *sábio*, the prestige swiftly acquired by Flamel as a scientist of renown turns him into a rival whose presence is intolerable. . . . Pelino's reputation as a *sábio* is based as much as anything on his propensity for correcting the grammar of the writers whose works he criticizes in his paper, as well as of those with whom he converses in Tubiacanga. On the other hand, as Prado notes, Flamel subscribes to numerous magazines and keeps up to date with his subject. Consequently, his relationship with language and with his chosen field of knowledge is dynamic, progressive, and substantial. Pelino functions clearly as Flamel's antithesis right to the end of the story. He is prominent in the battle of the bones. Flamel's science (or pseudo-science) shakes and overturns the passivity of the little town, tearing away Tubiacanga's mask of respectability. Flamel's progressive attitude to modes of communication triumphs over the conservative attitude of Pelino. Expressed in the jargon of applied linguistics, one might even say that in **"A Nova Califórnia"** prescriptive grammar is overthrown by descriptive grammar.

Flamel's ability to subvert the prevailing system in Tubiacanga lies in two factors: first, his apartness, his strangeness; and second, his energy. Flamel represents the alien force of modern science and technology, untainted by ideology of any persuasion. It is entirely appropriate that his origins are unknown and that the learned correspondence and magazines he receives in great quantities should come from all parts of the world and in various languages. Equally appropriately, his formal relations with his neighbours in Tubiacanga are quite neutral. Because of his complete independence and self-imposed isolation, he cannot be subjected to pressures of any kind. He is untouchable, impervious, an avenging angel perfectly adequate to the kind of fiction that Lima Barreto has created in **"A Nova Califórnia,"** for here we are in the world of fable, a brand of magic realism *avant la lettre*.

This is not to say that **"A Nova Califórnia"** is not susceptible to a Realist reading. It is a story which examines on one level the power of superstition—ultimately, the evil of superstition. **"A Nova Califórnia"** may be read as a Realist treatment of greed and gullibility in a backward and rural Latin-American environment. It is perfectly logical that the extremely superstitious populace of a small Brazilian town at the turn of the century should view Raimundo Flamel as some kind of magician or warlock. It is equally logical, in a Realist reading of the story, that the educated élite in this primitive community should come to admire him. Brazil, the land of the *feiticeiro*, was, and indeed still is, the land of the *doutor*. Flamel strikes fear into the untutored, irrational mind, while he excites grudging admiration in the educated section of the community which values, above all, outward signs of learning. However, it is one thing to describe how he might appear to the people of Tubiacanga, but it is quite another to assess the associations this extravagant figure could have for the reader. Reduced to its bare essentials, the story depicts a man's search for the Philosopher's Stone.

It is worth remembering that the search for the Philosopher's Stone was far from being a search for a key to untold wealth. It was quite the opposite. Following neo-Platonic doctrines that man was a microcosm of God's creation and, therefore, fitted not only to understand that creation but also to direct, control, and modify it, the activities of the theurgical alchemist were directed toward promoting virtue in man and encouraging the upward progress of the soul. Flamel's religious scepticism marks him out as a latter-day version of the magus of Renaissance theurgy. The conservative ideology of Tubiacanga is completely out of phase with the way of life represented by Flamel. It can comprehend his discovery only on its own terms: it cannot conceive of the creation of gold other than as a means for increasing personal wealth. In the same way, Afonso Celso and the apostles of the new Brazil can conceive of her only as some kind of utopian form of Eldorado or Promised Land. . . . They are inimical to Flamel's example of love and patient toil, his humble simplicity expressed in his ascetic existence and compassion for the children. Flamel is the man of action whose actions and way of life are rejected and totally misunderstood. In *Triste Fim de Policarpo Quaresma* Lima Barreto carries the same drama of the man of action who signifies possible change from the realm of fable into that of the Realist novel.

I suggested that Flamel's energy in **"A Nova Califórnia"** is fatal to Tubiacanga, whose vulnerability stems from its conservatism, stagnation, and inertia. For Flamel, Tubiacanga is no temporary refuge from the hostility of the world, as Policarpo Quaresma's small-holding is for him in the equally sleepy little town of Curuzu in *Triste Fim*. Flamel is more like a stone dropping into calm waters and creating eddies that turn into a tidal wave, engulfing Tubiacanga. Instead of the milieu closing in around him to restrict his field of action, nullifying his efforts (as happens to Quaresma the patriot when he endeavours to prove by personal example that Brazil is an agricultural paradise) Flamel's energy radiates outwards to destroy the social and political systems of Tubiacanga. The fabric of society beneath its placid, immovable exterior cannot withstand the presence of his symbolic discovery once it is converted into Bastos's equally symbolic *potosi*. Policarpo Quaresma is an amusing representative of *ufanista* ideas. He has none of the rigorously pragmatic, scientific approach of Flamel. His efforts towards the promotion of Tupi as the national language and resuscitation of interest in folklore are aimed at promoting a peculiarly telluric patriotism. This is confirmed when he is hounded from his job in the War Ministry, loses his reason, and then seeks solace in the country. His subsequent agricultural experiment is not prompted in the first instance by pursuit of knowledge for its own sake but to confirm the *ufanista* conviction that Brazil is a paradise of natural riches. He operates *a priori*, like Afonso Celso in his book, yet Quaresma's whole existence glows with a love of learning. Misguided and misunderstood, his life in its quiet way is one of action and energy right to the end. Consequently, he is of the same breed as Flamel.

The energy/inertia opposition is expanded to rich and varied effect in the novel, helping to shape the narrative just as it does in **"A Nova Califórnia."** Quaresma's studies in Brazilian history, geography, folklore, and Amerindian languages denote energy, enthusiasm, and passion. The old poet and folklorist he visits in his search for indigenous, truly Brazilian traditions, stories, and popular poetry turns out to be a man for whom Policarpo Quaresma shares briefly a fellow-feeling of intense enthusiasm. The old poet is a fleeting but significant analogue of Quaresma. Like the Major, he is convinced of the richness of Brazilian popular poetry. More significantly, he awaits the arrival on the scene of the great literary genius capable of fixing this richness for all time in a masterpiece. The old poet is, consequently, an analogue of Quaresma as he is at this early stage in the story. But since the poet, unlike Policarpo, has clearly completed his trajectory and realized that he himself is not the genius who could carry out this task, it is now his destiny to await the emergence of such a man. Quaresma, in turn, will experience a similar patriotic *échec*. He will go farther than the old poet, however, in that he will actually fall prey to the illusion of thinking that he has discovered the genius capable of achieving what he, Quaresma, has failed to achieve. The difference is that this figure will not be a "literato de gênio" but rather "Sully e Henri Quatre," as Policarpo transposes his bookish patriotism into the world of political action through his relationship with Marshal Floriano Peixoto.

Ricardo Coração dos Outros is another analogue of Major Quaresma in his enthusiasm for popular music: "Major, o violão é o instrumento da paixão." . . . Like Quaresma, the lover of all things Brazilian like the old poet, Ricardo's commitment is to something largely ignored or despised by many: "Todo ele fremindo de paixão pelo instrumento desprezado." . . . As happens in so many of the Major's relationships, he and Ricardo are brought together by a coincidence of enthusiasms. The motives behind the concentration of energies brought to bear on a specific area of experience coalesce and generate solidarity. Just as Quaresma will come to see Curuzu as a harsh and ungrateful land, Ricardo experiences the same sensation in his chosen field, where it is expressed in identical imagery: Ricardo feels himself to be "como um apóstolo em terra ingrata que não lhe quer ouvir a boa nova." . . . (pp. 840-43)

A series of figures in the novel express these qualities of passion and energy. Vicente Coleoni is the Italian father of Quaresma's goddaughter Olga. Through the Major's help he rises from street-seller to wealthy man. Quaresma is impressed by him and is drawn to help him in his hour of need by his energy: "Havia na sua afirmação uma tal *energia,* e um grande e estranho acento de ferocidade." . . . His daughter Olga is "menina vivaz," attracted to her godfather by his "ânsia de ideal, uma tenacidade em seguir un sonho." By way of striking contrast, there are those who embody inertia. There is General Albernaz, . . . whose only energy is provoked by his anxiety to marry off his five daughters, while the only energy of which he himself is aware is that which he evokes in his incessant descriptions of battles in which he himself never took part during the Paraguayan War. . . . Dr Campos, one of the two political-party leaders in Curuzu, is a man who "não gastava grande *energia* mental." . . . Olga's husband, Armando Borges, wants to advance his medical career, "mas faltava-lhe *energia* para o estudo prolongado." . . . Ismênia, pathetic daughter of General Albernaz, is brought up to believe that to marry is her only goal in life, "com uma preguiça de impressionar." . . . and "a sua aparência de bondade passiva, de indolência de corpo, de idéia e de sentidos." . . . (p. 843)

In Curuzu, Quaresma is appalled at the energy injected into political squabbles while the land lies neglected. However, when Olga visits Policarpo's small-holding, it is she who questions the nature of this neglect: "Não podia ser preguiça só ou indolência. Para o seu gasto, para uso próprio, o homen tem sempre *energia* para trabalhar." . . . Meanwhile, her godfather, despite setbacks and oblivious to such questions, "voltava com mais rigor e *energia* à tarefa que se impusera." . . .

Finally, Quaresma comes to see that it is his industry, and not the exceptional fertility of Brazilian soil, that makes his avocados flourish. The scales fall from his eyes. He sees the lack of energy in Curuzu as stemming from the immobility, the inertia of the system maintained by law and decree—a system that is paralysing and (like Pelino's grammar in **"A Nova Califórnia"**) prescriptive. . . . The panorama of lassitude and indolence around Curuzu passes before his eyes and is supremely exemplified in his hired hand, Felizardo: "homem bom, ativo e trabalhador, sem ânimo de plantar um grão de milho em casa e bebendo todo o dinheiro que lhe passava pelas mãos." . . . This description of Felizardo's plight synthesizes the whole problem of the incessant opposition of energy/inertia in Part II, the rural phase in Quaresma's patriotic adventures. The climax in the struggle between these two warring factors takes place in Part III, in which Policarpo Quaresma returns to Rio de Janeiro.

Quaresma's indifference to local politics in Curuzu is interpreted as simulated indifference. It is therefore ironic that the one thing for which Quaresma shows no enthusiasm brings him pain and anguish, and fatally shapes his destiny, for, in Curuzu, only politics matter. The fact that the Major had known Marshal Floriano Peixoto, the new President of the Republic after the resignation of Marshal Deodoro da Fonseca in 1891, causes

Quaresma to be regarded with awe and to be courted by the local party leaders, Dr Campos and Lieutenant Antonino Dutra. Even here, in the country, his past seeks him out. The shadow of power in the name Floriano falls across his path. The energy that Policarpo Quaresma employs disinterestedly in order to make the earth yield its fruits is employed by those around him in political intrigue. Here the parallel with the protagonist of "A Nova Califórnia" is instructive. Like Flamel he is totally indifferent to politics, but his innocence in this area is not so extreme that he is incapable of seeing that politics and agriculture are inextricably intertwined. Nor is it true, as John Kinnear claims . . . , that Quaresma asks no questions in Curuzu. Flamel has compassion for the rural poor, but asks no questions and seeks no remedies. Policarpo does both. He observes the lack of solidarity among the peasants, and endeavours to answer the question of why this poverty and abandonment exist by accusing the government of indifference. In his own small way, he finds an answer. His own industry brings some modest results. The ultimate reality that he never understood, surrounded by his colleagues at his office in the Ministry of War, and that he still cannot penetrate in Curuzu, is the reality of inertia.

Blinded by naive patriotism, Quaresma only gradually and painfully comes to see what his goddaughter Olga sees quickly and effortlessly, when she visits the Major on his small-holding: the inertia, the depression, the self-perpetuating demoralization of the small, dusty town and its miserable, broken-spirited peasants. Not understanding the nature of an ineluctable general inertia, Policarpo seeks to end at a stroke the evident state of apathy and to create the sense of solidarity lacking among the peasants, so that when news comes that the Navy has rebelled against the Republic, he sends his expressive telegram to Marshal Floriano: "Marechal Floriano, Rio. Peço *energia*. Sigo ja.—Quaresma." . . . It is noteworthy that other characters invest similar hopes in the new strong man of the Republic, but for more selfish reasons. The ambitious young accountant, Genelício, sets great store by the "*energia* e decisão de governo de Floriano: esperava ser subdiretor e não podia um governo sério, honesto e enérgico, fazer outro coisa." . . . (pp. 843-45)

Quaresma realizes that Floriano has assumed dictatorial powers. Having learnt of the invincible power of authority in the various forms it assumes in the Civil Service and, later, in the country, having seen it frustrate his patriotic schemes at every turn, he now appeals in desperation to the power of such authority. He sees in the so-called *Marechal de Ferro* the mailed fist that may be persuaded to impose by force from above his ideal of agrarian reform. Floriano signifies power, a power that he, Quaresma, must tap. The dictator also signifies energy to the little Major; for Floriano has assumed absolute power in the face of a national crisis, with civil war in the South and the Naval Revolt in the Bay of Rio. (p. 845)

Unfortunately, energy is precisely the quality in which Floriano is conspicuously lacking. That this fact is of considerable importance is clear, as I have shown, from the number of times the text alludes to energy or lack of it. Floriano's hand is limp, his gaze is lacklustre, and his indolence in despatching his duties is proverbial. . . . Known at the height of his power and popularity during the Civil War as *A Esfinge,* the Iron Marshal's celebrated taciturnity and monosyllabic conversation, legendary in his own lifetime, are turned against him. Interpreted by some as indicating a deep and subtle mind, these traits are

portrayed here as signs of his inveterate sloth. When Quaresma's turn for an audience with the dictator finally arrives, he steps forward to present Floriano with his report on agricultural conditions in the State of Rio de Janeiro. It is received ungraciously, and Policarpo finds himself assigned to a detachment of troops protecting the city against attacks by the naval insurgents in the Bay.

Marshal Floriano appears only once more in the novel, on the night he visits Quaresma's detachment at their posts. This scene, in which the Major steels himself to challenge Floriano on his agrarian reform, will confirm the total absence of energy and the reality of a massive inertia of which the *Marechal de Ferro* is the crucial embodiment in the novel. As officer commanding the detachment, Quaresma goes to meet him, reporting an attack on his post the previous day. Floriano "respondia por monossílabos preguiçosos." When Quaresma finally plucks up courage to ask if the president has found time to read his report on the state of the countryside, Floriano "respondeu lentamente, quase sem levantar o lábio pendente: 'Li'." . . . Having broken the ice, as he thinks, Policarpo becomes enthusiastic, even voluble. The brilliance of the moonlight, shining down on this final confrontation between energy and inertia in the novel, is emphasized, while, characteristically, the importance of the episode is underplayed. Also characteristically, the traditional romantic resonances that a moonlit scene suggests are submerged in the evocation of the coldness and neutrality of the moon's light—equally traditional associations. This last idea is manipulated to sinister effect. . . . In a setting in which men are traditionally moved to dream, Quaresma's dreams are being shattered. Here the grotesque duet between Quaresma's passion and Floriano's indifference can be seen. Here, in the moonlight, the little Major is oblivious to the fruitlessness of his actions. The cold, borrowed light of the moon merely underlines the ultimate sterility gradually emerging from his patriotic struggle.

At the close of his story, in prison, Quaresma himself finally sees the true extent of his failure. His extreme degree of lucidity, moreover, enables him to universalize it. If patriotism as it has hitherto been known is an illusion, there remains man's capacity for idealism. After all, Quaresma, despite his *ufanismo,* has striven disinterestedly for the betterment of his country and for the good of the community. Yet nothing has changed. . . . The profound despair of Quaresma's *triste fim* parallels in Realist terms the despair of *A Nova Califórnia.* Indeed, Part II of *Triste Fim de Policarpo Quaresma* repeats the *plot* of the short story in the Formalist sense. (pp. 845-47)

I have attempted to demonstrate that not only is *Triste Fim de Policarpo Quaresma* a novelistic elaboration of "A Nova Califórnia" in another key, but that a juxtaposition of the two texts helps to illuminate the novel from a fresh angle. To conclude, I would draw the reader's attention to one more parallel between the two narratives. Flamel and Quaresma are both, in their different ways, men of learning. The former dominates his learning, aware of its limitations. The latter is dominated by his, totally oblivious to its limitations. Yet both texts strive to make us associate energy with books and with the concept of the *sábio*. . . . For the society with which Quaresma is in conflict, books and learning are a fetish, expressed by the concept of the *sábio* who is in reality a false *sábio*, not a man like Quaresma whose learning, no matter how misdirected, has substance. (p. 848)

R. J. Oakley, " 'Triste Fim de Policarpo Quaresma'
and the New California," in The Modern Language
Review, *Vol. 78, Part 4, October, 1983, pp. 838-49.*

ADDITIONAL BIBLIOGRAPHY

Burns, E. Bradford. "The New Brazil and the Foundations of Twen-
tieth-Century Nationalism." In his *Nationalism in Brazil: A Historical
Survey,* pp. 51-71. New York: Frederick A. Praeger, 1968.
  Discussion of Barreto's satirical treatment of nationalism in *The
  Patriot,* with an excerpt from that work.

Teixeira, Vera Regina. "Lima Barreto: Dead or Alive." *World Literature Today* 53, No. 1 (Winter 1979): 36-40.
  Publishing history of Lima Barreto's work, with critical remarks.

Sigbjørn Obstfelder

1866-1900

Norwegian poet, novelist, dramatist, short story writer, diarist, and essayist.

Obstfelder is often considered the chief representative of the fin-de-siècle in Norwegian poetry, a reputation that he has gained as much by the romantic myth surrounding his emotionally troubled life and premature death as by his Symbolist-influenced verses. His debut collection, *Digte,* contains many of his best and most characteristic poems, which are praised for their inventive language, unconventional forms, and mystical, idiosyncratic symbolism. Characterized by a brooding sense of alienation and restlessness, his writings reflect his continuing desire to be united with society, with the universe, and, ultimately, with God. According to critic Harald Beyer, Obstfelder "had the newborn child's capacity for wondering at the world, a capacity which is the ultimate source of all religion and art. His original, moving, often hectic verse and prose poetry are the words of a man who feels that he is a stranger on earth, a melancholy pantheist, an inquiring dreamer."

Obstfelder was the eighth of sixteen children born to Herman Friedrich, a baker, and Serine Egelandsdal Obstfelder. The family home in Stavenger was dominated by Herman Obstfelder's stringent religious fundamentalism, and debts incurred through his speculative business ventures ruined the family financially. Emotionally, their lives were unhappy as well; less than half of the children survived into adulthood, and, in 1880, Serine Obstfelder died following childbirth. Biographers have noted that these overwhelming personal losses, especially the loss of his mother, profoundly affected Obstfelder, who even as a youth was introverted and emotionally unstable. His subsequent melancholia and eventual breakdown have been linked directly to the unhappiness of his childhood. Obstfelder later recalled his youth in "Isløsning": "It slipped away, it was partly dark, the glowing darkness of a constricted childhood where the joy of life was suppressed and whipped bloody, burned to coal so that all could be black." Obstfelder graduated from secondary school in Stavenger in 1884 and in 1886 began studies in philology at the University of Christiania (now Oslo). The following year he published his first essay, a characteristically ascetic proposition arguing for sexual abstinence in unmarried men and women. Obstfelder eventually left the university to study engineering at a technical school but, due to a nervous collapse in the spring of 1890, failed to complete his degree. That autumn Obstfelder traveled to Milwaukee to join his younger brother Herman, who had emigrated two years earlier. After working for a few months with Herman at the Wisconsin Iron and Bridge Company, Obstfelder moved to suburban Chicago, where he found employment as a draftsman and surveyor.

Disappointed with his life in America and determined to pursue a career as a musical composer, Obstfelder returned to Norway in August 1891. According to Obstfelder's diary of this period (known as the "America Journal"), he had become increasingly disillusioned and depressed in the United States. Most biographers attribute this unhappiness to his deteriorating emotional condition, for immediately upon his return to Stavenger, Obstfelder suffered a nervous breakdown and remained insti-

tutionalized until Christmas of that year. As his recovery progressed, he began to write again, and, although his devotion to music remained, he turned instead to a literary career. He visited Paris in 1892, beginning the extensive European and Scandinavian travels that continued until his death in 1900. In Paris he was encouraged and influenced by his friend, the Norwegian art historian Jens Thiis. Critics have noted that many of the most effective poems in *Digte* were written while Obstfelder and Thiis traveled together in France and Belgium. With the publication of that collection and subsequent works, Obstfelder was able to support himself primarily through writing, although he occasionally received government assistance in the form of travel grants. In 1898 he married Danish singer Ingebord Weeke, and during their two-year marriage the Obstfelders lived in France, Denmark, Norway, and Germany. In July 1900, Obstfelder became ill and died, reportedly of tuberculosis.

Writing in the 1890s, Obstfelder presented an idiosyncratic voice in the "New Romanticism" movement in Norwegian literature. An accomplished violinist, Obstfelder was enamored of the ability of music to communicate moods and feelings, and he hoped to achieve similar but even greater effects through his poetry. Many of his early poems celebrate his infatuation with language, a medium he believed held limitless possibilities. Early in his career, in an attempt to express "the inexpressible,'' Obstfelder renounced traditional poetic forms in favor of free verse; he later turned to prose poetry and eventually to prose. Critics have repeatedly compared his works with those of the Symbolist movement in European poetry. Mary Kay Norseng, for example, has defined characteristics common to both Obstfelder's works and to those of influential Symbolists, noting in particular that all are ''characterized by a quality of strangeness and mystery, an intent to communicate indirectly through mood and enigmatic symbol, an attempt to imitate music, and a decadent spirit, i.e., a spirit preoccupied with death.'' ''Jeg ser'' (''I See''), one of the most characteristic and undoubtedly the most popular of Obstfelder's poems, contains what Norseng has called ''the classic expression of modern alienation'': ''I see, I see . . . / I must have come to the wrong planet! / It's so strange here . . . .'' Similar feelings of isolation and estrangement, often accompanied by irrational anxiety, recur throughout Obstfelder's poems, dramas, and prose works. As in ''I See,'' Obstfelder was often preoccupied with his alienation from nature and from humanity and sought to connect himself with life through his writings. His erotic poems, especially, reflect his desire to participate fully in life, yet critics have noted that Obstfelder's protagonists rarely achieve a successful union or integration with others. He was equally disturbed by his separation from God, and the yearning for God subsequently became the central theme of his last project, the confessional novel *En praests dagbog,* the title of which has been translated as ''A Cleric's Journal.'' Largely based on the painful experiences of Obstfelder's breakdown in August 1891, the *Dagbog,* together with Obstfelder's tragic personal history, is believed to have served as an inspiration for Rainer Maria Rilke's *Die Aufeichnungen des Malte Laurids Brigge (The Notebooks of Malte Laurids Brigge).*

A number of Obstfelder's contemporaries were bewildered by his unorthodox poetry. According to Harald Beyer, Norwegian publisher John Grieg's reaction to Obstfelder's poetry expressed the initial opinion of many: ''Just as surely as [Vilhelm Krag's] poems were the wildest nonsense, these are absolute insanity''; and, in the *Oxford Book of Scandinavian Verse,* Sir Edmund Gosse dismissed Obstfelder simply as ''an eccentric and degenerate oddity not without talent.'' However startling it was to some observers, Obstfelder's poetry nevertheless received many favorable reviews from early critics, and a translation of Obstfelder's verses into English was praised by a reviewer in the *Times Literary Supplement:* ''Obstfelder clothed . . . vague and often incomprehensible ideas in a style of remarkable delicacy and fire, and the less distinct was the message which he felt impelled to deliver, the more beautiful is often the speech in which he proclaims it.'' More recent critics, including Arne Hannevik in Norway, Reidar Eknar in Sweden, and Norseng in the United States, have devoted lengthy critical studies to Obstfelder's works, contributing to periodic revivals of Obstfelder's international popularity among students of Norwegian literature and bolstering his reputation as a gifted writer with a unique vision who significantly influenced redevelopment of Scandinavian Modernism.

PRINCIPAL WORKS

Digte (poetry) 1893
To novelletter (short stories) 1895
Korset (novella) 1896
De røde dråber (drama) [first publication] 1897
Esther (drama) [first publication] 1899; published in journal *Samtiden*

En praests dagbog (novel) 1900
Om våren (drama) 1902
Poems from the Norwegian of Sigbjørn Obstfelder (poetry) 1920
Brev til hans bror (letters) 1949
  [''Sigbjørn Obstfelder's Letters to his Brother Herman'' (partial translation) in ''Sigbjørn Obstfelder and America'', published in journal *Norwegian-American Studies,* 1983]
Samlede skrifter. 3 vols. (poetry, short stories, drama, novella, diary, and essays) 1950
Breve fra Sigbjørn Obstfelder (letters) 1966

THE TIMES LITERARY SUPPLEMENT (essay date 1920)

[*In the following excerpt, the critic reviews the translation* Poems from the Norwegian of Sigbjørn Obstfelder.]

The last decade of the nineteenth century saw the passage of a group of Norwegian writers who were distinguished by the violence of their individualism. They followed the decay of the idealistic and moralizing generation of which Ibsen and Björnson were the figureheads; and they expressed, with imperfect utterance, various types of violent reaction against it. Three of these young men have left some mark on the literature of their country. Gabriel Finne, who died in 1899, was the author of a series of ugly but powerful novels, inspired by a hatred of social order. Arne Dybfest, who was a pronounced atheist and anarchist, flung himself out of a boat when sailing in the fjord, in order to escape arrest for having abetted the suicide of a friend. This was in 1892. There remained the most gifted and the least indignant of the trio, Sigbjørn Obstfelder, a selection from whose poems is now presented to English readers. . . . We welcome this modest publication, devoted to a curious figure, which will doubtless continue to attract attention not so much for its merit as for its romantic originality. In Norwegian literature there is nothing which resembles Obstfelder, who had no precursor and has inspired no disciples. . . .

He was a complete rebel in form, and his cadences are equally irregular and abnormal, whether broken into what looks like metre or not. He was neither poet nor prose-writer, but a rhapsodist of remarkable individuality.

The most human of Obstfelder's poems is **''Navnlos'' (''Nameless''),** of which Mr. Selver gives a careful translation. The poet wanders at night across a park in a city, and finds sitting on a bench a fallen woman, by whom he leans in silence while they weep together. The sentiment is that which the Russians, and particularly Dostoevsky, have made familiar to us, an aimless tenderness, a lachrymose, inactive pity. This poem ends thus:—

Mists of the darkness are sinking over trees, over souls;

The leafage has no colours, the grass no green,

But in the mist sink noiselessly black leaves,

And in the darkness sits hidden on a lonely bench one who is nameless,

And tends against her hot breast a sick man's countenance,

And tends in her soft hands a haunted man's
eyes,

And none but God hears his anguished sobbing,

And none but God hears her comforting whisper.

This is close to the original, except in twice translating *gjem-
mer*, "hides," as "tends." Mr. Selver's principal fault as a
translator is his tendency to use fine language, as when (in
"Venner") he translates what should be simply "the happier
heart, the warmer pulse" as "the joyouser heart, the fervider
pulse"; or (in the same piece) "the nights were so long and
bright" as "the nighttimes were so lengthy and lustrous"; or
(in **"Eva"**) "thy hands which rest in mine" as "thy hands
which cling to my own." This is unfair to Obstfelder, whose
extravagant and morbid mysticism is only made endurable by
the tact with which he enshrines it in language of extreme
directness.

The hectic and solitary life of Obstfelder was appropriate to
the fevered melancholy of his writings.... He journeyed in a
perpetual melancholy dream, a fugitive on the face of the earth,
plunged in the study of chaotic conceptions of life and death
and the soul. When he paused to write, he clothed these vague
and often incomprehensible ideas in a style of remarkable delicacy and fire, and the less distinct was the message which he
felt impelled to deliver, the more beautiful is often the speech
in which he proclaims it. But his temper, though not hateful
like that of Arne Dybfest nor hideous like that of Gabriel Finne,
is obscure and sterile. He is inspired by infinite longing and
the pain of finite hearts that yearn.

> *"Sigbjørn Obstfelder," in* The Times Literary Sup-
> plement, *No. 982, November 11, 1920, p. 730.*

GEORGE C. SCHOOLFIELD (essay date 1957)

[*Schoolfield is an American educator and critic whose works
include numerous studies of German and Scandinavian literature.
In the following excerpt, he discusses significant characteristics
of Obstfelder's works, examining in particular symbolism and
idealism in* A Cleric's Journal.]

The judgment which Edmund Gosse once passed upon Sigbjørn
Obstfelder is not very flattering. He called the poet "an eccentric and degenerate oddity not without talent"; and that,
we may presume, is the opinion held even today by the reader
whose knowledge of Scandinavian literature does not go beyond the Victorian introductions of *The Oxford Book of Scandinavian Verse*. Without having read a single line of Obstfelder
we can mistrust what Gosse has to say; the industrious translator
of Ibsen was not sympathetic to those he would call "unhealthy
writers" (although the reader of *Father and Son* may suspect
the author's own healthiness). Today of course we are not very
much upset by whatever degeneracy we may find in Obstfelder;
we should rather class him among the purest of the pure, especially when we contrast him with his French models, Baudelaire and Verlaine, his British contemporaries of the yellow
nineties, or even with the later and greater Englishman whose
literary character so much resembles Obstfelder's, D. H. Lawrence. Perhaps we should not be at all disturbed by Gosse's
remark, despite the fact that he, by dint of criticism as well as
translation, remains the chief agency through which nineteenth
century Danish and Norwegian literature are transmitted to the
general reader in England or America. At least some knowledge
of a poet is better than none at all.

Not only a late Victorian was able to achieve such a wonderful
misconception. Rainer Maria Rilke, whose spiritual affinity to
Obstfelder, and the relationship between *Malte Laurids Brigge*
and *En praests dagbog* [*A Cleric's Journal*], have never been
thoroughly studied, seems with all good will to have been guilty
of a subtler and more damaging lack of understanding. If the
report of Maurice Betz, Rilke's French translator, is to be
trusted, the poet altogether missed the point of the *Dagbog*.
Betz records what Rilke told him of the book. *"Son Journal
d'un prêtre est l'historie d'une âme qui, dans ses tentatives
désespérées d'approcher de Dieu, s'en éloigne au contrarie
de plus en plus, en proie à un fièvre cérébrale qui va en
s'exaspérant"* ["His Journal is the story of a soul who, in his
despairing attempts to approach God, actually becomes more
estranged from him, a prey to an intellectual fever that brings
him to despair"]. Whatever doubts Obstfelder may have felt
about the success of his book, he nonetheless comes to certain
conclusions in its final pages which have nothing to do with
a loss of God but rather with His attainment in a certain form.
As for the ambiguous *fièvre cérébrale* it is nonexistent if the
phrase is to be taken literally; if understood in a more general
sense, then almost any literary hero might be said to be in its
clutches, for are not Achilles and Stephen Daedalus, Egil and
Paul Morel, each *en proie à un fièvre cérébrale?* Rilke, in his
more intelligent and less moralizing way, has made once more
Gosse's charge of decadence. This is true not only of his conversation with Betz. The German poet, who admittedly took
(his own concept of) Obstfelder as a model for Malte, condemns his hero as a weak and defeated man, almost a Werth-
erian scapegoat. There is a warning in one of Rilke's letters:
the young reader should not concern himself too much with
"poor Malte," who has not been able to face up to the demands
of "das Übergrosse." It is in this form that Obstfelder, or a
distorted copy of him, has crept into the minds of other non-
Scandinavian readers, those who concern themselves with the
works of one of the great modern poets. Great poets, even in
the twentieth century, cannot be said to understand, perhaps
do not want to understand, the nature of their gifted contemporaries.

Thus we may condemn Obstfelder as a degenerate or become
faintly interested in him as a Norwegian impressionist, an unhappy poet early dead, a model for Malte Laurids Brigge; and
somehow the words degenerate, decadent still cling to these
nicer phrases. Whether we have come to know Obstfelder from
the brief notices in English and American histories of Norwegian literature, or have read the criticisms published in Norway, we still have to approach the poet as English-speaking
people, to place him in relation to our own and other literatures,
and to apply modern standards of criticism.

There are some absurd pieces in the collection of poems which
Obstfelder published in 1893. There are also lyrics which as-
tonish by the directness of their language and of their thought.
Their titles are almost always unnecessary. We do not require
notes, we must not seek out the meaning of the words or parse
them as if we were reading an ancient language. There is no
sheen of a personalized style: what style there is results from
the poet's intellect, his attempt to say something and not simply
to speak. The poems are without irony, either of attack or
protection; whoever is accustomed to American verse since the
twenties will be a little embarrassed at this. A sophisticated
reader might call the poems somewhat slipshod in style, somewhat lacking in milieu, somewhat naive in thought. That they
are not improvisations we know from accounts of Obstfelder's
mode of work; if anything he was too careful a craftsman. That

they lack a unified milieu is true, in that each poem creates its own atmosphere, part and parcel of the verse itself. They are without doubt naive. Only a naive poet could write about other people in the undisguised fashion of "**Venner**" and "**Genre**," or about nature in the overwhelmed manner of "**Orkan**" and "**Al skabningens sukker**"; not even Whitman could keep the message of purity so free from bombast as Obstfelder in "**Kan speilet tale?**" The eye would have been more than deep and wise, warm and dark blue, and the final questions would not have been put so straightforwardly: *Er du ren? Er du tro?* ["Are you pure? Are you true?"].

It is easy to believe that a poet of Obstfelder's openness was often parodied, just as it is easy to believe that such a cruel novel as Sven Lange's *Hjaertets Gaerninger* could have been written about him. The unhappy "**Fantasi**" with its too often repeated imperatives would make us smile, even if it did not bear the subtitle: "December, 1890, Milwaukee." The contrast of the poem's sultry "setting" and sultrier exhortations with the image "Milwaukee," a name which denotes the epitome of solid Middlewesternism in American life, may be too much for our sense of humor. There are also passages in the *Skovviser,* especially in the "**Pampassange**," which make us smile by their vocabulary alone: *tzar* and *tzarina* and *wigwam*. This is bad Whitman. Of course it is not fair to dwell upon those features of Obstfelder's poetry which may seem particularly ludicrous to American readers. But we dwell upon them because it is revealing to do so: Obstfelder's judgment is at fault, but underlying the mistake in taste is again Obstfelder's openness. Such poems as "**Orkan**," the often quoted "**Jeg ser**," or the single word outbursts of "**Drikkevise**" embarrass us for the poet, yet we must accept them just as we accept the beauty of "**Nu vaagner alle smaa vover**" or "**Har gaat og higet,**" because they stem from the same poetic trait, be it fault or virtue. Desire is the theme of "**Drikkevise**" as well as of "**Har gaat og higet**": the latter's directness is the former's bluntness. The difference between the failures and the successes among the poems is not the genuineness of the poet's feeling or his choice of subject: it is rather the control which he is able to exert over his manner of approach.

We have insisted perhaps too much upon the openness of Obstfelder's lyrics. For now we must contradict ourselves to a degree; the erotic poems, which make up not a small portion of the original collection, are honeycombed with poetic subterfuges, practised perhaps unconsciously by the writer. Not that Obstfelder indulges in trickery with respect to the reader; if trickery is present it is directed against the poet himself. The poems in their expression are as direct as any in the collection; their implication is however unnatural—might we use the word "decadent"? Here if anywhere in Obstfelder is opportunity for the Victorian attack, the Rilkean implication. In none of the erotic poems (those poems where a desire, an unconsummated relationship, is expressed) can we find the proper balance of things. Something seems to be wrong with Obstfelder's erotic nature; the desire, if present at all, goes so far and no farther. Josef Nilsson in his essay on Obstfelder's mysticism ["Sigbjørn Obstfelders Mystik," *Edda*, 1933] has presented the problem thoroughly and exactly. Obstfelder's capacity to desire fails him at the wrong moment. . . . Why, in the prose poem "**Natten**," does he hear the approaching footsteps of the desired one—and realize that he is not ready to receive her? What happens at the close of "**Nu vaagner alle smaa vover**"? After the awakening of the young girls we find the poet alone, unable to think of love. As Nilsson demonstrates Obstfelder's psyche is not a normal one. He concludes that two souls, a masculine

and a feminine, co-exist within Obstfelder. He might have drawn more unpleasant conclusions about the poet's feeling for woman. The prostitute ("**Navnløs**"), the blind woman ("**Den sortklaedte**"), the dying girl ("**Liv**") attract and receive him. We dare not say that they arouse him. The strong, almost brutal woman finds the most admiring portrait; she however remains less approachable—often the approach is not even suggested. The domineering tone of "**Piger**" . . . , the expostulations of Esther to the nameless man, even the unhappily named *tzarina* of the *Skovviser* imply an unhealthy interest in the masculine woman. The emotions of these commanding natures are of course close to the advances of the *terne,* of Tzjiolitzka in "**Fantasi**" who is impelled to kiss the sleeping man. In each case the woman plays the normal role of the man, seducing or commanding, while the man himself remains passive, completely at the woman's mercy. We do not intend to offer a psychological discussion of these tendencies; we should rather repeat, this time more definitely, that the words decadence, degeneracy might be applied here.

However we have spoken only of erotic poems. The erotic feeling of Obstfelder may certainly be called peculiar. We have not yet examined the love poems. When we do we find nothing strange; they are at worst—or at best—idealistic, almost Schillerian. What does Obstfelder look for in the woman? He really does not want the sensual, the bold, however much he may try to make himself believe it. He is rather "old-fashioned," more so than even a Gosse. (pp. 193-97)

Obstfelder married in 1898. His poems of marriage are included in the *Digte* of 1893, his nouvelle *Korset* on the essence of marriage appeared in 1896. It is both painful and suggestive to learn that marriage, which Obstfelder understood so well in the ideal, turned out to be such a tragedy in actual life. The woman for whom he seeks he knows completely. His knowledge of women in the flesh is less perfect. . . . Marriage in the ideal evidently busied the mind of the poet long before he thought of marrying any real woman. Yet the early marriage poem "**Genre**" is realistic, one might say practical. It describes marriage not as a spiritual problem (as we might have expected from the statements in "**Kval**") but as a social one. . . . (p. 198)

Skovviser, for all their faults, lead into another chamber of Obstfelder's marriage thought. The best of them, the first, compresses within a stanza what D. H. Lawrence has said at greater length in the beach scenes of *Kangaroo* and in the crockery battles of *The Rainbow:* that man and wife are as children, playing together and fighting (against one another) together. . . . But men and women, although married, are not always children and young. They grow old and the one or the other of them may die. The prose poem "**Hvepsen**," in its idyllic atmosphere, its vision of great in small, even in the profession of its chief human figure, reminds us of the Austrian Biedermeier, of Stifter, and of his story on marriage grown old, *Der Waldgänger.* In that story an architect and his wife, despite their happy marriage, decide to separate so that the man may marry a second time and beget the children denied him in his first union. The change ends in quiet tragedy for both members of the original couple. "**Hvepsen**" is not so detailed; the human actors appear as observers of a wasp which lingers by the body of its dead mate until it also dies. The watchers, grown old and forgetful in long companionship, remember one another once again. As so often in Obstfelder the story is open, almost to the point of sentimentality; but its theme is none the less true for that. It may seem strange to find a "moral" in a prose poem by an impressionist poet; this is another of the traits that make us hesitate to place Obstfelder in a certain category without more thorough investigation.

We have called Obstfelder's poems of marriage practical and realistic. They teach lessons in what one should do to keep a marriage happy. *Korset,* with its problematical hero and all too experienced heroine, is not quite so simple. Obstfelder ventures, in treating the relationship of *desire* between the narrator and Rebekka, to peer again into some of the unsavory facets of the soul which he had skirted and sometimes touched upon in his erotic poems. The reader becomes a little suspicious at the narrator's relationship to Bredo, at his musings on the sculptor's (professional?) knowledge of Rebekka, and, as we have said before, at his hesitancy to become Rebekka's lover. Yet these passages are not the deepest in the nouvelle, nor are those in which Bredo announces his somewhat puerile thoughts upon woman, which are simply: that a woman may be the making of one man and the ruin of another. The "moral" of the book (if we may once more be allowed that most appropriate word) is to be found in a passage first placed into the mouth of Bredo, then given variations by the narrator and by Rebekka: *Og vi kan pine andre til døde ved vor selvpinsel.* The message in itself is nothing very original, even when—or especially when—applied to marriage; it is only after we have learned, first from the narrator's own words and then from Rebekka's, what the narrator has been and could be for the woman, and after we have contrasted this with what has happened, that we see the real tragedy. The sensitivity which gave the hero the power to make Rebekka young once more (compare the transformation scene at the book's beginning) has also made him prey to doubts which destroy the union and cause Rebekka to take her life. Not that Rebekka did not give the man sufficient grounds for doubt; but, Obstfelder says, he should have been able to overcome all suspicions and all knowledge for the sake of the perfect union. What Rebekka writes in her diary invites comparison with other hymns of praise to the lover or husband in world literature. It is not at once erotic and metaphysical as the *Liebestod* is, it does not attain the mythological grandeur of the thoughts of Mrs. Leslie in *The Plumed Serpent,* it is not a simple catalogue of physical and more particularly sexual accomplishments such as Marie Morgan offers at the end of *To Have and Have Not.* While the supersensory thought of Tristan—the union of two complementary souls in a future world—is not lacking, the essence of what Rebekka has to say is "practical," is "realistic." One could draw up a balance sheet and calculate the gains, as well as the great final loss, that Rebekka has drawn from the love affair. . . . She has grown younger, she has grown better. The narrator may reckon his own gains and losses too. . . . There is mutual gain and, in the case of failure, mutual loss. Each of Obstfelder's couples partakes of this exchange: the hardly realized loves of the student and Liv, of Odd and Lili (in *De røde draaber*), the more elemental reciprocity of powers in *Skovviser,* in "**Esther,**" in "**Sletten,**" the hopeful-hopeless love of the couple in *Korset,* are each a giving and a taking, a gain and a loss.

We might presume a third and binding element in such unions, at least in the more complete, the less death-touched. The child often appears, but a ghostly one, sneaking in and out of the pages as if it had no right to existence. It lies in the cradle of "**Genre,**" it unites the *tzar* and *tzarina* of *Skovviser,* its implication within the mother's swollen belly torments the man of "**Bugen,**" it belongs only to the woman in *Korset* and helps to destroy rather than unite the pair, its presence is hinted at in the closing pages of *En praests dagbog;* yet it never really exists. If we believed in signs and portents we should be tempted to read a certain meaning, that of birth through death, into the coincidence that Obstfelder died on the day of his daughter's birth. We could continue our mystifications by demonstrating that Obstfelder does not allow the child to appear as a developed and influential figure in his works, that it is present only as a facet of womanhood, that he fears its coming may destroy his place in his beloved's, its mother's arms. However we prefer to follow a more prosaic course and to assume that while woman was very much a part of both the fact and the dream of Obstfelder's experience, the child intruded only upon the latter. Obstfelder did not know enough about the child, and had not thought enough about its place in the union to make any but the most vague allusions to it. The problem of birth, on the other hand, concerned the poet thoroughly, since he, not knowing what the future dicta of psychiatry would be, thought of the experience as having very much to do with the mother and relatively little with the baby. (pp. 199-201)

In the last of the *Skovviser* Obstfelder connects woman's act of giving birth to nature's, drawing the conclusion that nature, like the woman, suffers, that night, bearing day, is as much a producer of life, and as worthy of man's respect, as woman herself. This analogy is not an unusual one, nor is the mystery with which Obstfelder surrounds the equation of woman and nature peculiar to him. The originality (which is never a real aesthetic virtue) and the depth of the concept lie in what becomes of woman: having compared her to nature, made her nature in little, Obstfelder in his later writings brings her out, so to speak, on the other side of nature, and makes her woman again, but now woman as our connection with that which we cannot know. She has become a mediatrix, corresponding to Rilke's image of the *Vermittler,* the angel. (Curiously, Rilke's angels in the *Duiueser Elegien* are definitely masculine beings; if Obstfelder had lived would he also have made this transformation?) However the great rose become sun become woman at the end of *En praests dagbog* is not a surprising transition in Obstfelder's work. One of the most beautiful poems in the collection of 1893 starts us along this difficult path: the tragic epithalamium, "**Brudens blege ansigt.**" Its forerunner in the Germanic literatures and its equal in the musicality if not the delicacy of its speech, is the *Brautgesang* of Clemens Brentano, *Komm heraus, komm heraus, o du schöne, schöne Braut.* Where Brentano mourns only the loss of maidenhood and so approaches a common type of Central European folksong, Obstfelder begins with a much more exalted notion of the bride. Brentano, however slightly, mocks the bride; Obstfelder prays for her (and happily succeeds in avoiding sentimentality). In the refrain the prayer and its wishes give way to another tone, and we are tempted to say "bride" no longer, but rather "sacrifice," and sacrifice for the sake of us all:

> Vaar gaar, vaar dør,
> sne drysser over liljers lig,
> liv smiler, liv iler
> død imøde.
>
> ["Spring comes, spring dies,
> snow falls on the lily's corpse,
> life smiles, life flies
> toward death" (tr. by Mary Kay Norseng).]

Life and beauty, the beauty of maidenhood and the lilies, hurry toward death, the dream must die. . . . The bride's suffering and death will bring forth new life: this sacrifice, although one of necessity, inspires Obstfelder's most worthy treatment of the woman as life-bringer, whose only recompense is the poet's respect. Here again we might speak of a subterfuge in Obstfelder, although of a less distasteful type than those mentioned above. In the *Digte* Obstfelder admires woman as an object of desire (and sets up the most impregnable barriers between himself and her), woman as a wife, and woman as the sacrifice, the loser and giver of life. We might say that the poet's attitude in the first case is perverse, that in the second it is the most ''normal,'' partaking of both the actual and the ideal, and in the third has the most mysticism. Obstfelder is never able to combine all the attitudes, or does not want to. Does he really desire the wife? Does he feel any ''husbandly love''—indeed anything but awe—for the mother? We think not. The sacrificed woman can survive the birth and become an ordinary human, a mistress and a wife, again, without losing the sanctity she has won. Such a synthesis does not occur to Obstfelder in his early poems.

It is a little doubtful whether Obstfelder ever attained this view of woman, although the vision of the *Dagbog* admits of a number of interpretations.... Obstfelder as an artist shied away from the synthesis, preferring to deal with only one type of woman at a time; this type he varied not by adduction of new traits but by transformation. We have already mentioned the beginnings of the progression from woman to nature to woman, now in cosmic form, as they appear in *Skovviser.* Nor does ''Brudens blege ansigt'' lack the identification. How do we see the bride? Her head is bound around with myrtle, roses ornament her breast: the myrtle withers, the roses die, snow drifts upon the lilies. First the natural symbols of the bride, myrtle and roses, fade away, then the bride herself, become nature (the lilies), perishes. Woman is not only compared to nature, she becomes it. The *To Novelletter,* published in 1895, develope this idea, the one (''Sletten'') broadly and perhaps too obviously by Obstfelderian standards, the other (''Liv'') negatively, even incidentally, but all the more poignantly. (pp. 202-04)

''Liv,'' ... despite its end-of-the-century quality, its languidly resigned air that reminds us of the immature *Ene* ... is as an example of writing on the level of the prose poems. The story is compressed, almost bare, in the best Obstfelderian manner. A student comes to know the nature of his next-door neighbour, a lonely Icelandic girl, without ever having seen her. At last they meet and he attends her through her final illness. We cannot overlook the more banal implication of the story, ''of a love too pure and tender for this earth.'' ... In ''Liv'' the hackneyed theme is treated, if not so unusually, then so gracefully that we are not disturbed by the subject matter. Liv, like Lili in *De røde draaber,* gives the hero, by means of her love and death, not a new life, but a new vision of the old one. Like Naomi in ''Sletten'' (again in the last pages of the tale) Liv becomes the bond which joins the student to the cosmos; however it is not so much her love that accomplishes this as the fact of her death. She has, to use a Rilkean phrase, died the ''great,'' the ''meaningful'' death. At the tale's conclusion the student, going out into the night, seeks after the word of the mystery *(gaadens ord):* when all the grating sounds have fallen still, when people have forgotten and he himself has forgotten, will the word come, and all become clear, and his soul awake? This is the same result, more spiritually expressed, as that of ''Sletten.'' The only difference is that the heroine's part is less clear, less definitely bound to her quality as woman. In this the nouvelle is farther away than ''Sletten'' from the vision of the *Dagbog.* It fills in that middle step in our scheme, where woman becomes nature or is replaced by it. The tale's most impressive passage, and one of the most musically written scenes in Obstfelder, is that in which Liv retells her dream of

Iceland. Obstfelder has not chosen Liv's homeland at random; Liv is Iceland and Iceland Liv, a beautiful yet almost lifeless being alone in the northern seas, yearning toward the unattainable south and its sun. Iceland becomes no geographic entity but the essence of the northern landscape.... In Liv's dream Iceland moves every night a little toward the south. Someday, in a thousand years or so, the land will become warm and nature will burst into bloom. Liv, sick no longer, and the student will be there; they will talk and fall asleep ''while the northern lights are dancing.'' The transformation of nature (and of Liv) has taken place, but not into a world of simple voluptuousness. The old sense of mystery remains. Not only is Liv transformed in nature's transformation (for she is nature), but also in her transformation there is the mixture of the spiritual and the sensuous we later find in the minister's rose. It is necessary to go to the earlier works to find the meaning of *En praests dagbog.* Can we complain at the artistic rightness of this? All of Obstfelder's works have but one hero.

They have however many heroines, not all taking woman's form. Among the posthumous lyrics we find a poem, ''Traeet,'' (dated 1895) whose subject, nature personified and speaking, is isolated in Obstfelder. Nature often appears in other of the later poems, but as an expression of the writer's awakening (''Dag''), or as a mode of speech to his beloved (''Til dig''), or as an example of life's pitifulness (''Adieu''), or again as woman's transformation in the fragment ''Rosen.'' In ''Traeet'' nature speaks out of itself. (We might say that the conversation between man and dog in the prose poem ''Hunden'' is a variation upon the same device, but coarsened and sensationalized.) In ''Adieu,'' one of the delicately pretty pieces which Obstfelder wrote on occasion, the poet looks at the plant's death from outside. He speaks affectedly about it ... and we realize that a number of other poets might have written an identical poem. In ''Traeet'' Obstfelder is as open and direct as in any of the most successful lyrics of 1893. The tree, like the mother, has given birth, has created summer and now is dying; it has kept none of its blossoms for itself. Suddenly it begins to tremble. A new branch springs out (the woodsman's saw?). The tree is doomed.... The tree does not know whether the new branch points up toward the heights or inward toward the depths. *Da er millioner stjerner omkring.* The final experience, whatever its result may be, new life or total destruction, has been a meaningful one; the tree, like Liv, like Rebekka, like the bride, has died a ''great death.'' The tragedy lies within the fact that it can communicate its death to no one; and on this account we find the hopeless ending. But the tree ''has seen a million stars.'' In death it has profited from death, making its contact with the whole of nature and the *gaadens ord* beyond.

The hero of ''Liv'' says: ... ''There is something I must understand.'' The sentence is the core of Obstfelder's work. Impressionist he may be, even decadent, but the searching for an answer likens him to the greatest figures in Dano-Norwegian literature, to Kierkegaard and his true Christianity, to Jacobsen and his *vanskelige død,* to the Ibsen of *Brand*—and even Gosse must have approved of these. He is looking for something—heaven's his destination. Obstfelder was not a poser, and the search for the *gaadens ord* is not a mere literary device with him, as it is so often in *Gottessucherliteratur.* The tone in which he writes to Ellen Key of the conception of his novel should be proof enough. The few pages already composed contain more and are deeper than all he has ever written.... Of course the search did not begin in 1897 with the first draft of *En praests dagbog.* It is obvious everywhere in the earlier works of Obstfelder. Yet there is one difference. Elsewhere Obstfelder, forever occupied with woman, has made her serve as his means of approach. Even in the most sensual poems the "meaning" of the relationship cannot be forgotten (perhaps a cause of Obstfelder's tricks, his perversity? He feels the incongruity between agency and end.) In his early thirties, perhaps even before, he undergoes a change. Woman has lost, if indeed she possessed, any erotic meaning. Now in the diary she would seem to disappear altogether; Obstfelder seeks for the mystery through his own senses or with the aid of nature, nature whose relation to woman is for the time being not evident. He has become an idealist, in a more accepted sense of the term. The progression is not an uncommon one among so-called idealistic poets, poets never termed decadent in the histories of literature. (pp. 205-08)

If woman is gone, of what does the main body of *En praests dagbog* consist? Nature has already been mentioned (and in the essay of professor [Anathon Aall, "Sigbjorn Obstfelder," *Samtiden*, 1900] it is pointed out that Obstfelder's love of nature was not simply a cosmic one, but could become specific, even scientific.) We have not yet mentioned music except as an element of Obstfelder's verse style. It does not appear as subject matter either in the lyrics or the prose tales. However we know from every account of Obstfelder's life, from Vilhelm Krag and Johan Bojer and from Obstfelder's accounts of his life in America, that the poet was an enthusiastic and talented violinist, that during his American sojourn he planned to become a professional musician. Why he renounced this plan we do not know: perhaps because of a conciousness of his lack of technical training. It is curious that he refrained from treating music in the works written before *En praests dagbog;* it is even more curious that in the novel music assumes such strange forms. Obstfelder, the disappointed musician, never imagines himself as composer or performer in the manner of E.T.A. Hoffmann (*Kreisleriana, Kater Murr*) or Thomas Mann (*Doktor Faustus*). Music becomes instead a part of nature, a "sounding" of nature's movement: as in the case of Naomi in **"Sletten,"** from whom Obstfelder intentionally removed each individual trait, the poet likewise strips music of its practical, its real connections. No orchestras, no virtuosi play the music of Obstfelder. It is simply the music of the spheres. (pp. 209-10)

En praests dagbog opens with a question . . . which sets the tone of the book's first section. How true is faith, what is the meaning of suffering? . . . For the minister the divine in each of its manifestations inspires terror; he approaches the divine at times with fear and trembling, at times with a simulated confidence. He makes a typical transformation when he decides that Jehovah cannot love the seeker who comes creeping, pale with terror or broken with fatigue. Suddenly he allows himself to be cast into the very state of humiliation . . . that he has mocked. Why should precisely he be in correct relationship to the cosmos, as Obstfelder so geometrically puts it? He is unworthy, his mouth is full of slime, a yellow cast in his eye, his skin green—in a moment he has gone from the highest to the lowest, from interpreter, and so a chosen being, of God, to the vilest example of the flesh. . . . Much the same can be said about the other material in the book's first section. It consists of a hodge-podge of commonplaces that evidence wide and often ill-digested reading, but joined by passages of a wonderful musicality. (pp. 211-12)

Artistically we may complain at this crazy quilt; Obstfelder justifies it philosophically in the sentence: *Vi maa søge. Det er en naturlov.* In these opening pages *En praests dagbog* is

what its name implies, a diary—and one which hardly seems to have been intended for publication, with its grotesque juxtapositions of thought, its citations from the most varied collection of writers and thinkers. However we can find an artistic unity apart from the style itself; the mode of seeking. The most often quoted poem of Obstfelder is **"Jeg ser"**; Christian Claussen in **"Grundmotivet i Obstfelder's Digtning"** and **"Eiendomligheter i Obstfelder's Digtning"** makes much of the "eye," both inner and outer, in Obstfelder's works. And what has the verb been? *La mig se . . .! La mig skue!* The word is used in a metaphysical sense, of course: in the moments of ecstasy, when Obstfelder for the first time perceives the wonderful net of the cosmos . . . which God must also *see* from his vantage point, the minister remarks that he can *see* far better than otherwise with all his five senses. In this passage "to see" is used in a trifold meaning: the ordinary seeing of the senses (and even that is a more complicateed concept than the simple seeing of the eyes), the poet's mystical vision, and the vision of God, of which Obstfelder's own vision has been but an imitation, a supposition. But the connection between the physical seeing of **"Jeg ser"**—there too a seeing by more than the eyes—and the constant metaphysical seeing of the diary is clear. The change from the one to the other is indicated in a quotation from the Old Testament: the transition has something of that milieu about it, with its interweaving of sensuous and supersensuous experiences, its expression of the supersensuous experience in sensuous form, and more important, in a sensuous spirit. "And Moses concealed his face, for he feared to look upon God."

Among the many fragments we come upon one which begins: "The railroad station." We are surprised, as so often, by the sudden introduction of an entirely new thought, and the poet himself is surprised: here is a feature of life which seems to him to be a companion mystery to that which he has been pursuing. Once—in the Old Testament world, in the world of the diary's beginning—men stood still, now they have become like molecules in a shining gas, caught in movement and sound, caught in music. . . . At first the poet is frightened by his discovery; he seeks peace, stillness, the very state of standing still. In the next pages he makes his initial approach to the riddle of God, not merely supposing His acts but attempting to know Him. He fails, defeated by manifoldness of the divine, especially as it is represented in the Trinity, Father, Son, and Holy Ghost. . . . Then follows the terrible experience of degradation. Upon recovery the hero is seized by new visions, not of God but of nature in idealized form: the Himalayas in a burning sun which despite its fire remains pure light and does not disturb the mountains' calm. From this he turns to thoughts of the Mediterranean, the Atlantic, of his childhood, which last he wishes to experience once more. A regression has taken place: visions of nature without movement, thoughts of his youth, . . . *og da vilde der komme ro, den store ro.* The approach through sight alone, since contemplation presupposes rest, inaction, on the part of the seer and the object of his sight, has failed. The poet cannot deal with the element of motion in the world's mystery or the manifoldness of heaven's.

With the words *Jeg har hørt musik* a second section of the book begins. "The Parsifal overture. It was as if the very realm of heaven sang." The music which the man hears is a discovery, a new world, at once motion and repose. . . . The repose of the old world it is not, the repose of the stationary, but rather the repose of continuous and regular movement, of eternal repetition, of musical form. When we read farther, to learn that there is "a sun in the sea of tones, sun and suns, small beams in a thousand colors,'' in other words when the syn-aesthetic experience has taken place and the auditory impression has become a visual one, but without losing its original quality, then we are reminded that Obstfelder had been reading Dante at the time of the diary's beginning. . . . Obstfelder both seems to admire and without question employs Dante's concept of music. As the musical section progresses, the feeling of repose disappears; the Parsifal music, which has justly been called a series of *andanti*, gives way to a swiftly moving but still regular music of the spheres. . . . The basically musical description of the universe is continued throughout the diary's second section, and at its close we reach a first positive climax (as compared to the exhausting and fruitless climaxes of self-abasement in the earlier part of the book). The geometrical figures reappear near the end of the long crescendo, as if to state once more the structural element of music and of Obstfelder's universe; simultaneously ''rest,'' ''repose'' is reintroduced. . . . Rhythm is the repose of life; *stasis* the repose of death.

The exposition of the vision of the new life is stylistically astounding; prose has seldom been employed to such a completely musical and more precisely counterpuntal effect, with the constant intermingling of several themes, and what is more important, the constant sense of motion. But the idea is not new. The music of the spheres is an ancient and widespread concept in world literature, one of the most common ways of expressing the cosmos' movement. What is important is the use to which Obstfelder puts this marvelous and poetically a little threadbare music: the Norwegian allows it to form the background and central thought of an entire section of the diary, just as it forms the omnipresent background, finally crystallizing into the eternal rose, of Dante's *Paradiso*. . . .

The melody is circular; it has movement and at the same time a closed geometrical form (reminding us immediately of Obstfelder's passion for the globe, the *klode*); it is expressed synaesthetically, as in the *Dagbog:* ''and all the other lights made sound the name of Mary.''

After this Dantean climax the movement of Obstfelder's universe gently subsides with the repetition of the fugue's principal ideas, and rhythm and form, which from the beginning have had the upper hand over melody in the composition, now exclude all else. . . . From the concept of solitary rhythm a solitary god, the holder of the baton, as Obstfelder not too aptly puts it, is deduced. However the god remains only a deduction—and consequently a disappointment to the seeker. Thus the transition from the extreme ecstacy of the second section to the hopelessness of the third is accomplished. Obstfelder's depiction of the Primer Mover is much shorter and less concrete than that of Dante; Obstfelder can borrow substance but not vision and faith from the *Divine Comedy*. Now the poet has made two approaches to the Godhead, one through a helter-skelter of various methods (of which the scientific was perhaps the most important), one through music, which fails for lack of faith to carry it to its conclusion. In his state of exhaustion after the ''more than a week of thoughts and visions'' the poet falls prey to new torments. One night a rat appears in his room, a bearer of all the horror of the actual world. . . . The minister feels a horror very much like that felt by Rilke's hero in *Malte*. How can the cosmic dance and the world of darkness exist side by side? The hero of the Norwegian novel begins his march through the impurity and obscenity of the world—and ends in a condemnation of the *ville tentaculaire* and in a hymn of praise to the happy savage, a passage that demonstrates once again

the essentially diary-like quality of Obstfelder's book. (It should be compared with the carefully selected group of essays and letters which compose *Malte*.) The hero is again in the state of degradation which preceded the vision of music and the second section of the *Dagbog*, and again a new element is introduced, this time not an art form but a theory (suggested in the novel by a physician): that nothing is to be gained by seeking after heaven, that heaven is better created on earth, a theme which has been common in European literature and which can find its origin in Achilles' remarks in the *Nekuia*. Obstfelder seizes upon the hackneyed thought (we are reminded once more of his apology for *Korset*) and transforms it into a third vision. Nowhere is Obstfelder's relationship to the great idealists so clearly demonstrated as here. He takes up a basic tenet of the social reformer (as well as of the hedonist) in literature, embraces it, and then, employing devices from the last and most ethereal cantos of the *Divine Comedy*, renders it into the material of a vision—while never wholly giving up his connection with the actual, his acceptance of the original idea.

The doctor's preachments are typical of the reforming positivism of the late nineteenth century. . . . [The minister] characteristically envisions himself as a new Ignatius, whose aims however are not of heaven but of earth. This most ludicrous of all Obstfelder's ecstasies (yet honestly expressed as all of them) is of brief duration. It is destroyed by the question of his imagined disciples: but what of death? The awful contrast between his diverse visions, the ever-moving cosmos, the splendid heaven on earth, the undeniable wretchedness, physical and spiritual, of his fellow humans, leaves him desolate. All his efforts to understand *den store, den ene* have failed. The doctor's lesson has taught the *praest* the value of practical love, the searcher's attitude toward the cosmos (and God) has always been that of the lover, however shy his passion may at times have been. He cannot love all mankind or God himself: both forces are too great for him. . . . But he cannot deny the existence of any of these forces. Therefore he decides to begin to learn to love—again a striking resemblance to Malte.

We should not be too unprepared for what occurs. The final vision is based upon a triple foundation: the doctor's sound and all too practical (and so impractical) advice, Obstfelder's own weakness for the ideal, and finally the woman, who has been absent throughout the majority of the book. The poet is faced with a triply difficult problem; having decided that love is the only approach, however insufficient, to the *gaadens ord*, he must try to love, at least in their representatives, reality and the world beyond and inevitably the woman, who contains elements of both. But learning to love so much, even in the most simple fashion, is terribly difficult, and the poet goes out into the hills in search of a ''little center'' around which all the beams of life may order themselves. . . . Feeling a need for an intermediary, Obstfelder falls back first upon the symbols of Christianity, then upon the images of the greatest Christian poem, leaving forever the Old Testament world where the interplay between God and man was so direct and so impossible of long duration. First of all his hero finds a lamb. A host of Christian references occur to us: the Good Shepherd and the *Agnus Dei*, Christ the saviour of his flock and Christ sacrificed. Obstfelder does not intend any of these precise meanings: he wishes rather that the lamb be seen as a bearer and evocator of love, the first step in the minister's education in love. Looking up from the eyes of the lamb (''with their eternal lament at the separation of souls'') he sees the heaven filled with roses, of which one is burning brighter than all the rest. It is the sun, smiling at the man like a lofty mother who stands in infinitely luxuriant repose, children at her mature and heavy breasts. The sun become woman begins to speak and in the course of her speech assumes more and more a human image. All that system which the man has earlier discovered, in other words, the vision of music in geometrical form . . . is a grinning skeleton. What is all system, all abstraction, against the woman who stands with milk flowing from her breasts? . . . After the disappearance of the vision the *praest* runs off to the habitations of men, the smell of fresh coffee in his nostrils (!), determined to live for the beauty of life and to make his personal, this time less ambitious approach to the Godhead through the agency of woman.

We must ask ourselves two questions. How does the vision answer the long series of Obstfelder's wonderings? And where does it place Obstfelder in relation to the idealists, especially to Dante whose influence should be detectable to the reader of the summary above? The former question is more easily answered. Obstfelder has assumed, too abruptly perhaps, the logical and last position of his development. Woman, the central theme of the stories and the *Digte,* has returned: disappearing as nature in **"Liv,"** substituting nature in **"Sletten,"** revealing the miracles of union in *Korset,* she appears after a long hiatus as natural phenomena, the rose, the sun, and finally woman once more. She has become at once a more complete and a more idealized being than before. She has not only become a mother but has kept her beauty; the earlier idea of motherhood as sacrifice and death together with all perverse eroticism and "death-consecration" has disappeared. Woman, having passed through the stage of nature, has become more natural. The concept of woman, although "normalized," has at the same time remained ideal. We do not know, perhaps fortunately, what the success of a practical application of Obstfelder's new femininity would be, but must content ourselves with studying the ideal union of flesh and spirit. Our real disappointment should be at Obstfelder's denial of his abstract gains, of his theory of music, or more precisely, his employment of only a part of these gains in his final vision. We have mentioned before that Obstfelder has seen the universe in terms of geometrical figures, and that the stuff of these figures is music, a concept which the sun-woman denies in the bitterest words: *Benrade, abstraktioner.* However her form, as compared to that of the male principle, is the globe. . . . The lightning represents of course motion, again male, while she is roundness, in repose. The music of the spheres, the moving of the stars in their courses is circular; nevertheless it has motion. Likewise the music of Obstfelder, although first perceived in lines, becomes in the perfect vision the ball, the circle. Again it possesses motion, the sempiternal motion of rhythm. Obstfelder's music was therefore a perfectly good synthesis, in abstract form, of the masculine and feminine, and in this respect the poet approaches the final description of the Godhead in the *Comedy,* where the Prime Mover, while round, is also moving, His rhythm being the very life of the universe. But Obstfelder, with his inherent feminine bias and impelled to find some less abstract image of the *gaadens ord,* denies his earlier success and with it music, a primary force in his poetic work. Realizing this, we cannot wonder that Obstfelder before his death damned his work as a failure. Music and woman are the chief ingredients of his creations; he has removed one for the sake of the other.

Obstfelder had a model in other poets for such a union. Goethe couples the symbols of music and woman, although perhaps not in their Obstfelderian meanings, in the passage of *Faust*

where the hero, still old, examines the sign of the macrocosm. Dante makes the same connection, and repeatedly, in the final cantos of the *Comedy*. (pp. 212-20)

We wonder if Obstfelder, made susceptible to Dante's images by his own nature, had any further reason for employing them? They may seem incongruous in a book whose entire milieu is so little that of a Huysmans novel, of the Catholic revival, so much that of *Brand,* of the distinctly non-decadent North. We wonder too if at the close of the *Dagbog,* thus where Obstfelder has his last say, the poet again is guilty of the same type of erotic thought which tempted him in the *Digte,* this time however not seeking refuge with a blind girl or a prostitute, but with the mother? Has Obstfelder found a simple refuge (and so the charge of decadence for once strikes home) or has he discovered a possibility of union, in which both refuge and search have a part? The evidence is sparse. There is in the *Digte* a poem, **"Nocturne,"** which closes with the most obvious Mariolatry (certainly unnatural for a poet of Obstfelder's background). . . . The last line is particularly revealing: the picture of Mary rocking the cradle of the earth is in its coziness, its "family quality," remarkably close to the child-images of the *Divine Comedy* and thus to the great mother of the diary. There is no possibility of any faith on Obstfelder's part: in a letter to Ellen Key he reveals that he should like to fall down and worship at the roadside crosses of Bohemia but that he in all honesty cannot. Faith is simply lacking. Yet in the same letter he speaks of his desire to return to Norway, to become a village school teacher. Faith is supplanted by the home or, as in the poem **"Nocturne,"** is a part of it. We recall **"Juleaften"** (and its prose counterpart **"Amerikansk Juleaften"** with its nostalgia and its family bible) of the rebirth of the home in **"Hvepsen."** On this account we cannot wonder at Obstfelder's use of the mother images (the nursing similes) and the mother theme (the Mystic Rose) after Dante: Obstfelder combines thoughts of childhood (with their connotations of homeland) and the mother (with her divine as well as her earthly attributes) into the final scene—the son and lover adoring the sun-mother and turning, at her command, to the world of beauty, where nostalgia and search, or reality and the ideal, meet. Dante's final sight is of the two-fold nature of Christ, His divinity and humanity; he has come to the highest realm through the aid of woman, also human and divine. Obstfelder, a lesser poet and supported by no faith and no dogma, has stopped with the mediatrix, has made her into his goal, composed of both home and heaven. Religious faith is rejected, the refuge but half accepted. The ideal has not disappeared and the search not ended. Compromise is not satisfactory but the best a modern man can do.

For the literary histories Obstfelder may remain a representative of the *fin-de-siècle,* of Norwegian impressionism. But if we understand his aims, his difficulties, and his results, we must conclude that although a minor figure he is in reality an idealist, and as such deserves a place in the history of world literature. (pp. 221-23)

> *George C. Schoolfield, "Sigbjørn Obstfelder: A Study*
> *in Idealism," in EDDA, Vol. LVII, 1957, pp. 193-223.*

JAMES WALTER McFARLANE (essay date 1960)

[*An English critic, educator, and translator, McFarlane is a noted scholar of Norwegian literature. His numerous works include the eight-volume* Oxford Ibsen *(1961-77) and* Ibsen and the Temper of Norwegian Literature *(1960). In the following excerpt from that study, McFarlane discusses the relationship between Obst-*

felder's life and work, particularly as expressed in A Cleric's Journal.]

Sigbjørn Obstfelder's popular reputation in his native Norway is a cloak that conceals rather than clothes him, a thing made shapeless by anthologists and hagiographers acting with scant regard for the true configuration of his poetry. It spreads over the pages of the anthologies, in which a handful of poems repetitively and monotonously create an image of their author as one who—in the words of his best-known poem—had "surely come to the wrong planet"; and it is stretched in other ways by those among his admirers who demand that the other dimensions should be made to conform, who exaggerate his stature, inflate his importance. Obstfelder was too modest a man and too modest a poet to wear a garment so grotesquely misshapen. But in among the catchwords and the cults, there nevertheless resides a talent of a peculiarly fine but strangely limited distinction, a personality for which to be stereotyped and to be deified are fates equally disabling.

In spite of the attention Obstfelder has attracted in Scandinavia, there will be few in England or America who know his name, fewer still his work; of his admittedly modest output of published material—modest, that is, in comparison with the still unpublished manuscript material which his editor claims would fill a ten-volume variorum edition—only a selection of his lyrics have so far been translated into English. (p. 104)

Here and there outside Scandinavia, the name of Obstfelder may be recognized as that of the young man on whom Rilke modelled the diarist hero of *Die Aufzeichnungen des Malte Laurids Brigge.* The recognition tends to have two unfortunate consequences: in the first place, it prompts comparisons not only in style but in value between Rilke and Obstfelder, an undertaking that greatly flatters the latter, for the two poets are by any notation of values barely comparable; it has also led some into accepting *A Cleric's Journal* itself as a source for *Malte Laurids Brigge,* which seems hardly justified on the evidence. The most that seems justified is to find in their common ancestry the name of Kierkegaard.... [It] is rather the details of Obstfelder's life and personality—which Rilke might well have learned from Ellen Key, at different times the confidante of both men—that provided material for *Malte Laurids Brigge;* Obstfelder was an example of the *Früheentrückten,* of those who died young; for as Rilke later told his French translator Maurice Betz, two things had struck him about Obstfelder—that he too had lived as a Scandinavian in Paris, and that he had died at the age of thirty-three, without having given his work the full measure of his tormented and generous soul. (pp. 105-06)

The torment of soul that Rilke remarked in Obstfelder is conspicuous as the most obvious characteristic in his life and work, and particularly so in *A Cleric's Journal;* yet it determined his career and coloured his poetry not so much by the nature of the elements of which it was compounded, nor even by the intensity with which it manifested itself, as by Obstfelder's own awareness of and insight into it. The strife in his mind was a personal variant of the conventional *fin-de-siècle* malady of the conflicting claims of life and art: and in his case it took the form of how to resolve the individual's worth as a solitary, independent, creative spirit, questioning, brooding, uncertain, with the same individual's potentialities as an element in the social pattern, confident and purposeful. As he wrote in 1894:

> It is only when one sees the great cities, the beating hearts of the age, that one experiences

the urge to feel oneself *at one* with this working, suffering and sinning society of men, to understand what it does and what it leaves undone, to share sickness with the sick, and to understand it that one might be able to heal....

[Always] the main tension (with him, as with the fictional diarist of *A Cleric's Journal*) was that between what lies within the individual and what exists without, between solitary contemplation and social action. By his determination to implicate himself in life, by attempting to discipline what could be disciplined only at fearful cost, he kept at high tension the torment in his soul, driving himself to the point where his reason temporarily collapsed, and even ultimately to his death. (pp. 106-07)

What distinguishes him from the majority of his European contemporaries in art and literature is, however, not so much that the fluctuations of his soul were more violent, nor that the decisions in terms of daily conduct were more extreme, but that he was *fin-de-siècle* not as the result of self-indulgence but rather as the consequence of vain self-discipline. It is not often that one finds, in his articles or his correspondence, any hint that he felt himself in any way set apart from his fellows; but where phrases of this nature do occur, they suggest that he felt himself distinguished from others not by any greater sensitivity or more intense emotional life but by the measures he adopted to control and discipline himself. It cannot be denied that there was a strong streak of eroticism in his temperament; yet in 1887 he wrote on the question of sexual restraint among young men, priding himself on the fact that he was "one of the few who have really striven to be worthy of Woman in this respect." And he used similar phrases about his literary composition, claiming distinction not for his sensibility but for his strength of purpose, asserting that there was surely scarcely any other young author who had the strength of will *he* had to hold fast to a composition for years. Where others had seen their sensibility as a thing to be carefully fostered and nurtured, he saw it as a threat to the living of a full life, as something inimical to active participation in human affairs; where others sought to escape from actuality into a world of vivid and possibly exotic sensation, he knew that such an escape was only too fatally easy for one of his nature, and unceasingly sought to resist. There was no thrill in giving himself up to the ecstasy of the moment, but only a sense of betrayal and guilt; there was nothing in him of the *poseur,* for he feared rather than exploited the mystic strain in his make-up and lamented his inability to share in the material triumphs of honest labour. He was too painfully aware of what Walt Whitman had called "the hiatus in singular eminence," that sense of lack that possesses the poet when he feels he is too remote from common life, felt it perhaps even more acutely than Whitman who had not, as Obstfelder had, experienced the real impact of the machine on society. Engagement, not detachment, was what he asked from life.

The percipience that was his, he therefore employed not as a medium through which to experience ever more vivid and unusual sensation, but as an instrument to aid him in his quest for meaning in the universe. "I believe," he wrote to a friend in 1895, the year he began work on *A Cleric's Journal,* "that I have, as scarcely any other young author has, the urge to penetrate into the mystery of nature, to see Man in the light of what is eternal in time, space and energy, to see the changing forms of life, flower, larva, infusoria in great array as the song of Universal Life." Portentous though these phrases may sound when thus lifted out of their context in Obstfelder's life and art, it would nevertheless be false to think of him as an over-earnest and solemnly intense young man, destitute of all humour; it is true that he took himself seriously, true also that he showed no inhibitions about asking the big questions; but it is equally obvious from other evidence that he could on occasion write with much wit, and that satire came naturally to him. Indeed one wonders whether his refusal to indulge in this satirical form was not perhaps another piece of self-discipline, another act of controlled suppression in respect of something that he felt unworthy of a conscientious poet, something that was too often the refuge of those who were not wholly certain whether they were serious about things or not. Poets, he says in one of his shorter articles, are like those who lend us lenses, telescopes, microscopes, the better to see and comprehend what is all around us. His sensibility was thus put out to work, becoming a device for attempting to trace and record the connections between things, connections too tenuous and too fine for the coarser and less sensitive minds of his fellows to catch.

All this is clearly mirrored in *A Cleric's Journal*, that work which occupied him during the last years of his life. Rilke's summary of it—"the story of a soul who, in his despairing attempts to approach God, actually becomes more estranged from Him, a prey to an intellectual fever that brings him to despair"—is only true in part. A good deal of the book admittedly grew out of the mental turmoil that had accompanied his breakdown, and it is not without relevance that Obstfelder requested that certain letters written to his brother from the asylum should be returned to him. Moreover he tended, after this time, to see the problems of existence more and more as religious problems; and in *A Cleric's Journal* the application of a religious framework to those ideas which habitually preoccupied him is immediately evident. But the mysticism is only one aspect, just as the problem of practical living is another, of something much more crucial: the purpose of life itself, the search for some kind of certainty in this uncertain world, whether it concerns the nature of God or the patterns of community living. The bishop, the doctor and the worker all have, in this journal, their own kind of certainty, their own confident belief in some chosen faith, dogmatic, socialist, materialist, as the case may be; only the lonely poet has doubts and the compulsion to express them. It is a book with the courage of its lack of convictions.

Some have seen in Obstfelder's work an attempt to do with language what his great contemporary Edvard Munch tried to do with paint; and the judgement Obstfelder himself passed on Munch might be regarded as applying with almost equal validity to his own work. He stresses the fact that Munch was a receptive artist, whose greatness lay in the subtlety of his colour and not in any power of reshaping or manipulating the forms he saw in life; his talent did not run to the creation of new lines:

> But those lines that *are* [wrote Obstfelder], those he sees as no other man. And it is as if, from all that exists, from all existence with all its forms and all its chaos, he extracts *one* line which he constantly worked towards and which he endeavours to turn more and more beautifully. Is it the line of his inmost Self? Or is it the one drawn by the encounter between his soul's plan and that of the universe about him?

This surely applies equally to *A Cleric's Journal;* the course it follows—and would have pursued further if time and health had permitted—is that traced by the encounter between Obst-

felder's tormented soul and cosmic reality. What he was not endowed with was the ability to project his experiences, to give them the newly moulded form of poetic invention, to organize, to construct; instead he had the capacity for marvel, for standing and looking and listening and dreaming. In this work, he does not set out to create a poetic world complete with his own inner and inherent laws, but instead endeavours, with the utmost delicacy, to follow the twists and turns, the evasions, the withdrawals and the probings of a soul's progress in an exploration of this world.

To call his work symbolist, as is often done, is therefore true only in a very limited sense; visionary is rather the term that more exactly describes his idiosyncratic attempts to say the unsayable—"those feelings," as he wrote in his early student days, "that have not acquired the form of thought." Whereas Rilke, for example, built up a range of symbols (the angel, the puppet, the acrobat) to assist him in saying *das Unsägliche* ["the unutterable"], Obstfelder found that what he had similarly called *det usigelige* ["the inexpressible"] communicated itself in visions. Time and again in *A Cleric's Journal,* the sense of the mysterious oneness that fills the universe is translated into purely visual terms, into the things that a mystically endowed man might see: patterns, networks, nearly visible threads that link the things of life, these are the images that keep recurring; even music which meant so much to him and for which he showed so sensitive an understanding, is a thing to be watched, even rhythm is a little triangle or square drawn by the conductor's hand that wings out over the massed instruments of the orchestra. This prepotently visual sense, it is hinted, makes difficulties for a soul such as his: which is best able to contemplate and appreciate the ancient world when things stood still, when the universal design was a static and comprehensible thing, when the earth stood firm on its four corners; to trace a pattern in movement, to grasp the rhythm of things that are constantly changing, shifting position, rushing through space, that is something that makes demands on faculties other than the visual. For all Obstfelder's deep love and understanding of music, his imagination is one that feeds mainly on what the eye sees. This is possibly one of the reasons why, in spite of the studied simplicity of language, his prose has an ornamental quality, reminiscent of the earlier poetry of Stefan George who, as he himself implied, had to be content with a hot and decorative and bejewelled style because he was not mature enough to fashion it in a cool, metallic form, hard and smooth.

It is typical of Obstfelder that he should have oscillated between regarding *A Cleric's Journal* as his masterpiece and seeing it as a melancholy failure. At first it seemed like something momentous to him; in 1897, when he looked over what he had written, he felt that it was more profound than anything he had produced hitherto; and in the following year he was confirmed in this opinion—"the weightiest, the richest thing I have written." But shortly before his death, he viewed it with complete despair:

> This book has come to be my misfortune. At one time I approached it with the greatest of expectations. . . . And more and more a deep despondency has possessed me. I have misgivings about what I have done. It does not seem to me to correspond to what I had in mind, nor to what I still feel I was capable of. . . . And of late I have been and am seized by the deepest disgust for this book.

That the book in its present form is both unfinished and un-revised conditions to some extent one's valuation of it as a piece of literature. Where Rilke deliberately and for artistic reasons chose to leave *Malte Laurids Brigge* with its air of incompleteness, Obstfelder had no choice; not only does it lack its immediate concluding section—which Obstfelder had said would have taken a further three months' work—but even when thus completed, it was intended that it should serve only as the first section of a larger work. That it also lacks finish in another sense there is no need to dispute: some of its colours are crude, some of its extremely "lyrical" passages distressingly self-conscious, and some of its lapses into exaltation disconcerting. But the world can now only take it as it was left: as a work of extreme honesty, full of the immediacy of experience, and remarkable as much by its delicacy and power of expression as by the resonance of its courage; as something, in other words, rather less than a masterpiece, rather more than a literary curiosity. (pp. 108-13)

> *James Walter McFarlane, "Sigbjørn Obstfelder,"*
> *in his* Ibsen and the Temper of Norwegian Literature,
> *Oxford University Press, Oxford, 1960, pp. 104-13.*

MARY KAY NORSENG   (essay date 1982)

[*Norseng is an American educator and critic specializing in Scandinavian literature. Her critical biography* Sigbjørn Obstfelder *is the most comprehensive examination in English of Obstfelder's life and works. In the following excerpt from that study, Norseng surveys Obstfelder's poetry and prose.*]

Sigbjørn Obstfelder looked at the world and saw it staring back at him with strange eyes. They are everywhere in his writings. Sometimes they are magical, like the hepatica bouquets that beam at him in February from the face of a child, or the thousands of eyes of his lover's arm, shining as her soul. More often they are ominous. Gas lights peer at him in the night like huge, yellow pupils, and a warm, dark-blue eye meets his gaze in the mirror. God's eye, he fears, lives independently inside him, and a blind woman nearly suffocates him with her caressing, blinding hands.

The eyes of Obstfelder's works betray him. He was a haunted man, painfully self-conscious, never really at home anywhere, and seldom at peace with himself. He was also a very gifted writer with a vision as unique as it was contemporary and the daring to commit it to paper. The combination made him Norway's poet "par excellence" of the *fin de siècle,* one of the significant precursors of Scandinavian Modernism, and—all labels aside—a remarkable, often eccentric writer then and now. (p. 1)

Although he began writing as a teenager, his major works are confined to the 1890s, and, relatively speaking, they are few: a collection of poems in verse and a collection of prose poems, two short stories, a novella, three plays, a novel, and several essays and articles. A perfectionist, he wrote and rewrote, never satisfied, never finished. The works he published in his lifetime seemed mysterious to many and were often misunderstood or not understood at all. Yet even as he lived he became legend, particularly to his fellow artists.

To them he was the manchild, both terrified and in awe of existence. Sensitive and life-shy, he seemed barely able to protect himself from wind and weather, light and dark. (pp. 1-2)

The line separating his life from his fictions was very fine. In his poetry, his prose, and his dramas he generally used a protagonist obviously modelled on himself, a sensitive outsider searching for meaning; and he consistently wrote in first person, using the lyrical "I" more associated with poetry until it became one of the most popular voices of prose in the 1890s. Obstfelder was a pioneer of first person narration and certainly paid the price of often being taken for his protagonists. (p. 3)

Obstfelder began to write serious poetry in the year of 1890. He was twenty-three and not at all sure of himself. ". . . Words, no I can't use words," he commented in a letter to his brother in May. But he could and he was, writing poetry that was both inspired and boldly different from traditional Norwegian verse. These early poems seemed to well up from within and demand to be written: They are for the most part a celebration of life, from the sounds of the rain to the excitement of seduction. In a period of unusual exuberance—particularly through the spring and early summer of 1890—Obstfelder experimented with poetic language and form to find expression for what he called "the inexpressible," the unconscious life still innocent of conventional patterns of feeling and thought. Already in 1884 he had written in the short essay **"Allegro Sentimentale"**:

> What are you to do—with all the longings, all
> the memories—all the great things you catch a
> glimpse of, all the small things the scrutinizing
> microscope enlarges? The inexpressible, those
> feelings which have not taken the form of
> thought, you want to bring them forth—but oh!
> the soil is so cold, the climate so harsh. . . .

An experimenter with language, Obstfelder would, nevertheless, always be troubled by the inadequacy of the medium. Even in this year of 1890 he wrote, "Oh, are my words not deadeningly dry," imagining an art that would go beyond language, "an advanced pantomime that could capture the accidental, its bonds and links, the transitions, the play of the positions, the mysterious fluctuations of the lines" (**"Børn og kunst"** [**"Children and Art"** . . .]). (p. 17)

As a writer he continually strove to write a poetic language as akin to music as possible, believing such a language could communicate most directly. But what began for Obstfelder in the spring of 1890 as delight in the capability of language to convey "inexpressible" moods through sounds and rhythms ended a little over a year later in alienation from language and a mad flight into what he thought of as the more powerful, purer medium of music.

His deep distrust of language was shared by many poets of the nineteenth and twentieth centuries. Elizabeth Sewell has written of the Symbolists, Valéry and Mallarmé in particular, that "each of them would have preferred, absolutely, either music or silence above the 'impurity' of human language." Yet for them and for Obstfelder it was this very distrust of words that led to a new kind of poetry. And in this initial period of inspiration and experimentation Obstfelder was excited by what language could do, not discouraged by what it could not do.

Many Norwegian poets had written about spring, but few had written so unconventionally about it as Obstfelder did in 1890. As late as 1966 the prominent Swedish poet, Gunnar Ekelöf, spoke of the poem **"Vår"** [**"Spring"** . . .] as a moment of liberation in his own youth. Written while Obstfelder was studying engineering during those last weeks at the technical college, it betrays his desire to be studying something quite different; but more importantly, it delights in new ways of hearing, seeing, and using language.

> To hell with castironpiles!
> To hell with castironpiles!
> Sss . . . such heavenly laxness,
>   bles . . . sed lax . . . ness!
> Red in the green, green in the red,
>   green in the green!
> Abutmentstrengths?
>
>   To hell with abutmentstrengths!
>   To hell with abutmentstrengths!
> That woman walking over there,
>   has she sorrows?
> She should dress in blue, anemone blue,
>   her hat buttercup!
> Rollerbearings?
>
>   To hell with rollerbearings!
>   To hell with rollerbearings!
> Warmth and . . . barberries and . . . parasols and . . .
>   and butterflies and . . .
> and and and silver in the air and silver on the sea . . .
>   Waiter! Wine!
> Holes in my socks?
>
>   To hell with holes in my socks!
>   To hell with holes in my socks!
> I have sun, I have shade!
>   —the whole world!
> Should just have had . . . a little red-dressed
>   . . . blond darling . . .

"**Spring**" can quite rightly be called a little poetry revolution in the context of the Norwegian 1890s. First of all, it broke with the traditional uses of end rhyme and strict meter, seeking subtler relationships in rhythm and sound. Not all of Obstfelder's poems are written in free verse, but as the literary historian and critic Rolf Nyboe Nettum has said, ". . . the best of them are. It is this that makes Obstfelder the forerunner of 20th century Scandinavian Modernism." Second, it employs a most "unpoetic" vocabulary and the open-ended structure which would become characteristic of Obstfelder's work. (pp. 19-20)

Like much of Obstfelder's poetry, "**Spring**" may at first seem simple, but its apparent naiveté must not deceive us into dismissing it as unsophisticated. Here as elsewhere the ingenuous tone, the freer form, and the open ending are intended to make us see what we have not seen before. As Rolf Nyboe Nettum has written:

> . . . the apparent naiveté is a subtlety that forces the listener to pay close attention. The unconventional form—also characterized by abrupt outbursts and unequal line lengths—is ultimately rooted in Obstfelder's questioning attitude toward life.

Nettum goes on, however, to make the point that Obstfelder's style

> is a necessary expression of the spirit of the age, and not the result of accidental experiments. At bottom lies a profound feeling that the old picture of the world is crushed, that the world does not constitute a fixed, well arranged and meaningful structure.

The unfixed world view is cause for excitement in "**Spring**," but it was also cause, as Nettum suggested, for deep-seated fears and the growing sense of alienation which writers of the 1890s, Obstfelder in particular, sought to express. In much of his poetry, especially that written after his breakdown, he attempted to construct worlds—still landscapes, bare trees, fixed stars, motionless people—but the worlds continually threatened to collapse or to petrify.

Obstfelder lived with the paradox that his relative world view provided him with the surest means of discovering the "inexpressible" while at the same time giving rise to such anguish as to cost him his sanity. The struggle to resolve the paradox is implicit in nearly everything he wrote. His last work, *A Cleric's Journal*, focuses precisely on the human need for things to be in flux—for surely that is life—and the equally human need for things to be fixed—but is that not, he fears, death?

His concerns were seemingly not so serious, however, in the spring and early summer of 1890. In June he wrote one of his simplest, happiest, and best-loved poems, "**Regn**" ["**Rain**" . . .]. If in "**Spring**" he jostled expectations by avoiding traditional poetic devices, in "**Rain**" he accomplished the same thing by exploiting them.

> One is one, and two is two—
>   hopping on land,
>   trickling in sand.
> Zip zop,
>   dripping on top.
> tick tock, rain this o'clock.
> Rain, rain, rain, rain,
>   pouring rain,
>   drizzling rain,
> rain, rain, rain, rain,
>   delightful and rank
>   delightful and dank!
> One is one, and two is two—
>   hopping on land,
>   trickling in sand.
> Zip zop,
>   dripping on top,
>   tick tock,
>   rain this o'clock.

Written from the somewhat unusual point of view of the rain drops, the poem's intent is clear: as nearly as possible to reproduce in words the natural phenomenon of rain. It is an exercise in rhythm and onomatopoeia, the light, staccato beat and the tapping of the consonantal stops mimicking a gentle, steady shower. (pp. 22-4)

Several poems from this early period are best understood in light of Obstfelder's desire to recreate the elemental rhythms. Unlike "**Spring**" and "**Rain**," these poems are passionate, often strained attempts to become one with the rhythmic life force. They are not his best poems, but the visions they contain are central to his work.

"**Orkan**" ["**Tempest**" . . .], written sometime [during the spring of 1890], is the poet's frenetic exhortation of a storm, raging with all the power of the earth, the air, and the sea to free his spirit and join it with its own. (pp. 24-5)

As is so often the case in Obstfelder's writing, the poet interprets the physical universe as feminine, and he responds erotically to it. The storm is a wild, dancing woman in whose presence he is defenseless. He is naked and white; he throws himself down into the grass, his arms outstretched into space in a position of surrender. In effect he exhorts the storm to make violent love to him, to play with his hair, open up his wings, and plunge him into the sea. Through submission to this awesome feminine force the poet seems to grow equal to it and to merge with it in a frenzied dance of life. (p. 25)

There is no more central theme or symbol in Obstfelder's work than women. They appear as children and mothers, as lovers and whores. They are sensual, ephemeral, earthy, and divine. But though they have many faces, they are considered essentially one being. In *The Cross* the sculptor Bredo says:

> There are thousands, yes hundreds of thousands of men in the world. But there is only one woman, only a single one. It is the same woman who is in all women, the same slinking phantom,—that can make itself as small as a mouse—and as large and wonderful as a "fata morgana." . . .

The poet responds to the phantom woman in classically contradictory ways: as life-threatening when she appears as the mature, erotic woman, the seductress, or the vampire; as life-preserving when she appears as the virgin, the mother, or the madonna. Though such projections were common in the literature of the nineteenth century, particularly in the 1890s, they function in the extreme in Obstfelder's writing. There can be no doubt that he was very troubled in his response to women and to sex; nor can there be any doubt that this deeply affected his poetry. (p. 31)

The early erotic love poetry is remarkably direct and daring for its time, and provides a telling picture of Obstfelder's poet/lover.

"Elskovshvisken" ["Love Whispers" . . .], from March 1890, is written as a dialogue between two lovers whispering to each other, each repeating the other's words like two instruments repeating themes in a musical score. They whisper in rhythms suggestive of their excitement, the rhythms growing more pulsating as the lovers grow more passionate. (p. 34)

"Love Whispers" is one of the few poems in which the poet and the mature woman enter into a union of any kind. Although love between man and woman is one of the most common metaphors for the loss of the self in another, there is a marked absence of communion in the erotic poems in contrast to the nature poetry. On the contrary, in the love poetry there is often a reassertion of the poet's separateness. Even in **"Love Whispers"** the act of love seems only to have begun, and strangely the poet seems lost in himself. His sudden startled awareness of the woman's silent face only serves to emphasize not the union but the distance between the lovers.

The poem derives its tension from the man's ambivalence to the woman. He is seduced but under protest. Preferring to remain a child, he responds to her playful offer to hug and kiss him and hum him to sleep but fears her passion-filled eyes; he thinks of her kisses and the rhythm of his blood in terms of the rocking of a baby; and he uses a simple, child-like language. (p. 35)

Using a narrator more distant than the frightened lover of **"Whispers"** . . . , Obstfelder wrote a number of beautiful poems about young women, softer portraits than those of the seductresses. These are among the best of the early poems, Obstfelder achieving in them that marvelous sense of mystery—Baudelaire [in his "La chambre double"] called it "delicious

obscurity"—which has become the hallmark of Symbolist poetry in general and certainly of Obstfelder's poetry in particular. The mystery-making involves the careful selection of details and the withholding of information to create a simultaneous impression of sensuousness and obscurity. (p. 36)

> Can the mirror speak?
>
> The mirror can speak.
>
> Looking at you each morning,
>   studying,
> looking at you with its deep, wise eye,
>   —your own!
> welcoming you with its warm, its dark-blue eye:
>   Are you pure?
>   Are you true?

Obstfelder wrote **"Kan speilet tale?" ["Can the Mirror Speak?"** . . .] in the late winter/early spring of 1891 while he was in Washington Heights [Illinois]. The surreal eye, staring back at the poet, studying him, questioning him, seems to indicate the beginning of Obstfelder's intense, schizophrenic self-absorption that resulted in his breakdown in the late summer. The probing eye also foreshadows the writing to come, a writing preoccupied with seeing and understanding in a world of shadows. The poetry, plays, and prose are full of these eyes that stare into the self and out into the universe, strained, blind eyes comforted only by tears, eyes literally afraid both of the light and the dark, held defiantly open but longing to be closed.

Obstfelder wrote very few poems during his months in America. **"Friends"** and **"Can the Mirror Speak?"** were written there, and several others as well, but poetic language, for the most part, frustrated him, and he turned to music. Words became his nemesis. (pp. 38-9)

He had, however, written some very fine, unusual, and even revolutionary poetry. He had broken down rigid forms and substituted the mystery and the illogic of dreams. He attempted to use language to get beyond language. And he established the major themes of his later works: the poet as child, his need to see and understand, his love and his fear of women, his profound sense of separateness, and his desperate wish to be taken up into a superior being. (p. 39)

After a period of convalescence in the winter of 1891-1892, he slowly began to write poetry again; but he did not really regain the confidence or the will to devote his energies exclusively to writing until he met [the art historian Jens] Thiis in Paris in the fall and traveled with him in Belgium. From what Thiis has said, Obstfelder at last found peace of mind, and the poems simply came "gushing forth." (p. 40)

The later poetry shares a greater affinity with contemporary European Symbolist poetry than did that of 1890-1891. [Arne Hannevik, the author of *Obstfelder og mystikken (Obstfelder and Mysticism)*] suggested that Thiis had introduced Obstfelder to Verlaine and Baudelaire and possibly Maeterlinck. But even those poems most likely written before the trip to the Continent reflect the common moods and concerns of Symbolism. In her book *The Symbolist Movement*, Anna Balakian observed:

> With symbolism, art ceased in truth to be national and assumed the collective premises of Western culture. Its overwhelming concern was the non-temporal, non-sectarian, non-geographic, and non-national problem of the human condition: the confrontation between

human mortality and the power of survival through the preservation of the human sensitivities in the art forms.

Obstfelder's poetry is no exception, focusing on Symbolism's favorite themes: beauty, death, alienation, loneliness, and communication. (pp. 40-1)

The conception of the poet as one singled out by the demonic muse to be a stranger on earth is, of course, a commonplace in Romantic literature of all ages. Few took it so to heart, however, as did the writers of the 1890s. The Danish poet Johannes Jørgensen (1866-1956) asserted, for example, that Baudelaire was constitutionally incapable of being a part of life because at his birth a wicked fairy had touched his soul with a drop of sap from the Romantics' blue flower. "He is born in the sign of the moon; under its power his soul swells in the flow and disappears in the ebb." A similar stranger, marked by death, paradoxically owing his very life to it, becomes Obstfelder's predominant narrator in both the poetry and prose. Though he does not always speak of it he is nonetheless aware of death's constant presence, whether in the falling leaves or frightened flowers, in the lover's pale skin, or in the icy blue calm that settles over many of the later poems.

Much of the jubilation of 1890 is gone from the poetry, replaced in part by this fascination with death. Obstfelder by no means discounted the earlier poetry, however. It is apparent that when preparing the order of *Poems* he worked with an organizing principle of extreme contrast—radical fluctuations in mood—indirectly making the statement that the real mysteries of life lie in its extremes and its contradictions. The volume begins, for example, with "**Friends,**" the vision of transcendence now lost but perhaps someday to be regained; followed by the later poem, "**Eve,**" in which the terrified poet stares out into an empty universe; followed by "**Tempest,**" the mad, erotic dance with life. "I have done everything," Obstfelder wrote to a friend, "to find the naive expression to convey the movement between two different poles of my soul in its youth." The range in mood in the poetry of 1892 and after is expansive but plays in a darker register than the earlier poetry on wonderment, ennui, angst, alienation, and ominous bliss. Each mood has its opposite, the beautiful exposing the ugly, the leer revealing the smile. Through the contradictions Obstfelder hoped to conjure from life its beauties and its truths. (pp. 42-3)

In "**Julaften**" ["**Christmas Eve**" . . .] Obstfelder portrayed the poet as the motherless child, a metaphor for the outsider who will forever be excluded from the common community. Probably written in December 1892 in Stavanger, it is one of Obstfelder's classic poems both in content and form. . . . Typically naive in tone and simple in structure, it is nevertheless a poem of multiple meanings. As much as any of Obstfelder's poems, it presents his interpretation of the individual in the modern world. The myth of the man/child terrified by life—associated both with Obstfelder's private and poetic personae—grew out of the poems like "**Christmas Eve.**"

Like "**Agony,**" "**Alone,**" and "**All Creation Sighs,**" "**Christmas Eve**" is divided into scenes expressive of variations in the poet's moods. Here, however, there are no dramatic reversals but rather a movement toward alleviation of his despair as he attempts to exert some control over his world. The poem begins with his exclamation that it is Christmas Eve, but only in the

second verse do we realize that he is excluded from the warmth and abundance of the festival.

> Christmas Eve!
> Windows bright with Christmas candles,
> trees overflowing living rooms,
> carols through cracks in doors.
>
> I wander streets alone
> listening to children's songs.
> I rest on steps, I think
> of my dead mother.
>
> (pp. 49-50)

In part two the poet leaves the city to seek out a landscape more befitting his mood, one very much like the snow-covered landscape of death in "**Agony.**"

> I walk to the fields—
> out—among the stars.
>
> My shadow glides over shadows
> of dead-limbed trees.
>
> I find in the snow,
> glittering like Christmas candles,
> a body still trembling,
> a sparrow, dead of frost.
>
> (pp. 50-1)

In part three the scene changes once again to the poet's attic room, sparsely furnished and far above the full living rooms of the community. The structure of the verse changes as well, the poet using a stricter, two line metrical pattern—reminiscent of a children's jingle—in contrast to the more proselike verse of the earlier sections. . . .

> And I went home to my attic room
> and put a candle in my bottle.
>
> I put the candle in my bottle
> and lay the Bible on my trunk.
>
> I knelt down at my trunk
> and blew the dust from my Bible.
>
> I folded my hands over my Bible
> and cried.
>
> (p. 51)

The image of the man as child is one that Obstfelder used often to portray the individual in an alienating world in which the despair is profound and the control minimal. The longing for the mother is itself often an expression for the longing for a spiritual home, for peace, and the reconciliation of the self to the world. In "**Christmas Eve**" no such reconciliation takes place, although the poet's tears may momentarily ease his fear. In the poems that follow the poet participates in various tableaux of mother and child, longing to be protected from his growing sense of alienation.

The woman assumes a powerful cosmic role in relation to the poet's child persona. She appears as a mother goddess in the earlier works as well as the later. In poems from 1890 like "**Tempest**" and "**All Creation Sighs**" the universe itself is such a goddess. In the poem "**Nocturne**" . . . , from 1893, she seems to be the Catholic Virgin Mary, who is rocking all her children to sleep. "A woman hovers out in the blue, / the Lord's mother, Maria, Maria, / lovingly shutting the eyes of the soul, / carefully rocking the cradle of earth." In the Whitmanesque "**Pampassange**" ["**Songs of Pampas**" . . .], also written in 1893, she is the Indian goddess of the earth, "the earth's breast from which sighs rise to the stars," protectress of the night, the day, and of earth's children. In *A Cleric's Journal* she appears in a vision of sun and roses, bringing peace to the tortured priest.

The woman, however, is a goddess of both good and evil, life and death. As in the poems from 1890, she becomes the poet's universe; but in the best of the poems from this time she symbolizes a universe which is both life-giving and life-destroying. (p. 53)

Through landscapes shaped and colored by his moods, the poet conveys his feelings of loneliness, alienation, and despair. The poem entitled **"Without Name"** takes place in a pitch black park in which black leaves fall silently to the ground and gas lamps stare like dilating yellow pupils into the night. In **"Eve"** the entire landscape—as far as the poet's eye can see—is the same undifferentiated leaden gray, and in **"Barcarole"** sea and sky flow together in a silent, liquid universe.

At the same time, in each of these poems the mood of the landscape is made inseparable from the central symbol, the mothering woman to whom the poet goes for comfort, giving rise to the paradox that the woman is both goddess and devil. For although she embraces the poet, providing him with a place of refuge from his despair, she is also the very symbol of that despair and envelops him in it. (p. 54)

These poems are the reverse side of earlier poems like **"Tempest"** and **"All Creation Sighs"** in which the poet actively tries to lose himself in a primitive celebration of life. In these poems, too, the poet wishes to lose himself, but he expresses it as a strong wish to be totally passive, metaphorically to cry or to fall asleep in his mother's imprisoning arms.

The pervasive anxiety of so much of Obstfelder's poetry was undeniably a reaction to the growing sense of alienation felt in many quarters of late nineteenth-century society. (p. 58)

"Jeg ser" ["I See" . . .], written sometime in 1892, is the best-known and, according to many, the finest of Obstfelder's poems. In the context of the expressionistic mood poems discussed in the previous section, **"I See"** is somewhat unusual in that its landscape is the city and further there is no dominant feminine presence. The poet stands alone and unprotected in the city street, his vision—his only real connection with the outside world—threatened by an impending storm. . . .

> I see the white sky,
> I see the gray-blue clouds,
> I see the bloody sun.
>
> So this is the world
> So this is the home of the planets.
>
> A rain drop!
>
> I see the tall buildings.
> I see the thousands of windows,
> I see the distant church tower.
>
> So this is the earth.
> So this is the home of mankind.
>
> The gray-blue clouds gather.
> The sun is gone.
>
> I see the well-dressed gentlemen,
> I see the smiling ladies,
> I see the bowed horses.

> The lead blue clouds grow heavy.
>
> I see, I see . . .
> I must have come to the wrong planet!
> It's so strange here . . .
>
>   (pp. 58-9)

The degree of alienation the poet feels in **"I See"** can be gauged by looking back to two of the more joyful poems of 1890, **"Rain"** and **"Spring."** The poet was so in touch with his world then that he could physically feel it. In **"Rain"** he was content merely to convey the properties of the marvelous natural phenomenon, but in **"I See"** he is so distanced from the storm that he can barely comprehend it. . . . The joy of life he felt in **"Spring"** is replaced in **"I See"** by a paralyzing detachment, the things he sees about him no longer toys for his pleasure but surfaces that have little to do with him. His words, earlier a real source of inspiration, are now a monotonous litany of disinterested observations. "I see, I see," he repeats over and over again.

It would be misleading to imply through a comparison of **"Spring"** and **"I See"** a development in Obstfelder's poetry from joy in life to alienation. His moods, the prime determinants in his work, were cyclical, and therefore a comparison of the two poems most correctly conveys the emotional extremes found in his poetry.

The same is true of his work in general. Some things were written more under the influence of a certain mood than others, of course, but it is the fluctuation in mood that is constant.

Neither is there any major philosophical development. It is generally accepted that Obstfelder emerged from his breakdown with a belief in a personal God. This may indeed be true, but it did not generate any *fundamental* change. The concept of a superior being is to be found in his writing both before and after 1891. Obstfelder always had a mystic's yearning to "see God," whether he defined it as a raging storm, or a spiral of light and fire, or the Christian God. Nor does his writing indicate that he ever had an unshaken belief in such a God. Often, as in **"Christmas Eve,"** there is no divine presence, only a desperate longing for one; and in poems like **"Eve"** the longing itself is rendered meaningless. Again, doubt and longing are the constants in Obstfelder's works, not belief. The mood, of course, is often religious, but dogma is hard to detect.

Development in his authorship must be viewed in terms of experimentation with various forms. Already in 1892 he had written to his brother regarding some of his poems: "They don't satisfy me. . . . When one has something original to say it takes a long time to find the form." In retrospect we know he found it in the prose poem. (pp. 61-3)

Obstfelder's prose poems, only twenty-five in number in the collected works, comprise a small but superior part of his writing. The darling genre of many of the poets of the 1890s, the prose poem was also a favorite of Obstfelder's. . . .

The free, short form was well suited to Obstfelder's talent and artistic aims. He seems to have recognized in it the same possibilities as Baudelaire. (p. 64)

At his best, Obstfelder achieved Baudelaire's "ambitious" dream of a language both musical and sufficiently supple. Reidar Ekner [in his anthology *En sällsam gemenskap (A Strange Fellowship)*] used the Swedish term *mjuk*—meaning both soft and supple—to describe his language, the "softness" deriving most importantly, in Ekner's estimation, from the infrequent number of accented syllables. The prose poem allowed Obst-felder to use more freely the deceptively simple poetic language he had striven for in his poetry in verse, a necessarily more restrictive medium.

The prose poem's undefined form also easily lent itself to the conveyance of his intense moods. He could, first of all, make the poem as short as he wished; and, indeed, in many of them he proved Poe right in his assertion that "all intense excite-ments are, through a psychal necessity, brief." Also the poem did not have to function according to any fixed structure: there need be no beginning, middle, and end; other than logical or sequential relationships could bind one thought to the next; and the open or questioning ending which Obstfelder so often used provided a fitting "closure." Such freedom was an obvious advantage to a poet like Obstfelder who was trying to express new and still unanalyzed structures of mood, dreams, and the unconscious.

If he worked with any one structural pattern, it was a fugue-like structure—common already to the poetry in verse—based on the statement, repetition, and variation of themes. One of the most obvious applications of the structure in the prose poems can be seen in **"Roser"** [**"Roses"** . . .], originally com-posed in 1886 and rewritten in 1892. This rather long poem is like a dream in which the dreamer feels himself being buried in "roses and red and rose petals covered with snow." Three major themes repeat themselves, sometimes separately, some-times in combination with each other. The first is the poet's physical sensation of being covered in roses.

> *Massing* over him, falling, trickling, trickling,
> hurling, piling up, massing over him into a soft—
> white petals, red petals—soft rosekiss, rosepetalkiss.
> On his forehead, on his mouth, on his throat.

The second theme is the poet's wish to die in the arms of a mother figure whom he connects with the roses, and the third is his erotic fantasy of the woman and himself, their hearts beating together as they seem to merge into one.

> There are *two*. There are *two*.
>   It's dying.
> There are *two*. There are *two*.
>   Dying.
>   *
>   One.
>
>   (pp. 64-5)

The "musical structure" is seldom as transparent as in **"Roses"**; nevertheless, most of the poems function according to this principle of recurring themes, which, for Obstfelder, was a fundamental principle of life. In the "America Journal" he wrote:

> This, that changes tempo, this, that grows in
> strength, this, that suddenly stops, and thinks,
> this that returns, continually returns as some-
> thing else, in another form perhaps, weaker,
> stronger, becomes the principal voice,—all this
> is found in life. Fugued music is found in na-
> ture. . . .

In particular, the loose structure lent itself to the kind of indirect communication Obstfelder hoped might reveal "the inexpres-sible." Repeated words could gradually take on new meanings, repeated themes could be treated several times to bring out as many nuances as possible, various themes could be dialectically structured to bring out their meanings both in opposition and in contrast to each other.

The single most important technique used by Obstfelder in the prose poems was made possible by this structure based on repetition. The technique can best be described as the conscious withholding of information from the reader in order to create a strange or mysterious mood. More information is gradually supplied as certain themes are returned to, but only partially and usually after the fact, again heightening the mood. (pp. 66-7)

Although a sense of isolation and alienation is often the effect of much of Obstfelder's poetry, he nevertheless saw in the quality of mysteriousness the *possibility* of the opposite, i. e., the possibility to communicate precisely because not all is defined. Obstfelder believed in what T. S. Eliot would call the "objective correlative." The poet writes subjectively and the reader receives and interprets subjectively; but on a deeper level they communicate the psychological or emotional truth that has inspired their subjective interpretations. As personal or as strange as many of the prose poems are, they communicate with a psychological universality both remarkable and often disturb-ing. (p. 68)

Obstfelder's earliest writings had been short pieces of prose, biographical and fictional sketches, tales, travelogues, and sto-ries. Throughout his life he continued to work with prose, even during the most prolific of the poetry years; in spite of the fact that he is remembered as a poet, prose seemed to come most naturally to him. He brought poetic language closer to prose, and he truly excelled at the prose poem. It was therefore only a matter of time before he began to experiment with longer fiction.

Between the fall of 1893 and the summer of 1896 he wrote and published two short stories, **"Liv"** and **"Sletten"** [**"The Plain"**], and a longer novella, *Korset* [*The Cross*]. (p. 93)

[In] a way, Obstfelder wrote the same strange love story—with variations—again and again. All three stories involve sim-ilar haunted lovers, the irremediably lonely seeker and his beautiful soul-mate. Their story is an 1890s cliché. The young man, yearning to experience life's essence, has withdrawn from the community into the peace and isolation of his own soul; but he "accidentally" encounters a young woman, herself set apart from society in some way, and a mysterious, mood-filled relationship develops between them. Through his love for the woman the man experiences life more profoundly than ever before. She, however, dies or undergoes a death ritual in order that the poet might live.

Erotic love appears to play a more significant and succoring role, not in **"Liv,"** but in the later works, **"The Plain"** and *The Cross*. For the first time in Obstfelder's writing the man's love for the woman is made richer and more human, encom-passing feelings of an emotional, spiritual, and physical nature which complement rather than contradict each other. (pp. 93-4)

None of these is really a true love story, except in the most narcissistic sense, for they are all essentially concerned with one person, the poetic seeker. He is the protagonist, the nar-rator, and the sole determiner of reality in the story. All char-acters and all events exist only relative to him. He sees himself in everything and everyone, and thus all things, particularly the woman, become a reflection, an extension, a metaphor, or a distortion of himself.

There is no epic development, little tension, and virtually no action in these stories, the weak story line barely able to support a fictional structure at all. What little action takes place is generally told after the fact, the course of events being at all times secondary to sounding the emotional and spiritual depths of the protagonist. His character emerges not through personal *bildung* and dramatic encounters but through a mosaic of moods, reflections, reminiscences, projections, and ponderings, inspired most often by the woman fate strangely arranged for him to meet.

Like much of the poetry, the stories employ the fugue-like structure, themes introduced and then brought back in variation in order to bring out the overtones and undertones of the protagonist's personality.

Obstfelder felt strongly about this particular fictional form. (p. 94)

The article **"Jeg-formen i litteraturen"** [**"The I-Form in Literature"**] . . . was a defense of first-person narrative against prominent critic Edvard Brandes's accusation that it was confessional and easy. Obstfelder's contrary belief that first-person narration was artistically sophisticated, sound, and rich in possibilities inspired the article which has become an informal manifesto. It reads in part:

> Dr. Edvard Brandes writes a sentence that seems to me unworthy of a man of *his* sensitivity. It is a kind of word game: If only the I-form didn't exist, if only these people could keep their *I* out of their books!
>
> Herr Edv. Brandes knows full well that the pronoun doesn't decide it, *he* is more often a transposed I, a false *he*, than the I is the author's *I*. . . . The I-form is born of the need to go right to the bottom of that person or the specific state of mind one imagines. . . . No form demands such keen hearing. The he-form covers up, one can fill it up as one can a sack, with one's own personality, with what one has seen, with what one poeticizes—The I-form needs absolute metallic clarity, no alloying is tolerated. . . .
>
> The I-form is also a result of the need to go deeper. The drama presents characters through their external reflections, the novel combines, spins together persons, events. The I-form wants to reach what is between and behind all this. For that matter it is a monologue. But it is more.
>
> It is an independent art form.
>
> (p. 95)

Through this form Obstfelder could explore at length the "I" or the self familiar from the poetry. He is supremely sensitive, registering the slightest fluctuation in mood, the slightest change in nature, intuiting correspondences among himself, others, and the world, at brief moments penetrating life's mysterious, metaphysical dimension.

But the I-narrator was much more than a sophisticated literary device to Obstfelder. He clearly intended close identification among author, narrator/protagonist, and sympathetic reader. Together they would explore the depths of one fictional soul, and in the process reach into themselves and out to each other. Intense communication between poet and reader was possible, Obstfelder believed, through the "I-form.". . . The I-narrator

was intended to be a sort of metaphysical medium through whom "poet" and reader communicated their deepest feelings.

But in reality he functions as much as a negative as a positive force both on his surroundings and the reader. Like the haunted child of the poetry, he is a passive man. The woman, typically, is the active partner. He often speaks in a monotone and is totally uninterested in the normal course of events. And although he is intensely sensitive to life, he too is equally drawn toward death, finding in death's presence life's supreme moment. He can thus have a nearly paralyzing effect on the objects, both human and nonhuman, that he brings into his frame of reference.

The narrator's very personality seems to work against Obstfelder's intent. (pp. 95-6)

And indeed it may be that Obstfelder, though he never grew cynical toward the narrator-self, grew nevertheless more and more skeptical of him. There seems to be evidence for this if we take seriously the slight technical changes in point of view from the first story to the last, changes which serve increasingly to expose the narrator as a potentially destructive force. In **"Liv,"** narrator and implied narrator are essentially one, the protagonist being the most sensitive character and an absolutely innocent one. In **"The Plain"** there seems to be a momentary split between implied narrator and the protagonist, whose sensitivity is seen as possibly harmful to life. In *The Cross* Obstfelder deliberately sought to achieve distance between the two "voices," the narrator putting himself on trial, if only to determine he had "acted" properly. In each story the narrator/protagonist *is* found innocent and redeemed. But if narrative technique can be taken as an indication, Obstfelder grew increasingly suspicious of the sensitive poet, looking for more sophisticated ways of revealing his destructive side. Interestingly, *A Cleric's Journal* is told through a schizophrenic minister. As in the poetry, Obstfelder may have needed two voices, and particularly the voices of extremes, in order to tell his story. (p. 97)

In 1896 Obstfelder wrote to a friend, "It's very possible, by the way, that I'm becoming, more and more, a dramatist; there is no form that comes so naturally to me." It is curious that he should have been so enthused about the dramatic form in particular. For him the essence of life and literature lay in the invisible movements of the soul, in silences and obscurities. Drama, however, is not generally made of such sensitive stuff; but Obstfelder, if not under the influence of, then once again in the spirit of the Symbolists, attempted to make mood the real protagonist in the theater.

He completed three plays and the first act of a fourth. In the crucial year of 1892 when he started to think of himself as a poet again, he began his first legitimate play, *Esther,* and from then on he always seemed to have a dramatic work—more or less close at hand—that he was contemplating, beginning, reworking, or finishing. In this sense the plays span nearly the decade of his career. In terms of his enthusiasm for the drama, however, they figure most centrally in the years between late 1895 and 1900. (p. 114)

Obstfelder's plays are as successful, or unsuccessful, as most of the plays written in the tradition of the so-called "static" drama. He shared with the major Symbolist dramatists, of whom Maurice Maeterlinck was the major representative, a desire to communicate in the theater as they did in their poetry, through suggestion, mood, and deliberate obscurity. Their plays flew in the face of any traditional concept of dramatic action, replacing character, plot, and development with the favored musical structure of mood, theme, and variation. All elements of the drama were to contribute to the mysterious mood.

The motivation for the static drama was, as Maeterlinck himself defined it, to portray "the soul, self-contained in the midst of everrestless immensities." The intention was no less than to relocate the dramatic conflict, as the most universal drama was deemed present in the silent soul. Maeterlinck's often-quoted example is of the old man in the armchair.

> I have grown to believe that an old man, seated in his armchair, waiting patiently with his lamp beside him, giving unconscious ear to all the eternal laws that reign about his house, interpreting, without comprehending, the silence of doors and windows, and the quivering voice of the light, submitting with bent head to the presence of his soul and destiny—. . . I have grown to believe that he, motionless as he is, does yet live in reality a deeper, more human and more universal life than the lover who strangles his mistress, the captain who conquers in battle, or "the husband who avenges his honor."

Although direct influence is difficult to demonstrate, Obstfelder was undoubtedly aware of Maeterlinck's theories. In a letter to [Norwegian actress] Johanne Dybwad which accompanied the original manuscript of [*De røde dråber (The Red Drops)*] he formulated his dramatic method in terms not unlike Maeterlinck's. The details refer specifically to *The Red Drops*, but the general principles apply equally to [*Esther* and *Om Våren (In Spring)*]. He said he imagined a theater of poetry, a theater in which the audience would experience the play as it would a landscape painting or a piece of beautiful music; and he too spoke of the altered focus of the drama.

> One might think then that the dramatic conflict is that which takes place between [the protagonist] and [the characters which surround him]. This is not the case. What happens dramatically to [him] happens only in terms of himself. And that is what should be new and crazy or new and good, and for a good actor, the interesting task.

> These other people exist only as background, as "the chorus," in relation to which [the main characters] should stand out as large silhouettes, poeticized over some of life's great forces.

In the plays—as consistently elsewhere—Obstfelder sought to present not ordinary characters on an ordinary stage, but the "essential" human being in an eternal perspective. To this effect atmosphere overwhelms, dialogue is minimal but pregnant with meaning, silence is everywhere and movement—save for fleeing the stage—is slight. The individual characters seem pathetically small and fragile, prisoners of the mood that envelops them. Time and space, life and death, as projected through the mood, seem omnipotent; and thus the powerlessness of the individual could be dramatically portrayed, were the play successful.

There are obvious risks in this kind of theater. Silences, in and of themselves, are not dramatic. Too little action can be simply tedious. Striving for the "inexpressible," Obstfelder often employed the utterly simple, yet pregnant vocabulary of the poetry; but the effect could be melodramatic or banal.

Nevertheless, the plays are an interesting segment of Obstfelder's authorship. In particular, they demonstrate his constant fascination with the theme of rebirth cast in ever-changing symbols. The same ritualistic pattern, fundamental to the prose, of descending into the darkness in order to be spiritually reborn is also central to these plays, particularly *The Red Drops*. They provide, in fact, a review of Obstfelder's works from the early poetry to *A Cleric's Journal,* containing as they do the major symbolic constructs of his poetic universe. (pp. 115-16)

Obstfelder died with the manuscript unfinished, having written the first section and begun drafts of a second; but immediately following his death the first section was published as *A Cleric's Journal*. Obstfelder himself obviously felt it was not ready for publication; and some critics—Hannevik included—consider it flawed, in particular by its lack of concentration and resolution. Indeed, the *Journal* is an imperfect work; but by virtue of its serious intent, its aesthetic and psychological concerns, and its moments of real poetry, it *is* Obstfelder's major work. The *Journal* is a culmination in yet another new form—the diary novel—of the dominant themes of his authorship: the effort to see beyond the veil of reality; the relentless questioning of existence; the sensation of alienation, or homelessness, within the self and without; the vacillation between one emotional extreme and the other; and the search for peace and death. The *Journal's* lack of resolution, considered by some an aesthetic flaw, is in reality an aesthetic device: it is the essence of this novel more than any other of Obstfelder's works, making it his most fascinating, and at the same time, most frightening statement on the relativity of perception.

The line between biography and fiction was never thinner than in the *Journal*. Many of the cleric's visions can be traced to the "events," hallucinatory and real, of Obstfelder's illness which he recorded at the time in the "America Journal" and in letters and jottings from Frogner Colony.

The partial record of the events leading up to his breakdown, the "America Journal," seems to have provided Obstfelder with some of the most significant source material, both in regard to content and form. Specific images, such as the presence of God as the beating of great wings, appear in both journals. But there are also more general parallels. Obstfelder and the cleric fight the same battles, reaching desperately outward to discover the secret of the universe and inward to learn the secret of the self. Both risk insanity for vision. Music, which is Obstfelder's obsession in the "America Journal," is one of the cleric's principal metaphors. And, too, their manic/depressive personalities determine the nature of their quests and the vacillating format of both their journals.

That the protagonist is a cleric or a minister is also undoubtedly inspired by Obstfelder's illness which, at least in one of its manifestations, assumed the form of a religious crisis. . . . Obstfelder actually seemed in danger of being overwhelmed by the religious dimension of the *Journal,* however. He intended it to be both a psychological study of a modern soul and a religious/philosophical work of depth. As he wrote to Ellen Key in 1900, "Yes, I had the wildest dreams about probing deep into both the problem of God and the drama of life—. . . ." But the "problem of God" often overcame both Obstfelder and his minister. In a letter from 1898 he described the concerns of the *Journal:*

> I have for many years . . . wished to find an expression for religious brooding and battle . . . for the painful fumbling toward God and the

Innermost, for the magnificent sensation of God at certain moments, for the battle between God and man, for the appalling feeling of being distanced from the source, etc., etc.

These certainly are the obsessions of the brooding cleric. It is both his method and his madness to pose questions about the nature of God and Satan, goodness and evil, life and death, first from one philosophical vantage point, then another, and then still another, until hopefully he would reach clarity, what he calls "the little center" or the "innermost."

First of all, his *method* of questioning is dangerous, if not deadly; but this will concern all dimensions of the *Journal,* not simply the religious. Secondly, his religious philosophy is naive, as if deliberately oversimplified to be understood by a tortured mind. *Possibly* this was intentional on Obstfelder's part. The cleric's philosophical pretentions are mocked at the end by the mother goddess who appears to him in the setting sun, proclaiming that all his abstract thought is as nothing compared to her substance, color, and form. Fittingly, it is a triumph of the visual and the sensual over the intellectual, in other words, a vindication of Obstfelder's own poetry. Nevertheless, up until the end, both Obstfelder and his cleric are repeatedly overcome by the religious questions, and the *Journal,* as a work of literature, suffers. As if to deemphasize its religious aspect, Herman Obstfelder said in 1925 that his brother "regarded the work as an attempt to portray how a modern human being thinks and feels." And indeed, the *Journal* is at heart, and at best, Obstfelder's final portrait of the sensitive, soul-searching, religiously inclined poet caught in the nightmare of his own mind. (pp. 129-31)

Mary Kay Norseng, in her Sigbjørn Obstfelder, *Twayne Publishers, 1982, 162 p.*

ADDITIONAL BIBLIOGRAPHY

Arestad, Sverre. "Sigbjørn Obstfelder in America." *Norwegian-American Studies* 29 (1983): 253-92.
  Biographical sketch of Obstfelder centering on his reactions to America as expressed in a series of letters to his brother Herman in Milwaukee. Arestad provides eighteen of the letters in English translations.

Beyer, Harald. "The Neoromantic Reaction." In his *A History of Norwegian Literature,* edited and translated by Einar Haugen, pp. 251-64. New York: New York University Press, 1956.
  An introductory sketch cataloging prominent themes and characteristics of Obstfelder's principal works. According to Beyer: "He had the newborn child's capacity for wondering at the world, a capacity which is the ultimate source of all religion and art. His original, moving, often hectic verse and prose poetry are the words of a man who feels that he is a stranger on earth, a melancholy pantheist, an inquiring dreamer."

Hambro, C. J. Introduction to *Anthology of Norwegian Lyrics,* edited and translated by Charles Wharton Stork, pp. xv-xxxvi. Princeton: Princeton University Press, 1942.
  Briefly notes Obstfelder as one of the first Norwegian poets "to release poetry from, sometimes to dissolve, the old traditional and stricter lyrical forms." According to Hambro: "To a large extent, Obstfelder's attitude to the world was one of astonishment and wonder, often of confusion and bewilderment. He felt—and he was not the only one who felt it—that he had tumbled down on a wrong planet. He strove to attain a direct simplicity that discarded accepted forms. He tried to give expression to sentiments almost too vague and intimate for ordinary direct words."

Norseng, Mary Kay. "Obstfelder's Prose Poem in General and in Particular." *Scandinavian Studies* 50, No. 2 (Spring 1978): 177-85.
  Emphasizes the suitability of the prose poem form to Obstfelder's talent and temperament through a close examination of "Bugen." According to Norseng: "[Obstfelder] was one of the first writers in Scandinavia to liberate poetry from strict meter and rhyme, bringing it closer to prose and giving himself more freedom to play on the words, sounds, and rhythms he loved and hoped could equal the evocative nature of music."

Sjöberg, Lief, and Jensen, N. L. "Early Scandinavian Symbolism." In *The Symbolist Movement in the Literature of European Languages,* edited by Anna Balakian, pp. 575-86. Budapest: Akadémiai Kiadó, 1982.
  Brief introductory essay relying chiefly on Arne Hannevik's *Obstfelder og mystikken* and Reidar Ekner's *En sällsam gemenskap.* According to Sjöberg and Jensen: "As far as Symbolism is concerned, Obstfelder learned to conceive phenomena in a symbolic manner, perhaps primarily from his experiences of illness—but obviously Symbolism strengthened Obstfelder's belief in the use of symbols and dreams for artistic purposes. His development is, above all, a personal and logical development of himself rather than a theory of poetics."

Boris Pilnyak

1894-1937?

(Also transliterated as Pilniak and Pilnjak; pseudonym of Boris Andreyevich Vogau) Russian novelist and short story writer.

Pilnyak is considered one of the most representative literary figures of the era following the 1918 Revolution in Russia. His novels and short stories typically explore the meaning of the Revolution to Russian society, utilizing a fragmented, non-linear narrative described as a "blizzard of words" through which he sought to reflect contemporary social and political chaos. This unconventional style, labeled "Pilnyakism," became widely imitated, making Pilnyak one of the dominant influences on Russian prose fiction during the 1920s.

Pilnyak was born in Mozhaisk, near Moscow, to educated parents of the middle class. The elder Pilnyaks were active in the Russian Populist movement, and their son was strongly influenced by their liberal political views and association with leftist intellectuals. After completing secondary school in Nizhni-Novgorod in 1913, Pilnyak continued his formal education at the University of Kolomna and the Moscow Institute of Commerce, from which he graduated in 1920 with a degree in finance and business administration. During his years as a student he supported himself by writing feuilletons for provincial newspapers, and by 1915 his short fiction began appearing in leading Russian literary journals. His first collection of short stories, entitled *Bylyo*, was published in 1920 to critical indifference. Two years later, however, he achieved fame with the publication of *Goly god (The Naked Year)*, often considered the first important work to deal with the effect of the Revolution on Russian society. Thereafter Pilnyak rose rapidly to a position of influence in the Soviet literary community. Over the next decade he became one of the wealthiest individuals in the country, earning from royalties, according to his estimate, "at least twenty times as much" as Soviet leader Joseph Stalin. During the period of his greatest influence, he traveled extensively in the Soviet Union and abroad and composed numerous works based on his experiences.

In 1926 Pilnyak came into conflict with Soviet officials with the publication of his short story "Povest nepogashennoy luny" ("The Tale of the Unextinguished Moon") in the journal *Novyi mir*. The story concerns the murder of a political figure by surgeons under the direction of a powerful government official, a situation closely paralleling the death of military commander Mikhail Frunze, who died in 1925 after abdominal surgery allegedly dictated by government officials. Despite Pilnyak's introductory disclaimer that the story was not based on "genuine facts and living persons," the issue of *Novyi mir* in which it appeared was quickly withdrawn from circulation and the story was denounced as a "malicious slander on our party." Three years later Pilnyak became the object of a concerted governmental campaign of vilification, ostensibly in response to his publication in Europe of the novel *Krasnoye derevo (Mahogany)*, which was rejected on ideological grounds for publication in the Soviet Union. However, Western critics contend that the campaign against Pilnyak was primarily intended to enforce ideological conformity in the All-Russian Union of Writers, of which Pilnyak was chairman. Attacks on his reputation continued sporadically until 1937, when he was arrested

on charges of being a spy for the Japanese and a Trotskyite. Although circumstances surrounding his death are unclear, it is believed that he was executed shortly thereafter.

In his first novel, *The Naked Year*, Pilnyak established the characteristic style for which he became famous. Fragmentary and plotless, the work has often been described as "not a novel at all," composed as it is of scraps of original narrative, several previously published short stories, newspaper reports, legal documents, genealogical data, philosophical interpolations, statistical tables, folklore, and reflections on Russian culture. Pilnyak's prose style is similarly varied, juxtaposing documentary, lyrical, and naturalistic passages in his depiction of post-revolutionary famine and upheaval. According to Victor Erlich, this style "was designed to serve as a fictional correlative of a profoundly traumatizing historical experience. The manner and the matter, the medium and message, were made to cohere in their very incoherence, with the actual chaos rendered, or approximated, by seeming compositional anarchy." Throughout the novel the Revolution is depicted as a native, peasant uprising against the Western-style bureaucracy imposed on Russia by Peter the Great and perpetuated by his ideological successors. Commentators have observed the ambivalence with which Pilnyak viewed the Revolution, contrasting his support for the movement's indigenous, anarchic elements with his indifference to communism, which he perceived as essentially Western and therefore irrelevant to the problems of Russia. In 1923 he wrote: "Insofar as the Communists are with Russia, I am with them. I realize that the destinies of the Communist party interest me far less than the destinies of Russia. The Communist party is for me but a link in the destiny of Russia."

Pilnyak's preoccupation with the destiny of Russia recurs throughout his works. A related theme, the place of Russia in the conflict between East and West, dominates the novel *Tretya stolitsa*, in which he proclaimed: "A joyless dull sun rises over Russia, which has withdrawn into the steppes—but this is a sunrise, whereas in the West it is the sunset and the blood is thinning out." Nevertheless, Pilnyak remained indifferent to politics, convinced that constants of human nature and struggle for survival were of greater significance than ephemeral political concerns. Images of birth, death, and sexual love pervade his works, with nature and the power of instinct often placed in opposition to civilization and human reason. This dichotomy informs one of Pilnyak's most important works, *Mashiny i volki*, or "Machines and Wolves," which concerns the place of technology in society. Although the novel has traditionally been viewed as an apotheosis of primitivism and instinct, which are contrasted with the dehumanizing aspects of technology, at least one critic has taken issue with this assessment. According to Gary L. Browning, the novel also contains "a convincing reverse scale of values: the forward-looking and reliable machine as contrasted to the ignorant and perfidious wolf." Pilnyak's last important novel, *Volga vpadayet v Kaspiyskoye more (The Volga Falls to the Caspian Sea)*, has been subject to similarly conflicting evaluations. The work, which incorporates a reworked version of the proscribed novel *Mahogany* into the tale of a Soviet dam-building project, has frequently been dismissed by critics as a heavy-handed attempt by Pilnyak to regain favor with the regime. In the words of Max Eastman, "probably no work of art in the world's history was ever completed in more direct violation of the artist's conscience, or with a more unadulterated motive of self-preservation than Pilnyak's *The Volga Falls to the Caspian Sea*." Kenneth R. Brostrom, however, disputes this view, maintaining that the work actually constitutes a serious indictment of official Soviet doctrines. Browning likewise asserts that "Pilnyak in fact displayed uncommon courage in writing this novel," and adds that the novel is furthermore successful as a work of art.

Although Pilnyak's works have received increasing critical attention in recent years, opinion remains divided as to their literary merit. D. S. Mirsky has dismissed Pilnyak as "muddle-headed, fundamentally uncultured, . . . and devoid of ideas," and William A. Drake called him "so prone to imitation that he barely escapes the reproach of plagiarism," while other critics, including Irving Howe, consider him one of the master prose writers of this century. Nevertheless, critics unanimously find Pilnyak an important representative of modernistic trends in world literature, as well as a representative of, and decisive influence on, the literature of his nation and era.

PRINCIPAL WORKS

Bylyo   (short stories)   1920
Goly god   (novel)   1922
   [*The Naked Year*, 1928]
Ivan da Marya   (novel)   1922
Tretya stolitsa   (novel)   1923
Materialy k romanu   (novel)   1924; published in journal
      Krasnaya nov
Tales of the Wilderness   (short stories)   1924
Mashiny i volki   (novel)   1925
Mat' syra zemlya   (novel)   1926
"Povest nepogashennoy luny"   (short story)   1926;
      published in journal *Novyi mir*
   ["The Tale of the Unextinguished Moon" published in
      *The Tale of the Unextinguished Moon, and Other
      Stories*, 1967]
Krasnoye derevo   (novel)   1929
   [*Mahogany*, 1965]
Sobranie sochinenii. 8 vols.   (novels and short stories)
      1929-30
Volga vpadayet v Kaspiyskoye more   (novel)   1930
   [*The Volga Falls to the Caspian Sea*, 1931; also published
      as *The Volga Flows to the Caspian Sea*, 1932]
O'key   (travel essay)   1933
Ivan Moscow   (novel)   1935
Rozhdeniye cheloveka   (novel)   1935
Sozrevaniye plodov   (novel)   1936
The Tale of the Unextinguished Moon, and Other Stories
      (short stories)   1967
Mother Earth, and Other Stories   (short stories)   1968

LEON TROTSKY   (essay date 1923)

[*Considered the principal strategist of the Bolshevik Revolution in Russia, Trotsky was also a brilliant and influential political theorist who contributed thousands of essays, letters, and political*

tracts to the literature of Marxism. Described by Alfred Kazin as "the most brilliant, the most high-minded, the most cultivated of the Russian Communists," he was furthermore a highly regarded historian, biographer, and literary critic whose Literatura i revolyutsia (Literature and Revolution) *is considered a seminal work of Marxist literary theory and criticism. In the following excerpt from that work, Trotsky assesses the artistry and ideology of Pilnyak's works.*]

Pilnyak is a realist and an excellent observer with fresh eyes and a good ear. People and things are not old and worn out for him and always the same, and only thrown into temporary disorder by the Revolution. He takes them in their freshness and uniqueness, that is, alive and not dead, and he seeks support for his artistic order in the disorder of the Revolution which is to him a live and fundamental fact.

In art as well as in politics—and in some respect art is like politics and politics like art, because both are art—a "realist" may look only at what is under his feet, notice only obstacles, minuses, holes, torn boots, broken dishes. Then politics will be in fear, evasive, opportunistic, and art will be petty, eaten with skepticism, episodic. Pilnyak is a realist. The question is only as to the standard of his realism. And a large standard is needed for our time. (pp. 76-7)

"Yes, in a hundred or one hundred and fifty years men will yearn for the present Russia, as for the days of the most beautiful manifestation of the human spirit. . . . But my shoe is torn and I would like to sit abroad in a restaurant and drink a little whisky." (*Ivan and Mary*.) Just as a train of cattle cars, because of the confusion of hands, feet, bagmen and lights, cannot see a road 2,000 versts long, so Pilnyak tells us, because of a torn shoe and because of all the other discordancies and difficulties of Soviet life, one cannot see the historic turn made in these very days. "Seas and plateaus have changed places! For in Russia there is the beautiful agony of birth! For Russia is being divided into economic zones! For in Russia there is life! For the waters are muddy with high floods from the black earth. This *I* know. But *they* see lice in the filth." The question is put with very clear precision. They (the bitter Philistines, the deposed leaders, the offended prophets, the pedants, the stupid ones, the professional dreamers) see only lice and mud, when in truth above this there is also the agony of birth. Pilnyak knows this. Can he limit himself to sighs and convulsions, to physiologic episodes? No, he wants to make one feel birth. This is a great task to himself. But it is not yet time to say that he has solved it.

Pilnyak has no theme because of his fear of being episodic. True, he has a hint of two, three, and even more themes which are drawn in all directions through the texture of the story; but only a hint and without the central pivotal meaning which generally belongs to a theme. Pilnyak wants to show present-day life in its relations and in its movement and he grasps at it in this way and in that, making parallel and perpendicular cross-cuts in different places, because it is nowhere the same as it was. The themes, more truly the theme possibilities, which cross his stories, are only samples of life taken at random, and life, let us note, is now much fuller of subject matter than ever before. But Pilnyak's pivot is not these episodic and sometimes anecdotal subjects. But what? Here is the stumblingblock. The invisible axis (the earth's axis is also invisible) should be the Revolution itself, around which should turn the whole unsettled, chaotic and reconstructing life. But in order that the reader should feel this axis, the author himself must have felt it and at the same time must have thought it through.

When Pilnyak, without knowing at whom he was aiming, hits Zamyatin and other "Islanders" and says that an ant does not understand the beauty of a female statue because it sees nothing but small projections and grooves as it creeps over it, he has spoken to the point and sharply. Every great epoch, whether it is the Reformation or the Renaissance or the Revolution, must be accepted as a whole, and not in sections or in little parts. The masses, with their invincible social instinct, always participate in these movements. In the individual this instinct attains the level of a generalizing reason. But the spiritually mediocre are neither with the one nor the other; they are too individualistic to share in the perceptions of the masses and too undeveloped for a synthesized understanding. Their share is the bumps and grooves on which they bruise themselves with philosophic and aesthetic curses. How is it with Pilnyak in this matter?

Pilnyak scrutinizes very aptly and sharply a section of our life and in this lies his strength, for he is a realist. Beyond this he knows and proclaims this knowledge of his aloud, that Russia is being turned into economic zones, that the beautiful agonies of birth are taking place within her and that in the confusion of lice and curses and bagmen, the greatest transition in history is being accomplished. Pilnyak must know this since he proclaims it aloud. But the trouble is that he only proclaims it, as if he were contrasting these convictions with the vital and cruel actual existence. He doesn't turn his back on revolutionary Russia; on the contrary, he accepts it and even praises it in his own fashion. But he merely says so. He cannot acquit it artistically because he cannot grasp it intellectually. Therefore Pilnyak often willfully breaks the thread of his narrative with his own hands in order to tie the knots himself quickly, end to end, to explain (somehow or other), to generalize (and very badly) and to ornament lyrically (sometimes beautifully and much more often superfluously). Pilnyak tied a great number of such purposeful authors' knots. His whole work is dualistic, sometimes it is the Revolution that is the invisible axis, sometimes, very visibly, it is the author himself who is timidly rotating around the Revolution. Such is Pilnyak today.

As to subject matter, Pilnyak is provincial. He takes the Revolution in its periphery, in its back yards, in the village, and mainly in the provincial towns. His Revolution is a small town one. Still, even such an approach can be vital. It can be even more organic. But to be that you cannot stop at the periphery. You have to find the axis of the Revolution which is neither in the village nor in the district. You can approach the Revolution through the small town, but you cannot have a small town line of vision on it.

A district council of the Soviets—a sled road—"Comrades, help me in"—bast shoes—sheepskins—the waiting line to the Soviet house for bread, for sausages, for tobacco—Comrades, you are the sole masters of the Revolutionary Council and township—oh, sweetheart, you give little, so little! (this in reference to sausages)—it is the last decisive battle—the International—the Entente—international capitalism. . . .

In such bits of discussion, of life, of speeches, of sausages and of anthems, there is something of the Revolution; a vital part of it grasped with a keen eye, but as if in a hurry, as if rushing past. But something is lacking there that would tie these bits together from within. The idea which underlies our epoch is lacking. When Pilnyak pictures a cattle car, you feel the artist in him, the future artist, the potential future artist. But you do not feel the satisfaction which comes from solving contradictions, which is the greatest sign of a work of art. It is just as

perplexing as before, and even more so. Why the train? Why the cattle car, and what have they in them that is of Russia and for Russia? No one asks Pilnyak for an historical analysis of a cattle car in a cross section of life and a cross section of time, or even, what is more, for a prophetic announcement towards which he inclines so futilely himself. But if Pilnyak himself had understood the cattle car and its connection with the course of events, it would have been transmitted to the reader. But at present the foul cattle car moves along without any justification, and Pilnyak, who accepts it, only creates doubt in the reader's mind.

One of Pilnyak's latest works, **"The Snowstorm,"** proves the kind of great writer he is. The meaningless dreary life of the filthy provincial philistine perishing in the midst of Revolution, the prosaic senseless routine of everyday Soviet life, and all this in the midst of the October storm, is painted by Pilnyak not as a unified picture, but as a series of bright spots, of apt silhouettes and clever sketches. The general impression is always the same—a restless dualism.

"Olga thought that a revolution was like a snowstorm—and the people in it were like flakes." Pilnyak thinks the same, not without Blok's influence, who took the Revolution exclusively as an element, and because of his temperament, as a cold element; not as a fire—as a snowstorm, "and the people in it are like snowflakes." But if a revolution is only the might of an unbridled element playing with man, then where do the days of the most beautiful manifestation of the human spirit come in? And if the agonies can be justified, because they are the agonies of birth, *what is it, in fact, that is being born?* If you have no answer to this you will have a torn shoe, lice, blood, snowstorm and even leap-frog, but not revolution.

Does Pilnyak know what is being born from the agonies of Revolution? No, he does not. Certainly he has heard said (how could he not but hear!) but he does not believe it. Pilnyak is not an artist of the Revolution, but only an artistic "fellow-traveler." Will he become its artist? We do not know. But at present he is not. Posterity will talk about "the most beautiful days" of the human spirit. Very well, but what was Pilnyak in those days? Unclear, hazy, dual. Is it not for this reason that Pilnyak is afraid of the events and of the people who define strictly and who give a meaning to what is happening? Often Pilnyak passes the Communist by with respect, a little coldly, sometimes even with sympathy, but he passes him by. You seldom find a revolutionary workman in Pilnyak, and what is more important, the author does not see and cannot see with the latter's eyes the things that are happening. In *The Bare Year* he looks at life with the eyes of his various characters, who are also all "fellow-travelers" of the Revolution, and here is disclosed another remarkable manifestation: the Red Army does not exist for this artist of 1918-1921. How does that happen? The first years of the Revolution were, above all, years of war, and the blood rushed from the heart of the country to the fronts and peripheries, and there for several years it was spilt in great quantities. During those years the workers' vanguard put all its enthusiasm, all its faith in the future, all its renunciation, its clarity of thought, and its will into the Red Army. The urban revolutionary Red Guard at the end of 1917 and the beginning of 1928, in its fight for self-preservation, spread to the front in divisions and battalions. Pilnyak pays no attention to this. The Red Army does not exist for him. That is why the year 1919 is bare for him.

But somehow Pilnyak must answer the question, what is this all for? He must have a philosophy of revolution of his own.

Here is a most alarming disclosure. Pilnyak's philosophy of history is absolutely retrogressional. This artistic "fellow-traveler" reasons as if the road of the Revolution leads backwards, not forwards. Pilnyak accepts the Revolution because it is national, and it is national because it pulls down Peter the Great and resurrects the Seventeenth Century. To him the Revolution is national, because he thinks it retrogressional.

The Bare Year, Pilnyak's principal work, is marked absolutely by this dualism. The basis, the foundation, the ground of it is made up of the snowstorm, of witchcraft, of superstition, of wood sprites, of those sects which live in the same state of ages ago, and for whom Petrograd means nothing. On the other hand, in passing, "the factory became resurrected" owing to the activity of groups of provincial workers. "Is there not a poem here, a hundred-fold greater than the resurrection of Lazarus?"

The city is robbed in the year 1918-1919, and Pilnyak hails this, because it suddenly appears that even he has "no use for Petrograd." On the other hand, still in passing, the Bolsheviks, the men in leather jackets, are "the pick of the flabby and uncouth Russian people. In leather jackets—you can't dampen them. This we know, this we want; this we have decided, and no turning back." But Bolshevism is the product of a city culture. Without Petrograd there would have been no selection from the "uncouth people." The witches' rites, the folk-songs, the age-old words are the foundation. But the "Gviu, the Glavbum, the Guvuz! Oh, what a blizzard! How stormy it is! How good it is!" It is very good, but ends do not meet, and that is not so good.

Indeed, Russia is full of contradictions and of the most extreme contradictions at that. Side by side with sorcerers' incantations is the Glavbum. How the little literary men turn up their noses contemptuously at this new syllabic formation, and Pilnyak repeats: "Guvuz, Glavbum . . . how nice!" In these unusual temporary words—temporary as a camp, or as a bonfire on a river bank (for a camp is not a house and a bonfire is not a hearth)—Pilnyak sees reflected the spirit of his times. "How nice!" It is good that Pilnyak sees this. But how shall one deal with the city which the Revolution, though city born, has damaged so heavily? Here lies Pilnyak's failure. He has not decided, either intellectually or emotionally, what he will choose out of the chaos of contradictions. But one must choose. The Revolution has cut time in half. And though in present-day Russia, the sorcerers' incantations exist side by side with the Gviu and the Glavbum, they are not on the same historic plane. The Gviu and the Glavbum, no matter how imperfect, tend forward, while the incantations, no matter how "folklike," are the dead weight of history. The sectarian Donat is splendid. He is a stumpy peasant and a horse-thief with strict rules (he does not drink tea). He, if you please, is not in need of Petrograd. The Bolshevik Archipov is also very fine. He manages the district and at daybreak memorizes foreign words from a book and he is clever and strong and says, "foonction energetically," but what is more important, he himself functions energetically. But in which one of them is the Revolution? Donat belongs to the unhistoric, to the "green" Russia, to the undigested Seventeenth Century. Archipov, on the contrary, belongs to the Twenty-first Century, even though he does not know his foreign words well. If Donat proves the stronger, and if this sedate pious horse-thief carries away both capital and railroad, then it will be the end of the Revolution and at the same time the end of Russia. Time has been cut in two, one-half is living and the other half is dead, and one has to

choose the living half. Pilnyak cannot decide and hesitates to make his choice, and for the sake of conciliation, he puts a Pugachev beard on the Bolshevik Archipov. But these are all theatricals. We have seen Archipov—he shaves.

The sorcerer Egorka says: "'Russia is wise in herself. The German is clever, but his mind is foolish . . .'. 'And how about the Karl Marxes?' one asks. 'He is a German,' I say, 'and therefore a fool.'—and Lenin?—'Lenin,' I say, 'is a peasant, a Bolshevik, and you must be communists . . .'." Pilnyak himself is hiding behind the sorcerer Egorka, and it is very disturbing that when he speaks for the Bolsheviks he speaks openly and when he speaks against the Bolsheviks, it is in the half-witted tongue of a sorcerer. What has he that is deeper and more real? Might not this "fellow-traveler" change at one of the stations into the train going the other way!

The political danger here produces an immediate artistic one. If Pilnyak should insist on resolving the Revolution into peasant revolts and peasant life—it would mean a further simplifying of his artistic methods. Even now Pilnyak does not present a picture of the Revolution, but only its base and background. He has laid on the base with good, bold strokes, but what a pity if the master should decide that the base is the whole picture. The October Revolution is an urban one, a Petrograd and Moscow one. "The Revolution is still going on," Pilnyak remarks in passing. The entire future work of the Revolution will be directed towards the industrializing and modernizing of our economy, towards making more precise the processes and methods of reconstruction in all fields, towards uprooting the idiocy of village life, towards making human personality more complex and enriching it. The proletarian revolution can be technically and culturally completed and justified only through electrification, and not through a return to the candle, through the materialistic philosophy of a working optimism and not through woodland superstitions and stagnant fatalism. It would be too bad if Pilnyak should want to become the poet of the candle with the pretensions of a revolutionist! This, of course, is no political harm—no one would think of dragging Pilnyak into politics—but a most real and genuine artistic danger. The fault lies in an historic approach, which comes from a false point of view and from a crying dualism. This results in a deviation from the most important aspects of reality, and in a reduction of everything to the primitive, to the socially barbaric, to the further roughening of artistic methods, to naturalistic excesses, insolent but not courageous, for they are not carried to the end. Further on, before you know it, it will lead to mysticism and to mystic hypocrisy (as per the passport of a romanticist), which is the complete and final death.

Even now Pilnyak shows his romanticist passport every time he is in difficulty. This is especially true when he has to show his acceptance of the Revolution, not in vague and ambiguous terms, but quite clearly. Then he makes immediately (in the manner of Andrey Biely) a typographical recession of several quads and in quite a new tone announces: Do not forget, please, that I am a romanticist. Drunkards very frequently have to display great solemnity, but also sober people have often to pretend that they are drunk to escape from difficult situations. Does not Pilnyak belong to the latter? When he insistently calls himself a romanticist and asks that this should not be forgotten, does not the frightened realist who is lacking horizon speak in him? The Revolution is not at all a torn boot, plus romanticism. The art of the Revolution does not at all consist in not seeing the truth or in transforming the stern reality by an effort of the imagination into the vulgarity of the "legend in the making" for oneself, and for one's own use. The psychology of "the legend in the making" is contrary to the Revolution. With it, and with its mysticism and its mystifications, began the counter-revolutionary period which came after 1905. (pp. 78-88)

For all the significance and freshness of Pilnyak's manner, his mannerisms because they are frequently imitative, are troublesome. It is difficult to understand how Pilnyak could have fallen into artistic dependence on Biely, and on Biely's worst sides at that. There is the tiresome subjectivism which takes the form of frequently repeated nonsensical lyrical interpositions; the rabid and irrational literary argumentation which swings back and forth from ultra-realism to unexpected psycho-philosophical discourses; the arrangement of the text in typographic terraces; the unrelated quotations which are brought in by mechanical association; all of which are unnecessary, boresome and imitative. But Andrey Biely is cunning. He covers the holes in his teaching with a lyrical hysteria. Biely is an Anthroposophist, he acquired wisdom from Rudolph Steiner, he kept vigil in the German mystic temple in Switzerland, he drank coffee and ate sausages. And as his mystic philosophy is meager and pitiful, a half sincere (hysterical) charlatanism and a charlatanism strictly according to the dictionary have crept into his literary methods, for the sake of covering this up—and the farther he advances, the more this is true. But why should Pilnyak find this necessary, or can it be that Pilnyak is also preparing to teach us the tragi-consoling philosophy of redemption . . .? Does not Pilnyak take the world as it is in its corporeality and value it for that? Why, then, this dependence on Biely? Evidently, like a curved mirror, it reflects Pilnyak's inner need of a synthetic picture of the Revolution. The gaps in Pilnyak's spiritual grasp cause his weakness for Biely, the verbal decorator of spiritual failures. But for Pilnyak, this is a road downward, and it would be good for him if he could throw off the semi-buffoonish manner of the Russian Steinerite, and would move upward on his own road. (pp. 88-9)

Pilnyak is a young writer, but, none the less, he is not a youth. He has entered the most critical age, and his great danger lies in a premature and sudden venerability. He hardly ceased to be promising when he became an oracle. He writes like an oracle; he is ambiguous, he is obscure, he hints like a priest, he instructs, though really it is he who needs to study and to study very hard, because his ends are not socially or artistically correlated. His technique is unstable and uneconomical, his voice breaks, his plagiarisms strike the eye. Perhaps all these are the inevitable ailments of growth, but there must be one condition—no venerability. Because if self-satisfaction and pedantry lurk behind the broken voice, then, even his big talent will not save him from an inglorious end. (p. 90)

> *Leon Trotsky, "The Literary 'Fellow-Travelers' of the Revolution," in his* Literature and Revolution, *translated by Rose Strunsky, 1925. Reprint by The University of Michigan Press, 1960, pp. 56-115.*

D. S. MIRSKY (essay date 1926)

[*Mirsky was a Russian prince who fled his country after the Bolshevik Revolution and settled in London. While in England, he wrote two important and comprehensive histories of Russian literature,* Contemporary Russian Literature *(1926) and* A History of Russian Literature *(1927). In 1932, having reconciled himself to the Soviet regime, Mirsky returned to the U.S.S.R. He continued to write literary criticism, but his work eventually ran afoul of Soviet censors and he was exiled to Siberia. He disappeared in 1937. In the following excerpt, Mirsky briefly surveys Pilnyak's*

novels and short stories to 1924, offering a highly disapproving evaluation of these works.]

[Boris Pilnyak] began writing before the Revolution (1915), but his early work is unoriginal and reflects various influences—most of all, Bunin's. In 1922 appeared his "novel" *The Bare Year,* which created something of a sensation by its subject-matter and by its new manner. This novel is not a novel at all: the non-narrative tendency of modern Russian prose reaches in it its high-water mark. It is rather a symphony unfolded along laws invented by the author and purporting to be a vast panorama of Russia in the throes of Revolution and civil war. The principal literary influence discernible in it is that of Bely's *Petersburg.* Like *Petersburg,* it is, first of all, a piece of historical philosophy: the only real character in the book is Russia, Russia as an elemental force and an historical entity. The Revolution to Pilnyak is the rising of the mass of peasants and lower classes against the un-Russian polity of the Petersburg Empire. *The Bare Year* was followed by *Ivan da Maria . . . , The Third Metropolis . . . ,* and numerous shorter "stories" which may all be described in the same terms. The "novels" and "stories" of Pilnyak may be viewed as higher political journalism which has taken the form of a musical fugue. Unfortunately Pilnyak is too muddle-headed, fundamentally uncultured (in spite of a veneer of "Symbolist" culture), and devoid of ideas for his conceptions of Russian history to have any intrinsic interest. His manner, largely a further development of Bely's, is, however, in the details his own: it is based on vast sweeping panoramas and mass effects with a wealth of historical allusion and the deliberate utilization of "intersecting planes," so that the line of narrative (if it may be called narrative) is constantly broken abruptly and taken up at another point, geographically and constructively. He even goes so far as to quote, in the interest of "intersection" and "disjointure," passages from other people's books: *The Third Metropolis* contains long quotations from *The Gentleman from San Francisco* and from a story by Vsevolod Ivanov. As a whole, Pilnyak's manner is a complete impasse and is little more than a curio. His "novels" would be sorry stuff if he did not possess a genuine gift of vivid, realistic painting, which produces refreshing islands in the barren waste of his historical speculations. The chapter of *The Bare Year*—"Train No. 58"—describing travel in Soviet Russia in 1919, is an admirable example of his crude, unsweetened, and outspoken naturalism. The figure of Xenia Ordynina in *Ivan da Maria,* a girl of the gentry who has become an agent of the Cheka, and commits the worst cruelties on a basis of sexual perversion ("the Revolution," she says, "is all permeated with sex for me"), is a gruesome and convincing, though by no means attractive, figure. Pilnyak has been in England (in 1923) and written a book of *English Tales . . . ,* but the least said of them, the better—they are simply incredibly silly. (pp. 309-10)

> *D. S. Mirsky, "The New Prose," in his* Contemporary Russian Literature: 1881-1925, *Alfred A. Knopf, 1926, pp. 281-315.*

WILLIAM A. DRAKE (essay date 1928)

[*Drake was an American journalist, translator, and critic who served as foreign editor of the* New York Herald Tribune *literary supplement from 1924 to 1927. He was also an adaptor of European plays, including Franz Werfel's* Schweiger *(1923). In the following excerpt Drake responds to Leon Trotsky's analysis of Pilnyak's works (see essay dated 1923), discussing Pilnyak's expression of his political perspective through his fiction.*]

In that fiercely biased criticism of the writers of Soviet Russia, *Literatura i Revolutzia,* Leon Trotzky severely arraigns Boris Pilniak upon many counts of political and artistic evasion. Trotzky's accusations are, to be sure, dogmatic, and he presses them with an emphasis which rather engages our sympathies for his unfortunate subject than seduces our judgment against him. But his objections, in the main, are well founded. There is cause for the esthetic apprehension which admirers of the Russian genius feel in contemplating this stuttering verbal cyclone; and there is cause for Trotzky's political chagrin. And thus it appears that the most conspicuous member of the little band who have lately arisen to express, in their fiction, the character and ideals of Soviet Russia, is, in fact, not a Bolshevist innovator at all, but a realist properly stemming from the main stream of the Russian classic tradition; that, far from being a force of astounding originality, he is so prone to imitation that he barely escapes the reproach of plagiarism; and that he is fundamentally so conservative in his political instincts that the most acute publicist of the Revolution openly warns him lest the logical development of his present attitudes should ultimately set him against the very Russia which he now celebrates as an infant titan of prodigious birth and limitless destiny.

Trotzky's premise is, of course, dictated by the urgent political necessities of the new State. Trotzky is a communist and a politician. He sees his nation at the first triumph of a social movement as tremendous as the Reformation, with its ultimate fate still suspended precariously in the balance, and menaced by the armed hand of the very world whose saviour it hopes presently to become. Thus, in the new nation's perilous infancy, he would press every force into the service of its vindication and its survival. In the Russia of Trotzky, there is no time now for art; there is justification only for actively constructive forces. While this situation remains, those who will not lend their art to the service of propaganda, or who permit any reservations to obstruct their complete allegiance to the communist ideal, are simply traitors. But Pilniak is neither a communist nor a politician, nor yet even a pamphleteer. He is an artist, excited by the rapture of being alive in the epoch of such a tremendous event, and very much engaged by the singular contrasts which it has produced. He exults at beholding Russia in what appears to him as "a beautiful agony of birth." Yet one feels that he does so, not from conviction, but merely because he is of the Revolutionary generation, because the spectacle pleases him esthetically, and because there is nothing else to do about it. Certainly he is not a Bolshevist. The Workers' Revolution interests him but little, and it is clear that he does not understand all that it signifies. At heart, Pilniak remains, as he has always been, an instinctive anarchist.

The October Revolution is a workers' movement, localized in the great cities, Moscow and Petrograd. But to this major, identifying, communist phase of the Revolution, Pilniak is indifferent. To him, its colors are drab, its excesses commonplace. Like all the great realists of the past, Pilniak believes that it is only in the heart of the peasant that the artist or the seer shall ever find Russia. So, in all his tales, he writes of the peasants, of rural communities, of rustic affairs, envisaging the Revolution, not as a modern social movement, but as a logical culmination of the hundreds of peasant revolts which in turn gave their martyrs to the gallows and to the Siberian mines and their paragraphs to the dark annals of the Empire. The People alone exist for Boris Pilniak; the People who, try as the local Soviets may to fit them into the ordered scheme of the System, remain Oblomovs, serene and amiable, but utterly uncomprehending and indifferent. (pp. 176-78)

Pilniak's two earliest collections of short stories, *Bylyo* and *Ivan da Marya,* contain the germs of all that later came to flourish in outlandish bloom in his two great epics of the Revolution, *Goly God* and *Mashiny i Volki.* One notes at once that Pilniak writes as an observer of these events, and not as a participant; that his human and esthetic sympathies are with the peasants, and not with the workers; that, although he supports the Revolution, he is at heart an anarchist, and far removed from the Bolshevist point of view. One notes that, as a mocking-bird of literature, he makes Stevenson appear, by contrast, as a very zealot of originality. He has borrowed the dialectical virtuosity of his style from Aleksei Remisov; its typographical idiosyncrasies and its pseudophilosophical accent from Andrey Biely. His skepticism derives from Chekhov, and his treatment of sex from Rozanov and Aleksei Tolstoy. His debt to Ivan Bunin is likewise great. His major fiction is one long variation of Biely's great tour-de-force, the novel *Petrograd.* It represents, as Prince Mirsky somewhat cruelly remarks, "a sort of epitome of modern Russian fiction, a living literary history."

These allegiances, as Trotzky complains, link Pilniak to a past which a proper Revolutionary should have long since repudiated; but the complete divorcement which the Red prophet requires is unthinkable. Pilniak, in company with those of his contemporaries whom Trotzky patronizingly terms the "fellow-travelers" of the Revolution, has repudiated the whole technique and a large portion of the spirit of classic Russian fiction. He has gone artistically as far to the Left as it is possible for him to go, without becoming a mere eccentric or a downright propagandist. One feels that he has done these things, not for a political ideal, but because he has seen the necessities of Russian art alter with the rending of the Russian social fabric; and, from the remoteness of another land and language, we can better applaud this motive than its alternative. For the Volga and the Neva still flow to the sea as before the cataclysm, and the Kremlin lifts its selfsame Byzantine towers above the mummy of Lenin as above the catafalques of the Tsars. There is a point beyond which a literature cannot cut itself off from its main stream without depriving itself of the invigorating sap of the national substance. Trotzky would designate that point as the October Revolution, but Trotzky is a statesman. Pilniak, the artist, sets it at about 1904, thus linking the present revolutionary epoch with the revolutionary epoch which gave it birth. And in the same way, in his mind and in his art, he links the Workers' Revolution with the peasant struggles of two hundred years, insisting that the spirit which found its ultimate vindication in the October uprising is not as singular or as modern as Trotzky pretends, but represents the explosion of long accumulated resentments and the consummation of an ancient passion for freedom. (pp. 179-81)

Goly God . . . is a description of the famine year of 1918-1919. The scene is a small provincial city, Ordynin, which takes its name from the principal family of the place. There we see, mixed in a frantic medley and united alone by their common suffering, all the elements of the new Russia—the Ordynins, decayed and divided, going their several ways to destruction; the peasants, "still living in the Stone Age," their eyes turned in indolent adoration toward the past and utterly dazed and helpless before the sudden shifting of immediate events; the Bolshevist commissars, the "Leather Jackets," brusque, active, and arrogantly confident of the future. We see them all as Fate has molded them, in their fundamental separateness, the superstition of the peasants contrasting the materialism of their new masters, anarchy contrasting communism, and the two finding a common basis only in death, starvation, drunkenness, and sexual excess.

There is no plot, no unity of place or time, almost no coherence, in the novel. The protagonists are the classes—the peasants, the workers, and the bourgeoisie—who may be represented, from time to time, by any of their members. The theme is the contrast of these classes in the flux of the new order, and the action moves hither and there, into the present, the past, and the future, losing itself and finding itself again, or not finding itself at all, as chance and its creator will it—even as, in the bare year, those derelicts of life passed one another and were lost to view, like ships in a troubled night. Like the society which it annotates, the novel is tortured, diffuse, and unfinished. It ends without a true conclusion, and on the title page of the book appears the legend: "Volume One," as if to emphasize the necessarily unfinished state of this picture of a transitional society.

It is improbable that a second volume of *Goly God* was ever intended. Yet *Mashiny i Volki* appears as a direct continuation of the earlier narrative, inasmuch as it presents another exactly similar segment of the same society, at a further point of its development to the new order. The Kolomna of *Mashiny i Volki* is very like the Ordynin of *Goly God,* and its people are identical. The style is as violent and as vivid, and the abrupt transitions are but hardly relieved by the artifice of interjected notations from the supposed diary of a simple local historian, who bears the strangely significant name of Ivan Alexandrovich Nepomnyashtchy. The unfinished effect is stressed by the author's use of cross-references throughout the text and of notations for chapter-headings, and by his repeated designation of portions of the book as "fragments."

The story, or rather, the loosely connected anthology of episodes which does service for a plot, centers about the erection of a factory in the town by a Bolshevist commissariat. Pilniak sees this transition from peasant retrogression to Bolshevist progress as a struggle between the wolves and the machines, and as a resurrection more wonderful than that of Lazarus. "Our whole Revolution," he makes one of his characters say, "is elemental, like the wolves." It is clear to which side his sympathy tends, but it is also clear which the more definitely arouses his admiration. In this struggle, the wolf must needs be crushed and the machine emerge triumphant; but out of the Russian past, out of the past of blood and color, the wolf-cry of the great Piotr is still heard in the land. And it will take more than a Soviet manifesto to stifle that cry, or yet to misdirect the impulse of disinterested art in a writer whose instincts are fundamentally as strong and pure as those of Boris Pilniak. (pp. 181-83)

> *William A. Drake, "Boris Pilniak," in his* Contemporary European Writers, *The John Day Company, 1928, pp. 176-83.*

GEORGE SOLOVEYTCHIK   (essay date 1928)

[*In the following excerpt from an introduction to* The Naked Year, *Soloveytchik discusses the novel's literary merits.*]

The main feature of [the novel *The Naked Year*] is that it is not a novel at all; it has no plot, it does not endeavour to narrate anything in a consecutive way or deal with any particular sub-

ject. There are traces in it of two or three or even more plots, only jotted down, just hinted at and always left unworked-out, interlacing and somewhat chaotic. They are of secondary importance. The subject-matter is Russia, the Revolution, life in Russia during a ghastly year of terror, civil war and famine. Pilnyak tries to show that life in all its aspects, in its real relation to people and things. For that purpose he makes a number of "cross-sections," cutting into life from various angles and at different points. In using this method of writing, or of making his construction on "intersecting planes," he has resorted to a most ingenious device: could there, indeed, be anything more admirably concise and self-explanatory than such headings as:

> Through the eyes of Andrey
>
> Through the eyes of Natalia
>
> Through the eyes of Irina, etc. . . . .

What does he see through these eyes, what does he show us? Pilnyak is a realist, an excellent observer with a keen eye and a fine ear. He is refreshing too for he finds a new side, a new aspect to everybody and everything. To him people and things are not the old, well-known, worn-out, always the same people and things, only just slightly altered or temporarily upset by the Revolution. He takes them in their newness, in their unrepeatable freshness, as live people and not dead puppets, and the very chaos of the Revolution is to him something alive, something of the foremost importance and of definite artistic value. But a realist is always bound to see the negative side first, and sometimes only the negative side. Whether in politics or in art, the realist is handicapped by the very virtues of his realism; he is always looking for trouble, his eye as well as his frame of mind is directed towards discovering the defects rather than the advantages of people, things or even historical processes; his outlook is limited. The scope of an artist's realism, his talent, must be great indeed, to endow his creation with real artistic value. Pilnyak is not a champion of the Revolution, he is not its poet, but merely an artistic "poputchik" of it, a fellow-traveller. And that is why throughout his work there is this dual and alternating acceptance and rejection of the Revolution and all with which it is fraught. His book has, so to speak, no centre of gravity, no axis. Is it the Revolution, or its episodes, or the author himself? Pilnyak does not seem capable of making up his mind. Thus the bolsheviks accuse him of having written a book that is definitely one-sided, of looking through the eyes of Irina or Natasha or Andrey, but never through the eyes of, say, Arkhip, or the eyes of "the leather-tunics,"—in fact, of having entirely missed that aspect of the naked year. This accusation does not seem altogether warranted. To me, one of the most striking things in the book is that gradual and complete change of its spirit; in the beginning the author seems full of enthusiasm for the Revolution, this enthusiasm permeates every word of his, and only little by little it vanishes, dissolving in complete hopelessness and utter gloom. Pilnyak does not endeavour just to describe the Revolution; his attempt is far more ambitious, for by means of the written word he tries to translate it on paper in an almost architectural or even sculptural way. But to approach the Revolution from a purely artistic angle is fraught with great difficulties. Taken in its episodes, in its ever-changing and casual manifestations, the Revolution is rather apt to sink to the commonplace, it becomes trivial and insignificant. Yet to the reader this is considerably more interesting and more valuable than if the author were animated by some political idea and the book were reduced to the level of a piece of propaganda. For all its deficiencies and dangers, Pilnyak's method of approach results in a picture of life as it really is, and not as a political writer would see it or wish to see it. Thus, the book must be judged by purely literary and human, not political standards. Who but the bolsheviks care about Pilnyak's attitude to integral communism, or his conception of Russian history, or, again, his ideas about God, Karl Marx, Lenin, sex, etc. etc.? In Soviet Russia, the amazing aphorism of one of his characters, a sexually perverted person who says, "I feel that the whole revolution smells of sexual organs," created great popularity for Pilnyak. On the other hand, his wavering attitude towards the Revolution earned him some sharp criticisms from various communist leaders. To the reader outside Russia all this is a matter of comparative indifference. What matters is that Pilnyak is a writer of undoubted literary talent. His manner is often irritating, his style is rough and his "cross-sections" are in many places bewildering. There is the further encumbrance of a multitude of new words and incomprehensible abbreviations, now permeating the Russian language in Soviet Russia, together with a whole scale of noises invented by Pilnyak himself. It is a strange, weird, terribly uneven book. But its extreme crudeness never shocks, even the particularly daring passages could hardly be labelled as suggestive or pornographic. In spite of its faults, in spite of its manner, there is something in the book that brings home to the most critical reader the talent of Boris Pilnyak. The many beautiful passages in the book are a proof that whenever Pilnyak has a subject really congenial to him he can rise to the heights attained only by great masters. (pp. 23-7)

> *George Soloveytchik, in a preface to* The Naked Year
> *by Boris Pilnyak, translated by Alec Brown, 1928.*
> *Reprint by AMS Press Inc., 1971, pp. 23-7.*

MARC SLONIM (essay date 1953)

[*Slonim was a Russian-born American critic who wrote extensively on Russian literature. In the following excerpt, he discusses Pilnyak's literary influences, the philosophical basis of his works, and characteristic features of his prose.*]

[Pilniak's] attempts at establishing Symbolist-Populist prose have often been identified with that boldness of style which originated in the revolutionary spirit of his times, and his whims, mannerisms, and stylistic fancies were regarded as typical of a whole generation. The *émigré* critics displayed especial hostility toward this "incomprehensible, chaotic, and altogether horrid scion of Bolshevism."

The truth was that Pilniak did not represent Revolutionary prose or the Revolutionary mentality, and he was not a Communist. His style had been inspired by the Decadents and Symbolists and his ideas and political leanings by the Slavophiles and Populists. Born into a family of middle-class intellectuals with strong Populist leanings, Boris Pilniak (the pseudonym of Boris Vogau) had been greatly influenced by Gogol and Dostoevsky and by Rozanov, Remizov, and Bely. His fragmentary composition, his lack of plots, his "blizzard of words" deliberately let loose in a disorderly way, the use of characters as bearers of concepts, and his philosophizing—all linked him with the pre-Revolutionary tradition.

Until about 1928 Pilniak followed the principles of Bely's "poetic rhythmic prose." He wrote long, involved sentences burdened with incidental propositions, hints, allegorical turns, symbolic allusions, and all sorts of word play. The author's asides or divagations constantly broke the narrative; he con-

versed with the reader or made disclosures about his own techniques; he often interrupted a highly emotional scene by wondering whether this part of the novel really had come off as he had intended it to, or placed quotations from historical documents in the midst of a love dialogue. Like Dos Passos he loved to obstruct his narration with "newsreels"—excerpts from the daily press, the texts of law regulations, and legal documents. *The Naked Year,* or *Cow-Wheat,* and *Machines and Wolves* look like literary jumble-shops: poems in prose, reflections on Russian culture, genealogical trees of the main characters alternate with crude scenes of physical love and dynamic descriptions of staggering adventures. Yet the attentive reader can easily discover a continuous thread running like a rogue's yarn through the fabric. Although the author assembles heterogeneous elements in order to shock and bewilder, the succession of seemingly unrelated episodes and irrelevant digressions falls into a preordained pattern, and one even gets used to Pilniak's vocabulary—a mixture of archaisms and colloquialisms with regional or local expressions.

By the early 1930's Pilniak had given up many of his artifices, but although *The Volga Flows to the Caspian Sea* shows more directness and simplicity and is more readable, it still retains the basic features of his early manner: his rejection of objective narrative, his insistence on the "conventionality" of art, and his own conventions of fragmentary composition, of poetic technique, of intonation and mixed genres.

The underlying philosophy of his work was as eclectic as his style: it is a blend of Nietzsche, Rozanov, and Slavophile aspirations, with a peculiar brand of nationalistic Bolshevism. Pilniak welcomed the Revolution as the end of the artificial "Sanct Peter Burg period" and the recrudescence of seventeenth-century Moscow: "Mosk-va," he maintained, "means dark water." The dark waters (the peasantry) were going to flood the city and engulf the intellectuals and the bureaucrats. The wild primitivism of Revolutionary excesses was simply an outburst of national energies, proclaiming a resumption of a Scythian way of life. The whole system of symbols in *The Naked Year* indicates that famine and anarchy had been necessary to help the Russians rediscover themselves. The huts where bearded peasants live next to their cows, sheep, and pigs, the bonfires ignited by flint-lighters, the villages haunted in winter by hungry wolves, the exploits wherein lust and blood reign supreme—this is the true, primitive, savage Russia of anarchical peasant rebellions, the Russia of Stenka Razin and Pugachev. Wars and epidemics never undermine the physical strength and animal spirits of the people, and the pagan ritual of weddings and christenings go on throughout the country. Pilniak glorifies this bodily might (Blok called it "burning love") in scenes of sexual passion or sheer erotic revelry, and contrasts them with impotent and hypocritical Europe. In *The Third Capital* he writes: "A joyless dull sun rises over Russia, which has withdrawn into the steppes—but this is a sunrise, whereas in the West it is the sunset, and the blood is thinning out."

A sociological emotionalist, Pilniak had no precise political credo: sometimes he talked like a Slavophile of 1840, yet he interpreted the Revolution in terms of peasant anarchism and as a victory of the countryside over the city. This victory also assumed the character of a triumph of the subconscious and irrational over the conscious and rational in man and society. In his *Diary* for 1923 (published in 1924) he said: "In so far as the Communists are with Russia, I am with them. I realize that the destinies of the Communist party interest me far less than the destinies of Russia. The Communist party is for me but a link in the destiny of Russia.'' Yet in *The Naked Year* he identified the Bolsheviks with the city dwellers who wanted to guide the peasants and to channel the anarchical elements of the Rebellion—and glorified the ''men in leather jackets'' (commonly worn by the Communists at that time), since they were the ''steel-hard elite, the select from among the loose-sand Russians.'' They would rule because they had the will to power, the pluck and the strength to lead the primitive popular movement.

Although Pilniak had apparently accepted this situation, he often pointed out the rift between the anti-European Maximalism of the peasants and the planned efforts of the Communists. In *Mother Earth,* one of his best novelettes he depicts a forlorn region beyond the Volga, a region as changeless and dark as the centuries-old forests bounding it. Time has stopped in these villages, and the Communist Nekluyev, who had come there with a group of comrades, finds medieval customs and troglodytic natives who reek of blood and raw pelts. All his efforts to draw closer to them and make them understand the ideas of the Revolution are doomed to failure; they represent the Scythia of the seventeenth century, while he stands for the urban Communism of the twentieth. In none of his later works did Pilniak answer the question he had raised in all his stories of primitive Russia. He seemed to have recognized the mission of the Communists as that of enlightening and organizing the peasants, but at the same time he could not hide his anti-European and anti-rational feelings. He frequently reproached the Communists as ''mechanical rationalists,'' and often pointed to instinct and emotions as the basic elements of human behavior.

In *Spilled Time,* a collection of stories that did not deal with Revolutionary events, Pilniak concentrated on what in his opinion were the psychological constants of the ''game of life'': birth, growth, the struggle for survival, sexual possession, death. Human beings are part of nature, and wisdom lies in obedience to cosmic rhythms, which govern both animal passions and the movements of the stars. Thus nature is opposed to culture, and several tales resulting from Pilniak's extensive travels in Europe, the Far East, and America reflect this point of view clearly. These tales, incidentally, have a strong anti-Western flavor: Eurasia, or the union between Russia and Asia, particularly China, is envisioned as a powerful primeval force that will overwhelm rationalistic and agnostic Occidental Europe.

Pilniak's basic philosophy found its best expression in *The Tale of the Unextinguished Moon* . . . , which depicted the death of Michael Frunze, the Commander-in-Chief of the Red Army, and alluded to Stalin as ''the unbending man of steel.'' The novel deals with one Gavrilov, a Red Army man, who falls ill and is ordered by the central committee of the party to undergo an operation. Gavrilov feels instinctively that he ought to avoid the surgeon's knife. His thoughts on life and death are simple and profound; he reads Tolstoy with great delight, and he likes children; fictional heroes and his own feelings appear to him most real and important. The party machine, however, and the leader who wants Gavrilov to go on the operation table because ''a useful worker ought to be repaired for further functioning'' appear to him mechanical and hostile. Gavrilov, despite all party directives and medical science, dies under the knife—and life goes right on, triumphant over the smug trickery of poor reason. The robots of the party, with all their control boards, telephones, radios, Red guards standing at attention, and faultless aides-de-camp, had not treated Gavrilov as a hu-

man being; he had been no more than a tool to them. (pp. 284-87)

The psychological tales and historical novelettes Pilniak concentrated on after 1928, in the fallacious hope of avoiding the dangerous and slippery topics of Soviet actuality, did not save him from attacks. During the first Five-Year Plan he decided to prove his loyalty to the regime and wrote *The Volga Flows into the Caspian Sea*. . . . His intention was to show the building of a dam as a triumph of man's organized, purposeful activity in overcoming the traditional inertia of Russia and in conquering nature—a typical article of faith in the Communist credo. He even succeeded in drawing a few portraits of Communist enthusiasts, those very ''unbending men in leather jackets.'' But although the chapters on socialist industrialization were written brilliantly and reflected the sweeping dynamism of the period, a significant part of the novel (initially its first drafts), called ''Mahogany,'' revived the old anarchical-Populist tendencies of the writer. It depicted a somnolent provincial town deeply entangled in the mores of the ancient past: even the members of the Communist opposition talked and acted like Old Believers or the holy innocents of seventeenth-century Moscow. The heroes of the tale, two brothers who travel about in quest of antique mahogany furniture which they sell at a great profit, bore a resemblance to characters from Gogol's *Dead Souls*. The whole tone of ''Mahogany'' suggested Pilniak's doubts about whether the Asiatic indolence, the medieval ways of life, the whimsicality of old-fashioned eccentrics could ever be changed. It also implied that Communism was simply a façade for Byzantine rigidity, Muscovite isolationism, and national self-withdrawal.

The fact that ''Mahogany'' had been brought out by an *émigré* publisher in Berlin provoked a violent campaign against Pilniak, led by proletarian critics. He was expelled from all literary organizations, and his works were branded as examples of ''reactionary philosophy.'' It was not so much his anarchical tendencies that aroused the ire of Communist ideologists as it was his anti-social and anti-historical attitude, which glorified the ''constants of human nature'': what Pilniak was really concerned about were the organic processes of birth, love, and death, and his best pages dealt with solitude, sex, the torment and dread of annihilation, and the feeling of oneness with nature. He always intimated that beyond social upheavals there was something fixed, something immutable in the human heart, and that the downfall of emperors, the tumult of mobs, and the rebirth of society cannot alter man's basic sufferings and conflicts. (p. 287)

> *Marc Slonim, "Literary Trends of the NEP Period,"*
> *in his* Modern Russian Literature: From Chekhov to
> the Present, *Oxford University Press, 1953, pp.*
> *269-93.*

IRVING HOWE (essay date 1968)

[*A longtime editor of the leftist magazine* Dissent *and a regular contributor to* The New Republic, *Howe is one of America's most highly respected literary critics and social historians. In the following excerpt, Howe discusses Pilnyak's short fiction.*]

Among the Russian writers of the 'twenties few can have been more talented than Boris Pilnyak. . . . Though a literary modernist experimenting with abrupt narrative transitions, cryptic philosophical intermezzos, and a style that has been described as a ''blizzard of words,'' Pilnyak also had something in him of the ancient tribal bard. He was a marvelous storyteller, a spellbinder, an enchanted rhetorician. The surface of his fiction deals with revolutionary Russia, but beneath it, like a land buried under lava, there is always traditional sluggish Russia. Pilnyak is a romantic in that he is fascinated by experiences drawn to their breaking point, situations of extreme pressure and revelation; but also a romantic in that he likes to set his stories against a background of peasant timelessness, primitive survivals. (p. 72)

As a writer Pilnyak is obsessed with the contrasts between the rhythm of a generation trapped in a historical cataclysm and the larger rhythms of the life of an entire people. A man may suppose his life to be driven by conscious purposes, but in reality he is acting out part of a centuries-long national drama. Shattering change is set against flat changelessness. In stories like **"The Cheshire Cheese"** and **"Wormwood"** the Revolution is at the stark foreground, but behind it sweeps the anarchic fury of the Russian peasants.

Pilnyak believed that the Revolution, far from being the proletarian uprising that Lenin and Trotsky supposed, was actually an outburst of long-suppressed primitive Russian energies. As it now seems, he was quite as wrong as the Bolsheviks, for in reality neither the peasants nor the proletariat triumphed in Russia. But from a literary perspective it hardly matters that Pilnyak was wrong, since his point of view enabled him to dramatize the experience into which he had been thrust. Better than he realized, Pilnyak's stories show the ordeal of a people at a point where tradition has been ruptured, a culture contorted with the agonies of rebirth, and men enslaved to a masquerade of historical consciousness.

Some of his stories are simply magnificent. There is **"The Bielkonsky Estate,"** which describes the leave-taking of an old landowner, stoical and dignified, and his replacement by a nervous peasant leader: one feels as if one were thrust into the eye of a maelstrom. There is **"Above the Ravine,"** a virtuoso piece composed by Pilnyak at the age of twenty-one, in which he describes the life and courtship of a pair of eagles: a story written as if the earth were unpeopled and God were looking down upon the uncomplicated savagery of creation. There is **"The Tale of the Unextinguished Moon,"** which Pilnyak wrote in 1927: a tense and austere narrative about the death of a beloved Red Army commander whom the party leadership mercilessly orders to undergo a needless operation. When the story first appeared, it became immediately clear that it was based on an actual incident, the death of Mikhail Frunze, Trotsky's successor as Commissar of War, and that the character ordering the operation is Stalin, whom Pilnyak does not name but keeps describing as "the man who never stoops." It is one of the most terrifying pieces of prose ever written in the Soviet Union, and no amount of later obeisance—Pilnyak would not prove himself a hero in the 'thirties—could remove the sentence his boldness in publishing this story had surely brought upon him. In 1937, during the purges, he was shot. But now we can see that he was one of the prose masters of this century, as great a writer of short fiction as Isaac Babel. (pp. 72-3)

> Irving Howe, "The Continuity of Russian Voices,"
> in Harper's Magazine, Vol. 236, No. 1412, January,
> 1968, pp. 69-74.

ROBERT A. MAGUIRE (essay date 1968)

[Maguire is an American educator and critic specializing in Russian literature. In the following excerpt, he offers a general characterization of Pilnyak's works and a detailed analysis of Mater-

ialy k romanu. In an unexcerpted portion of his essay, Maguire discusses a critical article written in 1922 by Alexander Voronskii, an influential Bolshevik critic and editor of the journal Krasnaya nov (Red Virgin Soil). According to Maguire, Voronskii's article combined criticism of Pilnyak's unorthodox political views with assurance that "sincere evidence of a desire to change would bring sympathetic understanding and support." Maguire speculates that Pilnyak may subsequently have attempted to produce politically acceptable works, "or at least tried to create the impression that he was doing so," as his 1924 novel Materialy k romanu "looks like a deliberate attempt to court Voronskii's favor."]

Boris Pil'nyak is one of those writers who miss greatness but who alter the literary history of their country in a decisive way. He lacked a real gift for fiction—an incandescent vision capable of fusing good intentions, prodigious reading, and keen powers of observation into compelling art. He was instead a borrower, an eclectic, the diligent pupil of Belyi, Remizov, and Bunin. Yet his lack of originality determined his importance, for he adapted the techniques and strategies of his teachers to the new themes of Revolution and Civil War. Through him, they took on a respectability that they could no longer command by themselves; and because he was extremely popular and widely imitated during the early twenties, they left a deep and lasting impression on the new literature.

He began around 1915 as an allegorist in the "primitive" vein, which writers had been mining since the turn of the century in rebellion against reason, humanism, and esthetics. The cult of violence and death (Andreev), of sex and instinctual will (Artsybashev), of children, savages, and outlaws (Sologub, Gumilyov, Gor'kii), the attempt to destroy beauty with nonsense, dissonance, ugliness, formlessness, or artlessness—these had been but a few of the ways in which the theme displayed itself. Pil'nyak's palette in the early stories was subdued by comparison, his vision on the whole lyrical and benevolent, and his technical resources ruthlessly conventional. All these stories proceeded from the idea that nature knows best. **"An Entire Life" (Tselaya zhizn'),** for example, tells of two birds who mate, release their young into the world without regrets, and finally separate when the male can no longer provide. Sentiment, loyalty, even habit—the bases of human marriage— have no place in this superior realm of sheer instinct. **"A Year of Their Life" (God ikh zhizni)** unites the whole world in one vast procreative urge: the hunter Demid mates with Marina in the spring and fills her with child; a year later Makar, the bear who is Demid's constant companion, comes to maturity and goes off in search of a mate of his own. What is embarrassing in paraphrase does not come off at all badly in context. Pil'nyak works here in a quiet, subdued way with his animals and naturemen and does not overstate the simple and obvious moral of his tales—virtues that he unfortunately let atrophy as he went on.

But these excursions into exoticism were merely exercises; his ambitions reached higher. **"The Snows" (Snega),** another story from the same period, foreshadowed the direction they would take. Here the hero is an intellectual who has wearied of civilization and the deceptive importunings of the mind, and has finally unlocked the secret of life through a liaison with a simple peasant woman. "Yes," he muses, "a year closer to death, a year further away from birth"—that is all there is to it. His former mistress comes to understand this, even though she cannot accept it. "There have been hundreds of religions, hundreds of ethics, esthetics, science, philosophical systems; and everything has changed and is still changing, and only one thing does not change: that everything living—man, rye, a mouse—is born, breeds and dies. . . .''

The conflict which is merely implied in most of the other early stories is here stated outright: instinct versus intellect, nature versus civilization, chaos versus logic. It remained Pil'nyak's characteristic theme, no matter how intricately he embroidered it. Usually, however, he grants his heroes no such blissful repose in the arms of their discovery. He prefers to catch them at the moment when they have become aware of the conflict within them, and then watch it tear them apart. For man is both agent and victim, pulled by the competing claims of intellect, which wills toward consciousness and seeks it in a self-definition through system and order, and instinct, which is formless and timeless, and constitutes the ground of all being. Hence the paradox, which Pil'nyak contains in the recurring image of the caged wolf, that man builds higher and higher barriers to shut out what he yearns after. Nearly always, man tries to jump the walls of his self-made prison, but the serene and ordered life behind them has sapped his vitality. Once outside, he can never return; he has left all illusion behind. This is the truth that those impassioned seekers, the men of science, discover in the story **"Zavoloch'e."** Their journey to the Arctic is a journey back into time in quest of man's primeval state. But they find there only an endless universe of cold and ice without dimension. Their minds shout out across the empty spaces that planlessness must have a plan; but only the gelid wind replies. This is the answer to their quest. They cannot accept it, but they know it is true.

For his longer stories, Pil'nyak works this conflict into a whole cosmology. The aboriginal idyll now lodges in a vast and mysterious realm called "Asia," or "East," or "Mongol." Ranged against it is the world that man has created in order and symmetry, with urban machine civilization the pinnacle: this is called "Europe." There is nothing in the universe which does not serve one or the other. Each realm has agents carrying on ceaseless sabotage. Each has an army that wages tireless warfare with the other. Each also has its internal emigrés, men who look longingly at the other world, yet who do not really wish to leave their own; and it is on this divided and guilt-ridden souls that Pil'nyak focuses his gaze, watching the emotional balance tip now one way, now the other. It was when he began to set the history of Russia, particularly the recent history, into this cosmology that he found his true voice and won his fame. The Revolution of 1917 became, in his works, the decisive and final encounter in this vast cosmic struggle. It is the subject of his first novel **Bare Year (Golyi god . . .).** (pp. 101-04)

For Pil'nyak, the Revolution is not the conflict of proletariat and bourgeoisie, but of East, represented by the peasantry, and West, represented by urban Russia. And what of the Bolsheviks? The peasants cannot even pronounce the word "revolution" correctly; but they understand that it bears no resemblance to what the Bolsheviks claim to be doing. "Beat the Communists," they shout. "We're for the re-lo-voo-shun (*revolyukhu*)!" For the Bolsheviks, as the servants of a "scientific" ideology, are merely defending, under another name, that whole structure of civilization which true resolution has risen up to topple. Some of Pil'nyak's choicest sarcasm is reserved for them:

> In the Ordynin house, in the Executive Committee (there were no geraniums gracing these windows), people in leather jackets, Bolsheviks, would assemble upstairs. Here they were,

in leather jackets, every one of them erect, a lusty leather lad, every one of them sturdy, curls spilling down the back of his neck from under his cap, skin pulled taut over cheekbones, folds at the corners of the mouth, sharp-creased movements. The pick of Russia's soft-boned and misshapen folk. In leather jackets—there's no getting at them. Here's what we know, here's what we want, here's where we're put—and that's that.

They are actually counter-revolutionaries. But their prideful intellects must pay: Asia triumphs, sweeping everything away, even the peasantry; and the final vision opens up an austere and eternal Paradise, which is undefiled by man's presumptuous sin of mind:

> The forest stands austere, pillar-like, and against it the snowstorm hurls itself in fury. Night. . . . New, ever new snow-furies hurl themselves against the forest pillars, wailing, screeching, shouting, howling a female howl of frenzied rage, falling dead, and behind them more, ever more furies rush on, never relenting, ever increasing, like the head of a snake—two for every one cut off—but the forest stands like Il'ya Muromets.

Pil'nyak's universe was constructed from ready-made materials. To see the Revolution as a spontaneous upwelling of the peasantry was to express a commonplace of the time. As Blok said: "Bolshevism and the Revolution exist neither in Moscow nor in Petersburg. Bolshevism—the real, Russian, devout kind—is somewhere in the depths of Russia, perhaps in the village. Yes, most likely there. . . ." "Asia" called up a thousand years of history, first recorded as the chroniclers turned their eyes eastward on the hostile nomads of the far-reaching steppe; then battened into myth by the ingress of the Mongols; constantly renewed by the eastward-running expansion of Russian trade and military power; ornamented by the discovery, toward the end of the nineteenth century, of the philosophies of China and India and the literatures of Persia and Turkey; animated more recently by new religious enthusiasms that sprang from the rediscovery of Orthodoxy, the fascination with anthroposophy, and the authority of Vladimir Solov'yov. One of its offshoots, the two-Russias theme—"Asia" or "Europe," village or city, soil or salon—had absorbed intellectuals for a century or more. Pil'nyak's version owed most to the so-called Eurasians: in its contempt for the Russian intelligentsia as products of Western civilization; the rejection of Europe not so much for itself as for its irrelevance to Russian problems; the denial that capitalism (a European invention) could contribute to Russia's development; the interpretation of the Revolution as a cleansing, renewing event; and the assertion that Russians are neither Europeans nor Asians, but a mixture of both, or Eurasians.

Pil'nyak pulled these familiar ideas together into a single view of the world and set them in a new literary context. He rooted the themes of Easternism and primitivism specifically in the peasantry and recast the two-Russias theme in terms of the social conflicts of his time. The result was a version of the revolutionary experience that struck an immediate response in the twenties and has haunted Russian writers ever since. (pp. 104-06)

Materials for a Novel tells of the rise of industry in Russia. Like many other twentieth-century works with industrial themes—Gorkii's *The Artamonov Business,* for instance, or Leonov's *Road to Ocean*—it covers a large expanse of time, beginning with the first tentative efforts to tame nature and ending with a glimpse of a future ruled by the machine. Somewhat in the manner of Upton Sinclair, Pil'nyak treats his setting (Kolomna and environs) with such care and detail as to create a sense of documentary reality. He focuses on two periods of violent social upheaval in Russia—1905 and 1921—and, as usual, explores their impact on a variety of people and institutions. As in *Bare Year,* we are taken to the decaying country manor, the petit-bourgeois house, and the primitive socialist collective. But this time the fulcrum is different. Pil'nyak moves his story mainly on the inner life of a factory, which is spread out over a period of some sixty years. This much certainly seems to represent an advance toward acknowledging modern times. Pil'nyak goes even further, by making a distinction between the oppressive machine civilization of capitalism, and the liberating machine civilization of Communism which he wraps in a luxuriant lyricism reminiscent of the Smithy poets. The distinction is one that the Communists themselves make, of course. As Voronskii had reminded Pil'nyak:

> The progressive movement of the human spirit is measured by man's power over nature, and if this movement has at present been brought to a halt by "complete mechanization," the reason is to be found in social inequality, in the decay and disintegration of the [social] order based on man's sway over man, and not in the fact that technology as such has destroyed everything spiritual.

This very argument turns up in *Materials,* where it is put into the mouth of the Bolshevik hero, Andrei Kozhukhov. The sweeping condemnation of all technology in favor of a life of pristine simplicity is assigned to a most unattractive specimen of the old intelligentsia, the engineer Erliksov. Although pre-Petrine Russia remains the ideal, scarcely a trace remains of the "historiosophy" and "Asiaticism" that Voronskii had found so offensive in *Bare Year.* There is a new attitude toward the Bolsheviks as well. The portrait of Kozhukhov panders to the Bolshevik self-image, without the slightest tinge of irony: Pil'nyak makes him the only character to appear in both parts, fits him out with an Old Revolutionary past that was shopworn even in 1924, and endows him with the storybook qualities of resoluteness, vision, and humanity. Finally, Pil'nyak seems to play up those quirks of his style that Voronskii had singled out for special praise: the lyricism is lusher, the treatment of the various regional human "types" fuller and more detailed, the landscapes more colorful and precise. And he makes several authorial intrusions to assure the reader that the fragmentary nature of his work, which so many critics had complained about, is deliberate.

It is tempting to interpret these changes as calculated responses to the remarks that Voronskii had made in his silhouette. We cannot be sure whether they were or not; but the fact that *Materials for a Novel* was the first substantial piece of prose fiction by Pil'nyak that *Red Virgin Soil* ever published suggests at last the possibility that Voronskii saw them that way. If so, he was badly mistaken. Pil'nyak made no break with his earlier work but merely redeployed its components. The basic myth remained intact, only now we see it in the process of enaction: its unfolding defines history and creates the rhythm and movement of the story. Everything begins with "some men who yearned to walk along the swamp paths, who took it into their

heads to raise Rus' up on her hind legs, traverse the swamps, lay out roads with a ruler, fetter themselves with granite, iron and steel, cursing tranced Rus' of the wooden huts—and they set out. . . ." And so the towns, cities, factories grew, subduing raw nature. But what seems like progress is really a prideful flexing of the intellect and the will which in turn teach man to fear and then to abandon the very thing that makes him whole. It is the Eden myth. In fact, Pil'nyak locates it in a kind of garden:

> If you turn off the main road, drive through the field, ford Black Creek, make your way first through a dark aspen wood, then through a red pine wood, skirt some ravines, cut through a village, drag up and down dry valleys, jolt through another forest over the snags, then cross the Oka in a ferry, just as people did three hundred years ago, pass through meadows and willow groves, then where the path is lost, effaced, obliterated in the tall green grass—you will come to Kadanok, to the Kadanok swamps. Here there are no roads. Here the wild ducks cry. Here it smells of ooze, peat, swamp gas. Here live the thirteen Sisters Ague and Fever. Here on sandy islets the pines grow rank, here by the bog the alder thickets stand close together, by the bogs the heather has carpeted the earth—and at night, when the thirteen Sisters Ague and Fever roam, in the swamps over the water skim green swampfires, noiseless and cold, fearsome fires, and then the air smells of sulphur, and the frenzied ducks cry in terror. Here there are neither paths nor roads—here roam wolves, hunters and tramps. Here you can sink into a bog. . . .

It is a self-contained universe, perfectly harmonious (the language that evokes it is invariably rhetorical); yet because it holds the mystery of life and death, it is also sinister and terrifying. It asserts itself, again and again, through "rebellion, the rising of the masses" aimed at "shattering the iron horses and the roads"; it "smashes against the concrete and iron, against the steel of the cities" and once more "vanishes in the byways." . . . This savage dialectic ends just as the Marxists have predicted, with the triumph of technology. Man has won; happiness ensues.

But there is a catch. Just as the Utopias envisaged by Kirillov, in Dostoevskii's *Possessed,* or by Pozdnyshev, in Tolstoi's *Kreutzer Sonata,* depend upon the extinction of the human race—in the first case through mass suicide, in the second through sexual continence—so the Utopia envisaged by the Bolshevik hero of *Materials for a Novel* depends upon the sacrifice of man to the machine which he has created for the purpose of freeing himself from all dependence. The final scene of the story foreshadows the paradox:

> Behind the glass the turbines and the steam dynamo ran noiselessly in the glaring light. No people were to be seen. They peered in, they saw: leaning against the railing below the turbine, his head resting on his chest, slept a fitter, with a rag in his hand. A greaser entered, carrying a tea pot and a piece of bread, went over to the stairway leading to the boiler room, and walked down it.

"Look," Forst said to Kozhukhov. "It's night.
There's a long time to go yet before the change
of shift. . . . The machine is consolidated human genius. The fitter is asleep, the greaser has
gone to drink tea with the girls who haul the
coal. . . . The machine is running by itself,
without man. . . . Look closely, see how it's
running . . . it's running all by itself, without
man! . . . Remarkable. . . ."

Man has outsmarted himself. In the end he must face the annihilation he has tried to escape. History has come full circle.
The Eden he builds is a mocking copy of the Eden he has tried
to flee: smokestacks for trees, lamps for stars, generators for
suns, railroad tracks for rustic paths, machine oil for primeval
muck. And he settles for it with a sigh of relief, though it is
infinitely more terrible than what he has pulled against. But,
debrained, he can no longer appreciate the irony. He is the
issue of that tradition of anti-industrial fiction that Kuprin's
Moloch, Upton Sinclair's *The Jungle,* and Gor'kii's *Mother*
had helped create for Russian literature.

All Pil'nyak's works are allegories, none more obviously so
than *Materials for a Novel.* The events, settings, characters,
even the imagery are structured on opposing parallels that recapitulate the root myth: country/city; field/factory; soul/mind;
past/present; peasant/worker, and so on, with the second element representing a corruption or parody of the first. The characters serve as vehicles of the allegory. One polarity is represented by the peasant girl Dasha, the original Eve: "from
all her being wafted all the stupefying odors of her forest
habitation . . . and all of her seemed to be hewn out of a
cobblestone—a huge bosom, a huge stomach, a huge behind,
huge hands." . . . The other is represented by the Bolshevik
Andrei Kozhukhov, the pragmatic dreamer, who is dedicated
to making the peaceful mindless existence of the Dashas purposeful and useful by harnessing it to the factory. Dasha is so
far unspoiled; but her announcement that she plans to go to
work in the factory as a cleaning woman indicates that the
process of decay has already set in. What awaits her is painted
in the typically lurid colors of anti-industrial fiction:

> the machine would consume her simple mo-
> rality and ethics, consume her healthy flush,
> force her to push coal carts up to the furnaces,
> to inhale soot and the wisecracks of the fore-
> man. Then the foreman would have her come
> to his apartment or, on a holiday, to the Lurov
> woods on the other side of the Oka, and there
> she would make the rounds, just as all factory
> girls do; and in those lice-infested barracks,
> where people live stacked one on top of the
> other, where there is no joy and can be none,
> where the human rabble has gathered, she would
> consider it happiness that a foreman had taken
> her, because *that* and a bottle of vodka would
> be happiness. . . .

Between Dasha and Andrei moves Erliksov. He is an engineer
who designs and builds machines, yet understands their terrible
power, a man who yearns after the untrammelled state of the
natural man, yet distrusts and fears its anonymity. He is the
human version of the caged wolf he has seen at a bazaar.
Through a love affair with Dasha and through friendship with
Andrei, he hopes to resolve the conflict of reason and intuition
and emerge a whole man. But no resolution is possible; and
finally he is literally torn apart when, in expiation of the sin

of intellect, he throws himself into a huge flywheel on one of
those machines he has helped to create. The god that has been
brought into existence to serve man ends by subduing him.

The Russian reader, who for generations had treated the personages of fiction as flesh-and-blood individuals, found himself
balked and frustrated by Pil'nyak's people. They have no individuality. They never change or develop; they lack depth,
mind, motivation; they scarcely even possess a physical existence, so meager an allotment does the author give them of
his not inconsiderable powers of description. As Viktor Gofman has aptly observed, they do their acting behind the scenes,
and present us with the results in the form of letters, diaries,
and speeches. As mere emblems, mere vehicles of moods and
ideas, they can, at most, open windows onto events. Pil'nyak
is essentially a writer of situations and settings. He is at his
best in mass portraits: the proletariat, the peasantry, families,
villages, towns, periods in history.

History, for Pil'nyak, is neither a story nor a random succession
of incidents, but a myth that is central to all of life. Assuming
different forms but remaining essentially the same, it is immune
to time and to man's efforts to direct it. What looks like historical change is only an intensification of forces that have been
present all along. Thus *Materials for a Novel* really ends the
moment it begins back in what is conventionally called the
sixteenth century, with the act of self-enslavement performed
in the name of self-liberation. This concept of history is also
a concept of time. The attempt to blur the reader's sense of
past and present through sudden leaps in narration suggests the
workings of a "subjective" time such as we expect in literature.
But at bottom, a strict law operates even here. The order in
which events unfold is really always the same, regardless of
what men think or how the author may rearrange their components; the outcome is foreordained. Time, like history, is a
constant state of being, a unity which makes all events and
experiences simultaneous. We can neither allot it with our
calendars and clocks, nor manipulate it with our fancies.

Pil'nyak virtually defines that change in the concept of time
which went along with the decline of the novel toward the end
of the nineteenth century. It is intimated in Chekhov's sense
of the repetitiousness of life and in his predilection for circular
structures (as in "The Cart"); it is occasionally seen in Bunin
(*Brethren* is one of the best examples); but it is peculiarly a
theme of the Symbolists, whence Pil'nyak probably took it. In
the service of this concept, the usual strategies of narrative
prose are sacrificed. Pil'nyak works, as he described it, through
"associations of parallels and antitheses" . . . , not through an
unfolding of a story line in time and space. We must therefore
read him as we read so much modern poetry—vertically, as it
were, piecing together a picture from scattered clues. He deliberately destroys scenes or episodes that threaten to develop
even a rudimentary story interest. Thus he breaks off the pursuit
of Andrei Kozhukhov by the police just at the point where
most writers would begin to develop it. In this respect, he
stands apart from the writers of the Serapion Brotherhood, like
Kaverin, Grin, and Ivanov, who considered "plotlessness"
one of the more unfortunate characteristics of older Russian
fiction and tried to remedy it in their own writing. We are
reminded instead of Belyi's technique of evoking chaos through
sudden shifts of setting and perspective. But Belyi, at least in
Petersburg and *The Silver Dove,* uses a gridwork of traditional
plot to sustain his work. Pil'nyak does nothing of the kind in
Materials. Nor does he pay the slightest respect to the conventions of genre; in fact it is in this work that the breakdown

of those conventions, which had begun in the late nineteenth century, reaches its extreme. "Materials" is an apt description of the process: although "for a novel," the work is an assemblage of pages from a diary, letters, historical tracts, ethnographical sketches, anecdotes, dramatic monologues, political slogans, high rhetoric and obscene expletive, exquisitely crafted "literature" and unstructured babble. We have before us a compendium of virtually all the styles of prose language, whether literary or nonliterary, that were being produced at the time. They are juxtaposed in seemingly random fashion to support Pil'nyak's notion that all of human experience—not just what we traditionally reserve to the province of literature—serves a great timeless myth. It is his way of suggesting universality.

It was this appearance of unstructured artlessness verging on chaos that enhanced Pil'nyak's reputation at the time as a "realist," an observant chronicler of his age. Actually, art lurked beneath every utterance. *Materials for a Novel,* like all Pil'nyak's work, has a unity which is created not merely by the pervasive central myth, but also by a carefully crafted repertoire of formal devices.

Perhaps the most common of them is repetition. Here we find virtually a catalogue of the rhetorician's art: anaphora ("Gody shli: / Devyat'sot devat'nadtsatyi. / Devyat'sot dvadtsatyi. / Devyat'sot dvadtsat' pervyi...."); paramoion ("*prishol, poshol po shasham....*"); parachesis ("*davno narodam vosslavlennyi....*"); paragmenon ("Muzhiku nashemu kak dikar'—slavya-ni-nu,—reshat'sya, reshit'sya, reshat'." ...); homoioptoton ("zhili vmes*te*, v tesno*te*, smra*de*, p'yans*tve*, verili bog*u*, chort*u*, nachal'stv*u*, sglaz*u*...."); and many others.

Even more strikingly, Pil'nyak has at his command a basic fund of incidents, themes, and images which travel from one work to another, not as leitmotifs (for their meaning varies from context to context) but simply as bricks and mortar. Much of *Bare Year,* for instance, was assembled from an earlier collection of stories entitled *Grass (Byl'yo).* Within a single work, whole phrases, lines, paragraphs, and even scenes may be repeated at various points. Sometimes the repetition is subtle, as, for instance, where the basic structure of a scene is retained, but the contents strung upon it are varied—a kind of exergasia. Usually, however, we have to do with word-for-word recurrences, so much so that *Materials* looks like a pastiche of self-plagiarisms. This technique serves several purposes. For one thing, the repetitions act as stimuli, which condition the reader to react, in predictable ways, with pity, boredom, or anger: we soon learn what is expected of us, even if we refuse to satisfy the expectation. For another thing, they provide loci (in a kind of tautotes) around which individual scenes can be structured—as, for example, the word "stove-couch" (*lezhanka*) which organizes the otherwise chaotic interior of a certain house: "in the house there is a stove-couch—by the stove-couch . . . on the stove-couch . . . by the stove-couch . . . beside the stove-couch," and, at the end, "in front of the stove-couch." . . . (pp. 111-19)

Finally, the repetitions reinforce Pil'nyak's theme that all life is fundamentally the same because it exists in a timeless present and merely recapitulates, in different contexts, all that has ever happened. In effect, Pil'nyak was writing one great work throughout his career. It was never completed, but we see parts of it in the novels and stories he did produce.

Andrei Belyi uses repetitions as well; like Pil'nyak, he has a repertoire of images that travel from work to work. But there is an important difference: Belyi is a symbolist; Pil'nyak is

not. Each work of Belyi's represents an organic structure in which each symbol has a plurality of meaning that depends upon its position in the work as a whole and its interrelationships with other symbols, a meaning that reveals itself gradually, as the work unfolds, in a series of epiphanies. Pil'nyak's use of the image is nonsymbolic. His images carry no hidden meanings; they function as signs which refer directly to concepts, and their function never changes within one work, very often not from work to work either. They are a perfect illustration of a point that one of the characters in *Petersburg* makes: "Don't confuse allegory with the symbol: allegory is a symbol that has become common currency...." Wolf, peasant, wind, snowstorm, factory, Revolution are the emblems, the tags of Pil'nyak's world—a static world, in which appearance and reality are one, and things are shown after they have happened, not while they are in process. By naming something he fixes it forever. The "idea" of a Pil'nyak work becomes obvious fairly early, sometimes on the very first page, as in *Materials;* what follows merely elaborates or embroiders.

Closely related to repetition is the literary echo, which Pil'nyak, like Belyi, Remizov, and Bunin, uses lavishly. One of the most striking illustrations can be found in the description of the factory in *Materials.* Here Pil'nyak cannibalizes a stock nineteenth-century Russian literary landscape. "These places," we are told, "had everything in order not to be that poetry which for centuries was considered genuine." The landscape, in other words, does not lack anything; it contains all that the faithful reader of Turgenev or Goncharov might expect. But it is different. Surveying the environs, like the sensitive narrator of Karamzin's "Poor Liza," the author observes the "ancient Moscow river," now "choked with piles of wood, boxes of peat, barges on the water, a whistling steamer, and the water can't be seen...." The verdant hills along the river bank? Now "hills of slag." The winding rutted rural road? Now "two tracks of iron rails for carts." The endearing diminutives for nature beloved of Karamzin and Turgenev are here too—only now we find not "dear little birds" (*ptichki*) or "pretty little bushes" (*kustochki*), but a "dear little locomotive" (*parovichek*) and "pretty little carts" (*vagonchiki*). The rustle of leaves has become the hiss of the factory, which is "very boring"; the inevitable monastery on the distant hill is "unnecessary"; the sky is something one now "does not wish to look at"; the old estate set in the linden trees or acacias has undergone a transformation too: "before you, three chance linden trees, a poplar—and beyond the poplar, in the acacias, a 'guest house,' a 'house for bachelors,' cement houses with tile roofs in the style of Swedish cottages, houses for engineers—peaceful and solid." And the placid rural village, complete with idyllic mother and child, has turned into "little huts like bird houses, with front gardens rank with poppies and burdocks, with little boys covered in dust and with a woman by the gate and a suckling pig in a mud puddle...." The literary echo, besides serving the theme of corruption and decay, adds the dimension of memory and pathos to the story. And as an ironic statement, it hurls an accusation as well—an accusation that the writers of the nineteenth century were either too heavy-handed to pick out the thread of reality, or else deliberately lied about what they saw, using "fiction" to distort or conceal the truth. In this respect too, Pil'nyak carried on yet another theme of the literary generation before him.

Many of these devices, to be sure, are purely ornamental. That is to say, they do not serve the basic myth and fulfill no essential thematic or structural role: they can be moved from place to place, expanded or shortened, even done away with entirely.

Such, for example, are the imitations of peasant sayings that stud *Materials for a Novel:* "Two poods of bread is a horse, half a village of houses is a pood." . . . At one point, Pil'nyak weaves a whole long passage of such sayings, real and invented. . . . Or he may employ literary references in the same way:

> A thief, a plain fool and an Ivanushka the fool, a boor, a toady, a Smerdyakov, Gogolian, Shchedrinian or Ostrovskiian, type—and with them the fools in Christ's name, the Alyosha Karamazovs, the Juliana Lazarevas, the Serafim Sarovskiis lived together. . . .

Yet such devices—often mere catalogues—do make an essential contribution to the work as a whole; for they help create and sustain that rhetorical, highly artificial tone which permeates every part and confers a unity. Even the most careless and seemingly artless effects may be elaborate rhetorical constructs. Pil'nyak's sentence structure, for instance, which creates an impression of extraordinary randomness, is actually built upon the principle of parataxis, with the word "i" ["and"] serving (much as in Old Russian literature) both to link the paratactical units and to set them off, as relative pronouns do. The same point may be made of many of Pil'nyak's "realistic," even "naturalistic" descriptions. Consider the factory in *Materials:*

> smoke, soot, fire—noise, clang, shriek and iron's squeak—semi-darkness, electricity instead of sun—machinery, tolerances, gauges, cupola furnaces, open-hearth furnaces, smiths, hydraulic presses and presses weighing tons. . . .

Certainly, this is an effective piece of impressionism; but it is also highly artificial, with the rhythmic grouping (smoke, soot, fire—noise, clang, shriek), the careful contrasts of visual, audial, and light-dark effects, and the paratactical syntax. Even the machines are not so much functional pieces of equipment as brand names chosen for their exotic sounds.

This atmosphere of artificiality is deliberate. It asserts a principle of literariness which openly and defiantly manipulates the "material." Its motivation, in *Materials,* is provided by an author-persona who introduces and ends the story, makes the links between scenes and events, fades into the background when other narrators or "eyes" step forward, affects a helpless attitude in the face of experiences he pretends merely to be recording, and participates in the story himself, with his own distinctive manner of speaking. In these respects, he resembles the typical narrator of the *skaz.* But he is not that; he is too sophisticated, too conscious, too calculating a literary intelligence. Every move he makes is carefully planned. Even those passages that resemble free association are highly organized interior monologues. The author-narrator leaves us in no doubt about his function in the work, for he frequently resorts to what the Russian Formalists called "baring the device." "I came out of Belyi and Bunin," we are told, "many people do many things better than I, and I consider myself entitled to appropriate this 'better' or whatever I can do better (Oh Peregudov and Dal', I conceal from nobody what I have taken from you for this story!)." . . . The fourth "fragment" is introduced in the following way: "from the chapter entitled 'Rubbish,' which does not fit into the plan of the tale, but which nevertheless is essential before proceeding to the development of the spectacle." . . . (pp. 119-23)

It is this willful, often playful self-assertiveness that gives warrant to the great variety of styles and genres in the work. No attempt is made to conceal art. On the contrary, art is thrust in the reader's face, with all its underpinnings exposed. Through arbitrariness, through artificiality, through the exploitation of a range of material seemingly seized at random, the literary mind proclaims its right to do as it pleases. In many ways, the capricious literariness of this and other works by Pil'nyak calls to mind the verbal prestidigitation of the Old Russian writer, like Daniel the Exile and Ilarion, who worked in a period when literary talent was measured by the number of sources one could bring to hand and weave together into new tapestries. From the more recent past, it carried into the twenties that cult of artificiality which the Symbolists, in particular, had practiced ("Oh, books are more beautiful than roses!"), in their belief that the created world is superior to the world of nature, the inanimate higher than the animate. (pp. 123-24)

> Robert A. Maguire, *"The Pioneers: Pil'nyak and Ivanov,"* in his Red Virgin Soil: Soviet Literature in the 1920's, *1968. Reprint by Cornell University Press, 1987, pp. 101-47.*

ALAYNE P. REILLY (essay date 1971)

[*In the following excerpt, Reilly criticizes* Okei *as poorly-written propaganda composed solely for political purposes.*]

Pilnyak traveled across America for three months, going by train from New York to California and returning by automobile to New York. *Okay, An American Novel* is an account of life in America as he saw it during his travels. The work is not a novel, as the title might imply, but a long, rambling, publicist travel memoir that is unworthy of Pilnyak's talents as a writer. There is almost no sign of his earlier ornamental and rhythmic prose. The leitmotif technique that was so successful in *The Naked Year* has degenerated into Stakhanovite bathos in *Okay.* A few propagandist terms become heavy motifs, mournfully repeated throughout the three hundred pages of text: "flags," "philistine," "Nietzschean dollars," "American individualism," "advertising," and numerous "och's" and "ach's." The Ford conveyor belt turns into a negative metaphor for American life in general. The roads become "conveyor belts" of the capitalist society moving mechanically through a standardized life:

> Really, one cannot escape from the conveyor belts of America's roads, and really, to travel along the conveyor belts of the American roads is no less tiresome than to work on Ford's conveyor belts.
>
> Ford is the American god and savior.
>
> America! The genius of America! Ford! The genius of Ford! For this principle—the birth of machines on the conveyor belt—has been adapted everywhere now, even in restaurants and by many merchants.
>
> Man is not a human being but an addition to a conveyor belt.

Like Gorky and Mayakovsky before him, Pilnyak describes the American obsession with money:

> But "Unto Caesar. . . ." Truisms often happen to be true, and the truism that the dollar, and only the dollar is master, sovereign, dream, and

the delight of American morality is the truest of truisms.

American patriotism appears only when there is talk about the dollar or—the American flag!

Dear Nietzschean dollar!

Mister capitalism is the Nietzschean dollar.

The master of America and her leader is the Nietzschean dollar.

The prominent display of the American flag everywhere he went, "even in cemeteries," seems to have bothered Pilnyak. He sarcastically describes the "three whales" of American democracy as the Bible, the Constitution, and the national flag.

New York is described as "inhuman," although he seems to have felt a twinge of admiration for the buildings of the city when viewed from above: "From the sixtieth, the hundredth floor, New York is striking, indescribable, extraordinary, ominous, an ominously beautiful city—a city of the triumph of industry, of the scope of human skill." He continues his description of New York from below in somewhat different terms:

> But if you walk along the streets of New York, it is a terrible city, the most terrible city in the world, no matter whether you are on Park Avenue or on the Bowery. The city is deafened with noise. The city breathes gasoline instead of air. The city is victimized by the prostitute-like beauty of its electric advertisements. The streets are strewn with garbage, without a single leaf. . . . A city in which it is impossible for man to live.

Pilnyak reports visiting a millionaire on the thirtieth-floor roof garden of his skyscraper and looking down on the roofs of smaller neighboring buildings:

> The sunset was beautiful, the roof of the neighboring building was littered with orange peels thrown there no doubt from the roof of my poor millionaire's home, since the legend of heavenly manna, like the legend of heavenly oranges, cannot be explained by the laws of physics. Oh, how sinister and inhuman New York is from a skyscraper. Och, America! Ach, America of national flags that fly even over cemeteries! Ach, American Nietzschean individualism!

One wonders how the laws of physics would explain orange peels falling straight down for twenty-five stories—they might be more inclined to hit the roof from the hands of tenants sunning thereon. The emotional illogicality of the scene is typical of propagandist writings. The capitalist is by nature guilty. The inhabitants of the smaller buildings are by nature not inclined to leave garbage behind when they go up on their roofs. Also typical is the introductory sentence about the sunset. Such scenes seem more effective when contrasted to the beauty of nature.

Pilnyak visited America in 1931 in the midst of the depression, a time when America may indeed have seemed on the brink of collapse. Although curiously enough he does not dwell on the depression at any length. He concentrates instead on the usual propaganda themes: poverty of the masses versus the wealth of depraved millionaires; exploitation and the inhu-

manity of capitalism; mistreatment of Negroes and Indians; gangsterism and crime. He seems preoccupied with conveyor belts, national flags, and Nietzschean dollars. He makes only a few attempts to herald the coming of Communism.

But Pilnyak's heart apparently was not in his task. *Okay* is weakly written, with no real consistency of theme or content. Poor Pilnyak was writing for his life and apparently hoped he could make up for his lack of inspiration by persistent repetition of key propagandist clichés. The mood throughout is laboriously negative. His imagination is not fired either by America or by his commissioned exposé. The closest he comes to his earlier ornamental style is in a brief description of the only things in America that he liked: the cactus desert in the West and Niagara Falls. In these passages he is obviously moved—his writing becomes fresh, imaginative, and almost lyrical, especially in comparison with the awkward style and expression of the rest of the book. . . . (pp. 24-8)

Unlike Mayakovsky who forgot nature after he saw electricity, Pilnyak remains awed only by the grandeur of nature. This may also account for some of his negative reactions to the big cities of America. (p. 29)

> *Alayne P. Reilly, "Four Early Impressions: Gorky, Mayakovsky, Pilnyak, Ilf and Petrov," in his* America in Contemporary Soviet Literature, *New York University Press, 1971, pp. 3-45.*

KENNETH NORMAN BROSTROM　(essay date 1973)

[*Brostrom is an American educator and critic who has published several essays on Pilnyak. In the following excerpt, he examines the philosophical bases of Pilnyak's works, surveying his writings in order to trace the author's philosophical development.*]

> This is what fools people: a man is always a teller of tales, he lives surrounded by his stories and the stories of others, he sees everything that happens to him through them; and he tries to live his own life as if he were telling a story.

This declaration by Antoine Roquentin, the protagonist of Sartre's novel *Nausea*, contains the kernel of the epistemological judgment which preoccupied Pil'njak in one way or another throughout the twenties. Viktor Šklovskij had good reason to claim that Pil'njak was not a diversified writer and that he tended to repeat himself from work to work. But Šklovskij failed to perceive *what* it was that Pil'njak was repeating, and he is not alone. The misunderstanding, in my opinion, is general. Its cause may be the relatively cursory reading which many critics seem to have given his works. It may also derive from a tendency to impose upon more mature works conceptions gleaned from Pil'njak's early, rather simple short stories; this led to an initial disjuncture between writer and critic which eventually yawned into a chasm by 1930. It has continued little changed to the present.

My aim here is not to prove that Pil'njak was a precursor of the existentialists but to describe the conceptual matters which are the basis for the thematic organization of his allegories. Pil'njak's ideas themselves were hardly original, for not only were they old hat in the philosophical tradition of scepticism deriving from Hume and Kant, but they play an important role in the great nineteenth century masterpieces. What then does Roquentin suggest here that will prove so helpful?

"This is what fools people: a man is always a teller of tales, . . . he sees everything that happens to him through them. . . ." The simple word "story" is here manipulated into a metaphor which suggests the insight Isak Dinesen must have had in mind when she once stated, "All sorrows can be borne if you put them into a story or tell a story about them. . . ." The metaphor indicates the self-deceiving manner in which men understand the world about them and their place in it. It implies the human need for meaning, for coherence, form, and significance in living—man's need to feel not only that he *is,* but that he *is moving* from someplace to some other place, that his life is in this sense a "story." It is a "story" because it exists within the context of a greater story, the patterned, significant movement of the universe.

The metaphor of the story is serviceable if it is understood in terms of the Aristotelian definition of plot. Two rudimentary features of traditional plots are pertinent here: first, movement, the sequential passage of events which occurs in such a way that the audience is aware of some beginning, middle and end; and second, the elimination of accident, of random events or episodes which have no significant bearing upon the developing story. In short, the "story" represents a universe purged of contingency. Events are no longer meaningless but meaningful because they are part of a coherent and developing pattern.

Roquentin believes men are victims of the "plots" they impose upon their own lives, upon the world, and upon the universe. He cares not whether these stories come from the Pentateuch, the Gospels, the Koran or Buddha, from Marx or Locke, from family, tribe, nation, or private fantasy; they are all delusions, efforts to create meaning through form and pattern where there is none in fact. For him existence is chaotic, ruled by contingency, so that events have causes but no meaning, no teleology, much like the endless and meaningless collisions of gas molecules in Brownian motion. In such a random context human life simply *is,* possessing no inherent significance, for it is part of no genuine "story" which infuses it with meaning.

These conceptions are elaborated in one form or another extensively in existentialist thought, but that is beside the point here. It is important, however, that Pil'njak had access to much in the philosophical and literary traditions to which existentialism is indebted. He refers on several occasions, for example, to one of the precursors of the existentialists, Nietzsche, as well as to Kant, whose relevance in this context hardly requires elaboration. I suspect, although I cannot prove, that Pil'njak was influenced by both philosophers in his frequent assertion of the ultimate unintelligibility of much in this world and of the impossibility of proving the existence of any eternal and absolute Ideal.

It is unnecessary to make of Pil'njak a reader of philosophy, for we know without question that he was an avid reader of Russian literature. The best works of the nineteenth century, in their concern for the "great questions," could easily have provided him with the lineaments of his own vision. In fact, Dostoevskij had a profound influence upon Pil'njak's thought. Ivan Karamazov's proposition that "if there is no God, then everything is permitted" describes the implications of a universe without some transcendental story, while the Underground Man is a tireless story-teller who endlessly fantasizes tales about himself in an ever failing effort to generate a kind of literary shapeliness within his life in the random, hostile environment of St. Petersburg. (It is not for nothing that he is a great reader and prides himself upon it.) Tolstoj repeatedly dealt with the same issues; Levin, for instance, is finally ob-

sessed with a Kantian notion of the limitations of rational thought, that is, with thought processes which cannot provide him with the kind of story he needs to suffuse his existence with a sure sense of absolute, eternal significance. Although Levin gains everything that Anna Karenina loses in the course of the novel, her suicide and his own impulse to follow suit are parallel phenomena due to the loss of a "story," for both characters are deprived of their sense of an ordered context which validates, justifies, and informs their lives with meaning. The awareness of this loss leads them into the psychic state Sartre calls "nausea."

[Various] degrees of such "nausea" recur in Pil'njak's work, and here too he had literary models in the past. . . . It is indeed one of the recurrent motifs in modern literature to which Sartre simply applied a useful term.

In spite of the evolutionary development in Pil'njak's treatment of these philosophical issues, it can be said that he was generally concerned with elaborating metaphorically from various perspectives a conception which Langdon Gilkey has stated in the following manner:

> Our intellectual life seems to be founded on a creative and autonomous act of human knowing. The *motivation* of this act is a concerned drive or urge on the part of our rational consciousness for the truth; the ground for *what* is affirmed is the self-validating grasp by that consciousness of what it judges to be true; and thus the ultimate *basis* for this act is inescapably our commitment in the midst of risks to a fundamental vision that may well be in error. Our most fundamental notions seem to be validated and validatable only by the self-satisfaction of our intellectual powers, the self-accrediting act of our rational consciousness that *these* notions, and not some others, reflect the way that things actually are.

It will remain one of the remarkable singularities of Pil'njak's career that prior to expressing his distrust of all ideas in *Golyj god* and succeeding works, he was utterly devoted to a few simple conceptions. Whether one prefers "biologism" or "zoologism," Pil'njak's worldview as a young writer emphasized the physical and moral benefits to be derived from an elemental, almost mindless merging with the rhythms of the natural world. The pattern which informs existence with meaning for him was simple: birth—the struggle to survive and reproduce—death; man is an animal, and nature knows best. It is a vision whose general tenor comprises equal parts of Rousseau and Darwin. To live willfully in a manner that attempts to deny or ignore the necessities imposed by nature upon all life is to court failures ranging from frustration to extinction. Early in his career Pil'njak began to associate native Russian "byt" with an ideal lifestyle harmonious with the cyclical patterns of nature.

This last conviction was rooted in the intelligentsia's tradition of primitivism which derived in large part from the massive impact of the peasantry upon social thought and moral philosophy. For Pil'njak, as for us, the major figure here was Tolstoj. But there is no sophisticated comprehension of Tolstojan primitivism in his early works; primitive Tolstojanism would be a more accurate appellation. The story obviously derived from Tolstoj during this early period is **"Smerti,"** but the works most characteristic and often discussed are **"Nad ovragom"** and **"God ix žizni."**

In 1917 the quality of Pil'njak's Tolstojanism improved dramatically as he began to stress two issues which tended to undermine his simple, mechanistic vision: human intellect and contingency. In **"Snega"** he created a Levin-like character named Polunin who after years of spiritual struggle has managed to overcome the nihilism which proceeds from rational meditation upon death and to accept his own life and death as mysteriously good manifestations of the cyclical movements of the cosmos. But the fact of this acceptance indicates that Polunin is still guided in his merger with nature, not by raw instinct, but by a consciously apprehended conception. Pil'njak was now aware of a dominant idea of his mature work, the inevitable loneliness that the rational man must experience in confronting the material universe, of which his body is a part, the whole being governed by apparently aimless natural forces. This perception admits the possibility that nature's cycles are not inherently good, that the universe is governed by contingency, causation without meaning, and that ideas to the contrary are illusions. Contingency is a principal theme in the stories following **"Snega"** (**"Pozëmka,"** **"Smertel'noe manit,"** **"Vešči,"** etc.).

The theme of contingency may have derived from the rampaging disorder of revolution which must have seriously challenged Pil'njak's youthful philosophy. Previously carnage and violence had been understood as part of a fundamentally harmonious order wherein new life balanced death. Now chaos and death were predominant, and they were products of an enormous body of forces Pil'njak had completely ignored—history. His earlier inclination to assert an elemental, universal order now was transformed into a desire to seek out and to understand a new story, this time within the apparent chaos of historical upheaval.

Pil'njak's themes from 1918-20 are not entirely consistent, but the immediacy of events must have dictated a certain degree of confusion. **"Smertel'noe manit"** (March, 1918) I understand as a simple allegory postulating that the revolution is a return to the ancient Slavic past (the literal level of the story does not refer to the revolution). If this interpretation is correct, the story established Pil'njak's dominant understanding of the revolution during the next two years, repeated in works such as **"Arina"** and **"Prosëlki."** But this hypothesis was contradicted by another vision in which burgeoning chaos and meaningless death had enveloped rulers and ruled alike, denying the existence of any significant pattern in events (e.g., **"Imenie Belokonskoe"**). **"U Nikoly, čto na Belyx Kolodezjax"** (February, 1919), a story of considerable complexity, was Pil'njak's first attempt at combining these contradictory hypotheses to express uncertainty; this work was thus a harbinger of the period beginning with **Golyj god.** Certain stories from the years of War Communism also contain what appear to be furtive, ambiguous attacks upon the Bolsheviks (**"Ego Veličestvo, Kneeb Piter Komandor,"** **"Kolymen-gorod"**), although Pil'njak's attitude toward them became increasingly complex, tentative, and uncertain as time passed.

After **"U Nikoly, . . ."** Pil'njak began an artistically successful but intellectually unconvincing effort to understand the dynamics of the revolution through the conception of death and resurrection. This notion was grounded in his past preoccupation with the yearly cycle and biological proliferation and extinction, as well as in his knowledge of folklore and Christian traditions. But what precisely was to be resurrected is unclear

on the whole. Initially, Pil'njak associated this idea with the rebirth of ancient Slavic culture and spirit, and its corollary, the death in Russia of Western European culture and the city (**"Tysjača let"** and **"Polyn'"**). But in 1919 he began to utilize this same conception to suggest the possible birth in Russia of a new urban, technological society organized and guided by the Bolsheviks (**"Kolymen-gorod,"** **"Pri dverjax"**). Thus, a new source of uncertainty different from those in **"U Nikoly, . . ."** made its appearance in his work.

It is possible, I think, to view Pil'njak's earliest biological themes and his diverse efforts to depict the revolution's meaning as product of his initial understanding of the nature of artistic thinking. Implicit in these works is a quasi-Symbolist notion which is the source of a persistent conception in Pil'njak's more mature work . . .: the psychological similarities between faith and artistic endeavor. He apparently understood creative artistic thinking as a special kind of cognition which attempts to perceive, identify, and embody in aesthetic form the forces, the determining essences, that shape and propel reality. Artistic thinking derives its unique power from its kinship with those forces in the external world. (pp. 76-84)

The uncertainty which had manifested itself in Pil'njak's work during 1918-20 apparently led to a loss of faith in the resonance between artistic thought and the immanent structure of the external world, initiating the period of the "epistemological impasse." It was while he was composing **Golyj god** in 1920 that Pil'njak must have made the decision which altered radically the thematic organization of his art. He elected to embody his perplexity in the novel's structure by creating a principal narrator who would explore the apparent randomness of Russian life and meditate upon the three hypotheses noted above concerning the meaning or lack of it immanent in the revolution: that Russia was returning to her distant past, or beginning a new Bolshevik socialist machine age, or experiencing an explosion of meaningless chaos. This novel established the thematic concerns which characterized Pil'njak's work during the following two years (1921-22). For concentrated power of invention they were the best years in Pil'njak's brief, remarkable career. . . . In [Pil'njak's most successful efforts during this period] the general pattern of death and resurrection remained the revolution's hypothetical dynamic and the source of hope for the future. But the increasingly dominant mood during these two years was one of pessimism as Pil'njak's examination of the revolutionary era intensified his suspicion that meaninglessness might lie at the heart of the horrifying events of the civil war period. This generated a distinct thematic tension between two antithetical visions of existence, idealism and nihilism. [In a footnote, the critic notes: These two terms are not used in their rigorous philosophical meanings here. Rather, "nihilism" suggests a philosophy urging a world in which there are no principles of meaning, where events simply happen; "idealism" suggests the opposite view, that within apparent chaos there exist principles upon which one can build a reliable faith.] Pil'njak's narrators are now caught by this conflict which proceeds from the apparent lack of harmony between human belief with its consequent values and the elusive principles within external reality which validate that belief, whatever its nature. Two antagonistic feminine character types, the syphilitic whore and variations upon Turgenev's ethereal true believer, Liza Kalitina, now are employed in intricate correlation with this question. This irresolution reached its climax in *Tret'ja stolica* (June, 1922). (pp. 85-6)

Nihilism became the dominant philosophical orientation in Pil'njak's work following *Tret'ja stolica*. The salient indication of this was his abrupt desertion in all historical contexts of the vague but optimistic conception, death and resurrection. "**Lesnaja dača**" (September, 1922) still implies this principle but only in an individual procreative context. Pil'njak's next story, "**Volki**" (December, 1922), is perhaps the bitterest, most despairing work of his entire career. The revolution had been bloody anarchy in the name of brotherhood, and the idealists of 1917 had become the wolves of 1922.

Travel in Europe interrupted Pil'njak's writing after "**Volki**" for nine months, and his work during the next two years was a rather confusing melange of old themes and continuing pessimism. For example, "**Speranza**" (September, 1923), meaning "hope" in Italian, depicts the great faith in the revolution's promise held by sailors on a European coal transport. But their hope is unconvincing, for they perceive the meaning of events in Russia from a great distance and largely through wishful rumors. Pil'njak returned during these two years to his old zoological interests, but their implications were generally reversed. Vigor became violence, carnality became bestiality, and the pure "natural" life, an amoral struggle to survive. In works such as *Černyj xleb* and "**Storona nenašinskaja**," Pil'njak reexamined his concept of Russian "byt" and indicated here as well a substantial change of attitude. Not a trace remained of his former belief that it was the citadel of the natural man, the good Russian peasant. The peasant was now a wolf and his "byt," a vast psychological swamp from which Russia almost certainly would never extricate herself to build a better, more humane life. The frequent morbidity of Pil'njak's mood is suggested by the fact that the majority of his sensitive idealists in this period suffer from Sartre's nausea; they are assaulted by the repellent, disordered world surrounding them, and they are often depicted in the act of attempted flight from it.

This nihilistic vision was occasionally complicated by recurrences of the theme of uncertainty ("**Staryj syr**," "**Ledoxod**"). The tension between the two has its fullest, most intricate expression in *Mašiny i volki*, which draws together the concerns which had dominated Pil'njak's work since 1920. But the novel is more than a rehashing of old ideas, for in it Pil'njak turned to the Bolsheviks and technology with greater seriousness than ever before. His narrator ponders the Bolshevik faith and the possibility that it does not conform to the pattern endlessly reiterated by the innumerable illusory faiths checkering the human past; he views it as faith without mysticism, without a transcendent dimension, as a faith in man's will and intelligence and in his ability to force order and meaning upon the aimless flux of human life and history. That there are rumblings here of the Dostoevskian or Nietzschean superman is clear. But Pil'njak underplays Dostoevskij's understanding of the pride that goes before the fall in the superman, for he apparently saw this doctrine, born in the previous century and now exercising political power, as the only potential exit from the swamp of history. Later, near the end of the twenties, one can find treatments of the superman in Pil'njak's work which would have been more congenial to Dostoevskij, in *Ivan Moskva* and *Volga vpadaet v Kaspijskoe more*.

After *Mašiny i volki* (completed in June, 1924) there occurred a significant shift in focus in Pil'njak's work. His ideas were essentially unchanged, but his subject matter was new. The conundrum of history as a specific focus for meditation suddenly disappeared from his works and was supplanted by stories and tales in a Chekhovian vein dealing with individual psychology and the partiality of every man's understanding of

himself, of those around him, and of the world at large. Two important works, *Mat' syra-zemlja* and *Povest' nepogašennoj luny*, do possess a historical dimension, but it serves primarily as a context for the characters' conflicting world-views. Several works dealing with these themes are drawn from Pil'njak's travel experiences and their autobiographical elements are quite explicit, pointing directly to his important reportages of 1926-27. This new emphasis upon individual human fallibility represents a return to the questioning, tentative attitude toward human knowledge, including his own, characteristic of Pil'njak's post-*Golyj god* work; he indicated as much in partially autobiographical works such as "**Rasplësnutoe vremja**" and "**Neroždënnaja povest'**." Generally speaking, this period in Pil'njak's career, extending to the end of 1925 and *Povest' nepogašennoj luny*, is the most variable in quality of his mature work. This last tale, *Zavoloč'e*, and a few short stories are important achievements, but numerous others are of passing interest.

The partially autobiographical short stories written during 1924-25 are significant in that they provide a model for Pil'njak's reportages written after the scandal caused by *Povest' nepogašennoj luny*. In these works (*Korni japonskogo solnca* and *Kitajskaja povest'*), particularly the latter, Pil'njak treated himself as a semi-fictional protagonist who is caught in the psychological prison created by his native "byt," the cultural matrix which provides each man with the lineaments of his worldview.

The "prison of 'byt'" was one of Pil'njak's principal themes to the end of the twenties, finding one of its best expressions in *Ivan Moskva*. Travel in the Far East seems to have made Pil'njak aware of a new dimension to the Bolshevik-superman theme developed in *Mašiny i volki*. The Bolsheviks were not men apart who might be bold and clever enough to lift Russia out of the swamp of her "byt" and past; they themselves were products of that past and culture. In an act of overweening pride and confidence in their own intellects, they had declared they could transform themselves, Russian humanity, and eventually mankind. But their attempt was shaped by the very past they wished to escape. *Ivan Moskva* is, on this level, a pamphlet written against political egotists. But it is also a work which elaborates superbly the nihilism typical of Pil'njak's depiction of human life during the late twenties. Uncertainty had finally yielded to the conviction that human life is inherently valueless. But Pil'njak's fundamentally optimistic and hopeful nature apparently led him to the belief that contradictory human beings can create value in their lives by realizing their potential for virtuous behavior. Thus, Ivan's congenital syphilis is symbolic of inevitable human weakness and fallibility, but his capacity for decency and profound love redeems his life. One indication of the persistence of this understanding of the human condition is contained in a story written immediately before *Volga vpadaet v Kaspijskoe more*. Its title, "**Dvadcat' vosem' tysjač pečatnyx znakov**" (February, 1929), indicates the approximate number of spaces on the story's pages occupied by the individual letters of words and the spaces between them. The story itself depicts Dostoevskian dissonances in human behavior, while its title is an emblem of the inherently valueless base upon which all human "goodness" and "evil" rest.

In *Korni japonskogo solnca* Pil'njak made a grand historical distinction between "material" and "spiritual" progress which recurs in his work of the late twenties. *Ivan Moskva* incorporates the essentials of this dichotomy, wherein the former variety of progress is understood to advance ever more rapidly, the latter in the mass and on the whole, not at all. And the latter for Pil'njak was the only kind of progress that could be considered genuine human progress. In a very real sense this summarizes the pessimistic aspect of his historical views, for it implies the apparent inability of men to rise above their "byt," the contingency that governs the world they live in, and their own weak, fallible natures. Human history never changes.

The optimistic pole of Pil'njak's vision during the late twenties is indicated most directly by four stories from 1927 and 1928; the first three, **"Lord Bajron," "Vernost'," and "Mal'čik iz Trall,"** were written in rapid succession during December, 1927, and the last, **"Zemlja na rukax,"** in June, 1928. In these works Pil'njak described a series of values which he apparently conceived to be independent of history, of time, place, culture, and individual caprice: courage, fidelity, beauty, and love. Meaning in existence is generated by their realization in human behavior.

It is significant, I think, that these stories were preceded by **"Delo smerti,"** a work which focuses in a distinctly Tolstojan manner upon mortality, stressing the inability of science to provide any soothing response to this inevitability. By now Pil'njak had moved far beyond his early "primitive Tolstojanism," and he understood fully one of Tolstoj's principal convictions, that the modern Western mind as it has developed since the seventeenth century is itself the source of the faulty but logically irrefutable conception that a disjuncture exists between man's consciousness and the law-governed, purposeless natural world of which his body is inescapably a perishable part. Pil'njak, unlike Tolstoj, did not resort to the Transcendental to conquer the resultant awareness of estrangement from the self and the world. Rather, he attempted to find eternal and absolute human values in this earth, within the texture of human life. The fourth title noted above, **"Zemlja na rukax,"** suggests his response to that pain the existentialists have termed the anguished sense of "anxiety," "homelessness," and "estrangement" which men often feel within the context of their world. The title hints as well at the critical role earth imagery plays in Pil'njak's works throughout the twenties.

These issues achieved their fullest expression in *Volga vpadaet v Kaspijskoe more.* For the previous two years Pil'njak had devoted himself almost exclusively to the short story, and he now returned to the long form to deal with the First Five-Year Plan. Although it is a commonplace to view this work as Pil'njak's faltering attempt to redeem himself after the events surrounding the publication of *Krasnoe derevo* in Berlin, this is an opinion scarcely defensible, I think, in light of demonstrable facts.

This survey of Pil'njak's career ignores the caprice and fun which have so often influenced critics. That there are passages in his work which display such characteristics is undeniable, but the general tenor of Pil'njak's art is the antithesis of mirth and jocularity. In spite of his rhetorical flair and a liking for caricature which frequently induce delight, Pil'njak generally avoided situational humor. For him, situational absurdity was not a stimulus for laughter as it often was, say for Zoščenko, but rather the source of emotional responses ranging from disgust to horror; such entanglements were symptomatic of the purposelessness, the "plotlessness," of human existence. The fact that his humor is largely verbal and not situational is also related to the abyss which underlies the statement, "Words to me are like coins to a numismatist." In it Pil'njak expressed his uncertainty concerning his depiction of "Truth." Do words woven into a tale reflect some immanent truth in the external world, or are they toys, pieces of verbal coinage which possess

no more inherent value than the random hunks of metal which men shape and treasure? The revolution for Pil'njak was hyperbolic history which exaggerated the basic dilemmas of human existence; in it he sought and failed to find some resolution to the problem of faith. Like the great writers of the nineteenth century, he is often disconcerting, and sometimes depressing.

Pil'njak was very much aware of those great writers. Scattered comments in his work suggest that he felt himself to be part of the greatest literary tradition in history. His ambitions, I think, were very high. He hoped to carve out a lofty niche for himself in that pantheon of artists. How high he managed to climb remains to be seen. (pp. 87-94)

> *Kenneth Norman Brostrom, in his* The Novels of Boris Pil'njak as Allegory, *a dissertation submitted to The University of Michigan, 1973, 370 p.*

VICTOR ERLICH   (essay date 1983)

[*Erlich is a Russian émigré educator and critic who has written extensively on Russian literature. In the following excerpt he discusses themes and techniques in Pilnyak's works, focusing on his most important novels.*]

In a sophisticated essay published in 1927 Viktor Gofman characterized the thoroughgoing crisis of Russian artistic prose as the

> disintegration of the essential elements of narrative fiction and of their traditional interrelationships. . . . Plot, narration, style broke up into their constituent parts and acquired independent existence as elements of a potential construction, as illustrative (and approximate) samples of plot, narration and style—a *sui generis* literary inventory.

Not inappropriately, this cheerless diagnosis was offered in conjunction with an astute and harshly critical assessment of Boris Pilnyak, a prolific and resourceful writer, dubbed by D. S. Mirsky in 1925 "a sort of epitome of modern Russian fiction." In his unselective responsiveness to virtually all the styles, techniques, and quests available to an early-twentieth-century Russian prose writer and his near-obsession with the ultimate meaning of the Russian revolution, he is indeed one of the most representative literary figures of his era.

Pilnyak began his career on the eve of the revolution. His early stories, couched in the vein of somber poetic realism, owed more to Bunin than to either Bely or Remizov. By comparison with the novels that followed, **"Over the Ravine" ("Nad ovragom"), "The Lure of Death" ("Smertelnoe manit"), "Mother Earth" ("Mat syra zemlia"),** were relatively subdued and succinct performances. Yet the themes which were to become Pilnyak's trademark—nature versus civilization, the call of the wild, the indomitable power of the instinct—were unmistakably present in those tales as well as in his first small-scale attempts to portray post-October realities. Such narratives as **"At Nikola's" ("U Nikoly"), "Wormwood" ("Polyn"), "Arina," "The Belokonsky Estate" ("Imenie Belokonskoe")** . . . offer suggestive glimpses of the Russian countryside gripped by revolutionary fever.

It is a tribute to Pilnyak's hankering after the "large form" as a necessary vehicle for rendering the rhythms and textures of "Russia's terrible years" that, in spite of his demonstrable affinity for the shorter narrative, he should have promptly embarked on what became his most characteristic and most influential work, *The Bare Year* (*Goly god . . .*), a vivid, fragmentary, disheveled pageant of the year 1919, the year of famine and hope, of savagery and euphoria. By the same token, it is a symptom of the relative fluidity of genre boundaries in Russian narrative fiction of the early twenties that this, Pilnyak's first novel, should have been made up in large part of several of the post-1917 stories cited above. (Previously featured episodes and characters—the dreamy anarchist Andrei, the free and sensuous Arina, the idealistic young noblewoman Natalia, the archeologist Budek—surface again in *The Bare Year*.) This proclivity for self-quotation, for drawing heavily upon one's previous works, is still more apparent in Pilnyak's second novel, *Machines and Wolves* (*Mashiny i volki*), . . . which, in addition to multiple echoes from *The Bare Year*, incorporates several short narratives Pilnyak had produced in the intervening two years. "A Pilnyak novel," quipped Shklovsky, "is a cohabitation of several short stories. One can take apart two novels and paste together out of them a third one."

This potential of the early Pilnyak novel for absorbing what Robert Maguire has called "ready-made materials" is inseparable from its loose-jointed, permissive, not to say inchoate structure, its tendency to draw into its orbit in a seemingly unselective, random fashion elements of various literary as well as nonliterary modes. In his excellent study *Red Virgin Soil* [see excerpt dated 1968] Maguire speaks aptly of an "assemblage of pages from a diary, letters, historical tracts, ethnographical sketches, anecdotes, dramatic monologues, political slogans, high rhetoric and obscene expletives." No wonder the champion of the well-constructed Western novel, Lev Lunts, was moved by Pilnyak's novelistic debut to concern and dismay. Writing to Maksim Gorky, he dubbed *The Bare Year* "a characteristic and outrageous phenomenon. . . ." "This is not a novel," he insisted, "but a collection of materials."

Interestingly enough, Lunts's scornful reference anticipated by some two years Pilnyak's own designation. About one-third of his *Machines and Wolves* was a slightly reshuffled version of a fragmentary sequence featured in 1922 in the journal *Red Virgin Soil* (*Krasnaya nov*) and entitled "**Materials for a Novel.**" The collagelike quality of *Machines and Wolves* was further signaled by a facetiously long-winded subtitle: "About the Kolomna province, about the Wolves and Machines, about black bread and Ryazan apples, about Russia, Rasseya [a folksy, substandard variant], Rus, about Moscow and the Revolution, about people, Communists and quacks, about the statistician Ivan Aleksandrovich Nepomnyashchy [literally "nonremembering"] and many others. . . ." Elsewhere, incidentally, Ivan Nepomnyashchy, whose dry facts and figures bearing on matters such as demography and industrial production keep obtruding themselves on the narrator's lyrical meanderings, is described, somewhat misleadingly, as the chief hero of the novel, even though he makes his first appearance on page 148!

The generic implications of this modus operandi are not easily pinned down. The proliferation of the folkloric and journalistic materials, the grafting upon the narrative of excerpts from old legal codes, newspaper clippings, or statistical tables represent an "orientation toward the document" (V. Gofman), or, in Pilnyak's own words, a "getting away for good from traditional *belles lettres*." At the same time, the blatant manipulation of recognizable literary models (Pilnyak's short novel *The Third Metropolis* [*Tretia stolitsa*] . . . includes a lengthy excerpt from Bunin's "The Gentleman from San Francisco" ["Gospodin iz San-Frantsisko"]), elaborately Sternian chapter headings in *Machines and Wolves* (for example, "A section of the book which lies outside of the narrative frame"), authorial leanings out of that frame ("This is not Robert Smith, this is I. B. Pilnyak speaking")—all these appear to be designed to point up the "literariness" of the proceedings. In either case the distinction between fact and fiction is called into question and the fluidity of the boundaries of the novelistic enterprise "laid bare," in Shklovsky's famous phrase.

One of the inevitable consequences of subverting the novel's traditional structure is the relative weakness of its two essential components: plot and characterization. The frantic shuttling between different locales, the interweaving of disparate episodes, makes a sustained narrative impossible and saps the reader's interest in the crisscrossing subplots. Perhaps more importantly the multiple characters, which emerge from and dissolve back into the "stylistic blizzard" (Tynyanov) and migrate, under identical or different names, from one Pilnyak narrative to another, remain underdeveloped if not shadowy. Shklovsky notes shrewdly that Pilnyak's heroes are actually not so much heroes as vehicles for, or signals of, the quasi-autonomous fragments with which they are associated. One might add that their function is thematic as well as compositional. They are also epitomes of social settings or groupings, of recognizable socio-historical roles or plights. The cast of each Pilnyak novel, be it *The Bare Year, Machines and Wolves,* or *The Third Metropolis,* is apt to include a guilt-stricken, idealistic scion of a decaying aristocratic family reaching toward the new (Gleb Ordynin in *The Bare Year*, D. Roshchislavsky in *Machines and Wolves*), a crusty peasant wizard full of "saws and modern instances," an iron-willed Bolshevik, a lusty young woman in search of sexual fulfillment, as well as a pure maiden who seems to have stepped out of the pages of a Turgenev novel (Natalia Ordynina in *The Bare Year* or Liza Kalitina in *The Third Metropolis*), and, finally, a passive observer-chronicler steeped in the old Russian lore. In addition to embodying some of the standard predicaments of the revolutionary era, many of Pilnyak's protagonists serve to illustrate the author's pat generalizations, to help articulate his obtrusive, not to say obsessive, historiosophic concerns. For one of the characteristics of the early Pilnyak novel is the proclivity for what Boris Eikhenbaum in his *The Young Tolstoy* calls "generalizatsia," that is, for arguing—and emoting—in the large.

The tendency to subsume destinies of individuals under unwieldy cultural-historical entities looms especially large in *The Third Metropolis,* an avowedly "nonrealistic" narrative, pointedly dedicated to Aleksei Remizov: "I dedicate this thoroughly nonrealistic novel [actually Pilnyak uses the noncommittal term *povest*] to Aleksei Remizov in whose workshop I was an apprentice."

In its opening passage, a wedged-in bit of "reality," an advertisement for the "people's baths" is followed by a staccato statement of the time and place of the *agon*, and a cast of characters:

> Time: the Lent of the eighth year of the First World War and of the downfall of the European civilization and the sixth Lent of the Great Russian Revolution. Place: there is no place of action. Russia, Europe, the world. *Dramatis personae:* there are none. Russia, Europe, the world, faith, disbelief, civilization, blizzards, thunderstorms, the images of the Holy Virgin.

People—men in overcoats with collars turned up. Women—but women are my sadness, to me, a romantic, the only thing, the most beautiful, the greatest joy....

The passage is doubly characteristic of Pilnyak. Quite apart from the self-indulgent "romantic" effusion triggered by the mention of women, it highlights, indeed overstates, the nearly anonymous or illustrative quality of Pilnyak's protagonists, overshadowed as they are by the large cultural complexes, "Russia, Europe, the world." In fact, it is the pervasiveness in Pilnyak's fiction of historiosophic, or, if you will, historio-publicistic concerns—the authorial addiction to dichotomies such as Russia/Europe, East/West, Moscow/Petersburg, city/village, nature/civilization—which serves here as a sui generis organizing principle and prevents the seemingly anarchic mass of styles, genres, time levels, episodes that constitutes the Pilnyak novel from actually disintegrating. These antinomies provide discernible, if at times tenuous, links between the disparate elements of a gaudy mosaic whose only common denominator otherwise would have been carefully contrived incoherence.

Pilnyak's ideational leitmotifs have a counterpart in insistent verbal refrains. In a careful analysis of Pilnyak's early fiction, A. Schramm discerns in its tissue a high incidence of rhythmical-syntactical parallelism and alliteration as well as a strong predisposition for repeating opening words, "Here there are no roads. Here wild ducks cry. Here it smells of slime, peat, marsh gas" (*Zdes netu dorog. Zdes krichat dikie utki. Zdes pakhnet tinom, torfom, bolotnym gazom*), and indeed, entire passages.

No less pervasive are Pilnyak's favorite images, most notably the snowstorm (*metel*), which lends the title and the ambience to one of Pilnyak's best short stories and which sweeps or howls its way through many pages of *The Bare Year*. In a rather telling effect which proved too "Futurist" for the taste of Lvov-Rogachevsky, an aesthetically conservative critic, the all-Russian blizzard becomes an auditory correlative of social innovation as it is made to sing out bizarre-sounding early Soviet institutional abbreviations: "And today's song in the snowstorm. Snowstorm. Pines. Clearings. Terrors. Shooyaya, shooyaya, shooyaya . . . Gviuu, gaauu, giviiiuum, giviiiiiuuuu. And—Gla-vboom! Gla-bvooomm!! . . ." One hundred and thirty pages later the snowstorm sings again, and the persona clearly delights in the Tyutchevian "chaos of sounds": "Ah! What a storm when the wind eats the snow! Shoyaa, Shoy-oyaa! Shoooyaaa! . . . Giviiu, gaaum! Glav-bum! Glav-bum! Gu-vuzz! Ahh! What a snowstorm! How snowstormy! [*Kak metelno!*] How g-o-o-d!" As the novel closes, the snowstorm surfaces again as "it hurls itself like furies" against the indestructible, primeval Russian forest, which "stands firm like a stockade...."

The symbolic import of the image which dominates *The Bare Year* is as obvious as it is derivative. Pilnyak's *metel* comes in a straight line from the *vyuga* which blows snow in the faces of Alexander Blok's bloodstained apostles. (Pilnyak's indebtedness to the author of *The Twelve* [*Dvenadtsat*] is pointed up by the epigraph drawn from Blok's famous 1914 lyric, whose operative line is "We, children of Russia's terrible years.") In Pilnyak as in Blok the blizzard stands for the October Revolution, viewed by both as an elemental force, a purifying storm. In *The Bare Year* this notion is given a primitivist and nativist slant. The upheaval turns out to be an indigenous peasant rebellion which owes much more to Pugachov than to Karl

Marx and which threatens to shatter the painstakingly erected edifice of alien, post-Petrine bureaucracy, a resurgence of eternal, unreconstructed, rural, grass roots Russia. The theme is repeatedly sounded and variously orchestrated as it weaves its way from the impassioned monologues of upper-class intellectuals to the more pungent mutterings of canny rustic old-timers. The gentle dreamy Gleb Ordynin provides one of the most explicit statements:

> The Revolution set Russia against Europe.... Russia, in its way of life, customs and towns ... returned to the seventeenth century.... Popular rebellion is a seizure of power and creation of their own genuine Russian truth by genuine Russians.... Who will win this struggle—mechanized Europe or sectarian, orthodox spiritual Russia? ...

To the old peasant wizard Yegorka, the revolution is a throwback to Stenka Razin:

> There is no International, but there is a popular Russian revolution, rebellion after the image of Stepan Timofeyevich [Razin].... How about Karl Marx? He is a German, I say, so he must be a fool. As for the Communists, to hell with them! The Bolsheviks will manage without them!

Are we justified, one might inquire at this point, in reducing the polyphony, indeed cacophony, of the Pilnyak universe to a common ideological denominator? Can his disheveled literary chronicle, which passes in review the entire spectrum of contemporary attitudes toward the revolution from "decadent" aristocratic escapism through the neo-Slavophile and anarchist modes of acceptance to Bolshevism, be said to yield an unambiguous message? At least one recent student of the early Pilnyak, the already mentioned A. Schramm, thinks not. Calling attention to such structural characteristics of *The Bare Year* as mediating some sections of the novel through the consciousness of the individual protagonists (for example, the relevant chapter headings are "Through Andrei's Eyes," "Through Natalia's Eyes," "Through Irina's Eyes"), she posits the underlying pluralism and open-endedness of *The Bare Year* and *Machines and Wolves*. The choice of the optimal stance or perspective is allegedly left to the reader.... (pp. 157-62)

Schramm has a point, but she fails to make important distinctions. To be sure, ideological consistency was not Pilnyak's forte. It is a matter of record that through the 1920s, often to the dismay of the orthodox Soviet critics, he shunned doctrinal commitment and kept his sensibility wide open to the ambiguities and contradictions of the revolutionary process. Yet, the montagelike accumulation of heterogeneous detail, often resulting in a virtual orgy of enumeration, apparently designed to produce the impression of the bewildering multifariousness of the new reality, should not be mistaken for a pluralistic vision or a genuine sense of complexity. By the same token, toying with multiple points of view is not tantamount here to nondirective, let alone self-effacing, authorial stance. One of the reasons why Pilnyak's dramatis personae often fail to emerge as memorable or distinctive presences is the imperiousness or near-ubiquitousness of the author's preoccupations, the frequent obtrusion of the "monological" upon the seeming polyphony. ("The hero of these books," Pilnyak wrote in 1923, "is my life, my thought, and my actions.") The "pervasive historiosophic concept" that haunts his novels may not represent their unequivocal conclusion, but it does have the force of the privileged frame of reference. It seems to serve as a salient rationalization for the underlying gut reaction to the upheaval, a sense of exhilaration over the sheer sweep of events, a reveling in the chaos which plays havoc with normal inhibitions and constraints: "Ah! What a snowstorm! How snowstormy! How good!" In spite of his somewhat helpless attraction to ideas or rather to generalities, Pilnyak is not an intellectual novelist.

If this celebration of untrammeled and often destructive spontaneity (*stikhiinost*) is not always as full-throated as it might have been, that has, to my mind, less to do with Pilnyak's novelistic evenhandedness than with his deep-seated ambivalence toward the regime which emerged from the October Revolution and the mentality which presided over it. The section of *The Bare Year* dealing with the Bolshevik activists has drawn much comment. Robert Maguire is quite justified in calling attention to Pilnyak's sarcasm: "This is what we know, this is what we want, this is what we have stated—that's all there is to it." Yes, the "men in leather jackets" are single-minded, self-assured, know-it-all simplifiers. Moreover, they insist on using foreign words and on mangling them, to boot (*enegichno fuktsirovat*). But if Pilnyak's influential protector, A. Voronsky, missed the sarcastic note in this portrayal of the "new men," the American critic seems oblivious to Pilnyak's grudging admiration for the Bolsheviks' vigor, energy, and sense of purpose: "Of the Russian crumbly, rough nation, a topnotch selection." Nor do they merely "fuction enegetically." Some of them are clearly capable of love and tenderness, of delicacy of feeling. The nearly chaste encounter between the dedicated Communist Arkhipov and Natalia Ordynina is an oasis of "purity and intelligence" in the violence-ridden and brutally carnal universe of *The Bare Year.*

If ambivalence is one of the undercurrents in *The Bare Year,* it seems to lie at the core of Pilnyak's second full-length novel, *Machines and Wolves,* whose very title announces its central dichotomy. In the early portion of *Machines and Wolves* the wolf prowling in the Russian countryside, an all too obvious symbol of untamed, savage nature, cuts a glamorous, nearly heroic figure. This romanticization is promptly undercut by the luridly naturalistic portrayal of a savage struggle for survival between wolves and peasants, a struggle in which the moral boundary between the hunters and the hunted often appears fluid. As the disjointed narrative presses on, the myth of the proud, beautiful wolf—"terrible like Stenka Razin's rebellion"—is increasingly challenged by another brand of romanticism, that of the "machine revolution":

> Along with the peasant rebellion, hostile, like Pugachov's, to cities and factories, there marched on the romanticism of the proletarian revolution. . . . Communists, men of the machine, heretics . . . reached toward the truth of the machine . . . and toward a world stern like the diesel. . . . Russia is the first country to dare replace man by machine and in so doing to build justice. . . .

The paths of the Roshchislavsky brothers recall those of the Ordynins in *The Bare Year,* heirs to a decaying aristocratic family. They part tragically. The pure-of-heart but unhinged Yuri, who threw in his lot with the "wolves," perishes, overcome by madness. Dmitri espouses the gospel of the machine revolution: "Emancipated labor will dig canals, dry out seas . . . bring the good news to Man. This will be accomplished by genius, culture and the proletarian. Russia was the first to call

out to the workers of the world. This is the metaphysics of the proletariat and I am with the machine-minded Communists." Dmitri could proclaim the vision but it was not given to him to implement it. The gentle apostle of industrialization is vanquished by native backwardness and savagery; he is killed by village hoodlums. It falls to a dedicated foreign specialist, the English engineer Frost, to pick up the banner of liberation through the machine and wave it in the faces of the backsliders and neophilistines: "Only labor, only accumulation of values can save Russia."

Throughout the novel the status of the "metaphysics of the proletariat" remains precarious. The triumph of technology may liberate man, but it is no less likely to displace or supersede him. The finale of *Machines and Wolves* offers neither a denouement nor a resolution of the dilemma. The conflict between the two myths is smothered by the booming rhetoric of momentary nationwide consensus as the peasant and the proletarian join in the mourning of "the man who was an era," "a man who died in order to become a legend"—Vladimir Lenin. As the sirens of new Russia proclaim the ascendancy of the machine ("The human revolutions of machines and the world march on"), somewhere in the heart of rural Russia the tame, innocuous chronicler, the statistician Ivan Alexandrovich Nepomnyashchy, collapses in an epileptic fit and two ultra-Russian earth mothers hasten to his rescue.

It is symptomatic of Pilnyak's much advertised romanticism that his apparent inner conflict should have assumed the form of an uneasy shuttling between two rival utopias, those of the Noble Savage and of liberation through technology, rather than of a more common stalemate between nostalgia and a grudging recognition of new realities. Apparently, Pilnyak found it difficult to resist the lure of any ideology that could be construed as a myth.

This proclivity, indeed gluttony, for mythmaking, coupled incongruously with a measure of creative intransigence and a keen eye for stark realia, may well underlie what appears to me a still deeper, and more fundamental, Pilnyakian polarity. At times he seems to have been of two minds not only about the relative virtues of spontaneity and organization, of nature and technology, but also about the relative merits of truth and illusion. *The Third Metropolis* contains an astounding passage. Robert Smith, an affluent and smug yet perceptive English businessman visiting Russia in the early twenties, notes in his diary a striking discrepancy between what is being said and what is actually happening, a ubiquitous affinity for denial: "The lie is everywhere, in work, in social activity, in family relations. Everybody's lying—the Communists, the bourgeois, the workers, even the enemies of the Revolution, the entire Russian nation is lying. What is this?—a mass psychosis, an illness, a blindness?" Quite unexpectedly, the profoundly disturbing syndrome turns out to be a positive phenomenon. "I have thought much," continues Mr. Smith, "of the will to see and related it to the will to dare [literally, "to want"—*khotet*]; apparently, there is another will—the will not to see whenever the will to see clashes with the will to dare. Russia lives today by the will to dare and the will not to see. . . ."

It would be much too hasty to assume that Mr. Smith speaks here for Boris Pilnyak, the more so since in his nearly concurrent literary credo, **"Excerpts from a Diary,"** "the will not to see" is invoked in a pejorative context: "I do not acknowledge that a writer ought to live with the 'will not to see' or, to put it bluntly, the will to lie. I know very well that I am not able to write otherwise than I write now. . . . I do not know how, I will not. . . . There is a law of literature which prohibits, makes impossible, the violation of a literary gift.'' As a chronicler of the birth pains of the new Russia, Pilnyak neither ignored nor soft-pedaled the appallingly high human cost of social change, the "hunger, death and terror." (The justly acclaimed description, in *The Bare Year,* of freight train #57 "crammed with people, flour and filth," is a telling spectacle of human degradation, as well as human resilience.) Because of his habit of blurting out unauthorized, inconvenient truths, he repeatedly ran afoul of the powers-that-be, whether by hinting at the ruthlessness of the incipient Stalin rule in the poignant **"Tale about the Unextinguished Moon" ("Povest nepogash-ennoi luny")** . . . or by a sympathetic portrayal, in *Mahogany* **("Krasnoe derevo")** . . . , of the last Mohicans of revolutionary fundamentalism, including—horribile dictu!—a Trotskyite.

But this, it seems to me, is only part of the story. While *The Third Metropolis* is no more conclusive or ideologically coherent than *Machines and Wolves,* its central theme is the contrast between moribund, decadent, "Spenglerian" Europe and Russia, "destitute, hungry lice-ridden," but vital, throbbing, "on the march." May not the "blindness" observed by Mr. Smith, the "will not to see," be one of the essential sources of this dynamism, of this headlong thrust toward the future, a thrust which could well have been paralyzed or slowed down by undue awareness of the price exacted by it? As usual, one cannot be sure, but there is little in *The Third Metropolis* to offset this implication.

At times Pilnyak's frenzied rhetoric tends to blur the boundary between truth and untruth as it insists strenuously on the "greatness" of the mystiques which move men and women to heroic action. The above-quoted passage from *Machines and Wolves* where the narrator emotes about the "machine and truth about to be embodied in the world" is preceded by the statement that "a great lie, like a great truth, was being created in Russia." A critic such as Robert Maguire, who sees Pilnyak as a more or less consistent *Maschinensturmer,* might well interpret this bizarre phrase as "a great lie posing as a great truth." But to me the tenor of the sequence does not appear as straightforward as that. The issue here, one suspects, is not a willful distortion of reality by self-deceived or dishonest propagandists, but the fluidity of the boundary between truth and illusion in a realm where the scope, the "grandeur," of a social vision matters more than its validity.

It is no reflection, finally, on the integrity of Pilnyak's quest for the ultimate meaning of his profoundly bewildering era to say that his residual commitment to one of the Russian novelist's time-honored traditions, that of truth-telling, was jeopardized by his peculiar susceptibility to eschatological bombast, to the intoxicating fumes of utopian mystique. One can only speculate that his apparent moral confusion did little to prevent his hasty "reorientation" (*perestroika*) in the face of a vicious official campaign, as the pointed candor of *Mahogany* gave way to the essentially meretricious and hyperbolically celebratory tenor of *The Volga Flows to the Caspian Sea (Volga vpadaet v Kaspiiskoe more)*. . . . (pp. 162-67)

But this, as Dostoevsky might say, is the beginning of a new story. My concern here is with the place of Pilnyak in early Soviet fiction, with his role as one of the pioneers of the postrevolutionary Russian novel. Whether one sees his early large-scale narrative as a possible solution to the much-touted crisis of the novel, or one of its most acute symptoms, it was designed to serve as a fictional correlative of a profoundly traumatizing historical experience. The manner and the matter,

the medium and message, were made to cohere in their very incoherence, with the actual chaos rendered, or approximated, by seeming compositional anarchy. Even as the novel's structure contrived to emulate its subject, its imagery—a whirl of antinomies—embodied the underlying stance of a writer impaled on the horns of a dilemma he was unable to resolve. (pp. 162-67)

> Victor Erlich, "The Novel in Crisis: Boris Pilniak and Konstantin Fedin," in The Russian Novel from Pushkin to Pasternak, *edited by John Garrard, Yale University Press, 1983, pp. 155-76.*

GARY BROWNING (essay date 1985)

[*Browning is the author of the biographical and critical study* Boris Pilniak: Scythian at a Typewriter. *In the following excerpt from that work, he examines dominant themes and techniques of Pilniak's fiction and analyzes* The Naked Year, *detailing the author's presentation of four distinct themes and his use of various literary techniques and rhetorical devices.*]

Pilniak's theme for a given work emerges from his current thoughts and moods. This theme becomes a "focal point" for "disparate rays" of inspiration. It then determines form and style. The vast majority of Pilniak's works center on aspects and combinations of four themes: instinct, ideology, Russia's heritage and destiny, and culture and "barbarism." These themes are complex and dynamic.

Underlying and pervading all else in life, according to Pilniak, is man's deep and spontaneous allegiance to instinct, particularly to sexual love and propagation. Beyond time, history, philosophy, religion, and science stands one preeminent and immutable truth: all live to reproduce. Especially in Pilniak's earlier works, spring signals the reawakening of life through its solitary "law of birth." Frequently, in the spring, young virgin girls gather to perform ancient mating dances and songs. Other calendar customs, legends, rites, folk art, and medicine also acquire fullest meaning in the earthy joys of sexual reproduction. Both Pilniak's elemental, dangerously "wild," passionate maidens and his older and worldly-wise women intuitively understand that, whatever else life may require, their one fundamental instinct is to bear children, for a child is his parents' promise of eternity. Therefore, a woman, regardless of the abandon or restraint with which she has loved, is cloaked in the mantle of virtue and high solemnity as she conceives and gives birth. Pilniak likens the sensations evoked by the centuries-old Annunciation and Mother-of-God ikons to the purity and the sublime emotions swelling in his heroines, who rejoice in those same timeless glad tidings. Marriage is bonded through the blood of childbirth, and worthy mothers esteem their progeny above all social or even personal considerations. They may seek solace for their own matrimonial disappointments in boundless love for their children.

However, human love is fragile; it is rarely perfect or enduring in its joy. In many of his works Pilniak portrays love aborted by male lethargy or perfidy, misplaced priorities that draw the woman away from love, irreversible errors in the timing of one's impulse to bear children, and violence that tragically destroys the climate for loving. Further, love is easily perverted through debauchery as an individual wantonly indulges the sexual appetite without regard for universal standards of morality and the soul of one's partner. In this orgiastic abyss the sensual man, often an artist (writer or painter) or intellectual, is superficial and treacherous, while the wanton woman contracts a venereal disease, nature's vengeance for her sterile promiscuity.

Although man's instinct to love and bear children receives most of Pilniak's attention, he also treats an instinct beckoning man toward death. The author portrays death as an indifferent ineluctability, and man's appropriate response as dignified courage. When death comes at the natural time of the life cycle and when one's pledges to nature and humanity have been redeemed, death, like birth and propagation, possesses an attraction and a somber beauty. Together with the biological instincts of propagation and death, Pilniak emphasizes, late in his career, other "instincts" or ingrained behavior: social (equality and justice), moral-ethical (honesty and brotherhood), and, finally, aesthetic (refined artistic taste).

Pilniak's second major theme concerns ideology. In addition to life's meaning that springs from "man's unconscious, in instinct, in blood, in sun," another meaning arises from "the mind, duty, honesty, and the open blinds of consciousness." With his rational faculties, man searches for answers to questions about religion and ideology. Although Pilniak uses biblical images and quotations for titles and epigraphs to several of his early works, he professes no belief in God. He writes in 1921 that, for him, Christianity is a "mute charter," much less compelling in its appeal than paganism with its worship of nature. When Pilniak discusses the issue of belief in his early works, he portrays the anguish of disillusionment and faithlessness, leading some to seek "truth and God" in the simple folk, and others to contemplate or commit suicide.

A related strain from his earliest to his final works, but especially prominent from the revolution until the late 1920s, is the theme of relativism and pan-humanism in ideology. Most prominent is the Heraclitian assertion that "all flows, all passes," even in ideological systems. This philosophy prompts disdain for rabid ideologues, but tolerance for all who are sincere in their individual quests for truth. In moments of serenity and lucidity Pilniak's wisest observers acknowledge that beyond all ideological welter and flux remains a massive, bed-rock reality: all men everywhere are brothers, united much more by their common humanity than differentiated through transitory ideologies. Nevertheless, Pilniak genuinely admires the vitality, vision, determination, courage, honesty, the commitment to enriching man materially and culturally, and the devotion to brotherhood and justice of the "genuine" bolsheviks, who play a role in many of the author's works from 1920 to 1937. Pilniak is, however, outspoken in his criticism of bolshevism's "barbarity," the negative side of this ascendant ideology.

Beginning with the October Revolution, Pilniak engages a third broad theme: the heritage and destiny of Russia. In its earliest form this theme examines the question of national survival and suggests that, despite the violence and hunger threatening Russia during "Varangian" times, she will not perish. Vast inner resources will protect her essence. On the other hand, disease and death are the fate of many of the wealthy nobles who pervert love, squander a spiritual and intellectual heritage, and vitiate their physical powers through drunken excess. The first phase of the revolution appeared to Pilniak (and to many others of the time) as a spontaneous, rural, anarchic, peasant rebellion against everything "foreign" to the soul of Mother Russia, in the spirit of Sten 'ka Razin and Emel'ian Pugachev. Peter the Great served as a convenient symbol of all that is unnatural, unhealthy, and western. This encrustation had been forced upon a temporarily immobile but essentially much more powerful host, as melted wax poured onto a steel ball. When the ball is

again set in motion, the wax shatters and flies off at every contact, revealing once more the indestructible, pre-eighteenth century, "pure" Russian core.

Pilniak also seeks to understand Russia's place and role in the East-West (Rome-Byzantium) dichotomy, especially the relations of the third center (Russia) to the other two. Is a regenerated and revitalized Russia now preparing to assume her place of destiny as mankind's "third capital"? Gradually the "bolshevik builder" theme replaces all these issues concerning the revolution. The "builder" theme parallels that which culminates Pilniak's interest in ideology.

The final principal theme to agitate the writer throughout his career is culture and barbarism. Culture represents the liberating and ennobling features of civilization, often facilitated through the material abundance that advanced technology affords. The leading manifestation of barbarism is any form of violence. Force destroys both personal love and cultural or social progress when it is the means to the end. The "instinct of the bludgeon," one of man's oldest and most persistent impulses, must not compensate for incompetence or cowardice. And any "Utopia" that can succeed only by depriving man of his freedom, his individuality, his sensitivity, and his healthy instincts is a sterile and flawed *machine,* doomed to self-destruction. A form of barbarism particularly repugnant to Pilniak is material and cultural poverty, which, if sustained, deprives man of dignity, transforming him into a brutish animal. Pilniak vigorously pursues the culprits, tsarist and communist, who debase the powerless laborer through, most commonly, demeaning working conditions.

The last major component of Pilniak's conception of barbarism is *poshlost'*, a revolting blend of philistinism, incompetence, and hypocrisy. His preferred targets are "weekend bolsheviks" and petty Soviet bureaucrats who vulgarize all they do and ostensibly believe through their suffocating mediocrity.

These themes—instinct, ideology, Russia, and culture and barbarism—are often intertwined in intricate combinations; no two are ever mutually exclusive. For example, in *Naked Year* the "leather jacket" bolshevik Arkhip Arkhipov embodies elements of all four themes. His instinct for love and propagation is healthy and moves him to propose to Natal'ia, a fellow bolshevik, with whom he hopes to raise "intelligent kiddies" (*detishki razumnye*). He represents the vigorous and sincere young bolsheviks who appear capable of replacing both the insensitive commercial West ("Europe with a briefcase") and the stagnant East (the vapid "Heavenly Empire") with a third power characterized by energy and innocent exuberance ("mogét enegrichno fuktsirovat'" [*sic*]). Arkhip has a beard "like Pugachev's," which suggests that he is a reincarnation of the pre-Petrine folk, the custodians of Russia's and perhaps humanity's uncorrupted and untrammeled native soul. Finally, he is committed to battle barbarism, which binds man in the chains of "stupidity, falsity, and pain."

On the other hand, Olen'ka Kunts, also from *Naked Year,* represents the perverse side of the same themes. Her love is trivial, debauched, and without progeny. She is superficially a bolshevik, more from expectation of personal advantage than from conviction. Kunts (the name is foreign) has nothing in common with the aspirations of her fellow Russians. Her contribution to bridging the East-West schism is to play the role of a "virgin" who mates with a "westerner" (Ian Laitis from Lithuania) in order to conceive a "savior" for Russia. This trivial, mystical scheme is treated ironically and is a vulgarization of Arkhip's far less pretentious but ultimately much more grandiose resolution. Olen'ka mindlessly mimeographs and signs arrest warrants, although she whines sentimentally when one of these is used against her neighbor. She is "barbaric" in her hypocrisy, incompetence, and cultural poverty.

Pilniak is essentially a romantic writer, inclined to the exotic, the sensational, the decadent or transcendent, the astonishing and coincidental, and the concealed "truth." Even in his travel sketches, a preeminently realistic genre, Pilniak seeks meaning in apparent mystery, avidly focuses on the exceptional, and draws sweeping conclusions from "typical" manifestations of the national soul. And when he first writes about the role of the machine in human progress, he does so with a note of mysticism, for although the machine is "bloodless" it has a soul, the soul of regimentation, monotony, and death. Later, in the sketches praising the scientific and technological accomplishments of socialism, Pilniak is most attracted to the extraordinary heroism of the explorers and workers, the immensity and power of the factories, and the breathtaking contrasts between early production without mechanization and current, more technologically advanced methods. He views the new from as strikingly romantic a perspective as the superseded but tenaciously alluring old. Even "documents," ostensibly genuine and mundane, are selected and, if necessary, revised to reflect the unusual and hidden truth.

In his fiction Pilniak most often uses contemporary "reality" to demonstrate the cyclical nature of man's history and the primacy of "eternal," human concerns. He frequently devotes his energies to the unusual or even bizarre, the extremes of diseased debauchery and youthful vitality, the danger-fraught and tragic, and moments of personal epiphany and insight. The author relishes the dialectical, colloquial, and substandard language of his characters, for, as he often repeats in *Machines and Wolves,* "words to me are like coins to a numismatist." And he enjoys startling the reader by announcing in advance the fate and even death of a character who is just beginning to play a role in the work. On the second page of **"Damp Mother Earth"** Pilniak reveals that his heroine will perish, and in **"Zavoloch'e"** he discloses that, of the twenty-two men in the Arctic rescue party, only one, Lachinov, will survive.

Pilniak willingly distorts, exaggerates, and invents "reality" to serve his themes and ideas. This tendency arose, he later admits, when as a small boy with a surging fantasy he "lied so that I could bring nature and concepts into an order which seemed to me to be the best and most engrossing. I lied incredibly, and suffered because I was despised by those around me, but I could not help lying." This playful *mea culpa* could serve as an epigraph to Pilniak's entire artistic creation; it demonstrates that "fantasizing is far more interesting than rummaging around in reality."

Pilniak's style, frequently self-conscious and mannered, reflects above all a concern for euphony and rhythm. The author recalls that these tendencies also developed from his childhood. As a small boy, oblivious to all, he would sit on a toy horse in front of a mirror "many hours every day for whole months" and talk to himself as he pretended to battle the Pecheneg and Polovtsian enemy: "I know that I *reveled* there in front of the mirror, and I still remember that sitting in front of the mirror was *essential*." He further emphasized the importance of speaking out loud: "Until I was eighteen I talked to myself. I was ashamed of it, but it was a need I had. I used to go into the forest or to some deserted spot, and there I composed aloud,

by word, by sound, giving an organization to what I had seen, and fantasizing in order to organize."

On another occasion he explained that "every word has its own sound texture. One must not combine words of disparate sound textures just as one must not build houses by combining a row of bricks with a row of logs and then another row of bricks." Pilniak displays little notion of theoretical linguistics or literary theory; he composes naturally, by ear, according to what *sounds* best. In Pilniak's finest works the results are impressive, especially as the author describes nature. (pp. 79-84)

The preferred figures of speech (tropes) in Pilniak's works are metonymy, simile, and especially allegory, although, on occasion, he uses metaphor, hyberbole, and personification. By far the best known of Pilniak's metonymies is the use of the "leather jacket" for a bolshevik. The sections of *Naked Year* entitled "The Leather Jackets" were frequently published separately and eventually aroused the ire of Stalin himself, who, betraying his ignorance of Pilniak's method, objected to this image devoid of "revolutionary perspective." Pilniak more frequently uses simile through the instrumental case, although "as" or "like" are also common. In *Naked Year,* for instance, the author portrays the inscrutable and lethargic East as peering out with eyes "like soldiers' buttons" (*soldatskimi pugovitsami*), impassive yet frighteningly powerful.

But Pilniak's favorite trope is allegory. He rarely uses the rather obvious continuous allegory or openly propagandizing allegory, but he frequently employs the *implicit allegory* in which additional connotations unobtrusively complement and broaden the surface meaning. The primary feature of implicit allegory is a preference for "mannequin" characters, interesting mainly for the ideas which shroud them. In *Naked Year,* for example, members of the Ordynin family are far more allegorical than individual. Boris is implicitly associated with an early Russian saint and explicitly with the biblical Samson and the epic folk heroes, the *bogatyri.* And he stands for impoverished Russian noblemen who have squandered their many forms of wealth and are now bereft of faith or intellectual commitment.

Pilniak also uses symbols, albeit rarely, to suggest deeper meaning. Among the best examples are China Town in *Naked Year,* the Russian crone in *Machines and Wolves,* and the moon in the **"Tale of the Unextinguished Moon."**

Virtually all of Pilniak's tropes and symbols until 1924, and many even later, arise from his myth of the preeminence of the individual in nature's unchanging life cycle. This myth starkly conflicts with "scientific" communism's emphasis on the economics of the collective and on a dialectical development toward ever higher states in man's history.

Pilniak often links words of the same grammatical category in lengthy chains that provide semantic "nests" or catalogs of meaning. These series are rhythmical and allusive, as important for their symbolic connotations as for denotation. In his syntax Pilniak evolves toward an elliptical, paratactic, impressionistic, "dynamic" prose style characterized by a sparse use of grammatical or logical connectives, in which individual words suggest but do not amplify associations. Pilniak, a Scythian at the typewriter, explains that he prefers writing "not belles-lettres, but rather roughly, like pagan burial mound statues and soaked oak," which technique, he asserts, is for him far more demanding than conventional methods. The author's memorable description of the train carrying "baggers" in search of food in *Naked Year* illustrates: "People, human legs, arms, heads, stomachs, backs, human excrement,—people covered with lice like the freight cars were with these people. People, having collected here and defended their right to travel with the greatest brute force, for there in the starving provinces at every station tens of hungry people threw themselves at the freight cars, and over heads, necks, backs, legs they crawled along people inside—they were beaten, they beat back, tearing out and throwing off those already in, and the fighting continued until the train started, carrying those off who had lodged inside, and those who had just crawled in prepared for a new fight at a new station.''

Pilniak's composition often appears arbitrary or gratuitous. He frequently seems to include too much from too broad a thematic spectrum. One searches for connectives and relations among the diverse parts. Most often, however, Pilniak does have a general design and a relatively coherent message for the reader. Although, he observes, there may appear to be no ''apparent logical connection between these things, a whole picture is formed because that is how it was all perceived.'' His works may resemble a ''writer's notebook''—a random presentation of ''raw'' data, bare facts, summary points, unworked material, and snatches of everyday life which form an overall impression of the context. Using this compositional structure, the author frequently comunicates meaning through montage— the parallel arrangement of scenes leading, through juxtaposition and association, to significant ideas—and collage—the apparently incongruous placement of seemingly unrelated materials that finally yield suggestive relationships of meaning.

A recurring, aphoristic, accretive refrain (leitmotif, literary echo) typically provides a key to the montage or collage. The refrain often appears near the beginning and end of the work; any occurrence of the refrain is incremental in meaning as a result of the story's illustrative subject matter. In **"Snow Wind"** . . . , for example, the wolf pack ''howls pleadingly, pleading for the leader to return'' from mourning over his dead mate. In the course of the story this refrain is repeated with variations until the pleading becomes more clearly motivated by a desire to kill the emotionally crippled leader and establish another more fit in his stead. The meaning of some works, among them *Naked Year,* can only be understood by carefully examining such central, accretive refrains. Referring to his accretive refrain as an image, Pilniak confides: ''From the phrase to the paragraph, to the chapter, to the whole work I trace how the reader will follow the image. I offer the reader an opportunity to be with *me,* not with the classical hero. . . . I myself, as a reader, want to participate in the creation of the image, and I request that I not be bound by the author's raptures.'' Among the noteworthy facets of this statement are Pilniak's expectation that the reader be seriously engaged rather than passively content with mere entertainment, and the definition of his hero: himself, his experience, and his time. Rather than the carefully drawn and psychologically profound characters of a Tolstoi or Dostoevskii, Pilniak's reader encounters an author crafting an image or refrain that encapsules and provides the key to an important human truth.

In narrative technique and atmosphere Pilniak presents a picture of diversity. His authorial point of view is fluid, embodying variations of first-person, romantic-ironical, and objective-dramatic methods as appropriate to the work or section within a work. In *Naked Year* he combines many points of view, including the objective depiction of Ordynin City; the ironical portrayal of the superficial bolsheviks; the dramatic conversations between Gleb and the priest Silvester; the first-person and lyrical scenes ''in the eyes'' of various characters, especially Irina; the author's ''baring the device'' as he addresses his reader directly through a first-person testimony in defense of the genuine bolsheviks; and others. In some scenes the tone is strictly documentary, while in others it is ironic, lyrical, or oracular. Regardless of narrative voice and tone, Pilniak rarely describes anything, anyone, or any time with epic exhaustiveness. He prefers the ''leaping and lingering'' biblical narrative style, which inspires much of old Russian literature and allows him to traverse vast expanses in search of stable meaning. The most important exception, however, is his depiction of nature. In most nature descriptions he creates a sensuous atmosphere, with abundant attention to smells, sounds, color, and texture. Finally, in some works, especially *Naked Year,* Pilniak is considered naturalistic and overly physiological in certain of his descriptions, but by today's standards he appears restrained and distinctly unerotic.

For Pilniak, narrative time generally implies a grand sweep. He prefers to portray man briefly at several points of his life, often finally from the perspective of his mature years. From this vantage the hero then generalizes in his wisdom born of experience and trial. Here too Pilniak ''leaps'' over long periods of time and ''lingers'' on dramatic, critically important moments. He gives little detail at intermediate stages, only brief summaries of what is pertinent to the hero's crisis or revelation in the present. For example, in **"Things"** . . . Pilniak portrays a woman who, thirty years before, was engaged to be married. The reader knows nothing of her earlier life or of her fiancé. Something unspecified occurs and she never marries. Now she must move, and in her packing she discovers three notes reminding her of her moment of happiness and prompting her to take along several items connected with that time of promise, instead of leaving them behind as she had intended. The solitary ray of sunshine in her life of otherwise unfulfilled love is connected with these few, suddenly very precious ''things.''

Finally, Pilniak frequently takes the opportunity in his works to perform literary penance. In one typical approach he parodies or otherwise ridicules his own former ideas and positions. He also frequently repents of his narcissism and lack of sexual restraint by including in many of his works autobiographical characters who possess his weaknesses to an exaggerated degree. In **"Zavoloch'e,"** for instance, Pilniak enshrines several of Peter the Great's features which he had earlier branded negative in **"His Majesty Kneeb Piter Komandor."** And the author creates a double for himself in the artist Lachinov, a dissolute and trivial egotist who is finally reborn a human being in the distant Arctic. (pp. 85-9)

In *Naked Year* Pilniak depicts four main groups: the provincial nobility; priests, mystics and sorcerers; anarchists; and the bolsheviks. The author plumbs each group's intellectual and spiritual depths both at a single historical juncture (the revolution) and in relation to the eternal perspective (love and family) to discover aspects of the many-faceted Russian soul and culture. The two common touchstones that reveal the viability of a given group or individual are, first, relation to the revolution and second, the expression of human love. In *Naked Year* Pilniak views the revolution as a purifying fire or a cleansing blizzard that is ridding Russia of artificially introduced foreign encrustations of material and religious culture, while clearing the way for the reassertion of ancient, native-Russian spiritual and social values. Each of the novel's characters inhibits, promotes, or is indifferent to this elemental purging by the revolution. More important, each individual is judged according to whether his beliefs and behavior enhance or pervert human love—thus leading to wholesome sexual union and engendering healthy children. Throughout *Naked Year* the church bells peal, piercing the barriers of the particular and fleeting moment in time (revolution), signaling passing time and eternal movement, and reminding the reader that propagating the species through love and family is primary in the life of man.

The Ordynin family (presumably from *orda,* the Golden Horde)—mainly a diseased and impotent group in precipitous decline—represents the provincial nobility. The Ordynins' position is virtually hopeless, for, being princes and princesses, they reject and are rejected by the revolution. Further, the debauched excesses of their fathers have bequeathed hereditary syphilis to the children, thereby making healthy reproduction unlikely. . . . In general the Ordynin family is associated with debauchery, abortion, disease, and abuse of power.

Members of the provincial nobility nevertheless make significant ideological statements that contribute to the novel's polyphony. The idealistic Gleb, for instance, when speaking with his uncle, the deranged but at times intellectually incisive Archbishop Sylvester, assumes the position of a Eurasianist. Gleb considers the mechanized and acquisitive European culture detrimental to man's spiritual development: "And everything is dead, a mass of machines, technology and comfort. The path of European culture led to war, 'fourteen was able to create this war. The machine culture forgot about the culture of the spirit, the spiritual." . . . Gleb views the revolution as a popular liberating force that has rid Russia of the process and consequence of westernization that Peter the Great inaugurated on a broad scale in the eighteenth century. The reader also discovers that Gleb's view of beauty and love anticipates the reemphasis of the heroic-religious in art, formerly produced by Russian artists: "Our ancient craftsmen interpreted the image of the virgin as the sweetest of truths, the spiritual essence of motherhood—universal motherhood." . . . For Gleb, love is primarily an abstract ideal to admire from a distance.

Sylvester agrees that the revolution is a popular rebellion (not ideological but social) of the genuine Russians (peasants), but he rejects Gleb's contention that Russian Orthodoxy is an inherent element in the mentality of these "genuine" Russians. No, he asserts, "Orthodox Christianity arrived with the tsars, with an alien power" . . . , and is being overthrown and cast aside along with the tsardom. A naturalistic peasant faith ("water sprites and witches, or Leo Tolstoy, or, if you don't watch out, Darwin" . . .) is emerging. Sylvester also perceives that peasant power is asserting itself in the new government: "they've reached Moscow, seized their own power and have begun to build their own state—and they will build it. They'll build it in such a way as not to interfere with or encroach on each other, like mushrooms in a wood." . . . As is essential in polyphony, Pilniak refrains from directly commenting upon or identifying with either voice, but maintains a discreet distance while proceeding to introduce other representative voices of the times.

The second major group of characters that Pilniak depicts (after the provincial nobility) includes those who base their commitments on the mystical and miraculous. While the Russian Orthodox archbishop Sylvester has lost his faith and mind, a degraded Freemasonry maintains its hold on the shell-shocked mystic Semyon Matveev Zilotov. The latter has become convinced through a misinterpretation of Masonic literature that Russia is destined to suffer "hunger, sedition and murder" . . . for twenty years more. After this period a savior will appear,

the fruit of a potent union between Russia and "a strange nation." The irony is unmistakable as Zilotov maneuvers to bring two ludicrous bolsheviks, the "virgin" Ol'ga Kunts and the faithless but willing Ian Laitis, to "sacred" union. Pilniak does not restrain his sarcasm for these two mediocre and hypocritical perverts, for they denigrate the purposes both of the revolution and of love.

Other prominent exponents of the metaphysical include the rural folk sorcerers, whose voice is far more vital. Pilniak is at his artistic best as he portrays the exotic beliefs and hoary customs of the white-haired sorcerer Egorka. This wizard is steeped in pre-Christian folk wisdom, sayings, incantations, herbal medicine, and superstitions. His attitude toward the revolution is presumably typical of a significant portion of backwater Russia: "There's no Internashnal, but there is a popular Russian revolution, a rebellion—and nothing more. Like Stephan Timofeevich's.—'And Karl Marx?' they asked.— 'A German,' I say, 'so he must have been stupid.'—'And Lenin'—'Lenin,' I say, 'was of peasant stock, a bolshevik, and I suppose you are communests. . . . But get rid, too, of— the communests!—the bolsheviks, I say, will sort things out by themselves'." . . . Like Sylvester, Egorka insists that the Russian bolsheviks are peasants who reject European culture and advance native aspirations. The view was common in the early 1920s that the bolsheviks (the word is of Russian derivation) were of the folk, while the communists (this word is borrowed into Russian) were ideologically oriented and intellectually motivated internationalists, and foreign. While "bolshevik" in politics, Egorka is, with respect to love, an exponent of the free and spontaneous, as found in nature among wild animals. For example, his affair with the forest girl, Arina . . . , demonstrates his uninhibited passion. Yet this coupling will not produce progeny—at least the story mentions none. Nevertheless, Egorka's vigorous voice and the opulent nature it endorses are undeniably alluring.

The third important collection of voices belongs to the anarchists. For a brief time in 1918 Pilniak had himself lived with anarchists and listened carefully to the adherents of a small, rural, utopian commune. In the third chapter of *Naked Year,* the author presents various views of the anarchists' way of life "through their own eyes." As he joins a commune, Andrei Volkovich experiences an exhilarating emancipation: "Freedom, freedom! Having nothing, refusing everything— being poor!" . . . Andrei is an appreciative observer of the female anarchists Aganka, Anna, Natásha, and Irina, who are entirely liberated. Yet somehow, like the brothers Ordynin, he lacks both the commanding personal vision and the stamina to actively create his world and to form stable relations to love and the revolution.

The anarchist Natal'ia, on the other hand, is moving toward a firm position regarding both. She has come to the environs of Ordynin with the archaeologist Baudek to excavate ancient burial mounds and cities built by unknown, pre-Scythian peoples from the Asiatic steppes. Here civilization had arrived and then vanished without written history, and now "in the stone vaults it was deathly, there was no longer a smell of anything, and every time it was necessary to enter them, thoughts became precise and peaceful, and sorrow entered the soul." . . . (pp. 115-18)

Natal'ia views the Russian people (masses) as destitute and vulnerable to extinction, yet indifferent to physical needs and perhaps possessing an ageless inner wisdom that transcends definition and formal communication. For Natal'ia, their revolution is associated with the bitter smell of wormwood growing at the digs. The wormwood is "the sadness of our days," but also an emblem of purification, for with it "the peasant women chase out devils and unclean spirits from their huts." . . . In her heart she accepts the revolution and at the same time is drawing nearer to love for Baudek. Were she not killed when the anarchists destroy their own commune following an altercation, she presumably would channel great energy into creative efforts. Yet the logical extension of anarchy is destruction, not creation, and Natal'ia perishes unfulfilled.

The final adherent of anarchism is Irina, who praises the laws of nature, specifically survival of the fittest. She eventually abandons Andrei, her flaccid fiancé at the commune, to become the wife of a sectarian peasant (and horse thief), Mark. Irina subscribes to the notion that "men don't ask—men take! They take freely and willfully, like bandits and anarchists!" . . . She proudly becomes the "slave" of the powerful and resolute Mark, who is also her "brother, protector, comrade." . . . Mark is an extreme representative of anarchism; he illustrates the life of a vigorous, daring, unfettered "bandit and anarchist." Through him another alternative, paralleling that of the sorcerer Egorka—a life independent of government and revolution; a life of robust and unaffected love—finds its place in the polyphony.

The fourth and final major set of voices belongs to the bolsheviks, a group equally as diverse as the others. The superficial, yet momentarily powerful and therefore menacing, police chief Ian Laitis and his assistant Olen'ka Kunts have been mentioned above. They provide a chilling reminder of the shallow opportunism and gnarled justice which many bolsheviks represented, and they are mercilessly exposed by the author. On the other hand, Donat Ratchin . . . and Tonia Ordynin . . . are young bolsheviks, children of merchant and noble families respectively, who provide a glimpse into the psychology of those motivated by a hatred rooted in past abuses, and by a determination to destroy that which has warped their lives.

Much more humane and touching is the portrait of the serious, hard-working, but ideologically and culturally naive peasant, Ivan Koloturov-Kononov. The winds of the revolution lift and drop him willy-nilly into the position of bolshevik chairman of a Poor Peasants' Committee. When circumstances force Ivan to evict a lifelong friend, another Ordynin prince, from his estate, a paradox results. The prince Andrei is actually invigorated when freed from his bondage to the material side of life, much as was the anarchist Andrei. Ivan, on the other hand, becomes progressively more bound to his minor bureaucracy and is increasingly estranged from his family and the soil. Ivan's error in assessing the value and function of a beautiful, one-handed, eighteenth-century clock (which he finally turns into a cupboard) suggests bolshevik disregard for the beneficial aspects of cultural and social progress in the past centuries (including Peter's eighteenth century). The error also scores the wasteful turning back of the hands of time to an era of relative crudity. The mounting exasperation Ivan feels from the lumps of mud he and his comrades strew all over the mansion floor indicates how difficult it is for a rather primitive, peasant bolshevik to quickly assume the role of master. When the nobles lived in the mansion, the floors were, by contrast, always clean.

The pair that eventually appears to best satisfy the criteria of a selfless and affirmative attitude toward the revolution and of a promise of healthy love and family are Natal'ia Ordynin and Arkhip Arkhipov. Natal'ia is "the only human being" . . . in her aristocratic family, a converted bolshevik who works as a doctor in the town hospital. Arkhip, who is from a hardy, clever, and honest peasant family, is now a member of the local Party Executive Committee. The section of *Naked Year* that details the marriage proposal between these two (Pilniak entitles it "the brightest" chapter in the novel) is a "poem" . . . about the power of love to heal and to elevate, for "man is not an animal, to love like an animal." . . . Merging the purest of the aristocracy with the strongest of the peasantry through the media of revolution and love produces firm expectations of future happiness.

Naked Year, then, includes many voices, most of them occasional rather than continual throughout the work. As in Dostoevskii's polyphonic novel, these voices coexist in autonomous worlds. Like Dostoevskii, Pilniak also "heard both the dominant, recognized, loud voices of the age, that is to say, the dominant, leading ideas (both official and unofficial), and the still-weak voices, the ideas which had not yet reached full development, the latent ideas no one else had yet discovered, and the ideas which were only beginning to mature, the embryos of future *Weltanschauungen*." Yet significant differences between the aesthetic systems of Dostoevskii and Pilniak render the two authors more divergent than similar. In Pilniak's polyphony the voices coexist but, contrary to Dostoevskii's, rarely interact. They are separate entities that do not enter into dialogical polemics. Pilniak tends to employ "integral dislogical contrapositions," wherein one should view characters and ideologies in implicit relation to each other like thematically related but discrete panels in a hinged ikonographic triptych.

However, Pilniak does create a semblance of organization. And he suggests a thematic convergence and ideological center through his masterful use of accretive refrains. These refrains recur intact or segmented, unchanged or slightly modified, throughout the novel. The technique is to introduce a refrain, then illustrate it through episodes from the life of the times, while at intervals repeating the refrain or its elements. With each partial or full repetition the refrain accretes in significance and acquires a more precise meaning.

In *Naked Year* the first and most important accretive refrain is "China-town" (*Kitai-gorod*). Early in the novel Pilniak introduces this image through references to commercial or industrial activity in three areas of Russia: Moscow, Nizhnii-Novgorod and Ordynin. In Moscow:

> In daytime China-town stirred with a million human lives—in bowler hats, in felt hats and homespun coats—itself a bowler hat and with a briefcase of bonds, shares, invoices, bills of exchange—of ikons, skins, manufactured goods, raisins, gold, platinum, Martianich vodka—a virtual Europe, all bowlerized.—But at night the bowlers disappeared from the stone sidestreets and town houses, emptiness and silence arrived, the dogs roamed about, and the streetlamps shone funereally among the stones, and the people, as rare as dogs, and wearing peaked caps, walked only into and out of Zariadie. And then in this desert out of the town houses and from under the gates crawled: China without a bowler hat on. The Heavenly Empire, which lies somewhere beyond the steppes to the east, beyond the Great Stone Wall, and looks at the world with slanting eyes, like the buttons of Russian soldiers' greatcoats. . . .

This China-town in Moscow is paralleled by others on a descending scale of organized activity as one moves from Moscow east to Nizhnii-Novgorod and Ordynin. The refrain is a concentrated statement of what the various story lines illustrate, a basic contrast between the poles of motion and rest, civilization and primitiveness, progress and stagnation, order and anarchy, mind and spirit, city (merchant-worker-factory-police) and country (production and protection by the peasant), "foreign" ideological systems (orthodoxy, capitalism, Marxism-communism) and native systems (paganism, the *mir* and bolshevism). (pp. 118-21)

When Pilniak first introduces [the second principal accretive refrain, the "leather jackets,"] the reader can justifiably view the leather jackets either positively or as objects of derision:

> Leather people in leather jackets (bolsheviks),—all the same size, each one a leather beauty, each one strong, with curls in ringlets under his peaked cap pushed back on his head; each had, more than anything else, will power in his protruding cheek-bones, in the lines around his mouth and in his lumbering movements—and audacity. Of Russia's rough, crumbly nationhood—the best slice. It's just as well they wear leather jackets—you won't wet them with the lemonade of psychology, this is what we have stated, this is what we know, this is what we want, and—that's all there is to it! Incidentally, surely none of them has ever read Karl Marx. . . .

Yet as the novel progresses Arkhip is shown to be deeply committed to his beliefs and work, and sincere in his love for Natal'ia. A gradual refocusing occurs until, as the above description is repeated near the end of the novel, a broader meaning appears. Now the ambiguous leather jackets—at whom the more sophisticated readers have patronizingly smiled—appear in a considerably more positive light. Arkhip still mispronounces certain Russian and foreign words that he has incompletely assimilated, but this is because of his rapid and diverse activity:

> The Russian word *mogut*—he articulated—*magut'*. In a leather jacket, with a beard like Pugachev's.—Is that funny?—there's funnier to come: Arkhip Arkhipov used to wake up with the dawn and quietly away from everyone:— he studied his books, Kiselev's *Algebra,* Kistiakovskii's economic geography, a history of fourteenth-century Russia (published by Granat), Marx's *Das Kapital,* Ozerov's *Financial Science,* Weitsmann's *Bookkeeping,* a teach-yourself German textbook—and he also studied a small dictionary of foreign words which had come into Russian, compiled by Gavkin.
>
> Leather jackets.
>
> Bolsheviks. Bolsheviks?—Yes. So—that's what bolsheviks are like! . . .

Whereas earlier Arkhip had not read Marx, even in Russian, he is now engaged in a comprehensive program of self-education that would rival that of any of his critics.

Significantly, Pilniak completely lays bare all artistic devices and introduces an episode from his own life that implies respect for the bolsheviks. After the Whites had been defeated, Pilniak

took part in an expedition to the industrial regions of the country to determine the condition of the factories. On this trip he met a determined bolshevik, Lukich, who disregarded the obvious problems and set out to overcome the "insurmountable": "I, the author, thought that we would be returning to Moscow, since *it was impossible to do anything*. But we set off—to the factories, *for there is nothing that cannot be done*—for it was not possible to do nothing. We set off, because the non-specialist Bolshevik K., Lukich, very simply reasoned that if it were done, there would be no need to do it, and hands—will accomplish anything. Bolsheviks. Leather jackets." . . . (pp. 122-23)

Other supportive accretive refrains could be discussed, but the meaning of *Naked Year* is finally drawn together through the refrains of three folk motifs. The first is a reference to Ivanushka the Fool . . . , who embodies important aspects of the China-town refrain and of the "Asiatic" Russian. Ivanushka in Russian folk tales is stupid and sluggish, yet he invariably triumphs in the end, presumably because simplicity and truth (innocence) are on his side (versus his opponents' greed and duplicity). Pilniak implies that although there are abysmal depths of ignorance and stagnation in Russia, primal truth is nevertheless embedded in the Russian soul (as Natal'ia perceives regarding the peasant family at the railroad station) and must therefore be victorious at last.

The second folk motif relates to the "living and dead waters." . . . The magical living waters restore to life that which is dead. An inference is that Russia, now undergoing a period of soul-rending suffering and prevalent death, will be restored to full life by living water. One form of that life-giving water may be the genuine bolshevik represented by Arkhip Arkhipov and Natal'ia Ordynin, the first having been instrumental in the "resurrection" . . . of the "dead" factory, and the second being a doctor and healer by profession.

Although rejuvenation is inevitable, the third folk motif registers a lament. In this motif the impatient Ivan Tsarevich destroys the frog skin of his beautiful princess, hoping to prevent his mate from returning to her repulsive, enchanted form. If he could have persevered a short while longer, he would have achieved the same result without the cruel trials he subsequently had to endure. Russia, before the revolution, had slowly progressed toward the worthy goals of greater social justice and opportunity. Now the steady development has been upset by an unrestrained impulse to hasten the process, and the cataclysmic upheaval of 1917 has brought to nobility and peasants alike monumental and wasteful suffering through hunger, disease, and the bullet.

In summary, the three pairs in the novel who appear to have the most consistent (yet distinct) relations to the revolution and human love are the sorcerers Egorka and Arina, the anarchists Mark and Irina, and the bolsheviks Arkhip and Natal'ia. Each couple appeals to the reader in its own way and is characterized by a lack of hypocrisy. Their voices, together with many others', produce a polyphonic novel. Nevertheless, Pilniak structures the polyphony in *Naked Year* through the plot device of accretive refrains. These skeletal refrains steadily accrete in significance as the author gives them flesh through illustrations from the stories in the novel. The meaning of *Naked Year,* as suggested by the refrains, is essentially that the Russian people have violently and indiscriminately torn the European cultural overlay from a massive and durable "Asiatic" substratum. But Pilniak also queries whether the Arkhip Arkhipovs, the genuine leather jackets (as opposed to Laitis and Kunts), will not provide the living waters to restore and reshape the Asiatic Ivan-ushka the Fool Russia, now undergoing cruel torments. Will not these determined and inexhaustible men of the Russian soil, these native sons who wear Russian shirts under their leather jackets . . . and who are one with the people rather than imposed upon them from above, create a new order to fill the vacuum left by the rejection of Western cultural values? "So what then—surely China will not be replaced for a bowler hat in a tail coat and with a briefcase?!—will not the third one come in turn, the one that—cain enegetically fuction!'' . . .

Without insisting on this personal intuition (the two preceding chapters are called the first and second parts of a triptych—the final chapter, however, is not designated as the expected third part), Pilniak ends his novel with a hymn in praise of the long-suffering and steadfast Russian people who will bear all present and future assaults, as did the greatest Russian folk epic hero, Il'ia-Muromets:

> The forest stands stern like a stockade and the snowstorm hurls itself against it like furies. Night. Is the saga-legend about how the knights died not about the forest and snowstorm?—More and more snowstorm furies hurl them-selves against the forest stockade, howling, yelling, shouting, roaring like wrathful women; dead animals fall, and after them the furies still rush, they never decrease,—they increase like the snake's heads—two for each one cut off, and the forest stands like Il'ia Muromets. . . .

Regardless of current physical torments, the Russian people will persevere and endure, and perhaps with Arkhip and Na-tal'ia now in the forefront they will begin a new era of vitality and justice. (pp. 123-25)

> *Gary Browning, in his* Boris Pilniak: Scythian at a Typewriter, *Ardis, 1985, 259 p.*

ADDITIONAL BIBLIOGRAPHY

Alexandrov, Vladimir E. "Belyj Subtexts in Pil'njak's *Golyj God*." *Slavic and East European Journal* 27, No. 1 (Spring 1983): 81-90.
 Analyzes Pilnyak's incorporation into *Goly god* of themes and techniques from Andrey Bely's novel *Serebrianyi golub'*.

Alexandrova, Vera. "Boris Pilnyak (1894-?)." In her *A History of Soviet Literature*, pp. 156-73. Garden City, N.Y.: Doubleday & Co., 1963.
 Discusses Pilnyak's most important works.

Avins, Carol. "Ice and Icon: Spengler in Russia" and "The Loss of Home." In her *Border Crossings: The West and Russian Identity in Soviet Literature, 1917-1934*, pp. 35-47, 79-90. Berkeley: University of California Press, 1983.
 Discusses *The Third Capital* and "The Old Cheese."

Brostrom, Kenneth N. "The Enigma of Pil'njak's *The Volga Falls to the Caspian Sea*." *Slavic and East European Journal* 18, No. 3 (Fall 1974): 271-98.
 Disputes the allegation that the novel was written "as a faint-hearted attempt at self-preservation." Brostrom argues that in *The Volga Falls to the Caspian Sea* Pilnyak asserts the value of virtue and love and derides "the Bolsheviks' arrogant assertion that their policies would bring about the spiritual transformation of man—hardly the act of a coward."

———. "Boris Pil'njak's *A Chinese Tale*: Exile as Allegory." *Mosaic* IX, No. 3 (Spring 1976): 11-25.

Asserts that Pilnyak's early works are allegories on the problem of faith and that his writings after 1925 became increasingly ni-hilistic. Brostrom demonstrates *A Chinese Tale* to be a pivotal work "structured . . . upon the dual philosophical perspective of nihilism and epistemological uncertainty."

———. "Pilnyak's *Naked Year:* The Problem of Faith." *Russian Literature Triquarterly*, No. 16 (1979): 114-53.
 Contends that *The Naked Year* "and its successors challenge the reader to discover in a seemingly disordered narration a solution in meaning; in so doing the reader mimics the narrator's difficult quest, conducted in metaphor, to discover the teleology, if any, immanent in the revolution's apparent chaos."

Browning, Gary L. "Civilization and Nature in Boris Pil'njak's *Machines and Wolves*." *Slavic and East European Journal* 20, No. 2 (Summer 1976): 155-66.
 Acknowledges the novel's "dichotomy between the instinct-ori-ented and independent wolf on the one hand, and the cerebral and constraining machine on the other," but demonstrates that there also exists in the novel "a convincing reverse scale of values: the forward-looking and reliable machine as contrasted to the ignorant and perfidious wolf."

———. "Pil'njak's *Soljanoj ambar*: A Commentary on Its Unpub-lished Part." *Russian Language Journal* XXXII, No. 112 (Spring 1978): 89-100.
 Examines the background and content of Pilnyak's "final artistic and ethical statement," a novel completed six weeks before his arrest in 1937.

Eastman, Max. "The Humiliation of Boris Pilnyak." In his *Artists in Uniform: A Study of Literature and Bureaucratism*, pp. 104-25. New York: Alfred A. Knopf, 1934.
 Calls Pilnyak "Russia's leading expert in recantation, abjection, self-repudiation, sighs of repentence, and prayers of apology."

Edwards, T.R.N. "Pil'nyak: The Fatal Confusion." In his *Three Rus-sian Writers and the Irrational: Zamyatin, Pil'nyak, and Bulgakov*, pp. 87-136. Cambridge, England: Cambridge University Press, 1982.
 Examines irrational elements in *The Naked Year, The Tale of the Unextinguished Moon*, and the short stories "A Whole Lifetime," "A Year in Their Life," and "The Bridegroom Cometh."

Falchikov, Michael. "Rerouting the Train of Time—Boris Pil'nyak's *Krasnoye derevo*." *The Modern Language Review* 75, Part 1 (January 1980): 138-47.
 Asserts that Pilnyak's central theme in *Mahogany* is "the problem of time and memory" and maintains that "in his setting of this work on the eve of collectivization he was trying to capture a particular and unique moment in time and preserve it before it was committed to oblivion by the 'march of historical progress'."

Frankel, Edith Rogovin. "A Note on Pilnyak's *Tale of the Unextin-guished Moon*." *Soviet Studies* XXIV, No. 4 (April 1973): 550-53.
 Maintains that the story is "not merely a statement about Stalin's power, but about the nature of the society itself."

Hyman, Stanley Edgar. "Varangian Times." In his *The Critic's Cre-dentials*, edited by Phoebe Pettingell, pp. 241-47. New York: Athe-neum, 1978.
 Review of *Mother Earth, and Other Stories* maintaining that "at his best, Boris Pilnyak was a matchless captor of the historical moment in all its rich life, a master of the full range of comic rhetoric, and a unique poetic voice in fiction."

Jensen, Peter Alberg. *Nature as Code: The Achievement of Boris Pilnjak, 1915-1924*. Copenhagen: Rosenkilde and Bagger, 1979.
 Biography and analysis of Pilnyak's most important works to 1924.

Maloney, Philip. "Anarchism and Bolshevism in the Works of Boris Pilnyak." *The Russian Review* 32, No. 1 (January 1973): 43-53.
 Discusses Pilnyak's portrayal of the Revolution as a popular an-archic revolt against a centralized bureaucracy and examines the distinction in his works between anarchic "Bolshevik" values and "communist" opposition to these values.

————. "Heraclitean Themes in the Works of Boris Pil'njak." *Russian Language Journal* XXXII, No. 112 (Spring 1978): 101-06.

    Presents the Greek philosopher Heraclitus as a probable influence on Pilnyak's philosophical convictions.

Muchnic, Helen. "Stories of Intrigue and Love." In her *Russian Writers: Notes and Essays,* pp. 291-98. New York: Random House, 1971.

    Maintains that Pilnyak "loves vigor and also chaos, and is fascinated by decay; his whole being gravitates toward the passionate, the elemental, the bestial, and is attracted by death. His voice is tuned to anarchy. Dutifully, he believes in reason and progress, but emotionally he is with the ageless and subliminal."

Reck, Vera T. *Boris Pil'niak: A Soviet Writer in Conflict with the State.* Montreal: McGill-Queen's University Press, 1975, 243 p.

    Discusses the publication and content of Pilnyak's most controversial works and their reception by government officials.

————, ed. "Excerpts from the Diaries of Korney Chukovsky Relating to Boris Pilnyak." In *California Slavic Studies,* Vol. XI, pp. 187-99. Berkeley: University of California Press, 1980.

    Personal anecdotes.

Rinkus, Jerome K. "Mythological and Folkloric Motifs in Pil'njak's *Mat' Syra-zemlja.*" *Russian Language Journal* XXIX, No. 103 (Spring 1975): 29-35.

    Examines how mythological and folkloric motifs contribute to the story's thematic unity.

Semeka, Elena. "The Structure of Boris Pil'njak's *Povest' nepogašennoj luny:* From a Structure to a Determination of the Genre." In *The Structural Analysis of Narrative Texts: Conference Papers,* edited by Andrej Kodjak, Michael J. Connolly, and Krystyna Pomorska, pp. 145-71. Columbus, Ohio: Slavica Publishers, 1980.

    Denies that *The Tale of the Unextinguished Moon* is intended to portray actual events and attempts to demonstrate through structural analysis of the original text that Pilnyak sought instead to compose a work with broad philosophical implications, "which he coded in a complex system of varied symbols, allusions, and oblique references."

Swados, Harvey. "On Boris Pilnyak's *The Volga Falls to the Caspian Sea.*" In *Rediscoveries,* edited by David Madden, pp. 147-64. New York: Crown Publishers, 1971.

    Argues that although Pilnyak was partly successful in his attempt to "write a bad book in an effort to ingratiate himself and purchase at least a temporary personal security," the work nevertheless merits praise for the extent to which he failed in his effort to subordinate literary artistry to political aims.

Thompson, Boris. "The Difference of Art: Some Soviet Writers of the 1920s and 1930s." In his *Lot's Wife and the Venus of Milo: Conflicting Attitudes to the Cultural Heritage in Modern Russia,* pp. 98-122. Cambridge, England; Cambridge University Press, 1978.

    Examines Pilnyak's attitude toward the past, maintaining that he "welcomed the revolution not because he was a Marxist, or indeed for any social or political reasons, but because he saw it as restoring Russian culture to its true origins, from which it had been fatally diverted by the Western flirtations of Peter the Great, and the whole of subsequent Russian cultural development down to 1917."

Tulloch, A. R. "The 'Man vs. Machine' Theme in Pilnyak's *Machines and Wolves.*" *Russian Literature Triquarterly,* No. 8 (Spring 1974): 329-339i.

    Examines the thematic conflict of nature and instinct with civilization and rationality.

Kenneth (Lewis) Roberts

1885-1957

(Also wrote under the pseudonym of Cornelius Obenchain Van Loot) American novelist, journalist, nonfiction writer, essayist, autobiographer, dramatist, editor, and translator.

Roberts is best known for his extensively researched historical novels set in eighteenth and early nineteenth-century America. Marked by their fidelity to fact, vigorous style, and sometimes unconventional perspectives on the past, these novels present panoramic views of the Colonial and Revolutionary Wars and the War of 1812 while specifically focusing on actual historical figures such as Benedict Arnold and Robert Rogers. By combining vivid dramatizations of history with fictional adventure and intrigue, Roberts provided what Jane Harris has called "not only an enlightening account of early American history but also a very human and entertaining one."

Roberts was born in Kennebunk, Maine, into a family which had lived in the state for generations and figured in its history as pioneers and soldiers. Following his early education in Massachusetts, he attended Cornell University, where he was editor of the *Widow,* Cornell's humor magazine. He graduated in 1908, moved to Boston, and began working for the *Boston Post,* eventually becoming editor of the humor page. In addition, Roberts wrote for *Life* and *Puck.* During this time he developed a reputation as an accurate, truthful reporter, a notable humorist, and as a strongly opinionated man. In 1917 George Lorimer, the editor of the *Saturday Evening Post,* published Roberts's first short story, beginning a lasting professional and personal relationship between the two men. Near the end of World War I, Roberts left the *Boston Post* and served as captain in the Intelligence Service of the American Expeditionary Force in Siberia. Following his discharge in 1919, Lorimer hired him as a foreign correspondent for the *Saturday Evening Post,* and from 1919 through 1928 Roberts contributed over two hundred articles to the magazine. He also published seven books during this time, many of which were collections of his *Post* articles. Among them are *Europe's Morning After,* which chronicles the chaos in Europe following World War I, and *Why Europe Leaves Home,* which articulates his observations and prejudices regarding Central European immigrants to America and is credited with influencing Congress to establish immigration quotas. Others address subjects such as the rise of Mussolini and Hitler, antique collecting, and Florida real estate. Little known today, these books record some early twentieth-century issues and indicate the diversity of Roberts's interests.

While establishing an international reputation as a journalist, Roberts began to collect material for novels dealing with the experiences of one Maine family through three vital periods of the state's history. In 1928, with the encouragement of his friend and neighbor Booth Tarkington, he retired from journalism to devote his efforts to his first novel, *Arundel.* Although Maine is the primary setting of many of his novels, Roberts modified his original plan to write a series of novels about one family, instead focusing in *Arundel* and its sequel, *Rabble in Arms,* on the campaigns of the Northern Army during the Revolutionary War and on the career of Benedict Arnold prior to his treason. Roberts's two other novels in this series,

The Lively Lady and *Captain Caution,* are sea stories set during the War of 1812. Considered minor works, both have received favorable commentary for their graphic description of the lives of American seamen during this war. Together these four novels comprise Roberts's "Chronicles of Arundel," Arundel being an earlier name of Kennebunk. The popular success of his next novel, *Northwest Passage*—in which he surveyed the career of Robert Rogers both as a major in the French and Indian War and subsequently as an explorer—enabled Roberts to build his estate in Kennebunkport and relieved him of financial worries for the rest of his life. In 1940 he published his longest and last major novel, *Oliver Wiswell,* a compassionate and therefore critically controversial portrayal of the American Revolution from the Loyalist point of view. Clifton Fadiman has noted that in this retelling of a historical "lost cause," Roberts made traditional historical villains human and understandable to readers who had been taught that the Loyalist cause was "wrong." Although Roberts was sympathetic with the American rebellion, he considered it important to present the Loyalist view of this complex situation.

Most of Roberts's works published during the last ten years of his life were nonfiction, displaying, like his fiction, his strong opinions. Among them are his autobiography, *I Wanted to Write,* in which he discussed his career, and a number of books about dowsing. Included in these is *Henry Gross and His Dows-*

ing Rod, which promoted dowsing as a possible solution to the world's insufficient water supply. Although this book is generally criticized as unscientific and illogical, critics nevertheless acknowledge Roberts's sincere interest in this subject. Near the end of his life Roberts published another historical novel, *Boon Island,* basing his story on an actual shipwreck in 1710 off the New England coast. Roberts died at his estate in Kennebunkport in 1957.

Roberts's desire to be an accurate reporter was fundamental to his approach to novel-writing. *I Wanted to Write* discusses his search to discover more about the experiences of his ancestors—people who had fought with Washington, marched with Benedict Arnold to Quebec, and manned privateers in the War of 1812. As he researched both his own past and the various subjects for his novels, he concluded that history books in general did not contain the necessary details for a full, satisfactory understanding of the past, criticizing historians for overlooking or being "too slovenly to unearth" many important details. Eschewing commonly accepted historical truisms, Roberts whenever possible sought out original sources and contemporary accounts of the events he wrote about. For example, while researching the 1775-1777 campaigns of the Northern Army, which involved their march to and retreat from Quebec through the battles at Saratoga, Roberts became aware of what he described as the "shockingly raw deal" Benedict Arnold had received from his contemporaries and the "contemptibly raw deal" afforded him by historians and biographers. Among his source materials were Arnold's journal, which he later compiled into a reference book entitled *March to Quebec,* and the journals of soldiers in Arnold's expedition. In both *Arundel* and *Rabble in Arms* Arnold is portrayed as an inspiring leader, a military genius, and a significant contributor to the American cause. Critical opinion of Roberts's portrayal of Arnold has been varied. For example, while Herbert Faulkner West has described Roberts as a meticulous historian who found ample historical evidence that Arnold was "a man of the greatest generosity, unselfishness, bravery," Jane Harris has noted that because Roberts extolled Arnold's virtues and attributed few faults to him, he failed to create a well-rounded character.

Although Arnold figures prominently in both *Arundel* and *Rabble in Arms,* the primary focus of the first novel is its narrator, Steven Nason, while the men of the Northern Army are the principal concern of the second. Roberts's narrative style is typified in *Arundel* as Nason's first-person narrative intertwines his own experiences with those of actual historical figures. Although *Arundel* was not well received, one early anonymous critic noted that "Nason's own fortunes . . . are deftly and inextricably interwoven with the purely historical narrative," and praised the narration for its vigor, simplicity, and charming archaism. In addition, the novel has been recognized for its vivid, evocative descriptions and for Roberts's dramatization of the march to Quebec. *Rabble in Arms,* which chronicles the Northern Army's movement from Quebec to their victory over the British at Saratoga, is the most popular and highly praised of the Chronicles.

Northwest Passage, Roberts's most critically esteemed novel, dramatizes in two parts the brilliant military career of Robert Rogers as the leader of the Rangers during the French and Indian War and his subsequent failure as an explorer seeking a northwest passage to the Pacific. Critics have offered some sharply differing appraisals of this work. Allan Nevins, who considered the second part marred by disjointed narrative, in-

adequate backgrounds, and unconvincing characters, praised the treatment of Rogers's military career as "one of the classic stories of American adventure." West concurred with this view in noting that *Northwest Passage* would have been better as a work of art had it ended before the story of Rogers's downfall. In a contrasting appraisal, Bernard DeVoto asserted that the second part is superior to the first, stating that it is animated "with an imaginative warmth that [Roberts] has not shown us before," and that "it moves on a plane of understanding and perception that only the best kind of historical fiction achieves." The entire work has been described by Williams as a "great novel in the strict tradition of classic tragedy" featuring a "hero of moderate excellence, reduced to adversity through human weakness and error." Qualities of *Northwest Passage* commonly praised by critics are the graphically descriptive writing that offers readers an intimate view of the realities of war, and the characterizations of Rogers and of Langdon Towne, the fictional narrator whose fortunes become involved with those of an actual historical figure. In general, however, Roberts's fictional creations are regarded as inferior to his historical characters, and are sometimes dismissed as flat and unconvincing. Specifically, his one-dimensional portrayals of women and his extremely evil characterization of villains have been criticized. However, favorable recognition has been given to a number of his fictional narrators and to his comic characters—most notably Cap Huff, who appears in *Arundel, Rabble in Arms,* and *Northwest Passage,* and who is cited as an example of the humor with which Roberts enriched his novels. While his fictional characters are generally subordinate to his plots, critics note that they are memorable and that they realistically portray the experiences of early Americans.

Roberts's work has been criticized or ignored by most historians. For example, historian Adrienne Koch points out that Roberts's particular interpretation and compression of facts "cannot share with the audience the complex nature of evidence, the multifarious directions in which contemporary documents can point, the scrupulous qualifications that surely impede a 'story' even if they endow us with materials for a richer ultimate penetration of the past." Nevertheless, Roberts's ability to report, illuminate, and enliven history within engrossing narratives has been recognized since the appearance of his first novel, and near the end of his life he was awarded a special Pulitzer Prize for having "long contributed to the creation of greater interest in our early American history."

(See also *Contemporary Authors,* Vol. 109 and *Dictionary of Literary Biography,* Vol. 9: *American Novelists: 1910-1945.*)

PRINCIPAL WORKS

Europe's Morning After (essays) 1921
Sun Hunting (essays) 1922
Why Europe Leaves Home (essays) 1922
The Collector's Whatnot [with Booth Tarkington and Hugh McNair under the pseudonyms of Cornelius Obenchain Van Loot, Milton Kilgallen, and Murgatroyd Elphinsone] (essays) 1923
Black Magic (nonfiction) 1924
Florida Loafing (essays) 1925
Florida (essays) 1926
Antiquamania (nonfiction) 1928
Arundel (novel) 1930; revised edition 1956
The Lively Lady (novel) 1931
Rabble in Arms (novel) 1933
The Brotherhood of Man [with Robert Garland] (drama) 1934

Captain Caution (novel) 1934
For Authors Only and Other Gloomy Essays (essays) 1935
It Must Be Your Tonsils (essays) 1936
Northwest Passage (novel) 1937
March to Quebec: Journals of the Members of Arnold's Expedition [editor] (journals) 1938
Trending into Maine (essays) 1938
Oliver Wiswell (novel) 1940
The Kenneth Roberts Reader (essays) 1945
Lydia Bailey (novel) 1947
Moreau de St. Mery's American Journey (1793-1798) [with Anna M. Roberts; translators] (journals) 1947
I Wanted to Write (autobiography) 1949
Henry Gross and His Dowsing Rod (nonfiction) 1951
The Seventh Sense (nonfiction) 1953
Boon Island (novel) 1956
Water Unlimited (nonfiction) 1957
The Battle of Cowpens: The Great Morale Builder (novel) 1958

JULIAN STREET (essay date 1922)

[*An American novelist and essayist, Street was also the author of a number of books regarding wines, gastronomy, and travel. In the following excerpt, he favorably reviews* Why Europe Leaves Home. *Unexcerpted portions of the essay reveal the critic's sympathy with some of Roberts's more xenophobic feelings about East European Jews.*]

Keenly observant, vividly and breezily written, often humorous and always sound, [*Why Europe Leaves Home*] is as important to present-day Americans as notice of approaching hurricane to the captain of a ship at sea; indeed, it is more important, for whereas the captain cannot still the waves by writing to his Congressman, the foundering of the United States in a sea of South and Central European immigration may be prevented if we, the passengers and crew, have but the energy to tack a "No Admittance" sign upon the bowsprit.

That, in effect, is what Mr. Roberts has to tell us as the result of his observations during the last two years in Europe, and he tells it so convincingly, with such richness of color and anecdotal detail, that sane and disinterested readers will, I believe, find it impossible to disagree with him. Objections to Mr. Roberts's book will, to readjust the metaphor, be heard only in the steerage of our luxurious national craft, and from persons more concerned with getting their friends aboard than with maintaining a certain standard of desirability in the ship's company. It is claimed by Mr. Roberts's publishers that an article of his, first published in the *Saturday Evening Post* and here presented in revised and enlarged form, did more than anything else to impel Congress to rush through emergency immigration legislation, and, further, that the conclusions drawn in Chapter IV. of *Why Europe Leaves Home* form the basis for a permanent law now under consideration. May the day soon come when this book, having served its purpose, will sink to unimportance!

In emphasizing the importance of *Why Europe Leaves Home* I do not, however, wish to alarm those potential readers who regard important books as being as dry as a guest room inkwell. Mr. Roberts's tale of his interview with King Constantine of Greece is the most wickedly humorous thing of the kind I have seen since the late John Reed's interview with William Jennings Bryan was published a good many years ago in *Collier's Weekly*. Though one feels throughout this book the underlying intensity of the author, Mr. Roberts's manner is anything but heavy. Just when you think he has become so wrapped up in his message as to forget the requirements of a large American audience, he surprises you by turning a back somersault.

It is the opinion of the author if more immigrants continue to pour in and we fail as we have been failing to assimilate them the United States will develop large numbers of separate racial groups as distinct as those of Czechoslovakia, "where various people lie around in undigested lumps," or else that America will be populated by a mongrel race entirely different from the present American people. . . .

I strongly urge Americans whose children are to live in the United States to read Mr. Roberts's *Why Europe Leaves Home*. It ought at the present time to have the right of way over any other book I know.

> Julian Street, in a review of "Why Europe Leaves Home," in The New York Times Book Review, *July 30, 1922, p. 17.*

THE NEW YORK TIMES BOOK REVIEW (essay date 1930)

[*In the following essay, the critic offers a favorable review of Roberts's first novel,* Arundel, *noting especially the vigor and simplicity of the narrative.*]

Arundel, "being the recollections of Steven Nason of Arundel, in the Province of Maine," is an achievement—a really fine and stirring historical novel. It is a detailed and dramatic account of the secret expedition against Quebec, which Colonel Benedict Arnold, in the first months of the Revolution, led up the Kennebec River and over the impassable Height of Land to the St. Lawrence—a surprise attack ranking in heroism, if not in size and importance, with Hannibal's passage of the Alps and Bolivar's brilliant march over the Andes.

Steven Nason, son of the keeper of a garrison house at Arundel, was a trader and woodsman and a friend of Benedict Arnold. Washington and Arnold, through bad counsel, had rejected the proffered service of the Abenaki Indians, but Arnold—no traitor at the time, but a very gallant and able officer—called upon his friend Nason to guide his hazardous expedition. Nason's own romance is closely bound up with the success of the enterprise, since his youthful fiancée had been taken by the St. Francis Indians and held captive in Quebec. Thus Mr. Roberts has adroitly provided a framework of plot for a bit of military history which has hardly a dramatic equal in the annals of modern warfare.

The ascent of the Kennebec by bateau to the fork of the Dead River, the heart-breaking, month-long battle with rapids and floods and swamps, with discouragement and fever and starvation, and finally the brilliant attack upon the snow-clad cliffs of Quebec, provide as stirring a central action as any historical novel can boast. Nason's own fortunes, his secret enlistment of the aid of the Abenaki warriors, his work in defeating a system of British intrigue and his final, but unjust, exposure as a spy, together with the startling conclusion to his romance, are deftly and inextricably interwoven with the purely historical narrative.

Many novels dealing with the past falter before the difficult technical problem of idiomatic speech, and, in trying to achieve a correctly archaic grammar, they succeed, as often as not, in evolving a highly improbable synthetic mode of expression. Mr. Roberts has solved this problem at once, and in a fashion which does him infinite credit. The narrative, in Steven Nason's own words, has a vigor and simplicity seldom achieved, except by a writer working in the idiom of his own decade. At the same time it is charmingly archaic, full-flavored and, except for one or two isolated passages, wholly convincing. Mr. Roberts's descriptive writing is graphic and finely sensuous.

> There are a great number of fat eels that lie in each of the current riffles at low tide, so thick that in less than an hour's time one boy with a trident may take enough of them to fill a barrel, which is a feat that I have frequently accomplished, being passionately fond of smoked eel with a gallon of cider either before or after my meals, or during them, or late at night when the nip of Autumn or the bite of Winter is in the air, or indeed at any time whatever, now that I stop to think on it.

The same style, which conveys the very taste and fragrance of hot, buttered rum before an open fire, expands equally well to encompass the bleakness of the terrible march over the Height of Land.

> That Friday night the rain fell as I have never known it to fall before, in solid sheets, like water pouring out of a hogshead, and the wind rampaged very terribly among the trees, coming in bursts that increased constantly in strength, as the strength of a man's breath increases when he fails in an attempt to blow out a candle, though with each succeeding burst we said to each other that it could blow no harder.

In *Arundel* Kenneth Roberts has succeeded splendidly in capturing a fragrance belonging to the past, a faint but indispensable aroma which is the chief charm of a historical novel, and which most American historical novels have notably lacked.

> *A review of "Arundel," in* The New York Times Book Review, *January 12, 1930, p. 8.*

BOSTON EVENING TRANSCRIPT (essay date 1933)

[*In the following excerpt, the critic favorably reviews* Rabble in Arms.]

Nothing we have ever read has made us see and feel the American Revolution with the vividness of [*Rabble in Arms*]. In it history becomes alive. The actual purpose of the historical novel is that it shall translate fact into human experience and *Rabble in Arms* is a supreme justification of that. Much in Mr. Roberts's novel concerning the hardships suffered by the Americans we have known from childhood, especially the difficulty of their struggle against the trained soldiers of England, the differences of loyalty which complicate any revolution, the worthlessness of the currency, the problem of the leaders due to the fact that companies enlisted for short periods and were always leaving and going home at crucial moments, the lack of organization, and all the petty differences between the separate colonies. These things have been told us over and over again, but here they take on surprisingly fresh significance as

part of the stupendous panorama of war which Mr. Roberts spreads before us. Curiously, he fixes indelibly two opposing facts. The first is an amazement at the spirit of this rabble who were fighting against such odds, and the other is the conviction that though England's trained regiments might out-maneuver or defeat this rabble it would be impossible for England to hold so large a country when it was aroused to fight as these men fight. . . .

The protagonist of this story is Benedict Arnold, for whom already Mr. Roberts has expressed unbounded admiration. In its four great episodes Arnold remains the supremely brilliant leader. . . . Toward the end Mr. Roberts makes his personal plea for a better understanding of this leader who despite all he accomplished for the American cause has suffered the supreme ignominy in public opinion through the years. Though Mr. Roberts is doubtless right when he avers that it is unlikely he can change this public judgment of Arnold's career, it is at least certain that he has made clear why Arnold or any other intelligent man should have doubted the ability of the colonists at this time to rule themselves or to make of themselves a nation. No one reading this novel but must forever recall Arnold as a brilliant leader and a military genius to whom the country owes much.

> *D. L. M., "Benedict Arnold as a Colonial Leader," in* Boston Evening Transcript, *Part 4, November 29, 1933, p. 2.*

WILLIAM ROSE BENÉT (essay date 1934)

[*Benét was an American poet, editor, and novelist. Among his works are his Pulitzer Prize-winning autobiographical novel in verse,* The Dust Which is God, *and* Oxford Anthology of American Literature, *which he edited in collaboration with Norman Holmes Pearson. In the following excerpt, Benét praises the descriptive quality of Roberts's writing in* Captain Caution, *yet nevertheless finds the novel inferior to* Rabble in Arms.]

[*Captain Caution*] is a good historical novel for your money. Kenneth Roberts has now written the fourth of the Chronicles of Arundel, a town in the province of Maine that he first described in the novel *Arundel,* which told of a secret expedition during Revolutionary days, led by Colonel Benedict Arnold against Quebec. Then, in *The Lively Lady,* he gave us a yarn of the War of 1812, and followed it with *Rabble in Arms,* his best to date, again a story with the background of the War for American Independence and the figure of Benedict Arnold looming large in it. Now again, in *Captain Caution,* we are on the high seas during the War of 1812, and visit, incidentally, both France and England. . . .

[In] my opinion the description of the British hulks, the prison-ships, in the Medway, of the hero's pugilistic encounter aboard one, and of the escape over mud-banks by several of the prisoners, is as good writing in the field of the romantic historical novel as Mr. Roberts has led us to expect from him, and that is saying a great deal. There is plenty of ingenious episode thereafter; and the book has a hero, a heroine, a plausible villain, and several characters furnishing excellent comic relief. Then too, there is the prime invention of the Gangway Pendulum, together with that of a pretty good system for gambling at roulette; there is the appearance of no less a figure than Talleyrand himself; and there is always that combination of graphic narration with historical accuracy for which Mr. Roberts has by now become so well known.

If one compares *Captain Caution* with *Rabble in Arms* it is, frankly, far less important; though it does present to us aspects of the strife of nations in the early nineteenth century which are less-well-known and show the age very much as it actually must have been with a good deal of the gilt off the gingerbread. But there is small reason for setting it above a really good Sabatini, of which there are quite a number, taking into consideration the handling of different periods and backgrounds. As usual the critics have gone off the deep end about Mr. Roberts's work, and my own enthusiasm for *Rabble in Arms* was genuine, but in *Captain Caution* he has written a new novel neither of the scope of the former extremely powerful book nor of its depth and richness. Still I think the description of the British hulks and the prisoners and their escape will stand up with some of the best passages in historical fiction. One is inclined to compare it with certain of Dickens's best descriptions also, for its human qualities. That is a good deal to say, I know; but it is such powerful writing that sets Mr. Roberts's work apart from that of most historical novelists of our time.

William Rose Benét, "In the War of 1812," in The Saturday Review of Literature, Vol. XI, No. 17, November 10, 1934, p. 273.

BERNARD DeVOTO (essay date 1937)

[*An editor of the* Saturday Review of Literature *and longtime contributor to* Harper's Magazine, *DeVoto was a highly controversial literary critic and historian. A man whose thought enraged much of America's literary establishment during the 1930s and 1940s, he was frequently motivated by anger at authors he considered ignorant of American life and history. As a critic, he admired mastery of form and psychological subtlety in literature. His own work is characterized by its scholarly thoroughness and by its vigorous, infectious style. DeVoto was "profoundly interested" in American history and authored several historical works, notably the Pulitzer Prize-winning* Across the Wide Missouri *(1947). In the following excerpt, DeVoto offers a favorable review of* Northwest Passage, *particularly praising the second half of this novel.*]

Northwest Passage makes it necessary to take Mr. Roberts rather more seriously than before, for he has become a more serious novelist.

His earlier books, the stories of Arundel and the two sea stories, are conventional historical narratives, traditionally romantic in outline but original 'and realistic in detail, unreflective, rapid, and usually superficial in their feeling for history. By superficial I do not mean to derogate from Mr. Roberts's rich inventiveness nor to deny that he has a fine eye for the characteristic, the picturesque, and the historically appropriate; I mean that he has been indifferent to the energies and movements of which the events he describes were a specific expression, that he has not bothered about their relation to the age. Thus the chronicles of Arundel are first-rate action stories in a historical setting, swift and frequently absorbing stories of war and hardship, but they are not historical novels in the sense that, say, *Henry Esmond* and *The Scarlet Letter* are. *Arundel*, for instance, exhibits none of the collapsing colonial system and little of the emerging nation. *Northwest Passage* has much of the former and a good deal of the latter, and that is only one of the ways in which it departs from the type of the other books and gets into historical realization.

Through the earlier books Mr. Roberts steadily developed as a story teller and as an antiquarian. In the new one the antiquarian is quite willing to interrupt the story teller. . . .

Most of *Northwest Passage* just precedes *Arundel* in time, and several characters reappear, notably Cap Huff. The hero is Robert Rogers, the scout, explorer, Indian fighter, promoter, speculator, adventurer, soldier of fortune, and Tory recruiting agent whom readers of Parkman will identify as the most skillful commander of colonial rangers during the French and Indian War. Narrated by a young artist [Langdon Towne] who (in the Catlin manner and rather anachronistically) wants to paint the Indians, the first half of the novel deals with the raid of Rogers' Rangers on St. Francis and the return through early winter and without provisions across northern Vermont to the Connecticut. . . .

But there is an important change when Langdon Towne, the war ended, goes to London to study painting, and Mr. Roberts turns to Rogers's ambition to discover the Northwest Passage. The pace slackens, Mr. Roberts gets interested in challenging Thackeray, readjusting the verdicts of history, and pondering its less palpable forces—and the novel changes in kind and considerably improves. The challenge to Thackeray comes off very well. There are a few unnecessary displays of historical characters in walk-on parts, and an occasional cheap touch of the kind which has a character make a prediction which is grotesque in the light of what we now know, or has another one call James Boswell an ass and lament the time Johnson wastes talking with him. But, this granted, the London of the period comes variously and most amazingly, to life: the London of "characters," eccentrics, grotesques, Mohocks; of Hogarth, Clive, Reynolds, Benjamin Franklin, the young Burke, Sir John Fielding, the Royal Society; of gin-shops, debtors' prisons, slums, beggars, "monsters"; of Townsend and the Bute ministry and the Stamp Act and the skeptical Whigs. No communities lived so vividly in Mr. Roberts's earlier work, and you will read this evocation with as much satisfaction as you ever got from *The Virginian*.

Even so, it is not the best part of *Northwest Passage*. Rogers's efforts at length get him the governorship of Michilimackinac, Langdon Towne goes with him to paint the Western Indians, and suddenly Mr. Roberts is animating his material with an imaginative warmth that he had not shown us before. The hunger and desire of the nation just about to break westward into the untrodden lands, the tangle of cupidities and venalities and stupidities that in great part conditioned them—they are in *Northwest Passage* as they have not been in our fiction before. The soldiery, the traders, the *voyageurs*, and the first wave of the pioneers are done with fine versatility, and the Indians are done with genuine magnificence. Francis Parkman and a good many others are at the author's shoulder while he writes, but his treatment of the Western tribes displays historical imagination of a high order. And we are all likely to be in Mr. Roberts's debt: the signs point to an early extension to precisely that ground by the present wave of historical novels, and it is good to have a high and authoritative standard set at the beginning.

In short, the second half of *Northwest Passage* is not only a good story, it moves on a plane of understanding and perception that only the best kind of historical fiction achieves.

As a historian, Mr. Roberts is something of a revisionist. Jonathan Carver was not so scaly as he makes him out, and the specifications for a romantic hero have forced a lot of plastic surgery on Major Rogers. As a novelist, he remains conventional in all his detailed characterization and quite uninterested in psychology. No one in the book has much intellectual life, no one meditates much, no one is an introvert; there is no

Henry Esmond, there is not even an Athos or an Aramis. The love story is trite and Ann, its heroine, writes letters far less like an eighteenth-century gentlewoman than like a twentieth-century boarding-school girl. On the other hand, the book is not defaced by archaisms or self-conscious period work. Mr. Roberts wisely contents himself with an occasional touch of formality or floridity in dialogue, an occasional obsolete expression, and a mass of homely and appropriate details, so that the atmosphere passes off quite naturally. It is a first-rate job, a novel that is read with intent interest and is sure to be remembered with satisfaction, head and shoulders above most of the period pieces that have recently come into favor.

> *Bernard DeVoto, ''Roberts Rangers,'' in* The Saturday Review of Literature, *Vol. XVI, No. 10, July 3, 1937, p. 5.*

ALLAN NEVINS (essay date 1937)

[*An American historian and journalist, Nevins's major works are in the fields of biography and U.S. history after 1847. He was twice awarded the Pulitzer Prize—in 1932 for* Grover Cleveland: A Study in Courage, *and in 1937 for* Hamilton Fish: The Inner History of the Grant Administration. *In the following excerpt, Nevins favorably reviews the first half of* Northwest Passage, *while citing major flaws in the second half of the novel.*]

At first blush Robert Rogers the Ranger seems ideally fitted for the central character of Mr. Roberts's long novel of the French and Indian War. Two and a half centuries of border fighting produced no more striking figure. . . .

He is particularly suited to Mr. Roberts's pen in that he represents the American, the provincial, side of the conflict. . . . His command was for the most part made up of provincials, and he taught them to fight like himself. In short, while this is a story of a British war, it deals with a true American hero commanding American men and fighting primarily for American objects.

Yet if the subject has its advantages it also has its disadvantages—and grave ones at that. Mr. Roberts is too skillful and gifted a writer not to make the most of the advantages and to minimize the disadvantages, but he cannot wholly escape the latter. One of them affects the texture of the book—it is Rogers's character. He had very unheroic as well as heroic qualities, the vices as well as the virtues of the frontier. Smuggler, counterfeiter, heavy drinker, gambler, woman hunter, loading himself with debt and then looking desperately to the main chance, the Major had little morals and less principle. After placing him on a heroic plane it is a little hard to keep him there. This great disadvantage affects the structure of the book. Rogers had too long and varied a career for a single novel. Though Mr. Roberts takes him up in 1759 when his fame was well established, he requires more than 700 pages to bring him down to the Revolution; he has to treat of him in the French War, in London, as commander at Michilimackinac, and in London again. The book inevitably breaks into sections, and sprawls over too much time and territory. And in order to carry the narrator, a young soldier-painter, through all Rogers's wanderings, the author has to strain probability.

As a matter of fact, the book falls into two great parts, nearly equal in length, and bound together only by Rogers's dominating personality. The first part, a story that keeps the reader in breathless suspense for three hundred pages, centers in the most brilliant of Rogers's operations. This was his immortal expedition of 1759, under Amherst's orders, against the Aben-

aki capital on the St. Francis River, chief settlement of a Catholicized Indian tribe which for three generations had killed, kidnaped and tortured along the New England frontier. . . .

Detached from the volume . . . , the three hundred pages on this St. Francis expedition make one of the classic stories of American adventure.

But of the second and larger half of the book we cannot speak so highly. Its theme is the great dream which Mr. Roberts (with much sound historical reason) ascribes to Robert Rogers: the dream of pushing westward to the Pacific, of discovering that Northwest Passage for which the Crown had offered £20,000 reward, of bringing all America to the Shining Mountains, the River Ouragon and the Western Sea under the British flag. (p. 1)

Mr. Roberts's conception of Rogers's character is consistent, historically defensible and appealing. Of course defenders of Johnson, Gage and Carver could find evidence for a basically different and hostile conception. Since Rogers's private life was so vagrant, it is hard to feel certain of all his public aims. For the purposes of historical fiction, however, the figure of the great ranger is admirably done. The shifts between the heroic and base are disconcerting but not unreal. The real defects of the second half of the book lie in the disjointed narrative and the inadequate backgrounds. As the narrative swings from the fashionable world and Cabinet Ministers of London to the Minnesota Indians and back again to Fleet Prison in London it becomes unconvincing. We find vigorous narrative bits and spirited scenes. But when Mr. Roberts introduces Hogarth, Sir Joshua Reynolds, Benjamin Franklin and other London characters his dialogue begins to creak. He even presents an incredible letter from Edmund Burke to Rogers. His sketches of English society, which are curiously hostile, seem to come out of Smollett and the caricaturists. Also when the story swings west of Prairie du Chien, among the Sioux and Chippewa, it equally taxes our credulity. Mr. Roberts is authentically and vigorously at home in the valleys of the St. Lawrence and Connecticut, but it is evident that he moves less familiarly among the Minnesota tribes.

The unevenness of the volume points to a certain unevenness in the author's power. Mr. Roberts has few equals in the narrative of adventure. He can glue his reader's mind to his page. But he has little skill in depicting society, and little also in drawing any character who is not of a rough, elemental sort.

In brief, this book, like Robert Rogers himself, is a compound of masterly qualities and of limitations. To the first half, dealing with the French and Indian War, it would be difficult to give too much praise. The racing narrative will make the reader's blood throb in his veins. But the ill-articulated second half, with much excellent writing interlarded with very stagy scenes, is rambling in general effect, and often unpersuasive. Several characters, including the heroine, come straight out of melodrama. The best element in the book as a whole is the original and impressive presentation of Rogers himself. From first to last he is all of one piece. He is a powerful individual whose discipline in woods and war is perfect, but who in civilized circles has no discipline at all; who with a strength as rugged as the North Woods, an energy as uncheckable as a mountain torrent, succeeds brilliantly when the drum beats, but fails ignominiously when brought to the vicinity of drink, dice or women; fails—but does not capitulate. Even in Fleet Prison he remains ''the celebrated Major Rogers,'' with a wild dignity about him. His eagle eye, rough voice, hurried stride, wild blustering ways and grandiose ambitions dominate the whole action. He is the one real character in the book, and everywhere he is real. And as Mr. Roberts's main intention was a portrait of Rogers, the book as a whole may well be called a success. (pp. 1-2)

> Allan Nevins, "Rousing Tale of the French and Indian War," in New York Herald Tribune Books, *July 4, 1937, pp. 1-2.*

BURTON RASCOE   (essay date 1938)

[*Rascoe was an American literary critic who served on the staff of several influential periodicals during the early and mid-twentieth century. Noted for his perceptiveness in recognizing new or obscure talent, Rascoe was, at one time or another during his career, the chief literary critic of such publications as the* Chicago Tribune, New York Herald Tribune Books, *the* Bookman, Esquire, Newsweek, *and the* American Mercury. *In the following excerpt, Rascoe presents an unfavorable appraisal of Roberts's fiction, while expressing high regard for his ability to write nonfiction.*]

One of my numerous unorthodox and heretical opinions is that Kenneth Roberts has no particular talent for writing fiction. As a novelist he gets by, I think, as in the Arundel series and in *Northwest Passage,* wholly because he is primarily a most excellent nonfiction writer. He is always at war with the conventional historians, because most of them are slipshod, unenterprising, and likely to swallow whole the printed words of any other historian who has a Ph.D. and who is just as slipshod and unenterprising as they are.

Thus he gets some fire and force into his yarns out of pure resentment against the myths handed down, from one to another, by the academic historians. He happens to be extremely academic, in the true sense, himself, and so is ready to take a half year out of his life to verify or to prove wrong some insignificant statement he has encountered in the work of two dozen historians but which, nevertheless, seems phony to him. . . .

I say, if we are going to have history, let us have history; if we are going to have legend, let us have legend; and if we decide we are going to have history and put it into books as history, let it be history, not legend. Roberts feels that way about it, and I'm for him.

The thing that makes him good in this respect, of course, is the thing that militates against his being a very good writer of fiction. Fiction is a matter of the imagination, of the free range of the mind and spirit; it is not concerned with facts or even with the minor truths: it is concerned with the universal truths concerning human beings. No such person as Micawber ever existed. Charles Dickens' father, from whom Micawber was drawn, did exist in the flesh. Micawber is truer to the heart and spirit of any male you can name (you, if you are a male—no matter if you are Mussolini—and me included) than all the true facts you can adduce about Dickens *père*.

Roberts hasn't a Dickens talent in the creation of characters of the imagination. In all the fiction he has written that I have read, he has never made a single character come to life. He has told us all about them and what they did; but he has not made them breathe.

I like Roberts best when he is writing nonfiction. I have been absorbed by every word of *Trending into Maine.* . . . One chapter is called: "Maine Stories I'd Like to Write." He gives us

the gist. I hope he never writes them. We who have imaginations know all there is from his factual notes. Expansion would spoil them, especially the way Roberts goes about expanding. But *Trending into Maine* is, I want to tell you, far more in entertainment and information value than you have any right to expect out of 30-odd works of historical fiction, including all of Roberts'.

> Burton Rascoe, "'As Maine Goes'," in Newsweek, *Vol. XI, No. 25, June 20, 1938, p. 31.*

BEN AMES WILLIAMS   (essay date 1938)

[*Williams was an American novelist and short story writer who was a good friend of Roberts. In the following excerpt, Williams discusses Roberts's stature as a novelist and the praiseworthy qualities of his first five novels.*]

Today there stand five novels to Mr. Roberts' credit [*Arundel, The Lively Lady, Rabble in Arms, Captain Caution,* and *Northwest Passage*]. The public verdict on them has already been delivered, and the critics have applauded each book as it appeared; but it is now possible to make some appraisal not of the individual volumes, but of the stature and importance of the man's work as a whole. There has been too much emphasis, in the discussion of Mr. Roberts' works, on the fact that they are based on history. (pp. 7-8)

The result of this emphasis on the extent and accuracy of Mr. Roberts' historical research has been to becloud his merits as a novelist. It is conceivable that any first-rate reporter could have put together an account of the expedition against Quebec as complete and as accurate as that in *Arundel;* but only a first-rate novelist could have written the book which Mr. Roberts wrote about that expedition. If it were not so easy to say that Mr. Roberts is a profound student and a great historian, it would have been clear long ago that he is also a novelist whose stature and whose capacities are steadily increasing.

It is impossible to define a great novel. Probably only time can offer a final appraisal of any book. But from an examination of those novels which after half a century or more still appear to be first-rate—*Tom Jones, Vanity Fair, Bovary, War and Peace, Copperfield,* half a dozen others—it appears that they have some traits in common. They have gusto. They seem to have been written headlong, rushingly, the words tumbling over one another like those of a speaker so full of his subject that he cannot wait to pick and choose. They are long yet seem short; the novelist has so much to tell that the reader puts his book down while still hungry for more, still full of questions and inquiry. No man can read *War and Peace* and remain incurious about Napoleon. No man can read *Arundel* and *Rabble in Arms* without wishing to know more about Benedict Arnold. (pp. 8-9)

This quality of gusto in the great novels of the past was not a mere matter of piling words on words. It was the robust exuberance of overflowing genius, pouring out—sometimes without discretion or critical restraint—scenes and characters and chapters in a teeming flood, from which the reader might take what he chose and let the rest go by. And those great novels had another common quality. They were most often tragic in their theme; and their writers were more interested in failure than in success, in weakness than in strength, in vice than in virtue. The novelist exalted what was good by hating what was bad; he praised virtue by portraying the ugliness of vice. . . . Mr. Roberts as an individual and as a novelist hates sham, hypocrisy, littleness above all things. When he deals with the petty and the mean his words have a scalding bitterness; and seen through his eyes, the stupid follies, the selfish intrigues, the petty bickerings of the Continental Congress become as abominable as adultery.

His novels have these two qualities—the gusto, and the abhorrence of evil things and men—which appear to be common to all great novels. But merely to write many words does not make greatness in a novelist; nor to hate evil. The man must also be master of the tools of his trade. He must know how to handle humor, description, characterization.

Mr. Roberts since he began his career as a reporter has always been skilled in humorous writing, and humor enriches every page of his novels. Cap Huff as a character in whom humor was an inherent and persistent quality can face any comparison without flinching. The Harvard episode in *Northwest Passage* is Mr. Roberts at his humorous best; but there are single lines and brief passages here and there through all his novels which will make the reader smile or chuckle or laugh aloud before he reads on. Mr. Roberts' descriptive passages, especially when he writes about that region around Arundel which he knows and loves so well, evoke a deep peace and serenity, as though the reader looked upon the scenes which the author describes. These passages, by virtue of Mr. Roberts' skilful use of the first person form of narrative, are enriched by affection. The reader comes to love the land as Steven Nason loved it long ago.

Mr. Roberts has created a dozen characters which fix themselves in memory more deeply than the reader may at the moment realize. . . . Some of Mr. Roberts' characters have [the] trick of embedding themselves permanently in the reader's consciousness. In the more superficial matter of quick characterization, Mr. Roberts is adept. One line often serves to present an individual complete and recognizable. "She had the look of never having done anything that did not give her pleasure." "I have never known a man so proud of a weak stomach, or so desirous of discussing it." "Wyseman Clagett . . . stood there looking at me horribly." "High Sheriff Thomas Packer—the same who later hanged the school teacher, Ruth Blay." . . . Examples could be multiplied unendingly. In these technical respects, Mr. Roberts is master of the tools of his trade.

Of his books, four are written in the first person. The fine novels which have been written in the first person can be counted on the fingers of two hands. (pp. 9-10)

To write in the first person, to tell only what "I" saw or heard or thought, is perhaps the most severe of limitations. This form of narrative Mr. Roberts has made completely his servant. No one has used the first person so effectively since *Lorna Doone.*

To any reader of Mr. Roberts' successive novels it must be apparent that his capacities are steadily increasing. His most recent novel [*Northwest Passage*] is unquestionably his best thus far. I said in reviewing *Arundel* that it revealed Mr. Roberts "as a novelist of extraordinary powers." . . .

Seven years later, in reviewing *Northwest Passage,* I said: "When Kenneth Roberts wrote *Arundel,* he produced a novel which for most writers would have been a culmination. In *Rabble in Arms* and today in *Northwest Passage,* he has proved that *Arundel* was no more than a promise now bountifully fulfilled." (p. 11)

The Lively Lady followed *Arundel.* It was complete; it was in pleasant ways, for easy and delightful reading, perhaps the best of his books. But it lacked the grandeur of *Arundel;* and it was to be overshadowed presently by *Rabble in Arms.*

Rabble in Arms is the longest of Mr. Roberts' novels; and it is a sequel to *Arundel.* The reader of *Arundel* had felt that in some way hard to define *Arundel* demanded completion; but *Rabble in Arms* did not complete *Arundel.* It served to make clear that *Arundel* was in fact only the first part of a noble tragedy, the end of which still remains unwritten.

Mr. Roberts has said that the original plan of his novels was to set down the adventures of one family through certain vital periods in the history of Maine; and his earlier novels have been called "Chronicles of Arundel". As he began to write, he modified that original plan to the extent that he designed *Arundel* and *Rabble in Arms* as a record of the campaigns of the Northern Army.

But he was writing more than history; he was writing a novel, and a novel must have people in it, and the lay reader will inevitably be more interested in the people in any novel than in its historical background. No one could write a novel, or a series of novels, about the Northern Army without finding every page of his book dominated by the figure of Benedict Arnold. This is what happened to Mr. Roberts. Arnold captured these two books. *Arundel* and *Rabble in Arms* are as they stand the first two volumes of a great tragedy which remains unfinished so long as the rest of Arnold's story remains untold.

But to write the story of Benedict Arnold was not Mr. Roberts' plan; and to this extent, these two novels escaped from his grasp. In themselves complete, they are also incomplete. Mr. Roberts wrote the story of the Northern Army as it had never been written, and as no one else could have written it. Even though they may be considered as the beginning of an unfinished work, *Arundel* and *Rabble in Arms,* taken together, may justly be rated as the greatest historical novel written by an American—with one exception.

The exception is *Northwest Passage.* Here is not only an historical document of the first importance; here is also a great novel in the strict tradition of classic tragedy. It is great because in this novel Mr. Roberts had his plan; it was complete; he wrote it complete. It has those qualities of magnitude and order essential to tragic beauty. Mr. Roberts presents Major Robert Rogers in his heroic period, in those years when he was able to multiply himself, to make out of ordinary men giants able to do the impossible. But Mr. Roberts goes farther. He continues the tragic tale while the heroic figure of the leader of the Rangers begins to shrink and grow small; it dissipates itself; it withdraws into shabby shadows; it ceases to be heroic; it becomes in the end negligible. (pp. 12-13)

The Greek philosophy of tragedy held that the best fable is simple, without catastrophe; and that the hero should be a figure of moderate excellence, reduced to adversity through some great human weakness or error. The fable which Mr. Roberts chose to use in *Northwest Passage* fitted the classic tradition; it was the simple fable of a hero of moderate excellence reduced to adversity through human weakness and error. For a novelist to conceive the second part of *Northwest Passage* required a calm remoteness of mind. The novelist had to feel the pity and the terror which the mean end of Rogers must evoke without being shaken by them and rendered artistically inarticulate. To write the second part of *Northwest Passage* without the easy recourse to the devices of climax and catastrophe was a task incredibly difficult. Mr. Roberts undertook this task, and he accomplished it. He wrote what he planned to write. He saw the fable whole, and he wrote it whole.

In these eight or ten years of his career as a working novelist, Mr. Roberts has shown a steady growth and an increasing mastery of his plan and of his instrument. From such pens, greatness comes. (pp. 13-14)

> *Ben Ames Williams, "Kenneth Roberts," in* Kenneth Roberts: An American Novelist *by Ben Ames Williams and others, Doubleday, Doran & Company, Inc., 1938, pp. 7-14.*

ORVILLE PRESCOTT (essay date 1947)

[*Prescott was the daily literary critic for the* New York Times *from 1942 to 1966. His major critical work is* In My Opinion: An Inquiry into the Contemporary Novel *(1952). In the following excerpt, Prescott appraises Roberts's fiction in general and the novel* Lydia Bailey *in particular*]

[*Lydia Bailey* is] the most widely publicized book of the new year. . . . Admirers of Mr. Roberts's immensely popular brand of fiction will not be disappointed in this jumbo-size historical romance. It has all the characteristic Roberts merits, which are substantial, and all the faults, which are serious. In many re-

spects, it is the very archetype of the present decade's most popular variety of literature. It is an historical novel about America's own past; it is wildly melodramatic, filled with incredible heroics, fantastic coincidences, and savage violence; it is packed with evidence of conscientious research. And thus it is completely conventional.

Kenneth Roberts is a big, hearty, vital, opinionated, hasty-tempered man. He hates politicians, hypocrisy, corruption, cowardice, and tyranny. He loves food, action, valor, independence, and the very stuff of history itself. All this is plain as a pikestaff in his books. He is uninterested in, or incapable of, the subtleties of fiction as an art. His plots are crude and clumsy, his virtuous characters only stilted puppets. But he is a superb chronicler of violence, battle, massacre, rape, flight, and pursuit. He is wonderfully effective in his portraits of picturesque, eccentric, lusty men of action. And always his enormous relish for the life of the past endows his work with a living background of interest in itself.

Lydia Bailey, then, is a "grand tale" of the slave war in Haiti against the French and of America's almost forgotten war against the Barbary pirates. It can't be taken seriously as fiction, but it can be enjoyed for its lurid panorama of history. To point out its flaws of construction, characterization, and probability would be a waste of time. Mr. Roberts, although he worked for six years on this book, does not care a hoot about such matters, and neither do most of his readers.

> *Orville Prescott, in a review of "Lydia Bailey," in* The Yale Review, *Vol. XXXVI, No. 3, March, 1947, p. 573.*

Kenneth Roberts. The Granger Collection, New York.

JAY LEWIS (essay date 1947?)

[*Lewis was a literary critic whose reviews, according to Phillis Hanson—editor of Lewis's* Other Men's Minds—*"can be classified under the very general title of exposition. Though they were consistently appraisals rather than attacks, they often developed into various forms of the essay, lecture, monograph, editorial, sermon, concrete and abstract opinion, personal and impersonal reflection." In the following excerpt, Lewis surveys Roberts's works dealing with the Colonial and Revolutionary War periods.*]

Kenneth Roberts is one of the world's greatest writers, one of those immortals who weave words into tales and such tales! They abound in movement, they have vigor and color and they also have that mark of the master craftsman, comic relief. Moreover, they are flawlessly written. (p. 158)

That Kenneth Roberts is among the great masters you recognize at once. He has the splendor and sincerity of Scott, the simplicity of Stevenson, the sweep and scope of Sienkiewicz, yet differing as they differ one from the other. He has an individuality all his own, a personality embossed on the printed page as distinct as that of Dumas or Hugo. (pp. 158-59)

All authors put their personalities into their books.

They reveal their inner selves rather than their outward.

They may create characters, using the traits they see in others through their psychological studies of self, but the trend of their thoughts is unmistakable, plain as footprints in the sand. Their manner of thinking crops out like specks in a ledge. The lode itself may be gold or base metal, but its presence is revealed. (p. 159)

Without having met or ever seen Kenneth Roberts it is clear to me that he is not only a great writer but a man of rugged honesty and virile patriotism.

That superb trilogy, the first three books of the "Chronicles of Arundel," incidentally, compares favorably with the best three of "The Leatherstocking Tales" and still leaves *The Lively Lady* and *Captain Caution* to offset *The Red Rover, The Pilot,* or any other of Cooper's sea tales. *Oliver Wiswell* is a far more robust tale than *The Spy.* But, as Dogberry insisted, comparisons are odorous. (pp. 159-60)

[A] tale to have permanent value must have substance, and upon the quality of that substance depends the worth of the book. Some call it the texture of the tale, the warp and woof of the fabric; but the finished product, pattern as well as weaving, also counts, with the result that superior quality is recognized as easily as shoddy is known for what it is.

There is substance, a superior quality, about the books of Kenneth Roberts, such as you will find only in those of the accepted great masters of English literature. (p. 160)

Time alone is said to set an official seal upon the classics, whether fiction or otherwise; but there are established standards by which books may be judged, especially romances popularly called historical novels, among which are classed the "Chronicles of Arundel."

Background, construction, development of the story to a fitting climax, delineation of characters by dialogue, as well as by description, action, suspense, surprise and comedy, what the dramatists called comic relief, something to loosen the tension, relax the strain and afford contrast with the more dramatic situations, all have to be considered. (p. 161)

The comedy in the books of Kenneth Roberts runs from roaring farce and homespun humor to classic wit and irony, often with a sardonic grotesque exaggeration, characteristic of rural America and like the assumed innocence of Mark Twain, devastating in its effect.

The grim drollery of Tom Buell with his Perkins' Metallic Tractors, Sergeant McNab and his Indian spouse, Old Doc Means and his naïve seriousness are funny, but they only tend to emphasize the genuine, spontaneous humor of Cap Huff, the best comic character since Zagloba, probably the greatest in English literature, aside from Falstaff.

Cap Huff appears in *Northwest Passage, Arundel* and *Rabble in Arms,* reappearing in retrospect for a moment in *Captain Caution,* a regular Paul Bunyan in his gastronomical feats.

In many school lists the "Chronicles of Arundel" are required reading, but they are something more. They are necessary reading if you are to understand the true background of the Colonial, Revolutionary and War of 1812 periods, when the foundation for the building of the nation was laid.

We are apt to forget, in our joyous admiration of the Founding Fathers, that there were many great and good men who did not think separation from the mother country was necessary: that fear of France and of French intentions to regain control and dominate America influenced their minds. (pp. 161-62)

[In] the "Chronicles of Arundel," you will find [several] things reflected—the rise of democracy, the fight for freedom, the intolerance and violence of mobs, the dismaying thought that tolerance has won few victories and that fear is a force to be reckoned with. . . .

In the books of Kenneth Roberts you get more than a mere chronicle of [the] times. You get a true background with documented facts, for the tremendous amount of research, with the tediousness, the labor, the earnestness for accuracy implied is enough to exhaust a contemplative mind. (p. 164)

Bare bones of facts are clothed with romance and realism. His stories are more than mere historical romances, they are matter-of-fact [and] realistic. . . .

His backgrounds are real, his characters are real, his facts are real and he has that convincing quality that Dumas possessed.

And only the real masters possess that magic.

In most historical novels you are taken from the present into the past, where you feel as unreal as the Connecticut Yankee at the court of King Arthur; but Kenneth Roberts brings the past to the present and you become a part of it. Things as they were become things as they are.

You are given closeups of the people and the period, their problems, their motives, their attitude individually and collectively toward public questions, public opinion, pressure groups, political opportunists, idealists, patriots for profit, patriots through fear, false patriots and honest patriots. (p. 165)

History and historical novels based on conventional history present stories done in the accepted style; but Kenneth Roberts presents actual history, documented, backed by recorded evidence obtained by the most persistent and thorough research work.

His data for *Arundel* alone would be called a formidable volume were it not so full of interesting information from original sources that it became a book well worth publishing under the title, *The March to Quebec,* and which may well be called a collector's item.

There is no questioning the accuracy of Kenneth Roberts nor his fidelity to history. His facts are documented beyond any doubt. (p. 166)

It was not the most clamorous in the days of the "Chronicles of Arundel" who were the sincerest patriots, but rather the reticent, thoughtful and sometimes doubtful citizens who were the bulwarks of democracy, who followed Washington faithfully and with him were sorrowful over the apostasy of Arnold. It was they who were the real Founding Fathers, the builders of the nation, and Kenneth Roberts makes that fact clear to all.

In the "Chronicles of Arundel," Kenneth Roberts reveals the difference between conventional history and actual history. (pp. 166-67)

Only the bright side of war is presented in conventional history, the darker side is left to poets and novelists. Actual history may be found in the records and the records reveal the base as well as the beautiful.

The fact that deified heroes had their faults is often granted, but that those whom conventional history has condemned may have had redeeming qualities, even virtues, is generally ignored, or grudgingly admitted.

In his "Chronicles of Arundel" it has been the purpose of Kenneth Roberts to be just, to present the base as well as the beautiful, to set forth actual history against a background of truth. Not only to write realism into romance, but to show how far conventional history may be from the facts.

In doing so he presented two supermen with human failings and faults, victims of vaulting ambition, as well as victims of their unbounded imaginations. Thwarted, balked, calumniated, humiliated, the poison of ingratitude first numbed and then destroyed them.

Although *Arundel* was written first, *Northwest Passage* preceded it in the actual order of the Chronicles, including the trilogy that records the saga of Cap Huff, as well as its more important heroes.

Northwest Passage has Langdon Towne, American artist, for its historian; but its real story is the disintegration of a superman, Robert Rogers, leader of the Rangers who destroyed the St. Francis Indians and whose subsequent career is one of the most amazing known to mankind. (pp. 167-68)

In *Arundel,* second of the series, Stephen Nason is the hero, but Arnold pervades the book from the time he appears as captain of his trading brig, off the Maine coast, to its end, following the disaster at Quebec, where Stephen Nason discovers the truth about Mary Mallison and her abductor.

Of the march of Arnold's men through the Maine wilderness to the shores of the St. Lawrence, opposite Quebec, their sufferings, their endurance, their patriotism, much has been written, but it remained for Kenneth Roberts to make it real in a romance unmatched in American literature, save by such masterpieces as *Northwest Passage* and *Rabble in Arms,* third of the chronicles.

In that tale Arnold again dominates the story. He is pictured as an inspiring leader, generous, valiant, resourceful, unconquerable, never despairing, no matter how great the odds. Thwarted, hated, but carrying on despite his detractors, turning

calamitous failure into wonderful success, he is the incarnate patriot, the unconquerable soldier. (p. 169)

Grit and determination are no less in evidence in the stories of *The Lively Lady* and *Captain Caution,* both of which belong among the "Chronicles of Arundel," although of another generation and the War of 1812.

Yet [the protagonist] young Richard Nason is the son of Stephen Nason and Phoebe Nason and possesses qualities drawn from both, a sturdy patriotism and steadiness of purpose that recognizes no failure. (pp. 169-70)

There are seafights in both *The Lively Lady* and *Captain Caution,* realistic seafights and scenes ashore equally exciting. . . .

As romance it would be hard to choose between *The Lively Lady* and *Captain Caution.* . . . (p. 170)

Both stories, while romantic enough to suit the most sentimental, have a sturdy patriotism which shows that the supreme purpose is to make plain what sort of folk our forebears were.

Nor is that purpose absent from *Oliver Wiswell,* although that novel presents the loyalist side. (pp. 170-71)

Oliver Wiswell, without doubt, is Kenneth Roberts at his best. It would be hard to name a better novel in all English literature. There may be more popular books: many, perhaps, more attractive in theme to readers in general, and many readers may dislike the fact that Oliver Wiswell never saw the errors of his way or became converted to the patriotic cause. But that was not the purpose of the author. His idea was to show that there was another side to the conventional story of the American revolution and ably did he carry out his plan.

Regarded fairly, without prejudice, as the product of an American author, *Oliver Wiswell* is the finest work in the entire list of American fiction. (p. 171)

Legends of heroes and their heroic deeds are destined to become a part of the folklore of the American people; and the sturdy independence of those pioneers, may yet be remembered with a sigh for lost liberty. The future alone holds the spinning of that thread. . . .

[It] is in *Oliver Wiswell* and the "Chronicles of Arundel" that Kenneth Roberts is at his best, for in them is written himself.

Great writers write what they feel. The others merely feel what they write. (p. 172)

> *Jay Lewis, "Kenneth Roberts," in his* Other Men's Minds: The Critical Writings of Jay Lewis, *edited by Phyllis Hanson, G. P. Putnam's Sons, 1948, pp. 158-72.*

CARLOS BAKER (essay date 1956)

> [*Baker is an American critic, poet, novelist, and educator. Two of his most notable works, considered to be significant contributions to critical literature, are* Shelley's Major Poetry *and* Hemingway: The Artist as Writer. *In the following excerpt, Baker favorably reviews* Boon Island *and discusses the historical account on which Roberts based this novel.*]

Like most of Kenneth Roberts' books, *Boon Island* is fiction with a factual base. As all brine-soaked students of New England shipwreck-lore are aware, a real Nottingham galley, 120 tons, ten guns, fourteen souls aboard, with a cargo of English cordage and Irish butter and cheese, did indeed break up only a few leagues from the mouth of the Piscataqua that Arctic

December night, between 8 and 9 o'clock, over 200 years ago. Four of the castaways died, two by accident, two by illness; and one of the latter was eaten by his comrades, with the desperate hunger of men who had subsisted for weeks on a diet of rockweed, a handful of mussels, one raw seagull, a piece of minced rawhide and the slightly salty scale-ice which they chipped off the boulders.

Though Captain Dean himself seems to have been only a simple, God-fearing, seafaring man, he was made of hero's stuff. That he could write, as well, is shown by his short but remarkably graphic first-person account of the expedition: "A Narrative of the Sufferings, Preservation and Deliverance of Captain John Dean and Company." This narrative is Mr. Roberts' source. With some minor divergencies, he follows it meticulously. From it he derived in large measure his portrait of the captain—that firm, quiet and kindly man who used his authority only for the welfare of others, and who richly earned the right to his command by the expedient of doing more work than he required of any of his subordinates.

From the source-book also came hints and quick line-drawings on which Roberts based other characters. . . .

For a historian of Mr. Roberts' persuasion, the horrible fascination of such a sourcebook as Dean's narrative is that it raises more questions than it answers. Who, for example, was that "stout, brave fellow," a Swede by derivation, who, despite the loss by frostbite of both his feet kept insisting that the castaways' only hope of rescue lay in building a raft, of the most primitive materials, on which he and another would try to reach shore? . . . How did it happen that young Moses Butler, erstwhile boy actor and whitebait fisherman, should turn up among the crew as captain's apprentice? . . .

All of Mr. Roberts' historical fiction is built upon the premise that reality is better than daydreams. . . . [His] account of the situation of the mariners on Boon Island gleams with a combination of interest and authenticity such as only an accurate and responsible historical novelist could achieve. ***Boon Island*** is not a pretty story; but there is no law that says fiction must be made of sugar and spice. . . . After the lapse of nine years it is good to have Mr. Roberts back with yet another indication that the truth makes better reading than trumped-up romance.

> *Carlos Baker, "To Courage Belonged the Victory,"*
> *in* The New York Times Book Review, *January 1,*
> *1956, p. 3.*

ADRIENNE KOCH (essay date 1958)

[*Koch is an American historian and editor. In the following excerpt she favorably appraises* The Battle of Cowpens: The Great Morale Builder *as a vivid, telling depiction of the battle and of the period, while pointing out the limitations of Roberts's approach to historical reportage.*]

Kenneth Roberts's reputation for the writing of vividly conceived history will not be marred by this brief manuscript [***The Battle of Cowpens: The Great Morale Builder***], which he completed before his death last year. . . . The Battle of Cowpens, which was fought in a South Carolina grazing meadow five miles square, in 1781, by Banastre Tarleton's British veterans against Daniel Morgan's smaller backwoods army, lasted for exactly one hour. It does not require much more time than that to scan the hundred pages of this re-creation of the battle. But whether the reader only scans or stops to question an occasional dramatic exaggeration, and to enjoy a powerful phrase, it is

safe to say he will leave the book with a sharpened and more intimate sense of the remarkable encounter at Cowpens, of the nature of the Continental and British campaign in the South, and indeed of the character of the American Revolution as a human as well as military struggle.

Mr. Roberts, who made too much of his disagreements with professional historians, was correct at least in sensing that his powers of imaginative visualization could lend pungency to the recital of events and to the revelation of the human beings involved in them. Thus he provides artful sketches of the crude but seasoned and incomparably valiant Morgan and the young, Oxford-educated "hell-raiser" Tarleton, whose reputation as a cavalry leader was associated with his brilliant raiding tactics and his policy of sabering the enemy without mercy. The substance of the ensuing battle story is deftly chosen from the letters and reports of the principals and their contemporaries, so that the excitement of rapid orders and emotionally-charged speech reaches us in place of the nonvascular verbalisms of academic history.

There is not much, for example, that is labored about the contrast between Morgan's tough backwoods sharp-shooters in their broken shoes and torn clothing, and the "colorful line of British . . . bright with scarlet, blue, green, and white . . . the brass helmets of the dragoons," etc. But the incisive command Morgan gives his men: "Get the epaulettes" tells us more, in authentic tones, than a scad of sociological observation about the composition of the opposing forces. More revealing yet is a phrase like the following about the character of the Revolution: that after it moved to the South, it was "one of the dirtiest civil wars ever fought." By a few convincing examples Mr. Roberts is able to establish his point that the Loyalists considered themselves as patriotic as anyone and the rebels who called themselves Patriots were as likely as the former to shift sides, depending upon local prospects.

The extreme compression of narrative, however, favors an oracular and prophetic stance on the writer's part. He disputes the "truth" offered by "historians" on the ground of unconvincing details, inaccurate interpretations of the importance of the battle, and general flabbiness in visualizing what he so positively sees. He wills to capture the reader's assent, but he cannot share with that audience the complex nature of evidence, the multifarious directions in which contemporary documents can point, the scrupulous qualifications that surely impede a "story" even if they endow us with materials for a richer ultimate penetration of the past. In a word, he is carrying on a Tarleton *and* Morgan raid on the plane of the high popularization of history. On this plane, he successfully creates a sense of the Battle of Cowpens as a great morale builder, in its "enormous effect on Northern morale, and its awakening of public opinion in the North to the need of giving Greene the military assistance he so richly deserved." What is never made clear, however, is why the earlier battle at King's Mountain is not also credited with the "morale builder" role. If it is true that had there been no Cowpens, there could have been no surrender by Cornwallis at Yorktown, it is equally true that had there been no King's Mountain, there could have been no Cowpens. In short, history as the intense drama of selected episode is capable of contributing something valuable, but it is a partial phase, and a mode of presentation—not the larger substance, nor *the* way to truth.

> *Adrienne Koch, "'Get the Epaulettes'," in* The Saturday Review, *New York, Vol. XLI, No. 19, May 10, 1958, p. 15.*

HERBERT FAULKNER WEST   (essay date 1962)

[*West was an American critic, publisher, and educator whose special areas of expertise were book collecting, nature writers, and Western philosophers. In the following excerpt, West surveys Roberts's career as a journalist and historical novelist.*]

Kenneth Roberts' first books deal pretty much with his experiences as a traveling correspondent for the *Saturday Evening Post*. On looking over these books today, I find it difficult to believe that any of them have much lasting merit as literature, though they may have some interest for future historians in understanding a point of view prevalent in the early twenties, which I am sure Roberts reflected. For instance, a historian would not find it amiss to read Roberts' *Europe's Morning After*, published by Harper in 1921. This book represents material gathered during 1919 and the early months of 1920, during which time Roberts traveled through Poland, Austria, Czechoslovakia, Italy, France and England. He accurately described the European chaos, as he did also in his book the following year, *Why Europe Leaves Home*. This latter is a true account of many of the reasons which caused Central Europeans to overrun America.

Then Kenneth Roberts had an amusing bout with the amazing state of Florida. This left some ephemeral works in its train, such as *Sun Hunting* . . . , *Florida Loafing* . . . , a book about real estate, and another book on Florida published by Harper in 1926. Again, these books have interest only to the historian who is trying to find out what Florida was like during the boom days of the twenties before the very solid crash of 1929.

It might be interjected at this point that Kenneth Roberts came from an old Maine family, that his ancestors came over in 1639, and their lives became part of the state's history. It was inevitable that when he settled down to be a serious writer his thoughts would travel back to his parents, grandparents, great-grandparents, and those of them who had fought with Washington, who followed Benedict Arnold through the wilderness to Quebec, and who manned privateers in the War of 1812. So his interest in the past is perfectly understandable, and is reflected in his two books on collecting antiques: one, *Antiquamania*, 1928, the supposed collected papers of Professor Milton Kilgallen, indicating the difficulties in the path of the antique dealer and collector; the other, *The Collector's What-Not*.

It is pertinent here to mention that Roberts' most consistent mentor and helper as a writer was Booth Tarkington, to whom he dedicated several of his books. Tarkington was also interested in antiques and paintings, and it is easy to surmise that many of their conversations dealt with the passions and problems of collectors. (pp. 90-1)

Roberts also had a life-long interest in Italy. As a matter of fact, he lived there on and off, and wrote some of his novels there. The fascination of Mussolini and Fascism were powerful enough for him to write in 1924 his book, *Black Magic*. . . . This book, a plea for conservatism (Roberts was a dyed-in-the-wool Maine conservative), dealt with Mussolini and Hitler, then rising stars in the twentieth century firmament. The book is an account of the benefits that Roberts thought Mussolini brought to Italy and of the perverse qualities of the Nazi dictatorship then showing its power in Bavaria. The same year, speaking of conservatism, he wrote a little book on Calvin Coolidge. Reading this today makes one realize that Roberts let his enthusiasm for Coolidge bedim his judgment of him as a president. Indeed, looking back, one can excuse the rosy

optimism produced during the early twenties which resulted later in the nightmare of the 1929 crash and the second World War. (p. 91)

In the latter part of the twenties, he decided to devote his life to the writing of fiction. He already had trained himself as an accurate reporter, and he set for himself high standards as a writer of historical fiction. By this time, according to his close friend Ben Ames Williams, Roberts was the master of the tools of his trade.

His four novels about Arundel were all written in the first person, and, again according to Williams, "No one has used the first person so effectively since [Blackmore wrote] *Lorna Doone*" [see excerpt dated 1938]. It seemed, at least to Roberts, that for him the first person came more naturally than the third. The curious reader may find in the introduction to his last book, *Cowpens: The Great Morale Builder*, his credo as a writer of historical fiction. This came to me in the form of a letter in 1936 for a book of mine now out of print, which deals with writers and book collectors. I quote one or two important statements from this letter:

> I have a theory that history can be most effectively told in the form of fiction, because only in the writing of fiction that stands the test of truth do falsities come to the surface. Historians of the Northern Army have either ignored the most enlightening details of the campaigns or have failed to dig up the details which they should have possessed, or have refused to point out the misrepresentations and downright lies for which diarists, journalists, and so on were responsible. . . . The constant gauge of a conscientious novelist must be, "Is this true: is this the way it happened?" That gauge is applied to everything—conversation, characters, action. The historian isn't bothered by that gauge. He can accept a statement made by a reliable man. If St. Clair says in his court-martial that the moon was full on July 5th, 1776, Hoffman Nickerson naturally feels free to accept it. When I come to writing the action on the night of July 5th, however, I find that the night was clear with a hot wind blowing: that the Americans retreated beneath the screen of darkness and smoke, and that it wasn't until Fermoy's cabin burned that the British caught sight of the retreat . . . By consulting a calendar for 1776, I find that St. Clair was mistaken. The moon on July 5th, 1776, was a new moon. It went down shortly after sundown. There wasn't any moon at all during the retreat.

Readers of Roberts know that he spent many years rehabilitating, in a sense, the reputation of Benedict Arnold. He said once that on the evidence he was able to find, Arnold was "a man of the greatest generosity, unselfishness, bravery and good taste. People persist in thinking that in *Arundel* and *Rabble in Arms* I was writing Arnold's story; I wasn't at all. I was writing the story of the Northern Army. I wrote Arnold as I found him . . . as I tried to write everyone connected with that Army."

Whatever faults the future critic may find in Roberts' work, he certainly will never be able to deny that Roberts set a very high standard for himself as a writer. All over America and England he had research people checking on the most minute facts. That fidelity to fact does not necessarily make a great historical novel, I would be the first to admit. It needs, besides this, great creative ability in building up characters, as well as a sense of proportion which is able to see each event in its proper perspective. Some of these qualities Roberts undoubtedly lacked, particularly in his creation of women characters, but in his blunt honesty, in his untiring search for truth, and in his unbiased attitude toward his characters he must be highly praised. There is in all of Roberts' fiction a gusto, a vigor of style and an exuberance which set him apart as a writer of historical fiction in America. No one that I know of has written as well as he about the tremendous physical effort expended by the early followers of Arnold or by Rogers' Rangers. Let us consider the Arundel series of novels.

Arundel, his first novel, called one of "extraordinary strength and power," [see Williams excerpt dated 1938] appeared first in November 1929. This story is based on Benedict Arnold's secret expedition to Quebec, and deals most effectively with colonial frontier life, the fighters of the vanished Abenaki nation, the game-filled forests, ambushes, battles, and the struggles of a starving indomitable army of men attacking the snow-clad cliffs of Quebec. Using real characters such as Arnold, Burr, Morgan and Robert Rogers, he also created the immortal Cap Huff, "in whom humor was an inherent and persistent quality" [see Williams excerpt dated 1938] . . . , and Stephen Nason, through whose eyes we see the action. Nason's abhorrence of evil things and evil men, I am sure, was Roberts' own. (pp. 91-3)

The Lively Lady appeared in 1931. If this novel lacks the grandeur and scope of *Arundel,* it partly makes up for this in the interest it creates in the reader by showing the sufferings of thousands of American seamen imprisoned in the infamous Dartmoor Prison. The hero, Richard Nason, is the son of Phoebe and Stephen Nason of *Arundel.* Roberts succeeds better than anyone I know in exposing the miseries of American seamen during this war. Perhaps his villains are painted with too dark colors and his heroes with too light. Nevertheless, in King Dick, the giant negro ruler of Prison No. 4, and in Thomas Shortland, the commandant, Roberts makes real to many the horrors of this (or any other) war. Of Dartmoor he says: "For if ever there was a place that looked like an abode for devils and lost souls it was this swarthy, sinister moor."

In some respects, I think his novel *Rabble in Arms* is his best. A sequel to *Arundel,* it came out in 1933. If one is going to read only one of Roberts' novels I would suggest *Rabble in Arms.* This tale of the Northern Army, which begins where *Arundel* ends, and ends with the second Battle of Saratoga two years later, is a blend of romance, biography and history. The title comes from George Burgoyne's contemptuous statement of "a rabble in arms, flushed with success and insolence." Roberts paints in this book perhaps his broadest canvas of the American Revolution. His descriptions of the retreat of the half-dead Americans from Canada, of the Battle of Valcour Island, the flight from Ticonderoga before Burgoyne, and the final Battle of Saratoga, reach the highest standards of any American writer of historical fiction. Once again the reader becomes especially close to Cap Huff, Benedict Arnold, Stephen and Phoebe Nason.

When Roberts wrote the following about Benedict Arnold he was using his most considered judgment: "Benedict Arnold was a great leader! A great general! A great mariner! The most brilliant soldier of the Revolution. He was the bravest man I have ever known."

Captain Caution, 1934, is the last of the Chronicles of Arundel. It, too, deals with the War of 1812, and is a story of the romance of an Arundel mariner and the seafaring daughter of an Arundel shipmaster. Bootleggers, gangsters, grafting politicians, slavers, demimondaines, also hold the stage. Perhaps the most thrilling episode is the hero's imprisonment in the hold of a British gun-brig. His battle to retake the brig, a prize-fight aboard a British hulk, the escape to France, and the final Battle of Madeira against the enemy Slade, are other high points in the story.

In a letter written to Kenneth Roberts sometime in 1935, I deprecated *The Lively Lady* and *Captain Caution* as minor works compared to *Arundel* and *Rabble in Arms.* I have never forgotten his blast in a letter in which he told me that just as much labor had gone into these two as the other two. Though this is undoubtedly true, I still feel they are products of a lot of historical material he had left over and which fitted into his scheme of writing four books about Arundel. Most critics would agree, I think, that his masterpiece was yet to come. (pp. 93-5)

Northwest Passage . . . was a tremendous success, both as a novel and as a moving picture, and enabled Roberts to build his magnificent house in Kennebunkport and to be free from financial worries. . . .

The first part [of the novel tells of Major Robert Rogers] and his Rangers' attack against the St. Francis tribes on the Canadian border, in which Rogers proved himself one of the greatest of Indian fighters; then the retreat, after having burned the village down, through the Cohase intervals; and the final escape down the Connecticut River on rafts to the safety of Old No. 4, now the town of Charlestown, New Hampshire. (p. 95)

The first part of *Northwest Passage* seems to me to represent the high peak of Roberts' writing as a historical novelist. I know of no book written in this country that has conveyed so well the tremendous amount of physical effort, courage and indomitable persistence in that wilderness march through swamps to final safety on the river. I hope some day this may be published separately.

However, Roberts was interested in telling the whole story of Robert Rogers, the story of a man reduced to adversity through human weakness and error. He insisted on seeing the story whole, and he wrote it that way. It has been called a great novel "in the strict tradition of classic tragedy [see Williams excerpt dated 1938], and to a certain degree this is so. Yet, I have never been able to rid myself of the feeling that, as a work of art, it would have been better ended on the American scene and not continued to Rogers' last tragic years in England. (pp. 95-6)

The story is told from the viewpoint of a Harvard student named Langdon Towne, and well told it is. The novel has been translated into many languages, as have many other of Roberts' books, and I am sure it will continue to be read for a long time. (p. 96)

Kenneth Roberts' historical research has produced two other books which must be mentioned as vulnerable contributions to American history, for they make available to those interested much source material for a study of America's struggle for its place in the sun. One of these books was *March to Quebec* . . . , which contains the journals of the members of Arnold's expedition, including Arnold's own, as well as that of Lieutenant John Montressor. The second was a publication in 1947 of

Moreau de St. Méry's journey in 1793-98, translated by Kenneth and his wife, Anna Mosser Roberts.

Meanwhile, he had written two humorous books of essays: *For Authors Only* . . . , dealing with diets, the strange characteristics of Oxford, and so on; and an amusing comic piece, *It Must Be Your Tonsils*. . . . It might also be added that during his career he wrote several one-act plays. Regarding the first of these, *The Brotherhood of Man,* he says in a note to me: "Since you are going in all over, you had better have this too. It was written in the transport coming home from Siberia, and it is supposed to depict the last days of the royal family of Russia." His love for Maine, which was a constant force in his life, was also distilled in a book, *Trending into Maine,* which treats of travelers in Maine, shooting, shipbuilding, Maine cooking, etc. This was delightfully illustrated by N. C. Wyeth, and proved to be a popular book.

In 1940 *Oliver Wiswell,* the story of the royalists in the American Revolution, was written. Vivid pictures of Bunker Hill, the battles of Long Island, the political intrigues of the British, are all stirringly told, and Roberts does his best to write unbiasedly about the American Royalists. Lack of space prevents any longer analysis of this book, which was followed . . . by *Lydia Bailey,* a story of Haiti.

Neither of these books, at least for me, is as satisfying as the Chronicles of Arundel or *Northwest Passage*. It may be that they were written to satisfy a ready market, but in any case they are too long, too full of information, and some of the characters, particularly Lydia Bailey, somehow fail to ring true. (pp. 96-7)

Boon Island . . . is to me a failure if judged by the magnificent qualities of his earlier books. This is the story of a shipwreck of 1710 in which the British ship *Nottingham* struck the ledge known as Boon Island off the coast of Maine.

His last historical book appeared after his sudden death in July 1957, and is a reprinting of two articles he wrote for *Collier's* on the Battle of Cowpens. This seems to me to recreate once again some of his old vigor as a writer on American history.

Perhaps the less said the better about his period of defending the work of his friend, Henry Gross, in the use of the dowsing rod, though it does show his passion for justice and truth as he saw it. I personally have felt that his energies had been seriously drained by the creation of seven long historical novels, so that almost by necessity he turned to another interest, which was the subject of the national problem of sufficient water. With an intensity perhaps greater than the necessity, he defended against scientists and other experts "the working of the dowsing rod." Three books were written, *Henry Gross and His Dowsing Rod* . . . , *The Seventh Sense* . . . , and *Water Unlimited*. . . . Actually "Water Unlimited" was a corporation formed in 1950 to direct and develop Henry Gross's amazing ability to find water with a dowsing rod. Without getting into the merits or demerits of this situation, I do happen to know that he convinced Ben Ames Williams and many others, and perhaps one doesn't need to be convinced that water can be dowsed by the proper person with a divining rod.

I have always felt that this controversy somewhat embittered Roberts, and I have always regretted that he ever got mixed up with it. But if one remembers that the idea of spiritualism somewhat obfuscated Conan Doyle's vision during the last years of his life, so it might be said that water dowsing did the same with Roberts.

In conclusion, let me say that it is probably too early even yet to judge fully Kenneth Roberts as a writer of historical fiction. However, I think a statement may be made that so far in the history of American literature no one has painted so vigorously and with so much respect for fact some of the vast canvases of characters and scenes in American history. (pp. 98-9)

> *Herbert Faulkner West, "The Works of Kenneth Roberts," in* Colby Library Quarterly, *Series VI, No. 3, September, 1962, pp. 89-99.*

JANET HARRIS (essay date 1976)

[*An American political activist, historian, educator, and writer, Harris wrote a number of works on social revolution. In the following excerpt from her book-length study of Roberts's work, Harris examines the elements of his novels and surveys the critical commentary on his work, developing her thesis that Roberts merits recognition not only as a writer of historical fiction but as a significant American novelist.*]

Basic to understanding Roberts' purpose in [his] novels is his concept of history, summarized by John E. McManic: "Roberts has a theory of history which is epic in scope, and yet under his talented hand comes down to the ultimate individual. It is the history of this continent as you or you or you could have lived it had you been a man of action in those early stirring days." Roberts' concern for what would have happened to him or to some member of his family living during the American Revolution causes the reader to identify, if not with the main character or narrator, at least with the times. . . . Roberts' novels are more than stories; they are imaginative interpretations of history.

Roberts' works have been generally overlooked by students of American fiction, and only in studies concerned specifically with historical novels does he receive any major consideration. Though all critics give him credit for carefully accurate research, most overlook the literary quality of his novels. (pp. 7-8)

Studies dealing generally with historical fiction likewise evaluate Roberts merely as a re-creator of past events and times rather than as a novelist. (p. 10)

Even though critics have not yet recognized Roberts as a significant American novelist, the continuing popularity of his works indicates that readers see merit in his fiction. (p. 11)

Out of his desire to discover and express universal truth grow the themes he writes about—the futility of war, the existence in every age of men who deny change, the recurrent betrayal of the great man by petty men, and the forgotten courage of the common man. The skillful articulation of these themes through Roberts' fictional technique constitutes the literary excellence of his novels.

Since Roberts has not received the recognition his artistry merits, his novels should be reevaluated in the light of their literary excellence. . . . In addition to his skill in the reproduction of past times and events, Roberts' fictional technique deserves major consideration by students of American fiction. (pp. 12-13)

By limiting his cast of characters and isolating them on one small island, Roberts made his novel [*Boon Island*] "too simple" for readers who needed a marching army, dashing heroes, and farcical humor to entertain them. However, for a study of Roberts' fictional technique, the simplicity and limitations of

Boon Island provide an excellent opportunity to examine the basic elements of Roberts' method of presenting a story. (p. 19)

A basic element in any of Roberts' novels is his reliance on history for as many facts as can be authenticated. Although the incident that became the core of *Boon Island* remains minor if compared to the American Revolution or the War of 1812, Roberts describes an actual incident. . . . (p. 22)

Characteristically, Roberts preferred first person narration because the events, however inconsequential or significant in the course of history, assume monumental importance to a man whose personal fortunes are affected. From this angle of vision, a fictional narrator in the natural course of his life finds himself involved in situations that he sees as part of his daily existence but that the reader evaluates as a part of history. The character of the narrator determines his judgment of what he witnesses. Miles Whitworth, the son of a lawyer and insurance broker, begins his narrative by questioning the value of attending Oxford and the nature of an education. Like many youths in eighteenth-century England, he prefers the theaters and sailing on the Thames to studying the classics like the story of Ulysses. Throughout his journey, he weighs what he remembers from books and formal education against the common sense of his father and what he learns from the ordeal on Boon Island. (p. 23)

The other men in the novel share in Miles' odyssey from innocence to experience and from thoughtless acceptance of oneself to a testing of the essence of one's strength. Boon Island forces to the surface the basic qualities of each man. (p. 24)

Even though Roberts' technique involves developing historical facts into suspenseful plots, he goes beyond a mere adventure story to suggest some truth valid both in the past and in the present. Miles' question, "how many of us have our Boon Islands?" . . . , prompted reviewers to consider the book as an "historical allegory." *Boon Island* lacks the pattern of symbolism required for an allegory, but in a broad sense Miles' odyssey can be interpreted as a symbol of the struggle of life. Joseph Conrad in "Youth" writes "there are those voyages that seem ordered for the illustration of life, that might stand for a symbol of existence. *Boon Island* provides a good introduction to Roberts' fiction because he contrasts "roaring, amoral, and effete eighteenth-century London" . . . with simple, kindly, hardworking, pioneer America. (p. 25)

From the vantage point of 1976 the period of the American Revolution appears almost a mythological heroic age. Historians as well as writers of fiction have contributed to the myths by glorifying heroes and glossing over details. Some authors, however, have always demanded a realistic assessment of historical figures and events. Through his novels, Kenneth Roberts attempts to correct "the onesidedness of the conventional picture of certain aspects of American history" [according to Heinrich Straumann (see Additional Bibliography)]. He shows the fallacy of labeling a man either hero or traitor because of one act. For example, the treason of Benedict Arnold has become his mark in history, but his critics minimize or more often ignore his prowess as a military leader. In *Arundel* and *Rabble in Arms,* Roberts pictures a courageous Benedict Arnold, a man undaunted by adversity. In all of his novels, but especially in *Northwest Passage, Arundel,* and *Rabble in Arms,* Roberts attacks the romantic concept of war as a conflict of brave soldiers led by gallant leaders who fight for noble causes. To Roberts, war is a trap into which men fall thinking to solve one problem, only to find they have created a worse dilemma.

Because he felt historical facts alone could not convey the truth of past events, he chose the novel as his medium of communication. . . . (p. 26)

Because his treatment of the past transcends the limits of historical periods, his works should not be restricted to the category of historical fiction, a classification often used to indicate minimal literary merit, but should be regarded primarily as novels. . . . Characterization, theme development, and arrangement and balance of historical and fictional material are the matters on which [*Northwest Passage, Arundel,* and *Rabble in Arms*] . . . must be judged. The order of these novels follows the chronology of historical events depicted.

One of the outstanding features of Roberts' novels is the intertwining of the stories of the fictional narrator and the historical protagonist. In each of Roberts' three most important novels—*Northwest Passage, Arundel,* and *Rabble in Arms*—a narrator relates his own experiences including his association with historical figures. Within the framework of the narrator's consciousness, Roberts recreates events before and during the American Revolution in which the narrator, as well as the historical protagonist, becomes intimately involved. (pp. 26-7)

In *Northwest Passage,* Roberts' best novel, both the historical protagonist and the fictional narrator change and develop. For Langdon [Towne], *Northwest Passage* is a maturation process. As a boy he almost gives up painting to please Elizabeth Browne and her family. He joins the rangers expecting an entertaining experience because "'the summer campaign'll be over'." . . . He matures quickly, however, as he discovers he must equal the rangers' endurance. As a ranger leader, [Major Robert] Rogers performs amazing physical feats. He leads his men to St. Francis and overcomes all obstacles to survival and victory. This first half of *Northwest Passage* shows Langdon's hero worship for Rogers and Rogers' ability as an Indian fighter. A few critics argue that this first portion should have been the entire novel. For example, Herbert Faulkner West says the second part of the novel "detracts from the artistic whole which Mr. Roberts achieved so well in the first part of his novel" [see excerpt dated 1962]. If Roberts' intention had been merely to write an adventure story, he would have been satisfied with re-creating the exciting attack on St. Francis and the retreat that followed. His subject, however, was the dream of a northwest passage. . . . In the second part of *Northwest Passage,* Langdon becomes independent of Rogers. In contrast, the ranger leader slowly stagnates as a result of inactivity and loses his ability to act independently. While Langdon's career as an artist progresses, Rogers' position as a hero fades. To John Kitch, this half of *Northwest Passage* succeeds because Roberts no longer merely describes physical action but probes "the depths of one of his characters, thereby producing a pathetic portrait of a man who has lost everything, even his courage and self-respect." . . . (pp. 29-30)

The interweaving of Langdon's and Rogers' lives accomplishes what Roberts never achieves so well again—reader indentification with both the narrator and the historical protagonist. *Northwest Passage* is basically the story of two men who influence each other. Rogers gives Langdon his opportunity to paint Indians; through Rogers' secretary, Langdon meets his future wife, Ann Potter; and seeing Rogers in different situations forces Langdon to understand that even heroes have faults. The ranger leader learns of the northwest passage from Langdon at their first meeting, and on a visit to Kittery he meets Elizabeth Browne. Throughout their association, Langdon, as Rogers' confidant and friend, remains the one person with whom

Major Rogers can be completely honest. By creating a narrator involved in the events important in Robert Rogers' life, Roberts balances the plot between fictional narrator and historical protagonist.

Roberts followed the same basic pattern in the earlier novels *Arundel* and *Rabble in Arms* but failed to maintain an even balance between historical and fictional material. (p. 30)

Arundel tells the story of Steven Nason and the Northern Army: Benedict Arnold merits attention only as a part of the army. Technically, Arnold is not present for enough of the action to be a central protagonist. The story of Steven's maturation overshadows the story of Benedict Arnold because Steven's fate concerns the reader.... Although Roberts maintains an adequate arrangement of fictional and historical material, *Arundel* contains some weaknesses of a first novel. Perhaps too much space is devoted to establishing the narrator; early meetings between Steven and Arnold appear contrived; and the ending of the novel seems somewhat flat because Roberts returns Steven and his friends to Arundel. As [John Ira] Kitch suggests [in his 1965 dissertation], "*Arundel* is not brilliant, but interesting, not profound but solid, not captivating but moving."... (pp. 32-3)

Rabble in Arms provides a shift in emphasis and a more complex plot structure than *Arundel*. In *Northwest Passage* Roberts balances the stories of the fictional narrator and the historical protagonist; in *Arundel* the author focuses on the narrator; but in *Rabble in Arms* the fate of the Northern Army overshadows the personal fortunes of either the narrator or the historical protagonist. (p. 33)

Even though the balance between historical protagonist and fictional narrator differs in each of these three novels, the author suits the arrangement to his purpose for the work. *Northwest Passage* focuses on two men and their effect on each other. *Arundel* concentrates on one individual who exemplifies those involved in Arnold's march to Quebec. In *Rabble in Arms* the men of the Northern Army become the real heroes. The arrangement of his material to create the desired emphasis is one merit of Roberts' fictional technique.

Since in all three novels Roberts uses narrators, how effectively he handles first-person narration determines in part how successful his novels are.... [Since] Roberts uses first-person narration, none of his narrators claims to analyze himself; each tells only what he experiences. To the reader falls the task of objective interpretation and evaluation.... A reader, marching to Quebec with Steven Nason, sees the irony of a young man's determination to rescue Mary Mallinson and his blindness to his love for Phoebe. Steven cannot see this irony about himself until the end of the novel, but a perceptive reader not only identifies with Steven but also views him as a character who changes with experience. Thus all of Roberts' narrators are both participants and observers.

As reporters, Roberts' narrators give the novels at least technical unity, for only what lies within the consciousness of these characters can be related. The close association between fictional narrator and historical protagonist reinforces the unity of plot by allowing historical events to become a logical and necessary part of the narrator's experience.... In *Northwest Passage*, Langdon Towne, a youth entranced by a vigorous leader, sees Rogers through a mist of hero worship. Only something shocking, such as the attempted seduction of Ann, could awaken Langdon to Rogers' fallibility. Steven Nason in *Arundel* and Peter Merrill in *Rabble in Arms* view Arnold only as

a leader. Both are aware he possesses human weaknesses, but both expect prodigious feats from him. A reader who expected the narrators to evaluate Benedict Arnold objectively would be asking them to violate the consistent point of view which the author carefully maintains. Each narrator must see his experiences as only a man with his background would. In *Northwest Passage,* therefore, Langdon Towne observes everything, even Major Rogers, as an artist would.... Using believable narrators with whom the reader can identify and who rarely violate their consistent viewpoints, Roberts demonstrates his mastery of the first-person narrative. Making history live through his narrators enriches Roberts' fiction.

To re-create and explain the past, Roberts employs both historical and fictional characters.... Although critics have generally pointed to Roberts' "inability to create living characters" as his greatest weakness, they have at the same time praised him for his vibrant depiction of history.... The discrepancy here is that people make history, and only through real, vigorous characters can Roberts transform historical facts into a story so adventurous that a reader proceeds with urgency to the conclusion. (pp. 36-8)

[In] his treatment of historical figures Roberts makes his narrator's first impressions prophetic. When Langdon first sees Robert Rogers, he describes the ranger leader's primary quality as "solid thickness: not mental thickness, but physical—a kind of physical unkillableness."... This ability to endure but not to succeed makes Rogers a tragic figure. As Ben Ames Williams suggests, Roberts portrays Major Rogers as an Aristotelian hero. While a ranger leader, Rogers accomplishes what only a man with courage, foresight, and self-discipline can do. But as a peace-time governor he falters. Approaching all problems primarily with physical courage, he lacks the ability to discriminate "between great hazards and minor ones".... Sir William Johnson and General Thomas Gage hasten Rogers' fall by doing everything in their power to thwart Rogers' success as a governor and his dream of discovering a northwest passage. Thus Rogers does not completely fit the pattern of an Aristotelian hero, but even so he is a tragic figure.... The most fully developed of any of Roberts' historical characters, Rogers is a dynamic figure.

In dealing with Benedict Arnold, Roberts fails to achieve the same round characterization that makes Robert Rogers a major protagonist. Arnold appears as a man of inexhaustible energy who will go to any extent to accomplish his goal.... Combined with this craving for activity is Arnold's ability to inspire action in his men.... A determined man, he becomes irritated by anything that stands in his way. In *Arundel,* for example, he hears rumors that Steven Nason is a spy. Rather than risk any danger to the mission, Arnold angrily dismisses Steven, allowing him no opportunity for defense and calling him "nothing but an innkeeper and a trader—a man who'll take money for almost anything he owns."... As a military commander, however, Arnold is a genius. He outmaneuvers the British at the battle of Valcour and defeats them with sheer courage at Saratoga. But unlike Rogers in *Northwest Passage,* Arnold, as a fictional character, possesses few faults to aid in his downfall. Even his hasty judgment of Steven Nason grows out of concern for his expedition. Kenneth Roberts has been criticized for this vindication of Benedict Arnold in *Arundel* and *Rabble in Arms.* He sees Arnold as a man treated unjustly by Congress and deliberately restricted by jealous peers. In the novels, Arnold merits none of this abuse. At the end of *Rabble in Arms,* Peter Merrill suggests that Arnold's treason was motivated by patriotism—the fear of French domination of the colonies. Chilson H. Leonard says he once thought Roberts was just "making out an ingenious case for his hero" until he examined some of the author's sources and discovered that many people in the colonies felt as Roberts believes Arnold did. Walter Rideout notes, however [in his *The Radical Novel in the United States: 1900-1954*], that Roberts' attempts to justify Arnold's acts "ultimately smash up against the hard fact of the hero's subsequent treason." Whether or not Roberts' explanation is sound, the basic consideration must be Arnold's effectiveness as a character in *Arundel* and *Rabble in Arms*. In this regard, Roberts vividly portrays a dashing leader. To Peter Merrill, Arnold is a man—perhaps the only man—who can save the Northern Army and the colonies. What else can Peter do but defend Arnold? It is only logical that Peter, who is not involved with Arnold at the time of the treason, will project what he knows about the hero into the future. From this standpoint Arnold succeeds as a character; his treason lies outside the scope of the novel. (pp. 39-41)

Minor historical figures in Roberts' novels usually do not appear as rounded characters. Richard Eastman in *A Guide to the Novel* summarizes their function: "Flat minor characters, easy to judge because the novelist has pictured them in black and white, may serve as contrast to define major characters in a moral sense." For example, in *Arundel* and *Rabble in Arms,* as Bertram indicates, minor characters are divided between good and bad depending on how they view Arnold. General Washington, for instance, appears a dignified, reserved leader who appreciates Arnold's abilities. General Gates, in contrast, remains at headquarters while Arnold fights and then refuses to mention Arnold at all in his report of the battle to Congress. Thus these minor characters emphasize Arnold's virtues. (p. 41)

Bringing to life historical figures supplies one of the pleasures of Roberts' novels, but he also creates memorable fictional characters; his narrators are the most dynamic. Each matures as he faces physical, mental, and emotional tests. . . . Although the narrators possess many similarities and are basically the same type of man, Roberts never allows them to lose their individuality. Even after having read all three novels, a reader distinguishes clearly between Langdon Towne, the artist, Steven Nason, the innkeeper and woodsman, and Peter Merrill, the sea captain. Because each character never forgets what he is, the reader remembers also. . . . They become real people.

Although important as motivation for the narrators, the female characters in Roberts' novels are usually one-dimensional. Marie de Sabrevois of *Arundel* and *Rabble in Arms* appears as a beautiful but cunning spy. Her every word and gesture contribute to this impression. In *Northwest Passage* Elizabeth Browne, even as a girl demanding everyone's attention, becomes the unhappy, nagging wife of Robert Rogers. Always forgiving and understanding, Ann Potter seems too perfect. (pp. 42-3)

Roberts' most delightful creations are his humorous figures such as Cap Huff, Sergeant McNott, and Doc Means. Each of these men displays some peculiar distinguishing trait. Cap, whose name is really Saved from Captivity, appears in all three novels. His special interest is buttered rum, usually someone else's. Adept at borrowing, often without the lender's knowledge, Cap provides what Nason's scouts need but what the army does not supply. Jay Lewis labels Cap Huff as a comic character, "probably the greatest in English literature, aside from Falstaff" [see excerpt dated 1948]. Red-haired Sergeant McNott of *Northwest Passage* has a wooden leg which his

Indian wife removes and threatens to burn when he misbehaves or attempts to leave her. Doc Means of *Rabble in Arms* carries an asafoetida bag and always appears in the last stages of feebleness. Yet he marches with the army using his unorthodox medicinal remedies to doctor Nason's scouts. In addition to providing humor, these characters often comment on the action, voicing opinions that the narrators cannot bring themselves to express. . . . Through an artistic intermingling of tragedy, humor, and suspense Roberts provides not only an enlightening account of early American history but also a very human and entertaining one. . . . In Roberts' novels humor offers one means of maintaining sanity in situations which appear insane to individuals experiencing them.

Even Roberts' fictional characters have some basis in history. His narrators frequently possess qualities that Roberts' ancestors had. Steven Nason, for example, is a composite of Stephen Harding, Jr. and Edward Nason, Roberts' maternal great-grandfathers. . . . [The] historical facts which Roberts uses as a basis for his figures give only the outline for characters. Creating the personality, the moral nature, and the speech of these people and relating them to each other stand out as Roberts' creative accomplishment. (pp. 43-5)

In *Northwest Passage, Arundel,* and *Rabble in Arms* all three narrators discover that war is a futile, senseless madness from which few men escape untainted. (p. 45)

A second theme important to Roberts' fiction is the betrayal of great men by petty ones. In *Northwest Passage* Robert Rogers recognizes this situation, although he seems unable to control it: "'You don't know what men in the highest positions will do when they see rivals coming too close! They'll steal, lie, buy votes, break their promises and go back on their friends! War's hard business, but politics is worse." . . . Benedict Arnold also understands that often his worst enemies are not the British but his own officers: "'I've come to believe that jealousy's the motive that accounts for almost everything that's bad and wrong. No human being, I do believe, can achieve any unusual success—display any marked ability—without being attacked by jealous people. Nearly every man, after he passes his thirtieth year, is sour with jealousy." . . . Despised for their ability and fame, both men face defeat, not at the hands of the British or the Indians but the Americans. (p. 46)

In wars there are frequently not two clearly defined ideological positions but numerous shades of loyalty and rebellion. To Kenneth Roberts, the American Revolution was such a conflict. . . . In an effort to complete the story of the American Revolution, Roberts wrote *Oliver Wiswell* . . . presenting the Loyalists' view of the war. This unique perspective gives the Revolution the aspect of a civil war, emphasizing the division in the American people. (p. 48)

In *Oliver Wiswell,* Roberts uses more historical characters than in any other novel. . . . From the Loyalist point of view, Roberts' historical characters are separated into three classifications—rebels, Loyalists, and British. Individual characterizations reinforce the picture of each group as a whole.

To Oliver Wiswell, rebels are essentially undisciplined men who do not know the control of reason. . . . Through their actions, Roberts establishes the rebels as men determined to tolerate no opinion but their own. For daring to oppose them, clergymen, physicians, lawyers, and numerous other educated and honorable men are driven from their homes. The rebels eagerly encourage wealthy Loyalists to abandon their property which can then be confiscated. As individuals the rebels are almost inhuman. . . . Oliver's characterization of rebels as men without principles is a general one, for he quite naturally has little personal contact with them.

In contrast to the rebels, the Loyalists shun war. . . . At first, the Loyalists, educated men accustomed to intellectual freedom, cannot comprehend that the rebels who cry for liberty refuse that very liberty to their countrymen. . . . Once the Loyalists realize that they must fight, however, their courage is beyond question, as the defense of Ninety-Six demonstrates.

Over and over, Roberts portrays the British as bunglers. From the beginning they insist on using European military tactics. . . . As a result of the mismanagement and obstinacy of the British, the Loyalists become the third side of the American Revolution.

To include this vast array of historical figures and still portray them individually presents problems for any novelist. By allowing each characterization to add one more fragment of evidence to the general picture of a group, Roberts has clearly defined the three major forces involved in *Oliver Wiswell*. For the purpose of creating a story with such a broad scope, these characterizations, though of necessity somewhat flat, reinforce the plot. Only through repeating the qualities of each group could Roberts make such a strong impression on his readers.

Fictional characters in *Oliver Wiswell* are really subordinate to the story of the Loyalists. . . . Oliver, an historian, serves as a reliable reporter of the Revolution. . . . Although not as forceful as Langdon Towne or even Steven Nason, Oliver surpasses these two in one respect: he can immerse himself in a cause rather than in personal loyalty to a hero. As a narrator, he both comments on and participates in the events he describes. (pp. 51-4)

To dramatize adequately the American Revolution in one novel challenges any writer of fiction. In *Oliver Wiswell,* however, Kenneth Roberts successfully limits the viewpoint to one person and yet covers events from 1775 until 1783. Through the narrator's presence in Boston, New York, London, Paris, Ninety-Six, and Nova Scotia, the author unifies his plot. Although as Kitch indicates, a few of the episodes, particularly those in France, do not "ring true," the reader willingly overlooks such weaknesses because the events have great significance for the Loyalist cause, the primary focus of *Oliver Wiswell.* Roberts also keeps the reader's attention by maintaining suspense through his use of time and foreshadowing. (p. 55)

Because Roberts presents the Loyalist viewpoint, he has been criticized for changing the nature of the American Revolution "to make it appear an inexcusable revolt by inferior races against good masters . . ." [according to Charles William Thompson]. In reality, he merely focuses on a forgotten phase of the Revolution. His thesis in *Oliver Wiswell* is that "in any upheaval the values in what is forever lost must be balanced against whatever is gained." . . . The important consideration remains not that *Oliver Wiswell* may contain misinterpretations of the Revolution, but that unfortunately it contains too much truth.

As a novel *Oliver Wiswell* does not equal *Northwest Passage* in unified plot structure nor in character study. It does, however, arouse an intense indignation at injustice and intolerance. Roberts combines characterization of historical figures, sustained suspense, and condemnation of war to produce a novel which clearly strengthens the author's position as a significant American novelist. (p. 57)

Kenneth Roberts did not want to write "historical" fiction. In fact, he says he always had a "profound aversion to most historical novels, because the people in them aren't real people, and neither act nor talk like anyone I've ever known." While writing **Rabble in Arms** he insisted "I wish it could be distinctly understood that I do *not* write historical novels." . . . The occasion for his protest was a passage in a historical novel in which "the hero explains how pure he is, not even allowing himself to touch the heroine's skirt." . . . At the other extreme, historical accounts supplied only the outline of events and frequently not an accurate outline. Searching histories of Maine for information about his ancestors, Roberts discovered the shortcomings of supposedly factual records:

> I had tried to get some of these things straightened out in my mind by reading histories that purported to explain them; but in every case—not in most cases, but in *every* case—I found that the books explained nothing fully or satisfactorily. They were drab, dull, unconvincing, rich in omissions, and crowded with statements that couldn't possibly be true. The people in them were generals and statesmen and important personages: cardboard people, flat, unreal, bloodless, lifeless, behaving without rhyme or reason. The little people like my great-great-grandfathers and all those other men from Maine, who sailed the ships and stopped the bullets and cursed the rotten food and stole chickens and wanted to get the hell out of there and go home—they just didn't exist at all. . . .

Such men seemed "soldiers in a snapshot, silent and stiff." . . . Out of his desire to refute the romanticized, sentimental, unrealistic treatment of past events in novels and his passion to combat the lifeless, staid, inaccurate historical chronicles, Roberts created what he believed to be an innovation—novels based on history which tell the truth. If what Kenneth Roberts wrote are historical novels, then the term deserves new respect.

An examination of these novels clearly demonstrates that Kenneth Roberts has made a lasting contribution to American literature. Long recognized for his vivid recreation of historical periods and events, he has been classified as a writer of historical fiction, a label which minimizes his artistic talent. However, a revaluation of his works with regard to fictional technique establishes the author's position as a significant American novelist.

Foremost among the merits of Roberts' fiction is his emphasis on an interesting plot dramatized by vigorous characters. . . . [Roberts'] readers experience a sense of urgency as they are drawn forward by the action. . . . Roberts' characters, both fictional and historical, add to the excitement of his novels. Depicting figures as they would seem to an ordinary man unaware of their historical significance, Roberts provides a refreshing approach to the past. His fictional characters, especially the humorous figures, enliven his plots. For his readers, Roberts' novels are intriguing adventures.

Through first-person narration, the author makes history a vital part of the suspense in his novels. Although his imagination may not have been extraordinary, it is notable that out of the mass of facts Roberts collected should come solid novels; "a man with no imagination could have produced only the same facts and trivia at greater and more gruesome length" [according to Kitch]. In short, he created literature out of historical facts. Scrupulous in his adherence to historical accuracy, Roberts nevertheless comprehends that a reader must become so absorbed in a story that he forgets he is reading about actual events. . . . Because the reader identifies with the narrators, he too can relive historical events. . . . The immediacy of the past is a forceful quality of Roberts' fiction.

Roberts' works cannot be restricted to the classification of historical novels, however, because he goes beyond merely recreating a certain period; he presents themes of universal significance. For him, history represents more than a record of events; it is also a study of human nature. . . . While examining a specific historical event, Roberts notes implications for all men in all times. Thus war is a barbaric experience regardless of causes or results. In any age men who deny change betray the men of vision. Those preoccupied with personal power often undermine the work of great men through jealousy and pettiness. The impact of these themes springs from Roberts' "sincerity, a real desire to say something to others," [according to Harold P. Scott, in his *On Writing Well: Selected Reading from Two Centuries*]. His fiction is an effective method of expression because his themes grow naturally out of the plots; he is never merely preaching.

Kenneth Roberts' fictional technique, including exciting plots, memorable characters, vivid portrayals of history, and universally significant themes, earns him a position as an important American novelist. However, his works do have certain limitations, such as loose plot organization, little symbolism, rapid incidents, and flat characterization. With neither the imagination of Mark Twain nor the perfected style of Henry James, Roberts is admittedly not a classic American author. . . . In brief, he is more concerned with what he says than with how he says it. Consequently, at a time when the very nature of the United States is being examined, Roberts speaks to Americans, affirming that patriotism is not shameful while at the same time deploring the "consistent" men who refuse to question any accepted institution or tradition. Reason, justice, honor—these qualities are sought today just as they were in the American Revolution or during the War of 1812, and Kenneth Roberts demonstrates the continuum of the American past and present. He recognizes with T. S. Eliot that "Time present and time past / Are both perhaps present in time future, / And time future contained in time past." Reliving the past through Kenneth Roberts' fiction provides insight into the relevant relationships between past, present and future. (pp. 75-8)

> *Janet Harris, in her* A Century of American History in Fiction: Kenneth Roberts' Novels, *Gordon Press, 1976, 101 p.*

ADDITIONAL BIBLIOGRAPHY

Bagger, Eugene S. "Ethnology by Ear." *The New Republic* XXX, No. 389 (17 May 1922): 349.
  Unfavorable review of *Why Europe Leaves Home* in which Bagger criticizes Roberts's views on immigration and prohibition.

Cary, Richard. "Inside Kenneth Roberts." *Colby Library Quarterly*, Series VI, No. 3 (September 1962): 130-32.
  Brief character sketch of Roberts, including some reminiscences about his wife, Anna Mosser Roberts.

————."Roberts and Lorimer: The First Decade." *Colby Library Quarterly*, Series VI, No. 3 (September 1962): 106-29.
  Discusses the writing careers of George Lorimer and Roberts, focusing in particular on the professional association and friendship which developed between these two men. The essay includes many excerpts from their correspondence.

Coffin, Robert P. Tristram. "Homer Didn't Tell Lies." *The Saturday Review of Literature*, New York XXXIV, No. 1 (6 January 1951): 15-16.
  Favorable review of *Henry Gross and His Dowsing Rod*, a work by which, according to Coffin, "the cause of folklore as a basis of the science of living has been vastly advanced." Coffin also expresses his personal belief in water dowsing.

Commager, Henry Steele. "A Breathless Vista of Forgotten History: Kenneth Roberts Brings to Life the World of 1800." *New York Herald Tribune Weekly Book Review* (5 January 1947): 1-2.
  Plot summary and mostly favorable review of *Lydia Bailey*. Commager praises Roberts in general for his "narrative talent, . . . passion for authenticity, and . . . marked independence of judgment that place him in the forefront of our historical novelists."

Coyle, Lee. "Kenneth Roberts and the American Historical Novel." In *Popular Literature in America*, edited by James C. Austin, pp. 70-7. Bowling Green: Bowling Green University Popular Press, 1972.
  Survey of Roberts's novels, expressing high regard for Roberts as both a novelist and historian. Coyle notes that the low status of the historical novel among scholars has had an adverse effect on Robert's critical standing.

Devree, Howard. "Journalistic Kaliedoscope of the Florida Boom." *The New York Times Book Review* (13 June 1926): 10.
  Review of *Florida*, Roberts's account of the Florida real estate boom of the 1920s.

Fadiman. Clifton. "A Little Theorizing." *The New Yorker* XVI, No. 41 (23 November 1940): 75-7.
  Notes that the popular appeal of *Oliver Wiswell* is similar to that of Margaret Mitchell's *Gone With the Wind*, in that each novel appealingly presented a lost cause with which few readers had hitherto been in sympathy.

Gardner, Martin. "Dowsing Bugs and Doodlebugs." In his *In the Name of Science*, pp. 101-15. New York: G. P. Putnam's Sons, 1952.
  Discounts dowsing as a legitimate means of locating water and criticizes the unscientific basis of Roberts's promotion of dowsing in his book *Henry Gross and His Dowsing Rod*.

Marsh, Fred T. "Kenneth Roberts's Huge and Lively Novel: A Bold Presentation of the Tory Side of Our Revolution." *New York Herald Tribune Books* (24 November 1940): 1-2.
  Plot summary and review of *Oliver Wiswell*, that acknowledges Roberts as a leading historical novelist but notes that the novel is "neither candid nor dispassionate," and that "never was there a more bigoted history even from the rebel side."

Nevins, Allan. "Young Man in a Revolution." *Saturday Review of Literature* XXIII, No. 5 (23 November 1940): 5.
  Plot summary and review of *Oliver Wiswell*. Nevins also briefly summarizes what he regards as the strengths and weaknesses of Roberts's fiction in general.

Nichols, Lewis. "A Visit with Mr. Roberts." *The New York Times Book Review* (1 January 1956): 3, 21.
  Describes Roberts's Maine estate and quotes Roberts regarding his home, his novel *Boon Island*, and his interest in dowsing.

"Pussyfoot Propaganda." *The Saturday Review* 134, No. 3496 (28 October 1922): 630.
  Review of *Why Europe Leaves Home*. The commentator disagrees with some of Roberts's views on prohibition and immigration, but commends him for writing "with gusto," and an entertaining, humorous style.

Straumann, Heinrich. "The Quest for Tradition." In his *American Literature in the Twentieth Century*, pp. 48-70. New York: Harper & Row, 1956.

Commends Roberts for the unconventional, enlightening perspectives of his novels and discusses *Oliver Wiswell* as a good example of his "unobtrusive introduction of a fundamental human problem" in his novels—"namely the clash of the attitude of loyalty with independent pragmatic judgment in one and the same person."

Tarkington, Booth. "Europe's Grand Tour since the War." *The New York Times Book Review and Magazine* (10 April 1921): 14.
Favorable review of *Europe's Morning After,* described by Tarkington as "a valuable and entertaining book." He commends Roberts's use of the English language, his clear presentation of the European situation following World War I, and the humor in this work.

Van Gelder, Robert. "When the Republic Was Young: Kenneth Roberts' Novel Roams the Map in the Familiar Picaresque Tradition." *The New York Times Book Review* (5 January 1947): 1, 25.
Review of *Lydia Bailey.* Van Gelder considers the book to be marred by an uneven plot and forced dialogue, but enriched by its basis in history.

Williams, Ben Ames. Introduction to *The Kenneth Roberts Reader,* by Kenneth Roberts and Anna M. Roberts, pp. vii-xi. Garden City: Doubleday, Doran and Co., 1945.
Personal reminiscence by a friend of Roberts.

Ybarra, T. R. *"Europe's Morning After." The New York Times Book Review and Magazine* (27 March 1921): 12.
Largely unfavorable review of *Europe's Morning After,* in which Ybarra criticizes Roberts's humorous tone as inappropriate and somewhat forced.

Romain Rolland

1866-1944

French novelist, biographer, historian, critic, and dramatist.

Considered one of the foremost French authors during the early twentieth century, Rolland was an ardent pacifist and humanist whose many works of fiction were written primarily as a vehicle for the dissemination of his philosophical views. His most comprehensive and sustained exposition occurs in the ten-volume novel *Jean-Christophe,* wherein Rolland explores the fundamental unity of all things and delineates his conception of humanity's proper role in the universal scheme. Although Rolland's works were highly esteemed during his lifetime and earned him the 1915 Nobel prize for literature, his idealism and sweeping style are more closely linked to nineteenth-century Romanticism than to the trends of modern fiction, and as a result his novels have not retained their popularity. He is, however, still regarded as an able historian and critic and as a courageous and prophetic political observer.

Rolland was born in Clamecy, in the pastoral Burgundy region of central France. Although Rolland's father was a local official and a prominent citizen of Clamecy, the family moved to Paris in 1880 so that Rolland could be educated at the finest schools in France. Attending the Lycée Saint-Louis and later the prestigious Ecole Normale Supèrieur, Rolland's course of study was primarily history and philosophy, but his passionate devotion to music eventually led him to concentrate upon the origins and nature of that art. Throughout his life, Rolland would insist that his writings were nothing more than an outlet for a creative energy frustrated by the inability to compose music.

In 1899, upon completion of his studies at the Ecole, Rolland was offered the opportunity to do postgraduate research in Rome, and it was the artistic influence of that city which inspired the creation of his first works, a cycle of dramas based on themes and subjects derived from classical literature. In 1890 Rolland wrote, ''I would not be a professor for anything in the world . . . I am an artist at heart''; but within a few years his lack of literary success and his desire to marry had forced him to accept a teaching position in Paris. Rolland's drama *Saint-Louis* was published in the *Revue de Paris* in 1897, and while critical response to the play was not favorable, Rolland immediately began work on a second cycle of dramas based upon the events of the French Revolution, and these fared somewhat better among critics.

Following the dissolution of his marriage in 1901, Rolland took a small apartment in a run-down section of Paris and began work on *Jean-Christophe,* a project he had been formulating since his trip to Rome twelve years earlier. Living alone and rarely going out, Rolland spent the next ten years writing the life story of a German musician who embodied all of Rolland's own ideals. Although he began the novel in relative obscurity, by the time the final volume was published in 1912 Rolland had become internationally renowned, the early sections of *Jean-Christophe* having been so successful that they were immediately translated into English, German, Spanish, and Italian.

Photopress, Zurich

Always concerned with moral and social issues, Rolland felt compelled to use his newly-acquired stature in the service of humanity, and with international tensions threatening the tenuous peace of Europe, he became an outspoken advocate of pacifism and internationalism. In June 1914, Rolland left France to settle in Switzerland, where he hoped to inspire the creation of a new, cosmopolitan society free from the fierce nationalism he felt had become all too common in other European nations. Throughout the first World War he published a number of antiwar essays, but his efforts were poorly received. In his most famous antiwar essay, ''Au-dessus de la mêlee'' (''Above the Battle''), Rolland denounced violence absolutely and refused to recognize any distinction between those who resorted to its use for aggressive purposes and those who did so in their own defense. The people of France, feeling that they had been unjustifiably attacked by Germany and had responded in the only manner possible, were outraged by their compatriot's denunciations, and Rolland, whose adulation of German artists was already well known through his novels and biographies, was accused of pro-German sympathies.

The antipathy which developed between Rolland and the French people as a result of his refusal to approve their efforts during the war lingered long after the fighting had ceased, and Rolland remained in Switzerland until 1936. Suspecting that the peace secured by the Treaty of Versailles had settled nothing and had in fact created more tension among European nations, Rolland continued his appeals for international fraternity throughout the 1920s and 1930s in the hope of averting another war. In addition, he established contact with prominent intellectuals of other nations as part of his plan to organize an international community whose power would rival that of sovereign states and so facilitate the initiation of an era of peace and rationality. In 1932, Rolland successfully orchestrated an International Congress Against War and Fascism, but as the decade progressed, it became clear that the territorial ambitions of the German state would eventually require a military response, and Rolland himself began to admit the inevitability of such a necessary evil.

Rolland returned to France in 1937 and purchased a small villa near his birthplace in Clamecy. Disillusioned with politics by the outbreak of war in 1939, he devoted his final years to compiling his memoirs, writing a biography of his friend and former publisher, Charles Péguy, and adding some concluding sections to his seven-volume study of Beethoven. He died in December of 1944.

Believing strongly that human beings possess enormous potential for virtuous and noble behavior, Rolland considered it the duty of art to instruct and inspire humanity, and his works were written with this end in mind. In *Jean-Christophe*, for example, Rolland created his ideal man: a sensitive, courageous individual who possesses not only genius but also a freedom of mind that allows him to perceive the world fully, clearly, and objectively. Like any human being, he is occasionally tempted to abandon his high ideals in favor of proximate pleasure or gain, but he never succumbs to what Rolland considered the petty materialism of his age, much as Rolland himself refused to retract his unpopular opinions in the face of fierce opposition. In writing *Jean-Christophe*, Rolland sought not only to present a comprehensive moral view of life but also to introduce innovative literary techniques derived from his studies of music. However, while critics agree that the novel successfully utilizes such symphonic elements as crescendo, coda, and recurrent motifs, they point out that Rolland's use of these devices does not represent a true innovation, since the arts have always been united and guided by the same general principles and practices. The most successful literary technique employed in *Jean-Christophe* is Rolland's use of the river as his dominant thematic motif, reflecting his belief that existence is a temporal flow of phenomena whose components—humanity and the natural world—are formed of the same essential materials, governed by the same laws, and inherently interdependent. The theme of the river of life is continued throughout Rolland's second novel cycle, *L'âme enchantée*, in which the central character is in fact named Annette Rivière. *L'âme enchantée* is generally regarded as Rolland's attempt to create a female Jean-Christophe, though critics agree that the later novel is inferior, not because Annette Rivière fails to attain the heroic stature of her predecessor, but because the author introduces political polemics to the detriment of the narrative.

Although Rolland based his portrait of Jean-Christophe upon the kind of man he himself wished to be, he also drew heavily from the life of one of his personal heroes, Ludwig von Beethoven. Rolland's reverence for German artists, a guiding force in both his ideology and his work, has been the subject of much attention, particularly since it led to his renowned estrangement from the French people. Critics generally agree that Rolland, who admired above all the robust, idealistic individual, was quite naturally impressed by the metaphysical orientation and sheer power of German Romantic art. Moreover, although Rolland proclaimed himself a citizen of the world, he also admitted to feeling a definite affinity for the Teutonic people. His reverence for the subjects of his biographies did not, however, mar the quality of those works. A trained historian and critic, Rolland presented accurate and objective accounts of his subjects' lives and works, and as a result his critical biographies are frequently considered his finest work.

Rolland's dramatic works, on the other hand, represent his least successful literary endeavors. Inspired by Shakespeare's plays, Rolland planned early in his career to create a series of dramas which would, like *Jean-Christophe*, constitute a comprehensive statement of his faith in the human spirit. The first cycle, unofficially titled "Tragedies of Faith," included *Saint-Louis* and was eventually abandoned. The second cycle, *Théâtre de la Révolution*, recounts the events of the French Revolution, and while several of these dramas were performed, they were not popular with audiences. Rolland's goal in creating the *Théâtre de la Révolution* was to bring to the stage scenes of ardent revolutionary idealism in which the audience would actually participate by serving as the Parisian mobs or spectators to the proceedings of the Tribunal. The overly didactic quality of his plays was, however, unpalatable to French theatergoers, who preferred to be entertained rather than instructed during their evenings at the theater.

Although Rolland is not as well known today as he was during the early decades of the century, specific aspects of his work continue to draw attention. Writing in 1967, Anthony Burgess judged *Jean-Christophe* "the best musical novel there is," and several subsequent studies have focused on musical elements in the novel. Yet most critics consider *Jean-Christophe* as a whole unsuccessful, finding the work vigorous and perceptive in the early volumes but increasingly diffuse in the later ones. Furthermore, the novel's extreme length is discouraging to many modern readers. Rolland's most popular work of fiction is the much shorter *Colas Breugnon, bonhomme vit encore! (Colas Breugnon)*, which is a humorous and colorful evocation of rural Burgundy. Many critics, however, consider all of Rolland's fiction to be secondary in importance to his criticism and biographies, particularly his incisive analysis of the life and work of Beethoven. Several commentators have noted that Rolland's renown is not the result of his literary achievements at all, but rather of his creation of a larger than life persona and of his adherence to a set of Utopian ideals which collectively have been called "the credo of a modern Romantic."

PRINCIPAL WORKS

Saint-Louis   (drama)   1897
Aërt   (drama)   1898
*Les loups   (drama)   1898
   [*Wolves*, 1937]
*Le triomphe de la raison   (drama)   1899
*Danton   (drama)   1900
   [*Danton*, 1918]
*Le quatorze juillet   (drama)   1902
   [*The Fourteenth of July*, 1918]
Beethoven   (biography)   1903
   [*Beethoven*, 1917]
Le théâtre du peuple   (essay)   1903; published in journal
   Cahiers de la Quinzaine
   [*The People's Theater*, 1918]
**L'aube   (novel)   1905
**Le matin   (novel)   1905

**L'adolescent* (novel) 1905
Michel-Ange (criticism) 1905
**La révolte* (novel) 1907
**La foire sur la place* (novel) 1908
**Antoinette* (novel) 1908
Musiciens d'aujourd'hui (nonfiction) 1908
   [*Musicians of Today*, 1914]
Musiciens d'autrefois (nonfiction) 1908
   [*Some Musicians of Former Days*, 1915]
**Dans la maison* (novel) 1909
Haendel (criticism) 1910
   [*Handel*, 1916]
Jean-Christophe (novel) 1910; published in England as
   John Christopher. 2 vols.
**Les amies* (novel) 1910
Jean-Christophe in Paris (novel) 1911; published in
   England as *John Christopher in Paris*
La vie de Michel-Ange (biography) 1911
   [*Michelangelo*, 1915]
**Le buisson ardent* (novel) 1911
Vie de Tolstoï (biography) 1911
   [*Tolstoy*, 1911]
**La nouvelle journée* (novel) 1912
Jean-Christophe; Journey's End (novel) 1913; published
   in England as *John Christopher; Journey's End*
Au-dessus de la mêlée (essays) 1915
   [*Above the Battle*, 1916]
Colas Breugnon, bonhomme vit encore! (novel) 1919
   [*Colas Breugnon*, 1919]
Liluli (drama) 1919
   [*Liluli*, 1920]
Voyage musical aux pays du passé (nonfiction) 1919
   [*A Musical Tour Through the Land of the Past*, 1922]
*Clerambault, histoire d'une conscience libre pendant la
   guerre* (novel) 1920
   [*Clerambault, the Story of an Independent Spirit during
   the War*, 1921]
Pierre et Luce (novel) 1920
   [*Pierre and Luce*, 1922]
***Annette et Sylvie* (novel) 1922
   [*Annette and Sylvie*, 1925]
Les vaincus (drama) 1922
***L'été* (novel) 1924
   [*Summer*, 1925]
Mahatma Gandhi (biography) 1924
   [*Mahatma Gandhi: The Man Who Became One with the
   Universal Being*, 1924]
**Le jeu de l'amour et de la mort* (drama) 1925
   [*The Game of Love and Death*, 1926]
**Pâques fleuris* (drama) 1926
   [*Palm Sunday*, 1928]
****Mere et fils*. 2 vols. (novel) 1927
   [*Mother and Son*, 1927]
Beethoven: Les grandes époques créatrices. 7 vols.
   (criticism) 1928-45
   [*Beethoven the Creator*, (partial translation) 1929-37]
**Les leonides* (drama) 1928
Essai sur la mystique et l'action de l'Inde vivante. 3 vols.
   (essays) 1929-30
   [*Prophets of the New India*, 1930]
Goethe et Beethoven (criticism) 1930
   [*Goethe and Beethoven*, 1931]
****L'annonciatrice, Anna Nuncia: La mort d'un monde*
   (novel) 1933
   [*The Death of a World*, 1933]

****L'annonciatrice, Anna Nuncia: L'enfantement*. 2 vols.
   (novel) 1933
   [*World in Birth*, 1934]
Par la révolution, la paix (essays) 1935
Quinze ans de combat, 1919-1934 (essays) 1935
   [*I Will Not Rest*, 1937]
Compagnons de route (essays) 1936
**Robespierre* (drama) 1939
Le voyage intérieur (autobiography) 1942
   [*Journey Within*, 1947]
Péguy. 2 vols. (biography) 1944
Mémoirs, et fragments de Journal (journal) 1956

All dates listed for dramas above are first publication dates.

*These plays comprise the dramatic cycle *Théâtre de la Révolution*.

**These ten volumes comprise the cyclical novel *Jean-Christophe*.
The individual volumes are listed sequentially in order of publication. The English translation of the novel was published in the three
installments listed above—*Jean-Christophe, Jean-Christophe in Paris*,
and *Jean-Christophe: Journey's End*—each of which collects several
volumes of the French original. The translated installments are listed
here separately under their English titles.

***These volumes comprise the cyclical novel *L'âme enchantée*.

CLEVELAND PALMER (essay date 1911)

[*In the following excerpt, Palmer discusses the merits and flaws
of* Jean-Christophe.]

A perusal of parts of [**Jean-Christophe**], in the French, did not
produce a very favourable impression upon the present reviewer, and it was difficult to understand the unstinted praise
that had been poured out upon it by Mr. George Moore, Mr.
Edmund Gosse and others of the critical confraternity. This
was partly due to the fact that, having no external events of
importance, and depending for its interest altogether upon the
progressive development of a single character, **Jean-Christophe**
must be read consecutively from the start. It is decidedly a
book not to be dipped into. Readers must be warned, in view
of its formidable length, that here it is a case of all or nothing.
Also, the original seems to suffer from the utter slovenliness
and lack of distinction of its style. Any one who has come to
seek in French a certain precision, elegance and clarity of
expression, as well as a feeling for artistic restraint, for form
and for structure, cannot but be offended by the chaotic shapeliness and by the enormous volubility of the present work. To
tell the whole story of the life of a man, omitting nothing, is
a tempting experiment for the modern novelist trained in the
school of naturalism. But in throwing over so many aids to the
arousing and holding of attention, in seeking to make art imitate
life in the most literal sense, is to run a great risk of producing
that impression of boredom and disgust which life itself so
often produces. It requires a great artist to court such a danger
successfully. On a relatively small scale, Flaubert did this in
Une Vie. But not even that writer would have dared to attempt
a **Jean-Christophe**.

That M. Romain Rolland should deliberately plan to tell the
story of his hero in ten volumes would argue, on the face of
it, either sublime conviction or fatuous self-confidence. He has
none of the literary skill and power of a Flaubert, or even of
a Zola. That he writes a bastard French style is perhaps nothing,

since Stendhal's style has also been loudly and universally decried. But Stendhal at least registered his ideas and impressions concisely and with pungent precision. M. Rolland, on the other hand, is rhetorical and redundant, he conceals none of the tentative steps by which he strives after—and sometimes attains—the right word or phrase, and he indulges in passages of heightened and ejaculatory prose that represent a return to the most turgid type of the *roman lyrique* of the early nineteenth century. He moralises, rhapsodises, digresses, proceeds from the psychological analysis of the individual to that of the race, discusses poetry and music in their national manifestations, and, in short, makes of the novel a medium for the expression of the whole of modern life and the modern spirit.

Yet the fact remains that, in spite of all these antecedent grounds for probable failure, *Jean-Christophe* is an impressive, and often an extraordinarily interesting piece of fiction. . . . [If] M. Rolland has, in a measure, succeeded where even Flaubert would have failed, the reason is that the former has chosen a subject quite different from that which would have attracted the latter. Like Stendhal in his *Julien Sorel,* M. Rolland has set out to depict, not a commonplace character, but a type of the *homme superieur.* The comparison is misleading, for if Julien was superior through intelligence, Jean-Christophe is superior rather through his soul. He is, indeed, a musical genius, as well as a man of heroic cast and proportions, morally and spiritually. He performs many acts that are unheroic enough, his natural kindliness is frequently eclipsed by the cruelty of youth or the egoism of genius. But he remains sympathetic and even noble because he is passionately and vividly alive, because he feels remorse for what he does that is wrong, because he himself suffers, and because he is impatient with lies and seeks unremittingly the truth. He is no charlatan, he is sincere. He is even a little god-like, and this is intentional on the part of his creator, for M. Rolland regards life as spiritual energy, and its manifestation in man as true divinity. He glorifies life, and sings pæans in its praise. It is not life that is bad. It is the things that obstruct the flow of its forces. Men go down because they cling to these obstructions. Jean-Christophe survives, and even triumphs, because he detaches himself from them, one by one, in his search for truth.

Naturally, as this is a novel with a musical hero, the criticism of conservatism and the classical spirit is carried out largely in the field of music. And as the hero is also a German, the specific object of the attack is the German national character as divined in its musical expression. It is the German lie that Jean-Christophe first detects and exposes—to his own sorrow—the lie of the shallow German idealism and "terrible tenderness." Later on, we are told, Jean-Christophe, who leaves his little Rhenish town for Paris at the end of the present volume, discovers the French lie. Whether we are to have the rest of this story in English—only seven of the projected ten parts have yet appeared in French—depends, the translator remarks in his preface, upon the reception accorded to the present volume. It will be interesting to see what this reception will be like. It is no longer necessary to take the apologetic tone for the psychological novel that Taine took in his article on *Rouge-et-Noir* in the '60's. The fact that *Jean-Christophe* is a musical novel should help it to reach a certain class of readers, but a stronger and wider appeal lies in the breath and sympathy with which the emotional experiences of the hero are handled.

M. Rolland is a biographer of Beethoven, and his study of the various phases of the character of that composer has given him

an insight into the operations of genius from its earliest manifestations. The boyhood part of the book is particularly well done. The child of six is trained by a drunken father for the part of the infant prodigy. Drilled at the piano, forced, at dictation, to pen an obsequious dedicatory letter to the local Duke, he is finally presented upon the stage in a paroxysm of shyness and awakened resentment at the indignity of the whole proceeding. The episode has a pathos that is almost painful. But there is charm, too, in these early pages, as when pride and affection prompt the grandfather to take down the notes of the airs the little boy hums in his play, and to draw up "Op. I" of Jean-Christophe's musical compositions: "The Pleasures of Childhood." The old man is a musician and an unsuccessful composer, and he cannot resist adding a trio of his own to his grandson's minuet, so that something of himself will not altogether perish. For one who makes almost a gospel of the insolent glory of youth, M. Rolland has a profound and sympathetic insight into the secrets of broken old age. Louisa, Jean-Christophe's peasant mother, inarticulate in her sorrow of living, is a portrait filled out with tender and understanding touches. But the book is a perfect gallery of portraits. One would say that all the types of contemporary German life were contained in this gallery, and though they are introduced in the most casual fashion—scarcely delineated before they are dismissed to make way for others—they remain in the memory with sharpness and clearness of detail. For they are, in the majority of instances, human types, as well as German, and if they are interesting and memorable, it is because they are immediately recognised as universally true. Take, for example, another of the old men, Justus Euler, who illustrates the author's paradox that most men die at twenty or thirty, and thereafter are but pale and mechanical reflections of what they were when they were alive:

> On every subject he had ideas ready-made, dating from his youth. He pretended to some knowledge of the arts, but he clung to certain hallowed names of men, about whom he was forever reiterating his emphatic formulæ: everything else was naught and had never been. When modern interests were mentioned he would not listen and talked of something else. He declared that he loved music passionately, and he would ask Christophe to play. But as soon as Christophe . . . began to play, the old fellow would begin to talk loudly to his daughter, as though the music only increased his interest in everything but music. . . . There were only a few airs—three or four—some very beautiful, others very ugly, but all equally sacred, which were privileged to gain comparative silence and absolute approval. With the very first notes the old man would go into ecstasies, tears would come into his eyes, not so much for the pleasure he was enjoying as for the pleasure he once had enjoyed.

It is this intimate knowledge of the human heart that gives the work of M. Romain Rolland its true distinction. His sympathetic understanding of vague impulses and promptings enables him to carry his hero without indignity through the rather undignified and ridiculous adventures of adolescence, and to gild even a vulgar love with a kind of glory. Perhaps his chief danger lies in this direction, and another age or generation, less in love with youth, may spurn much of his work as of a spurious sentimentality. Certainly his art, so solidly based upon observation and insight, would gain with greater restraint in expression. But M. Rolland shares in that spirit of revolt of which he makes his hero the embodiment. Jean-Christophe's onslaught upon the composers and virtuosi of Germany, and the petty personalities of his native town, is not more fierce than that which his creator makes by implication against the conventions of French fiction. And while it is not always possible to praise, it is impossible to deny that he has brought back the spirit of youth, or some semblence of it, into the desiccated French novel of to-day. (pp. 495-97)

> Cleveland Palmer, "Romain Rolland's 'Jean-Christophe'," in The Bookman, New York, Vol. XXXII, No. 5, January, 1911, pp. 495-97.

THE NATION   (essay date 1911)

[*In the following excerpt, the critic condemns* Jean-Christophe *for stylistic reasons.*]

The six hundred pages of [*Jean-Christophe: Dawn, Morning, Youth, Revolt*] are presumably little more than half of the French edition, in which there are three additional parts. It is also stated that *Jean-Christophe,* if the public so desires, will be followed by two more works with which to round out a trilogy. Hence this English translation may be regarded as a sample asking for a specially serious judgment. The book will probably be taken, at first sight, for a very full realistic account of a musical genius from the day of his birth to the time when, at twenty years of age, he is compelled by an act of rebellion against the military to flee from his country; he is last seen taking the train for Paris, where his éxperiences are recorded in the three parts not yet translated.

The plot is not worth mentioning, since the action is fragmentary and episodic, with only that slight unity which must result from following the thread of a single life. Sheer artlessness this method, we believe, has been pronounced in France, which, confident of a mission, disarms and possesses. The method needs to be examined. It differs entirely from what is generally called realism, in that it never presents anything like a full cross-section of the hero's life at any given time, and also in the fact that character and action are not related to each other in a natural way. These peculiarities can be illustrated best together. Although the setting remains almost constantly the same, new persons keep appearing, and old ones, when once they have served the author's purpose, disappear for great stretches of time, if not forever. Even of Jean's two brothers we get no accurate picture. The younger returns momentarily from oblivion to steal away the hero's mistress when it is desirable that this chapter in Jean's life shall close. Previously the youthful Frau Sabine, whom the reader has seen but a moment, is stricken dead of a trivial cold after she has stirred Jean with first desire. And Uncle Gottfried, the peddler, passes like Pippa and changes events with a word. A student of Tolstoy, M. Rolland has failed to grasp Tolstoy's way of editing. He presents a series of incomplete scenes, which are all too obviously created to carry and crystallize spiritual action; action does not grow inevitably out of character and setting.

The result is what might be expected. Robbed of a natural framework, the inner life, no feature of which seems to the author too trivial to mention, loses any real meaning and sorely lacks interest. Imagine this method applied to the intangible realities of Becky Sharp or Diana, and the futility of Jean-Christophe becomes apparent. The author is not a novelist, he is a psychologist, though it must be said that he has uncommon

power to phrase the most transitory sensations. On this spiritual side, the hero's relentless search, in defiance of all conventions, for what he conceives to be the truth, carries one back to the early days of German romanticism. (pp. 62-3)

> A review of "Jean-Christophe: Dawn, Morning, Youth, Revolt," in The Nation, Vol. XCII, No. 2377, January 19, 1911, pp. 62-3.

THE NEW YORK TIMES BOOK REVIEW   (essay date 1913)

[*In the following excerpt, the critic explains and assesses the compositional method employed in* Jean-Christophe.]

The epic novel seldom fails to attract attention; it may fall short of being great or popular, but it is rarely unimportant. It crashes, en bloc, into the field of public attention by reason of its sheer force, if by nothing else. Thus, it is inevitable that two continents should be discussing the Gil Blas of the hour, the Wilhelm Meister of to-day, *Jean-Christophe*. Books VIII., IX. and X. are now ready in the third volume of the English translation of M. Rolland's great work, and the completed *Jean-Christophe* is at last in print. It is unfortunate that the work was published, and hence reviewed, piecemeal. The first four books, carrying the reader just across the threshold of the young musician's turbulent life, were all too prematurely discussed and tagged with assorted adjectives. It was judgment of the opera from the overture, the prologue for the play. But now M. Rolland has put down his pen, and the ten-volume work may be viewed in its entirety.

M. Rolland shows the life of his hero from the very first stirrings in the cradle to the shadow at the road's end, or, as he himself significantly spaces it, from dawn to dawn again, from birth to rebirth. He spreads out the entire fabric of this man's life, sadly soiled here and there, but the warp and the woof are strong. Jean-Christophe is no mock hero; he is genuinely large and virile enough to carry the weight of material with which M. Rolland burdens him. The choice of a daimonic personality for one's hero, the irresponsible man of genius who is a law unto himself, always obviates many difficulties for the author; it makes the incredible seem happily inevitable though inexplicable.

There is no stone in Jean-Christophe's life which is left unturned; we live his life through and indeed grow old along with him. Born in a stuffy little German town, of parents miserably differing in station and temperament, he embarks on life equipped with a curious mixture of ideal tendencies and sordid appetites. He makes his public appearance as a composer and a pianist at the age of seven. From that time his struggle begins; commercialized while he is little more than a baby, fighting his way through the unlovely wrangles of his home life, cramped by the commonplace existence of his provincial town, maturing all too rapidly under the restraint of unnatural responsibilities, Christophe at sixteen is anything but juvenile. Sturm-und-Drang catches him early and terrifically; with the awakening of the desire to create he chokes in Germany, goes to France, where one finds him, bewildered in the streets of Paris, seeking a place for his art.

We follow him, almost microscopically, through the ensuing years of disappointment. He is amazed at the French life. The German life made him impatient and irritated him, but he stands appalled at French decadence, at the sham of the market place where art is prostituted for art's sake. Unhealthfulness is beyond Christophe's comprehension.

"What ails you that you think such evil things?" he cries in his lumbering French at the litterateurs, the pseudo-artists whom he is led to believe represent France. They smile at his im-

Rolland in 1888.

potence and go on their way belittling Bach and Wagner to the glorification of some upstart of the moment. Often these clever Parisians trick the uncouth musician cruelly; Christophe is like the keen blade smiting at feathers and raging when they snow him under and are likely to suffocate him.

Struggling, passionately despising and hating, now and again bursting into laughter, Christophe plunges his way through these little people who swarm like Lilliputians under his heels. He gathers many friends along the road; they fill a place in his life and drop away. It is through one of these wayfarers, whose hand touched Christophe's for a moment, that he is able to realize his early ideal, to find the France in which he had believed, the substance behind the empty shell which, like all that is best and noblest in the life of any nation, is concealed by the glitter and blare of the clique, the "artistic circle."

The end of Christophe's life finds him at last coming face to face with all these people, good, bad, and despicable, recognizing that he is one among them and by some good fortune speaking to them through the symphonies which he has builded out of his life. We read a noble record of a common experience; the revelation that may come to any man, pointing out to him that he is indeed the servant of the future. Little by little the curious transposition takes place for Christophe by which one's work becomes the real, the tangible and actual, and one's life the vision and the dream. The two mediocre young people, Georges and Aurora, standing on either side of Christophe's bedside at the end, are but symbols. The vision passes—and Christophe has slipped away.

Confronted with the problem of making life understandable, of interpreting its complexities and its contradictions, M. Rol-

land has seemingly despaired and turned to the only open door, mere reproduction of the whole affair. He refuses to edit life. He has, of course, experienced the terrifying importance of the trivial things of life, and he has quailed before the chance which every artist takes of choosing the non-essential. Rather, he sets all life before us with an earnestness and a care which must, nevertheless, be admired, saying: "There's how the whole thing stands. If it isn't right, blame the Creator."

The method is not brave. Neither is it fair to the reader. His imagination is shackled hand and foot. There is nothing about Jean-Christophe or the three generations through which Christophe passes which the reader does not know and see and feel in abundant detail. M. Rolland is engrossed with the joy of creation and the exercise of his excellent power of observation and analysis, but he forgets that there is an active audience, and that Jean-Christophe as a safety valve for his own energy is small justification for his ten volumes. M. Rolland comes by this mania for writing all or nothing by his great-grandfather, whose immense journal recording the trivialities of every day of his life formed much of one of his earlier works, a drama, *I Juliet*. But explanation does not excuse.

A demand for editing, however, does not imply that *Jean-Christophe* is a formless mass of material, justified by volume only, and valuable in parts as a searching and pungent commentary on the continental thought of—we must say it—yesterday. Romain Rolland is no callow youth, thirsting for self-expression and placing himself outside a technique of whose bounds he is ignorant. On the contrary, he has been a life-long student of that highly technical form of art, the drama. There is little from the best of to-day's work to compare with the "Antoinette" of Jean-Christophe; it is a finished and a lovely thing which will stand for a long time. The whole novel, if novel we may call it, is obviously no running narrative; it is a rounded whole, conceived, as its author declares, end and beginning, before it was written. The attempt to produce in it a positive rhythm by massing of material and emphasis has succeeded; the same themes occur over and over again, growing, shaping, and changing as the whole symphony shapes and changes. The bare technique of *Jean-Christophe* is that of a symphony rather than a novel; but the transposition carries.

The work is admittedly epic. *Jean-Christophe* has none of the sentimental sickliness of *Wilhelm Meister*. Much as we love the young Goethe, we are too often put out of touch with him by having to stop to laugh at him. We cannot find Christophe ludicrous; we can neither jeer nor remain indifferent to him. But we cannot laugh with him. Christophe himself we see bursting into roars as he views these absurd poseurs in motley, but M. Rolland's earnestness commands the book and us, and we dare not smile. M. Rolland holds his Wagner and his Goethe, his Tolstoy and his Beethoven too close and too seriously. Commendable his gravity is, but oppressive it also is.

Yet we come from the book with the refreshment of contact with a live and healthy force. We feel a tightening of the muscles such as comes from watching magnificent horses, or responding to the virility of an able demagogue on a cart tail. And when we have turned the last page and some one asks us, "What is life, anyway?" we know no more than Jean-Christophe, and it is good if we can cry with him:

"A tragedy. Hurrah!"

"M. Rolland's Epic," in The New York Times Book Review, *March 16, 1913, p. 142.*

HERMANN HESSE (essay date 1915)

[Recipient of the Nobel Prize in literature for 1946, Hesse is considered one of the most important German novelists of the twentieth century. Lyrical in style, his novels are concerned with a search on the part of their protagonists for self-knowledge and for insight into the relationship between physical and spiritual realms. Critics often look upon Hesse's works as falling into the tradition of German Romanticism, from the early bildungsroman Peter Camenzind *(1904) to the introspective* Steppenwolf *(1927) to the mystical* Das Glasperlenspiel *(1943;* Magister Ludi*), his last major work.* Magister Ludi *is generally held to epitomize Hesse's achievement, delineating a complex vision which intermingles art and religion to convey a sense of harmony unifying the diverse elements of existence. This work, along with such earlier novels as* Siddhartha, *established Hesse's reputation as an author who to many readers and critics approximates the role of a modern sage. In the following essay, which first appeared in German in 1915, Hesse praises* Jean-Christophe *and commends Rolland's personal integrity.]*

In . . . extensive works of fiction it can easily happen that the beginning enchants us without the whole being able to sustain the same high level. In *Jean Christophe* too, naturally enough, not every page is of equal value. Artistically, poetically, I consider the first part, the account of his childhood and early youth, the most significant. But in any case there will not be a reader who will not love the whole of this work, who will not admire in addition to the conception and intuition of its most successful parts the patience and faithful work, the understanding and sense of fairness of the subsequent chapters. In the purely artistic sense a beautiful lyric poem of four lines is more perfect and valuable than any novel, including *Wilhelm Meister*. A novel like *Jean Christophe* is not only art, it is not only the behavior of a soul, it is also the attempt of a mind to comprehend intellectually and to some extent with a sense of collective justice the temper of a time, of a culture, of a section of mankind. The musician Jean Christophe is not only a character, the past vision of a poet, he is at the same time an abstraction, a bearer of rich meanings, almost a myth. He is the spirit of music, the spirit of German originality and sluggish German tortuousness, for whom the mirror, the charm, the spur, the paradisal enchantment, the lovely, dear, depraved, clever, childish, mad, splendid Paris is essential for his fate. Romain Rolland, the Frenchman, has portrayed his German hero with a love that is apparently greater than his own love for his native Paris. For a thousand pages our affectionate sympathy is steadily on the side of the struggling musician against blind, evil, mendacious Paris. Apparently almost everywhere Paris customs, Paris art, Paris manners and lack of them are treated with inexorable harshness, while the hero Christophe is the object of unvarying love. Apparently Christophe is right and Paris wrong. In reality it is not so at all, and this is one of the great charms of the book. In reality this externally wicked and corrupt Paris is the object of a deep, holy love, stands far higher than any criticism or love could place it, exists cool and mighty and becomes fateful for everyone who touches it. Frenchmen, especially those of the war years, have still very little conception of what a song has here been sung to their holy of holies. For very many Frenchmen up to the time of the war, Rolland was a poet who had converted his minor weakness of a fondness for the German character into his strength. We too thought the same thing about him. In reality Rolland is a Frenchman through and through, the true essence of the French spirit, and for that very reason it is doubly significant and valuable that this Romain Rolland was among the few who during the war took human love seriously

and who in time of peace takes the so universally acknowledged international ideals seriously. This man has not only written many very intelligent and fine books, he has also forborne to take part in the hue and cry for the sake of cheap laurels. Just as he unobtrusively donated to the International Red Cross in Geneva the Nobel Prize money he had won, so he relinquished fame, friendships, his treasure of a hard-won home, and love in order to remain true to his heart. . . . The time will come when the values of such persons and such actions, which today seem purely passive, will prove themselves actively. Then it will be seen that Rolland's attitude during the war was the most Christian that can be conceived of. And people will admire in his great musical novel not simply the critical intellect and great ability but also the by no means passionless love of justice, the courageous and reverent love for mankind as a whole. (pp. 331-33)

> Hermann Hesse, "Romain Rolland (1922, 1915)," in his My Belief: Essays on Life and Art, *edited by Theodore Ziolkowski, translated by Denver Lindley with Ralph Manheim, Farrar, Straus and Giroux, 1974, pp. 329-33.*

ELIZABETH SHEPLEY SERGEANT (essay date 1916)

[In the following excerpt, Sergeant discusses the objective rationality displayed in Above the Battle.*]*

[Romain Rolland] is one of the few important European thinkers who have actually kept their mental and moral perspective since Europe went to pieces. Much was to be expected from the author of *Jean-Christophe*. Even while the winds of nationalism were rising he dedicated his life and his art to an

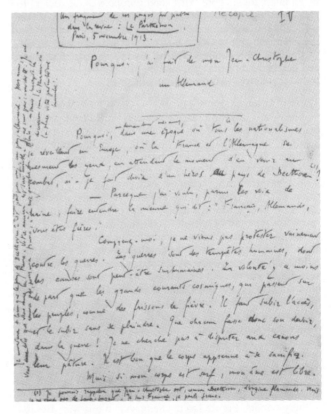

Holograph copy of a note on Jean Christophe.

effort to see France unflinchingly and to look into the heart of her great neighbor. Yet even Rolland has been able to achieve clearness of head and calmness of heart only by retiring to neutral Switzerland. The articles and letters which make up [*Au-Dessus de la Mêlée*] appeared for the most part in the Geneva *Journal*. They brought the wrath of both France and Germany on the author's head. The reason is not far to seek. France and Germany wish to believe the worst of each other— Rolland insists, even in these dire days, on repudiating national hatreds and cultivating international understanding.

Rolland has always claimed "the consent of reason." To him all sanctions are personal, all battles must be fought in the individual soul. Soul is a word he has a liking for, and the reason in which he believes is not the affair of intellect alone. "The intelligence of thought is nothing without that of the heart." This is very like Vauvenargues' famous phrase, "les grandes pensées viennent du coeur" ["great thoughts come from the heart"]; and indeed Rolland seems, by his combination of profound human tenderness with a solid and stoical strain of character, to belong to the same French line as the seventeenth century moralist—broadly speaking, to the protestant and liberal, as opposed to the Catholic and traditionalist line. "I believe," said Jean-Christophe, "that a vigorous and healthy man must remake his own philosophy, as he remakes his life, his art, as he decides in action, and as he loves." What could be more Emersonian, more remote from the theories of M. Barrès? Probably Barrès would say that Rolland could not now be living in Alpine detachment if his youth had not been perverted by foreign influence. Wagner, Tolstoi, Dostoëvsky, became his spiritual masters in the 'eighties, and he began to dream of that "good Europe," as Nietzsche called it, where the best of the culture of all lands should be shared by an international élite. This good Europe was, of course, the real fatherland of Jean-Christophe; and again in the new volume we read that the élite has "two cities: our earthly country and the other, the city of God. Of the former we are the occupants; of the latter the builders. Let us give to the first our bodies and our faithful hearts. But nothing of what we love—family, friends, country—has a claim on our spirits."

The article which gives its name to the volume was the one that most aroused the French press against Rolland, though it begins with a poignant invocation to the *jeunesse héroique du monde* ["heroic youth of the world"], especially to the youth of France who "for years have been confiding your dreams to me." "How you avenge us for the years of skepticism, of weak pleasure-seeking when we were growing up. . . . War 'of revenge,' . . . indeed, but not as a narrow chauvinism understands it: faith's revenge upon all the egoism of senses and spirit, absolute gift of oneself to eternal ideas." Even if France should perish, such a death would be the supreme victory of a race. Yet if the hands of the combatants are clean, by what right have the guardians of European civilization sacrificed such living riches? All the spiritual forces are marshalled behind the armies. Eucken against Bergson, Hauptmann against Maeterlinck, Hervé under the flag of Austerlitz. Rolland recognizes that the tragedy of the conflict is that every one of the peoples is really menaced in independence, life, and honor. The original fault, in his opinion, belongs to the "three rapacious eagles," Austria, Russia, and Prussia; and as between the two latter he maintains that Russia is "the lesser evil," not only because her modern art is more vital, but because her thinkers have always protested against the violence of their military tyrants. France has the *beau rôle* in this war. But that is precisely why he wishes her to conquer not only by right,

but by "the superiority of her generous heart." That is why he pleads for charity, lucidity, and calm. While the soldiers fight without hatred, the writers at home brandish bloody pens and cry "Kill! Kill!"

The article on "**Idols,**" a fierce arraignment of intellectualism, is perhaps the most powerful of the collection. Humanity, he moans, in spite of the efforts of forty centuries, remains enslaved to the phantoms of its own mind. In the fabrication the intellectuals surpass the common herd. They weave the web more closely and produce monstrous chefs-d'oeuvres. So we get the idol of Kultur—this is the worst and greatest—but Rolland attacks also the new French idol of "race," of "civilization," of "Latinity." "Try to forget your ideas," he adjures both nations, "and look in each others' eyes. 'Don't you see that you are me?' said old Hugo to one of his enemies."

For nearly a year Rolland's articles could get into the French papers only in fragmentary form, "deformed" by his enemies. Even to these enemies he turns the other cheek, and every "friend of Jean-Christophe," as his readers all over the world have been called, will respect him for proclaiming his right to keep his old friends in Germany; for protesting against what he believes to be both a political and a moral error—the total crushing of the enemy nation; for pointing out the dawnings in Germany of discontent and right reason; for urging that the two nations must not burn the bridges of a future friendship. There is an illuminating chapter on German war literature; the tone of a few "young reviews" being distinctly critical of their military leaders. Young France is not writing for publication— war has struck deeper into her body—her works are her acts and also her letters. For certain of these Rolland "would give the most beautiful verses of the most beautiful of poems."

It is quite clear, however, from the development of this book— which is arranged in chronological order and evolves, as the preface points out, from indignation to pity—that to Rolland the war ends by becoming wholly terrible and unendurable. From his post in Geneva, one of service to an international society for the benefit of civil prisoners, he welcomes all documents which show the uprising against war of too supine public opinion, neutral and other, and urges upon the élite the need of a supreme court of conscience. Nobody who reads him at this distance can doubt the ardor of his patriotism, though one cannot help feeling that his absence from France has somewhat tempered the reality of what he has to say. Once already, at the time of the Affaire Dreyfus, he has refused to take sides, apparently from an instinctive recoil from the angers of the warring camps. Now he shrinks from the grim passions of Paris in wartime. This is the other face of his human tenderness, as his clinging to Tolstoian hopes in the midst of the international shipwreck is the other side of his immovable stoical idealism. Even Jaurès, whose death he laments as an irreparable loss to European democracy, modified his views with the times. Not so Rolland; and one regrets that the entreaties of his friends have driven him into silence. It is strong proof of how far, in the country where one has hitherto found the human spirit most free, a tragic necessity has subordinated thought to action, and free will to obedience. (pp. 49-50)

> *Elizabeth Shepley Sergeant, "Above the Mêlée," in*
> The New Republic, *Vol. VI, No. 67, February 12,*
> *1916, pp. 49-50.*

THE SPECTATOR (essay date 1916)

[*In the following excerpt, the critic takes exception to Rolland's condemnation in* Above the Battle *of all belligerents in World War I.*]

English readers will turn with the liveliest curiosity to [*Above the Battle*] to see why they excited so great a commotion in Paris and why M. Romain Rolland's book was boycotted. Probably the first feeling of the reader will be surprise that the indignation should have been so great, or even that there was any indignation at all, for he will find directly he opens the book a denunciation of German crime as bitter and searching as any that can have been written in French. It has the sort of quality, this first essay addressed to Hauptmann, that we should like to see in all pro-Ally arguments about the war which are likely to come under the eyes of neutrals. It is so vivid that it is impossible not to read every word of it, although the English translation, excellent though it is, is necessarily but a ghost of M. Rolland's glowing French. So much for the first impression. But a little more reading of the essays, or at least a very short reflection upon them when they have all been read, will show why they caused anger in France, and why it was perfectly natural that they should do so. Although they denounce Germany, they assume that all the nations engaged in the war are alike steeped in a madness which has quite unnecessarily brought civilization to the verge of destruction. The ultimate cause of the war, M. Rolland implies, is a universal unreason. He writes in the manner since adopted by Mr. Bertrand Russell, who has told us that the nations are fighting with no better reason, in the final analysis, than that of two dogs who are infuriated by each other's smell.

The plain man who reads this kind of thing, particularly if he is insensible to beauties of language—and even those who are not insensible may think the offence the greater for the literary skill—is simply goaded to madness. He remembers that Germany was prepared for war and that the Allies were unprepared; he remembers that very late in the negotiations before the war Russia was willing to refer the whole dispute to a fresh series of negotiations and that Germany refused; he remembers that Britain proposed a Conference and that Germany refused; and he remembers that at the eleventh hour Sir Edward Grey declared that he would accept any plan within reason which promised peace, even though France and Russia should not approve—and that even then Germany insisted on having war. When he remembers these things he has not a scrap of patience left for the man of letters, or political philosopher, who argues as though the responsibility of the Allies were of the same character and degree as that of Germany. In our opinion, his anger is not only not to be wondered at, but is hardly to be condemned. These men of letters often try us too high. If M. Rolland had written all the sentiments in this book, in almost the same language, before the war began, his readers, we undertake to say, would have listened to him with great respect, even though they disagreed. Those who were capable of appreciating such things would have been chiefly conscious of the beauties of his style. There would have been no exasperation. It is possible that a time may come after the war when these essays may still be read with calmness and pleasure. But in the France of this hour it is impossible. M. Rolland's error, in fine, is his extraordinary inopportuneness. If this is the kind of give-and-take support he has to offer his country in her desperate extremity, and he is yet astonished that he should be denounced, he has not, after all, begun to understand that human nature which it has been the aim of his life to study. He goes off to Switzerland. He talks of looking down from the high plateaus of that mountainous country on the strife of nations. It is a most unfortunate phrase. It is precisely this "looking down" from a height, whether it be a physical, moral, or philosophical height, which enrages a man who is conscious that he is playing his own honest, humble, and dangerous part

in a great cause, while his lecturing philosopher is less perilously engaged. Such a feeling as this is very cogently expressed by a French officer who has written a hot condemnation of M. Rolland in a small pamphlet that lies before us—*Romain Rolland Parle.* . . . (pp. 631-32)

Let us look at some specimen passages of what M. Rolland says well against Germany, and also of what he says so inopportunely as to spoil the effect of his good words. The following is from the letter to Hauptmann:

> Not content to fling yourselves on living Belgium, you wage war on the dead, on the glories of past ages. You bombard Malines, you burn Rubens, and Louvain is now no more than a heap of ashes—Louvain with its treasures of art and of science, the sacred town! What are you, then, Hauptmann, and by what name do you want us to call you now, since you repudiate the title of barbarians? Are you the grandsons of Goethe or of Attila? Are you making war on enemies or on the human spirit? Kill men if you like, but respect masterpieces. They are the patrimony of the human race. You, like all the rest of us, are its depositories; in pillaging it, as you do, you show yourselves unworthy of our great heritage, unworthy to take your place in that little European army which is civilisation's guard of honour. It is not to the opinion of the rest of the world that I address myself in challenging you, Hauptmann. In the name of our Europe, of which you have hitherto been one of the most illustrious champions, in the name of that civilisation for which the greatest of men have striven all down the ages, in the name of the very honour of your Germanic race, Gerhart Hauptmann, I abjure you, I challenge you, you and the intellectuals of Germany, amongst whom I reckon so many friends, to protest with all your energy against this crime which is recoiling upon you.

The essay entitled **"Pro Aris,"** which is an apology for those who talk even more of the shattering of cathedrals and grand buildings than of the loss of precious lives, is a noble and imaginative piece of writing, steel-girded with scorn and horror at German acts. **"The Idols,"** again, is an extraordinarily powerful indictment of German *Kultur*.

But what are we to say of the ineptness of the following passage addressed equally to all the nations concerned?

> And thus the three greatest nations of the West, the guardians of civilisation, rush headlong to their ruin, calling in to their aid Cossacks, Turks, Japanese, Cingalese, Soudanese, Senegalese, Moroccans, Egyptians, Sikhs and Sepoys— barbarians from the poles and those from the equator, souls and bodies of all colours. It is as if the four quarters of the Roman Empire at the time of the Tetrarchy had called upon the barbarians of the whole universe to devour each other. Is our civilisation so solid that you do not fear to shake the pillars on which it rests? Can you not see that all falls in upon you if one column be shattered? Could you not have learned if not to love one another, at least to

tolerate the great virtues and the great vices of the other? Was it not your duty to attempt— you have never attempted it in sincerity—to settle amicably the questions which divided you—the problem of peoples annexed against their will, the equitable division of productive labour and the riches of the world?

M. Rolland has written a note to these lines in order to disavow all intention of disparaging the non-Europeans fighting with the Allies. We unreservedly believe him, but surely the words still condemn themselves. This is not the way to write of the decision of the Allies that, as the future of the world depended upon Germany being beaten, no single race in the world could be held unaffected by the war. Perhaps the worst passage of all for inopportuneness is the following:—

> The real tragedy, to one situated in the midst of the conflict and able to look down from the high plateaus of Switzerland into all the hostile camps, is the patent fact that actually each of the nations is being menaced in its dearest possessions—in its honour, its independence, its life. Who has brought these plagues upon them? brought them to the desperate alternative of overwhelming their adversary or dying? None other than their governments, and above all, in my opinion, the three great culprits, the three rapacious eagles, the three empires, the tortuous policy of the house of Austria, the ravenous greed of Tsarism, the brutality of Prussia. The worst enemy of each nation is not without, but within its frontiers, and none has the courage to fight against it.

It may be asked whether M. Rolland, having laid the blame on nearly every one, has no remedy for every one's ills. He has. He says that our first duty is to form "a moral High Court, a tribunal of consciences, to watch and pass impartial judgment on any violations of the laws of nations." What is the Hague Court, we should like to know, but a tribunal of consciences? And with what authority does he propose to endow his tribunal? Is it to have the authority of force—enough force to compel Germany? Or does he suggest that the grand protest of many united consciences will melt the heart of Germany? M. Rolland complains that "the neutral countries are too much effaced." But who has effaced them? Have they not effaced themselves? Has any Power violently forbidden them to stand up for international law and honesty and humanity? M. Rolland finally appeals to Switzerland to stand forth amid the tempest. It is all very unreal and extremely unhelpful.

We cannot refrain from saying, in conclusion, at the risk of appearing shockingly Philistine, that throughout the war most men of letters have served the world badly. Words master them even while they are hailed as masters of words. They look on from their studies, or the tops of mountains, and they elegantly give unpractical, and too often fantastic advice to men who are covered with the dust and heat of battle. They have earned, we fear, the resentment they have provoked. We feel inclined to exhort them all at least to get embroiled in a street fight, if they are unable to serve with the colours, and then to ask themselves how far their ideas really protect them against the ways of natural men or assuage the temper of a crowd. (p. 632)

A review of "Above the Battle," in The Spectator, *Vol. 116, No. 4586, May 20, 1916, pp. 631-32.*

BARRETT H. CLARK   (essay date 1918)

[*Clark was a Canadian-born American drama critic who, in his various editorial and advisory capacities, was particularly interested in gaining wider recognition for the work of young, unknown playwrights and in retrieving forgotten plays from earlier periods, as in his twenty-volume anthology* America's Lost Plays *(1940-41). In the following excerpt, Clark discusses Rolland's dramatic works.*]

It is perhaps a little surprising to learn that the author of *Jean-Christophe* has written at least sixteen full-length plays. Most of these, it is true, antedate the publication of the first parts of his epoch-making novel, but since nothing that comes from the brain of Romain Rolland can fail to possess significance and interest, a brief inquiry into his dramatic writings and theories on the drama will reveal an aspect of the man which has hitherto strangely enough scarcely been touched upon. His plays for a people's theater, and his book of projects, are as integral a part of his development as *Jean-Christophe* itself.

The life of M. Rolland seems to have been a perpetual struggle between conflicting mental forces: for years he read philosophy, and suffered agonies before he at last found himself spiritually; until the completion of *Jean-Christophe* he was a prey to doubts regarding the utility of art and the end of life. He applied in turn to the great master-minds of the world—Empedocles, Spinoza, Michelangelo, Shakespeare, Beethoven, Tolstoy—seeking for a satisfactory philosophy of life. Small wonder, therefore, that his work should bear the imprint of the masters who have at one time or another been his guides and inspiration.

His two years' sojourn in Rome, from 1890 to 1892, awakened a passionate interest in the Italian Renaissance, which he immediately translated into plays. It is likely that *Orsino, Les Baglioni,* and *Le Siège de Mantoue,* plays of the Renaissance, were inspired by Shakespeare, for whose historical dramas M. Rolland professes a decided partiality. The plays are not published, but if we can judge from the fact that Mounet-Sully wished to produce *Orsino,* they must have shown some of the power of the later plays. At Rome he was associated with the aged revolutionist Malwida von Meysenburg, whom he had met at Versailles some time before, and doubtless the story of her eventful life had its part in shaping his ideals. Four other plays—three of them on classical subjects—belong to this period: *Niobe, Caligula, Empédocle,* and *Jeanne de Piennes.* It is probable that these also belonged to the writer's period of apprenticeship. At the end of M. Rolland's stay in Rome he went to the Wagner Festival at Bayreuth, in company with Malwida.

Even at this time he was already dreaming of a new theater in France, and his theoretical writings of later times bear unmistakable proof of the impression made upon him by the Bayreuth theater and Wagner's epoch-making ideas on art and the people.

After his marriage in 1892 Romain Rolland returned to Italy, where he gathered material for his thesis, which he presented and successfully upheld at the Sorbonne in 1895. His subject was *The Origins of the Modern Lyric Theater. History of the Opera in Europe Before Lully and Scarlatti.* This he published in book form in 1895. But in addition to his university studies and his lectures, he found time to experiment with the dramatic form, and in 1896 he published his *Saint Louis.* As this was later included in a volume called *Tragedies of Faith—Les Tragédies de la Foi*—together with two other plays, he evidently conceived it as one of a series of works based upon a single underlying idea.

Saint Louis depicts, in the author's own words, "religious exaltation." In *Saint Louis* and the two other plays which accompany it—*Aërt* and *Le Triomphe de la Raison*—"One can observe the presence of the main currents and passions of the French youth of to-day." All three show "the ardor of sacrifice, but a sacrifice which is courageous, militant: a double reaction against cowardice of thought and cowardice of action, against skepticism and against the relinquishment of the great destiny of the nation." But in spite of this "program," M. Rolland is an artist far too austere to write thesis-plays; he has often spoken in contempt of them. Nor did he in the least appeal to the great public; for his plays have as yet not proved acceptable to them. *Saint Louis* is a beautiful poem, not a tragedy after all, but a triumph, for no hero may see the fruits of his labor, and if a temporary failure seems for a moment to cloud the sky, it is only temporary. This is the message of *Saint Louis.* The good monarch who, "dying at the foot of the mountain, sees Jerusalem only through the eyes of his army," is a figure of hope. *Aërt* takes us from the time of the Crusades to "an imaginary Holland of the seventeenth century." Aërt, the son of a murdered patriot, is imprisoned by his father's assassin; he makes a vain effort to rally the forces of the opposition, and at last, free from all that is vile in life, he throws himself from the window. *Le Triomphe de la Raison* belongs, so far as the subject is concerned, to the Revolutionary plays. As an after-piece to *Le 14 Juillet, Danton,* and *Les Loups,* it shows the Revolution "devouring itself"—to translate literally the author's own comment. So far as it depicts the excesses into which faith can lead men, it is a tragedy, but there is an implication of progress in the characters whose fate is bound

Playbill for Les Loups.

up with that of the Revolution, even those who fell prey to the blood-lust of the Girondist massacres.

The *Théâtre de la Révolution* includes the three Revolutionary plays I have just mentioned. They were written not as experiments for some vague stage dreamed by the author, but for theatrical production before the people, the masses of France. That they were not wholly successful matters little; Romain Rolland might well refer us to the "moral" of *Saint Louis:* he has opened a new field and laid before his countrymen—perhaps the world—an ideal which may well require half a century to bear fruit. The idea of writing a series of plays on the French Revolution was suggested to M. Rolland by a decree of the Committee of Public Safety, dated March 10, 1794:

> 1. That the Théâtre-Français shall henceforward be solely dedicated to productions given by and for the people at stated intervals each month:
>
> 2. That the building shall bear the following inscription on its façade: PEOPLE'S THEATER, and that the various troupes of actors already established in the Paris theaters shall be requisitioned in turn to act in these popular productions, which are to take place three times in every decade.

A few weeks later there appeared another decree, inviting the poets "to celebrate the principal events of the French Revolution, to compose Republican plays, and picture for posterity the great epochs of the regeneration of the French, and give to history that solid character which is fitting for the annals of a great people who have fought victoriously for their liberty, in spite of the opposition of all the tyrants of Europe."

"All these projects for Republican art," says M. Rolland, "fell, on the 9th of Thermidor, together with the chiefs of the Republic."

When, early in 1903, Romain Rolland and a few associates began writing for the *Revue d'Art Dramatique* a series of articles on the people's theater, they were merely "following the tradition interrupted by the events of the Revolution; and it was but natural that one of them was led to select the Revolution itself as the natural subject for popular productions. The three plays were to have been part of a dramatic cycle on the Revolution—a sort of epic comprising ten plays. *Le 14 Juillet* was the first page, and *Danton,* the center, the decisive crisis, wherein the reason of the chiefs of the Revolution seemed to waver, and their common faith be sacrificed to personal hatred. In *Les Loups,* where the Revolution is depicted on the field of battle, and in *Le Triomphe de la Raison,* where it goes out into the provinces in pursuit of the Girondin proscripts, it devours itself." Thus M. Rolland.

The remaining plays are three in number, and inferior in dramatic and literary quality to the six just discussed. The first of these is an anti-war propaganda piece, *Le Temps viendra,* published in 1903, and inspired by the Boer war. *La Montespan,* a French historical drama, followed in 1904, and *Les Trois Amoureuses,* also based upon history, in 1906.

In order to grasp the full significance of Mr. Rolland's plays it will be necessary to consider his interesting book, *Le Théâtre du Peuple.* Ever since the early eighties M. Rolland had been a staunch admirer and in some ways a disciple of Tolstoy. The young Frenchman, however, expressed his doubts to the Russian, and in 1887 Tolstoy wrote a long letter which was, according to one of M. Rolland's biographers, a sort of preliminary sketch for *What Is Art?* And when that astounding book appeared, with its iconoclastic attacks on M. Rolland's idols, he was at first prone to disagree, but *Le Théâtre du Peuple* is ample proof that "literature for the people" had sunk deep into the Frenchman's heart. The theater, in common with most modern art, is a whitened sepulcher, rotten to the core, affected, aristocratic, anti-democratic. The evil is not only in the plays, but in acting and the physical arrangement of the playhouse itself. New plays must be written for the masses, plays which they can understand, plays which bring them together as a class and in which they can participate. M. Rolland briefly considers the dramatic masterpieces of the world, from Sophocles to the comedies of the boulevard, and finds them, with rare exceptions, unsuited to the people. Even Shakespeare and Schiller are lifeless: they belong to past epochs, and express ideas foreign to the French workingmen of the twentieth century. The playhouses, too, are built for a society divided into classes; these must be altered to suit the workingmen. Says M. Rolland in the preface to the first edition: "Of late there has been an attempt to found a People's Theater in Paris. Already personal and political interests have begun to make themselves evident. But we must unflinchingly destroy the parasites who seek a living at the expense of our theater. The People's Theater is not a fashionable toy; it is no game for dilettanti. It is the imperious expression of a new society, its voice and thought; it is, as a result of circumstances, the war-machine against an ageing and fossilized society. Let there be no misunderstanding: we must not merely open up new old theaters, bourgeois theaters endeavoring to appear new merely by calling themselves people's theaters. We must found a theater by and for the people, a new art for a new world."

Having tested the plays of the past and found them wanting, M. Rolland set himself the task of supplying plays for his projected people's theater. As we have seen, he went to the Revolution, and wrote plays which would appeal to the masses. But these plays must also be acted *by* the people, and M. Rolland proceeded to make the people a character, a great composite crowd, participating as The People. In *Le 14 Juillet,* The People are the protagonist, and the taking of the Bastille afforded him ample opportunity for utilizing them. In *Danton* they are rather implied until the last act, while in *Les Loups* and *Le Triomphe de la Raison* they hover in the background and determine the course of events: they are always near at hand, although they do not appear on the stage. M. Rolland must of course be a confirmed enemy to our star-system, and there is, even in the hero-play of *Danton,* a fairly even distribution of parts. The effect is at first somewhat disconcerting, and the plays seem a trifle discursive and rambling, but this is doubtless due to the fact that we are accustomed to the Sardou method of handling historical themes. There is no conventional plot, and the love-interest, as developed in such a play as *Patrie,* is conspicuously absent. In its stead there is greater breadth of touch, a solider framework, a broader canvas; and the artist, we instinctively feel, is better able to depict a great movement like the Revolution than if he were confined to raveling and unraveling a plot. Possibly M. Rolland's ignorance of or disdain for the tricks of the dramatist's trade has lessened the purely dramatic tension of occasional scenes, but, on the other hand, he has drawn characters—Hoche, Desmoulins, Danton, Robespierre, among others—which Sardou and the rest could scarcely have conceived. The lovable weakness of Desmoulins, the dynamic and superhuman power of Danton, have never been so vividly set forth as in these plays, and the

Revolution, so often exposed as a series of more or less exciting events, stands forth as the most human of all stories.

While it is true that M. Rolland recognizes the motive power of the people in the first two plays of his Revolutionary cycle, and while they direct and influence practically every event, he is not blind to the excesses into which they fell, and the last two plays, *Les Loups* and *Le Triomphe de la Raison,* to some extent show the degeneration of the people. *Les Loups* is perhaps, from the purely theatrical viewpoint, the best play M. Rolland ever wrote; it treats of the moral decay of the Revolutionists, and the situation developed is as gripping as any of Henry Bernstein's famous second acts. A former nobleman is suspected of treachery by his fellow officers, and a pretext readily found to kill him. At the last moment one of his comrades discovers that he is innocent; however, in order to conceal the treachery of a successful Revolutionary general, he is sacrificed. *Le Triomphe de la Raison* is similar in theme.

No attempt at dramatic reform, no theory, no ideal—whatever its eventual worth—ought to obscure the fact that all of M. Rolland's plays are unsuccessful from the viewpoint of production. Good reading they undoubtedly make; literature they assuredly are, but they have not pleased audiences for consecutive days, weeks, and months. This does not of necessity damn them, but it should cause us to ask whether or not they belong to that class of hybrids, the closet-drama. M. Rolland's first mistake was in writing plays for a hypothetical and practically nonexistent public. The first edition of *Le Théâtre du Peuple* concludes with these words: "Do you want a people's art? Then begin by having a people!" France is in many ways an aristocratic country with an aristocratic art; it is but natural, therefore, that all reform should be slower than in younger countries; and M. Rolland in his impatience attempted the impossible. In trying to avoid what was conventional in the French drama, he restricted himself to a more or less formless medium, and the people who saw his plays missed what they were accustomed to see: a well-defined story.

What success would have attended his innovations in another country it is hard to say; what success will attend him if he perseveres, seems easier to predict. The past five years have witnessed a profound change in French thought and art, and perhaps Romain Rolland will once more find his faith justified in a new France where the people shall have a theater of their own. Meantime, his ideas have spread to other lands and there borne the fruit he had hoped would flourish in his own beloved France. (pp. 3-12)

        Barrett H. Clark, "Romain Rolland and the People's Theater," in The Fourteenth of July and Danton: Two Plays of the French Revolution by Romain Rolland, translated by Barrett H. Clark, Henry Holt and Company, 1918, pp. 3-12.

A. G. H. SPIERS (essay date 1919)

[In the following excerpt, Spiers praises Colas Breugnon.*]*

Rolland's *Colas Breugnon* is certainly one of the best novels to come out of France in the last twelvemonth. This is a good book, amusing, healthy and, in both form and spirit, decidedly original.

Rolland is getting older. *Colas Breugnon,* though printed (but not issued) fully five years ago, shows traces of a change not uncommon in those persons who have passed the halfway mark of life. Forty is, as Péguy once remarked, an implacable age, an age after which "bluff" is impossible, when our blood reasserts its rights and our ancestors come into their own. Romain Rolland's experience testifies to the truth of this remark. He was planning, so he himself tells us, to continue writing in the vein of *Jean-Christophe;* but suddenly he felt it impossible to carry on the spirit of his younger days; and, a visit to his native country, *la Bourgogne nivernaise,* having awakened within him all the Colas Breugnons that *"je porte dans ma peau"* ["I carry within me"], he composed instead the present *"oeuvre insouciante"* ["carefree work"].

As was to be expected, this new work is unlike any of Rolland's preceding writings. It is not an historic study, a critical appreciation, a philosophic essay, nor yet even, in the strictest sense of the word, a novel. It is rather a volume of reminiscences as told by a man of fifty; and the very aimlessness with which this man talks is in itself a pleasure; for Breugnon is himself the one subject of the book, holding our attention by the display of a wayward, sympathetic, and aggressive personality.

In a desultory fashion he tells us of many things—this virile and jovial fellow. A walk with his little granddaughter Godie gives him an opportunity to introduce the pretty story of the three birds—the wren, the robin, and the skylark—who each year bring down from heaven the warmth needed alike by man, beast, and plant; an exchange of banter with his married daughter Martine brings in the amusing conditions on which the *bon Dieu* agreed that children should be born able to walk; and an account of his love of roaming ends with a really beautiful description of the first visit paid by Breugnon to his onetime sweetheart, la Belette, thirty-five years after she had married another.

It is true that these events, like Breugnon himself, belong to a period none too close to our own—the first years of the seventeenth century. But we constantly forget the fact. The old fellow is a man of such tact and of such infinite foresight! What he tells us is precisely the thing in which we of today are interested, and he leaves untold whatever might seem strictly local. Even those things which by their nature would seem exclusively connected with the epoch in which he lives, contain a peculiar charm for us; for, as he describes it, that epoch appears far more delightful than ours and its contemplation strangely apt to release our repressed desires.

In those days a man's contact with the world he lived in was saner, more direct, more satisfying than now. Physic had not yet taken the place of physique, a strong arm might still prod a tardy justice, and many a good thing fell to the lot of him whose heart was stout and whose imagination was fertile. Breugnon feasts for the sheer joy of eating and drinking; he fights lustily for the satisfaction of his instinctive desire to punish those who have injured him; he plies his chisel and his plane (he is a master wood-carver) not for the remote and characterless reward of money, but for the immediate delight of the hand that shapes and the fancy that plans, for the happiness of the artist who loves his productions *"de la bonne manière, voluptueusement, de l'esprit et des membres"* ["well, sensually, in body and soul"]; and, for the satisfaction of an instinct scarcely less fundamental—the instinct of irreverence—he plays tricks on the nobles, is by no means enthusiastic in his allegiance to *"la grosse dondon de Florence"* ["the chubby wench from Florence"] (the queen regent!), and casts doubt—whether in earnest or in jest, neither he nor we can tell—upon the reality of the Deity.

Cruel indeed is the contrast for the unwary reader who, shaking off the spell of Breugnon's words, compares that life with our flesh-mortifying, spirit-deadening life of today. Yet the comparison is inevitable. (pp. 166-67)

That this contrast was intentional on Rolland's part, that it should be looked upon as the purpose that led him to write *Colas Breugnon,* is improbable: this book is anything but a direct criticism or pointed satire upon our modern times. But that this contrast was present, if not in the mind, at least in the feelings of the author, there can be no doubt. Have we not Rolland's own statement that this book was written as *"une réaction contre la contrainte de dix ans"* ["a reaction against the constraint of ten years"] spent in the *"atmosphère un peu tragique"* ["slightly tragic atmosphere"] of our contemporary Jean-Christophe? To live in the company of Breugnon is a tonic: for all his faults, he appeals to us as a favored individual privileged to indulge, vigorously and in the harmlessness of health, those feelings and instincts which have been so cramped by our modern civilization as to die within us or to degenerate into unlovely and maleficent impulses. Rolland too, before ourselves, has felt the effect of this tonic—has loved it, reveled in it; and this fact explains two things: it explains why Rolland has described the life of Breugnon in a peculiarly lyric style in which the sentences and paragraphs have a rhythmic swing of which the effect is heightened, now and again, by assonance and rhyme; and it explains also why we must consider these reminiscences of a hero living three hundred years ago, as an expression of the feelings of a man of our day.

Colas Breugnon is, therefore, a thoroughly up-to-date work, modern in inspiration and written in accordance with the ideas of the most recent type of novelist. Its author, ignoring the scruples of the slaves of environment, is primarily interested in reproducing, not the scientifically correct picture of a bygone age, but a mood which he himself is feeling. Finding certain elements of this mood in the life of a past century, he strips them of whatever would remind us too strongly of their date, fuses them with other elements belonging more particularly to his own times and, out of this diverse material, creates a work of art, vital and compelling, possessing an originality all its own. (pp. 167-68)

A. G. H. Spiers, "The Art of the Younger French Writers," in The Bookman, *New York, Vol. L, No. 2, October, 1919, pp. 166-73.*

RENÉ LALOU (essay date 1922)

[*Lalou was a prominent French essayist and critic and the author of a comprehensive history of modern French literature entitled* La littérature française contemporaine (Contemporary French Literature, *1922; revised edition 1941). As a critic Lalou was noted for his impartiality and frankness (he had no strong ties to any literary movements), for his historical discrimination and perspective, and for the balance and clarity of his critical judgments. Lalou's works include studies of such modern authors as André Gide, Paul Valéry, and Roger Martin du Gard, as well as essays on such classic literary figures as C. A. Sainte-Beuve, Charles Baudelaire, and Gérard de Nerval. In English translation, Lalou's critical works have been credited with introducing the works of leading modern French writers to the English-speaking world. Lalou also helped to make the works of numerous English authors accessible to the French through his translations of the works of Shakespeare, Edgar Allan Poe, and George Meredith, and through critical studies of modern English authors, the best known of which is his* Panorama de la litterature anglaise contemporaine*

(1927). In the following excerpt from Contemporary French Literature, *Lalou surveys Rolland's literary career.*]

Internationalism . . . is for Romain Rolland the faith of a moralist. No doubt "divine music" was for him as for his hero "the light which was to illumine his life"; but Gourmont's analysis was none the less incomplete when it stopped short at "his musicographic logic." The music preferred by Rolland is that the beauty of which assumes a moral significance. He ends his study on Monteverdi with this distinction: "Monteverdi was certainly one of the great Latin artists who can always adapt their talent to practical circumstances, very different in this from the great German composers who write without bothering whether what they write can be played or not." Between those who utilize the resources of their epoch and those who force upon it "a music of the future," it is felt where his sympathies lie. Hence his affection for the Romantics, for Berlioz, Wagner and Hugo Wolf. He himself has explained his own position at the end of an article on *Pelléas et Mélisande:* "Not that Debussy's art, any more than Racine's, suffices to represent French genius. There is quite another side to this genius, which is in no wise represented here. It is heroic action, the intoxication of reason, laughter, the passion for light, the France of Rabelais, of Molière, of Diderot, and, in music, we shall say (for want of better) the France of Berlioz and of Bizet. To tell the truth, it is this I prefer; but God forbid I should repudiate the other!" All Rolland is contained in these lines written in 1907. He has exalted in Beethoven, in Michelangelo, in Tolstoï, the apostles of this "heroic action" of which he found no such highly characterized representative in the art of his own country. He has tried, in *Colas Breugnon* and *Liluli,* to renew the laughter of Rabelais and of Diderot. He has consecrated the protagonists of his novels, Jean-Christophe and Clérambault, to "the passion for light." He has become one of the respected voices of Europe. To be a great French writer he has lacked the ability to enjoy without effort that France of Racine and Debussy, all delicate shades and supplenesses, the triumph of a refined intelligence before which his heart has remained cold. He has rendered it full justice; but, not having loved it, he has never penetrated the secret of this perfection. He certainly admires "the gentle, luminous, veiled sky of the Ile de France"; but this harmony—the harmony of *Pelléas* and of *Bérénice*—is wanting in his work.

This is seen in reading his plays. In *Le Théâtre du Peuple* he shows the illusions of the managers of popular theatres and concludes, like a moralist: to have a new theatre, we must have a new people, a people of free minds. His last sentence is a repetition of Goethe's "in the beginning was Action." He employs the stage then for convictions in action. The three *Tragédies de la foi* and the three dramas of the *Théâtre de la Révolution* are above all valuable as a lesson in enthusiasm. Now Rolland's talent is not one of those which dissemble the arbitrariness of such an attitude. He attempts it however and combines the portrayal of Saint Louis, the hero of "religious exaltation" endeared to him by their common hatred of scepticism, with an intolerable melodrama in which clumsy psychology falls into the conventional and in which the style wavers between blank verse and the most prosaic form. Double stumbling-block of the purely ideological theatre: either the characters will, as in *Le Triomphe de la raison,* be symbols deprived of personal life; or else the desire of interest his public will deform the original conception of *Aert* and his drama of "national exaltation," of virile energy, will end by presenting us on the boards a young woman in fancy dress lost in a petty love plot. The eloquent intentions of *14 Juillet* and *Les Loups*

are not sufficient to animate flesh and blood. As for *Danton,* this glorification of the tribune could not help taking on the stage the violent relief of a popular print. Rolland's merits and defects combined to forbid him theatrical expression. This experience was however not lost, if it taught him what subjects suited his temperament. There was, between 1895 and 1905, a revival of hero-worship borne witness to by writers as different as Maeterlinck and Georges Sorel. The [Dreyfus] Affair had required certain men to take a virile stand, with enormous risks. Even for the sceptical Anatole France, Colonel Picquart was a hero. Rolland will invoke this example and that of the Boers in the preface to his Beethoven. Was not the best of his dramatic work an evocation of heroic figures, Saint Louis, Aert, Danton? Hampered by scenic requirements, this psychology, this exaltation of heroism were to unfold themselves at leisure in the book. A sure instinct inspired Romain Rolland with his lives of illustrious men. The introduction to the *Beethoven* states his plan: "Old Europe is lying benumbed in a heavy, vitiated atmosphere. A sordid materialism weighs down thought. . . . The world is suffocating. Let us open the windows. Let in free air. Let us breathe the breath of heroes." We can measure the distance covered from Symbolism when the hero was for some Mallarmé, for others Ruysbroeck or Novalis. At present he is called Beethoven. Rolland chose him because "there emanates from him a contagion of courage, a joy in battle, the intoxication of feeling God in one's consciousness," because his *durch Leiden Freude* is the "motto of every heroic soul." The passionate biography which celebrated at the same time "the foremost musician and the most heroic force of modern art," is certainly Romain Rolland's most finished work. Its publication in 1903 was, in Péguy's words, "not only the beginning of Romain Rolland's literary success and of that of the *Cahiers de la quinzaine,* but infinitely more than a beginning of literary fortune, it was a sudden moral revelation, an unveiled, revealed presentiment, the revelation, the flowering, the sudden communication of a great moral fortune." Continuing to fly the red flag of the heroes, Rolland wrote a *Vie de Michel-Ange,* based upon the "poignant contradiction between a heroic genius and a will which was not heroic"—an antithesis which suggested to him these characteristic reflections: "Let it not be expected of us after so many others to see there one more grandeur! We shall never say it is because a man is too great that the world does not suffice him. Mental disquietude is not a sign of greatness." This Sorbonne professor of the history of art had nothing of the æsthetic dilettante about him. Ten years after the *Beethoven* he wrote a *Vie de Tolstoï:* "The light just extinguished has been, for those of my generation, the purest illumining their youth." He saw in Tolstoï "the one true friend in all contemporary art." Alone, indeed, he had then demanded of the artist that religious and moral message which Rolland demanded in his turn.

The *Vies des hommes illustres* were passionate recreations. Rolland undertook at the same time an original creation. Choosing the subject where his critical knowledge could best nourish his inventions, he imagined the life of a great musician. In eight years he published the ten volumes of *Jean-Christophe* which conduct his hero from his birth in a city of Rhenish Germany to his death evoking the beloved stream which murmurs to him: "Hosanna to life! Hosanna to death!" The author describes step by step this road with its succession of revolts, failures, renewals of energy, where friendships, loves, artist quarrels, social cares interrupt a career which genius ends however by magnifying and which finds its reward in a noble appeasement.

Jean-Christophe is then a monument of the contemporary French novel. It resembles a little those enormous constructions of

Strauss or of Mahler whose weakness Rolland has himself pointed out. Parts of the work are already crumbling, such as the *Foire sur la place* in which the polemic had but a timely interest and the descriptions of the workingmen's movements in *Le Buisson ardent* which gave an unfortunate melodramatic turn to the narrative. Moreover this story of Jean-Christophe Krafft is weighed down with digressions. The whole book entitled *Antoinette* is a *hors-d'œuvre*. There are too many women in Krafft's life, from Sabine and Ada to Anna and Grazia. They encumber the novel all the more for the reason that Romain Rolland has never been able to draw a feminine character. He lacks precisely for this the delicate qualities of the Racinian and Debussyist France. In the *Dialogue de l'auteur avec son ombre* he has claimed the right to have France judged by a German musician. He nevertheless felt the difficulty of this point of view and, to obviate it, placed next to Jean-Christophe a Frenchman, his friend Olivier Jeannin; but beside the vigorous Krafft Olivier appears pale and theoretical. The contrast brings out irrefutably the natural bent of Rolland's talent which once again goes to the representative of "heroic action." A last reproach and the gravest: moments when no impassioned sentiment inspires him with those eloquent formulas which are the successes of the enthusiastic moralist, *Jean-Christophe* contains whole pages of formless writing, of what Gourmont called "his chalky style." Here is an example: "The family, having vainly imposed its veto, closed completely for him who ignored its sacrosanct authority. The city, all those who counted, showing themselves, as usual, one with regard to what touched the moral dignity of the community, banded solidly against the imprudent couple." This quotation will suffice. It would be profitless to continue.

For examination of what Rolland lacks is really useful only to define more clearly what he possesses. His virtues are absolute sincerity, hatred of every baseness and every hypocrisy, love of heroism and of divine music. All this he has incarnated in Jean-Christophe Krafft and his creation lives. In spite of the childhood memories of celebrated musicians which Rolland has levied upon in the first volumes, Jean-Christophe lives from *L'Aube* where, in excellent pictures full of Germanic sensibility, he discovers the world, injustice, the majesty of "our Father Rhine" and luminous music. He lives, "a little fifteen-year-old Puritan," in *Le Matin;* and, in *L'Adolescent,* he spends his impetuosity "in a succession of insane forces and falls into the void." He lives intensely in *La Révolte* where he rebels against the stupidity of the German town and also against "the false idealism" with which his childhood's idols are tainted and which Wagner did not escape. The plebeian element in him, deeply rooted in life, manifests itself equally amid the disorders of Parisian society and in his revolt against the stupid suicide proposed to him by Anna Braun. He bears in his soul the artist who wishes to express himself and who will succeed. His fevers, his sensuality, his mystic union with Grazia, his grief after Olivier's death are all transformed into music. Rolland has made this power of creative genius magnificently sensible. In describing it, this man who is less a writer than an apostle of heroism has sometimes achieved a moving literary beauty, as for example the account of the resurrection of the musician at the end of *Le Buisson ardent* and the passage in *L'Aube* where the genius of Beethoven haunts Jean-Christophe asleep: "This gigantic soul entered him, distending his members and his soul, and seemed to give them colossal proportions. He walked on the world. He was like a mountain, and storms raged in him. Storms of fury! Storms of grief! . . . Ah! what grief! . . . But that did not matter! He felt

so strong! . . . Suffer! To keep on suffering! . . . Ah! how good it is to be strong! How good it is to suffer when one is strong! . . .''

Colas Breugnon was not published until 1919. It had been in print since 1914. Rolland invites us to see in it the reaction against ten years' constraint in *Jean-Christophe's* armour which, "fitting me at first, had ended by becoming too tight"—a work of relaxation which none the less involves a sufficiently clear intention revealed by this sentence from *Clérambault:* "He was currently called sentimental by his adversaries; and certainly he was; but he knew it and because he was French he was able to laugh at it, make fun of himself." In telling this tale of a loquacious Nivernais of the time of Louis XIII, Rolland wished to divert his contemporaries. He does not seem to have succeeded. He renewed the attempt in *Liluli,* the triumph of the Illusion which subdues to his ruinous designs a Master-God disguised as an Arab merchant, a Truth heavily clad and gagged, a Reason which has stolen its bandage from Love. It causes the death of the inoffensive peasants Janot and Hansot as well as of the noble friends Altaïr and Antarès, it provokes war between the Gallipoulets and the Hurluberloches and drags Polichinelle himself down in the final catastrophe. To heighten the jest, Rolland, justifying himself by a quotation from Rabelais, saw fit to write *Colas* and *Liluli* in an extraordinary style strewn with more or less assonant *alexandrins* and octosyllables. One will judge by these two examples whether this treatment increases or destroys the comical effect he was after:

> "Breugnon, mauvais garçon, tu ris, n'as-tu pas honte?
>
> —Que veux-tu, mon ami, je suis ce que je suis. Rire ne m'empêche pas de souffrir; mais souffrir n'empêchera jamais un bon Français de rire. Et qu'il rie ou larmoie, il faut d'abord qu'il voie . . .''
>
> (*Colas Breugnon.*)

> ["Breugnon, you bad boy, you laugh, aren't you ashamed?"
>
> "Well, my friend, I'm what I am. Laughing doesn't prevent me from suffering; but suffering will never prevent a good Frenchman from laughing; and whether laughing or crying, he must first of all see. . . ." (*Colas Breugnon.*)]

> "Tout doux! tout doux! soufflez un peu! quels dératés! vous ruisselez! Gare au déluge! Vous le fuyez, de la vallée, et sur les monts, dans vos paniers, vous l'apportez! . . . Mon ami, tu vas éclater.''
>
> (*Liluli.*)

> ["Gently! gently! Take a breath! What lively chaps! You stream! Look out for the deluge! You flee it, from the valley, and on the mountains, in your baskets, you bring it! . . . My friend, you'll burst." (*Liluli.*)]

In *La Nouvelle Journée* Rolland had written that "Europe resembled a huge armed vigil." In 1914 the war broke out. He was then in Switzerland, better situated than many for keeping an open mind but less well perhaps for discerning exactly where the heart of France beat. His enemies were able, with a certain show of truth, to accuse him of being so easily *au-dessus de la mêlée* because he was outside it. As usual however his attitude was loyal and courageous. As early as August 29, his open letter to Hauptmann virulently denounced German barbarism guilty of burning Louvain; but in his famous article, **"Au-dessus de la mêlée"** (which has given its title to the volume in which it is included), Rolland deplored and seemed to disapprove of "these singular encounters, Eucken against Bergson, Hauptmann against Maeterlinck, Rolland against Hauptmann." One week after the battle of the Marne he proclaimed his internationalism: "Our duty is to build, both broader and higher, dominating injustice and national hatreds, the walls of the town where the free and fraternal souls of the whole world should assemble." When to-day we reread these articles several sentences only of which, malevolently interpreted, then filtered into France, it is easy to see that the misunderstanding was caused above all by interested enmities and the stupidity of the censorship. A closer contact with the realities of his country would have warned Rolland that his image, "it is then a matter of waiting, guarding oneself as far as possible against the madness of Ajax," had not the same meaning in Paris and in Geneva. The simple publication of the noble **"Lettre à ceux qui m'accusent"** would have dissipated every suspicion by showing that Rolland accused not the peoples but their leaders, the intellectuals, of having failed in their most sacred duty. *Les Idoles* affirms this continuity in his meditations as a moralist. He reproaches the chiefs of European thought with not having been "characters." Faithful even in the storm to the ideal of **Beethoven**, of **Jean-Christophe** and of **Tolstoï**, this scrupulous honesty which had made him one of the counsellors of the European soul was incapable of admitting an excuse for repudiation.

Perhaps this admirable rigidity of a moralist's conscience has been partly responsible for that want of flexibility which is his real artistic failure. His first post-war book was awaited impatiently. *Pierre et Luce* is merely a brief Parisian love-story under the menace of the Gothas, terminated by the catastrophe at St. Gervais on Good Friday, 1918; but *Clérambault,* the "story of a free conscience during the war," written between 1916 and 1920, is a compact work. Unfortunately it brings no rejuvenation. Rolland maintains his conclusions. To the false ideal of unanimous life which, confronted with the war, ended in abdication, he opposes the heroic revolt of individual consciences. He condemns equally "the insanities of the German thinkers and the extravagances of Parisian talkers." Without refusing his homage to Lenin and Trotzky, "the heroic woodsmen," he rejects the proletarian dictatorship as completely as the ancient tyranny. For the moralist knows that the blemishes are in us as well as in our governments. On the plane of action we are always coming up against a dilemma of injustice: "We find there a bronze *Dikè* recognized by the mind, which it can even honour as a Law of the universe; but the heart does not accept it. The heart refuses to submit to it. Its mission is to revoke the Law of eternal war. Will it ever be able to do so? . . . Who knows? In any event, it is clear that its hope, its will, spring from the natural order. Its mission is supernatural and, properly speaking, *religious.*" The writer insists that this adjective which he prints in italics be given its full meaning. Clérambault's last word is, in fact, an identification of Jesus and the free spirit, both eternally insurgent, eternally crucified, eternally renascent.

Eloquent pages do not, however, form an artistically living work. "This book," says the preface, "is not a novel but the confession of a free soul in the midst of the storm . . . Let nothing autobiographical be sought in it." Yet the whole leaves a very equivocal impression. All the end of the book, at least, is purely romantic, and it is the law of the novel which forces the author to kill Clérambault. If it contains nothing autobio-

graphical in point of facts, it is none the less difficult to admit that in his numerous discourses Clérambault alone is "occupied with expressing his overflowing and diffuse ego." Clérambault is but an idea of man. Jean-Christophe was a living man. Will Romain Rolland remain the prisoner of his own apostolate or will he liberate himself from it? Will he see the burning bush and, without our respect for his high "religious probity" being diminished by it, will he give us the book in which he will finally reconcile the two Frances which are not opposed in the music where the elusive Melisande receives the solemn kiss of the sage Arkël? (pp. 183-90)

> *René Lalou, "Traditionalism and Internationalism,"*
> *in his* Contemporary French Literature, *translated by*
> *William Aspenwall Bradley, Alfred A. Knopf, 1924,*
> *pp. 159-207.*

STEFAN ZWEIG (essay date 1924)

[*Zweig, a prominent Austrian biographer, novelist, essayist, and critic, was a fervent humanist and a strong believer in internationalism as the potential salvation of the human species. Through his fiction and nonfiction, Zweig endeavored to promote an atmosphere of tolerance and sought to increase humanity's understanding of itself as a means of attaining harmonious coexistence. Most of his fiction deals with violent emotions, and while critics unanimously praise his sensitive exploration of individual psychology, many believe that his failure to adequately treat social dynamics results in an incomplete portrayal of human behavior. Nevertheless, Zweig's writings, his high degree of personal integrity, and his intellectual zeal have earned wide respect. In the following excerpt, Zweig, who was Rolland's friend and biographer (see Additional Bibliography), compares* Annette et Sylvie *to* Jean-Christophe.]

The heroes of Romain Rolland's novels are never really isolated figures. His true subject is always a collectivity, an entire generation. So that Rolland, like Balzac and Zola among his predecessors, like Marcel Proust and Martin du Gard among his successors, needs more than one of the traditionally novel-lengthed volumes to express such powerful visions. He always needs a cycle to encompass a whole life-process, which is what the Greek word cycle itself signifies. His first attempt was in the drama. Twenty years ago he wanted to write ten tragedies depicting the French Revolution in its rise, crisis, and fall; he wanted to grasp as a single unit that entire generation, with all the ideas and contradictions in character which it manifested from 1792 until the triumph of Napoleon. This *Théâtre de la Révolution* was never completed. But he did finish *Jean Christophe:* the story of a different generation, one contemporaneous to him and already past history for us who are younger, the generation of Germany and France between the two wars of 1870 and 1914. And history has shown how accurately by this choice of theme he has touched on the most burning problem of our age, the European problem. During the war he devoted himself more to the times and its ills than to matters of art and form. And it is only now, after laying down in art, as it were, the tragic realization of those war years, that he returns with a vast new novel cycle. It is called *L'Ame Enchantée,* and the first volume, *Annette et Sylvie,* has just appeared.

But the artist merely seems to alter his problems: in reality every poet retains some one fundamental problem which moves him and which he develops again and again in changing forms, under changing circumstances, by what are apparently contradictory figures. In all his works, both the artistic and the polemical, Rolland's fundamental problem remains the same: the problem of the free man, the *homme libre,* who holds his ego, his personality, his self-earned beliefs staunchly in opposition to the world, the times, and mankind. To preserve one's freedom, in Rolland's sense, is to fight unceasingly against the world; and to suffer for such freedom without relinquishing it constitutes for him the only genuine heroism on earth. The men of the Revolution fight for their freedom as for their personal ideas, so that each is victorious after his own manner, Danton differently from Robespierre, Saint-Just, or Marat. They seem to be enemies of one another, and they are enemies, since each wants to misuse his personal idea of freedom to enslave the others; they fall, each a victim of the world and each a victor in his own cause. Similarly Jean Christophe struggles for freedom in the sphere of art, Olivier for freedom in the sphere of justice; and even that seemingly quite ordinary middle-class Colas Breugnon finds his strength solely in the feeling of his independence from princes and counts, from poverty and fate, through an inner stability, through the clarity and genuineness of his nature. Again, Clerambault fights for the independence of his idea of humanity over against the militaristic madness of a whole epoch; he too triumphs, though despised and conquered, for he remains *l'un contre tous,* the one against the many, the eternal rebel, like all harbingers and prophets. For some deep revolutionary vein is common to all Rolland's heroes.

This motif of inner freedom is also the theme of Romain Rolland's new novel. This time however it is not a man who is fighting for freedom, but a free woman, the representative of a new coming era whose destiny bears upon our own time, upon the world war, and beyond it to the present hour. Jean Christophe dies before the war; his character was a presentiment and a prophecy of the frightful catastrophe. His friendship with Olivier was almost a philosophic attempt to keep the two countries Germany and France united in affection. The heroine of this new novel no longer lives under a clouded sky with lightning flashes in the distance, but in the midst of the storm, in the tumbling chaos of Europe.

A woman's battle for freedom must necessarily be different from a man's. The man has his work, some belief, conviction, or idea, to defend against the world. The woman defends herself, her life, her mind, her feelings, defends them against unseen powers, against cupidity, against custom, against the invisible restrictions which are opposed to her free development in this civilized, moralistic, and Christian world. Thus, the problem contains unsuspected potentialities; it is more intimate, to be sure, but this does not make a simple, nameless, anonymous woman's struggle in defence of her personality any the less important than that of the artist defending some work, the politician some idea, the scientist some conviction.

Only the first volume, **Annette et Sylvie,** the prelude to this massively proportioned work, has appeared at present. It is like a delicate *andante* which is frequently interrupted by a gentle *scherzo.* But towards the end we already feel the approach, the rumbling clash of passionate excitement, the tragic ascent into the profoundly symphonic (for like all his works, this great novel of Romain Rolland's is built on musical principles). Annette, who is a good, middle-class girl, intact and mediocre, learns after the death of her father that he has left an illegitimate daughter, in poor circumstances. More from an instinctive curiosity, but also from a feeling of duty, she decides to visit her. In this she has already destroyed an initial restriction, an invisible law which was shackling her. Almost unconsciously, she has made her first step towards freedom. In Sylvie she becomes acquainted with a new form of freedom;

not the noblest form, but yet the very pure, clear, spontaneous freedom of the submerged proletarian classes. The young girl does as she likes, gives herself to a lover if she is so inclined; she lives outside of society, and thus has the natural security of an almost animal existence; she is cheerful, carefree, with unhampered impulses, open in her speech, untroubled in her actions. All this is foreign to the middle-class girl, but alluring. Magically attracted by this new element of freedom, she comes nearer to her sister, who refuses with a sure instinct to be transplanted into a *bourgeois* atmosphere; and from this first contact Annette, despite all rivalries and petty conflicts, becomes aware of what a vast possession freedom is. And when a young man with whom she is in love, of *bourgeois* family, approaches her and wants to marry her in the usual *bourgeois* fashion and make her his life companion, some deep presentiment warns her that this entering into marriage would also be a loss of the precious thing which she has just been on the verge of grasping—namely, her personal freedom. She discusses this with her fiancé, and asks him whether he is willing, after marriage, to leave her a part of her nature, the most secret and intangible part, her freedom; he must not ask her to subject herself completely and without reserve to his will. "This desire, the most profound yearning of my life, is probably not easy to express," she tells him, "because it is not precise enough and is too far-reaching. It has to do with a right demanded by the living soul, the right to develop, to change." She requires that some ultimate part of herself must not become subordinate to him, not be lost completely in the solidarity of marriage. Here we are strongly reminded of Goethe's remarkable epigram, written in one of his letters: "My heart is an open city which any one can enter; but somewhere inside there is a closed citadel, and here no one dare penetrate." This citadel, this last mysterious reach of her freedom, she wishes to preserve in order to be true to her love in a higher sense than in the disintegration and surrender demanded by marriage. Now the fiancé, completely entangled in his *bourgeois* attitudes, misunderstands this yearning, and thinks (since he has no feeling for the profoundest elements of love) that she does not love him. So the engagement is broken; but after it is broken she shows in a wonderful and truly heroic manner that if she cannot give her soul completely to the man she loves, she can give her body. She abandons herself to him in the flesh, and then leaves him; he is perplexed, for it is the tragedy of mediocrity that it cannot understand greatness. Here a most daring step has been taken, away from the *bourgeois* world and into a free, bold existence of her own. She has given up the quiet secure world which she was accustomed to, and must now go her way through the world alone—or even more than alone, for the fruits of that surrender is a child, an illegitimate child, which she must now lead beside her in the struggle for herself, for the truest, most essential part of her life.

Rolland takes his heroine through this first step in the prelude, **Annette et Sylvie.** Psychologically, in the delicacy of feeling, the fineness of the transitions, this work is equal to the best volumes of **Jean Christophe.** But so far it still lacks that richness of characterization which gives his other novels their sea roar, their current and fulness, their symphonies. It is only a promise, an opening chord, a single incident. And the next volumes, presumably, will bring with them that plastic fulness which differentiates Rolland's novels so gratifyingly from the psychological monographs of most contemporary writers. (pp. 445-48)

Stefan Zweig, "Romain Rolland after the War," in
The Dial, *Vol. LXXVI, May, 1924, pp. 445-48.*

BEN RAY REDMAN   (essay date 1934)

[*Redman was an American novelist, poet, and critic. In the following excerpt, he laments the negative effect of Rolland's overt
polemics in the seven-volume novel cycle* L'âme enchantée.]

And so it ends, the long novel which Romain Rolland wrote
between 1921 and 1933; the long novel that began as an intimate story of the two daughters of Raoul Rivière, Parisian
architect, and that has overflowed its banks to sweep forward
as the history of a world enduring the agonies of apparent death
and possible resurrection. We have been almost a decade reading it, for the first volume, **Annette and Sylvie,** appeared here
in translation early in 1925, while the fifth and final volume
has only just come from the press. And, having read it, what
do we make of it all? Yes, of it all; for there is no judging the
last instalment alone, despite the publisher's assurance that it
constitutes an independent novel. We are confronted by a single
narrative of more than two thousand pages, of which the action
covers thirty-odd years,—pre-war, war, and post-war. A big
work, certainly. But what quality is there in the bulk? Is there
greatness here as well as size. The questions pose themselves.

They pose themselves, for here is a work that is conceived on
the grand scale, with vast ambition, and executed with an
independent disregard of conventional patterns, but one that
evokes many controversial issues; that begins as a simple story,
moving at a leisurely pace through the quiet days of an orderly
world, and reaches its climax and its end in political pamphleteering that is at once eloquent and furious.

The wise reader would, perhaps, have foreseen this end. But
I failed to do so. I had no suspicion of the volcano of passionate
prophecy and propaganda that was to erupt from the last six
hundred pages of M. Rolland's novel. I did not anticipate the
sudden outburst of proselytizing energy born of a lethal hatred
for one class in the class struggle, and of an almost mystical
love for the opposing class.

Fiction that turns into pamphleteering? Then this long narrative
is not homogeneous; it begins as one thing and ends as another.
So it would seem at first glance. But M. Rolland can advance
cogent reasons in opposition to this judgment. He can argue
that Annette and Marc, having begun their careers as individuals, were necessarily caught up in the great battle of their
generation, and submerged in it, while contributing to it; and
that, this being so, their historian was compelled to become a
kind of pamphleteer, being unable, in any other role, to enunciate the true significance of their lives. He can even argue
that in such a day as ours fiction which is not pamphleteering
is devoid of force and meaning. Message is everything; let art
take care of itself.

> Individualism, the free spirit, since the other
> war, has had its army of Metz and its Sedan.
> It has surrendered. What is left of it? A few
> shreds of flags, hidden in pockets, which are
> exhibited at private gatherings; or in safe pa-
> lavers.
>
> There is only one sacred cause today. The cause
> of Labor, alone. All the rest, faith and culture,
> pure reason, social state—all must be rebuilt,
> from the beginning, upon the unshakable foun-
> dations of organized Labor. [Oh ye, of mighty
> faith, who can believe in unshakable founda-
> tions!]

Ponder these quotations well, and I think you will understand
that M. Rolland will not be much disturbed by a charge of
artistic failure, so long as his powers as a prophet and a pamphleteer are recognized. Romain Rolland sees himself at once
in a castigating and a messianic role. With furious blows he
belabors the exploiters of the old order: and simultaneously he
exalts labor in all lands, and the glorious future which labor
will create with its hands and brain, its humanitarian vision,
and its uncompromising faith.

He comes before us, carrying a whip in one hand and a book
of revelations in the other. But he also comes before us as a
novelist, and so long as literature has a life of its own, so long
as it has not been made entirely subservient to some form of
social service, it is fair to judge him as a novelist. Here he
must be judged, specifically, as the author of **The Soul Enchanted.** And so judged, his stature shrinks. The writer of
fiction is less than the preacher, less than the propagandist. He
has power, but it is an intermittent power which is scornful of
artistic bonds and bounds. Few writers are possessed of greater
eloquence, but he often displays a lack of simple skill. The
threads of his long narrative frequently fall slack, and he is
sometimes clumsy in patching (as when he introduces a railway
accident, and an important character, into his fifth volume, of
which and of whom we should have heard in his fourth volume). His principal characters, with all their slowly awakening
passion for humanity, seem strangely removed from the common clay we know. Their emotions are a little larger than life,
verging too often on hysteria; their spiritual experiences too
often escape from the realm of the explicable; their most casual
conversations are frequently too cryptic or too highfalutin; and
in too many of their aspects and actions they appear to have
been imagined rather than observed. Another curious fact is
that they are not solidly planted in any recognizable group of
friends and acquaintances; they are singularly detached, they
float. The great background of Western civilization is painted
in bold strokes behind them, but their immediate background
lacks definition. Because of all these facts they fail perfectly
to incarnate the message their creator would deliver; now that
the whole work is before us we can see that the integration of
the novelist's fiction and the preacher's truth is faulty and
incomplete. And there is one odd mistake which M. Rolland
makes in **A World in Birth** that cannot be allowed to pass
without comment. Suddenly he introduces himself, in his own
person, into the narrative, thereby stepping down from his post
of auctorial omniscience, and rending the veil of illusion asunder. The moment that he refers to Annette and Marc as real
persons, capable of meeting the indubitably real Romain Rolland in the flesh, the gossamer web of fiction is rudely violated.
This is the kind of blunder that could be made only by an
author who had grown supremely, and fatally, careless through
confidence in his own genius.

One can understand how he might be so confident, for that he
has genius of a kind, as differentiated from talent, there is no
doubt. But in his latest work it has been made to serve two
masters, and it has served the one better than the other. Rolland,
the fiery prolocutor of Revolution and the Rights of Man, has
been well served. Rolland, the novelist, has to a certain extent
been betrayed. Saying this, I know that I am judging a man
who believes in a new world, and in new literary values, by
the standards of an old world whose values have been long
established. The time may come when **The Soul Enchanted**
will hold an honored place as one of the great pioneer works
of Revolutionary fiction. But it is not for us to anticipate the
brave new judgments of a brave new people.

Ben Ray Redman, "Romain Rolland's Prophetic Novel," in The Saturday Review of Literature, *Vol. XI, No. 16, November 3, 1934, p. 257.*

ROMAIN ROLLAND   (essay date 1937)

[*In the following excerpt from an introduction to a series of letters written to Leo Tolstoy, Rolland presents his mature view of the nature and importance of art.*]

I loved Tolstoy deeply—I have never ceased to love him. For two or three years I had been living enveloped in the atmosphere of his thought [i.e., for two or three years before his first letter to Tolstoy, that is since 1884-1885—*translator's note*]; I was certainly more familiar with his works, *War and Peace, Anna Karenina,* and the *Death of Ivan Ilyitch,* than with any of the great French writers. The kindness, the intelligence, the absolute truth of this great man made him my surest guide in the moral anarchy of our times.

But on the other hand I loved art passionately; since childhood I had nourished myself on art, especially on music; I could not have done without it; I can say that music was as indispensable a food for my life as bread.—Therefore, how disturbed I was when I read those violent diatribes against the immorality of art, in the works of the man I was accustomed to respect and to believe! I felt however that nothing was purer than the impression conveyed by the work of a great artist. In a symphony of Beethoven, in a picture by Rembrandt one not only forgets one's ego, but one also finds the strength of understanding and of kindness which flows from these great hearts. Tolstoy spoke of the corruption of art which depraves and isolates men. Where had I been so refreshed, where had I fraternized more with men than in the universal emotions of an *Oedipus-Rex,* or of the *Symphony with Chorus*? But I distrusted myself, and I was deeply disturbed lest perhaps I was wasting my life, at its very beginning, in the service of a bad cause, whereas my wish was to make myself useful to others.

I wrote to Tolstoy. He replied the fourth of October, 1887. His letter does not need any comment. It reflects the tranquility and lucidity of his soul,—a soul in which all is reason and charity. It is written with the evangelical simplicity of this artist, not concerned with style but solely with making himself clearly understood, not fearing to repeat his thought in order to impress it on one's mind. One hears his familiar words; he does not write, he converses.

I only wish to say how completely in agreement with his thought I feel today,—even more than when I received that letter. If I am sorry that Tolstoy sometimes erred in his judgment of one great man or another, such as Beethoven or Wagner; if I am sorry that he was wrong in judging them without knowing them, or at least without knowing them well enough,—if I regret too that he passed judgment on French art on the strength of a handful of ridiculous decadent artists (with very few exceptions),—and this judgment is explained by the fact that he was nauseated by their pretentious poems and morbid reviews,—on the other hand, I find that his general judgments of art are absolutely true.

Yes, *"The products of true science and of true art are the products of sacrifices and not of material advantages."*—and it is not only ethics, it is art itself which demands that art be no longer the sole property of a privileged social class. An artist myself, I am the first to call for the time when art will again become the common wealth of the nation, stripped of all its privileges and subsidies, its decorations and official glory. I call for this moment in the name of the dignity of art, sullied by the thousands of parasites who live shamefully at its expense. Art must not be a career; it must be a vocation. Now in the present civilization, it is only the truly great artists who make real sacrifices; they alone confront harsh obstacles, because they are the only ones who refuse to sell their thoughts, who refuse to prostitute themselves for the pleasure of corrupt patrons who pay the procurers of intellectual debauch. By suppressing the privileges of art, by making access to it increasingly difficult, there is no danger that the real artists will suffer more; only the multitude of those idlers will be removed who become intellectuals in order to abandon the people and avoid more disagreeable toil.

The world has no need, year in and year out, of ten thousand works of art (or works which make this claim) in the Salons of Paris, of its hundreds of plays, of its thousands of novels. There is a need for three or four geniuses per century, and a need for a people in whom reason, kindness, and the understanding of beautiful things are widespread, a people whose heart is whole, whose intelligence and outlook are healthy, who is capable of seeing, feeling, and understanding every thing beautiful and good in the world, and who works to embellish life.

It would not displease me, I admit, if all artists were obliged to participate in the common condition, and that the total manual labor necessary to sustain and maintain the social edifice be divided up among everybody, with no exceptions. Shared by all, the labor would not be sufficiently oppressive to keep true artists from creating their art works in addition; but it would suffice to take away from false artists the desire to use their leisure hours in intellectual occupations—And how much better art would be.

Goethe said somewhere: *"Continuous writing or reading of books finally makes one a book."*—The artificial, morbid, weak character of our art today is the result of its being no longer rooted in the life of the earth; it is no longer the work of living men, but of phantoms of living men, shadows of beings, larvae fed by words, colors of paintings, sounds of instruments, fragments of sensations. How many true artists, in order not to have to sell their art, have had to live and must still live by another intellectual craft, besides their art! And how much more hampering for the imagination this intellectual craft is than manual work, which tires the body, but leaves the mind free!

But will the beauty of a work of art not lose by this? Is art not exclusive? Does art accept sharing with anything else? Does it not require the whole day, an entire life?—"But," I ask all artists of good faith: "Does one produce a great deal more when one has the entire day free than when one has only two hours a day?" I have often had the opposite experience myself. Hardship is not without value for the mind. Too much freedom is a poor inspiration; it leads the mind into apathy and indifference. Man needs a goad. Were life not so short, man would not be in such haste to live. If he feels himself enclosed within the narrow limits of a few hours, he will act with more passion. Genius yearns for obstacles, and obstacles form genius. As for persons with talents, we have only too many of them. Our civilization swarms with talented people, who are in fact quite useless, and indeed harmful. If most of these people would disappear, if there were fewer painters, fewer musicians, fewer writers, fewer critics, fewer pianists, fewer stage-struck actors, fewer journalists, it would not be a great loss, but a very great

Rolland at the time he wrote Jean Christophe.

good fortune. And even though art might lose in its precision, in its style, in its technical perfection, I would not worry much about it, if it gained in moral strength and health. There are days when I think without indignation about the burning of the Library of Alexandria. What does this dead past, this scaffolding of sciences, arts, and civilizations heaped upon our lives, mean to us? Who will liberate us?

"The first science of the earth is the science of living so as to cause the least evil possible and the most good. The first art of the world is the art of knowing how to avoid evil and to produce good with the least possible effort." (pp. 325-26)

> *Romain Rolland, "Introduction to Tolstoy's Letter of October 4, 1887," in* Earth: A History, *edited by Joseph Niver, Sr., translated by William T. Starr, KTO Press, 1977, pp. 325-26.*

GUSTAVE SAMAZEUILH (essay date 1945)

[*In the following excerpt, originally published in France in 1945, Samazeuilh surveys Rolland's writings on music and musicians.*]

The music of the masters, and that of all those who pursue a noble ideal with sincere enthusiasm, no matter from whence they come nor to what school they are considered to belong, have lost in Romain Rolland one of their most understanding and highly-qualified supporters. A great mind and a great heart, he spent his whole existence in following the promptings of a generous and disinterested conscience, without any concern for comment. He was not only one of the masters of French musicology, but also a person of rare qualities who, from his earliest youth remained closely connected with an art which was for him, throughout the trials of life, a tonic and a consolation. It is for this reason that the numerous and vital pages which he devoted to music, and which alone concern me here at present, have such a special ring about them, which distinguishes them from so many works, the interest and utility of which are beyond dispute, but which belong to the realm of what is properly termed exegesis or documentation, than to that of creation proper.

As long ago as the thesis he wrote for his doctorate on *Les origines du théatre lyrique (The Origins of Opera)* . . . Romain Rolland gave evidence of the lofty principles which were to inspire his actions. In it he underlined music's powerful contribution to general history, since its aim is to express the very essence of the human spirit and its infinite diversity. Music adapts itself to the characters of all nations and of all times; since its birth in Italy it has appeared by turns in Germany, in France, in Russia, in Spain, indeed even in England. It is not necessarily confined by any formula or theory. In a way it is humanity's dream, which runs its course in spite of conflicts. Rolland made a study, already in a masterly way, of its successive manifestations at the epoch of the beginnings of opera. He was soon to return to the same questions again in the series of studies collected together under the title *Musiciens d'autrefois (Musicians of the Past)*, and added chapters full of substance on the Florentine School, Luigi Rossi's *Orfeo*, Lulli, Gluck, Grétry, and Mozart, whose respective characters and parts in the history of music were evoked with a penetration and breadth of ideas all too rare in this subject, in which too often the spirit of prejudice creates its havoc. These essays were written almost forty years ago. Read them again: you will see that they have lost none of their relevance.

I am tempted to say the same for the *Voyage musical au pays de passé (A Musical Tour through the Land of the Past)*, which is less widely known, and which forms a natural complement to *Musiciens d'autrefois*. Firstly you will find in it, under the title *Le roman comique d'un musicien au XVIIe siécle*, a lively summary of a curious book by the composer Johann Kuhnau: *Der musikalische Quacksalber*, which was published in Dresden in 1700, and which describes the convalescence of musical Germany after the Thirty Years' War, and the formation of its great classical style. An analysis of the diary of Samuel Pepys, an enlightened amateur of the time of Charles II, makes us understand the true essence of the English musical spirit at the time of the Restoration. These are followed by studies on the origins of classical style and music in the eighteenth century,— on Telemann and on Metastasio, whose value and importance, not often enough recognised, are underlined by Romain Rolland. The *Voyage musical à travers l'Europe du XVIIIe siècle (A Musical Tour Through Eighteenth-century Europe)* then transports us successively to Italy, the cradle of opera and of the musical theatre, and to Germany, where instrumental and symphonic music made the great strides with which we are all familiar. I must be careful not to overlook the vigorously sketched and concise portrait of Handel, which serves in a way as a preparation for the book which Romain Rolland devoted a few years later to the author of the *Messiah* in the *Maîtres de la musique* series published by Alcan, and which is still today the most complete and solid work which we have in France on this subject. In it, before examining the works themselves in all their many aspects, he gives prominence to the great objectivity, the lofty impersonality, and the grand style which, no doubt owing to a life of travel, combines in itself so many other intimately assimilated styles, which characterize Handel's genius. He praises the force, the passion, the humour in him, combined with a sense of form and with a power of communication which, without in any way losing caste, is able to reach the soul of the masses. Finally, amongst other similar works which Romain Rolland has left, it will be sufficient for me to recall the full accounts of *L'Opéra au dix-septième siècle en Italie (Opera in Italy in the Seventeenth Century)*, the *Origines de l'Opèra allemand (The Origins of German Opera)* and *L'Opéra au dix-septième siècle (Seventeenth-century Opera)* which are among the best chapters of Albert Lavignac's *Encyclopédie de la Musique*, as well as the masterly introduction to the *Histoire de la musique* by the late Henry Prunières which, alas, remains unfinished.

I come now to *Musiciens d'aujourd'hui (Musicians of Today)* which dates from about the same period as the *Musiciens d'autrefois*. It must be regretted that Romain Rolland, absorbed as he was to the end of his days by so many different tasks, was not able later to find the leisure to complete this work. In it he first of all discusses Hector Berlioz. Rolland praises to perfection that audacious genius coupled, as we know, to a vacillating and troubled soul; he stresses Berlioz's liberating

rôle in French music of his epoch, and he praises his high poetic aspirations, doubtless superior to his gift of musical invention proper. Next comes Richard Wagner, in whose work Rolland does not gloss over certain incongruities of style and the lack of balance which, in his opinion, results from the predominance of the musical over the dramatic element proper in Wagner's works. This does not prevent him from having the highest opinion of the heroic dash, the happy joyousness, and the youthful force of *Siegfried*, the overflowing passion of *Tristan* —"a monument of sublime power which dominates all other poems of love—as Wagner dominates all other artists of the century—from the mountain heights." In his opinion *Tristan* remains "the highest summit of art since Beethoven." It is not surprising that the pages which follow, devoted to Camille Saint-Saëns, are more moderate in tone. But they do do justice to the works, which are extensive, of this competent representative of the French classical spirit, to the perfect clarity of his message, in which something of the spirit of Mendelssohn and of Spontini survives. Vincent d'Indy likewise, in spite of the intransigence of some of his ideas, is appreciated by Rolland, both as a composer and as an animating spirit, with a remarkable independence of outlook and concern for fairness, and an all too rare sympathy for his powerful creative temperament, which is so often at odds with his aesthetic theories. Did not Romain Rolland himself make that "faith in action," which he values and praises in the author of *Fervaal*, one of the principles of his own life? So far as Richard Strauss was concerned, he had the same understanding; he was the first in France to recognise, to describe the character of Strauss's strong personality, of his proud independence, before rendering full justice, at the end of his life, to the extraordinary vitality which gives to the octogenarian master's recent works, sent him by a mutual friend at his own request, a renewed and passionate youth. Nor must I forget those pages written with emotion which revealed to France the infectiously attractive works and the tragic destiny of Hugo Wolf, or the soothing freshness of the Abbé Perosi's oratorios, and which also stated the profound reasons for the French triumph of Claude Debussy's *Pelléas et Mélisande:* the close synthesis of the score with the text, without one overlapping the other, as is sometimes the case with Wagner; the originality of the declamation closely moulded to the words; the subtlety of the harmonic language; the finely-shaded leavening of the orchestra; that "essence of taste" which, in Romain Rolland's opinion represents, as do celebrated works by a Berlioz or a Bizet, one of the aspects of the musical face of France.

Two essays of a general nature conclude *Musiciens d' aujourd'hui*. The first, motivated by an international festival held in Strasbourg, states certain truths, which unfortunately more often than not are still valid, about French music and German music, and about the way in which they were represented and defended on that occasion. In spite of the unfavourable conditions of the contest, in spite of the presence of such men as Richard Strauss and Gustav Mahler conducting the *Sinfonia Domestica* and the *Second Symphony in C Minor*, Romain Rolland points out that the experience was of an encouraging nature for French music "which is silently engaged in taking the place of German music." Romain Rolland devoted a long study, which first appeared in a foreign publication, to this cheering *Revival*, which dates from immediately after the war of 1870, and the principal cradle of which was the *Société Nationale*, to the disinterested efforts of which he does full justice. This study still has its appeal today. In it he successively examines the rôle of opera houses, of symphony concerts, of the Conservatoire, of the *Schola Cantorum* (the fertile work of which he stresses, without concealing that its spirit is sometimes too particularist), of chamber music societies, and of the University, which held out longer against the introduction of music into its curriculum than did institutions of elementary education. Then he points out how excellent was the state of French music at that time, but also how shaky its prospects of duration were.

> The battle is not won for it. It will not be for a long time to come—so long as the taste of the general public remains unchanged—so long as the nation is not musically educated—so long as the links, which should unite the élite of a nation with the people, if the élite wishes to survive and to preserve its thought, are not re-established. It is the duty of the historian to point out to French artists that they must never disarm against the common enemy, which is more dangerous in a democracy than anywhere else: mediocrity. The road that stretches before us is still long and difficult. But when, turning round, with a glance we take stock of the path already trodden, we can have confidence. Who of us can contemplate without pride the task accomplished during the last thirty years? . . . A town in which out of nothing there has arisen one of the foremost symphonic schools of Europe, in which one of the keenest concert publics in existence has been formed, as well as an élite of great connoisseurs with catholic curiosity and all-embracing and free minds, who are the pride of France. . . . It is impossible not to admire the nation which its very defeat has resuscitated, and the generation which has accomplished this magnificent work of the musical revival of the nation with unflagging perseverance and the faith which removes mountains.

A moving tribute, and one which, almost at the same time, the episodes in *Jean-Christophe* relevant to French music were to confirm and develop, notably in *La Foire sur la place* which, too, has lost nothing of its flavour. In it there are—on the spirit of musical production of the epoch, on the monotony of the programmes of Parisian concerts, on the recruitment of critics, on the blunders of musical snobbery, on the excesses of choirs—appraisals the caustic implications of which equal those of the criticism with which, in the first part of *La Révolte,* Romain Rolland did not spare the German romantics and certain of their immediate successors. From it I glean in passing this profound view:

> Until then Christophe had believed that great ideas carry their light with them everywhere. He now became aware that no matter how ideas might change, men remained the same; and in the last resort nothing counted but men: ideas were what men were. If men were born mediocre or servile, genius itself became mediocre in passing through their souls, and the cry of liberation of the hero breaking his fetters became the act of servitude of generations to come.

(pp. 219-25)

But it was the appeal of the genius of Beethoven—who, according to that same Paul Dukas "remains one of the most dazzling signs of the greatness of human destiny on the earthly horizon"—that was to enslave the passionate spirit of Romain

Rolland from his youth onwards, and made him worship him unflaggingly until his dying day. In 1903 he published in Charles Péguy's *Cahiers de la quinzaine* the work which brought the *Cahiers* their first important success—his *Vie de Beethoven,* so packed with thought in its voluntary conciseness, and which later became famous. In the very first pages he states its significance: "I give the title of hero only to those who were great in heart." As one of the greatest amongst these, the man whose life we are describing in this very article, said himself:

> I acknowledge no other sign of superiority than goodness. Where the character is not great, there is no great man, there is not even a great artist, nor a great man of action; there is nothing but a hollow idol for the vulgar mob: time destroys them together. Success is of little importance. It is a question of *being* great, and not of appearing to be so.

Twenty-five years later he was completing the first volumes of the vast work devoted to *Les grandes époques créatrices (The great creative periods)* of the master of Bonn, the plan of which he had long been maturing, and which originally was to have consisted of five parts: the formative period, the heroic years, the acme of classical art, the great crisis, and the last Testament. But the length of time which the accomplishment of a task of this scope, as he conceived it, would have necessitated, and the demands of his numerous other activities and of his health which was, unfortunately, often frail, led him to concentrate first of all on essentials, in the hope of later summing up, in substantial comprehensive surveys, the history of the periods of formation or of maturity—a project which in the end he was unable to carry out. In the brief introduction to the first volume, he stressed how perennial is Beethoven's message, in his view so profoundly representative of an European age belonging to the past. He could only smile at the disapproval which he encountered amongst those newcomers

> who, tied like us to the turning wheel of time, imagine that only the past passes, and that the clock of the mind stops at their noon—who cherish the illusion that the new formula alone wipes out for ever the old formulas, and will not itself be wiped out, without seeing that even while they are speaking the wheel is turning and that the shadow of the past is already twining around their legs.

Have things changed a great deal in this respect? I leave it to you to decide. . . .

It would, unfortunately, be impossible for me here to summarise adequately or in detail his *Les grandes époques créatrices,* and all the problems of aesthetics and of technique which they raise, and the fruitful lessons in ethics which they contain. That would call for a whole book . . . . They show us to what an extent the powerful temperament, the great soul of a man like Beethoven remains representative of his century, and of the generous passions which shook it. In the immense output with which you are familiar and which includes all styles, Rolland does not only pick out the highest summits, the most significant turning-points, the most finished achievements. He also depicts the man as he was at the moment when he conceived them, and the environment which saw their birth. Thus, he opens with a striking portrait of Beethoven at the age of thirty, full of vigour and fervour, ready to obey the imperious voice of his inner genius, and who already, in certain of the piano sonatas, had fully shown of what he was capable. Next he describes the decisive crisis of 1802, and its glorious consequences; the *Eroica*, the *Appassionata*, *Fidelio*, the four *Leonora* overtures, the genesis of which Romain Rolland studies in detail with the assistance of Nottebohm's valuable *Sketch Books;* Rolland also added passages of no less import on Beethoven's deafness, on the influence of the sisters Josephine and Theresa von Brunswick, and of their cousin Giulietta Guicciardi.

Next, that concern for synthesis which was so characteristic, and which gives rise to so much protraction in his writings, led him, in connection with Beethoven's relationship with Bettina Brentano, that young and fascinating Egeria of great men, to consider the question of the relations between Beethoven and Goethe, which until then had been rarely studied, and to devote an intermediary volume to this question which, although closely linked to the others, is complete in itself. You will see, in *Goethe et Beethoven,* why two geniuses of the breadth and scope of those we are discussing can pass close to one other without seeing one other. "And the one who loves most (Beethoven), only succeeded in wounding the other. And the other, who understands most, will never know the person closest to him, the greatest, his only peer, the only person worthy of him." An interesting letter from Bettina, fully imbued with the Beethovenian spirit, completes this part of the work. It exalts the powers of genius which are freely expressed, and contrasts them with the empty formulas of the epigones and reasoners. Music must, by concentration of thought, free itself from the mechanism of the mind, and be nothing but the direct expression of the ultimate flow of life.

In 1937 there appeared in their turn the two volumes of *Le Chant de la Résurrection,* which opened with a new portrait of Beethoven at the age of fifty, at grips with the difficulties of life, with political crises, and foreign occupation. It illuminates, as it were, the psychological and musical analysis of those sample works which Romain Rolland selected as being particularly representative of this epoch of the great musician's troubled existence; prior to this he had given a masterly summary of the preceding period (1806-1809), prolific in masterpiece such as the Fourth, Fifth and Sixth symphonies, the last piano concertos, the Violin Concerto, the Trios (Op. 70), and the *Coriolan* overture. These sample works are, first of all, the Sonata for piano, op. 101, the song cycle: *An die ferne geliebte* (Op. 98), the song *Resignation*, the importance of which, too often disregarded, is fully brought out,—then the monumental Sonata for piano, op. 106, which dates from the same period as the first sketches for the Ninth Symphony, the Mass in D, and the three last sonatas, which are examined fully in chapters which, owing to the copiousness and soundness of their documentation, their breadth of tone, and the richness of views which abounds in them, are true models of their kind. I cannot do better than refer you to them, as well as to the short supplementary passages on the Eleven Bagatelles, the Brentano family, and the letter to the Immortal Beloved, which throw significant light on certain points which hitherto had remained obscure.

Lastly, before his death Romain Rolland was able, as he desired, to revise the final proofs of his commentary on *La cathédrale interrompue*—what human work is ever really finished?—which, in his view, is formed by the Ninth Symphony, the last Quartets, and the multifarious plans which haunted Beethoven's inspired brain to his last days, of which Rolland gives a striking account in the last volume: *Finita Comoedia.*

In this final triptych, which itself constitutes the last panel and the worthy crown of the vast triptych of *Les grandes époques créatrices*, Romain Rolland does not only give us historical and technical studies worthy both of these imperishable monuments of musical history and also of a writer of his own high rank, but proves to us, by means of a detailed study of the successive sketches, how the Ninth Symphony, the final Quartets and the *Variations on a theme by Diabelli* at the same time evoke the past, illustrate the present, and foreshadow the future. He makes us feel, beneath the external categories of notes, of equivalent forms, the stirring of the inner forces which animate them, and which give them so great a power over our reason and our hearts. By reproducing Beethoven's opinions on the most diverse subjects and individuals, he pays a final tribute to that power of concentration, that natural generosity, that inexhaustible faculty of poetic invention and,—no matter what may have been said about it—of melodic invention—that power of a mind over which reason and the mastery of a great constructor hold sway. He sees in the force radiating from the heart of a man like Beethoven the secret of the unlimited powers of his art. On the ethical as on the aesthetic plane, he notes the phases of a Herculean struggle between the man and his destiny. To Beethoven's so often affirmed religious convictions he gives the space they merit, thereby giving proof of his respect for freedom of opinions, and he also gives space to the extraordinary understanding which a man like Wagner showed from his youth onwards for the very essence of Beethoven's genius. He praises that truth and simplicity progressively won, and that uprightness, that never-lacking sincerity, that invincible attraction towards the sublime art, "the supreme aspiration of which is to dissolve in the Awakening."

The future of a work such as this, the faithful reflection of the great figure it evokes and of the fine spirit which was pregnant with it for so long, is assured. Will not the works of Beethoven, which are above fashions, because of the unity of their conception, the prodigious variety of their aspects, the high level of their style which always stems from creative thought, and their continual progress towards new poetic horizons, remain eternal? (pp. 226-31)

> *Gustave Samazeuilh, "Romain Rolland and Music,"
> in* Richard Strauss & Romain Rolland: Correspondence, *edited and translated by Rollo Myers, University of California Press, 1968, pp. 219-32.*

E. M. FORSTER (essay date 1945)

[*Forster was a prominent English novelist, critic, and essayist, whose works reflect his liberal humanism. His most celebrated novel,* A Passage to India *(1924), is a complex examination of personal relationships amid the conflicts of the modern world. Although some of Forster's critical essays are considered naive in their literary assessments, his discussion of fictional techniques in his* Aspects of the Novel *(1927) is regarded as a minor classic in literary criticism. In the following excerpt originally published as an obituary in 1945, Forster discusses changing attitudes toward Rolland's work.*]

There died a couple of months ago a French writer who is of international importance. Whether he was a great writer is debatable, but he did address all humanity, not merely his own nation. Romain Rolland is not as celebrated today as he was a quarter of a century back, when he seemed to be of the first rank, and to have almost the stature of Tolstoy. There are two reasons for this decline in reputation. He did not fulfil his early promise as a novelist, the world did not fulfil his hopes; and he started out with passionate hopes. He became isolated, he was partly forgotten.

He was born in 1866. Although he came from the heart of France, and became a professor at Paris, he had strong Teutonic sympathies, which we must bear in mind if we are to understand him. He had an enormous admiration for German music, and for much German literature, and he cherished a rather Teutonic cult for the great man. With him, the cult was beneficent, for greatness, in his vision, meant not power over others, not dictatorship, but creation, exploration. All the same, his life-long insistence on the Hero is not very French, and it has its distant parallel in the sinister cult which has produced Hitler. He combined hero worship with belief in the people, and by "the people," he meant not the stodgy "common man" who is being so boosted by our administrators today, but the people as a fiery instinctive emotional force, the people who made the French Revolution. The "hero" and the "people" were his twin stars, and whenever they shine he sees his way through the uncongenial tangle of his century.

His most important work is the enormous novel, *John Christopher*. The theme of it is the hero as musician. There are ten volumes, and I can remember our excitement at the beginning of the century when they were coming out. We were full of hopes then, easily held hopes, we did not know the severity of the problems which Fate was reserving for us, and the volumes were both civilised and inspiring, and how few books are both! They were intensely human, they had integrity, they possessed the culture of the past, yet they proclaimed that culture is not time-bound or class-bound, it is a living spirit to be carried on. "Have you read the latest *John Christopher?*" we were saying. "Has he got to Paris yet?" As the series proceeded, our excitement slackened. However, the author pushed his great achievement through, and was awarded the Nobel Prize for literature in 1916. Romain Rolland had entered the first world-war.

He was shattered by it to an extent which we can scarcely comprehend. Today we are all of us tougher, and though we still cherish hopes they are protected by a very necessary crust of cynicism. We are no longer surprised. He—who had known what was best in Germany, and there was much good in that Germany—he, who was an inheritor of France, saw the two precious civilisations destroying each other, and the imperialism of Russia slinking up behind. While loyal to France, he became an internationalist, and a precursor of the League of Nations, and addressed to the youth of his country a pamphlet entitled *Above the Battle*.

> For the finer spirits of Europe there are two dwelling places: our earthly fatherland, and the City of God. Of the one we are the guests, of the other the builders. To the one let us give our lives and our faithful hearts; but neither family, friend nor fatherland nor aught that we love has power over the spirit. The spirit is the light. It is our duty to lift it above tempests, and thrust aside the clouds that threaten to obscure it: to build higher and stronger, dominating the injustice and hatred of nations, the walls of that city wherein the souls of the whole world may assemble.

The title *Above the Battle* was unfortunate. It suggested that the writer felt himself superior to his fellows, and it annoyed people who were brave or vulgar-minded or both—and it is

possible to be both. He became unpopular in his own country, and stayed for the rest of the war in Switzerland working on prisoners' relief. When peace came he had some further success as a dramatist. He had always been interested in a People's Theatre, where the people could be given what they understood and could participate in, and not what the upper classes thought nice for them. He had longed for the popular stage of ancient Greece to be reborn in the modern world. And he had himself written plays, dealing with mass-revolution and freedom (a play on Danton, for instance), and some of these were performed, under the direction of Reinhardt. But it is as the author of *John Christopher* and *Above the Battle* that he is best remembered.

Romain Rolland knew and understood a great deal about music, and whatever he says is worth reading. He wrote a long and important work on Beethoven, also on Handel; he could appreciate composers as diverse from one another as Berlioz and Hugo Wolf. He did not like Brahms—most Frenchmen and many Germans do not—and he had only a contemptuous tolerance for Debussy. What he demanded was vitality, robustness from which alone the mysterious filaments of the spirit can sprout. He felt music as a breath from the vanished centuries, to be transformed by our lungs into the song of the moment and the prophecy of the future; music is the god which each generation must make into flesh. It was the deepest thing for him, and anyone who has felt its depth is bound to join in homage to him. I am not qualified to say whether he is a sound musical interpreter. He is certainly a thrilling one, and here is the heart of him, without doubt. There is a scene in the opening volume of *John Christopher* where the hero, still a baby, touches the piano for the first time, and experiments in the marriage of sounds. I have never come across a scene like it in literature, for it is not merely poetic, not merely good child psychology: it seems to take us inside a special chamber of the human spirit, and make us co-creators.

The opening volumes of *John Christopher* are the best. They take place in a little princely city of the old Germany, on the banks of the Rhine. The child's forbears have been musicians here for generations in a quiet way, but he himself is anything but submissive and he does not fit in. The young Beethoven is in the writer's mind, and he has supplied other details from his own youth. Explosive, moody, inconsiderate, uncouth, John Christopher is all the same good, affectionate, generous, trustful. He suffers atrociously from poverty, and the cruelty of his drunken father, and from fear of death which is only tempered by his disgust at life. Violent longings, powers outside him shake him. His genius is recognised, but not fully recognised: he is too large for the little town, and when he is actually rude to its Grand Duke he is expelled and escapes to France. In these early volumes we get, besides the impression of genius and character, a brilliant and sympathetic account of the old Germany which will never return; we sit in little shops and go for Sunday walks or to a performance at the local opera; we make love, with discretion, to this girl or that; we are narrow-minded and serious, and past us all the time flows the Rhine. *Dawn* and *Morning* (volumes one and two) are delightful. In volume five we get to Paris and the interest rather flags. John Christopher's comments and escapades are less exciting and his surroundings have lost their vividness. He discovers, after a good deal of grumpiness, that Paris is not France, gets into touch with the people, and makes close friends with a fine-natured Frenchman, Olivier. By now he is famous, and there is a touching episode when he visits a provincial admirer—a humble and sincere old man whom he has never seen. The visit is a success—just a success; we are on tenterhooks all the time lest it be a failure, for the great musician is extremely irritable and the humble old man is an admirer of Brahms, and a bit of a bore.

The final volume, *The New Day,* passes into mysticism. The hero, mortally sick, finds himself fording a river which is partly the Rhine of his youth, partly the river of death. The crossing is hard, and on his shoulder is seated a child. Heavier grows the burden, and from the bank he has left come cries of "You'll never succeed." He stumbles, he is drowning—and then the water becomes shallow. The sun rises. Bells burst into music, and he reaches the further shore. John Christopher is saved. And he has not merely saved himself. He is not just the artist. He is Christopher the saint. He has carried on his shoulders, through the troubles of our century, the divine spirit of man, so that it may live and grow. "Child, who are you?" he asks. And the child answers, "I am the day which is going to be born."

I don't think the work will live like another French panorama-novel of the period—the novel of Proust. It is too episodic and diffuse, the conception sags, the satire is often journalistic and the style flat. But Romain Rolland was a far bigger person than Proust from the social and moral point of view; he cared about other people and tried to help them, he fought for a better world constantly and passionately, and he moved across frontiers towards internationalism as surely as the Rhine moves through Germany to the universal sea. He may be forgotten today, but insight and sincerity such as his will return to a world which needs them badly, and through other lips he will inspire youth once more and clarify its hopes. (pp. 234-38)

> E. M. Forster, "Romain Rolland and the Hero," in his Two Cheers for Democracy, *Harcourt Brace Jovanovich, Inc., 1951, pp. 234-38.*

WILLIAM H. McCLAIN   (essay date 1948)

[*In the following excerpt, McClain discusses the evolution of Rolland's attitude toward the Soviet Union.*]

"Brothers of Russia," wrote Romain Rolland in 1917, "we have not only to congratulate you on your great achievement but to thank you as well, for in winning liberty you have labored not for yourselves alone but for us as well, your western brothers."

These are the opening lines of the essay, **"A la Russie libre et libératrice"** in which Rolland hails the Russian Revolution as opening a new era for all humanity and announces to the world his decision to become its champion.

Like the great eighteenth-century writers who had contributed so much to his spiritual formation—Rousseau, Herder, Voltaire, Goethe—Rolland had always been a firm believer in social progress and in world peace. With these men he had felt that love of one's own country should not blind one to the achievements of other nations, and with them he hoped that all men in all nations would one day arrive at the stage already reached by many thinkers in the past and by a few in the present era, where "one no longer knows nations, where one feels the happiness of one's neighbors as one's own." Such was the outlook of Jean-Christophe, the *Weltbuerger*, and such, too, was Rolland's own outlook in 1914.

The Great War was a rude awakening from these dreams of peace. At first Rolland was in despair, for in those early days

of the war it seemed to him at times as though all of his hopes and efforts of the Christophe years had been in vain. For Rolland, however, such feelings of personal frustration generally lasted only until a new course of action had presented itself. The war was not long in indicating one. As early as 1915 Rolland writes that he will not only continue to pursue his campaign against war and hatred but will embark on a new campaign against the great evil underlying all of the world's recent conflicts, capitalism. It was quite evident, he felt, that the world could not exist after the war, save at the risk of new and deadlier conflicts, unless the existing social system, "dominated by monstrously overgrown capitalistic imperialisms," were radically changed. It was this conviction which led Rolland the evolutionist, the believer in gradual social change, to hail the Russian Revolution in 1917 as heralding the advent of a new social order for all mankind.

Even while greeting the Revolution enthusiastically, however, Rolland warned its leaders at the same time of the dangers confronting it. "Remember the mistakes of the French Revolution," he tells them, "and be tolerant. May your revolution be one of a great, humane people, and may it avoid the excesses of which ours was guilty."

It is clear from the rather admonishing tone of this first communication to the newly born Soviet state that Rolland was not free from doubts concerning the revolution even in the moment of his first enthusiasm.

When the allies directed an economic blockade against Russia in 1919, Rolland spoke ardently in her defense. Yet, even while he defended her, he reprimanded her for her harsh treatment of her intellectuals. It was indispensable to the ultimate success of the revolution, he felt, that workers and intellectuals should iron out their differences, for both, he thought, had an important role to play. He liked to think of the new Russia as an edifice under construction where workers and artisans should labor side by side, as they did in the Middle Ages while building the great cathedrals.

He refused absolutely to subscribe to the view held by Henri Barbusse and certain other French sympathizers with Russia, that the intellectuals should surrender their independence entirely and become mere slaves of the revolution. His stand on this issue and his objections against the violence of the revolution culminated finally in a controversy with Barbusse which it might be interesting to consider briefly here.

In reply to one of Barbusse's articles in *Clarté,* December 1922, Rolland published an open letter in the Belgian review, *L'Art Libre,* challenging Barbusse's contention that the ends justify the means in revolutions. It is not true, Rolland maintained, that the ends justify the means or are more significant than the means. If anything, he argued, the means are of even greater importance, "for the end (so rarely reached, and always incompletely) but modifies external relations between men, whereas the means shape the minds of men according to the rhythm of justice or the rhythm of violence."

Moral values should therefore be even more carefully safeguarded during a revolution than in ordinary times, he insisted. He for one, he continued, was of the opinion that no "raison d'état" was great enough to warrant the sacrifice to it of humanity, truth, and liberty; and he declared that he could never bring himself to condone militarism, violence, police terror, and brute force merely because they were "instruments of a communist dictatorship rather than of a plutocracy."

Later, to be sure, Rolland admitted that violence must intrude in the earlier stages of a revolution and even went so far as to criticize his earlier stand against it as "hollow and ineffective." That he admitted this somewhat grudgingly, however, we can sense from a later remark that violence, "though perhaps necessary, is nevertheless regrettable."

His feelings concerning the importance of intellectual and spiritual freedom were even more positive. "Our present problem," he wrote in 1922, "is to find a harmony in which the legitimate exigencies of the socio-economic revolution and those not less legitimate of spiritual liberty are reconciled."

The quest for this harmony was to occupy Rolland for many years to come. In these years, to be sure, Russia was not always in the immediate foreground in his mind, for much of his energy and effort was devoted to organizing the struggle against fascism, which was just beginning to emerge as the new and even deadlier reincarnation of his old arch-enemy, nationalism. At all times, however, he kept a watchful eye out for any danger threatening Russia and did not hesitate to lash out boldly in her defense when he sensed that her position was in any way imperiled.

When England severed diplomatic relations with Russia in 1927, Rolland immediately entered the lists in her behalf. Once again he reminded artists and intellectual leaders everywhere that the Russian Revolution represented the greatest social advance in the history of modern Europe and called upon them to see that it was not crushed, assuring them that if it were, the proletariat of the whole world was doomed.

Lunatcharsky, the People's Commissary for Public Education, responded warmly to Rolland's defense of Russia in a letter in which he assured Rolland that his name was respected in Russia and invited him to submit an article to the new review, *Revolution and Culture*, which was appearing in conjunction with *Pravda*. Shortly afterward Rolland received an invitation to attend the celebration of the tenth anniversary of the October Revolution. Ill health forced him to decline, but he wrote assuring his friends that he would be among them in spirit.

On November 4, 1927, he sent a second message, communicating his most cordial greetings and best wishes upon the occasion of this "greatest anniversary of social history," but reminding the leaders of the new Russian State once again that the Russian Revolution would continue to be successful only if it avoided the errors and excesses of the French Revolution.

The growing feeling that a conscious effort was being made in the capitalistic states to stir up ill-will toward Russia caused Rolland to declare in 1930 that he would make common cause with her, although he himself was not a communist. "We cannot tolerate," he writes, "that under the deceitful cloaks of religion, justice and civilization, the foulest forms of reaction: that of gold, that of the sword, and that of the tiara, enslave our West and fling our peoples against the great friendly peoples of the Russian Revolution." This was in reality an open declaration of war against the "International of Business" which he accused of arousing public opinion against Russia through an organized press campaign, and of attempting, in this manner, to force the hands of governments "which are asking only that their hands be forced."

With this declaration Rolland aligned himself irrevocably with the forces of the Revolution. Yet the disquietude, the earlier objections on humanistic grounds still persisted. Rolland's readings in Karl Marx were most helpful in overcoming these objections, for, as he tells us, Marx "tore away the illusions we in the bourgeois states allow ourselves to be wrapped in and thus ruthlessly laid bare the bourgeois ideology."

The most important "illusion" which Marx dispelled for Rolland was the illusion of liberty in the bourgeois state. In his *Zur Judenfrage,* Rolland informs us, Marx points out that the much vaunted liberty of the bourgeois state is in reality but the freedom to do anything that does not infringe upon the rights of others. What Marx finds most objectionable in such a concept, Rolland continues, is that it defines liberty in terms of the limits within which one is free to move and that, in so doing, it causes each man to see in every other man a limitation to his liberty. This emphasis on the right of the limited individual to live unto himself alone has made of man in bourgeois society a fundamentally selfish and unsocial being, an "abstract citizen," as Marx phrases it, whose only concern is for his own interests. The limits within which one can move, Marx argues, are set by a fence. Man is "penned up," and the right of man "is based not on the liberty of union of one man with another, but rather on separation, the right of the limited individual, limited to himself."

Communism alone, Marx thought, could make a human being of the "abstract citizen" of the bourgeois state. This it would do by making him a truly social being again. For, Marx held, once the barrier of private property is removed, man is no longer separated from his fellow men and can find his true "human" self again through co-operation with others. Carrying his argument a step further, Marx concluded that communism, in thus helping man to "find himself" as a human being, might truly be said to coincide with the humanistic ideal of the past:

> Communism, in so far as it is . . . the return
> of man to himself, in so far as he is social man,
> that is to say, human man, a complete return,
> a conscious return, and preserving all the wealth
> of anterior development—this Communism,
> being an accomplished naturalism, coincides
> with humanism.

Rolland's resistance to communism was all but broken by this assurance that communism as a way of life was completely compatible with the vision of social harmony he shared with Goethe, Schiller, and Beethoven. To break it entirely, there was necessary only some assurance that the liberty and integrity of the individual would remain inviolate in the communistic state. This assurance Marx furnished as well in his statement that the development of the communistic state as a whole depends on and is conditioned by the free development of the individuals which make it up.

Rolland required no further proof. As early as 1934 we find him writing that he considers the harmoniously functioning socialistic state the realization of the ideal society envisioned by the great humanists of the past, and that he looks upon Soviet Russia as the living example of such a state.

As evidence that the humanistic values are not being neglected in the new proletarian state, Rolland cites the observance there of the centenaries of Goethe and Beethoven and the plans to celebrate the centenary of Pushkin and the 750th anniversary of the Georgian poet, Roustaveli.

In every way, he concludes, both in commemorating the work of the world's past spiritual leaders and in assimilating to herself the finest elements of foreign cultures, the Russia of today has shown herself a fitting heir to the spiritual traditions of the Western world. In a letter to Fedor Gladov and Ilya Selvinsky, he speaks of his hope that Russia will serve as a repository where the spiritual treasures of the West may be safely stored. Just as in Shakespeare's *Antony and Cleopatra* the cortege of Dionysus deserts Antony's camp and passes over into the camp of his enemies, so today, he tells them, the gods of the old world, particularly the god of liberty, are forsaking Russia's enemies to enter her camp. Faithful ever to these gods, Rolland joins them in their passage into the new camp. "They have passed over to the new order," he declares, "and we who were, who are faithful to them, we follow them; to serve them, we serve the order they animate."

Rolland concludes the "Panorama" of his *I Will Not Rest* with the fervent wish that the torch borne by these gods—that same torch whose flame has lighted his path in days past—may become in Russia a beacon light whose rays will illuminate the path of all humanity in its march forward.

During the period of his orientation toward Russia, Rolland's banner, he informs us in his *Compagnons de route,* was Goethe's phrase: *Das Ideelle sei im Reellen anzuerkennen* ["the ideal is recognizable in the real"]. It is not surprising that Rolland should choose a motto in which both real and ideal are represented, for in seeking a positive course of social action—and this has been the goal of his striving in recent years—Rolland did not wish to abandon the idealism of his youth. What he hoped rather was to find a synthesis of real and ideal, a philosophy of social action in which the dream would still have its place.

Both Shakespeare and Goethe, Rolland believed, were singularly successful in striking the proper balance between real and ideal in their art. Each, however, arrived at this equilibrium in a different manner, according to Rolland: Shakespeare, through rising above life and its passions, Goethe by identifying himself completely with it. Shakespeare, the lofty Olympian who dominated life and its passions, had no desire to modify the world. He saw it as immutable in its joys and sorrows, in its tempests, "telle une mer" ["such a sea"]. Goethe, on the other hand, could not share this static world-view, for he and his era had made the discovery that the very essence of life is eternal change, that life is a process of eternal becoming, a "Devenir éternel."

Rolland connects this concept of the "Devenir éternel" in a very interesting fashion not only with the revolutionary spirit of Goethe's own period but with the recent upheavals of the present era as well. Even during Goethe's lifetime, Rolland demonstrates, the concept of the "Devenir éternel" was formulated into a dialectic system by Hegel. Almost immediately after it had been formulated into a definite theory, it was taken up by Marx and his followers and given its social application. Thus we may say, Rolland concludes, that Goethe unwittingly prepared the way for Lenin!

Lenin, Rolland finds, is, like Goethe, an outstanding example of a man who has identified himself completely with the spirit of his age. In every way, he points out, Lenin was in intimate contact with those life forces which express themselves in the masses, so that one might in truth say of him that he moved with that "élan vital, qui lance et qui soutient la montée perpétuelle de l'humanité" ["vital force, which advances and which supports the perpetual ascent of humanity"].

It was Rolland's most ardent wish to identify himself with the spirit of his age as Goethe and Lenin had done, and, at the close of *I Will Not Rest,* he seems to have made great strides in this direction by turning to Russia and communism.

We have seen, however, that even Rolland's final acceptance of Russia was to a large extent dependent on the assurance that the human values in which he believed were beginning to come into their own there once more. In fact, so great was the importance of these human values for him that we might almost say Rolland accepted Russia primarily not as a bold, new, social experiment but as a step forward toward the realization of his ideal of enlightened co-operation among all men in all nations.

In connection with this latter fact, another interesting point should be mentioned: the fact that Rolland, for one reason or another, never visited Russia in person. In view of his admiration for Russia's achievements and his cordial relations with so many of her leaders, this cannot but strike one as curious. Why did he not accept one of the numerous invitations to go there? Did he perhaps fear that his ideal would be hopelessly shattered, if he confronted the reality of Soviet Russia?

This fear doubtless explains in part his failure to go to Russia. There was, however, a more important reason still: the fact that even in 1935 Russia was no longer the final answer.

For some time Rolland's thought had been turning eastward toward India, "la Burg de l'âme" ["city of the soul"] where in Vivekananda, Ramakrishna, and Gandhi he had found new "compagnons de route" ["fellow travelers"]. The fruit of this pilgrimage to the "spiritual stronghold of the East" was a new synthesis which brought Rolland once again to the more purely humanistic and idealistic outlook of the Christophe years. For from this spiritual contact with the East a new ideal was born—the ideal of panhumanism which transcended communism in envisioning the ultimate incorporation of all races and creeds into one great union.

The first great task confronting the builders of this new union was, Rolland thought, to effect a rapprochement between Occident and Orient through the union of India and Russia. Until this objective was achieved no union would be possible, he felt. Accordingly, in the introduction to his volume of essays, *Par la Révolution, la Paix,* which appeared in 1935, he informs us that his chief preoccupation henceforth will be to harmonize the two forms of revolutionary action represented by India and Russia: non-violence and revolution.

Universal peace is still the ultimate goal as in the Christophe years. Rolland himself, however, has changed. No longer the idealistic pacifist of the years preceding World War I, he is now militant and aggressive. It is no longer enough merely to desire peace, he tells us. We must be willing to struggle to obtain it and to fight, if necessary, to maintain it. Above all, he warns us, it is important to want the proper kind of peace. Peace which is but the absence of war will bring us nothing, he maintains. The true peace which must be our goal is the peace which rests on the harmonious co-operation of all peoples and all creeds. Such a peace, he assures us, can be realized only if we are willing to change the existing social order and create a new one in which a proper existence will be guaranteed to all human beings everywhere.

"Par la Révolution, la Paix!" ["Through Revolution, Peace!"] becomes the new battle cry. The revolution to which it refers, however, is something far greater than the mere overthrowing of a regime or even of an entire social order. It is, he later tells us in *Compagnons de route,* that permanent revolution, "qui monte à l'assaut éternel du destin, et par la force lui ravit, jour après jour, un lambeau de plus de la vérité" ["mounts an unending attack upon destiny, and wrests from it, day after day, another shred of truth"].

These lines remind one, perhaps more than anything Rolland has written, of the aging Faust whom Rolland so resembled in his ceaseless quest for something higher and better. For, like Faust, Rolland too was above all a perfectionist and a seeker after truth, even though he realized, as Faust did, that the ideal toward which he was striving was one which he could realize only in anticipation—"im Vorgefühl." It was inevitable, then, that Russia should represent in his eyes at best only the promise that his far higher, almost transcendental ideal of international harmony and universal peace would one day be realized.

The keynote of Rolland's nature was a certain dynamism, and he wrote, as he tells us in the "Epilogue" of his *I Will Not Rest,* for those "who are on the move." Life for him was nothing, if not movement, and he admired Russia in the years before World War II because he felt that she was a vital part of that movement. He believed then, he informs us in the "Epilogue," that the Soviet Union was being carried forward "by the irresistible surge of historical evolution," and that the Communist party was the only party of social action which was making its way forward toward the final goal—his goal— of a human community without frontiers and without classes. It was because of this belief alone that he supported Russia until his death in 1944.

One can scarcely resist the temptation at this point to speculate as to what Rolland's attitude toward Russia might have been, if he had lived into the present period. Doubtless he would have found it difficult, if not impossible, to reconcile his earlier idealistic view of Russia with the Russia of today. It is even possible that he would have withdrawn his support altogether. Of this, naturally, we cannot be certain. We may be certain, however, that he would not have continued to support Russia, if he had felt that he could no longer look upon her as part of the "vanguard of humanity's great marching army," for it was only as such that he supported her in the pre-war years, when he looked to her and to the other members of this vanguard to lead humanity in its endless march forward. (pp. 122-29)

William H. McClain, "Romain Rolland and Russia," in The Romanic Review, *Vol. XXXIX, No. 2 (April, 1948), pp. 122-29.*

JOHN CRUICKSHANK (essay date 1954)

[*Cruickshank is an Irish critic who has written extensively on French literature. In the following excerpt originally published in* Hermathena *in 1954, he examines the psychological origins of Rolland's political thought.*]

Romain Rolland saw life as presenting two main aspects: process and unity. He shaped his own thinking in accordance with the picture which he had established, so that the structure of his thought possesses a double movement. It is progressive and it is reconciliatory. This suggests the pattern of the Hegelian dialectic, for his thought moves through opposites to a superior harmony which embraces both. Descotes, in his book on Rolland, goes so far as to claim a direct influence, but it is difficult to find any specific evidence in support of this view.

Given this emphasis on process and unity, the main principles of Rolland's political thinking at once emerge. His social theory is dynamic and progressive. He regards social change as both

inevitable and desirable. In some societies the natural rhythm of political evolution must be recognized and implemented. In other societies—for example those faced by the "unnatural" situation of European supremacy and exploitation—the more violent tempo of revolution must be accepted as the only means of initiating a forward movement. In both cases, the goal toward which movement is made will be a fuller realization of equality of rights arising from that underlying unity which a static social theory tends to conceal. All *a priori* theories of social or racial supremacy run counter to that spiritual view of the world which makes unity its basis. Social and racial differentiation, in so far as they exist, cannot affect the undifferentiated spiritual reality which underlies them. These, then, are the broad principles which maintained Rolland's position on the political left. The instinct to keep his thinking mobile and unitary ultimately determined his political attitude.

The double pattern of Rolland's thought—its combination of flexibility with an assimilative tendency—not only decided the general orientation of his political theory, but imparted certain distinguishing features to it. These features, which follow from his preoccupation with process and unity, are: independence of party ties, belief in artistic commitment, tolerance, insistence on the dignity and uniqueness of the individual person. A short discussion of each will complete the picture of how Rolland's mental characteristics molded the contours of his political convictions.

In the first place, Romain Rolland's attitude is characterized by independence and the capacity to change his point of view. His thinking was too flexible to become insistently dogmatic or narrowly doctrinaire. An awareness of movement and a desire to synthesize introduced into his thought a measure of restlessness which rebelled against the limiting demands of group loyalty. He steadfastly refused to join any political party. He preferred to remain unaccountable to a disciplinary system which, on occasions, would inevitably tend to place considerations of party solidarity above truth. Furthermore, an intellectual insistence on the underlying unity of life means that the purest form of mental activity must concern itself with universals. This is another argument for refusing any reduction to the arbitrary dimensions of a prearranged system. And so, Romain Rolland persisted in assuming entire responsibility for his political views, emphasizing at the same time his unwillingness to commit himself to a particular policy of future action.

Rolland's refusal to become a party politician is to be taken as a measure, not of his indifference, but of his deep and serious concern with those problems which political activity seeks to solve. This concern led him to adopt a position which many would regard as suicidal in a serious artist. He attempted, both through his imaginative writings and in articles and manifestos, to exercise political influence. When art and polemics consciously seek to live in harmony, art frequently suffers most from the experiment, and many critics would say that Rolland provides an example. Yet whatever one's point of view, one can understand how the unitary tendency of Rolland's thought shaped his attitude. He believed that no man, whether an artist or not, can abstract himself completely from political and social life. The individual lives within a group of some sort, and those theories which seek to separate him entirely from his social context ignore evident facts. The artist, in particular, possesses special vision and has at his disposal a unique means of communicating his perceptions. A privileged gift for language, which is his by definition, involves him in serious responsibility

Rolland and Mahatma Gandhi in 1931. Photograph by Rod Schlemmer.

toward his readers. While he has a clear duty to extend and enrich his own spiritual and intellectual life, he must not allow his attitude to harden into complete egotism and indifference. He should renew his vision mainly in order to communicate it with new and persuasive power to others.

Also, Rolland considered it his civic duty to make his views publicly known, but he regarded his theories as being of little value until he had tested them in a practical way. Although reacting against what he held to be the moral degeneracy of much professional politics, he was not content to remain aloof. It was his constant concern to harmonize theory with practice, and he therefore sought to divert into practical and fruitful channels that objectivity which his independence of party ties made possible.

A third characteristic of Rolland's political thinking is his capacity for tolerance. The virtue of tolerance is a further consequence of mobile and unitary thinking. Both the temporal and spatial movements of Rolland's mind introduce broadness of vision and an awareness of relativity. The relationships which result, based either on similarity or contrast, can only be rightly judged by reference to that ultimate unity which they suggest and which transcends them. Rolland's tolerance therefore arose from his desire to reach an essential unity underlying apparent diversity. He considered that while many systems of belief contain partial truth, no creed offers infallibility. This was the

basis of his reconciling activity. He conceived it as his duty not to reject out of hand an alien system of belief. He attempted rather to discover what was true in all creeds, defending and extending their common fund of wisdom. This was the cast of mind which he brought to bear on the tensions and conflicts of the Third Republic in France.

An insistence on the unique importance of each individual is the fourth consequence of Romain Rolland's capacity of mobile and unitary thinking. His monistic beliefs rendered the relationship between man and deity that of the mode to its substance, and a wholly spiritual view of man resulted. It is part of Romain Rolland's significance as a writer on social and political matters that he fought unceasingly for a fully dimensional view of the individual. He was the determined opponent of any force seeking to enslave human personality or diminish the complexity of human needs and aspirations. He realized the presence, in our modern unbalance, of tendencies which threaten to dehumanize human life. It is from this viewpoint that one must judge his tireless campaigning on behalf of colonial peoples; his championship of Gandhi against the British in India; his appeals on behalf of Sacco and Vanzetti, Norris and Patterson; his denunciation of fascism and nazism. In fact, Rolland gave to the fraternal idea its full, logical extension. He accepted the brotherhood of man as a spiritual reality, relegating the brotherhood of some men with common beliefs and interests to the realm of convenience and expediency. Here his awareness of process is again important. It means that no particular communal grouping can be regarded as final. It allows for man's further growth in spiritual understanding. It recognizes that no terrestrial organization can be a complete substitute for that identity between men which can be fully attained only in the godhead. In a word, it not only realizes the manifest difficulties of the fraternal idea but, despite these obstacles, it emphasizes the need for a sustained effort to approach this ideal more nearly. (pp. 181-85)

> John Cruickshank, "Romain Rolland: The Psychological Basis of Political Belief," *in* The Literary Imagination: Psychoanalysis and the Genius of the Writer, *edited by Hendrik M. Ruitenbeek, Quadrangle Books, 1965, pp. 169-85.*

DAVID SICE (essay date 1966)

[*Sice is an American critic and educator. In the following excerpt, he analyzes those qualities which led Rolland to describe* Jean-Christophe *as a "musical" novel.*]

Why consider the idea of music in Romain Rolland's pre-World War I *roman-fleuve?* The novel, which had an international vogue of some importance at the time of its publication, and which in the decades following gave rise to a considerable amount of scholarly and non-scholarly examination, today has been relegated by the critics to comparative obscurity. It remains, on the one hand, a curious, monumental specimen, and indeed the original, of its genre; and, on the other, a splendid example of the ideals and limitations of its era, that strangely distant never-never land of pre-war Europe. If it continues to be particularly successful on the eastern side of the Iron Curtain, along with the rest of Rolland's works, and to arouse critical interest there, that is due in some measure at least to the direction the author's political ideas took after the First World War. Indeed, a good proportion of the attention *Jean-Christophe* receives today, on either side of the "curtain," is of a political or sociological, rather than a literary nature.

But *Jean-Christophe* is essentially a novel about music; and even more basically, the novel of the Musician. The political ideas which Rolland expresses throughout the work either form part of the "realist" counterpoint to the heroic ideal of the composer's life, or participate in the hero's constantly changing view of the world around him—the series of intellectual and moral zigzags which characterize Rolland's conception of the artist's life. Although Rolland intended from the beginning, and especially in the middle volumes of the work, to extend the optic of the novel, in the best tradition of realism, beyond the limits of his hero's personality into the complex problems of contemporary society, his talents and the nature of his initial inspiration were focused on the life of the creative artist. What gives the novel its peculiar personality is in fact its very persistent attention, through the space of ten volumes, to the character and the "becoming" of its musician-hero. Even the examination of the "politics" of the musical world of his time is a function of this becoming.

Jean-Christophe is an attempt to synthesize the personality of the musical artist, the idea, and the creation of music. In its conception and structure, it attempts to create a literary form closely related to the esthetics and architecture of music. Thus discussion of *Jean-Christophe* as a "musical" novel must center around Rolland's approach to refocusing the definition of the novel into musical terms; although much has been written concerning Rolland as a "musical" writer, there seems to be

a good deal of confusion as to what the term really signifies—if anything.

About Rolland's qualifications to write on music there can be no question. But it is not enough to say that Rolland, as a musicologist, biographer, critic, and profound lover of music was capable of writing a novel about music, or the novel of the musician. Nor could *Jean-Christophe's* more or less enduring success as a work of literature, based to a great extent on its musical focus, be sufficient for us to consider it, *de facto,* a "musical novel." And yet, it is a fact that since its publication the work has been so termed by a variety of critics and appreciators. Citations from a few of these will indicate the divergency of their definitions of the term.

The musicologist Leo Schrade, in spite of his reservations concerning later developments in Rolland's thought, speaks of the author's *Jean-Christophe* and *Vie de Beethoven* in generally flattering terms; but his attempts to characterize the "musicality" of Rolland's style remain somewhat vague: "Musical language seems with Rolland an inborn medium. It appears that he drew poetical inspiration, now from the rhythm of music, now from contemplating music; throughout his life he paid tribute to this art" [Leo Schrade, *Beethoven in France*].

In a statement by J. B. Barrère, on the other hand, we find an attempt to assimilate the musical and the literary experience on other grounds: "C'est un poète qui a fait de la musique avec des images. Et même, la musique, il la comprenait et transposait en images" ["He was a poet who made music with images. Also, he understood and transposed music in images"]. Here we find the implication that both music and literature, in Rolland's sensibility, were functions of the more central quality of imagery, in which they found their common ground. Rolland's writing is imbued, as Schrade states, with his musical culture. Frequently Rolland feels it necessary to insert lines of musical themes into the text, in the guise of epigraphs or illustrations of his message: *An die Musik* of Schubert, Bach's *Bleib bei uns,* the *Seid umschlungen, Millionen* from the finale of Beethoven's *Ninth,* etc. As Jean-Christophe undergoes his numerous modifications of viewpoint, the "background music" changes accordingly; we can almost hear it. As Barrère claims, it is true that in attempting to express musical creations in terms of a literary form (cf. young Buddenbrook's improvisations on the harmonium), to translate the musical experience of his hero into words, Rolland resorted to descriptive passages which evoke images present either in the mind of the composer as he created, or in the mind of a sensitive listener. In that sense, what Rolland wrote consists of images which lie midway between music and literature, and in which the two arts might find some common ground of experience. It is also true, as we can see from numerous passages of Rolland's personal writings, that he felt music emanating from nature as he observed it, completing the process of vision. Conversely, he entertained visions of nature, plastic images, while absorbed in the auditory experience of the concert hall, or in the reading of a musical score. The effort to evoke the experience of Christophe's music during the course of the novel is evidence of Rolland's belief that this interplay of the arts, which he, like many others, experienced, might be utilized by the literary artist in recreating musical works.

But this is the least satisfactory and, I believe, the least important aspect of *Jean-Christophe's* "musicality." Rolland himself, in criticizing his friend Strauss's *Sinfonia Domestica,* hinted at the futility of such a procedure, in the inverse sense, when he blamed the composer for tying his music too closely to a program. He felt that the two "languages" were too dissimilar for such cooperation: the program tended to limit the freedom of the music, and the music did not seem to substantiate the logic and the explicitness of the words used to describe it. Alain, in an article for a special edition of *Europe* honoring Rolland's sixtieth birthday, likened the author's descriptions of music to Proust's, and characterized the procedure used by both as invalid. This is especially true of non-existent music, as opposed to descriptions of familiar works.

Others have attempted to explain the impression of musicality which the novel gives by claiming that Rolland wrote literature in musical, rather than literary *forms;* that the construction of the novel is consciously musical: rather than resort to traditional novelistic techniques, the author made use of his competence as a music critic and musicologist to build it on traditional musical structures. Rolland did frequently use the word "symphonic" to describe the structure of his novel, and the imagination quickly passes from the use of the word in a metaphorical sense to application of it in a more literal way. Rolland lent a certain air of validity to this assumption, when he asked Louis Gillet, who was editing a volume of selections from his works shortly before the First World War, to emphasize the musical procedures pursued in the construction of the novel:

> Je souhaiterais notamment qu'on mît en lumière (ce qu'on n'a guère fait, jusqu'à présent) la personnalité, non seulement morale, mais artistique, de *Jean-Christophe,*—ce que l'oeuvre peut avoir d'original, au point de vue littéraire,—et notamment, ses procédés symphoniques:—Préludes et Postludes,—thèmes conducteurs,—développements et crescendo symphoniques et rythmiques (comme dans l'ouragan de foehn et la révélation nocturne, à la fin du *Buisson ardent*), (ou dans l'orage de la création artistique au début de *la Révolte*)—coda—etc. Je me rends compte que ç'a été, en composant ces livres, ma constante forme de pensée. . . .

> [Particularly I should like to see emphasized (which has not so far been done) not only the moral but the artistic character of *Jean-Christophe*—what originality the work may have from the literary point of view, and notably its symphonic procedures: preludes and postludes, guiding themes, symphonic and rhythmic development and crescendo (as in the foehn storm and the revelation in the night, at the end of *Le buisson ardent,* or the storm of artistic creation at the beginning of *La revolte*), coda, etc. I realize now that this has been my constant form of thought while composing these books. . . .]

There are indeed examples of individual "musical" forms to be found in the text of *Jean-Christophe*—if we accept Rolland's assimilation of musical and literary terminology. They are, for the most part, "set pieces" which distinguish themselves from the current of the work, interrupting its progress momentarily. They form summations, landmarks in the flow of the hero's development. The passages cited by Roland in his letter are excellent models of this procedure: a kind of self-contained tone-poem in which a theme is developed rhythmically and lyrically, which attempts to give some sort of direct intuition, through images, of the internal nature of the composer's creative faculties at work. But it is not the *form* of these passages, their strictly external resemblances to corresponding musical structures like the prelude, the symphonic crescendo, or the coda, which makes them "musical" in any profound sense. The same procedures exist in strictly literary terms, under different names, as preface or prologue, dramatic development, and conclusion or epilogue. Even if Rolland categorized these formal divisions under musical names, the nature of the procedure is not necessarily non-literary.

Stefan Zweig, in his biography of Rolland, comes closer to isolating the element in the author's writing which gives it its musical nature. He sees it as a necessity for breadth of scope, for cyclical development along a winding, complex path rather than along rigorously logical lines. But Zweig misses the point in attributing this tendency to an ethical, rather than to an essentially esthetic necessity on the author's part: "For Rolland, breadth of scope is a moral necessity rather than an artistic [*sic*]. Since he would be just in his enthusiasm, since in the parliament of his work he would give every idea its spokesman, he is compelled to write many-voiced choruses."

Zweig's explanation is valid, to an extent, for the procedure in *La Foire sur la place* and *Dans la maison,* where Rolland has Jean-Christophe embrace successively two opposing sides of the same central issue (the musical "health" of France), in order to do justice to the case. But these two volumes represent a break in the development of the novel (inasmuch as it reflects the life-flow of its composer-hero), by their essentially polemical nature. They seem to me to be the least "musical" of all the parts of the novel, for this reason, and useless as demonstrations of the basic technique employed by the author.

However, breadth of scope seems to me to be a significant attribute of the essential musical quality of the novel. A central idea of the *roman-fleuve* is the attempt to seize being in its duration, to put the author and reader into direct and continuing communion with its ceaseless movement, to embrace the universe in its becoming instead of cutting across its flow by a process of analytical dissection. Such an aspiration necessitates breadth and a certain apparent lack of incisiveness. This is the quality in Rolland's prose which several critics have chosen to emphasize. A typical example is found in Charles Baudoin's introduction to "Le Seuil," one of the chapters of *Le Voyage intérieur:* "Pour qui pense en mouvement, en dynamisme, en musique, comme Bergson et comme Jean-Christophe, les méandres même 'errants' du chemin contiennent plus de vérité qu'une 'position' même solide" ["For those who think in movement, in dynamism, in music, like Bergson and like Jean-Christophe, the very 'errant' meanderings of the path contain more truth than a solid 'position'"].

This following of every involution of the stream of movement, whatever its relationship to the more logical pattern which is supposed to dictate literary creation, is also referred to by Jean Bonnerot in describing the style and the construction of *Jean-Christophe:* "Ce style uniforme et sans éclat, ce style journalier qui paraît fuir au courant de la plume sans râtures" ["This uniform and unremarkable style, this journalistic style which seems to flow speedily from the pen without revision"]. Such a conception of the creative process followed by Rolland implies, however, a variety of automatic writing ("sans râtures"), in which the artist delivers himself over to the spell of his intuition, living and transcribing simultaneously the experience of his vision. (pp. 862-67)

One may, of course, accept such a definition of the process of musical creation. It is an idea which has had many antecedents in German philosophy, as in the discussion of "Dionysian" and "Apollonian" art in Nietzsche's *Birth of Tragedy*. One of Rolland's letters to Sofia Guerrieri-Gonzaga, dating from the era of *Dans la maison,* apparently accepts it: "Heureux Christophe! Il est musicien, il n'a qu'à s'abandonner à son flot intérieur" ["Lucky Christophe! He is a musician, he has only to abandon himself to his interior flow"]. But the remainder of this passage takes pains to distinguish clearly between music and literary art—specifically that of Rolland himself in *Jean-Christophe:* "Mais pour contempler l'univers et pour tâcher de le pénétrer par la pensée, pour être écrivain, il faut une autre nature, qui ne s'abandonne jamais, qui n'est jamais inconsciente, qui a toujours les yeux ouverts, même dans la passion" ["But to contemplate the universe and to attempt to penetrate it through thought, to be a writer, it takes another nature, which never abandons itself, which is never unconscious, which always has its eyes open, even in the midst of passion"].

But this, like many other statements to be found in Rolland's writings, is only a partial truth, a truth in passage. Rolland was fascinated by Beethoven's sketch-books, in which he could follow the mind of the musician as he painstakingly worked out the ideas dictated to him by his inspiration, transforming the original themes frequently almost beyond recognition. He underlines the essential role of conscious artistry in the works of Handel, Bach, and all the great musicians prior to the Romantic movement. And his enduring appreciation of Wagner was based on a conviction that the composer's greatest works, such as *Tristan and Isolde,* were essentially "classical" in this sense. Thus Rolland's conception of the workings of the musical mind can in no way be limited to the purely intuitional process ascribed to Christophe in the above letter.

A more definitive statement of Rolland's, moreover, dating from some time after the termination of *Jean-Christophe,* indicates the extent of the author's identification of his own writing with musical creation: "Je suis, de nature, un musicien qui, détourné de son art, s'exprime en littérature" ["I am, by nature, a musician who, diverted from his art, expresses himself in literature"]. Rolland leaves no doubt, even at this point when his focus of attention has been turned from music by four years of war, that he continues to identify his creative process with that of the composer. (pp. 867-68)

If Rolland's novel is musical in its intrinsic nature, it is because he conceived it *in the way he felt to be that of the symphonic composer.* Like the symphony, the novel was for him an immense structure, complex and simple at the same time, built on certain themes, on certain rhythms, on certain dominant sentiments, dictated from the author's intuition of formless substance, having its own internal laws, but conceived in its architectural whole, in its grand lines, from the beginning; having a shape, a direction and a final goal which were imagined before anything was put into its material form; and constantly directed, in the midst of its apparent wanderings, by the overall conception, its internal relationships, and the laws of its development (which were neither those of the traditional novel, nor those of "la logique raisonneuse").

If there are imperfections in the detail of his working-out of the novel, it is not because the work took shape in haste, or from day to day; it is because it was conceived on a monumental, monolithic scale, and was not meant to be "regardé à la loupe" ["viewed under a magnifying glass"]. Rolland cites the words of Gluck, answering criticism of his operas:

> Supposez un homme qui pour mieux voir les peintures de la coupole du Val-de-Grâce monte dans la coupole, et, le visage appliqué au mur, crie au peintre qui est en bas: "Eh! Monsieur, est-ce un nez? est-ce un pied? qu'avez-vous prétendu faire?" Le peintre lui répondrait: "Eh, Monsieur, descendez, vous le verrez aussi bien que moi."—Certaines oeuvres sont faites pour être vues de loin, parce qu'il y a en elles un rythme passionné qui mène tout l'ensemble et subordonne les détails à l'effet général. Ainsi Tolstoï, ainsi Beethoven. . . .

> [Suppose a man, in order to better see the paintings of the Val-de-Grace cupola, goes up to the cupola, and, his face pressed to the wall, cries to the painter below: "Hey! sir, is this a nose? is this a foot? what did you think you were doing?" The painter would say to him: "Sir, come down, you will see it as well as I."—Some works are made to be seen from afar, because there is in them a passionate rhythm which leads the entire ensemble and subordinates details to the general effect. So it is with Tolstoy, so it is with Beethoven. . . .]

Thus Beethoven and Gluck, who represent to Rolland "grandes âmes" ["great souls"], compose carelessly, not because of any lack of ability to do correct work—but because the nature of their vision, the scope of their imagination, demanded such a large-scale, coarse-grained technique. Viewed from close up, this coarseness and lack of correct detail seems a senseless, untidy jumble. (That is why Rolland insisted that the "purists" in the musicological and critical world of Paris would never be capable of understanding great music.) Seen on the other hand from the viewpoint intended by the composer or the author himself, from which his eye could embrace the extent of the entire structure, all of the dissonant or confused detail becomes clarified, as part of the larger pattern, rhythmic or plastic, of the work. In essence, this is the way in which the great productions of nineteenth-century symphonic literature must be appreciated: the nature of such music, such architecture, requires that the listener submerge himself in the stream, the duration of the work; that he exist in unison with it, and experience the composer's intuition in the same rhythm in which it dictated itself to him. But at the same time, part of the listener's consciousness must remain separate from this submerged intuition, analyzing and organizing the experience which the rest of the mind is undergoing, tracing direction and development, relating and balancing rhythms, and synthesizing the apparently unrelated or dissonant, antithetical experiences which occur from moment to moment. This emergent segment of consciousness is, in part, the ear of memory. But it is also another ear, a tension toward the future, which relates the end of the work to all the parts as they are immediately experienced.

This is certainly the quality which Alain found in the sections of *Jean-Christophe* which to him seemed truly "musical": "Tout le livre est musique par un mouvement épique qui va selon le cours du temps, et par un genre de souvenir en avant de soi, et aussitôt passé, aussitôt recouvert. Même un lent Adagio n'attend pas; il nous emporte; on sent d'autant mieux l'inflexible loi par ce mouvement majestueux, sans violence ni faiblesse" ["The entire book is musical through an epic movement which goes according to the march of time, and by a kind of memory in advance of itself, recovered as soon as it has gone. Even a slow Adagio doesn't pause; it carries us; we perceive so much better the inflexible law by this majestic movement, without violence or weakness''']. It is the power of memory, of foresight, of emergent reason, rising above the turmoil of discords, dissonances, false resolutions, modulations, enharmonics, and all the mysteries of detail which make up the musical experience, that Rolland considered as the essence of the musical mind. It is that same power which he felt to be in himself the focus of the act of literary creation, the transcendent force which emerges from the turbulence of internal conflicts, of passions and events, and remains clear and omniscient through everything which absorbs the intuition and the senses. . . . (pp. 872-73)

It is as a function, and as an expression, of this power, the attribute of the great symphonists, that the heroic life of *Jean-Christophe* was to take shape, passing through the contradictory stages of his development, seeming to lose its direction and to change its nature from chapter to chapter, from volume to volume, but always returning, inevitably, to the route which the author had plotted, always embodying the law of development upon which his character was constructed; and always, somehow, retaining the original given substance of his personality, through profound changes in environment, age, esthetic doctrine, and political belief. Rolland's vision of music, and his vision of the novel's effect in a world on the brink of its great struggle, was one in which the inflexible law of becoming, through its resolution of all the intermediary stages of dissonance, would eventually bring humanity to the level of exaltation which marks Christophe's final stage: the bright peace above the battle. Like Rolland's Empedocles, Christophe was to sing ''son chant d'espoir et de paix, la splendide symphonie de la Vie universelle, dont les dissonances cruelles périodiquement se résolvent en des accords de lumière'' [his song of hope and peace, the splendid symphony of universal life, whose cruel dissonances periodically resolve themselves in harmonies of light'']. . . .

If both music and the novel took another direction in the years following the creation of *Jean-Christophe,* that was due, to a great extent, to the birth of a new era, growing out of the upheaval of the first World War. Christophe remains as a summit of the idealistic novel, and as the summation of a concept of art which still has its nostalgic attractions today. (p. 874)

> David Sice, '''Jean-Christophe' as a 'Musical' Novel,'' in The French Review, Vol. XXXIX, No. 6, May, 1966, pp. 862-74.

J. KOLBERT (essay date 1968)

[*In the following excerpt, Kolbert discusses Rolland's biographies of prominent German artists.*]

Romain Rolland, who received his Doctorat ès Lettres in Paris in 1895 and who inaugurated the program of musicology at the Sorbonne, pours into his biographies all of the erudition and scholarly precision that we have come to expect from the most distinguished musical historians. This point is stressed by one of Rolland's most ardent admirers, André Maurois, who claims that Rolland's passion for historical verity derives not only from his own temperament but also from his training at the Ecole Normale Supérieure and at the Ecole Française de Rome. . . . Though Rolland injects into his biographies the warm lyricism and the poetic fervor of an unabashed hero-worshiper, he succeeds in temporizing his zeal with his scrupulous adherence to research documents. Maurois, himself a systematic and scholarly biographer, once referred to Romain Rolland's biographies as ''lyrical poems that sing their tribute

to heroes.'' Yes, to a large extent, these are poems of sorts, but the exuberence in them is counterbalanced by the biographer's devotion to truth and fact. (p. 381)

No genre occupies in Rolland's total productivity a more vital place than his biographies. They give cohesiveness to the various parcels of his lengthy and active literary career. In his inspired introduction to *Compagnons de route* he discloses that all of his heroic subjects ''participent à l'unité profonde d'un même destin, qui, sous des masques variés, s'est poursuivi, toute la vie'' [''share in the profound unity of a destiny, which, under various guises, pursues them all their lives''].

We should note another striking unity: the one which, through an amazing series of affinities and coincidences, ties Rolland to his subjects. Undoubtedly the portraitist selected for biographies only those models with whom he had much in common, with whom he could engage in a symbiotic relationship. We can conjecture that had Beethoven, Goethe, or Mozart lived during the holocaust of World War I, they would probably have shared his views and would have soared with him loftily ''au-dessus de la mêlée.'' As Rolland wrote his life of Handel or of Beethoven he transformed himself into a modern Handel or Beethoven. Insinuating himself into their minds and spirits, he attempted to react to outer reality as they had done. Zweig quotes Rolland as he discloses his rapports with his heroic subjects: ''The bliss and the pain, the desires and the dreams of Mozart and Beethoven, have become flesh of my flesh and bone of my bone.''

These German heroes attracted Rolland because, in the main, they were musicians; and he had a feverish need for music—especially German music—a need which he characterized as ''mon premier amour'' [''my first love'']. Out of this unquenchable thirst for music grew some of his finest biographies. Music is that staunch force which enabled him to transcend the national frontiers, which transported him into those realms where we realize once and for all that all men are brothers, citizens of humanity, where political circumscriptions hardly exist. In a letter to Clara Collet (April 25, 1906), Rolland confesses that ''Ma vraie langue est la musique. C'est elle qui a fait de moi un Weltbürger'' [''My true language is music. It is she who made of me a citizen of the world'']. Even as a fourteen-year-old youth he utilized music as an antidote against the bitter disappointments he found at the Lycée Saint-Louis, where he was repelled both by the positivistic materialism espoused by so many of the professors and also by the crudeness and insensitivity of his fellow students. So, as an evasion from what he regarded as the overly brutal Paris of 1880 he turned instinctively to the beauties of the natural landscape and to literature and music, largely those of Germany. Furthermore, he was irresistibly drawn into the passionate web of Nietzsche and Wagner by his strange and fascinating, lady-companion, Malwida von Meysenbug, with whom he spent countless hours during his Roman sojourn discussing her ebullient personal contacts with the giants of a preceding generation in Germany.

Romain Rolland could thus sincerely believe himself to be as much a product of German culture as were many enlightened young Germans of this generation. In *Au-dessus de la mêlée* he disclosed to ''Mes Amis Allemands'' [''My German Friends''] that ''Vous savez combien j'aime votre vieille Allemagne. Je suis fils de Beethoven, de Leibnitz et de Goethe, au moins autant que vous'' [''You know how much I love your old Germany. I am the son of Beethoven, of Liebnitz and of Goethe, at least as much as you'']. . . .

If there is a quite obvious unity between Rolland and his models, there is an even more striking commonness that ties all of the biographies into an integral corpus of literature. First, all of them follow the contours of the biographer's candid propensity for hero-worship. Rolland never attempted to conceal his unbridled enthusiasm for the men he admired so passionately. In our age of widespread cynicism, of embarrassment before the overt display of zeal, his biographies rise like isolated sentinels apart from the greatest mass of literary compositions. His very vocabulary is tinted with the glaring colors of joyous praise. "Respirons le souffle des héros" ["Let us breathe the air of heroes"], he jubilantly broadcasts in the 1903 preface to the *Vie de Beethoven*. . . . These five words adequately summarize the heroic atmosphere that pervades his biographical and fictional literature. Quite clearly, in his *Haendel,* he prefers the virile, powerful, energetic, and overflowing creator of the *Messiah* to the effete Henry Purcell, whom he describes as "ce charmant artiste, maladif, de tempérament débile . . . féminin . . . frêle" ["this charming artist, sickly, of feeble temperament . . . feminine . . . frail"]. He admires Wagner's titanic powers in an era when men tend to be "enfermés, étiolés et livresques à l'excès, loin de l'action" ["shut in, ennervated and bookish to excess, removed from action"]. . . . The ability to translate indomitable willpower into massive acts, this is the prerequisite of the hero, for whom no dreams are unrealizable. So Beethoven's biography is treated not only as that of idealist imbued with faith in the brotherhood of man, but it is also an ode to limitless energy. Rolland's life of Richard Strauss bathes in verbal pyrotechnics that equal the musical heroism of *Ein Heldenleben*. Rolland opines that "C'est par ces côtés héroïques qu'il [Richard Strauss] est l'héritier d'une partie de la pensée de Beethoven et de Wagner" ["It is in these heroic aspects that he is the heir to a portion of the thought of Beethoven and Wagner"]. Even the congenial and gracious Mozart is treated as though he had been a tireless Promethean dynamo: "La grande joie pour lui, c'est de créer" ["For him, the great joy was to create"]. (pp. 382-84)

Besides belonging to a breed of titanic men, these German heroes share several other impressive qualities. Most, although of German or Austrian extraction, are above all Europeans, in the most exalted sense. Romain Rolland, the fervent believer in European oneness, emphasizes the European-ness of his idols. Glück he treats more as a product of French thought and as a phenomenon of the continental Age of the Encyclopedists than as a narrowly German composer. The German Handel was not only the most beloved composer of England, but he was fluent in French and wrote his entire correspondence in this language. More than once he refused to return to Germany simply for reasons of patriotism. For Romain Rolland he was the incarnation of a citizen of Europe "Par sa culture universelle, sa connaissance des théories artistiques du passé, sa familiarité avec les oeuvres importantes de l'Italie et de la France, ses relations avec les principaux maîtres allemands" ["Through his universal culture, his knowledge of artistic theories of the past, his familiarity with the important works of Italy and France, his relations with the principal German masters"]. . . . The biographer even extols Handel's lack of patriotism: "Mais il faut bien dire: le patriotisme allemand, Haendel n'en avait guère. Il avait la mentalité des grands artistes de son temps, pour qui la patrie, c'était l'art et la Foi" ["But it must be said: of German patriotism Handel had scarcely any. He possessed the mentality of the great artists of his time, whose native land was art and Faith"]. Even Richard Wagner, so often considered during the era of the Nazis as a supernationalist, is depicted as a continental figure, a European. Rol-

land prefers his operas "Siegfried" and "Tristan" mainly because they are not poisoned by what he calls "Bismarckisme." Another super-German spirit, Richard Strauss, is transformed by the pen of Romain Rolland into a European artist, a human crossroads in whose soul merge the best of the music of the north and the finest qualities of the Latin or Mediterranean cultures. In the case of Strauss' music Rolland notes that "Il serait facile et oiseux de relever des réminiscences précises de France et d'Italie, jusque dans les oeuvres les plus avancées: dans *Zarathustrâ*, dans *Heldenleben*" ["It would be easy and useless to point out precise reminiscences of France and Italy, even just those in the most advanced works: in *Zarathustra,* in *Heldenleben*"]. While Richard Strauss' musical genius represents the quintessence of European inspirations, Rolland concludes his study of this composer on a note of regret; he laments that this once European musician has fallen prey to the hollow illusion of German nationalism and the stupid, drunken obsession of European conquest. Hugo Wolf, on the other hand, was an inveterate European by taste and temperament: "Il fut de ces jeunes Allemands qui aimèrent passionnément Berlioz, et grâce à qui la France devra plus tard d'être glorifiée dans ce grand artiste" ["He was of those young Germans who passionately love Berlioz, and thanks to whom France should one day be glorified in this great artist"]. . . . But of all of these great Europeans it is Beethoven who reigns supreme as the internationalist par excellence. Romain Rolland's Beethoven is no puny patriot: he is the noblest expression of the continental ideal. The product of the Napoleonic era in Europe and of the French revolutionary spirit, he is depicted as being disinterested in Germanism in its narrow nationalistic sense. Rolland takes obvious pleasure in demonstrating that Beethoven is not even a pure German: by his paternal grandfather he was partially Flemish. In a footnote on the same page the biographer reminds his readers that "Il ne faut pas oublier ce fait" ["One must not forget this fact"]. Thanks to the human loftiness and the total intellectual independence of this figure, he refuses in his *Vie de Beethoven* to classify him under the restricted rubric of a German composer. The biographer makes much of the fact that following the completion of the Ninth Symphony, Beethoven longed to see, perhaps even settle in, the dazzling light of southern France and Italy. "Südliches Frankreich, dahin! dahin!" ["Southern France, to there! to there"], Beethoven scribbled in one of his notebooks.

Most assuredly the European state of mind is a precondition for any man to reign in the gallery of heroes of Romain Rolland. He himself once wrote that "Je suis d'autre part un intellectuel d'Europe" ["I am, on the other hand, a European intellectual"]. This Frenchman, born in the heartland of France, in provincial Nièvre, never forgot the odors and natural beauty of the countryside near Auxerre. This Frenchman, who loved France so deeply, yearned for a unity of Europe more than anything else in the world. His cult of men like Mozart, Goethe, Beethoven, Glück, and Handel nourished so effectively his appetite for things European. Their poetry and their music were the words and sounds not of nations but of an entire continental humanity.

Romain Rolland the biographer approached the hero-subject from two vantage-points. He studied them as artist-creators; but, above all else, he studied them as superior human beings, exalted members of the human race. This dual confrontation reflects his personal esthetic philosophy: he hardly interested himself in art for art's sake; nor did he believe that art could be divorced from human life and be studied as an entity unto itself. On the contrary, he contended that art is supreme only to the extent that it can serve humanity and only when imbued with the warm substance of the artist's personal experience. "J'appelle héros, seuls, ceux qui furent grands par le coeur" ["I call heroes only those made great by the heart"], Rolland wrote in his preface the the *Beethoven*. . . . Artists, he opined, should refuse to address themselves to the few snobs of their immediate *confrérie;* they must speak to the popular masses. In his essay on Glück he wrote in favor of this popular conception of art: "Un art ne vaut d'être honoré et aimé des hommes que s'il est vraiment humain, s'il parle pour tous les hommes, et non pour quelques pédants" ["Art is not worthy of being honored and loved by men unless it is truly human, unless it speaks for all men and not for a few pedants"]. And he added: "Ce fut la grandeur de l'art de Glück qu'il fut essentiellement humain, et même populaire, au sens le plus élevé du mot" ["It was the grandeur of the art of Glück that it was essentially human, and even popular, in the highest sense of the word"].

The biographies of Romain Rolland thus inevitably focus attention on two aspects of a hero's existence: the creative experiences an artist has lived and the drama of human life. Almost always in the second category Rolland emphasized that the hero had invariably suffered from excruciating pain and torment. Unless one has suffered one cannot truly dwell in the Rollandean pantheon of heroes. Only through pain can the hero fulfill the demands of the human condition. The biographer quotes from Beethoven, who in 1815 wrote to the Countess Erdödy; "Durch Leiden Freude"—"La Joie par la souffrance" ["Joy through suffering"]. It is a fact that virtually all of Rolland's models experienced some form of tragic suffering during at least one stage of their life. Occasionally, the hero has suffered for so long that his presence on this planet can be regarded as something of a supreme sacrifice in behalf of the whole human race. Sometimes the suffering derives from an almost solitary and humiliating struggle by the hero against collective stupidity and intolerence as he seeks to enunciate such unpopular positions as world peace, human justice, and the brotherhood of all men. The suffering may also come in the form of terrible physical pain. Usually the more unbearable the torments of body and soul, the more determined becomes the hero's resolve ultimately to achieve a victorious dénouement. Since these figures eventually survive the pains of tragic destiny, Rolland uses their example to demonstrate that we ordinary mortals can also survive similar moral and physical crises.

Except for Goethe, the figures in Rolland's repertory of German heroes all experienced what he called, in his essay on Mozart, a "lutte sans répit contre la misère et la maladie" ["a constant struggle against misery and malady"]. Adversity inspires formulation of some of the most exalted examples of art, as was the situation in the life of Handel: "Qui croirait," Rolland asks, "que cette oeuvre, robuste et saine entre toutes, était écrite en vingt jours, comme en se jouant, au milieu des tristesses, à deux doigts de la ruine et d'une maladie grave, où la raison de Haendel faillit rester engloutie?" ["Who could believe that this work, robust and healthy above all, had been written in twenty days, as though for sport, in the midst of sorrows, on the brink of ruin and grave illness, wherein Handel's reason must be swallowed up"]. Rolland dramatizes the painful struggle of Handel, during much of his career, to compose in spite of the curse of growing blindness from cataracts. His most moving chapters in the *Vie de Beethoven* portray the composer's bout with the tragedy of deafness. In fact, he described twenty-five years of Beethoven's life as little more than

"une plainte d'agonie" ["a wail of agony"]. Rolland emphasized both the fear of public humiliation as Beethoven tried to conceal his deafness from his audiences and also the tragedy of a great musician unable to hear the sounds pouring forth from his soul. But this was not all. The biographer pointed to the irony of Beethoven's almost unceasing solitude. In the case of Hugo, the suffering derived principally from the five-year period during which he collapsed with a nervous breakdown (1890-95), a breakdown which of course stifled his creative forces at the precise moment when he was starting to develop his ultimate formula for the lied as an art form. (pp. 385-89)

The preface to the *Vie de Beethoven* serves as one of the most significant esthetic pronouncements by Rolland, as Zweig so aptly claimed. It is here that the biographer declared that we readers need heroic examples of illustrious men to console us during our most trying physical and moral battles of life. Rolland also tries to console the humblest of us by implying that any one may be endowed with the potential qualities of heroism, that anyone may, in his limited way, become a Beethoven of sorts. We can thus utilize his biography as a guide for the formulation of the cardinal principals of our own existence. Rolland refers to Beethoven as "Celui qui nous apprit à vivre et à mourir" ["He who taught us to live and to die"]. Here then is the fundamental raison d'être of great biography as a legitimate artform. It is that branch of literature that brings us face to face with the most exemplary destinies of the human kind. (p. 389)

J. Kolbert "Romain Rolland: Biographer of German Heroes," in Revue de littérature comparée, Vol. 42, No. 3, July-September, 1968, pp. 380-89.

HAROLD MARCH (essay date 1971)

[*In the following excerpt from his book-length study of Rolland, March discusses the evolution of Rolland's concept of heroism.*]

In common parlance a hero is one who bravely faces death, usually on behalf of a person, a country, a cause. Success on some level is normally expected of him, but it may be posthumous. As a matter of fact for the spectator who has no personal aspiration to heroism, a dead hero is productive of loftier emotions.

Rolland's earliest idea of the hero was a simplification of the popular prototype: the sufficient cause of the hero's defiance of death was life itself, so that survival was at a premium. Death was by definition a failure, however splendid.

But the hero who is successful in the sense of mere animal survival belongs to the period of childish fantasy; in Rolland's literary work he is soon replaced by the paradoxical hero, he who loses, yet wins. An early example is Orsino with his dying cry, "Death does not exist!" By the time we get to *Les Loups,* which ignited the Revolutionary cycle, moral heroism is in full swing. There are three conceivable candidates for number one hero: Teulier, whose physical description fits Rolland himself, as he no doubt intended: cold, correct, neat, buttoned up from head to foot, very tall, very straight, with the air of an energetic fanatical Puritan, speaking in a peremptory fashion, without gestures. Second there is Quesnel, Commissioner of the Republic; third, Verrat, the former butcher (surely a symbolic occupation) who wins victories and is the idol of the populace. He is presented so unfavorably, physically and morally, that he could not be the hero, however many victories he may win. Quesnel is presented respectfully and his patriotic dishonesty is given a hearing, but it is Teulier, with his "Let justice be done, though the heavens fall," the man who looks like Rolland, who stands out as the hero. And Rolland, be it noted, adopted the pseudonym "Saint-Just" for the first night.

In *Beethoven* . . . he disavowed success, whether physical or moral: "I do not call heroes those who have triumphed by thought or by might—only those who were great at heart. . . . What does success matter? It is a question not of seeming but of being great." . . . (pp.68-9)

The preliminary theme of *Michelange* . . . is the hero disenchanted with victory, bodied forth by a statue called "The Victor":

> Standing erect he has one knee on the back of
> a bearded prisoner, who is bending and ex-
> tending His head like an ox. But the victor is
> not looking at him. At the moment of striking
> he checks and turns away, sadly and indeci-
> sively . . . he cares no more for victory. . . .
> This image of heroic Doubt, this broken-winged
> Victory . . . is Michelangelo himself, and the
> symbol of his whole life. . . .
>
> (p. 69)

The evolution of Rolland's hero from physical to moral courage led naturally enough to the problem of pacifism and related issues. The occasion was furnished by the Boer War at the turn of the century; the statement of position came in the play *Le Temps viendra*. In previous works war had been accepted as inevitable, or even (in a righteous cause) as glorious. But in *Le Temps viendra* Rolland for the first time attacks war—or perhaps it would be more accurate to say that his play contains an attack on war, since the author's own position, as in the Dreyfus case, is a little ambiguous.

The British Commander-in-Chief, Lord Clifford, is presented sympathetically, though unheroically; the real enemy is neither England nor the Boers but imperialism, and the villain is Lewis-Brown, the representative of the mining interests.

There are two candidates for the hero. One of them is an Italian prisoner who has been fighting with the Boers. At his interrogation Clifford asks, "Why didn't you stay at home?" The prisoner (impertinently): "How about you?" Clifford: "Italy is not an enemy of England." Prisoner: "Everything unjust is my enemy. My country is wherever liberty is violated. What do I care about your nations? I am a citizen of the world!"

Later the Italian in attempting to escape shoots and is shot by a British soldier, Alan. Both are mortally wounded but have time for farewell speeches. Other soldiers crowd around. The consensus is put by one of them: "It's not our fault. It is fate." The Italian will have none of this: "There is no fate. There is only ourselves. If we do what we should all will go well." He and Alan embrace and die, Alan crying, "I have done wrong."

The incident opens the eyes of Owen, one of the bystanding English soldiers, and he declares: "I shall kill no more." He refuses duty and at the close of the play is led away, paraphrasing the Old Testament prophets and giving the play a name: "The time will come when all men shall know the truth, and they shall beat their swords into plowshares, and their spears into pruning hooks, and when the lion shall lie down by the lamb. The time will come."

The sentiments of the Italian sound like Rolland, but Owen is, both dramatically and by the standard applied to Clifford, more

the hero than the Italian. While he was working on the play Rolland wrote to Malwida [von Meysenburg] (August 31, 1901): "The great tragedy of human actions seems to me to be that they are usually accomplished against men's will, by an irresistible fate which leads them to ruin. And I should like to make of this play an action against war." . . . (pp. 69-70)

The dedication of the play is somewhat enigmatic: "This play arraigns, not a European people but Europe. I dedicate it to—Civilization. Romain Rolland. February 1902." In the body of the play he seems to be attacking uncivilized civilization—the imperialism denounced by Clifford; consequently we can assume that the Civilization (with a capital C) of the dedication is not the existing but the ideal civilization, the Peaceable Kingdom to come. (p. 70)

> *Harold March, in his* Romain Rolland, *Twayne Publishers, Inc., 1971, 168 p.*

DUSHAN BRESKY (essay date 1973)

[*In the following excerpt, Bresky discusses* Jean-Christophe *and assesses its importance in modern literature.*]

Born in an era of waning naturalism, *Jean-Christophe* is a neo-Romantic reaction against both the socially oriented rationalism of Zola, and the epicurean dilettantism of Anatole France. In a way, the work is a literary *compagnon de route* of the Bergsonian cult of intuition. His incursions into satire in *La Foire sur la place* notwithstanding, Rolland is a grave and sentimental genius whose concept of art is tragi-heroic and whose treatment of subject matter is dominantly melodramatic, often lyrical. The framing of the novel by an introduction, "The Author's Dialog with his Shadow," and an epilog, "Good-bye, Jean-Christophe," points to a typically Romantic *culte du moi*. The same Bergsonian neo-Romanticism is evident in *Le Voyage intérieur* and in Rolland's correspondence and even in his monographs on the great musicians.

In the novel's introduction, Rolland firmly proclaimed in 1904 that he was not writing a work of art but a work of faith; the rather complacent epilog confirms this, but its implications are somewhat contradictory:

> J'ai écrit la tragédie d'une génération qui va
> disparaître. Je n'ai cherché à rien dissimuler de
> ses vices et de ses vertus, de sa tristesse pe-
> sante, de son orgueil chaotique, de ses efforts
> héroïques et de ses accablements sous l'écra-
> sant fardeau surhumaine; toute une *Somme* du
> monde, une morale, une esthétique, une foi,
> une humanité nouvelle à refaire.—Voilà ce que
> nous fûmes.
>
> [I have written the tragedy of a generation which
> is going to disappear. I have sought to hide
> nothing of its vices and of its virtues, of its
> heavy sorrow, of its chaotic pride, of its heroic
> efforts and of its prostration under the crushing
> superhuman burden; a sum total of the world,
> a moral, an aesthetic, a faith, a new humanity
> to be made.—That is what we were.]

Rolland's correspondence also contains many contradictions, some of which may be attributed to his intuitive rather than rational approach to art and to its techniques. In one of his literary epistles, Rolland protests that he is not a "man of letters," but a man, plain and simple. Another letter, however, suggests the contrary: here, Rolland leaves no doubt that in his eyes, *Jean-Christophe* is a unique work of art and that he as an author developed new literary techniques and achieved an unprecedented synthesis of music, poetry, prose and architecture. However, Rolland's contradictions and his Romantic semantics should not be overemphasized. In his personal alliance of art and faith, art simply does not play first fiddle, but there is after all no reason why a work of faith cannot at the same time be a work of art, or the reverse. Nor does being an *homme de lettres* preclude being a man: using the term in its technical sense does not imply that writers necessarily lack virility. One does not have to go back to Archilochos or to Agrippa d'Aubigné to find *humaniores litterae* combined with rugged heroism. The generation of Malraux and Hemingway cherished a somewhat similar cult, trying not only to write but also to live like men.

Examining the nature of Rolland's faith and its role in his art, one cannot ignore the striking parallels which exist between the author's spiritual and his esthetic orientations. His personal religion is syncretic. If Christophe can preach a simple monotheism, "On n'aime pas vingt choses à la fois, on ne sert pas plusieurs dieux!" ["One does not love twenty things at the same time, one does not serve many gods"].... Rolland's own all-embracing intuition leads him to reconcile various creeds and gods: Judaism with Christianity, Judeo-Christianity with Spinozian and various other sorts of pantheism, with Zoroastrian dualism, with the Nietzschean concept of a heroic *Übermensch*, and all this with Marxist materialism. In Rolland's novel the portrait of God is developed gradually together with Christophe's spiritual experience. As a child Christophe discovers Him in the heroic tones of Beethoven's overture.... To the young composer He appears as a vital power, relentlessly creating and recreating life, its joy and its beauty. During his second exile in Switzerland, after the death of his friend Olivier, the now middle-aged composer weighed down with the absurdity of life meets his God again. This time they talk with each other and Christophe learns that God is not omnipotent but that He Himself has to defend life, including his own eternal life, against the forces of death and nothingness. To live meaningfully, man has to elevate himself to divine heights by suffering, struggling and constant creating. In moments of creation, Christophe's muse occupies the divine pedestal. Only in his final reunion with God does the musician realize that his Maker is a Harmony governing the two conflicting powers. He is the God with two powerful wings, he is Life and Death. Only by maintaining a steady balance in His inner dynamism can He be "le jour qui se lève" ["the day that dawns"], the eternal resurrection. Life without Death would be a stale affair.

The syncretism which characterizes Rolland's religious beliefs is also at the basis of his conception of art. "One has to embrace everything with courage and joy and throw it into the glowing metal of one's own heart, negative and positive forces, friendly and hostile, all the raw of life. There will come of this a statue which will shape itself within us, the divine fruit of our spirit," says Rolland. "I for my part accept everything in life." The affirmation is typical of Rolland's Don Quixotism, its noble aspirations and its folly. What may be feasible in metaphysical contemplations and dreams—who knows?—presents certain difficulties in practical literary creation where so much depends on elimination, rigid selection and density. Rolland invokes dramatic discipline to improve the art of prose. He claims to have lent the cyclical structure of epic poetry to *Jean-Christophe*, which he characterizes as a lyrical poem in prose. In addition,

he tells his readers that he has used musical techniques in the novel, adapting devices such as leitmotiv, *thème conducteur*, preludes, postludes and codas to the needs of literary art. Finally, for the amalgam is not yet complete, Rolland encourages critics to look for the plan of an austere medieval cathedral in the foundations of his novel. The content of the novel betrays an urge to embrace the greatest possible variety of subject matter. Rolland does not limit himself to telling Christophe's colorful life story from the cradle to the grave; together with the destiny of an individual and his psychological conflicts, he wants to embrace the "macrocosm," the whole life of French society at the turn of the century. He satirizes the mediocre *monde* and glorifies the anonymous Faustian elite of scientists, humanists and artists. And in many fragmentary dialogues he tries to embrace several centuries of French cultural achievements. Such an artistic goal is ambitious, though not unattainable, as Thomas Mann demonstrated in *The Magic Mountain*. With more sobriety and discipline, Mann dealt with a comparable range of subject matter by using a limited number of character-types and a more economical setting. His microcosm and macrocosm are united in the Davos sanatorium, where most of the carefully selected, very genuine yet symbolic characters play their rôles from the outset to the climax of the novel. This is far from being the case in *Jean-Christophe*. Externally, the ten volumes of text are rather symmetrically divided into two parts, with an equal number of chapters in each, but there are a multitude of characters and episodic actions, and their epical integration is extremely loose. Many minor characters pop up never to appear again. Once Christophe leaves home, the dramatic unity begins to crumble. The only cohesive force in the second half is Christophe's destiny and his meetings with God. The novel's inner structure is neither a symphony, nor a cathedral, nor an epical cycle, but rather an artistically uneven sequence of melodramatic adventures and dialogues. The hero's causeries and polemics form a sketchy panorama of the flaccid French *monde* with all its glamorous pretentions, of the economic, artistic and intellectual establishment, confronted with anonymous rebels and idealists from every sector of French life. Perhaps this "horizontal mosaic" was intended to stylize the cross-nave of Rolland's cathedral, perhaps it imitates a symphonic movement in which all the instruments shrill the counterpoints of human passions, of low interests and noble dreams. But whatever Rolland's artistic intention, the sudden changes of tone and topic weaken the dramatic unity of the narrative. And the belated refocusing on a fresh outburst of Christophe's erotic passion in exile in Switzerland, far from saving the novel's structure, simply weakens it further. Finally, Rolland's rhetoric is the last but not the least example of his propensity to extend or magnify every feeling, every action. He tries to express more with his words than they convey. His insatiable delight in metaphorical hyperbole, his pathetic epanaphoras, pleonastic explanatory appositions, redundant parenthetical humor, long gradations, Rabelaisian enumerations all help to overstylize the multitude of subjects treated.

As a champion of overstatement, Rolland has many illustrious ancestors: Mme. de Lafayette, Jean-Jacques Rousseau, Balzac, Hugo, Tolstoy and particularly Rabelais, who was one of his favorite writers and models. Christophe's composition of an operatic version of *Gargantua* is an indirect tribute to Rabelais; and scholarly works on musical history, essays, dramas, novels, monographs on oriental thinkers and religions, political crusading and petition signing, newspaper articles, a vast correspondence—all this is a replica of Rabelaisian energy. But it is not enough to make Rolland the Rabelais of the twentieth century. He is too much the Romantic puritan who takes himself very seriously and who, unlike the happy monk, preaches too much. He lacks Rabelais' mocking irreverence and his pithy medieval vulgarity. He lacks the Renaissance polyhistor's humanist range—theology, law, medicine, philology. Where Rabelais talks lightly, Rolland talks with florid pathos. Despite his proverbial verbosity, Rabelais sums up his appetite for encyclopedic knowledge and *joie de vivre* with one word, "Trink!" To express the same thing, Rolland "embrace[s] everything, positive and negative values, friendly and hostile, all the ore of life." The differences between the two men are vast. "La farce est finie" ["The farce is over"], says the dying Rabelais; and *Jean Christophe's* last words are: "Tu renaîtras. Repose! Tout n'est plus qu'un seul coeur. Sourire de la nuit et du jour enlacés. Harmonie, couple auguste de l'amour et de la haine! Je chanterai le Dieu aux deux puissantes ailes. Hosanna à la vie! Hosanna à la mort!" ["You will be reborn. Rest! You are only a single heart. Smile of the night and the day intertwined. Harmony, august couple of love and hate! I will praise God with his two powerful wings. Hosanna to life! Hosanna to death!"]

Rolland's passion for bridging gaps and taming hostile powers in his heart also colored his political orientation. During World War I, because he wanted to choose "everything" he was unable to support either of the two main belligerents and went into exile, remaining above the hatred, above the turmoil, *au-dessus de la mêlée*. He worked as a militant pacifist on the soil of a neutral Switzerland. Following the war, while extending his religious sympathies to Hindu pantheism and Ghandi's pacifism, he also tried to embrace Communism and reconcile his faith in God with revolutionary Marxism. The Marxist tenet that any faith in any creator is an opium for the people did not seem to affect either his faith or his new-found sympathy for Stalin. He sincerely believed that decadent Western society had little hope of survival, and that it could only be saved by an alliance with the vital raw forces that launched the Russian revolution. Rather than giving up, as did Gide, his rôle of intellectual matchmaker between Bolchevism and Western democracy, at a time when thousands of Russians were being liquidated in jails and forced-labour camps, the elderly *Prix Nobel* applauded Lenin and Stalin as two "experienced gardeners." Seen in historical perspective, his snubbing of the "martyred Russian writers," Konstantin Balmont and Ivan Bunin, or his endorsement of the Communist establishment in the mid-thirties exemplify the practical pitfalls of Rolland's syncretism. Naturally, Rolland's political life does not concern us here, regardless of what indirect influence his moral support may have had on the general atmosphere at the Yalta conference or on the present enslavement of Central Europe, for example. Like the political activities of Picasso, of Bertrand Russell, Sartre, Arthur Miller, Brecht, Tynan and many others, this chapter, without being forgotten, is irrelevant to an esthetic judgement of his literary work. Just as no-one will judge Churchill's statesmanship on the basis of the impressionistic canvases he produced on the French Riviera following his retirement, it would be inappropriate to bear a grudge against the young Schillerian *Schwärmer* who began *Jean-Christophe* at the turn of the century and who much later, as a famous writer, applied his Romantic naïveté to politics.

Critics sympathetic to Rolland's ramified eclecticism describe it as a harmony of contrasts, but for some these contrasts may seem strikingly similar to contradictions. Rolland's attempt to establish a spiritual and esthetic harmony in *Jean-Christophe* falls far short of the classical harmony of Goethe's life-work.

Goethe succeeded in reaching a balance between Apollonian and Dionysian inspiration, between classicism and romanticism. *Jean-Christophe* is a work of dominantly Romantic inspiration and because of this it will inevitably suffer from the ups and downs of critical appraisal. It will always appeal to Romantically oriented critics and it will stir up those with a Voltairean turn of mind or who, like Gide, are uncompromising esthetes. Nevertheless, finding *Jean-Christophe*'s place in the history of the French and European novel is less difficult today than in 1916 or 1917 when Gide so reservedly and so reluctantly admitted in his journal that in spite of its serious esthetic flaws, *Jean-Christophe* was the "most significant or at least the most typical" piece of literature of its generation. At that time, Gide, no doubt surprised that this particular novel had been awarded the Nobel Prize, may well have judiciously weighed up all Rolland's French contemporaries, Bourget, Barrès, Claudel, Proust, Valéry, himself and perhaps the older writers who were still publishing in 1900, Zola, Huysmans and Anatole France. He had doubtless had no time to reassess his first judgement of *A la Recherche du temps perdu*, which as a reader for the *Nouvelle Revue Française* he had not found worthy of publication, and was no doubt reluctant to compete himself in his own private literary rating (his own works were not extensive at that time in any case). Psychologically oriented, and possessing a different type of lucidity from Anatole France's, he would not be likely to compare the esthetic standards of a novel like *Les Dieux ont soif* with *Jean-Christophe*, which appeared in the same year of 1912. In giving priority to *Jean-Christophe*, he could not disregard its experimental qualities, its ardent humanism and the melodramatic accents which so much appealed to the broad public. He may also have admired Rolland's courage in working for international peace alone in exile while his country was fighting against Germany. Today, one may ask whether the patina of sixty years has dated or enhanced the art of *Jean-Christophe*. For a variety of reasons, many critics will find Gide's conclusion debatable. Some will consider Proust's and Gide's own literary heritage artistically far more significant. An intimate literary cathedral such as *La Symphonie pastorale* appears esthetically more stimulating than Rolland's "symphony-cathedral." Other critics may look back with melancholy on the last successful wedding of modern and classical art and favor *Les Dieux ont soif* or France's minor prose works, such as "Le Chanteur de Kymé."

In the history of the European novel, Thomas Mann's *The Magic Mountain* may well be the milestone in the construction of a musical novel, and Joyce's *Ulysses* the most significant example of truly experimental techniques. But no matter what rank individual critics may attribute to *Jean-Christophe*, it will remain forever the rare credo of a modern Romantic. If book sales can be taken as proof that books are read, the sale records indicated by J.-Barrère prove that *Jean-Christophe* has maintained its appeal to today's reading public. This is an achievement which for its scope alone cannot be overlooked. The novel belongs in the same category as those literary marathons successfully completed by Balzac, Zola, Duhamel, Jules Romains or Roger Martin du Gard. In addition, *Jean-Christophe* stands out as a Romantic counterpoint to Zola's naturalist materialism, to France's epicurean scepticism, to Gide's tragic soul-searching and blasphemous doubt. Because of its length, future generations will probably not read it from cover to cover, but the unified melodrama of the first four volumes, the satire of the Parisian cultural scene in the early 1900's and various comments on music and literature will always stimulate and entertain the reader, whatever his field of interest. In days when absurdity, nihilism, lack of taste, cool materialism and charlatanism celebrate their triumphs, reading *Jean-Christophe,* with all its excesses, may be a blessed tonic for the soul. (pp. 89-95)

Dushan Bresky, in his Cathedral or Symphony: Essays on "Jean-Christophe," *Herbert Lang Bern, 1973, 109 p.*

HELENE KASTINGER RILEY   (lecture date 1981)

[*In the following excerpt, Riley examines similarities and differences in the political thought of Rolland and Stefan Zweig.*]

The friendship between Stefan Zweig and Romain Rolland had its basis in the unusual similarity of their political and personal beliefs, and in the configuration of an idealistic humanism, a cultural elitism, and an energetic pacifism which characterized the thinking of both men. Rolland's quest for understanding between people of different nations and races emerged first in the correspondence of the 21-year-old with Leo Tolstoy in 1887, after the Russian has publicly assailed two of Rolland's idols: Tolstoy had called Beethoven a seductive sensualist and Shakespeare a fourth-class poet. The young man's challenge brought Tolstoy's response: he did not deplore real art, but intellectual creativity was of value only if it involved personal sacrifice for the progress of humanity, if it was useful in uniting mankind and delivering it from false gods. Rolland's future artistic endeavors show the impact of Tolstoy's advice. While still practically unknown in France, he published his ten-volume novel *Jean-Christophe* in installments between 1904 and 1912 in the *Cahiers de la Quinzaine,* and became a well-known figure in European intellectual circles long before his native country recognized his political and historical significance. *Jean-Christophe* made its impact outside of France because of its theme and its prophetic spirit. Its protagonist depicts a gifted young German musician who perceives Rolland's native country through the foreigner's observant and critical eye. There was much in this self-analysis which angered the French, but Rolland also depicted what he considered the spirit of the true artist and Frenchman in Jean-Christophe's friend Olivier. Thus the critical aspect has a didactic core, and Jean-Christophe's symbolic crossing of the Rhine may be interpreted as a gesture of friendship and understanding between two historically antagonistic nations. Rolland was idealistic, but not naive. In the tragedies he wrote on historical subjects and in the novel he warned Europe of the alternative to rational dialogue between the nations, and in the last volume of *Jean-Christophe* he predicted in 1912 the imminent catastrophe: "The fire which smoldered in the European forest began to break out into flames. Extinguished in one place, it emerged in another. . . . In the East there were already skirmishes—the upbeat to the great war of nations. All of Europe, yesterday still skeptical and apathetic, was ravaged by flames like a dead forest."

Rolland foresaw the advent of the First World War, but he was not a pessimist; rather he exuded strength in the belief that ultimately reason would prevail, and that unity among the intellectual leaders of the European nations was an achievable goal. For this he fought with his pen and through contacts with like-minded individuals across the borders. Stefan Zweig wrote in his "Thanks to Romain Rolland": "I had already known him earlier; I had loved him earlier . . . but the entire and incomparable greatness of his intellectual presence I experienced only in the darkest days of my life: indelible, terrible days in the abyss of war—I shall not forget you." Zweig, who had met Rolland in Paris shortly before the outbreak of the war, renewed his contact with the Frenchman after the latter

had fled to Switzerland, treated as a traitor by his own country because of his attempts to preserve a semblance of reason in the madness of the warring nations. "I do not attempt to fight the war," Rolland wrote to Zweig in March 1915, "because I know that it is impossible—now more than ever! I attempt to fight hate. I attempt to save everything which may be saved from it: clear judgment, human mercy, Christian charity—or at least what is left of it; and for each of my miserable attempts I must pay dearly." Two months later, in May 1915, he writes Zweig again: "You are indeed that multifaceted and honorable European spirit which our time needs and whose appearance I have awaited for 20 years. We have in our Latin countries no critic of your dimensions." He writes of his isolation, of the loss of his French friends, of the sheeplike public who misunderstand his attempts at peacemaking; yet he immediately proceeds to the promise of the future: "I ponder much what we must do after the war—if we are still of this world then; a large work which shall surpass all political or artistic endeavors; an apostolic work of worldwide communion; the great heart of Tolstoy combined with a richer and stronger intellect—with more peace, too, and more light; a church above all churches; an elite of the elite (and from all classes) . . . in all parts of the world I have brethren who are closer to me than if they were of my own flesh. A powerful religious era is commencing ("religious" in its truest sense: that which unites man)."

In Rolland's efforts to maintain a semblance of reason and understanding among the intellectuals of Europe during the devastating crisis of 1914-1918; in his attempts to establish a Pan-European community of outstanding minds which could provide moral strength and political guidance above the battle, Zweig saw in the somewhat-older Rolland the incarnation of that humanistic enthusiasm and heroism which he felt was needed to replace the petty nationalistic patriotism of the warring nations. In his biography of Rolland, which continues to retain its place among the outstanding characterizations of the Frenchman, and in his presentations and lectures, Zweig examines Rolland's creed in the light of his own beliefs. In his address at the *Meistersaal* in Berlin on January 29, 1926, he speaks of Rolland and his functional idealism. The war, Zweig maintains, destroyed not only cities and nations, but the belief in humanity: "Like the contents which run out of a broken vessel, so the inner essence, the creed vanished with the stable foundations of the state and the ideology of bygone days, and each of us must attempt to renew in himself a viable belief in the future." No man has exuded such strength, is such a living example of far-reaching consequences in our time as Romain Rolland, Zweig asserts, and attempts to explain Rolland's charisma: some had read his *Jean-Christophe* and their youthful search received direction, passion, suspense; others had never read the novel but felt during the war that perhaps not everything was as simplistic as newspapers and propaganda had protrayed it, and suddenly the first essays of Rolland appeared and strengthened their inner convictions and conscience; again others had experienced his lectures in music history at the Sorbonne and told how he had instilled in them the "idea" of art; some had written Rolland in their hour of need and insecurity and had received a letter from him which conveyed and intensified in them his idealistic spirit. There was opposition to Rolland's mission, of course, particularly from the political left which considered his ideology impractical and naive. Henri Barbusse's scathing article "A propos du Rollandisme" in the *Clarté* (1921), for instance, led to a widespread controversy in which Rolland himself took part. "I am at a loss," Zweig says, "to explain the intrinsic nature of his creed. There is no Rollandism," he says in rebuttal to Barbusse's mockery, "there is no formula, which could be written down and asserted''; rather it is the unity of work and personality as evidence of Rolland's security and goal-oriented spirit which evokes enthusiasm and belief in his followers. Zweig then outlines the development of Rolland's creed as he sees it. Music first taught Rolland to ''perceive all peoples as a unit of emotion, but he perceived music not only with the senses but also with his intellect, his ardor, his passions.'' In Rome he encountered his second world—that of the ancient edifices, the art of Leonardo and Michelangelo. ''But the third voice, Germany, was still lacking in the grand triad which our European culture essentially is''; this missing element he encountered in the person of Malvida von Meysenburg, for whom the death of Goethe in 1832, the revolution of 1848 were memorable experiences, the friend of Richard Wagner and Nietzsche, the last confidante of their great, world-encompassing ideas. Rolland had experienced the nations not from below, as a tourist perceives them from his vantage point in small hotels with petty discomforts, but from above, in the visions of the great and creative individuals. ''He learned to view heroically—each nation in her elite''; and from this knowledge of excellence inherent in all peoples he derived his strength and his calling to proclaim it to others. In the great times of disappointment, desolation, and despair he said to himself: ''Just as I am disappointed in the real world, so millions are disappointed: here one, there one in a room, a village, a city; and they know nothing about each other. They must be united now, these many lonely, disappointed people, in a new kind of community.'' He envisaged it as a community of spirits, of an elite of intellectuals from all nations—a community above petty political differences, nationalistic prejudices, personal advantage. This idea Zweig called ''our collective nation,'' or ''European destiny,'' and credits Rolland with having shaped it and nurtured it in a time of war when it was not possible to achieve it legally. ''Only recently I read that famous book again, *Au dessus de la mêlée*,'' Zweig writes about Rolland's war essays, ''that document of this battle, and I was surprised how little of an exciting nature it contained. How was it possible that this book was so inflammatory? Those are things which today everyone is saying, any statesman at any given hour, and no one finds it particularly daring or unwise''; but it must be remembered that at that time anyone with similar declarations was ''completely finished in his own country and in most others as well.'' (pp. 20-3)

Despite the many similarities of belief between the two men, there surfaces a fundamental difference of attitude in the acceptance of and in the adaptation to political change, which culminates in their differing reception of the Second World War, a disaster which they had both expected and attempted to prevent. Zweig heeded Rolland's call and sounded the warning of one crying in the wilderness. In 1919 he wrote about the ''Tragedy of Forgetting.'' One year has passed, he says, and already the truths learned in such bitter lessons are forgotten. 'More than ever the nations barricade themselves against each other; the generals, even the conquered ones, have become heroes again; the mouldy phrases serve again as bread of life.'' Tirelessly Zweig writes, travels, lectures for peace, reason, and understanding. He writes Rolland's biography, translates his works, edits the *Liber amicorum,* an homage to Rolland to which the famous and like-minded of many nations and professions contributed. He searches philosophy and history for examples to be held up against the powers of destruction. Portraits of Tolstoy, Ramuz, Jaurès, Rathenau, Montaigne, Chateaubriant, Weininger, and many others bring indirectly the message for the need of unification. In 1928 he travels to Russia at the invitation of the Russian government and returns to write

a long essay about his impressions. He finds much praise for the endurance of this people, but his concern belongs to the fate of the Russian intellectuals: ''They have not risen in their quality of life and into a higher freedom, but rather they have been thrown back into even more depressed and oppressed means and conditions of existence, into more restricted sphere of physical and emotional freedom. They are still the ones paying the highest and most unrecognized bitter tribute of this transition.'' It cannot be maintained that Zweig was inactive or remained passive, but his activity was of an essentially inbred, innate nature. He appealed to a large, but geographically diffuse group of intellectuals on their own terms and in their own sphere, largely removed from the political forces which wielded power. On May 10, 1933, his books were publicly burned, and in 1936 he reads in his lecture at Rio de Janeiro his ''Thanks to Brazil.'' ''I am speaking the truth when I say that it is difficult not to be happy here,'' he says, but the bitterness, the pain of his exile is evident in his closing words: ''And if I may ask something further of life in addition to the inexhaustible beauty I have seen and experienced here, it would be: to be permitted to return to this wonderful land.'' It is a pregnant sentence, a double-edged thanks, for he asks not to stay but to return—on a visit perhaps, in better days; yet he returned to stay. While working on his essay on Montaigne in Petropolis, Brazil, shortly before his death, he writes: ''If one can't dispose of these sufferings, one must make an end of it bravely and quickly. That is the only medicine.''

Rolland, too, knew the passions and the pain; he, too, was an idealist and a pacifist; but Rolland was also a political activist. Intrigued by the Indian nonviolent movement for independence, he wrote his biography of Mahatma Gandhi (1924) and the three volumes of *Essai sur la mystique et l'action de l'Inde vivante*. . . . He met with Gandhi and Tagore and urgently attempted to establish an international house of friendship, a ''center of intellectual resistance against the coming storm, to retain a connection between the European and Asian elite''; but for the Indians time had little meaning and Rolland lost patience. His sense of urgency heightened by the rise of the fascist element in Germany and Italy, Rolland saw only one power in Europe strong enough to conquer it. He, who had written in 1922, ''the neo-Marxist communist doctrine is incompatible with true human progress'' turned to it now in the hope that it would foster international unity and prevent war. In 1932 he presided in absentia at the International Congress Against War and Fascism in Amsterdam, and became honorary member of the Academy of Sciences in Leningrad. A year later he turned down the Goethe medal as a form of protest against the rise of Nazism in Germany. He engaged in writing ''open letters'' to German newspapers and fought literary battles with the intellectuals who chided him. His essay of 1934, **''Those Who Die in Mussolini's Prisons,''** immortalized the Italian communist leader Antonio Gramsci, and in 1935 he visited Gorki, returning convinced that Russia's example had to be emulated: ''In the chaos of all these conflicts only one great people . . . have realized the proletarian state . . . USSR.''

Rolland was nearly seventy years old then and he, too, was unable to change the events that shaped Europe for years to come; and not unlike Zweig he went into exile, although he remained in France. Shortly before the outbreak of the war he moved to a little village near his birthplace and remained secluded. In November, 1944, shortly before his death, he wrote his friend Jean-Richard Bloch: ''From our high walls which kept us prisoner without defending us, we have seen these days the beginnings of the pitiful exodus, then the invasion. . . . For

a long time we were occupied, under strong surveillance."
Like Zweig, Rolland suffered from this inner exile. In the same
letter he asked the friend to visit him: "One is so deprived of
true and faithful friends! We need each other to remain alive."
Rolland died a few weeks later in December 30, 1944 without
having seen Bloch again.

The exhortations of these two idealistic men seem strangely
naive in modern times. It is difficult to fathom that they were
persuaded that proclamations of a utopian philosophical goal
could effectively counteract the concrete economic, political,
and militaristic forces which united in preparation for the new
effort; but neither Rolland nor Zweig was unaware of these
realities. They were simply representatives of a unique era
which dealt in the realization of dreams—an era which fought
a war to end all wars, which offered idealism in the political
sphere with the League of Nations, and in science with the
Monist movement. They knew well that materialistic endeavors
alone would not rouse the nations to a new exchange of hostilities, and it must be remembered that it was the force of an
opposing ideology of hate, that of Hitler, which eventually
conquered the minds and led to the Holocaust. Zweig and
Rolland catered to the prevalent international yearning for a
creed, a sense of direction, a strong ideology, and in that
perspective their undertaking was a realistic attempt to gather
the scattered humanitarian forces. Perhaps economic necessity
will accomplish in future what moral concern failed to yield
in the past. (pp. 24-7)

> *Helene Kastinger Riley, "The Quest for Reason: Ste-*
> *fan Zweig's and Romain Rolland's Struggle for Pan-*
> *European Unity," in* Stefan Zweig: The World of
> Yesterday's Humanist Today, *edited by Marion Son-*
> *nenfeld, State University of New York Press, 1983,*
> *pp. 20-31.*

ADDITIONAL BIBLIOGRAPHY

Alden, Douglas W. "Proustian Configuration in *Jean-Christophe*."
The French Review XLI, No. 2 (November 1967): 262-71.
    Contends that, despite strong antipathy between Proust and Rol-
    land, their styles bear a mutual resemblance.

Baudoin, Charles. "Romain Rolland." In his *Contemporary Studies*,
pp. 62-78. Freeport, N.Y.: Books for Libraries Press, 1969.
    Discussion of Rolland's principal works to 1919.

Beiswanger, George W. "Artist, Philosopher, and the Ideal Society."
Journal of Philosophy XXVIII, No. 21 (8 October 1931): 574-80.
    Comparison of Rolland's aesthetics to those of Plato.

Boyd, Ernest. "Romain Rolland." *Saturday Review of Literature* II,
No. 7 (12 September 1925): 119.
    Negative review of *Summer*. Boyd concludes that "here is no
    promise of another *Jean-Christophe,* but rather a confirmation of
    the feeling that Romain Rolland had only that one great novel in
    him."

Browne, Waldo R. "Inter Arma Caritas." *The Dial* LX, No. 714 (16
March 1916): 277-79.
    Commends Rolland's pacifism as expressed in *Above the Battle.*

Cruickshank, John. "The Nature of Artistic Creation in the Works of
Romain Rolland." *The Modern Language Review* XLVI, Nos. 3 & 4
(July & October 1951): 379-87.
    Examines Rolland's attitude toward didactic art.

Cunliffe, J. W., and De Bacourt, Pierre. "Romain Rolland." In their
French Literature during the Last Half Century, pp. 190-201. New
York: Macmillan Co., 1927.
    Discussion of Rolland's life and major works.

Fisher, David James. "Romain Rolland and the Ideology and Aesthetics of French People's Theatre." *Theatre Quarterly* IX, No. 33
(Spring 1979): 83-103.
    Comprehensive discussion of Rolland's theory and practice of
    theater for the mass audience and an examination of the socio-
    political environment which influenced him.

Francis, R. A. "Romain Rolland and Jean-Jacques Rousseau." *Nottingham French Studies* VIII, No. 1 (May 1969): 40-53.
    Examines some similarities and differences in the backgrounds,
    personalities, and ideas of Rolland and Rousseau, concluding that
    "Rolland was the lesser artist because he was the greater man."

——. "Romain Rolland and Science: Parts I and II." *Nottingham
French Studies* X, Nos. 1, 2 (May 1971; October 1971): 21-32, 74-86.
    Explores the impact of contemporary natural science on Rolland's
    ideas.

——. "Romain Rolland and Gandhi: A Study in Communication."
Journal of European Studies 5, No. 4 (December 1975): 291-307.
    Chronological account of the contact between Rolland and Gan-
    dhi.

——. "Romain Rolland and Some British Intellectuals during the
War." *Journal of European Studies* 10, No. 3 (September 1980):
189-209.
    Historical account of Rolland's relations with prominent British
    intellectuals, including Bernard Shaw and H. G. Wells, and of
    his efforts to enlist their support for his pacifist cause during World
    War I.

Guérard, Albert Leon. "Romain Rolland." In his *Five Masters of
French Romance,* pp. 252-96. New York: Charles Scribner's Sons,
1916.
    Discussion of Rolland's life, *Jean-Christophe,* and *Above the
    Battle.*

Hanley, David. "A Marriage of Convenience? Romain Rolland's First
Encounters with Socialism." *European Studies Review* 9, No. 2 (April
1979): 211-36.
    Points to those aspects of Rolland's thought which led him nat-
    urally to embrace socialism.

Harris, Frederick John. *André Gide and Romain Rolland: Two Men
Divided.* New Brunswick, N.J.: Rutgers University Press, 1973, 282
p.
    Study of the attitudes Gide and Rolland "adopted toward each
    other and of the impressions they formed of each other as persons
    and as artists."

Kahn, Lothar. "Romain Rolland and the Jews." *Chicago Jewish Forum*
26, No. 3 (Spring 1968): 201-04.
    Examination of Rolland's Jewish characters.

Moore, Charles H. "Rolland and Hauptmann before the Melee."
Romanic Review LI, No. 2 (April 1960): 103-14.
    Discusses the reasons for the public dispute between Rolland and
    German playwright Gerhart Hauptmann, which centered on the
    morality of war.

Price, Lucien. "Romain Rolland Converses." *Atlantic Monthly* 156,
No. 6 (December 1935): 718-26.
    Account of Price's conversations with Rolland in 1919.

Sapir, Edward. "*Jean-Christophe:* An Epic of Humanity." *The Dial*
LXII, No. 742 (17 May 1917): 423-26.
    Praises the comprehensive nature of *Jean-Christophe.*

Scales, Derek P. "Feeling for Nature in Romain Rolland." *Australian Journal of French Studies* IX, No. 1 (January-April 1972): 40-54.
> Textual analysis focusing on Rolland's reverence for the natural world.

Sice, David. *Music and the Musician in "Jean-Christophe."* New Haven: Yale University Press, 1968, 185 p.
> Study of *Jean-Christophe* which focuses on the impact of music theory upon both the style and content of that work.

Review of *Jean-Christophe,* by Romain Rolland. *Spectator* 110, No. 4425 (19 April 1913): 656-58.
> Laudatory review of *Jean-Christophe* in which the critic finds that the work "has given to the world something definitely new in form, in spirit, and in ideal."

Starr, William T. "Romain Rolland and Some Italian Contemporaries." *Symposium* VIII, No. 2 (Winter 1954): 273-88.
> Discusses the influence of Giovanni Papini, Benedetto Croce, and Gabriele D'Annunzio in Rolland's life and works.

———. *Romain Rolland and a World at War.* Evanston, Il.: Northwestern University Press, 1956, 223 p.
> Examines in depth the nature, origins, and effects of Rolland's pacifism.

———. "Water Symbols in the Novels of Romain Rolland." *Neophilogus* LVI, No. 2 (April 1972): 146-61.
> Discusses the importance of water imagery in Rolland's fiction.

Stephens, Winifred. "Romain Rolland" and *"Jean-Christophe."* In her *French Novelists of Today,* pp. 97-136, pp. 139-76. London: John Lane, 1915.
> Discussion of the major influences and events in Rolland's life and a summary of *Jean-Christophe* which focuses in particular on Rolland's "Teutonism."

Strauss, Harold. "Rolland's Novel of Disillusion." *The New York Times Book Review* (15 October 1933): 6.
> Review of *The Death of a World* in the *L'âme enchantée* novel cycle. Strauss considers *L'âme enchantée* an attack on "the four complacent bourgeois strongholds: the family; morality (so called); the political State; and greed, the evil of property."

Watson, G. "Socialism and Revolution in *Jean-Christophe.*" *Essays in French Literature,* No. 2 (November 1965): 30-42.
> Examines Rolland's ambiguous attitude toward socialism.

Weinberg, Albert K. "The Dream in *Jean-Christophe.*" *The Journal of Abnormal Psychology* XIII, No. 1 (April 1918): 12-16.
> Thorough analysis of Ada's dream in *L'adolescent,* which the critic considers an unintentional affirmation of Freudian theory.

Zweig, Stefan. *Romain Rolland.* New York: Thomas Seltzer, 1921, 377 p.
> Biography written by a friend and colleague.

Sait Faik (Abasıyanık)

1906-1954

(Born Sait Faik; last name Abasıyanık added in accordance with the Surname Law passed in 1934 by the Turkish Republic. The author published his works as Sait Faik, and he is correctly referred to by this name used in full, since Faik does not serve as a last name. Today, many Turkish publications list him under Abasıyanık.) Turkish short story and novella writer, novelist, poet, journalist, and translator.

Sait Faik is accorded great importance among Turkish short story writers for his highly individual use of this form when it was still new to his country's literature. Prior to the late nineteenth century, Turkish literature was primarily composed of either poetry written by and for the Ottoman elite or of stories modelled after an oral tradition of folktales. With the expanding influence of Western European culture in the 1870s, literary forms in Eastern nations underwent a corresponding transformation, and in Turkey the influence of such French novelists as Guy de Maupassant, Gustave Flaubert, and Emile Zola was very strong. In the 1920s, during the process of radical Westernization which took place under the regime of Mustafa Kemal Atatürk, social realist fiction of the type encouraged in the Soviet Union came to dominate the Turkish literary scene. Contrasting with this trend, Sait Faik practiced a more intimate and subjective manner of expression by writing autobiographical short stories which are nonetheless considered adept portrayals of life in his society. Combining a realist's powers of observation with a romantic's sensibility, Sait Faik's stories provide what William C. Hickman has termed "snapshots" of life, especially among the lower classes, in the city of Istanbul.

The son of a prosperous lumber merchant and his wife, Sait Faik was born and grew up in Adapzarı, a city of northwest Anatolia. In 1923, the family moved to Istanbul, where Sait Faik later attended the Bursa Lycée. After receiving his degree in 1928, he began post-graduate studies at the University of Istanbul, and the following year published his first story, "Kites," in an Istanbul daily. He left the university to study economics in Lausanne, Switzerland, but almost immediately changed his plans and traveled to Grenoble, France, studying French at the Champollion Lycée. Sait Faik traveled throughout France for several years in the early 1930s, during which time he also published his short stories in the Turkish literary journal *Varlık*. In 1934 he returned to Istanbul, where he taught briefly in a school for orphans and undertook a business venture which failed. After these two attempts at conventional occupations, along with a short-lived career as a court reporter for an Istanbul newspaper, Sait Faik supported himself by his writing and by income from property bequeathed by his father. Sait Faik's first collection of stories, *Semaver,* appeared in 1936, and he continued to publish his work at regular intervals until his death. Otherwise, he led the life of an idle wanderer in the streets and coffeehouses of Istanbul, associating more often with common people and social outsiders than with Turkish literary society. For the last five years of his life his health deteriorated from cirrhosis of the liver, the result of longtime heavy drinking. He died at the age of forty-seven.

In a retrospective essay on his literary career, Sait Faik wrote: "[It] does not matter much, in the writing profession, if a

man's writings are not that good. It is enough to be honest, not to sell our pen either to the government or to the boss, not even to the people." It is from this precept of artistic honesty that the major qualities of Sait Faik's work derive, most apparently his plainspoken prose style and his unaffected portrayals of the poor and outcast. Throughout his career, Sait Faik depicted the harsh lives of beggars, orphans, small merchants, thieves, fishermen, prostitutes, and various ethnic minorities, but he did not sentimentalize them or reduce their suffering to a literary protest for political reforms, as was the prevailing custom among his contemporaries. Such figures were part of Sait Faik's daily life, and he found these people far more real and interesting than any abstract platform of values which would attempt to improve their lot. He was consequently censured by socialist critics for what they considered the morally uncommitted nature of his writings; ironically, it is the force of his judgments of the people and events around him that constitutes a primary interest of his work. Concerned above all with honest personal expression, he was not averse to an unpatronizing view of his subjects, as in the story "I Kept Grumbling," where the narrator writes: "You tell yourself that you like poor people. That's a lie. Deep down, you don't believe in what you're saying. Which poor people? What sort of poor? That monstrous beggar woman? The fisherman who goes on his knees before any worthless person? Or that rowdy chestnut peddler at the street corner who dumps his rotten chestnuts on a man whose face mirrors hunger, loneliness, a touch of madness, and world-weariness?'' While this outburst is an example of the splenetic undertone which critics find throughout Sait Faik's fiction, its message qualifies rather than negates the author's sensitivity to the suffering of others. According to Talat Sait Halman: ''The central theme of Sait Faik's fiction might well be summarized as *the happiness of ordinary people thwarted*.'' This statement is especially well exemplified by one of Sait Faik's earliest stories, ''Samovar,'' which begins with the symbolic title object appearing to the main character ''like a factory where there was no suffering, no strikes, no accidents,'' and concludes with the simile: ''Steaming like brass samovars, blond workers—their noses running, minds bent on strike, hearts heavy. . . .''

In Sait Faik's stories, the first-person voice predominates and often wanders into private dreams and escapist visions as it tells of the banal or grotesque vicissitudes of Istanbul's lower classes. Poetic impressions of Istanbul life accumulate from one story to the next, creating a scrapbook of characters, places, and atmospheres. In ''The Neighborhood Coffeehouse,'' for instance, the central drama of the story remains fragmentary, without resolution or message, and does not take precedence over the narrator's aesthete-like perceptions of the scene before him. As William C. Hickman states: ''There is a tension . . . in Sait Faik's stories between the worlds of work and art, action and reflection. The author had a dream of their reconciliation, a dream made manifest on the one hand in his enduring interest in and feeling of solidarity with the common people whom he neither idealized nor romanticized. On the other hand the author's dream or vision finds its way into the stories in the form of fantasy or daydream. It is this which, perhaps more than anything, is a mark of Sait Faik's short fiction.'' For this individual method of literary expression, Sait Faik is considered one of the most important short story writers in Turkish literature.

PRINCIPAL WORKS

Semaver (short stories) 1936
Sarnıç (short stories) 1939
Şahmerdan (short stories) 1940
Medâri maişet motoru (novella) 1944; also published as
   Birtakım İnsanlar [revised edition], 1952
Lüzumsuz adam (short stories) 1948
Mahalle kahvesi (short stories) 1950
Havada bulut (short stories) 1951
Kumpanya (novella) 1951
Havuz başı (short stories) 1952
Son kuşlar (short stories) 1952
Kayıp aranıyor (novel) 1953
Şimdi sevişme vakti (poetry) 1953
Alemdağda var bir yilan (short stories) 1954
Az şekerli (short stories) 1954
Tüneldeki çocuk (short stories) 1955
A Dot on the Map: Selected Short Stories and Poems
   (short stories and poems) 1983

SAIT FAIK (essay date 1949?)

[*In the following excerpt, Sait Faik looks back on his career as a writer.*]

If a person could truthfully measure himself, how many people would be left in the field of literature and journalism? Good or bad, I have been writing for twenty years. I neither believe it if they praise me, nor do I let it bother me too much if they attack me. And, as far as I am concerned, it does not matter much, in the writing profession, if a man's writings are not that good. It is enough to be honest, not to sell our pen either to the government, or to the boss, not even to the people. I am saying this thinking of demagoguery, of the microbe called ''public opinion.'' There is more to it. I do not know if I have the right to consider myself a writer, since I do not write with the intention of pleasing that creature we fear most—the critic—and not even the reader. Once I was asked what my profession was. To tell the truth, with considerable hesitation, but proudly, I said ''writer.'' This was to fill in my profession in the proper space in a document. The officials asked me for an official paper to prove that I was a writer. ''Sir,'' I almost said, ''I am the author of a few books of short stories,'' but I realized quickly that these could not be used as proof.

Once I used to write stories and do reporting for a certain paper. I used to get ten liras for my interviews and features, and five for the short stories. My mother, bless her, kept the house going and food on the table with money left by my father. I used to get five to ten liras a week from that place I mentioned. I could go to the café, and I lived a contented life.

Was it improper to turn to that place that published my writings? My business would have been taken care of if they had been kind enough to give me a short note saying: ''We confirm that the gentleman called Sait Faik writes for us; short stories for five liras, interviews and features for ten. He is a fool.'' No sir, they did not give it to me. No, my friend, they did not. ''We cannot give you a letter. If that office wants it, let them call. We will tell them over the phone,'' they said. Was I to say, ''Please, I beg you''? I cannot say that, damn it. I took my poor self out of there and went to Gülhane Park [a park near the Palace of Topkaı in Istanbul]. There I remembered something. Once I was a member of a society. Since I was late with my membership dues, they had asked for them in a letter. And they had written that if I paid my monthly dues, they would be honored to have me again among their members. I felt ashamed, borrowed the twenty-five liras from my mother—never to be repaid—and paid my dues. I was probably still a member of that society. After all, I had paid my debt, right? And an official letter from that society would not only have proved that I was a writer, but would have convinced the world even if I had never touched a pen.

They asked me to bring the receipt they had given me for the dues paid. I turned the house upside down, found the receipt and took it to them. They found another excuse. Somehow they just could not say that I was a writer. They could not bring themselves to verify my profession as a writer.

There it is. From that day on I realized that I was a writer, I was really a writer; and that is why I cannot write.

This is because there is a great responsibility on the writer of today. This responsibility is only to see the truth and write the truth. I never wrote as a favor to anybody nor for anybody's pleasure, but I have written a lot of sentences for my own pleasure. When I remove them from my writing, I will still write for *Yeditepe* [a literary magazine published in Istanbul]. Now, if you'd excuse me. . . .

Oh yes. . . . They wrote "none" in the place for profession in that document. The Turkish word did not bother me too much. But there was also a French section to that document. There too they wrote *sans profession*, and that made the blood rush to my head. (It is a long story to tell the reason, and it is unnecessary.) The friends to whom I tell the incident die laughing. What can I do? I go along with them; so we laugh together.

But now, whoever asks me "What do you do?" I answer proudly, "I am a writer." Previously I used to be ashamed. I'd falter and say, "I am an author," which sounded pretty suspicious even to me. What a fool I was. Look, I am a pure, unadulterated writer. If I wasn't one, I would have certainly gotten a pretentious letter from both of these places. Because in both places there is not a single person who has held a pen in his hand, or, if he has, who has not at least thought of making money with it.

Thank God, now *Yeditepe* doesn't pay its writers. I would have asked for at least five liras for this piece. And then, when I got the five liras I would have worried and wondered, "Why did I cheat poor Hüsam? Is this piece worth five liras?" (pp. 21-3)

> *Sait Faik, "In the Twentieth Year of Being a Writer,"*
> *translated by Stoyan Peycheff, in his* A Dot on the
> Map: Selected Stories and Poems, *edited by Talat*
> *Sait Halman, Indiana University Turkish Studies,*
> *1983, pp. 21-3.*

KEMAL H. KARPAT   (essay date 1960-61)

[*In the following excerpt from an essay on modern Turkish literature, Karpat offers a brief, general discussion of Sait Faik's fiction.*]

A specialist in those moods of "spleen" that once inspired such nineteenth century masters as Baudelaire, Gogol, Stephen Crane or Arthur Schnitzler, Sait Faik—departing from the formalistic, tortuous, over-idealized writing of the past—has left us some wonderfully tender and dreamlike vignettes that reveal odd aspects, sections and characters of Istanbul, a city that deserves as great writers to unravel its complex mysteries as Paris or old St. Petersburg, Vienna or New York. The undisputed master of Turkish prose, Sait Faik's work reveals few traceable literary influences. (p. 298)

His short stories find lovable aspects in every incident and every human being, however insignificant. "If men are not to love each other, why do they build such crowded cities?" he said—an expression which epitomizes his philosophy. Sait Faik chose all his subjects from the lower classes of the Istanbul scene—peddlers, fishermen, small merchants, petty white collar workers—and he presented them without idealization or even dramatization, yet his short stories, when taken together, are the drama of the little man who tries to earn a living and lives from day to day with his dreams and worries. Sait Faik does not pity him because he is insignificant, rather he admires him, for his unimportance neither crushes nor prevents his being happy and having his own personality and his own, to him, important pursuits. This precisely is what endears all his heroes to the reader. Sait Faik's style and insight have left a deep impact upon the younger generation. In this respect, without intending it, he has been a school of his own. (pp. 298-99)

> *Kemal H. Karpat, "Contemporary Turkish Litera-*
> *ture," in* The Literary Review, *Vol. 4, No. 2, Winter,*
> *1960-61, pp. 287-302.*

WILLIAM C. HICKMAN   (essay date 1976)

[*Hickman is a critic and translator of Turkish literature. In the following excerpt, a slightly revised version of an essay originally published in 1976, Hickman provides social and literary background pertinent to Sait Faik's fiction and examines the author's technique of blending reality and fantasy in his stories.*]

In a country and among a people where the oral tradition of storytelling is demonstrably old, the literary short story in Turkey is a product only of the twentieth century. . . . The short story . . . had no immediate predecessor in Turkish literature, being neither anecdote nor simply a shortened version of the novel. It is for this reason perhaps that the short story, in the true sense of the term, appeared somewhat later than the first Turkish novels and the "Westernized" poetry. It is something of a curiosity then that while the novel is known even today by its French name, *roman*, the short story, a genuinely new creation in Turkish literature is called—from Arabic—*hikâye* (sometimes also *küçük hikâye:* "narration," "relation" or even "episode"), a term which only in recent years has begun to give way to the Turkish neologism, *öykü.*

Despite its novelty the Turkish short story, in the brief span of three-quarters of a century, has had several outstanding practitioners. Sait Faik is by no means the least among these. (p. 25)

Born in the waning years of the reign of Sultan Abdül Hamid II, the last sovereign to assert vigorously the leadership of the Ottoman dynasty, Sait Faik grew up at a time when Turkish prose literature was moving in new directions. The influence of Guy de Maupassant, Emile Zola and other French realist writers was strong. Even before he graduated from high school—in the year that Mustafa Kemal (Atatürk) introduced the Latin-based modern Turkish alphabet and launched a sweeping program of language reform—the young Sait Faik was probably reading the works of Ömer Seyfettin, Refik Halid Karay, Reşat Nuri Güntekin and Halide Edip Adıvar, prominent among the writers of the early twentieth century who tried to bring Turkish literature into closer touch with Turkish society at all levels. Their works tended to deal more with the petty bureaucrats, townspeople and middle class population than with the sometimes cosmopolitan upper class Istanbul society which had figured prominently in the works of their predecessors. On the other hand the generation born in the 1880s, a prolific decade for Turkish literature, became increasingly caught up, in the years of full maturity, in the strongly nationalist direction of Turkish politics. Some also found themselves in exile as a result of opposition to the policies of the new Republican regime. All told, their influence on Sait Faik is minimal.

As the young Republic turned to the problems of Anatolia and its rural population, an overwhelming majority in the country, "social realist" writing emerged. It was not the young man from Adapazarı, however, but another young writer, Sabahattin Ali, born in the same year as Sait Faik, who became one of the early, and perhaps best known, outspoken champions of the illiterate and largely unseen and unheard masses. His classically structured stories, with dramatically defined plots, a powerful emotional appeal and straightforward, uncluttered style, bring home forcefully the plight of the rural citizenry. Sabahattin Ali skillfully and succinctly described the thoughtless injustice perpetrated and perpetuated by a strongly centralized national government, the tyranny of local gendarmes and the hopeless grinding poverty which wore down the villagers and drove them into bitter life-and-death struggles with one another. The social realist school of writing which emerged in Turkey in the 1930s and gained added impetus in the 1950s after the publication, by the young schoolteacher Mahmut Makal, of the eye-opening personal account *Bizim Köy* (Our Village, 1949; English translation: *A Village in Anatolia,* translated by Wyndham Deedes, 1954), continues strongly down to the present time. The works of such writers as Fakir Baykurt, Samim Kocagöz and Kemal Tahir are adequate testimony as much to the persistence of basic social and economic problems, rural backwardness and the need for land reform, as to the continuing dedication of writers of great idealism and zeal.

The literature of social protest in Turkey has produced a number of solid works of fiction. Not surprisingly, however, that movement has tended to dominate and to arrogate to itself the mainstream of Turkish literature. Literary criticism has been affected as well and an observer from outside the country senses that the message of protest is sometimes valued as highly as the artistic accomplishment. It is not strange, therefore, to find Sait Faik judged, on occasion, as a representative, if eccentric, of the social protest movement. While there is no doubt that he was a champion of the common man, an ardent defender of justice, honesty, integrity, and simple human decency, it is a mistake to view Sait Faik's writing solely, or even primarily, from that point of view. To do so is to circumscribe sharply a just appreciation of his life's work. While there are occasional digressions into social polemic in his stories—and these should be kept separate from his non-fiction writings, a division not always as clear as one would expect—Sait Faik wrote with an unmistakable sense of the artistic. Too solitary a man to have cared much for doctrinaire interpretations of class struggle, Sait Faik was nevertheless an unstinting champion of human dignity, and thought of himself as such. Speaking of an earlier generation of writers—perhaps the one immediately preceding his own—he is reported to have said:

> They did not become involved in life. Speaking from the heights, they desperately wanted to remake society. But for ourselves, we have no such pretensions. We only want to live the same life, in society, with our fellow men.

As Tahir Alangu has commented, it seemed that "Sait Faik had appeared on the scene to save the short story from the hands of 'those who make literature'." But paradox is clear enough and did not escape the Turkish critic: "We find (in him) a man who, while at first sight appearing to give no value to art and literature, in fact devoted his whole life to that end."

To put it only slightly differently, Sait Faik was a man with a utopian dream whose idealism was tempered by a strong introspective bent and a penchant for daydreaming. If that latter weakness diminished by one the ranks of social reformers, it undoubtedly contributed to the development of a brilliant, although erratic, writer and stylist, and helped boost the author to his enviable position among the leading prose artists of Republican Turkish literature.

A son of Anatolia, Sait Faik left the provincial, landlocked city of his childhood at age seventeen and later went to Istanbul. He never returned. While Ankara had become the center of nationalist political fervor and the gathering place of a growing number of young intellectuals and writers, it is not hard to

understand the influence which the sprawling, cosmopolitan, former Ottoman capital had on a young man perhaps with vague literary, but no political or social aspirations. As temperamental as the weather and waterways which surround and envelop it, the city had a strong attraction for Sait Faik. The settings for his stories are seaside cafés, the coffee shops and taverns of working class districts, trams, "the bridge" (Galata Bridge over the Golden Horn), boat landings and above all the sea itself with its Princes' Islands, especially the lesser Kınalı, Burgaz and Sivriada. That world is animated by the keepers of small shops, roving street sellers, the "unemployed," and of course the fishermen, mostly Greek.

A picture emerges, and for one who knows the city it evokes strong memories. But Sait Faik does not present a "whole" city. The Istanbul which stands out in relief from his stories is both literally and figuratively a city without skyline. Neither the Byzantine nor the Ottoman heritage provides any source of point of reference for the author. There is no echo of history here. Sait Faik is concerned not with majestic and towering structures, but with the lives of ordinary people who crowd the streets in their shadows below. The immediate events and issues of his own time are similarly ignored. A sense of timelessness prevails. Only the seasons change while the years stand still. As Kemal Karpat has very aptly observed, Istanbul "deserves as great writers to unravel its complex mysteries as Paris or old St. Petersburg, Vienna or New York," but Sait Faik was not—and certainly would not have imagined himself to be—the man for that task, having no panoramic view of the city. The stories, to use Karpat's phrase, have the character of "tender and dreamlike vignettes" rather than the grand appearance of tapestry.

If the wide-angle lens was not part of Sait Faik's working equipment, the candid camera was. And what we have in his stories, one might suggest, is a collection of snapshots some of which, at first sight, appear out of focus, and others taken off balance or at odd angles. Here and there the composition and cropping seem hasty and unfinished. Above all the photographer, or a remarkable likeness, seems constantly to have placed himself in front of the camera just before the shutter was released. In the same way that a single figure may appear time after time in the pictures of a snapshot album, so Sait Faik steps out at us again and again as we turn the pages of his stories. But to carry the analogy one step further: while the author reappears in his own "pictures" these are only oblique self-portraits.

If we approach Sait Faik's works expecting classic short story development, certainly we will be put off. The stories seem loosely constructed and meandering. There is little development of plot in the familiar sense. We reach the end of a story with the impatient feeling that "nothing happened." True: "action" is held to a minimum. But then Sait Faik, from all we know, was never a "man of action." The events of his stories are meditations, events of the mind. The fishermen whose boats the narrator shares—Kalafat, Barba Antimos, Barba Vasili—and the others, the casual acquaintances and vendors, all of them, however deftly sketched, remain in the last analysis vague and ill defined as fictional characters.

Frank O'Connor, the Irish critic and author himself of several volumes of short stories, has suggested that what identifies the short story, as distinct from the novel, is its "submerged population group"—a phrase he apparently coined but admittedly didn't like—whether officials, serfs, prostitutes or provincials. "Always in the short story," he wrote, "there is this sense of outlawed figures wandering about the fringes of society. . . . As a result there is in the short story at its most characteristic . . . an intense awareness of human loneliness." Outlawed or not, and O'Connor of course meant the term in its broadest possible sense, including particularly social and economic exclusion, the country of Sait Faik's stories has its own well-defined "submerged population": the fishermen, sellers and the rest. Nevertheless the "little people," whom the author sensitively and sympathetically sketches, for the most part fail to emerge in their own right. The narrator, too, plays a prominent role, and the stories, it turns out, are often as much about him as about them. The narrator as artist-writer becomes the representative of another submerged population group, although not at all the same one to which the other characters belong. The "lonely voice," again to appropriate one of O'Connor's apt phrases, is as much that of the artist-narrator as of the common man.

It may be worth pointing out, although the reader will surely discover it for himself, that once the narrator is identified with the writer-artist figure it is only one more step to the equation: narrator = author (Sait Faik). It is difficult to resist taking that step since Sait Faik generally insisted on a first-person narrative. But that association serves mainly to distract, for any writing is an extension of the writer, a part of his life, and hence autobiographical. It may be interesting to read Sait Faik's stories for clues to the author's biography, but we should remember that what he intended was fiction, not autobiographical snippets.

The common man and the writer-artist, these were the two fascinations of the author. It is a rare story in which both are absent. The two, however, do not coexist naturally, and while the narrator, simply by his physical presence, bridges the gulf which opens up between their two worlds, an intellectual and emotional gulf remains. It is that distance, the separateness—real or imaginary—of those worlds which preoccupied Sait Faik.

The subjects from which he drew inspiration for his stories, which provided the keys to unlock stored up treasures of imagination and fantasy, and which offered the absolutely essential strength and nourishment of comradeship and company to a man who otherwise lived somewhat aloof, these people in the end could neither appreciate the subtlety of his reflection nor verbalize a response to them. The company that he kept was fundamentally important for the author-narrator, but fell short of providing that completely meaningful communication which he demanded. The stories provided that necessary outlet. In the stories, then, the narrator remains a man apart, an exile by choice, ironically, in his own adopted land. He felt he was not understood and therefore had to return, over and over again, to his pencil and paper which were at the same time passion and refuge. In an often-quoted passage from the story **"Haritada Bir Nokta"** (**"A Dot on the Map"**) he gives a compelling description of his commitment to writing:

> I had promised myself: I wasn't going to write a thing. What was writing anyway but a passion and greed? Here in the company of honest, upright people I was going to await death, quietly. What need did I have for greed and rage? But I couldn't do it. I ran to the tobacconist and bought pencil and paper. I sat down. I took out the pocketknife that I carried for whittling little sticks in case I got bored walking along the deserted roads of the island. I sharpened

> my pencil. Then I held it and kissed it. I'd go crazy if I couldn't write.
> (translated by William C. Hickman)

There is tension, then, in Sait Faik's stories between the worlds of work and art, action and reflection. The author had a dream of their reconciliation, a dream made manifest on the one hand in his enduring interest in and feeling of solidarity with the common people whom he neither idealized nor romanticized. On the other hand the author's dream or vision finds its way into the stories in the form of fantasy or daydream. It is this which, perhaps more than anything, is a mark of Sait Faik's short fiction. And not only that. It becomes a fundamental element in his technique of fictional narrative. In its most generalized form this illusory device can be seen in the identification of author with narrator, especially when the narrator is cast in the role of storyteller, as he often is. Thus many of the stories immediately have the character of story-within-a-story. The author takes pains, on occasion, to confuse further the narrator's identity, playing a kind of verbal hide-and-seek with the reader, as for example in the opening of his **"Balikcisini Bulan Olta"** (**"The Line Which Found Its Fisherman"**). Taking a different tack, the author relates, in a number of stories, an undisguised fantasy or reverie. In so doing he explicitly delineates two levels of reality. Sometimes an entire story has a dreamlike cast, as for example **"Bir Kaya Parcası Gibi"** (**"Like a Bit of Rock Cliff"**). The fog closes in and the "real" world of familiar landmarks disappears, for a time at least. A perfect symbol of the creative thought process in which ties to concrete realities are loosened and the imagination drifts on waters where charts are of no value, the fog is a recurring image in Sait Faik's stories.

The technique of confusing or juxtaposing reality and fantasy is entirely too consistent, at least in the later stories, to be fortuitous. Sait Faik seems bent on a game of systematic deception. In whatever particular form it takes, the technique is a convenient mirror, stylistically, to the underlying existential conflict between the worlds of thought and action. This antagonism is perhaps nowhere more vivid—nor the use of the dream technique more straightforward—than in **"Sivriada Geceleri"** (**"Sivriada Nights"**).

First published in 1952, **"Sivriada Nights"** is a fine example of the care and craftsmanship of which the author was capable. The death of a seagull, a brief dramatic moment midway through the story, serves to trigger the narrator's imagination, and divides the narrative neatly between observation of the routine activities of the fishermen and description of his own response to the bird's death. The harmony and rhythms of work and nature are disturbed. The vigorous, gruff Kalafat, preoccupied with the tiring tasks of earning a living from the sea, and Sotiri, the young friend and helper, are indifferent to the bird's last agony. For the narrator, however, whose physical contribution to the fishing trip is significant, the death becomes a total distraction. Disoriented, he loses touch with the reality of his companions' presence. His utter preoccupation with the bird and his tender, compassionate care for it at the moment before death are worthy of a human friend, as indeed the author makes clear through the traditional Moslem death-bed ritual of offering drops of water to slake the thirst of temptation and ward off the devil. This sensitivity irritates Kalafat who sharply mocks his uselessness by accusing him of being "a poet." How to explain to them his mourning, inner confusion, and nagging sense of guilt and physical inadequacy? The narrator takes the reader on an imaginary journey, foreshadowed by a passing reference earlier in the story, back to the "days of creation" where we see a primordial, even archetypal enactment of the clash of human natures. Then emerging from this reverie with a new-found strength he tries to prove his worth by spinning a yarn which will both entertain and explain his feelings. The "story-within-a-story" is a failure, but the narrator has found his way. Toward morning the sight of a boat passing in the dark waters stimulates the narrator's imagination once again. Wanting to share his excitement, to try again to convey the thrill of emotion, and perhaps now to offset at the sight of a simple thing of beauty, the earlier morbid fascination with death and loss, he awakens Kalafat, only to be rebuked again for his foolishness.

Sait Faik sets aside completely the tight development of the preceding story in the composition of **"Sevgiliye Mektup"** (**"Love Letter"**). Here we have a meditation, a monologue so to speak, on the conflict between simple, hedonistic enjoyment of pleasure and the demands of the real world in a time of war and violence. The tension between the two is suggested at the outset in the references to "the world situation" and "my feelings about you" and runs on through the story like a thread. The writer recalls an incident from the Turkish War of Independence during his childhood. The pleasure of the experience—the gathering of the family, the physical closeness and the long-remembered sensation of garish facial color in the lightning flashes—outweighs the fright of the moment. From recollection to fantasy, the letter writer leaps through time. Spinning a delicate daydream, he proposes a reunion with his beloved to put out of mind the loneliness of winter months, and in a single long meandering sentence—it takes up nearly a quarter of this very short story—lyrically describes his idyllic vision: a boat ride in shallow, placid waters. The miracles and simple marvels of nature are an image of love, exquisite yet transient as the gossamer of the daydream itself. The mood changes again, as imperceptibly as the breeze, and the idyll becomes the reality of a world of aggressions and pretense.

Having posed the terms of his own private debate—the one to whom the letter is addressed might well be the writer's conscience personified—he is free to indulge in polemic and speculation, and here the letter, as story, threatens to collapse under the sheer weight and artlessness of his argument. In a series of short, choppy paragraphs the writer lashes out bitterly against the "war-makers" who in the end seem to be broadly, if vaguely, identified with philosophers, critics and, generally, the world at large. As if aware that his strident tone can only further antagonize, he brings the letter to an abrupt end. Assuming a defensive posture he returns once again to the promise of an outing, to be put off now until the summer. And not everything, we note, will be exactly as promised.

While **"Love Letter"** is perhaps technically flawed by the intrusion of a disconcerting polemic, the story again shows clearly the author's preoccupation with reality and fantasy. The writer's tender profession of love, in the form of a vision, is a lyric tour de force, and contrasts sharply with austere wartime conditions of the early forties when the story was written. Less the artist than in other stories, the narrator here seems to speak for all men for whom the idealized realization of love is a far different matter from the workaday world. Steering a clear course between the dangerous shoals of banality and sentimentality the writer leaves us with a convincing picture of human sensitivity, frustration and hurt.

Sait Faik was fond of the character sketch and his collected works include several examples of this sort: **"Birahanedeki**

Adam" (**"The Man in the Pub"**), **"Baba Oğul"** (**"Father and Son"**), **"Hayvanca Gülen Adam"** (**"The Man with the Idiot Smile"**). A sub-group among these is a smaller number of stories which utilize as their characteristic narrative style the interview; one such is **"Diş ve Diş Ağrısı Nedir Bilmeyen Adam"** (**"The Man Who Doesn't Know What a Tooth or a Toothache Is"**). An acquaintance of the narrator, Bay Ferit Yazgan—otherwise Ferit Bey—is a man without a tooth in his head. He is, in fact, a man who never had any teeth. An oddity of nature, Ferit Bey strikes us as a more likely candidate for inclusion in the strange collection of characters in *Ripley's Believe It or Not* than the subject of a short story. The interview proceeds apparently without aim. The writer-interviewer prods Ferit Bey on matters of diet and expands on the unimaginable good fortune of never knowing the traumas of the dentist's chair. In his turn Ferit Bey is determined to remind us of a recent history of digestion difficulties. Then sensing the interviewer's interest in his life history, he jots down a brief autobiographical account. The interview ends with Ferit Bey's suggestion that they get together again over a beer, if only they can talk a little less about teeth!

Is Sait Faik simply having a good joke at our expense? Is this all an innocuous put-on? The "man who doesn't know what a tooth or a toothache is" is not such a unique figure after all. The author insists that reality is not what it appears to be. In purely physiological terms Ferit Bey's remarkable jaw bone will tell us nothing about his digestion, while his conversation is anything but remarkable. The author provides the story with an added twist in his parting comment, a direct clue to his purpose in case the intentionally unpretentious character of the narrative has lulled us into unresponsiveness.

Sait Faik was fascinated by the extraordinary characters whom he created. But he makes us see immediately that these, including even the grotesque among them, are only the reflections of "ordinary" human beings in the curved mirror of our own minds. It is we who turn Ferit Bey into a curiosity, we who rob him of a rightful anonymity. By setting our own terms it is we who misjudge and consequently misunderstand.

Seemingly disinterested in the narrow but penetrating mainstream of Turkish language "reform" or "purification" (*özleşme*), Sait Faik used the established well-accepted vocabulary to make Turkish an extremely flexible vehicle for the writing of fiction. At once the least and the most that can be said is that by refining and defining the language in the manner of a poet, he created a style very distinctively his own. Unfortunately this aspect of his writing can scarcely be conveyed in translation. But the language, the narrative style and the content of his stories bind together to create a homogeneous body of work—any part of which can quickly be identified as his—which, despite a recurring moodiness or spleen, constitutes a penetrating view of the individual in and against society. (pp. 26-35)

William C. Hickman, "Dream and Reality in Three Stories by Sait Faik," in A Dot on the Map: Selected Stories and Poems *by Sait Faik, edited by Talat Sait Halman, Indiana University Turkish Studies, 1983, pp. 25-35.*

YAŞAR NABİ NAYIR   (essay date 1981?)

[*Nayır was a prominent Turkish essayist, translator, and editor. From 1933 to 1981 he published* Varlık, *the influential Turkish literary journal in which many of Sait Faik's stories first appeared.*]

It is not an easy task to account for the specific qualities that constitute the strength of Sait Faik's work. Very few of his stories have a tidy plot or solid structure. He had no interest in suspenseful, complex, engrossing story-lines. His style and concentration as well as plot development are not always flawless. Nonetheless, his stories wield such magic that they captivate the reader, filling his head with evocations. He startles us with unexpected flashes of how human reality—man's fate—manifests itself in the lives of ordinary people.

The writers he read and the influences he absorbed are almost impossible to ascertain. As a matter of fact, he had probably neither read enough to acquire any solid cultural orientation nor thought his readings through. He was a *sui generis* writer in whose work no specific influences may be found. This constitutes an important factor in the striking power of his work. Throughout his life, Sait Faik worked like a trail blazer. But just as he absorbed few, if any, influences from other writers, the fiction he produced is too special for others to draw upon.

Sait Faik was a man of integrity: he maintained his dedication to his principle of honesty throughout his life. His integrity was not conditioned by traditional mores, but emanated from logic and rational principles. For him honesty meant refraining from perpetrating evil unto others, from willful deception. In his eyes, a poor woman who sold her flesh or a starving man who stole were honest. But he would never forgive anyone who forced them to commit such acts or who exploited them.

Integrity was a hallmark of his writing as well. He never stooped to shock effects, bombast or pompousness. He did not pose as an advocate of great causes or as a social revolutionary for the purpose of expanding his readership or to get a round of applause. His statements employ no tricks designed for easy popularity nor any gewgaws or embellishments. Sait Faik was forthright, even blunt.

If he dressed poorly, frequented the wrong places, consorted with streetwalkers, never held a job, drank, gambled, and squandered his money, and, even if these are regarded immoral, these acts hurt no one but himself. Some people might argue that these cut his life short and thereby deprived all of us. To them I would respond by indicating that we owe most of his works to his particular life-style, that thanks to him we have come to realize the significant experiences and the inner life of ordinary people whom we had scarcely known before.

In his last stories, Sait Faik demonstrates a tendency toward obscurity. Critics who regarded this to be an attempt at innovation or an attention-getting device are mistaken. In my opinion, he wrote those particular stories in reaction to a misguided but prevalent realism which happened to be at the level of newspaper reporting during Sait Faik's last years. He had never cared for debates on art and literature, but as his friends witnessed in the years immediately preceding his death, he made harsh and devastating statements against the movement of doctrinaire realism. (pp. 18-19)

Sait Faik lived his own modest life among us as a dreamer. He did not leave many books behind. But his fiction has value and strength. Few authors have made a more estimable or impressive contribution. (p. 20)

Yaşar Nabi Nayır, ''Remembering Sait Faik,'' translated by Talat Sait Halman in A Dot on the Map: Selected Stories and Poems *by Sait Faik, edited by*

Talat Sait Halman, Indiana University Turkish Studies, 1983, pp. 17-20.

TALAT SAIT HALMAN (essay date 1983)

[*A former Turkish Minister of Culture and Ambassador for Cultural Affairs, Halman has written extensively in English on Turkish literature. In the following excerpt, he discusses characteristic themes and stylistic traits of Sait Faik's stories.*]

Sait Faik lived the life of a flâneur—wandering through the city of Istanbul, absorbing its vivid impressions, eavesdropping on its people, and observing its daily drama. Standing *media vitae,* he was a reluctant voyeur who frequently found himself dragged into the comic episodes and the tragedies enacted on the street scene. This sensitive and often cynical idler-about-town gave his narrative accounts of Istanbul's human landscape in about 170 stories, two short novels, numerous interviews, and a handful of poems.

Immediately after Sait Faik's death in 1954 at the age of 47, a newspaper reporter interviewed some of his non-literary friends and found that these ordinary people—fishermen, youngsters, loiterers, the owners, and patrons of coffeehouses—with whom he had spent a great deal of time through the years, had little or no idea about his fame and stature as a writer or even about his having been a writer at all. Sait Faik's persona, so dominant in his fiction, scrupulously shunned intrusion into the lives of his favorite characters in life. In a poem he expressed an aspect of the way he dealt creatively with his dramatis personae: ''Some days at dusk I would sit / And write stories / Like mad / And the people in my mind / Would sail out to sea for fishing.''

Turkish critics have often stressed Sait Faik's concern for the common man, for the man in the street, or—to use the term which was fashionable in the 1940s and 1950s—''the little man.'' In the case of many writers such an infatuation results from a romantic attitude or an ideology. Sait Faik's stories seldom betray this type of romantic attitude or reveal any social cause per se. His characters are authentic individuals he knew on a personal basis. He did not set them up as symbols or metaphors: he refused to think of any of these as an *eidos* or *topos.* The way he saw and depicted them was free and clear of ideological bias. In transposing them from life to fiction, he preserved the integrity of the individual characters, making them live according to their own attributes, idiosyncrasies and psychological motives. (pp. 3-4)

Sait Faik, who was once referred to as ''Turkey's Balzac,'' an analogy that is difficult to endorse, approached his fiction as essentially a miniaturist and allowed his stories to create a broad panorama of the life of Istanbul. Although no unified structure emerges, it can safely be argued that his work is larger than the sum of its parts. This does not mean that the constituent parts lack inherent strength. A number of his stories can actually be counted among the best of their genre produced in Turkey.

According to the Turkish critic Mustafa Kutlu, who published a study of Sait Faik's short stories in 1964, ''Sait Faik, like his contemporaries, projects the image of a realist, but is a romantic in terms of style and the empathy, even love, he feels for the characters he delineates.'' In his textual analyses of short stories published in 1979, Professor Mehmet Kaplan, one of Turkey's leading academic critics, comments: ''Sait Faik is a realist in terms of his world-view and narrative style. But he does not merely deal with the external aspects of reality. . . . Behind the exterior, he finds a kind spirit and a deep significance. . . . His realism avoids shallowness, encompassing myth, poetry, sentiment, and fantasy; it has a unified view of ugliness and beauty, good and evil—it embraces all of humanity and the world as a whole. It is this profound, wide-ranging, sympathetic and tolerant view of life that makes Sait Faik's stories as richly endowed, complex and lovely as life itself.''

Sait Faik's career, which spanned barely twenty-five years from about 1929 to 1954, yielded an output that displays considerable variety of themes and techniques although virtually all of his stories have certain similarities—his unmistakable style, the focal importance of the narrator, the preoccupation with social outcasts and marginal groups, an unfaltering ear for colloquial speech, etc. His stories, in their range of feeling and creative strategies, can be likened to many disparate works by some of his predecessors, contemporaries and successors outside Turkey. Occasionally one finds plots worthy of a de Maupassant, moods reminiscent of a Chekhov, and sometimes the lucidity of a Maugham, although none of these writers—not even some of the French writers he presumably read during his stay in Grenoble—seems to have had any direct influence on him. In some stories, the Turkish writers gives us a blend of fantasy and concrete fact, and the interplay of different levels of reality in the Faulknerian manner. In others, one finds a structual clarity and a crispness of language typical of Hemingway. Sait Faik's later stories occasionally read like Donald Barthelme's early work, sharing the same eery sensations of a foray into the realms of fantasy.

In his perceptive references to Sait Faik's work, Professor Kemal Karpat, a foremost political scientist, has described him as ''a specialist in those moods of 'spleen' that once inspired such nineteenth century masters as Baudelaire, Gogol, Stephen Crane or Arthur Schnitzler.''

His introspective and whimsical qualities stand in sharp contrast against the stark depictions of beleaguered peasants and factory workers in the fiction of socialist realism produced by many of his prominent contemporaries and successors, including such major figures as Sabahattin Ali (d. 1948), Orhan Kemal (d. 1970), Yashar Kemal (b. 1922), Fakir Baykurt (b. 1929), et al. Although Sait Faik has enjoyed estimable praise and has remained widely popular, he has sometimes been berated by various champions of socialist realism. Interestingly, it was a confirmed conservative who first leveled criticism at Sait Faik—essentially for bourgeois attitudes: Peyami Safa (d. 1961) wrote that he found in the author's work ''the stammerings of a likeable melancholy child,'' and added elsewhere that, in him, ''a completely aristocratic sensitivity stands in contrast to a shabby, barefooted, and impudent narrative style. This is not unlike the clash between the personality of a rich bourgeois and the role he plays in a stage production for the benefit of a charitable organization.''

The most strenuous criticism came from a group of socialist writers who took Sait Faik's work to task for its bourgeois origins and concerns. A widely read novelist and short-story writer, Bekir Yıldız (b. 1933) wrote: Sait Faik was a writer who did not involve himself with the change of the established order, but rather dabbled in the consequences of that order. Instead of settling accounts with the bourgeoisie, he chose to run away like a hippie and take shelter in nature and among the poor. Although he fled from real life, he still maintained his sincerity and integrity as a creative artist to the very end. . . . Having come from bourgeois origins, he never managed to

break away from his own class. We must rectify a widespread misconception: It is assumed that by using the man in the street as his subject he renounced his class. In reality, the nature of his affection for the common man was precisely the factor that impeded his identification with the poor.''

The advocates of socialist realism were judging him by criteria that were hardly applicable, bacause Sait Faik, although he shared their basic concerns, had mapped out a different aesthetic strategy for himself: ''Moral values,'' he once stated, ''have been undergoing an extensive change in our society. The old guard of our literature used to look down on life and society. They still do. They do not get involved in life. They are enamored of the ideal of improving the social order by shouting down from the top. As far as we are concerned, we make no claims for reforming or transforming society.''

Many authors who came to Sait Faik's defense stressed that he had effectively upheld the dignity and the inherent rights of the man in the street, and that his subtle approach had just as much intrinsic strength as the naked force of socialist literature. In his apologia, Hilmi Yavuz, one of Turkey's most accomplished students of fiction, made the following observation: ''I have always regarded Sait Faik as a moralist, but his moralism is not in the old-fashioned sense of deriving a moral from a story or putting on airs as a preacher. . . . His moralism lacks philosophical foundations. We could therefore call him a Camus who is not a philosopher.''

Sait Faik represents a subtle humanism which affirms each person's worth while refusing to treat him or her as a pat symbol of social and economic injustice. He was not a snob, but stood against the naive and simplistic aspects of socialist realism. Given his insistence on the subjective voice, with its inscapes and dolorous moods, it easy to understand why some of the firebrand critics in the 1970s came to regard him as a self-indulgent aesthete whose patronizing attitude bordered on noblesse oblige.

Sait Faik was a restless narcissist par excellence. A confirmed non-conformist, he saw himself and his characters as anti-heroes—alienated, disenchanted, forgotten or disenfranchised. Virtually all of his major figures are on the fringes of society. Like Sait Faik himself, they are the idlers, the mavericks, people who have chosen not to become ''someone'' (When one of his teachers asked him to write an essay on ''What I want to become,'' his one-sentence composition asserted: ''I don't want to become anything''), the outcast and the jobless, but also poor people. His gallery of characters includes innumerable members of the ethnic minorities.

A cursory glance might give the impression that Sait Faik was a solipsist raised in the tradition of Proust, Gide, or Duhamel. Certainly his fiction contains enough absorption with his own persona and enough private musing to lend credence to such a view. One could even detect a touch of good-natured decadence. But his work is hardly confessional or self-serving. For all his commitment to individualism, Sait Faik wrote uncompromisingly as a man of conscience to make exposés of injustice. His plea for human justice, for a higher morality, and for a good society went far beyond some of the less than audacious statements he made, e.g., ''The creative artist should not remain blind; he should observe everything around him,'' or ''For writing, I need, not the freedom of flowers and birds, but the freedom of my inmost love, frenzy, and irrepressible thoughts.'' It is conceivable that the author was disenchanted with his private commitment to the betterment of his society.

As if to add grist to the mills of his detractors, he uttered the following words of disquietude near the end of his life: "To tell the truth, I have grown weary of relating human suffering . . . after having endeavored to restructure the world."

His stories constitute an odyssey into the realm of innocence lost. As in most of Tennessee Williams' plays, characters in his stories "always depend on the kindness of strangers," but can even be victimized by some of their loved ones. Acts of cruelty and instances of deprivation form the basis of the poignancy that permeates many of his best short stories.

Empathy is the dominant attitude of Sait Faik as narrator and protagonist. The heartrending scenes he observes sometimes become the extensions of his self or even of his fate. Like himself, his despairing peasants, sickly women, abandoned children, pitiable thieves and prostitutes, and outcasts of all sorts are presented as occasionally enjoying life's simple pleasures but often suffering in a continual drama which gives glimpses and intimations of tragedy. There is no outright indictment or any rebellion in Sait Faik's plots. As narrator, he seldom passes judgment let alone engage in denunciations or fulminations. His tone is almost always subdued, unpolemical, pliant, and only occasionally plaintive.

The central theme in Sait Faik's fiction might well be summarized as *the happiness of ordinary people thwarted*. If the critic must single out one prevalent mood, that would be *elegiac*. The stories masterfully juxtapose the lament for shattered lives with a dirge for the big city contaminated and the vast sea polluted. Together, the inscapes of suffering and the landscapes in agony create the panorama of the tragedy of the modern age. Often, it is the old Greek fisherman and his seagull who survive as a metaphor of human innocence. Sait Faik's vision of life is based on the human predicament. In this sense, he is akin to William Faulkner. In fact, a Turkish critic, Adnan Binyazar, has observed that "Sait Faik created a human tragedy. In him we find the sustained tragic voice of William Faulkner."

Particularly in the last ten years of his life, Sait Faik witnessed the evolution of modern humanism in Turkish intellectual life. Although he never became an active member of this movement, which gave its best output after his death, he was temperamentally linked with it. Like most humanists, Sait Faik not only upheld the proposition that man, being endowed with dignity and inherent worth, is the measure of all things, but he also maintained a strong sense of optimism about the human capability of building a better society. He was essentially an ameliorist. The allusions in his stories are almost always the expression of hope, if not faith, in a better world—and reality often comes, sometimes quite abruptly, as a rude awakening. In fact, one finds in most of his highly effective stories a pattern of violence breaking out in the midst of a passage of serenity or a harsh episode jarring lyrical tranquillity.

His death, as captured by the prominent poet Fazıl Hüsnü Dağlarca (b. 1914), who knew him well, seems to have occurred in similar fashion: "Sait died / Earlier than the blue of the sea; / After so many loves / He died while kissing his mother. / He died, his hands and feet far away, / With windowpanes still blanketed under smoke, / He died without leave of absence from the little boys, / His blond childhood lingering on his face." (pp. 4-8)

Some of Sait Faik's stories have homosexual characters and episodes. In a very few cases these are overt, in others extremely guarded. Occasionally, as in **"Fear of Loving,"** the author takes advantage of the fact that there is no gender in Turkish and makes it impossible for the reader to ascertain the sex of a principal character. (p. 8)

A recurrent criticism has centered around Sait Faik's hasty, even slapdash, writing. One of his friends, the prominent and prolific writer Aziz Nesin, was a witness to the extreme speed with which Sait Faik would write his pieces and rush them to a newspaper or magazine to pick up his fee of a few liras. Tarık Buğra, a well-known fiction writer, who edited a volume of Sait Faik's selected stories for publication by the Ministry of Education (1972), notes in his introduction that "these extraordinary stories are far from meticulous, given their occasional sloppy twists of syntax, phraseology, punctuation and composition, but virtually all of their paragraphs are teeming generously, almost prodigally, with perceptions, insights, intuitions, and sentiments, each one notable for its revelations."

The notoriety of carelessness attached to some of Sait Faik's writing seems justified. He actually wrote many stories in a mad hurry, sitting at a café or on a ferryboat, and never bothered to reread them before rushing them to a publisher. He said, however, that a number of his stories took as long as three months to finish. Although some of them seem so spare and precise that it would be difficult to change a single word or edit a single sentence, others are blatantly diffuse. A notorious example is one of his novellas which had one name for a protagonist in the first half and a completely different name in the second half—an error that was only corrected in the second edition of the book. (p. 9)

Melih Cevdet Anday, one of Turkey's major poets, has advanced the argument that Sait Faik's so-called "carelessness" was the "hallmark of his style, and his style was unique." Anday wrote: "As far as I am concerned, he was not sloppy in his use of the language. Whatever he did stylistically, he did for deliberate effect." Anday's apologia has a certain validity, because Sait Faik wrote the way he lived—spontaneously, sensually, impressionistically, experientially, always stressing the authentic touch and the ring of truth. He probably felt that a story is a microcosm or slice of life and cannot be, should not be, any more perfect than life itself. Above all, he was conscious of human frailty, foibles and follies. In exploring human situations, his stories reflected, not only in substance but in form as well, the flaws of life.

Muzaffer Uyguner, a well-known critic who published a book on Sait Faik in 1964, stressed that "in his stories, Sait Faik dealt with the fundamental themes of human beings and his love of humanity. Nature, too, is dealt with in conjunction with human beings and other living creatures."

Sait Faik's work is marked by a restless quest. His stories have the flâneur's alternating concentration and listlessness. "I am addicted," he once asserted, "to walking. I follow my nose and go wherever it leads me, getting instantly bored with any given place. I discover animals, people, gardens, desolate shores. Then I am born again."

This flâneur's stories have a special magic of their own. For decades, most readers in his own country have regarded him as the master of his genre. (pp. 9-10)

A very touching tribute was paid to Sait Faik by his friend Bedri Rahmi Eyuboğlu (d. 1975), a celebrated Turkish painter and poet, in a long, sprawling poem entitled "The Saga of Istanbul." The segment on Sait Faik evokes, in an effective and quintessential way the life and fiction of a captivating flâneur:

Say *Istanbul* and Sait Faik comes to mind:
Pebbles twitter on the shore of Burgaz Island,
While a blue-eyed boy grows up in circles of joy
A blue-eyed old fisherman grows younger and tinier,
When they reach the same height they turn into Sait
And they roam the city hand in hand,
Cursing bird and beast, friend and foe alike!
On Sivriada they gather gulls's eggs,
By midnight they're in the red-light district,
In the morning they go through Galata:
At the café they kid around with a harmless lunatic,
"Whaddya know," they say. "You're holding the
    paper upside down."
Then they set the poor guy's newspaper on fire,
Then they sit and weep quietly.

Say *Istanbul* and Sait Faik comes to mind:
All over this town's rock and soil and water,
A friend of the poor and the sick,
Whose pencil is as sharp as his heart is wounded,
Bleeding for the lonely and yearning for the pure and
    the good.

Say *Istanbul* and Sait's last years come to mind:
At his best age he's told he has just a few years to live;
How could Sait bear the thought of it?
The blue-eyed boy doesn't give a damn,
But the old fisherman broods like hell;
And a green venom bursts out of the sea
Piercing the heart that feels, ravaging the mind that
    knows.

(pp. 10-11)

> Talat Sait Halman, *"Introduction: Fiction of a Flâ-
> neur,"* in A Dot on the Map: Selected Stories and
> Poems *by Sait Faik, edited by Talat Sait Halman,
> Indiana University Turkish Studies, 1983, pp. 3-11.*

SAAD EL-GABALAWY (essay date 1986)

[*The following essay is a review of a recent English translation
of Sait Faik's stories and poems.*]

Sait Faik, one of Turkey's most important writers of fiction,
typifies a strange trend of realism, wavering between nature
and art, action and contemplation. In *A Dot on the Map,* a
collection of some fifty very short stories, he reveals a remarkable familiarity with the masses in the slums and meandering alleys of Istanbul, which makes him feel at home with
common people without a trace of intellectual snobbery or
condescension. They are observed closely, in a spirit of compassion and tenderness, against their natural settings in seamy
cafés, workingclass taverns, boat landings, small shops or fishing villages. With his empathetic perception of "the little man,"
Faik often ensnares the truth of life among the lower class in
highly significant moments of illumination. For subjects of his
stories, he turns to the poor, the oppressed, the underprivileged,
the outcast and the delinquent, so that the protagonists are
sickly women, abandoned children, degraded servants, petty
thieves or pathetic whores, who have failed to find their spiritual home in civilized society. Without melodramatic sentimentality or ideological bias, the writer maintains their integrity as authentic individuals, focusing preeminently on vibrations
of feeling and thought at heightened moments of crisis.

In **"The Head and the Bottle"** . . . the narrator says at the
beginning: "I seem to be registering all the unnecessary aspects
and the minutest details of many happenings. . . . I notice something that might be faintly relevant or utterly absurd." The
statement aptly describes a predominant trait in the stories of
Sait Faik, who usually derives his material from seemingly
trivial or insignificant incidents of everyday life, but endows
them with a sense of strangeness and beauty. In fact, he attempts to recreate in the sophisticated mind of the adult the
sense of wonder and mystery felt by ignorant and naive characters. In his fiction, the familiar seems peculiar and unfamiliar, seen in a new light by a sensitive writer of exquisite
taste. Thus, a dot on the map, the death of a seagull, a sizzling
simovar or a bundle of clothes can trigger perceptions and
meditations of profound significance.

The reader who expects classic story development, with a tidy
plot, is bound to become frustrated and irritable, because actually nothing happens in terms of well-defined action. The
stories have the character of "tender and dreamlike vignettes,"
designed to focus on events of the mind. Through the magic
of evocative words and images, the writer releases the imagination from boundaries of time and space, stimulating vague
feelings and unsettling insights which have a haunting quality.
They linger in the reader's memory and tend to expand gradually, suggesting different dimensions of meaning. The power
of ambiguity is manifest vividly in such stories as **"Sivriada
Nights"** and **"Love Letter,"** in which the storyteller relies on
the juxtaposition of reality and fantasy with a striking effect.
There are several other pieces where the familiar landmarks of
the real world are shrouded in a cloud of mystery. It is no
accident that fog is a recurrent image in the stories, enhancing
the atmosphere of fantasy or daydream.

The prevalent mood is plaintive, almost elegiac, with intimations of tragedy strongly reminiscent of Faulkner. The author dwells on such themes as the loss of innocence, the frustration of hope, the shattered lives of ordinary people, the brutal
abuse of poor children, the denial of love or the contamination
of the big city. Some of the stories convey subtle suggestions
of homosexuality—presumably a reflection of the writer's sexual inclinations—which are redeemed from vulgarity by passion. It should be noted, however, that Faik's tender compassion for the sufferings of the common man has no philosophical
foundations. He is not an exponent of committed realism,
preoccupied with radical analyses of the economic basis of
social malaise. Yet, without indulging in revolutionary rhetoric, he appears to hold out the hope of change and amelio-
ration. It is interesting in this regard that champions of socialist
realism in Turkish literature refer to his "aristocratic sensitivity" and "bourgeois origins." . . .

> Saad El-Gabalawy, *in a review of "A Dot on the
> Map: Selected Stories,"* in The International Fiction
> Review, *Vol. 13, No. 2, Summer, 1986, p. 101.*

ADDITIONAL BIBLIOGRAPHY

Blasing, Mutlu Konuk. Review of *A Dot on the Map: Selected Stories
and Poems,* by Sait Faik. *World Literature Today* 59, No. 1 (Winter
1985): 155.
    Calls Sait Faik "a major Turkish short story writer" who "stands
    out as a special case: his work does not show obvious influences
    and has not particularly influenced younger writers, yet he has
    achieved a personal vision, a distinctive style, and considerable
    popularity."

Leslie Stephen

1832-1904

English critic, biographer, historian, editor, and philosopher.

Stephen was a distinguished man of letters and a member of Victorian England's intellectual elite. While his prestige stemmed largely from his skillful editorial direction of the *Dictionary of National Biography* and *Cornhill* magazine, he was also highly respected for his literary criticism, histories, and biographies. Stephen's writings all display his affinity with the rationalist thought of the eighteenth century and clearly exhibit the religious skepticism and confidence in scientific method so characteristic of the later nineteenth century. As a result, his work is often considered the quintessential expression of the Victorian spirit and is read for the valuable insight it provides into the thought of that era. In addition, Stephen was the father of several remarkable children, including the novelist Virginia Woolf, and their fame has generated much interest in both his character and his ideas.

Born in London, Stephen was the son of James Stephen III, a high-ranking royal official who was also known for his frequent contributions to the *Edinburgh Review*. Both of Stephen's parents were prominent members of the Clapham Sect, a group of Christian political reformers who primarily sought to abolish slavery, and while he later rejected their Christian sentiments, he retained throughout his life the strict moral sense and concern for social responsibility they impressed upon him in his youth. Stephen displayed a strong interest in literature as soon as he was able to read, but his parents were somewhat shocked by the intensity with which their frail and sensitive child responded to the emotional transports of poetry, and they confined his lessons to more prosaic subjects. After being tutored at home, Stephen was sent to Eton and then to Cambridge, where he studied mathematics and eagerly sought to improve his health by hiking and rowing. The spirit of intellectual vigor and unimpeded inquiry at Cambridge was so pleasing to Stephen that, after being awarded his degree, he chose to stay on as an instructor. He taught for ten years, enjoying the celibate, scholastic life enormously and making frequent trips to the continent for Alpine hiking expeditions, which he later described in *The Playground of Europe*.

Although Stephen began composing essays for publication while still at Cambridge, he did not consider writing as a career until circumstances forced him to resign his teaching post. One of the primary requirements for university teachers in Stephen's day was ordination in the Church of England, and Stephen, the son of devout parents, had willingly complied. Eventually, however, he began to realize that he did not believe the tenets of Christian theology, and his position as an ordained minister gradually became untenable. Ultimately, when Stephen refused to perform the duties of his ministerial office, he was asked to resign his tutorship, and in 1865 he agreed. The doctrinal doubt which led to Stephen's agnosticism centered primarily on what he perceived to be certain logical flaws inherent in Christianity, particularly those involved in the problem of evil. Finding utterly ridiculous the idea that evil had been visited upon humanity by an allegedly just and benevolent creator as punishment for its sins, Stephen wrote: "The potter has no right to be angry with his pots. If he had wanted them different,

he should have made them different." Unlike the many religious skeptics who agonized over their loss of faith, Stephen was troubled very little by his, and with the teaching profession closed to him, he simply chose another career.

Determined to become a journalist, Stephen settled in London, where his brother Fitzjames was already a regular contributor to the city's newspapers. Stephen began writing literary criticism, and his essays were of such high quality that they were readily accepted and frequently solicited by the *Saturday Review, Cornhill,* and the *Pall Mall Gazette*. By 1871, the year in which he was appointed editor of *Cornhill*, Stephen felt ready to attempt something more comprehensive, and he began work on the *History of English Thought in the Eighteenth Century,* originally intended as a history of the deist controversy but later expanded to include all philosophical thought of the period. Stephen's intense interest in rationalist thought led him to concentrate on the primary exponents of rationalism in his biographies and to devote several volumes to his own philosophical speculations, most notably in *The Science of Ethics* and *An Agnostic's Apology, and Other Essays*.

Although Virginia Woolf portrayed her father as the self-absorbed pedant Mr. Ramsay in *To the Lighthouse,* Stephen in fact derived much pleasure and inspiration from involvement in family life. His first wife, who was the daughter of author

William Makepeace Thackeray, died in 1875, but Stephen remarried a few years later and soon became the patriarch of the large family loosely described in Woolf's novel. The early years of his second marriage were extremely productive for Stephen, and it was during this period that he wrote many of his major works.

From 1882 through 1890, Stephen was occupied primarily with the editorship of the *Dictionary of National Biography,* a compilation which grew to twenty-six volumes under his editorship, and would eventually reach sixty-three volumes under his successor. With only one assistant, Stephen commissioned the writing of articles, choosing to write 378 of them himself, and edited every word of the manuscript. The task was enormous and took its toll on Stephen, whose health was deteriorating rapidly. Nevertheless, even after he retired from the *DNB,* too ill to perform the work required, Stephen produced several biographies and oversaw the publication of numerous works he had produced in earlier decades. He died of cancer in 1904.

When Stephen announced his agnosticism in print, he also noted, "I do not the less believe in morality." Thus, two factors—a firm belief that right and wrong exist independently of theology and that reason and science should be used as the guide to their definition—form the central paradigm of Stephen's thought. He was unconcerned with metaphysics, believing the unknowable to be just that and hence unworthy of attention, and preferred to consider questions of ethics. In "An Agnostic's Apology," Stephen argued that Christianity not only fails to satisfy the demands of reason, but also provides insufficient moral guidance as a result of its cryptic and frequently contradictory teachings. He preferred the philosophical constructs of the English Utilitarians Jeremy Bentham and John Stuart Mill, who attempted to base their ethical valuations upon empirically derived conclusions of the natural and social sciences. This preference can be clearly seen in *The History of English Thought in the Eighteenth Century,* wherein Stephen not only explains the ideas of such thinkers as John Locke, David Hume, and Jeremy Bentham, but also supports the arguments of eighteenth-century rationalists with nineteenth-century scientific theories. It was, however, in *The Science of Ethics* that Stephen presented his most comprehensive and most systematic analysis of the moral implications of both rationalist philosophy and newly-discovered phenomena such as biological evolution. Nevertheless, critics agree that despite a concerted effort, Stephen failed both to answer the most obvious and pressing moral questions, and to reconcile Utilitarian thought with that of intuitive moralists.

Although Stephen's concern for morality pervades his literary criticism, he was not ignorant of aesthetic considerations. He did, however, reject the pure aesthetics espoused by the European Romantics earlier in the century and exemplified in John Keats's lines: "Beauty is truth, truth beauty—that is all / Ye know on earth, and all ye need to know." Stephen found the experience of literature not a sensory encounter with beauty but a form of intellectual communication, and while he understood the importance of artistry, he preferred a work to carry an important message as well. "Even a novel," Stephen wrote, "should have a ruling thought." This is not to say that he endorsed didacticism in fiction, for he found such writing abhorrent. Rather, Stephen recommended the creation of works so thoroughly infused with healthy moral attitudes that overt didacticism would be superfluous.

Believing firmly in the materialist view of history developed by Karl Marx, Stephen was convinced that ideas could only

be fully understood in the context of the place and time in which they developed, and this fact accounts for his interest in biography as well as the much-discussed biographical dimension of his literary criticism. If literature was a form of communication, Stephen wished to know as much as possible about his correspondent in order to properly interpret the message. Moreover, for Stephen, one of the most pleasant aspects of reading fiction was the feeling of becoming acquainted with a great mind he would not otherwise have the opportunity to know. Many modern critics, tending toward a more aesthetic view of literature and regarding a work as distinct from the circumstances of its creation, denigrate this aspect of Stephen's criticism, but, as Edwin Sheen has pointed out, his attitude was in fact consistent with the prevailing literary theory of his day.

While Stephen was not reticent about announcing his personal preferences in literature or passing judgment on the works he discussed, his criticism did not generally display overt biases. Indeed, one of his major recommendations was the application of objective standards in literary criticism in order to remove the impressionistic, subjective elements that had come to dominate the field. As a result, his essays are characterized by a quality of fairness and a general tone of tolerance.

Critical assessment of Stephen's work is distinguished by enormous diversity. Some critics find his most important contribution in his shaping of the editorial policies of the *Dictionary of National Biography* and judge his writings to be interesting only insofar as they reveal the mind of a Victorian intellectual. A large number of commentators consider Stephen's literary criticism his best and most lasting achievement, while others contend that his lack of aesthetic sensibility rendered him incapable of good criticism and that he was at his best in his histories and biographies. There are, however, areas of consensus. *The History of English Thought in the Eighteenth Century* is generally considered the definitive work on that subject, and Stephen's bold step in discussing the novel as serious literature is regarded as an important development in the history of literary criticism. In addition, critics unanimously praise Stephen's lucid and elegant prose and applaud the obvious erudition displayed in his work. Moreover, despite the controversy which surrounds his talents, Stephen's work is considered the most articulate and comprehensive expression of the Victorian positivist spirit and is regarded as a valuable key to understanding that period.

PRINCIPAL WORKS

Sketches from Cambridge (essays) 1865
The Playground of Europe (essays) 1871
Essays on Freethinking and Plainspeaking (essays) 1873
Hours in a Library. 4 vols. (essays) 1874-1907
The History of English Thought in the Eighteenth Century. 2 vols. (history) 1876
Samuel Johnson (biography) 1878
Alexander Pope (biography) 1880
The Science of Ethics (nonfiction) 1882
Swift (biography) 1882
The Life of Henry Fawcett (biography) 1885
An Agnostic's Apology, and Other Essays (essays) 1893
The Life of Sir James Fitzjames Stephen (biography) 1895
Social Rights and Duties. 2 vols. (lectures) 1896
Studies of a Biographer. 4 vols. (essays) 1898-1902
The English Utilitarians. 3 vols. (essays) 1900

THE SPECTATOR (essay date 1874)

[*In the following essay, the critic discusses the literary assessments presented in* Hours in a Library.]

Readers of the *Cornhill,* of *Fraser,* and the *Fortnightly* will be already familiar with the contents of [*Hours in a Library*]. In these days, the magazine or review takes precedence of the book. A writer's thoughts appear first in a serial, and afterwards, if considered worthy, are republished in a more permanent form. The mischief is, that a charming magazine article often ceases to charm when placed between the covers of a book. We read periodical literature partly, no doubt, to be instructed, and for the sake of the mental stimulus it affords, but chiefly for the amusement of an idle hour. What we want in it is lightness of touch, a freshness of expression if not of thought, picturesque description, rapidity of movement, a perspicacity of style, and at least as much knowledge as may place the writer in advance of his readers. The literary man who meets the public in this way soon learns to know the kind of material with which to supply them, and is careful to avoid all prolonged arguments, all elaborate and parenthetical sentences, all criticism that cannot readily be grasped, and all details that are likely to impede the flow of the composition. The literature thus produced is not wholly deserving of praise. No doubt it suits exactly the pages for which it is designed, but it will be often deemed wanting in power and permanent worth when it claims a place upon our library-shelves.

These remarks have been suggested to us by a perusal of Mr. Stephen's essays, some of which are really admirable specimens of periodical literature. Good taste, sound judgment, competent knowledge, and an occasional vivacity of expression,—these literary virtues are evident throughout, and will attract and please the reader as he turns over the pages. On the other hand, we do not find in this work the subtle criticism, the fine imagination, or the perfect beauty of utterance, which so attract us in some volumes of biographical and literary criticism that we are drawn towards them again and again, to receive every time some new intellectual impulse, or the pleasure derived from sonorous melody of expression. This is merely saying in other words that Mr. Leslie Stephen, although an admirable writer, does not stand in the front rank of authors or critics. His work is thoroughly well done, but we do not detect in it that vitality which is likely to render it of permanent value. What matter! If these essays be not read twenty years hence, they are certain to be read now, and cannot fail to raise the reputation of the writer. Five of the papers are devoted to novelists,—De Foe, Richardson, Sir W. Scott, Hawthorne, and Balzac; there is also an essay on De Quincey, one on Pope as a moralist, in which character, it may be remembered, he has been specially praised by Mr. Ruskin, and another on Mr. Elwin's edition of the poet. It will be seen that the table of contents is attractive, and there are few readers who care for

what may be called "pure literature" (let no one imagine that we use the words in the sense attached to them by subscribers to the "Pure Literature" Society), who will not be interested in Mr. Stephen's comments and criticism.

To begin at the beginning. The judgment here given of Defoe is, we think, a true one in the main, though we question whether the writer does sufficient justice to this novelist's transcendent power. The morality of Defoe's minor novels, *Roxana* and *Moll Flanders,* is very questionable, for the association with mean people and mean vices can have no wholesome tendency. These tales are coarse and often repulsive, and they are all the more repulsive as the work of a comparatively old man; but their intense realism and minute Dutch painting take powerful hold of us as we read, and they contain passages which of their kind are unsurpassed in fiction. Mr. Stephen allows that in *Roxana, Moll Flanders,* and *Colonel Jack* there are some forcible situations, but he considers that these novels possess "no higher interest than that which belongs to the ordinary police-report given with infinite fullness and vivacity of detail." We might object that this "vivacity" would of itself go far towards destroying any resemblance to the police-report, but the secret of Defoe's power is not to be explained by Mr. Stephen's criticism. The novelist, hard, and dry, and cold as at times he seems, without passion, without ideality, without that love of the beautiful which has inspired many a smaller writer, possessed a strong imagination, and enchains his readers' attention by the aid of it. To this, and not to any mere accumulation of details, however vivaciously given, is due the enthralling interest of his *Journal of the Plague,* and still more of his incomparable fiction *Robinson Crusoe.* Defoe was not a poet, but that story excites the mind in the way in which a great poem excites it. The author's tricks and strange artifices for giving verisimilitude to his details are but a part, and comparatively a mean part of his art; his realism has been rivalled, perhaps, by some modern novelists, but the combination of realism with imagination as displayed in *Robinson Crusoe* is rare indeed. Mr. Stephen is quite ready to allow that Defoe possessed a powerful imagination, but it appears to us he does not do justice to it as the secret of his strength. Nevertheless, there is some truth in the following statement:—

> Defoe was above the ordinary standard, in so far as he did not, like most of us, see things merely as a blurred and inexplicable chaos, but he was below the great imaginative writers in the comparative coldness and dry precision of his mental vision. To him the world was a vast picture, from which all confusion was banished; everything was definite, clear, and precise, as in a photograph; as in a photograph, too, everything could be accurately measured, and the result stated in figures. . . . The result is a product which is to Fielding or Scott what a portrait by a first-rate photographer is to one by Vandyke or Reynolds, though, perhaps, the peculiar qualifications which go to make a Defoe are almost as rare as those which form the more elevated artist.

Further on in the volume, Mr. Stephen writes with carefully measured praise of Scott himself, and from many of his remarks on that great novelist we must express our dissent. He thinks that the "Wizard" has already lost very much of his power; hints, or observes he has heard it hinted, that Scott is dull; asks whether the decay of interest in his novels is not due to something more than the lapse of time, and other similar questions, which, he says, it is a painful task to examine impartially. The writer's remarks appear to be suggested by Mr. Carlyle's celebrated essay, which, if we accept Mr. Carlyle's criticism, is no doubt extremely derogatory to the genius of Scott. Mr. Stephen is far from receiving it without objection. He thinks that what the essayist says of Shakespeare might in his earlier years have applied as well to Scott. He does not allow that Scott wrote with preposterous haste, or merely for money; but he seems to accept the statement that the Waverley Novels are addressed entirely to the every-day mind, and that "for any other mind there is next to no nourishment in them." If Mr. Carlyle and Mr. Stephen, so far as he follows him, are right here, then Goethe, and Coleridge, and Hawthorne, and Keble, and Robertson of Brighton, and other notable men, were utterly mistaken in their opinions. But were they thus mistaken? We think not, and that Mr. Carlyle's error lies partly in expecting to find in these romances what cannot be found in them. What if Scott had no "great gospel" to deliver? All poets are not prophets. Some surely may be allowed to sing for the joy of singing, and so benefit the world indirectly by increasing the stock of harmless pleasure. Much more than this might be said in defence of Scott, and we might venture to hint our gratefulness that Scott did not, *as a story teller*, attempt to write what was "profitable for doctrine, for reproof, for correction." Scott's rivals in the art of novel-writing have multiplied since his death. We have had greater novelists in one department or in another, but we question whether Scott is not as dear as he ever was to Englishmen and Scotchmen all the world over; and the variety of editions of his works now publishing justifies us in the belief that he is still one of the most popular of authors,— he is certainly one of the healthiest and most delightful.

We must not attempt to follow every line of thought suggested by Mr. Stephen's *Hours in a Library.* An able and elaborate article on Balzac will interest many readers; others will appreciate and thoroughly enjoy the estimate of Hawthorne, to whose peculiar and exquisite genius Mr. Stephen does ample justice. Of Richardson, so much has been said of late years, that little is left to say. Mr. Stephen is not quite accurate in his remark that this novelist's works never enjoy the honours of cheap reprints, and despite of much in them that is stilted, wearisome, and twaddling, we believe that they will always retain a high place in the literature of fiction. Whether *Pamela* is or is not moral, no doubt that author intended it to be so,— in any case, we cannot agree with Mr. Stephen that it is not amusing, and *Clarissa Harlowe* is assuredly the most pathetic tale ever written. Richardson, says Mr. Stephen, has invented two characters, Clarissa and Sir Charles Grandison, which have still a strong vitality; he might have added Lovelace, whose name is familiar everywhere as the type of an attractive libertine. Mr. Stephen, however, regards him as a "fancy character, who has every merit but that of existence." Two noticeable articles in the volume are devoted to Pope. The critic is severe in his remarks on Mr. Elwin's edition of the poet, and wonders, as others have done, that a writer who finds so much to denounce and so little to admire in Pope should have spent so much exhausting toil in editing his works. On one point we entirely agree with Mr. Stephen. Pope was neither a philosopher nor a theologian, and we do not read his poetry either for its philosophy or theology. We may regret that there is much in the poetry which we cannot admire or even approve, but an elaborate argument to expose the unsoundness of his views is labour thrown away. With this quotation we must close our notice of Mr. Stephen's pleasant volume:—

Nothing is more vexatious than to find oneself launched in a vast philosophical and theological controversy when we expected a judicious criticism; to have a learned and laborious editor treating Pope as if he were Strauss, Renan, or Comte; to be told that his arguments are childish, and at the same time to be treated to elaborate refutations of them as though they were likely to be dangerous to our faith; to find that the editor has forgotten the critic in the sound divine, and mixes sermons with his notes; and to be wearied out with the one question about Pope, which is utterly uninteresting to every reasonable human being at the present day, namely, how far he was or was not sound in his theological views.

(pp. 857-58)

"Mr. Leslie Stephen's Literary Essays," in The Spectator, *Vol. 47, No. 2401, July 4, 1874, pp. 857-58.*

THE NATION (essay date 1878)

[*In the following excerpt from a review of* Essays on Freethinking and Plainspeaking, *the critic explains the intellectual value of that work.*]

[The essays which appear in *Essays on Freethinking and Plainspeaking*] (with an exception or two) first apeared in *Fraser's Magazine* and the *Fortnightly Review,* and in the interval between the first and the last there seems to be a change from a rather cautious to a very outspoken position, though the latter is plainly enough foreshadowed in the earlier writings. The first four and the concluding essay especially form a series which either attempts, with extraordinary care, to lead the reader quietly on to a positivism more and more pronounced at each step, or else, as seems much more probable from Mr. Stephen's temperament, shows a development of his own convictions. The deliberate moderation with which he questions the fairness of the position of the Broad Church in retaining the old forms while rejecting the old substance, ripens into harsher criticism upon those who would cultivate religion as a fine art when they can no longer yield it their faith; the relation of modern science to the older faiths emphasizes more distinctly his radicalism, and at last he ends by stoutly refusing the name of Christian, and vigorously asserting the duty of avowing his radicalism. His position is so extreme that he is no doubt right in expecting the approval of few Englishmen but those who already agree with him; but they will appreciate the vigor of his thoughts and the straightforwardness of their utterance, while those who take the other side will find little that is absolutely new to trouble them. The allusion . . . to "some contemptible French author," who explains the origin of modesty by referring it to a savage instinct, is an unnecessary bit of sentimentality from any point of view. M. Littré, who is the author of the suggestion, is well known as the greatest of Comte's followers; and his theory, or something closely akin to it, is essential to every natural theory of man's intellectual rise from savagery. But sentimentalism is not at all one of Mr. Stephen's faults. He is indeed very English, and the atmosphere in which he writes is always to be borne in mind. The social influence of the Church, and the partial ostracism which radicalism has to meet there, make concealment much commoner than here; and render it less extraordinary that a man of Mr. Stephen's ability should think that he must discard the name of Christian in order to preserve his honesty.

In this country the position of the English Church has always been different from its native one. From the first it has been essentially a missionary church among the heathen, and it is to-day more marked for the extraordinary intensity with which it preserves its faith in beliefs that are quietly fading from the creeds of its competitors, and the warm zeal with which it seeks to draw the unbeliever into its fold, than for its liberalism or progress. Of course there are broad thinkers within its borders, as every great city can show, but they do not form as prominent and influential a party here as in England. The rejection of the political compromise from which the Church sprang seems to have given it a fresher life here; and in religion new life generally means firmer hold of doctrine, and stronger conviction that only faith can save. There have been comparatively few representatives of that section of the Broad party which, when the old methods seemed to be failing, boldly ventured to essay the new, and profesed to bring the best light of historical criticism and of scientific investigation to be upon the old dogmas only the better to exhibit their strength. As a movement it was scarcely in accord with the Church here, or indeed with our national instincts, from which the taste for the intellectual discussion of dogmas that our fathers felt so strongly has nearly departed.. But even in England it did not succeed. The new wine was too effervescent. It was not, as Mr. Stephen says, because the English creed was, like the English constitution, ''the product of a series of compromises, accidents, and bit-by-bit reforms, carried out by no definite principle, but by a sort of indefinite rule of thumb.'' However true it may be of the constitution, this does not at all represent the growth of the Church. When the Protestant creeds first took shape, the profoundest and subtlest thought of the time still found its best field in such topics. If we consider them unassisted by inspiration, we must still the more acknowledge the transcendent genius of the creation, for each of the great creeds is a perfect logical whole. Starting with its primal assumption that the collective voice of the Church was the voice of God, there was no assailable point in the Catholic creed. And when the stern facts compelled our fathers to doubt the purity of the Church's conscience and reject its authority, they still felt the need of an unquestionable source, and naturally sought and found it in the written Word. They did not go to history or science for evidences of Christianity. The ''thus God spake'' was final, and the Protestant creed which they built up on it (which, despite a few anomalies, is the creed of the English Church) is harmonious and complete. There would have been an impossible anachronism in supposing that the certainty of these *à priori* foundations could be replaced by any abstruse metaphysical probabilities or vague analogies from natural science. And to-day, much as philosophy and science may do, the certainty of the old faith they cannot give. Modern science has sadly shaken the belief in this infallibility of the holy text, both as to facts and laws. Modern thought has moved away from the creeds, but, however we may regret it, we cannot bring it back by scientific formulas with which they had nothing in common. The Broad Church has not been able to restrain the power it invoked, and again, as in the old legend, the dwarfs cry out that the Siegfried hammer has struck with such crushing energy that metal and anvil are driven into the earth.

The other liberal movement, which asserted that the creed was full of insoluble mysteries, was successful here. This position had great advantages. It easily disposed of any troublesome points by calling them inscrutable. Of course antiquarians knew well enough that the great thinkers who worked out the creed would have stared in holy horror at the idea that they had left anything spiritually unintelligible or obscure, but modern thought has swept away from them so far that many thinkers, some even of the leading philosophers of the time, have easily followed the suggestion of the Church, and indolently asserted the impossibility of understanding them; and naturally the method has found great favor in this country, especially in the more liberal sects. In the end, however, this movement, too, must fail, for the great creeds are great wholes from which no part can be servered without perilling the whole. The old legend comes back of the vigil in the valley of St. John, where the knight waits long before the enchanted castle, and at last in impotent, desperate uncertainty dashes his axe against the charmed rock, and finds that with the fall of a single turret the charm has broken and the whole castle lies open. The great creeds were the life of the Christian Church, and it is vain to hope that the Church can retain its influence when it does not insist upon the exclusive power of its creed to save. If the dogmas are acknowledged to be unimportant, men will give but a lax and indolent support to the church which so acknowledges its impotence. Belief must be in something definite and something certain, and it must be all-important. This is what has made Episcopacy and its offspring, Methodism, so successful of late years in this country. It has been perfectly sure. With all our loose breadth we crave sometimes something firmer, right or wrong, or rather something about which there can be no question of right or wrong. Keen as our artistic perceptions are, we are not always satisfied with ''that beautiful but shadowy region where romance takes the places of history and poetry of reasoning.''

For those who are unable to retain the old faith, but afraid to relinquish it, there is little satisfaction in books like Mr. Stephen's, which only try to show the untenableness of a foothold that they fear to change. The half conviction of insecurity they do not wish to recognize. They dislike to be told that ''the division between faith and reason is a half measure till it is frankly admitted that faith has to do with fiction and reason with fact.'' Yet it is exactly against these half-way believers that Mr. Stephen's book is aimed. He has nothing to say against those who can still adhere fully to the old faith. He is too far away from them to meet them. He half unwillingly recognizes for a moment or two the other extreme of philosophical theism, the doctrine that the God-intoxicated Spinoza gave the clearest form to, but which is as old as the oldest thought—that philosophy which retains the direct personal knowledge of the divine essence, the all-informing eternal substance, ''path, motive, guide, original, and end,'' while it drops all other dogmas. But he touches it only for an instant, for he himself goes further and keeps nothing. But still the old beliefs cover the whole ground, and one watches with interest the close approach of the modern positivist to the ancient stoic; a likeness of thought rather than feeling it is true, but still a striking one. Both worship the Universal Nature, refusing any further step in Divine definition. Both seek the true life in harmony with universal order. Both make their aim the universal good. ''Never repent,'' says Mr. Stephen, ''unless by repentence you mean drawing lessons from past experience. Beating against the bars of fate you will only wound yourself and mar what yet remains to you.'' The love of those we have lost ''is at best an enervating enjoyment, and a needless pain. The figments of theology are a consecration of our delusive dreams; the teaching of the new faith should be the utilization of every emotion to the bettering of the world of the future.'' Instead of the utter self-surrender of Christianity Mr. Stephen puts the dignity of self-culture; instead of asceticism, the training one's instincts ''into harmony with the interests of the whole social organism.'' Resignation where there is a choice is but an ''ignoble yielding to evils which might be extirpated.'' Suffering is an evil to be conquered, or at least stoically withstood, not a punishment to be submitted to; and our reward lies not in any immortality of personal bliss but in the good we have done, ''spreading in widening circles to all eternity.'' We have but to clothe these thoughts in Latin to transport ourselves to that early time when Christianity was still struggling for existence, and stoicism seemed the only resource. (pp. 79-80)

''Stephen's Freethinking and Plainspeaking,'' in The Nation, *Vol. XXVI, No. 657, January 31, 1878, pp. 79-80.*

THE NATION   (essay date 1893)

[*In the following excerpt, the critic commends* An Agnostic's Apology, and Other Essays *for its style, clarity, and strong argumentation.*]

Mr. Stephen collects in [*An Agnostic's Apology and Other Essays*] articles which have before seen the light in various periodicals, though their recasting and expansion here have left on them few marks of the particular occasions which called them out; while affinity of theme and a certain order and progress of thought make the whole go well within a single cover. No mind of his generation has penetrated more deeply than Mr. Stephen's into the questions relating to the limitations of knowledge, the nature of belief, the methods of science, the rationale of toleration and of the propagation of truth; and his discussion of them is an intellectual treat even to those who remain unconvinced by his reasoning. He is as far as possible from being one who ''disbelieves heavily'' (to adapt Renan's phrase), and many a deft touch—as, for example, where he speaks of allowing creeds ''to expire by the method of explanation''—gives the added point of humor to his acuteness.

The long chapter on ''Poisonous Opinions,'' which is really an essay on toleration, furnishes an excellent instance of his power to wind himself into a subject like a serpent, as Goldsmith said of Burke. Starting out with Mill's position in the essay on Liberty, he points out the need of correcting and expanding the doctrine of toleration therein laid down. He challenges Mill's concession that truth may be suppressed by persecution. First catch your truth. It is only a ''happy thought'' conception of scientific discovery which allows one to suppose that, if Newton, for example, could have been caught and ''stamped out'' when on the point of announcing his theory of gravitation, the truth would have died with its discoverer. Mill does not go far enough in claiming that truth has a ''tendency'' to triumph. It is bound to triumph unless the whole system of civilization of which it is an organic part is blotted out. Where can you draw the line? If gravitation is heretical, then you must not only condemn that doctrine, but all those studies in astronomy and navigation and physics which are so many fingerposts pointing to it. To stamp out a particular thought you must stamp out all thought. Mill's historical instances of the strangling of nascent Protestantism in Spain Mr. Stephen examines only to come to the conclusion that it was not Spanish persecution, but the entire constitution of the Spanish mind, which prevented the spread of Protestantism in the Peninsula. There is no good reason for supposing that the Protestant religion would have made any more headway in Spain in the sixteenth century, if not hindered by persecution, than it does in the nineteenth, when it is not hindered by persecution.

The entire chapter is marked by the highest qualities of thought and literary expression, and the volume as a whole is well worth the attention of those who would know what a singularly fair and frank and acute thinker has to say on the most important subjects of human thought. (pp. 203-04)

A review of ''An Agnostic's Apology, and Other Essays,'' in The Nation, *Vol. LVI, No. 1446, March 16, 1893, pp. 203-04.*

JAMES ASHCROFT NOBLE   (essay date 1896)

[*In the following excerpt, Noble praises Stephen's ''common sense'' critical style, noting both the strengths and weaknesses inherent in his critical approach.*]

When, a hundred years hence, some one sets himself to write the history of English critical literature in the nineteenth century, he will probably regard Mr. Leslie Stephen as a transition figure, and see in his work a bridge spanning the gulf between two important and sharply differentiated schools. There were certain years during which Lord Macaulay and Mr. Walter Pater were contemporaries; but to pass from the purely literary essays of the former to those of the latter is like passing from one age into another. It seems as if something of the nature of a revolution were necessary to account for the amazing change in matter and manner, in tone and atmosphere; and yet the student of the entire literature of the time sees no violent cataclysm of portentous cleavage: he sees nothing but a series of natural and orderly stages of development. One of these stages is represented in a most delightful and interesting fashion by [Mr. Leslie Stephen]. . . . There is no doubt that, in the main, Mr. Leslie Stephen's critical work has more in common with the Edinburgh than with the Oxford school. It is, to use words which are in some danger of becoming terms of literary slang, ''judicial'' rather than ''aesthetic;'' its conclusions are based rather on general principles than on particular sensibilities or preferences; it strives after impersonal estimates rather than personal appreciations. Nevertheless there is, in addition to all this, a constant admission, explicit or implicit, of the fact that even the critic cannot jump off his own shadow, and that, though he must appeal to the common reason, his appeal must in the nature of things be made on behalf of some individual approval or disapproval which it is his business to justify. Macaulay made it a charge against Southey that what he considered his opinions were in fact merely his tastes. If I understand Mr. Leslie Stephen—and misunderstanding of so lucid a writer is all but impossible—he would say that, in matters of criticism at any rate, Southey was right; that a man's tastes *must* become his opinions, but that because opinion is a power, a factor in the world's progress, he must spare no pains to assure himself that the taste is not a mere personal whim, but that it has behind it a persuasive justification.

Thus, in the opening paragraph of his essay on Charlotte Brontë, Mr. Stephen remarks that ''our faith in an author must, in the first instance, be the product of instinctive sympathy instead of deliberate reason. It may be propagated by the contagion of enthusiasm, and preached with all the fervour of proselytism. But when we are seeking to justify our emotions, we must endeavour to get for the time into the position of an independent spectator, applying with rigid impartiality such methods as are best calculated to free us from the impulse of personal bias.'' That such a critical method has a number of admirable qualities is a fact too obvious for indication, but the qualities have their inevitable defects, and there is something in Mr. Leslie Stephen's temperament which brings them into prominence. He is so much afraid of the ''contagion of enthusiasm'' and the "fervour of proselytism" presenting themselves in the wrong place that it often seems as if he deliberately excluded them from their right place. Emotional fervour should not be substituted for exact statement or logical argument; but the one is necessarily more telling, the other more persuasive, when it has emotion behind it. Enthusiasm should never outrun *reason*, but it may and must outrun *reasoning*, for no mere argument can justify the passionate admiration of any masterpiece—say the *Confessions of an English Opium Eater*, or Keats's lines "To a Grecian Urn"—to any person by whom that admiration is unshared. Mr. Leslie Stephen's intellect is a trifle over-dominant; he forgets too absolutely what some younger critics remember too exclusively, that whatever intellectual bravery criticism may arrogate to itself, it is, in the last analysis, an affair of taste, of sensibility, and that (though the saying may be pushed to unwise applications) *De gustibus non est disputandum* ["There is no accounting for taste"].

Mr. Stephen's suspicion of violent feeling as liable to be overcharged, of strong language as liable to be exaggerated, is in itself so natural and healthy that one could wish it made itself more manifest in contemporary critical literature; but his maintenance of the guarded attitude is a little too persistent. He says very truly, of a somewhat hysterical phrase of Kingsley's, that it "requires a little dilution"; but he has such a horror of intellectual intoxication that he keeps the diluting water-bottle always within reach, and does not fail to use it. Many people, I daresay, feel that Mr. Stephen's work would be not merely more telling, but more helpful, if every now and then he would let himself go. Partly in virtue of this very moderation—this instinct for sobriety and balance of judgment—Mr. Stephen is a more trustworthy critic than Macaulay; but he does not assist readers in the same way that Macaulay was wont to assist them.

> Homer is not more decidedly the first of heroic poets, Shakespeare is not more decidedly the first of dramatists, Demosthenes is not more decidedly the first of orators than Boswell is the first of biographers. . . . Though there were many clever men in England during the latter half of the seventeenth century, there were only two minds which possessed the imaginative faculty in a very eminent degree. One of these minds produced the *Paradise Lost*, the other the *Pilgrim's Progress*.

No reader of these sentences can feel any uncertainty about Macaulay's view of the place in literature occupied by Boswell's biography and Bunyan's allegory; but it is by no means so easy to be sure of Mr. Stephen's view of such other notable books as *Robinson Crusoe, Clarissa*, or the *Religio Medici*. Every one remembers Lamb's delightful story of the worthy citizen who asked Wordsworth if he did not think that Milton was a great man. If we ask Mr. Leslie Stephen whether Sir Thomas Browne, Sterne, and Coleridge were great men, he at once devotes to them a number of shrewd, instructive, and illuminating remarks, and having thus provided us with materials for a reply, leaves us to formulate it for ourselves.

Now that is, of course, a method tantalising to the youthful student, who wishes to be told without any ambiguity what he is to think of this or that noble writer. Criticism, however, is not written exclusively for youths in search of a literary creed, any more than fiction is produced solely for the consumption of the famous or notorious young person; and I think there are few mature lovers of letters who do not return again and again to the work of Mr. Leslie Stephen with a sense of refreshment

and stimulation such as they derive from the utterances of hardly any contemporary critic. He is, to use a good old-fashioned word, honoured by Lamb's employment of it, so satisfyingly matterful. He will not write a single sentence unless he has not merely something to say but something which he is *impelled* to say; witness his declaration with regard to the poetry of Shelley—"I feel no vocation to add to the mass of imperfectly appreciative disquisition." A man of letters who has the courage to confess that he has nothing of value to add to Shelley criticism may be trusted not to lapse into chatter; we may be quite sure that whatever be the theme, his treatment of it is a response to some unmistakably audible call.

As a rule the men in whose writings this note of impulsion is most manifest are lacking in the matter of catholicity. In one set of ideas, one class of minds, they are genuinely and deeply interested, and their interest in a favourite theme gives to their utterance warmth, vigour, and arrestingness; but on other themes they write flatly or not at all. There is nothing of this flatness in the writing of Mr. Leslie Stephen. He has no raptures; he could not, and perhaps would not if he could, write of any one as Mr. Swinburne writes of Victor Hugo and Charlotte Brontë; but there is something almost as marvellous as it is delightful in the range of his discriminating appreciation. I do not slur the epithet, for the masterpiece in the presence of which Mr. Stephen would not discriminate has yet to be created; but the appreciation, with all its refinements, is really genuine; and admirers of such diverse writers as Defoe, Massinger, Crabbe, Hawthorne, and Lord Beaconsfield will probably agree that he has said things of these favourites which they would have been much pleased to say themselves.

There is a certain grip in Mr. Stephen's work, due to the fact that he is as much interested in life as in literature; or perhaps it would be truer to say he is interested in literature mainly because it is an outcome of life. There are critics who seem to consider it a fine thing to write about a book as if it had no personality behind it, but were a sort of literary Melchizedek that had sprung into being without any preliminary process of generation. This is what is called "disinterested" criticism; it is really criticism that is truncated, impoverished, devitalised. Mr. Leslie Stephen is content to be a man first, and a literary connoisseur afterwards; and whether it be a merit or a defect of his critical estimates, it is their unfailing character to regard literature as preeminently an *expression*. This is a point upon which I should speak without hesitation even had I no guide but more or less vague inferential evidence; but while writing the foregoing sentences accident has led me to an explicit statement which renders doubt impossible. At the opening of his essay on **"Dr. Johnson's Writings,"** Mr. Stephen sets himself to combat the opinion entertained by Macaulay that the qualities of a man's written work provide no trustworthy indication of the quality of the man himself. Mr. Stephen admits that there may be obvious differences which impress the imagination,—that the man who "writes like an angel" may at times be heard to "talk like poor Poll"; but after contending that even then we may "detect the essential identity under superficial differences" he utters the emphatic manifesto: "The whole art of criticism consists in learning to know the human being who is partially revealed to us in his spoken or written words." There is no difficulty in placing the author of such a definition.

Mr. Leslie Stephen's style is the style which his substance makes inevitable. The manner of the seer or the rhetorician would indeed be an ill-fitting vesture for the thought of a shrewd, humorous observer who knows how to admire wisely, how to condemn sanely, but who, neither in eulogy nor condemnation, will allow himself the perilous luxury of excitement. Wordsworth once in his life took too much to drink, and Mr. Leslie Stephen evidently thinks that it was a good thing for him. Perhaps if this distinguished critic would allow himself a single bout of literary intoxication—if he would only indulge in just one blatant extravagance—we might feel him nearer and dearer than before. In a mad world there is a certain high degree of sanity which is a trifle irritating. On the other hand, there are certain kinds of insanity which are more irritating still. It may be a sign that I am rather a poor creature, but I am more than content to take Mr. Leslie Stephen as I find him. I once wrote an essay in which I expressed my appreciation of what I called ''the poetry of common sense,'' and a lady who is herself a most charming poet, professed to regard it as an elaborate *jeu d' esprit,* on the ground that poetry and common sense are antipodal. Of course she spoke with authority, and she may have been right; I cannot tell. But if common sense be expelled from poetry, I hope the poor outcast may find a home with criticism, and so long as Mr. Leslie Stephen lives and writes, this shelter at least is assured to her. The common sense—or what is called such—of the vulgar is not a thing of price, and I give it up to the tormentors; but the native shrewdness which is reinforced by wide knowledge and keen humour is a treasure indeed, and there is no page of Mr. Leslie Stephen's from which it is absent. (pp. 399-401)

> *James Ashcroft Noble, ''Living Critics III—Leslie Stephen,'' in* The Bookman, *New York, Vol. II, No. 5, January, 1896, pp. 399-401.*

FRANCIS THOMPSON   (essay date 1898)

[*Thompson was one of the most important poets of the Catholic Revival in nineteenth-century English literature. Often compared to the seventeenth-century metaphysical poets, especially Richard Crashaw, he is best known for his poem ''The Hound of Heaven'' (1893), which displays Thompson's characteristic themes of spiritual struggle, redemption, and transcendent love. Like other writers of the fin de siècle period, Thompson wrote poetry and prose noted for rich verbal effects and a devotion to the values of aestheticism. In the following excerpt from an essay originally published in the* Academy, *July 30, 1898, Thompson expresses admiration for Stephen's skills as a biographer but questions his ability as a critic.*]

A various and (in its way) influential career has been Mr. Leslie Stephen's in modern English literature. His *Hours in a Library* have given him deserved reputation as an essayist. His *History of English Thought in the Eighteenth Century* has given him reputation in the more solid walks of literature. In Mr. John Morley's ''Men of Letters'' series, his studies of Pope, Swift, and especially his admirable Johnson, have exhibited his power as a biographer—a biographer on the minor scale. As editor of the *Cornhill* he attained success and prominence in yet another line. Seldom does a successful *littérateur* make a good editor; but under Mr. Leslie Stephen's direction the *Cornhill* took a new lease of vitality such as it had not done since the days of its start by Thackeray, though its brilliance was on different lines from those followed by the great novelist. Under Mr. Stephen the immortal initials R.L.S [Robert Louis Stevenson] lit up its pages; he, too, if we recollect rightly, gave asylum to Mr. Henley, destined himself to be a famous editor. Both these writers might have sought in vain the recognition of the conventional editor. Homage to the man who helps others up the ladder which he has climbed himself. But with energies

unexhausted, his last adventure was his most memorable. He became the editor and the inspiration of that monumental work, the *Dictionary of National Biography,* and not only went through all the labours of its editing, but contributed numbers of articles to its first volumes. It has now been relinquished to the control of Mr. Sidney Lee; but its inception must ever be associated with Mr. Leslie Stephen. For he not only edited it, wrote for it, but he impressed on it—in style and plan—his own character. The numerous contributors who supported and continue to support the undertaking wrote as they have written because Mr. Stephen set them the model. And the model was his own.

What that model is may be learned from his new volumes, *Studies of a Biographer,* which represent most of the characteristics to be found in his life's work, except, perhaps, such more lengthy and set work as the *History of Eighteenth Century Thought.* The title, *Studies of a Biographer,* almost disclaims the name of essayist, though we have called him essayist. Yet there are some things in this work which justify that name, and these let us consider first. From this aspect, among his many aspects, Mr. Leslie Stephen is peculiar and difficult to estimate aright. Let it be said frankly, and in general, that the essay (properly so called, and exercising the widest latitude in the interpretation of the term) is not Mr. Stephen's province. Yet it is impossible to refuse him respect in it. The essay is not his province by birthright; yet he makes it his by force of arms. In the essay on Matthew Arnold (delivered as a lecture before the Owens College, but really an essay) he modestly sets himself down a Philistine. ''Humility is truth,'' said St. Bernard. Humility here is truth. Mr. Leslie Stephen, from the standpoint of Matthew Arnold, is a Philistine. That reminds us how the word has shifted its meanings since the days of Arnold. It has come to mean a man who cares nothing for literature. Nay, its uttermost degradation has been reached by a writer in the daily press, a writer belonging to the class of ''young barbarians'' whom Arnold contemned, and who has used it to designate those that do not dress according to the highly tailored canons of the ''Johnnies'' and ''Chappies.'' After this, the spiritual children of Arnold have nothing left but to abandon the word, as cast-off clothing, to the *valets* of language. Arnold intended it for those—inside or outside literature—who were natively prosaic and unimaginative. Now to these Mr. Stephen belongs. One is loath to endorse his self-claim of that ugly word ''Philistine.'' One is loath to abandon him to the enemy—he does too much honour to them. He is a literary Panther:

> So poised, so gently he descends from high,
> It seems a soft dismissal from the sky.

Yet throughout his writing one cannot but be conscious of a certain hardness, a lack of moist light. He appreciates poetry—particularly the poetry of men such as Wordsworth and Arnold. But his appreciation is intellectual. Poetry, or the appreciation of poetry, requires in its fulness both intellect and emotion. Nevertheless one may have it without intellect, but not without emotion. Mr. Stephen does seem in a certain way to reach an intellectual appreciation even of the aesthetic side in poetry. If he does not reach it directly, he seems, by a certain strenuous fairness of mind, to reach it in a reflex way, through considering and appreciating its aesthetic effect on others. In the same manner he succeeds in forming an intellectual image of much else, in diverse directions, which has no personal appeal to him. So he becomes the most cultivated of non-aesthetic writers; of all Philistines, the one whom those of the opposite camp can read with pleasure and placidity.

All this comes out remarkably in his discourse on Arnold. It is the best essay ever written by a critic on an author with whom he was in no native sympathy. That is to say, an author whose root-principles are the destructive opposite of his own. Over and over again one exclaims: "He should have belonged to us!" Yet we are simultaneously aware that he never could have been one of us; that he is a born antagonist, with a superbly chivalrous recognition of his adversary's merit and strength. His judgment of Arnold is admirable, his sympathy refused or unwilling. That is a paradox which runs through Mr. Leslie Stephen's whole nature. His mind is that of the "scientist," but a glorified scientist. The scientist professes to examine everything without *a priori* bias; but when he confronts something alien to his own province, resting on principles other than his own, he becomes the most partisan and bigoted of critics. Mr. Stephen really tries to carry out the principles which the brethren of his cause only profess. To perceive this, compare his methods when he confronts an idealist with the methods (in a like situation) of Professor Huxley. Take as a specimen of his thoughtfully candid spirit this passage on Arnold, with which we might have some quarrel in a detail or so, but surely none in essence:

> We—for I may perhaps presume that some of you belong, like me, to the prosaic faction—feel, when dealing with such a man as Arnold, at a loss. He has intuitions where we have only calculations. . . . He shows at once a type where our rough statistical and analytical tables fail to reveal more than a few tangible facts; he perceives the spirit and finer essence of an idea where it seems to slip through our coarser fingers, leaving only a residuum of sophistical paradox. In the long run, the prosaic weigher and measurer has one advantage—he is generally in the right as far as he goes. [Quite true.] His tests may be coarser, but they are more decisive, and less dependent upon his own fancies ["fancy" is an erroneous word in the case of a *true* master of intuition]; but when he tries to understand his rival, to explain how at a bound the intuitive perception has reached conclusions after which he can only hobble on limping feet, he is apt to make a bungle of it; to despise the power in which he is so deficient; and probably to suggest unreasonable doubts as to its reality and value.

Was ever such recognising criticism from an avowed demi-adversary? Throughout, Mr. Stephen admits the value of being "shaken up" by Arnold's keen assaults on the rigid Philistine position. *Fas est ab hoste doceri* ["It is allowable to learn even from an enemy"] is the burthen of his essay. Yet there is a suggested reason for his avowed half-protesting sympathy. Arnold and he are really one in cause. They are both Agnostics, though their Agnosticism is so diverse in pattern. And many of his strictures on Arnold would be admitted—nay, applauded—by idealists who were not Agnostics.

Mr. Stephen's limitations as essayist are better seen in his comments on the recent *Life of Tennyson*. He takes up the position which many of us take—that the later Tennyson is not equal to the earlier. He takes it up with characteristic modesty and apology, fearing that he may be "Philistine." But when he comes to the reason of the faith that is in him, he flounders. He shelters himself behind the allegory of "The Idylls," and

his dislike of allegory; behind his dislike of philosophy, so shadowily and indirectly conveyed. One may almost assert with confidence that the real reason of his abated enthusiasm is one with ours. Ruskin expressed it when he said that he felt the art and finish in these poems a little more than he liked to feel it. To this Tennyson replied that "The Idylls" were really rapidly written. Mr. Stephen feels the answer to be insufficient, but goes into all manner of roundabout considerations in the endeavour to explain *why* the answer is unsatisfactory. If his strength had lain in discussion, comment, analysis, he would have struck the direct answer at once. Mr. Ruskin was right. It matters nothing at all *how* a poem was written: it matters everything what is its effect. If the effect be one of downright inspiration, it is insignificant whether the poet spent months upon it. If the effect be one of self-conscious elaboration, without fire or fervour, or spontaneous richness, it does not signify though it were written in an hour after supper. Tennyson's earlier poems were full enough of highly wrought diction (whether he actually lingered over them or not); but this was carried off by the underlying *spirit* of inspiration. In "The Idylls" this magic is apparent only in passages, in images, in lines, in phrases: the general tissue has an air of mere artistry, without magic, without inevitableness. The allegory is neither here nor there; one's tastes as to the poetic expression of philosophy are neither here nor there. One comes to perceive that Mr. Stephen's power hardly lies in criticism. Even in the case of Arnold he makes no illuminative remarks; says nothing that in substance has not been said before. Neither, most certainly, does it lie in making a subject the theme for his own flights of thought or fancy. Where does it lie?

If one had read nothing else that Mr. Leslie Stephen had written; if one had read neither his "Men of Letters" volumes nor his contributions to the *Dictionary of National Biography*, the answer would yet be apparent in [*Studies of a Biographer*.] The reader may find it writ large in the "Johnsoniana," the "Byrom," the "Gibbon's Autobiography," the "Importation of German," above all, in "Wordsworth's Youth." The "Johnsoniana" deals with Dr. Birkbeck Hill's "Johnsonian Miscellanies," and in masterly manner impresses into its few pages a sketch of the un-Boswellian Johnson; bringing out by contrast the debt we owe Boswell, the true genius of that much-sneered-at writer. Yet with all its compression it is not dry. Even more typical is the article on Wordsworth. Mr. Stephen is here treating a book of M. Legouis—a book singularly interesting and unexpectedly excellent as coming from a French writer. With some dissent in minor matters (as he mentions), he does yet give the reader, in effect, an admirable and clear synopsis of what M. Legouis takes a book to set forth. The detailed examination by which M. Legouis brings out and enforces his conclusions is, perforce, absent; but the pith of the book is there. So that, having read Mr. Stephen, you could almost work out the French writer's demonstration for yourself.

That, in a phrase, is Mr. Leslie Stephen's peculiar function and excellence—to extract the square root of a book, or of many books. Clearly, we cannot call such a production an essay, or such a writer an essayist, in the original meaning of the terms. Not, indeed, according to any sense of these terms, with all their modern latitude of application. He does not make a book or a theme a nucleus of his own discourse; he macerates a subject; he scoops the pulp of the fruit, and throws away the skin. Essentially, no matter what he writes, at his best and most characteristic he is, in fact, a biographer. Whether writing *Johnson* for the "Men of Letters," or the "Johnsoniana" in these volumes, which is professedly more or less an essay, he

Stephen at the age of twenty-eight.

is equally a biographer. A biographer, but a biographer in little. And thus all his tasks have been really an unconscious preparation for the crowning task by which he will chiefly live—the *Dictionary of National Biography.* There his gift of scholarly and felicitous compression, his power to fuse multifarious information without dulness and with perfect proportion, found its fitting exercise. It does not matter that only a certain portion of the innumerable articles in that work are actually from his pen. The credit of an architect is not lessened because the details of his work must needs be executed by subordinates. And Mr. Leslie Stephen is the architect of the Dictionary; though, like Michelangelo, he has had to leave to another architect the task of continuing and completing his conception. Every article therein is framed under laws and upon a model laid by him. And those laws, that model, are derived from his own practice; from that method of cultured, perspicuous, symmetrical condensation, exhibited in this book as in those which have gone before it. One or two papers there are, it is true, in the beginning of the book, both desultory in structure, and frequently slipshod in grammar. But the bulk of it is as well-knit in style as in substance. The Liebig of biography—that is our final verdict on Mr. Leslie Stephen. (pp. 3-9)

> *Francis Thompson, "The Liebig of Biography," in his* Literary Criticisms, Newly Discovered and Collected, *edited by Rev. Terrence L. Connolly, S.J., E. P. Dutton and Company Inc., 1948, pp. 3-9.*

THE NATION (essay date 1904)

[*In the following review of* English Literature and Society in the Eighteenth Century, *the critic discusses those qualities that earned*

What were the qualities which made Leslie Stephen, towards the close of his career, the first among living English critics? *English Literature and Society in the Eighteenth Century* supplies for any intelligent reader the answer to our question. His preëminence among the writers of his time was not due to any single talent; it was not due to his mere literary gifts, great though they were. It was due to the obvious presence, in every work which he has produced, of four qualities rare in themselves and hardly ever found in combination—sincerity, individuality, humor, and the scientific spirit.

"So far as my reading has gone," writes Leslie Stephen in the *Science of Ethics,* which to some of us constitutes the most impressive and weightiest of all his works, "I have found only two kinds of speculation which are absolutely useless—that of the hopelessly stupid, and that of the hopelessly insincere." Of stupidity he can never have felt himself in danger, and there is not a book he has written which does not show the determination that, whatever else it should lack, it should possess the merit of sincerity. Let it be noted that sincerity includes a good deal more than the honesty of a teacher who is determined to say nothing which he does not believe to be true, and even to state on every topic which he handles the whole truth as it is seen by him. This is much, but for complete moral and intellectual sincerity something further is needed. The perfectly sincere man will instinctively aim at a certain kind of simplicity; he will not be led astray by the dictates of vanity, or even by the innocent egotism which attaches unbounded importance to a writer's own watchwords or phrases. Stephen was free at once from the conceit, and from the conceits, of your man of letters. His abhorrence of vanity and his sense of humor led him, indeed, greatly to undervalue the worth and the effect of his labors; he was a teacher who possessed far more disciples than he knew of.

> I do not believe (though again I cannot be certain even of this negative statement) that there is a single original thought in the book from beginning to end. By original, I mean, of course, a thought which has not occurred to others; though I, of course, also claim to have made every thought which I utter my own by reflection and assimilation.

These words, taken from the *Science of Ethics,* show how little he claims for himself as a teacher of ethics.

> I hope and believe that I have said nothing original. I have certainly only been attempting to express the views which are accepted, in their general outline at least, by historians, whether of the political or literary kind.

This is his humble claim as Ford lecturer when handling a topic of which he was the acknowledged master. Humor, it may be allowed, here takes the form of gentle irony. Still, it is manifest that Stephen had no conceit of his own powers He was preëminently a man of letters, but he did not even overrate the importance of literature. "Nations," he reminds his readers, "have got on remarkably well, and have made not only material but political and moral progress, in the periods when they have written few books, and those bad ones; and, conversely, have produced some admirable literature while they were developing some very ugly tendencies." He never dreamed that the writers of books were the modern priesthood, commissioned to supply mankind with spiritual guidance. Throughout his works are scattered memorable sentences which embody some profound truth admirably, because lucidly, expressed; but rarely, if ever, does he use what have been called sacramental terms. He never attempts to popularize a doctrine by embodying it in some expression, such as "sweetness and light," and "grand style," the "dismal science," and the like, which undoubtedly are for the moment effective, but which substitute words for argument, and, by becoming a sort of literary slang, vulgarize the ideas which they are supposed to embody.

If the power of our author's criticism is due to its sincerity, its charm arises from a quality which, for want of a better name, we may call "individuality." By whatever word this quality be called, it is nothing else than the capacity of a writer to stamp his work with the impress of his own individual character. This is an entirely different thing from egotism, and is a gift in which many powerful and interesting thinkers are deficient. Many are the men who, though endowed with much personal and much conversational charm, leave in their books no trace of the brilliancy, the sympathetic humor, or the easy play of intellect which was the delight of their friends. Readers who have felt something like personal affection for Dr. Johnson fancy that they know him from his works. This is in the main a delusion. If Boswell had never lived, is it certain that even Dr. Birkbeck Hill would have revelled in the writings of Johnson? We doubt it. We trace Johnson's character in his books, if indeed we ever read them, but we in fact read into the writings on which Johnson's fame is supposed to rest, the personal traits which have been revealed to us by Boswell. John Austin, again, delighted his friends by his exalted character, by the charm of his conversation and the wisdom of his thoughts. A passage in the Autobiography of John Mill is now the only memorial of Austin as he appeared to the circle of friends who knew and admired him. The *Province of Jurisprudence Defined* tells us nothing of Austin but his logical power, and contains nothing but the dogmatic utterances of a logical jurist; it utterly lacks individuality. Stephen, on the other hand, is himself to every line that he has written. His *Hours in a Library* and his Ford Lectures recall at any rate the conversational charm which no one who has ever come under its influence will forget. In this matter, as in some others, he resembles Bagehot, for when Bagehot explains the mysteries either of Lombard Street or of the English Constitution, readers feel that they are not so much reading a treatise as listening to a most interesting talker. With Stephen, criticism turns into an hour in a library with the most delightful of companions.

> I will confess that the last time I read *Clarissa Harlowe* it affected me with a kind of disgust. We wonder sometimes at the coarse nerves of our ancestors, who could see on the stage any quantity of murders, and ghosts, and miscellaneous horrors. Richardson gave me the same shock from the elaborate detail in which he tells the story of Clarissa; rubbing our noses, if I may say so, in all her agony, and squeezing the last drop of bitterness out of every incident.

Here we have acute criticism, but its interest is immensely enhanced by our keen sense of the critic's personality.

This individuality stands, of course, in the closest connection with that humor which gives a peculiar flavor to Stephen's works, and is itself bound up with his intense delight in biography. Sir George Trevelyan writes of Macaulay and his sisters that "when they were discoursing together about a work

of history or biography, a bystander would have supposed that they lived in the times of which the author treated, and had a personal acquaintance with every human being who was mentioned in its pages." These words equally apply to Stephen; he was not a mere student, but he lived with the people of the past as if they had been his intimate friends or associates. He would grow warm over a slander on Hobbes in the way in which most of us are heated by a libel on a living friend; he neither forgot, nor wished to forget, that Hazlitt, eminent as he was as a critic, was from some points of view a cad.

We have seen somewhere imputed to Stephen a want of insight into character. A more curious mistake on the part of a critic can hardly be imagined. The charm of literature was to our author the study of human beings, and he studied human nature with extraordinary acuteness. If any one wishes to test Stephen's gift for analyzing character, let him consider carefully the various passages in the Ford Lectures where reference is made to Pope. Nowhere do we get anything like so fair an estimate of the greatest of English satirists. We have brought before us, on the one hand, the absurdity of the notion adopted by Pope and accepted by his age, that "Homer was in the sphere of poetry what Lycurgus was supposed to be in the field of legislation," and "had at a single bound created poetry and made it a vehicle of philosophy, politics, and ethics." But, on the other hand, we are not suffered to forget that

> Pope manages to be really impressive, and to utter sentiments which really ennobled the deist creed—the aversion to narrow superstition, to the bigotry which "dealt damnation round the land," and the conviction that the true religion must correspond to a cosmopolitan humanity. I remember hearing Carlyle quote with admiration the "Universal Prayer":
>
> > Father of all, in every age,
> > In every clime adored,
> > By saint, by savage, and by sage,
> > Jehovah, Jove, or Lord,
>
> and it is the worthy utterance of one good legacy which the deist bequeathed to posterity.

Sincerity, individuality, a sense of humor, are, in Stephen, combined with the scientific spirit. He never for a moment forgets, or lets his readers forget, that, while every man is a distinct individual, marked by traits peculiar to himself, yet every man, however eminent, is influenced by the spirit of his time. To perceive this general truth and to accept it, is nothing; there is no one who now does not know that every one is in a sense the creature of his age. But vague generalizations of this kind are in themselves excessively worthless and often excessively delusive. No one proclaimed the platitudes or truisms of so-called scientific history in more sounding language than Buckle, but no writer of any eminence ever threw less light on the relation between men's character and the circumstances of their age. Stephen has no tremendous laws of progress to announce; he entertains no great belief in wide generalizations; but in the Ford Lectures, as in most of his writings, he insists again and again upon the consideration that

> the philosophy of an age is in itself determined to a very great extent by the social position. It gives the solutions of the problems forced upon the reasoner by the practical conditions of his time. To understand why certain ideas become current, we have to consider not merely the

ostensible logic, but all the motives which led men to investigate the most pressing difficulties suggested by the social development.

But he does much more than enounce this principle: he traces out its actual working as exhibited in the literature of the eighteenth century. Take, as one example of this extraordinary capacity for blending philosophy with the history of literature, the account given of the "Wits" and their influence. We seem at first to be hearing a series of anecdotes or epigrams about the leading writers of a brilliant age, but we are made gradually to see that all the men of that age, however different their talents and their opinions, held in common a belief in the supremacy of common sense. This faith was shared by Locke, by Berkeley, by Pope, by Addison, by Steele, and by Swift; it marked a revolution in the opinions of educated men, and separates the eighteenth from the sixteenth and seventeenth centuries.

> Politically, the change means toleration, for it is assumed that the vulgar can judge for themselves; intellectually, it means rationalism, that is, an appeal to the reason common to all men; and in literature it means the hatred of pedantry and the acceptance of such literary forms as are thoroughly congenial and intelligible to the common sense of the new audience. The hatred of the pedantic is the characteristic sentiment of the time.

And this state of things gave predominance to the "Wits," who were "scholars and gentlemen, with rather more of the gentlemen than the scholars," who lived in London and formed a kind of island of illumination amid the surrounding darkness of the agricultural country, who met at coffee-houses in a kind of "tacit confederation of clubs to compare notes and form the whole public opinion of the day."

But to detach our author's philosophic ideas from the epigrams, the anecdotes, and the quotations by which they are illustrated, is of necessity to spoil them, for his possession of the scientific spirit is manifested not by the enunciation of abstract principles, but by showing every reader how in fact the general ideas of an age, whether sought for in the lives, in the conversation, or in the writings of actual men and women, blend with and govern its literature. The true answer, in short, to the question with which this article opens is, that Leslie Stephen was the most eminent critic of his time because he was much more than a mere critic; he was at once a man of letters, a biographer, and a truth-loving and subtle thinker. (pp. 293-94)

> *"Leslie Stephen as a Critic,"* in The Nation, *Vol. LXXVIII, No. 2024, April 14, 1904, pp. 293-94.*

JANET E. COURTNEY (essay date 1920)

[*In the following excerpt, Courtney discusses Stephen's agnosticism and its impact upon his philosophical writings.*]

[In *Essays on Freethinking and Plainspeaking*] Stephen raises the question which Arnold had also raised, how best to effect the transition from the old world of unquestioning faith to the new world of scientific questioning. And his answer to it is very different from Arnold's.

> We are passing through a great change, of which no living man can expect to witness the end, or even the beginning of the end. How is it to

be brought about with the least shock to morality and lofty sentiment; and how are the ideas already familiar to educated people to be propagated through less cultivated classes with the least possible injury to the vital parts of their faith? . . . Am I to say, for example, openly, that the history of the promulgation of the Jewish Law is nothing but a popular legend, when ignorant persons will suppose that I mean to strike at the very foundation of morals? Is not silence in such a case better than a rash proclamation of a bare truth? . . . I imagine that one conclusion is plain enough in theory, though not always carried out in practice. Whatever reticence may be desirable, we ought not to tell lies, or to countenance the telling of lies.

Stephen is very clear that whoever believes that he cannot "at the same time officiate as a clergymen and speak the truth" is bound to officiate no longer. He is equally clear, with Bradlaugh, that "one of the superstitions against which we have specially to contend in England is the excessive idolatry of the Bible." Are the Broad Churchmen, who accept so many of the conclusions of the Higher Criticism, right in continuing to read in church passages of doubtful authenticity and still more dubious morality "with a solemnity calculated to impress their sacred character upon the minds of their congregations"?

His answer, put shortly, is that this cannot be right. He recognises that though "the Broad Church party are in the main honest and able men," their vain efforts to reconcile the irreconcilable "involve a waste of honesty and ability." Maurice's writings seemed to him "a melancholy instance of the way in which a fine intellect may run to waste in the fruitless endeavour to force new truth into the old mould. A new chaos, and not a new order, is the result of such manipulation of the raw materials of faith." But Maurice was a mystic and a metaphysician. Stephen was a disbeliever in the value of ontology—he regarded it as the ghost of theology—and there is no trace of mysticism in any of his writings, except perhaps a hint in *The Alps in Winter,* where he speaks of "pure undefined emotion, indifferent to any logical embodiment, undisturbed by external perception."

But for the most part he was by no means indifferent to logical embodiment. To him the first duty of a thinker was "saying what he thinks in the plainest possible language." He would scarcely tolerate even the use of a foreign word. No το τι ην ειναι or *Ding an sich* for him. What was clearly apprehended could be expressed in its simple English equivalent. No wonder that Maurice seemed to him "muddle-headed, intricate, and futile," though this he said in a private letter only. In the *Essays* he merely indulges in a half-tender, half-humorous reminiscence of the days when he sat among those who could not come "within the range of (Maurice's) personal influence without being profoundly attracted by the beauty of his character. The lads who, with the advantage of hearing his teaching before the authorities of King's College discovered that he did not believe that hell was as hot and as durable as could be wished, generally went through a curious intellectual stage in after life. Some, indeed, have never emerged from it." Others, like Leslie Stephen, retained "only the moral lesson that candour and toleration were excellent things, whilst refusing to admit that they implied acceptance of two contradictory theories at the same time."

Even in this first volume of *Essays,* and still more clearly in the later *An Agnostic's Apology,* Stephen attacked the problem, which Arnold had shirked, of the divinity of Jesus Christ. Much had been said from Colenso's time onwards against the credibility and authenticity of the Old Testament stories. People were beginning to be accustomed to hear these questioned with equanimity. But the New Testament was a different matter. Even Arnold had not ventured beyond a suggestion that the more miraculous events, such as the Resurrection, were not unmixed with legend, and, as *Aberglaube,* need not be regarded as "of faith." Stephen did not stop there. He will have nothing to say to such glozing over of difficulties.

> It is the product of intellectual indolence, though not of actual intellectual revolt. We have not the courage to say that the Christian doctrines are false, but we are lazy enough to treat them as irrelevant. . . . To proclaim unsectarian Christianity is, in circuitous language, to proclaim that Christianity is dead. . . . No! the essence of the belief is the divinity of Chirst. . . . To be a Christian in any real sense you must start from a dogma of the most tremendous kind, and an undogmatic creed is as senseless as a statue without shape or a picture without colour. Unsectarian means unchristian.

To his own question, "Are we Christians?" he replies in effect that most men of intellect are not. Many still call themselves by the name, some for lower reasons, some

> for the higher reason, that they fear to part with the grain along with the chaff; but such men have ceased substantially, though only a few have ceased avowedly, to be Christian in any intelligible sense of the name. How long the shadow ought to survive the substance is a question which may be commended to serious consideration.

The *Essays* end, therefore, with a negative conclusion. By 1878 he was prepared to speak more definitely. In the interval his life had been broken by a great sorrow. On his forty-third birthday (28th Nov., 1875) his wife died suddenly in Switzerland, where she had gone for her health, and where she was happily looking forward to the birth of a second child. To a man so affectionate and so dependent upon affection the blow was terrible, coming as it did not long after the death of his mother, to whom he had always been so tenderly attached. That loss he could take with resignation. Lady Stephen had died in the fulness of years. "I only feel that something is taken out of my life," he wrote to Norton, "which can never come back to it, and that I am one stage nearer the end. . . . I hope that it may help to make me a better man in some sense," though not (as a pious uncle had hoped) to make him a Christian.

But his wife's death was different—"some things won't bear talking about"—and what he had to say he could only say by inference in his writings. His convictions were unflinching. "Is there a more cutting piece of satire in the language than the reference in our funeral service to the 'sure and certain hope of a blessed resurrection'?" Even in the Christian churches themselves, are there not strange puzzles? Do they not claim essential continuity with the Jewish creed, a creed which pointedly omits all reference to a future state? Is not the *Book of Job* "a splendid declamation in favour of Agnosticism"? And

Ecclesiastes "a treatise of 'melancholy scepticism'"? Yet these are read in the churches. Compare again the Psalm, "Lord, thou hast been our refuge," with the passage from Paul's *Epistle to the Corinthians,* appointed to be read in the Burial Service.

> Which is the most congenial sentiment at a moment when our hearts are most open to impressions? Standing by an open grave, and moved by all the most solemn sentiments of our nature, we all, I think—I can only speak for myself—with certainty must feel that the Psalmist takes his sorrow like a man . . . while the Apostle is desperately trying to shirk the inevitable. . . . I would rather face the inevitable with open eyes.

This was Stephen's attitude always. He would face the inevitable. As an agnostic he must assert that there are limits to human intelligence, and that metempirical knowledge, which includes theology, lies beyond those limits and is therefore, for him, no knowledge. Of Christ he says,

> I hold that Christ was a man. I regard the character of Christ as within the range of human possibilities. . . . Why should I be forced to postulate an incarnation of deity to account for goodness, even in a superlative degree? . . . The belief in God is simply the opposite pole of disbelief in man.

Of the Bible he says,

> The Bible has been made an idol and therefore made grotesque. . . . The grotesque in art and religion is merely a proof that the infantile imagination has no grasp of realities. Floods drowning the world, rivers turned to blood, and the sun standing still to light a massacre, are toys of an arbitrary fancy, which can join incongruities without a sense of absurdity.

So much for his negative conclusions. What had he to give on the positive side? In a long analysis of Newman's theology, especially the super-subtle *Grammar of Assent,* he grants Newman's thesis—which was also Arnold's—that the test of a creed is its vitality. "It proves its right by exercising its power. That is true which will work." But when Newman listened with awe to the voice in his soul, *Securus judicat orbis terrarum,* was it necessary, was it even reasonable, to limit *orbis terrarum* to the lands which had embraced Catholicism? And when Arnold said of the secret of Jesus that "it worked," was it incumbent on him to believe that the secret was of divine origin, was more than the moral teaching of a man of the finest moral perceptions? Faith is certainly an assumption, and assumptions—hypotheses—are a necessity of intellectual progress.

> The whole history of human belief is a history of the growth and decay of such assumptions. . . . To assume a doctrine may be the best or only way of testing its truth. . . . But whilst this is perfectly true of belief, it is not true of right belief.

That depends on the verification of assumptions. We must not believe more than the evidence warrants, no matter how comforting, how fortifying, how fertile in good such beliefs may seem to be!

The *depositum* of faith which we must accept is not that which is guarded by any single Church, however august in its history and imposing in its pretensions. It is that body of scientific truth which is the slow growth of human experience through countless ages and which develops by the labour of truth-loving men and under the remorseless pressure of hard facts. . . . Those opinions have the most authority which are most rational; and the safest test of rationality is that they have commended themselves to independent inquirers, who themselves acknowledged no law but reason.

How does Christianity stand the test? In Stephen's opinion, very imperfectly.

In its origin it proposed a remedy no longer appropriate to modern wants; and greatly as it has been developed it has not been developed in the required direction. The old doctrine, for example, makes poverty sacred and inevitable, instead of regarding it as an evil to be extirpated; it places all our hopes in a world differing from this in all its conditions, and to be reached only through a supernatural catastrophe, instead of hoping everything from gradual development.

Christianity must be discarded, therefore, as both untrue and definitely harmful, because contradicting the belief in human progress which has gradually dawned upon reasoning men. But, when asked, "What is to be the religion of the future?" Stephen, true to his agnostic principles, answers, "I have not the slightest idea. I am perfectly certain of my own ignorance, and I have a strong impression that almost every one else is equally ignorant." Still he gives some faint indications of the possibilities. Science, he thinks, "has the key of the position. The common-sense of mankind, as well as their lower passions, would crush any open attack upon the tangible material results of modern scientific progress." (pp. 183-91)

The Science of Ethics . . . represents the maturity of [Stephen's] thought, his effort to state as lucidly as might be what were those principles of morality in which he believed, and which were to help him, as an agnostic, "to live and die like a gentleman." The book owes, of course, a good deal to Herbert Spencer, who had done so much to revise philosophy in the light of Darwin's discoveries. But though Stephen acknowledges the debt fully, it is clear that he was repelled by Spencer's metaphysical speculations. "The unknowable . . . is not made into a reality by its capital letter." As regards the theory of knowledge, the last word for him was with Hume. His greatest debt was to John Stuart Mill and, on the scientific side, to Darwin direct. Spencer's work seemed to him derivative, and Sidgwick's view of the relation of evolution to ethics did not commend itself to him.

His aim he defines in words which recall Spencer, "to lay down an ethical doctrine in harmony with the doctrine of evolution." Metaphysics are to be ruled out. Metaphysical reasoning, he appears to think, is quite distinct from scientific reasoning (an odd conviction!), and knowledge can be obtained in the region of the physical sciences "entirely independent of the metaphysician's theories. . . . May we not discover propositions about the relations of men to each other, and the internal relations of the individual human being which will be

equally independent of metaphysical disputes?" He strives, therefore, to get moral questions into the region of science— "a region in which all metaphysical tenets are indifferent"— and proceeds to an examination of the facts, which are the subject-matter of ethics, viz. the emotions and the reason in relation to conduct, the motives actuating men in social relations, the forms which the moral law has assumed, the virtues, their connexion with happiness, the conscience, the moral sanctions. The tone of the whole treatise is severely scientific. Its outcome is an enlightened utilitarianism. A moral rule is "a statement of a condition of social welfare," proved to be such by scientific observation and comparison. Moral problems "can only be examined when we have some knowledge of the organisation of man and of society, which is unattainable by any other than the scientific method." To prove, for instance, drunkenness to be socially mischievous is to prove it to be wicked. "Morality is a product of the social factor."

Ethics, then, is the child of sociology, and sociology is a science to be studied by the historical method and the method of experiment. It is a somewhat arid creed. No wonder that Leslie Stephen was disposed to belittle the influence of the moralist.

He accepts human nature as it is, and he tries to show how it may maintain and improve the advantages already acquired. His influence is little enough; but, such as it is, it depends upon the fact that a certain harmony has already come into existence. . . . It is happy for the world that moral progress has not to wait till an unimpeachable system of ethics has been elaborated.

It is, perhaps, also happy for the world that there have been moral teachers more inspired, if less conscientiously scientific, than Leslie Stephen. One suspects that he was a philosopher more from a sense of duty than from an irresistible impulse to philosophising. Had it been otherwise, he would, perhaps, have been less content to turn his back upon metaphysics without a more searching examination of its claim. But he was the product of an age, and of a university, inclined to exalt scientific method almost above scientific discoveries, and to allow more play to scientific analysis than to scientific imagination. It is curious that Oxford, dogmatic in its theology, has always been more inclined to metaphysical speculation, whereas Cambridge makes up for the fluidity of its divinity by restricting its moral philosophy within very narrow limits.

Stephen's more human and imaginative qualities he gave to literature, not to philosophy. It is as a biographer that he has the greatest claim to remembrance, and biography needs human insight and human sympathy, qualities in which this most lovable of friends was in no way deficient. His Lives of his brother, of Fawcett, of Swift, Johnson, Pope, George Eliot, are models of their kind, the last especially sympathetic and discriminating in its criticism. And the literary essays, which he republished as *Hours in a Library* and *Studies of a Biographer,* prove his gifts as a critic of letters.

Why, then, did he philosophise? In the first place, no doubt, because the study of the eighteenth century deists led on naturally to rationalism and to the nineteenth century utilitarians. But, secondly, because he firmly believed that every man should think out his own creed, that moral problems "require to be discussed in every generation with a change of dialect," and that it is much "if one can communicate the very slightest impetus to the slowly grinding wheels of speculation.'' More he did not hope to do, and perhaps more cannot be claimed for him. His greatest achievement as a freethinker is just his clear thinking and plain speaking. He did not greatly advance ethical or sociological theory. He deliberately did nothing for the other branches of philosophy. Where religion and theology were concerned, he was destructive, not constructive. But he did for the cultured classes what Bradlaugh had done for the uncultured. He was, in his way, quite as much of an iconoclast without any of the coarseness of attack which would have revolted those he sought to help.

Now and again a phrase escaped him, which was perhaps unnecessarily wounding, as, for instance, that Christianity had "to provide a God-man; to bring together into some sort of unity two conceptions so heterogeneous as that of the ground of all existence and that of a particular peasant in Galilee.'' But, for the most part, whilst fully exemplifying his own principle that "every man who says frankly and fully what he thinks is so far doing a public service,'' he contrived to render that service without any unnecessary or offensive scorn. He did not seek to proselytise. Conversion, in the religious sense, appeared to him an absurdity. He had no anxiety to thrust his views upon others, but neither would he conceal them. Free himself and the defender of freedom for others, he believed that toleration was unconditionally and necessarily conducive to happiness, and that Christian orthodoxy, with its inevitable tendency to ally itself with the conservative forces of society, was a real danger to human progress. And, by his own life, and by the courage and serenity of spirit, with which he faced a long and painful illness that could have but one end, he impressed upon all who came near him, that Christianity was not needed to help a man "to die like a gentleman.'' (pp. 192-96)

> Janet E. Courtney, "Leslie Stephen," in her Free-thinkers of the Nineteenth Century, E. P. Dutton & Company, 1920, pp. 171-97.

DESMOND MacCARTHY (essay date 1937)

[MacCarthy was one of the foremost English literary and dramatic critics of the twentieth century. He served for many years on the staff of the New Statesman and edited Life and Letters. A member of the Bloomsbury group, which also included Stephen's daughters Vanessa Bell and Virginia Woolf among its number, MacCarthy was guided by their primary tenet that "one's prime objects in life were love, the creation and enjoyment of aesthetic experience, and the pursuit of knowledge." According to his critics, Mac-Carthy brought to his work a wide range of reading, serious and sensitive judgment, an interest in the works of new writers, and high critical standards. In the following excerpt, MacCarthy describes Stephen's critical perspective and assesses his importance. For a response to MacCarthy's comments, see the excerpt by Q. D. Leavis dated 1939.]

Judged by the influence upon men's minds alone, the writings which Leslie Stephen collected in **Essays on Free-thinking and Plain-speaking** . . . , and in **An Agnostic's Apology** . . . , must be considered the most important part of his life's work. One reason why, as we shall be presently reminded, he wrote disparagingly of literary criticism, was that it seemed so trivial compared with criticism of thought and religion. What if he had induced some readers to take a clearer view of the merits and limitations of Fielding or De Quincey, or if he had succeeded in giving a tolerably true account of some man's life? Of what importance was that compared with helping men to a truer conception of the nature of things, or with the work of a man of science? This reflection, which often visited him, robbed him of retrospective satisfaction in his books, though while writing them he derived keen pleasure from knocking nails on the head. He knew that his controversial writings had made an impression on the public, who think by fits and starts, but before the end of the nineteenth century his controversial work was over. He could have only repeated himself. (pp. 7-8)

[The] most comprehensive description of Leslie Stephen as a critic would be to call him an expert in character, if that is also taken as implying connoisseurship in defining points of view. It is his conception of the writer that gives unity to most of his literary essays; not the relation of a book to the history of literature or to some standard of perfection. What he investigated with greater interest was the relation of a book to its author. Of course, this did not preclude his pointing out with great acuteness, as he went along, an author's successes or failures as a craftsman, or reminding us of the pertinence or the folly of a work as a commentary on life; but as a critic he directed our attention chiefly to the sort of man the author had apparently been; to the man who saw and felt things thus and thus, and expressed himself in this way and no other.

The title of his last four volumes of criticism, **Studies of a Biographer,** is in no small degree applicable to his first collection of critical essays, **Hours in a Library.** In his essay on **"Shakespeare the Man,"** we find him writing:

> Now I confess that to me one main interest in reading is always the communion with the author. *Paradise Lost* gives me the sense of intercourse with Milton, and the *Waverley Novels* bring me a greeting from Scott. Every author, I fancy, is unconsciously his own Boswell, and, however "objective" or dramatic he professes to be, really betrays his own secrets.
>
> (pp. 9-10)

Now a critic who approaches his subjects in this spirit will inevitably discourse more about human nature and morals than about art, and Leslie Stephen is the least aesthetic of noteworthy critics. In this connection his strenuous evangelical upbringing must not be overlooked; through both his father and his mother his home was affiliated to the Clapham Sect. He is constantly harping on "sincerity." Sincerity is a condition of all satisfactory personal relations, and therefore a condition of the communion between writer and reader which he valued most. In his essay on Sterne, whom he finds deficient in that respect, he says:

> The qualification must, of course, be understood that a great book really expresses the most refined essence of the writer's character. It gives the author transfigured and does not represent all the stains and distortions which he may have received in his progress through the world. In real life we might have been repelled by Milton's stern Puritanism, or by some outbreak of rather testy self-assertion. In reading *Paradise Lost*, we feel only the loftiness of character, and are raised and inspirited by the sentiments without pausing to consider the particular application.
>
> If this be true in some degree of all imaginative writers, it is especially true of humorists. For humour is essentially the expression of a per-

sonal idiosyncrasy. . . . We love the humour in
short so far as we love the character from which
it flows.

He could not bring himself to love Sterne, which I (though
love may be too strong a word) find no difficulty in doing. He
examined his life, especially his married life and his flirtations,
with severity, and he concluded that ''Sterne was a man who
understood to perfection the art of enjoying his own good
feelings as a luxury without humbling himself to translate them
into practice'' (Stephen's definition of a sentimentalist). The
judgment pronounced by Thackeray on Sterne seemed to him
substantially unimpeachable. He strongly reprobated Sterne's
trick of inclining our thoughts (before we realise it) gently
towards indecency. With that sense of fun which delights to
trip up the dignity of the reader, trusting to his smiling afterwards, he had no sympathy. Leslie Stephen did not smile at
that sort of mischief; nor did he make any comment on the
really penetrating humour of the opening of *Tristram Shandy*.

Nevertheless, it must not be supposed that this essay, perhaps
more likely than any other in ***Hours in a Library*** to strike our
contemporaries as missing the point, is without warmly appreciative passages. Referring to Sterne's touches of exquisite
precision, he says that ''they give the impression that the thing
has been done once for all.'' Two or three of the scenes in
which Uncle Toby expresses his sentiments struck him as being
''as perfect in their way as the half-dozen lines in which Mrs
Quickly describes the end of Falstaff; and Uncle Toby's oath,''
he declares to be ''a triumph fully worthy of Shakespeare'';
but he adds, ''the recording angel, through he comes in effectively, is a little suspicious to me.'' While admitting the
felicity with which the scene is presented, he suggests that it
would have been really stronger had the angel been omitted
(by stronger, he means more moving), ''for the angel seems
to introduce an unpleasant air as of eighteenth-century polite-
ness; we fancy that he would have welcomed a Lord Chester-
field to the celestial mansions with a faultless bow and a dexterous compliment.''

Perfectly true. But to wish on that account the angel away is
surely to miss the point of Sterne, whose attitude towards all
emotions was playful. No doubt Sterne thought that here, or
in the bravura passage on the dead donkey, he was achieving
the acme of pathos. But his temperament was stronger than
any conscious intention; consequently what in effect we enjoy,
as everywhere in Sterne, is an elegant ambiguity. As with some
other Irishmen known to fame, Sterne's heart was in his imagination. The infection we catch from him is, as Goethe noticed,
a light fantastic sense of freedom; a state of mind (Shandyism)
in which we enjoy together the pleasures of extravagant sensibility, and a feeling that nothing much matters.

Leslie Stephen's attitude towards Sterne's pathetic passages
was the same as Dr Johnson's who, when Miss Monckton said:
''I am sure they have affected me,'' replied smiling and rolling
himself about, ''That is because, dearest, you are a dunce.''
Johnson set no store by airy detachment, nor could he believe
that posterity would cherish its products. Did he not point to
Sterne as an instance of the ephemeral nature of all reputations
founded on the fantastic? Leslie Stephen had no sense of the
fantastic, or of the charm of the artificial; it is one of the dumb
notes on his piano. He wanted to be moved; and more—he
wanted to be certain that the author had been moved himself.

We are always pursued in reading Pope . . . by
disagreeable misgivings. We don't know what

comes from the heart, and what from the lips:
when the real man is speaking, and when we
are only listening to old commonplaces skilfully vamped. . . . A critic of the highest order
is provided with an Ithuriel spear, which dis-
criminates the sham sentiments from the true.
As a banker's clerk can tell a bad coin by its
ring on the counter, without need of a testing
apparatus, the true critic can instinctively estimate the amount of bullion in Pope's epigrammatic tinsel. But criticism of this kind, as
Pope truly says, is as rare as poetical genius.
Humbler writers must be content to take their
weights and measures, or, in other words, to
test their first impression, by such external evidence as is available. They must proceed cautiously in these delicate matters, and instead of
leaping to the truth by a rapid intuition, pa-
tiently enquire what light is thrown upon Pope's
sincerity by the recorded events of his life, and
a careful cross-examination of the various witnesses to his character.

Leslie Stephen did not trust himself to tell good coin by its
ring, or perhaps it would be truer to say he thought he ought
not to. Certainly, investigations into the genuineness of an
author require a testing apparatus, even when conducted by a
critic of rapid intuitions. In the case of Pope that investigation
ended unfavourably. I will not consider at this point how far
that verdict ought to modify our estimate of Pope's poetry, but
will turn to an instance where the results of a similar enquiry
were so overwhelmingly favourable that they reversed a judgment based on the written word. In his first essay on Johnson,
Leslie Stephen wrote:

The whole art of criticism consists in learning
to know the human being who is partially revealed to us in his spoken or his written words.
Whatever the means of communication, the
problem is the same. The two methods of enquiry may supplement each other; but their substantial agreement is the test of their accuracy.
If Johnson, as a writer, appears to us to be a
mere windbag and manufacturer of sesquipe-
dalian verbiage, whilst as a talker, he appears
to be one of the most genuine and deeply feeling
of men, we may be sure that our analysis has
been somewhere defective.

Johnson was the man after Leslie Stephen's heart. Of his five
biographical monographs in the ***English Men of Letters,*** his
Johnson is the best, and it is equal to the very best in that
excellent series. Johnson was the man he loved most in literature, though not (need it be said?) the writer he admired most,
which incidentally throws some doubt on his critical method.
Johnson as a writer seemed to him ''a great force half wasted
because the fashionable costume of the day hampered the free
exercise of his powers''; but Johnson as he is known through
the records of his life and his talk, embodied nearly all the
qualities which Leslie Stephen admired most in other writers.

We cannot be in Johnson's company long without becoming
aware that what attracts us to him so strongly is that he combined a disillusioned estimate of human nature, sufficient to
launch twenty little cynics, with a craving for love and sympathy so urgent that it would have turned a weaker nature into
a benign sentimentalist, and in a lesser degree this is what

attracts us in Leslie Stephen. His raciest passages might often be described as cynical. There are also evidences of deep feeling. There is a Johnsonian contempt for those who look only upon the bright side of life or human nature, equalled only by a contempt for those who adopt a querulous or dainty tone.

> Good sense . . . is one of the excellent qualities to which we are scarcely inclined to do justice at the present day; it is the guide of a time of equilibrium, stirred by no vehement gales of passion, and we lose sight of it just when it might give us some useful advice.

But he is aware of its limitations. "Like all the shrewd and sensible part of mankind," he says of Johnson, "he condemns as mere moonshine what may be easily the first faint dawn of new daylight." That is an important admission.

But Leslie Stephen was born in 1832, not 1709, which implies considerable differences, and allowing for those, it is tempting to describe his critical work as an attempt to go on writing, in the nineteenth century, Johnson's *Lives of the Poets*. He was more at home with prose writers; but the poets he did study were Pope, Crabbe, Coleridge, Wordsworth, Tennyson and Matthew Arnold; Shelley in so far as his poetry is related to the ideas of Godwin; Cowper in so far as he could be compared with Rousseau, and Donne—but only in relation to his times. He sees Pope as "the incarnation of the literary spirit," and as the complete antithesis to the evil principle of dullness which generates an atmosphere in which literature cannot thrive; but he would be the last man to see in such a phrase as "die of a rose in aromatic pain" the best evidence of Pope's genius.

The essays on Tennyson and Matthew Arnold contain little literary criticism. The former gives an account of what Tennyson's poetry meant to Stephen's generation, and shows a strong preference for the earlier poetry. (pp. 11-21)

He utterly repudiated (and how rightly!) Taine's verdict on *In Memoriam* as the mourning of a correct gentleman wiping away his tears with a cambric handkerchief; but he regretted that the poet should be always haunted by the fear of depriving his "sister of her happy views" ("a woefully feeble phrase, by the way, for Tennyson"), and perpetually be praising the philosopher for keeping his doubts to himself. (pp. 21-2)

In the essay on Arnold he expresses the same impatience at being told again and again, however melodiously, that the wisest of us must take dejectedly "his seat upon the intellectual throne," keeping as our only friend "sad patience, too near neighbour to despair." (p. 22)

It is impossible to imagine a Matthew Arnold who had never been at Oxford and a Leslie Stephen who had never been at Cambridge. The stamp which this University left on him was lasting. The fourteen years he spent here as an undergraduate and a fellow of Trinity Hall, from 1850 to 1864, decided what he was to admire and trust in men and books throughout his life. A famous definition might be modified to fit him: Criticism is the adventures of the soul of Cambridge among masterpieces. Souls like bodies change. Perhaps that of Cambridge has changed or its changing; from time to time indications of that possibility have lately reached me. All I can say is that the spirit of Cambridge in the late 'nineties was very like indeed to that which Leslie Stephen knew and carried away with him. He was well aware that some of these adventures might cause outsiders to blaspheme, and there is a recurring note in his criticism—I will not call it apologetic, it was often humorously

defiant—which amounts now and then to an admission that possibly the soul of Cambridge had no business at all to embark on such adventures; to risk perdition in regions where reason is at a disadvantage compared with intuition, and the habits are encouraged of skimming over intellectual difficulties, and deviating into the delicate impertinences of egotism. As a practising critic he limited himself as far as he could to that aspect of his subject about which it was possible to argue. He was a man of letters who would have preferred to be a philosopher or a man of science. (pp. 23-5)

Perhaps this is the place to say something about his intellectual ambitions. Their nature as well as the direction of them had an effect on his criticism. Apparently he was not ambitious, but he was only not ambitious because, in literature at any rate, he thought only the highest achievement worth while; and that was out of his reach. One friend attributed to him the opinion that on the whole books ought *not* to be written; and there is occasionally something in the tone of his comments on authors which lends plausibility to that exaggeration. He would have gladly extended the condemnation of mediocre poetry ("In poetry there is no golden mean; mediocrity there is of a different metal") to every branch of literature. Yet he lived in a period of hero-worship, and was himself extremely susceptible to emotions of enthusiasm and reverence. His horror of gush was partly due to fear of failing to do justice to those almost sacred feelings. He held (and this was one of his first principles as a critic) that "a man's weakness can rarely be overlooked without underestimating his strength". Some of his studies in human nature might seem grudging, owing to the number of reservations they contain, until the reader has grasped that praise from Leslie Stephen, which he always strove to make precise, meant a very great deal.

His essays are an effective protest against the contemporary habit of debasing the currency of praise. He was absurdly humble about his own writings, partly, as I have said, because he would have far rather been a philosopher or a man of science, partly on account of this sense of the width of the gap between work of the first order and the next. It is possible that a tendency to dwell on that gap was self-consolatory; if he could be by no means reckoned among writers of the first order, others of no mean merit were likewise excluded. (pp. 34-6)

In the core of his emotional nature he gave preference to the private virtues. It is sometimes even disconcerting to find how much this influenced him in deciding the value of an author's works to the world. He is, as might have been anticipated, severe towards Rousseau; and in so far as he relents, it is due to his discovering in Rousseau "a redeeming quality," namely the value he set on the simple affections, on "an idyllic life of calm domestic tranquility," perhaps not unlike Cowper's delight in taking tea with Mrs Unwin, though streaked (oddly as it appears to Stephen) with "a kind of sensual appetite for pure simple pleasures." In Hazlitt he cannot stomach the *Liber Amoris;* in Coleridge, his having left Southey to look after Mrs Coleridge and the children; and in De Quincey he cannot overlook that the source of the awe-struck sense of the vast and vague which De Quincey communicated so magnificently, was opium. In Thackeray, one of his favorite novelists, he sees no faults that seriously matter, since "his writings mean, if they mean anything, that the love of a wife and child and friends is the one sacred element in our nature, of infinitely higher price than anything which can come into competition with it; and that Vanity Fair is what it is because it stimulates the pursuit of objects frivolous and unsatisfying just so far that they imply indifference to those emotions." He is also lenient to Kingsley, partly because he detects in Kingsley the belief that "the root of all that is good in man lies in the purity and vigour of the domestic affections." In short, there are times when we are left wondering if a critic, in whom the exercise of the intellect was a passion, is not saying in effect: "Be good, sweet maid, and let who will be clever." There are passages scattered through his books which indicate that, compared with qualities of heart, all others seemed to him like a row of figures preceded by a decimal point and incapable of rising to the value of a single unit. That he underrated the value of his own work, there is no doubt. Even his masterly **English Thought in the Eighteenth Century** failed to satisfy him. He knew it was well done, but he doubted its value, since thought and imaginative literature were only by-products of social evolution, "the noise that the wheels make as they go round," and therefore no history of thought could be complete by itself. It was because Sainte-Beuve had taken such pains to place every author in his social setting and his times that he respected Sainte-Beuve's work so much. The view held in France by some critics, and advocated in England by Oscar Wilde and Walter Pater, that criticism was the quintessence of literature appeared to him too absurd to discuss. All the critic could do for his fellow-men was to stimulate their interest in literature by pointing out what he had himself enjoyed or not enjoyed, and by giving names to the qualities he perceived in them. He could appeal to the reader and say: Are not these, when you come to think it over, the strong points of this book, and these the weak ones?

Stephen himself was deficient in the power of transmitting the emotions he had derived himself from literature; he seldom, if ever, attempted to record a thrill. But he excelled in describing the qualities of authors, whether he summed up for or against them; and this is a most important part of the critic's function. By focussing in a phrase our scattered impressions, the critic confers an intellectual benefit which increases our interest when we think over an author's works. True, we can enjoy Defoe without noticing that his method of producing an impression of reality is the same as that of the circumstantial liar, who introduces details so fortuitous that it is hard to believe he could have invented them; but when Leslie Stephen says this, it brings suddenly together in our minds a number of instances. And the same effect is produced by his remark that knowledge of human nature in Fielding is based on observation rather than intuitive sympathy. Leslie Stephen's critical essays are crammed with illuminating comments of this kind. Of course, they do not help us to decide whether the fiction in question is good or bad, any more than a naturalist's description of a beast necessarily throws light on its value to man. But criticism must be in great part a Natural History of Authors, in which are set forth their distinctive features, their adaptation to their environment, and their relations to other species. When it comes to judgment, the test which Leslie Stephen applied was the relation of a work to life, the extent to which it ministered, in one way or another, to all human good. (pp. 42-7)

> *Desmond MacCarthy, in his* Leslie Stephen, *1937. Reprint by Folcroft Library Editions, 1972, 47 p.*

Q. D. LEAVIS (essay date 1939)

[*Leavis was an English critic who served as co-editor of the literary journal* Scrutiny *for a number of years. Like her husband, critic F. R. Leavis, she adopted what has been called a conservative approach to literature, seeking to preserve the "great tradition" of such authors as George Eliot and Henry James. In*

assessing a work of literature, Leavis was particularly concerned with its moral character, and recommended the creation of fiction that would not only entertain but also subtly and skillfully edify the reader. In the following excerpt, Leavis responds to what she perceives as Desmond MacCarthy's objections to Stephen's critical methods (see excerpt dated 1937).]

The reputation of Leslie Stephen as literary critic seems to have been at its lowest ebb when Mr. Desmond MacCarthy in his lecture on *Leslie Stephen* [see excerpt dated 1937] . . . nailed down the coffin. No contrary demonstration was provoked among the audience or the Press. However, some of us may feel that the last word has not yet been said, on our side, and on the other—the corpse's—that these bones can still live. Those of us who can remember the barren state of English literary criticism before *The Sacred Wood* reached the common reader and before *The Problem of Style* and *Principles of Literary Criticism* appeared remember also their debt to Leslie Stephen: for after Johnson, Coleridge and Arnold who was there who was any help? (Certainly not Pater or Symons or Saintsbury or. . . .) We were grateful to Leslie Stephen not so much for what he wrote—though that was considerable—as for what he stood for, implied and pointed to. He seemed to us to be in the direct line of the best tradition of our literary criticism, to exemplify the principle virtues of a literary critic, and to exhibit a tone, a discipline and an attitude that were desirable models to form oneself on. This, to us, would have seemed the obvious starting-point for any contemporary littérateur speaking on that subject. Mr. MacCarthy, however, was entirely apologetic and deprecatory. This—he said, as it were—is what Leslie Stephen was, these were his scraps of abilities (and a poor showing they make, I grant you), of course he had none of the essential qualifications for a literary critic (we know what they are) and he had all these disabilities, but still there it is and I've done my duty by him.

I think it owing to Leslie Stephen to scrutinize Mr. MacCarthy's critical values and to state, in greater detail than I have done above, what Leslie Stephen stands for and what his criticism consisted of. For apart from Mr. MacCarthy's unfortunate testimonial and the chatty informal *Life and Letters* by Maitland, there is nothing; except Stephen's own *Some Early Impressions,* which even in Cambridge no one seems to read. On the other hand, everyone has read *To the Lighthouse,* and the portrait-piece of Mr. Ramsay by Leslie Stephen's gifted daughter elicited immediate recognition from the oldest generation. Yes, that's Leslie Stephen, the word went round; and that brilliant study in the Lytton Strachey manner of a slightly ludicrous, slightly bogus, Victorian philosopher somehow served to discredit Leslie Stephen's literary work. But it is obvious to any student of it that that work could not have been produced by Mr. Ramsay. However, Stephen seems fated to be known only as the original editor of the *D.N.B.* (pp. 404-05)

Let us recapitulate the grounds of dispute between Mr. MacCarthy and Leslie Stephen. Stephen, misguided man, thought the critic should confine himself to what is discussible about a work of art instead of recording his thrill at experiencing it: the youngest hand will have the answer ready that it is the critic's business to advance the profitable discussion of literature, substitute-creation ("transmitting the emotions derived from literature") being indefensible egotism. His detailed analyses of writings, focussing on the writer's idiom and technical devices, do not help us to decide whether the work is good or bad, says Mr. MacCarthy; we on the contrary who believe that literary criticism can be demonstrated and so argued about find Stephen's procedure—starting from the surface and working inwards to radical criticism—obviously right and convincing. We believe with Stephen that literary criticism is not a mystic rapture but a process of the intelligence. No doubt the environment of Clerk Maxwell and Henry Sidgwick was peculiarly favourable to the development of such an attitude to literature, but we recollect that Arnold and Coleridge also practised this method when they were most effectual. His feeling that the character of an author was a factor in his art to be reckoned with was, we are assured, a demerit in a critic, it interfered with his judgment of a piece of literature. We reply that Stephen had evidently a finer critical sense than Bloomsbury; if we mean by art something more profound than an "aesthetic" theory can explain we have to agree with Henry James, that in the last event the value of a work of art depends on the quality of the writer's make-up. Art is not amoral and everything is not as valuable as everything else. Stephen did not apply a moral touch-stone naïvely. In practice the question at issue is, can we or can we not diagnose Sterne's limitations and George Eliot's only partial success as artists in terms of these writers' make-up? Stephen thought he could and we think he did. The position we share with Leslie Stephen has been admirably stated by Mr. L. H. Myers in the Preface to *The Root and the Flower,* where he says that

> Proust, for instance, by treating all sorts of sensibility as equal in importance, and all man-ifestations of character as standing on the same plane of significance, adds nothing to his achievement, but only draws attention to himself as aiming at the exaltation of a rather petty form of aestheticism. For my part, I believe that a man serves himself better by showing a respect for such moral taste as he may possess.

Unless we adopt this position, says Mr. Myers, we "are likely to be satisfied with art that is petty." Stephen had no use for art that is petty; Mr. MacCarthy wants to be allowed to rebuke him for describing Sterne as "a systematic trifler" representing "a shallow vein." Of course the academic attitude to literature is much the same as Mr. MacCarthy's. "It appears that you prefer some authors to others, Mr. Graves" is the classic rebuke of authority to criticism. Stephen was not academic—it is only one of his virtues but it is the fundamental one for a critic— he was not conventional, timid or respectable in his findings. "It is tempting to try to clear away some of the stupendous rubbish-heaps of eulogy which accumulate over the great men when admiration has become obligatory on pain of literary renunciation" he wrote. (pp. 407-08)

[Stephen's] belief in reason (as opposed to "intuition") de-plored by Mr. MacCarthy did not lead to crass blindness. He was not ignorant of the fact that a work of art has its own internal logic; but he did not consider that this exempted the author or poet from intellectual scrutiny. He expected a poet who deployed philosophic views to have sound ones, and he realized, in spite of his great "intuitive" admiration for Words-worth, that Wordsworth's were not always sound. For Shelley's intellectual lights he had the greatest disrespect, and was able to make a corresponding case against Shelley's poetry—he protests to J. A. Symonds that he cannot agree with his praise of Shelley in the Men of Letters volume, there is "a certain hollowness" about the Prometheus, an "insubstantial mist" in much of Shelley's most admired poems. His use of "reason" is in the Johnson tradition. Since it led him to explore Lamb's sophistical defence of Restoration Comedy and Hazlitt's of Wycherley, it was evidently a useful critical technique. His

cautious examination of what a writer has to offer will seem to many of us, in spite of Mr. MacCarthy, worth more than a cartload of records of thrills. (p. 411)

His style was no doubt precipitated by the conditions of work-ing as journalist, editor and biographer, but it is a genuine expression of personality and an effective weapon. Aspects of it were registered in the contemporary mots: "No flowers by request" and "Stephen's ink was never watery" (or purple, it might have been added). He had the right to come down on Arnold for his rhetoric about the dreaming spires and to object to his mannerisms. Stephen was the type of the critic who makes no parade of personality, has no studied attitudes, whose manner consists of an absence of manner but is felt as the presence of a mature personality. He himself described his style modestly as "short-winded and provokingly argumen-tative," and says that whereas X "can keep up a flow of eloquence" he himself cannot keep on the rhetorical level be-cause he "must always have some tangible remark to make." Unlike his contemporaries we cannot consider this in any way unfortunate. His habitual tone and style are represented by this from the essay on Jowett: "To a distinct view of the importance of some solution he seems to have joined the profound con-viction that no conceivable solution would hold water. 'He stood,' says one of his pupils, in a rather different sense, 'at the parting of many ways,' and he wrote, one must add, 'No thoroughfare' upon them all." As a critic he stood for out-spoken criticism all round; "I like his [Huxley's] pugnacity— a quality I always admire. The more hard-hitting goes on in the world, the better I am pleased—meaning always hard-hitting in the spiritual sense." His critical credo is constantly implied in the essays *Hours in a Library* (four volumes), *Studies of a Biographer* (four volumes) and the fragmentary *English Literature and Society in the Eighteenth Century.* It corresponds generally to the position that we hold to-day. (p. 412)

I hope I have made it plain not only what Leslie Stephen's strength as a literary critic was, but why I have chosen to describe him as a Cambridge critic. His is not (unfortunately) the invariable kind of criticism practised at Cambridge or by Cambridge products, but it is what the world of journalism and *belles-lettres* means when it refers with respect or malice to "Cambridge Criticism." His style, his tone, his mental attri-butes, his outlook are what are considered the most admirable, or objectionable, or at any rate, whatever your opinion of it, the most characteristic features of the Cambridge school. Cam-bridge has not by any means produced only Leslie Stephens; it is sufficient to name Rupert Brooke and Housman as evidence that dug-outs exist as refuges from the prevailing wind, that east wind which Elton, I think, says might have done Pater so much good if he had been placed in the other university. In contemporary Cambridge where one section still holds literary criticism to be a charming parasite and sends its soul, with Mr. MacCarthy's approval, adventuring among masterpieces, while another holds semasiology to have superseded literary criticism along with philosophy and the rest—it is high time for those who look back with respect to Leslie Stephen as the examplar of a sound position and a profitable practice to put it on record why they honour his memory. (pp. 414-15)

Q. D. Leavis, "Leslie Stephen: Cambridge Critic," in Scrutiny, Vol. VII, No. 4, March, 1939, pp. 404-15.

NOEL GILROY ANNAN (essay date 1951)

[Annan is an English historian, biographer, and critic who has written extensively on Stephen, including the definitive biography

Stephen (right) with his Alpine guide, Melchior Anderegg.

to date, Leslie Stephen: The Godless Victorian *(1984). Annan's analyses are strongly influenced by his rationalist, humanist philosophy, generally emphasizing the logical connections between modes of thought and their historical and cultural antecedents. In the following excerpt from his first book-length study of Stephen, Annan assesses Stephen's importance in nineteenth-century English literature and philosophy.]*

[Leslie Stephen] is a man to respect. His virtues were the simple virtues that deserve praise wherever they are found. He was proud of his own country but despised jingos: he hoped to leave some reflections in his books to benefit, not only Englishmen, but all men of good will. He was proud of his family, but nothing of a snob: he wished to leave a memory which his children might honour. This quiet patriotism and domestic piety flowed from a magnanimous spirit. Revenge, envy, and malice were beneath him; he loved his friends and scorned to injure his enemies. With that solid worth and intolerance of impostors, which invests so many of his contemporaries with the grandeur of hoary oaks, *nil admirari* ["being astonished at nothing"] was his precept, the salute to genius his practice. He pitied the weak—he had suffered as a weakling—but he exhorted them to master their frailty, and his own feats of endurance and daring live in the Alpine records as clearly as his moral courage and intellectual honesty are printed in the history of his times. Courage is sometimes tainted with arrogance or brutality, but Stephen was scrupulous in controversy,

modest of his attainments, and candid in his agnosticism. His was the purest kind of renunciation, not inspired by hatred of priests or by the desire to destroy the temple and build it in three days. He wanted to change men not destroy them.

Historically he is no more than a representative figure. He was not a seminal mind, but an eminent controversialist and a literary journalist who expounded the liberal-rationalist tradition which he neither modified like Mill nor criticised like Arnold. He was not an original philosopher, but an historian of thought. Nor was he a great figure in the development of the social sciences like Alfred Marshall or James Frazer. If he saw the errors of Comte and Taine in applying the scientific method and gave as many happy examples of what this method cannot achieve as what it can, he did not realise, as Mill did, that the imperative task facing rationalists was to discover how induction and deduction can be applied in the treatment of social phenomena. (Can change in society be measured in other fields than theoretical economics; if not, how far do the social sciences consist of justifications of different arrangements of facts; and how far are these arrangements determined by implicit judgments of value?) A great rationalist introduces a new technique of enquiry; or creates a new department of knowledge; or changed by his discoveries the very nature of the facts on which men previously had worked. Stephen was not in this class; he swam strongly with the stream instead of turning it to irrigate new country. Partly because he lacked supreme originality and partly because he was too anxious to teach the tenets of the faith, he remained an incomparable *vulgarisateur* unable to revise the premises on which he based his teaching. And Stephen knew his own measure. Did he not say that his place would be at most a footnote in history?

Yet, perhaps, there is more to be said for footnotes than Stephen imagined. Stephen was not merely a scholar but a good scholar. In a limited way he said certain things about certain matters or people—on Hoadly, or Richardson, or Paley—which were *right*. He was an intellectual in the sense that other men have followed his judgments. A good scholar is one who not only produces order in some field of human knowledge, but does not obscure the thought of future generations. Great minds, driven by powerful imaginations, construct new systems and change the thought of their generation; but their books have a curious way of being disregarded after a short passage of time. Frazer's *Golden Bough* was an epic; but do modern anthropologists seriously build on that work to-day? Stephen's *English Thought in the Eighteenth Century* is not an epic; but because Stephen says plainly what he is doing, sets himself a limited objective and does not declare, for instance, that some thinker is of a greater *intrinsic* value by reason of his *literary* value, scholars to-day are helped by his book. They continue to take Stephen's works from the shelves because he made his own approach so clear. Though they may be working from another angle, they find Stephen useful because, as a good positivist, he does not disguise his method nor his personal interpretations. He despised obscurity and practised clarity. As a result, those who disagree state the grounds of their disagreement with the respect of men talking to their equal. No serious explorer of eighteenth century thought and literature can ignore Stephen's pioneer work. American scholarship has analysed minutely Defoe's treatment of his sources; but Stephen's essay is still worth reading. He may not perceive that Clarissa is in love with Lovelace, but his dissection of Richardson remains a classic. He had read so widely in eighteenth century prose and entered so completely into the minds of those writers that the points he makes are too numerous and sensible to be disregarded. His judgments outside the eighteenth century also repay study. John Plamenatz in his admirable critical study of the Utilitarians takes Stephen rather than more recent critics as a reference for manoeuvre. Even theologians benefit from the clarity of Stephen's arguments: he gives them every opportunity to confound them, there are no weasel-words, no camouflage or deception.

And this is true of Stephen's literary criticism. Not only F. R. Leavis and his disciples praise him warmly. T. S. Eliot in his famous essay on Massinger calls Stephen's work on this playwright ''a piece of formidable destructive analysis,'' though he adds that Stephen has not put Massinger ''finally and irrefutably into a place.'' Eliot agrees that Massinger's characterisation is weak and that Stephen's objection to Massinger's method of revealing a villain has great cogency, though perhaps the objection is stated in too *a priori* a fashion. No two critical sensibilities could be more obviously opposed than those of Leslie Stephen and Raymond Mortimer. Mortimer owes little to Stephen and his scale of values differs greatly. Yet if their essays on Balzac are compared, the measure of agreement is startling. They both make some two dozen points (Stephen in over eleven, Mortimer in under five thousand words). Both agree that Balzac lived vicariously in an imaginary world and that for him dream and reality were the same; that his view of human nature was nonsensical and that society cannot be divided in Balzac's fashion into virtuous fools and clever knaves; that his stories are improbable but thrilling and that while his ceaseless explanations are intolerable, the incredibilities do not matter since his vigour and intensity sweep the reader away. In other words, Stephen did more than his share to establish that consensus of opinion about numerous topics which is held by most educated men. Positivists would say that Stephen increased knowledge, and anyone who welcomes the increase of knowledge should pay his tribute. True, the knowledge he increased makes little stir in the world; but then scholars should expect tribute from none but scholars and should be well satisfied if they obtain even that.

Here a distinction must be drawn. Stephen was not a professional but an amateur scholar, a Victorian gentleman such as Darwin or Acton, who sat in his own library and digested its contents without much recourse to the British Museum. He read his sources, memorised their arguments, pondered, and then sat down and wrote without the apparatus of card indexes and cross-references. It is a way of sowing knowledge which invites armed men to spring up from the soil. Mistaken judgments which could have been rectified by yet wider reading are but one part of the harvest, and, naturally, subsequent research has corrected Stephen's work, particularly in the *D.N.B.* In his own lifetime Stephen had to admit that, curiously enough, he had leant too heavily on what orthodox critics had said of the anti-clerical revolutionary, Tom Paine; and this error was typical of Stephen's fondness for subtle and logical thinkers, and his antipathy to far more influential, but cruder, writers. Yet how great are the gains of the amateur! With what sweep, with what concentrated control, what a work of expert craftsmanship has he written! How his style in *English Thought in the Eighteenth Century* shames that of our own generation, how pellucid and natural, how solid without being heavy, ironical without being flashy, how it coaxes the reader from point to point on an easy gentle rein! Stephen teaches a lesson to all scholars in his field. Analytical history to be read must be readable. The scholar must subdue that spirit of egoism which tempts him to write for himself and to forget his reader. He must not only subdue the desire to turn his work into a battle

of the books in which the author turns from his task to bite other scholars; he must also assimilate his technique of criticism into the blood-stream or his work will be indigestible. He must put truth first; but over-scrupulous regard for truth can bring a double-edged reward. Determined that every sentence shall say neither more nor less than the truth, the professional literary scholar too often creates a forest of abstract nouns, intersected by critical approaches, in which the reader for sheer weariness lays himself down and dies. Scholars who properly base *own* write solely for other scholars; but historians of thought and literature, and biographers, should settle questions of method, approach and disputed material, in articles in the learned periodicals, leaving themselves free to write for that wider public which it is their duty to consider. Stephen would have rejected the modern priggery which regards wit as a sign of insincerity and style as something which ''gets between'' the reader and the truth.

Nevertheless, Stephen was more than a good scholar, though when it is asked where he stands in the history of nineteenth-century thought, the answer at first sight is unimpressive. He was an exponent of a tradition of thought which was stricken as he himself lay dying. A rationalist is always a bad life if one wants to insure against the short memory of posterity: his ideas soon become so remote that they are remembered only for their quaintness. Muddlers like the imaginative Coleridge, intricate minds like F. D. Maurice, who meet a crisis by developing a highly personalised dialectic, prophets, seers, even charlatans, have a longer life than the rationalist whose reputation is soon spotted with the death-tokens of a rare article or reference in a work of learning. Nearly everything Stephen wrote which could claim to be a contribution to thought would have to be reinterpreted to-day. But a positivist, such as Stephen, welcomes the extinction of his reputation: to him his future insignificance is a sign that others have built on his work and profited by his blunders. The life, which is unimpressive to posterity, is in his view a life well spent in destroying superstition and selflessly working for the future.

It is an error to consider rationalism as an icy, unemotional creed, hostile to all that is poetic, imaginative, generous and ardent; the spare and lean athlete is also graceful and vigorous. While watching the greatest rationalists at work, the image forms in the mind of a hurdler who glides forward with felicitous ease scarcely seeming to rise or fall. What is condemned as mechanical is in reality an exquisitely co-ordinated mental effort; what is disliked as metallic is the strength of body and mind developed by exacting training; what is despised as unsubtle is that simplicity of the athlete who has mastered his technique and deludes by his concinnity. To succeed means to renounce trivial delights and to dedicate the coming years to the pursuit. It is this spirit of self-sacrifice, the challenge to succeed where others have failed, the intense difficulty of excelling and of conquering matter by mind, that inspires youth to follow the calling. The discipline is severe, the mood cool and calm, but the reward is beyond price. The discipline eschews all devices which enable the trick to be performed without hard work and declares war upon rhetoric, phrase-making, hypnotism, and on all those contrivances which spell-binders and mountebanks employ to seduce and impose upon a credulous world. The mood is that of a man, a tiny figure, standing on the beach, the vast uncharted sea of facts stretching before him to the horizon; but who turns to his fellows with noble self-assurance: *cras ingens iterabimus aequor* [''tomorrow we go out upon the boundless sea.''] The reward is no less than the possession of a part of truth itself. Not the appearance of encompassing the whole of truth which an artist creates and persuades others to accept as an exquisite *aperçu* of life; not the subtle impression of experience which, by its very restraint and horror of drawing conclusions, leaves us nevertheless with an uncanny awareness of how events and people are shaped; but of truths that are independent of personal vagary, solid and substantial, capable of acceptance by all dispassionate men of good will. And if this is an illusion—if in fact such truths can never be proved to exist and if all truth is interpretation, all reality appearance—then it is an illusion absolutely necessary for the increase of knowledge and the dissipation of envy, hatred and fear, the enemies of man's happiness and greatness. The rationalist temper is one of moderate optimism and even exaltation. The discovery of truths, tangible and in some degree immutable, obtained by relentless analysis, satisfies the self-esteem; and the belief that these truths will light the path to a wiser, happier future inspires the rationalist in his labours, comforts him for the loss of those spiritual analgesics which deaden the senses to unpalatable facts, and fires him with the ardour and eloquence that he is popularly supposed to lack. He too has his vision: the vision of the present forging the shape of the future. And it is a mistake to dismiss his dream as facilely optimistic. The rationalist vision is also tragic. His hopes are blighted by the cancers that breed about the heart: the crassness of human stupidity, the degradation of the evils corrupting society, the dreary aimless courses of peoples and governments, exasperate and frustrate him and whisper that tyranny, misery and calamity are the eternal lot of man. And so, unable to remould the scheme of things nearer to his heart's desire, the rationalist labours on, now in this vineyard and in that, striving to bring order into one small corner of the chaos which surrounds him and to which he inescapably belongs. The belief that order can be created, and the realisation that his own efforts will change little in the world, are the two central facts in his experience that dignify and ennoble him.

Leslie Stephen held to this faith and was proud to acknowledge his debt to the past. He reminded his contemporaries that not they, but their eighteenth-century forebears, had mapped the paths to truth. "I would never abuse," he wrote, "the century which loved common sense and freedom of speech, and hated humbug and mystery; the century in which first sprang to life most of the social and intellectual movements which are still the best hope of our own; in which science and history and invention first took their modern shape; the century of David Hume, and Adam Smith, and Gibbon, and Burke, and Johnson, and Fielding, and many old friends to whom I aver incalculable gratitude. . . ." This historical sense of belonging to a tradition of thought, in which each man had contributed something, but had also erred, and in which philosophical speculation was kept close to earth by common sense and a generous morality, saved Stephen from the vices of ratiocination; he was a rationalist but never a progressive. The progressive shovels all human experience into the machine of the mind and processes it with a scientific method; he has invested in reading and wants a quick return from his money, and hence searches about for a few fashionable theories which will explain all facets of life; indeed without theories he would be unable to progress. Stephen was sceptical of theories but believed in methods which put the individual in the right relation to the facts; he thought that books widened the mind but that quality of mind depended on character and moral education; and progress for him was an incalculable and slow-motioned operation. He not only believed in, but knew how to use, reason.

Some of the steps he took in using reason naturally appear to us in retrospect to be fallacious. Like almost all his contem-

poraries he drew certain conclusions, which he thought to be logical, and which we should not agree were inferred logically; and he demanded, which we do not, that every true proposition should be shown to be logically necessary. When Stephen said that theology was unreal and had no right to exist, he confused an ethical reflection (that theology is a waste of time) with a logical inference (that theology is logically improper). Theology, however, is a mode of reasoning as valid as other modes of reasoning; as a human activity it is not unreal, nor are its rules dissimilar from those which govern other activities such as jurisprudence; and there is no *logical* reason why men should not use this mode of reasoning, if they please. Yet Stephen was arguing only as his clerical opponents argued when they declared in ethics that the ultimate justification for preferring one course of action to another was that the former accorded with the will of God. To believe that we are acting in accordance with the will of God may comfort and give us strength to act even though the action and its consequences are unpleasant to ourselves; but it is not integral to the logic of *ethics*. Stephen was determined to separate ethics from religion for two reasons. Firstly because to admit enthusiastic exhortation as part of the logic of ethics is to agree with Newman that "the logic is felt not proved." Secondly because the acceptance of dogmatic systems of thought cause men to make wrong ethical judgments: the wrong course of action may be chosen because it appears to accord with some dogma or saintly *obiter dictum*, and hence persecution or poverty is justified on grounds which purport to be ethical but are in fact religious. And this was his most valuable contribution to the controversy. (pp. 278-86)

> *Noel Gilroy Annan, in his* Leslie Stephen: His Thought *and Character in Relation to His Time,* MacGibbon & Kee, *1951, 342 p.*

SIDNEY A. BURRELL   (essay date 1951)

[*In the following excerpt, Burrell discusses the evolution of Stephen's personal philosophy and his evaluation of the history of thought.*]

It has been said by at least one authority that the career of Sir Leslie Stephen epitomized in its intellectual manifestations and its chronology all that was distinctly Victorian in nineteenth-century England. In that there is a great deal of truth. His life span antedated the reign of the queen by five years and exceeded it by three. All of his intellectual attitudes were in a direct and almost too simple way a reflection of certain patterns of thought generally looked upon by historians as peculiar to the Victorian age. He was a liberal in the tradition of J. S. Mill during the late heyday of the liberal fashion in the sixties, and though his later enthusiasm waned, his basic faith did not. He was a zealous Darwinian during a period when not to be one was to court excommunication by the intellectual hierarchy of the seventies and eighties. To list his friends and the contemporaries he admired is to recite the roll call of Victorian liberal thinkers—Morley, Sidgwick, Spencer, Darwin, and Huxley among many—whose interests encompassed every sphere of intellectual activity. His religious experiences recall the contemplation, the struggle, the renunciation of Christian theology by the typical Victorian "agnostic," an appellation which in itself is helpfully illustrative, since Stephen lent his aid in making it a permanent part of the language. All of his intellectual interests were firmly grounded in that confident respect for the natural sciences, which was perhaps the commonest characteristic, not alone of his generation, but of almost the entire century.

To say this much may seem to imply a wider wisdom in the twentieth century, since it has become increasingly fashionable to belabor the Victorians, not for their rigid loyalty to social custom as was the case a generation or so ago, but precisely because of their predisposition to an intellectual libertinism which did not take into consideration the ultimate implications of unrestricted freedom. It should be remembered, however, that the expression of a kind of optimistic confidence in the final ends of the universe was something very nearly akin to a confirmation of belief in the Trinity by orthodox Christians and did not always reveal the inner questionings or the mental trepidation of the affirmant. The heresy of quiet doubt was more often to be found in unexpected places. Philosophical pessimism was something to be denied when directly charged, even though it seemed to be confirmed by events and trends of thinking during the eighties and nineties. The movement from a confident to a doubtful security was also a characteristic of the age.

Here too Stephen was a kind of microcosm of his generation—the typical figure whom historians find useful for purposes of illustration. He was so patently the "go-between thinker" of a later literary critic's description that it is almost impossible to find in his writing an idea or an opinion that did not belong to the public domain of Victorian thought. Like Voltaire in another time and place his was the task of making clear what others had thought or observed first. His also was the skill of the highly literate and talented journalist rather than that of the original thinker or artistic genius. It was a skill which he used well and which was to win for him a high reputation among his contemporaries, though none knew more clearly than he that it might not outlast his own lifetime.

The attitudes of his age, then, pervaded and permeated everything he wrote, not in any subtle manner but clearly and discernibly. They were as evident in his speculative writings as they were in his literary criticism. His historical writings, too, bear witness to their influence. It is, for this reason, extremely difficult to separate any of his published works into distinct categories, though they clearly indicate the wide diversity of his interests. Each in its own way was intended to exhibit one aspect of a coherent and cohesive system of thought. His interest in philosophical matters led him to the study of history; the problems raised there led back to philosophy; both, in their turn, governed his attitude toward literature and were reflected in his critical writings. To attempt, then, to distinguish him as a historian apart from the variety of his other interests is very nearly impossible, nor can he be understood as such without reference to the numerous other concerns that occupied his attention throughout his life. These diversified interests further add to the difficulty of classification, since they ultimately made it possible for him to pursue more than one career. Very probably the best description of his life's work is to be found in the phrase "man of letters," since it alone is comprehensive enough to encompass all that he did as historian, philosopher, critic, and editor. (pp. 111-13)

The first of his important historical writings, *The History of English Thought in the Eighteenth Century,* appeared in 1876. It was not the result of any great love for historical scholarship, *per se,* but was rather the culmination of his interest in the eighteenth-century deists and their sceptical contemporaries, whose religious outlook was similar to his own. He was afterwards to admit that he was unprepared for the problems

involved in writing a work of this sort, and that he might not have undertaken it had he been prepared. By training and temperament he was ill-equipped for the kind of "scientific" historical research that was only beginning to make its way in England at about this time. Stubbs and Freeman were completely unknown to him, and he afterwards recorded his feeling of humiliation at the "calm and honourable self-devotion" of S. R. Gardiner, whom he came to know while editing the *Dictionary of National Biography.* Pure research never attracted him except at intermittent periods, though, as will be seen, he was capable of great scholarly effort when necessary.

The introduction to the *History of English Thought* revealed at once the scale of his intellectual values in dealing with the past. It was contained in his affirmation of a typically Victorian faith in the validity of scientific truth: "Our knowledge," he wrote, "has, in some departments, passed into the scientific stage. It can be stated as a systematic body of established truths. It is consistent and certain. The primary axioms are fixed beyond the reach of scepticism. . . ." For Stephen, then, the whole history of human intellectual development appeared to have led to this certainty. It was implicit not only in his assumptions but in the assumptions of all whom he regarded as most advanced among contemporary thinkers. His task as a historian was the devious one of tracing out the tortuous course of that gradually emerging truth which had made this certainty possible and to explain, at the same time, why its complete victory over "superstition and error" had not yet been attained. His explanation was one which, within the limits of its premises, appealed to the notions of historical plausibility held by most of his like-minded contemporaries. He was aware at the outset of the continuing distinction in the categories of human thought between the cumulative knowledge of the natural sciences and the non-cumulative knowledge contained in areas of speculation unrelated to the pure sciences. It was a distinction, however, which troubled him quite as much as it troubled other respectful devotees of scientific thought in the nineteenth century. He felt quite simply that the separation could not and, in the last analysis, did not exist. One category must, of necessity, depend upon the other. As he wrote long afterwards in attempting to answer Newman's troublesome contention that "science does not give certainty": "The scientific doctrines must lay down the base to which all other truth, so far as it is discoverable, must conform. . . . The man of science advocates free inquiry precisely because it is the way to truth, and the only way, though a way which leads through many errors." It was clearly the way which Leslie Stephen himself attempted to follow in all of his intellectual endeavors.

His desire to apply the methods of scientific analysis to the historical development of ideas involved him deeply in the ancient dilemma of historians. How much should be attributed to the individual and how much to deterministic forces beyond the individual's control in attempting to explain the history of human thought? Once again his own deepest convictions helped to solve the problem, though it was first of all necessary to make it plain why men continued to wrangle over "metaphysical problems substantially identical with those which perplexed the most ancient Greek sages." The reason was clear enough. There were still lacking sound postulates for dealing with man as a moral and social being. Without them there could never be a true study of "sociology" as understood in the terms of the natural sciences. Erroneous postulates were not destroyed merely because they came under the scrutiny of careful and thoughtful analysis. So long as they were not so "mischievous as to be fatal to the agent" who made use of them they would continue to have a kind of social validity. Outmoded doctrines (among which Victorian Christianity was quite clearly included) only gradually dissolved by contact with facts. The role of philosophers in the historical development of ideas was clearly that of all individual men when faced with the problem of controlling or directing the impersonal forces of history. All that they might hope to do was to struggle everlastingly toward certainty and harmony where ideas were involved, constantly striving to square the phenomena of the material world with the postulates of philosophical theory. Though the pursuit was, by implication, not entirely hopeless, it was one which, because of the weakness of man's "speculative impulse," individual great minds could not win by their own unaided efforts. The great determinants of intellectual evolution had, very often, to be sought outside the sphere of individual human effort. The acceptance of controlling ideas by society as a whole depended on something more than the evangelizing attempts of the speculative thinker.

Stephen's explanation of these forces placed him, at least partially, in that tradition of English thought which was at least as old as Hobbes. It was to be found only by examining those factors in the human environment that forced men to accept new creeds in a kind of involuntary way. The most important of them, as he saw it, could be summed up in the phrase "scientific utility." It was the efficacy of the scientific method that most evidently influenced men's thinking by assisting them in the struggle to control their physical environment. The effects of this method could be observed directly by masses of human beings completely untouched by the "logical implications" of philosophy. The instant that a race abandoned the use of charms in dealing with wild beasts, for example, and became aware of the rudimentary uses of iron in extirpating its enemies, it was already well on its way to accepting the credibility of science. It was clearly demonstrating the effectiveness of a crude scientific method by its victories in the "great game of life." Not only would it flourish materially, but it would come to believe in science. It would thus begin the slow process of evolving a set of beliefs which could be correlated with its existing institutions, since the ideals of a society were, in a sense, only forms of justification for the existing social order. It was, in fact, this correlation of institutions and ideals that made difficult the emergence of newer, more scientifically accurate doctrines, since men seldom challenged the validity of older creeds until the "natural order" of society, be it kingship or priesthood, had become unfitted for its social tasks and thus made possible the questioning of that faith which had sustained its existence. It was the social environment, then, which very often determined the acceptance or rejection of ideas by most men. Successful creeds had to appeal to more than the intellect alone. They must control disorderly passions and provide "a vivid imagery for the expression of the emotions." The distrust of the mass mind implied in Stephen's argument was more clearly indicated by his conclusion that a majority in any society might not be educated up to the degree of culture necessary for the acceptance of new beliefs. Most men appeared to him to prefer ideas more easily assimilable by the ordinary intellect, and it was for this reason that the "utility" of an idea was ultimately important in explaining its acceptance on a wide scale. If it worked, it would be difficult for a "truer" belief to replace it and might, indeed, stifle an idea that had emerged prematurely only to be rejected by the generation which had brought it into being. The material conditions of a society were in this instance then the ultimate determinants of a society's ideals: here was a doctrine which,

barring conflict over detail and method, reflected the most widely held "scientific" assumptions of the century.

To assume, however, that Stephen saw the relationship between social conditions and their intellectual end products as expressible in terms of a simple and direct causal relationship would only distort his views. In this respect he was not in the rather overstressed tradition of Marx or Comte. His awareness of the complexity of the whole process of intellectual change as seen, for example, in the history of literature—in fact, his very awareness of the diversity of literature as an art form—prevented his drawing any overly simple conclusions in a dogmatically "scientific" manner. He seemed to retain a kind of faith that his assumptions on this score had to be true without ever satisfactorily explaining why. This feeling grew with him as he advanced in years, and, undoubtedly, some of his later literary and scholarly researches greatly influenced it. Though he continued to repeat the old canons of his vague, deterministic faith in this matter to the end, there was a marked difference between the intellectual confidence expressed in the *History of English Thought* and that of the Ford Lectures on *English Literature and Society in the Eighteenth Century*, which were published nearly thirty years later. Despite the softening of assumptions and the acknowledgment of the difficulty involved in explaining the relationship between ideas and their environment, the credo remained fixed, and, in both works, he continued to view the intellectual history of eighteenth-century England in much the same way.

The eighteenth century, as he first explained it in the *History of English Thought*, was, by implication, a period of great promise. It had opened with a resolute challenge to Christian orthodoxy, first by the deists and then by the sceptics of David Hume's school. It was also a century of profound disappointment. The greatest thinkers of the time had fallen short of the duty required of them by the rigid standards of intellectual honesty so dear to the liberal Victorian tradition. Frightened by the devastating analyses of Hume, they had retreated before the disintegrating implications contained in his conclusions. Their recourse to political controversy or sheer antiquarianism was, in Stephen's opinion, the measure of their failure; the English age of reason had eddied out in a period of speculative sterility. Men had allowed themselves to become too terrified at their own audacity in attacking those doctrines that seemed to offer the only lasting consolation to suffering humanity, "the only sound basis of morality." . . . This failure of eighteenth-century intellectual leadership had abandoned the masses to a resurgent, emotional orthodoxy which found its leaders in Wesley and the evangelicals. Once again ordinary human beings had accepted a less complete, less true belief in favor of others that more nearly fulfilled their social and emotional needs. The problems of religious orthodoxy remained to trouble Leslie Stephen and his Victorian contemporaries.

During the years following the appearance of the *History of English Thought* Stephen's attention was increasingly drawn to a consideration of the question that he felt to be the most important raised by his study of the eighteenth century. It was that question which, as we have already seen, seemed to have taken the heart out of that century's attack on Christian orthodoxy: how could men found a system of morals upon a body of objective, scientific truth completely divorced from the postulates of traditional theology? The problem had assumed particular importance in view of his increasing conviction that the discoveries of Darwin constituted the outstanding contribution of his generation to the history of modern thought. In a published article, which appeared in May 1880, he contrasted Henry Thomas Buckle's philosophy of history most unfavorably with the hypotheses of Darwin and then went on to declare, "We classify the ablest thinkers by the relation which their opinions bear to it [Darwin's theory] and, whatever its ultimate fate, no one can doubt that it will be the most conspicuous factor in the history of modern speculation." In Stephen's opinion it provided the necessary basis for an understanding of that which was significant and fundamental in historic development as distinct from the merely transitory and temporary. The great shortcoming of that school of historians which had come into existence in Britain at the end of the eighteenth century and of the English utilitarians from Bentham through J. S. Mill had been their failure to understand or appreciate the significance of evolution as an elemental force in explaining the development of human societies. Both of these groups had utilized the historical method, but they had neither understood nor applied it properly. In spite of this he viewed the contributions of the utilitarians as particularly important in at least one respect. Bentham and his disciples had provided a part of the method necessary to construct an ultimately harmonious and universal system of certain knowledge. The attempt of the Benthamites to reduce human motivation to a pain-pleasure hypothesis as broadly expressed in the formula of "the greatest happiness of the greatest number" was at least an approach towards a true science of sociology. Their tendency to think of the "individual as a unit of constant properties" had obscured for them the importance of history (and for "history" here one could easily substitute the phrase "biological evolution") in explaining the complex development of the social organism. Bentham, however, had recognized the necessity for separating ethics from theology and was striving toward that end. If the separation appeared difficult, it was the duty of the speculative thinker to resolve the difficulty. Stephen hoped that his own particular contribution to the history of thought would take the form of completing Bentham's task by utilizing the scientific theories of a later generation.

This was the purpose that engaged most of his intellectual effort in the period between 1878 and 1882. His interest in it was not unique, for, in one way or another, it might almost be called the most important speculative problem of the Victorian age. In its broadest aspects it involved the troublesome question, once again, of the individual's relation to his environment as expressed in terms of the "cosmic process" of evolution, and, further, it carried with it implications that reached directly into diverse fields of social and political theory. The apparently explicit emphasis upon struggle as a means of determining the "survival of the fittest" in Darwin's theory of natural selection had forced the formulation of an entirely new set of questions for those who wished to deal with the problem of morality on the basis of scientific inquiry. How might a balance best be struck between the claims of the individual pursuing his own ends and the ends of society as a whole? Did society have the right to curb the individual in the interests of a group morality? In Stephen's case the point of view expressed by T. H. Huxley when he spoke of a perpetual warfare between "microcosm and macrocosm" was an insufficient answer to these questions. The implications in this argument were uncomfortably reminiscent of political views which were already discrediting faith in the unrestricted scope of individual freedom. His own solution as contained in *The Science of Ethics,* which appeared in 1882, was an attempted synthesis of the ideas of Bentham and Darwin in such a way as to resolve the seeming conflict between them into a philosophical harmony. As a substitute for the "final" Benthamite end of "happiness" he wished to

establish the "practical" Darwinian moral aim of "social preservation" and thus fuse the aims of the individual and society as a whole. It was the unhappy duty of his philosopher friend, Henry Sidgwick, to point out to him that the two were not necessarily compatible and that, in fact, the desire to "preserve the social organism" might not inevitably lead to "the greatest happiness of the greatest number." Sidgwick was clearly aware of the difficulty of attempting to solve intellectual problems by ignoring logical or actual contradictions. What Stephen had done was to reformulate and restate the strong presuppositions of his original faith. His hoped-for contribution to the history of thought was one of the major disappointments of his life. (pp. 114-21)

While working on the *Science of Ethics* [Stephen] also produced four titles for the "English Men of Letters" series, and though he published relatively less while serving as editor of the *Dictionary,* his personal bibliography during the time when he was writing *The English Utilitarians* continued to grow rapidly. In the meantime, too, his interest in the Ethical Society forced him increasingly to assume the role of platform speaker. For a critical evaluation of his historical writing, however, the last two major works of his life, *The English Utilitarians,* which appeared in 1900, and *English Literature and Society in the Eighteenth Century,* which was published in 1904, far outweigh his other later works.

For some years he had projected an extensive study which was intended to do for the nineteenth century what he had already done for the eighteenth. The result was *The English Utilitarians,* which, though one of his more ambitious pieces of writing, fell far short of this original intention. It was undertaken at a time when the liberal ideals to which he had subscribed as a young man were coming under increasing attack from the protagonists of state intervention and outright socialism during the last years of the century. Stephen's enthusiasm for the teachings of J. S. Mill, though somewhat cooler than in his youth, had by no means disappeared. He remained convinced that the "individualism" expressed in the writings of the early liberals had not been intended to sanction "the selfishness of wicked capitialists." Even in the eighteenth century it had not been the unmitigated evil that its detractors were attempting to make it appear. Individualism, particularly in its economic aspects, had made England a great power with world-wide interests and had led to that involuntary progress, the motivation for which Bentham and the early utilitarians had only tried to define.

His study of the origins of Bentham's movement was a labor of love, then, that had its roots in the deepest influences of his youth. It also reflected some of the marked changes that had come over him with the advancing years. In his introduction to *The English Utilitarians* it was clear that he was willing to grant what seemed to be a position of greater importance to the speculative thinker in promoting new ideas than he had been in the *History of English Thought* twenty-odd years before. The influence of such men was, however, still indirect and obscure, but "a solid core of ascertained and verifiable truth" was the "fixed pivot upon which all beliefs must ultimately turn." The confidence in a scientific explanation of utilitarianism was virtually abandoned and had very nearly given way to a feeling that any kind of scientific scholarship might well be impossible. On the other hand, however, he continued to hold rather firmly to his belief that Bentham and his followers had been the true founders of that philosophy which justified the freedom of the individual and which, in its turn, had given rise to the liberal doctrines of the early nineteenth century. He was not, as has sometimes been thought, completely unaware of the implications in utilitarian thinking which might permit state action in restriction of the individual. Like his cousin, A. V. Dicey, however, he tended to brush aside this objection by pointing out that "Utility [in Bentham's writings], therefore, will, as a rule, forbid the action of government: but, as utility is always the ultimate principle, and there may be cases in which it does not coincide with the 'let alone' principle, we must always admmit the possibility that in special cases government can interfere usefully, and, in that case, approve the interference." For Stephen, then, the basic element in Benthamite thought was always "individualistic," while restrictive action on the part of the state remained an exception. His certainty on this aspect of Benthamism was to contrast rather painfully with the analysis of Elie Halévy, who saw the contradiction between Bentham's assertion that the interests of the individual and society as a whole had to be harmonized "artificially" by the legislator and the assumption of Adam Smith and the classical economists that the harmony could be achieved by allowing free play to the forces of individualism in a "natural" way.

Stephen's alarm at the decline of liberal individualism was further heightened by a growing fear that the influences of mass democracy might hasten its disappearance. For him the popular "mandate" which was supposed to express the "infallible" judgment of a majority that could not "in point of logic be erroneous" constituted a dangerous portent for the future. It might, in fact, lead to "errors and hasty judgments and deviations from the true line of progress," requiring "exposure the more unsparing in proportion to their temporary popularity." In this his feelings were again shared in some measure by Dicey and also reflected in somewhat the same way J. S. Mill's own discovery of this possibility after reading Tocqueville's *Democracy in America* in the 1830's. It was for this reason, as Stephen saw it, that the early disciples of Bentham had been inconsistent with their own principles in promoting democracy and the elimination of "sinister interests" by reform after 1832. They had, indeed, only created a Frankenstein for themselves, since they were "not limiting the sphere of government in general, only giving it to a new class which would in many ways use it more energetically. . . . The old system had tended to keep the poor man down. The Chartist system had tended to plunder the rich. The right principle was to leave everything to 'supply and demand.'" Stephen feared the implications of the bitter lesson contained in neglect of what for him was an obvious fact.

His growing depression at the changing attitudes of late Victorian society did not, in the main, affect his views on philosophy and history. The last of his published works, *English Literature and Society in the Eighteenth Century,* though it brought to the study of literary movement the techniques and insights of Stephen's experience in other fields of study, was essentially a rather more modest reiteration of his earlier convictions. The professional historian, however, could only agree with his suggestion "that a literary history is so far satisfactory as it takes the facts into consideration and regards literature, in the perhaps too pretentious phrase, as a parfunction of the whole social organism." The problem of interrelating ideas and literary forms to the phenomena of history had become even more complex than it had appeared to be thirty years before.

In many respects Stephen was not a great historian. As a writer his technical skill showed at its best when he was dealing with the materials of biography, though often, as in his contrasting descriptions of James Mill and Coleridge in *The English Utilitarians,* his pictures were too sharply drawn and too clearly analyzed according to his own canons to be exact. His assumptions were too simply and markedly Victorian. Hobbes, for example, was praised by implication as a "Herbert Spencer of the seventeenth century"; Toland was guilty of "insincerity" because he continued to accept "the dying metaphysical system" of Locke's theology; Gibbon, whatever his shortcomings as a historian, had "struck by far the heaviest blow which [Christianity] had yet received from any single hand" and was worthy of remembrance for that fact. Only as past systems of thought approximated to his own Victorian agnosticism or his own intellectual aspirations were they found worthy of praise. This is not to imply that he failed in the obligation to understand the point of view of those with whom he disagreed. Within limits he invariably attempted to present their arguments in what he regarded as the best possible light, though he was often unaware that by so doing he was only recasting them in terms of his own. Nor did he lack what might be called a sense of scholarly curiosity. It was A. V. Dicey, again, who once wrote that "Leslie whether successful or not is always trying to ascertain the truth." The quality is admirable, but what both Stephen and Dicey overlooked was the obvious difficulty of agreement upon the terms by which truth should be sought. A later generation is, perhaps, more keenly aware of the dilemma, but even by the standards of his time, Stephen's approach to it was patently oversimplified. His historical studies were intended to amplify a preconceived notion of truth, and at no time in his life did he completely overcome the temptation to view scholarly research as a means to serve his own intellectual ends. He was not, of course, unique in this shortcoming, but he held to it with a stubbornness that forced him to ignore many of the questions raised by his own speculation. His agnosticism, persisted in, became in time very like the kind of faith he so often condemned in orthodox theologians. The same was true of his firmly held utilitarian-Darwinian convictions. His constant reiteration of the same judgments, as in the case of many other like-minded Victorians, finally became very like the "flogging of a dead horse." It is for this reason that his historical writings are, in many ways, more valuable as period pieces than as definitive examples of a kind of timeless scholarship. The *Dictionary of National Biography* remains his greatest intellectual monument. It is not, however, an unworthy one. (pp. 123-27)

Sidney A. Burrell, "Sir Leslie Stephen (1832-1904)," in Some Modern Historians of Britain: Essays in Honor of R. L. Schuyler, Herman Ausubel, J. Bartlet Brebner, and Erling M. Hunt, eds., The Dryden Press, 1951, pp. 111-27.

GERTRUDE HIMMELFARB (essay date 1952)

[*Himmelfarb is a prominent American historian who specializes in studies of Victorian society. In the following excerpt, originally published in the November 1952 issue of* Partisan Review, *she discusses Stephen as he typifies the Victorian scholar-gentleman.*]

The professional bearing of the Victorian intellectual is so conspicuous that his amateur status is apt to be overlooked. This professionalism is exhibited in the regularity and facility of his writing—the normal accreditation of a genuine, working intellectual. There cannot have been many writers like Anthony Trollope, who kept a schedule and a watch in front of him to make sure that he turned out his 250 words every quarter of an hour for a minimum of three hours. But the sense of writing as a regular occupation, not beholden to inspiration or creative impulse, was and still is typical among English intellectuals. Stephen himself was no more productive than many others; he averaged three or four 8,000-word articles a week (each at one sitting, it is, incredibly, reported), apart from incidental writing tasks. This was the sportsmanlike way of writing: no fuss, no anguish, the game played at the appointed time, so many minutes to the period, so many periods to the event.

As a writer, then, the Victorian intellectual was very much the professional; it was as a thinker that he tended to be amateur, and largely for the reason that he was so professional in his writing. No one could write profoundly on subjects worked up for the occasion at the rate of 25,000 words a week. And even if he could, the writer would not have wanted to enter too profoundly into his subjects. There was something unsporting, to his mind, in the way a German philosopher (or these days, the English complain, an American academician) worried an idea, strained for a meaning, deliberately cultivated the difficult and obscure. The Victorian essayist was sensible and urbane, preserving the amenities of discourse, the manners of a gentleman in the presence of ladies. A book or theme was explored, with not unseemly haste or heat, until the contracted number of pages were filled. Where there was a show of passion it was against those who, by affronting common sense, had ruled themselves out of the company of gentlemen. The German philosophers were most objectionable: Hegel was, Stephen confided in his diary, "in many things, a little better than an ass"; and he refused to believe that Coleridge could have stolen his Shakespeare criticism from Schlegel, "partly at least, for the reason which would induce me to acquit a supposed thief of having stolen a pair of breeches from a wild Highlandman."

For the most part, the Germans excepted, the tone was mild and agreeable. It was as if the essayist had entered into a compact of friendship with his subject, so that Morley could be equally tender toward Rousseau and Burke, or Stephen toward almost all the great writers with whom he dealt. As a biographer, Stephen prided himself on not revealing all that an inquisitive reader might like to know, and as a critic he praised the Memorials of Charles Kingsley for its reticence. He was widely read in the literature of the eighteenth and nineteenth centuries, but he managed, as English reviewers say in praise, to carry his learning lightly. He was thoughtful yet never argumentative, sensitive but not precious, sympathetic without being committed. He had all the virtues of the gentleman—amiability, broad-mindedness and a high tolerance—which meant that he had the great vice of the essayist—literary promiscuity.

Stephen's essay on Jonathan Edwards is instructive. Here was a man who was as unlikely a candidate for his sympathy as is conceivable—a religious zealot, mystic, witch-hunter, and hairsplitting theologian. Yet Stephen never lost his temper: Edwards "is morbid, it may be, but he is not insincere"; "there is something rather touching, though at times our sympathy is not quite unequivocal. . . ." Stephen was able to be good-tempered because he never really believed that a man could honestly believe in sin and hellfire as Edwards professed to. Himself a gentleman, he was generous enough to ignore these distressing lapses of taste and to assume that Edwards too was at heart a gentleman. So casually and smoothly that the reader is almost lulled into acquiescence, Stephen worked up to the remarkable judgment:

> That Edwards possessed extraordinary acute-
> ness is as clear as it is singular that so acute a

man should have suffered his intellectual activity to be restrained within such narrow fetters. Placed in a different medium, under the same circumstances, for example, as Hume or Kant, he might have developed a system of metaphysics comparable in its effect upon the history of thought to the doctrines of either of those thinkers. He was, one might fancy, formed by nature to be a German professor, and accidentally dropped into American forests.

The Victorian essayist had the temperament which Americans associate less with the literary critic than with the cultural anthropologist. A variety of beliefs, styles, and personalities came under his purview, and, in the fashion of the anthropologist, he gave them each the best of his understanding and sympathy. But he never made the mistake of believing them or accepting them at face value, much as the anthropologist takes care neither to be contemptuous of the Zulu nor deferential toward the Christian. To all his subjects he displayed the same gentle irreverence, with only the slightest hint of the superciliousness that betrays the superior man who is above the battle. Thus Stephen could say, of the greatest mind of his time: "Newman is good enough as a writer and ingenious enough as a sophist to be worth a little examination. I only consider him as a curiosity." Or he could refer to Hobbes as "a Herbert Spencer of the seventeenth century," and describe philosophy in general as a by-product of social evolution, "the noise that the wheels make as they go round."

But like the anthropologist, who often harbors behind his façade of impartiality a whole armory of beliefs and assumptions, the essayist too had his stock of prejudices which every now and then emerged in the rhetoric of the essay. In Stephen's case, they were expressed by his favorite invectives, "morbid" and "unmanly." Morbid and unmanly were anything tainted with excessive sentiment, sensibility, emotion, or exoticism. Donne's love poetry was morbid. Rousseau had a morbid tendency to introspection and a morbid appetite for happiness. Balzac's lovers were morbidly sentimental and morbidly religious. Keats, Shelley, and Coleridge were unmanly. Charlotte Brontë's Rochester and George Eliot's Tito and Daniel Deronda were all feminine. (A reviewer of Stephen's book on Eliot corrected what he took to be a typographical error in the description of a male character as womanly.)

Stephen was confident that he himself could never be charged with unmanliness. His philosophy, such as it was, was a sound, English utilitarianism. His religion was a healthy agnosticism. His esthetic principles were common sense and good nature. His highest praise of a young man was to call him "a manly and affectionate young fellow." If all of this sometimes added up to Philistinism, then he admitted to being a "thorough Philistine who is dull enough to glory in his Philistinism." Besides, Philistinism was a word that "a prig gives to the rest of mankind." He disclaimed any comprehension of the non-literary arts; "artistic people," he once told his artistic children, "inhabit a world very unfamiliar to me." And he was only so much of an intellectual as his compulsive sense of manliness permitted him to be—and manliness drove a hard bargain. The result was that Stephen, who, as Maitland put it, had a "lust for pen and ink" so great that he begrudged the time spent at the dinner table, could be found uttering, and, what is more, believing, such crude philistinisms as: "To recommend contemplation in preference to action is like preferring sleeping to walking." Or: "The highest poetry, like the noblest morality, is the product of a thoroughly healthy mind.'' Writing itself, if conducted in the properly casual and sportsmanlike spirit, was not unmanly. But thinking was suspect. It was for this reason that Stephen, as he once confessed, found that he could write when he could not read—and a fortiori when he could not think. (pp. 212-16)

There are different habitats of madness suitable for different varieties of intelligence and sensibility. There are the super-rational heights of madness on which may be found a science-ravished spirit like Comte; and there are the irrational depths in which a Dostoevski or Nietzsche may find refuge. Victorian intellectuals dwelled, for the most part, upon the plains of madness—that deceptively peaceful countryside where philosophers paraded as journalists and writers showed off their Rugby Blues more proudly than their Oxford Firsts. Here lived those scientists and rationalists (Darwin, Huxley, Spencer) who suffered from lifelong illnesses which defied medical diagnosis and cure; novelists of domestic manners and morals (Bulwer Lytton, Thackeray, Meredith, Dickens) whose marriages were tragically unhappy; religious libertarians (Harrison, Stephen, Morley) who were zealous puritans; successful and wealthy writers (Macaulay, Dickens, Darwin) who were obsessed with the fear of bankruptcy; moral critics (Carlyle, Eliot, Mill, Ruskin) who lived in the shadow of sexual aberrations and improprieties; and in general an intellectual community suffering a larger proportion of nervous breakdowns, it would seem, than almost any other (Maine, Lecky, Kingsley, Symonds, Mill are the names that come most readily to mind, although the list can be expanded almost indefinitely). In this company of ''manly and affectionate fellows,'' Stephen was a member in good standing. (pp. 218-19)

> Gertrude Himmelfarb, "Leslie Stephen: The Victorian as Intellectual," in her Victorian Minds, Alfred A. Knopf, 1968, pp. 198-219.

S. O. A. ULLMANN   (essay date 1956)

[*Ullmann was a Hungarian-born English critic. In the following excerpt from an introduction to a collection of Stephen's essays, he assesses the quality of Stephen's work, praising in particular the judiciousness of his literary criticism.*]

Seldom has a gifted writer tried as hard as Leslie Stephen to court neglect or been as successful in achieving that aim. Although specialists know his *History of English Thought in the Eighteenth Century* and lovers of mountaineering literature still enjoy his *Playground of Europe,* many well-educated readers remember him, if at all, only as the first editor of the *Dictionary of National Biography* or as the father of Vanessa Bell and Virginia Woolf. (p. 7)

Surprisingly, Stephen himself was largely responsible for the neglect accorded his work. He made it difficult for critics to look upon him as really first-rate because he habitually scoffed at his own works. His innate hypersensitivity and his almost morbid awareness of his slightest shortcomings led him to deny all claims to originality and consider himself a failure and even at times an imposter. Although he loved poetry and as a boy had literally become so intoxicated by it that doctors had prescribed a diet of prose, in his criticism he pretended to be a prosaic person, humbly feeling his way amid the mysteries of high poetic art. He insisted that he was only a sensible man of the world writing for other sensible men, subscribers to *The Cornhill Magazine* and *The National Review.* This approach to literature was well suited to win the confidence of his read-

ers. By posing as an ''outsider'' instead of a man of letters, he not only could attack the excesses of æstheticism, but also could snipe at the Philistines themselves, who were quite willing to listen to friendly criticism from one of their own number. (p. 8)

Stephen's most consistently entertaining essays are probably those on mountaineering. Climbing was a passion with him for more than thirty years. By the time that his health had forced him to lead a more sedentary life, he had many difficult ascents to his credit and had long ago been honoured by election to the presidency of the Alpine Club. In his mountaineering essays he gave literary distinction to a new genre. By turns exciting and ironic, exalted and whimsical, these essays have never been surpassed. **"A Substitute for the Alps,"** his last and one of his best, is more timely today than when it first appeared some sixty years ago. Now that teams of experts, employing hundreds of porters carrying tons of equipment, have at last painfully hoisted themselves to the top of Mount Everest and Mount Godwin Austen (K-2), it is amusing to read Stephen's mock onslaught upon these ''new-fangled monstrosities.'' He writes as a vacationing amateur for whom mountain-climbing means a pleasant day's perpendicular jaunt up an alp in the company of a friend and two or three congenial guides. His essay good-naturedly pokes fun at Asian mountaineering, which seems to him much more like a military expedition or a Gargantuan scientific experiment than like a sport. (pp. 9-10)

Stephen's essays on social questions have kept their freshness and show us a side of him seldom as clearly revealed elsewhere. In 1869-1870, during his early days with *The Cornhill Magazine* before he became its editor, he wrote a series of twelve essays signed ''A Cynic.'' He never reprinted any of them, although the first, **"A Cynic's Apology,"** has appeared in several anthologies. **"Vacations"** belongs to this series, and **"International Prejudices"** is in a similar vein. They are not earnest attempts to reform society, but merely playful though dexterous thrusts at contemporary cant. Many of the follies that Stephen pokes fun at are, alas, still with us: our self-deception, our blind worship of science, and our tendency to make superficial and hasty generalizations about other nations and other races.

What passes for cynicism in these early essays is only an attempt to expose conceit, hypocrisy, and sentimentalism. Even though he calls himself a cynic, his prevailing tone is ironic rather than cynical. This irony is a counterpart of his agnosticism and implies that to go too far in any direction is to get into an area where one can talk only nonsense. Stephen turns his brand of irony to particularly good use in his only literary satire, **"Did Shakespeare Write Bacon?"** In it he examines an ingenious hypothesis which, as he remarks with deceptive gravity, ''should only require a brief exposition to secure its acceptance by some people.''

Most of his literary essays, however, are somewhat more serious. . . . [It] is as a critic that I believe Stephen will be remembered longest. Except for Matthew Arnold, no other Victorian produced so large a body of distinguished criticism. Although critics as different as Carlyle and Swinburne have written an occasional essay that is finer than any of Stephen's, none of his contemporaries maintains so uniform a standard of excellence. Nor does any inspire as great confidence in his judgments, for none is so careful to explain the basis for his opinions. Stephen is sensitive yet incisive, sympathetic yet ultimately disinterested. He knows what he wants to say and says it without obscurity, without arrogance, and without trying to substitute bombast for critical insight. when literary historians sum up Stephen's criticism as rationalistic, utilitarian, agnostic, positivistic, their sweeping generalisations overlook the sources of his vital strength: his keen sensibility, his critical impartiality, his breadth of view, and his lively and vigorous style. (pp. 10-11)

Stephen was wrong when he said that the best critic is the one who "makes the fewest mistakes." By modern standards he made fewer "mistakes" than Arnold and far fewer than Dr. Johnson; yet his criticism is not therefore superior to theirs. Like all good prose, the best criticism possesses the kind of literary excellence that transcends mere utility. Such excellence depends far more upon the qualities of mind and sensibility which the critic displays than upon the ultimate validity of his judgments. I am not trying to excuse Stephen for exercising bad judgment. He needs no such excuse, since he probably wrote a larger number of judicious critiques than any other Victorian. But far more important, all of them bear the personal stamp of an alert and sensitive mind, without which criticism has little permanent value.

Although usually not an innovator, Stephen was the first to give serious consideration to most of the major English novelists. He was also among the first to emphasize the influence of social structure upon literature. He pointed out the many ways in which a writer's sense of his audience affects his work, and by so doing Stephen helped prepare the way for the modern school of sociological criticism. Still more important, he played a leading part in the rehabilitation of the eighteenth century. He admired it because by temperament and intellectual heritage he was almost as much a man of the Enlightenment as of his own age. He shared the eighteenth-century's hatred of pedantry, its distrust of "enthusiasm" and fanaticism, its respect for common sense, its tolerance. His knowledge of intellectual history made him realise how much he owed to the ideas of men like Burke and Hume. His own *History of English Thought in the Eighteenth Century* was primarily an attempt to make his contemporaries as aware as he was of their intellectual debt to their predecessors. It is easy enough now to point out the limitations of Stephen's appreciation of men like Pope and Swift, but measured by the standards of his day, as set by Carlyle and Arnold, Stephen's praise of the Augustans seems generous indeed. Moreover, his criticism helped to convince many of his contemporaries that there was no justification for superciliously dismissing the eighteenth century as an age without imagination or literary distinction.

Stephen's own interest in the historical method as applied to philosophy, religion, and government antedated his career as a writer. It was thus natural for him to make use of this method once he began to write about literature. Not only in his historical essays but also in his criticism he conveys the impression that he sees literature in relation to society as a whole and fully understands the relation of any particular work to the history of literature. His unusually harsh review of Taine's *History of English Literature,* however, shows how strongly he disapproved of criticism which seemed to him to abuse even a sound method. He had no respect for Taine's *a priori* theories, his hasty generalisations, and his pseudo-scientific pretences. Stephen was quite aware, moreover, as some modern scholars are not, of "the vast difference between what is called knowing a thing's history and knowing the thing itself." Although generally more interested in understanding works than in passing judgment on them, he was careful to treat the historical method simply as a useful auxiliary, not as a substitute for critical judgment and individual taste.

He had his weaknesses, of course, particularly his inability to discuss poetic technique, a subject on which usually he remained wisely silent; his frequent failure to distinguish between an author and his work; and, by modern standards, his excessive attention to "the moral element in literature," though in this respect he was far more temperate than most of his contemporaries.

Stephen was, nevertheless, a remarkably fine critic. Neither dilettante nor pedant, he approached literature as a cultured man of the world. Although making use of many of the insights provided by advances in history, science, and sociology, he avoided becoming overcommitted to any one of them. His criticism holds a middle course between critical extremes. It tries to be both sympathetic and impartial, and refrains from using either a blackjack or a censer. Stephen never attempts to bludgeon readers into agreement or to awe them by dogmatic assertions. When he finally pronounces judgment he speaks with assurance, because he knows his own mind and never pretends to be speaking for anyone but himself. Stephen claimed that criticism was not his "proper line," but a friend came nearer to the truth when he called him "a critic blind to no literary merit save his own." (pp. 11-14)

S. O. A. Ullmann, in an introduction to Men, Books, and Mountains: Essays *by Leslie Stephen, edited by S. O. A. Ullmann, The Hogarth Press, 1956, pp. 7-14.*

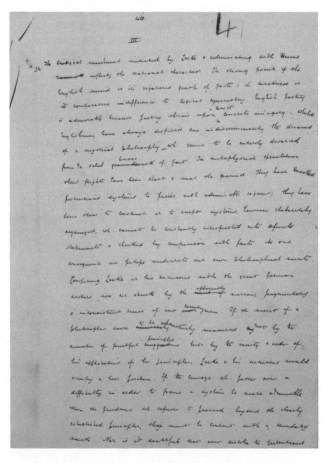

Holograph copy of a page from The History of English Thought in the Eighteenth Century.

RENÉ WELLEK (essay date 1957)

[*Wellek's* History of Modern Criticism *(1955-1986) is a major, comprehensive study of the literary critics of the last three centuries. Wellek's critical method, as demonstrated in the* History *and outlined in his* Theory of Literature *(1949) is one of describing, analyzing, and evaluating a work solely in terms of the problems it poses for itself and how the writer solves them. For Wellek, biographical, historical, and psychological information is incidental. Although many of Wellek's critical methods are reflected in the work of the New Critics, he was not a member of that group, and rejected their more formalistic tendencies. In the following excerpt from an essay originally published in the journal* Victorian Studies *in 1957, Wellek explains why he considers Stephen's critical method limited.*]

No one can doubt the general distinction of Leslie Stephen in various fields: he was the first editor of the *Dictionary of National Biography* who alone contributed 378 articles; he wrote five volumes (Johnson, Pope, Swift, George Eliot, Hobbes) for the English Men of Letters series; he was a moral philosopher who expounded agnosticism and an evolutionary *Science of Ethics* . . . , and finally and most eminently he was an intellectual historian whose *History of English Thought in the Eighteenth Century* . . . and the *English Utilitarians* . . . put him possibly first among the neglected band of Victorian intellectual historians: Buckle, Lecky, John Morley, Flint, Merz, Adamson, to name only a few.

Strictly from the point of view of literary criticism Stephen's position and importance are debatable. Desmond MacCarthy in a lecture on Leslie Stephen . . . called him "the least aesthetic of noteworthy critics" and complained that he is "deficient in the power of transmitting emotions he had derived himself from literature; he seldom, if ever, attempted to record a thrill" [see excerpt dated 1937]. Q. D. Leavis, on the other hand, thought such deficiency an asset, as criticism is "not a mystic rapture but a process of intelligence" [see excerpt dated 1939]. Stephen for her is a great critic precisely because he is a sturdy moralist, the true "Cambridge critic," presumably a spiritual ancestor of her husband. Noel G. Annan, in his excellent book on Stephen . . . , tried to strike a balance. He admits Stephen's limitations but still claims him as "Arnold's disciple" who "did for English fiction what Arnold had tried to do for poetry."

The comparison with Arnold will not, however, withstand inspection. Stephen does not share his faith in classical humanism, either ancient or Goethean. He does not advocate culture, criticism, or an opening of doors to Continental winds of doctrine, and he does not believe in the future of poetry. As the review of Taine shows, he doubts the value of racial types, Celtic, Teutonic, and Latin, so prominent in Arnold's criticism. He never uses touchstones. In a lecture on Arnold . . . Stephen himself says that Arnold's intellectual type was different from his own. "Had Arnold been called upon to pronounce judgment upon me, he must, however reluctantly, have put me down as a Philistine." Philistinism surely means here Stephen's own basic utilitarianism, which he tried elaborately to reconcile with Darwinian evolutionism. It means, in literary criticism, a frank intellectualism and moralism.

The essay on **"Wordsworth's Ethics"** begins characteristically: "Under every poetry, it has been said, there lies a philosophy. Rather, it may almost be said, every poetry is a philosophy." Anticipating the very phrasing of A. O. Lovejoy's statement that "ideas in literature are philosophical ideas in dilution," Stephen studies literature because "it holds a number of intellectual dogmas in solution." He tries to extract from Wordsworth's poetry an ethics which, he confidently believes, will "fall spontaneously into a scientific system of thought."

Stephen, however, is well aware of the difference between a philosophical treatise and a piece of imaginative literature. The whole aesthetic doctrine seems to him "a misstatement of the very undeniable and very ancient truth, that it is the poet's business, to present types, for example, and not to give bare psychological theory." The poet must incarnate his thought in concrete imagery. "The morality, for example, of Goethe and Shakespeare appears in the presentation of such characters as Iago and Mephistopheles." The role of criticism, or at least one of its roles, will be a translation into intellectual terms of what the poet has told us by characters and events. The title of one of Stephen's essays, **"Pope as a Moralist,"** could analogously be given to almost all his other articles.

Of course Stephen is not content with this role of translator: he judges and ranks his authors according to their implied moral philosophies. The standard is that of a secular, social morality which teaches us to recognize the "surpassing value of manliness, honesty, and pure domestic affection" but still has a sense of evil and a feeling for man's impotence and of the mystery around him. Shakespeare, Wordsworth, George Eliot, Scott meet these specifications, and of all writers Dr. Johnson appeals to Stephen most by his morality and his sense of personal doom. On a lower level are the good common-sense moralists like Pope and Fielding, who have their limitations. "We scarcely come into contact with man as he appears in presence of the infinite." And then there are the writers whom Stephen calls morbid, great, and bitter men like Swift, warped, protesting women like Charlotte Brontë, extravagant cynics like Balzac, cloudy idealists such as Shelley, and insincere buffoons such as Sterne.

This is, no doubt, moralistic criticism, but it is literary criticism because it is concerned with the "world" of the poet, with his characters and events as they affect the characters, and with the literary value of the books, for Stephen is convinced of the basic identity of moral and aesthetic value. "The highest poetry must be that which expresses not only the richest but the healthiest nature," and "vicious feeling indicates some morbid tendency, and is so far destructive of the poetical faculty." "The vigour," he asserts, "with which a man grasps and assimilates a deep moral doctrine is a test of the degree in which he possesses one essential condition of the higher poetical excellence." Within the limits of this conception Stephen analyzes the psychology of characters and the implicit morality of the chief English novelists from Defoe to Stevenson and applies the same procedure to dramatists like Shakespeare or Massinger, to poets like Pope, Gray, or Shelley and to essayists like De Quincey or Hazlitt. The criticism of books quite naturally passes into biography, into a judgment of the man rather than the work, for Stephen does not believe in the distinction. He can say that "the whole art of criticism consists in learning to know the human being who is partially revealed to us in his spoken or his written words." He can identify the study of the life of Charlotte Brontë with the study of her novels, and he can become involved in the most awkward conundrums about Pope's "sincerity," since he admires him as a moralist and still has to accept the evidence, accumulated by Elwin, of his "lying on the most stupendous scale."

Though Stephen has a professional grasp of British empirical philosophy, he shies away from an analysis of the metaphysics, ontology, or even theory of knowledge of the writers he discusses. He brushes off Wordsworth's "mysticism," sneers at Coleridge's philosophy, and treats Shelley's Godwinian sensationalism and Platonic idealism as mere romantic moonshine. Nor do we get, of course, any analysis of technique, language, or composition, whether in poetry or in fiction. He does on occasion recognize that "the technical merits of form can hardly be separated from the merits of substance," but usually he "leaves such points to critics of finer perception and a greater command of superlatives." The essay on Sterne has nothing whatever to say about *Tristram Shandy* as a novel—its parody of the novel form, its handling of time, etc. The essays on Shelley and Coleridge shirk any discussion of the poetry. When Stephen recommends the address to Chaos from *The Dunciad,* he quotes other people's opinions but carefully refrains from endorsing their praise. Occasional comments on Defoe's devices to enhance credibility or Richardson's difficulties with the epistolary form or Massinger's prosaic blank verse are so rare that MacCarthy's conclusion about Stephen's criticism as the "least aesthetic" seems amply justified.

The moralistic point of view overrides also the historical and social point of view in Stephen. At first sight he seems imbued with the historical method of his time. Certainly *English Thought in the Eighteenth Century* contains passages that define the character of imaginative literature as a "function of many forces"—the current philosophy, the inherited peculiarities of the race, its history, its climate, its social and political relations. The late lectures *English Literature and Society in the Eighteenth Century* . . . treat literature "as a particular function of the whole social organism," and Stephen's biographer, F. W. Maitland, reports that "I have heard him maintain that philosophical thought and imaginative literature . . . are but a sort of by-product of social evolution, or, as he once put it, 'the noise that the wheels make as they go round.'" But however closely Stephen studies the relations between literature and history or between literature and the audience to which it was addressed, he is never willing to embrace the consequences of a sociological method—its complete determinism, its moral indifference, its relativistic suspension of judgment, its elimination of the individual. He complains that the "exaltation of the historical method threatens to become a part of our contemporary cant" and ridicules the historical method if it means "accepting beliefs as fact without troubling about their reasons." Even while he strongly recommends the study of English history and intellectual currents to the student of English literature, he recognizes that there is "a vast difference between what is called knowing a thing's history and really knowing the thing itself." He holds firmly to a fixed standard of morality which alone lifts him above the flux of history and allows him to judge literature, even though he himself, paradoxically enough, in his *Science of Ethics* tried to explain even ethics as a result of the process of evolution.

But apart from morality and truth Stephen has no standards or theory for literature. He expressly denies that there can be a science of aesthetics or any general rules or principles of criticism, even though he recommends that the critic proceed in a scientific spirit, with due regard to facts, dispassionately, with "a certain modesty in expression and diffidence in forming opinions." At most, he grants "that there is surely no harm in a man's announcing his individual taste, if he expressly admits that he is not prescribing to the tastes of others." He can even say that "all criticism is a nuisance and a parasitic growth upon literature." "The one great service a critic can render is to keep vice, vulgarity, or stupidity at bay." It seems significant that we hear nothing of ugliness or bad art.

Ultimately Stephen simply distrusts art. Like his utilitarian and evangelical friends he concedes that "there is a good deal to be said for the thesis that all fiction is really a kind of lying, and that art in general is a luxurious indulgence, to which we have no right whilst crime and disease are rampant in the outer world." He defends the author's comments in the novels of Fielding and Thackeray with an argument which makes him hardly a safe guide to fiction. "A child dislikes to have the illusion broken, and is angry if you try to persuade him that Giant Despair was not a real personage like his favourite Blunderbore. But the attempt to produce such illusions is really unworthy of a work intended for full-grown readers."

This basic skepticism and even nihilism about the value of literature and the rights of criticism are the reasons for the present neglect of Stephen as a critic. His certainties are purely moral, not metaphysical or aesthetic, and even his acute moralistic criticism will be felt today narrowly circumscribed by his view of human nature and history. His moral vision, earnest, public-spirited, upright as it is, seems cramped by the complacencies and facile assumptions of his positivistic and utilitarian creed. We can fully recognize his great historical merits, especially in his defense of the kindred values of 18th-century literature. We can admire the sober analytical skill of many of his essays (especially in *Hours in a Library,* a collection greatly superior to the *Studies of a Biographer*). But we must admit the grave limitations of a sensibility that treats literature either as a moral statement in disguise or as a social and psychological document. It is hard to believe that Stephen's criticism can be made to speak to our time. (pp. 185-90)

> *René Wellek, "Arnold, Bagehot, and Stephen," in his* A History of Modern Criticism, 1750-1950: The Later Nineteenth Century, *Yale University Press, 1965, pp. 155-90.*

EDWIN D. SHEEN (essay date 1958)

[*In the following excerpt, Sheen considers Stephen's approach to literature in relation to modern critical theory.*]

Commenting on non-historical methods of criticism, Leslie Stephen once mentioned a certain critic who "condemned a republication of Johnson's preface to his dictionary, because, as he truly observed, it showed that the author was not familiar with the latest researches of the nineteenth century." Stephen himself, on those rare occasions in our time when notice is taken of him as a critic, is often put at a similar disadvantage, being roundly condemned for his unfamiliarity with the lore of the latest schools, or apportioned the subtle damnation of faint praise for being thoroughly and avowedly in harmony with the empirical scientific *Zeitgeist* of the era in which he lived and with the objective, fact-worshipping, anti-metaphysical spirit of the university which shaped his intellect. As a matter of fact, it would be difficult to find a more direct antithesis to the modern spirit than Leslie Stephen, and the modern who attempts to judge him according to mid-twentieth-century standards is likely to arrive at conclusions which are either obvious or not necessarily so. I shall point out only a few instances of this antithesis, based principally on certain observations by Desmond MacCarthy [see excerpt dated 1937], as a representative of the modern spirit, and Noel Annan, Stephen's latest biographer—since to marshall all the evidence would be impossible within any reasonable space.

MacCarthy, for example, did not like Stephen's interest in "communion with the author," and Annan indicates a similar point of view when he holds that in Stephen's criticism "the reader's eye is too often taken off the work of art by the shift in emphasis from the work to the author's life and the relation of both to his times." Under the influence of a critical tradition which tends to fix the eye so steadily upon the work that the work often begins to take on colors and shapes more directly traceable to the critic's eye than to the writer's mind and soul, these critics imply, as a self-evident truth, that Stephen's interest in the man who made the book is an injudicious preoccupation and a regrettable shift in emphasis. Stephen, on the other hand, would be somewhat puzzled at the implication that book and man are such separate and distinct phenomena that in talking about the one a critic must be careful not to become preoccupied with or shift his emphasis to the other. To him an experience with a book was not essentially an experience with words, phrases, and clauses; or figures of speech and rhythms and rhymes; or irony and ambiguity; or "variations of pace" "texture of language," or moods created by a skillful choice of materials. It was primarily an experience with a man, and with various creatures of that man who must necessarily bear the stamp of his image and (consequently) the image of his times. If pertinent observations about the author's personality and his life and times and their relationship to his work are to be considered a "shift in emphasis," then Stephen would certainly hold that unless such a shift were made constantly and searchingly, neither the author nor the work could be fully appreciated and interpreted. He did not deny, of course, that children and careless readers may derive a great deal of pleasure from a book like *Gulliver's Travels* without any supplementary knowledge of any sort; but he held that such enjoyment must remain on a relatively superficial level. (pp. 1-3)

We need not insist that Stephen is right and the New Critics wrong—perhaps irony and images and ambiguity and the other objects of modern inquiry are indeed all that one need be interested in—but if so, Stephen is to be refuted, not summarily condemned for his unfamiliarity with modern aesthetics.

The New Critics are likewise disturbed because of Stephen's apparent inability to criticize poetry to any purpose. MacCarthy saw him as "the least aesthetic of noteworthy critics," who was "more at home with prose writers," seldom, if ever, attempted to record a thrill, and "limited himself as far as he could to that aspect of his subject about which it was possible to argue." Annan again agrees in principle, asserting that "Stephen rarely criticized poetry and when he did he left off where he should have begun," which he counts as a defect because "a great critic should move with ease between prose and poetry." He disagrees, however, with "the common explanation . . . that Stephen had no touch of poetry within himself." Stephen, he held, "had, not too little, but too much poetry in him and drank it in such draughts that he could not savour the delicacies or tell the vintages."

This is a generous admission and probably quite close to the truth. Stephen was congenitally shy of temperament, with an almost morbid tendency to underrate his abilities and achievements, especially when there was other work of some excellence with which his own might be unfavorably compared. Thus he would naturally shrink from the kind of criticism involving the self-exposure which his family and his set did not consider quite respectable. And as Annan suggested, his love of poetry was no ordinary love—it had affected his young spirit more strongly than was deemed best for him by an eminent physician and was intimately tied up with recollections of his mother and his sister. Any attempt, then, to reconstruct,

record, and transmit the intimate feelings and sacred associations which made poetry great to him might well have struck him as indecent if not sacrilegious. Certainly he would fear that what seemed wonderfully beautiful to him might sound vapid and silly to others of a different background and point of view.

It must be admitted, then, that Stephen, though he criticized some poets, avoided the kind of criticism which records thrills and attempts a thorough anatomization of the poet's effect on the reader. Habitually, when the opportunity to take such a flight presented itself, he confessed to a prosaic mind unfit for such delicate and sensitive operations. "I do not wish," he said characteristically, "to examine the justice of [Swinburne's] assaults [upon the rivals of Charlotte Brontë], and still less to limp on halting and prosaic feet after his eloquent discourse." It was undoubtedly a pose, but it was a pose that he could not help. He was haunted constantly by the fear that he was an imposter and a misfit in the field of criticism; and this feeling must necessarily have been intensified when he contemplated invading—even for a moment in order to preserve a proper balance—the province of his betters—like Lamb or Hazlitt or Arnold—who knew instinctively the right things to say and could say them in a criticism that read like poetry itself.

It is not clear, however, why this legitimate Horatian tendency to recognize the limitations of his talents should be regarded as a defect. Is a critic necessarily required to move with ease between prose and poetry? It might be argued with equal cogency that Arnold, with whom Annan was comparing Stephen at this time, rarely criticized prose and never dealt with the novel and the biographical forms, to which Stephen gave a great deal of attention with considerable insight. The concentration upon poetry to the neglect of prose is characteristic not only of Arnold, but of most other great critics from antiquity to Stephen's time—those that come most readily to mind showed interest in prose only as it was associated with oratory and persuasion, or as it related to the fitness of the vernacular for the expression of poetic ideas. Certain critics, indeed, who have gained some attention since Stephen's time move—whether with ease or not—among all forms of writing, and their forerunners among Stephen's contemporaries took for their province not only all forms of writing, but painting and music and all other types of creative expression as well. Whether such diffusion is to be taken as a sign of genius or merely as the sophomoric self-confidence of the intellectually immature prig (the conception is Stephen's) must remain largely a matter of opinion. Stephen was trained in the Cambridge tradition of limited but thorough competence. It is not strange that he ultimately decided to confine his criticism to those forms which lent themselves most naturally to his favored methods of analysis and which he felt were best fitted for his temperament.

Moreover, if we look beyond the *Cornhill Magazine* and the later biographical and critical pieces to which Stephen appended his signature, and dip into the lively pages of the *Saturday Review,* where he published anonymously much of what he called his "subterranean work," we may be surprised to find that in the early days of his journalistic career he did try his hand at criticizing poetry from a more or less aesthetic point of view. Certain essays on style and taste show very convincing signs of his hand, and though there is nothing startlingly original in them, they nevertheless reveal a mind that was capable of some significant thought on these subjects. Also apparently from his hand are reviews of the works of Christina Rossetti and Matthew Arnold, and of a host of unknowns seeking name and fame who were intermittently dealt with, usually unkindly, in groups of half a dozen or so, under the repeated general title of "Minor Poets."

Reviewing *The Prince's Progress and Other Poems,* he spoke of the "lightly tuneful meditativeness about most of Miss Rossett's verses" and added:

> They have the delicious and truly poetic effect of striking us as things overheard, as if they were the unconscious outcome of the most harmonious moods, in which the hearer is neither suspected nor wished. They are like the piping of a bird on a spray in the sunshine, or the quaint singing with which a child amuses itself when it forgets that anybody is listening.

He found in these verses not much thinking, or high or deep feeling, or passion, "and no sense of the vast blank space which a great poet always finds encompassing the ideas of life and nature and human circumstances"; nevertheless the poems "are melodious and sweet and marked with that peerless calm which lay at the root of Shelley's notion of happiness as an essential condition of poetry."

"To have written *Sohrab and Rustum,*" he said in a review of Arnold's *New Poems,* "was to win the lasting admiration and gratitude of every lover of poetry. The fine harmony of the verse, the stately imagery, the nobly tragical manner of the story, its sombre yet elevated pathos, fill the mind with that joy which it is the poet's chief glory to give." He deplored the dearth of "light and brightness" and of "the cheerful inspiration of poetic joy"; but noted the "gracious harmony of verse, delicately pensive moods, stately and grave thoughts," and here and there "glimpses of the old calmness and luminous objectivity."

This is not sociology or history. It is, in fact, pretty much like the stuff out of which many an aspiring modern critic has attempted to fashion a reputation as an aesthete. We might guess that had the aesthetic type of criticism been respectable among the members of Stephen's circle, and had he turned his hand seriously to it, he could have gushed about the beauties of poetry and the variations of pace and texture of prose as well or as badly as the next man. To understand why he did not we might note the difference between the Cambridge and the Oxford mind, which Stephen often pointed out. Oxford, he held, encouraged the development of metaphysicians, dreamers, prophets; Cambridge, where poets were never happy, aimed to develop a disciplined, practical mind interested in facts, neatly turned arguments, and matters capable of demonstration. Stephen, the embodiment of the Cambridge ethos, was terribly ill at ease in any Zion that suggested the Oxford atmosphere. He adhered to his father's belief that criticism was "generally a self-sufficient, insolent, superficial and unedifying style of writing." He had learned from his own experience that if a critic wanders into aestheticism, he is likely to talk of "light and brightness" and "the cheerful inspiration of poetic joy," and of "lightly tuneful meditativeness" and "the piping of a bird on a spray in the sunshine"—distinctly un-Cantabrigian expressions of undisciplined emotion and odiously suggestive of certain Oxford gentlemen who were recognized as the leading aesthetes of the time.

Unlike the New Critics, however, Stephen did not believe that to eschew aesthetics meant necessarily to eschew criticism altogether. With Cambridge efficiency and an equally Canta-

brigian interest in genus and species, he divided critics into two classes—the heaven-born aesthetic and the pedestrian journeyman scientist—each with its limited field of competence. Critics of the first type—Lamb, Hazlitt, Ruskin, and Arnold were representative examples—could reach pertinent conclusions about writers by trusting only their personal feelings and intuitive impressions. Not so with those of the second class, in which Stephen placed himself. They must confine themselves to statements verifiable by historical data or derivable from the text. "A critic of the highest order," he said in an essay on Pope,

> is provided with an Ithuriel spear, which discriminates the sham sentiments from the true. As a banker's clerk can tell a bad coin by its ring on the counter, without need of a testing apparatus, the true critic can instinctively estimate the amount of bullion in Pope's epigrammatic tinsel.

Critics of the lower orders, on the other hand, "must be content to take their weights and measures, or, in other words, to test their first impressions, by such external evidence as is available." They must "proceed cautiously," and substitute "patient inquiry" for the "rapid intuition" by means of which the heaven-born critic leaps to his correct conclusions.

These heaven-born critics were naturally rare—Stephen thought we could hardly expect more than one or two in a generation. The earth-born breed, on the other hand, represented by the workaday journeymen constantly grinding out hasty reviews of current works in order to meet deadlines, were a numerous and not insignificant race. In spite of the disparaging remarks he was constantly making about criticism, including his own, Stephen took quite seriously his work as a member of this pedestrian clan and seems to have devoted a good deal of thought to its *modus operandi.* A *Saturday Review* article which we can assign to him with some degree of certainty traced the development of critical reviewing from its beginning with a seventeenth-century French journal to his own day. Here he listed several useful services that critics of the lower orders have performed for the reading public: notably the exposure of folly and fraud, and the simplification of the process of book selection for the man of taste who wishes to read the best but does not have the time to examine and evaluate each work as it comes off the press. In a later *Saturday* article he drew up a code of ethics for the reviewer intended to insure fairness to the author and at the same time adapted to the trying conditions under which the reviewer must arrive at his judgments. In other "subterranean" works he defended the critic from the enemies necessarily created by candid judgments and preached the necessity of honest opinion untainted by the bias of the prevailing clique. His more respectable *Cornhill* contributions also deal frequently with the defense of periodical criticism, the responsibilities of the critic to his authors and his public, and the methods to pursue in order to insure scientific accuracy where the intuitive inspiration of the first-rate critic is necessarily lacking.

This being the case, Annan is hardly on solid ground when he suggests that Stephen in avoiding the seas of aesthetic criticism was not only guilty of a fatal deficiency in his method and a craven neglect of his own responsibility, but was also frustrated by a too stinging awareness of his limitations and employed compensatory methods that were not quite legitimate. He accuses Stephen of trying "to bluff the reader"; of satirizing Arnold's fine perception of "ethnological nuances . . . in English literature''; of crying aloud in desperation ''for an Ithuriel spear to distinguish true sentiments from false'' and resorting to vague, naïve, and pointless escapes when his cry went unheeded; and of finally ''shaking his head,'' apparently in hopeless confusion, as he admitted that all his tests ''were as personal as any he had condemned in Arnold.'' ''Ithuriel had come on parade without his spear,'' Annan cries triumphantly as he pictures Desmond MacCarthy seeing at a glance, ''like a martinet inspecting troops,'' the deficiencies in Stephen's critical equipment.

These observations stem from the conviction, characteristically modern, that a critic must reflect the prevailing tradition and speak the familiar language or be read out of the profession; and are based upon the argument by assertion, also characteristically modern, which demolishes the opposition by meticulously demonstrating the manner and extent to which it constitutes opposition. Stephen avoided the ''bright green marshes of aestheticism'' (or was pretty careful not to wade in above his knees) for reasons of his own which we have already briefly noted. There is no need to read unjustifiable inferences into his modest conception of his powers. His statement that ''the value of all good work ultimately depends upon touches so fine as to elude the sight'' must appear necessarily to be evidence of maundering, hesitation, and despair (the interpretation is Annan's) only to those (of the Oxford mind) who are certain that they can themselves delineate the exact ingredients of beauty and their proper proportions. The figure of the Ithuriel spear, which we have already seen in its context, was grossly misinterpreted. There is no cry of desperation involved—only a rather interesting analysis of two different types of critical mind. If Annan wishes to contend that the pedestrian critic is no critic at all, he may do so; but he cannot justly suggest that Stephen cried out for the spear which he never dreamed of being able to wield, or aspired to strut spearless on parade in the ranks of his betters. (pp. 3-10)

The extent to which Stephen's critical principles were antithetically at variance with those of certain modern schools is perhaps most interestingly revealed in his comments in the *Saturday Review* on the less durable works which came under his scrutiny. Here he is seen to have been in constant conflict with practices which are now more or less taken for granted, but which in his time, it seems, were manifested principally in the works of obscure hack poets. A severe criticism of one ''Ellis,'' for example, cites the ungrammatical use of *thine* to refer to a plural antecedent, the stumbling metre, and the bad rhymes, such as of *morn* with *dawn* and of *arm* with *calm*. Another particularly savage review attacks one ''E.D.S.'' not only for bad rhyme and for being generally an egregious ass, but also because the lines of his ''heroic poem in four books . . . do not even begin with capital letters so that that which is commonly looked upon as the clearest indication of poetry is absent.'' He was also annoyed by the obscurity of some of the current poetic efforts. Even in Browning, ''the only great living poetic master'' of ''bright, wide, large-eyed thought,'' the obscurity was a handicap. ''It is not every one,'' he wrote, ''who likes that his poetry should be rather more difficult to understand than a treatise on Chinese metaphysics''; and though he derived ample reward from the mastery of Browning's poems, he was still tempted ''in moments of laziness, to turn impatiently from *Sordello* to the study of such comparatively transparent works as *Hamlet* or *Faust*.'' A little later he introduced his discussion of the ''Minor Poets'' with a similar reference to Browning:

It was once safe for a man of any culture to infer, in reading a poem, that what seemed to have no sense was senseless. But since Mr. Browning began to write we are no more expected to understand at first sight a modern poem than a chorus in a Greek play.

Even before the comparatively early date when Stephen severed his connection with the *Saturday,* he realized that he was fighting a losing battle in behalf of eighteenth-century correctness and good sense. As we have noted, he was willing to accept as normal a certain amount of obscurity in poetry; it was not long before he also admitted that such rhymes as *arm-calm* and *morn-dawn* were becoming too common to be successfully opposed. From the perspective of our present position we can see how much all that he fought against was actually the trumpet of a prophecy, whether we consider it a prophecy of good or evil. For in our day, at least so far as criticism in some of its more obvious manifestations is concerned, obscurity after Browning's worst example is more likely to attract than to repel followers, who will eagerly plunge into any morass of unintelligibility in the hope of coming up with some previously undiscovered pearl of subtle significance. Likewise it appears that forgotten minor poets like ''Ellis'' and ''E.D.S.'' deserve to be resurrected and belatedly hailed as pioneers: for rhyme that is pure and obvious either to the eye or to the ear is almost obsolescent, and its place has been taken by intricacies of sound-juggling of which a prosaic reader (like Stephen) could hardly even notice the existence—let alone understand—without the aid of an analysis by a baptized expert in the cultish lore; and such devices as the eschewing of capital letters, and a lofty freedom and independence in, or of, matters of grammatical and structural convention, far from being regarded as reprehensible, are lauded and imitated as evidence of profound conception and bold technique.

The influence of Leslie Stephen in the field of criticism was not inconsiderable during his lifetime. By no insignificant number of the literati he was placed among the foremost English critics of his time, able to compete on even terms with Arnold, Ruskin, and Pater. Whether modern criticism could profit by a revival of the critical spirit that he represented is a question to be left to posterity; but a few closing observations may be in order. Obviously, of course, the journeyman critic is still in the majority and might advantageously study Stephen's methods and ethics of reviewing; but there is yet another point. We are in the midst of an age of strong, aggressive leaders and weak, hero-worshipping followers; when the tendency of the rank and file to accept and believe, to attach themselves to a clique and pledge uncritical allegiance to its total gospel, is becoming alarmingly manifest. The rise of the great dictators and near-dictators in the first half of this century has indicated how readily whole nations can be influenced by this spirit in their political beliefs; and the evidence that it is exerting an undue influence in other fields—not only in criticism, but in the labor movement, race relations, and the methods of education, for example—is far from negligible. For those grovelling enthusiasts who cannot enjoy a healthy feeling of security unless they are seated at the feet of some powerful and able prophet, imbibing his nonsense along with his wisdom—for these Stephen has a message. Above everything else he preached independence in tastes and judgments. He would be sycophant to no scribbler, dead or alive; and he constantly warned both author and critic to beware of the debilitating incense of the cult or mutual admiration society. You cannot really appreciate the true worth of your great man, he would tell the disciples of schools, until you have taken his measure and tested his doctrine by the dry light of reason. "Spiritual guides," he wrote in his essay on Jowett, "are troublesome personages. A prophet, perhaps we [of Cambridge] thought, is apt to be a bit of a humbug, and at any rate a cause of humbug in others." He was merely putting into Cantabrigian words the excellent advice of another Oxford gentleman whom the New Critics at least respected: that in following the best light that we have we must be sure that our light is not darkness. I know of no advice of which certain modern critics—and I would include many who consider themselves disciples of Stephen—stand in greater need. (pp. 11-14)

> *Edwin D. Sheen, "Leslie Stephen and Modern Criticism," in CLA Journal, Vol. II, No. 1, September, 1958, pp. 1-14.*

RICHARD STANG (essay date 1959)

[*In the following excerpt, Stang explores Stephen's concept of morality in literature.*]

Leslie Stephen, in his essay **"Art and Morality,"** has given us what will probably remain the classic attack on didactic fiction and the convention of poetic justice.

> Novels with a purpose are proverbially detestable, for a novel with a purpose means a book setting forth that a villain is hanged and a good man presented with a thousand pounds—that is silly and really immoral; for in the first place the imaginary event is no guarantee for the real event; secondly, a particular case does not prove a rule; thirdly, it is not true that virtue is always rewarded and vice punished; and fourthly, virtue should not be inculcated with a simple view to money or the gallows.

"The highest morality of a great work of art," Stephen asserts in his essay on Fielding, depends not on the way an author rewards and punishes his characters but "on the power with which the essential beauty and ugliness of virtue and vice are exhibited by an impartial observer." Iago is an ugly character and does not have to come to a bad end to repel the reader. When Fielding, who is a great writer by virtue of his "seriousness of purpose," loses this impartiality and becomes angry with Blifil, "he simply reviles" and ceases to understand. The resulting character is a blur, rather than a consistent portrait. With the consequent loss of insight, due to the overpowering of his judgment by his moral sense, he ceases to be an artist at all.

But Stephen's cool and logical demolition of the simple-minded novel with a moral purpose does not mean that literary art can ever be divorced from morality, "a system of rules for regulating our passions." It was folly to underestimate the danger to society of such "brutalizing and anti-social instincts" and habits of mind as "cynicism, prurience and voluptuous delight in cruelty." These, for Stephen, were "simply abominable," and "he who keeps them alive is doing harm, and more harm if he has the talent of a Shakespeare, a Mozart, or a Raphael. . . . Nobody should compose poems for human beasts." A novel or poem, Stephen writes, should not attempt like a Chinese vase to exist for no purpose except to please the aesthetic sense, but must have "a ruling thought, though it should not degenerate into a tract; and the thought should be one which will help to purify and sustain the mind by which it is assim-

ilated; and therefore tend to make society so far healthier and happier." Like all the major Victorian novelists and critics, Stephen demanded of fiction a definite social and moral function, not to be realized by direct preaching. Instead, the reader should be "affected by the morality which permeated the whole structure and substance" of the book. Bulwer-Lytton, a favourite whipping boy of the Victorian critics, was thus condemned because "his moral is not embodied in his works, but exhibited with all the emphasis of sententious aphorism." His works could have no real effect on their readers, moral or otherwise, because they lacked "spontaneity and vigour," because he had "no firm grasp of real life . . . no imaginative intensity." And all the serious purpose in the world could not make one a first-rate novelist if he lacked these gifts.

Stephen evidently felt that he had somewhat oversimplified the whole problem in his **"Art and Morality,"** for his ideas appear in a more fully developed form in **"The Moral Element in Literature,"** which was also published in the *Cornhill Magazine*. Here the morality of a work has nothing to do with anything specific that the author says; rather the influence of a work "depends upon a man's total power, upon his intellectual and emotional vigour, upon the strength of his passions, the clearness of his reason, the delicacy of his perceptions, the general harmony of his faculties. . . ." In short, there could be no divorce between literary standards and moral standards; they were one and the same thing, so that the idea of "a Shakespeare, a Mozart, or a Raphael" creating immoral works was impossible. The very qualities which were responsible for their genius—strength, clarity, harmony—were *ipso facto* moral. Morality Stephen now sees as health, "the whole organisation working soundly," and this quality, if it is in the man, must be in his work. Any moral degradation would be immediately perceptible by the literary critic as a literary fault. "The literary equivalent of moral degradation is blunted feeling, the loss of delicate perception which enables a man to distinguish between exalted passion and brutish appetite, and disqualifies him from dealing with the highest problems of human nature. . . ."

Morality for Stephen could never be merely passive, a "spontaneous obedience to a certain code of rules—a dislike to lying, stealing, drunkenness and so forth." Such an idea he found "an utterly inadequate measure of a man's total excellence," rather it is something active, "the amount of energy he represents and . . . the vigour of his impact on the world of thought." As a result, the ultimate value of any book was dependent on the nature of its author. "I measure the worth of any book by the worth of the friend whom it reveals to me. . . . The worth of an author is in proportion to his whole intellectual force." George Eliot had come to a very similar conclusion about the relationship between a novel and its novelist. "Don't you agree with me that much superfluous stuff is written on all sides about purpose in art? A nasty mind makes nasty art, whether for art or any other sake. And a meagre mind will bring forth what is meagre. And some effect in determining other minds there must be according to the degree of nobleness or meanness in the selection made by the artist's soul."

It was in his penetrating analysis of Charlotte Brontë that Stephen showed how he would apply the ideas he worked out in his more theoretical essays. *Jane Eyre* was a result of two wholly conflicting aims: one, stated in the preface, was a "protest against conventionality," and the other was a most "unflinching adherence to the proper conventions of society." "At one moment . . . we seem to be drifting towards the solution that strong passion is the one really good thing in the world . . . ," and at another that "Duty is supreme," duty to the moral conventions of society. If one asked the rather awkward question: "What would Jane Eyre have done, and what would our sympathies have been, had she found that Mrs. Rochester had not been burnt at Thornfield?" it becomes apparent that Charlotte Brontë has left "an unsolved discord" in her book and "an inharmonious representation of life." Stephen finds the same symptoms in her style, "a certain feverish disquiet" marked by strong mannerisms. "At its best, we have admirable flashes of vivid expression, where the material of language is the incarnation of keen intuitive thought. At its worst, it is strangely contorted, crowded by rather awkward personifications, and degenerates towards a rather unpleasant Ossianesque. More severity of taste would increase the power by restraining the abuse."

In *Villette* Stephen finds the same qualities that he found in *Jane Eyre.* "She is between the opposite poles of duty and happiness, and cannot see how to reconcile their claims, or even . . . to state the question at issue. She pursues one path energetically, till she feels herself to be in danger, and then shrinks with a kind of instinctive dread. . . ." Stephen here, in Charlotte Brontë, is, of course, giving the classic description of neurosis, a conflict engendered by alternate attraction and withdrawal without any possibility of a resolution. "Undoubtedly such a position speaks of a mind diseased, and a more powerful intellect would even under her conditions have worked out some more comprehensible and harmonious solution." Her only possible position is the one she is left with at the end of her novel: "that life is a mystery, but that happiness must be sought by courting misery." As a result, any claims made for Charlotte Brontë as a novelist of "the highest rank" must be denied, because she is not "amongst those who have fought their way to a clearer atmosphere, and can help us to clearer conceptions. . . ."

In the same essay Stephen tries to define precisely the ideal critical approach to novels: "to feel strongly, and yet to analyse coolly." Even though our reactions are necessarily at first strongly emotional, "the product of instinctive sympathy [or antipathy], instead of deliberate reason," "when we are seeking to justify our emotions," we must become as objective as we can, "applying with rigid impartiality such methods as are best calculated to free us from the influence of personal bias." His notion of a kind of scientific objectivity in criticism, like Arnold's, has very strong affinities with the main stream of French criticism in the nineteenth century, especially Taine and Saint-Beuve.

> Though criticism cannot boast of being a science, it ought to aim at something like a scientific basis, or at least proceed in a scientific spirit. The critic, therefore, before abandoning himself to the oratorical impulse, should endeavor to classify the phenomena with which he is dealing as calmly as if he were ticketing a fossil in a museum. The most glowing eulogy, the most bitter denunciation have their proper place; but they belong to the art of persuasion, and form no part of the scientific method.

And one can search in vain through all Stephen's critical writings for the purple passages of impressionistic critics like Swinburne and Pater. It is important, though, to remember that Stephen never treated a piece of literature as purely a historical artifact, a fossil, that has no power to influence our lives. The value of any novel lay in the fact that it was an extension of the reader's world, and as such, should have a very definite influence on him. To read a novel in the true sense "is to lay aside for a moment one's own personality, and to become a part of the author. It is to enter the world in which he habitually lives—for each of us lives in a separate world of his own—to breathe his air. . . ." It was Stephen's ability to project himself into a novel, identify himself with its author, and, at the same time, to maintain his objectivity that gives his best criticism its special quality. "To be an adequate critic is almost to be a contradiction in terms; to be susceptible to a force, and yet free from its influence; to be moving with the stream, and yet to be standing on the bank." (pp. 75-9)

> *Richard Stang, "The Sacred Office: The Critics,"*
> *in his* The Theory of the Novel in England: 1850-1870,
> *Columbia University Press, 1959, pp. 46-90.*

JOHN GROSS (essay date 1969)

[*Gross is an English literary scholar and the author of several critical studies, including the highly regarded* Rise and Fall of the Man of Letters *(1969). In the following excerpt from that work, Gross discusses Stephen's most significant contributions in the field of literature.*]

Although Stephen himself took it for granted that after his death posterity would quickly consign him to the learned footnotes, few Victorian prose-writers of the second rank have in fact worn as well. His accomplishments as editor, biographer, historian of ideas, essay-writing alpinist are still fairly common knowledge, while his criticism has a tart flavour which recommends it to modern tastes, and marks him off from all but a tiny handful of his contemporaries. It is true that latter-day admirers have sometimes paid too much attention to his purely negative virtues as a critic, but it must also be conceded that these are an essential part of his appeal. He knew how to make short work of mawkishness or affectation. He was expert at showing up impostors for what they were. In an age of histrionics he kept a cool head, and his lack of enthusiasm can be infectious.

Stephen's astringency has often been put down to the intellectual nip in the Cambridge air. He himself was proud to belong to a university which favoured mathematics rather than mysticism, a university where a Newman, let alone a Jowett, would have been judged by the dry light of reason—and found wanting. A follower of John Stuart Mill, in a looser way he can also be thought of as a product of Cambridge rationalism. It is possible, however, to make too much of the *genius loci.* One of Stephen's most ardent modern defenders, Q. D. Leavis, has even gone as far as to label him "Leslie Stephen, Cambridge Critic" [see excerpt dated 1939]. There seems to be some question of faking a pedigree here, so it is perhaps worth pointing out that "London critic" would be at least as appropriate a description. If Stephen had remained a don, pushing generations of students through the Tripos, coaching the college eight, presiding over bump suppers, he might never have become a writer at all. As it is, he shouldered the burdens of journalism without complaining—deliberately opted for them, in fact, after his loss of faith had led to him resigning his fellowship. And journalism in turn was able to offer a man of his calibre far better openings than would have been the case twenty years earlier.

His first important connection, secured for him by Fitzjames, was with the *Saturday Review,* which according to Mrs Leavis "seems to have been a congenial extension of the Cambridge

Talland House, the Stephens' summer home (described by Virginia Woolf in To the Lighthouse).

ethos.'' Bearing in mind Female Strangulation and much else, we may well feel that if this were altogether true, so much the worse for Cambridge. Fortunately, however, Stephen found the *Saturday* a good deal less congenial than Mrs Leavis suggests. He may have caught the superficial tone of the paper, but he disapproved of most of its policies, and like another dissident contributor, his friend John Morley, he was barred from writing about politics or religion in its pages. Nor was he a reviler by nature. It is true that on one side of his character he was rather impressed by what he praised Bagehot for demonstrating—''the real value of good, sweeping, outrageous cynicism.'' When he first began writing for the *Cornhill*, he chose to sign himself ''A Cynic.'' But no one can have been taken in for very long. At heart he was an affectionate man, easily bruised, with none of his brother's truculence. His agnosticism, too, gave him a certain dry detachment, which kept him from committing himself too belligerently to the common assumptions of his class. For a Victorian moralist he was tactful, even circumspect. But whatever his private misgivings may have been, he was not prepared to fly in the face of established convention, and his literary work was to some extent a means of gently disengaging himself from the fray. Starting out as an energetic Liberal, by the 1870s he was ready to settle for political quietism. He did not expect to change the world by writing essays, and there was nothing particularly heroic, in his view, about being a man of letters. Rather, it was a career which called for a decent regular dose of humorous self-depreciation.

The writers who meant the most to him—the only writers, one sometimes feels, who really touched him deeply—were those like Dr Johnson or Wordsworth who offered, as he saw it, fairly direct lessons in fortitude and stoical wisdom. For the rest, he was content with the role of judicious biographer. The one modern critic whom he praised unreservedly was Sainte-Beuve, but he himself approached authors less as a ''naturalist of souls'' than as a seasoned judge of character. His curiosity was hemmed in by orthodox taboos, and the deeper riddles or contradictions of a personality were liable to strike him as merely irritating and perverse. However, he was far from being the head prefect which his concern with character-building may make him sound. The judgements are worth having; the clear, effortless style, with its beautifully marshalled detail and glancing ironies, represents in itself a notable mastery of experience.

Furthermore, Stephen's interest in biography goes well beyond that of the miniaturist: his figures are always firmly set down in a landscape. Primarily a historian of ideas, he also pioneered the sociological study of literature in England. Today this method can hardly be considered a blinding novelty: every A-level candidate knows how to examine Tom Moore's slightest lyric in the light of the Industrial Revolution. There is still something to be learned, though, from Stephen's flexibility and natural caution. He might refer to literature as ''the noise that the wheels make as they go round,'' which sounds as mechanistic an image as anything in Taine, but he was keenly aware of the dangers lurking in over-simplified analogies and monocausal explanations. His long review of Taine's *History of English Literature*, which appeared in the *Fortnightly* in 1873, is one of the most devastating things he ever wrote: on page after page he shows how brutally the Frenchman had had to torture the facts in order to make them fit his preordained theories. The demonstration is all the more convincing in view of his complete agreement with Taine's fundamental doctrine, that "we ought to study the organism in connection with the medium." Scientific literary history was both possible and desirable, but to get very far it would require precision instruments which still had to be developed. What was objectionable was Taine's brash assumption that his home-made gadget—*race, milieu, moment*—was already fully adequate to the task.

A contemporary reader who accepted Stephen's detailed criticisms of Taine might nevertheless quite reasonably have felt that his overall severity was out of place. By being so resolutely hostile, he was in effect trying to stifle a new subject in its infancy. What, after all, were the alternatives? How would *he* have set about relating writers to their social background? Thirty years later, in *English Literature and Society in the Eighteenth Century,* he took up the challenge. The lectures which make up this book—they were delivered at Oxford on his behalf by his nephew H. A. L. Fisher, while he himself lay dying—are modest and tentative in their conclusions, but admirably clear-headed; they sketch out, as no previous English criticism had done, the right lines on which to explore the literary consequences of changes in the economic status of authors and the composition of the reading public. Admittedly this is as far as Stephen ventures. He had very little sense of the subtler ways in which consciousness might be transformed by environment; compared with a modern account like Ian Watt's, for instance, his treatment of the eighteenth-century novel seems two-dimensional. But at least he provided foundations on which others could build.

If the book were no more than a scholarly blueprint, however, it would have been superannuated long ago. What keeps it alive is Stephen's essential sympathy with his material. Ostensibly the only point he sets out to prove is that the literary history of any period gains by being seen as one strand in a complex social tissue; he does not offer to revise established rankings or pass judgement on the phenomena which he studies. No one could read him for long, though, without detecting a strong undercurrent of regret for lost virtues. He admires the dominant temper of eighteenth-century civilization, and looks back with nostalgia on its relative homogeneity. Where he really warms to his theme is discussing Dr Johnson and the Club. Educated society in Johnson's day had still been compact enough for him to be accepted as literary dictator in the tradition of Ben Jonson, Dryden, Pope. But he was the last of his line— "men like Carlyle and Macaulay, who had a similar distinction in later days, could only be leaders of a single group or section in the more complex society of their time, though it was not yet so multitudinous and chaotic as the literary class has become in our own." Stephen believed in facing the facts. He was a modern man, who lectured to Ethical Societies and tried to keep up with modern thought. But his heart lay in the past. Maitland, in his biography, recalls seeing a list of books which Stephen ordered from the London Library during his last illness:

> It began with the names of Réville, Martineau, Brunetiére, Flint, Vauvenargues, Vandal, Sabatier, Chateaubriand, Sorel, Pater, Ostrogorski, W. Watson and Dostoieffsky. Some of our biblical critics are there, and Emile Zola. Then, when other books failed, he fell back on the old, old story. Need I name it? He told his

nurse that his enjoyment of books had begun and would end with Boswell's "Life of Johnson."

(pp. 83-7)

In this failure to get to grips with the literature of his own time Stephen shows up to disadvantage beside the man he ridiculed, Taine. Taine's picture of nineteenth-century England is lurid and frequently grotesque, but hardly more so than the actual scenes which he was describing; if he goes quaintly wrong on points of detail, he also succeeds in conveying, with a gusto that was quite beyond Stephen, the sheer turmoil of Victorian life, its extravagance and squalor and superabundant energy. His account of the London docks, for instance, has all the murky power of a Doré engraving. And looking at the English business class from the outside, he could appreciate to the full the forces embodied, say, in the unyielding pride of a Mr Dombey. ("To find a parallel we must read again the *Mémoires* of Saint-Simon.") By contrast, Stephen was lukewarm. He had something of his brother's notorious distaste for Dickens; in his article on him for the *Dictionary of National Biography* he makes the Fitzjamesian observation that "if literary fame could be measured by popularity with the half-educated, Dickens must claim the highest position among English novelists." This is the son of Sir James Stephen, K.C.B., speaking, and he is *not* prepared to forgive the Circumlocution Office.

Stephen's attitude to Arnold is equally revealing. He admired him and learned a great deal from him, but he insisted on drawing the sting from his social criticism. However trenchantly Arnold had satirized the ugliness and coarseness of the Philistines, he had done so in the spirit "of one who recognized the monster was after all a most kindly monster at bottom." It would be difficult to put the matter more complacently. On the other hand Stephen's own "philistinism" has its sympathetic side. Certainly it saved him from self-righteousness and the wrong kind of critical intransigence. The more irreconcilable modern opponents of mass culture are fond of quoting his remark that "really the value of second-rate literature is nil"; they conveniently overlook the fact that on another occasion he could reflect that "all books are good, that is to say there is scarcely any book that may not serve as a match to fire our enthusiasm." Must one point out that neither statement is meant to be taken entirely literally, or treated as absolute dogma? Yes, I suppose one must—as though it were not the most natural thing in the world to feel in certain moods that only a handful of writers are ultimately worth bothering with, and at other times that a diet of nothing but the classics would be intolerable.

In any case, it would have been unbecoming for the editor of the *Cornhill* to have campaigned too vigorously against second-rate literature, since that, after all, was the staple commodity in which he dealt. During Stephen's term of office, which lasted from 1871 to 1882, the magazine continued to publish work by most of the leading writers of the day: Arnold, Hardy, Henry James were among his contributors. But this is very far from saying that every number contained fiction of the quality of *Washington Square* or *Far From the Madding Crowd.* Much more characteristic were such offerings as *Zelda's Fortune* and *White Wings: A Yachting Romance.* No doubt Stephen would ideally have preferred to print masterpieces, but he soldiered on; and though he might grumble about having to blue-pencil Hardy ("delete 'amorous' substitute 'sentimental'") in order to placate his public, for the most part he went along quite happily with their views on the proprieties. Nor was he at all averse himself, as a reader, to a nice old-fashioned romantic wallow, with wedding-bells ringing out in Chapter the Last. The level of non-fiction in the *Cornhill,* on the other hand, was kept as high as he could afford under the middlebrow circumstances. As high, or higher: an audience which thrilled to the fortunes of Zelda was easily bored by John Addington Symonds on Italian art or Birkbeck Hill's Johnsonian studies or Stephen's own *Hours in a Library,* and the magazine's circulation, which was around 25,000 when he became editor, had been more than halved by the time he resigned. His successor, James Payn, an old friend from Eton and Cambridge days, was a popular novelist without any intellectual pretensions who was called in by the publishers in an effort to win back lost readers. Although the editorship had never been more for Stephen than a part-time job, a respectable source of income while he got on with his own books, he was irked at the thought of failure. True, before leaving he had at any rate managed to discover one new contributor of real promise in Robert Louis Stevenson. But even he was not an author whom he could take all that seriously. Looking back near the end of his life, he disagreed with critics like Henry James who had praised the deepening psychological penetration of Stevenson's later stories, and plumped firmly for *Treasure Island* as his finest work.

Did he recognize at the same time that the whole mainstream Victorian literary tradition was drying up? Whatever forebodings he may have had he kept to himself. For ten years, after giving up the *Cornhill,* his energies had largely been devoted to organizing the *Dictionary of National Biography,* and his thoughts largely fixed on the past. The *D.N.B.* remains his most enduring achievement. It is also a monument to the more attractive side of Victorian private enterprise: a sixty-three-volume colossus, mainly written by freelance scholars and financed by George Smith out of his own pocket. (Not that Smith didn't have the money to spare: quite apart from his publishing ventures, he is supposed to have made over £1,000,000 out of the British concession for Apollinaris.) A generation earlier, Matthew Arnold, in his essay on Academies, had been able to cite the shoddiness of English biographical dictionaries as a self-evident example of how much better they ordered these things in France. After Stephen and his team had done their work, such a reproach would have been impossible. Scholarship is cumulative, and inevitably the *D.N.B.* has been overtaken by research in the course of eighty years. But it is still one of the most serviceable of all reference-books, and—as anyone who has ever been side-tracked by it will testify—one of the most beguiling.

For Stephen himself it represented both a triumph and a retreat. In 1882 he had published his most ambitious book, *The Science of Ethics.* It was not a success; and in embarking on the *Dictionary* he was putting his gifts to more appropriate if less adventurous use. He might preach post-Darwinian ethics, but he felt more at home with the limited certainties of the obituary column. As Noel Annan has pointed out, for an evolutionary thinker he was strangely indifferent to the actual mechanisms of social change; and the whole self-defeating idea of a science of ethics, although it may have answered the immediate emotional needs of men who had only just shaken off their religion, seems completely at odds with his own traditional practice as a moralist. There is nothing very obviously scientific about the flexible common sense which informs most of his literary work. He rode with the positivist tide, but he was too sane to suppose that irrefutable moral judgements could ever be arrived at by looking them up in a ready-reckoner. Nietzsche might have had him in mind when he wrote, in *Beyond Good and Evil,* that

moral sensibility in Europe today is just as subtle, ancient, manifold, sensitive, and refined as the "science of morality" that goes with it is young, raw, clumsy, and inept. This is a fascinating opposition which occasionally takes on colour and flesh in the person of some moralist.

Which is another way of saying that Stephen himself was often more impressive than his ideas. There is a constant hint about him of unused capacity, reserve power. Thomas Hardy sensed it when he wrote the sonnet comparing him to the "spare and desolate" Schreckhorn which he had been the first to climb. Meredith sensed it when he put him into *The Egoist* as the laconic tutor Vernon Whitford, with his "sunken brilliancy." To such men he was potentially a hero. But the hints remained hints, the reserve was never to be lowered. Fifty years after Meredith, Stephen's daughter portrayed him as Mr Ramsay in *To the Lighthouse*—a Vernon Whitford grown old and querulous and hypersensitive, a disappointed man. Mr Ramsay is the utilitarian as he appeared to a generation of aesthetes, forever going on about "reality" as though it were a hard, angular, well-scrubbed kitchen table, blind to the flamingo clouds of the imagination. In his cut-and-dried fashion he thinks of philosophy in terms of the alphabet. He can run through the letters up to Q (and "very few people in the whole of England ever reach Q"). But there he sticks. "Z is only reached by one mind in a generation. Still, if he could reach R it would be something." On then to R. But it eludes him, and by his own marking-system he is a failure. He is also the prisoner of his own critical habits of thought. When he goes to bed after the dinner-party which marks the climax of the first half of the novel, he picks up a volume of Scott. Downstairs they have been saying that nobody reads Scott any more, and all he can think of as he opens the book is that they will soon be saying the same about him. He is feeling thoroughly sorry for himself. Then, as he reads on, he is completely absorbed, slapping his thighs at the humour. The book entrances him—and "now, he felt, it didn't matter a damn who reached Z." He is reading for the love of it, all thoughts of the professional critic put to one side. But not for long. A few reflections about morality and English novels and French novels and the contrast between Scott and Balzac start to intrude, and though he tries to keep his mind on the story he is soon fretting again over whether or not his own books are still admired by the Young.

To the Lighthouse is a work of fiction, not an autobiography; equally, Mr Ramsay is an irritable paterfamilias seen through the eyes of childhood, not a public man studied by an impartial observer. Virginia Woolf herself was capable of appraising her father's character far more favourably, as she was to show in the tribute (reprinted in *The Captain's Death-Bed*) which she wrote on the centenary of his birth. Still, the fact remains that Mr Ramsay *is* Stephen, at one remove: a Stephen who could never get beyond Q. A little more personal resonance, one feels, a higher degree of social involvement, and his criticism might have ranked beside Arnold's. As it is, he played safe: he is the Gentleman in the Library, content not to ask too many embarrassing questions. This sets a definite limit on his value to posterity. Unlike Arnold, he never seems an indispensable critic—except, that is, in the sense of there being no finer example of his type available. Without him, we should scarcely have guessed quite how formidable a Gentleman in a Library could be. (pp. 88-93)

John Gross, "The Higher Journalism," in his The Rise and Fall of the Man of Letters: A Study of the

Idiosyncratic and the Humane in Modern Literature, *Weidenfeld & Nicolson, 1969, pp. 62-97.*

DAVID D. ZINK   (essay date 1972)

[*Zink is an American critic and the author of* Leslie Stephen, *a study of the author's life, thought, and writings. In the following excerpt from that work, Zink discusses Stephen's skill as a critic, maintaining that he has been misunderstood by both his supporters and his detractors. Zink also provides an assessment of Stephen's biographies.*]

Stephen's rationalism and his commitment to agnosticism had spurred him to writing which earned his distinction as a pioneer historian of ideas. At the same time, the pleasure he found in English literature motivated a more esthetic phase of his career which established him among the leading Victorian literary critics and biographers—a phase of his career that may prove to have been the more successful. His sincerity, dedication, and intellectual power are clearly evident as a historian. Yet the main thrust of his rationalistic writing was destructive. Although every age needs its doubters, men seldom build enduring reputations in this fashion; the Voltaires of history are few. As Stephen himself noted in his "Cynic" series for the *Cornhill,* the disparager's role is generally not an exalted one. On the other hand, when he devoted his energies to literature, his insights were more constructive and therefore probably more lasting. Though not a Matthew Arnold, he merits serious consideration as a pioneer critic of the English novel, as a leader in the Victorian rehabilitation of the Augustan age, and as one who early recognized the consequences of the social matrix for literature. (p. 109)

Stephen's performance as a literary critic is clearly understood only in the light of the general nature of the critical task as it evolved during the nineteenth century. The emergence of the English middle class as a political and economic force in 1832 was accompanied by a need for the establishment of esthetic standards acceptable to that class. Neo-Classical principles of the previous century were in a sense tainted by their association with aristocratic patronage. Consequently, middle-class intellectuals began to evolve their own esthetic. As various commentators on the period have noted, their esthetic was largely a moral one. Variations on the theme—great art is produced by those with profound moral visions—pervade the thought and practice of the important Victorian artists and critics. Whatever beauty may be created, to them the final end of art is to teach important human truths. And, while such a view may strike the reader as "typically Victorian," he is reminded that, as Jerome H. Buckley has observed, such an esthetic is hardly unique since it was grounded on the basic assumptions of most Classical esthetic theories.

At the same time, the moral esthetic held a powerful appeal for the middle class. The art critic, John Ruskin, for example, first experienced a phenomenal success largely as a result of his ability to explain painting and architecture in terms acceptable to the middle-class reader. Although Ruskin's esthetic was dominated by moral and religious considerations, his position developed from about 1840 to 1860 to include the psychological, social, and political implications of art for his countrymen. As he grew more critical of English society, especially of the ills created by rapid industrialization, his message became less palatable to his countrymen. His criticism hearkened back to the Middle Ages when, as he saw it, a sound society allowed whole men to create great architecture. Despite its

efficiency, the division of labor in an industrial society destroyed the worker.

Victorian literary criticism itself dealt increasingly with the relationship of literary art to its roots in society, and such an approach often led to the criticism of society. Matthew Arnold's view of poetry as a criticism of life, for example, was extended in his own practice to delineate the functions of the critic whose province included both the interpretation of literature and the critique of society. Arnold's love of Classical literature led him to compare the ancient Greek's feeling for beauty with the lack of imagination and the smug materialism of his own class whom he attacked as "Philistines" in *Culture and Anarchy* (1869).

Stephen himself assumed the additional burden of eighteenth-century scholarship in addition to the dual role of social and literary critic. The first result should be an appreciation of the fact that Stephen was handicapped both by having, to a considerable extent, to function as a scholarly pioneer, and by assuming the dual role of social and literary critic. The neglected state of eighteenth-century studies and criticism of the English novel made the first inevitable, but the second handicap was, perhaps, a mistake of judgment. If so, it was a common one in the Victorian period, as is illustrated in Arnold's own career. At any rate, Stephen's task was enormous but worthwhile. Stephen began with general evaluations of eighteenth-century novelists, then worked out the intellectual history of the period in *English Thought,* expanded the subject with biographies of key Augustans, all the while continuing to develop an esthetic theory which would be relevant to Victorian fiction.

The corollary of this development as a literary critic was an increase in his objectivity as a critic of society. . . . Basically, the task of the scholar was apparently more congenial to Stephen than some aspects of the literary critic's domain—especially that of poetry. While he showed real skill in vivifying abstract ideas as an intellectual historian, his analysis of poetry revealed far less discrimination than that of his famous contemporary, Arnold. The comparison of the two as critics began with Stephen's friend, John Morley, who regarded Arnold as the more cosmopolitan and able in his examination of the relationship between literature and its social background. Although subsequent comparisons have continued this view, the fact that Stephen is compared with the foremost critic of the Victorian period suggests the intrinsic value of his criticism.

Stephen had met Arnold early in his London days, but the two men were never close friends, despite Stephen's early admiration of the older man, especially because of his brashness as a social critic. By 1884, a letter of Stephen's to his friend Norton reveals that he had begun to be irritated by the smugness he saw in Arnold's social criticism. . . . He particularly resented Arnold's critical terminology, even though he later admitted in his essay on Arnold that the term "Philistine" was probably descriptive of himself—but we have already observed the dogmatism of Stephen's own social criticism. And the distance between smugness and dogmatism is surely not great.

After Arnold's death, Stephen delivered a lecture on the poet in 1893, one later reprinted in Volume II of *Studies of a Biographer,* in which he expressed strong approbation of Arnold as a poet and as a literary critic. Stephen was particularly impressed by the soundness of Arnold's critical intuitions. Arnold's poetic sensitivity, which made him surer and more graceful in his criticism, caused him to select passages from the great poets as touchstones in his criticism in a way superior to Stephen's; and the younger man's essay on Arnold reflects his own awareness of this superiority. Indeed, Stephen described himself as having a prosaic mind when compared with the poetic sensibility of Arnold. The difference in their imaginations is suggested by the historical periods to which they were most strongly attracted: Arnold found Hellenic grace congenial; Stephen preferred the common sense of the Augustans.

Is Stephen to be considered Arnold's disciple? He often follows Arnold in his feeling that the critic is to judge and rank literature, but in his essay on Arnold, Stephen stated that the function of the critic was simply to "distinguish between the sham and the genuine article"; it was not to rank writers in a hierarchy. In this respect, Stephen is closer to appreciation than judgment. Still, as we shall see, the net effect of Stephen's criticism of the English novel was to help to bring order out of chaos. Although Stephen certainly accepted Arnold's opinion that great literature functions as a criticism of life in the largest sense, Stephen's criticism concentrated more on the moral quality of the writer and less on purely esthetic aspects of his work than did Arnold's. However, a close examination of Stephen's moral esthetic reveals that it does not differ essentially in kind from Arnold's own.

In our century a continuing debate over Stephen's merits as a critic also illuminates the general nature of his performance. The debate began with a quarrel between two English critics, Desmond MacCarthy and Q. D. Leavis. In his undergraduate days MacCarthy had been an acquaintance of Leonard Woolf, later the husband of Stephen's most famous daughter, Virginia. In those days MacCarthy was also an intimate of the Stephen family, and in 1937 he criticized Stephen as deficient in esthetic standards [see excerpt dated 1937]. Because Stephen's response to literature was also too intellectual, it lacked emotional depth. MacCarthy further asserted that Stephen's criticism was impaired by his moralistic approach, his rationalism, and his failure to regard literary criticism as a kind of creativity. MacCarthy, who represents the impressionistic and personal response to literature in English criticism, writes criticism that is appreciative, not judicial. Rather than attempting to establish a hierarchy of artists, he stresses the uniqueness of the writer's personal vision; he prefers also to emphasize the writer's ambiguity of statement instead of his moral gravity.

MacCarthy was answered two years later by Q. D. Leavis [see excerpt dated 1939] who shared Stephen's belief that the critic must proceed with a systematic appraisal. To her, Stephen's rationalism was not a weakness but a strength, particularly when he employed it to examine the moral sense and general philosophy of a writer. In short, Mrs. Leavis regarded Stephen as a judicious critic who was bound to document his pleasure in a writer's work by demonstrating his moral seriousness, his intellectual depth, and his craftsmanship. Her defense linked Stephen with Henry James because of the concern for the moral seriousness of the writer which they both reflect in their work.

In 1951, Stephen's second biographer, Annan, sought a middle ground and demonstrated both the strengths and weaknesses of his subject [see excerpt dated 1951]. He appreciated Stephen's accomplishments as a judicious critic, but he finally granted Stephen's failure to subject the novel to the close technical analysis customary in our century. Fourteen years later René Wellek, who amplified MacCarthy's position, insisted that Stephen was seldom aware of esthetic criteria; instead, he had judged literature on intellectual and moral grounds. Furthermore, the ethical values of Stephen were characterized by Professor Wellek as a narrow social morality, one essentially

utilitarian [see excerpt dated 1957; Zink is referring to the republication of *A History of Modern Criticism* in 1965].

I suspect that the Platonic triad—Truth, Beauty, and Goodness—which is implicit in Wellek's judgment may have unduly influenced his appreciation of Stephen's work. If criticism is extended beyond questions of pure form, some concern for the ends of art seems inevitable. In that case, certainly the intellectual and ethical aspects of a particular work of art also become relevant topics for the literary critic. It should be noted that Wellek praised Henry James for a concept of fiction which, to a considerable extent, parallels Stephen's idea that poetry might be assessed in terms of its implicit philosophy. The novel, to James, is vicarious experience which can lead the reader to self-knowledge because the artist has presented his own synthesis which, in the best writers, can be dignified as a philosophy. Professor Wellek justifiably saw in this the implication that the artist speaks not only as an esthetic man but also as one who is rational and ethical.

Stephen was also criticized by Wellek for his application of the sociological approach; it was deficient because his moralistic tendency prevented him from admitting the relativistic values of the method. Finally, Wellek doubted that Stephen as a literary critic had anything to say to the modern reader. Although we find much truth in these remarks, I believe that they are not entirely fair to Stephen's achievements. His critical stance, despite its Puritan overtones, was more broadly humanistic than Wellek was willing to grant.

Stephen's seemingly cavalier attitude toward the practice of literary criticism is yet more deeply disturbing to modern commentators. In 1900, he said, "I always feel that a critic is a kind of parasitical growth, and that the best critic should come below a second-rate original writer." . . . A similar statement appeared in *English Literature and Society in the Eighteenth Century,* and it reflects an attitude toward criticism which from the first he held consistently. While the general reader may be sympathetic to this point of view, it represents a treasonable position to many professionals. Despite this apparent contempt for criticism, in 1876 Stephen defended the function of the critic in a *Cornhill* essay, **"Thoughts on Criticism."** In it, he said the critic's business was to promote "a critical spirit such as raises instead of depressing the standard of literary excellence." Deploring the tendency of Victorian critics to assume that their personal taste corresponded to universal taste, he echoed David Hume's "Of the Standard of Taste" (1757) by insisting that individual taste must be validated by that of cultivated individuals with the passage of time. As he said of the critic, "The fact given him is that he is affected in a particular way by a given work of art; the fact to be inferred is, that the work of art indicates such and such qualities in its author, and will produce such and such an effect upon the world."

In theory, at least, Stephen seems to have the best of both worlds—judicious and appreciative criticism. As he explained the best stance for the delivery of judgments produced by his method, it is easy to see that his diffidence results from a very real sense of the hazards that attend the act of judgment. His ideal critic would avoid dogmatism through his recognition that he is but an individual speaking. On the other hand, his position, that "of a presumably cultivated individual . . . should give at least a strong presumption as to that definitive verdict which can only be passed by posterity." Such caution is refreshingly sane when we recall the occasional modern critic whose work suggests the feeling that criticism is more important than creative work, especially when his criticism is accompanied by the conviction of an invincible ignorance and an incurable want of taste on the part of the reading public.

In practice, Stephen is apparently more limited. His approach seems to be that of the typical mid-Victorian critic who demands moral instruction from art. When the exact nature of this moral instruction is clearly understood, however, Stephen is less parochial. He produced his most valid insights when he faced a writer who could profitably be subjected to ethical and rational scrutiny. He therefore preferred not to emphasize purely esthetic problems but, at the same time, did not deny their importance. It is hard to imagine the humanist of today who would be unable to sympathize with the spirit of a statement made by Stephen in 1881: "It is impossible ever really to exclude moral considerations from esthetical judgments; though it is easy to misapply them, or to overlook the importance of other aspects of a man's total influence. To make a poet into a simple moralist—a teacher of a certain definite code of ethics, is to put him into a wrong place, and judge him implicitly by an inappropriate criterion; but it is equally true that he can only be deprived of moral quality if he takes no interest in the profoundest and most comprehensive topics of human thought and faith.'' (pp. 111-17)

In an era of official biographies which eulogized their subjects, Stephen was instrumental in helping to bring a judicious quality into the genre. The kind of biography he wrote occupies the middle ground between the biographies of his day which produced an image suitable for public tastes and that type of modern biography which reduces archives to reference books stuffed with a welter of facts barely subdued to a recognizable design. Stephen's most successful biographies are soundly grounded on the life and works of his subject. At the same time, an identifiable personal vision of the subject pervades the biography. Uncritical adulation was foreign to his rationalistic temperament. Since his own biographical studies began with eighteenth-century figures, he had been free to exercise greater objectivity than was customary in official biographies of Victorians.

Readers of twentieth-century biographies who are accustomed to psychological analysis in depth will not, of course, find it in Stephen. And sometimes what Stephen calls "psychological" will, for twentieth-century readers, be "moral." But, granting him his own ground rules, how successful was his analysis of the moral quality of those writers he studied? The answer to this question depends upon Stephen's moral vision which, as we have seen, was the basis for his esthetic views. For the agnostic, the meaning of literature, and especially of biography, was to be found in its capacity to perpetuate an ethical sense in society. Literature was to furnish illustrations of the results of a breadth of moral vision and thus enhance the reader's sensitivity to value questions. Religion was to be replaced by literature as a conveyer of ethics.

But what can be said of Stephen's own values? The question is paramount when such values become the principle of selection for the biographer. Stephen's vision of human nature is more broadly humanistic than that modern view which, after Freud, has tended to reduce man to a mere sexual animal; but his ethical sense is not finally sophisticated enough for twentieth-century readers. This crucial matter was thoughtfully analyzed by Professor Annan in his biography, particularly in the chapter entitled "Moral and Immoral Man." Annan felt that Stephen tended to oversimplify character by stressing the distinctions between masculine and feminine traits. To be manly was, most importantly, to subdue one's lusts; to be feminine

was to assist such restraint by existing as a model of innocence. More generally, to be manly was to work at those worthwhile pursuits which improve society and to be undaunted by the defeats all men sustain. When a male writer failed to live up to Stephen's idea of the manly, he was called morbid, although this term, too, was often applied to any emotional behavior by a man.

Such emphasis upon conduct generated a more subtle deficiency: Stephen was often blind to the total moral quality of a person which, after all, is composed of good and bad tendencies. The urge to classify a man as bad or good deadens one to the contradictions of human character, and Annan explained this fault of Stephen's by two factors. One was his liberal sensibility, dominated as it was by the rationalistic desire to bring logical order into the chaos of human experience. Such a sensibility is more at home with categories. A more important factor was Stephen's lack of knowledge of human behavior, which was explained by Annan as the consequence of his fear that more knowledge would make moral judgments impossible.

The general truth of Annan's conception of Stephen's moral vision is evident, but, as Stephen's work is considered, it must be qualified. His treatment of Pope, for example, suggests full awareness of the contrary impulses of human nature. And, in the treatment of his esthetic views above, it became clear that Stephen's tastes were broader than they have been generally thought to be. As for the implications of his sexual attitudes, the sexual license which has begun to pervade the Western world in the latter part of our own century indicates that sex is more than a psychological problem. For some, sexual fulfillment has become a kind of ethic of its own, one to be pursued regardless of the consequences for others. Stephen and his age wrongly feared sex, but is it any more sensible to make it a god? Whatever the crudities of Stephen's ethics, however, his own concern with human values was certainly appropriate in view of the fact that his biographies often dealt with figures who regarded themselves as moralists.

Stephen's most important work as a biographer was his editorship of the *Dictionary of National Biography,* which began in 1882. Within two years, individual volumes were appearing quarterly. The labor of the next six years on the huge project took its toll. When Stephen's health began to fail from overwork and he turned the *Dictionary* over to his assistant, Sidney Lee, in 1890, Stephen was responsible for the first twenty-six volumes; Lee prepared the next thirty-seven. The sixty-three volumes contain nearly 30,000 articles from 654 contributors. Stephen himself wrote 378 articles, the research for which would have provided the basis for as many twentieth-century master's theses. His contributions included philosophers and literary men of the seventeenth, eighteenth, and nineteenth centuries. Predictably, Stephen's emphasis was on eighteenth-century figures.

His other biographical work includes the official biographies, *The Life of Henry Fawcett* . . . , his college friend; *The Life of Sir James Fitzjames Stephen* . . . , his brother; the books in the English Men of Letters series, *Samuel Johnson* . . . , *Alexander Pope* . . . , *Jonathan Swift* . . . , *George Eliot* . . . , and *Hobbes* . . . , and finally, a number of essays which first appeared mainly in the *National Review*. The best of these were later collected in four volumes as *Studies of a Biographer,* which were published in 1898 and in 1902. The life of Fawcett, typical of those which are commemorative in intent, is yet a restrained account which shows its subject as a man of principle active in the vital political issues of the day, the solutions of which tended to broaden democracy. This biography of a popular figure went through five editions in two years.

The pieces collected in *Studies of a Biographer,* are more gentle than the earlier *Hours in a Library;* they reveal a greater sensitivity to the emotional qualities of the literary personality being examined. Also, the tendency is more biographical than critical. Of these essays, the twentieth-century reader will probably enjoy most the ones about Ralph Waldo Emerson and Robert Louis Stevenson. The Emerson essay is a remarkably fair estimate of a writer whose temperament was radically different from Stephen's. Emerson emerges as a man who legitimately earned the admiration of his contemporaries through his cosmic optimism.

George Eliot . . . is the most readable of Stephen's biographical studies. It is an account of her work as a novelist which treats only those events of her life which have a demonstrable relation to her fiction. Roughly chronological in approach, the book is structured by her major works. Stephen's point of view is essentially that of his *Cornhill* essay which we have already discussed: the early Eliot with its vigorous evocation of the rural characters of her Warwickshire youth gave way after *Silas Marner* to fiction made uneven by her increasing thoughtfulness about philosophical and psychological problems. Stephen felt strong admiration for her craftsmanship in the early novels. As might be expected, he was also keenly appreciative of her intellectual courage as she awakened at Coventry from her Evangelical heritage to a full participation in the attacks of Victorian rationalism upon historical Christianity. He dwelt upon her spiritual and intellectual history, one which was made dramatic by a strong religious feeling in conflict with an intellectual rejection of Christian dogma. Out of this dilemma emerged an ever more subtle analysis of the practical consequences of possessing ideals in a world inhospitable to them. The moral problem held great appeal for Stephen, but he recognized that even the soundest ideas are useless unless executed artistically.

The handling of one particular biographical problem, a matter of general concern to Victorians, once again illustrates the moral esthetic in action. The novelist presented conflicting images to her public: her novels made her the great moral teacher; the novelist herself lived with another's husband for many years. Her relationship with George Henry Lewes, which began about 1854, was handled with great objectivity by Stephen: he accepted her position as she herself explained it. Under the circumstances, the arrangement represented the moral equivalent of a legal marriage, a position validated by the pair's conduct during the balance of their lives. At the same time, Stephen recognized an important consequence of the union for the novelist. The famous Sunday afternoon receptions, begun after their move to the Priory in 1863, quickly became audiences for those who wished to pay homage to the genius of Eliot. The affairs were directed by the devoted Lewes whose vivacity saved them from undue solemnity. Yet perhaps they were finally harmful to the artist, for Stephen felt that it was "not altogether healthy for any human being to live in an atmosphere from which every unpleasant draught of chilling or bracing influence is so carefully excluded. Lewes performed the part of the censor who carefully prevents an autocrat from seeing that his flatterers are not the mouthpiece of the whole human race." . . . Eliot herself deliberately avoided reading criticism of her novels, and the insulated quality of the later portion of her life helped to account for those artistic flaws which Stephen saw in her novels.

Eliot's novels were also strongly affected by her intellectual interests. Stephen himself, however, did not condemn her work for didacticism of the usual sort. He observed that critics often lost their objectivity in the face of any didactic intent which they might detect in a work of fiction. He himself did not wish to be preached to with moral platitudes; on the other hand, how could the writer prevent the influence of his reading from being felt in his fiction? Were not his philosophy and his psychology parts of his mental equipment? Stephen felt that they were. When the novelist creates characters to illustrate his conceptual knowledge, he has gone astray; but it is legitimate to create characters from his own experience which also happen to illustrate general human behavior as formalized by philosophy or psychology. Eliot was not at first guilty of building her character from theory. Maggie Tulliver of *The Mill on the Floss* "is profoundly interesting—not because her character has been constructed from psychological formulae, but because when presented it offers problems to the psychologist as fascinating as any direct autobiography." In her early novels such psychology and philosophy as Eliot possessed led the reader to feel "that we are looking through the eyes of a tender, tolerant, and sympathetic observer of the aspirations of muddled and limited intellects." . . . (pp. 138-43)

The close relationship of ethics to art which Eliot insisted upon was, predictably, acceptable to Stephen. He was at pains to explain that, in Eliot's case, beauty includes moral beauty, or beauty of character: "The novelist must recognize the charm of a loving nature, of a spirit of self-sacrifice, or of the chivalrous and manly virtues." No moral relativist, Stephen held "that there is some real difference between virtue and vice, and that the novelist will show consciousness of the fact in proportion to the power of his mind and the range of his sympathies." . . . But again, as in Stephen's treatment of Jonathan Edwards and Wordsworth, his study of Eliot reveals a broader humanism than moderns are prone to grant the Victorians. A Victorian moralist might logically be expected to praise art which advanced moral causes regardless of its esthetic qualities. Stephen, on the contrary, was critical of the later Eliot novels in which he detected the presence of theories which distorted experience. He preferred the early novels, whose interest stemmed from their fidelity both to rural England and to Eliot's own psychological and intellectual development.

He was most critical of her work in the genre of the historical novel. As a literary historian, he could give her credit for attempting to develop the historical novel. Scott had been successful in creating lively action and memorable characters, but his novels had been blotted with anachronisms. Despite her careful homework, however, Eliot was unable to bring to life the excitement of that Renaissance Florence in which *Romola* (1862-63) was set. An authentic reproduction of the period would have been striking to the Victorian reader: "The combination of artistic inspiration, intellectual audacity, gross superstition, and supreme indifference to morality, gives the shock of entering a new world where all established formulae break down, or are in a chaotic state of internecine conflict." . . . When the reader is to move in the society of the Borgias and Machiavelli, he expects to observe a scene in which "the elementary human passions have been let loose, when violence and treachery are normal parts of the day's work, where new intellectual horizons have opened, and yet the old creeds are still potent, and there is the strangest mingling of high aspirations and brutal indulgence . . . so . . . that the ruffian is still religious, and the enlightened reformer fanatically superstitious.''. . . Unfortunately, such a world does not emerge in *Romola*.

The appeal of the novel for Stephen was based upon the appearance of Eliot's typical heroine, for Romola is a high-minded girl who is denied expression of her ideals because of the ruthless society in which she found herself. ''Romola was, I take it, a cousin of Maggie Tulliver, though of loftier character, and provided with a thorough classical culture. The religious crisis through which she had to pass was not due to Savonarola, but to modern controversies.'' The actual subject of the book is, then, ''the ordeal through which Romola has to pass, and the tragedy of a high feminine nature exposed to such doubts and conflicting impulses as may still present themselves in different shapes.'' . . . George Eliot's success in the portrayal of such psychological conflicts is an important basis for her reader appeal in the twentieth century, a fact which verifies Stephen's judgment.

Of all of Eliot's heroines, Maggie Tulliver attracted Stephen most powerfully. The reason for this was that Maggie transcended the type. She was given ''such reality by the wayward foibles associated with her noble impulses'' that her character ''glows with a more tender and poetic charm than any of her other heroines.'' . . . Dorothea Brooke, the heroine of *Middlemarch*, intended by her creator to be the most poignant example of the female type represented by Maggie, failed to attract Stephen's sympathies. As he had earlier argued in the *Cornhill*, Dorothea's story amounted to a satire of the young woman whose demands on life are impractical. Stephen also sensed that Eliot's attitude was not entirely ironic. Both compassion and irony were evident to him in the handling of Dorothea's life. Nonetheless, he was more attracted to Lydgate and to the story of his defeat, a character whose energies and ambitions were thwarted by the limits of his shallow wife Rosamund. Despite Eliot's failure to carry out her intentions, accomplishments of this order compelled Stephen to acknowledge her great achievement as a novelist in *Middlemarch*.

Stephen's characteristic independence appears in his judgment of the multiple-plot structure of *Middlemarch*. One of the most surprising features of Victorian criticism is the conscious adherence to the theory of structural unity, a theory which had emerged as early as 1868. Critics urged organic unity upon the diffuse Victorian novel, which were often structured by the stories of many characters. The four-element plot of *Middlemarch* was, in Stephen's opinion, admirably suited to the creation of a realistic portrayal of human relations in English provincial society. His judgment, then, represents a challenge of a fashionable theory, a challenge whose validity has been confirmed by twentieth-century studies of the novel.

Twentieth-century scholarship on *Middlemarch*, as well as the whole modern critical approach to fiction, informs a recent commentary on the novel by David Daiches. Yet he agrees that the Prelude which introduces the St. Theresa theme is misleading. The Prelude establishes the characteristic ambiguity of tone: compassion and irony. Yet the novel is not Dorothea's, for her story is seen as a successful means of drawing the reader into the larger story, which is ''the author's mature vision of the mutual interaction between different lives in a given society.'' Thus, while the twentieth-century student of Eliot may, for instance, smile to himself about Stephen's fondness for Maggie, he must finally admit the validity of many of Stephen's initial judgments of the novelist's work. (pp. 143-45)

David D. Zink, in his Leslie Stephen, *Twayne Publishers, Inc., 1972, 169 p.*

STUART HAMPSHIRE   (essay date 1978)

[*Hampshire was an English critic and philosopher. In the following excerpt, he discusses the style and merit of* The Mausoleum Book.]

''Certainly I will admit that I am not a 'failure' pure and simple. . . . The sense in which I do take myself to be a failure is this: I have scattered myself too much. I think that I had it in me to make a real contribution to philosophical or ethical thought.'' The confessional outpouring of the *Mausoleum Book*, short as it is and addressed only to his family, will probably do more to preserve Sir Leslie Stephen's name than any of his other writings; more even than the *History of English Thought in the Eighteenth Century*, an assured classic, still readable, but apt to make only a pale impression alongside this book, which glows with strong feeling, powerfully and strangely expressed. Any possibility of failure is erased.

The strangeness is in the elevated language in which the story of two marriages and two bereavements is told for the benefit of the descendants of these marriages. Stephen is proud of his own emotions and glories in the excess of his devotion to his second wife, Julia, and in the black depth of his despair when she dies. The baring of the breast, an urgent sincerity, goes together with a very high moral tone; and, as Alan Bell remarks in his introduction, the vocabulary of this resolute free-thinker becomes ecclesiastical when he carefully explains the degree and kind of his love to his children. Yet one never doubts the genuineness of the confession, or doubts that one is following closely the movement of his thought and feeling mirrored in his extraordinarily direct style, which is that of an intimate letter. The book is a literary triumph.

The *Mausoleum Book* follows Stephen's emotional development as an adult—harshly self-critical and unsparing, the story of a ''silent, cold and sarcastic man,'' dominating, self-pitying, privileged, imposing, disdainful of the common run of things, fiercely honest and always serious. With his brilliant brother, Fitzjames, he belonged to an established intellectual aristocracy from the moment that he left Eton for Cambridge. His peers formed a loose group, all well known to each other, which probably has had no equal elsewhere, as, for example, in nineteenth-century France, for intellectual power and variety; nor has there been any subsequent period in England when so many men of letters of comparable intellectual distinction might be, and often were, gathered formidably in one room. In the context of his brooding on his own achievement, quoted above, Stephen mentions the admiration that he earned from his friends, Sidgwick, Morley, Pollock and Maitland. Elsewhere in the book Huxley, Lowell and, of course Thackeray, appear as close friends: also Meredith, G. H. Lewes, George Eliot, Trollope, Herbert Spencer, Froude, J. R. Green, were in varying degree friends also, and, on an outer circle, Browning, Tennyson, Carlyle, Mill, Matthew Arnold; the painters Burne-Jones, Millais, Watts, Holman Hunt, were all closely involved with Stephen's family. There were dining clubs and Pollock and Stephen founded yet another club, ''Sunday Tramps,'' at which these strenuous and productive men exchanged ideas. Mammoth walks and Swiss mountains were essential to Stephen. The first editorship of the *Dictionary of National Biography* was the great, and vastly laborious, achievement of Stephen's life, and precluded any possibility of being thought a ''failure,''

Stephen with his daughter Virginia in 1902.

even by the most exacting standards set by his circle. He was the founder of a glorious institution and thereby became an institution himself, even apart from his journalism and history of ideas.

But still in the *Mausoleum Book* he repines and bears down on his children with a bitter insistence on self-examination. The tone is very close to that of Mr. Ramsay in *To the Lighthouse;* it must have been stifling and oppressive for children in real life to be addressed with the full weight of this passionate man's demands for sympathy, admiration and forgiveness. He cannot let go, and he must explain exactly why he loved Minny Thackeray and why he was shattered by her death and why he could fall in love with Julia Duckworth, and why he worshipped her and why he can never say enough about her and about the extent of his loss when she died. It is as if he stood accused, in his own eyes, of the incapacity to love. So monstrous and overgrown is his conscience, his ideal self, that he seems, in this confession to his family, to be addressing a deity within the breast in self-justification. He is dedicated to moral perfection, and he cannot be sure that he comes close to it, although he knows that his wife, Julia, did; so there is a noble discontent expressed in his writing, which sometimes lapses into a rather ignoble grumbling about his difficulties and trials.

Lytton Strachey, now temporarily and absurdly underrated, emphasized the romantic remoteness of eminent Victorians,

who usually did not talk and write, and therefore apparently did not feel, in ways that seem to us natural and unforced. This fascinating book supports him. The screen of privacy and of reticence is not lowered in front of declarations of love, and in front of inner doubts and intimate reflections, which would now be found unfitting and unnatural in the cold print of deliberate and well-written autobiography, even though one would expect them in a Victorian novel, and particularly in Charlotte Brontë. Perhaps the most novelistic passage in the book is the description of the tense waiting that followed Leslie Stephen's proposal to Julia Duckworth, and her declared readiness to become his most intimate friend, while her attachment to her dead husband left her incapable of love and of another marriage. The tension is very definitely conveyed, but abstractly, without any concrete details or picturing of what actually happened between them and of how Julia changed and of what incident occurred in this restless interval. The screen of privacy and of reticence comes down in front of concrete incident and of the details of living, and of course in front of explicit sexual feeling. Yet the brooding, irritable, self-willed, long-striding, mountain-climbing, heavily male presence is brought massively before the reader, with his impatient demands and his commanding talents and energies.

Perhaps the root of the difference between present styles of feeling and expression and this intimidating Victorian model is to be found in the importance which Stephen confidently assumes that his emotions and his family history retain. He seems to be sure that he is at the center of the world, and that the events in this individual consciousness must be placed on record, this soul's history probed. There is very little protective irony. His evangelical background comes forward into the style of his thought, if not into its content. "The pathetic romance" of his life, as he calls it, must have a moral and must have a meaning for his children. It is not difficult to understand why his children felt a need for a radical change of style, nor why Virginia Woolf was set free by his death to live among her friends, unshadowed by the lowering presence in Hyde Park Gate, and set free to develop a style that disowns the evangelical inheritance.

Stuart Hampshire, "The Heavy Victorian Father," in The Times Literary Supplement, No. 3959, February 10, 1978, p. 159.

HAROLD OREL (essay date 1984)

[Orel is an American critic whose area of special interest is the Victorian period. In the following excerpt, he discusses Stephen's critical theories.]

[Leslie Stephen maintained], in numerous contexts and at moments when such declarations were unnecessary, that literature as an aesthetic experience was somehow less worthy, less defensible, than literature seen as related to moral and ethical issues, than literature based upon a philosophical premise. We have heard before the notion that one main interest in reading "is always the communion with the author." Stephen's stress on biographical concerns—whether incidental or quite irrelevant to the main purpose of a book—suggests that often he is less concerned with art, with the shaping of form or with the relationship between form and content, with the aesthetic principles that were becoming so critical to a large number of men of letters in the final decades of the century, than with elements of literary works not always uppermost in the minds of their creators. A literature that depends for acceptance on its reader's approval of the man behind the work or of the doctrine held by the writer is being judged on extra-literary principles.

Is literature in itself important enough to Stephen to justify Stephen's choice of vocation? Stephen often enough considers the possibility that it is not. A sensible man, such as Stephen thought himself to be, and such as he portrayed himself to others, is not necessarily the guide we choose for ourselves when wandering through the labyrinths of art; and matters are not improved when Stephen employs repeatedly, and perhaps in a more idiosyncratic sense than is justifiable, the term of "Cynic" for himself. (For example, he wrote twelve essays for the *Cornhill Magazine* in 1869-70, and signed them "A Cynic"; Stephen was ridiculing various forms of sentimentality and cant; but the notion that he was cynical and sneering in all his views, self-deprecating and unconvinced of the importance of his reviewing, damaged his reputation for fully a century.)

Stephen did not enjoy some kinds of literature, those written by authors he could not like personally: Walt Whitman ("I am hopelessly unable, for example, to appreciate Walt Whitman. . . . The shortcomings still stick in my throat . . . ."); Ossian ("I cannot read him. Nobody can read him"); Matthew Arnold's melancholic heroes, the Obermanns and Amiels of other writers as well as the protagonists of his own poems ("excellent but surely effeminate persons, who taste of the fruit of the Tree of Knowledge, and finding the taste bitter,

go on making wry faces over it all their lives; and, admitting with one party that the old creeds are doomed, assert with the other that all beauty must die with them''); the quarterly reviewers ("a mere combatant in a series of faction fights, puffing friends, and saying to an enemy, 'This will never do'''); the second part of Goethe's *Faust* ("intolerably allegorical"); and a discreetly brief list of writers, many of them poets. One inevitably comes to suspect that Stephen's dislike of what he called the "mere moonshine" element in poetry, an element that bulked large in the poetry of his century, prevented him from writing at length about most of the Romantics, and many of his contemporaries, though the shyness which had afflicted him as a day student at Eton and as an undergraduate in Trinity Hall undoubtedly contributed to his desire not to give needless offence.

He had serious reservations about the right of a critic to legislate. Though he seriously doubted that art had ever been "perfectly spontaneous," or had ever lacked critics to bother the artist who sang or recited by instinct, he was convinced that Spenser and Shakespeare had thought about the principles of their art as much, or almost as much, as their modern critics. "But as the noxious animal called a critic becomes rampant," Stephen wrote in an essay on Gray,

> we have a different phase. . . . The distinction seems to be that the critic, as he grows more conceited, not only lays down rules for the guidance of the imaginative impulse, but begins to think himself capable of producing any given effect at pleasure. He has got to the bottom of the whole affair, and can tell you what is the chemical composition of a "Hamlet," or an "Agamemnon," or an "Iliad," and can therefore teach you what materials to select and how to combine them. He can give you a recipe for an epic poem, or for combining the proper mediaeval or classical flavour to your performance. . . .

The only improvement that modern critics offered over the "noxious animals" of previous ages was a useful emphasis on "the necessity of an historical study of different literary forms." Stephen was rendering judgement on Addison's criticism of Milton; Longinus, Aristotle and M Bossu wrote for different audiences in different centuries; surely, Stephen implied, there were many different types of art; surely, too, a critic must study how they evolved before he could argue that they needed to live up to an "absolutely correct and infallible code of art, applicable in all times and places." The changeability of genres and artistic interests means, inevitably, the fallibility of a critic who assumes he speaks not merely for his own of for his contemporary audience's taste, but for all posterity. In commenting on Ruskin's critical judgments, which Stephen politely noted were "certainly not always right," Stephen went on to say, "No critic can always judge rightly, unless at the cost of being thoroughly commonplace." Ruskin's discussion of the "theoretic" faculty or imagination might not pass muster with later psychologists any better than his theory of the beautiful with professors of aesthetics. The message, therefore, was that critics in general would do well to cultivate humility. As Stephen says elsewhere (in an essay on Johnsoniana), a critic who defines his duties as those of finding fault ("shortcomings") will never be guilty of unprofessional conduct, or (horrors!) an unbecoming enthusiasm.

This variety of modesty did not arise from the fact that Stephen had much to be modest about. But what may have endeared the critic of the Victorian Age, who after all was simply repeating the common refrain of his profession, has more than a slightly chilling effect to modern readers. In fairness, Stephen concentrated on his subject-matter rather than on himself as the peculiar sensibility through whose filter any writer's talent had to pass; he did not conceive his duty to be remaking the writer's achievement in terms of what might be suitable for a cultural context decades or even centuries removed from the era in which that writer worked; nor did he cull flowers of selected passages at the expense of their contexts. It is therefore unrewarding, for the most part, to read Stephen hoping to learn more about the whims and biases of the critic; Stephen's eye is usually on the sparrow.

Still, there are moments that one might wish extended. We can gather from an essay on Godwin and Shelley that Stephen despised extremism in all its forms; the comment that Shelley was, "in one aspect, a typical though a superlative example of a race of human beings, which has, it may be, no fault except the fault of being intolerable," leads inevitably to the conclusion that Shelley, had he not been a poet, would have been "an insufferable bore." Shelley had "a terrible affinity for the race of crotchet-mongers, the people who believe that the world is to be saved out of hand by vegetarianism, or female suffrage, or representation of minorities, the one-sided, one-ideaed, shrill-voiced and irrepressible revolutionists." Unlike Bagehot, who admired Shakespeare for understanding and sympathising with the stupid and the boring elements of England's population, Stephen, with a very deep-rooted distaste, confessed, "I believe that bores are often the very salt of the earth, though I confess that the undiluted salt has for me a disagreeable and acrid flavour." Moreover, the din arising from the devotees of some of Shelley's "pet theories" had become "much noisier" in modern times; in much of Shelley's poetry one could hear "the apparent echo of much inexpressibly dreary rant which has deafened us from a thousand platforms."

Many modern readers agree with Stephen's argument that an effort to separate the poet from the man "as though his excellence were to be measured by a radically different set of tests" is "either erroneous or trifling and superficial." Stephen is simply paying homage to a view expressed by Carlyle: "The poet who could merely sit on a chair and compose stanzas could never make a stanza worth much. He could not sing the heroic warrior, unless he himself were an heroic warrior, too." But the line drawn by Stephen between his own opinion and that of Carlyle is worth stressing. Carlyle emphasised conscience as "not only the supreme but the single faculty of the soul," and morality as not only a necessary but the sole condition of all excellence; and an ethical judgement as "the sole essence and meaning" of any aesthetic judgement. The view, Stephen believed, is too harsh; it has "a certain stamp of Puritanical narrowness." The distance measured here may be taken as witness to a saneness or wholeness of spirit. Although we of the late twentieth century have no Carlyle-like figure to repudiate in quite the same way, Stephen's position provides useful documentation against the view, widely accepted by readers bemused at Virginia Woolf's portrait of her father as Mr Ramsay in *To the Lighthouse*, that Stephen could not divorce ethical considerations from aesthetic judgements.

There is also in Stephen's writings a rueful, rather attractive willingness to write himself down as someone who failed to make the most of special occasions, and one who perceives clearly enough the chasm between personal ambition and worldly achievement. In an essay on Matthew Arnold, Stephen confessed that he had known Arnold personally, though he could not honestly say that he could pass on "reminiscences." "At one of my meetings with him, indeed, I do remember a remark which was made, and which struck me at the moment as singularly happy. Unfortunately, it was a remark made by me and not by him. Nothing, therefore, should induce me to report it . . . ." This honesty carries over to his description of the way in which Tennyson's poems became the centre of an admiring circle of undergraduates at Cambridge. Stephen memorised large swatches of his work: "It was delightful to catch a young man coming up from the country and indoctrinate him by spouting *Locksley Hall* and the *Lotus Eaters*." For Stephen, "poet" in those years turned into a phase equivalent to "Tennyson." He knew then that such enthusiasm, though partly obligatory, was in large measure "warm and spontaneous." "For that one owes a debt of gratitude to the poet not easily to be estimated. It is a blessing to share an enthusiasm . . . ." This could be said without elevating to a height higher than their merits deserved such later poems as *Idylls of the King*. Stopford Brooke's admiration of the *Idylls*, accompanying such hosannas as those heard from Thackeray, Macaulay and Gladstone, was "cordially reverential." But Stephen failed to appreciate Tennyson's best-seller, despite his careful study of Brooke's critique.

> Even a knowledge that one ought to be enthusiastic is a different thing from enthusiasm. Not to recognise the wonderful literary skill and the exceeding beauty of many passages would, of course, imply more stupidity than any one would willingly admit; but I am afraid that from the publication of the *Idylls* I had to admit that I was not quite of the inner circle of true worshippers.

That may, of course, be no more than the declaration of independence that a mature man makes after reviewing the fad-following excitements of his adolescence; still, there is wistfulness in the admission.

Nevertheless we seldom find in the essays of literary criticism the vigorous outburst of personal feeling—the admiration for "the heroes of the river and the cricket-field" of Stephen's youth who are still surrounded by the halo "who surrounded them in the days when 'muscular Christianity' was first preached and the whole duty of man" was said "to consist in fearing God and walking a thousand miles in a thousand hours," a remark that enlivens the essay **"In Praise of Walking"**—and the autobiographical candour that Stephen enjoyed in the writings of other men. (pp. 106-10)

Stephen's influence on his contemporaries and juniors grew primarily from the fact that he was so often correct in his judgment on the virtues and weaknesses of writers. Though not as witty as Bagehot in his assessment of Shakespeare, Stephen's essay seems closer to the truth of the man. *English Literature and Society in the Eighteenth Century* was not only a pioneering clearing-away of rubble, enabling Victorians to see the full dimensions of what the preceding century had accomplished; it remains today the most readable and informative introduction to an age that provided one of England's richest intellectual feasts. In his evaluations of nineteenth-century writers, the emphasis on the human being behind the art is firmly grounded on considerations of form and content. For example, Stephen may announce that Charlotte Brontë is the heroine of all her novels, that Lucy Snowe "is avowedly her own likeness, and Lucy Snowe differs only by accidents from Jane Eyre; whilst her sister is the heroine of the third novel; "but Stephen then goes on to define, with almost scientific care, the nature of the realism to be found in her fictional portrait-painting. He may have thought more highly of Grant Allen and a few others than subsequent generations have done. Still, it is difficult to find in the pages of the many volumes of *Hours in a Library* or *Studies of a Biographer,* or of the periodicals to which he contributed so frequently, literary judgements that have since been overturned or seriously modified, despite the accumulation of data, and despite the devising of new critical methodologies. He wrote with vigour, style and intelligence about the kinds of literature that he enjoyed reading. His critical essays retain to this day their power to interest, and to convince. (pp. 122-23)

> Harold Orel, "Leslie Stephen," in his Victorian Literary Critics: George Henry Lewes, Walter Bagehot, Richard Holt Hutton, Leslie Stephen, Andrew Lang, George Saintsbury and Edmund Gosse, *St. Martin's Press, 1984, pp. 90-123.*

ADDITIONAL BIBLIOGRAPHY

Annan, Noel Gilroy. *Leslie Stephen: The Godless Victorian.* London: Weidenfield and Nicolson, 1984, 432 p.
  The most comprehensive biography to date.

"An Agnostic's Apology, and Other Essays." *Athenaeum,* No. 3413 (25 March 1893): 401.
  Review of *An Agnostic's Apology, and Other Essays* in which the critic praises the logical coherence of that work while disagreeing with its central theses. The critic notes: "If, as Mr. Stephen states . . . , the ultimate test of a belief is its vitality; if that is true—and we are bound to consider the needs, not of solitary philosophers, but of mankind in general—it is hardly probable that agnosticism will have vitality enough to outlast a brief period of transition, or ever supplant some definite form of religious belief as a satisfaction of human needs."

Bell, Alan. "Leslie Stephen and the DNB." *The Times Literary Supplement,* No. 3951 (16 December 1977): 1478.
  Traces the history of Stephen's involvement in the *Dictionary of National Biography.*

Bell, Quentin. "The Mausoleum Book." *Review of English Literature* 6, No. 1 (January 1965): 9-18.
  Biographical data concerning Stephen's family.

Bicknell, John W. "Leslie Stephen's *English Thought in the Eighteenth Century:* A Tract for the Times." *Victorian Studies* VI, No. 2 (December 1962): 103-20.
  Discusses Stephen's fascination with the logical constructs of eighteenth-century thought.

———. "The Unbelievers." In *Victorian Prose: A Guide to Research,* edited by David J. DeLaura, pp. 470-527. New York: The Modern Language Association of America, 1973.
  Comprehensive bibliographical information.

Birrell, Augustine. "Hours in a Library." In his *Essays about Men, Women, and Books,* pp. 189-98. London: Elliot Stock, 1894.
  Laudatory review of *Hours in a Library*

Donoghue, Dennis. "A First-Rate Second-Class Mind." *The New York Times Book Review* LXXXIX, No. 53 (30 December 1984): 8.

Review of Noel Annan's 1984 biography in which Donoghue concludes that Stephen's primary significance for contemporary readers is that "many aspects of his day are more clearly visible in him than in greater figures, precisely because his relation to them was exemplary rather than dominant."

Gosse, Edmund. "Leslie Stephen." In his *Silhouettes,* pp. 319-26. New York: Charles Scribner's Sons, 1925.
  Biographical essay written by a friend.

Greenwood, Frederick. "Sir Leslie Stephen." *The Living Age* CCXL, No. 3115 (19 March 1904): 764-67.
  Memorial tribute written by a friend.

Grosskurth, Phyllis. *Leslie Stephen.* London: Longman's, Green, and Co., 1968, 36 p.
  Biographical and critical information intended as a brief overview.

Harrison, Frederick. "Sir Leslie Stephen." *Cornhill* 89, No. 94 n.s. (April 1904): 433-43.
  Personal reminiscences of a friend.

Hyman, Virginia R. "The Metamorphosis of Leslie Stephen." *Virginia Woolf Quarterly* II, Nos. 1-2 (Winter-Spring 1975): 48-65.
  Compares and contrasts Stephen with Virginia Woolf's Mr. Ramsay.

Maitland, Frederic William. *The Life and Letters of Leslie Stephen.* New York: G. P. Putnam's Sons, 1906, 510 p.
  Comprehensive biography which includes extensive excerpts from Stephen's correspondence. Maitland was the biographer selected by Stephen himself and was a close friend.

Maurer, Oscar. "Leslie Stephen and the *Cornhill* Magazine." *Studies in English* XXXII (1953): 67-95.
  Discussion of the effect of Stephen's editorship on the *Cornhill* magazine which maintains that his high intellectual standards improved the quality of the journal.

Rosenbaum, S. P. "An Educated Man's Daughter: Leslie Stephen, Virginia Woolf and the Bloomsbury Group." In *Virginia Woolf: New Critical Essays,* edited by Patricia Clements and Isobel Grundy, pp. 32-56. London: Vision, 1983.
  Discusses the impact of Stephen's thought on Bloomsbury, maintaining: "the work of Stephen was part of their education as it was Virginia Woolf's, and it influenced not only her criticism, biographies, and polemics, but also the literary and historical writings of Leonard Woolf, the biographies of Lytton Strachey, the essays of Keynes, the criticism of Desmond MacCarthy, and the biographical and critical writings of Forster."

Smith, Gregory. "Belief and Conduct." *The Theological Monthly* I, No. 1 (January 1889): 120-24.
  Refutes Stephen's contention that Christian doctrine provides insufficient and ambiguous moral guidance.

Von Arx, Jeffrey Paul. "Leslie Stephen: Inventing the Progressive Tradition." In his *Progress and Pessimism,* pp. 11-219. Cambridge: Harvard University Press, 1985.
  Extensive discussion of Stephen's rejection of religious orthodoxy.

Williams, Stanley. "Leslie Stephen Twenty Years Later." *The London Mercury* VIII, No. 48 (October 1923): 621-34.
  Assesses Stephen's achievements, concluding that his literary criticism was his most important contribution to English letters.

Woolf, Virginia. "Leslie Stephen." In her *The Captain's Death Bed and Other Essays,* pp. 69-75. New York: Harcourt, Brace and Company, 1950.
  Some biographical comments by Stephen's daughter.

S. S. Van Dine

1888-1939

(Pseudonym of Willard Huntington Wright) American novelist, poet, essayist, critic, and editor.

Under the pseudonym of S. S. Van Dine, Wright became one of the most successful detective writers of his time, and his novels featuring the brilliant and exotic Philo Vance resurrected the detective story as a vital popular form in American literature. Before his success as a genre novelist, however, Wright's creative ambitions were at the farthest pole from commercial fiction: pre-Van Dine works include treatises on aesthetics, a study of German philosopher Friedrich Nietzsche, and a serious novel portraying the tribulations and ultimate failure of a would-be artist. His own inability to gain favorable recognition or a sufficient living from these works, along with a fortuitous set of circumstances in his life, led to the creation of an eccentric fictional character whom Wright invested with his own taste for erudition and his coldly theoretical turn of mind.

Wright was born into a well-to-do family of Charlottesville, Virginia. A precocious child and youth, he received a degree from Pomona College in California at the age of sixteen, proceeding to Harvard University for postgraduate studies. He travelled to Munich and Paris to study art, intending to become a painter, and during this time also memorized musical scores as preparation for a potential career as an orchestra conductor. Eventually, however, Wright decided to pursue a career as a writer. He worked as a journalist, writing literary and art reviews, and in 1907 became the literary editor of the *Los Angeles Times*. In 1912, he moved to New York to accept a position as literary and dramatic editor for *Town Topics,* and in the same year the new owner of the *Smart Set* hired him as editor of the magazine. It was during the year of Wright's editorship that the *Smart Set* gained its renown as a provocative publication offering serious and sophisticated writing rather than the traditional light entertainment of its competitors. With H. L. Mencken and George Jean Nathan as regular contributors, the *Smart Set* became a refuge for elitist art and opinions that by their nature challenged the values and assumptions of American readers. After twelve months as editor, Wright had created one of the finest journals of the period; unfortunately, the tone and content of the *Smart Set* also alienated many subscribers and advertisers. The magazine was nearly bankrupt in 1913, when Wright's refusal to temper some of his more advanced editorial policies led to his removal as editor. Subsequently, with Mencken and Nathan as coeditors, the periodical thrived in a somewhat moderated form, which nevertheless earned Mencken and Nathan their reputations as leading iconoclasts in American letters, while leaving Wright in relative obscurity.

In the four years following his dismissal from the *Smart Set,* Wright published a number of works in various genres, including the poetry collection *Songs of Youth,* the critical study *What Nietzsche Taught,* a study in aesthetics entitled *The Creative Will,* the critical survey *Modern Painting,* and the novel *The Man of Promise.* While the first two books received little notice, subsequent publications were more widely reviewed and for the most part condemned. The studies of painting and aesthetics were criticized as elitist and unconvincing in their promotion of a distinctly modernist art, although a later ap-

praisal by Carl Richard Dolmetsch celebrates *Modern Painting* as a landmark work in American art criticism. Similarly, *The Man of Promise* was dismissed as a repellently sympathetic portrait of an intellectual snob and indulgent sensualist who regards his relationships with women as a hindrance to his development as an artist. Among the few offering their approval of the work was H. L. Mencken, who praised it largely for those elements that were hostile or indifferent to the prevailing literary values of the day. Compounding Wright's difficulties as an antagonist of the American literary scene were health problems, alcoholism, and drug addiction, all of which ultimately led to a complete physical and emotional breakdown in 1918.

During his first few years as an invalid, Wright was forbidden by his doctor to engage in the strain of literary activities, either by reading or writing. When he finally gained permission to read, it was on the condition that his reading matter consist entirely of light fiction. Choosing detective stories as literary diversion, Wright amassed a library of over 2,000 volumes representing the best examples of the genre. He read these works with the intention of one day writing a short study of the mechanics and development of detective fiction, an analytical survey which was later published as the introduction to his anthology *The Great Detective Stories.* As Wright explained in his essay "I Used to Be a Highbrow but Look at Me Now": "I think it is safe to say that I have read more detective novels, and have made a closer and more careful study of them from the technical, literary, and evolutional standpoint, than any other man living. . . ." Seeking a source of income in a potentially lucrative popular genre, Wright began writing detective novels, the first of which, *The Benson Murder Case,* was published in 1926. The book was phenomenally popular, as were its dozen successors which Wright published under the name S. S. Van Dine. Profitable screen adaptations of the novels enhanced "Van Dine's" success. Wright died of heart failure at the age of fifty-one.

Wright did not view the detective story as a serious literary form, either in fact or in its potential. As is evident from his introduction to *The Great Detective Stories* and his "Twenty Rules for Writing Detective Stories," he considered this type of fiction an exercise in "puzzle-making," and he wrote his own novels according to the formulas he had observed in works by the most successful detective writers of the past. Perceiving detective stories as purely intellectual diversion, he avoided engaging the reader's emotions or creating suspense, literary effects that he believed more properly belonged to the popular genres of romantic and adventure fiction. In the detective story, Wright maintained, all fictional elements—plot, characterization, setting, language—should serve only to present the fragments of the puzzle, challenging the reader to assemble them correctly before the solution is revealed at the end. Wright was extremely adept at providing unexpected solutions, and this was the source of the popularity of his novels during the 1920s and 1930s. In addition, his series detective, Philo Vance, is a memorably odd character. One of the most exotic offspring of the Sherlock Holmes line of detectives, Vance is an authority on art and aesthetics, an amateur pianist, chef, breeder of Scottish terriers and Siamese fighting fish, an Egyptologist, a Europeanized American whose speech combines a haughty professorial patois with fashionable Britishisms of the period, and in general an unlikeable yet fascinating personality. As a detective, Vance offers a distinctive method of solving murders based on understanding the psychology of the murderer. This criminological technique is founded on the assumption that, like a work of art, a given murder displays a definite style which gives away the perpetrator. All that remains is to discover the suspect whose particular psychology fits the style of the deed. This methodology is employed in all twelve Vance novels, the first six of which are considered superior to the last six. Early in his fiction career, Wright in fact claimed that an author has no more than a half-dozen good detective plots latent in his or her imagination.

Extremely successful at the time of their publication, the novels of Van Dine received far less attention after Wright's death. The character of Philo Vance, whose mannerisms had always irritated readers to some degree, was replaced in American readers' affections by such hard-boiled private eyes as Dashiell Hammett's Sam Spade and Raymond Chandler's Phillip Marlowe. Nevertheless, Vance remains one of the best-remembered among exotic fictional sleuths, and novels of S. S. Van Dine hold a conspicuous place in the history of detective fiction.

(See also *Contemporary Authors,* Vol. 115.)

PRINCIPAL WORKS

AS WILLARD HUNTINGTON WRIGHT

Songs of Youth (poetry) 1913

Europe after 8:15 [with H. L. Mencken and George Jean Nathan] (travel essays) 1914
Modern Painting (criticism) 1915
What Nietzsche Taught (criticism) 1915
The Creative Will (criticism) 1916
The Forum Exhibition of Modern American Painters, March Thirteenth to March Twenty-fifth, 1916 (criticism) 1916
The Man of Promise (novel) 1916
Informing a Nation (nonfiction) 1917
Misinforming a Nation (nonfiction) 1917
The Future of Painting (criticism) 1923

AS S. S. VAN DINE

The Benson Murder Case (novel) 1926
The "Canary" Murder Case (novel) 1927
The Great Detective Stories [editor] (short stories) 1927
The Greene Murder Case (novel) 1928
"Twenty Rules for Writing Detective Stories" (essay) 1928; published in journal *American Magazine*
The Bishop Murder Case (novel) 1929
I Used to Be a Highbrow but Look at Me Now (essay) 1929
The Scarab Murder Case (novel) 1930
The Kennel Murder Case (novel) 1933
The Casino Murder Case (novel) 1934
The Dragon Murder Case (novel) 1934
The Garden Murder Case (novel) 1935
The President's Mystery Story [with Rupert Hughes, Samuel Hopkins Adams, and others] (novel) 1935
The Kidnap Murder Case (novel) 1936
The Gracie Allen Murder Case (novel) 1938; also published as *The Smell of Murder,* 1950
The Winter Murder Case (novel) 1939

H. W. BOYNTON (essay date 1916)

[*Boynton was an American critic who wrote several studies of American literature and literary figures. In the following excerpt from a review of* The Man of Promise, *he derides the abilities and aspirations of the novel's protagonist.*]

There is a . . . striking resemblance between [*The Man of Promise*] and Mr. Dreiser's *The Genius.* Like the alleged hero of that dreary chronicle, Stanford West is a paltry figure from beginning to end. It is idle for his author to try to persuade us that he is a man of remarkable personality and achievement, "the ablest novelist in England," and what not. He is a wretched human insect, the slave of his momentary lusts, and if in the end we leave him pinned under his wife's thumb, we can only feel that it is the best place for him. Whether or not (as has been suggested) Mr. Dreiser had his tongue in his cheek when he painted his latest caricature of manhood, it is clear that Mr. Wright takes his portrait and his subject seriously. The idea is that poor Stanford West cannot fulfil his promise because he is always being smothered by some woman or other. For example, there is the mistress of his college days, whom he occasionally beats and drags about by the hair; if she had not been a female, he would not have been obsessed by her, and he would have taken his degree at Harvard a year earlier. As if it were not bad enough to have to keep a mistress, he possesses, at the same time, a fiancée out West, and is presently constrained to let her marry him and support him. Even then women will not let him alone, and he is continually being hampered by the necessities they thrust upon him. At intervals, when they give him time, he does, or prepares to do, great things: "His eyes were fiery and confident. When he talked, his language was exuberant, his gestures spirited. His brain overflowed with discoveries and intuitions, expectant aspirations and organised energies." But they do not give him time enough. If he leaves his wife, there is always somebody to step into her place. Occasionally they are useful to him for the moment. There is Evelyn Naesmith, for instance: "She compensated him for the absence of his wife and, in a measure, furnished him with a justification for having deserted his legal obligations. His nature was such that he required a sexual and social complement; and no woman had ever gratified his material and chemical needs with such intelligent understanding." But the handy Evelyn proves faithless, and our hero, subduing "an instinct to strangle her" sends her out of his life. Alas, the conspiracy of woman against him has by this time done its deadly work. That "gigantic ethic of culture running to ten volumes, which would cover every branch of aspiration" is given up, and the fellow knuckles under and is disposed of,— not a little to one reader's relief and satisfaction. (p. 203)

> *H. W. Boynton, in a review of "The Man of Promise," in* The Bookman, *New York, Vol. XLIII, No. 2, April, 1916, pp. 202-03.*

H. L. MENCKEN (essay date 1916)

[*From the era of World War I until the early years of the Great Depression, Mencken was one of the most influential figures in American letters. His strongly individualistic, irreverent outlook on life and his vigorous, invective-charged writing style helped establish the iconoclastic spirit of the Jazz Age and significantly shaped the direction of American literature. As a social and literary critic—the roles for which he is best known—Mencken was the scourge of evangelical Christianity, public service organizations, literary censorship, boosterism, provincialism, democracy, all advocates of personal or social improvement, and every other facet of American life that he perceived as humbug. In his literary criticism, Mencken encouraged American writers to shun the anglophilic, moralistic bent of the nineteenth century and to practice realism, an artistic call-to-arms that is most fully developed in his essay "Puritanism as a Literary Force," one of the seminal essays in modern literary criticism. A man who was widely renowned or feared during his lifetime as a would-be destroyer of established American values, Mencken once wrote: "All of my work, barring a few obvious burlesques, is based upon three fundamental ideas: 1. That knowledge is better than ignorance; 2. That it is better to tell the truth than to lie; and 3. That it is better to be free than to be a slave." In the following excerpt, Mencken praises The Man of Promise as an exceptional novel which contrasts in several ways with much of the American fiction being produced at the time.*]

All the qualities that make the average American novel the sweet, caressing, gaudy thing it is are absent from *The Man of Promise,* by Willard Huntington Wright. I have searched it from end to end for any trace of what is called Optimism, and in vain. There is no mention in it of sex hygiene, the Biltmore roof, German spies, Palm Beach, Wall Street, or the *corps diplomatique.* The hero, though of agreeable physique and respectably dressed, bears no resemblance whatever to a Leyendecker collar model. He has no low, flashy racing-car to convey him upon his libidinous enterprises—nor, indeed, any other internal combustion vehicle—and never either makes or loses so much as a single dollar in the stock market. His polygamy is confined, over a stretch of nearly twenty-five years, to but four women, all of them unmarried when he meets them,

and not one of them ever saves him from drink, or helps him to escape the police by hiding him in her bed-room, or gets him the secretaryship at Rome by making love to a United States Senator. His own conduct in matters of amour is singularly heretical. He never hugs any of his four loves in a taxicab after the opera, or drags any of them to a sinister roadhouse in Westchester, or addresses any of them in such terms as "You are like wine, little woman!" He is never wounded in France, or anywhere else, and thus lures none of the four into the Red Cross. He is never suspected of felony. He is never indicted or elected to office. He wins no prizes and makes no fortune. And as we leave him at last he is not rolling his eyes in ecstasy but grinning sardonically, and not heated up by love but cooled off. . . .

In brief, a hero of quite unusual kidney, a hero almost unprecedented in latter-day American fiction. And in a book no less uncommon than he is—a book that challenges curiosity at the very start by appearing without the customary cigar-band slipcover, and in cloth of a sombre maroon. (Even Dreiser's novels, remember, were bound by the intelligent Harpers in a figured cloth that might have made a Mother Hubbard for a charwoman.) And within? Within one finds, instead of the familiar journalese, a style that is careful, and graceful, and austere; and instead of the familiar looseness and incoherence, a delicate and accurate sense of form; and instead of the familiar prodigality of external action, an almost uninterrupted presentation of inward struggles; and instead of the familiar cheap mouthing of platitudes and imbecilities, an intelligible and interesting idea, competently worked out. The net result is a novel that, after the other fiction of the day, seems almost arctic in its restraint and aloofness, its elaborate avoidance of the maudlin, but that still leaves upon the mind an impression of curiously poignant drama, a conviction that something human and significant has been depicted in just the right way, a sense of genuine artistic achievement. There is, indeed, a touch of the Greek spirit in it. It is straightforward, clearly-designed, economical in its emotions, deft in its means. It makes its appeal, not to the tear ducts and the midriff, but to the centres of reflection, and they respond to it with a joyousness that is the product of long disuse. . . . Such novels are as rare in the United States as good music. They come but little oftener than the American symphony which so perversely never comes at all. Even when, as in this case, they fall a bit short of their apparent aim, they yet must give delight as evidences of a serious purpose that may yet bring in a great harvest, and that, in any case, is of value and dignity on its own account. Before fiction of the first rank may be written among us it must be tried again and again by men who are willing to fail. I think that Wright, barring Dreiser, has failed less than any other of the new generation. . . .

The idea underlying the book is neither very startling nor very new, though its appearance in an American novel is both. You will find it in Nietzsche, and in Max Stirner before him, not to say in Arthur Schopenhauer. It is, in a few words, the idea that the influence of women upon a man of any intellectual enterprise and originality, far from being inspirational, as the ladies themselves would have us believe, is often cruelly hampering, and that in this business of holding him down what are conventionally called good women may be quite as potent and quite as relentless as what are conventionally called bad women. (pp. 490-92)

Wright has done his story with great painstaking, and it shows a symmetry and bears a polish that are very rare in American fiction, or, for that matter, in English fiction. John Galsworthy works in somewhat the same fashion, but there are important points of difference. For one thing, *The Man of Promise* is harder and more formal in structure than any novel of Galsworthy that comes to mind and for another thing it lacks Galsworthy's mellowness, his middle-aged toleration, his visible feeling that nothing really matters. Wright is a far younger man, and the fine fieriness of youth is still in him: he takes even a work of fiction seriously. There is, indeed, almost too harsh an earnestness in his book, and, by the same token, too meticulous a finish. As a document in psychology, it is too well-made, as the plays of Scribe were too well-made on the side of mere intrigue. One gets a sniff of the laboratory.

But this, after all, is a merit as well as a defect, for the thing that the current American novel most sorely needs, even above that uncompromising intellectual honesty which Dreiser is almost alone in showing, is a greater sense of logic in structure, a more careful thinking out, a better management of rhythm and organization. Our novels are too often mere collections of materials, ill-selected and wholly undigested. They aim in one direction and proceed in another; they are full of inconsistencies, impossibilities, absurdities; the impression they leave is vague and uncertain. Wright, with his constant interest in the problems of aesthetic form, has planned his book with much more care and skill. There is in it an unaccustomed air of the studied, of the sophisticated, of the well reasoned. As an essay in form, indeed, it is almost as interesting as it is as a social document. (pp. 494-95)

A first novel which suggests a first novel almost not at all, its defects are yet those inherent in the work of a beginning novelist. It is, as I have said before, just a shade too relentless and scientific in its manner; the author has hung to his text with a pertinacity which might have been relaxed now and then without loss. You will find the same fierce gusto in the earlier novels of George Moore, and even in those of his middle period. Moore is now rewriting them, conditioning them, mellowing them. Perhaps Wright, in twenty years, will do the same with *The Man of Promise*. But even as it stands, it is incomparably above the common run of fiction in English. It hangs together, it gets somewhere, it is an authentic work of art. The very excess of zeal in it makes for a subtle charm; it radiates a sort of eloquence. . . . Such novels are too rare among us to be passed over lightly. This one deserves all the praise it is getting from the discriminating. Even more, it deserves all the abuse it is getting from the stupid. . . . (p. 496)

H. L. Mencken, "America Produces a Novelist," in
Forum, *Vol. 55, April, 1916, pp. 490-96.*

THE NEW REPUBLIC (essay date 1917)

[*The following negative review of* The Creative Will *represents typical critical reaction to Wright's studies in aesthetics.*]

Mr. Wright is a sensitive person who appears to be tremendously upset by the world's neglect of the artist. He cannot endure the cold indifference of the pure intellectual or the sneers of the scientist. In *The Creative Will* he mobilizes all his references and all his extensive surface knowledge of the arts for a defense of the sacred domain. Without discerning the causes of contemporary attacks he feels their force. The unflattering Freudian picture of the artist as the neurotic who is constantly curing himself he would scornfully repudiate, if he adverted to it. He is deeply perturbed at that vast and massive popular judgment which persists in taking the artist as the creator of

fables for play-time or as the skilful technician of sensuous thrills. He wishes to protect the artist in his rôle of high priest at the altar of human experience. In an older tradition Mr. Wright's fervor would perhaps have attached itself to the dogmas of some conventional religion. But that solacing object around which to gather one's enthusiasm is denied the sceptical and alert modernist. He is, obliged, perforce, to find some other refuge from the onslaughts of specialized knowledge. So Mr. Wright makes art the ultimate and highest of human interests, and those who, like himself, understand the deep science of aesthetics he considers the most important and most significant of those geniuses who roam an imperceptive world.

The Creative Will is thus a sort of challenge to those who are at all sceptical of the high dignity or essential greatness of the artist. For Mr. Wright gives to art the precision of mathematics, the validity of science and the insight of philosophy—the values of these separate disciplines are here fused in a higher harmony which includes them all. One thinks of Sainte Beuve's famous definition of a humanist as one who mediates between extremes, thus occupying all the space between them. To the artist Mr. Wright says, "Tremble not before the discoveries of science or the patient experiments of a realistic psychology; they cannot dispute your leadership. You as the artist are, by definition, the scientist and philosopher. You cannot be harmed by what you yourself have transcended." How can you doubt this when art "is a philosophic system based on concrete forms and objective experiences"; when "it is the mouthpiece of the will of nature, namely, the complete, unified intelligence of life"? Consider, too, how all folk-art is but the generous fairy-story of well intentioned democrats, when the truth of course is that all art sprang solely from individual genius. Fear not, "any attempt to democratize art results in the lowering of the artistic standard."

This pleasantly self-satisfying picture of art as the culmination of all that is highest in human activity enables Mr. Wright to smite with equal cleverness the artist who practices mere representation (one who can give only the external effects of life instead of life's underlying causes) and the artist who divorces himself from life in sterile abstractions. The deepest realities of life—according to Mr. Wright, the recurrences of plastic and spring rhythms—can only be focused adequately in consciousness by a great work of art. And only the mind of the great artist is capable of the necessary organization and insight for pulling the seemingly disconnected and unrelated strands and wisps of life into a single organic unity. Furthermore, only the critic trained in the "science" of aesthetics can recognize the great work of art and appraise it. Everyday critics can only see in art the stirrings of sentiment or the representative images which have some special emotional aura. With just and considerable skill Mr. Wright sharpens his dagger of wit against the flinty stupidity of the average art critic. But the outcome is disappointing. His so-called science of aesthetics leaves us with no more specific criterion for judgment than all-round intelligence.

Certainly a respectable case can be made out for the contention that art is the final goal of human endeavor. In thrilling and memorable phrases Mr. Clive Bell has done just that in his impassioned book, *Art*. Such a contention may or may not be valid, but at least it can be supported by a body of psychological experiment and ethical generalization that cannot be dismissed with a shrug. Mr. Wright, however, is not the man for so severe a task. He is less the able defender of a cause before the court of reason than the errant knight sallying forth with dramatic flourishes of the sword to the rescue of his besieged lady. Deliberately, he has selected the form of epigram and aphorism—smooth little paragraphs that abound in such flashing insights as "great art, whether music, literature or painting, is great because of its ability to permeate every part of the spectator's being," and "the medium of music is sound." These, if you please, are, according to the paper cover of the book among "the most important contributions to the philosophy and science of aesthetics which have appeared in any language."

Once Mr. Wright wrote a book called *What Nietzsche Taught,* but he neglected to learn one of that philosopher's most pungent lessons, which was, not to attempt a volume of metaphysical epigrams unless you are a genius. The power of such an achievement when successful should have taught Mr. Wright to be wary of its inevitable feebleness when a failure. For plodding or industrious or merely clever minds cannot here take the risk of near-success. The author must be perfect, as Nietzsche was perfect in *Beyond Good and Evil.* One cannot endure the random movements of a mind struggling for the complete epigram. The dazzle and clap-trap of surface brilliance or verbal antitheses are twice as annoying as in the more formal or conventionally moulded argument. One demands always the just, always the keen and vivid insight. And in *The Creative Will* the supply is pitifully inadequate to the demand. It is mostly will, and very little creation. (pp. 382-83)

> *H. S., "To the Rescue of Art," in* The New Republic, *Vol. X, No. 130, April 28, 1917, pp. 382-83.*

CARTY RANCK   (essay date 1926)

[*In the following excerpt the critic unfavorably reviews the first Philo Vance novel,* The Benson Murder Case.]

Mr. Van Dine's first attempt at detective fiction introduces a new detective, Mr. Philo Vance, and we are promised other adventures of this crime debutante, who is introduced on the jacket in these fulsome words: "Philo Vance, we believe, will inevitably find a literary niche alongside of that triumvirate of immortal sleuths, Monsieur Le Coq, Auguste Dupin and Sherlock Holmes."

We can only say that if Philo ever finds such a niche it will prove most uncomfortably large for him. Also he would be rather embarrassed, for we are certain that Messrs. Le Coq, Dupin and Holmes could never tolerate for a moment such a complacent ass.

Discounting the jacket "blurb" we found ourselves woefully disappointed in *The Benson Murder Case.* It is a conventional murder mystery, togged out in meretricious garb, and we found it much ado about nothing. It is old stuff, cunningly disguised with paprika and French dressing and served with a sauce of fine writing and many Latin and Greek quotations, all intended to show what a devil of a fellow is Philo Vance. But the picture that finally emerges from the woods of words is not that of a great detective but a tedious dilettante. Some one has called "Dr. Watson," the fatuous commentator of Sherlock Holmes, "the greatest fool in Christendom," but the soft-minded friend of Philo Vance goes him one better.

> *Carty Ranck, "An Old Sleuth and Two New Ones," in* New York Herald Tribune Books, *November 21, 1926, p. 16.*

DASHIELL HAMMETT   (essay date 1927)

[*An American novelist and screenwriter, Hammett is recognized as the first great writer of the hard-boiled school of detective fiction. In contrast to genteel, "country-house" mysteries, his novels, including* Red Harvest *(1929) and* The Maltese Falcon *(1930), introduced tough private eyes such as Sam Spade, who move among the sordid subclasses of urban America. In the following excerpt, Hammett ridicules various aspects of* The Benson Murder Case.]

[In *The Benson Murder Case*] Alvin Benson is found sitting in a wicker chair in his living room, a book still in his hand, his legs crossed, and his body comfortably relaxed in a lifelike position. He is dead. A bullet from an Army model Colt .45 automatic pistol, held some six feet away when the trigger was pulled, has passed completely through his head. That his position should have been so slightly disturbed by the impact of such a bullet at such a range is preposterous, but the phenomenon hasn't anything to do with the plot, so don't, as I did, waste time trying to figure it out. The murderer's identity becomes obvious quite early in the story. The authorities, no matter how stupid the author chose to make them, would have cleared up the mystery promptly if they had been allowed to follow the most rudimentary police routine. But then what would there have been for the gifted Vance to do?

This Philo Vance is in the Sherlock Holmes tradition and his conversational manner is that of a high-school girl who has been studying the foreign words and phrases in the back of her dictionary. He is a bore when he discusses art and philosophy, but when he switches to criminal psychology he is delightful. There is a theory that any one who talks enough on any subject must, if only by chance, finally say something not altogether incorrect. Vance disproves this theory: he manages always, and usually ridiculously, to be wrong. His exposition of the technique employed by a gentleman shooting another gentleman who sits six feet in front of him deserves a place in a *How to be a detective by mail* course.

To supply this genius with a field for his operations the author has to treat his policemen abominably. He doesn't let them ask any questions that aren't wholly irrelevant. They can't make inquiries of anyone who might know anything. They aren't permitted to take any steps toward learning whether the dead man was robbed. Their fingerprint experts are excluded from the scene of the crime. When information concerning a mysterious box of jewelry accidentally bobs up everybody resolutely ignores it, since it would have led to a solution before the three-hundredth page.

Mr. Van Dine doesn't deprive his officials of every liberty, however: he generously lets them compete with Vance now and then in the expression of idiocies. Thus Heath, a police detective-sergeant, says that any pistol of less than .44 calibre is too small to stop a man, and the district attorney, Markham, displays an amazed disinclination to admit that a confession could actually be false. This Markham is an outrageously naïve person: the most credible statement in the tale is to the effect that Markham served only one term in this office. The book is written in the little-did-he-realize style.

> *Dashiell Hammett, "Poor Scotland Yard!" in* The Saturday Review of Literature, *Vol. III, No. 25, January 15, 1927, p. 510.*

S. S. VAN DINE   (essay date 1928)

[*In the following excerpt, Van Dine sets forth his twenty rules for writing detective stories.*]

The detective story is a kind of intellectual game. It is more—it is a sporting event. And for the writing of detective stories there are very definite laws—unwritten, perhaps, but none the less binding; and every respectable and self-respecting concocter of literary mysteries lives up to them. Herewith, then, is a sort of Credo, based partly on the practice of all the great writers of detective stories, and partly on the promptings of the honest author's inner conscience. To wit:

1. The reader must have equal opportunity with the detective for solving the mystery. All clues must be plainly stated and described.

2. No willful tricks or deceptions may be placed on the reader other than those played legitimately by the criminal on the detective himself.

3. There must be no love interest. The business in hand is to bring a criminal to the bar of justice, not to bring a lovelorn couple to the hymeneal altar.

4. The detective himself, or one of the official investigators, should never turn out to be the culprit. This is bald trickery, on a par with offering some one a bright penny for a five-dollar gold piece. It's false pretenses.

5. The culprit must be determined by logical deductions—not by accident or coincidence or unmotivated confession. To solve a criminal problem in this latter fashion is like sending the reader on a deliberate wild-goose chase, and then telling him, after he has failed, that you had the object of his search up your sleeve all the time. Such an author is no better than a practical joker.

6. The detective novel must have a detective in it; and a detective is not a detective unless he detects. His function is to gather clues that will eventually lead to the person who did the dirty work in the first chapter; and if the detective does not reach his conclusions through an analysis of those clues, he has no more solved his problem than the schoolboy who gets his answer out of the back of the arithmetic.

7. There simply must be a corpse in a detective novel, and the deader the corpse the better. No lesser crime than murder will suffice. Three hundred pages is far too much pother for a crime other than murder. After all, the reader's trouble and expenditure of energy must be rewarded.

8. The problem of the crime must be solved by strictly naturalistic means. Such methods for learning the truth as slate-writing, ouija-boards, mind-reading, spiritualistic séances, crystal-gazing, and the like, are taboo. A reader has a chance when matching his wits with a rationalistic detective, but, if he must compete with the world of spirits and go chasing about the fourth dimension of metaphysics, he is defeated *ab initio*.

9. There must be but one detective—that is, but one protagonist of deduction—one *deus ex machina*. To bring the minds of three or four, or sometimes a gang of detectives to bear on a problem, is not only to disperse the interest and break the direct thread of logic, but to take an unfair advantage of the reader. If there is more than one detective the reader doesn't know who his co-deductor is. It's like making the reader run a race with a relay team.

10. The culprit must turn out to be a person who has played a more or less prominent part in the story—that is, a person with whom the reader is familiar and in whom he takes an interest.

11. Servants must not be chosen by the author as the culprit. This is begging a noble question. It is a too easy solution. The culprit must be a decidedly worth-while person—one that wouldn't ordinarily come under suspicion.

12. There must be but one culprit, no matter how many murders are committed. The culprit may, of course, have a minor helper or co-plotter; but the entire onus must rest on one pair of shoulders: the entire indignation of the reader must be permitted to concentrate on a single black nature.

13. Secret societies, camorras, mafias, *et al.*, have no place in a detective story. A fascinating and truly beautiful murder is irremediably spoiled by any such wholesale culpability. To be sure, the murderer in a detective novel should be given a sporting chance; but it is going too far to grant him a secret society to fall back on. No high-class, self-respecting murderer would want such odds.

14. The method of murder, and the means of detecting it, must be rational and scientific. That is to say, pseudo-science and purely imaginative and speculative devices are not to be tolerated in the *roman policier*. Once an author soars into the realm of fantasy, in the Jules Verne manner, he is outside the bounds of detective fiction, cavorting in the uncharted reaches of adventure.

15. The truth of the problem must at all times be apparent—provided the reader is shrewd enough to see it. By this I mean that if the reader, after learning the explanation for the crime, should reread the book, he would see that the solution had, in a sense, been staring him in the face—that all the clues really pointed to the culprit—and that, if he had been as clever as the detective, he could have solved the mystery himself without going on to the final chapter. That the clever reader does often thus solve the problem goes without saying.

16. A detective novel should contain no long descriptive passages, no literary dallying with side-issues, no subtly worked-out, character analyses, no "atmospheric" preoccupations. Such matters have no vital place in a record of crime and deduction. They hold up the action, and introduce issues irrelevant to the main purpose, which is to state a problem, analyze it, and bring it to a successful conclusion. To be sure, there must be a sufficient descriptiveness and character delineation to give the novel verisimilitude.

17. A professional criminal must never be shouldered with the guilt of a crime in a detective story. Crimes by house-breakers and bandits are the province of the police departments—not of authors and brilliant amateur detectives. A really fascinating crime is one committed by a pillar of a church, or a spinster noted for her charities.

18. A crime in a detective story must never turn out to be an accident or a suicide. To end an odyssey of sleuthing with such an anti-climax is to hoodwink the trusting and kind-hearted reader.

19. The motives for all crimes in detective stories should be personal. International plottings and war politics belong in a different category of fiction—in secret-service tales, for instance. But a murder story must be kept *gemuetlich*, so to speak. It must reflect the reader's everyday experiences, and give him a certain outlet for his own repressed desires and emotions.

20. And (to give my Credo an even score of items) I herewith list a few of the devices which no self-respecting detective-

story writer will now avail himself of. They have been employed too often, and are familiar to all true lovers of literary crime. To use them is a confession of the author's ineptitude and lack of originality. (*a*) Determining the identity of the culprit by comparing the butt of a cigarette left at the scene of the crime with the brand smoked by a suspect. (*b*) The bogus spiritualistic séance to frighten the culprit into giving himself away. (*c*) Forged finger-prints. (*d*) The dummy-figure alibi. (*e*) The dog that does not bark and thereby reveals the fact that the intruder is familiar. (*f*) The final pinning of the crime on a twin, or a relative who looks exactly like the suspected, but innocent, person. (*g*) The hypodermic syringe and the knockout drops. (*h*) The commission of the murder in a locked room after the police have actually broken in. (*i*) The word-association test for guilt. (*j*) The cipher, or code letter, which is eventually unraveled by the sleuth. (pp. 129-31)

> *S. S. Van Dine, "'I Used to Be a Highbrow but Look at Me Now',"in* The American Magazine, *Vol. 106, September, 1928, pp. 14-31.*

GILBERT SELDES   (essay date 1929)

[*Seldes was an American critic and journalist who published a variety of works on the theater, motion pictures, radio, and television. In the following excerpt, he objects to the "pedantry" of Philo Vance.*]

The amazing success of S. S. Van Dine about four years ago has given new life to detective fiction. (p. 125)

The singular thing about this success is that it was achieved in spite of the author, who created a disagreeable pedant for his detective and treated him as if he were the most admirable and amiable of men. Crotchety detectives are no novelty; Cuff, in *The Moonstone*, anticipates them as he does nearly everything interesting. Van Dine's Philo Vance, with his implausible English accent, his unparalleled erudition, and his swank, would be enough to turn anyone away from the stories after five pages were it not that the stories, by that time, are more interesting than the detective. The first two novels, ***The Benson*** and ***The "Canary" Murder Cases,*** were based on incidents not yet gone from the public mind, those of Elwell and Dot King; they were the best of the lot. The third, ***The Greene Murder Case***, was a compilation of nearly all the strange murders noted in criminology, and the solution of the mystery was properly found in two or three dozen German textbooks in the library of the half-dozen victims. The basis of the latest in the series, ***The Bishop Murder Case,*** is a mixture of Mother Goose and higher mathematics, with such an exposition of the theories of Einstein as I have not discovered in the daily press.

Van Dine is in the good tradition of the detective novel because his interest is in deduction. In his early stories his detective insisted that every murder was, in a sense, a work of art, and the murderer, like the artist, left his imprint on his handiwork. In the latest book he returns to more ordinary reasoning, suggesting that the murderer commits his crimes in the way he does because of his character—in this case, because he is an adept of interstellar mathematics and holds finite life in contempt. But what he now omits is the entirely human interest of motive. The first two cases were fairly motivated; but as Van Dine grew more and more anxious to conceal his criminal, he gradually deprived him of any plausible motive, so that in the latest version we have a man putting seven or eight of his nearest friends to death in order to cast suspicion on someone

else. It is true that he is professionally jealous of this last person.

What constitutes fair dealing with the reader in this type of story has never been well defined. It is, however, considered desirable that the actual criminal should be more or less in plain sight while the detection is going on—the fact that in actual murders he usually manages not to be, is put aside—and nothing is more irritating, or bad form, than the introduction of an unknown at the end to shoulder the blame. The excellent *Bellamy Trial* [by Frances Noyes Hart] gave each character exactly its due because each appeared before the jury, the criminal included, and each received just the importance the trial would give him. It would also be fair dealing to make the motive adequate. To complicate mysteries, authors have assigned adequate motive to three or four characters, and it is almost obligatory that several of them should have opportunity as well. Van Dine has built up motive for each of a series of characters, killing them off just as the motivation becomes convincing, and then has had nothing left for his murderer.

This is, of course, the pedantry of murder, and it leads to an interesting speculation. People generally assume that bad work in literature comes from being too conscious of one's public; here is a case where bad work is due to contempt of the public. Van Dine knows perfectly that if twelve human beings are capable of understanding the Einstein theory, only two or three thousand times as many can understand his reduction of it. He knows that all of Philo Vance's vaporings will be skipped, by those who are impressed as well as by those who want to get on with the story. Yet there they are, with the affectations of the detective which are not part of the character, with a type of lordly writing which actively holds up the narrative. One feels that these things are deliberate, even willful, that the author, in full consciousness of his hold over the public, writes badly "and makes them like it." It may not detract from the popularity of the series, for people are impressed by pedantry and false characterization, but the naïve shag tobacco and the love of the violin of Sherlock Holmes strike us as being more honest and in the end contribute to making him a "character" in every sense. The pedantry in Van Dine's character is, as I have suggested, eating its way into the plots. The technical skill of the books is so great that the author may be able to dispense with credulity, especially of motive; but here again he is despising his public, to the detriment of his work.

The general intelligence, the superior style, the careful construction of the Philo Vance series have, without doubt, brought thousands of readers to a formerly despised type of fiction, and they, in turn, will bring more intelligence and care to the detective story itself. I share Mr. Alexander Woollcott's weakness, which he confessed recently in a violent and reasonable attack on Van Dine: I would rather read a poor detective story than none at all. But I hope that the followers of Van Dine—and he himself before he makes good his threat to stop writing—will profit by his excellences and avoid his mistakes. For the detective story ought to keep its purity, approaching the serenity and the perfection of the mathematical formula; and it ought to be written in complete and honest respect for the reader. With that respect, pedantry is always at war. (pp. 125-26)

> *Gilbert Seldes, "Van Dine and His Public," in* The New Republic, *Vol. LIX, No. 759, June 19, 1929, pp. 125-26.*

H. DOUGLAS THOMSON   (essay date 1931)

[*Thomson's* Masters of Mystery: A Study of the Detective Story *was one of the earliest book-length studies of mystery fiction. In the following excerpt from that study, Thomson considers the psychology of murder and plot devices in the Philo Vance novels.*]

A murder from the Van Dine point of view is akin to a work of art. *In primis* it is a thing created of thought. Also it has a technique in the execution, and bears the impress of its author's character. De Quincey might have agreed with Van Dine on the last point, but he certainly did not have occasion to argue about it. Let us wrestle with this idea for a minute. We start with the statement that any given murder will have the stamp of the murderer upon it—the brand of Cain, so to speak, in reverse. From this you may conclude that the psychologist will be able to pick out the murderer from a study of those characters connected with the crime. As far as the detective story goes the psychologist will have to be infallible; one cannot allow his psychology to be in any sense experimental. Very well then, let us have Philo Vance's own succinct explanation:—

> Having determined the exact psychological na-
> ture of the deed, it only remained to find some
> interested person whose mind and temperament
> were such that, if he undertook a task of this
> kind in the given circumstances, he would in-
> evitably do it in precisely the manner in which
> it was done.
>
>   (pp. 263-64)

The technique of the crime is therefore the investigator's lode-star. It is possible that the psychologist might have as much difficulty in settling the authorship of a murder as the literary critic in deciding who wrote *The Poems of Ossian*. The psychologist would more than likely go astray in such cases as the following:—

> (1) Where a person killed some one in mistake
> for some one else.

> (2) Where a person murdered another in a mo-
> mentary fit of aberration or of seeing red.

Does the aesthetic-psychological argument hold water where much has been committed in a *Kubla Khan* trance? It is hard to believe that such a murder would betray a tell-tale technique. We would not accept the psychologist's retort that it would be possible to name the person prone to this form of mania. You will notice too, that Van Dine's murders are all premeditated; the stamp has time to make the impression.

The solutions in the Van Dine novels are based on a study of this technique. In *The Benson Murder Case* Vance argues that the nature of the crime proves that it was committed by a bold, fearless gambler, by an aggressive, brutal man with no subtlety or imagination about him. He casts his eye round the circle of suspects and finds the head to fit his cap. A novel game of poker resolves his doubts in *The Canary Murder Case*. He knows the kind of man who committed the crime, but he does not know the suspects well enough to pin, as it were, "the psychological indications" of the crime to the culprit's nature. So a game of poker is arranged, because Vance believes with "Doctor George A. Dorsey" that: "Poker is a cross-section of life. The way a man behaves in a poker game is the way he behaves in life." Clergymen have said the same thing about golf; and we wait for the detective story wherein the detective stymies his suspects one after the other in order to observe how their physical organisms respond to "the stimuli supplied by the game." The poker game is pre-arranged so that Vance may discover the real gambler in the party of suspects.

In *The Greene Murder Case* it is rather different. There is a whole series of murders, and Vance has to regard these murders as a composite whole. Here there is an extremely interesting digression on the difference between a photograph and a painting. Vance is determined to regard the murders as a painting, but at first he has to be content with the unrelated facts of the photograph. How he manages to do this is surprisingly ingenious. He catalogues the facts, selects certain of them, numbers them and by shifting these numbers about he is able to arrive at a grouping which satisfies his aesthetic, or rational, or psychological, sense. Once he is satisfied with this arrangement he can put his old formula to the test. He returns in *The Bishop Murder Case* to the simpler process. As in *The Greene Murder Case* there is again a series of murders. But this time the solution is much less intricate, for Vance reasons from "the psychological aspects of the case" that the murders were committed by a man who would scoff at human values, but would play with infinity, e.g., the mathematician; and his eye lights on Professor Dillard.

It must not be supposed that Vance's thoughts are all in the clouds of psychology. The application of psychology is the final master stroke, but the data and the classification of the various unrelated facts have to come first. It usually happens that the police experts, the doctors, the camera-men, the fingerprints and firearms specialists produce the several items of evidence. Markham and Heath, Vance's foils, fail to group these facts in the right order or to inter-relate them correctly. They attempt "to reduce human nature to a formula," a formula which makes room for circumstantial evidence. Quite often, however, Vance himself is not above trick exhibitions. One recalls the "bit of clever criminal mechanism"—the twine and the tweezers—employed to open the door from the "other" side in *The Canary Murder Case;* and in *The Benson Murder Case* the substitution of the cartridges, detected owing to the peculiar brightness of one cartridge amongst its six tarnished fellows.

A word about the structure of the Van Dine plots. In *The Benson Murder Case* and *The Canary Murder Case* we note the following points:—

> (1) The victim is a double-dyed villain, and a
> blackmailer to boot.

> (2) There are, therefore, several people who
> would have a motive for the murder.

> (3) The suspects are all mustered near the scene
> of the crime at the critical moment. These fea-
> tures are introduced so that Vance can play
> about with his ideas of the technique of the
> crime.

In *The Greene Murder Case* and *The Bishop Murder Case* the composition of the plot is widely different. Psychology is not at so highly valued a premium. In both stories there is a series of murders. In *The Greene Murder Case* a family is wiped out, and one after the other the erstwhile suspects become victims. It is worth mentioning that in many points *The Greene Murder Case* bears a close similarity to the unsolved Croydon Poisoning Case. The solution in *The Greene Murder Case* is really reached by a process of elimination. Similarly in *The Bishop Murder Case*. Both these novels are incidentally interesting studies in criminology. The murders in the former are imitations of historical murders described in the tomes of Tobias Greene's lurid library. In *The Bishop Murder Case,* as already mentioned, we have a study of a mathematician whose sense of values has become distorted. Thus in these two novels we have the abnormal murder, which means a certain deficiency in motive. To make our problem still harder, Van Dine peoples these stories with neurotic chess champions, neurotic mathematicians and neurotic young women (not to mention the rather cranky old women capable of doing anything).

In *The Scarab Murder Case* . . . Van Dine reintroduced the subject of Egyptology into the detective story. The killing is done in the darkness of the Bliss Museum, and the murderer turns out to be, as we rather expected, the antiquarian Bliss. There is nothing startling in the plot; it is a simple example of "double bluff." Bliss, our first real suspect, tried to give people the impression that he was the victim of a plot, and built up a nice little case against himself. As this was an American case, he was confident of acquittal from lack of *real* evidence against him. Van Dine is careful in his first attempt at a "double bluff" plot to preserve his reputation for fair play with the reader. Thus he makes Vance claim:—

> "I did not say one word to give you the definite impression that I exonerated Bliss. Not once did I say he was innocent."

(pp. 264-67)

Philo Vance is delightful company. He belongs to no school, but has a certain affinity to Lord Peter Wimsey. He is the aristocratic dilettante, a master of refined badinage. (p. 268)

> *H. Douglas Thomson, "The American Detective Story," in his* Masters of Mystery: A Study of the Detective Story, *Wm. Collins Sons & Co. Ltd., 1931, pp. 257-73.*

RALPH PARTRIDGE (essay date 1935)

[*In the following excerpt, Partridge unfavorably compares* The Garden Murder Case *to earlier Philo Vance stories.*]

The new Philo Vance story suffers by comparison with many of its predecessors. I do not think *The Garden Murder Case* will gain Mr. Van Dine new admirers, although it may very well not lose him any of his old brigade. It is disappointing to have to say this, as I had been counting on Mr. Van Dine to provide detective readers with a merry Christmas. But, presumably, as *The Purple Murder Case* will not be forthcoming for the usual six months or so, we must take this—and like it. So to begin with the book's merits: Mr. Van Dine's work is always cast in a classical mould; he never relaxes his grip on the detective unities, a single criminal, a single motive and a singular solution. In *The Garden Murder Case* the crime is committed in one of those New York penthouses which seem to have been built to the plans of intending murderers. The victim is one of a betting set, who are listening in to the broadcast of a race in which all are financially interested: and naturally he meets his fate during the broadcast. The technical background, which always bulks large in Mr. Van Dine's cases, will have little appeal for English readers, seeing it consists of American horse-racing jargon, which may be genuine or spurious for all I know. There are two complaints to be lodged against the book. The first is technical, and therefore very unusual in a Van Dine; the criminal is highly conspicuous from the very outset. Anyone who likes spotting the villain as they go along will find this one almost too easy. The second objection is aesthetic; that admirable mental automaton, Philo Vance, is credited with an emotion. Until I saw *The Dragon Murder Case* on the films I never realised what an absolute

neuter that man was bound to be for the purposes of Mr. Van Dine's plots. The only human features an actor could evolve out of him were dropping his 'g's and smoking *Régie* cigarettes; otherwise he had to play the difficult rôle of a superhuman needle of intelligence. The consequence is that I can't even remember who acted the part. Naturally, therefore, one asks oneself what on earth has come over old Philo in *The Garden Murder Case*—can it be Love? Oh, no, it is only a new idea of Mr. Van Dine's to round off his story elegantly, and a shocking one, as in fact it ruins the plot by indecent exposure. (pp. 941-42)

> *Ralph Partridge, "Crime for Christmas," in* The New Statesman & Nation, *Vol. X, No. 251, December 14, 1935, pp. 941-42.*

CARL RICHARD DOLMETSCH (essay date 1969)

[*Dolmetsch is an American critic, educator, and author of* The Smart Set: A History and Anthology *(1966). In the following excerpt, he surveys Wright's literary career prior to writing the Van Dine novels.*]

Though the annals of American literary history are studded with many a bizarre career, none is more wondrously enigmatic than that of Willard Huntington Wright, known to *aficionados* of detective fiction by his pseudonym, "S. S. Van Dine." . . .

Wright (alias "Van Dine") looked upon himself as a *poète manqué*, or at least an underrated and misunderstood virtuoso in belles-lettres and criticism who, in order to make a decent living, resorted to casting pearls before swine. Whether or not he was in truth a potentially great writer whose highest creative faculties were thwarted by an indifferent public and hostile critics—which is the way he seems to have viewed his fate— is at least debatable. In several respects a brilliant editor, in all regards an incisive, well-informed critic of the arts (painting and music as well as literature), in fiction a superb craftsman and stylist, it may also be argued that Wright was his own worst enemy, one whose talent for alienating his peers and his public was perhaps as great as his other abilities. On balance, therefore, Wright must be judged a writer of considerable merit and power whose failures and shortcomings, as well as attainments, reveal significant aspects of the relationship of the American literary artist to the democratization of letters that occurred on a massive scale in the United States at the turn of this century. Perhaps more important, the schizothymic career of Wright-"Van Dine" offers an intriguing case history (in the judicial, not clinical, sense) from which we may comprehend some of the attitudes by a certain type of American writer, past and present, toward the profession of authorship and toward himself as he confronts the exigencies of a changing society.

Willard Huntington Wright came upon the American literary scene at the close of a period of frenzied revolution in literary taste created by what, for want of better terms, may be called the "magazine explosion." (p. 153)

Town Topics and the *Smart Set,* in which Willard Wright made his literary debuts before a national audience, were both products of the "magazine explosion" even though their announced programs were antithetical to the democratization of literary taste that that development introduced. (p. 154)

Wright was barely twenty-two when he began contributing book reviews to *Town Topics* and just twenty-four when he became editor-in-chief of the *Smart Set* whose attitudes of "smartness," "cleverness," and aristocratic *hauteur* became central to his entire subsequent career. Like his illustrious contemporaries on the *Smart Set,* H. L. Mencken and George Jean Nathan, Wright was particularly ill-suited by nurture and temperament to the prevailing conditions of the American literary marketplace, situated then as now in mid-Manhattan, when he arrived from the Far West in 1912 like a Young Lochinvar come to rescue the American Muse from the clawings of the simian rabble. Steadfastly reared in "the European tradition" (so they thought) by intellectual parents of some means if not great wealth, Willard Wright had been a precocious learner, speaking French and German fluently by the age of ten, taking his degree in literature from Pomona College at sixteen and breaking off graduate studies in philosophy at Harvard at eighteen because, he insouciantly claimed, they had nothing more to teach him there. From Harvard he returned West to marry and become, at the astonishing age of nineteen, the literary editor of the *Los Angeles Times.* Already, however, he had found a philosophy to espouse passionately in Nietzsche's *Der Wille zur Macht* (was he not embodying it in his own life?) and had fallen under the spell of an essentially anti-democratic Germanophilia which he shared with most of the brightest American intellects of his generation. (pp. 154-55)

A few months before he was untimely felled by cancer (in December 1911), [Percival] Pollard published *Masks and Minstrels of New Germany,* his most significant work, though it has been overlooked by most American literary historians despite ample evidence of its importance to the thinking of young intellectuals of Wright's generation. Though the readers of *Masks and Minstrels* may not have been numerous, it was widely and lengthily reviewed in enthusiastic essays by young critics who found it a veritable Book of Revelations. (p. 155)

Here, in Pollard's glowing account, the young *literati* of a provincial land could discover and sample the wit of the iconoclastic German magazines, *Simplicissimus* and *Jugend,* and could learn for the first time of the social satire of the *Überbrett'l* movement in the literary cabarets of Berlin, Munich and Vienna. Pollard's "new Germany" was, of course, a metaphor for the Hohenzollern and Hapsburg empires of the post-Bismarck era where, he somewhat myopically claimed, the old, repressive *Junkertum* was giving way to a free, enlightened *Geistesaristokratie* of artists and intellectuals (including especially writers) who were successfully counterattacking the kinds of vulgarization of the arts that, like DeTocqueville long before him, he alleged to be an inevitability of Western-style democracy. (pp. 155-56)

[Willard Wright, H. L. Mencken and George Jean Nathan] yearned to start, if not precisely "an *Überbrett'l,*" at least a magazine with the thrust of *Simplicissimus* or *Jugend* to cleanse their land of the results of literary democratization—puerility, provincialism and puritanism. (p. 156)

[Wright], Mencken and Nathan (the drama critic of the *Smart Set*), began earnestly discussing practical ways to realize their desire to introduce a Nietzschean anti-bourgeois bias into American literary journalism by collaborating upon a new periodical or, failing that, by reorganizing the *Smart Set.*

Meanwhile, early in 1911 the *Smart Set* had been purchased by a self-made magazine entrepreneur, John Adams Thayer, who fancied himself to be heterodox and "advanced" in his thinking. In reality, Thayer had little education and less taste despite his rather considerable business acumen. Casting about for an editor who could revitalize his magazine with new ideas,

he was easily persuaded (largely by Mencken and Nathan) to engage Wright and give him *carte blanche* in the editorial policies of the *Smart Set.* In the twelve months of his editorial control (1913), Wright very nearly bankrupted Thayer and his magazine, though he rescued it from being merely a literary sideshow destined for obscurity and made it what it was to remain for most of the next decade—one of the most important American journals of its day, and, indeed, in the literary history of the United States.

The particular measures and editorial decisions by which Wright accomplished this need not detain us here. In sum, he did so by introducing more European contributors in a single year (including a great many of the writers cited in Pollard's *Masks and Minstrels*) than had any other American commercial magazine before then (or probably since), he published a large amount of unconventional writing by novice American writers (much of it sexually "daring" by the standards of 1913), and most important, in collaboration with Mencken and Nathan he began a satirical attack upon bourgeois American life and letters which, with an interruption during the war years (1917-1918) when free expression was throttled, was continued as a hallmark of the *Smart Set* until 1923. To this attack, in addition to their regular critical articles, Mencken contributed dozens of cynical epigram fillers and his acid dissections of American speech and folkways (the basis of his later monumental study, *The American Language*), Nathan produced a seemingly endless succession of parodies of cheap Broadway plays and popular fiction, and Wright solicited satirical stories and poems and added his razor-sharp editorial commentaries.

Despite the laurels that Wright won in some quarters for these achievements, he soon overplayed his hand and, as a result, he must ultimately be judged a brilliant failure as an editor. Although he proclaimed in his first editorial manifesto the hour of liberation for American letters from commercial mediocrity and timorous puritanism to be at hand, the readers of the *Smart Set* were too often shocked, dismayed and disaffected by such an abrupt shift in the tone and contents of their magazine. The American reading public of 1913—even the "civilized minority" to whom the *Smart Set* catered—were not yet ready to support a serious commercial magazine (though they would plenty of "little" ones) that flouted prevailing literary taboos and flaunted the social criticism advanced by Wright. (pp. 156-57)

[If] Mencken and Nathan finally turned Wright's failures to success in the *Smart Set,* it was simply because, though no less tolerant than he of prevailing American shibboleths, they profited from his mistakes, heeded their own counsel of moderation and found a receptive audience by becoming popularizers. It may, in fact, be claimed that the chief contribution made to American letters and the theatre by this enigmatic pair was in their collective role of popularizer of ideas, of a kind of literature and a kind of theatre that hitherto had been considered *avant-garde* and the exclusive province of an intellectual elite in the United States. As an editor, Wright sought to cultivate this elite, not necessarily to enlarge it. Therein lay his greatest failure and Mencken's and Nathan's greatest success.

His departure from the *Smart Set* (in late December 1913) closed Wright's career as an editor and turned his energies wholly toward the profession of authorship. The next four years, while he supported himself by writing art criticism for the *Forum* and *International Studio* magazines and book reviews for a daily newspaper, the *New York Evening Mail,* comprised literarily the most productive period of his life. During this time he produced five books of his own and collaborated in a sixth. Meanwhile, while editing the *Smart Set* in 1913, he had brought out a collection of verse, ***Songs of Youth,*** containing twenty poems he had contributed to newspapers and magazines. Like Mencken's juvenile *Ventures Into Verse,* these "songs" are easy to forget—full of *"ubi sunt"* plaints, hedonist exhortations, fashionable bittersweet despair, and faint echoes of Swinburne, Dowson and the later French Symbolists. They are conventional rather than inspired, showing craftsmanship rather than poetic talent of any high order, and their lukewarm critical reception apparently discouraged Wright from pursuing his Muse much further.

Europe After 8:15, in which he collaborated with his erstwhile *Smart Set* colleagues (Mencken and Nathan) is, therefore, the first of Wright's books to merit much attention today. Ostensibly a "guide book" to European nocturnal haunts for the sophisticated American, it is really almost a parody of such books and its appearance in August 1914, even as Europe was erupting in blood, is surely one of the unluckiest mischances in American publishing history. As a result, ***Europe After 8:15*** sold too few copies to pay the printer's bills and was forgotten almost before its ink was dry. Nevertheless, it remains one of the most ingratiating collections of European travel sketches yet published in the venerable American tradition inaugurated by "Geoffrey Crayon, Gent". (p. 159)

A better title might have been *Personal Impressions of Selected European Cities* inasmuch as the sketches are not concerned solely with "after 8:15" life and only five cities are surveyed: Vienna, Munich, Berlin, London and Paris. It is no accident that so many of the cities included are German-speaking, and there is a brief, wonderfully satirical introduction ("Preface in the Socratic Manner") by Mencken in which two typical American tourists meet by chance on "the brow of the Hungerberg at Innsbruck" where, utterly ignoring the breathtaking beauty that surrounds them, they solace each other with mutual denunciations of virtually everything European.

The sketches that follow this "Socratic" dialogue have an amazing unity of style and viewpoint for a collaborative effort. Each is an impressionistic vignette of urban leisure activities: theatres and cabarets, cafes and *biergärten,* soubrettes and other delicacies of the eye, ear and palate—a veritable catalogue of *Wein, Weiber und Gesang!* The German and Austrian cities are made particularly attractive and, in the rhapsodic tones (larded with German words and phrases) with which Wright hymns the delights of Hapsburg Vienna, Mencken those of Munich and Nathan those of Berlin, it would scarcely be exaggeration to call this a thoroughly Germanophile work. By contrast, Paris and London come off distinctly second-best if only because they had, so the authors of these sketches claim, succumbed to the lure of the dollar, catering to vulgar American tastes. Nowhere in ***Europe After 8:15,*** however, is mention made of the great monuments—palaces, churches, museums and other public edifices—of these European cultural capitals; no Baedeker-like descriptions for the Grand Tour mar the tone. Everything is done with a light touch, with just the right balance of sentimentality and humor. . . . (pp. 159-60)

Wright's next work, also published in 1914, was an essay on the philosophical ideas of Friedrich Nietzsche, ***What Nietzsche Taught.*** Chronologically speaking, it is the second important book about Nietzsche that appeared in the United States, the first having been Mencken's *The Philosophy of Friedrich Nietzsche* (1908), Wright's laudatory review of which (in the

Los Angeles Times) had occasioned the correspondence between the two which ripened into friendship. Many students of American philosophical writing (as well as admirers of Nietzsche) have pronounced Wright's the better of the two books, claiming that he explicated Nietzsche's ideas with more precision and made them at once more accessible to the Anglo-American mind. Whatever the case, this book (like its predecessor, ***Europe After 8:15***) appeared in a most unpropitious hour when poor Nietzsche, simply because he was a German who glorified things Teutonic, had become suspect among an increasing number of the very readers in the United States that Wright's book might have reached a few years earlier. Already, in late 1914, the American intellectual community was beginning to feel the impact of what Mencken dubbed "Anglomania"—the results of an enormously successful campaign of cultural propaganda which, with considerable help from the German High Command, would eventually involve the United States in World War I.

Modern Painting, Its Tendency and Meaning, which Willard Wright completed in Paris in the summer of 1915 while visiting his older brother, Stanton Macdonald-Wright (he had hyphenated his middle and last names), a leading painter of a post-impressionist movement called "Synchronism," was his fourth book (including ***Songs of Youth***) written or compiled within two years. It was published in New York, in October 1915 and sold well enough to warrant a reprinting ten years later. It is unquestionably the finest work of Wright's early period, judged from a stylistic viewpoint and from the mastery it shows of his subject. Like his brother, Willard Wright had studied art for several years, had seriously considered making his career as a painter, and had given it up at last only reluctantly, perhaps concluding that he could not compete successfully with his talented sibling. However, the brothers had remained close at this period of their lives and the younger had derived from his elder a passion for "modernism" in art and a great deal of intimate knowledge of contemporary artistic movements. All of this is vigorously displayed in ***Modern Painting,*** whose tone as well as title recalls John Ruskin at his best.

Whether or not he did so intentionally, Wright capitalized in his book on modernism in art upon the enormous interest in the subject engendered in the United States by the historic Armory Show in New York in April 1913—an event often cited as the "watershed" in American art history, dividing past from present. Marcel Duchamp's Cubist painting, "Nude Descending a Staircase," had created an unprecedented furor in American artistic circles and on the question of approving or condemning Cubism and allied post-impressionist schools the issue had been joined. Of course, Wright enlisted himself squarely on the side of the Cubists and their multifarious contemporaries and, in fifteen erudite and persuasive chapters, he eloquently pled the cause of the modernists, demonstrating the continuity of twentieth century art with that of past ages and defending on grounds of historical necessity (as well as technical advancement) the innovations in art that seemed so shocking to many Americans in 1915. With admirable thoroughness he discussed in detail the work of some fifty "revolutionary" artists: Manet, Renoir, Cezanne, Gauguin, Matisse, Picasso, Braque, Kandinsky, *et al.*—treating each as if he were (as we now take for granted!) the peer of Da Vinci, Titian and Michelangelo. Along the way he made intelligent comments on dozens of others, including such then-obscure American painters as Kroll, Childe Hassam and what was disparagingly called the "Ash-Can School", and he treated his readers to extensive introductions to the theories and techniques of Impressionism,

Neo-Impressionism, Cubism, Futurism, Synchronism and a host of other brand new "-isms" in painting. In short, as the first book on this hitherto-recondite subject by an American, subsequent art history may have rendered it somewhat obsolete today, but it remains a highly readable exposition and anyone who encounters it must conclude that, in such a subject, Willard Wright found his true *métier*. It is an impression that his later works, *The Future of Painting* . . . and an admirable anthology, *The Forum Exhibition of American Painters* . . . , serve to reinforce.

The thesis of *Modern Painting,* if it may be said to have one, is that what separates the "modern" artist from his predecessors and makes him an exciting innovator is that he has discovered how to apply the force of his "creative will." Just what this force is remains somewhat vague in this work, but it is clear that Wright means it to signify some kind of auto-suggestion or self-intoxication by means of which the artist transcends Nature. The artist, in other words, creates his own world from within himself, he is in no way dependent upon the external world of Nature and natural forms. To expound and develop this thesis into a coherent theory of aesthetics, Wright immediately set to work composing a companion volume to *Modern Painting* which he published in the following year (1916) under the title, *The Creative Will.* But if he thought this theoretical work was in any real sense an original contribution to aesthetics, he was soon disabused. Even his friend Mencken had to point out in his review that the essay was as embarrassing *mélange* of warmed-over ideas lifted whole-cloth from Schopenhauer, Nietzsche and Bergson.

In order to exemplify the operation of the "creative will" in an individual artist's life, Wright then undertook a novel, *The Man of Promise* . . . , his first venture into sustained fiction (he had earlier contributed a few short stories to the *Smart Set*) and his only one outside the detective genre. Like Theodore Dreiser's *The "Genius"* (1915), to which this novel bears many striking parallels, *The Man of Promise* concerns an aesthete-hero's unsuccessful struggles to create an important revolutionary work of art against the debilitating and constricting influences of environment—the claims of filial obligation, of hostages to fortune (a wife and child) and the artist's own sensual nature. Stanford West, the central character, is easily recognizable as Willard Wright himself in this disguise and, if we know anything at all of Wright's personal life, we are soon aware that we are reading fictionalized autobiography—the more interesting for all that.

Stanford West's father (like Wright's), the president of a small college, has marked his son for an academic career—a fate against which West (also like Wright) rebels, deciding to become a great writer. The driving force of his life is his dream of producing a neo-Aristotelian tragedy full of "the Greek spirit" that is large, radical and free and will at once revolutionize the modern theatre and modern philosophical thought. In time he comes to realize that he cannot create his *magnum opus* while he is fettered by the two women who dominate his life—his mother and, later, his wife. He flees from their influence, turning to two emancipated women for understanding and encouragement. Again he is disappointed, finding that an intelligent and sensitive mistress may satisfy his physical passions and give him companionship, but her claims upon his soul will sap his creativity and fetter his will. At last he yields to the importunings of Seminoff, his alter-ego (apparently based upon Wright's brother, S. Macdonald-Wright) and good conscience, and returns to his forgiving wife to accept the college

professorship he once scorned so that he can provide for his small daughter. In the end, West knows that he has failed his "creative will" and that he will probably never produce more than pedestrian works, but he knows and accepts the reasons why.

As a *bildungsroman* and a novel of ideas treating the relations of the artist to his society, *The Man of Promise* is greatly inferior to either D. H. Lawrence's *Sons and Lovers* or Joyce's *Portrait of the Artist* . . . , two contemporaneous novels known to Wright and with which his work immediately challenges comparison. Its too-meticulous melodramatic plot structure (Mencken likened it to Scribe's "well-made" plays [see Mencken excerpt dated 1916]) and Wright's failure to make Stanford West a really sympathetic character—like Dreiser's Eugene Witla (in *The "Genius"*), which is also autobiographical, he remains simply an egoistic prig—brought unfavorable criticism from almost every reviewer. Yet, *The Man of Promise* is no worse than a host of similar novels produced in the United States in the second and third decades of this century and it is an interesting precursor of such works as F. Scott Fitzgerald's *This Side of Paradise* (1920), the novels of Thomas Wolfe in the '20's and '30's and, more recently, Salinger's Seymour Glass stories. As a first novel by an author still in his twenties, it gave earnest of a talent for serious fiction that was destined to remain unfulfilled.

Wright was frustrated and infuriated by the generally hostile notices accorded both *The Creative Will* and *The Man of Promise.* He suspected, perhaps rightly, that some of the fault-finding was motivated by antipathy toward his known pro-German sympathies in an hour when the United States were edging ever closer to open belligerency as an ally of Great Britain. In revenge upon his Anglophile critics, therefore, he composed a monograph, *Misinforming a Nation,* attacking the newly-published first American edition of the *Encyclopedia Britannica.* It was a brilliant if untimely polemic which, despite its intemperate and indiscreet tone, accurately pinpointed dozens of factual errors, slantings and downright distortions tending to prove that the authority of the *Encyclopedia Britannica* was vitiated by its Anglophile bias. To say these things in the Untied States in 1917, however accurate they might be, was to invite calumny and vituperation. This Wright received in full measure from Stuart P. Sherman and a host of likeminded critics who vilified him as, at best, tactless and unpatriotic, at worst, a paid agent of the Wilhelmstraße. (pp. 160-63)

In time, "S. S. Van Dine" made Willard Huntington Wright a rich man and a celebrity, pointed out in public places and sought-after as a lecturer, a judge in detective-story contests, and an authority on the history, techniques and future of detective fiction.

But for Wright it was a success tinged with bitterness. What he could do so well he valued little. To be lauded as the peer of Mary Roberts Rinehart was, he ruminated, a hollow and ironical honor. Even as he enjoyed the wealth these books brought him, he loathed the "easy" fame he had won as "Van Dine"—a fame that could never wholly belong to Willard Wright himself. Surrounded by luxurious appointments in a Fifth Avenue penthouse apartment, amid the paintings and *objets d'art* he at last could afford to collect, "Van Dine" ordered his butler to set at his elbow each waking half hour a pony of cognac. It was, he reflected as he spun off another Philo Vance adventure, "by far the pleasantest way to commit suicide." The final irony was that it was a sudden heart seizure, not alcohol, that brought the release he longed for.

What can we make of the strange case of this writer who seemed so determined to fail? Perhaps he is an object lesson of what happens in a democratic society to an author who estranges himself from that society, who will neither come to terms with it nor agree to combat it by rules other than those of his own making. At all events, those who argue that genius will out, that the talents of an artist or a writer will prevail against all odds, would do well to take a close look at the case of Willard Huntington Wright, alias "S. S. Van Dine," before they dismiss the jury and pass sentence. (p. 164)

> Carl Richard Dolmetsch, "The Writer in America: The Strange Case of 'S. S. Van Dine'," in Literatur und Sprache der Vereinigten Staaten: Aufsätze zu Ehren von Hans Galinsky, Hans Helmcke, Klaus Lubbers, Renate Schmidt-v. Bardeleben, eds., Carl Winter Universitätsverlag, 1969, pp. 153-64.

WILLIAM RUEHLMANN (essay date 1974)

[Ruehlmann is an American critic and journalist. In the following excerpt from his A Saint with a Gun, a study of American detective fiction, he compares Philo Vance and Sherlock Holmes with respect to their actions outside the law.]

Although Holmes was made to say on one occasion that "it's every man's business to see justice done," unlike his future American heirs he appeared to be more interested in mercy than in justice. His extralegal activities usually extended to preventing prosecution rather than personally carrying it out. The detective suppresses evidence in "The Boscombe Valley Mystery" (1891) that would convict an aging murderer in order to protect the reputation of a dying man. In "The Adventure of Charles Augustus Milverton" (1904), Holmes witnesses the killing of an extortionist and refuses to pursue the woman who did it. In each instance the victim was a blackmailer; blackmail had to be the unforgivable Victorian crime in a society surviving on the appearance of rectitude. Although he saw the law and its defenders as flawed, the English private eye was more protector than enforcer.

Not so the American version. S. S. Van Dine's dilettantish Philo Vance was an unlikely minister of vengeance, but even in the drawing-room novels that made him the best-selling favorite of Franklin Roosevelt rough justice prevailed. Van Dine (the pseudonym of Willard Huntington Wright) wrote that "all good detective novels have had for their protagonist a character of attractiveness and interest, of high and fascinating attainments—a man at once unusual and unusual, colorful and gifted." Philo Vance was Van Dine's idea of such a character. He bore a disturbing resemblance to Holmes:

> He was just under six feet, slender, sinewy, and graceful. His chiselled regular features gave his face the attraction of strength and uniform modelling, but a sardonic coldness of expression precluded the designation of handsome. He had aloof gray eyes, a straight, slender nose, and a mouth suggesting both cruelty and asceticism.

He was bloodless like Holmes—and, like Holmes, a man with a passion for arcane minutiae:

> He was something of an authority on Japanese and Chinese prints; he knew tapestries and ceramics; and once I heard him give an impromptu causerie to a few guests on Tanagora

figurines which, had it been transcribed, would have made a most delightful and interesting monograph.

Also like Holmes, Vance's exploits are recounted by a biographer, "Van Dine" himself, who, as the detective's legal and financial adviser, follows him slavishly about. More effacing even than Watson, "Van Dine" never in the course of a dozen novels utters a single word. Rather, he restricts himself to a meticulous recounting of Vance's movements and comments. These comments are delivered in an accent which is labeled Oxonian, but which, upon examination, resembles no recognizable tongue in the civilized world. An example:

> "By the by," he said, slipping into his coat, "I note that our upliftin' press bedecked its front pages this morning with head-lines about a pogrom at the old Greene mansion last night. Wherefore?"

Another: ". . . I'm happy to note that crime is picking up again. It's a deuced drab world without a nice murky murder now and then, don't y' know." A smoker of rose petal-tipped Régie cigarettes, eater of truffes gastronome with Madeira sauce, devotee of the Hispano-Suiza and translator of Delacroix, the monocled Vance is a caricature of Poe's Dupin given the mobility and function of Doyle's Holmes. He shares their mutual passion for cold reason: "Until we can approach all human problems . . . with the clinical aloofness and cynical contempt of a doctor examining a guinea-pig strapped to a board, we have little chance of getting at the truth." And he shares as well their supreme confidence in the application of analysis to crime: "Just as an expert aesthetician can analyze a picture and tell you who painted it, so can the expert psychologist analyze a crime and tell you who committed it. . . ."

Vance first appears in *The Benson Murder Case* . . . and is immediately placed in a position superior to the police. As a friend of District Attorney Markham, Vance is called in whenever a crime is committed that defeats the ratiocinative powers of the authorities—that is to say, he is called in all the time. Vance's opinion of his official rivals is predictably scornful: "I say, Markham, . . . it has always been a source of amazement to me how easily you investigators of crime are misled by what you call clues. You find a footprint, or a parked automobile, or a monogrammed handkerchief, and then dash off on a wild chase with your eternal *Ecce signum!*" Pontificates Philo: "The only crimes that are ever solved are those planned by stupid people." The Law is usually represented by the stolid Sergeant Heath, who pursues the obvious with the unrelenting assiduousness of a process server in a one-reeler. Heath in moments of indecision is prone to divest himself of outbursts like these: "What's on the cards? Where do we go from here? I need action." Vance is moved at such junctures to grieve: "And it's stubborn, unimaginative chaps like Heath who constitute the human barrage between the criminal and society! . . . Sad, sad."

It is perhaps even sadder that the only intervening supportive bulwark is Vance, for he takes some little time to catch his man—often at the cost of numerous lives in the interim. At the outset of *The Greene Murder Case* . . . , Vance is summoned to investigate a murder and shooting at the home of a decadent upper-class family. By the time he uncovers the killer a further assault has occurred and three more murders, reducing his viable list of suspects to three. These executions proceed as Vance commits himself to musings such as the following: ". . .

Some deep, awful motive lies behind that crime. There are depths beneath depths in what happened last night—obscure fetid chambers of the human soul. Black hatreds, unnatural desires, hideous impulses, obscene ambitions are at the bottom of it." . . . When he does at long last corner the killer he withholds his knowledge that she is in possession of cyanide capsules; this permits her to kill herself in the very presence of the district attorney. The two surviving suspects then embrace and sail for the Riviera.

Vance's tendency to help justice along is at its apogee in *The Bishop Murder Case*. . . . Here he does not assist a suicide—he engineers one. Before breaking into one suspect's home, Vance engages in this discussion of legal procedure:

> Markham rushed forward and caught him round the shoulders.
>
> "Are you mad?" he exclaimed. "You're breaking the law."
>
> "The law!" There was scathing irony in Vance's retort. "We're dealing with a monster who sneers at all law. You may coddle him if you care to, but I'm going to search that attic if it means spending the rest of my life in jail.—Sergeant, open that door!"

His haste may in part spring from the usual concatenation of killings in the course of a lingering Vance investigation, but some of it is vendetta as well. When Vance arranges for the murderer to quaff a dram of poison—again in the presence of the D.A.—Markham exhibits growing impatience.

> "You took the law into your own hands!"
>
> "I took it in my arms—it was helpless. . . . But don't be so righteous. Do you bring a rattlesnake to the bar of justice? Do you give a mad dog his day in court? I felt no more compunction in aiding a monster like Dillard into the Beyond than I would have in crushing out a poisonous reptile in the act of striking."
>
> "But it was murder!" exclaimed Markham in horrified indignation.
>
> "Oh, doubtless," said Vance cheerfully.

What Markham has overlooked is the initial stricture Vance demanded on his first appearance. If the authorities wanted his help, Vance warned, "I must have your word you'll give me every possible assistance, and will refrain from all profound legal objections." The principal difference between Vance and his quarry seems to reside only in the number of victims; under the dandy's mask is a killer as cold-blooded as the major who murders bald Alvin Benson or the heiress who thins out the Greene family or the "bishop" who bumps off his rivals with a bow and arrow. (pp. 39-43)

> *William Ruehlmann, "The Sleepless Knight," in his*
> Saint with a Gun: The Unlawful American Private
> Eye, *New York University Press, 1974, pp. 19-54.*

ROGER ROSENBLATT (essay date 1975)

[*Rosenblatt is an American journalist and critic who has worked as literary editor and columnist for the* New Republic *and as editorial writer and columnist for the* Washington Post. *In the following excerpt, he presents an analysis of the character Philo Vance.*]

Philo Vance returned to New York from a trip to Egypt in the summer of 1936. He had "thrown himself into Egyptological research," in order to forget the lovely Zalia Graem of *The Garden Murder Case,* and now, understandably, was near exhaustion. Starting in 1926 he already had solved the *Benson, Canary, Greene, Bishop, Scarab, Kennel, Dragon* and *Casino* murder cases and was about to dig into the *Kidnap.* (The *Winter* and *Gracie Allen . . .* murder cases were yet to come.) His friend and narrator, S. S. Van Dine, feared for Vance's health, but it was only "a short time before I recognized the old vital Vance that I had always known, keen for sports, for various impersonal activities, and for the constant millings of the undercurrents of human psychology." The confident silliness of that description gives us Vance and Van Dine in a shot.

Vance's manner of talking was more vivid than Van Dine's, but no less preposterous—"I'm in a perfect Erebus of tenebrosity." What Van Dine consigned to pseudo-scholarly footnotes, Vance said aloud. More show-off than pedant, he disguised his mockery of others in self-parody, which became ludicrous itself when tied by Van Dine to Vance's supposed deep nature. Van Dine wanted us to believe that Vance was more mysterious than the murders he dealt with; but good detectives, including Sherlock Holmes, cannot hold us by their characters. The most interesting thing about Vance was money. (p. 32)

In 1929 [Van Dine] collected and wrote a long introduction to an anthology of *Great Detective Stories*. . . . Wright's rules for good mystery writing are interesting [see Van Dine excerpt dated 1928], but his knowledge of the growth of the detective story as a genre is extraordinary, and explains much about his creation of Vance. Clearly Vance was a deliberate invention, discovered as Dupin or Holmes often discovered criminals, through a process of elimination. He was a fusion of Holmes, Gaboriau's M. Lecoq, G. K. Chesterton's Father Brown, H. C. Bailey's Dr. Fortune, A.E.W. Mason's Hanaud, Anthony Wynne's Dr. Haily and Melville Davisson Post's Uncle Abner—the virtue common to all being a preeminence of intuitive genius over fact arrangement. Wright believed that "the cooperation extended by the reader to his favorite detective is wholly a mental process." At the same time he knew that no reader wants to be part of purely logical mental process, which would merely associate him with the bungling police.

Van Dine's great feat with Vance is that we are not permitted to like him. Chandler and Hammett, for all their self-conscious hard-boiledness, made their detectives lovable; they kicked them in the mud to win our hearts. "Down these mean streets a man must go who is not himself mean," said Chandler in "The Simple Art of Murder," an essay propelled by sentimentality. Van Dine on the other hand, who manufactured the "fragrant world" which Chandler condemned, where only the rich bump each other off, came much closer than Chandler to creating a truly hard-boiled egg. In *The Benson Murder Case* Vance ridicules the D.A., Markham, his close friend, in front of a suspect. Neither Sam Spade, Phillip Marlowe or even the shady Ned Beaumont would have done that.

Nobody loves a man who wears a monocle. Vance is not despicable; it is merely impossible to like him actively. Unlike Holmes or Nero Wolfe he has no interesting assistant to warm the narrative. Van Dine, the family lawyer, is too pompous and corny to make Vance attractive in any sense deeper than the Abercrombie and Fitch catalogue. Vance's aloneness conveys no feeling of underlying melancholy, precisely because Van Dine is always, and deliberately, pushing the possibility too hard. Vance's elaborate independence from the world is in fact reassuring; we don't worry for his mental health between cases. Even the love touch of *The Garden Murder Case* is just a touch.

His solitariness is essential to these stories, nevertheless, because over half the murders occur in families: brothers knife brothers; children poison parents. Like the Greeks, Van Dine knew that families are dangerous. Vance stands outside both the story and the institution of the family, which he implicitly criticizes. He is the most important person in the story—he puts it in order by solving the crime—but he is also free of the participants, free of connections. By ending the mystery, he restores his bachelorhood.

Like other detectives, Vance imposes order on disorganized events. His loneliness is also like a god's, whose sense of order is higher than and hidden from that of ordinary people. Vance is rich but no conservative; he creates his own systems. As the only one on the case with the power to make his system work, he is relied upon by others. Yet he does not give his sense of order to anyone for future use, certainly not to the police who must start from scratch at every murder.

He stands outside the law as well, openly contemptuous and covertly supportive, in the American way. He does not think the law is evil or unnecessary, merely beside most points: "No. Legal technicalities quite useless in such an emergency. Deeper issues involved. Human issues, d'ye see." He is so confident in his knowledge of human issues that he refers to these murders as "unnatural" and "grotesque" because they jostle his theories of behavior. Vance's idea of justice is purely poetic. More often than not he allows the culprit to cheat the State.

Of course it is not his capability for organization that we seek in these stories, but the assurance, in the distance, that that capability exists. What we wish for and indulge in, here and in all mysteries, is the thrill of unknowing, unknowing who the murderer is, and particularly who is going to get it next. By using devices which keep Vance unlikable, Van Dine extended this thrill to fine lengths, without stalling. Vance's knowledge of fish or rare coins is always pertinent to the crimes. His foppish presentation of information makes us as impatient as Markham, but like Markham we hear him out on the suspicion that the information will be valuable, and allow us to beat both Markham and Vance to the killer.

This is a set up, in fact, because Van Dine's killers are not detectable by information alone: "The material indications of the crime don't enter into my calculations. . . . I have other, and surer, ways of reaching conclusions." The detective tells us outright in every story that he will expose the guilty person by determining temperament and likely action in given circumstances. From then on, however, he piles on motives and clues, non irrelevant, and gulls us into using deduction as a method; in effect, he turns us into Markhams. He meanwhile remains psychological, which is what any logician in his right mind would prefer to be. While we struggle with chess moves (the *Bishop*) and lines of trajectory (the *Benson*), he announces (usually with a third of the novel to go) that he already knows who the murderer is—indeed that he has known for some time—but needs to slum in facts in order to prove it. Thus at the end we concentrate almost totally on Vance, which allows the suspects to dwindle down to a precious few (two in the *Greene*) without our being certain about the murderer.

Van Dine's other diversionary tactic is his precision with details. He loved maps and diagrams, and insisted on telling us

all the street routes taken. Superficially realistic, this is a wildly romantic touch; it presents an imaginary New York, like Fitzgerald's in *Gatsby*, with great pastoral space and elegant silences. It also tightens suspense; the layouts of vast apartments and brownstones make vivid both the scenes of the crimes and the crimes themselves. This is the fancy stuff of which Chandler disapproved in the name of realism, but again Chandler missed the point. Van Dine's details are not meant to divert us from the reality of the world (which is no more accurately captured by describing sheets in a whorehouse), but from the identity of the killer.

In the infamous "Who Cares Who Killed Roger Ackroyd?" Edmund Wilson said that "the reading of detective stories is simply a kind of vice that, for silliness and minor harmfulness, ranks somewhere between smoking and crossword puzzles." The judgment is too cute to mean anything. A crossword puzzle in fact was what Van Dine had in mind when he planned his novels, "an extended puzzle in fictional form." He was not creating fiction, but a kind of riddle.

This probably is why he went out of style as soon as Hammett, Chandler and others established themselves. Hammett and Chandler could (and did) breed imitators because they were toying with small-scale tragedy—always easier to imitate because if the crime is gripping enough, one can leave out other essential parts of tragedy with minimum risk. Van Dine, who was working more with an architectural than literary form, was difficult to re-create or revive. Scribner tried to reissue the murders a few years ago, and got nowhere. Fawcett Publications redid the first four books in paperback, with few sales.

Yet people might be ready for Philo Vance again. For one thing, our economic state is making class differences so blatant that snobs and dandies may come back into cultural favor. For another, public interest in serious fiction is waning, and readers increasingly prefer things like riddles which free them of the understanding of other men's hearts. For a third, these stories are good—clever and intricate, expertly paced, particularly effective as summer reading, in an electric storm, when the car is gone and something seems wrong with the phone. (pp. 32-4)

Roger Rosenblatt, "S. S. Van Dine," in The New Republic, *Vol. 173, No. 4, July 26, 1975, pp. 32-4.*

ADDITIONAL BIBLIOGRAPHY

Angoff, Charles. "The Mystique of *The Smart Set*." *The Literary Review* 11, No. 1 (Autumn 1967): 49-60.

> Contains information on Wright's yearlong editorship of the *Smart Set,* a period that "set a new tone for quality journalism in the United States."

Bartlett, Randolph. "The Man of Promise." *The Saturday Review of Literature* XIII, No. 1 (2 November 1935): 10.

> Overview of Wright's works published under his own name and as S. S. Van Dine. Regarding the Van Dine novels, Bartlett sees a decline in quality after *The Green Murder Case*.

Boyd, Ernest. "Willard Huntington Wright." *The Saturday Review of Literature* XIX, No. 26 (22 April 1939): 8.

> Boyd's reminiscences of his acquaintance with Wright. Boyd comments: "He was the most interesting and attractive *unlikable* man I have ever known."

Dueren, Fred. "Philo Vance." *The Armchair Detective* 9, No. 1 (November 1975): 23-4.

Biographical data on the characters of Philo Vance and S. S. Van Dine.

Gidley, M. "William Faulkner and Willard Huntington Wright's *The Creative Will*." *The Canadian Review of American Studies* IX, No. 2 (Fall 1978): 169-77.
Discusses the influence of Wright's aesthetic theories on Faulkner, who, Gidley concludes, "definitely absorbed ideas which Wright, among others, was advancing. It may well be that some of Wright's teachings filtered deeper into Faulkner's psyche, there to be transmuted into the art that Wright himself seems always to have just failed or failed utterly to achieve."

Gilman, Lawrence. "Woman: The Enemy." *The North American Review* CCIII, No. 726 (May 1916): 769-72.
Condemns the negative view of women held by the protagonist of *The Man of Promise*.

Hagemann, E. R. "Philo Vance's Sunday Nights at the Old Stuyvesant Club." *Clues: A Journal of Detection* 1, No. 2 (Fall/Winter 1980): 35-41.
Concerns a series of articles by Van Dine based on true crime stories.

Hale, Edward E. Review of *The Man of Promise*, by Willard Huntington Wright. *The Dial* LX, No. 720 (8 June 1916): 552-54.
Analysis of the protagonist of *The Man of Promise*. Hale calls Stanford West a "muddle-headed sensualist" who is misrepresented by Wright as a man of ideas.

Haycraft, Howard, "America: 1918-1930 (The Golden Age)." In his *Murder for Pleasure: The Life and Times of the Detective Story*, pp. 159-80. New York: D. Appleton-Century Co., 1941.
Biographical sketch and brief discussion of Van Dine's place in the development of the detective novel. Haycraft concludes that the Philo Vance novels "were epochal in the sense that they raised the detective story to a new peak of excellence and popularity in the land of its birth; they were American in the narrow sense that their milieu and subject matter were American; yet in method and style they departed no whit from the well established English tradition."

Mather, Frank Jewett, Jr. "The Artist as Superman." *The Dial* LXII, No. 733 (11 January 1917): 15-17.

Describes an attack on Wright's aesthetic theories in *The Creative Will*. Mather summarizes that "Mr. Wright's groundwork is a rather crass romantic individualism. He imagines a creative art *in vacuo*, by an anti-social superman."

Mellquist, Jerome. "The Lift of New Ideas." In his *The Emergence of an American Art*, pp. 243-53. New York: Charles Scribner's Sons, 1942.
Account of Wright's career as an art critic. Mellquist states: "As critic he was admirable. . . . Like a lion he tore into the enemies of art."

Mumford, Lewis. "The Future of Painting." *The New Republic* XXXVI, No. 458 (12 September 1923): 79-80.
Argues against the principal points of Wright's study *The Future of Painting*.

Murch, A. E. "The Golden Age." In his *The Development of the Detective Novel*, pp. 218-43. 1958. Reprint. Westport, Conn.: Greenwood Press, 1968.
Brief characterization of Van Dine's novels and of his sleuth Philo Vance. Of Vance, Murch remarks: "In his 'institutional' methods, his sensitiveness to psychological clues, he is sometimes faintly reminiscent of Reginald Fortune, but he lacks the saving graces of modesty and a sense of humour."

Pate, Janet. "Philo Vance." In her *The Book of Sleuths*, pp. 61-3. London: New English Library, 1977.
Character sketch of Philo Vance. Pate concludes: "As a character study he has little or no substance—for who can believe in a personality built only on a set of gimmicky affectations and the constant airing of intellectual prowess."

Symons, Julian. "The Golden Age: The Twenties." In his *Mortal Consequences: A History—From the Detective Story to the Crime Novel*, pp. 100-17. New York: Harper & Row, 1972.
Sketch of Wright's career and description of the twelve Van Dine novels. Symons considers *The Greene Murder Case* and *The Bishop Murder Case* the best of these, and says of them: "In their outrageous cleverness, their disdainful disregard of everything except the detective and the puzzle, they are among the finest fruits of the Golden Age."

Simone (Adolphine) Weil

1909-1943

(Also wrote under pseudonym of Emile Novis) French philosopher, essayist, dramatist, and poet.

Weil is regarded as one of the most brilliant and enigmatic Christian thinkers of the twentieth century. Her ascetic life and ambivalence toward the Catholic Church have become as well known and as much a part of her influence as her written works, most of which were collected posthumously from her notebooks. Often paradoxical and contradictory, Weil's writings convey her intense compassion for the suffering of others, her repudiation of modern nihilism, and her longing to be united with God.

Weil was born in Paris, the daughter of a prosperous doctor and his wife. Her childhood was marked by intellectual precociousness and a sensitivity to human suffering. At the age of five, for example, she refused to eat sugar because none could be supplied to the soldiers at the front during the First World War; at the age of six, she was able to quote passages of seventeenth-century French dramatist Jean Racine from memory. Although she earned her high school degree at fifteen, she felt extremely inferior to her brother André, who was a mathematical prodigy, and as a consequence she seriously considered suicide and nearly suffered a nervous breakdown. Between 1925 and 1928, Weil studied at the Henri IV Lycée under the philosopher Alain (Emile Chartier), whose influence intensified her innate antipathy toward the unequal social order and her self-questioning search for truth. She continued her education at the Ecole Normale, receiving her diploma in 1931, after which she began to teach philosophy. During this period she also engaged in activities with various revolutionary groups: she picketed with striking workers, published articles in such leftist journals as the *Révolution prolétarienne,* and lived on an amount of money equal to the relief given to the unemployed, giving the rest of her salary away to the poor. Weil's activism brought her into conflict with school authorities, and as a result she taught at five different schools between 1931 and 1938. During this period she also took a year's leave from teaching to work in factories in Paris, an experience that convinced her of the brutality and debasement of factory life, the necessity to break the barrier between intellectual and manual labor, and the meager chance for a proletarian revolution. She felt contempt for the rhetoric of revolutionary politicians such as V. I. Lenin, who she was sure had never seen the inside of a factory. She became further disillusioned with the possibilities of revolution during her service in the Spanish Civil War with the anarchist group *Confederación nacional del trabajo,* observing enough brutality on both sides of the conflict to reject the justification of violence for any purpose.

Between 1936 and 1938, Weil underwent a spiritual conversion that began with an attraction toward Christianity, which she considered the "religion of slaves" with whom she identified herself, and culminated in several mystical experiences. In a cathedral in Assisi in 1937, for example, she was driven to her knees while alone in the chapel of St. Francis, having been compelled "by something stronger than myself." In 1938, Weil met an Oxford undergraduate who introduced her to the work of the seventeenth-century Metaphysical poets; she was

From Simone Weil: A Fellowship in Love, by Jacques Cabaud. Courtesy of Oxford University Press.

especially attracted to George Herbert's "Love," which she would recite and concentrate on during her periodic and intense migraine headaches. In the middle of November, while she was reciting this poem, the most pivotal of her mystical experiences occurred. As she wrote, "Christ Himself came down and took possession of me." She had formerly believed that God did not directly reveal himself to individuals, but since she had never read the mystics and was not expecting the experience to occur, she became convinced that it was genuine. From this time on, Weil turned from an emphasis on social and political action, which she called "ersatz divinity," toward a search for spiritual truth.

In 1940, since both she and her father were unemployable in Paris under the Vichy government, Weil moved with her parents to Marseilles. There she met the Dominican Father J. M. Perrin, with whom she cultivated one of her few close friendships and who nearly succeeded in persuading her to be baptized into the Roman Catholic Church. Weil expressed to Perrin her desire to experience the life of an agricultural laborer, and in 1941 Perrin introduced her to Gustave Thibon, a farmer who employed Weil during the fall grape harvest. Thibon was also a noted Catholic philosopher and writer, and while Weil worked for him, they developed a deep mutual respect. When she emigrated to America with her parents in 1942, Weil left her notebooks with Thibon, urging that he use her ideas in his own writing. Weil soon afterward traveled to England to work with the Free French forces and pleaded unsuccessfully to be parachuted into France to join the Resistance, even though this action would have been almost certainly fatal to her, given her poor health and Jewish background. During this period she contracted tuberculosis while limiting her food to the amount that the French obtained during rationing. Refusing treatment for her illness, she died in a sanatorium in Ashford, Kent, of "voluntary starvation." It is still a matter for debate whether her death was a result of anorexia, actual suicide, mental illness, or a self-imposed martyrdom due to her unbending asceticism.

Weil published only magazine articles and poems during her lifetime. Of these, "*L'Iliade; ou, Le poème de la force*" ("The *Iliad;* or, The Poem of Force") has gained the greatest attention. To Weil, the *Iliad* illustrated pacifism by presenting the absolute futility of the Trojan War. In her essay on Homer's epic she developed the thesis that violence degrades the victim and the victor alike, and that it makes both into selfless "things." Weil considered this a supreme sin, because the self, once destroyed from without, could never be sacrificed to God from within, a sacrifice which Weil considered central to atonement and redemption. Aside from these few articles, the bulk of her work was collected from her notebooks by Perrin and Thibon and published posthumously. Of these works, only the essay *L'enracinement (The Need for Roots)* was prepared by Weil for publication. Composed in response to a request by French Resistance workers to write an essay on her perception of the causes for France's capitulation to Germany in 1940, *The Need for Roots* contends that spiritual decay among the French people left nothing but a superficial patriotism to defend France against Germany. Weil suggested a radical restructuring of French society based on a work ethic that stressed personal responsibilities rather than rights, corrected injustices to workers, and abolished political parties and centralized government. The rest of Weil's published works are selections from her notebooks, letters, and articles.

Although Weil's philosophy was not systematic and did not follow the structure of philosophical argument, several concepts recur and are crucial to an understanding of her thought. One of Weil's most basic tenets was the necessity of destroying the self in imitation of Christ's self-sacrifice in the Crucifixion. In Weil's religious philosophy, God had first abandoned the universe in the act of creating it, and with the incarnation of himself into the person of Jesus Christ, he made it possible for humanity to come to him. Weil did not, however, regard the crucifixion of Christ as a substitutionary sacrifice for humankind, but rather as a model for people to follow. Weil's philosophy centers on the abandonment of God by God, signified by Christ's cry, "My God, My God, why hast Thou forsaken Me?" Weil felt that it was at such a point of total abandonment, when one experiences the utter absence of God, that one must continue to love devoid of an object of love in order for redemption to become accessible. This redemption depends on the destruction of the self, sacrificing the will to God in order to be reunited with him. Since only God is uncorrupted and thus worthy of perfect love, according to Weil, he loves us insofar as we become a clear channel through which he can love himself. The self must be destroyed in order for the individual to become that clear channel. This view of life implies a Manichean duality, one that Weil expressed by the tension between "gravity" and "grace." All of the physical universe is drawn downward by gravity, or necessity, an unmitigated

evil according to Weil. Physical laws illustrate the conspicuous absence of God, as well as the inherent evil of everything on the material plane, and no effort within this plane can bring a person nearer to God. One must simply wait for a visitation of grace, as God manifests himself to the waiting soul and lifts it to himself.

Another basic precept of Weil's thought is that elements of Christian faith, including the possibility of salvation, exist to some degree in all religious systems, and had existed even in myths which long predate the birth of Christ. Weil found prefigurations of Christianity among many ancient religions, and particularly among those of the ancient Greeks. The *Iliad*, Plato, and the drama of Aeschylus and Sophocles seemed to her of the highest inspiration. It was the rejection by the Catholic Church of the validity of other religions, which thus excluded many people from the ranks of the redeemed, that kept Weil from accepting baptism. She felt that the Church had inherited too many of the traditions of Rome and Israel, civilizations which she unequivocally attacked. Rome she felt to be as horrific in its cruelty as Nazi Germany; the Jews she condemned for their fierce nationalism, charging that they did nothing but exterminate other peoples until they were themselves conquered by the Babylonian Empire. She also rejected the Old Testament as spiritually uninspired.

Criticism of Weil has taken three principal approaches to her life and writing. As her work was first being published during the 1950s, critical discussion centered on Weil's objections to the Catholic Church. The tendency was either to accept Weil as an unbaptized saint, or at least as a person with great spiritual enlightenment, or to reject her as having compassionate and brilliant, but ultimately heretical, ideas. Eventually she received cautious acceptance by Catholic critics, though not as one who should be followed as a spiritual or intellectual model. A second approach tended to ignore questions of orthodoxy in favor of interpretations of various aspects of Weil's thought. Often critics tried to identify consistent threads throughout her apparently contradictory and often paradoxical statements. This was difficult, partly because Weil felt that the pursuit of transcendent truths required expression in the form of paradoxes, and partly because Weil never ceased her intense self-questioning, always reexamining earlier beliefs. More recently, some critics are reevaluating her influence, pointing out the impracticability of her utopian vision and dispelling what they consider a falsely mythic perception of her life, one which interferes with objective criticism. These critics point out that her reported self-denial at an early age was not uncommon for French children during the First World War and was encouraged by parents, and that her highly touted experiences as a laborer lasted less than six months, cumulatively. Her extreme anti-Semitism has been attacked as well, a portion of her thought that has often been ignored by Weil's defenders. Nevertheless, most critics concede that she demonstrated frequently penetrating insight and an unquestionable integrity in all of her writings.

Although there has been much dissent and controversy surrounding her work, Weil is regarded among the most important contributors to modern religious thought. She combined a most profound faith with intellectual skepticism, an intense love for the Catholic Church with criticism of its doctrines and practices, a deep compassion toward the suffering of others with indifference toward her own suffering, and a logical mind with a mystical spirit. Few have been able to so successfully challenge orthodox belief and make so honest an attempt to revive the original ideals of that belief. As both apologist and critic, Weil is one of the most influential Christian philosophers of the twentieth century.

PRINCIPAL WORKS

"L'Iliade; ou, Le poème de la force" [as Emile Novis] (essay) 1940; published in journal *Cahiers du Sud* ["The *Iliad;* or, The Poem of Force" published in journal *Politics*, 1945]

La pesanteur et la grâce (essays) 1947 [*Gravity and Grace*, 1952]

L'enracinement (essay) 1949 [*The Need for Roots*, 1952]

L'attente de Dieu (letters and essays) 1950 [*Waiting for God*, 1951]

La connaissance surnaturelle (notebooks) 1950 [*New York Notebook* and *London Notebook* published in *First and Last Notebooks*, 1970]

La condition ouvrière (essays) 1951

Les intuitions pré-chrétiennes (essays) 1951

Lettre à un religieux (letter) 1951 [*Letter to a Priest*, 1953]

Cahiers. 3 vols. (notebooks) 1951-56 [*The Notebooks of Simone Weil* (partial translation), 1956]

La source grecque (essays) 1953

Oppression et liberté (essays) 1955 [*Oppression and Liberty*, 1958]

Venise sauvée (drama) [first publication] 1955

Ecrits de Londres et dernieres lettres (essays and letters) 1957

*Intimations of Christianity (essays) 1957

Leçons de philosophie de Simone Weil (lectures) 1959 [*Lectures on Philosophy*, 1978]

Ecrits historiques et politiques (essays) 1960

Pensées sans ordre concernant l'amour de Dieu (aphorisms) 1962

Sur la science (essays) 1965

Poèmes, suivis de "Venise sauvée" (poetry and drama) 1968

First and Last Notebooks (notebooks) 1970

**This work is composed of translated selections from *La source grecque* and *Les intuitions pré-chrétiennes*.

GUSTAVE THIBON (essay date 1947)

[*Thibon was a French Catholic writer and philosopher who knew Weil during her life and, with J. M. Perrin, edited and published selections from her notebooks after her death. In the following excerpt from his preface to* Gravity and Grace, *translated from the 1947 French edition, Thibon offers a personal evaluation of Weil's thought and warns against an unqualified condemnation or affirmation of her work as a whole.*]

I am a Catholic, Simone Weil was not. I have never doubted for a second that she was infinitely more advanced than I am in the experimental knowledge of supernatural truths, but outwardly she always remained on the borders of the Church and was never baptized. One of the last letters she wrote me shows very clearly her attitude with regard to Catholicism: "At this moment I should be more ready to die for the Church, if one day before long it should need anyone to die for it, than I

should be to enter it. To die does not commit one to anything, if one can say such a thing; it does not contain anything in the nature of a lie. . . . At present I have the impression that I am lying, whatever I do, whether it be by remaining outside the Church or by entering it. The question is to know where there is less of a lie. . . ." As to whether Simone Weil was a heroic lover of Jesus Christ, my conviction has never changed; all the same her doctrine, though it is within the orbit of the great Christian truths, contains nothing specifically Catholic and she never accepted the universal authority of the Church. Now a Catholic who has to assess the thought of a non-Catholic has difficulty in avoiding two opposite extremes. The first consists of applying the principles of speculative theology to the thought in question and mercilessly condemning everything which, seen from outside, does not appear to be strictly orthodox. This method has the advantage of railings, which are always necessary on the bridges leading to God, but used without understanding or love, it is in danger of degenerating into an abuse of the evangelical precept: "If thine eye offend thee. . . ." For my part, as I am neither a theologian nor specially entrusted with the defense of the deposit of Christian faith, I do not feel myself in any way qualified for such an undertaking. The last thing I want to do is to set myself up as an official theologian who, armed with a sort of Baedeker of divine things, presumes to pronounce final judgment on the report, even incomplete, of a heroic explorer. . . . The second danger consists of trying, at whatever cost, to bend the thought one is studying into conformity with Catholic truth. That is a manifest abuse of the text, "Compel them to come in." We think that whatever is true or pure in a human life or work finds its place naturally in the Catholic synthesis without being forced or twisted in order to do so. We have no need to grasp everything for ourselves like a miser trying to increase his treasure, for everything already belongs to us who belong to Christ. . . .

It is not for me to decide how far the ideas of Simone Weil are or are not orthodox. I will confine myself to showing—on purely personal evidence—how far a Christian can interpret these ideas in order to find nourishment for his spiritual life.

I shall be particularly careful not to pick a quarrel with Simone Weil about words. Her vocabulary is that of the mystics and not of the speculative theologians: it does not seek to express the eternal order of being but the actual journey of the soul in search of God. This is the case with all spiritual writers. When in the *Dialogue* of St. Catherine of Siena Christ says to her, "I am that which is, thou art that which is not," this formula which reduces the creature to pure nothingness cannot be accepted on the plane of ontological knowledge. It is the same with the expressions used by so many mystics who speak of the poverty of God, of his dependence in relation to the creature, etc.: they are true in the order of love, and false in the order of being. Jacques Maritain was the first to show, with perfect metaphysical precision, that these two vocabularies do not contradict each other, for one is related to speculative and the other to practical and affective knowledge.

Two things in particular in Simone Weil's work have shocked the few friends to whom we have shown her manuscripts. First, the absolute division which she seems to establish between the created world and a transcendent God, who has tied his own hands in the presence of evil and who abandons the universe to the sport of chance and absurdity: there is a danger lest this clean cut should lead to the elimination of the idea of Providence in history and of the notion of progress, and as a result to a misunderstanding of the values and duties of this present world. In the second place, her fear of the social element is likely to lead to the isolation of the individual in a proud self-sufficiency.

We repeat that Simone Weil speaks as a mystic and not as a metaphysician. We are prepared to admit, and we do so readily, that the tendency of her genius, which inclines her constantly to stress the irreducible nature of supernatural reality, often leads her to overlook the meeting places and transitional stages between nature and grace. Nothing is more certain than that she has misunderstood certain aspects of Christian piety. But that does not authorize us to assert that the aspect she describes is not Christian. No human experience—if we except that of Christ—has ever embraced supernatural truth in its totality. St. John of the Cross, for instance, does not emphasize the same divine realities as St. Bonaventura. There are several schools of spirituality, and if we substitute the word "God" for "world," we can say of the mystics what the poet said of men in general:

> Dass jeder sieht die Welt in seinem Sinn
> Und jeder siehet recht, so viel ist Sinn darin!

If, as the Gospel says, there are many mansions in heaven, there are also many roads which lead to heaven.

Simone Weil chose the negative road: "There are people for whom everything is salutary here below, which brings God nearer; for me it is everything that keeps him at a distance." Is not this royal road of salvation, which consists of finding and loving God in what is absolutely other than God (the blind necessity of nothingness and evil . . .), strangely like the bare mountain of Carmel where man has as his guide just one single word: nothing? And does St. John of the Cross speak in less absolute terms of the nothingness of created things and of the love which binds us to them? "The entire being of the creatures compared with the infinite being of God is nothing, and thus the soul, which is a prisoner of what is created, is nothing. All the beauty of creatures is supreme ugliness before the infinite beauty of God. All the grace, all the charm of creatures is insipid and repulsive before the divine beauty. All the goodness the creatures contain is only the height of malice when it is in the presence of divine goodness. Only God is good. . . ."

Moreover, though the theology of Simone Weil rejects the idea of popular imagination, of a God who governs the world like the father of a family or a temporal sovereign, it does not in any way exclude the action of Providence in the higher sense of the word. There is no doubt that here below matter and evil exercise "all the causality which belongs to them"; the spectacle of the innumerable horrors of history is enough to prove that the kingdom of God is not of this world. (Does not Scripture describe the devil as the prince of this world?) Nevertheless, God remains mysteriously present in creation: without in any way changing the calamities which weigh upon us, his grace plays upon the laws of gravity like the sun's rays in the clouds. This God "who is silent in his love" is not indifferent to human misery after the manner of the God of Aristotle or Spinoza. It is out of love for his creature that he appears to efface himself from creation; it is in order to lead him on to the supreme purity that he leaves him to cross the whole expanse of suffering and darkness, abandoned and alone. In tying his own hands in the presence of evil, in stripping himself of everything which resembles earthly power and prestige, God invites men to love nothing but love in him. "He gives himself to men either as powerful or as perfect—it is for them to choose." But here below infinite perfection is infinite weak-

ness: God, in so far as he is love, hangs wholly and entirely on the Cross. . . .

Simone Weil is not in any way mistaken about the dignity and necessity of temporal values. She sees them as intermediaries—*metaxu*—between the soul and God. "What is it a sacrilege to destroy? Not that which is base, for that is of no importance. Not that which is high, for we cannot touch that. The *metaxu*. The *metaxu* form the region of good and evil. . . . No human being should be deprived of these *metaxu*, that is to say of those relative and mixed good things (home, country, traditions, culture, etc.) which warm and nourish the soul and without which, short of sainthood, a human life is not possible." But these relative and mixed good things can only be treated as such by those who, out of love for God, have passed through the total stripping; all others make them more or less into idols: "Only he who loves God with a supernatural love can see means simply as means."

Whatever she may have said about "choice, a notion of a low level" and about the absolute fruitlessness of voluntary action in the spiritual domain, Simone Weil does not, for all that, fall into quietism. On the contrary she constantly recalls that without strict diligence in our practice of the natural virtues, mystical life can be nothing but an illusion. The *cause* of grace dwells outside man, but its *condition* is within him. Simone Weil's hatred for illusion, above all when it takes the form of sensible devotion and a kind of religious "*Schwärmerei*," counterbalances everything which in so purified a spirituality might flatter the imagination or the pride. She liked to repeat, after St. John of the Cross, that inspiration which leads us to neglect the accomplishment of simple and lowly obligations does not come from God. "Duty is given us in order to kill the self. . . . We only attain to real prayer after we have worn down our own will by keeping rules."

She regarded with such suspicion any religious exaltation unsupported by a strict fidelity to the daily task, that the infrequent negligences of which she was guilty in the accomplishment of her duties—largely as a result of her delicate health—caused her to have bitter doubts about the truth of her spiritual vocation. "All these mystical phenomena," she wrote at the end of her life, with heart-rending humility, "are absolutely beyond me. I do not understand them. They are meant for beings who, to start with, possess the elementary moral virtues. I speak of them at random. And I am not even capable of telling myself sincerely that I speak of them at random."

Fully sharing the political ideas of Simone Weil as I do, I think it more becoming that I should not dwell on them at great length. Any other person but myself might make something very moving out of the story of this life in which, through the influence of reflection and faith, an essentially revolutionary temperament was gradually impregnated with the cult of tradition and the past. For Simone Weil never ceased to be a revolutionary. She was not, however, pledged to a chimerical future leading men away from reality, but devoted herself more and more to revolution in the name of an unchanging and eternal principle—a principle which has to be constantly re-established because it constantly tends to be degraded by time. Simone Weil did not believe in an indefinite perfecting of humanity: she even thought that the unfolding of history gave proof of the law of entropy rather than that of unlimited progress after the style of Condorcet. There is no need to defend her on this point. I do not see how it can be heretical to hold (in conformity with the great Greek tradition) that "change cannot be anything but limited and cyclic." As for her invectives against the "social Beast,'' however excessive a form they may sometimes take, we only have to put them back into their context in order to be assured that they do not in any way constitute an apology for anarchy. ''The social order,'' she writes, ''is irreducibly that of the prince of this world. Our only duty with regard to the social is to try to limit the evil of it. . . . Something of the social labeled divine; an intoxicating mixture which brings about every sort of license—the devil disguised.'' But she adds immediately: ''And yet what about a city? But that is not of the social order—it is a human environment of which we are no more conscious than of the air we breathe—a contact with nature, the past, tradition. A man's roots are not of the social order.'' In other words, social influence is both food and poison. It is food in so far as it provides the individual with the inner equipment necessary for living as a man and for approaching God; poison, in so far as it tends to rob him of his liberty and to take God's place. The perpetual encroachments of the social order upon the divine—that incessant degradation of mystical conceptions into politics—afford strong enough evidence, today more than ever, of the seriousness of this last danger.

Mutatis mutandis, the same remarks are applicable to the Church. Obviously a spirit so hungering for the absolute as was that of Simone Weil would necessarily be somewhat lacking in a sense of historical relativity: the words *nolite conformari huic a seculo* [''be not conformed to this world''] were for her a commandment allowing of no reservations. She found it very hard to understand that certain concessions of the Church to temporal exigencies did not in any way involve its eternal soul: The beatification of Charlemagne, for instance, seemed to her a scandalous compromise with the social idol. Somewhere she speaks of the Church as ''a great totalitarian beast.'' What does that signify? Totalitarianism is characterized at the same time by a refusal of the all and by the claim to be all. As the Catholic Church is the messenger of the All here below it does not need to be totalitarian. The accusation made by Simone Weil, in so far as it is well founded, can therefore only be applicable to certain members of the body of the Church who arbitrarily bolt the doors of love and truth, thus failing to understand the universal vocation of Catholicism. There is no question of reopening here—especially at a time when so many Catholics do not hesitate to provide whips with which to beat their Master—the discussions formerly caused by the idea of ''the Church as a body marked by sin.'' We will only state that when Christ said that ''the gates of hell should not prevail,'' he did not promise that everything in the Church would remain eternally pure, but that the essential deposit of faith would be saved, come what might. The Church is rooted in God: that does not exclude the possibility that the tree may bear dried up or worm-eaten branches. To have faith is to believe that the divine sap will never fail. The preservation of this ''incorruptible core of truth,'' to use the actual expression of Simone Weil, in the midst of all the impurities mixed into the body of the Church, constitutes, moreover, one of the strongest proofs of the divinity of Catholicism. The Church could only become a ''great totalitarian beast'' in so far as its human body were totally separated from its divine soul. This is an impossible hypothesis for the gates of hell shall never prevail. . . . Today it is seen as the last refuge of the universal faced with rampant totalitarianisms.

Thus with Simone Weil the expulsion of the social idol does not lead to religious individualism. ''The self and the social are the two great idols.'' Grace saves from the one as from the other. That is doubtless what Célestin Bouglé was trying

to express in his own manner when he saw in Simone Weil while she was still a student ''a mixture of anarchist and cleric. . . .''

Simone Weil can only be understood on the level from which she speaks. Her work is addressed to souls who, if they are not stripped as naked as her own, have at least kept deep within them an aspiration for that pure goodness to which she devoted her life and her death. I am not unaware of the dangers of a spirituality such as hers. The worst forms of giddiness are caused by the highest summits. But the fact that light may burn us is not a valid reason for leaving it under a bushel.

It is not a question of philosophy here but of life. Far from claiming to set up a personal system, Simone Weil strove with all her power to keep herself out of her work. Her one wish was to avoid getting in the way between God and men—to disappear ''so that the Creator and the creature could exchange their secrets.'' She cared nothing for her genius, knowing only too well that true greatness consists in learning to be nothing. (pp. 32-42)

> *Gustave Thibon, in an introduction to* Gravity and Grace *by Simone Weil, translated by Arthur Wills, G. P. Putnam's Sons, 1952, pp. 3-43.*

GABRIEL MARCEL   (essay date 1949)

[*Marcel was a French philosopher, dramatist, and critic who is generally described as a ''Christian Existentialist.'' Like atheist philosophers of the Existential school, such as Jean Paul Sartre and Albert Camus, Marcel saw the loneliness of the individual as central to human suffering, but unlike them he did not accept this loneliness as irremediable, nor did he accept the idea of an absurd universe without absolute meaning. Instead he believed that personal alienation could be transcended by the grace of God and through fully realized human relationships. Marcel felt that experiences involving faith, hope, and love which occur as a result of two people revealing themselves to each other unreservedly would lead to a true knowledge of God. In the following excerpt, Marcel is largely critical of Weil's religious convictions and concepts.*]

[*Gravity and Grace*] created no great stir when it first appeared, but it has made its way to all parts of the world. . . . A writer such as François Mauriac does not disguise his admiration for the book; a high destiny is undoubtedly in store for it. It is certainly the most ''non-conformist'' book ever written! Simone Weil was a Jewess and integrally so; but she is very far from sparing her co-religionists. ''Israel,'' she wrote, ''it is utterly horrible and made foul—one would say, deliberately—ever since Abraham, inclusively (well, save for a few prophets). As though to proclaim as clearly as possible—''Give heed! *That* is where evil is! Nation elect to be blinded! elect to be the executioner of Christ!'' And, a little further on, ''The Jews, that little handful of uprooted men, have been responsible for the uprooting of the whole round world. Their role, so far as Christianity is concerned, has been to root up Christendom from the whole of its own past. . . . The tendency of the Enlightenment, 1789, secularism, etc. . . . has increased immeasurably this uprooting by means of the myth of 'progress.' And an uprooted Europe has uprooted the rest of the world by its colonial conquests. Capitalism, totalitarianism are part and parcel of this uprooting movement. And anti-semitism inevitably propagates the influence of the Jews.''

There are grounds for thinking that Simone Weil, when she left Europe, was not without sympathy for Communism: but she was going to have her eyes opened as to what Communism in fact became, and would express herself about that, too, without the least hesitation. In Plato's footsteps (see *The Republic* bk. vi), she proceeded to denounce the Great Beast as "the only real idol; the only *ersatz* of God, the only imitation of That which is both my self and infinitely distant from my self." Moreover she inherited from her master, the moralist writer Alain, an invincible distrust of power, whatever it might be, and no matter who possessed it. "Always regard men in power as dangerous *things:* retire within yourself so far as you can without despising yourself. And if, one day, you see that you must either play the coward or go and crash yourself up against their power, you must regard yourself as conquered by the nature of things and not by men. One can be imprisoned or enchained; but one can also be stricken with blindness or paralysis—it makes no difference." Possibly we would not misinterpret Simone Weil if we said that in her eyes power is a principle of interior mental collapse: that it ultimately tends to drive him who possesses it into madness, and thus runs the risk of making him lose precisely what makes him human. The only way to preserve your dignity when you are the victim of violence, is to consider the man in power as a *thing.* But the discredit which she considers inseparable from the being the man in power, weighs also on the *social fact* as such. "Only one thing, *here below,* can be accepted as an end, for it is indeed in some sense transcendent so far as the human person goes: the collectivity." But what follows shows as clearly as possible that the "transcendence" spoken of here is a false and evil one, just as, for Hegel, there exists an evil Infinite. "The 'collectivity' is the object of every idolatry; that is what chains us to the earth. . . . 'Society' is invincibly the dominion of the Prince of this world. The only duty that is ours, so far as 'society' goes, is to limit its evil effects. (Richelieu said: 'The well-being of the State is a this-worldly affair.')"

This might tempt us to think that Simone Weil was strictly an individualist. Would that be just? No; for evidently in her perspective this word could bear no exact meaning, and this becomes clear when we see how she treats the "I." "We possess nothing in this world—for chance can strip us of everything else—save the power of saying 'I.' And that is what we must give to God—that is what we must destroy. Quite definitely, no other free act is allowed us save the destruction of one's 'I.'" These are sentences so tragic as to appal us; words written in blood. "Nothing in the world can take from us the power of saying 'I.' Nothing save the uttermost disaster, and nothing is worse than that uttermost disaster that destroys the 'I' by some outside force—for then one can no more destroy it for oneself." When this destruction is in fact produced by some exterior force, it produces within us a violent indignation. "But if one denies to oneself this indignation for the love of God, then the destruction of one's 'I' is not caused from without but from within." I think that we can fairly say that there is noticeable here a *transposition* of the great Christian principle that there is an affinity between Grace and the Cross—provided that I fully recognize the freedom of my act in taking up my cross and carrying it. Simone Weil would certainly refuse to admit—and would be right in doing so—that suffering even when extreme has value which is spiritual as such. Everything depends on the spirit *in which* the suffering is endured. "In hours of disaster," she admirably well writes, "our vital instinct survives the severing of our attachments and twines itself blindly round anything that can serve it as support, as a plant grips hold with its tendrils. . . . From this point of view disaster is always hideous, as life stripped naked always is, as a stump is, as the swarming of insects is. Life without form. There,

survival is the only attachment left—having no other object than itself—a Hell!"

It would seem to be no exaggeration to say that such phrases reveal a mental attitude which is hard enough to define, but which really amounts to a genuine hatred for existence as such. And then the problem consists in how Simone Weil can harmonize such an attitude with her belief in God—I hardly dare say in God the Creator, for I gravely doubt whether in her case those words can receive the meaning which Christianity assigns to them. But one can say that the whole of her mentality is under the domination of two opposing forces—grace, and the "down-drag" (*pesanteur*). "Every natural movement of the soul is controlled by laws analogous to those of material *weight.* Grace alone is an exception." But what exactly must one understand by this "weight" or down-drag? There is, in actual fact, a "human mechanic." Thus "anyone who suffers tries to communicate his suffering to another—either by ill-treating him, or by provoking him to pity—in order to lessen his own pain, and he does in fact so lessen it. But as for the man who has sunk to the deepest depths—who has no one to be sorry for him and who has not the power to hurt anyone—if he has no children and no one who loves him—ah! his suffering remains shut up within him and poisons him." Nor will Simone Weil deny—admirable sincerity!—that this tendency to extend one's torment out beyond oneself, is to be discovered still in the bottom of her own heart. "Living beings, and things, are not sacred enough to me: may I not filthy anything, when I shall have been wholly transformed into mire!" And she adds what seems to probe deep: "If one is so feeble that one can arouse no pity nor do any harm to anyone, well, one does do harm to the inward picture of the universe in oneself." We might at first be tempted to discern some sonorous echo of Spinoza in this kind of dialectic of suffering and abasement; but perhaps the analogy would be rather superficial. In Spinoza, the tendency of Being to persevere *as* Being presents itself as something indisputably and metaphysically true, but Simone Weil would certainly be strongly tempted to refuse such a quality in Being. Between her and Spinoza there was Schopenhauer, though perhaps he did not directly influence the author of "Grace and the Down-drag": it seems fairly clear, in fact, that she would have detected in him a sort of intellectual dilettantism. It is perfectly patent that the sense of man's wretchedness and that of the whole world takes precedence, in her, over any perception of creation in its beauty and glory, though she was far from insensitive to that beauty if not to that glory. But one has the impression that she did not recognize in herself any right to appreciate it in full freedom so long as so many of her fellow-men remained fettered and in tears. It seems to me perfectly impossible to form a true estimate of her mind unless one recognizes in it as something quite fundamental this "bias"—the sense of fraternity which in no way interfered with that clear sight of hers that at times one might almost feel implacable.

Grace is what sets itself in opposition to this dead mechanical force that Simone Weil calls *pesanteur* or the "down-drag." "Extinction of Desire (as in Buddhism); detachment; *amor fati*—or the desire for the Absolute Good—it always comes to the same thing: the emptying out of desire; the finite-ism of all 'contents'; desire without an object; desire without wishing. Detaching our desire from all 'goods' and then waiting. Experience proves that the void of this 'waiting' is filled: and then one is in contact with the Absolute Good." And elsewhere: "Renunciation: to imitate God's own renunciation in creating: there is a sense in which God renounces being All. We must

renounce being 'something.' That is our only 'good'. . . ."
"We possess only what we renounce; what we do not renounce, escapes us. In this sense one cannot possess anything save by way of God."

But had Simone Weil a truly clear idea of God? In spite of everything, we may doubt it. One cannot help feeling that she wavers between a notion which is still fairly close to Spinoza's and a definitely Christian one. In illustration of the former point I quote, for instance, the following: "At every moment, our existence is the love of God for us. But God can love only Himself; so His love of us is love for Himself through the *medium* of ourselves. So He who gives us being loves in us our consent to not-be." I confess to finding it difficult, from a Christian standpoint, to admit these two phrases. . . . God can love only Himself: His love for us is love for Himself through the medium of ourselves. At the heart of the Christian mystery, do we not meet with something that—in our poor human language—we can interpret only as the Will to proceed forth from Self, to create some non-Self in order to love it? To say that God can love only Himself is to go counter to the meaning of creation understood according to its deepest values; in fact to transform it into a bad joke. Other statements may be found elsewhere, as I have indicated, which seem much nearer to Christianity grasped in its essential bearing. One cannot but acknowledge, however, a certain lack of prudence in Simone Weil, a certain lack of moderation in her expression of the highest truths. Without going so far as to say that she

Weil in uniform of Confederación Nacional del Trabajo *during the Spanish Civil War. From* Simone Weil: A Fellowship in Love, *by Jacques Cabaud. Channel Press, 1964.*

was formally heretical, I should be inclined to say that she was constantly on the fringe of heresy; and that, in certain quite essential matters she uses expressions that a believer can but reject with a sort of horror. I will quote two examples. Here, to begin with, is a passage where it is rather the wording itself which jars on us and shocks us; the roots of her thought may be regarded as outside of criticism. "Inflexible necessity, destitution, distress, the crushing weight of poverty and of exhausting labour, cruelty, torture, violent death, brute force submitted to, terror, sicknesses—all is the divine love; it is God withdrawing Himself from us so that we may love Him. For were we exposed to the direct rays of His love, without the overshadowing of space, time and matter, we would evaporate like water under the sun; there would not be enough 'I' in us to sacrifice that 'I' through love. Necessity is the screen placed between God and ourselves to enable us to subsist. It is for us to pierce that screen so as to cease to *be*." I say that it is not prudent to express oneself like that; for such a way of speaking can but arouse a hatred for God in anyone who has not yet attained to the apex of mysticism. If the love of God is cruelty, torture, violent death, etc., may we be preserved from any such form of loving! One might suppose that we had been reading a thing written in jest. But I think a real metaphysical error lurked in the very form of words. It may be true to say that horror lays the soul bare and renders it, consequently, capable of grasping a reality which never would have got through to it if denudation had been spared it. But this certainly does not allow us to say that horror *is* the divine love. Much more delicate distinctions are here demanded which only a subtle theology could exhibit; these alone would avoid the unpleasant shock that the passage I have quoted would inflict upon a sensitive mind. But what seems to me much graver still is Simone's way of speaking about immortality. Here again there is the intrusion of a totally Spinozist way of thinking and of condemning the imagination. "We must set aside all beliefs that seek to fill the void, which sweeten what is bitter; belief in immortality; belief in the utility of sins—*etiam peccata;* belief in the providential ordering of events—in short, the *consolations* that men usually seek in religion." Elsewhere she says that "belief in immortality is harmful because it is not within our power to represent the soul to our mind as truly incorporeal. Such a belief is, then, really a belief in life simply *going on,* and it prevents our making any use of death." How fail to find grounds for anxiety in such formulas? How not detect in them a certain being in love with death which is radically incompatible with Christianity undefiled and true? "To love truth," she writes, "means to endure the void and consequently to accept death. *Truth is on the side of death.*" The italics are my own; and it is in those last words that I feel we find, seeping up in spite of all, the element in Simone Weil's spirituality which most demands that we should be on our guard. "There are those for whom everything, here below, which brings them nearer God, is helpful: for me, it is all that takes us further away from Him." This avowal is moving and beyond words revealing. It enables us to understand how Simone Weil could write in her paradoxical way that "the complete absence of mercy upon earth is itself a witness to divine mercy." But such a statement, however much it rends and pierces the heart, does not "ring Catholic"—and of course I am here taking the word "catholic" in its etymological sense of "universal." It is impossible not to turn back, for our necessary succour, to Claudel (I do not think Simone Weil liked him) and beg him to let us listen to the all-inclusive music of his mighty organ which alone can genuinely integrate the pathetic, agonizing voice of this partially de-judaised Jewess, so refractory to hope—with that patience which humanity owes to its own self. (pp. 12-18)

Gabriel Marcel, "Simone Weil," *in* The Month, *n.s. Vol. II, No. 1, July, 1949, pp. 9-18.*

G. L. ARNOLD (essay date 1950-51)

[*Arnold was a German social historian and critic. In the following excerpt, he discusses Weil's social and political thought as set forth in* The Need for Roots.]

A candid attempt to assess the significance of Simone Weil's thought must start from the admission that her work is too fragmentary to bear the weight of specialist criticism. It belongs to the class of utterances which draw their effect from the production of a kind of shock upon the reader. This is true even of *L'Enracinement,* her most considerable piece of work and the only one that approaches systematic form. Although largely concerned with the causes of the French collapse in 1940, it is an essay on morals—even on metaphysics—as much as an attempt at analysis. Historical and psychological insights, often of astonishing force and brilliance, are scattered throughout its 250 pages, but the emphasis is upon the moral choice before the individual rather than upon the functioning of society. Simone Weil is a moralist in the classic French tradition, the last of a great line which begins at the opening of the modern era and has ever since produced an unbroken succession of writers concerned with the whole duty of man towards eternity and his fellow-beings. Her tone, moreover, is almost as polemical as that of Péguy (whom she resembles in more than one respect), and her emphasis, where she deals with public matters, is commonly upon the moral and intellectual degradation of the élite which led France to destruction in 1940. It will scarcely be supposed that the literary product of this relentless quest for the sources of material disaster and spiritual corruption is of the kind which is commonly preferred in this country—a careful weighing of arguments and a tolerant attempt to be fair to all concerned. It must also be conceded to the critics, who have already made their voices heard, that there are occasions when she comes close to absurdity, e.g. in proposing that newspapers (as distinct from periodicals) should be forbidden to put forward any kind of editorial opinion, lest the reading public continue to be benumbed by paid propagandists; or in suggesting that special tribunals should watch over the factual truth of everything asserted in print. It may or may not be desirable that some means should be found to bring gross errors to the notice of the public. But when the argument is pushed to the point of suggesting that anyone should have the right to arraign e.g. M. Maritain for having overlooked the existence of those Greek thinkers who, unlike Aristotle, condemned the institution of slavery—it becomes plain that what is proposed is not merely objectionable but impossible. Or to take another instance, the suggestion that political parties in their present form should not be tolerated is frankly utopian and fundamentally undemocratic as well, even when backed by the unimpeachable argument that all modern mass organizations are potentially totalitarian. The tendency of these and similar arguments, scattered throughout the first part of *L'Enracinement,* is towards a sort of idealized 'Christian corporatism', of which it is sufficient to say that whatever the intentions of its more democratic proponents, its practical application so far has resulted either in the grotesqueries of the Dollfuss-Schuschnigg régime, or in frankly provisional and makeshift institutions such as those of Portugal under Salazar. Neither, incidentally, is mentioned by Simone Weil and the whole direction of her thought is towards something far more closely in tune with the historic traditions of French socialism, notably as represented by Proudhon and the "Fédérés" of 1871. It is, however, not without significance that although passionately attached to the cause of Free France she seems to have contemplated the disappearance of the Third Republic with a good deal of equanimity. Vichy, she thought, was merely profiting from the hopeless corruption of the Republican régime, an opinion undoubtedly shared by many radicals at the time but which led them to underestimate the fundamental attachment of the French people to the self-governing institutions, however eaten-away and discredited, of which in 1940 they suddenly found themselves deprived. In her conviction that the pre-war régime must on no account be permitted to re-establish itself after Vichy's sham-corporate experiments had been swept away, she doubtless reflected the prevailing mood of the resistance movement, or at any rate of its intellectuals. *L'Enracinement* is very much a document of this period of soul-searching, out of which have come so many things, some hopeful, others sterile, which have helped to make the Fourth Republic different from its predecessor. But it is only on the left wing of the M.R.P., among the more radical representatives of "Christian democracy" and "Christian socialism," that her pronouncements are likely to find a ready echo. And these friendly critics will inevitably be the first to note that the all-important question of forging a political instrument for carrying out the proposed institutional changes is hardly considered at all. Simone Weil is indeed weakest on the point on which the practitioners of politics are strongest: she obstinately refuses to face the problem of power. She takes it for granted that some authority or other exists and can be relied upon to decree fundamental changes for which majority consent may not be available. The confusion is not improved by demanding that the central government should abdicate its functions as far as possible in favour of local, regional and professional associations. For, since the workers' movement is explicitly described as unable to effect the necessary changes, the political parties are to be dissolved, and the State itself is to surrender the excessive power it has acquired, no adequate authority is left. We are, it seems, back with the utopians, and it is impossible not to remember that Proudhon, who anticipated much of Simone Weil's political and social programme, left his followers face to face with problems they had never thought of solving, and thus helped to bring on the colossal disaster of the Commune. Even Marx's subsequent declaration that the programme of the Communards, if given a chance, would have regenerated French society and introduced genuine self-government in the place of centralized bureaucracy, cannot alter the fact that the catastrophe was chiefly due to the inability of the "Fédérés" to make use of such authority as they possessed.

L'Enracinement is, however, more than a sketch of a Christian-socialist utopia, with industry decentralized, factories transformed into model institutions, village life ennobled, prostitution abolished, and education directed towards non-utilitarian ends. It contains all this and a good deal besides, e.g. a brilliant thumb-nail sketch of French history and a passionate onslaught on the nationalism of Maurras. But its primary significance is moral. If it fails as a statement of aims, it succeeds as an indictment of the *status quo* and of the intellectuals among its defenders. The indictment, moreover, is delivered not in abstract terms but in the form of a challenge to established values. It is, after all, a fact that France broke down in 1940, and to say that the disaster occurred because 'patriotism is not enough' and Frenchmen had nothing else to fall back upon, is to question some very deep-rooted national traditions. Again, a writer of the resistance movement who does not hesitate to assert that France was the aggressor in 1870, that the defeat of 1940 was deserved, and that the cult of Jeanne d'Arc between the wars was a species of nationalist idolatry designed to take the place of the forgotten Christian religion—is not an everyday phenomenon. Nor is it customary for French writers to denounce the imposition of French culture upon Provençals, Bretons, Flemings, Arabs, Negroes and Malays as spiritual murder. If Simone Weil had written nothing but the pages in *L'Enracinement* which describe the extention of French sovereignty to the provinces south of the Loire a slight tremor must have been caused in the realm of French letters on this account alone. (pp. 330-32)

[Both] the Right and the Left have found it difficult to discover a suitable label for Simone Weil. She has a disconcerting habit of cutting across familiar lines of approach, as when she enlivens an exposition of the socialist faith by rounding upon the Marxists. . . . In this, as well as in her social and moral judgments, she comes closest to Péguy, to whom she has inevitably been compared. But Péguy was orthodox in religion and a nationalist, though of the anti-Maurrassien stripe, in politics. Worst of all from Simone Weil's point of view, he thought highly of the institutions and traditions of classical Rome, for which she entertained an aversion equalled only by her dislike of the Old Testament. It is thus extremely difficult to 'place' her—and that is just why her writings have had such an impact upon young people impatient of the stale dispute between clericals and anti-clericals which has now been going on for more than a century, and eager likewise to break away from the traditional political feuds. There is a puritanical rigour about her judgments which sets her apart from other post-war writers. After pondering her impassioned indictment of the Ancien Régime, of Richelieu and Bossuet and Louis XIV, and then coming upon her half contemptuous, half pitying attitude towards the Enlightenment and the Revolution, one begins to wonder what French intellectual life would have been like if the Reformation had not been aborted. To be an unorthodox Christian in a country neatly split between Catholics and anti-clericals, a Proudhonist socialist in a century of mass organization, a moralist contemptuous of Latinity, and a mystic more attached to Plato and the Upanishads than to the Bible, requires at the very least an unusual capacity for going one's own way. Dr. Inge, one fancies, would approve of her metaphysics. One cannot imagine any French theologian doing so, just as one cannot see any organized body of opinion taking up what might be called her "programme," though some Catholics are probably in sympathy with it. (pp. 333-34)

> *G. L. Arnold, "Simone Weil," in* The Cambridge Journal, *Vol. IV, October, 1950-September, 1951, pp. 323-43.*

GRAHAM GREENE   (essay date 1951)

[*Greene, an English man of letters, is generally considered the most important contemporary Catholic novelist. In his major works, he explores the problems of spiritually and socially alienated individuals living in the corrupt and corrupting societies of the twentieth century. Formerly a book reviewer at the* Spectator, *Greene is also deemed an excellent film critic, a respected biographer, and a shrewd literary critic with a taste for the works of undeservedly neglected authors. In the following excerpt from a 1951 essay, he discusses* Waiting for God, *drawing attention to differences between orthodox Christian belief and Weil's belief.*]

Simone Weil was a young Jewish teacher of philosophy who died in exile from her native France in 1943 at the age of thirty-four. Since that time knowledge of her has spread by word of mouth, like the knowledge of some underground leader in wartime. [*Waiting for God*] is her first book to be published in English, the first message to reach us, though we had known that she had been acclaimed by both Catholics and Protestants in France. We read with excitement as the signals are handed in: contact at last has been made: and with a growing doubt. Here is a moment of vision: this we understand; but this?—surely the message must have been mutilated, for it seems to contradict what went before; and this?—the phrases seem jumbled, they mean little to us.

The most important part of the book, apart from the essay **"Forms of the Implicit Love of God,"** does literally consist of messages, letters written to a Father Perrin, a Dominican in Marseilles, the first three explaining why she is hesitating to be baptized, the last three giving her spiritual autobiography, an account of her intellectual vocation, and her last thoughts before leaving North Africa for England and being finally separated from her spiritual adviser (if one can so call one whose advice was never taken, and who was more often than not the victim of her preaching). It is a great pity that we cannot read Father Perrin's replies. From her references to them we can imagine their careful sympathetic approach to her problems, the vain attempt to guide the wide wash of her mystical thought into a channel where it could increase in depth.

Her abiding concern was her relationship to God and the Church. She had come to believe in the Christian God, in the Incarnation, and the dogmas of the Roman Catholic Church (of its social functions, perhaps naturally, as one who had experienced for some weeks the hardships of the Catalonian front, she remained suspicious), but she had no will to take the next step. She expected God to intervene, to push her into the Church if he so desired. She would not act except under orders. "If it is God's will that I should enter the Church, He will impose this will upon me at the exact moment when I shall have come to deserve that He should so impose it." But how can one deserve without some action, if only of the mind? She pays lip-service occasionally to free-will, but we cannot help feeling that she unduly restricted its scope. There are traces of Gnosticism in her postponement of baptism until she could be certain of perfection. "I think that only those who are above a certain level of spirituality can participate in the sacraments as such. For as long as those who are below this level have not reached it, whatever they may do, they cannot be strictly said to belong to the Church."

It was a strange attitude for a woman who wished ardently to share the labours of the poor, working with broken health in the Renault works, and who in safe England confined herself to the rations of those she had left in France. The Church was for the perfect. She could not see it as a being like herself, anxious to share the sufferings not only of the poor but of the imperfect, even of the vicious. She speaks to us in terms of "abandonment," but her abandonment always stops short of surrender, like a histrionic marble figure caught in a gesture not far removed from pride.

Her claims on our submission to her thought, and on our credulity, too, are vast. She tells us how once when she was reciting George Herbert's poem "Love," "Christ Himself came down and took possession of me," and again, referring to the Our Father, "sometimes also, during this recitation or at other moments, Christ is present with me in person, but His presence is infinitely more real, more moving, more clear than on that first occasion.'' We cannot help comparing this blunt claim with the long painful obscure journey towards the Beatific Vision described by St John of the Cross and St Teresa of Avila. But perhaps the greatest claim she makes is to a kind of universal inclusiveness:

> The degree of intellectual honesty which is obligatory for me, by reason of my particular vocation, demands that my thought should be indifferent to all ideas without exception, including for instance materialism and atheism; it must be equally welcoming and equally reserved with regard to every one of them.

One cannot deny, however, that these claims are sometimes supported by moments of vision: passages of great power and insight capable of drawing many enthusiasts to her side. The essay on Friendship is the most sustained of these passages, but again and again they flash through the contradictions and the muddled thought:

> The outward results of true affliction are nearly always bad. We lie when we try to disguise this. It is in affliction itself that the splendour of God's mercy shines; from its very depths, in the heart of its inconsolable bitterness. If, still persevering in our love, we fall to the point where the soul cannot keep back the cry, ''My God, why hast thou forsaken me?'', if we remain at this point without ceasing to love, we end by touching something which is not affliction, which is not joy; something which is the central essence, necessary and pure; something not of the senses, common to joy and sorrow; something which is the very love of God.

What makes us in the end unwilling to accept her claims? What is it that more often than not distorts her genuine love of truth? Is it that confusion arises first from her pride, and secondly—because she was a woman of great nobility—from the tension and pain in her own mind caused by that possessive demon? She claims too much (St Joan heard rightly when she was told to tell no one of her visions), and sometimes too stridently. She talks of suffering ''atrocious pain'' for others, ''those who are indifferent or unknown to me . . . including those of the most remote ages of antiquity,'' and it is almost as if a comic character from Dickens were speaking. We want to say, ''Don't go so far so quickly. Suffer first for someone you know and love,'' but love in these pages is only a universal love. She strikes out blindly in her personal pain, contradicting herself, allowing herself to believe that an ''infinite'' mercy can be shown in its entirety in a ''finite'' world. She no sooner seizes a truth than she lets it go in the pride of a too startling image. We leave her at the end on the edge of the abyss, digging her feet in, refusing to leap like the common herd (whom she loved in her collective way), demanding that she alone be singled out by a divine hand on her shoulder forcing her to yield. (pp. 372-75)

> *Graham Greene, ''Simone Weil,'' in his* Collected Essays, *The Viking Press, 1969, pp. 372-75.*

LESLIE A. FIEDLER   (essay date 1951)

[*Fiedler is a controversial and provocative American critic. While he has also written novels and short stories, his personal philos-* ophy and insights are thought to be most effectively expressed in his literary criticism. Emphasizing the psychological, sociological, and ethical context of works, Fiedler often views literature as the mirror of a society's consciousness. Similarly, he believes that the conventions and values of a society are powerful determinants of the direction taken by its authors' works. In the following excerpt from his preface to the English translation of Waiting for God, Fiedler discusses the dominant rhetorical devices evident in Weil's writings.]

Simone Weil's writing as a whole is marked by three characteristic devices: extreme statement or paradox; the equilibrium of contradictions; and exposition by myth. As the life of Simone Weil reflects a desire to insist on the absolute even at the risk of being absurd, so her writing tends always toward the extreme statement, the formulation that shocks by its willingness to push to its ultimate conclusion the kind of statement we ordinarily accept with the tacit understanding that no one will take it *too* seriously. The outrageous (from the natural point of view) ethics of Christianity, the paradoxes on which it is based are a scandal to common sense; but we have protected ourselves against them by turning them imperceptibly into platitudes. It is Simone Weil's method to revivify them, by recreating them in all their pristine offensiveness.

''He who gives bread to the famished sufferer for the love of God will not be thanked by Christ. He has already had his reward in this thought itself. Christ thanks those who do not know to whom they are giving food.'' Or ''Ineluctable necessity, misery, distress, the crushing weight of poverty and of work that drains the spirit, cruelty, torture, violent death, constraint, terror, sickness—all these are God's love!'' Or ''Evil is the beautiful obedience of matter to the will of God.''

Sometimes the primary function of her paradoxes is to remind us that we live in a world where the eternal values are reversed; it is as if Simone Weil were bent on proving to us, by our own uncontrollable drawing back from what we most eagerly should accept, that we do not truly believe those things to which we declare allegiance. ''. . . every time I think of the crucifixion of Christ I commit the sin of envy.'' ''Suffering: superiority of man over God. We needed the Incarnation to keep that superiority from becoming a scandal!''

Or sometimes it is our sentimentality that is being attacked, that *ersatz* of true charity which is in fact its worst enemy, ''[Christ] did not however prescribe the abolition of penal justice. He allowed stoning to continue. Wherever it is done with justice, it is therefore he who throws the first stone.'' ''Bread and stone are love. We must eat the bread and lay ourselves open to the stone, so that it may sink as deeply as possible into our flesh.''

Or the paradox may have as its point merely the proving of the *impossibility* of God's justice, the inconsequentiality of virtue and grace. ''A Gregorian chant bears testimony as effectively as the death of a martyr.'' ''. . : a Latin prose or a geometry problem, even though they are done wrong, may be of great service one day, provided we devote the right kind of effort to them. Should the occasion arise, they can one day make us better able to give someone in affliction exactly the help required to save him, at the supreme moment of his need.''

Corresponding to Simone Weil's basic conviction that no widely held belief is utterly devoid of truth is a dialectical method in which she balances against each other contrary propositions, not in order to arrive at a synthesis in terms of a ''golden mean,'' but rather to achieve an equilibrium of truths. ''One must accept all opinions,'' she has written, ''but then arrange them in a vertical order, placing them at appropriate levels.'' Best of all exercises for the finding of truth is the confrontation of statements that seem absolutely to contradict each other. ''Method of investigation—'' Simone Weil once jotted down in a note to herself, ''as soon as one has arrived at any position, try to find in what sense the contrary is true.''

When she is most faithful to this method, her thought is most satisfactory; only where some overwhelming prejudice prevents her from honoring contradictions is she narrow and un-illuminating—as for instance, toward Israel, Rome, Aristotle, or Corneille. These unwitting biases must be distinguished from her deliberate strategic emphases, her desire to ''throw the counterweight'' on the side of a proposition against which popular judgment is almost solidly arrayed; as she does most spectacularly by insisting, in the teeth of our worship of happiness and success, that ''unhappiness'' is the essential road to God, and the supreme evidence of God's love.

One can see her method of equilibrium most purely in her remarks on immortality of the soul, in her consideration of the rival Protestant and Catholic theories of the Eucharist, and especially in her approach to the existence of God. ''A case of contradictories, both of them true. There is a God. There is no God. Where is the problem? I am quite sure that there is a God in the sense that I am sure my love is no illusion. I am quite sure there is no God, in the sense that I am sure there is nothing which resembles what I can conceive when I say that word. . . .''

There are three main factors that converge in Simone Weil's interest in the myth (this is yet another aspect of her thought with which the contemporary reader of Jung and Joyce and Eliot and Mann feels particularly at home): first, there is the example of her master, Plato, who at all the great crises of his thought falls back on the mythic in search of a subtle and total explication; second, there is her own belief in multiple reve-lation, her conviction that the archetypal poetries of people everywhere restate the same truths in different metaphoric lan-guages; and third, there is her sense of myth as the special gospel of the poor, a treasury of insights into the Beauty of the World, which Providence has bestowed on poverty alone, but which, in our uprooted world, the alienated oppressed can no longer decipher for themselves.

To redeem the truths of the myths, they must be ''translated.'' Sometimes this is a relatively simple process of substituting for unfamiliar names, ones that belong to our own system of belief: Zeus is God the Father, Bacchus God the Son; Dionysus and Osiris ''are (in a certain manner) Christ himself.'' In the fragment of Sophocles, Electra is the human soul and Orestes is Christ; but in this latter example we are led, once we have identified the protagonists, to a complex religious truth: as Electra loves the absence of Orestes more than the presence of any other, so must we love God, who is by definition ''ab-sent'' from the material world, more than the ''real,'' present objects that surround us.

In a similar manner, other folk stories and traditional poems can lead toward revelations of fundamental truths: the ''two winged companions'' of an Upanishad, who sit on a single branch, one eating the fruit of the tree, the other looking at it, represent the two portions of the soul: the one that would contemplate the good, the other (like Eve in the Garden) that would consume it. Or the little tailor in Grimm's fairy tale who beats a giant in a throwing contest by hurling into the air a bird rather than a stone teaches us something about the nature

of Grace. And finally, we discover from ''all the great images of folklore and mythology'' what Simone Weil considers to be the truth most necessary to our salvation, namely, ''it is God who seeks man.''

The fate of the world, she knew, is decided out of time; and it is in myth that mankind has recorded its sense of its true history, the eternal ''immobile drama'' of necessity and evil, salvation and grace. (pp. 29-33)

> *Leslie A. Fiedler, in an introduction to* Waiting for God *by Simone Weil, translated by Emma Craufurd, G. P. Putnam's Sons, 1951, pp. 3-39.*

DORIS GRUMBACH   (essay date 1952)

[*Grumbach is an American novelist, critic, and biographer. She is best known for her novel* Chamber Music *(1979), a fictional memoir which depicts aberrant sexual relationships, such as in-cest, lesbianism, and homosexuality, as well as a decidedly fem-inist vision, in elegant, archaic language. Grumbach first received wide critical attention for her controversial biography of novelist Mary McCarthy,* The Company She Kept *(1967), in which she attempted to show that McCarthy's fiction is extremely autobio-graphical. Grumbach's harshest critics considered the book gos-sip-laden and unscholarly, while her defenders praised its bold-ness and, in the words of Granville Hicks, ''Grumbach's refusal to beat around [the] bush.'' Grumbach is a widely respected reviewer who has been a frequent contributor to many periodicals and has been the author of a column on nonfiction for the* New York Times Book Review *since 1976. In the following excerpt, she presents an orthodox Catholic refutation of Weil's religious thought.*]

If [Weil's] life and her writing (as Leslie A. Fiedler says in his acute introduction to *Waiting for God*) speak ''to all of us with special authority, outsider to outsiders, our kind of saint'' what does she say to those who paused, considered, and then entered the Church?

Far from threatening their faith (as Father Reinhold suggests she might), I think she provides us with material for positive statement of our faith, an opportunity we do not often have on Simone Weil's high level. The strength of the reply lies mainly in the nature of the philosophical system she devised; her sys-tem of beliefs was so complete because, for all its seeming universality and pitying humanism, it omitted potent factors which raise the scale on Father Perrin's side.

In all her careful spiritual calculations Simone Weil somehow overlooked (or completely dismissed) the existence and the power of the Devil. To attribute to all acts and all things existent an equal measure of good (because God made them all) is wishfully attractive but realistically untenable. God's will, it would seem, works through us in proportion to the purity of the medium. But God's will is not an absolute agent, simply because He has given us the power to deny it, pervert it, ignore it—or follow it. It is our birthright to do so; unfortunately it is often the occasion of our eternal damnation.

The rejection of God's will is the work of the Prince of Dark-ness, who is the agent of perversity, and of whose existence Simone Weil seemed unaware. The dichotomy which exists in all things; the part that belongs to God and the part that the Devil would retrieve from Him, could not exist under the uni-versality of all values, but in the real world it *does* exist.

It is curious that in all the hundred pages of her autobiography Simone Weil mentions the Devil only twice, once to attribute the social structure of the Church on earth to ''the Prince of this World,'' and again to define her own pride as ''Lucifer-ian.''

If it were true that only good exists on the earth, because the earth is God's, there would indeed be no earthly need for the Church, or for the convert's inner struggles about joining it. All existence would be united in one universal worship. But the Devil works hard and relentlessly to propagate his faith, and the Church exists as a barricade against his tirelessness.

Then, too, I wonder if her concept of will was not defective in the Christian sense. As one reads her beautiful prose one is aware of a certain Hebraic stringency and sternness in her view of God's will and her relational obedience to it. She is even capable of supposing Him to exert it paradoxically: ''If it were conceivable that in obeying God one should bring about one's own damnation while in disobeying Him one could be saved, I should still choose the way of obedience.'' Her ideal was the destruction of all will and the substitution of God's will in her, with nothing of her own personal being remaining, not even the will to desire God more perfectly.

Thomas Merton, in *Seeds of Contemplation*, makes the same point about the true contemplative: ''Less and less conscious of themselves, they finally cease to be aware of themselves doing things, and gradually God begins to do all that they do, in them and for them. . . .''

But Merton's account takes into consideration the contempla-tive's need of a guide or director, and he shows that primarily obedience must be to him. The true humility of the saint is involved in ''a passion for obedience itself and for renunciation of his own will . . . he does not obey his director merely because the commands or the advice given to him seem good or prof-itable and intelligent . . . (or) just because he thinks the abbot makes admirable decisions. . . . Sometimes the decisions of his superior seem to be less wise; but with this he is no longer concerned, because he accepts the superior as mediator between him and God and rests only in the will of God as it comes to him through the men who have been placed over him by the circumstances of his vocation.''

This was the flaw in Simone Weil's ''perfect obedience.'' With almost Protestant pride she refused a mediator. When Father Perrin thought her objections which she had confided to him ''were not incompatible with allegiance to the Church'' she still would not abandon her position. In a most literal sense she awaited *direct* word from God, and would never have admitted that a director could ever have been anything but an interruption in this perfect reception! ''For as to the spiritual direction of my soul I think God *Himself* has taken it in hand from the start. . . .''

Thomas Merton points out that ''the most dangerous man in the world is the contemplative who is guided by nobody. . . . He obeys the attractions of an interior voice but will not listen to other men.'' Simone Weil's danger was not to other men, but to herself because by refusing to listen to all but an ''interior voice'' she laid her decisions open to error. Granting the au-thenticity of the voice, it is possible she may not have under-stood completely the instructions it issued, may not have heard it entirely, or may have thought she heard too much. (pp. 169-70)

Father Reinhold points out that Simone Weil might have been liable to the charge of quietism. (''We do not obtain the most precious gifts by going in search of them but by waiting for them.'') Again the danger of her threshold state is personal.

Can it not be that atrophy sets in when all spiritual ''search'' or activity is abandoned? Those who progress or ''ascend'' (in Merton's graphic term) are in the very least motile. The di-rection they choose (or have chosen for them by their directors) may be erroneous but, this must be true: that any movement is good when it is directed to the soul's salvation, and that all journeys under guidance along all paths to God are good. (p. 171)

Doris Grumbach, ''The Vestibule State of Simone Weil,'' in The Catholic World, *Vol. CLXXV, No. 1047, June, 1952, pp. 166-71.*

T. S. ELIOT (essay date 1952)

[*Perhaps the most influential poet and critic of the first half of the twentieth century, Eliot is closely identified with many of the qualities denoted by the term Modernism: experimentation, formal complexity, artistic and intellectual eclecticism, and a classicist's view of the artist working at an emotional distance from his or her creation. He introduced a number of terms and concepts that strongly affected critical thought in his lifetime, among them the idea that poets must be conscious of the living tradition of liter-ature in order for their work to have artistic and spiritual validity. In general, Eliot upheld values of traditionalism and discipline, and in 1928 he annexed Christian theology to his overall con-servative world view. In the following excerpt, he discusses* The Need for Roots.]

In trying to understand [Simone Weil], we must not be dis-tracted—as is only too likely to happen on a first reading—by considering how far, and at what points, we agree or disagree. We must simply expose ourselves to the personality of a woman of genius, of a kind of genius akin to that of the saints.

Perhaps ''genius'' is not the right word. The only priest with whom she ever discussed her belief and her doubts has said, *''Je crois que son âme est incomparablement plus haute que son génie.''* That is another way of indicating that our first experience of Simone Weil should not be expressible in terms of approval or dissent. I cannot conceive of anybody's agreeing with all of her views, or of not disagreeing violently with some of them. But agreement and rejection are secondary: what mat-ters is to make contact with a great soul. Simone Weil was one who might have become a saint. Like some who have achieved this state, she had greater obstacles to overcome, as well as greater strength for overcoming them, than the rest of us. A potential saint can be a very difficult person: I suspect that Simone Weil could be at times insupportable. One is struck, here and there, by a contrast between an almost superhuman humility and what appears to be an almost outrageous arro-gance. There is a significant sentence by the French priest whom I have already quoted. He reports that he does not re-member ''ever having heard Simone Weil, in spite of her vir-tuous desire for objectivity, give way in the course of a dis-cussion.'' This comment throws light on much of her published work. I do not believe that she was ever animated by delight in her own forensic skill—a self-indulgence to which I suspect Pascal came dangerously near, in the *Letters*—the display of power in overcoming others in controversy. It was rather that all her thought was so intensely lived, that the abandonment of any opinion required modifications in her whole being: a process which could not take place painlessly, or in the course of a conversation. And—especially in the young, and in those like Simone Weil in whom one detects no sense of humor—egotism and selflessness can resemble each other so closely that we may mistake the one for the other.

The statement that Simone Weil's "soul was incomparably superior to her genius" will, however, be misunderstood if it gives the impression of depreciating her intellect. Certainly she could be unfair and intemperate; certainly she committed some astonishing aberrations and exaggerations. But those immoderate affirmations which tax the patience of the reader spring not from any flaw in her intellect but from excess of temperament. She came of a family with no lack of intellectual endowment—her brother is a distinguished mathematician; and as for her own mind, it was worthy of the soul which employed it. But the intellect, especially when bent upon such problems as those which harassed Simone Weil, can come to maturity only slowly; and we must not forget that Simone Weil died at the age of thirty-three. I think that in *The Need for Roots* especially, the maturity of her social and political thought is very remarkable. But she had a very great soul to grow up to; and we should not criticize her philosophy at thirty-three as if it were that of a person twenty or thirty years older.

In the work of such a writer we must expect to encounter paradox. Simone Weil was three things in the highest degree: French, Jewish, and Christian. She was a patriot who would gladly have been sent back to France to suffer and die for her compatriots: she had to die—partly, it would seem, as the result of self-mortification, in refusing to take more food than the official rations of ordinary people in France—in 1943 in a sanatorium at Ashford, Kent. She was also a patriot who saw clearly, as this book shows, the faults and the spiritual weakness of contemporary France. She was a Christian with an intense devotion to Our Lord in the Sacrament of the Altar, yet she refused baptism, and much of her writing constitutes a formidable criticism of the Church. She was intensely Jewish, suffering torments in the affliction of the Jews in Germany; yet she castigated Israel with all the severity of a Hebrew Prophet. Prophets, we are told, were stoned in Jerusalem: but Simone Weil is exposed to lapidation from several quarters. And in her political thinking she appears as a stern critic of both Right and Left; at the same time more truly a lover of order and hierarchy than most of those who call themselves Conservative, and more truly a lover of the people than most of those who call themselves Socialist.

As for her attitude toward the Church of Rome and her attitude toward Israel I wish . . . to make only one observation. The two attitudes are not only compatible but coherent, and should be considered as one. It was in fact her rejection of Israel that made her a very heterodox Christian. In her repudiation of all but a few parts of the Old Testament (and in what she accepted she discerned traces of Chaldean or Egyptian influence) she falls into something very like the Marcionite heresy. In denying the divine mission of Israel she is also rejecting the foundation of the Christian Church. Hence the difficulties that caused her so much agony of spirit. I must affirm that there is no trace of the Protestant in her composition: for her, the Christian Church could only be the Church of Rome. In the Church there is much to which she is blind, or about which she is strangely silent: she seems to give no thought to the Blessed Virgin; and as for the Saints, she is concerned only with those who attract her interest through their writings—such as St. Thomas Aquinas (whom she dislikes, perhaps on insufficient acquaintance) and St. John of the Cross (whom she admires because of his profound knowledge of spiritual method).

In one respect she has, at first sight, something in common with those intellectuals of the present day (mostly with a vague liberal Protestant background) who can find their way toward

the religious life only through the mysticism of the East. Her enthusiasm for everything Greek (including the mysteries) was unbounded. For her, there was no revelation to Israel, but a good deal of revelation to the Chaldeans, the Egyptians, and the Hindus. Her attitude may appear to be dangerously close to that of those universalists who maintain that the ultimate and esoteric truth is one, that all religions show some traces of it, and that it is a matter of indifference to which one of the great religions we adhere. Yet she is saved from this error— and this is a matter for admiration and thankfulness—by her devotion to the person of Our Lord.

In her criticism of the Jewish and the Christian faiths, I think that we have to try to make for ourselves a threefold distinction, asking ourselves: How much is just? How much is serious objection that must be rebutted? And how much, in the way of error, can be extenuated on the ground of the immaturity of a superior and passionate personality? Our analyses may differ widely, but we must ask and answer these questions for ourselves.

I do not know how good a Greek scholar she was. I do not know how well read she was in the history of the civilizations of the Eastern Mediterranean. I do not know whether she could read the Upanishads in Sanskrit; or, if so, how great was her mastery of what is not only a very highly developed language but a way of thought, the difficulties of which only become more formidable to a European student the more diligently he applies himself to it. But I do not think that she shows, in this field, the mind of a historian. In her adulation of Greece, and of the "wisdom of the East," as in her disparagement of Rome and Israel, she seems to me almost willful. In one quarter she sees only what she can admire; in another, she repudiates without discrimination. Because she dislikes the Roman Empire, she dislikes Virgil. Her admirations, when not motivated by her dislikes, seem to be at least intensified by them. One may sympathize with her horror at the brutalities of expanding or imperialistic peoples (as the Romans in Europe and the Spanish in America) in crushing local civilizations. But when, in order to enhance her denunciation of the Romans, she attempts to make out a case for the culture of the Druids, we do not feel that our meager knowledge of that vanished society gives any ground for her conjectures. We can share her revulsion from the atrocities committed in the suppression of the Albigensian heresy, and yet speculate whether the peculiar civilization of Provence had not come to the end of its productivity. Would the world be a better place today if there were half a dozen different cultures flourishing between the English Channel and the Mediterranean, instead of the one which we know as France? Simone Weil begins with an insight; but the logic of her emotions can lead her to make generalizations so large as to be meaningless. We may protest that we are so completely in the dark as to what the world would be like now if events had taken a different course, that such a question as that whether the latinization of Western Europe by Roman conquest was a good or bad thing is unanswerable. Her flights of fancy of this kind must not, however, be taken as invalidating her fundamental concept of *rootedness,* and her warnings against the evils of an overcentralized society. (pp. vi-x)

[*The Need for Roots*] was written during the last year or so of Simone Weil's life, during her employment at French Headquarters in London; and it issues, I understand, from memoranda which she submitted in connection with the policy to be pursued after the Liberation. The problems of the moment led her to much larger considerations; but even those pages in which she is concerned with the program to be followed by the Free French during the war and immediately after the Liberation show such foresight and maturity of judgment that they are of permanent value. This is, I think, among those works of hers already published, the one which approximates most closely to the form in which she might herself have chosen to release it.

I have dwelt chiefly upon certain ideas which are to be met with in all her writings, with some emphasis upon her errors and exaggerations. I have taken this course in the belief that many readers, coming for the first time upon some assertion likely to arouse intellectual incredulity or emotional antagonism, might be deterred from improving their acquaintance with a great soul and a brilliant mind. Simone Weil needs patience from her readers, as she doubtless needed patience from the friends who most admired and appreciated her. But in spite of the violence of her affections and antipathies, in spite of such unjustified generalizations as I have instanced, I find in the present book especially a balanced judgment, a wisdom in avoiding extremes, astonishing in anyone so young. It may be that in her conversations with Gustave Thibon she profited more than she knew from her contact with that wise and well-balanced mind.

As a political thinker, as in everything else, Simone Weil is not to be classified. The paradoxicality of her sympathies is a contributing cause of the equilibrium. On the one hand she was a passionate champion of the common people and especially of the oppressed—those oppressed by the wickedness and selfishness of men and those oppressed by the anonymous forces of modern society. She had worked in the Renault factory, she had worked as a field laborer, in order to share the life of people of town and country. On the other hand, she was by nature a solitary and an individualist, with a profound horror of what she called the *collectivity*—the monster created by modern totalitarianism. What she cared about was human souls. Her study of human rights and human obligations exposes the falsity of some of the verbiage still current which was used during the war to serve as a moral stimulant. Not the least striking example of her shrewdness, balance, and good sense is her examination of the principle of monarchy; and her short review of the political history of France is at once a condemnation of the French Revolution and a powerful argument against the possibility of a restoration of the kingship. She cannot be classified either as a reactionary or as a socialist. (pp. x-xii)

[*The Need for Roots*] belongs in that category of prolegomena to politics which politicians seldom read, and which most of them would be unlikely to understand or to know how to apply. Such books do not influence the contemporary conduct of affairs: for the men and women already engaged in this career and committed to the jargon of the market place, they always come too late. This is one of those books which ought to be studied by the young before their leisure has been lost and their capacity for thought destroyed in the life of the hustings and the legislative assembly; books the effect of which, we can only hope, will become apparent in the attitude of mind of another generation. (p. xii)

> *T. S. Eliot, in a preface to* The Need for Roots: Prelude to a Declaration of Duties toward Mankind *by Simone Weil, translated by Arthur Wills, G. P. Putnam's Sons, 1952, pp. v-xii.*

J. M. PERRIN (essay date 1952)

[*Perrin is a French Dominican priest who knew Weil during her life and, with Gustave Thibon, edited and published selections from her notebooks after her death. In the following excerpt, Perrin summarizes what he sees as the essential points of Weil's "message."*]

"I am separated from truth." Simone Weil allowed herself to say this in order to explain her desire for death and her hope that in it she would find the truth she craved. Could any words be more poignant or more heart-rending?

In a sense it is true of every human being. The great Newman asked that the words *"Ex umbris et imaginibus in veritam"* ["Out of the shadows and fancies into the truth"] should be inscribed on his tomb, and Saint Paul wrote: "We see now through a glass in a dark manner: but then face to face. Now I know in part: but then I shall know even as I am known" (I Cor. xiii. 12).

With Simone Weil there was, in addition, her sense of incompleteness, and the suffering of a mind torn in opposite directions; at the same time within the Church and outside it, anxious to obey and afraid of illusion; struggling in an impasse due to her adherence to the Catholic faith, her inability to conceive of it as an object of affirmation for her intellect, her inclination to jump to universal systematizations before testing the objective value of her material, and her scrupulous sincerity which drove her to give expression to every idea which came into her head before she had been able to check its value. Is it possible to speak of a message in the case of a mind which was still trying to find its way? Moreover this mind is scarcely known to us apart from rough notes which were never revised and upon which we have no light from any outside sources, confidences of friends or circumstantial details. Under these conditions is there not a danger of misrepresenting her thought and of attributing to her ideas which were never hers? Do we not risk giving the authority of her mind and spirit to what was perhaps nothing but the changing foam thrown off from reading or conversations (for she gives none too many references), objections to be refuted or material to be transformed in the process of assimilation?

It is necessary to do some careful sorting out in order to know her thoughts and also the truth of her thoughts. She herself invites us to do so. Those who would give her the authority of a master, either by accepting everything which comes from her as completely true, or, on the other hand, by contesting it all as a false doctrine, forget that she herself was only a traveller, journeying towards the truth. (pp. 99-100)

I want to help to bring out what is positive in her and what is valid, in so far as this word can be applied to human thought.

It would, however, be rash to claim to make a complete inventory of the spiritual discoveries of Simone Weil, or even of those most definitely connected with Christianity; in her everything is connected with Christianity and the word discovery is hardly suitable, for the truths in question have been heard "from the beginning," but she has said them again with a genius which is all her own and lived them with all the depth and force of her personality.

Perhaps at the head of the list we should put her doctrine of attention, whether applied to facts, ideas or persons (**"Thoughts on the Right Use of School Studies with a View of the Love of God"**). Once the importance has been stressed of preliminary enquiry, knowledge stored in the memory, the attentive study of documents and examination of all the facts necessary to avoid rash, unreal or erroneous systematizations, once all these prerequisites have been stressed (although this was neither the object of the essay nor the main concern of the author), this attitude of opening to the truth makes the soul utterly transparent to the light, prepares the way for the most beautiful vocations and enables human eyes to become as the eyes of Christ. While most thinkers want to invent their truth, attention disposes us to receive it.

In spite of the difficulties which attended such a method for Simone Weil on account of her intellectual temperament, if I may put it in this way, I am convinced that she would have been able to reduce and, as it were, burn up from within most of the prejudices—chiefly of an historical nature—which hindered her search.

It is useless to insist upon it; many consider this paper to be Simone Weil's masterpiece:

> Attention consists of suspending our thought, leaving it detached, empty and ready to be penetrated by the object, it means holding in our minds, within reach of this thought, but on a lower level and not in contact with it, the diverse knowledge we have acquired which we are forced to make use of. Our thought should be, in relation to all particular and already formulated thoughts, as a man on a mountain who, as he looks forward, sees also below him, without actually looking at them, a great many forests and plains. Above all our thought should be empty, waiting, not seeking anything, but ready to receive in its naked truth the object which is to penetrate it. . . . We do not obtain the most precious gifts by going in search of them but by waiting for them. Man cannot discover them by his own powers, and if he sets out to seek for them he will find in their place counterfeits of which he will be unable to discern the falsity. . . . This way of looking is, in the first place, attentive. The soul empties itself of all its own contents in order to receive the being it is looking at, just as he is, in all his truth. Only he who is capable of attention can do this. . . .

(pp. 101-02)

Another of the most beautiful features of Simone's doctrine is the attentive understanding of the individual in affliction: misfortune has made him like a thing, he is the nameless casualty, lying inert and bleeding by the wayside. We should respond to such affliction with compassion full of respect and attention, of devotion and insight, of self-loss through love of the sufferer, with compassion which is God's compassion in our human hearts.

That was one of her most cherished thoughts and one of the most generous motives of her life. Even those who feel obliged to censure her intellectual faults and her resistance to the words of Christ cannot help admiring the reckless devotion and heroism of her charity.

"That which you have done to the least of these my little ones. . . ."

We can dispute this or that of her formulae: but she had been able to see for herself that only too often acting ''for God'' went side by side with a complete lack of attention to the afflicted and the outcast: hence her concern. Moreover, when we read her closely we see what she meant, and understand that, from her point of view, to love the man in affliction and relieve him as we should, in a spirit of service and without a shadow of condescension, is not possible except supernaturally under the inspiration and through the very action of Christ.

It is obvious that the present time is ripe for such a message; the advance of laws and technics which aim at planning for everybody and relieving all poverty makes each being into a number, an anonymous individual, classified by government officials. Is it possible to see what will happen if this technical progress is not accompanied by ''an extra ration of soul,'' if the ''Great Beast'' is not carried off by a huge pair of wings?

This love of Simone's for human beings tended, alas, to screen the divine light, but it finds, or rather it is waiting for, its place in the Christian synthesis, for the true Christian loves men and respects the human values brought to light by the Saviour ''who took his delight among the children of men.''

It was this attitude which made it possible for her to converse, and to converse on deep matters, with people who were totally different from herself. Have we sufficiently noticed how she formed friendships with simple folk despite their lack of culture? With X or Y, in spite of their political differences? In a world where men shut themselves up in their circles and their parties, pass their time in labelling others without reference to what they really have in them but for the mere pleasure of classifying, judging, condemning, separating and opposing, is it not worth remembering this characteristic of Simone's?

Her conception of the duty of sanctity and of the ideal of evangelical purity should also be studied and placed among her most beautiful thoughts.

Apparently forgetting what she had said elsewhere, and recognizing the moral superiority of Christianity (she puts conscience above ideas, especially when she is systematizing), she says: ''It seems to me that in reality, if I dare to say so, saintliness is the minimum for a Christian. It is for the Christian what honesty in money matters is for the merchant, bravery for the soldier, a critical mind for the scholar. The specific value of the Christian is saintliness—if not, what is it?''

She formed a very high idea of this saintliness; she frequently repeated that all illusion must be excluded, whatever its name. ''We must be careful about the level on which we place the infinite. If we place it on the level which is only suitable for the finite, it will matter very little what name we give it.'' . . . (pp. 102-04)

But she also described its positive aspect: ''Truth which becomes life, that is the testimony of the spirit, truth transformed into life.'' . . . ''Sanctity is accompanied by an uninterrupted welling up of supernatural energy which acts irresistibly upon its surroundings. The other state (deceptive semblance) is accompanied with moral exhaustion, and often—as in my own case—exhaustion which is both physical and moral.'' . . . She did not forget that fidelity is a gift of God and that all confidence in ourselves is a denial. Concerning Saint Peter's presumption she said: ''This was to deny Christ already for it was to suppose the source of fidelity to be in himself and not in grace.'' . . . She tried elsewhere to explain the part played by effort and the gift of grace: ''For a man to be really inhabited by Christ as the host is after consecration, it is necessary that his flesh and blood should previously have become inert matter, and, what is more, food which his fellows can consume. Then, by a secret consecration, this matter can become the flesh and blood of Christ. This second transmutation is the affair of God alone, but the first is partly our own affair.'' . . . (pp. 104-05)

This brings us to her sense of God. It is perhaps the centre of her message. No doubt there are conceptions which might be disputed, exaggerated formulae, such as the one against hope, deviations and resistances, since she rejects some of the divine commandments and seems sometimes to make the divinity impersonal, but for her God is truly God: "The object of our desire must be none other than the one and only good, pure, perfect, total, absolute, inconceivable for us." Many label with the word God a conception invented by their own soul or provided by their environment. Simone thirsted to contemplate God himself, to be "in contact" with him, to depend upon him, to be transformed into him, whereas only too often religion becomes bogged in human elements and puerile conceptions.

Moreover, she knew that we can only go to God through the Mediator, and throughout the *Intuitions Pré-Chrétiennes* she insists upon this necessity: "If we had chlorophyll we should feed on light as trees do. Christ is this light." . . . She readily looked upon him as the model to be reproduced, or rather, as the life that animates us and the centre from which all the truth and light of the world proceed. At times some of her formulae seem to be slipping into syncretism, but it must not be forgotten that she eagerly affirms the historical reality of the Incarnation and of the life of Our Lord and that if she searches for traces of him in all places it is because she wants to bring all things to him. (p. 105)

> *J. M. Perrin, "Her Message," in* Simone Weil: As We Knew Her *by J. M. Perrin and G. Thibon, translated by Emma Craufurd, G. Routledge & Kegan Paul, 1953, pp. 99-105.*

BRADFORD COOK   (essay date 1953)

[*In the following excerpt, Cook explores the effect that Weil's religious belief exerted on her perception of the purpose and function of art.*]

[Simone Weil's] interest in artistic creation, both good and bad, sprang from her concern for the faculty of *attention,* or a subtle combination of the active and passive in mental concentration. Composition of any kind, by any mind, constituted a spiritual exercise leading eventually, she hoped, to the perfect concentration of prayer. Thus literature was to be respected as a means to transcendent ends, but strictly speaking, a means of neither more nor less importance than other forms of mental activity.

In addition to her diaries, articles, letters, and the commissioned work *L'Enracinement,* Simone Weil attempted a little verse, began a play, and wrote translations, most of which remain unpublished. She had, then, first-hand experience with literature; and despite her generally scornful attitude toward it, she surely found a far greater comfort and beauty in it than she dared admit. In this apparently superhuman soul there were longings and secrets which she never showed (save once or twice to her intelligent and kindly biographers, Perrin and Thibon), for fear of seeming even more imperfect to her God.

"Literature is important only as a symptom," she coldly observed. We must go even further with her to see that, from a purely theoretical point of view, literature had really no importance in her divinely governed world. Faithful to her beliefs and to her personality, Simone Weil was forced to this extremity. For art in that world, however else we may define it or invest it, remains a luxury, an embellishment, the Pascalian

divertissement, the Mallarmean *jeu,* which have no part in the divine necessity so dear to Simone Weil. Obsessed by man's gravity, his blessed and accursed closeness to the earth, his fated obedience to the laws of original sin, she could accept no beauty, no sublimation, no escape other than grace itself; no paradise on earth, no pleasurable sensations made captive in the Proustian work of art. These were echoes, of course, from the stern Catholicism of a Pascal or a Bossuet. But Simone Weil gave them a newer, stronger, and more pitiful voice, for she was pitifully lacking in the lyric and comic senses. It is significant that she saw the tragic in Molière, Bach, and Mozart. But she largely neglected their comic or joyful natures. It was to be expected that *Le Misanthrope* and the *Passions* should appeal to her principally. Again, art was not merely treachery against the gravitational nature of man, but useless as well, she thought, because all necessary beauty already exists. It is to be contemplated, not created; it has always been of a quality so pure, so evident, that all life can enjoy it. Her "practical" solution for the workers' and farmers' entertainment consisted merely of turning their thoughts, as they worked, to the planetary rotations (imitated by the spinning machine wheel), or to the hydrogen cycle, as they sowed. In this, too, Simone Weil had been gloriously preceded: her favorite St. Francis had spent his life in the worship of God-given beauties. Nor must she be denied too quickly when she affirms that songs "to our sister water" are more lastingly excellent than all the revolutionary alexandrines of Victor Hugo. From the literary point of view such judgments may seem doubtful. They are understandable if we remember that water simply meant more than verse to her Christian sensibility. Finally, to this tragically serious mind, literature meant falsehood. The writer's position is untenable, condemned as he is by art to the imaginative; yet, by his God, to the strictest of truths. Simone Weil often described imaginative literature as either immoral or boring: immoral in its rendering of evil and pain, since it sublimates or "treats" them in a thousand different tones, whereas they are earthly, supremely monotonous, never to be treated, but only accepted and absorbed as on the Cross (hence her respect for the monotonousness of Bach, Gregorian chant, and the epic); or boring in its portrayal of the good, because the true and therefore interesting good of God is inexpressible by man. The only answer, she concluded, is silence: the actual silence of Rimbaud, the longed-for silence of Mallarmé (often called sterility), two men (and, incidentally, two apparent atheists) who understood that the writer is, in fact, in a false position with respect to a divinity.

Simone Weil's theoretical abolition of art can be explained in the foregoing ways, but its true origin is something centrally uncreative in herself. From a detailed study of her religion and psychology, one is bound to observe that she had the self-destructive instinct more fully, more constantly than any thinker of our time. From her dowdy clothes, her hard labor, her fighting and starvation, to her theories on man's duty to de-create himself, to be absorbed in God, and to her longing for the Cross, she clung to as much mental and physical torture as this life can give. What sort of sublimation can we hope to find in the author of such coldly passionate, magnificent, and pitiful statements as these: "Wherever I am, I soil the silence of heaven and earth with my breathing and with the beating of my heart"; or "Even if we could be like God, it would be better to be mud which obeys God"; or "We must try to avoid misfortune as much as we can, so that when we do meet it, it may be perfectly pure and perfectly bitter." Joy and beauty she attributed so fully to her God and to the life which came before and will come after this, that there was almost nothing left of them in man and his devices.

And yet, for all her ideals and her will, she read and wrote, and could not forever repress her instinct for the beautiful. The saints had written and sung; Plato and Homer were not to be dismissed; tragic or not, Mozart and Bach were almost more undeniably a part of God than the mountains she watched in France. And so she compromised with the life she had, and made a truce which would be favorable to God but also leave a little something to the earth. She would turn the earth, its beauty, and its writers to some account, as Pascal had "used" his sickness. When she had so decided, she saw that the writer had a place in the creation after all. It has been observed that he exercises his faculty for attention, that art is a rudimentary form of prayer and commendable to that extent; so much so, indeed, that the usually careful Simone Weil could occasionally compliment even the worst of writers for honorable, if fruitless, efforts in this direction. Again, the writer and musician are reproducers of time and space, silence and absence, elements especially pondered by this mystic, who felt that God was absent from Himself in man. The most vivid of her sensations was that of convergence. Headaches were the convergence of pain and the joy of seeing Christ in their very midst; running through the branches of the Cross came time and space; the past and future of man lay finally on the heart of the Cross, with God infinitely distant from Christ and man. The book too, she felt, might act as a converger, as an infinitely unworthy Cross. So that her apparently catholic tastes in art can often be ascribed to a certain intensity in her spiritual thinking. The same mind that worshipped the vastness of the *Iliad* was almost equally fond of the smaller miracles in Mozart and Mallarmé. The sinking ship and corresponding notation of the *Coup de Dés*, the ethereal descents in the introduction to the 39th symphony or to *Don Giovanni*, figured the rise and "dying fall" of grace through gravity.

Simone Weil would also agree in principle (with Gide, for example) that beauty can be a guide to belief. The most ecstatic moments of her otherwise cold, clear style are to be found in her reaction to the Lord's Prayer. Yet her ecstasy, she would maintain, was founded on its truth; seconded, no doubt, by Biblical style, but not centered, as Gide would have it, on "the esthetic value of the Bible." Only a certain beauty was truth for her; had it not been so, she would have approved all excellent stylists, however satanic their substance.

In the final analysis, however, her praise was for the works that faithfully mirrored life on earth in its essentials of banality, pain, misery, fatigue, hunger, and force; works in which "the bones of human suffering are exposed." Chief among her faithful were Homer, Aeschylus, Sophocles, Shakespeare (but only in *King Lear*, the "tragedy on gravity" . . .), Molière in *L'Avare* and *Le Misanthrope*, Racine in *Phèdre,* Villon ("greatest of French poets" . . .), and d'Aubigné. Some of these, as the list shows, were faithful only for a moment; she states that Shakespeare was second-rate save for *Lear*, Racine third-rate save for *Phèdre*. And yet these judgments are perhaps not totally fantastic. Ramon Fernandez, speaking of the French genius in general, and of Racine in particular, had already noted the "liberties he takes with life." Simone Weil, in turn, refers intelligently to the 17th century as "a strange century indeed, which took the opposite view from that of the epic period and would only acknowledge human suffering in the context of love, while it insisted on swathing in glory the effects of force in war and in politics." . . . We might well be surprised that

she admired even *Phèdre*, were it not that we sense once again all that we do not know about her own jealousies or loves, and remember *Phèdre*, despite the quantities of life which it omits, for its perfect distillation of inward pain. In what is probably her greatest single composition, **"L'Amour de Dieu et le Malheur,"** . . . she insists that all *malheur* must spring from a *douleur physique* and that the latter is absent from Racinian tragedy, a "court tragedy," as she says, comparing it to Homer's work, in which characters do not "run toward death," but rather suffer death despite their ferocious desire to live. "It is not surprising," she adds, "that Racine led the most peaceful of private lives. His tragedies are cold, after all; they lack *douleur*. . . . Inhuman poet."

How strict she was with regard to the perfect literary expression of pain can be seen in her comments on Mauriac: "*Thérèse Desqueyroux:* almost a great book (but, in fact, a negligible book). There is something monstrous in (writers') ideas of life in those years (1918-1940). The book lacks the true color of evil, the monotony and facility of evil, the sense of emptiness and nothingness." . . . Would she have said as much of the naturalists, of Sartre, Camus, Malraux? Undoubtedly so. For if literary success depended only on the communication of reality in unpalatable forms, her list would hardly be exclusive. But, more important, she felt that these writers, whose "ideas of life were monstrous," had no proper perspective on human evils and misfortunes: they succeeded in making them clear to readers, without understanding their spiritual significance. In short, they were not divinely inspired.

Without such inspiration, and without several other qualities, no writer can please her completely. First, he must find a perfect compound of detachment and passion (the lifelong search of any artist). Second, it is preferable to have the *tête épique* of a Homer in order to give an adequate portrayal of monotony, fate, and allied conditions; in order to communicate universally. Hence her contention that writers appealing to an elite are inevitably second-rate, or worse, when compared to the supreme. Third (and perhaps most disturbing to certain French poets), divine inspiration implies facility in composition. Simone Weil did not always avoid the common delusion that artistic greatness is "measured by the pound," as Poe mockingly observed. It was her good fortune that Mozart, Bach, and Monteverdi, her leading illustrations of artistic facility, did, in fact, possess it in abundance and were at the same time three of the greatest musicians. Fourth, the writer had to be "involved" (it is only in this sense that she might have enjoyed the Existentialists): that is, not merely in close contact with his time, but responsible for his writings. She attacked Gide not so much for his "corruption of youth," as because he tended to avoid the consequences of his doctrines by "taking refuge behind the sacred privilege of art for art's sake." . . . Indeed, so-called esthetes, like men of letters, had always been a source of fear and disgust for her. But how are they to be distinguished from the true artists? "The word beauty," she remarks, "does not mean that things religious should be considered in the manner of the esthetes. Their point of view is sacrilegious. . . . They amuse themselves with beauty, handle it, look at it. But beauty is . . . nourishment." . . . The distinction is perhaps impossible to make in practice. But Simone Weil attempted it as anyone must: by sensing the point beyond which beauty is "cultivated," "handled," somehow given precedence over the spiritual substance of the work of art. Would we not agree with her in this, when we recall our contacts with a Homer, a Bach, a Mozart, whose works of infinite beauty we instinctively call "noble," "spiritual," or other words equally inadequate, but none the less corresponding to a precise feeling which is self-sufficient proof? Works in which the spirit has been gently, miraculously touched and healed, while their beauties, were they separable, would hover around it and never oppress. Yet, on the other hand, can we entirely agree with her conclusion that the "impure in heart" are incapable of purity in art? Here again Gide stands in her way and says: "There is no work of art without the collaboration of the Devil." The reader may have wondered why she considered Villon the "greatest of French poets." His wonder will increase at her answer that Villon was the "purest in heart"; for, she adds in desperation, we really know nothing of Villon's life. The fact is that we know, if not much, at least enough to determine that the life of Villon was not perfectly blameless. If he was a great poet, it was in spite of his private life or, in devious and Gidean ways, because of it. Clearly, Mozartean and Racinian purities tell us nothing of their personal lives. Actually, the debate is needless and arises from a confusion in Simone Weil's mind between the personal life of the artist and an incorruptible area of the spirit which is fertilized and repurified whenever he creates. It is this last (as she was aware) which makes the greatness of Villon, who may well have been a thief or worse at all other times, or the greatness of a Mozart, whose correspondence is not to be recommended to the pure in heart.

Such, then, were her main views, offered with her characteristic mixture of lofty thought, common sense, good taste, aggressiveness, and plain error. She wrote no epics, yet neither was she guilty of any sort of fakery in her writing. True to her principles, she poured her spirit into every word and action, revealed the naked realities of the world with a most convincing combination of detachment and passion, and communicated to her readers (as they will testify) with a matchless simplicity of language. Doubtless that language had been born not merely from a native simplicity, but from her continual readings in the Bible and folk tales; and here at last she joined hands with Gide, assured that art was a question of litotes and "overcome romanticism." A study of her style will some day reveal the kind of monotonousness, plainness of expression, and almost total absence of the decorative which most pleased her. Like her distant but very close spiritual father, Pascal, she had neither cause nor time for the artist's life; but she must have known that it was essential for her very sanity and for the satisfaction of the creative instinct (however small it may have been in her), to gather daily tortures to her mind and inscribe them for some brother or sister spirit of a later day. (pp. 74-80)

Bradford Cook, "Simone Weil: Art and the Artist under God," in Yale French Studies, No. 12, Fall-Winter, 1953, pp. 73-80.

ALFRED KAZIN (essay date 1955)

[A highly respected American literary critic, Kazin is best known for his essay collections The Inmost Leaf (1955) and Contemporaries (1962), and particularly for On Native Grounds (1942), a study of American prose writing since the era of William Dean Howells. In the following excerpt, he praises the integrity of Weil's life and spiritual convictions.]

[Simone Weil] was not the sort of "brilliant mind" who can comfortably add to our philosophy, nor was she exactly one of those "great souls," like Gandhi and Albert Schweitzer, who by their ethical example can inspire millions. She was a fanatically dedicated participant in the most critical experiences of our time, who tried to live them directly in contact with the

supernatural. Her real interest for us lies less in what she said than in the direction of her work, in the particular vision she tried to reach by the whole manner of her life. What she sought more than anything else was a loving attentiveness to all the living world that would lift man above the natural loneliness of existence.

This urge was her essential quality, her gift—not merely intellectual or ethical but remarkably open to all human experience at its most extreme, neglected, and uprooted. It was this that kept her outside the Catholic Church, on the ground, as she explained in *Waiting for God,* that "so many things are outside it, so many things that I love and do not want to give up, so many things that God loves, otherwise they would not be in existence"; that led to her distress at the Catholic formula of excommunication and compelled her, though a Jew who had fled for her life from Hitler, to protest indignantly against the belief that God could have "chosen" any people for any purpose whatever; that still gave her a sense of outrage at the Romans' contempt for their slaves, which, she thought, had carried over into the brutalities inflicted on workingmen, heretics, prisoners, and the colored races; that drove her to the factories, to Spain during the Civil War, and at the very end, when she was not permitted to join her own people under the Occupation, to starve herself in one last desperate expression of solidarity with them.

Everything that is fundamental in her life and thought radiates this closeness to pain, her need to know directly the rending misery of the universe, to imitate the Passion of Christ. "Those who are unhappy," she wrote in *Waiting for God,* "have no need for anything in this world but people capable of giving them their attention. . . . The love of our neighbor in all its fullness simply means being able to say to him, 'What are you going through?' " "Attention" she called "the contrary" of contempt. By it, she meant "a recognition that the sufferer exists, not only as a unit in a collection, or a specimen from the social category labelled 'unfortunate,' but as a man, exactly like us, who was one day stamped with a special mark by affliction. For this reason it is enough, but it is indispensable, to know how to look at him in a certain way." "Attention" was one of her major themes, and some of the most profound pages in *Waiting for God* are devoted to it. "We do not obtain the most precious gifts by going in search of them but by waiting for them. How can we go toward God? Even if we were to walk for hundreds of years, we should do no more than go round and round the world. Even in an airplane we cannot do anything else. We are incapable of progressing vertically. We cannot take a step toward the heavens." We can only wait, with an attentiveness that has no particular object to gain, that is the "highest form of prayer," that exposes us to the full affliction of being alive, but through which we can gain the integral significance of the universe in which we are placed.

When a French apprentice who is new on a job complains that the work hurts him, the older men usually say that "the trade is entering his body." This saying, which Simone Weil picked up in the Renault factory, had a special pathos for her. It expressed her belief that there is a particular closeness we can reach with the world, that the truth is always something to be lived. In *The Need for Roots,* commenting on the impersonal and detached "love of truth" on which science prides itself, she wrote that "truth is not an object of love. It is not an object at all. What one loves is something which exists, which one thinks on. . . . A truth is always the truth with reference to something. Truth is the radiant manifestation of reality. . . . To desire truth is to desire contact with a piece of reality.'' This ''direct contact'' was the one aim of her life, and her ability to find it in the darkest, most unexpected places is her special gift to a generation for whom, more than for any other, the living world has become a machine unresponsive to the human heart. (pp. 211-13)

> Alfred Kazin, ''The Gift,'' in his The Inmost Leaf: A Selection of Essays, *Harcourt Brace Jovanovich, Inc.*, 1955, pp. 208-13.

KENNETH REXROTH   (essay date 1957)

[*Rexroth was one of the leading pioneers in the revival of jazz and poetry in the San Francisco area during the 1940s and 1950s. Largely self-educated, he became involved early in his career with such left-wing organizations as the John Reed Club, the Communist party, and the International Workers of the World. During World War II he was a conscientious objector, and since that time has become anti-political in his work and writing. Rexroth's early poetry was greatly influenced by the surrealism of André Breton, but his later verse has become more traditional in style and content, though by no means less complex. However, it is as a critic and translator that Rexroth has gained prominence in American letters. As a critic, his acute intelligence and wide sympathy have allowed him to examine such varied subjects as jazz, Greek mythology, the works of D. H. Lawrence, and the Kabbal. As a translator, Rexroth is largely responsible for introducing the West to both Chinese and Japanese classics. In the following excerpt, Rexroth attacks various aspects of Weil's thought.*]

Simone Weil is one of the most remarkable women of the twentieth, or indeed of any other century. I have great sympathy for her, but sympathy is not necessarily congeniality. It would be easier to write of her if I liked what she has to say, which I strongly do not. . . .

One of her books, *The Need For Roots,* is a collection of egregious nonsense surpassed only by the deranged fantasies of the chauvinist Peguy. Written for De Gaulle it was a program for the moral rehabilitation of France when our side had won. It attempts to enlist on our side the same dark irrational spirits who seemed then to be fighting so successfully for the other side. Luckily, as it turned out, they lost and we won without much effective intervention from the spirits on either side. Realities of the kind called harsh rule France today rather than any vestige of Simone Weil's odd ideals. . . .

I have the greatest respect, indeed veneration, for any tortured soul seeking peace and illumination. But, in 1934 Simone Weil wrote this:

> War in our day is distinguished by the subordination of the combatants to the instruments of combat, and the armaments, the true heroes of modern warfare, as well as the men dedicated to their service, are directed by those who do not fight. Since this directing apparatus has no other way of fighting than sending its own soldiers, under compulsion, to their deaths— the war of one State against another resolves itself into a war of the State and the military apparatus against its own army. War in the last analysis appears as a struggle led by all the State apparatuses and general staffs against all men old enough and able to bear arms.

When war actually came she was writing things like this:

> In civil society, penal death, if death is used as a punishment, ought to be something beautiful. Religious ceremonies would be necessary for it to be made so. And there ought to be something to make it felt that the man who is being punished, on receiving death, accomplishes something great; contributes, as far as he is able in the situation in which he has placed himself, to the orderly state of the community. Let him remain in his cell until such time as he himself accepts to die?

What would Thomas Aquinas have made of this? Or any Sicilian peasant or Irish teamster? Very much, I fear, the same as you or I. This girl killed herself seeking salvation, a salvation she identified with Catholicism. This, and there are hundreds of remarks like it in the notebooks, is far from Catholicism, in fact from any religion. It has a horrible similarity to one theory of the Moscow trials, but it is a sick kind of agonized frivolity. There are other things: a captious, misinformed playing with Hinduism and comparative mythology, worse than the confabulations of Robert Graves; a toying with modern mathematics of infinitudes and incommensurabilities—a kind of post Cantor-Dedekind Neo-Pythagoreanism.

In her last years Simone Weil seems to have sought enlightenment by a systematic cultivation of maximum hypertension. Her thought proceeded by no way other than paradox. This is not new. There is a good deal of it in Pascal, that least Catholic of Catholic thinkers, and of course in Kierkegaard. In Chesterton it sinks to the level of a vulgar journalistic trick. Paul Tillich has created, beyond the ''theology of crisis'' of Barth, Niebuhr and the Neo-Lutherans, a ''theology of tension''— perhaps the most viable expression of that ancient science for a modern man. But there is the tension of life and the tension of death. Simone Weil was a dying girl. Hers was a spastic, moribund, intellectual and spiritual agony. We can sympathize with it, be moved to tears by it, much as we are by the last awful lunacies of Antonin Artaud, but we imitate it, allow it to infect us, at our peril. This is a Kierkegaard who refuses to leap. *Angst* for *angst*'s sake. Anguish is not enough. When it is made an end in itself it takes on a holy, or unholy, folly.

It is one thing, like John Woolman, to refuse sugar because it was made by slave labor, it is another thing to refuse to eat more than the starvation rations of occupied Paris when one is dying in an English sanatorium. (What sort of doctor permitted this?) It is touching, even tragic, but it is the farcical tragedy of Lear, equally distant from the tragedy of Prometheus on his rock or Christ on His Cross.

What was wrong with Simone Weil? Our grandparents used to say of learned girls who broke down, ''She studied too hard. She read too many books.'' And today we laugh at them. I think Simone Weil had both over- and under-equipped herself for the crisis that overwhelmed her—along, we forget, immersed in her tragedy, with all the rest of us. She was almost the perfectly typical passionate revolutionary intellectual woman—a frailer, even more highly strung Rosa Luxemburg.

Rosa was saved from personal, inner disaster during the great betrayals of the First World War by several, all rather toughminded, characteristics: a tenacious orthodoxy—she was perfectly confident of the sufficiency of Marxism as an answer, though she was more humane about it than Lenin; a warm, purely human love of people—physically, their smell and touch and comradeship; a kind of Jewish indomitable guts—that ultimate unkillability which comes only from grandparents in *yarmulke* and horsehair wig. Simone Weil had none of this. She made up her revolution out of her vitals, like a spider or silk worm. She could introject all the ill of the world into her own heart, but she could not project herself in sympathy to others. Her letters read like the more distraught signals of John of the Cross in the dark night. It is inconceivable that she could ever have written as Rosa did from prison to Sophia Kautsky. People to her were mere actors in her own spiritual melodrama. I doubt if she was ever aware of the smell of her own armpits. She may have called her fantasy "the need for roots," but *yarmulkes,* rosaries or plain chewing-tobacco atheism, none had ever existed in her past. She was born a *deracinée* and she insisted on remaining one. She was constitutionally disengaged—Renault, Spain and the Free French to the contrary notwithstanding. Faced with the ordinary but definite engagement of becoming a baptized Catholic she panicked.

Religion has been called the gap between the technology and the environment. When her intellectual and psychological environment blew up in her face, Simone Weil discovered that she had no technology whatever, and the gap was absolute. She never permitted herself access to anyone who could help her. If I were planning to enter the Catholic Church the last person I would approach would be the kind priest who could make head or tail of her *Letter to a Priest.*

Father Perrin and M. Thibon may have been wise men in their generation, but they both fell into the trap of her dialectic of agony. They took her seriously—in the wrong way. They lacked the vulgar but holy frivolity of common sense of the unsophisticated parish priest who would have told her, "Come, come, my child, what you need is to get baptized, obey the ten commandments, go to Mass on Sundays, make your Easter duties, forget about religion, put some meat on your bones, and get a husband." Simone Weil knew the type, and she avoided them as a criminal avoids the police, and probably secretly disdained them as much.

Only such advice could have saved her. Only the realization of the truth, so hard to come by for the religious adventurer, that no one is "called" to be any holier than he absolutely has to be, could have given her real illumination. To anything like this she was defiantly impervious. She went to John of the Cross when she should have gone to plain Father Dupont, or Father Monahan, or Father Aliotto. Even Huysmans, with all his posturing, had sense enough to make St. Severin, that humble slum church, his home parish. Simone Weil assaulted the Garden of Gethsemane, and as is so often the case, was broken on the gate.

But at least she speaks, again and again, of her absolutely sure sense of the suddenly descending, all-suffusing presence of God. So we know that somewhere, somehow, in all her agony, she did find some center of peace—a peace which, unless we believe in God, we may find hard to explain. (pp. 42-3)

> Kenneth Rexroth, "The Dialectic of Agony," in The Nation, *Vol. 184, No. 2, January 12, 1957, pp. 42-3.*

HANS MEYERHOFF (essay date 1957)

[*In the following excerpt from an essay originally published in* Commentary *in September, 1957, Meyerhoff discusses Weil's anti-Semitism.*]

[The private *Notebooks of Simone Weil*] throw a new and sharper light upon an aspect of her thought and personality that has been rather neglected so far, and which has a special significance for the Jewish reader. I mean her extreme religious anti-Semitism. "Her anti-Semitism," M. Thibon writes, "was so violent that the continuity established by the Church between the Old and New Testament was one of the chief obstacles to her becoming a Catholic. She was fond," he continues, "of saying that Hitler hunted on the same ground as the Jews and only persecuted them in order to resuscitate under another name and to his own advantage their tribal god, terrestrial, cruel, and exclusive." T. S. Eliot observed that it was Simone Weil's "rejection of Israel that made her a very heterodox Christian," and that, in this respect, she fell "into something very like the Marcionite heresy" [see excerpt dated 1952].

Marcion was a Christian theologian of the first half of the second century whose thought belongs to the religious phenomenon known as Gnosticism. (pp. 71-2)

Gnosticism takes its name from the Greek word for knowledge. But *gnosis* meant knowledge in a special sense—a higher, mysterious, esoteric kind of knowledge primarily designed to obtain personal salvation. . . .

Gnosticism was a typical product of Hellenism. Gnostic movements and sects arising in Persia, Greece, Rome, Egypt, Syria, and elsewhere mingled with each other in the great cultural and ideological melting pot of Hellenism. (p. 72)

Most Gnostic thinkers, including Marcion, combined their synthesis of Christianity and Hellenism with a radical attack upon the religious tradition of Judaism. It is this aspect of Gnosticism which comes to life again in the writings of Simone Weil.

The early history of the Church is haunted by a dilemma which must have had a special poignancy for Jewish converts. How should they reconcile the old faith of their fathers with the new gospel of the Son of God? Beginning with Paul, the foremost Jewish convert to Christianity, two attitudes may be distinguished in this matter. The attitude which won out in the doctrinal struggle is embodied in the official Catholic dogma that the teachings of the Old Testament are restored and preserved in the new faith. . . .

The other attitude was to reject and repudiate the authority of the Old Testament, which is what the Gnostics did. (p. 73)

The common element in the Gnostic trend was the belief that the essence of the new faith lay in its break with the world of man's fall depicted in the Old Testament, and by its triumph over the God of Israel who had created this world of sin, suffering, and death. Thus the view developed, as Adolf Harnack wrote, that "the believers in Christ were the only true community of God . . . and that the Jewish Church, persevering in its stubborn unbelief, was the synagogue of Satan."

Marcion—who, unlike St. Paul, was a Gentile—developed these views to an extreme. The ideas contained in his *Antitheses* throw into sharp relief the significant features of the Gnostic revolt ("antithesis") against the Old Testament.

The Christian gospels reveal a God of love, mercy, and compassion; the God of the Old Testament is jealous, cruel, and revengeful; hence they cannot be the same. Since Jesus proclaimed redemption through faith and love, he cannot be the son of the malign, cruel God of the Old Testament; hence he is the son of the new "unknown" God whom Paul hailed in the market place of Athens. This is confirmed by Jesus himself, who declared war on the Pharisees and constantly broke the old Law in words and deeds; hence he repudiated the old God behind this Law and asserted that new wine should not be poured into old vessels. The Old Testament is the record of man's history in the state of fall, sin, despair, and death; it is, in fact, the reign of Satan on earth. This history has come to an end with Jesus who redeemed mankind and destroyed the power of the old evil God. Hence the new faith and its sacred scriptures must be purged of all Jewish influences (which Marcion set out to do) lest it be distorted and contaminated by them. Textual revisions, finally, were used to defend doctrinal differences. Thus Marcion distinguished between the spirit of Christ that dwelled everlastingly with God, and the man Jesus who was born and died on this earth; he also repudiated, as did other Gnostics, the dogma of the resurrection in the flesh, and the early Christian faith in the return of Jesus and the establishment of his kingdom on earth.

These Gnostic ideas, as we have said, were defeated in the struggle for official supremacy within the Church, but they have lived on as undercurrents in the history of Christian theology and heresy. Simone Weil's religious struggle represents, as it were, a violent "return of the repressed." It seems almost as if the Jew faced with the crisis of conversion to Christianity relives a historical drama. He must come to terms with his religious heritage, and perhaps can do so in only one of two ways: either he must feel that the Apostolic Church represents the natural fulfillment and fruition of the religious seeds contained in the Jewish faith (this seems to have been the solution adopted by contemporary converts like Alfred Stern and Edith Stein) or he must radically and violently repudiate that faith. This was what Simone Weil did.

What makes her case so dramatic is that she launched her Gnostic revolt against the Jewish *religion* at a time when the Jewish *people* were suffering the worst agonies and tortures they have ever undergone within the Christian world. Staking her whole life on the hope and faith of salvation in Jesus, she was driven to indict the religion of her own people in the language of their worst enemies and persecutors.

Reading this indictment one sympathizes with the writer who protested against the review of *The Notebooks* which appeared in the *New York Times* on December 16, 1956. The reviewer called Simone Weil "Jewish, supremely and proudly so," praised "everything" she wrote as "new-minted, pure gold," and hailed her as "one of the greatest minds of our time." It is odd how such reviews make their appearance, but it is perhaps more disturbing to see how Simone Weil is presented to the public as *nothing but* a spiritual hero—a woman endowed with a restless, brilliant mind, who wrote about Homer, Plato, politics, mythology, and mathematics, a woman who explored the mysteries of divine love and transformed herself into a "pilgrim of the absolute." This transfiguration of Simone Weil has now become the conventional public portrait. Perhaps she was all these things, but she was more: she was also blind, cruel, and almost delusional, and she indulged in orgies of self-laceration. Did she draw up the terrible indictment of the religion of her people in order to inflict yet deeper wounds upon herself, and did she believe this new agony would make her more pleasing in the eyes of the new God?

In her discussion of the *Iliad,* Simone Weil perceived, and partly admired, a supernatural quality and magnificence behind the inhuman, wasteful violence which she assumed to be the main theme of Homer's epic. But the bloodshed, violence, and brutality she reads of in the Old Testament inspired in her only

horror. "Moses—starts off with a murder—Joshua—then a host of 'Judges' (murders, betrayals)—Samuel—Saul—David—Solomon—Kings of Judah and Israel. . . ." For Simone Weil the history of the ancient Hebrews is a unique record of murders and massacres. "Practically the only thing the Hebrews did was to exterminate." She duly notes "Abraham's cruelty towards Hagar and Ishmael"; the "horrible crime" committed by Jacob's children against the Hivites; "Joseph's atrocious conduct towards the Egyptians"; she counts the number of deaths caused by battle, plague, and earthquakes; and she dwells with horror and disgust upon the "deceitful," "barbarous" actions enjoined in Deuteronomy 20:10-18: and "thou shalt utterly destroy them, the Hittites, the Amorites, the Canaanites, the Perrizites, the Hivites and the Jebusites"—as if the Greeks she so admired had not sacked and ravaged Troy. Or, more importantly, as if these dark and stark injunctions of the Old Testament did not have a meaning in the natural evolution of the Jewish faith and people beyond their overt cruelty. For Simone Weil there was but one conclusion: Israel was an "artificial people, held together by a terrible violence." "What about the human sacrifices made to Baal?" Her answer: "The extermination of whole peoples is something far more appalling." Thus "everything [in the Old Testament] is of a polluted and atrocious character . . . beginning with Abraham, right down through all his descendants . . . as though to indicate perfectly clearly: Beware! That way lies evil."

Israel's "pollution" lies in its immorality and materialism. Here the record, according to Simone Weil, is, if anything, worse than that of the atrocities. The books of the Old Testament reek of carnal lust, incest, prostitution, defilement, drunkenness, deceit, theft, and fraud. There are but a few among the patriarchs who escape this charge. "Abraham defiles himself" and "hands his wife over to Pharaoh out of cowardice." Thus "the history of Israel begins with a prostitution. It is Israel's original impurity." And the original impurity was multiplied on a grand scale: Isaac "repeats Abraham's sin of cowardice. He allows himself to be deceived by Jacob, blinded by gluttony and foolishness. . . ." Jacob, in turn, "obtains the rights of the first-born by a cruel form of blackmail, and his father's blessings by lies and fraud. At Bethel he practices blackmail on God. He swindles Laban about the cattle. . . . Reuben (his eldest son) cohabits with his father's concubine. . . . Judah lies with his son's widow taking her to be a prostitute." There is nothing overlooked in Simone Weil's violent outbursts of moral indignation—not even the "excessive prosperity of the children of Israel in Egypt."

This is not the first time (nor will it be the last) that such accusations have been made against Israel, and against Israel alone—as if the civilizations of Greece, India, Egypt, and other peoples, among all those in whom Simone Weil discovers sparks of divine incarnation, did not reveal the same primitive morality of nature. Or, more importantly, as if we were not here (as elsewhere) dealing with stories, myths, and memories which recapture the dramatic origins of and transitions toward the so-called civilized morality which she applies in judging them. For Simone Weil there is but one conclusion: "The Hebrews, having rejected the Egyptian revelation, got the God they deserved—a carnal and collective God, who never spoke to anyone's soul, up to the time of exile." They were "too carnal-minded for any other God but Jehovah."

Hence Jehovah is Satan in disguise; and the religious mission of Israel is, at best, a warning that "this way lies evil," at worst, a terrible fraud and deceit. The only good thing that can be said for Israel is that it "represents an attempt at a supernatural form of social life," that "it succeeded in producing the best example of its kind"; but that "the result shows the sort of divine revelation of which the Great Beast (this is Simone Weil's way of designating the world of nature and man) is capable." Both Israel and ancient Rome are incarnations of the Great Beast. And the Famous Law of the Old Testament "was a sort of curse, as St. Paul says."

Thus, in the Pauline-Gnostic tradition, no good, let alone salvation, can come from the Law, or from this attempt to infuse social life with a supernatural or divine spirit. "Israel's spirituality was exclusively collective," and to ascribe any divine mission to the Jewish people is a mockery in view of their carnal and cruel nature. They were "*chosen* in order to be rendered blind, to be the executioner of Christ." (Perhaps Simone Weil, too, remembered taunts heard in childhood that she belonged to the people of "Christ-killers.") Rome and Israel "are perhaps the only two people to be ignorant of incarnation," and "it is for this reason that everything in Israel is contaminated with sin, because there is nothing pure without a participation in the incarnate divinity."

This passionate Gnostic denial of any trace of divinity or spirituality in the sacred Scriptures of Israel caused Simone Weil considerable trouble. After all, the Old Testament did preach an undeniably pure monotheism and did contain many specific injunctions against idolatry, and it was equally undeniable that the prophets, at least, displayed a "Messianic mentality." But, alas, this mentality "blinded them to the truth of the Messiah." It is pathetic to see how Simone Weil twists and distorts the Old Testament to make it all appear as pure deficit on her balance sheet. "The belief in a one and only God," of course, is incompatible—at least, for non-Christians—with religious dogmas like the Trinity or with faith in a divine mediator. But for Simone Weil, this striving for a pure monotheism was precisely "the cause" of what she called the "moral blindness" or the "tribal collectivism" of Israel. "There cannot be any contact as from one person to another between man and God except through the person of the Mediator. Apart from him, the only way in which God can be present to man is in a collective, a national way." The divine spirit without mediation turns into the "demoniacal." Hence, paradoxical as it may sound, their opposition to idolatry was the greatest misfortune of the Jewish people. In the first place, this opposition made an *eidolon*—and not a holy people—out of Israel itself: "no statue used to be created for Jehovah; but Israel is the statue of Jehovah"; and, in the second place, it caused Israel's doom: "The Jews were not allowed to be 'idolaters,' because otherwise they would not have killed Christ. If some ancient Hebrews were to come amongst us, the images of Christ crucified, the worship of the Virgin, and above all the Eucharist, God's real presence in a piece of matter, would be regarded by them as being that very thing which they were accustomed to name idolatry." The refusal to submit to this idolatry, then, constitutes Israel's religious failure; for the problem of "monotheism" can be "solved" only, as in Christianity, "through the Incarnation, and . . . the Virgin and Saints."

The specific accusations rise to a veritable paroxysm of religious anti-Semitism in the terrible summing up of the indictment: "It is not surprising that a people composed of fugitive slaves, or rather of the children of fugitive slaves, led forth to take possession by a series of massacres of a land whose soft climate and natural fertility gave it a paradise-like quality, and which had been organized on a flourishing basis by civilizations

in whose labors they had taken no part, and which they proceeded to destroy—that such a people was unable to produce anything very good. . . . To speak of 'God as educator' in connection with this people is a heinous sort of joke. Is it surprising that there should be so much evil in a civilization—our own—which is corrupted at its roots, in its very inspiration, by this atrocious lie? The curse of Israel weighs upon Christendom. The atrocities, the extermination of heretics and of unbelievers—all this was Israel. Capitalism was Israel. . . . Totalitarianism is Israel (more particularly so among the latter's worst enemies)." There is only one poison in the modern world—"the notion of progress"—which is "specifically Christian." "The other poisons mixed up with the truth of Christianity are of Jewish origin" and must be purged, as Marcion before her believed, from the body of Christian faith and dogma. "Jehovah, the Church of the Middle Ages, H[itler]—all these are earthly Gods"—in short, incarnations of Satan.

Reading this terrible outburst, one is moved to hope that Simone Weil attained in death what she did not attain in life: the peace that passeth understanding, and that she did not take the voices of demons for the silence of God. But these are matters on which we cannot cast any light. We can ask a more modest question and wonder, on a human plane, what sources may have contributed to this revival of Gnosticism, to this individual recapitulation of a historical crisis. Why could Simone Weil believe in a God of love and grace only through converting the God of the Jewish people into an incarnation of Satan? *The Notebooks* reveal that she inflicted this deep wound upon herself and committed this slander upon her own people as a last desperate measure of defense against total despair. The Christian faith (into which she was never baptized) was her last hope among the ruins of existence. For Simone Weil's "reading of reality"—as she called the struggle raging in her soul—yielded a pattern of alienation from the world, man and God.

"The world is uninhabitable"; and everything in it is evil. "That is why we have to flee to the next." The natural order of things, according to her, was subject to an inexorable, meaningless necessity—the force of "gravity," and gravity produced nothing but suffering and pain, disgust and despair. It is Kafka's world: "Our life is nothing but impossibility, absurdity. . . . Contradiction is our wretchedness; and the feeling of our wretchedness is the feeling of our reality. . . . That's why we must love it." It is the world of Ivan Karamazov: there is no reason, "absolutely none," by which the intellect can answer Ivan's doubt and despair at all the senseless and unjustifiable evil in this world—or, "one only": that it is an inscrutable, unintelligible manifestation of "supernatural love; that it is God's will. And for this last reason I would just as readily accept a world which was only evil and whose consequences could only be evil as a child's tear."

The world as it is, then, is utter darkness, and to think that a God could illuminate or "sanctify" it, in the language of Jewish tradition, blasphemes the faith that Simone Weil sought to embrace. Such Gnosticism voices an anguished protest and revolt against the sufferings of the human race throughout history, and against the hypocrisy by which it has often tried to cover over its misery. But when dark despair saps the marrow of the self, such a revolt is condemned to remain a pathetic, futile, impotent gesture that delivers human fate all the more completely into the hands of the mysterious, incomprehensible powers responsible for the suffering and the evil endured by mankind.

It is the estimate of man and of his powers vis-à-vis the world and God that decides the quality and direction of the Gnostic revolt. In Simone Weil, the curse of "gravity" or heaviness laid upon the world produced a painful excess of self-mortification. "Everything which is in me, without exception, is absolutely valueless.... Everything which I appropriate to myself becomes immediately valueless. *Ouden eimi:* I am nothing." *The Notebooks* develop ingenious variations on this theme: "I have to love to be nothing. How horrible it would be if I were something. I have to love my nothingness, love to be nothingness." Or, in the moments of greatest despair: "Leprosy—that is me. All that I am is leprosy. The 'I' as such is leprosy."

The Need for Roots—Simone Weil's political testament—to the contrary notwithstanding, these attitudes toward the world and the self do not create genuine possibilities in the sphere of social action. Simone Weil, as we have seen, participated in social movements and political affairs, but "what she cared about," as T. S. Eliot put it, "was human souls" [see excerpt dated 1952]—more specifically the salvation of human souls, not social blueprints or political manifestoes. For "the social is irremediably the domain of the devil." "Man is a social animal, and the social element represents evil.... It follows that life cannot be anything else but a spiritual laceration." Simone Weil's social ethics was as simple and severe as her personal ethics: unconditional surrender to the inscrutable will of God. "Even if one could be like unto God, it would be preferable to be a handful of mud that is obedient to God."

That the spirit of God may prevail, the body must die. Simone Weil lived to die unto the body. Most of the Gnostic sects, too, subscribed to an extreme asceticism and other-worldliness. Spiritual existence, especially for the elect, was incompatible with the desires of the flesh. The Marcionites, it is said, required married people to submit to divorce in order to be eligible for baptism. Somewhat analogously, Simone Weil believed that the church was even too lax in its taboo against all sexual intercourse not serving the purpose of procreation. According to her, one should "utterly renounce" the sexual act as such, and then "resort to it on the few occasions in the course of a lifetime" that were unavoidable lest the race become extinct. "In this way there would scarcely be any difference between the father of a family and a monk, so far as chastity is concerned." A casual remark like this is worth pondering in order to appreciate the kind of revulsion Simone Weil must have felt when reading the early books of the Old Testament—or when contemplating her own sexuality.

A reading of reality like Simone Weil's is prelude to a religion of absurdity. Like Kierkegaard, the solitary Danish thinker of the nineteenth century who has come to mean so much to the distraught minds of our time, Simone Weil leaped into faith on the wings of the absurd. "Extreme justice combined with the appearance of extreme injustice ..."; "God both One and three ..."; "Christ both God and man ..."; "The Host both earthly matter and body of God ..."—these are some of the religious paradoxes over which Simone Weil brooded and suffered. But, as we have seen, human existence itself is absurd: "Contradiction is our wretchedness; and the feeling of our wretchedness is the feeling of our reality." Crushed by contradictions, she made "contradiction" the criterion of faith. "Contradiction is our path toward God because we are creatures, and because creation is itself a contradiction." Or: "Contradiction experienced right to the very depths of the being means spiritual laceration, it means the Cross." The two realms

of being, nature and the spirit, body and soul, the world and God, loomed in her mind as absolutely incommensurable and irreconcilable. True to the Gnostic tradition, Simone Weil tried to overcome the terrible strain between these two dimensions, which she could not reconcile by human powers, by an appeal to mysterious, supernatural powers of mediation. She searched frantically for signs of mediation, and discovered mediating incarnations everywhere: in the religion of the Chaldeans and of the Egyptians, in the Upanishads and the Bhagavad-Gita, in Greek mythology, poetry, and drama, in Plato, Homer, and the Orphic mysteries, in Norse mythology, in Taoism and Zen Buddhism, in music and in mathematics—everywhere, she believed, there were signs and indications which anticipated man's final delivery from sin and death in the incarnation of Jesus as the Christ: everywhere—except in Israel and Rome.

Perhaps it is not so difficult to see now why Israel remained the great offense and stumbling block in this desperate pursuit of personal salvation. And perhaps the terrible curse Simone Weil laid upon the religion of her own people is a blessing in disguise. For what makes her shrink back in horror from "the goodly tents of Jacob and the tabernacles of Israel" upon which Balaam bestowed a reluctant blessing? What else but the purity of its monotheism gradually cleansed of all traces of magic and idolatrous imagery; the simple faith that the ordinary life of man, the intractable Adam, the mighty Leviathan, the great Earth Mother, the flesh, society, and nature, might be infused with a spirit of civilized humanity, or, in religious language, might be hallowed and sanctified; the prophetic faith that peace, love, and justice might transform man into a being pleasing in the sight of God; the human faith that the divine word is a gift to man in this life, not a promise of blessedness beyond; that the *Shechinah* is imprisoned in this world, not enthroned in the next; hence, the stubborn faith that this world is unredeemed; and perhaps the most creative of all ideas of religion, that which is born of the tension between the faith that the world is not redeemed and the resolve that it be redeemed by man's works and love. I don't know what the learned rabbis say, but speaking for myself, I find these "offenses" to be Israel's great and lasting contribution and the basis for my own private belief that it is worth being a Jew in a Christian world.

Simone Weil chose to condemn these "offenses" in the name of divine love and grace at a time when the prophetic faith of Israel was being gassed out of existence. She was not satisfied with such simple roots of faith as Israel's, but it is at least an open question whether she herself was not more uprooted—by *her* faith, which left her dangling in the No Man's Land of theological obscurantism—than the people to whom she offered *The Need for Roots*. Since she ultimately despaired of man, she could not believe that there might be a *human* life beyond despair. And thus her struggle for a new faith, powerful, passionate, and poignant as it is, is ultimately the expression of a desperate nihilism. The last message of hope is that of *The Grand Inquisitor:* magic, mystery, and authority. And perhaps this is the message that will prevail in our time.

Why did the God of Israel become the incarnation of Satan? Why did Simone Weil choose to condemn only the Jewish people? As we have seen, she discovered divine incarnations among a great many peoples of the ancient world—even though their historical and religious records (not to speak of that of the Christian peoples) were likewise filled with lust, incest, rape, cruelty, violence, and murder. Why the exception in the case of Israel? Why the one terrible curse amid the many generous blessings? And why did she even misread the text of the Hebrew Bible in order to make the curse stick? Thus, Jacob's wrestling with the angel is seen as another instance of "Israel's original impurity." What offends her so deeply in this story is the fact that Jacob is not destroyed by the angel, but seems to emerge victoriously from the struggle. Hence her accusing question: "Isn't it the greatest possible calamity, when you are wrestling with God, not to be beaten?" It is indeed—when the encounter between the human and the divine cannot be envisaged in any other terms but those of unconditional submission, obedience, and impotence on the part of man. The Biblical tale is much more subtle, however, than Simone Weil could perceive. Jacob does not emerge simply as the victor; or his alleged victory has quite a different meaning. The episode ends with these words: "And Jacob asked him, and said, Tell me . . . thy name. And he said, Wherefore is it that thou dost ask after my name? And he blessed him there" (Genesis 32:29). In other words, Jacob receives a blessing from, but not the "name" of, the angel; or the power of the blessing does not derive from Jacob's gaining possession of the *magic* name of the God. The characteristic religious significance of this incident—the conflict of magic and monotheism—escapes her altogether, just as she is completely blind to the Hebrew Scriptures' depiction of the slow, painful transformation of tribal hordes into a holy people making a covenant with God.

It is difficult to think, against the background of contemporary history, that such blind spots are due only to a Gnostic theology; or to avoid the suspicion that personal factors must have contributed to this revival of Gnosticism. *The Notebooks* reveal despair and self-hatred *in extremis;* they cry out in anguish over the absence of perfection and love in this world. Perhaps the faith of her fathers assumed such monstrous shape in the mind of Simone Weil because she demanded from them—her fathers and her people—a degree of perfection and a purity of love which are inhuman. Because they were not pure and perfect, her incapacity to love them as they were—or her incapacity to be loved as she was—turned into hatred and despair. Because her people were tainted with the flaws of our common mortality, she despaired at ever erasing these flaws in herself. And thus she came to curse those she may have loved most—and herself for the failure of perfection and love in their lives and hers. Perhaps this helps to explain the wild Gnostic "antitheses" that took shape in her mind: either absolute perfection and pure love or complete wretchedness and total despair—either all or nothing.

"What does it matter that there should never be joy in me, since there is perpetually perfect joy in God." What does it matter, indeed, if the lovelessness of one's own existence is ultimately the only condition for believing in the infinite love of God. "The attentive contemplation of misery, without compensation and consolation, drives us into the supernatural, and then we cannot do otherwise than love the source of it." We cannot do otherwise, because the only proof of God's perfection "is that we love him" precisely because of the misery he has inflicted upon us. The deepest roots of such a theology, all verbal protestations and overt actions to the contrary notwithstanding, are nourished by contempt, hatred, and cruelty toward man. "Contempt of human misery is the only source of supernatural felicity." Where did she find these bitter words in the sayings of Jesus? Perhaps she had to be so cruel and unforgiving to those she loved because she could not forgive herself for the contempt and cruelty in her own love. And thus she exalted to the level of supernatural grace what she could not resolve on the level of human gravity. Faith is the last refuge from despair at the failure of life: "Relentless necessity,

Type of machinery operated by Weil in Paris. From Simone Weil: A Fellowship in Love, *by Jacques Cabaud. Channel Press, 1964.*

misery, distress, the crushing burden of poverty and the exhausting labour, cruelty, torture, violent death, constraint, terror, disease—all this is but the divine love. It is God who out of love withdraws from us so that we can love him."

Thus God withdraws from a world that is doomed; he becomes the "absent God," *Deus absconditus*—because of the total absence of love and hope on earth. "Life," according to Simone Weil, was but "an ersatz form of salvation." Perhaps the salvation she sought was but an ersatz form of life. (pp. 74-85)

> Hans Meyerhoff, "Contra Simone Weil: 'The Voices
> of Demons for the Silence of God'," in Arguments
> and Doctrines: A Reader of Jewish Thinking in the
> Aftermath of the Holocaust, edited by Arthur A. Cohen,
> Harper & Row Publishers, 1970, pp. 70-85.

RICHARD REES (essay date 1958)

[An English critic and translator, Rees was an authority on Weil and translated several of her works. In the following excerpt, he discusses Weil's unfinished drama, Venise sauvée.*]*

Simone Weil's play [*Venise Sauvée*] is based upon the Abbé de Saint-Réal's narrative, upon which Otway also drew for *Venice Preserved*. It is the story of an unsuccessful Spanish plot to overthrow the Venetian Government, in the year 1618. The historical facts are obscure but are almost certainly more or less as given in Saint-Réal's semi-fictional narrative. The Spanish ambassador at Venice is said to have entrusted to some Provençal adventurers and corsairs the task of carrying out a *coup d'état* which would deliver Venice to the King of Spain. The plot failed because one or more of the conspirators betrayed it to the Venetian Council of Ten. What is certain, at any rate, is that:

> On a fine May morning in 1618 the citizens of
> Venice saw some corpses, disfigured by tor-
> ture, hanging between the pillars of St. Mark's;

and the rumour quickly spread that they were some foreign officers who had conspired to deliver the city to the Spaniards.

Simone Weil made use of this episode to illustrate, somewhat in the manner of the Greek tragedies with which her mind was penetrated, the theme of redemptive suffering. Her hero, Jaffier, is the outstanding figure among the conspirators, the one whom all admire as the perfect leader—and he is suddenly stricken with pity for Venice. Having obtained the promise that if he reveals information of vital import to the State of Venice, a free pardon will be granted to twenty persons whom he will name, he reveals to the Secretary of the Council all the details of the plot. His information is verified and the twenty leading conspirators, Jaffier's friends, are arrested. This happens on the eve of the great Ascension Day festival of the marriage of Venice with the Adriatic.

The Council of Ten are horrified on discovering the extent of the unsuspected danger, for it is clear that the conspiracy would infallibly have succeeded; and in their panic they revoke the promise of pardon. Jaffier's friends are tortured and executed. It was the council's intention to reward Jaffier with a high office in return for his service, but knowing he would refuse after the breaking of their promise, they offer him money instead, with banishment in perpetuity from the State of Venice. He at first refuses the money, but when the full horror of his position dawns upon him his spirit breaks and he accepts. While he is waiting under guard for the escort which will conduct him across the Venetian frontier, it is learned that there is still a pocket of resistance where the conspirators' troops are fighting in the centre of the city. The guards make no effort to prevent Jaffier when he rushes out to join the fight and die with the remaining conspirators. Thus they avoid a tiresome duty and are left free to enjoy the festival.

The working out of this drama enables Simone Weil to illustrate a number of her fundamental ideas, and above all her interpretation of the Christian theory of redemptive suffering. The conspirators, who are the tools of a great power, are all of them "uprooted" men, who have become corsairs and adventurers after banishment from their home countries. Their chief supporter in Venice is a Greek courtesan of noble birth who has been seduced and betrayed, and whose father has been put to death, by the Venetian governor of her native island. The Spanish empire is an example of Plato's "great animal," the social monster which automatically obeys the law that every being always seeks to expand and to exercise all the power at its disposal; the *ersatz* divinity whose service makes men believe themselves to be supermen and therefore dispensed from the normal obligations of humanity.

Venice, by contrast, represents the kind of good that men may hope to enjoy, in an imperfect form, in this world. A city, however wicked, is not a social monster to the same extent as an empire or a state. It is a human environment in which men can be rooted and can find nourishment for their souls. Men identified with a social monster come to think of themselves as "we" rather than as individuals. The Romans and the ancient Hebrews, according to Simone Weil, always thought in terms of "we"; and "we," she believed, is an even more dangerous obstacle to enlightenment than "I." She considered that even membership of a church is liable to create such an obstacle; and in her play the conspiracy itself represents a social monster for the conspirators. They are uprooted and homeless men, and the conspiracy gives them a sort of status, converting them from isolated individuals into members of an organisation who can think of themselves as "we."

Moreover, Venice is beautiful and can be loved for its beauty. Violetta, the daughter of the Secretary of the Council, symbolises this beauty, which is, as always, a precarious harmony of chance and the good, and her happy innocence is as fragile and vulnerable as a spray of apple blossom. At the end of the play Jaffier rushes out to die in a street fight. His sacrifice of friends, honour, ambition and happiness has at least saved Violetta's city and made it possible for her to enjoy the festival she so much looks forward to. Violetta knows nothing about the conspiracy, nor that Jaffier, whom she admires, is about to die. She comes on to the empty stage and speaks a few simple lines, like a Greek chorus, evoking the early morning light on the canals and palaces of Venice, bride of the sea, and her own excitement and joy at the prospect of the celebrations to come. So the play ends.

The Spanish ambassador's chief representative among the conspirators is a Frenchman, Renaud, who is the mouthpiece of traditional power politics. In his terms, the action of Spain against Venice is a necessity dictated by the objective European situation; and Simone Weil stresses in her notes that the behaviour of all the actors in the drama is similarly dictated by their situation in life. Evil is automatically transmitted by a process which continues indefinitely until someone, by a recoil of pity and imaginative vision, takes the evil to himself in the form of suffering. Such a recoil reverses the psychological law of gravity, and is therefore supernatural. In his discourses on the art of governing a conquered people, Renaud emphasises the supreme importance of uprooting them psychologically, so that they feel the ground has fallen away beneath their feet and that henceforth their only security lies in obedience to their conquerors—whom for this reason they will in the end come to love. When Jaffier says that the prospect of absolute power which will be his on the morrow makes him feel he is dreaming, Renaud replies that men who raise themselves to the plane on which history is made are indeed dreamers. But great men of action prefer dreams to reality; a great conqueror compels his victims to dream what he dictates, to dream his own dreams. It is, however, Renaud's speeches which prick Jaffier awake.

When we imagine evil, we imagine it as something romantic and exciting; but in reality it is common, monotonous and boring and also, above all, it is unreal—it is a state of dreaming. When we imagine good, we imagine it as tedious; but in reality it is always miraculously fresh and exciting—but also it is abnormal and infinitely rare. Jaffier awakens to the reality of Venice, and it therefore becomes *impossible* for him not to do whatever is necessary to save it. (*"Fallait bien,"* as the Breton sailor said.) In this way he becomes, as it were, the lightning conductor for the whole charge of evil which, by automatic transmission, would include the ruin of Venice in its unending sequence of dream-events; and in him all this great mass of evil is transmuted into suffering. He has not merely to suffer but also to be disgraced, and not merely in the eyes of the world but in his own. He must lose his self-respect. He has betrayed all his friends, including his best friend, Pierre, to whom he was closer than a brother; and finally he accepts the money reward so that he may have somewhere "to hide himself and sleep and eat." In her notebook Simone Weil quotes "Niobe also, of the beautiful hair, thought of eating" and comments: "That is sublime in the same way as space in Giotto's frescoes. A humiliation which forces us to renounce even despair." In her terminology, this is to "accept the void," and it is only when a man accepts the void that grace can enter in.

Some will find it self-evident that when Simone Weil uses this kind of language, she is speaking of what she knows. Others will disagree. But even those who are entirely sceptical, in a general way, of the assertions of all the great mystics and, in particular, of Simone Weil's experience described earlier in this book, might ponder her sketch of the last judgement and her "wager." In the former she imagines that at the moment of death the soul will be convinced that all the ends, including God, towards which its actions were directed during life were illusions; and her wager assumes that it is better to act as if God existed because in that case "no revelation at the moment of death can cause us any regret; for though chance or the devil ruled all the worlds we should still not regret having lived as we did," and in any case "to say that this world isn't worth anything, that this life isn't worth anything, and to adduce evil as the proof, is absurd; for if it isn't worth anything, of what exactly does evil deprive us?"

As to Jaffier, we are not told in the play whether he felt himself to be in a state of grace at the end. All we know is that he died ignominiously in a street fight. But clearly his actions are intended as an example of perfection. "I, if I be lifted up from the earth, will draw all men unto me," and those who have been lifted up have usually come to an ignominious end. We cannot lift ourselves, we can only be lifted:

> If I say to myself every morning: "I am courageous, I am not afraid," I may become courageous but with a courage which conforms to what, in my present imperfection, I imagine under that name, and accordingly my courage will not go beyond this imperfection. It can only be a modification on the same plane, not a change of plane.
>
> Contradiction is the criterion. We cannot by suggestion obtain things which are incompatible. Only grace can do that. A sensitive person who by suggestion becomes courageous hardens himself; often he may even, by a sort of savage pleasure, amputate his own sensitivity. Grace alone can give courage while leaving the sensitivity intact, or sensitivity while leaving the courage intact.
>
> The metaphor of altitude corresponds to this. If I am on the side of a mountain, from a certain spot on a level path I can see a lake; from another spot, after making a few steps, a forest. I have to choose: it has to be either the lake or the forest. If I want to see both the lake and the forest at the same time, I have got to climb higher.
>
> The only thing is, here the mountain doesn't exist. It is made of air. One has to be drawn upward.

This is the principle of what Simone Weil calls the experimental ontological proof. We have no capacity to raise ourselves, and no imaginary perfection can raise us, for it must be on the same level as we who imagine it. "What draws us up is directing our thoughts towards a veritable perfection." (pp. 191-200)

Venise Sauvée . . . which appears to be a classic tragedy of personal heroism is in fact concerned with the impersonal. Jaffier is not a free agent. Once the supernatural has taken

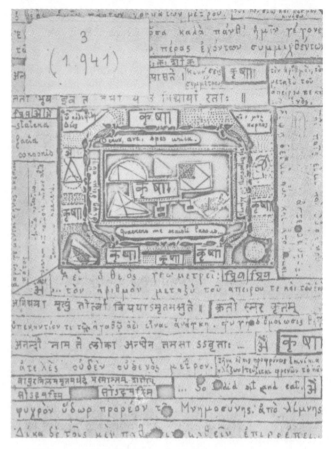

Weil's hand-illustrated cover of her 1941 notebook. From La vie de Simone Weil, *by Simone Petrement. Librairie Arteme Fayard, 1973.*

possession of him he has no choice but to act as he does. Whether this would have enabled him to withhold under torture the names of his fellow conspirators cannot be known. In the play, the Venetians believe he has such strength of mind that it would be useless to torture him. But it is unlikely that the author thought the same. In her notebooks she wrote:

> The "I" is killed all the faster the weaker the character of the person who undergoes affliction. Or, to be more precise, the affliction-limit, the "I"-destroying point of affliction varies according to the nature of the person; the limit is situated more or less far along the road of affliction, depending on the character, and the farther along it is situated the stronger we esteem the character to be. But this limit, whether it be situated here or there, exists in the case of all human beings, and if they are borne along by fate to the point of affliction which constitutes their limit, the "I" in them is caught up in the process of destruction.

But the personal tragedy of Jaffier is in a sense irrelevant. He has been the instrument of the supernatural and Venice has been saved; moreover, for Simone Weil, personal tragedy is almost always the inevitable condition of enlightenment, of freedom from the bondage of the "I," and of release for the impersonal element in the soul which is the chief source of whatever is sacred in every human being. (pp. 203-04)

Richard Rees, in a chapter in his Brave Men: A Study of D. H. Lawrence and Simone Weil, *Victor Gollancz Ltd., 1958, pp. 191-206.*

CZESŁAW MIŁOSZ (essay date 1960)

[*The winner of the 1980 Nobel Prize in literature, Miłosz is often called Poland's greatest living poet, although for political reasons his work was not published in Poland for over forty years and he has been in exile since 1951. In his work, Miłosz has for the most part avoided the experimentation with language that characterizes much modern poetry, concentrating instead on the clear expression of ideas. As he stated in his critical study of Polish literature: "When a poet is overwhelmed by strong emotions, his form tends to become more simple and more direct." Much of Miłosz's work is indeed strongly emotional and communicates a transcendent spirituality. Critics have commented on the influence of his Roman Catholic background and his Manichean fascination with good and evil. In addition to poetry, Miłosz's writings include literary studies, philosophical essays, and works examining the historical events of twentieth-century Eastern Europe. In the following excerpt from an essay which was first published in 1960, Miłosz discusses the spiritual and intellectual importance of Weil's work.*]

France offered a rare gift to the contemporary world in the person of Simone Weil. The appearance of such a writer in the twentieth century was against all the rules of probability, yet improbable things do happen. (p. 85)

Tactless in her writings and completely indifferent to fashions, she was able to go straight to the heart of the matter which preoccupies so many people today. I quote: "A man whose whole family died under torture, and who had himself been tortured for a long time in a concentration camp. Or a sixteenth-century Indian, the sole survivor after the total extermination of his people. Such men if they had previously believed in the mercy of God would either believe it no more, or else they would conceive of it quite differently than before." Conceive of it how? the solution proposed by Simone Weil is not to the taste of those who worship the goddess of History; it may be heretical from the Thomist point of view as well.

A few words should be said about Simone Weil's road to Christianity. She was imbued with Greek philosophy. Her beloved master was Plato, read and reread in the original. One can notice a paradox of similarity between our times and the times of decadent Rome, when for many people Plato—that "Greek Moses," as he was sometimes called—served as a guide to the promised land of Christendom. Such was the love of Simone Weil for Greece that she looked at all Greek philosophy as eminently Christian—with one exception: Aristotle, in her words "a bad tree which bore bad fruit." She rejected practically all Judaic tradition. She was never acquainted with Judaism and did not want to be, as she was unable to pardon the ancient Hebrews their cruelties, for instance the ruthless extermination of all the inhabitants of Canaan. A strange leftist, she categorically opposed any notion of progress in morality, that widely spread view according to which crimes committed three thousand years ago can be justified to a certain extent because men at that time were "less developed." And she was making early Christianity responsible for introducing, through the idea of "divine pedagogy," a "poison," namely, the notion of historical progress in morality. She says: "The great mistake of the Marxists and of the whole of the nineteenth century was to think that by walking straight ahead one would rise into the air." In her opinion, crimes of the remote past had to be judged as severely as those committed today. That is why she had a true horror of ancient Rome, a totalitarian

state not much better than the Hitlerian. She felt early Christians were right when they gave Rome the name of the Apocalyptic Beast. Rome completely destroyed the old civilizations of Europe, probably superior to the civilization of the Romans who were nothing but barbarians, so skillful in slandering their victims that they falsified for centuries our image of pre-Roman Europe. Rome also contaminated Christianity in its early formative stage. The principle, *anathema sit,* is of Roman origin. The only true Christian civilization was emerging in the eleventh and twelfth centuries in the countries of the Langue d'Oc, between the Mediterranean and the Loire. After it was destroyed by the Frenchmen who invaded that territory from the north and massacred the heretics—the Albigensians—there has not been any Christian civilization anywhere.

Violent in her judgments and uncompromising, Simone Weil was, at least by temperament, an Albigensian, a Cathar; this is the key to her thought. She drew extreme conclusions from the Platonic current in Christianity. (pp. 90-1)

The Albigensians were rooted in the old Manichaean tradition and, through it, akin to some sects of the Eastern Church of Bulgaria and of Russia. In their eyes God the monarch worshiped by the believers, could not be justified as he was a false God, a cruel Jehovah, an inferior demiurge, identical with the Prince of Darkness. Following the Manichaean tradition, Simone Weil used to say that when we pronounce the words of the Lord's Prayer: "Thy kingdom come" we pray for the end of the world as only then the power of the Prince of Darkness will be abolished. Yet she immediately added that "Thy will be done on earth" means our agreement to the existence of the world. All her philosophy is placed between these two poles.

There is a contradiction between our longing for the good, and the cold universe absolutely indifferent to any values, subject to the iron necessity of causes and effects. That contradiction has been solved by the rationalists and progressives of various kinds who placed the good in this world, in matter, and usually in the future. The philosophy of Hegel and of his followers crowned those attempts by inventing the idea of the good in movement, walking toward fuller and fuller accomplishment in history. Simone Weil, a staunch determinist (in this respect she was not unlike Spinoza), combatted such solutions as illegitimate. Her efforts were directed toward making the contradiction as acute as possible. Whoever tries to escape an inevitable contradiction by patching it up, is, she affirms, a coward. That is why she had been accused of having been too rigid and of having lacked a dialectical touch. Yet one can ask whether she was not more dialectical than many who practice the dialectical art by changing it into an art of compromises and who buy the unity of the opposites too cheaply.

Certainly her vision is not comforting. In the center we find the idea of the willful abdication of God, of the withdrawal of God from the universe. I quote: "God committed all phenomena without exception to the mechanism of the world." "The distance between the necessary and the good is the selfsame distance as that between the creature and the Creator." "Necessity is God's veil." "We must let the rational in the Cartesian sense, that is to say mechanical rule or necessity in its humanly demonstrable form, reside wherever we are able to imagine it, so that we might bring to light that which lies outside its range." "The absence of God is the most marvelous testimony of perfect love, and that is why pure necessity, necessity which is manifestly different from the good, is so beautiful." She allows neither the Providence of the traditional Christian preachers, nor the historical Providence of the progressive preachers. Does it mean that we are completely in the power of *la pesanteur,* gravity, that the cry of our heart is never answered? No. There is one exception from the universal determinism and that is Grace. "Contradiction" says Simone Weil, "is a lever of transcendence." "Impossibility is the door of the supernatural. We can only knock at it. Someone else opens it." God absent, God hidden, *Deus absconditus,* acts in the world through persuasion, through grace which pulls us out of *la pesanteur,* gravity, if we do not reject his gift. Those who believe that the contradiction between necessity and the good can be solved on any level other than that of mystery delude themselves. "We have to be in a desert. For he whom we must love is absent." "To love God through and across the destruction of Troy and Carthage, and without consolation. Love is not consolation, it is light."

For Simone Weil society is as subject to the rule of necessity as all the phenomena of the world. Yet if nature is nothing but necessity and therefore innocent, below the level of good and evil, society is a domain where beings endowed with consciousness suffer under the heel of an ally and tenant of necessity, the Prince of Darkness. She says: "The Devil is collective (this is the God of Durkheim)." Her stand in politics is summed up in a metaphor she used often, taken from Plato. Plato compares society to a Great Beast. Every citizen has a relationship with that Beast, with the result that asked what is the good, everyone gives an answer in accordance with his function: for one the good consists in combing the hair of the Beast, for another in scratching its skin, for the third in cleaning its nails. In that way men lose the possibility of knowing the true good. In this Simone Weil saw the source of all absurdities and injustices. Man in the clutches of social determinism is no more than an unconscious worshiper of the Great Beast. She was against idealistic moral philosophy as it is a reflection of imperceptible pressures exerted upon individuals by a given social body. According to her, Protestantism also leads inevitably to conventional ethics reflecting national or class interests. As for Karl Marx, he was a seeker of pure truth; he wanted to liberate man from the visible and invisible pressures of group ethics by denouncing them and by showing how they operate. Because of that initial intention of Marx, Marxism is much more precious for the Christians than any idealistic philosophy. Yet Marx, in his desire for truth and justice, while trying to avoid one error fell into another which, argues Simone Weil, always happens if one rejects transcendence, the only foundation of the good accessible to man. Marx opposed class-dominated ethics with the new ethics of professional revolutionaries, also group ethics, and thus paved the way for a new form of domination by the Great Beast. This short aphorism sums up her views: "The whole of Marxism, in so far as it is true, is contained in that page of Plato on the Great Beast; and its refutation is there, too."

But Simone Weil did not turn her back on history and was a partisan of personal commitment. She denied that there is any "Marxist doctrine" and denounced dialectical materialism as a philosophical misunderstanding. In her view dialectical materialism simply does not exist, as the dialectical element and the materialist element, put together, burst the term asunder. By such a criticism she revealed the unpleasant secret known only to the inner circles of the Communist parties. On the contrary, class struggle, filling thousands of years of history, was for her the most palpable reality. Meditations on social determinism led her to certain conclusions as to the main problem of technical civilization. That problem looks as follows.

Primitive man was oppressed by the hostile forces of Nature. Gradually he won his freedom in constant struggle against it, he harnessed the powers of water, of fire, of electricity and put them to his use. Yet he could not accomplish that without introducing a division of labor and an organization of production. Very primitive societies are egalitarian, they live in the state of "primitive communism." Members of such communities are not oppressed by other members, fear is located outside as the community is menaced by wild animals, natural cataclysms, and sometimes other human groups. As soon as the efforts of man in his struggle with his surroundings become more productive, the community differentiates into those who order and those who obey. Oppression of man by man grows proportionally to the increase of his realm of action; it seems to be its necessary price. Facing Nature, the member of a technical civilization holds the position of a god, but he is a slave of society. The ultimate sanction of any domination of man by man is the punishment of death—either by the sword, the gun, or from starvation. Collective humanity emancipated itself. "But this collective humanity has itself taken on with respect to the individual the oppressive function formerly exercised by Nature."

Today Simone Weil could have backed her social analyses with many new examples; it is often being said that underdeveloped countries can industrialize themselves only at the price of accepting totalitarian systems. China, for instance, would have provided her with much material for reflection.

The basic social and political issue of the twentieth century is: "Can this emancipation, won by society, be transferred to the individual?" Simone Weil was pessimistic. The end of the struggle between those who obey and those who give orders is not in sight, she argued. The dominating groups do not relinquish their privileges unless forced to. Yet in spite of the upheavals of the masses, the very organization of production soon engenders new masters and the struggle continues under new banners and new names. Heraclitus was right: struggle is the mother of gods and men.

This does not mean we can dismiss history, seeing it as eternal recurrence, and shrug at its spectacle. Willing or not, we are committed. We should throw our act into the balance by siding with the oppressed and by diminishing as much as possible the oppressive power of those who give orders. Without expecting too much: *hubris,* lack of measure, is punished by Fate, inherent in the laws of iron necessity.

The importance of Simone Weil should be, I feel, assessed in the perspective of our common shortcomings. We do not like to think to the bitter end. We escape consequences in advance. Through the rigor exemplified by her life and her writing (classical, dry, concise), she is able to provoke a salutary shame. Why does she fascinate so many intellectuals today? Such is my hypothesis: If this is a theological age, it has a marked bias for Manichaeism. Modern literature testifies to a sort of rage directed against the world which no longer seems the work of a wise clockmaker. The humor of that literature (and think of Beckett, Ionesco, Genet), if it is humor at all, is a sneer, a *ricanement,* thrown in the face of the universe. Professor Michael Polany has recently advanced the thesis that the most characteristic feature of the last decades has been not a moral laxity but a moral frenzy exploding in the literature of the absurd as well as in revolutionary movements. Political assassination has been practiced in the name of man's victory over the brutal order of Nature. Yet the belief in the magic blessings of History is being undermined by the very outcome of that belief: industrialization. It is more and more obvious (in the countries of Eastern Europe as well) that refrigerators and television sets, or even rockets sent to the moon, do not change man into God. Old conflicts between human groups have been abolished but are replaced by new ones, perhaps more acute.

I translated the selected works of Simone Weil into Polish in 1958 not because I pretended to be a "Weilian." I wrote frankly in the preface that I consider myself a Caliban, too fleshy, too heavy, to take on the feathers of an Ariel. Simone Weil was an Ariel. My aim was utilitarian, in accordance, I am sure, with her wishes as to the disposition of her works. A few years ago I spent many afternoons in her family's apartment overlooking the Luxembourg Gardens—at her table covered with ink stains from her pen—talking to her mother, a wonderful woman in her eighties. Albert Camus took refuge in that apartment the day he received the Nobel prize and was hunted by photographers and journalists. My aim, as I say, was utilitarian. I resented the division of Poland into two camps: the clerical and the anticlerical, nationalistic Catholic and Marxist—I exclude of course the *aparatchiki,* bureaucrats just catching every wind from Moscow. I suspect unorthodox Marxists (I use that word for lack of a better one) and nonnationalistic Catholics have very much in common, at least common interests. Simone Weil attacked the type of religion that is only a social or national conformism. She also attacked the shallowness of the so-called progressives. Perhaps my intention, when preparing a Polish selection of her works, was malicious. But if a theological fight is going on—as it is in Poland, especially in high schools and universities—then every weapon is good to make adversaries goggle-eyed and to show that the choice between Christianity as represented by a national religion and the official Marxist ideology is not the only choice left to us today.

In the present world torn asunder by a much more serious religious crisis than appearances would permit us to guess, Catholic writers are often rejected by people who are aware of their own misery as seekers and who have a reflex of defense when they meet proud possessors of the truth. The works of Simone Weil are read by Catholics and Protestants, atheists and agnostics. She has instilled a new leaven into the life of believers and unbelievers by proving that one should not be deluded by existing divergences of opinion and that many a Christian is a pagan, many a pagan a Christian in his heart. Perhaps she lived exactly for that. Her intelligence, the precision of her style were nothing but a very high degree of attention given to the sufferings of mankind. And, as she says, "Absolutely unmixed attention is prayer." (pp. 92-8)

> *Czesław Miłosz, "The Importance of Simone Weil,"*
> *in his* Emperor of the Earth: Modes of Eccentric
> Vision, *University of California Press, 1977, pp.*
> *85-98.*

JOSEPH BLENKINSOPP (essay date 1961)

[*Blenkinsopp is an English Catholic theologian, translator, and critic. In the following excerpt, he discusses Weil's belief that the essence of Christianity was prefigured in the myths of more ancient religions.*]

Most of the thirty-five queries [in *Letter to a Priest*] which [Simone Weil] puts to the French priest (did he ever answer?) are drawn from history and, for Simone, history means religious history, that of the spirit, of the enquiring and adoring mind of man, a kind of extension of man's spiritual being. She

speaks of her "concept of history," and although looked at objectively her treatment of ancient history is at times disastrously lacunous, to say the least, a concept certainly emerges. The religious history of the Old Testament was certainly her blind spot. She contrasts unfavourably the Hebrew will to power—national power—with the "sweet spirit" of the Egyptian Book of the Dead, an infelicitous contrast in any case, since these magic litanies were no more than an "Open Sesame" to the world of Osiris, and no indication of moral character. The "current of pure spirit" which began in Egypt and passed on through early Orphism to the great Greek tragedians and philosophers missed Israel somehow, and the Hebrews were far worse even than the taurolotrous Canaanites since the object of their worship was the nation in whose name any kind of atrocious conduct could be justified. Daniel was "the first absolutely pure character appearing in Jewish history" ("Jewish" for Simone includes "Hebrew")—a fairly drastic reappraisal. We have to remember her view that "society is essentially evil," and is indeed none other than the "Great Beast" since it is the depository and vehicle of that force which is at the opposite pole from spirit. We also must remember that she spoke and wrote as a victim—indirectly at least—of Nazi racialism. It is rather sad, just the same, that she so mis-read her Old Testament, and that she failed to see in it the story of the *discovery* of the true Israel. In the Israel of history something perished and was lost in the past, but something else, a part, a *remnant,* survived or rather was taken up into the forward-looking plan of God. After all, the call of the true Israel occurred before the nation came into existence, just as its fulfilment came when the nation had already been destroyed, and even as an appendage of a world-empire was about to be eclipsed. In the New Testament, where she spelt out the religion which she felt instinctively to be hers (she read from it every day) the true Israel is revealed as identical with the Church whose measurements, in the Apocalypse from which she so often quotes, are identical with those of the reborn city of Ezechiel. Simone Weil never contemplated sufficiently this unique and unparalleled movement in history, and consequently never came to understand the historical character and mission of the Church, and never felt herself justified in asking for baptism.

It is strange how often she refers to the mysterious and quite unprepared-for appearance of the Canaanite priest-king Melchisedek in Genesis. His service and knowledge of God were "infinitely superior" to anything then existing in Israel. He is a clear Biblical witness to such knowledge and service of God in a non-biblical religious tradition, and was probably a preincarnation of the Son of God, a view proposed also, apparently unknown to her, by St Cyprian, and suggested by other writers of the early Church. He reappears in her little essay on **"The Three Sons of Noah and the History of Mediterranean Civilization,"** where she is very impressed by the important place he has in Jewish and Christian tradition. The fact is that he illustrates perfectly her basic problem of the relation of the Christian religion to the pre-Christian and non-Christian worlds of religious experience. She sees this, and how justly, as one of the most pressing items on the religious programme of our age, but rather stultifies her case by over-statement:

> The extreme importance *at the present day* [her
> italics] of this problem comes from the fact that
> it is becoming a matter of urgency to remedy
> the divorce which has existed for twenty centuries, and goes on getting worse, between profane civilization and spirituality in Christian
> countries. Our civilization owes nothing to Is-

rael and very little to Christianity; it owes nearly
everything to pre-Christian antiquity . . . for
Christianity to become truly incarnated, for the
whole of life to become permeated by the Christian inspiration, it must first of all be recognized
that, historically, our profane civilization is derived from a religious inspiration which, although chronologically pre-Christian, was
Christian in essence.

There are, of course, many things that we would have to disagree with here, but she does recognize (as always) that the
Christian phenomenon must somehow be given the central place
in the history of the spirit following her view of the prophetic
unity of history; and it is our greatest concern that Christianity,
as an extension of the temporal mission of Christ, must become
incarnate in men of different upbringing, environment and culture. More urgently, towards the end of her questionnaire:

These problems are today of capital, urgent and
practical importance. For since all the profane
life of our countries is directly derived from
"pagan" civilizations, so long as the illusion
subsists of a break between so-called paganism
and Christianity, the latter will not be incarnate,
will not impregnate the whole of profane life
as it ought to do, will remain separated from
it and consequently nonactive.

As a contribution to this *rapprochement,* she asks: what is the
unique, central and irreducible point about the Christian religion? and finds that, in order to answer this question, she must
ask another: in what sense *is* Christianity a religion in the first
place? In the beginning there was only the word, the good
news, the proclamation of what had taken place. The denom-
ination "religion" is not found among the many that are used
in the records to describe the first followers of Christ. Those
nearest at hand took it for a Jewish *hairesis* or sect, since they
worshipped in the same temple, took the same vows, used the
same prayers and the same Scriptures without demur. For some
farther away it was a *superstitio;* for the Christians themselves
it was "The Way" (Acts xxiv, 14, etc.). When, then, did it
become a "religion?" when it came into competion or collision
with other "religions." Justin, Clement, Eusebius and other
apologists found that they had to justify their stand against the
well-organized world of Greek mythopoeic and rational thought
by answering the age-old questions in a different way. The
first reaction was to take the easy line and affirm that anything
of validity the Greeks possessed was either derived from Old
Testament revelation or was the creation of the devil, the ape
of God. The polemic broadened out but continued, and still
continues. For Simone Weil, Christianity is a religion because
it follows the basic pattern revealed by the study of comparative
religion, and it is unique because it alone fulfils it. If myth,
understood rightly, is the search of man for God, Christianity
records the search of God for man; and she would vehemently
have endorsed Chesterton's dictum that after Christ there are
no mythologies, since mythology is a quest. Several times,
and lovingly, she quotes the verse from the *Dies Irae* which
she sees as the epitome of the religion of Christ, *Quarens me
sedisti lassus,* and sees this intuition as foreshadowed (St Paul's
metaphor) by the Greeks. In *La Source Grecque,* . . . she sees
in the quest of Elektra a figure of that of the divine wayfarer
who sat weary on the lip of the well at Shekem. Antigone also
is a figure or prefigure of the divine lover. The theme of
redemptive suffering and the Saving Hero she traces back to

the primitive Orphic theology, and Prometheus, an Orphic saint,
is a precursor of Job and of the suffering and redeeming Lord
of the Christians. His lament: "Do you see what wrongs I
suffer?" finds its echo in the *Attendite et videte* of the liturgy
of the *Triduum Sanctum.* She writes:

Outside the New Testament itself, and outside
the liturgy of Holy Week, nowhere could there
be found words so poignant as those of certain
passages of this tragedy [*Prometheus Bound*],
words to express the love God bears us and the
suffering linked to this love.

If this cathartic view of suffering is indeed of orphic origin,
passing thence into a warp and woof of the great tragedians,
whose theme is *tô pathei mathos*—learning, experience through
suffering—we have the same said of Christ who "learned obedience through what he suffered" (Heb. v, 8); and is it too
remote a possibility to conceive that He was using an audacious
and not unfamiliar comparison when He spoke of casting fire
on the earth? "The Greeks," concludes Simone in *Les Intui-
tiones pré-chrétiennes,* "were haunted by the thought that caused
a saint of the Middle Ages to weep: the thought that Love is
not loved."

Her esteem of the great religious themes of Plato is so high
that she cannot see how they can be explained apart from some
supernatural revelation, in this case by means of earlier religious teaching, especially of the Mysteries and Pythagoras. It
interested her to observe that the formative influences on the
latter were oriental, and that his teacher was Pherecydes, a
Syrian. According to Plato, creation both in its initial act and
its subsistence is a product of harmony which is itself a re-
flexion of divine love, since both consist in the bringing together of extremes which are constituents of a new unity. But
there is an antithetic love which results in disorder and is
demonic in character—*eros,* the overriding passion. This love
has something of the nature of divine love, in so far as it is a
tendency to unite and a recognition that the only evil is absence,
but it seeks union at the price of its own identity; it is charged
and loaded to its own annihilation. Only in God can the *One*
be the absolute *Other*—go beyond, yet remain Himself; that
is, identity and union are only possible together in the divine
being. We are being, we exist, only in so far as we participate
in the divine and perfect being; that region of us which at any
moment is outside that Being is where we practise at love but
cannot achieve or consummate it. For Plato, as Simone Weil
recognized, love is the only thing that escapes the determinism
of nature, but it is also a *via crucis;* in his Perfectly Just Man
is the shadow of the Passion of Christ where the world of
necessity and the world of perfect justice meet. Her recognition
of the identity of Plato's *to agathon* with the God of Christianity
opened up for her new and deep springs of spirituality:

There is no other object of love for men save
the Good. Consequently none but God. We
need not search how to put the love of God in
us. It is the very foundation of our being. If
we love anything else, we do so by error as the
result of mistaken identity. We are like someone who runs joyfully down the street towards
a stranger whom at a distance he mistook for
a friend. But whatever is mediocre in us, by
an instinct of self-preservation and by means
of all sorts of lies, tries to hinder our recognition
of the truth: what we perpetually love from the
first to the last instant of life, is nothing else

than the true God. Because as soon as we recognize this, all the mediocrity in us is condemned to death.

She also draws the complementary and antithetic conclusion from Plato's doctrine in the Symposium, with important consequences for the contemporary world:

> Instead of seeing the love of God as a sublimated form of carnal desire, as many people in our wretched epoch do, Plato thinks that carnal desire is a corruption, degradation of the love of God.

The Greek quest for harmony and the Christian quest for union with God are therefore in the same line of thought; and just how far down this line she was prepared to travel can be seen in her view that it was love and the desire of Christ the Son of God which was at the origins of Greek science; their quest for perfect proportion and the messianic expectation of the Jews are in the same order of being. This thought she finds "inexpressibly intoxicating." And yet is not *all* history and *all* human destiny in view of and intimately connected with the Incarnation? "The world was not created but only for the Messiah"—the rabbinical saying would have met with Simone Weil's complete approval.

With the mention of the Incarnation we come to a nodal point of the attempt to find a common ground for a *rapport* between Christian and non-Christian spirituality. Far from being a mere debate or dialogue between men of different persuasions, that is today a missionary problem of the first magnitude, and was felt keenly by Simone Weil to be so. Just as the Platonic concept of mediation in creation and the ruling of the world and that of the divine lover and the object, derived from pre-existent religious tradition, were in essence "intuitions" of the supreme reality of the Trinity, so the Incarnation is prepared for in the religious soil of "pagan" spirituality. She does not explain in what way she considers Melchisedeq and, with more insistence, Osiris as pre-incarnations of the Son of God; but it is at least plain that she fully accepts the uniqueness of the *avatara*, the descent, of the divinity in a well-defined person known to history—Jesus of Nazareth. This is the crucial point—the point of acceptance and rejection, as the fact that all early heresies were christological shows. It follows that we should give high priority to the missionary task of preparing minds for this unique phenomenon; and since, from the standpoint of their relation to it, the pre-Christian world and this present non-Christian world are in the same position, it cannot be without interest for us to know whether God did, in fact, prepare minds for the Incarnation of His Son outside the Hebrew and Jewish milieu. Christ Himself, when the Greeks sought an interview with Him, spoke of His passion in a familiar religious idiom, with reference to the vegetation-god prototype, the corn that dies and yet bears fruit, and His passion and death, at the moment when they become part of sacred history and liturgical recitation, play out and fulfil the drama of the Dying and Rising God. Early Church writers who read history as providential and prophetic have no difficulty in seeing the vast shadow of the Incarnation cast backward over all history, and Augustine goes so far as to say that the Christian religion had always been in the world but that with the coming of Christ it began to be called Christianity. The great need today is for a theological study of the history of religions, either extinct, dormant or still active; a study which will be at the same time phenomenological, able, that is, to take the great themes of our own faith—incarnation, redemption, justification, etc.—studying their

meaning in the light of the total religious experience of mankind both past and present. The scattered efforts made so far—among Catholics we might mention Père de Lubac and Fathers Johanns and White, to whom reference has been made above—are encouraging but only an indication of the line along which our efforts must lie. We should be grateful to Simone Weil for having drawn our attention so forcibly to this need.

But, while seeing the need so clearly, she does not suggest an acceptable or even, in the last analysis, consistent remedy. For her, any man of any race, colour or religion who sincerely and humbly calls on God—his God—receives the Spirit of God (so far so good!), but this can never result in God inspiring him to quit his own religious tradition. "It is useless," she writes to her priest, "to send out missions to prevail upon the peoples of Asia, Africa or Oceania to enter the Church." The categorical command of Christ to go and make disciples of all nations cannot mean uprooting Europe from her religious traditions and imposing upon her an alien, semitic holy book. In fact, any change of religion must be bad. She complains that on the subject of *extra ecclesiam nulla salus* one gets different and mutually contradictory answers from different priests claims that this doctrine has now been jettisoned and that "the belief that a man can be saved outside the visible Church requires that all the elements of faith should be pondered afresh, under pain of complete incoherence." In a world in which the great majority of the population, increasing of geometrical progression, have no foreseeable possibility of active, sacramental contact with Christ, the Church is keenly conscious of the position of those without faith, but the problem calls not for any dogmatic re-statements but rather an understanding of the extent of the underlying unity of religious experience and taking advantage of all points of contact and convergence. (pp. 278-84)

> *Joseph Blenkinsopp, "The Frustrated Pilgrim: Afterthoughts on Simone Weil," in* The Wiseman Review, *Vol. 235, No. 489, Autumn, 1961, pp. 277-85.*

ELIZABETH JENNINGS (essay date 1961)

[In the following excerpt, Jennings discusses Weil's Jewish heritage and her rigorously questioning intellect.]

The most important thing to remember about Simone Weil is that she was Jewish. In the many books and articles which have been written about her, I do not think that this fact has been sufficiently emphasized. She was a Jewess uprooted from her own religion, so that in a double sense she was a wanderer: she had the instinctive Jewish need to wander and she also felt lost because she *was* uprooted, both from her own past and her own race. It was no chance matter that one of her books was concerned with man's "need for roots." Péguy said that Jews were either "merchants or prophets" and that one of their major characteristics was always to be "elsewhere." Simone Weil certainly had something of the prophet or seer in her temperament but this was qualified by an extraordinarily fine intellect. In many ways, she regarded the intellect as man's highest faculty and it is not surprising that when in *Waiting on God* she wrote about humility, she suggested that thoughts of one's own stupidity were more likely to induce humility than reflections on one's wickedness.

Simone Weil was a Jewess who hated Judaism. The religion of the Old Testament seemed to her a bloodthirsty and barbaric thing. Yet one of the contradictions in her nature (and she was full of contradictions) was that, like many orthodox Jews, she was obsessed with the idea of sacrifice; the scapegoat was something much more vivid than a mere symbol to her. Firmly established in her mind too was the idea of election or choice. Most of the books and essays which have been written about her, particularly those by Fr. Perrin and Gustave Thibon, are concerned with why she would not be baptized until she felt that God had personally and unmistakably indicated to her that she should be. Myself, I believe that this particular aspect of "waiting on God" was part of her Jewish inheritance; it went much deeper than arrogance or egotism and was, perhaps, something beyond her conscious control.

And this is the all-important fact to bear in mind in any examination of Simone Weil's life and thought—that, precise and luminous as her intellect was and assured as she herself was of its paramount efficacy, she was by no means always guided by it; her mind often moved more by intuition than by rational argument. It is here that Simone Weil enters the world of the poet and the mystic, who have this in common—that their experience, while it does not deny the rational faculty, transcends the rational faculty. It is true that Simone Weil was not a poet in the strictly literal sense but, in those parts of her writing where images took over, she approximated to poetry. On the other hand, there appears to be very little doubt that she had had mystical experience. In the following passage in *Waiting on God,* she gives an account of it:

> In my arguments about the insolubility of the problem of God I had never foreseen the possibility of that, of a real contact, person to person, here below, between a human being and God. I had vaguely heard tell of things of this kind, but I had never believed in them. In the *Fioretti* the accounts of apparitions rather put me off if anything, like the miracles in the Gospel. Moreover, in this sudden possession of me by Christ, neither my senses nor my imagination had any part; I only felt in the midst of my suffering the presence of a love, like that which one can read in the smile of a beloved face.
>
>   (pp. 131-32)

Like so many people who have been the recipients of some form of mystical experience, Simone Weil *questioned* her experience; she was eager to know its meaning and purpose. She shared with Teresa and John of the Cross that distaste for the sham that is so often the purest indication of a genuine and humble apprehension of the presence of God. (p. 133)

Simone Weil's intellect could never be wholly pacified but must forever be examining, appraising and drawing conclusions. Her intense seeking out of personal and often physical suffering was, I believe, partly a half-conscious attempt to abandon the demands of her intelligence. She *knew* that she was dazzled by the brilliance of her own intellect and so she sought darkness and oblivion in outward affliction, in the anonymous lives of factory workers and peasants, in the rejection not only of material pleasure but also of material necessities. Her way of life led to sickness, though it was something much deeper than sickness only that she was searching for. What she was seeking is revealed in the following words:

> It is not that I feel within me a capacity for intellectual creation. But I feel obligations which are related to such a creation. It is not my fault. Nobody but myself can appreciate these obligations. The conditions of intellectual or artistic

creation are so intimate and secret that no one can penetrate into them from the outside. I know that artists excuse their bad actions in this way. But it has to do with something very different in my case.

The note of protest here, the half-aware eschewing of authority, the wish for an autonomous world created by the mind *for* the mind, are more consonant with the attitude of the poet or artist than with that of the dedicated person of prayer.

It does seem, then, that the conflict in Simone Weil's life was something much more subtle than the force of Christian teaching invading a very Jewish mind, or even than the wish for assurance and truth at odds with an appetite for uncertainties. There is something *manqué* about all Simone Weil's work and I think the explanation for this is that she was both a writer *manqué* and a mystic *manqué*. What one senses most powerfully in her work is a profound duality, a duality which she herself was perfectly conscious of when she wrote,

> If still persevering in our love, we fall to the point where the soul cannot keep back the cry "My God, why has thou forsaken me?" if we remain at this point without ceasing to love, we end by touching something which is not affliction, which is not joy; something which is the central essence, necessary and pure; something not of the senses, common to joy and sorrow; something which is the very love of God.
>
> We know then that joy is the sweetness of contact with the love of God, that affliction is the wound of this same contact when it is painful, and that only the contact matters, not the manner of it.

These words, which could so easily be paralleled in the writings of Julian of Norwich or Teresa of Avila, describe an experience which is valid, honest, pure and indisputable; and yet the attitude of Simone Weil towards the experience, her desire for a perilous balance of opposites, her acceptance which has in it the note of despair (like hunting horns heard far off) as well as resignation, reveal that even in apparent serenity she could find anguish and uncertainty. For the truth is that when the saints and mystics have cried out to God in a language that sounds like despair, there has always been a profound and humble acceptance at the heart of their suffering—something very different from anxiety or doubt. What Simone Weil did was to assign to the moment of prayer the kind of anxiety which, in human experience, is only proper to the artist—the anguish of the poet, whenever words seem to fail his experience. It is as if Eliot's "intolerable wrestle with words and meanings" were transferred to the life of prayer, the communication of man with God. This, I am sure, was the conflict which prevented Simone Weil's request for baptism. It was not humility that she lacked but rather that she possessed the wrong kind of humility—a humility which is proper to the poet when he moves in the world of language and symbols, but wrong for the mystic who knows that pride and humility can work in the intellect as well as in the will: and who, therefore, acknowledges that both intellect and will must be placed in God's hands and resigned to his purposes.

These reflections are, to a certain extent, corroborated in the brief biography which Gustave Thibon wrote about his friend. He is expressly concerned with the central conflict in Simone

Weil's nature and attempts to reconcile her humility with her apparent aloofness, her intelligence with her passion, and, most subtle of all, her desire for detachment with her inability to be detached from detachment itself. For her, he says, "genius meant . . . the opening of the intelligence of man to the wisdom of God." He goes on to examine the contradictions in her character and says, "On the one hand there was a longing for absolute self-effacement, an unlimited opening to reality even under its harshest forms, and, on the other, a terrible self-will at the very heart of the self-stripping; the inflexible desire that this stripping should be her own work and should be accomplished in her own way, the consuming temptation to verify from within, to test everything and experience everything for herself."

"To verify everything from within"—this admirably sums up Simone Weil's attitude to philosophy, art and religious experience. . . . [There] have for many centuries been in the West two streams of mystical literature—that which embodies the affirmation of images (exemplified by writers like Traherne), and that which approves the rejection of images, the way of which the prose of St John of the Cross is the supreme example. But Simone Weil's experiences and writings do not fit completely into either of these categories; she *wished* to reject images and yet could never quite manage to relinquish them. As she said, "Perhaps . . . it may be given me, at least for a few moments, to receive the reward attached to work on the land and to none other, the feeling that the earth, the sun, the landscape really exist and are something more than mere scenery." There is, surely, more than a suggestion of pantheism in this sort of speculation.

In spite of her penetrating intellect and her uncompromising honesty, there does seem to have been an element of self-deception in Simone Weil's thought; so often she seems to cling to the *means* when it is the end that she really desires. In this she resembles the poet who, when the poem is written, the end achieved, is no longer interested but only desires the means towards yet another end, another completed work. M. Thibon touches on this dilemma when he compares Simone Weil with Rimbaud: "Someone has described Rimbaud as 'a mystic in the wild state.' Such a judgment can only be applied in a very indirect manner to Simone Weil. I have, however, often wondered how far certain very subtle values of Western civilization had penetrated to the deepest levels of her nature. What she lacked was that suppleness with regard to destiny . . . that spontaneous and actual sense of proportion which makes it possible to see everything in its right relationship. . . ." This lack M. Thibon ascribes, rightly I am sure, to her Jewish blood and temperament. "Is there," he asks, "anything more Jewish than the perpetual tension and uneasiness, the urge to examine and test the great realities?" The Jews, for centuries, have been notable for their artistic and creative qualities and perhaps it is not too farfetched to suggest that there is some connection between a race which needed to wander and which could never find a resting-place and the artist's own personal, and never satisfied, quest for a perfect work of art. Gustave Thibon quotes some highly relevant reflections on this matter from a letter which Simone Weil wrote to him about his own writing: "You have already experienced the dark night, but it is my belief that a great deal of it still remains for you to pass through before giving your true measure; for you are far from having attained in expression, and hence in thought, to the degree of utter stripping, nakedness and piercing force which is indispensable to the style which belongs to you." Here, she puts the language of mysticism at the service of literature and it

seems clear that, divided as she was in so many other ways, she was convinced of the unity of prayer and poetic experience. Thomas Merton has written, in his diary *The Sign of Jonas,* of the difficulty of living the life of prayer with the equipment of the artist. I think that Simone Weil always had this difficulty in mind. The reason why she seems to have been unable to resolve it was that while affirming intellectually the possible union of prayer and poetry, she could not herself live out this possibility. Her great respect for the intellect tended to make her underrate the power of the imagination.

M. Thibon makes some profound remarks about this problem when he discusses the nature of her genius. It was, he says, "of a philosophic and religious order," and was therefore founded on the intellect. Yet the play of the imagination and of the senses seldom ceased with her, even when she refused to recognize it. M. Thibon suggests that many of Simone Weil's writings should be taken on the level of "myths"—in other words, as analogies and images which are valid as adumbrations or glimmerings of experiences which soar *above* the intellect though they do not deny it.

In Simone Weil we are presented with an unquestionably complex character. Hers was a world of contradictions in which there was room both for the ideal human beauty of Greece and for the most austere ascetical practices of northern Europe. Such ideas, such opposites were accepted by her even while they could never be reconciled to each other. Philosophic and speculative as her cast of mind was, there is no system or method in her thought: there are footnotes and foreshadowings only. She longed to surrender herself completely yet lacked the ultimate confidence which hands over everything, even contradictions, into God's care. (pp. 135-39)

                    Elizabeth Jennings, "A World of Contradictions: A Study of Simone Weil," in her Every Changing Shape, *Andre Deutsch, 1961, pp. 131-39.*

JOHN J. McMANMON (essay date 1964)

[*In the following excerpt, McManmon discusses Weil's rejection of the goals and values of modern society.*]

Simone Weil had the audacity to tell this age that "the man for whom the development of personality is all that counts has totally lost all sense of the sacred. . . ." The statement, one of the first propositions in [*Selected Essays, 1934-1943*], is audacious because it implicitly challenges the value of the quest for personality, which is, in fact, the chief value upon which this age operates, and also because it implicitly attributes value to the sacred, which this age scorns.

Miss Weil's objection to the obsession with the quest for personality is two-fold. First, the quest itself is inner directed and thus carries with it the cause of its eventual failure: "The person in man is a thing in distress; it feels cold and is always looking for shelter." That shelter, outside the person and for which the person is always looking, is good: "At the bottom of the heart of every human being, from earliest infancy until the tomb, there is something that goes on indomitably expecting, in the teeth of all experience of crimes committed, suffered, and witnessed, that good and not evil will be done to him." Secondly, the quest for personality too often becomes a selfish neurosis which, when made *the* standard of life, opens "the door to every kind of tyranny." Ironically, this can be seen in the obsession of the age for rights: "Thanks to this word, what should have been a cry of protest from the depth of the heart

(I want my rights) has been turned into a shrill nagging of claims and counter-claims, which is both impure and impractical.'' The impurity and impracticality of the claims result from the attempt to base morality upon an effect of human nature—that man *does* have rights—rather than upon human nature itself. The whole of man, ''the arms, the thoughts, everything,'' and not merely his personality, should be the principle from which the individual, and thus society, orders his life. Even those artists who most wish to think of their work as a manifestation of their personality ''are in fact the most in bondage to public taste.'' And, most serious of all, the quest for personality has made society available to the tyranny of the collective, especially the state, the chief symbol of which is Rome, ''the Great Beast.''

In his introductory remarks to [*Selected Essays*], Richard Rees, the editor and translator, observes that Simone Weil's ''philosophical opinions . . . can be studied without reference to her view of history.'' The converse of this observation, that her view of history can be studied without reference to her philosophical opinions, does not hold. For she sees history as the narrative of man's failure to reach the impersonal, to heed the sacred, that ''reality outside the word, that is to say, outside space and time, outside man's mental universe, outside any sphere whatsoever that is accessible to human faculties.'' The cause of this failure she attributes to man's refusal to rise above the demands of personality—rights, wealth, property, power, the useful—to the level of the impersonal and sacred. The result is history, the study of tyrannies—of Rome over Greece, of Toulouse over Avignon, of the Church of Rome and the West over the Church of the East, of the Baroque over the Gothic, of the France of Louis XIV and Napoleon over Europe, of the Germany of Hitler over Europe. These tyrannies, however, are really symbolic of the tyranny of man's self over his spirit, which is the root-cause of all tyranny and which has led man into a state where ''he finds the opposition of good and evil an intolerable burden.'' At one time he tries to resolve the opposition by denying its reality. This leads to ''the theory that all objectives are equal'' and is repelled finally with horror. ''That is what happened in Europe (after World War I). The reaction of horror has been felt by each nation in turn, as misfortune overtook it.'' At another time man tries to resolve the opposition by finding substitutes for the sacred, especially in ''the adoration of the social under various divine names,'' as state, church, society:

> This method is frequently employed. Scientists and artists often make science and art a closed area within which there is no place for virtue or vice, whence they conclude that in their capacity of scientist or artist they are absolved from all moral responsibility. Soldiers and priests sometimes do the same, and in this way they justify the devastation of cities or the Inquisition.

The one means left, mysticism, man has consistently shunned, for it demands ''passing beyond the sphere where good and evil are in opposition, and this is achieved by the union of the soul with the absolute good,'' or placing God ''at the centre of life, whether of a people or of an individual soul.'' This is the lesson which Simone Weil passes on to us from her study of history.

Isaac Rosenfeld was right when he castigated Leslie Fiedler for referring to Simone Weil as ''the Outsider as Saint in an age of alienation'' and ''our kind of Saint.'' Simone Weil is not the outsider: it is the hero of our age—the solipsist, the neurotic seeker after personality—who is the outsider. To refer to her as ''our kind of saint'' is to reduce her life-effort to our kind of barren, frightened, compromise that never really tries to resolve the mysterious opposition of good and evil but merely denies its existence. The only possible result of such a position is a moral paralysis that immerses the whole individual beneath the floods of solipsism, so that eventually there is neither responsibility nor the ability to be happy because there is no communication or the belief in the possibility of happiness; every man becomes an island unto himself.

Miss Weil's solution—to rise to the sacred—is conventional. In one way, it is also irrelevant: how *does* one achieve the sacred? By seeking the true, the good, the beautiful, by pure love. Isolated from context, all these terms become platitudinous. However, the rhetorical force of Miss Weil's essays gives relevance to these seeming platitudes. Her writing has a way of making one believe that these generalizations *are* relevant, and practical, and attainable. It convinces not by force of logic or evidence, but by the wealth and sublimity of its content and conception: it ''transports'' the mind and emotions. It seems to induce the kind of attention or overpowering intuitive experience which Miss Weil herself advocates in order to become aware of the sacred:

> The mind which has learned to grasp thoughts which are inexpressible because of the number of relations they combine . . . such a mind has reached the point where it already dwells in truth. It possesses certainty and unclouded faith. And it matters little whether its original intelligence was great or small, whether its prison cell was narrow or wide. All that matters is that it has come to the end of its intelligence, such as it was, and has passed beyond it.

Nevertheless, when such moments of truth wear off, the terms again become seeming platitudes. Does Simone Weil, then, fail after all? I think not, because her writing has the power to bring about, however briefly and unconsciously, an *experience* of belief, and consequent hope. This experience itself could be impressive enough to shock a Meursault out of his solipsism and turn him into a Pierre who still wonders: why evil? what evil? what is life? where is it going? It is impressive enough to shake the solpsist out of one faith—that there is no faith because there can be no extra-personal object—and into another—that there *is* something outside the self. In other words, it is impressive enough to undermine the faith of unbelief, and give momentary consciousness to the fearful and pressed-down hope which is at the bottom of despair. (pp. 189-92)

> *John J. McManmon, ''Simone Weil and the Tyranny of Self over Spirit,'' in* Chicago Review, *Vol. 16, No. 4, Spring, 1964, pp. 189-92.*

THOMAS R. EDWARDS   (essay date 1971)

[Edwards is an American educator and critic. In the following excerpt from the section entitled ''Epic and the Modern Reader: A Note on Simone Weil'' in his Imagination and Power, *he discusses Weil's essay ''The* Iliad; *or, The Poem of Force.'']*

Epic . . . implies the dramatic situation in which a bard sings to men who may be strangers but who share with him a general cultural identity, a common language (with all this implies) and some prior awareness of the matter of his song. (p. 10)

It associates us gratifyingly with past greatness, with heroes who are *our* heroes; yet it also reminds us soberingly that it all *is* past, that we are less than our heritage. It allows us an imaginative association with greatness even as it makes us recognize that we are ordinary men—and it allows us some comfort in this rueful understanding. And it gives a perspective on our mixed relation to our own public world and its powerful creatures, our dependence on them, our suspicion of their "superior" purposes, our pleasure and horror at what they do in our name.

The substance of epic action is of course war. But I suppose that war is less the subject of epic than a metaphor for a larger subject, which is power itself, the ways in which men impose their will on other men. Battle, in this light, is only a concentrated image of the conflict of purposes that must (we assume) always characterize human relations if life is to be more than solitary and self-centred; it is no original observation to say that war, like business and games and family quarrels, is a form of politics and a mirror of its nature. But war is more than this. Though in many ways it shares the annoying but useful indecisiveness of other political modes, it yet is utterly decisive in another way—it makes men die who would prefer to live. War is both an image of politics and a destroyer of men, a dreadful literalizing of the aggressions politics keeps in discreet disguise. Here the complexity of epic becomes most evident and crucial, and hardest for modern men to respond to as men once did.

Simone Weil's brilliant essay, **"The *Iliad*; or, The Poem of Force,"** is a compelling expression of this difficulty. It is not a difficulty that in any way questions the value of epic; indeed, for Simone Weil the *Iliad* is "the purest and loveliest of mirrors" reflecting the pervasive and dreadful effect of force on men's lives. The essay deserves attentive reading in its entirety, but for convenience I will summarize its argument briefly.

Force, according to Simone Weil, is "that *x* that turns anybody who is subjected to it into a *thing*"; its denial of the individual life of its object leads to turning that object into a corpse, literally a thing, to be dragged around Troy behind a chariot. More subtly, force can turn a man into a thing, a "stone," while he is still alive, by stripping him of his weapons and armour to leave his life hanging on his conqueror's whim, or by making him an irrelevant object like Priam in Achilles' tent or a slave who has lost all memory of freedom. But force is not simply what the strong possess and the weak succumb to. In the *Iliad* "there is not a single man who does not at one time or another have to bow his neck to force" or who is "spared the shameful experience of fear." Winning hinges on destiny, not strength or valour, and this creates a kind of ironic justice, though neither the strong nor the weak perceive it until too late. War is in fact a shifting balance, which no one is moderate or virtuous enough to stabilize while he still can. By making men face every day the imminence of their own death, war "effaces all conceptions of purpose or goal, including even its own 'war aims.' It effaces the very notion of war's being brought to an end." The mind simply cannot accept "the idea that an unlimited effort should bring in only a limited profit or no profit at all"; having become a thing, the warrior is unresponsive not only to the life in other people but to the operation of reason itself. There are moments of insight in the *Iliad*, recognitions of love and mutual respect, but they serve mainly to sharpen regret for the pervasive violence and helplessness. And this regret is endorsed by the poet's bitterness about the action he sings of, his pity for victims, his painful recollections of the world of peace, his amazing sense of "equity."

Thus for Simone Weil the greatness of the *Iliad,* as of Attic tragedy and the Gospels, is that it reveals the relation of human suffering to its cause, "the subjections of the human spirit to force, that is, in the last analysis, to matter." Justice and love can grow only from a recognition that all men are fellow creatures, not members of distinct species, none of them "exempt from the misery that is the common lot." And such recognition is not to be found in western literature, except flickeringly in a few great writers:

> Nothing the peoples of Europe have produced is worth the first known poem that appeared among them. Perhaps they will yet rediscover the epic genius, when they learn that there is no refuge from fate, learn not to admire force, not to hate the enemy, nor to scorn the unfortunate. How soon this will happen is another question.

I have paraphrased Simone Weil at such length because I think her view of force is morally almost inescapable in our time and yet also imaginatively limiting. It would be foolish to pretend that she has simply misread Homer, and self-deceiving to insist too hopefully on the special circumstances of the essay—how the *Iliad* looked in 1940, in a conquered and occupied country, to a woman whose cultural heritage was Jewish, political views leftist, religion Catholic and increasingly mystical. It is hard not to feel that we all live in occupied countries, conquered (as she helps us to see) by the appalling force of a history whose consequences we are just beginning to understand. And her moral resistance predicts our efforts to resist, whether through politics or insurrection or inward withdrawal from public concern. It looks as if her experience of force and its meaning will for a long time remain our conception of our case, beset by forces that threaten our humanity by creating in us—in our very resistance to them, perhaps—something like their own indifference to everything that makes a man more than a manipulable object. As for Homer, one can see the risks of contemporizing the past (the idea of an "absurdist" Shakespeare and the like) without wanting to deny that unless art has meaning for living people it has no meaning, and that our life, our sense of our own condition, is what reaches out to the work and measures its relevance.

I have no doubt that "Homer" knew what Simone Weil knew about force. The trouble is that he knew other things too, as Shakespeare knew things that Beckett and Ionesco and Professor Kott don't. And the dominant moods of an age—what we mean when we say that Simone Weil speaks for "our" sense of things—have more than diagrammatic value only when they can be qualified and expanded into some further perception. For Simone Weil, war is only the ultimate literalization of the tendency of any life that is "materially" rather than "spiritually" oriented. War, when looked at steadily and whole, as Homer does, makes us see what we risk by permitting ourselves to be unmoved by suffering:

> He who does not realize to what extent shifting fortune and necessity hold in subjection every human spirit, cannot regard as fellow-creatures nor love as he loves himself those whom chance separated from him by an abyss. The variety of constraints pressing upon man give rise to the illusion of several distinct species that can-

not communicate. Only he who has measured the dominion of force, and knows how not to respect it, is capable of love and justice.

War, this seems to say, is ethically necessary. It is the concentrated image of our subjection to necessity and constraint, and only by enduring and learning to abhor it can we appreciate our bonds of suffering with other men and so come to brotherhood with them. If there is a scent of Manichaeanism in this, it is nonetheless persuasive and moving. But by implication it cancels out a great deal that the *Iliad* also expresses in its thorny complexity; though one participates in Simone Weil's feelings, hers is not the only conceivable view.

Her idea of force cancels out all but the minatory value of the "material" world, the world that includes not only war but politics, business, legislation, litigation, all secular exercises of power to any end at all. (She of course means to do just this.) But for Homer and his audience, the war at Troy was a public event that summed up, without denying the dangers, the ability of individual glory to confirm one's national and cultural identity. One must agree with Simone Weil that it is well that Homer saw the cost of glory. But her formula—that the moments of glory and grace measure the bitterness of the vision of force—could as well be turned around: does not the bitterness also measure and enhance the glory, by suggesting that great suffering may be needed to achieve great enterprises? However unpalatable this is to an age that has known suffering of a magnitude that threatens to make *any* great enterprise, any idea of public greatness at all, seem hollow and fake, it's hard to believe that such scepticism adequately comprehends the literary reality of the *Iliad* and its effect on the European imagination. It is not surprising that Aristotle and Virgil, Chapman and Pope and Fénelon, Keats and Arnold and Andrew Lang, saw Homer differently; but it may be important to remember that they did.

Epic literature grows out of the belief—or the desire to believe—that heroism is a possible and valuable image of man. It assumes that collective exercise of power may encourage great individual achievement, and that great individual achievement may confirm the worth of group enterprises. Rachel Bespaloff, without denying the grim perception of Simone Weil, adds what may be a salutary qualification of the idea of force:

> Force revels only in an abuse that is also self-abuse, in an excess that expends its store. It reveals itself in a kind of supreme leap, a murderous lightning stroke, in which calculation, chance, and power seem to fuse in a single element to defy man's fate. Herein lies the beauty of force. . . . In the *Iliad*, force appears as both the supreme reality and the supreme illusion of life. Force, for Homer, is divine insofar as it represents a superabundance of life that flashes out in the contempt for death and the ecstacy of self-sacrifice; it is detestable insofar as it contains a fatality that transforms it into inertia, a blind drive that is always pushing it on to the very end of its course, on to its own abolition and the obliteration of the very values it engendered.

There is an alternative to the picture of a man turned to a stone by exercising or submitting to force, and that is a picture of a man possessed (briefly) by a strength and purpose that seem superhuman and imaginatively liberating to men who are only

Weil's handwritten copy of George Herbert's "Love." From La vie de Simone Weil, *by Simone Petrement. Librairie Artéme Fayard, 1973.*

human. This picture is I hope no more comforting to me than to Simone Weil; in literature it is a short step to mindless patriotic hagiology, in life an even shorter step to the posturings of an American political convention or the Nuremberg Rallies. It is easy to agree with her that the *Iliad* is the greatest epic poem because it is the most suspicious in its scrutiny of how "great men" behave and its computation of the human cost of great achievements. But the poem and the tradition it governs are troublingly less easy to understand than that. To suppose that it or any authentic epic writing exists only to assess the ironies, to show the world of power only so that we may save our own souls by despising and rejecting it, does some damage to history and—much more important—to our capacity for a literary experience (to say nothing of life) that may for all its difficulty be uniquely valuable. (pp. 11-16)

> *Thomas R. Edwards, "The Disappearance of Heroic Man," in his* Imagination and Power: A Study of Poetry on Public Themes, *Oxford University Press, 1971, pp. 7-46.*

CONOR CRUISE O'BRIEN   (essay date 1977)

[*An Irish politician, historian, and critic, O'Brien served as Ireland's representative to the United Nations from 1955 to 1961 and has since held positions in the Irish government and in academia. He has written numerous studies of Irish history, of the United Nations, and of modern politics, and his works are often praised for their iconoclasm as well as their insight. Although O'Brien has concentrated his attention primarily on political and historical matters, his literary opinions are also highly esteemed and he has written important studies of Catholic writers and the influence of politics on literature. In the following excerpt, O'Brien discusses the antipolitical nature of Weil's later writing, particularly* The Need for Roots. *For a rebuttal of O'Brien's ideas, see the essay by Raymond Rosenthal (1977).]*

The concept of "applying" Simone Weil's thought in practical politics is I think contradictory to the main direction of that thought itself, which is that politics—and indeed social life generally—is the domain of the Beast, or of the devil, something to be suffered, something to be cried out against and struck back at, not something that can be set right. She is not entirely consistent in this. In Part One of *The Need for Roots* ("The Needs of the Soul") she sketches the kind of reconstruction of French society which the Free French might carry out after the liberation. It is a rather disconcerting sketch. A France reconstructed on Weilian lines—or as I think pseudo-Weilian lines—would have had no political parties, no trade unions, no freedom of association. It would have had a rigid, primitive, and eccentric form of censorship—one which would permit Jacques Maritain to be punished for having said something misleading about Aristotle. It would be organized on hierarchical lines, although we are not told just what these lines would be. There would be liberty, or something so described, coming second after "order" and just before "obedience" among the needs of the soul, but the guarantees of liberty in no way indicated. "Liberty," we are told, "consists in the ability to choose" but "when the possibilities of choice are so wide as to injure the commonweal, men cease to enjoy liberty." The text bristles with peremptory and often cryptic affirmations.

The atmosphere she evokes is that of a state to be governed by a spiritual and moral elite, a rule of the saints. In practice an effort by mortal and fallible men to "apply" *The Need for Roots* would probably have resulted in something quite like Vichy France—the resemblance to which she acknowledged with characteristic courage and integrity—but minus collaboration with Nazis and with de Gaulle at the top instead of Pétain. This is the rather discouraging outcome of a hypothetical effort to apply in politics the thinking of a writer who was essentially nonpolitical, and even antipolitical.

As I have indicated, I think the programmatic parts of *The Need for Roots* are a kind of lapse: they seem to have been elicited from Simone Weil by the demands of the war effort, rather than shaped by the necessities of her own lonely thinking. She herself was unable to take seriously the idea of applying them. "It is no use asking ourselves whether we are or are not capable of applying [this method of political action]. The answer would always be no!" She did think they might influence political decisions, and that their influence would be benign. As far as her "method of political action" was concerned—as distinct from more personal and profound aspects of her thought to which I come later—I think she was wrong on both counts. I think politicians made no use of her method, and if they had made any it would probably have been bad. General de Gaulle—presumably the politician most intended to be influenced—thought that she was out of her mind. He was of course quite wrong, but the verdict does set rather clear limits to the possible influence of her method on the politics of post-Liberation France.

Politics proceeds by associations of people, and Simone Weil had a deep-rooted aversion from such associations. This is why I call her antipolitical. On this matter the key passage is the following, from the section on "Freedom of Opinion" in "Needs of the Soul":

> The intelligence is defeated as soon as the expression of one's thoughts is preceded, explicitly or implicitly, by the little word "we." And when the light of the intelligence grows dim, it is not very long before the love of good becomes lost.

> The immediate, practical solution would be the abolition of political parties. Party strife, as it existed under the Third Republic, is intolerable. The single party, which is, moreover, its inevitable outcome, is the worst evil of all.

Elsewhere she speaks of "we" as positing an illegitimate middle term between the soul and God. (p. 23)

Simone Weil, the antipolitician, is a pure intellectual. Those intellectuals who seriously engage in politics (no matter what kind of politics) are impure intellectuals, necessarily committed to the Burkian economy, and doomed, according to Simone Weil, to the dimming both of their intellectual and of their moral sense. The political intellectual—who is of course the only politician now at all likely to know or want to know about Simone Weil—will necessarily feel reluctant to accept her view about his predicament. He will wish to claim that, even though he practices an economy of truth, he still brings into circulation more truth than, without him, would be in circulation in a vital domain of social life, and one which stands in need of as much truth as it can tolerate. But he will nonetheless be uncomfortably conscious of the force of Simone Weil's observations.

The effect in politics of the pure intellectual, such as Simone Weil, is normally exerted through the impure intellectuals, the only kind that that domain will tolerate. Save in exceptional circumstances the pure intellectual can only, in consequence, be a small influence, indirect, filtered, and perhaps distorted. Even so it would often work as an antipolitical influence, dissociative rather than associative, tending at times to the liberation of an individual conscience and to the extinction of a politician who might, just possibly, have been useful in his chosen domain if he had not fallen victim to the vertigo of intellectual purity. There are however wider and more permanent aspects of her potential influence which I shall discuss later.

In relation to politics, as to so much else, Simone Weil is the outsider, the lonely stranger. Her observations are detached, aloof, unfriendly, often very penetrating, sometimes perverse. Her best political sayings are aphorisms in the classical French hit-and-run tradition. She is especially vigilant, as one would expect, on that suspect frontier between the life of the intellect and political action. In a few pithy remarks about Marx and about Lenin, she sees intellectual disasters transforming themselves into political ones: "Marx worked out the conclusions before the method. He insisted on making his method into an instrument for predicting a future in accordance with his desires." As for Lenin he went in for "thinking with the object of refuting, the solution being given before the research." "The stifling regime which weighs at present upon the Russian people was already implied in embryo in Lenin's attitude towards his own process of thought. Long before it robbed the whole of Russia of liberty of thought the Bolshevik party had already taken it away from their own leader."

Her comments on Marx are I believe both pithy and true. Those on Lenin are brilliant, but illustrate the intellectual limitations of pure intellectuals. The idea that Lenin's method of thought was imposed on him by the Bolshevik party will not stand examination. Lenin by his technique of "split, split and split again" ensured that his party agreed with him, not vice versa.

In putting the blame on the party, Simone Weil's bias against the first person plural is visible again; in reality an unusually imperious first person singular had much more to do with the matter. The concept also shows the intellectual's characteristic overemphasis on the importance of thought. The nature of Russian society as it existed before the First World War, and the disastrous impact on that society of that war, followed by collapse and foreign intervention, did much more to produce the stifling regime than did the exiled Lenin's treatment of his thought processes.

Elsewhere indeed Simone Weil shows her awareness of such limitations of thought, and it would be useless to look for consistency in her writings on revolution. Immediately after the passage on Lenin, in her essay on "Lenin's Materialism and Empirico-criticism," she contrasts Lenin unfavorably with Marx. "Marx fortunately went about the process of thinking in a different way." But in the passage on Marx from which I have quoted—from an apparently later essay **"On the Contradictions of Marxism"**—she shows that Marx abused the process of thought in precisely the same way as Lenin did, by finding the solution first and then looking for arguments to buttress it, rather than means of testing it. This intellectual history is continuous; it is the history of the growth of a religion, not a science—and this Simone Weil saw—and it is because it was a religion that its fanatical and ruthless leaders were capable of taking over the bankrupt and devastated Russian Empire. Lenin's attitude to his processes of thought was in fact a symptom of his capacity to fill that vacuum.

Simone Weil's dissociative bent and her exaltation of the claims of the intellect do not, then, always stand her in good stead in her consideration of political processes. It is a different matter when she deals with the basic political bonding itself—in tribe, nation, state—and what might be called the original sin of that bonding—the notion of the inherent superiority of the entity constituted by it. In her consistent witness against that concept, in all its manifestations, lies the great and permanent value of Simone Weil's political writing.

"To love the little platoon to which we belong in society," wrote Edmund Burke, "is the first, the germ as it were, of public affections." Simone Weil was conscious of a countertruth to this; that it is possible to love the little platoon too much, so much that wider or higher affections fail to germinate. Of Jewish origin herself, she was profoundly repelled by the concept of the chosen people. This repulsion is a fundamental and abiding element in her mind and character. It could both carry her to strange extremes and stop her dead in her tracks. At one time it made it possible for her to counsel the acceptance of an anti-Semitic state in France as a lesser evil than war; at another it made it impossible for her to accept baptism into the Catholic Church. Both that acceptance and that refusal are significant expressions of what I call her antipolitics; her radical rejection of all limited associations.

The "acceptance" is contained in two letters of the spring of 1938, one to Jean Posternak, the second to the writer Gaston Bergery, later a Vichy diplomat. In the letter to Posternak she wrote:

At the moment, there are two possibilities. One is war with Germany for the sake of Czechoslovakia. Public opinion is scarcely interested in that remote country, but the Quai d'Orsay resolutely prefers war to German hegemony in central Europe; and as for the Communist party, any Franco-German war suits its book. . . . What may prevent violent measures is the generally recognized weakness of the French army. The other possibility is an antidemocratic *coup d'état* supported by Daladier and the army and accompanied by a very violent outbreak of anti-Semitism (of which there are signs everywhere), and by brutal measures against the parties and organizations of the left. Of the two possibilities I prefer the latter, since it would be less murderous of French youth as a whole.

In the letter to Bergery, developing the theme of German hegemony preferable to war, she added: "No doubt the superiority of German armed forces would lead France to adopt certain laws of exclusion, chiefly against Communists and Jews—which is, in my eyes and probably in the eyes of the majority of Frenchmen, nearly an indifferent matter in itself. One can quite well conceive that nothing essential would be affected."

Madame Pétrement makes the just comment: "She continued to think that nothing would be worse than a war. Moreover, her disinterestedness made her prefer, of the two evils, the one of which she personally would be the victim."

Three further points need to be made here. The first is to notice the intellectual courage with which she recognizes the terrible alternatives: war or acceptance of German hegemony. Most intellectuals at the time wanted to think they could reject *both* war *and* German hegemony. The second point concerns the coldness, even the apparent callousness, with which she refers to the probable fate of a minority to which she herself belongs: it would have been impossible for Simone Weil to refer to the "exclusion" of a minority as "nearly an indifferent matter in itself" if she had not herself belonged to that minority.

The third point is that "the certain law of exclusion" which she envisaged would have most directly affected people like herself: middle-class Jewish intellectuals of left-wing views. That was the "little platoon" to which she could not help belonging, but which she tried to sacrifice, because she belonged to it, in favor of the wider loyalty to humanity as a whole. Hitler's entry into Prague appears to have convinced her, however, that sacrifices of this kind could not in fact avert the greater evil of general war. Once the war was there she wanted to take the fullest possible part in its sacrifices, and did so, to the point of self-inflicted death by hunger. (*L'Enracinement* was written shortly before her death, and after her abandonment of the "lesser evil" concept.)

While Judaism repelled her, basically because of the concept of the chosen people, Catholicism strongly attracted her, because of the proclaimed universality of its message. But those who are drawn to Catholicism by that appeal are doomed to a degree of disillusionment when they encounter actual Catholics, in their local and national groupings, no more immune than others to tribal pride and prejudice. It was with French Catholics that Simone Weil had to do, and French Catholic traditions have been among the most exuberantly jingo in the world. The God of Charles Péguy for example was not out of tune with French Catholic opinion when he made his famous declaration:

> Quand il n'y aura plus ces Français, dit Dieu,
> il n'y aura plus personne pour me comprendre.
>
> [When there are no longer any French, spoke
> God, there will be no one to understand me.]

For Péguy this was in part a joke, a tender in-joke, but nonetheless to be felt as conveying a truth. Simone Weil, who was not particularly good at jokes, could see nothing but blasphemy in this kind of cozy tribal Catholicism. She had not rejected the Jews as chosen people in order to accept the French, or any others, in that capacity. That *seems* easy enough: there are plenty of people who are opposed to nationalistic hubris, or think they are. But Simone Weil's antinationalism was real, in a sense in which most people's was not, and its reality reveals itself in the thoroughness, the consistency, and intellectual daring with which it finds expression. These qualities are at their most remarkable near the end of her life, when she was working for the Free French in England. There is an apparent paradox here, but it is a superficial one. Many, probably most, of those with whom she was working—and not least their chief—were nationalists, even ultra-nationalists. But Simone Weil was not there for nationalistic reasons. On the contrary she saw Nazi Germany as the supreme contemporary embodiment of triumphal nationalism. (pp. 25-6)

Perhaps the greatest tragedy, in Simone Weil's life and death, is that she died, of a kind of self-inflicted wound, just as the time was coming when her spirit and her voice would be most desperately needed. Obviously no single person could have averted the French decision to reconquer Indochina, or to hold Algeria by force, or the needless horrors which followed from these decisions, or the inheritance by America of France's Indochina disaster, and the prolonged further aggravation of that disaster which followed. Yet any reader of Simone Weil knows with certainty that, if she had lived, her voice would have been lifted up against these things; and that the opposition to them would thereby have gained immensely in intensity, determination, and integrity.

Her capacity for dissociation would have served her well, when what people were pressed to join was a Gadarene rush. At a time when everybody in the West was being harangued about the dangers of communism, she would have seen those dangers—as she did see them, clearly, in the Thirties—but she would also have seen the dangers of *anti*communism, and stressed them not only because they were nearer, but for the fundamental reason that, for us in the West, they were the dangers *within us,* the means for the moment of exalting our triumphant group feelings, and our tendency to see evil as something external to us.

She could never have fallen in, as Albert Camus and so many other gifted intellectuals did, with the convenient localization of slavery "over there" and liberty "over here." She could not—as Solzhenitsyn to the grief of many of his admirers has done—have ever identified the "loss" of Indochina to the West with the "loss" of something called liberty to Indochina. Just possibly the fire and honesty of her witness might have helped to shorten the war, as Albert Schweitzer, for example, probably helped to bring nuclear testing to an end. We cannot know, and she herself would have been the last to exaggerate the capacity of anyone like herself to influence the action of the enormous beast, which is human society.

We are left with her example and her warnings. Few of us are likely to follow the example of this strange ascetic, and certainly no politician who claimed to follow it would be believed, and rightly so. Most of us, for obvious reasons, would sympathize with the advice given to her by her friend Dr. Louis Bercher:

> The basic thing here seemed to me to be the desire for purity. It is the source of all heresies, I told her. Remember the Cathars! Man is not pure but a "sinner." And the sinner must stink a bit, at the least.
>
> Simone didn't deny this, but she didn't give in to my point either.

But one does not need to be convinced by her mystical intuitions, or propose to imitate her life, in order to see that her warnings about nationalism, in all its multiform disguises, possess not only moral force but great practical shrewdness and permanent political value. She was a true prophet who foresaw the "appalling adversity" which certain tendencies present in the movement to which she adhered were capable of bringing on her country and on others.

That is the kind of insight of which practicing politicians in every country are in most need. Simone Weil's contribution to politics is not in system or method, or even in analysis, but in her lucid sensitivity to the dangerous forces at work in all collective activities, and her refusal to localize these forces exclusively in some other nation, or among the adherents of some other faith or ideology. One may, as I do, feel that there is something inhuman about her. Yet it may be that what we feel to be inhuman in her is that which made her capable of turning away from those aspects of our own all-too-human attachments which put our neighbors, our environment, our world, our children, ourselves all in deadly danger. (p. 28)

> *Conor Cruise O'Brien, "The Anti-Politics of Simone Weil," in* The New York Review of Books, *Vol. XXIV, No. 8, May 12, 1977, pp. 23-8.*

RAYMOND ROSENTHAL (essay date 1977)

[*Rosenthal is an American poet, critic, and editor. Among his most influential studies are* The Modern Poets *(1960) and* The New Poets *(1967), which analyze the verse of some of the most important poets of the twentieth century. In the following excerpt, Rosenthal attacks Conor Cruise O'Brien's view (see excerpt dated 1977) that Weil's political theory in* The Need for Roots *is untenable in actuality.*]

Mr. Conor Cruise O'Brien . . . accepts and even praises Simone Weil's criticisms of the collectivity when they are applied to nationalistic and cult groupings—he knows from bitter experience in Ireland how destructive of social peace such collectivities can be, how impervious to the appeals of reason—and yet the same criticisms when applied to other associations and collectivities, such as political parties and trade unions, strike him as incomprehensible, impractical, and even inhuman. But Simone Weil's idea that political life can be carried out without political parties, though an ideal and certainly not an immediately practicable one, is not foreign to a certain kind of thinking about politics. Marx himself expressed a rather similar point of view in his early works, and the ideal was both implicit and explicit in all of his subsequent writings. Not to mention Thoreau, Coleridge, Rousseau, John Jay Chapman, and a long line of anarchist writers and thinkers from Kropotkin to Paul Goodman.

Simone Weil's chief difference with this tradition lies in the fact that what they—including Marx—were usually content to state in general terms, she discussed in detail and even went to the trouble of trying to codify. Hence her rather complicated picture of an ideal political and social situation in which both political parties and trade unions—which are not, in her terminology, "natural associations"—would be subjected to controls by the community in order to modify and correct the bad effects of the inevitable ideological propaganda that emanates from such "collectivities." Mr. O'Brien's description of this codification, as presented in her book *The Need for Roots,* appears to me to be less than adequate. It certainly cannot be considered anti-social in its essence, or even in its details.

But what is most amazing in his essay, which sets out to sift the usable from the unusable in Simone Weil's political thinking, is his complete lack of response to her research into the nature of factory work and, allied with this research, her revolutionary conception of the relation of modern science and technology to both factory work and the social program of any group which has a better world in view and is working toward it. For Mr. O'Brien is no mere literary figure; he represented a working-class constituency in the Irish Parliament, he professes a belief in socialism, and so he must surely know something about what goes on in the factories in which his constituents worked, and also something of the general moral situation of factory workers all the world over, whatever the political and social setup may be. I hate to think that his curious blindness to the urgency of these problems is but a symptom of the further decadence of the working-class movement and would prefer to ascribe it to an understandable reluctance to pick up a "hot potato." But the potato is still there, whether he acknowledges it or not. (pp. 45-6)

Raymond Rosenthal, "Simone Weil's Politics," in The New York Review of Books, Vol. XXIV, No. 18, November 10, 1977, pp. 45-6.

JEAN AMÉRY (essay date 1979)

[In the following excerpt from an essay originally published in German in 1979, Améry challenges what he calls the Weil "myth" and criticizes her for unrealistic absolutism and self-inflicted suffering.]

In God all contradictions are resolved, claim the theologians along with Nicholas of Cusa. But on this miserable earth they are by no means resolved. They tear apart the individual and society. Simone Weil is the tragic example for the impotence of the *deus absconditus* in the face of the world's contradictions. Her thirst for the absolute literally withered her. Everything relative—origins, social station, education—was her downfall. She wanted to live wholly for others; her hardly surpassable egocentrism enveloped her as though she had been poured into amber. She aspired toward the eternal but the times formed her and finally turned her into a sacrificial animal. Her spirit dwelt aloft somewhere in the thinnest air of purity; her physical appearance was neglected and gave some people the impression that she was dirty. She hated Judaism, and externally as well as in her character make-up, she was extravagantly Jewish. She wanted to be a worker, but she was incapable of satisfactorily performing even the most rudimentary manual task. She felt that she was destined to be a hero, but when she went to Spain in order to take part in the Civil War, she clumsily

scorched herself with boiling oil and had to be returned home straightaway by her caring parents. She succeeded only in dying. And when this passionate Christian mystic was buried in Ashford, England, she was not baptized and not even a priest was there to bless her remains. Because of an air-raid alarm, the man of God had missed his train.

To make her out is no easy matter, for legends have obscured her being and work. Hagiography took the place of critical biography. Charles de Gaulle, who was no mean judge of people, said tersely that she was *folle,* crazy. But Camus, oppressed by the transcendent and transcendental basic human condition, spent an hour of meditation in her Paris room before he boarded the plane to Stockholm in order to accept the Nobel Prize. The philosopher Alain saw in her by far the most gifted of his pupils. Among those for whom she sparkled as a star in the darkness of time were T. S. Eliot, Gabriel Marcel, Maurice Schumann, Dietrich von Hildebrandt. She was, and has remained until today, a rare jewel that it would be blasphemous to touch. The prestige of her death has shielded her from criticism. But difficult as such an attempt may be, it is high time to penetrate the overgrowth of legend and get to the person—because what she was and did fits all too well into a neo-irrationalist trend whose grim consequences cannot yet be foreseen.

The circumstances of her birth already contained those possibilities of her life and tragic dying that became reality. She was born in Paris in 1909. Social drama was bursting forth in a land that in its length and breadth was still yearning for a pastoral idyl. Jaurès was already at work. The waves of the Dreyfus case had hardly subsided. A young man named Léon Blum had just renounced his estheticism and allied himself with those who truly were still the damned of this earth.

Bernard Weil, her father, a respected and prosperous physician from an old Jewish-Alsatian family, was practicing in Paris. Salomea, her mother (also called Selma and "Mime"), was born in Rostov-on-Don and was of Austrian-Galician background. Thus does one become an outsider in the heart of France. Alsatians and Jews are never quite genuine *Français de France.* One bears a double taint when, in addition, the Alsatian element is mixed with the elusive Jewish element. It doesn't matter if you were born and grew up in the capital city a hundred times over. I agree for the most part with the Franco-Jewish author Paul Giniewski, who in a recently published book interprets Simone Weil's existence as having been essentially determined by her origins. One need only read her writings and the secondary literature alongside the memoirs of the one-year-older Simone de Beauvoir, and one immediately perceives a difference that reaches into existential depths. In the case of the indisputed "Française de France," Beauvoir, everything is natural, down to her exaggeratedly extreme leftist and feminist protest. In the case of the Jewess, born of Alsatian-Galician family, even what is seemingly most natural becomes problematic. The being of the one is credible whether you admire her or not; but even those who wildly overestimate the other will perforce have their doubts about her.

The least one can say is that Simone Weil was ill at ease with herself, and this state affected almost all who knew her. "I have the suspicion," T. S. Eliot wrote, "that Simone Weil was unbearable at times." In fact, she was unbearable not only "at times" but almost always and everywhere. A lyceum superintendent reproached her for the "diffuseness and confusion" of her courses—rightly, as is known. Her friend and host Gustave Thibon, for whom she wanted to work as a farm-girl (which, of course, miscarried, since she was of no help in either house or field), suffered from her presence, despite the respect he showed for her intelligence and her assiduous search for God. Her pupils were bored during her classes, which she conducted as passionately as she did monotonously, and the majority of them failed the final examination. At the grape harvest, in which she felt compelled to participate in order to experience the living conditions of the rural proletariat, she plagued a fellow worker with the wisdom of the Upanishads—something the girl sufferingly endured. Her most important work to my mind bears the title *The Need for Roots*. But she herself was unable to take root, either among her colleagues at the Ecole Normale Supérieure, or as a teacher, or as a factory worker and syndicalist. As a Jew, as a homely girl (who almost ingeniously made herself even more unattractive than she already was through sloppy dress and a messy hairdo), as a poor teacher and hopelessly inept worker, she forever stood "outside," before the gates, hungering. The God after whom she yearned also held her at a distance.

Three characteristics determined the existence of this extraordinary woman: her uncanny, penetrating intelligence, her fierce determination to cleanse mankind of its earthly smut, and a boundless longing to suffer. Having grown up with a brother three years her senior, who early in life was already regarded as a scientific genius, she competed with him; and while she didn't catch up with him, she reached the point where she could understand quantum physics and even write on this most difficult subject. Her knowledge of ancient languages, particularly Greek, far exceeded the requirements of the Ecole Normale Supérieure, which in themselves were already excessively demanding. When she immersed herself in East Asian wisdom, she studied Sanskrit. After her turn to Catholicism she acquainted herself so thoroughly with the field of theology that she was able to discuss the problems of patrology and scholasticism with any scholar.

Her intelligence was also strikingly Jewish. Contrary to a widespread belief, Jews are very often very stupid. At the same time, however, they are endowed as a group with a store of talent that causes embarrassment even to a philosemite. For if he enumerates the Jewish geniuses, even against his own will the ugly word "egghead" will occur to him. Less would be better, one thinks when reading Simone Weil. Even in her *Letter to a Priest,* which ostentatiously places *humility* at the core of all thought, she argues—against herself—in a hairsplitting manner that not only a malicious antisemite would characterize as "talmudic."

Also her passion for social reform went to the very extreme and even beyond. She saw social misery more clearly than others; the social injustice in France, which was alleviated only under Léon Blum's short lived Popular Front, hurt her more than any of her contemporaries. But her reactions were far removed from both meliorist naïveté and rational-revolutionary methodology. Her social involvement, with all its estimable humaneness, brought nothing but trouble for her and burdens for her fellow fighters. In 1932 she took part in a strike in Le Puy; she managed to get arrested but had to go without the martyrdom to which she aspired—since the philosophy teacher was viewed as a harmless fool and immediately set free. Half in jest and half in scorn, she was called "la vierge rouge." During a miners' strike in Saint-Etienne she carried the red flag, a Joan of Arc without her Dunois and La Hire. But when she met Leo Trotsky shortly thereafter in her parents' home, he had the impression that she was a distraught person. He

later remarked in a letter that it was hardly worth discussing her.

Precisely this "blind" involvement, as it were, contributed to the creation of the legend. Or had she really been a pioneer: in her criticism of the Soviet Union and the Comintern as well as in her anarcho-syndicalist rebellion? Was she a forerunner of those who today see salvation only in the economic self-management by the workers? Was she the presaging prophetess of the "nouveaux philosophes," who sees everywhere only the "prince," the "maitre," and take the side of the plebs, whom all of the organized parties had arrogantly overlooked? She was, and then again she was not. For there exist texts, written by her in English exile, that bear witness to a frightening tendency toward authoritarian social systems of class character.

Actually, she was unpolitical. She saw in society, *every* society, only Plato's "Great Beast." She was always concerned only with pursuing her own salvation. No, not even that, but rather her own disaster; and at this, to be sure, she succeeded tragically. Wherewith we have touched the heart of her biography, her passion of passions. *She wanted to suffer,* absolutely and at any cost, even if she caused others pain by it— above all her parents, who were constantly fearful for her. She nourished herself poorly, wore garments of haircloth like a penitent, renounced a portion of her teacher's pay for the benefit of the unions, and finally died of hunger in England because she wanted to eat no more than the amount allotted in France to the "normal consumers," who had been placed on miserable rations—though, of course, even the poorest in that country naturally increased his food supply with illegal purchases. Was she a "masochist," as has often been said? That is a question of terminology. I prefer to apply the term only to a definite sexual deviation and would rather speak of her *self-torment*. Her Lord's Prayer would logically have had to end with the words: Forgive me never my debts and send me all that is bad, now and in the hour of my dying. Amen.

For years, since 1938 almost unceasingly, she suffered from agonizing headaches—Adrian Leverkühn's "head ache"—but I've never read that she ever submitted to serious medical treatment or even took analgesics. And above all: she imposed on herself the obligation to do physical labor although she was about as fit for it as she was for ballet. That was heroic, no doubt, even if here too a few remarks that will diminish the Simone Weil myth are imperative. Her work—first in a factory, then on a farm—lasted altogether a total of a half-year. Because she apparently wanted it that way, she was an *échec*, a failure: as a teacher, revolutionary, and worker. Even as a Christian.

Her Christianity, Manichean to the point of heresy, was nothing but suffering for God, and not salvation. What Weilian theology was, she herself described roughly in an opaque reflection on philosophy; in her work *La Connaissance surnaturelle,* whose very title contains an unresolvable contradiction, she wrote: "The characteristic method of philosophy consists in comprehending the problems as insoluble and in observing them, for years without end, expectantly, without any hope." Just as she denied herself sensible nourishment and modest everyday pleasures, she also denied herself every kind of intellectually positive accomplishment. The passionate Christian, who reminds us of Kierkegaard, also did not permit herself baptism, partly because she did not deem herself worthy of the sacraments, partly because she saw in the church less the mystical body of Christ than the *ecclesia triumphans* with its potential evil. Constantly in search of "perfect purity, perfect beauty, perfect justice," but aware that they are unattainable, she lost sight of all real beauty, good, and justice (since they can, after all, never be perfect). She was indeed "not of this world."

Her theological Manicheanism, whose roots we can explain only on the basis of her psychic constitution, extended deep even into her writing on completely profane subjects. In her notes on the "condition ouvriére," she penned very clever though not exactly overwhelmingly new thoughts on the alienation of female assembly-line workers. What she left out—because she hadn't experienced it—were the tiny compensations that enabled her fellow workers to endure: the fun of the Saturday dance, the short chat during work breaks, their love affairs. She herself, God's bride, was so chaste—and surely not only because her disposition and mournfully Jewish intellectual's face did not exactly attract droves of suitors—that she felt revulsion at any sort of physically tender communication. She regarded herself as a discard, a "slave," as she literally wrote. But absurdly, at the same time, as a genius of the absolute. To the extent that Simone Weil was really a clinical "case" (a thesis that can be confirmed), her condition would have to be diagnosed as that of an autodestructive megalomaniac. "Whatever I do," she wrote in *La Connaissance sur-naturelle*, "I know with perfect clarity that it is not the Good. For what I do cannot be the Good once I do it. . . . Whatever one does, one accomplishes the Bad, and it is the unbearably Bad." Thus she proceeds from "I" to "one": Whenever she castigates her lamentable self she is carrying out morbid autodestruction; as soon as she says "one" and thus also includes others, she is setting herself up as a judge of mankind altogether, she is deifying herself. Delusions of personal insignificance and of grandeur become absurdly congruent.

If the concept of the absurd, in the theological and philosophical sense, can be used at all, it hardly applies to anyone as accurately as to Simone Weil. Absurd were not only her unsuccessful teaching career, her attempt to force her way into the world of labor, her search for the undiscoverable God; her conduct during the storms of the epoch was also absurd. She was a radical pacifist at a time when even a child could see that what mattered was to destroy Hitler and his ignominious empire at any price. She protested, by the way, in an extraordinarily and admirably bold letter to the Commissioner of Jewish Affairs of the Vichy regime, Xavier Vallat—but not as the Jew she was and as which the others designated her and had already sentenced her; rather she protested by referring to the fact that she had never visited a synagogue and that she was rooted in Hellenistic Christian culture—an argument that, given the historical moment, was both heroic and naïve. *A la fin du compte*, after she had tossed her pacifism overboard after all and had become a determined patriot, she wished to remain in France. But in June 1942, at the last moment, she emigrated with her parents to America, not in order to stay there, however, but rather in order to get to England and from there to return to France, a little detour she could have reasonably spared herself. But what did reason mean to her? "God created us free and intelligent so that we can give up our will and our intelligence. . . ." . . . Thus she actually did offer up reason and life on the sacrificial altar of her God. In the process, she often had "more luck than brains," as the saying goes: The officials regarded her as an uninteresting case! Misfortune and martyrdom refused to materialize, even when one day, through pure clumsiness, she dropped a suitcase with Résistance documents, which then lay scattered on the street.

She was also an "uninteresting case" for the Free French Forces in London, where she had gone from America. Thanks above all to her friend Maurice Schumann, they barely let her have her way but never at all considered assigning her real tasks. *How* important for her the actual battle really was, is a question that must be asked. By this time she had long since given up her belief in the antifascist struggle as well as in the revolution, the hope of all those who, espousing the motto of the clandestine newspaper *Combat,* said: *De la résistance à la révolution!* "Marx declared that religion is the opium of the people," she wrote. "No, the revolution is opium. The revolutionary hopes are a stimulant. All final systems are utterly wrong." We know that there is truth in this pronouncement. But obviously, it could only be half-true, since it was written at a time when the antifascist struggle possessed at least a *relative* finality. However, she was not interested in the world, but in God.

The conversion of this Jewess, who had grown up in a free-thinking milieu, had begun in 1938 while she was listening to a Gregorian mass at an Easter service; during this mystical experience the convert suffered from raging headaches. This moment of suffering determined the five next years still granted her. Her posthumous writings, especially *Waiting for God* and *Letter to a Priest* (addressed to the Dominican priest Perrin), lend both moving and dismaying testimony to the long passion of these years. The process of her detachment from reality can be followed like a case history, and the subtlest theological interpretations—the analogy with gnosis, with St. Teresa of Avila and Pascal—change next to nothing. Simone Weil shirked not only the demand of the day, not only common sense, but logic in general, which is the reflection of existence. Christ did not become her "favorite dish," as Heine puts it with revealing cynicism, but he did become the oxygen of her mental respiration. She didn't argue; instead she contented herself with brusque claims such as this: "Only the presence of Christ can explain the phenomenon of thoughts or supernatural acts, of justice, the comprehension of misfortune, of benevolence, altruism. To believe that they can be present where Christ is absent is godless, even blasphemous." Thus, there can be no salvation in this world. Not with God; for he can only be eternally awaited—in vain; but he cannot be reached through patient approximation. Utopia is a sacrilege. There remains only a sacrificial death.

Simone Weil died in an English hospital on August 24, 1943, according to the coroner from "heart failure due to myocardial insufficiency caused by hunger and pulmonary tuberculosis." His down-to-earth business did not permit him to say: "Suicide resulting from a religious compulsion neurosis."

Her essential writings appeared after her death, which, as the end of a national martyr, silenced the beginnings of any criticism in France. The shadow of death became a halo, and this not only in her own country but in the entire world. Thus it would have been in bad taste or, worse, blasphemy to disparage the unsystematic nature of her oeuvre. For who could demand of a mystic, chosen to suffer, that she systematize her experience of God like some academic theologian or other? One dared even less to examine her political statements. After all, she had carried the red flag at strikes, had been in Spain, wanted to risk her life for the Résistance. That sufficed in those days. Today it does not; for as Voltaire says: "One owes consideration to the living, to the dead only the truth."

Simone Weil *lived,* beyond her earthly sojourn, in the early postwar years. Only now is she, the deceased, truly dead, and truth is attaining its full due. From the incense that surrounded her there now emerges quite a bit that does not show up so well at all in full light, especially since it oddly forbodes what is being proposed in our own time by a Left that has become estranged from itself. The spirit of the estates, *"l'esprit des corporations,"* must be reawakened, we read in **The Need for Roots**. In those days that was the influence of Pétain's "revolution nationale." In a liberated France, she said, the great industrial complexes would be dissolved. Small manufactories, archaic in character and strewn far across the land, were to nourish and also clothe the nation as productive resources and capital goods. That too was Vichy, and since then the Left has probably abandoned itself a hundred times over to similar notions of a retrogressive utopia. While work—manual, but above all agricultural work—is to be limited in time, it is to have a quasi-sacred character. Is this the surmounting of alienation, or is it reactionary homesickness for something historically outmoded? The latter, naturally; not the former. "If the young worker thinks of settling down," she writes, "he would then be ready to take root."

In the dry fields of human reason there grows no nature cure for such revelations. In any case, let all those civilization-weary hyperintellectuals who project their personal nausea into the social sphere be warned of an influence that can produce no good. One can love Simone Weil the human being. One certainly must pity her. But Weil the thinker is of no concern to anyone who cares about the enlightenment of mankind. (pp. 109-17)

> *Jean Améry, "Simone Weil: 'Beyond the Legend',"* in his *Radical Humanism: Selected Essays, edited and translated by Sidney Rosenfeld and Stella P. Rosenfeld, Indiana University Press, 1984, pp. 109-17.*

ADDITIONAL BIBLIOGRAPHY

Blumenthal, Gerda. "Simone Weil's Way of the Cross." *Thought* XXVII, No. 105 (Summer 1952): 225-34.
    A summary of Weil's philosophy, analyzing her attempt to reconcile Christian and non-Christian elements of her belief.

Buber, Martin. "The Silent Question: On Henri Bergson and Simone Weil." In his *The Writings of Martin Buber*, pp. 306-14. New York: New American Library, 1956.
    Compares the reactions of Henri Bergson and Simone Weil to the Judaism which they both rejected for Christianity.

Chaning-Pearce, Melville. "Christianity's Crucial Conflict: The Case of Simone Weil." *The Hibbert Journal* XLIX, No. 4 (July 1951): 333-40.
    Discusses the difficulties the Roman Catholic Church encounters when dealing with Weil, and advocates a more universal acceptance by the Church of personal, albeit idiosyncratic, belief.

Chiaromonte, Nicola. "Simone Weil's *Iliad*." In his *The Worm of Consciousness and Other Essays*, pp. 183-90. New York: Harcourt Brace Jovanovich, 1976.
    A discussion of Weil's "The *Iliad*; or, The Poem of Force."

Cliff, Michelle. "Sister/Outsider: Some Thoughts on Simone Weil." In *Between Women: Biographers, Novelists, Critics, Teachers and Artists Write about Their Work on Women*, edited by Carol Ascher, et al, pp. 311-25. Boston: Beacon Press, 1984.
    Discusses the themes of oppression and violence in Weil's work.

Frénaud, Georges. "Simone Weil's Religious Thought in the Light of Catholic Theology." *Theological Studies* XIV, No. 3 (September 1953): 349-76.
    Evaluates Weil's work and its relation to orthodox Catholicism.

Friedman, Maurice. "Simone Weil." In his *To Deny Our Nothingness: Contemporary Images of Man*, pp. 135-45. Chicago: University of Chicago Press, 1967.
    An interpretation of Weil's work as a modern expression of Gnosticism.

Godman, Stanley. "Simone Weil." *The Dublin Review*, No. 450 (1950): 67-81.
    An early discussion of Weil's life and thought.

Harper, Ralph. "The Beauty of This World." In his *Human Love: Existential and Mystical*, pp. 83-8. Baltimore: Johns Hopkins Press, 1966.
    Contrasts Weil's view of love with those of Fedor Dostoevski, Martin Buber, and Gerard Manley Hopkins.

Little, J. P. "Albert Camus, Simone Weil, and Modern Tragedy." *French Studies* XXXI, No. 1 (January 1977): 42-51.
    Compares Weil's play *Venise sauvée* to Camus's dramatic work.

Loades, Ann. "Simone Weil—Sacrifice: A Problem for Theology." In *Images of Belief in Literature*, edited by David Jasper, pp. 122-37. London: Macmillan, 1984.
    Compares Weil's conceptions of suffering and sacrifice to those of other writers and philosophers.

Merton, Thomas. "The Answer of Minerva: Pacifism and Resistance in Simone Weil." In his *The Literary Essays of Thomas Merton*, pp. 134-39. New York: New Directions, 1981.
    Discusses Weil's analyses of pacifism and war.

Murdoch, Iris. "Knowing the Void." *Spectator* CLXXXXVII, No. 6697 (2 November 1956): pp. 613-14.
    A review of *The Notebooks of Simone Weil*.

Pierce, Roy. "Simone Weil: Sociology, Utopia, and Faith." In his *Contemporary French Political Thought*, pp. 89-121. London: Oxford University Press, 1966.
    Considers Weil's utopian political philosophy both before and after her religious conversion.

Smock, A. "Doors: Simone Weil with Kafka." *Modern Language Notes* LXXXXV, No. 4 (May 1980): 850-63.
    Discusses Weil's and Franz Kafka's use of the image of the door.

Veto, Miklos J. "Simone Weil and Suffering." *Thought* XL, No. 157 (Summer 1965): 275-86.
    Discusses Weil's concept of suffering as decreation to unite humanity with God.

White, George Abbot, ed. *Simone Weil: Interpretations of a Life*. Amherst, Mass.: University of Massachusetts Press, 1981, 207 p.
    A volume of essays devoted to various aspects of Weil's life.

Oscar (Fingal O'Flahertie Wills) Wilde

1854-1900

Anglo-Irish dramatist, novelist, essayist, critic, poet, and short story writer.

The following entry presents criticism of Wilde's drama *The Importance of Being Earnest*, first performed in 1895 and first published in 1899. For a complete discussion of Wilde's career, see *TCLC*, Volumes 1 and 8.

Perhaps more than any other author of his time, Wilde is identified with the nineteenth-century "art for art's sake" movement, which defied the contemporary trend that subordinated art to ethical instruction. This credo of aestheticism, however, indicates only one facet of a man notorious for resisting any public institution—artistic, social, political, or moral—that attempted to subjugate individual will and imagination. In contrast to the traditional cult of nature, Wilde posed a cult of art in his critical essays and reviews; to socialism's cult of the masses, Wilde proposed a cult of the individual in "The Soul of Man under Socialism" and other works; and in opposition to the middle-class facade of false respectability, Wilde encouraged a struggle to realize one's true nature.

Wilde was born and grew up in Dublin, though unlike other expatriate Irish writers, he did not draw upon his homeland as a subject for his works. He began his advanced education at Dublin's Trinity College and concluded it with an outstanding academic career at Oxford. In college Wilde discovered the writings of Walter Pater, a major figure of the aesthetic revival in English arts and letters. Pater advocated the pursuit of intense aesthetic experience, a doctrine which became widely influential. Pater's keenest student, Wilde, exaggerated this doctrine into a way of life and was often parodied in the English press as the paradigm of the lisping aesthete in velvet breeches. Using his reputation as a self-declared saint of artistic beauty, Wilde promoted himself and his ideas with successful lecture tours of the United States, Canada, and Great Britain. In the late 1880s he continued to crusade for aestheticism as a book reviewer and as the editor of *Lady's World,* whose name he immediately changed to *Woman's World.* Wilde's first collection of prose, *The Happy Prince, and Other Tales,* further displays his singleminded efforts toward ornamentation and stylistic grace in his writings.

Wilde arrived at his greatest success through the production of four plays in the 1890s. The first three—*Lady Windermere's Fan, A Woman of No Importance,* and *An Ideal Husband*—are well-made comedies of manners revolving around social codes of the English upper classes. The fourth play, *The Importance of Being Earnest,* marked the height of Wilde's popularity and is considered his best and most characteristic drama. Dispensing with the more realistic characters and situations of its predecessors, *Earnest* represents the apogee of Victorian drawing-room farce. Its stylish characters, stylized dialogue, and elegant artificiality are for many readers and critics the ultimate revelation of Wilde's identity as both man and author. Although it has often been compared to the farcical comedies of the Restoration, as well as to the works of the eighteenth-century dramatists Oliver Goldsmith and Richard Brinsley Sheridan, modern critics regard *Earnest* as an important pre-

cursor of the twentieth-century existential drama. According to Katharine Worth: "As well as being an existential farce, *The Importance of Being Earnest* is [Wilde's] supreme demolition of late-nineteenth-century social and moral attitudes, the triumphal conclusion to his career as revolutionary moralist."

Upon its completion in late 1894, Wilde offered *The Importance of Being Earnest* to George Alexander, the actor-manager of the St. James's Theatre, who rejected the play as unsuited to the style of production normally presented by his theater. In January 1895, at a time when Wilde's *An Ideal Husband* was playing to enthusiastic houses at London's Haymarket Theatre, Henry James's extravagantly produced drama *Guy Domville* opened unsuccessfully at the St. James's and was immediately withdrawn. Consequently, Alexander, in need of a replacement play, reconsidered his earlier judgment, and arranged to stage Wilde's comedy. When asked by a journalist if the production would be a success, Wilde characteristically responded: "My dear fellow, you have got it wrong. The play *is* a success. The only question is whether the first night's audience will be one." Originally four acts, the play was condensed by Wilde into three at the request of Alexander, who triumphantly premiered *The Importance of Being Earnest* on February 14, 1895. In the weeks after the opening of *Earnest,*

Wilde was at the center of a scandal involving Lord Alfred Douglas, the son of the Marquis of Queensberry, and was arrested in April. Charged with committing homosexual acts, he was convicted and sentenced to serve two years hard labor at Reading Prison. Following Wilde's arrest, in a futile effort to keep *Earnest* running, Alexander removed Wilde's name from advertisements and programs, but attendance continued to fall. The play closed on May 8, 1895 after only eighty-six performances and was not financially successful until its revival almost fifteen years later. Before the scandal interrupted its run, however, *The Importance of Being Earnest* had been a popular success. Allan Aynesworth, "Algernon" in the original production, later recalled: "In my fifty-three years of acting, I never remember a greater triumph than the first night of *The Importance of Being Earnest*. The audience rose in their seats and cheered and cheered again."

Considered the embodiment of the aesthetic theories Wilde had proposed in the essay collection *Intentions, Earnest* is recognized as the quintessential Wildean comedy. W. H. Auden has suggested that Wilde made dialogue the supreme dramatic element of *Earnest*, thereby creating "a verbal universe in which the characters are determined by the kinds of things they say, and the plot is nothing but a succession of opportunities to say them." While critics have acknowledged that the plot is slight, they have agreed that it is nevertheless an imaginative rendering of a traditional scenario. Wilde took humorous liberties with many dramatic plot conventions, while offering, essentially, the story of a foundling who, grown into adulthood, is reunited with his family. However in Wilde's version the scenario is reduced to absurdity as the foundling, Jack Worthing, learns that he was separated from his family as a baby when his nurse confused him with a voluminous romantic novel and mistakenly deposited him and the handbag he was in at the baggage counter of a railway station. Jack lives in the country, where he is the guardian of a young lady, Cecily Cardew, but when he visits London he pretends to be his own nonexistent brother "Ernest." A similar deception is practiced by his friend Algernon Moncrieff, who visits a perennially ill acquaintance named Bunbury, also nonexistent, whenever he desires to escape the watchful society of his relations in London. In town, Jack falls in love with Gwendolyn Fairfax, who is Algernon's cousin. Gwendolyn's mother, Lady Bracknell, declaring that she will not allow her only daughter "to marry into a cloakroom, and form an alliance with a parcel," refuses the couple her permission to marry unless Jack can "produce at least one parent, of either sex, before the season is quite over." In the meantime, Algernon travels to the country to meet Jack's young ward, Cecily. Posing as Jack's invented brother "Ernest," Algernon becomes engaged to Cecily, but Jack will not allow their marriage unless Lady Bracknell relents and permits Gwendolyn to marry him. In a farcical recognition scene in which all is resolved, Cecily's tutor, Miss Prism, is discovered to be the confused nurse who left Jack in Victoria Station, and Jack proves to be Algernon's long-lost elder brother, Ernest.

Critic Ian Gregor has concluded that *Earnest* is "the dramatic expression of a precise aesthetic ideology, where Art is seen as the supreme ordering and perfection of life," and others have concurred, observing that in the elegant, ordered world of *Earnest*, truth means little and style, all. In such a world, a perfectly phrased lie is preferable to a graceless statement of fact. "In matters of grave importance," one character states, "style, not sincerity, is the vital thing." Such an attitude is considered perfectly suited to a particular breed of Wildean character, the dandy. As Arthur Ganz has emphasized: "The

essence of the Wildean dandy's code is the substitution of aesthetic values for moral values.... The essential point of the dandy's creed is always the exaltation of form over content, of externals over internals." Represented in Wilde's society comedies by individual figures such as Lord Darlington in *Lady Windermere's Fan* and Lord Goring in *An Ideal Husband,* the traits of the dandy—elegance, wit, aestheticism, intelligence, individualism, and social prominence—are distributed among the dramatis personae of *The Importance of Being Earnest*. According to Joseph Wood Krutch: "Wilde's greatest achievement in [*Earnest*] consists in his perfect imaginative realization of the ideal toward which the fashionable exquisite is tending and his creation of a realm in which his dandies can flutter through life successfully."

Wilde subtitled this work "A Trivial Comedy for Serious People" and described it as "exquisitely trivial, a delicate bubble of fancy," but most critics have shown reluctance to dismiss *Earnest* simply as an amusing, though meaningless entertainment. "Farce" is often regarded as too narrow a term to encompass the scope of humor in the play and the underlying social commentary of *Earnest*. Comprised of many types of humor—farce, parody, romantic comedy, comedy of manners, and burlesque—*Earnest* is particularly praised for its refined, yet whimsical comic dialogue. It is often described as a "verbal opera" and compared with the comic operas of Gilbert and Sullivan. Max Beerbohm has observed that Wilde's characters "speak a kind of beautiful nonsense—the language of high comedy twisted into fantasy. Throughout the dialogue is the horse-play of a distinguished imagination—a horse-play among words and ideas, conducted with poetic dignity." Highly stylized and artificial, the language of *Earnest* accounts for much of the humor of the play; the ubiquitous paradoxes and epigrams are typically Wildean, many of them echoing the celebrated conversation of their author. "In married life three is company, and two is none," according to Algernon; and, "Divorces are made in Heaven." Similarly, Jack's interview with Lady Bracknell is filled with comic reversals. When he affirms, in response to her inquiry, that he does indeed smoke, she says: "I am glad to hear it. A man should always have an occupation of some kind"; but when she later learns that he has lost both his parents, she warns: "To lose one parent, Mr. Worthing, may be regarded as a misfortune; to lose both looks like carelessness." Lady Bracknell is viewed as the most conventional character in the play and functions as the obstacle to the intended marriages. She has been called a Wildean masterpiece of characterization for her literal-mindedness and comic understatement: "I must say, Algernon, that I think it is high time that this Mr. Bunbury made up his mind whether he was going to live or not. This shilly-shallying with the question is absurd. It shows a very ill-balanced intellect and a lack of decision that is quite lamentable."

Like Lady Bracknell, the other characters in *Earnest* seem at first only exaggerated renderings of types who would have been easily recognizable to London theatergoers in 1895, but Wilde's characters are not meant to be representatives of reality. The personae themselves embody paradoxes as they reflect the philosophy of the play—that "we should treat all the trivial things of life very seriously and all the serious things of life with sincerity and studied triviality." Some recent observers have interpreted the characters in twentieth-century terms, recognizing that the invented personae, Bunbury and Ernest, ultimately indicate a search for identity in their creators. Those who advance this opinion emphasize that all of the problems in the play are resolved in the eventual identification of Jack

Worthing as Ernest Moncrieff. According to Worth: "It is a modern moment for an audience brought up on Pirandello and Beckett when Jack, turning from one character to another in search of the truth about himself, is directed by Miss Prism to Lady Bracknell . . . and asks her the question that has been causing existential tremors throughout the play: 'Would you kindly inform me who I am?'"

Much of the satire in *Earnest* is concentrated on Victorian class society and its conventional economic and moral values. Alan Bird has concluded that Wilde "made fun of everything the English held—and hold—sacred, not least money, baptism, birth, religion, food, and property—and in so nonsensical, light-hearted and fantastic a way that the comedy never fails to amuse." The idealism inherent in Victorian notions of love and marriage are also mocked by Wilde. For example, the two young ladies, Gwendolyn Fairfax and Cecily Cardew, each desire an "ideal" husband—that is, one who is named Ernest. As Gwendolyn explains: "We live . . . in an age of ideals. The fact is constantly mentioned in the more expensive monthly magazines, and has reached the provincial pulpits I am told: and my ideal has always been to love some one of the name of Ernest." In the same way, the romantic convention of love-at-first-sight is trivialized when Gwendolyn further confesses to "Ernest": "For me you have always had an irresistible fascination. Even before I met you I was far from indifferent to you. . . . The moment Algernon first mentioned to me that he had a friend called Ernest, I knew I was destined to love you." Similarly, Cecily recounts to a surprised Algernon, her courtship, engagement, and subsequent break-up with "Ernest Worthing," the man he is impersonating—a man who exists, and whom Cecily has agreed to marry, only in her imagination. Throughout the play, fantasy and imagination are celebrated, and critics have stressed that two of its characters—the conveniently ailing Bunbury and Jack's "wicked" younger brother Ernest—are wholly imaginary. The recurrent elements of nonsense and absurdity in *Earnest* have also led several recent observers to interpret it as a prophetically modern drama. David Parker has asserted that the comedy expresses "a preoccupation which the twentieth century cherishes," the contemplation of Nothingness; and Dennis J. Spininger has agreed, declaring the play "[Wilde's] most serious step toward the twentieth century."

Traditionally, critical evaluation of Wilde has been complicated, primarily because his works have to compete for attention with his sensational life, and *The Importance of Being Earnest* is no exception. Most early critics of the play, however, agreed that Wilde's *Earnest* is a perfectly constructed comedy in a completely original style. More recent critics have stressed the absurdist nature of *Earnest*, regarding the comedy as a forerunner of existential drama. According to Spininger, *The Importance of Being Earnest* is "a play which is also an anti-play, a drama that is a parody of its own conventions and terms of existence." Nevertheless, some critics continue to recommend *Earnest* simply as a well-constructed, brilliantly witty theatrical entertainment and Wilde's most characteristic work. According to E. B. Partridge, *The Importance of Being Earnest* "defends the life of the imagination in the subtlest of all ways—by embodying it in a play so trivial and absurd that it makes fun of itself—and defends it with the sunniest *sprezzatura* that even Wilde achieved. Here, as in the best parts of his essays and life he makes us realize . . . the vital importance of not being earnest."

(See also *Contemporary Authors*, Vol. 104; *Something about the Author*, Vol. 24; *Dictionary of Literary Biography*, Vol.

10: *Modern British Dramatists, 1900-1945*; Vol. 19: *British Poets, 1880-1914*; and Vol. 34: *British Novelists, 1890-1929—Traditionalists.*)

H. G. WELLS   (essay date 1895)

[*Wells is best known today, along with Jules Verne, as one of the fathers of modern science fiction and as a utopian idealist who correctly foretold an era of chemical warfare, atomic weaponry, and world wars. His writing was shaped by the influence of Arnold Bennett, Frank Harris, Joseph Conrad, and other contemporaries with whom he exchanged criticism and opinions on the art of writing. In the following excerpt from an essay originally published in the* Pall Mall Gazette *in 1895, Wells offers a favorable review of* The Importance of Being Earnest.]

It is, we were told last night, "much harder to listen to nonsense than to talk it"; but not if it is good nonsense. And very good nonsense, excellent fooling, is this new play of Mr. Oscar Wilde's. It is, indeed, as new a new comedy as we have had this year. Most of the others, after the fashion of Mr. John Worthing, J.P., last night, have been simply the old comedies posing as their own imaginary youngest brothers. More humorous dealing with theatrical conventions it would be difficult to imagine. To the dramatic critic especially who leads a dismal life, it came with a flavour of rare holiday. As for the serious people who populate this city, and to whom it is addressed, how they will take it is another matter. Last night, at any rate, it was a success, and our familiar first-night audience—whose cough, by-the-bye, is much quieter—received it with delight. . . .

It is all very funny, and Mr. Oscar Wilde has decorated a humour that is Gilbertian with innumerable spangles of that wit that is all his own. Of the pure and simple truth, for instance, he remarks that "Truth is never pure and rarely simple"; and the reply, "Yes, flowers are as common in the country as people are in London," is particularly pretty from the artless country girl to the town-bred Gwendolen. . . .

How Serious People—the majority of the population, according to Carlyle—how Serious People will take this Trivial Comedy written for their learning remains to be seen. No doubt seriously. One last night thought that the bag incident was a "little far-fetched." Moreover, he could not see how the bag and the baby got to Victoria Station . . . while the manuscript and perambulator turned up "at the summit of Primrose Hill." Why the summit? Such difficulties, he said, rob a play of "convincingness." That is one serious person disposed of, at any rate.

On the last production of a play by Mr. Oscar Wilde we said it was fairly bad, and anticipated success. This time we must congratulate him unreservedly on a delightful revival of theatrical satire. *Absit omen* ["May the omen be averted"]. But we could pray for the play's success, else we fear it may prove the last struggle of its author against the growing seriousness of his dramatic style. (pp. 187-88)

H. G. Wells, in an extract in Oscar Wilde: The Critical Heritage, *edited by Karl Beckson, Barnes & Noble, Inc., 1970, pp. 187-88.*

BERNARD SHAW (essay date 1895)

[*Shaw is generally considered the greatest dramatist to write in the English language since Shakespeare. Following the example of Henrik Ibsen, he succeeded in revolutionizing the English stage, disposing of the romantic conventions and devices of the "well-made play" and instituting the theater of ideas, grounded in realism. During the late nineteenth century, Shaw was also a prominent literary, art, and music critic. In 1895 he became the drama critic for the* Saturday Review, *and his reviews therein became known for their biting wit and brilliance. During his three years at the* Saturday Review, *Shaw determined that the theater was meant to be a "moral institution" and "elucidator of social conduct." The standards he applied to drama were quite simple: Is the play like real life? Does it convey sensible, socially progressive ideas? Because most of the drama produced during the 1890s failed to approach these ideals, Shaw usually assumed a severely critical and satirical attitude toward his subjects. In the following excerpt, originally published in the* Saturday Review, 23 February 1895, *he unfavorably reviews* Earnest, *calling into question the modernity and importance of the play.*]

However [*The Importance of Being Earnest*] may have been retouched immediately before its production, it must certainly have been written before *Lady Windermere's Fan.* I do not suppose it to be Mr. Wilde's first play: he is too susceptible to fine art to have begun otherwise than with a strenuous imitation of a great dramatic poem, Greek or Shakespearian; but it was perhaps the first which he designed for practical commercial use at the West End theatres. The evidence of this is abundant. The play has a plot—a gross anachronism; there is a scene between the two girls in the second act quite in the literary style of Mr. Gilbert, and almost inhuman enough to have been conceived by him; the humor is adulterated by stock mechanical fun to an extent that absolutely scandalizes one in a play with such an author's name to it; and the punning title and several of the more farcical passages recall the epoch of the late H. J. Byron. The whole has been varnished, and here and there veneered, by the author of *A Woman of No Importance*; but the general effect is that of a farcical comedy dating from the seventies, unplayed during that period because it was too clever and too decent, and brought up to date as far as possible by Mr. Wilde in his now completely formed style. Such is the impression left by the play on me. But I find other critics, equally entitled to respect, declaring that *The Importance of Being Earnest* is a strained effort of Mr. Wilde's at ultra-modernity, and that it could never have been written but for the opening up of entirely new paths in drama last year by *Arms and the Man.* At which I confess to a chuckle.

I cannot say that I greatly cared for *The Importance of Being Earnest.* It amused me, of course; but unless comedy touches me as well as amuses me, it leaves me with a sense of having wasted my evening. I go to the theatre to be moved to laughter, not to be tickled or bustled into it; and that is why, though I laugh as much as anybody at a farcical comedy, I am out of spirits before the end of the second act, and out of temper before the end of the third, my miserable mechanical laughter intensifying these symptoms at every outburst. If the public ever becomes intelligent enough to know when it is really enjoying itself and when it is not, there will be an end of farcical comedy. Now in *The Importance of Being Earnest* there is a good deal of this rib-tickling: for instance, the lies, the deceptions, the cross-purposes, the sham mourning, the christening of the two grown-up men, the muffin eating, and so forth. These could only have been raised from the farcical plane by making them occur to characters who had, like Don Quixote, convinced us of their reality and obtained some hold on our

sympathy. But that unfortunate moment of Gilbertism breaks our belief in the humanity of the play. Thus we are thrown back on the force of daintiness of its wit, brought home by an exquisitely grave, natural, and unconscious execution on the part of the actors. . . . On the whole I must decline to accept *The Importance of Being Earnest* as a day less than ten years old; and I am altogether unable to perceive any uncommon excellence in its presentation. (pp. 32-5)

> Bernard Shaw, "An Old New Play and a New Old One," in his Dramatic Opinions and Essays, Vol. 1, *edited by James Huneker, Brentano's, 1906, pp. 32-40.*

WILLIAM ARCHER (essay date 1895)

[*A Scottish dramatist and critic, Archer is best known as one of the earliest and most important translators of Henrik Ibsen's plays and as a drama critic of the London stage during the late nineteenth and early twentieth centuries. Archer valued drama as an intellectual product and not as simple entertainment. For that reason he did a great deal to promote the "new drama" of the 1890s, including the work of Ibsen and Bernard Shaw. Throughout his career he protested critical overvaluation of the English dramatic heritage, claiming that modern works were in many ways equal to or better than Elizabethan or Restoration drama. In the following excerpt, originally published in the* World, 20 February 1895, *Archer offers an appreciative review of* Earnest.]

The dramatic critic is not only a philosopher, moralist, aesthetician, and stylist, but also a labourer working for his hire.

Illustration of Allen Aynesworth as Algernon Moncrieff.

In this last capacity he cares nothing for the classifications of Aristotle, Polonius, or any other theorist, but instinctively makes a fourfold division of the works which come within his ken. These are his categories: (1) Plays which are good to see. (2) Plays which are good to write about. (3) Plays which are both. (4) Plays which are neither. Class 4 is naturally the largest; Class 3 the smallest; and Classes 1 and 2 balance each other pretty evenly. Mr. Oscar Wilde's new comedy, *The Importance of Being Earnest,* belongs indubitably to the first class. It is delightful to see, it sends wave after wave of laughter curling and foaming round the theatre; but as a text for criticism it is barren and delusive. It is like a mirage-oasis in the desert, grateful and comforting to the weary eye—but when you come close up to it, behold! it is intangible, it eludes your grasp. What can a poor critic do with a play which raises no principle, whether of art or morals, creates its own canons and conventions, and is nothing but an absolutely wilful expression of an irrepressibly witty personality? Mr. Pater, I think (or is it some one else?), has an essay on the tendency of all art to verge towards, and merge in, the absolute art—music. He might have found an example in *The Importance of Being Earnest,* which imitates nothing, represents nothing, means nothing, is nothing, except a sort of *rondo capriccioso* ["whimsical rondo"], in which the artist's fingers run with crisp irresponsibility up and down the keyboard of life. Why attempt to analyse and class such a play? Its theme, in other hands, would have made a capital farce; but "farce" is far too gross and commonplace a word to apply to such an iridescent filament of fantasy. Incidents of the same nature as Algy Moncrieffe's "Bunburying" and John Worthing's invention and subsequent suppression of his scapegrace brother Ernest have done duty in many a French vaudeville and English adaptation; but Mr. Wilde's humour transmutes them into something entirely new and individual. Amid so much that is negative, however, criticism may find one positive remark to make. Behind all Mr. Wilde's whim and even perversity, there lurks a very genuine science, or perhaps I should rather say instinct, of the theatre. In all his plays, and certainly not least in this one, the story is excellently told and illustrated with abundance of scenic detail. Monsieur Sarcey himself (if Mr. Wilde will forgive my saying so) would "chortle in his joy" over John Worthing's entrance in deep mourning (even down to his cane) to announce the death of his brother Ernest, when we know that Ernest in the flesh—a false but undeniable Ernest—is at that moment in the house making love to Cecily. The audience does not instantly awaken to the meaning of his inky suit, but even as he marches solemnly down the stage, and before a word is spoken, you can feel the idea kindling from row to row, until a "sudden glory" of laughter fills the theatre. It is only the born playwright who can imagine and work up to such an effect. Not that the play is a masterpiece of construction. It seemed to me that the author's invention languished a little after the middle of the second act, and that towards the close of that act there were even one or two brief patches of something almost like tediousness. But I have often noticed that the more successful the play, the more a first-night audience is apt to be troubled by inequalities of workmanship, of which subsequent audiences are barely conscious. . . . Mr. Wilde is least fortunate where he drops into Mr. Gilbert's Palace-of-Truth mannerism, as he is apt to do in the characters of Gwendolen and Cecily. Strange what a fascination this trick seems to possess for the comic playwright! Mr. Pinero, Mr. Shaw, and now Mr. Wilde, have all dabbled in it, never to their advantage. . . . (pp. 56-9)

> William Archer, "'The Importance of Being Earnest'—'Thorough-Bred'—'An M. P.'s Wife'," in his

The Theatrical "World" of 1895, Walter Scott, Ltd., 1896, pp. 56-61.

MAX BEERBOHM (essay date 1902)

[*Though he lived until 1956, Beerbohm is chiefly associated with the fin de siècle period in English literature, more specifically with its lighter phases of witty sophistication and mannered elegance. "Entertaining" in the most complimentary sense of the word, Beerbohm's criticism for the* Saturday Review—*where he was a long-time drama critic—everywhere indicates his scrupulously developed taste and unpretentious, fair-minded response to literature. In the following excerpt from an essay originally published in the* Saturday Review (London), 18 January 1902, *Beerbohm praises Wilde's achievement in* Earnest, *citing especially the polished dialogue of the play and the enduring quality of its humor.*]

Of a play representing actual life there can be, I think, no test more severe than its revival after seven or eight years of abeyance. For that period is enough to make it untrue to the surface of the present, yet not enough to enable us to unswitch it from the present. How seldom is the test passed! There is a better chance, naturally, for plays that weave life into fantastic forms; but even for them not a very good chance; for the fashion in fantasy itself changes. Fashions form a cycle, and we, steadily moving in that cycle, are farther from whatever fashion we have just passed than from any other. The things which once pleased our grandfathers are tolerable in comparison with the things which once pleased us. If in the lumber of the latter we find something that still pleases us, pleases us as much as ever it did, then, surely, we may preen ourselves on the possession of a classic, and congratulate posterity. Last week, at the St. James', was revived *The Importance of Being Earnest,* after an abeyance of exactly seven years—those seven years which, according to scientists, change every molecule in the human body, leaving nothing of what was there before. And yet to me the play came out fresh and exquisite as ever, and over the whole house almost every line was sending ripples of laughter—cumulative ripples that became waves, and receded only for fear of drowning the next line. In kind the play always was unlike any other, and in its kind it still seems perfect. I do not wonder that now the critics boldly call it a classic, and predict immortality. And (timorous though I am apt to be in prophecy) I join gladly in their chorus.

A classic must be guarded jealously. Nothing should be added to, or detracted from, a classic. . . . Mr. Wilde was a master in selection of words, and his words must not be amended. (pp. 188-89)

In scheme, of course, it is a hackneyed farce—the story of a young man coming up to London "on the spree," and of another young man going down conversely to the country, and of the complications that ensue. In treatment, also, it is farcical, in so far as some of the fun depends on absurd "situations," "stage-business," and so forth. Thus one might assume that the best way to act it would be to rattle through it. That were a gross error. For, despite the scheme of the play, the fun depends mainly on what the characters say, rather than on what they do. They speak a kind of beautiful nonsense—the language of high comedy, twisted into fantasy. Throughout the dialogue is the horse-play of a distinguished intellect and a distinguished imagination—a horse-play among words and ideas, conducted with poetic dignity. What differentiates this farce from any other, and makes it funnier than any other, is the humorous contrast between its style and matter. To preserve its style fully, the dialogue must be spoken with grave unction. The sound and the sense of the words must be taken seriously, treated beautifully. If mimes rattle through the play and anyhow, they manage to obscure much of its style, and much, therefore, of its fun. They lower it towards the plane of ordinary farce. (p. 190)

Max Beerbohm, "'The Importance of Being Earnest',' in his Around Theatres, *Simon and Schuster, 1954, pp. 188-91.*

JOHN DRINKWATER   (essay date 1925)

[*An English dramatist, poet, biographer, and critic, Drinkwater also directed and performed in numerous stage productions while serving as general manager of the Birmingham Repertory Theatre. He wrote his most notable play, the historical drama* Abraham Lincoln, *for that company in 1918. In works such as* Lincoln *and the verse drama* X = o: A Night of the Trojan War *(1917), Drinkwater espoused his fervent antiwar sentiment and "lifelong intolerance of intolerance." While these plays brought him popular renown on both sides of the Atlantic, critics were generally more enthusiastic toward his light comedy* Bird in Hand *(1927), which has been praised as a well-crafted departure from his didactic historical dramas. In the following excerpt, Drinkwater asserts that* Earnest *is Wilde's sole dramatic masterpiece.*]

The Importance of Being Earnest is not really a comedy of manners in the sense of being primarily a criticism of the follies into which a society is betrayed by its conventions, and a tearing off of the masks. Nor is it primarily a comedy of wit, sure and sustained as the wit is. Attempts have been made to derive the play in some measure from the Restoration masters, but without

A page from Wilde's handwritten manuscript.

much conviction, and while the manner employed by Wilde has clearly influenced some later writers, notably St. John Hankin, *The Importance of Being Earnest* really forms a class in English drama by itself. It is in mere simplicity that one says that it seems to be the only one of Wilde's works that really has its roots in passion. Every device of gaiety and even seeming nonsense is employed to keep the passion far back out of sight, and if it were otherwise the play would not be the masterpiece it is. But the passion is there. That is to say that the play is directly an expression of that part of Wilde's own experience which was least uncontaminated and in which he could take most delight. And this meant that all his great gifts as a craftsman were for once employed in work, where with insincerity almost as the theme, there was more sincerity than in anything else he did. Plays like *Salome* and *A Florentine Tragedy* are at best little more than virtuosity, while *A Woman of No Importance, Lady Windermere's Fan,* and *An Ideal Husband,* although they may have many of the qualities that mark Wilde's one great achievement, are on the whole frank surrenders to a fashion of the theatre which Wilde had too good a brain not to despise. But in *The Importance of Being Earnest* there is neither virtuosity nor concession. It is a superb and original piece of construction with several moments of stage mastery which can hardly be excelled in comedy, and packed throughout with a perfect understanding of dramatic speech. One has only to recall any scene in the play and place it beside almost any of the successful comedies that one sees in the ordinary run of theatre production to see how definitely apart that greatness is set which comes of having not three words in seven dramatically right but seven in seven. But when art comes to this excellence of form it can only mean excellence of life at the springs, and flowing through *The Importance of Being Earnest* is the surest and clearest part of Wilde's life. There was much, perhaps everything, in the more profoundly moving story of man that Wilde saw always imperfectly or not at all. But he did see, with a subtlety that can hardly be matched in our dramatic literature, that the common intrigues of daily life are not really the moralist's province at all, but interesting only for the sheer amusement that can be got out of them. Shakespeare gave to the English stage a comedy as full of poetic passion as great tragic art, Ben Jonson the comedy of humours, and Congreve and his fellows the true comedy of manners, but Wilde in his one masterpiece brought into the same company of excellence the comedy of pure fun. (pp. 227-29)

John Drinkwater, "Wilde's 'The Importance of Being Earnest'," in his The Muse in Council, *Sidgwick and Jackson Limited, 1925, pp. 225-29.*

JOSEPH WOOD KRUTCH   (essay date 1939)

[*Krutch is widely regarded as one of America's most respected drama critics. Noteworthy among his works are* The American Drama since 1918 *(1939), in which he analyzed the most important dramas of the 1920s and 1930s, and* "Modernism" in Modern Drama *(1953), in which he stressed the need for twentieth-century playwrights to infuse their works with traditional humanistic values. A conservative and idealistic thinker, he was a consistent proponent of human dignity and the preeminence of literary art. In the following excerpt, Krutch briefly assesses the durability of* Earnest.]

The Importance of Being Earnest has reached that dangerous age at which literary works are unmistakably outmoded without having become, so far at least, unquestionable classics. . . .

On the whole, the epigrams may be left to look after themselves, since time has tarnished them remarkably little. But the danger is that a modern audience may disallow even the slender claims which *The Importance of Being Earnest* makes to being a play, and that it will become no more than a series of bright remarks. If it is to be saved from this fate, it must be given an artificial style; but if it is also to be saved from another and worse fate, this style must be recognized as one inherent in the play itself, not one imposed in condescension by a modern director.

One cannot, in other words, successfully play it as a period piece. Oscar Wilde is "sophisticated" or nothing. He cannot be made quaint and survive; any tendency to laugh at rather than with him is utterly fatal; any silliness must be obviously the kind of silliness he intended. . . .

Wilde played at being a socialist. *The Importance of Being Earnest* is fantasy rather than satire in the graver meaning of the term because Wilde, like Congreve before him, had a sneaking admiration for the dandies whom he ridiculed, and infinitely preferred such irresponsible exquisites to dull though useful citizens. The fact, nevertheless, remains that the charm of his fools and the charm of all the dandies from Congreve on is subject to an economic interpretation. The privilege which they enjoy of "treating serious things trivially and trivial things seriously" is the result of the enviable freedom which their security confers upon them. If (*pace* Veblen) one wears gloves to indicate that one does not have to work, one talks nonsense to prove that one does not even have to think. Wilde's greatest achievement in this particular play consists in his perfect imaginative realization of the ideal toward which the fashionable exquisite is tending and his creation of a realm in which his dandies can flutter through life successfully. (p. 128)

> *Joseph Wood Krutch, "Cucumber Sandwiches," in*
> The Nation, *Vol. 148, No. 5, January 28, 1939, pp.*
> *128-29.*

EDOUARD RODITI (essay date 1947)

[*Born in France, Roditi is a poet, short story writer, biographer, translator, and critic whose works reflect his interest in Jewish thought and culture. In the following excerpt, he expresses a depreciative view of* Earnest.]

Like most modern plays that have any lasting value, Wilde's comedies transcend the average of our dreary age of commercial drama only by virtue of qualities that they share with other forms of literature, less popular or commercial, or with the drama of less commercial ages. But in his eagerness to make money, Wilde made too many concessions to the bad dramatic tastes and habits of his own times; and he failed throughout *A Woman of No Importance* and *An Ideal Husband,* and in several aspects of *Lady Windermere's Fan* and *The Importance of Being Earnest,* to achieve the lasting perfection of the true classic rather than the ambiguous survival of works that are treated as classics for lack of any better examples of their genre. (p. 126)

Wilde's three first comedies were, as John Drinkwater has pointed out [see excerpt dated 1925], "frank surrenders to a fashion of the theater which Wilde had too good a brain not to despise." Wilde had learned that the public, like Shylock, demands its pound of fleshly problem, of informative facts or of moral instruction, to allay the guilt of sheer enjoyment, before it will acclaim a new dramatist. Later, once captivated by his magic, it may forget its demands or begin to find, for

its pleasure, some justification in his mere art. And Wilde had reached the point, in *The Importance of Being Earnest,* where he could at last, it seems, rely on his earlier success, as an author of problem-plays, to carry him ahead, as an author of light comedies, on the crest of a wave of sheer popularity. In his last comedy, we find no fallen women, whether anxious to regain their lost respectability or to undermine the reputations of more worthy characters, no good women who must learn, through bitter experience, that sin and virtue are not clear-cut absolutes. Instead of the moral problem which the author must solve, Wilde now uses, as plot, a purely farcical intrigue, though perhaps still too much of an infernal machine, too loudly ticking beneath the light dialogue and too well timed, with all its happy couples paired off in the last act, to achieve the less obviously contrived or less self-conscious perfection of one of Sheridan's comedies of manners.

Between *The Importance of Being Earnest,* with all its plot and sub-plots, and Sheridan's *The Critic,* which is all situation and no plot, a happy mean can be found; and Wilde might have found it, had not the catastrophes of his private life smashed his popularity with the public and killed his desire to write any more. (pp. 134-35)

[In] Wilde's three first comedies, the light dialogue of the satirical comedy of manners was not yet properly fitted to the heavier plot of the problem-play. In *The Importance of Being Earnest,* the remarks and the character of Lady Bracknell seem far more appropriate, less affected and less unrealistically stylized, against their background, than those of the Duchess of Berwick in *Lady Windermere's Fan,* where Lady Windermere's unrelieved earnestness contrasts too violently with the frivolity of most of the other characters. We thus seem to be witnessing, in some scenes of Wilde's three first comedies, the improbable commerce of two different species of imagined humanity, *homo moralis* and *homo immoralis,* who could not conceivably live together on such amicable terms in the same small society: one of them would surely expel the other very soon, by some Gresham's Law such as that which drove fallen Adam and Eve out of the angels' Garden of Eden or which later caused the aboriginal Tasmanians to die out as soon as Victorian Englishmen appeared on their shores.

Though the characters of Wilde's farce are all of the same species, its plot is at times too heavily contrived, especially in the last act: the sudden revelation of Miss Prism's past solves too conveniently the problem of the hero's origin, and too many of the embarrassing lies of the play are too neatly resolved into truth. Such reliance on the whimsies of chance weakens the satire of a comedy of manners; its plot should seem to grow more directly out of the follies of its characters, mirroring the irrationality of an absurd society of human beings responsible for their own predicaments rather than the irresponsible tricks of a contemptibly frivolous destiny.

In spite of the polished brilliance of its paradoxical dialogue and the sure pace of its surprising action, *The Importance of Being Earnest* thus never transcends, as a work of art, the incomplete or the trivial. Its tone is that of satire, but of a satire which, for lack of a moral point of view, has lost its sting and degenerated into the almost approving banter of a P. G. Wodehouse. Satire, whether in the comedy of manners or any other genre of satirical literature, must be founded on more than a dandy's mere tastes and opinions; from some sounder moral philosophy, it must derive a necessary bitterness without which the satirist remains ineffectual while the manners of his comedies, not yet structurally integrated, seem superimposed as mere ornament on an arbitrary plot of farce. (pp. 137-39)

> *Edouard Roditi, in his* Oscar Wilde, *New Directions Books, 1947, 256 p.*

SIR JOHN GIELGUD (essay date 1949)

[*A highly acclaimed actor and director, as well as an autobiographer and critic, Gielgud has appeared in plays by many classic and contemporary dramatists. In the following excerpt, he discusses the mechanics of a successful production of* Earnest *from a director's point of view.*]

The comedies of the Restoration period, and those of Oscar Wilde, are less imaginative, less free, both in conception and execution, than the comedies of Shakespeare, and written, of course, for a picture stage. Their performance demands, both from actors and directors, a considerable understanding of the period in which they were written, and some degree of urban sophistication from the audience. They are city plays, and, though there are country scenes in them, those scenes represent the country seen very much through city eyes.

Shakespeare lived, probably, as much in the country as he did in London. Many of his comedies are pastoral in scene and atmosphere, but in his day the cities were so small compared to ours, that the juxtaposition in his plays of scenes of town and country life, court and woodland, inn yard, castle and seashore, give to their action—especially on the unlocalised stage for which he was writing—a wonderful freedom of movement and variety of atmosphere.

After the Restoration, with the introduction of picture stage, front curtain and proscenium, plays came to be written which could be sustained throughout in a single mood. Long acts took the place of short scenes. Audiences became increasingly delighted in seeing people on the stage behaving exactly as they themselves behaved at home (only saying more amusing things) against backgrounds of painted scenery and realistic accessories of every kind.

But playwrights of poetic genius cannot be kept down by convention. The mad scene of Valentine in Congreve's *Love for Love,* Worthing's interview with Lady Bracknell in **The Importance of Being Earnest,** and his arrival in mock mourning in the second act of the latter play, these are flights of poetic imagination—though, of course, they are comic scenes as well. The author, in each case, seems to blossom into a kind of inspired lunacy which is light, poetic, exquisitely original. These moments lift the plays in which they occur to a brilliant peak of nonsense. They are incomparable examples of their kind. They are scenes of classic farce.

We shall never know whether Wilde wrote his last play meaning to keep it as a perfectly "straight" realistic picture of high life as he knew it. It may be that the touches which make the play most memorable only occurred to him as an afterthought. He is known to have been the most wonderful extempore talker, but it is possible, too, that before he went to a party he did a little homework first (as an actor does), and was ready with some of the good things he proposed to say, even if he was not sure of the order in which he was going to say them. No doubt, too, he was stimulated by his own wit, and one good remark suggested another, till the best one, the cherry on top of the cake, came to him suddenly in a flash of inspiration. Certainly the construction of this his best play is careful and precise, though the author does not hesitate to make use of a set of stock characters and several well-worn devices of farce to carry his plot to a satisfactory conclusion. Similarly, Shakespeare and Congreve were not above a good deal of borrowing of plots, slapstick, and conventional misunderstandings, to keep their comedies spinning along to the usual pairing off of all the characters at the end.

The Importance of Being Earnest begins in a quite realistic atmosphere. The characters behave and talk in the languid, pointed, conscious manner of their day. They are witty, cultured, idle and wealthy. Even Lane, Algernon's manservant, has caught some of his master's wit, added a pinch of his own, and replies to questions with epigrams uttered in tones of deferential gravity. Everybody is solemn, correct, polite. The bachelors only loll or smoke or cross their legs when they are alone. In company they sit with straight backs and conduct themselves with irreproachable exactitude, hitching their trousers before they sit down, stripping off their gloves, shooting their cuffs. Their hats are worn at exactly the right angle, their canes carried with an air of studied negligence. They have never been seen in Piccadilly without top-hats and frock-coats.

Algy, in the country, is dressed to kill. But he must not kill the comedy by a costume verging upon caricature. A correct country suit of the period will be quite amusing enough to modern eyes. Miss Prism and Doctor Chasuble are stock figures of farce, the spinster governess and the country rector, but they must be simple and sincere in their playing, not exaggeratedly ridiculous. Well acted, they have great charm—Prism, at the end, has even a touch of pathos. The comedy verges upon fantasy and occasionally spills over into farce: it must never degenerate into knockabout. In act two it is the tradition of Worthing to produce from his breast-pocket a black-edged handkerchief. (We do not know if this was the invention of Wilde, or of George Alexander, who created the part. I suspect the latter, for there is no mention of it in the printed text.) This must not be flourished or handled continually to distract from the dialogue and force the laughter of the audience. Used twice, it is legitimate. Shaken once too often, if becomes a cheap "prop" which may destroy the whole beauty of the author's exquisite invention. The scene with the muffins, at the end of the second act, should be played deliberately and with great seriousness. Here again, the actors must not enjoy themselves too much, nor must they snatch and fight and talk with their mouths full. The decorum, the deadly importance of the triviality, is everything—they are greedy, determined, but exasperatedly polite.

Cecily is first cousin to Alice in Wonderland—the same backboard demureness, the same didactic manner, the echoes of remarks she has copied from her elders and her governess. Gwendolen is perhaps more difficult for an actress to hit off correctly, but we may find her prototype in the cartoons of George du Maurier in *Punch*. But her affectations must be of society, not the "Greenery Yallery Grosvenor Gallery" airs which Gilbert satirised in *Patience*. She is bored and elegant, with an occasional flash of individuality peeping out under overwhelming layers of her mother's condescension and snobbishness, which she frequently echoes in her own remarks.

Lady Bracknell is not called Augusta for nothing. She is never put out or surprised. She is never angry. But she is frequently disapproving and almost always annihilating. If the author were anyone but Wilde, she would be unanswerable. She moves slowly and seldom. She is beautifully dressed and carries herself superbly. Her every accessory—veil, gloves, parasol, chatelaine, bag and shoes—must be worn with a perfection of detail that has become second nature to her. It is impossible to conceive her (or her daughter either) except *en grande tenue.*

The pace of the comedy must be leisurely, mannered; and everybody must, of course, speak beautifully—but the wit must appear spontaneous, though self-conscious. The text must be studied and spoken so as to arouse a cumulative effect of laughter from the audience. That is to say it may be sometimes necessary to sacrifice laughs on certain witty lines, in order that a big laugh may come at the end of a passage, rather than to extract two or three small ones in between, which may dissipate the sense and retard the progress of the dialogue. There are, if anything, too many funny lines, and the actor may easily ruin a passage by allowing the audience to laugh in the middle. For instance, the following sally in the first Act:

> JACK. My dear Algy, you talk exactly as if you were a dentist. It is very vulgar to talk like a dentist when one isn't a dentist. It produces a false impression.
>
> ALGERNON. Well, that is exactly what dentists always do.

If the actors leave time for the audience to laugh after the words "It produces a false impression," Algernon's reply will fall flat and seem redundant. Actors with expert pace and timing will hurry the dialogue, Algernon breaking in quickly with his line, so that the audience may not laugh until he has spoken it. (pp. vii-x)

It is not easy to achieve the style, the lightness, the apparent ease which the play demands. Above all it is hard to act it with a deadly seriousness, yet with an inner consciousness of fun— the fun with which one plays seriously a very elaborate practical joke.

The play must originally have been thought funny because it tilted so brilliantly at society as it then was. The people who laughed at it were many of them laughing at themselves, reproduced with only very slight exaggeration upon the stage. To-day we laugh at the very idea that such types could ever have existed; at the whole system—the leaving of cards, chaperons, proposals of marriage, ceremony of meals, the ridiculously exaggerated values of birth, rank and fashion.

But there is a danger that the actors of to-day, lacking real types to observe, will turn the comedy into wild caricature, and the audience, even if they may not know the reason, will then find the piece contrived, silly and overdrawn. The performance needs to be correct though not dry, leisurely but not dragged, solemn yet full of sparkle. Above all it is an agreeable play. The brittle crackling staccato of Noel Coward, the smart rudeness of Frederick Lonsdale, this was not wit as Wilde conceived it. In his plays nobody is nervous, impatient, catty, or ill-natured. The "lower classes" are spoken of patronisingly but not contemptuously. Even Lady Bracknell's stern summons of "Prism!" in the final scene is firm without being cruel. The girls conduct their elegant quarrel with the highest good breeding. Everything depends on no one losing their tempers or their poise. The movement throughout must be smooth, stylish (but not balletic, as often occurs when actors and directors try to create a period sense) and the more elegantly the actors give and take, the more will the intrinsic quality of the wit emerge, as the grave puppet characters utter their delicate cadences and spin their web of preposterously elegant sophistication. (p. xi)

> *Sir John Gielgud, in an introduction to* The Importance of Being Earnest *by Oscar Wilde, William Heinemann Ltd., 1949, pp. vii-xi.*

John Gielgud as John Worthing, Gwen Frangeon-Davies as Gwendolen, and Edith Evans as Lady Bracknell in the 1939-40 Globe Theatre production. Photo by Angus Mc-Bean. Mander & Mitchenson Theatre Collection.

OTTO REINERT (essay date 1956)

[*In the following excerpt, Reinert traces Wilde's satiric targets and techniques in* The Importance of Being Earnest.]

Almost everyone agrees that *The Importance of Being Earnest* is good fun, but few have tried to show that it is also a good play. To say that Wilde has written a brilliant farce is not to say why it seems both funnier and more significant than other superior farces, and to say that the farce satirizes Victorianism is not, at this late date, to tell us why it amuses at all. From some of the incidental comments one gets the impression that the play is untouchable, so exquisite that criticism would be fatal—stupid abuse of something bright and fragile. A few critics, who take their business more seriously, refuse even to be charmed. The play "never transcends . . . the incomplete or the trivial," Edouard Roditi writes in his generally perceptive book on Wilde [see excerpt dated 1947]: "Its tone is that of satire, but of a satire which, for lack of a moral point of view, has lost its sting and degenerated into the almost approving banter of a P. G. Wodehouse."

But only a curious form of critical blindness can dismiss *Earnest* as a trifle of dialogues. It merits attention both as satire and as drama. The farce is meaningful. Tone and plot have been successfully integrated, and the whole is more truly comic— because normative—than a well-made play to end all well-made plays, a vehicle for the utterance of witty nonsense. Awareness of its satirical strategy precludes the criticism that it is elusive of reasoned analysis for lack of any kind of rationale.

Wilde first employed a pattern of ironic inversion in *An Ideal Husband,* the play immediately preceding *Earnest.* Its hero, Lord Goring, is not the irresponsible dandy he seems to be, the surface frivolity is not the real man, and his flippant paradoxes emphasize the irony of his moral position relative to that of Lord Chiltern, the pretended pillar of society. (p. 14)

But though the brand of wit is similar in *Earnest,* such an attitude cannot be attributed to any one or several of the characters in the later play, simply because it has no hero (or heroine) in the sense in which Lord Goring is the hero of *An Ideal Husband.* The characters in *Earnest* never stop being flippant; their flippancy is their whole nature and not, like Lord Goring's, the mocking mask of enlightened irony in a pompous society. The only ironist in *Earnest* is Wilde himself, who not only has abandoned the simple ethics of thesis melodrama but also has deliberately sacrificed the illusionistic conventions of naturalism in order to gain what Francis Fergusson calls (in *The Idea of a Theater*) . . . a "limited perspective, shared with the audience, as the basis of the fun," showing "human life *as* comic . . . because . . . consistent according to some narrowly defined, and hence unreal, basis."

That is why there is no reason to be embarrassed by the farce label. The play's merit is that it is *all* farce, capable of serving as a lucid image of the non-farcical reality that is kept strictly outside the play. Wilde has respected his paradoxes. He is no longer putting them to menial service as bright spots in sentimental thesis plays or as devices of crude melodramatic irony. *The Importance of Being Earnest* is one sustained metaphor, and esthetic detachment is the only mood in which it can be intelligently enjoyed. It insists on being acted straight, for if we should feel, even for a moment, that the characters are aware of what absurdities they are saying, the whole thing vanishes. Once object and image are confused there is a blurring of vision. No one in his right mind gets emotionally involved with the destinies of Algernon and Cecily, Gwendolen and Jack. But it is precisely their emotive neutrality as figures of farce that allows Wilde's characters to establish his "limited perspective": Wilde's basic formula for satire is their assumption of a code of behavior that represents the reality that Victorian convention pretends to ignore.

Algernon is explaining his reluctance to attend Lady Bracknell's dinner party:

> She will place me next Mary Farquhar, who always flirts with her own husband across the dinner table. That is not very pleasant. Indeed, it is not even decent . . . and that sort of thing is enormously on the increase. The amount of women in London who flirt with their own husbands is perfectly scandalous. It looks so bad. It is simply washing one's clean linen in public.

To say that Algernon's tone here is consciously flippant is to miss the joke altogether. The quip is not a quip; it means what it says. Algernon is indignant with a woman who spoils the fun of extramarital flirtation and who parades her virtue. He is shocked at convention. And his tone implies that he is elevating break of convention into a moral norm. He is not the first figure in English satire to do so; among his ancestors are Martin Scriblerus, other assumed identities in Pope and Swift (including Gulliver), and the apologist for Jonathan Wild. What they all have in common is that they derive their ideals for conduct from the actual practice of their societies, their standards are the standards of common corruption, they are literal-minded victims of their environments, realists with a vengeance.

Here is Algernon on conventional love institutions:

> I really don't see anything romantic in proposing. It is very romantic to be in love. But there is nothing romantic about a definite proposal. Why, one may be accepted. One usually is, I believe. Then the excitement is all over.
>
> (pp. 14-15)

The girls, too, implicitly accept this inverted code. In the proposal scene between Jack and Gwendolen the latter acts out reality: girls about to be proposed to quite realize the situation and are annoyed by their suitors' conventionally bungling approach. In the second act Gwendolen explains to Cecily that she always travels with her diary in order to "have something sensational to read in the train." One of Cecily's first speeches expresses her concern for "dear Uncle Jack" who is so "very serious" that "I think he cannot be quite well." When Algernon, at their first meeting, begs her not to think him wicked, she sternly replies:

> If you are not, then you have certainly been deceiving us all in a very inexcusable manner. I hope you have not been leading a double life, pretending to be wicked and being really good all the time. That would be hypocrisy.

Paradoxical morality cannot be argued much further than this, and the speech upsets even Algernon. In context it cuts down to the very core of the problem of manners with which Wilde is concerned. It epitomizes the central irony of the play, for the Bunburying Algernon, in escaping the hypocrisy of convention, becomes a hypocrite himself by pretending to be somebody he is not. (Even Miss Prism participates. She is telling Cecily about her youthful novel: "The good ended happily, and the bad unhappily. That is what Fiction means.")

Only Jack and Lady Bracknell seem at first glance to be outside the pattern of inversion, expressing shock when confronted with the code of cynical realism. But their conventionality is not genuine. Jack is a confirmed Bunburyist long before Algernon explains the term to him, and Bunburyism is most simply defined as a means of escape from convention. He occasionally acts the role of naive elicitor of Algernon's discourses on Bunburyism and is not such a consistent theorist of the realist code, but his behavior is certainly not conventional.

One of Lady Bracknell's main plot functions is to be an obstacle to Jack's romance with Gwendolen, but a systematic analysis of her speeches will show, I think, that she has no illusions about the reality her professed convention is supposed to conceal: ". . . I do not approve of mercenary marriages. When I married Lord Bracknell I had no fortune of any kind." To her the speech is neither cynical nor funny. It represents that compromise between practical hardheadedness and conventional morality that she has worked to her own satisfaction and behind which she has retired in dignified immunity. In other speeches she advocates Algernon's code with as much sanctimoniousness as he:

> Well, I must say, Algernon, that I think it is high time that Mr. Bunbury made up his mind whether he was going to live or to die. This shilly-shallying with the question is absurd. Nor

do I in any way approve of the modern sympathy with invalids. I consider it morbid.

She moralizes on behalf of people who take it for granted that
illness in others is always faked and that consequently sympathy with invalids is faked also, a concession to an artificial
and—literally—morbid code. The frivolous banter accomplishes something serious. It exposes the polite cynicism that
negates all values save personal convenience and salon decorum. Life and death have become matters of *savoir-vivre*.

The following speech presents a somewhat more complex case,
because Lady Bracknell is here simultaneously deferring to
convention and exposing its sham:

> French songs I cannot possibly allow. People
> always seem to think that they are improper,
> and either look shocked, which is vulgar, or
> laugh, which is worse. But German sounds a
> thoroughly respectable language, and indeed,
> I believe is so.

To laugh at presumably improper songs is to fly in the face of
convention and break the delicate fabric of social decorum.
But the opposite reaction is hardly less reprehensible. To register shock at indecency is indecently to call attention to something people realize the existence of but refuse to recognize.
In her last sentence she quietly gives away the polite fiction
that people in society know foreign languages.

When the pattern of inversion operates the characters either
express or assume a morality that is deduced from the actual
behavior of high society, though the existence of conventional
morality is sometimes recognized as a fact to come to terms
with. What the accumulation of paradox adds up to is an exposure both of hypocrisy and of the unnatural convention that
necessitates hypocrisy. In elegant accents of pompous bigotry
Wilde's puppets turn moral values upside down. "Good heavens," Algernon exclaims when Lane tells him that married
households rarely serve first-rate champagne. "Is marriage so
demoralizing as that?" We are made to share Wilde's view of
the ludicrous and sinister realities behind the fashionable façade
of an over-civilized society where nothing serious is considered
serious and nothing trivial trivial.

But *Earnest* is, before anything else, a play, an imitation of
action, and no discussion of tone apart from its dramatic setting
can account for the extraordinary impact of the play as play.
It is rather odd, therefore, to notice that even critics who have
been aware of serious satiric implications in the dialogue have
been prone to dismiss the plot as negligible, as, at best, "inspired nonsense." "The plot," writes Eric Bentley, in *The
Playwright as Thinker* . . . [see *TCLC*, Vol. 1], "is one of
those Gilbertian absurdities of lost infants and recovered brothers which can only be thought of to be laughed at," and he
defines the function of "the ridiculous action" as constantly
preventing the play from "breaking into bitter criticism." There
is truth in that, but the action has another and far more important
function as well: it informs the satiric dialogue with coherent
meaning.

The action of *The Importance of Being Earnest* is about just
that—the importance of being earnest. The title is as straightforward a statement of theme as any literalist could ask for.
Specifically, the play deals with the consequences of that way
of not being earnest that Algernon calls Bunburying, and it is
Bunburying that gives the plot moral significance. The key
speech in the play is Algernon's little lecture to Jack:

> Well, one must be serious about something, if
> one wants to have any amusement in life. I
> happen to be serious about Bunburying. What
> on earth you are serious about I haven't got the
> remotest idea. About everything, I should fancy.
> You have an absolutely trivial nature.

Bunburying means to invent a fictitious character, who can
serve as a pretext for escaping a frustrating social routine,
regulated by a repressive convention. The pretended reason for
getting away is perfectly respectable, even commendable, according to convention: to comfort a dying friend, to rescue a
fallen brother. Thus defined, Bunburying is simply the mechanism that sets in motion the preposterously elaborate plot of
mistaken identities. But the word has also a wider meaning.
Significantly, Algernon *happens* to be serious about Bunburying—that is, it is not the subterfuge itself that is important,
but the commitment to a course of action that will provide fun.
The Bunburyist in the wider sense is serious about not being
serious, and Bunburyism is the alternative to a convention that
fails to reckon with the facts of human nature. It stands for
behavior that will give experience the shading and perspective
that convention denies it. To be serious about everything is to
be serious about nothing; that is, to trifle. Algernon charges
Jack (unfairly, as it happens) with a failure to discriminate
among life values, to see that monotone of attitude blunts the
spirit and deadens joy. And this is precisely Wilde's charge
against Victorianism.

The Bunburyist lives in a world of irresponsibility, freed from
the enslavement of a hypocritical convention. He enjoys himself. But life beyond hypocrisy is life in a dangerous climate
of moral anarchy, and, like most states of revolt, Bunburyism
is not ideal. The escape from convention is itself a flagrant
instance of hypocrisy: pretense is the price the Bunburyist pays
for freedom from the pretense of convention. In his title pun
Wilde catches the moral failure of dandyism. Just as the conformist pretends to be, but is not, earnest, so Algernon and
Jack pretend to be, but are not, Ernest.

What Wilde is saying, then, is that all normal Victorians who
want to retain the respect of their conventional society are,
perforce, Bunburyists, leading double lives, one respectable,
one frivolous, neither earnest. Bunburyism, as Algernon confesses in the opening of the play, is the application of science
to life, to the exclusion of sentiment. Sentiment properly belongs to art. The science is the science of having a good time.
These are obviously false distinctions, and all that can be said
for Bunburyism as a way of life is that it offers relief from a
social round where, in Lady Bracknell's words, good behavior
and well being "rarely go together," and where, according to
Jack, "a high moral tone can hardly be said to conduce very
much to either one's health or one's happiness." Bunburyism
marks one of the extreme points in the swing of the pendulum,
Victorianism the other.

Neither of the two Bunburyists is either earnest or Ernest—
before the very end. [The critic adds in a footnote that: "It is
the one flaw in a superbly constructed play that Algernon remains Algernon at the end and thus ineligible as a husband for
Cecily. To say that she does not seem to mind at that point or
that Dr. Chasuble is quite ready for the christening cannot
conceal the flaw. It staggers the imagination to try to think of
any way in which Wilde could have turned Algernon into a
second Ernest, but, given the plot, he ought to have done so."]
It is only [at the end that the two Bunburyists] become, and
in more than a single sense, themselves. When the action begins

George Alexander as John Worthing. Mander & Mitchenson Theatre Collection.

they have already escaped the mortifying seriousness of convention, but it takes them three acts and the movement from town to country—the movement has symbolic relevance as a return to "naturalness"—to regain their balance and become earnest, that is, neither conventionally nor frivolously hypocritical. At the end of the play the respectable (though amorous) Miss Prism (her name suggests "prim prison") has been unmasked, the four young people are romantically engaged, Jack has discovered his Bunburying identity to be his true self, and Lady Bracknell must recognize the contemptible orphan of Act I, "born, or at any rate, bred in a handbag," as her own sister's son. The plot, as it were, makes a fool of respectability and proves the two Bunburyists "right" in their escapade. But it also repudiates Bunburyism. Algernon, who as a Bunburyist spoke cynically about proposals and matrimony in Act I, is happily proposing marriage to Cecily in Act II, and at the end his initial false dichotomies between life and art, science and sentiment, have been resolved in romance. The radical remedy of Bunburying has effected a cure, the pendulum rests in the perpendicular, and we share Jack's final conviction of "the vital Importance of Being Earnest." The two adjectives have not been chosen lightly. (pp. 15-18)

Otto Reinert, "Satiric Strategy in 'The Importance of Being Earnest'," in College English, *Vol. 18, No. 1, October, 1956, pp. 14-18.*

RICHARD FOSTER　(essay date 1956)

[*In the following excerpt, Foster maintains that in* The Importance of Being Earnest *Wilde created a masterpiece of parody through the transformation of stock comedic techniques, plot devices, and characters.*]

The Importance of Being Earnest is apt to be a stumbling block both to the detractors and admirers of Oscar Wilde as a man of letters. Those who want to dismiss him as the greatest ass of aestheticism may be troubled to find themselves, in this play, laughing with rather than at Wilde. Those few, on the other hand, who see in the whole of Wilde's work the same revolutionary quest for new means and materials of literary expression which characterized the poetic innovators of nineteenth-century France sometimes find it hard to laugh at all. Meanwhile, the play continues to flourish as one of the world's most robust stage classics. Part of the critics' difficulty—an inadequacy frequently experienced by critics, never by audiences—is that they cannot accurately name its type. The terms "farce" and "comedy of manners," the labels most frequently applied to *Earnest,* are neither of them adequate designations of the especially subtle and complicated artistic "being" that the play has.

Farce, first of all, depends for its effects upon extremely simplified characters tangling themselves up in incongruous situations, and upon a knowing audience gleefully anticipating their falling victim, in their ignorance, to some enormous but harmless confusion of fact or identity. We think of *The Comedy of Errors,* of *She Stoops to Conquer,* of Uncle Toby about to show "the very place" to the breathless Widow Wadman. Wilde's characters are certainly uncomplicated, and he makes use of some farce situations, such as Jack's mourning scene and his recognition scene at the end of the play. But the comedy of *Earnest* subsists, for the most part, not in action or situation but in dialogue. The dialogue, furthermore, is everywhere an exercise of wit—a subtler comic effect than farce can comfortably take very much time for. This is only a tentative claim, to be expanded on later, that the play is a very intellectual kind of comedy, too intellectual, certainly, to be described simply as a farce.

The Importance of Being Earnest is more often, and perhaps somewhat more accurately, regarded as a comedy of manners. Ridicule and exposure of the vanities, the hypocrisies, and the idleness of the upper classes is, to be sure, the main function of its verbal wit. Moreover, the stock patterns of Restoration and eighteenth-century manners comedy are evident in various characters: Jack and Algernon, though in quest of love rather than riches or intrigue, are unmistakably brothers to the opportunistic young wits that hunted in pairs through the social jungles of earlier comedy; Cecily and Gwendolen are their quarry; Lady Bracknell's is the dowager role, though she is more dominant and more shrewdly financial than her shrill, physical Restoration forebears; but perhaps Miss Prism's middle-aged sexuality, only just contained by the strictures of Victorian propriety, makes her, after all, a more direct descendant of Lady Wishfort.

But *Earnest,* in spite of these qualities, is not a true comedy of manners either. It is not even nearly one. A comedy of manners is fundamentally realistic: it requires the audience to accept the world presented on the stage as a real world, a possible world; and its human foibles, even if heightened and exaggerated in the play's satirical exposure of them, are nevertheless laughed at as representations of real excesses. A clear sign of the realism of manners comedy is the fact that there are characters in it that can always recognize a fool. The laughter that the witty young bucks of the older comedy share with the audience at the expense of a fool or fop unites the "real" world and the world of the play by showing that the same criteria for reason and unreason are valid in both. But Jack and Algernon are strangely respectful of Prism and Chasuble—two clear fools—because fools must be taken seriously in the extra-rational world of Wilde's play. When we recognize this extra-rational quality of Wilde's play, we begin to see that its satirical effects are less close to *The Way of the World* and *The Rivals* than to *The Rape of the Lock* and *Patience*. Where Congreve and Sheridan created a pretty close, if heightened, imitation of that world, Wilde and Gilbert and Pope performed an alchemic *reductio ad absurdum* of it. Folly is *represented* in the comedy of manners, *essentialized* in Pope's mock epic, Gilbert's operettas, and Wilde's play.

Wilde accomplishes this essentialization of folly by creating an "as if" world in which "real" values are inverted, reason and unreason interchanged, and the probable defined by improbability. The structure and materials of this "as if" world become especially interesting when we remember that the English theater was, at this time, just beginning to get over a century-long siege of melodrama and sentimentalism. Gwendolen's observation, for example, that "in matters of grave importance, style, not sincerity, is the vital thing" has the effect of ridiculing the "poetic" manner of contemporary melodrama, which Robertson and Jones had already rebelled against. Early in Act I, just after Jack has confessed "the whole truth pure and simple" about Cecily and his fictional brother Ernest, Algernon delivers an even more direct and sweeping critical dictum: "The truth," says Algy, "is rarely pure and never simple. Modern life would be very tedious if it were either, and modern literature a complete impossibility." From this point on, Wilde's play is to be a satiric demonstration of how art can lie romantically about human beings and distort the simple laws of real life with melodramatic complications and improbably easy escapes from them. Wilde has accomplished this by purloining from the hallowed edifice of romantic literature certain standard characters, themes, and plot situations in order to build out of them a comedy that fuses contemporary social satire with a straight-faced taking-off of the usages of the popular fiction and drama of Wilde's time, and, inevitably, of other times as well. (pp. 18-20)

Wilde's first technique is to spoof the timeless romantic fictions of love's inception. The myth of love at first sight undergoes a kind of superparody in the scene where Cecily does Algernon's punctual love-making one better by recounting from her "diary" the story of their engagement, his love letters (which she has written), the breaking of their engagement according to the demands of romantic love ritual, and their re-engagement. Cecily's notation of the broken engagement, in its casually incongruous juxtaposition of values, is reminiscent of Pope's satiric method in "The Rape of the Lock," where the deaths of lap-dogs and of husbands are of equal consequence: "Today I broke off my engagement with Ernest. I feel it is better to do so. The weather still continues charming." Gwendolen's love for Jack is sympathy itself; it is the old romantic idea of spiritual love based on simplicity and Platonic sensibility:

> The story of your romantic origin, as related to me by mamma, with unpleasing comments, has naturally stirred the deeper fibers of my nature. Your Christian name has an irresistible fasci-

nation. The simplicity of your character makes you exquisitely incomprehensible to me.

In a more sacred context, Desdemona, who saw her lover's visage "in his mind" just as Gwendolen sees Jack's in his name, fell in love with Othello for somewhat similar reasons. "My story being done," says Othello, "she gave me for my pains a world of sighs. / She swore, in faith, 'twas strange, 'twas passing strange, / 'Twas pitiful, 'twas wondrous pitiful." Othello sums up the nature of her love, and of Gwendolen's, when he says, "She loved me for the dangers I had passed. . . ."

Wilde reinforces his parody of the beautiful innocence of love at first sight and the spiritual impregnability of Platonic love by short-circuiting what our expectations would be if this were either the usual romantic melodrama or a real comedy of manners. Lady Bracknell's cupidity has arisen suddenly as an impediment to both marriages. But while the two young men—who ought to bounce away with a witticism or else do something dashing—are prostrate with devotion, the two young ladies are already making other plans. Gwendolen, the exponent of ideals and ideal love culled from "the more expensive monthly magazines," promises Jack, with superbly hardheaded double vision, that "although [Lady Bracknell] may prevent us from becoming man and wife, and I may marry someone else, and marry often, nothing can alter my eternal devotion to you." And though Algernon, the true voice of cynicism, is preposterously ready to wait seventeen years until his beloved legally comes of age at thirty-five, Cecily, the unspoiled country lass, belies her simple kind by declining his devotion: "I couldn't wait all that time. I hate waiting even five minutes for anybody. It makes me rather cross."

A standard complication of the literature of love that is parodied here is the love breach or "misunderstanding"—the lie, the secret sin out of the past, the error in judgment, the buried flaw of character that rises unbidden to the surface—which threatens to destroy love's ideality. But as the cases of Red Crosse and Una, Tom Jones and Sophia, Elizabeth and Darcy, and dozens of others have demonstrated, the breach can usually be healed if the offending party undergoes some penance or performs some act of selfless generosity or courage, whether psychological or material, in order to prove himself. In *Earnest* the love breach occurs when Gwendolen and Cecily discover that their Ernests are impostors named, respectively, Jack and Algernon; and the restoration of love is made possible when Jack and Algernon declare themselves ready to face the horrors of a christening. The situation at this point is so patently ludicrous, and the sentiments expressed by the two girls are at once so absurdly didactic and so resounding with the bathos of melodramatic reconciliation that we can hardly miss, amid the satire of manners, Wilde's strong undercurrent of literary satire.

But perhaps the most impressive evidence that Wilde's play is, in part at least, an elaborate literary lampoon, lies in the circumstances of the two pairs of lovers. The relationship of Algernon to Cecily, first of all, is essentially that of Rochester to Jane Eyre, of Mr. B. to Pamela. It is the situation of the jaded, world-weary, cynical, and preferably dissolute male being reformed, regenerated, and resentimentalized by the fresh, innocent, and feeling girl reared in isolation from the "world," preferably in the country. Algernon's cynicism is obvious enough in his nastily witty observations on life, and in his boredom with all amusements. The sign of his dissoluteness, one of Wilde's most brilliant comic strokes, is his constant hunger, his entire inability to resist stuffing himself at every opportunity. By this means Wilde has reduced the roué figure to a man of straw—or muffins. And he thrusts him through in the bit of dialogue where Algernon-as-Ernest learns from Cecily that Jack is going to banish him, and that he will have to choose between Australia and "the next world." Cecily questions whether he is good enough even for "this world," and Algy admits that he isn't: ". . . I want you to reform me. You might make that your mission, if you don't mind." "I'm afraid I haven't time, this afternoon," Cecily responds unfeelingly. (pp. 20-1)

The point of Wilde's satire is found in the nature of Algernon's reformation. Before his first interview with Cecily is over, Algernon is engaged to be married and reconciled to getting christened. But he had already been exploded in his very first exchange with Cecily, when his supposedly irretrievable sophistication is bested by the supposedly artless and sheltered country girl's supersophistication: "I hope you have not been leading a double life, pretending to be wicked and being really good all the time. That would be hypocrisy." With this the wit has passed from Algernon to Cecily, and he never regains it at any time when she is on the scene. The moral of Wilde's parody: the rake is a fake, girlish innocence is the bait of a monstrous mantrap, the wages of sin is matrimony.

Jack's troubled pursuit of Gwendolen embodies still another stock situation of romantic love fiction. As classic as *The Winter's Tale*, as old-fashioned as *Caste*, and as modern as last night's television play or last week's movie, it is the problem situation of two lovers separated by a barrier of class difference. Sometimes it is a matter of money, sometimes of blood. But in the majority of cases true love is saved by some last minute miracle, usually a surprising revelation of someone's real identity. The most impressive exercise of this kind is probably in *The Conscious Lovers*, where Steele relieves the long-suffering young Bevil by allowing his indigent sweetheart to prove to be the long lost daughter of Mr. Sealand, the fabulously wealthy parent of the girl Bevil had been unhappily scheduled to couple with in a purely business marriage. The enormity of Steele's resolution is only a little less notable than Wilde's parody of the type. After herding all his characters down to Shropshire to witness the marvels of his *deus ex machina*, Wilde parades before their eyes an extraordinary succession of coincidental revelations culminating in Jack's discovery not only that he is Algernon's brother but that his name really *is* Ernest.

Wilde delicately frames his recognition scene as a theatrical take-off by making Lady Bracknell say, with lofty aesthetic dread, "In families of high position strange coincidences are not supposed to occur. It is hardly considered the thing." Gwendolen, however, is having a splendid time: "The suspense is terrible. I hope it will last." (pp. 21-2)

Mr. Roditi, a critic who takes Wilde very seriously, has mistaken his most celebrated work for an inchoate comedy of manners and has therefore drawn the unfortunately academic conclusion that it is formally imperfect and artistically trivial [see excerpt dated 1947]. The play's "flaws"—the contrivances of plot, the convenience of its coincidences, and the neatness of its resolution—are, of course, its whole point. The subtlety of Wilde's art is such that it is easy to mistake *Earnest* for something it isn't, or else to dismiss it as a charming but inconsequential frill. But if intelligent laughter is better than mere laughter, it is worth understanding what kind of comedy Wilde has achieved by wedding social satire with literary burlesque.

Nothing in the play, first of all, is quite what it seems. The characters seem to wear badges of their natures; yet their sentiments and actions continually revoke and deny them. Jack and Algernon, tagged as clever young worldlings, are really sentimentalists and fussbudgets at heart. Algernon, it has already been pointed out, is quite fully exposed early in Act II. And Jack, though he waves once or twice the flag of cynical wit or clever pretense, worries and perspires through most of the play, muttering pettishly against Algernon's "nonsense" and appetite. He is a fuddled incompetent from the moment, early in Act I, when Algernon first challenges him on the matter of Cecily; and Gwendolen's wooing, only a little later, very nearly shatters him.

This same phenomenon in reverse is true of the two girls. Both of them bear the marks of the romantic Female. Both are pleased, first of all, to represent themselves as "better" than their world: Cecily because she has been preserved, unspoiled, in countrified isolation, and Gwendolen because she is, in Jack's phrase, "a sensible intellectual girl" whose nature has been enriched by heavy reading and brave thinking. But both also deport themselves as proper young ladies who appear to submit to the wishes of their parents and guardians when the plot requires them to; this is because the true romantic Female is never a stickler for rebellion. Yet these rarefied and genteel girls are the worldliest of schemers. They manipulate their lovers like men on a chess board, and one cannot escape the feeling, furthermore, that even Lady Bracknell prevails ultimately because they permit her to.

The dramatic effect of the comedy, then, is not of foolish but real people flaunting the real world's laws of reason, but of archetypal roles being gravely travestied. The characters know they are in a play, and they know what kind of play it is. Cecily and Gwendolen "do" parodies of themselves as they assist their lovers in their own self-ridiculing transformation from cynical wits to true men of feeling. The same is true of Prism and Chasuble, even of Lane, who knows perfectly well that he is the type of the wry butler-confidant who is smarter than his employer. Lady Bracknell is the only exception: her mind's eye, steadily on the funds, sees other matters—love, literature, virtue—exactly for what they are. She is a kind of choric ballast that weights the satire's indirection with direct scorn.

Wilde's society dramas, which try to come to grips realistically with real problems, are very nearly ruined by the fact that so many of the characters "talk like Oscar Wilde." But Wilde's specialty, the squinting epigram that is at once murderous and suicidal, is perfectly at home in *Earnest*. It is the verbal function of that queer double consciousness that permeates the whole play and transforms it into a kind of parody. It is quite right that Cecily, who maneuvers under the aegis of wide-eyed innocence, should say of her own journal of unspoiled reactions, "It is simply a very young girl's record of her own thoughts and impressions, and consequently meant for publication." Here burlesque of the Miranda character fuses with exposure of a grotesque type of littérateuse. A similar satiric fusion takes place when Cecily discovers that her innocent "nanny," Miss Prism, is, surprisingly, one of the three-volume ladies of Richardsonian sentiment and sensation. Cecily hopes that her novel did not end happily. "The good," answers prim Miss Prism, with shrewd business prowess, "ended happily, and the bad unhappily. That is what fiction means."

Such passages, deftly worked into the total fabric of the comedy, hold the key to Wilde's methods and purposes. By exposing and burlesquing the vacuities of a moribund literature

Wilde satirizes, too, the society that sustains and produces it; he has given us an oblique perspective on a society's shallowness through direct ridicule of the shallow art in which it sees its reflection. It is this subtle merging of matter and form that helps to make *The Importance of Being Earnest* an intellectual tour de force of the first order as well as one of the great comic masterpieces of the theater. (pp. 22-3)

> Richard Foster, "Wilde as Parodist: A Second Look at 'The Importance of Being Earnest'," in College English, *Vol. 18, No. 1, October, 1956, pp. 18-23.*

VINCENT F. HOPPER AND GERALD B. LAHEY (essay date 1959)

[*American educators and critics, Hopper and Lahey have edited several volumes of comedies by English and Irish dramatists, including William Congreve, Oliver Goldsmith, Richard B. Sheridan, and Oscar Wilde. In the following excerpt, Hopper and Lahey discuss satiric devices of plot, characterization, and dialogue in* Earnest *and offer a brief examination of the four-act version of the play.*]

We must not worry overmuch upon what peg to hang [*The Importance of Being Earnest*]: whether that of broad farce, comedy of manners, a specimen of the "well-made" play. It touches upon all of these and is none of them. Perhaps *The Importance of Being Earnest* is best regarded as a unique specimen of the comedy of cleverness, standing between Sheridan's comedy of manners and Shaw's comedy of ideas. As Wilde developed his dramatic talent, he more and more dramatized his own conversational cleverness. He accused Whistler, the noted wit and painter, of spelling Art with a capital "I." But critics have before now observed of Wilde's literary progress that his characters became *de plus en plus Oscarisé* ["more and more Oscarized"]. Generally a novel or play of Wilde's contains a character especially representative of its creator's temperament and views, such as Lord Henry in *The Picture of Dorian Gray,* Cecil Graham in *Lady Windermere's Fan,* Lord Illingworth in *A Woman of No Importance,* Lord Goring in *An Ideal Husband.* They are all the type of the suave, supercilious dandy. But in *The Importance of Being Earnest,* despite the variety of roles, the voice of the characters is that of Oscar. The play is almost entirely *Oscarisé.*

Like his own personality the play is a blend of antithetical elements. Wilde's personal manner was to deliver facetious, paradoxical, or trivial declarations in a spirit of formal, measured gravity—being neither too pontifical or affectedly pompous, nor yet too archly or consciously cute and comic. The lines of the play must be delivered in that way. In the composite texture of the play we have brilliant, copious, elaborately sophisticated dialogue whose tone is one of elegant flippancy and restrained mock-seriousness. This highly self-conscious verbal wit rests upon a plot that is broadly farcical, boisterously improbable—something that might have been the production of Tony Lumpkin, the practical joker and inventive prankster in Goldsmith's *She Stoops to Conquer.* The play as a whole is a blending of the high-comedy spirit of Congreve or Sheridan with the farcical spirit of the Marx Brothers. Yet there is an element of continuity between the dialogue and the plot, that of cleverly contrived nonsense. In the dialogue, conventional thought—and in the plot, conventional conduct—are equally turned topsy-turvy. The characters do not say what they think; what they say has little connection with what they do. Jack and Algernon, posing as cynical bachelor dandies, discreetly allude to surreptitiously irregular lives, yet there are no facts to convict them of anything unvirtuous; they deplore the doldrums of marriage and domesticity even as they cheerfully become engaged. The Rev. Chasuble exalts the celibacy of the Primitive Church even as he is entering the marital sanctuary of the primitive urges. The articulate Miss Prism, a pillar of propriety, is actually more rejoiced at the recovery of her handbag than at the restoration of the child whose infancy she had abandoned to a railway terminal cloakroom.

Despite the essentially artificial world of the play, there are elements of realistic satire. The Bunburying bachelors, for example, constitute a playful satire on the Victorian double-standard. The Rev. Chasuble is a light thrust at the High Church movement within the Established Church and its pre-occupation with a restoration of primitive church practices, its reintroduction of vestments, etc. His name is suggestive of the latter, the chasuble being an ecclesiastical vestment. Lady Bracknell is a caricature of the Victorian *grande dame* in her plenipotentiary and peremptory manner; she is repeated with variations in Shaw's *Major Barbara* in the person of Lady Britomart (the trick ending in Shaw's play turning upon a sudden disclosure concerning birth is also reminiscent of Wilde's comedy).

In both plot and dialogue there are also elements of satire; satirically, however, these elements are not related—and this may be a weakness in the construction of the play. The object of the satire of the plot has little or nothing to do with that of the dialogue. The plot is a pleasant parody of plots (of the type of Fielding's *Tom Jones*) which turn upon the dramatic discovery of the long-lost heir, the sudden restoration of the long-lost brother. Moreover, the long leg of coincidence upon which such plots uncertainly balance is pulled remorselessly in the situation of the absentminded interchange of the manuscript of a novel and a baby on the part of a maid who afterwards quite unknowingly becomes part of the domestic establishment of the lost baby—now grown to manhood. A further satiric ingredient of the plot is its parody of the traditional obstacle that stands between the union of loving souls: primarily—the imperious necessity of two young men possessing the given name of Ernest before they can be accepted as husbands. A secondary obstacle to union is parodied in the class-barrier, represented by the firm-minded Lady Bracknell, who refuses to allow "our only daughter—a girl brought up with the utmost care—to marry into a cloak-room, and form an alliance with a parcel." Simultaneously parodied is the reverse side of this conventional obstacle of romantic fiction, the psychology whereby the obstacle intensifies the love of the young people and fortifies their loyalty: "The story of your romantic origin, as related to me by mamma, with unpleasing comments, has naturally stirred the deeper fibers of my nature. . . . The simplicity of your character makes you exquisitely incomprehensible to me." The farcical convention of mistaken identity is amusingly played with in the confusion existing between Gwendolen and Cecily as to who possesses the mythical "Ernest," and in Miss Prism's being mistaken by Jack for his mother in the disclosure scene. Love-at-first-sight is lightly mocked at in the scene in which the contents of Cecily's diary are revealed to Algernon; romantically heroic sacrifice of lover for lady is parodied in the scene in which the gentlemen announce their reckless readiness to undergo baptism, the ladies alternately exclaiming: ". . . you are prepared to do this terrible thing. . . . To please me you are ready to face this fearful ordeal?" Indeed, deliberately or by inadvertence Wilde's plot parodies itself, for at the end the author fails to supply Algernon with the name of Ernest, despite the fact that Cecily has not waived her insistence on this point; moreover Wilde makes no comment on the fact that "Jack" as Ernest is to marry his own first-cousin.

In a larger sense, Wilde handles the plot so as to make it a parody of conventional dramatic farce; it is a mock-drama in something of the sense in which that other finely wrought triviality, Pope's *Rape of the Lock,* is a mock-epic. In *The Importance of Being Earnest* the characters do not react to events as they do in ordinary farce; their behavior is the conventional behavior inverted: they respond flippantly to the solemn and with mock-solemnity to the trivial. Traditionally the dramatic justification for farcical construction is that the extraordinary circumstances dominating the characters provoke from them emotionally intense responses. Such was the spirit of Congreve, Goldsmith, and Sheridan in the handling of farcical situations in *The Way of the World, She Stoops to Conquer, The Rivals,* and *The School for Scandal.* . . . But in Wilde's plot, the characters are not immersed in the action; they transcend the action and stand outside of history, as it were. Regardless of the crucial implications of their situation, they respond with studied self-possession, with bland detachment, or nonchalant brightness.

Illustrations of the foregoing will occur to any reader. Dr. Chasuble on hearing that Jack's brother has died in Paris of a chill has not more than concluded his warm condolences (adding a clinical footnote: "I myself am peculiarly susceptible to draughts"), than Algernon's sudden arrival and impersonation of the fictional brother upsets the report; his miraculous restoration to life is thereupon greeted by Dr. Chasuble with congratulatory blandness: "These are very joyful tidings." In the revelation scene in which Jack Worthing's true identity is dramatically disclosed by the evidence of the handbag, Miss Prism's outrageous negligence in having originally mislaid the baby generates no remorse. She is more interested in the recovery of lost property than in the restoration of the lost child; instead of anguished confession of error and astonishment at the circumstances that had brought the truth to light, she says in grey neutrality of voice: "The bag is undoubtedly mine. I am delighted to have it so unexpectedly restored to me. It has been a great inconvenience being without it all these years." (pp. 40-4)

In his characterization, where emotion is usually displayed, Wilde underplays it, as the instances just cited indicate, or reverses it. For example, one expects some delicacy of compassion for the condition of poor Bunbury. But Lady Bracknell exclaims: ". . . I think it is high time that Mr. Bunbury made up his mind whether he is going to live or to die. This shilly-shallying with the question is absurd." (p. 45)

There is still another reversal of conventional construction in the characterization of Dr. Chasuble and Miss Prism. Traditionally the middle-aged couple, or the elderly bachelor or spinster, or the elderly seekers of love are made game of. They take part in the comedy as a foil and off-set to the gay, young, witty couples. In Wilde's play there are no Lady Wishforts, no Mrs. Malaprops, no Sir Peter Teazles to be made ludicrous or deceived or revealed as obtuse. Chasuble and Prism are pitched in mood and key much as are the other characters. Miss Prism may in name be a telescoping of "prim" and "prissy"—the traits of the Victorian spinster. Still, she is as pert and saucy as the others; on the reversal of the news of brother "Ernest's" death, she says: "After we had all been resigned to his loss, his sudden return seems to me peculiarly distressing." As the pursuing woman, she manifests none of the shy retirement expected of the Victorian female. Dr. Cha-

suble's reverence for the celibate life, he confides, is owing to the fact that "the precept as well as the practice of the Primitive Church was distinctly against matrimony." To this the purposeful Miss Prism replies tartly: "That is obviously the reason why the Primitive Church has not lasted up to the present day." Finally, the dowager Lady Bracknell, although exaggerated, is likewise a commanding and imposing presence.

A final departure from conventional construction in the play is the omission of the slow-witted or the awkward or the pretentious or affected clown or buffoon. There are no Bob Acres, no Petulants or Witwouds, no Sir Benjamin Backbites in the play. There is within the framework of the play no specific chopping block against which the witty satiric speeches of the play may direct themselves. But the clown or fool is there by implication. It is the scheme of Victorian values for which there is no concrete representative in the play as, for instance, there is in Ibsen's *Ghosts, Enemy of the People,* etc. And this brings us back to our original observation that the satire of the dialogue has little to do with the parody of the plot. The former is directed for the most part against the values that were revered by the eminent pillars of Victorian society.

In title and texture, *The Importance of Being Earnest* is a playful satire on the old-fashioned, mid-Victorian character already obsolescent by Wilde's time. The good man of the pre-revolutionary eighteenth century, such as Squire Allworthy of Fielding's *Tom Jones,* approved of what was virtuous, honorable, and able. The good man of the mid-Victorian period, as presented in Tennyson's *Idylls of the King* and elsewhere, was noble, manly, and pure. (In our time, the good "personality" is normal, healthy, and adjusted.) The eighteenth-century man's virtue had nothing mystical about it; it called for fulfilling one's duty to family, friends, and neighbors. His honor was simply that code of conduct prescribed by his class. (The twentieth-century man aims at being just like everyone else—only more so?) But the ideal mid-Victorian character embodied aspirations towards a superior inner fineness of feeling, a purity of motive, a loftiness of aim, an elevation of mind. . . . The chief outward sign of this Victorian ideal man was his earnestness. In a letter of 1881, Matthew Arnold, one of the minor prophets of the Victorian period, said of Carlyle, one of the major prophets: "He was always 'carrying coals to Newcastle,' . . . preaching earnestness to a nation that had it by nature, but was less abundantly supplied with other things." The preoccupation with it was excessive because to the Victorian earnestness was a quasi-sacramental trait—an outward sign or manifestation of the inward graces of nobility, purity, manliness of character. Its opposite, the sure index to a subtle inner corruption, was a habitual flippancy of tone and frivolity of attitude. In 1851, Ruskin, another leading Victorian prophet and teacher, in his discussion of the new pre-Raphaelite movement in art, observed, "We are intended, as long as we live, to be in a state of intense moral effort. . . . Our energies are to be given to the soul's work—to the great fight with the Dragon. . . ." Ruskin was especially severe towards artists who "are expected, and themselves expect, to make their bread *by being clever*—. . . and are . . . for the most part, trying to be clever, and so living in an utterly false state of mind and action." Wilde's play from its title to its last line ("I've now realized for the first time in my life the Importance of Being Earnest.") is an unabashedly clever, an ironically flippant, and a gaily frivolous burlesque of this Victorian life-attitude. The earnest old prophets are gently nudged aside in favor of London's Playboys of the West End World. Hence Jack weary of being a pillar of society—a guardian—invents a brother Ernest as a relief from having "to adopt a high moral tone on all subjects."

In one way and another, most of the personal, domestic, and social sanctities of the Victorians are subjected to Wilde's light bantering satire. For example, no institution was more exalted in mind by the Victorian than the family; the fireside was his altar; to question the values of family life was to stand before the temple and scoff. Wilde was at it constantly. The impeccable servant Lane defines marriage as "a misunderstanding between myself and a young person." He apologizes for having introduced the topic of family life into conversation: ". . . not a very interesting subject. I never think of it myself." The Bunbury ruse exists because "in married life three is company and two is none." (pp. 45-8)

Another of the obvious Victorian preoccupations was that of reform and improvement, social and personal. The ubiquitous Victorian diary, for example, was a record to be used for self-examination with a view to ascertaining one's backslidings and advancements. Wilde refers to it merely as a record of purple passages meant for publication. . . . Gwendolen says of her diary: "I never travel without my diary. One should always have something sensational to read on the train."

The great Victorian invention, the social conscience, is treated lightly. Miss Prism observes: "I am not in favour of this modern mania for turning bad people into good people at a moment's notice." Perverse mention is made of a "Society for Preventing Discontent among the Upper Orders." Lady Bracknell, misunderstanding a report that Bunbury had been "exploded," exclaims, "I was not aware that Mr. Bunbury was interested in social legislation. If so, he is well punished for his morbidity."

Victorian social standards demanded of the proper female that she acquire refinement and respectability. Lady Bracknell, seeking a clue to the identification of the Miss Prism mentioned in her presence, asks whether she is a "female of repellent aspect." On being admonished that Miss Prism is "the most cultivated of ladies, and the very picture of respectability," Lady Bracknell retorts, "It is obviously the same person."

The Victorians wanted their art to contain a message, to provide guidance and support for right living. Hence Wilde makes Miss Prism, the governess, the embodiment of their conventional notions; she is a writer of three-decker novels in which "the good ended happily, and the bad unhappily. That is what Fiction means." Just as Wilde flicks his satiric whip at didactic art, so does he invert the "innocence" that Victorians demanded in their young ladies. He makes Cecily prefer distinctive manners to sound morals when she says to Algernon, "Yes, you've wonderfully good taste, Ernest. It's the excuse I've always given for your leading such a bad life."

To attempt to enumerate all or most of the instances in which the bubbling, effervescent dialogue touches with absurdity serious Victorian conventions would be to quote most of the play. To carry the analysis further would be to break the butterfly on the iron wheel, to dust the powder from the moth's wing with a clothes brush. Wilde's great contemporary Shaw fundamentally disapproved of what he considered to be Wilde's amoral nature, his too happy, irresponsible gaiety. Yet he greatly admired Wilde's supreme gifts as an entertainer. On hearing of Wilde's death, Shaw stated that he had gone straight to heaven, adding, "He is too good company to be excluded." It is his gift for light, bright amusement that constitutes the aesthetic center of the play, not the satire, which is merely the

channel for the expression of the wit. Wilde perhaps best characterized the play when he referred to it modestly as a clever little thing "written by a butterfly for butterflies."

Our discussion of the divergent satiric aims of plot and dialogue ought not to be closed without reference to the four-act version, somewhat longer than the present one which has been the basis of the acting tradition in English-speaking countries from the beginning. . . . The longer text contains amusing scenes and dialogue not appearing in the now traditional version. There may be some difference of opinion as to which is the more entertaining version. Despite the interesting additional material, many will feel that the present version is superior in artistic neatness and verbal economy, that the action moves more smoothly and that the wit snaps and crackles a little more sharply—that it is a little less elaborately mannered in style.

There are, however, two scenes in the plot of the original text that add to the parody of conventional farce such as we have already adverted to. . . . [The first of these is] an amusing scene turning on mistaken identity in which officers of the law arrive at the Manor House to arrest "Ernest Worthing" for a debt of several hundred pounds incurred at the luxurious Hotel Savoy in London. . . . The scene, of course, is handled with Wilde's usual bland indifference to implications and the everyday logic of human conduct. The second parody is a "take off" on another cliché of traditional comedy, the well-worn convention of the screen scene, such as we have in Goldsmith's *She Stoops to Conquer* and Sheridan's *The School for Scandal*. Algernon, supposedly paying a charity visit to the invalid Bunbury, is embarrassed by the sudden arrival at the Manor House of his aunt Lady Bracknell; he and Cecily retire behind a screen so that Wilde can burlesque this conventional stage situation.

As for the dialogue of the original text, it contains much more satire of the High Church movement towards restoring the precepts and practices of the Primitive Church. Most readers of today have forgotten how much the second half of the last century was troubled by "surplice riots" in churches and with court actions in restraint of those who were attempting to revive ancient rubrics and vestments, etc. Hence Dr. Chasuble (and with him, Miss Prism) has considerably more to say than in our version. At times the dialogue takes on a theological color as it turns on the spiritual merits of "baptismal regeneration" as opposed to more dramatic revivalist "conversions." Modern readers will have forgotten the sensational "Gorham case," a national scandal dealing with these ideas.

Some of the original humor becomes at moments sufficiently broad. For example, Dr. Chasuble enters to announce that the time has arrived for the christenings. Lady Bracknell, now present but unaware of all the fuss over the name of "Ernest," experiences a dignified but searching misgiving; she solemnly interrogates the assembled company as to the proper time-sequence in such matters, the propriety of christening babies before the marriage ceremonies have been performed. Obviously too much of this sort of humor can be overburdensome to the delicate fabric of the play as we have it; perhaps it is as well omitted. (pp. 48-52)

*Vincent F. Hopper and Gerald B. Lahey, "The Play,"
in* The Importance of Being Earnest *by Oscar Wilde,
edited by Vincent F. Hopper and Gerald B. Lahey,
Barron's Educational Series, 1959, pp. 40-52.*

E. B. PARTRIDGE   (essay date 1960)

[*An American educator and critic, Partridge is the author of studies of Ben Jonson and Oscar Wilde. In the following excerpt, he examines the targets of satire in* Earnest.]

Too often *The Importance of Being Earnest* is dismissed as a light farce whose loveliness fades as soon as anyone finds any meaning in it. Presumably the play is like ignorance to Lady Bracknell: "a delicate exotic fruit; touch it and the bloom is gone." Its beauty seems to come from its senselessness. Now, that there is a deep vein of nonsense in it I should not deny: Wilde can be as ethereally empty as Edward Lear. I should also agree that such brainlessness liberates—and especially liberates one from any obligation other than that of enjoying it.

Yet the play does make some sense, part of which Wilde himself suggests in his remark that it is "exquisitely trivial, a delicate bubble of fancy, and it has its philosophy (that we should treat all the trivial things of life seriously, and all the serious things of life with sincere and studied triviality)." So lightly does it carry its meaning within its bubble of fancy that one scarcely feels the weight it has. Only recently have critics come to see the play as a parody of literature and drama. Richard Foster [see excerpt dated 1956] has pointed out that Wilde uses many stereotyped situations in *Earnest*. Werner Vordtriede [see Additional Bibliography] has suggested that the second act of *Earnest* probably echoes Martha's garden scene in *Faust*. Indeed, the play reverberates with echoes of previous plays because it parodies not merely nineteenth-century drama but also—and more especially—classical drama. Lady Bracknell's coming down to Hertfordshire to prevent the marriage of Gwendolen and Jack is a classic *peripeteia* because it succeeds in bringing the lovers together, for in Hertfordshire she sees that least likely of all Theban shepherds, Laetitia Prism, to whom she asks the tragic question—"Prism, where is that baby?" Jack, like Oedipus, all his life had not known who he was until he learns that Miss Prism had left him in the cloakroom of the Victoria station (Brighton Line). Since a prism is a transparent body used for decomposing light into its spectrum, "Prism" is as optically accurate a name for an agent of *anagnorisis* ["recognition"] as even Aristophanes could invent. (Of course, one could think of Miss Prism, more geometrically, as a solid figure with plain surfaces.) Jack's being left in a hand-bag in a railway station seems a wild way of making fun of the foundling motif frequent in Menander and Plautus, as well as the motif of substituting one child for another (here one child is a "manuscript of a three-volume novel of more than usually revolting sentimentality"). The play even has a Terentian parent or *lena* in Lady Bracknell, who at first disapproves of the antics of youth and forbids any marriage she does not find profitable, but finally changes her mind when she discovers Cecily's wealth and Worthing's real identity. The play ends with the three marriages typical of Italianate comedy.

So light is its touch, so nearly meaningless its action that one may fail to see that this bubble of fancy is one long burlesque of the serious aspects of life. Everything receives the same slight dislocation into absurdity. For instance, the burlesque of falling in love. Jack's "irresistible fascination" is not his personal attractiveness or his fame or notoriety or power or money—indeed, none of the conventional reasons for being fascinating; it is his name, Ernest. Gwendolen's "ideal has always been to love some one of the name of Ernest. There is something in that name that inspires absolute confidence. The moment Algernon first mentioned to me that he had a friend called Ernest, I knew I was destined to love you." Is there a less rational explanation of falling in love than this—or a more convincing one? To say, as Cecily later does, that it had always been "a girlish dream of mine to love someone whose name was Ernest" is to suggest that the usual explanations for falling

in love (which are not much different from Cecily's) are quite as absurd as hers. Here as elsewhere Wilde shows us how delightful it can be to treat all the trivial things of life seriously and all the serious things trivially.

Lady Bracknell is almost the perfect figure of burlesque (though she, whose name is, after all, Augusta, must never be acted simply as a caricature of the snobbish aristocrat lest the tone of delicate mockery be destroyed). When Jack accuses Algernon of being untruthful, she answers in a way that perfectly expresses the Establishment: "Untruthful! My nephew Algernon? Impossible! He is an Oxonian." Her reasons are usually the world's reasons stated quintessentially. "A hundred and thirty thousand pounds! And in the Funds! Miss Cardew seems to me a most attractive young lady, now that I look at her. Few girls of the present day have any really solid qualities, any of the qualities that last, and improve with time. We live, I regret to say, in an age of surfaces." The blended voices of the calculating mother, the realist, and the snob are given to us pure, with great art, in the subtlest comic speech since Congreve. Lady Bracknell is a great innocent, one of Art's noble women. She is absolutely unaware of how naked of euphemism and hypocrisy her speech is. And, being unaware, she does not know how witty her remarks sometimes are:

> LADY BRACKNELL. Is this Miss Prism a female of repellent aspects, remotely connected with education?
>
> CHASUBLE. (*Somewhat indignantly*) She is the most cultivated of ladies, and the very picture of respectability.
>
> LADY BRACKNELL. It is obviously the same person.

To her it is obvious that a person connected with education would be cultivated, respectable, and repellent. But we who presumably do not think quite as Lady Bracknell does about teachers find the inter-connections of cultivation, respectability, and ugliness witty (because startling and illuminating). We enjoy the comic sight of two so opposite opinions about the same person suddenly equated by the word "obviously." Since we can find various reasons why a woman remotely connected with education might be at once the picture of respectability and a "female of repellent aspects," the passage is true, even if unconscious, wit. We might even go so far as to think of the repellency being caused by the cultivation or, more probably, the respectability. Is too much learning especially dangerous for pretty young girls? Cecily seems to think so when she says that she looks "quite plain" after her German lesson, apparently because German is not a "becoming" language.

The glorious and deliberate brainlessness of the young lovers, especially Cecily and Gwendolen, must be distinguished from the innocent brainlessness of Lady Bracknell, Miss Prism, and Chasuble. To adopt the pose of being completely without sense, as the young ladies do, requires real intelligence, just as to keep it pure requires great sensitiveness. Only a remarkably perceptive and articulate person with an exquisite sense of nonsense could be so wildly absurd as Gwendolen in her reception of Jack's proposal:

> GWENDOLEN. I adore you. But you haven't proposed to me yet. Nothing has been said at all about marriage. The subject has not even been touched on.
>
> JACK. Well . . . may I propose to you now?

GWENDOLEN. I think it would be an admirable opportunity. And to spare you any possible disappointment, Mr. Worthing, I think it only fair to tell you quite frankly beforehand that I am fully determined to accept you.

JACK. Gwendolen!

GWENDOLEN. Yes, Mr. Worthing, what have you got to say to me?

JACK. You know what I have got to say to you.

GWENDOLEN. Yes, but you don't say it.

JACK. Gwendolen, will you marry me? (*Goes on his knees*)

GWENDOLEN. Of course I will, darling. How long you have been about it! I am afraid you have had very little experience in how to propose.

(pp. 152-56)

The dialogue dances with sunny lightness over the surface of life, burlesquing at times with mock-solemnity, at times with arch-nonsense, many of the most serious aspects of life—birth, parentage, baptism, marriage, sin, death, love, deception, pain, morality, classes. After moving from one enormous and theatrically conventional conflict to another—lovers against forbidding mother in Act I; jealous women against each other at first, then women against deceiving men in Act II—the play finally resolves itself with a recognition scene to end all recognition scenes and an absolutely incredible explanation of what happened to the hero in his perambulator.

This unique fusion of wit, nonsense, parody, and burlesque gives *The Importance of Being Earnest* its light-hearted joyfulness and makes it the finest expression of *sprezzatura* in English comedy. Its wit alone breathes the very spirit of outward grace and inward truth, apparent carelessness and underlying responsibility, which is the attitude of Castiglione's courtier. Almost alone in English comedy, Wilde's wit can be gay and kindly without losing its sharpness, effortless and spontaneous without losing its artificial style.

What is the importance of being earnest? In the first act we see a distinction between Jack who, Algernon claims, must really be named Ernest because he is "the most earnest-looking person I ever saw," and Algernon, who to Jack is "hardly serious enough" to understand Jack's motives as a guardian. To be earnest is apparently to be serious, sincere, and sober— that is, moral; and since a "high moral tone" is not conducive to either health or happiness, to be earnest and moral is to be dull and even unhealthy. Furthermore, because Jack had found earnestness in the country so depressing, he invented a younger brother whose scrapes in the city could be used as a means of getting away from the high moral tone required of a guardian. In other words, he lied, though he does not use quite so harsh a word for it any more than Algernon calls his Bunburying lying. Algernon's feeling about telling the truth may be inferred from the way he described one of his sententious remarks: "It is perfectly phrased! and quite as true as any observation in civilized life should be." He implies, as Molière does in *The Misanthrope,* that to tell the truth is ill-bred, and to hear it told is usually uncomfortable. Jack makes the same point when he answers, hesitantly, Gwendolen's question about his brother, Ernest: "It is very painful for me to be forced to speak the

truth. It is the first time in my life that I have ever been reduced to such a painful position." (pp. 156-57)

For such earnestness he asks Gwendolen's forgiveness because he knows that it is ill-bred to speak the truth, the whole truth, and nothing but the truth all the time. She forgives him because she knows that, being human, he is sure to change. We see, then, the value not of truth, but of lies. By lying about his name and his having a brother, he made himself more attractive to Gwendolen (as Algernon did to Cecily). The lies were gay, imaginative, frivolous—anything but earnest. If either lover had been earnest—that is, sober, sincere, and truthful—he would have been dull and unsuccessful in his courting. Cecily finds Algernon fascinating because he is frivolous—quite unlike Uncle Jack, who seems to her often so serious that he can't be quite well. Health, she assumes, makes one perceptive enough to be cheerful and frivolous.

Both Cecily and Gwendolen agree with their lovers about the importance of imaginative lying, as one can see from the crucial passage at the opening of Act III. When Cecily says that Algernon's answer to her question seems satisfactory, Gwendolen says, "Yes, dear, if you can believe him."

CECILY. I don't. But that does not affect the wonderful beauty of his answer.

GWENDOLEN. True. In matters of grave importance, style, not sincerity, is the vital thing. Mr. Worthing, what explanation can you offer to me for pretending to have a brother? Was it in order that you might have an opportunity of coming up to town to see me as often as possible?

JACK. Can you doubt it, Miss Fairfax?

GWENDOLEN. I have the gravest doubts upon the subject. But I intend to crush them. This is not the moment for German skepticism.

All see the ironic point that the vital thing to have in civilized society is "style," not earnestness. (Lord Illingworth in *A Woman of No Importance* reveals the same connection between being sincere and being earnest when he warns Kelvil against taking sides in anything: "Taking sides is the beginning of sincerity, and earnestness follows shortly afterwards, and the human being becomes a bore.") To be sincere is to be dull— a depressing fate for a civilized person. To have style, as the young people in the play do, is to be carefree, cheerful, witty, charming, and irresponsible: in a word, imaginative.

The importance of *The Importance of Being Earnest,* then, is that it defends the life of the imagination in the subtlest of all ways—by embodying it in a play so trivial and absurd that it makes fun of itself—and defends it with the sunniest *sprezzatura* that even Wilde achieved. Here, as in the best parts of his essays and life, he makes us realize (probably not for the first time in our lives) the vital importance of not being earnest. (pp. 157-58)

E. B. Partridge, "The Importance of Not Being Earnest," in Bucknell Review, Vol. IX, No. 2, May, 1960, pp. 143-58.

HAROLD E. TOLIVER (essay date 1963)

[*An American educator and critic, Toliver is particularly concerned with issues of form and structure in literature. In the following excerpt, he examines the paradox of serious triviality and its function in* The Importance of Being Earnest.]

A proposal that *The Importance of Being Earnest* is genuinely in earnest is likely to evoke—perhaps with justice, certainly with indignation—Algernon's pronouncement, "Literary criticism is not your forte, my dear fellow. Don't try it. You should leave that to people who haven't been at a University." But the play itself is capricious enough to dress its seriousness in the bangles of absurdity and to imply that the costume is more important than what lies underneath. It is called *A Trivial Comedy for* Serious *People,* and judging from Wilde's own comments, the earnestness and the triviality are meant to reinforce each other. The play "is exquisitely trivial, a delicate bubble of fancy," Wilde once remarked to a reporter, but "it has its philosophy." The philosophy is "that we should treat all the trivial things of life seriously, and all the serious things of life with sincere and studied triviality." This, it is true, may not seem the sort of philosophy calculated to reward critical analysis; and if this is not enough, there is the additional warning that Wilde has Gilbert make in **"The Critic as Artist"**: "there are two ways of disliking art. . . . One is to dislike it. The other, to like it rationally." But I suggest quite solemnly that the play asks us to resist the inclination to bask uncritically in the wit and to examine closely the paradox of serious triviality. By its sheer abundance, the wit tends to be cloying, and if left without gravitational center, to spin off under its own dazzling energy.

The wit and the seriousness, then, contribute to each other. In terms of character, this means that Jack, Algernon, and others must come to reconcile truant pleasure and seriousness. In John Worthing's case, the crisscrossing of names may seem to imply that he embraces the paradox from the beginning: "Ernest" (like "Worthing," a name suggesting seriousness and stability) is the town delinquent while "Jack" (suggesting the rake) is the conservative moral guardian of a country niece. Actually, however, until his comic *anagnorisis* ["recognition of his true identity"], he is lacking in "proper" values and requires instruction in the pursuit of the trivial from Algernon. (Algernon in turn ultimately assumes the role, and proposes to assume the name, of "earnestness," whereas he has previously lived by the "science" of Bunburying and reserved sentiment for the piano.) Even in town Jack is conservative. He does not care about Bunburying and is quite willing to kill off his "brother" Ernest; in other words, despite the fact that he has his own brand of humor, he does not sufficiently understand the importance of being trivial. His upstage position consistently gives Algernon the initiative:

> JACK. For Heaven's sake, don't try to be cynical. It's perfectly easy to be cynical.
>
> ALGERNON. My dear Fellow, it isn't easy to be anything nowadays. There's such a beastly competition about. . . .

He is against divorce, and at times even against eating, while such things can be special arts when performed with style, as Algy performs when devouring the muffins:

> JACK. How you can sit there, calmly eating muffins when we are in this horrible trouble, I can't make out. You seem to be perfectly heartless.
>
> ALGERNON. Well, I can't eat muffins in an agitated manner. The butter would probably get

on my cuffs. One should always eat muffins quite calmly. It is the only way to eat them. . . .

The style is everything and the situation exists to make the style possible. As Wilde notes in **"Phrases and Philosophies for the Use of the Young"** and has Gwendolen comment in the play, "in matters of grave importance, style, not sincerity, is the vital thing." . . . It is this lesson that Jack must learn, and does learn eventually, even though, until the resolution, he frequently retreats behind established values.

But Lady Bracknell finds him lacking in other regards as well. He is disqualified from wedding Gwendolen because he is *not* respectable enough. Being the child of an "ordinary" handbag from Victoria station, Brighton line, is bothersome and bourgeois; to be so born shows "a contempt for the ordinary decencies of family life that reminds one of the worst excesses of the French Revolution." He is in the embarrassing position of being respectable in moral outlook and yet unfit for good society, whereas precisely the opposite is required if one is to live "earnestly," that is, to put into practice and into daily manners the philosophy of the play.

Jack is not alone in failing to grasp the paradox immediately. Miss Prism (whose name, as critics have pointed out, is a combination of prim, prissy, and perhaps prison) also errs on the side of over-seriousness. "Idle merriment and triviality" she finds out of place in those sensible of high duty and responsibility. Her moral outlook is uncompromising at times: the good should end happily and the bad unhappily, as they do in fiction. Yet like Jack she has an obvious charm and a sense for the trivial that requires only the right kind of stimulation. As the conductor of German lessons, she is, of course, a formidable obstacle to joy, or "laetitia." (The Rev. Canon Chasuble at one point calls her "Egeria" after the mythical patron of Roman law and order.) But she shows signs of living up to her given name. The chief difference between her triviality when it comes forward and that of Algy or Lady Bracknell is its moral and sentimental nature. Informed that the profligate "Ernest" is dead, for example, she finds it "a blessing of an extremely obvious kind." But she undermines her arch solemnity by unconsciously making a game of it, as in the remark, immediately following this one, that "After we had all been resigned to his loss, his sudden return seems to me peculiarly distressing." . . . The latter comment is doubly ironic since she herself has lost "Ernest" at the station, or rather, substituted for him "the manuscript of a three-volume novel of more than usually revolting sentimentality" and, even while the lighter side of "earnestness" keeps intruding upon her, wishes to be disembarrassed of it altogether.

Cecily comes much closer to embodying consistently the proper mixture of seriousness and triviality required of earnestness. She is said to be innocent and overly "natural" but can behave with ingratiating lightheartedness. Her taste for the incongruous is unsurpassed even by Algernon's. Nature and artifice are fused in her but completely inverted: nature is sacrificed to artifice. Her fertile imagination absorbs nature and transforms it into a delicate and witty fantasy, the quality of which is set off by contrast to Lady Bracknell's less spontaneous artifice and Miss Prism's less gracious sense of duty. While possessing the banter and illogic of a Mrs. Millamant, she is never forced to grow up as Millamant is. We could imagine her equally well pinning up curls with love letters in verse, but the rougher edges of experience are missing, just as Mirabell's depth and realism are missing in Algernon. The essence of Congreve's wit as Mirabell and Millamant exemplify it, is an ambivalent sensibility and an extremely fine intelligence which fuses opposites in a spirit of resignation. The essence of Wilde's wit as Cecily illustrates it is lightness, brilliance, and a refusal, on the surface at least, to concede anything to reality. The masks worn by Millamant and Mirabell are necessary to survive in the naturalistic environment of the Marwoods and Fainalls. Cecily's mask is worn in the sport of self-creation; no real enemy exists to guard against, unless perhaps boredom. Algernon is absorbed into her extravagant dream like a Prince Charming in Dandy-clothes.

Yet Cecily's world, like Belinda's in the *Rape of the Lock,* is fragile, "a delicate bubble of fancy." With the entrance of Gwendolen, Cecily is made aware of its precarious existence. A more enduring and satisfactory marriage of serious romance and lightheartedness must await the conclusion. The balance which must be maintained in the world of artifice remains upset until the final pairing off. Lack of balance, in fact, replaces, or rather lies behind, the stock comic obstacles to harmonious resolution. Cecily and Gwendolen speak of their respective loves "meditatively," "thoughtfully and sadly," yet attack each other "satirically," and "superciliously." Decorum is shattered in the brutal frankness of their exchange, as it is in the parallel clash between Jack and Algernon. The potential ugliness of social relations comes just close enough to the surface to set off the value of taking things less seriously. Jack's summary of Algernon's overdressed flippancy, while he himself stands ludicrously dressed in black, is the most extreme point of divergence: "Your vanity is ridiculous, your conduct an outrage, and your presence in my garden utterly absurd," he remarks. . . . Equilibrium and social tact are seemingly destroyed; Bunburying is over, even though Algernon still stands by it in principle and reassures us that somehow the artifice will be salvaged: "Well, one must be serious about something, if one wants to have any amusement in life. I happen to be serious about Bunburying. What on earth you are serious about, I haven't got the remotest idea. About everything, I should fancy. You have such an absolutely trivial nature." . . . (pp. 389-93)

Cecily and Algernon, then, like Jack and Gwendolen, seek a means to reconcile play and "real life." The frequency of remarks such as the one just quoted from Algernon is too great to suppose that the wit is meant to be merely embellishment. The very persistence of the trivial testifies to its importance and to its durability. It is a quality not of single characters or particular dialogues but of the entire play; it will not be purged or chastized. It has a metaphysical and metalogical order of its own which asserts itself against other kinds of order. As Johan Huizinga writes in *Homo Ludens,* "Play only becomes possible . . . when an influx of *mind* breaks down the absolute determinism of the cosmos. The very existence of play continually confirms the supra-logical nature of the human situation." Dandies such as Algernon are *play*-boys whose function is to view culture *"sub specie ludi"* ["under the appearance of a game"] and to fight off encroachments of moral and practical affairs. . . .

The play reshapes conventions, then, to fit the central action (learning to live the basic paradox) which dictates language, plot, and character. There is no place for the usual comic types and objects of satire which imitate and exaggerate the incongruities and ugliness of low or "worse than average" men, in Aristotelian terms. Few of the characteristics of comedy stressed by Aristotle, Cicero, Quintilian, Donatus, and other theorists find a place in the play. Low and high are remarkably alike.

Obscenity, or the risible in any of its cruder, realistic aspects, is sifted out completely. (Even Algy's overeating is admitted only to be translated into a social game: "I believe," he remarks stiffly to Jack's criticism, "it is customary in good society to take some slight refreshment at five o'clock.") . . . (p. 393)

The Importance does, of course, utilize conventional comic techniques, including those proper to farce (in the sense of carefree abandon), burlesque, romantic comedy, and even satire. But it uses them in special ways. In romantic and satiric comedy, iconoclasts and revelers such as Algernon are either relegated to the subplot and reoriented at the conclusion or else ostracized from the hero's society and subject to correction. (Thus Toby Belch marries Maria; Malvolio is turned out, at least momentarily; Benedict stops Beatrice's mouth with a kiss; Proteus in the *Two Gentlemen of Verona* ceases to be protean; Shylock is totally subdued; and so forth.) Farce has no particular structure; burlesque must aim at specific targets. But Wilde does not return the comic rebels chastized to the fold or drive them out completely—this would involve endorsing institutions for which he had no excessive liking. Nor does he satirize or burlesque conventions with any seriousness; to do so and to do nothing else would be to destroy the paradox of serious triviality, in effect, to leave the romantic action unresolved, whatever satisfaction burlesque might have in itself.

Hence Jack's discovery of identity parodies inherited, institutional respectability, to which romantic plots inevitably return hero and heroine, but it does not stop there. Algernon, who, as we have seen, undercuts Jack's sense of propriety throughout, is discovered after all to be his brother. The earlier reconciliation made at Cecily's whim has been entirely factitious:

> CECILY. Uncle Jack, if you don't shake hands with Ernest I will never forgive you.
>
> JACK. Never forgive me?
>
> CECILY. Never, never, never!
>
> JACK. Well, this is the last time I shall ever do it. (*Shakes hands with Algernon and glares*)
>
> CECILY. I feel very happy. (*They all go off except Jack and Algernon*)
>
> JACK. You young scoundrel, Algy, you must get out of this place as soon as possible. I don't allow any Bunburying here. . . .

But the bond established in the final reconciliation, despite the lighthearted tone, is of a more "earnest" kind:

> JACK. . . . Algy, you young scoundrel, you will have to treat me with more respect in the future. You have never behaved to me like a brother in all your life.
>
> ALGERNON. Well, not till to-day, old boy, I admit. I did my best, however, though I was out of practice. (*Shakes hands*) . . .

And inversely, upon being found to be Ernest, the brother of Algernon, Jack becomes less hostile towards flippancy. Lady Bracknell feels called upon to chastize ("My nephew, you seem to be displaying signs of triviality"), though even as she does so, she owns up to her new relative. As Algernon recedes to the background, Jack perceives at last the equilibrium of sport and seriousness which the play attempts to demonstrate:

"On the contrary, Aunt Augusta, I've now realized for the first time in my life the vital Importance of Being Earnest."

Some of Wilde's less successful plays reveal reasons why he should thus have wanted to make the King of Misrule equal to the King of Order. To recall them briefly may help to define the achievement of *The Importance*. The primary reason for Wilde's strategy would seem to be that this is the best and perhaps the only way of keeping the smudge of conventionality from comic structure without sacrificing the sense of self-discovery and well-being proper to comedy. Unfortunately, as critics of the melodramas have pointed out, Wilde did not always realize this. His typical plot revolves around moral questions treated in ways fundamentally at odds with the wit. Whatever the motives, Wilde attempts to wear the mask of cynicism while at the same time drawing upon stock moral responses. Consequently the wit is usually static and not essentially involved in the action. In the first act and throughout most of the second of *A Woman of No Importance,* for example, nothing happens but conversation, and when dramatic revelations are finally brought about, the wit ceases to matter. In *The Importance of Being Earnest,* the attitude of serious triviality moves the action and in turn is developed by the action; conflict is expressed in it and the resolution grows out of it. The masks, and with them, the spirit of farce and reveling, remain as the means by which the romance, such as it is, is given "style." But plays like *Lady Windermere's Fan* attack too blatantly the "hard and fast rules" and are ineffective at precisely those points when wit is abandoned for explicit demonstrations of thesis. Wilde is apparently not willing to let the philosophy of the Lord Darlingtons prevail, though it usually finds expression in terms which suggest his deepest sympathy:

> DUCHESS OF BERWICK. Dear Lord Darlington, how thoroughly depraved you are!
>
> LADY WINDERMERE. Lord Darlington is trivial.
>
> LORD DARLINGTON. Ah, don't say that, Lady Windermere.
>
> LADY WINDERMERE. Why do you *talk* so trivially about life, then?
>
> LORD DARLINGTON. Because I think life is far too important a thing ever to talk seriously about it. . . .

The melodramas as a rule shift from this kind of exchange to straightforward assertions that the good are in part bad and the bad in part good, which is an education in moral cliché rather than in earnestness. That Mrs. Erlynne is "a very clever woman" is a penultimate statement; that she is "a very good woman" is final and emphatic.

More broadly than simply breaking free of such restrictions, however, *The Importance* reflects the desire of all *fin de siècle* aesthetes to locate breathing space outside the rationalism and ossified social and religious customs of the times. (pp. 393-95)

Social satire and parody Wilde found to be effective weapons with which to achieve artistic freedom, but they seldom exist for themselves. *The Importance* succeeds where his other works fail because it is founded upon an insight into an "earnestness" capable of *making use* of orthodox social bonds without rejecting or endorsing them. Edouard Roditi [see excerpt dated 1947] has clearly missed the importance of the burlesque when he writes that *The Importance* relies on "an infernal machine, too loudly ticking beneath the light dialogue and too well timed,

with all its happy couples paired off in the last act." But he has also noticed something more easily overlooked, namely, that *The Importance* is resolved by the mechanisms which it mocks. While the wit by itself is primarily divisive, it takes coherence from that which it attacks. Undoubtedly this is a characteristic of most witty plays, but *The Importance* pushes the strategy to extremes: its laughter is always bounced off something, but makes no real attempt to knock anything over. The surprise of its paradoxes is not so much the discovery of unexpected truths about orthodox opinions as delight in verbal play. (The unwritten constitution of Dandyism, Baudelaire writes, asserts above all "a burning need to acquire originality, *within the apparent bounds of convention*"; it demands a "*serious* devotion to the frivolous.") (p. 396)

The burlesque of *The Importance* is . . . absorbed into a special kind of comic order which I believe is not quite like any other in English comedy. Wilde's attitude is fundamentally that of the ironist who brings two apparently opposed points of view into dialectical fusion. The irony does not reside in any particular character or speech, as I have indicated; it lies in the fundamental and continued interaction of values throughout the play. To put this another way—for the play's basic mode of operation is not as simple as this may make it seem—the relationship of values is roughly analogous to that of metaphor when an element of shock is present in the interaction of "tenor" and "vehicle," as in those metaphysical images in which, as Dr. Johnson complained, disparate things are yoked "by violence" together. As Wilde discovered in exile after leaving Reading Gaol and lapsing into comparative silence, the Dandy requires a more or less normal audience as the opposite side of his personality. He is the "tenor" (if a pun may be forgiven) riding on society's "vehicle," singing a gay, sometimes mocking, counterpoint; he accomplishes nothing if not the transformation of basic concord into *concordia discors.* Unlike such comic rebels as Falstaff, he is never a serious threat to the society he mocks. . . . (p. 397)

Most of all, the world of artifice which the wit creates does not mind being absurd. In such a world, it is not gentlemanly to read a friend's private cigarette case, but one is expected to publish one's secret diary. To speak like a dentist of "having the thing out at once" is vulgar unless one is a dentist because it produces a false impression; but to pass as "Ernest" when one is "Jack" is necessary for peace of mind. The game involved in most of these pronouncements is to make of serious moral questions—the rightness of reading certain kinds of literature or of playing false roles—a catalyst for creative wit. Any question will do and all questions work in much the same way: by reversing the orthodox, wit, like poetry and other forms of lying, gives one a sense of liberation. Philistines and Pharisees cannot tolerate, or be tolerated by, the absurd.

The Importance, then, has good reason to insist that only sustained irony and skepticism are properly earnest. Whatever the final validity of that idea as an idea, it is skillfully engineered and brought to a convincing dramatic embodiment. In the last scene, mistaken identities—Prism as unwed mother, for example—are piled up and then taken off with the usual trappings of suspense (parodied in Gwendolen's remark "this suspense is terrible. I hope it will last"). Jack's quest for a name in the old army lists is brought off with nonchalance and supreme "style" as he pauses midway through the frantic search to clear the air: "Mallam, Maxbohm, Magley—what ghastly names they have—Markby, Migsby, Moncrieff!" The relationship of the couples is based on love and truth—love and truth taken, of course, with an offhand gesture and tongue in cheek. Underlying romantic bonds save Algernon from extreme flippancy and cynicism without destroying his sense of freedom. (Cynicism has social value, Wilde writes elsewhere, "but in itself it is a poor affair, for to the true cynic nothing is ever revealed.") His love for Cecily is proper and conventional retribution for trying to avoid "sentiment." Taken all together, the couples are complementary and symmetrical: Gwendolen, who never calls a spade a spade and in fact, as she carefully points out to Cecily, has never seen one, embraces "Ernest"; Cecily, innocent and natural, embraces the professional Bunburyist; everyone takes the primrose path:

> JACK. It is a terrible thing for a man to find out suddenly that all his life he has been speaking nothing but the truth. Can you forgive me?
>
> GWENDOLEN. I can. For I feel that you are sure to change.
>
> CHASUBLE. (to Miss Prism) Laetitia! (Embraces her)
>
> MISS PRISM. (enthusiastically) Frederick! At last!
>
> ALGERNON. Cecily! (Embraces her) At last!
>
> JACK. Gwendolen! (Embraces her) At last! . . .
>
> (pp. 397-98)

Word and gesture reflect the play's *sprezzatura* (in Mr. Partridge's apt phrase) [see excerpt dated 1960] in balanced and masque-like movements, each couple embracing and repeating the phrases with belief and disbelief at the same time. The

A typed page of manuscript with Wilde's changes.

"delicate bubble of fancy" is made "impure" but not shattered by the burlesque. The total impression is that of a somewhat reserved and stylized Sybaritic dance, both vitally trivial and charmingly serious—in the play's own paradoxical phrase, gracefully "earnest." (pp. 398-99)

> *Harold E. Toliver, "Wilde and the Importance of 'Sincere and Studied Triviality'," in* Modern Drama, *Vol. 5, No. 4, February, 1963, pp. 389-99.*

MORRIS FREEDMAN   (essay date 1967)

[*Freedman is an American educator and critic whose works include several studies of modern drama and American literature. In the following excerpt, he focuses on despair and escapism in* The Importance of Being Earnest.]

The plays of Oscar Wilde tempt facile formulation. Louis Kronenberger, for example, in his survey of English comedy, speaks of *Lady Windermere's Fan* as "fashionable trash." Even Shaw [see excerpt dated 1895], who seemed uneasily aware that there was more to Wilde than met the common eye, called him "heartless." Mary McCarthy, who came close to suggesting that Wilde was touching on some of the themes of existential drama [see Additional Bibliography], echoed Shaw's charge of heartlessness and concentrated on Wilde's manner. Wilde's manner does blind one, but as in any valid art, manner is ultimately matter. (p. 63)

Wilde's matter is obviously concerned with the individual in a particular society, of course, a society obsessed by status, identity, limits of behavior. *The Importance of Being Earnest* is, among other things, an account of the search of several young persons for meaning in a society extraordinarily reluctant, even impotent, to assign importance to anything except the superficial. The dominant atmosphere, as in Sartre's *No Exit*, as in the settings of Beckett, is boredom, emptiness, a despair of experiencing genuine feeling. And because the characters rarely know what to do with themselves, other than indulge their impulses, the compulsion to wisecrack becomes pathological, onanistic, a substitute for feeling, thought, and behavior. The very cleverness becomes the action of the play, as when the principals pause in the repartee to comment on it.

The motivating force of the action is the absurd. The two young ladies insist on falling in love with and marrying young men who bear the name of Ernest; no other name will do. With "other babies," to quote one of them, the young men are ready to go off to be rechristened. Jack Worthing, when an infant, was exchanged for a three-volume novel. And if this is not enough to indicate to us the "literary" source of the action, we have the two young ladies arranging the events of their world in the diaries they keep. In short, the characters, while serving within the heart of conventional society, determine their own identity and fate, whenever possible, on the basis of self-indulgent whim, but a whim strictly confined within the value limits of that society. This is the sort of absurd hell Shaw described in *Man and Superman,* an "infernal Arcadia," as Mary McCarthy called it, a domain where the merest and shallowest longing is at once lavishly gratified.

Naturally, then, all things in the Wildean world have to be glorious, richly damasked, royally colored, elegantly arranged, sumptuously detailed, everywhere candied. . . . The film of *The Importance of Being Earnest* was an elaborate exercise in the delights of color, of cultivated lawns and trees, extravagant costumes, beautiful young people. And always, obviously, there is the dazzle in Wilde of the sheer text, of words and phrases meticulously arranged to shine and flash. Wilde's text has been perceptively called verbal opera, and we do regularly hear the melody of sheer language. Lady Bracknell not only rings the bell with a Wagnerian authority; her speeches sound like the arias of a Wagnerian contralto (or maybe tenor).

But Wilde is better than Maugham or Coward or Pinero or Jones or Kaufman, all of whom could write bright dialogue or construct intricate plots, because there lurks in the Wildean text a consciousness of the hellishness of all the activity and talk. In *The Importance of Being Earnest,* the two young men expect to find no pleasures in conventional society; they must go "Bunburying"; that is, they must leave their world and seek elsewhere for private satisfactions, which are never specified. They are required by the social trap to go through various motions, including courtship, and they sacrifice their private needs, wiping out their independent identity, willingly immolating themselves, causing themselves to assume new names, new identities. They move into the heart of a society which they despise, which they have for years been escaping, which they help depict for us as tawdry, dishonest, tyrannical, stupid, superficial. (pp. 63-5)

Wilde's despair in his world was instinctive and, one would venture, unconscious; it never rose to the level of an informed bitterness. The tragicomedy in Wilde comes from his acceptance of his world as a man, an acceptance violated by his rejection of it as an artist, that is, as someone who must actually people that world with characters outside himself. Wilde's characters, like Wilde himself, build a vast defense system about themselves to survive; they even claim, like Wilde, to give their genius to living, only their talent to art. Certainly one must survive first as a man, which may well take the greater energy under some circumstances, to function as an artist. The seeming lack of heart in Wilde should be a sign for us, perhaps, of how much heart had to be expended in finding a way through the cold climates of Wilde's world. The impotent, strained joshing of Wilde's people, amiable though it is, is akin to the wisecracking that accompanies abandonment of hope. (pp. 72-3)

> *Morris Freedman, "The Modern Tragicomedy of Wilde and O'Casey," in his* The Moral Impulse: Modern Drama from Ibsen to the Present, *Southern Illinois University Press, 1967, pp. 63-73.*

ROBERT J. JORDAN   (essay date 1970)

[*In the following excerpt, Jordan examines the nature of satire and fantasy in* The Importance of Being Earnest.]

The efforts of critics to rescue *The Importance of Being Earnest* from the triviality that Wilde claimed for it have led in recent years to two approaches. On the one hand Wilde's epigrammatic wit is analysed as an instrument of social criticism and the play is elevated to seriousness as a satire [as in the excerpts by Otto Reinert and Richard Foster dated 1956]. On the other hand its fantasy is viewed as an expression of the author's aesthetic creed and so is accorded the dignity of a philosophy [as in the excerpt by Harold E. Toliver dated 1963]. (p. 101)

The form of wit that lends particular support to the claim of social significance is that used to describe Lady Harbury's widowhood, "I never saw a woman so altered; she looks quite twenty years younger." In such a comment the platitudinous phrases embodying some conventional sentiment on morality or social behaviour are taken, one or two words (preferably

towards the end) are altered, and the whole thing is blown sky-high. A sense of security is created as the tired, familiar words roll out and then suddenly comes the jolt. Instead of the conventional sentiment comes, more often than not, its complete negation, and the shock is all the greater because this inversion of the platitude often sounds just as plausible a record of human attitudes as the platitude itself. Since the very existence of the *cliché* in the first place implies a standard and largely unquestioned attitude to the particular subject it deals with, this explosion of the *cliché* becomes an attack on the illusions and the hypocrisies of men.

As a trick of speech this device, no matter how recurrent, is open to the criticism that it has merely an incidental role in the play. By its means, touches of satire appear in the dialogue but the overall fabric (the manoeuvres of the plot and the behaviour of the characters) is unaffected. It can be argued, however, in *The Importance of Being Earnest,* that the trick extends beyond the dialogue, for an analogous device does appear at the broader level. The most striking manifestation at this level is to be found in the treatment of the relationship of the sexes. In this play are two sophisticated young gentlemen and two respectable young ladies. The normal expectation is that the young ladies will be delicate, romantic, dependent, and the young men will be sufficiently practical and experienced in the ways of the world to act as protectors for the young ladies—that they will have all the talents that high society demands of the escorts for its young women. Moreover, such an expectation does not seem unwarranted. Jack's serious manner and Algy's slightly cynical, slightly rakish worldliness seem to confirm that in their different ways these young men will have this social masterfulness.

But these expectations are completely flouted. The refined young ladies turn out to be hard-headed, cold-blooded, efficient and completely self-possessed and the young gentlemen simply crumple in front of them. Jack attempts a proposal of marriage, fluffs it, and finds Gwendolen taking the whole proceeding out of his hands and telling him what to do. Algy arrives in the country to have a flirtation with a country innocent and finds himself peremptorily assigned a role as *fiancé* in a relationship that the lady has organized for herself. It is the expectation of both women that their loved ones will be called Ernest and on this issue they are completely inflexible. The men wilt before their determination and are forced to scuttle around looking for a way of satisfying them.

This inverted relationship is the norm of the play. It is repeated in the Chasuble-Prism relationship where Chasuble is completely passive, and Prism the (somewhat bumbling) pursuer. The clearest example, however, is provided by the predicament of Lord Bracknell who, of course, never appears—whose nonappearance is indeed fitting, almost symbolic, since he is practically a non-person. He is the complete cypher, so dominated by his female relatives that Gwendolen can use the trick of the inverted platitude and describe him in the phrases that customarily justify the stay-at-home woman:

> Outside the family circle, papa, I am glad to say, is entirely unknown. I think that is quite as it should be. The home seems to me to be the proper sphere for the man. And certainly once a man begins to neglect his domestic duties he becomes painfully effeminate, does he not? . . .

We are taught that female submissiveness was one of the bulwarks of Victorian upper-middle-class society and here we see that article of faith being mocked as a sham. If the inverted platitude at the level of dialogue can be claimed as part of a satiric vision then so too can the comparable inversion in the very fabric of the play.

But even if this satiric device is structural in the play it can hardly be said to provide a satire of any great power. The main objection is that the particular inversion that is offered to us here is a common-place of social criticism at the time the play was written. *The Importance of Being Earnest,* after all, is a product of the age of the New Woman—the suffrage movement, the rational clothes movement, women in sport, women at the universities and so on. . . . In the case of Gwendolen, moreover, we appear to have not only this general situation but also specific echoes of the New Woman. Gwendolen apparently attends university extension lectures . . . and she talks glibly of "metaphysical speculations" . . . and "German scepticism" . . . so that Jack, who is in some awe of her, can speak of her as an "intellectual girl." . . . This erudition, together with her cold masterfulness, strongly suggests the standard satire on one variety of the New Woman.

Social criticism, then, though it is present in the action as well as the dialogue of the play, is still of no great power. In spite of it the heart of the work is elsewhere. If at one level the play is a social satire and at another it is a farce, at the most important level it seems to be a fantasy in which unattainable human ideals are allowed to realize themselves.

The most obvious ideal presented in the play is the dream of elegance, of effortlessly achieved grace and formal perfection. The aspiration here is stated explicitly in a whole series of paradoxes in which form or style is elevated above truth or virtue, notably in the exchange in the first few minutes of Act Three. . . . It is realized dramatically in the delicate symmetry of the plot, with its balanced characters and situations, and in the polish of the dialogue and the elegant chiselling of the epigrams. Many of these epigrams may use social comment as their material but it can be argued that in such cases the brilliance of the effect is ultimately more striking than the pungency of the criticism.

This element in the play has been much analysed, especially in relation to the cult of the dandy and the aesthetic creed that underlies him [see the excerpt by Harold E. Toliver dated 1963]. There is, however, another aspect of the idealization. One of the things about the world of the play is its innocence. This is a world many of whose characters seem completely indifferent to morality, but at the same time it is a world without evil. The absence of a moral sense, then, does not let loose sin and degradation, because to a large extent these things do not exist, except as unemotional abstractions. Miss Prism may have to warn her charge not to read certain "sensational" parts of a book but what endangers Cecily in this innocent world is not corrupting sexual outspokenness. It is the fallen Rupee, not the fallen woman, that threatens to disturb her. . . . (pp. 101-05)

Now if the play's opening situation were being treated realistically, innocence is one of the last things to be expected, for what we are presented with are two young men who are leading double lives, lives of outward social conformity coupled with lives devoted to secret pleasures. In the normal course of things this would almost inevitably imply sexual licence cloaked by Victorian hypocrisy, and at least two of the standard centres for the gentleman debauchee, Paris and the Empire Music Hall, receive passing mention in the text. But whatever the normal expectation the behaviour of Jack and Algy that we actually witness is infinitely removed from this world of sexual corruption. By taking up the "secret life" pattern the play is in a sense flirting with the possibilities of sex but when it comes to the point all such areas of experience are rigorously excluded. We watch as Algy goes on what might well be a sexual adventure, his descent on Jack's country house, but what results is completely innocuous.

However, while Algy may be a sexual innocent, he does reveal appetite in another form. In Act I he indulges himself with an entire plate of cucumber sandwiches, and in Act II the barrier breaks again and he wolfs the greater part of a plate of muffins. The role of this food-lust as a vice appears more clearly in the four-act version of the play where Dr. Chasuble declares that Jack should not pay "Ernest's" supper debts because it "would be encouraging his profligacy," while Miss Prism, having declared on the same page that "There can be little good in any young man who eats so much, and so often," later remarks that "to partake of two luncheons in one day would not be liberty. It would be licence." In a sense, then, Algy is lustful, but his lust is innocence itself.

This innocent vice does, however, suggest something. It is the vice, the wickedness of the child. Algernon is the naughty little boy who eats all the goodies. And in this lies a clue to this innocence which is central to the play as fantasy. All the young people are terribly elegant, exquisitely sophisticated adults. But much of their behaviour and many of their attitudes are redolent of the world of the child.

Consider, for example, Cecily. To begin with, we first hear of her as "little Cecily" who has given a present to her dear uncle. . . . Then, when we first meet her it is in the presence of her governess. It is quite possible that a girl of her age would still be studying under a private tutor, but uncle, tutor and the adjective little all suggest something of the child. Furthermore the main impression that is made in that scene in which we first see her is that little Cecily doesn't like school. . . . It can also be argued that her impatience and the way it is expressed is evocative of the child. At the prospect of having to wait seventeen years to marry she declares, "I couldn't wait all that time. I hate waiting even five minutes for anybody. It always makes me rather cross." . . . (pp. 105-06)

In Cecily's case the childlike qualities are omni-present. Elsewhere they are not so persistent, but if this idea of the characters as child-adults is considered, a point of reference may be found for many of their most characteristic responses. Much of the quarrelling in the play, for example, has the quality of children's tiffs, and a childlike petulance is a recurrent note. It is illustrated in the lovers' quarrel at the end of Act II and the beginning of Act III, while the petulance by itself is perfectly revealed at the end of Act I where we see Jack and Algy trying to decide how they will amuse themselves that evening:

> ALGERNON. What shall we do after dinner? Go to a theatre?
>
> JACK. Oh, no! I loathe listening.
>
> ALGERNON. Well, let us go to the Club?
>
> JACK. Oh, no! I hate talking.
>
> ALGERNON. Well, we might trot round to the Empire at ten?
>
> JACK. Oh, no! I can't bear looking at things. It is so silly.

ALGERNON. Well, what shall we do?

JACK. Nothing!

ALGERNON. It is awfully hard work doing nothing. . . .

This is extraordinarily like the *cliché* of a spoilt child sulkily refusing to play the various games suggested by a friend. Indeed, children's games are evoked by a whole series of features in the play. A significant part of the action is the playing of "pretend" games—Algy's Bunbury, Jack's Ernest, Cecily's *fiancé*—all involving imaginary characters who can, if need be, be killed off when they begin to get in the way of the game. There is also a great concern with the rules of the game—Algy insisting on telling Jack how to play Bunburying, Gwendolen instructing Jack how to propose properly, Cecily insisting on the correct forms and procedures from Algy. Moreover not only because of these games but also because of the general attitude to life the one sin that is more frequent in the play than gluttony is the equally childish one of "telling fibs." When Jack makes his grave charges against Algy's moral character to Lady Bracknell this is the substance of them . . . , and yet earlier Jack himself had been made to squirm when caught out in a major lie—indicating at the time that lying was his unvarying practice. . . . Throughout the play there is a scattering of bland falsehoods on minor issues (the unavailability of cucumbers, little Aunt Cecily of Tunbridge Wells) and there is always, of course, the series of paradoxes referred to earlier, in which the stylish lie is said to be preferable to the truth. In view of all these intimations of childhood, then, it is significant that some of the broader jokes in the play spring directly from the involvement of the characters in childish situations—the preoccupation with christening, for example, or Jack rushing into the arms of Miss Prism with a cry of "mother." . . . (pp. 107-08)

Of course not everybody in the play has these qualities of the child. Lady Bracknell, for example, is very much the adult—the person of irresistible authority and power who interrupts the games to demand what is going on. Jack in particular is in complete awe of her and looks on her as the immensely older person—to him she is someone who must be well over one hundred and fifty. . . . The other adults in the play are Chasuble and Miss Prism, the latter being for a few fleeting seconds Jack's mother. With these two, adulthood is characterized partly by authority and age but much more so by the way the aura of innocence does not extend to them. Their conversation, particularly in the scene in which they are first established on stage, is marked by its uneasy undertones of sexuality—"hang upon her lips," . . . "metaphor . . . drawn from bees," . . . "young women are green." . . . Indeed Miss Prism's pointed reference to an unmarried man as a "permanent public temptation" . . . cannot even be dismissed as an undertone.

There is, then, an atmosphere of innocence and freedom from corruption in this play that is in part created by insinuations of the child-like into the manners and attitudes of the characters. The child as embodiment of innocence and of the creative imagination is one of the obsessive nineteenth-century symbols and that Wilde himself has an interest in the world of children is implied in his experiments with the fairy-tale as a literary form. It might even be possible to claim that the element of the childlike in this play is an extension of the cult of youth that is a significant part of his thinking and that dictates sayings such as "The condition of perfection is idleness: the aim of

perfection is youth." . . . In any case children have a quality apart from their innocence that might well recommend them to Wilde, their ability to approach their own fantasies and their own trivial pastimes with intense gravity and seriousness. Part of the play's philosophy, after all, is allegedly that "we should treat all the trivial things of life seriously."

In this analysis of the play's fantasy two strands, elegance and innocence, have been distinguished. In fact they are not without relevance to one another. The perfection of elegance is best achieved in the absence of strong human emotion or of moral intensity since the presence of such fervour is likely to ruffle the elegance or make it appear, by comparison, trivial and futile. The pint-sized passions of Wilde's characters (petulance, hunger, impatience), together with their lack of moral concern thus create an atmosphere congenial to the flowering of the sophisticated manner. But at the same time some down-to-earth awareness of the tensions or weaknesses of humanity can serve a useful purpose in such a context and it is here that the social satire, the material of much of the elegant wit, has its place in the fantasy world. This conjunction of mild satire and fantasy in fact represents a fairly basic piece of literary tact. It enables the author to have his fantasy and at the same time to indicate his awareness of the imperfection of the world as it really is, to prevent the charge of *naiveté* by demonstrating an acute sense of things as they are and to brace the self-indulgence by surrounding it with laughter. (pp. 108-09)

Robert J. Jordan, "Satire and Fantasy in Wilde's 'The Importance of Being Earnest'," in Ariel, *Vol. 1, No. 3, July, 1970, pp. 101-09.*

DAVID PARKER   (essay date 1974)

[*In the following excerpt, Parker examines Wilde's concerns with identity and nothingness in* Earnest, *contending that the play is an antecedent of the twentieth-century Theater of the Absurd.*]

Farce is not necessarily trivial, and even when it is, through its very nature it usually makes assertions and raises questions about human identity; that is what makes the same situations enduringly popular. The hero of farce is usually a cunning rogue who, in order to gratify some impulse, spins an elaborate deception, which his victims seem constantly on the verge of exposing, so that he is constantly threatened with defeat, punishment, or humiliation. We admire the hero because he has the courage to obey his impulses and because his tricks render him protean—free from imposed identity. We despise his victims because they are prisoners of manners, which repress impulse and forbid deception. They seem narrow and timid. A more highly wrought and expressive sort of farce is that in which all (or most) of the protagonists are rogues, who compete to satisfy their impulses. The moral independence of the most versatile, the most protean, is endorsed by success. **The Importance of Being Earnest** belongs to that sort.

Moreover, Wilde consciously exploits the concern of farce with human identity. The joke in the title is often thought of as a mock-pompous piece of frivolity, but it is more than that. The play might as justly be named "The Importance of Being." The whole thing is comically addressed to the problem of recognizing and defining human identity; we are made to see wide significance in Jack's polite request, "Lady Bracknell, I hate to seem inquisitive, but would you kindly inform me who I am?" . . . The pun on *earnest* and *Ernest* merely makes the title more suitably comic. Neither being earnest nor being Ernest is of much help when confidence is lost in the substantiality of human identity. The concern with identity is repeatedly underlined in the text of the play, where statements that seem superficially only to poke fun at upper-class frivolity continually edge the mind toward a contemplation of the insubstantiality of identity. "It isn't easy to be anything nowadays," complains Algy in the first act. "There's such a lot of beastly competition about." And only a few lines later, Gwendolen feels obliged to deny that she is perfect: "It would leave no room for developments, and I intend to develop in many directions." . . . (pp. 175-76)

More than most writers of farce, Wilde was conscious of this concern with identity, so natural to the form, and he uses it to express a preoccupation which the nineteenth century gave birth to, and the twentieth century cherishes. Lurking always in the depths of the play is a steady contemplation of Nothingness, of *le néant,* which is all the more effective for its being, in contrast to most of its manifestations, comic in mode. Instead of making Nothingness a pretext for despair, Wilde finds in it a challenge to the imagination. For him, Nothingness in human identity, in human claims to knowledge, in the organization of society, becomes a field to be tilled by the artist—by the artist in each of us. (p. 176)

If *The Importance of Being Earnest* looks back to the French nineteenth century it also looks forward to the twentieth century and the drama of the absurd. The plot is absurd, in an obvious sense, and many critics have argued that it should be dismissed as a Gilbertian fantasy. It seems to me, however, that it is important, in the negative way that plots are, in the drama of the absurd. Everyone responds to preposterous situations in a way that is crazily systematic, defending his responses with absurdly sententious generalizations. Besides being used as a symbol for sensual vitality, eating becomes a subject for absurd imperatives. Algy, for instance, declares that "One should always eat muffins quite calmly. It is the only way to eat them." . . . People's behavior and sentiments act as a parody of the real world; such, it is suggested, is the nature of all action, all moralizing. But Wilde carries off this parody better than most of the playwrights whom we now describe as dramatists of the absurd. He is never obvious. His parody always works at two levels, which enrich each other: it pokes fun at the manners of a particular class, and it satirizes the human condition. To my knowledge, only Pinter and Albee do anything at all like this, with comparative success.

Nothingness is repeatedly evoked in the verbal texture of the play in a way that prefigures techniques of the drama of the absurd. Characters are always using words like *serious* and *nonsense* in a manner that sends out little ripples of significance. "If you don't take care," Jack warns Algy,

> your friend Bunbury will get you into a serious scrape some day.
>
> ALGERNON. I love scrapes. They are the only things that are never serious.
>
> JACK. Oh, that's nonsense, Algy. You never talk anything but nonsense.
>
> ALGERNON. Nobody ever does. . . .

Serious was recognized as a canting expression in the nineteenth century. "No one knows the power," wrote "F. Anstey" in 1885, "that a single serious hairdresser might effect with worldly customers" *(OED).* Algy's quasi pun works as a protest against the importance attached by the Victorians to the very business of attaching importance (parodied more broadly

in Miss Prism); for them, it is often apparent, this was a means of imposing form and stability on a world whose evanescence they half-suspected, a procedure of course unacceptable to Wilde. The joke is parallel to the one about *earnest.*

The play on the word *nonsense* expresses a sensibility that is recognizably modern, though it lacks the anguish that is now usually part of it. The sense of futility that arises out of the contemplation of Nothingness is felt only by those whose belief in human dignity requires support from a religious mythology, or a quasi-religious mythology, such as that subscribed to by many humanists. When his mind was at its most creative, Wilde felt no such need, willingly abandoning intellectual comfort and security for intellectual adventurousness in the unknown and unknowable. Algy's perception of universal nonsense is cheerful; it has the gusto of quick intelligence; and because it also works as a gibe at Algy's class, it has a quality of immediate practical shrewdness that makes it the more acceptable.

In the middle of the play, *absurd* itself is used repeatedly to evoke a sense of immanent Nothingness. Jack cannot understand how he should have a brother in the dining-room: "I don't know what it all means. I think it is perfectly absurd." . . . Algy will not deny that he is Jack's brother: "It would be absurd." . . . Jack says the same about the notion that Algy should lunch twice . . . , and he thinks Algy's presence in the garden at Woolton "utterly absurd." . . . (pp. 177-78)

These words are used in jokes and casual comments that do not stand out in the text and are likely to be delivered in a carelessly cynical manner, as bits of flimflam designed simply to gain the speaker a tactical advantage in the argument; but they crop up repeatedly and affect the whole flavor of the play.

The use of paradox performs the same function much more obviously. Each paradox is a sort of miniature stylistic enactment of the notion expressed in one of the boldest: "In matters of grave importance style, not sincerity, is the vital thing." . . . This pokes fun at the beau monde, of course, but it also hints at an answer to the problems raised in the jokes about *earnest* and *serious.* Once belief in epistemological certainty is abandoned, style, liberally interpreted, is more important than sincerity. By imposing a consciously provisional order onto evanescent reality, it makes practical decisions possible. Paradox imposes this order in a particularly striking way. It confounds conventional notions about order, identity, and dissimilarity, synthesizing new orders out of the confusion it exposes. Far from concealing chaos and disharmony, it rejoices in them, embraces them courageously, and takes them as a challenge to human wit and ingenuity. Wilde's rapid sequences of paradox after paradox picture for us a world in which men make, undo, and remake reality with almost every sentence they utter.

Of course, not all the paradoxes in *The Importance of Being Earnest* are purely verbal or confined to one remark. There is a sustained effort in the play to dissolve conventional notions of order in fields where they tend to hypertrophy. Wilde depicts a world in which the socially endorsed certainties are continually evaporating; values respecting social class, education, the Church, money, love, and the family undergo constant metamorphosis. Attitudes toward the family, in particular, are grotesquely transformed. Algy cheerfully dismisses the sentiments associated with kinship: "Relations are simply a tedious pack of tedious people, who haven't got the remotest knowledge of how to live, nor the smallest instinct about when to die." . . . Others invert the normal sentiments. Lady Bracknell speaks of an acquaintance whose husband has died: "I never saw a woman so altered, she looks quite twenty years younger." . . . (pp. 178-79)

In plot and action, too, conventional notions about family life are broken down. The handbag in Jack's family history excites Lady Bracknell's famous protest: "To be born, or at any rate bred in a handbag, whether it had handles or not, seems to me to display a contempt for the ordinary decencies of family life that reminds one of the worst excesses of the French Revolution." . . . The comedy is enhanced, of course, by the oddity of Lady Bracknell's own notions (or at least her way of expressing them). She seems to conceive family as something subject to human volition, and can advise Jack "to make a definite effort to produce, at any rate, one parent, of either sex, before the season is quite over." . . . Though we may see parody of upper-class snobbery here, others do will relations into—and out of—existence, without there being any feeling of parody. Jack invents a brother; the girls invent ideal husbands. (Algy's Bunbury is only a friend, but the effect is much the same.) At the other extreme, the characters accept the family relationships revealed at the end of the play, with an absurd eagerness that is just as effective in ridiculing conventional notions. This is particularly evident in Jack's outburst, when he mistakenly assumes Miss Prism to be his mother. She indignantly reminds him that she is unmarried. "Cannot repentance wipe out an act of folly?" he cries. "Why should there be one law for men and another for women? Mother! I forgive you." . . . The family is a category of everyday understanding that is one of the first to crumble before the vision of Nothingness. That is what enables Wilde's characters to adopt such a variety of postures with respect to it.

Individual identity, too, dissolves before the vision of Nothingness. That is why farce, and its traditional concern with human identity, was so useful to Wilde. Each character in *The Importance of Being Earnest* is a sort of vacuum that attains to individual identity only through an effort of the creative imagination. They are like Sartre's famous waiter in *L'Être et le Néant*, except that they make their decisions consciously, and that we are pleased rather than nauseated by the process. Each attains to identity in the mode of *being what he is not*.

It is a sense of the insubstantiality of human identity which causes Wilde to place such emphasis on impulse (on selfishness, if you like). Admit all the problems of epistemology, and impulse still remains. Obedience to impulse is a defiant way of asserting some sort of basic identity. Algy's obsession with food is an example. "I hate people who are not serious about meals," he complains. "It is so shallow of them." . . . Beneath the parody of manners, we can detect in this a perception, truthful within the terms of reference the play allows. Algy is prepared to use the word *serious* here because there is something fundamental to relate it to. When appetites are all that is substantial in human identity, all else must seem shallow. (pp. 179-80)

Changeability . . . is a corollary of obedience to impulse. As impulses vary, so must the attitudes of the individual. The protagonists of Wilde's play recognize this, particularly the girls. "I never change, except in my affections," Gwendolen announces. . . . Their changeability is most amusingly demonstrated in the first meeting of Gwendolen and Cecily, when, in the course of a single scene, they proceed from mutual suspicion to mutual affection, thence to mutual detestation, and finally to mutual affection again, all the time firmly maintaining that they are consistent. The audience is likely to laugh

at this sort of thing because it realizes that literary and social conventions are being ridiculed, but there is more to the comedy than that. There is a core of truth in what we are presented with: human beings do change. The joke lies in the way the characters are neither distressed nor surprised at their own changeability. In Wilde's world nothing else is expected.

Love might seem a surprising ingredient in such a world, but it is a play of courtship, and love does have importance in it. Love is based on impulse, after all, and for Wilde it is action, not object; a courageous creative effort of the will, not a substantial inner something; the free play of the imagination, not a faculty. The characters of the play constantly deny the substantiality of love, in speech and action. Their courtships consist in patterns of interlocking fantasy and wit; they woo through imposture and fancy; they pursue and fly; they test and torment each other. Never is there anything static or certain about their relationships. "The very essence of romance is uncertainty," says Algy. "If ever I get married, I'll certainly try to forget the fact." . . . (p. 181)

Because the characters live in a world in which order is constantly vanishing, they scorn theory, consistency, and the appearance of simplicity. "The truth," as Algy says, "is rarely pure and never simple." . . . Certainly, in matters of identity, seeming intelligibility is to be distrusted. "The simplicity of your nature," Gwendolen tells Jack, "makes you exquisitely incomprehensible to me." . . . The characters are alert, not to a harmonious universal nature, but to a proliferation of separate, deceptive, and contradictory sense-impressions. Knowledge comes only through the imagination. Gwendolen laughs at Jack's misgivings over her delight in his being called (as she thinks) Ernest. He cautiously inquires how she might feel were his name not Ernest, but she will not listen. "Ah, that is clearly a metaphysical speculation," she says, "and like all metaphysical speculation, has very little reference at all to the actual facts of real life, as we know them." . . . This is an ironic node. The observation by itself fits in with the general theme of the play, but in the immediate context the joke is against Gwendolen (and Jack, when we think how he must feel). He has only assumed the name of Ernest; her notions are just as "metaphysical"; and what seem to be the actual facts of real life thoroughly justify such a speculation. Yet at the end of the play, Gwendolen's faith in the name, her conviction that she will marry an Ernest, and her insistence that her lover conform to her ideal are all justified; we learn that Jack's true name is Ernest. One effect of all this is to satirize faith in ideals by having it vindicated absurdly, but there is more to it than that. We feel delighted at the outcome, not like the recipients of a warning. We are made to feel that confident fantasies justify themselves, that a bold imagination is more useful than plodding attention to apparent facts. (p. 182)

Jack and Algy certainly attain their ends through lying. They are true rogues, impulsive, lovers of deception and imposture. They fulfill themselves in the way of all rogues: by discovering human freedom in protean identity. Doubtless what they do permits us to laugh at the mad antics young gentlemen get up to, even to disapprove mildly, but the candid spectator will admit that their tricks inspire above all else a feeling of moral liberation. Jack's double life may be exposed, Algy's Bunbury may be deprived of his existence, but these deceptions serve their purpose, and part of us at least is glad.

Gwendolen and Cecily rely on beautiful untrue things as much as their suitors do, but instead of deceiving the world through imposture, they demand that the world accept the pleasing fantasies they choose to project onto it. The heroes adopt identities to suit the occasion; the heroines imagine identities to suit the persons with whom they choose to associate. Gwendolen explains her principles in love: "We live, as I hope you know, Mr. Worthing, in an age of ideals. The fact is constantly mentioned in the more expensive monthly magazines, and has reached the provincial pulpits, I am told. And my ideal has always been to love someone of the name of Ernest. There is something in that name that inspires absolute confidence." . . . She is very firm about this, and Cecily, whose words on the subject are almost identical . . . , is nearly as firm. The comic parallel generates a certain irony against the girls; we are tempted to laugh at them for sharing a folly, yet we cannot help admiring the strength of their resolution, absurd though it is. Though idealism is burlesqued, we are made to admire the wit and courage required to impose a pattern on the world, even such a one as this.

The women in the play are generally stronger and more resourceful than the men. The latter are forced to prevaricate in a way that at times seems shuffling, even abject, whereas the former are always perfectly poised and move with imperturbable grace from one contradictory posture to another. I suspect that this has something to do with Wilde's own personality and personal history, but the pattern makes sense on its own terms. The play may be seen as a disquisition in favor of a set of attitudes more normally associated with women than with men. It commends the sort of character that accepts experience, with all its confusions, and accommodates itself through provisional opportunist adjustments—through style, in short. It pokes fun at hard and fast ideas about reality, at that aggressive kind of intelligence which seeks to control reality through theory. Rightly or wrongly, women are thought of as conforming more often to the subtle stereotype; men are thought of as conforming more often to the aggressive stereotype. Wilde was not simplistic about this. The embodiment of aggressive masculine intelligence in the play is Miss Prism, but that is part of the joke against her. The other women are naturally more at home in Wilde's world than the men.

Lady Bracknell, of course, is the character that most thoroughly exemplifies feminine strength. Delightful though she is, she is likely at first to baffle the audience's expectations because she is cast in the role of obstructionist to the lovers; in a conventional romantic comedy she would have to be defeated and humiliated. Yet that is not what happens to her, and it is difficult even to imagine it happening. The critics have recognized that she rises above this role; she has even been called a goddess. Satisfaction is what Lady Bracknell requires, not defeat, because, irrespective of her role, she is the character that embodies most forcibly Wilde's notions about the creative power of the imagination. Out of the nebulous material of society fashion, she wills into being a world of rock-hard solidity, obedient to her dispensation, before which all other worlds, real and imagined, fade into ghostly insubstantiality. The audience may laugh at the burlesque of a fashionable hostess, but there is reverence in the laughter. Her directives on the acceptable and the proper are not empirical observations on the state of fashion; they are the utterances of a lawgiver, endowed with all but divine afflatus. . . . In contrast to the characters of farce who are imprisoned by manners, Lady Bracknell makes manners, and all the trivia of fashion, the building material of a world in which her will is law. She obtains freedom through manners, and she is powerful because she can impose her world on others.

Miss Prism and Dr. Chasuble are funny because they fail to impose their worlds on others, and in failing weakly parody the central characters. Their trouble is that they do not realize what they are doing and think that their rules and theories represent a real, substantial, unchanging world. Dr. Chasuble calls Miss Prism Egeria (an appellation much better suited to Lady Bracknell), but though she enunciates laws and definitions, they are tamely borrowed, not her own. Her paradoxes are amusing, not because they represent an attempt through wit to impose order on confusion, contradiction, and human folly, but because they indicate an unawareness of these things. Indeed, she does not realize that they are paradoxes. The audience laughs at her, not with her, when she describes her novel thus: "The good ended happily, and the bad unhappily. That is what Fiction means." . . . Clearly she is a fit partner for Dr. Chasuble, who is thoroughly insensitive to the present moment (he is always misinterpreting the situation) and given to forcing an all-purpose moral onto any situation. His famous sermon is an example: "My sermon on the meaning of the manna in the wilderness can be adapted to almost any occasion, joyful, or, as in the present case, distressing. I have preached it at harvest celebrations, christenings, confirmations, on days of humiliation and festal days." . . . Both Miss Prism's novel and Dr. Chasuble's sermon, it is clear, recommend an ordered picture of the world, which excludes the sense of absurdity behind order, central to Wilde's vision, a sense that *The Importance of Being Earnest,* in its entirety, practically demonstrates. (pp. 183-85)

What I have tried to do is to provide an interpretation fitting in with notions concerning farce, the drama of the absurd, and existentialist theories of identity, all of which have been fashionable in recent years. This can certainly help us like and understand the play, but I do not wish it to be thought that I am suggesting it be admired because it is "relevant" (whatever that word might mean nowadays). It seems to me that it should be admired, not simply because it expresses a characteristically modern sensibility, nor even because it does so before its time, prophetically, but because it does so supremely well. It is possible to dislike the play, on grounds similar to those set out by Mary McCarthy [see Additional Bibliography], if only because it is possible to dislike the sort of sensibility it expresses. Its vehicle, the literary tradition to which I suggest the play belongs, is one that readily allows the writer to sink into self-indulgence. Some feel it permits little else nowadays. But I think that if we are prepared to accept the sensibility and the tradition as capable of producing excellence (if, in other words, we are prepared to adopt appropriate standards in judging the play), we are compelled to recognize the excellence of Wilde's play. To the contemplation of Nothingness, of the absurd, Wilde brings qualities of wit, intelligence, and (not least) appetite for life, rarely found so abundantly in such a context. *The Importance of Being Earnest* is a great farce because it transcends the normal limitations of the form. Wilde used the form to make a play that is sparkling, but profound as well. (p. 186)

David Parker, "Oscar Wilde's Great Farce 'The Importance of Being Earnest'," in Modern Language Quarterly, *Vol. 35, No. 2, June, 1974, pp. 173-86.*

CHRISTOPHER S. NASSAAR (essay date 1974)

[Nassaar was born in Lebanon and is a critic and educator. According to Nassaar, his chief aim as a critic is "to establish Oscar Wilde as a major literary figure and to show the importance

of the Rossetti-Pater-Wilde line in nineteenth-century literature."
In the following excerpt, he discusses The Importance of Being
Earnest *as the reductio ad absurdum of Wilde's previous works.*]

The two most prominent words in [*The Importance of Being
Earnest*] are *nonsense* and *serious,* or their synonyms. This is
entirely appropriate, since the play itself is a reduction of all
seriousness to the level of nonsense. In it, Wilde pauses for a
space, takes a hard look at his career to date, and has a good,
long laugh at himself. The play is absolutely devoid of sober
content, and any attempt to find serious meaning in it must of
necessity fall wide of the mark.

To say that the play has no serious meaning, however, is not
to say that it has no meaning at all. Its very message, paradoxically, lies in its lack of seriousness, for here Oscar Wilde
has a hearty laugh at his own expense. The target of the fun
is Wilde's work up to this time. **"Lord Arthur Savile's Crime,"**
*The Picture of Dorian Gray, Salome, A Woman of No Impor-
tance,* even *An Ideal Husband*—Wilde singles out these works
and, one by one, destroys their intellectual content, reducing
them to the level of harmlessness and absurdity. Quite earnestly, he informs us that every serious thought he has had to
date is nonsense—and very laughable nonsense at that.

The Importance of Being Earnest is essentially a private joke,
though the source of its great popularity is Wilde's ability to
translate the joke into public terms. By achieving and maintaining a perfect balance between the public and the private,
Wilde managed to write one of the most brilliant comic masterpieces of the nineteenth century.

Oscar Wilde's works are often based on earlier ones. *The
Picture of Dorian Gray* carefully counterpoints **"Lord Arthur
Savile's Crime"** while providing *Lady Windermere's Fan* with
its basic theme. *A Woman of No Importance* is thematically a
repetition of *Salome,* while its wit is borrowed largely from
Dorian Gray. An Ideal Husband harks back to the fairy tales
in theme. *The Importance of Being Earnest* is the least self-
contained of Wilde's works, for it is rooted not in one but in
practically all of them. It is, moreover, an entirely original
play. (pp. 129-30)

If *Earnest* has exasperated the critics, it is because of this
complete originality. Without doubt, it widened the range of
the drama. Drama had been used subjectively before, by the
Romantics, but Wilde here carried it to the outer limits of
subjectivity and thus provided us with probably the most personal, private play in existence—a play that is basically a self-
parody. Forever a lover of paradox, he took the most objective
form known to literature and treated it entirely subjectively.
The opening lines suggest what sort of a drama this is going
to be:

> ALGERNON. Did you hear what I was playing,
> Lane?
>
> LANE. I didn't think it polite to listen, sir.
>
> ALGERNON. I'm sorry for that, for your sake.
> I don't play accurately—any one can play ac-
> curately—but I play with wonderful expres-
> sion. As far as the piano is concerned, senti-
> ment is my forte.
>
>   (pp. 130-31)

Like Algy's piano-playing, *The Importance of Being Earnest*
aims purely at creating a mood, and it succeeds so brilliantly
that audiences have been applauding since 1895. It is the object
of this analysis to show that the play also has a private meaning

that is wholly consistent with its humorous trivial mood. The
meaning—not necessary to an enjoyment of *Earnest*—reinforces the mood and adds an extra comic dimension to the play.
To see the play's dialogue as constituting an anti-Victorian
barrage—as Eric Bentley does [see *TCLC,* Vol. 1]—or to condemn it as depraved—as Mary McCarthy does [see Additional
Bibliography]—is really to be untrue to its tone and unappre-
ciative of its originality. Even Richard Ellmann misses the
mark—though not by much—when he sees the play's theme
as being sin and crime, treated indifferently and rendered harmless.

Wilde parodies his earlier works haphazardly in *Earnest,* but
in examining the play it is more organized to discuss these
works in order of their composition. In **"Lord Arthur Savile's
Crime,"** Sybil was the erotic personification of all perfection,
and Arthur had to undergo a symbolic baptism and murder the
evil within himself in order to marry her. Gwendolyn and
Cecily exist in this play partly—even entirely—as parodies of
Sybil. Both dismiss any attempt on the part of their suitors to
consider them perfect. For example:

> JACK. You're quite perfect, Miss Fairfax.
>
> GWENDOLYN. Oh! I hope I am not that. It would
> leave no room for developments, and I intend
> to develop in many directions. . . .

Algy has a similar experience with Cecily:

> ALGERNON. I hope, Cecily, I shall not offend
> you if I state quite frankly and openly that you
> seem to me to be in every way the visible per-
> sonification of absolute perfection.
>
> CECILY. I think your frankness does you great
> credit, Ernest. If you will allow me, I will copy
> your remarks into my diary. . . .

Cecily comically undercuts the notion of her perfection by
vainly dashing off to copy Algy's remarks into her diary. (pp.
131-32)

Indeed, any idea we may have had about the perfection of
Cecily and Gwendolyn is dispelled by their verbal duel in act
2. Furthermore, they both end up with wicked husbands. Sybil—or Lady Chiltern, for that matter—would have died as a
result, but Cecily and Gwendolyn remain quite happy and un-
harmed at the end of the play. Vice is a delightful, harmless
thing in *Earnest*: it cannot destroy. Besides, a touch of wickedness in a man makes him all the more attractive, and Cecily's
interest in Algy had begun when she heard how bad he was.

Arthur had to kill Podgers before he could marry Sybil, and
both Jack and Algy find themselves forced to "commit murder" before they can marry the women they love. Jack says:
"If Gwendolyn accepts me, I am going to kill my brother,
indeed I think I'll kill him in any case." . . . Similarly, Algy
"kills" Bunbury. In both cases, the person "killed" exists
only in the imagination of the murderer, whereas Podgers existed both within and outside of Arthur. In neither case, moreover, does the "murder" lead to the purification of its perpetrator. Arthur's crime, hilarious to begin with, is here rendered
entirely harmless and dissolves into complete nonsense.

Like Lord Arthur, Jack and Algy seem to have to undergo a
baptism of sorts before marriage can become possible. Unlike
Arthur's bathtub baptism and its subsequent torments, however, theirs does not involve a spiritual rebirth but simply a
change of name. Their baptism is a reductio ad absurdum of

Arthur's. Arthur's agony of rebirth is mocked in the following passage:

> JACK AND ALGERNON. We are going to be christened this afternoon.
>
> GWENDOLYN. (*To Jack*) For my sake you are prepared to do this terrible thing?
>
> JACK. I am.
>
> CECILY. (*To Algernon*) To please me you are ready to face this fearful ordeal?
>
> ALGERNON. I am!
>
> GWENDOLYN. How absurd to talk of the equality of the sexes! Where questions of self-sacrifice are concerned, men are infinitely beyond us. . . .

Nor does baptism turn out to be necessary in the end. It is discovered that Jack *is* Ernest, after all, and that Algy *is* his younger brother, known to Cecily as Ernest. Both escape the agony of a sprinkling by Chasuble.

In *Earnest,* **"The Soul of Man under Socialism"** is cut to pieces in a few brief lines. In the essay, Wilde had advocated the abolition of private property and had tried to win over the rich by writing: "Property not only has duties, but has so many duties that its possession to any large extent is a bore. It involves endless claims upon one, endless attention to business, endless bother. If property had simply pleasures we could stand it; but its duties make it unbearable. In the interest of the rich we must get rid of it." . . . In *The Importance of Being Earnest,* the wealthy Lady Bracknell agrees with Wilde but finds a nonsocialistic solution to the problem:

> LADY BRACKNELL. What is your income?
>
> JACK. Between seven and eight thousand a year.
>
> LADY BRACKNELL. (*Makes a note in her book*) In land, or in investments?
>
> JACK. In investments, chiefly.
>
> LADY BRACKNELL. That is satisfactory. What between the duties expected of one during one's lifetime, and the duties exacted from one after one's death, land has ceased to be either a profit or a pleasure. It gives one position, and prevents one from keeping it up. That's all that can be said about land. . . .
>
> (pp. 133-35)

If private property is a bother, then by all means eliminate it—invest the money! As for the lower classes, whose poverty Wilde had seen in the essay as poisoning the lives of the rich, they are summarily dismissed at the beginning of the play when Algy says: "Lane's views on marriage seem somewhat lax. Really, if the lower classes don't set us a good example, what on earth is the use of them? They seem, as a class, to have absolutely no sense of moral responsibility." . . . Nor does Lady Bracknell seem at all upset about the existence of the lower classes. After all, they are not on her list of socially acceptable people—the same list as the duchess of Bolton's, no less! If Jack cannot produce socially acceptable parents, he cannot marry Gwendolyn, and that is the end of that.

The idea of determinism is prominent in both **"Lord Arthur Savile's Crime"** and *The Picture of Dorian Gray.* In *Salome,*

too, Iokanaan, without understanding, correctly prophesies an evil Apocalypse. In *The Importance of Being Earnest,* Wilde has a good laugh at the expense of this concept. When Algy proposes to Cecily, he finds that he has already been engaged to her for three whole months and that the courting has already taken place. His future, he discovers, did not wait for him to bring it about but occurred without him:

> CECILY. I accepted you under this dear old tree here. The next day I bought this little ring in your name, and this is the little bangle with the true lovers' knot I promised you always to wear.
>
> ALGERNON. Did I give you this? It's very pretty, isn't it?
>
> CECILY. Yes, you've wonderfully good taste, Ernest. It's the excuse I've always given for your leading such a bad life. And this is the box in which I keep all your dear letters. (*Kneels at table, opens box, and produces letters tied up with blue ribbon*)
>
> ALGERNON. My letters! But, my own sweet Cecily, I have never written you any letters.
>
> CECILY. You need hardly remind me of that, Ernest. I remember only too well that I was forced to write your letters for you. I wrote always three times a week, and sometimes oftener. . . .

This goes on and on, as the concept of determinism is reduced to hilarious nonsense. (pp. 135-36)

The Picture of Dorian Gray is also heavily parodied in *The Importance of Being Earnest.* Dorian led a double life. The picture of his soul was locked safely away in a dark room while the innocent face he presented to respectable society was only a mask. As society began to suspect the real Dorian, he found himself shunned and avoided. His total unmasking—a horror he is spared during his lifetime—would have meant his irrevocable social ruin. Jack and Algy also lead double lives. As with Dorian, their real self is the wicked one. Jack explains to Algy that he wears a mask in the country for the sake of his ward, Cecily: "When one is placed in the position of guardian, one has to adopt a very high moral tone on all subjects. It's one's duty to do so." . . . (pp. 136-37)

Algy, on the other hand, assumes this façade in the city, where he is constantly under the gaze of Lady Bracknell and other respectable personages. The mask drops only when he goes Bunburying. As the play moves to its climax, the respectable identities of Jack and Algy are discovered by all to be fictional. Jack is found out—he is Ernest. Algy is also found out—he is Jack's wicked younger brother Ernest. For both Ernests, however, the result of this revelation is not ostracism but marriage. By reducing Dorian's situation to the level of farce and turning the unmasking into a happy event, Wilde dismisses the protagonist of his novel with a roar of carefree laughter.

The idea that paradoxes and epigrams have the power to corrupt—prominent in *Dorian Gray*—is also ridiculed here. Much of the wit of *The Importance of Being Earnest* is sparkling, hilarious nonsense, as for instance:

> JACK. Everybody is clever nowadays. You can't go anywhere without meeting clever people. The thing has become an absolute public nui-

sance. I wish to goodness we had a few fools
left.

ALGERNON. We have.

JACK. I should extremely like to meet them.
What do they talk about?

ALGERNON. The fools? Oh! about the clever
people, of course.

JACK. What fools! . . .

(p. 137)

Not all the play's wit is harmless, though. Some of it has the
potential to corrupt too, and this is especially true of Algy's
comments about marriage. "Divorces are made in Heaven," . . .
Algy remarks, then soon afterward observes that "in married
life three is company and two is none." . . . In the mouth of
Wotton, such comments would have had a disastrous effect on
Dorian. In *Earnest,* however, the comments are amusing but
harmless. They have no effect on Jack, to whom they are
addressed, or on Algy, who utters them. Both pursue the goal
of marriage in the play and end up happily married. At one
point, Algy repeats a famous epigram of Wotton's:

ALGERNON. All women become like their
mothers. That is their tragedy. No man does.
That's his.

JACK. Is that clever?

ALGERNON. It is perfectly phrased! and quite
as true as any observation in civilised life should
be. . . .

In this brief exchange, Wilde concisely sums up his attitude
toward Wotton in *The Importance of Being Earnest.* Wotton's
corrupt, immoral epigrams are now seen as toothless. Wit exists
because it is perfectly phrased, and for no other reason. The
play is full of witty comments whose only purpose is to be
perfectly phrased and therefore highly amusing—wit for wit's
sake, so to speak.

In *The Picture of Dorian Gray,* Wotton existed literally as a
Victorian devil, a modern-day Satan. This is parodied when
Jack says of Lady Bracknell: "Never met such a Gorgon. . . .
I don't really know what a Gorgon is like, but I am quite sure
that Lady Bracknell is one. In any case, she is a monster without
being a myth, which is rather unfair. . . . I beg your pardon,
Algy, I suppose I shouldn't talk about your own aunt in that
way before you." . . . The monster, we are immediately reminded, is only our good friend Algy's aunt. It is all very
funny and very absurd. And she is, after all, a harmless monster
whose attempt to keep Jack and Gwendolyn apart fails.

When it first appeared, *The Picture of Dorian Gray* evoked a
tremendous amount of hostile criticism in the press because of
its immorality. Replying to one of his critics, Wilde wrote to
the editor of the *St. James's Gazette:* "The sphere of art and
the sphere of ethics are absolutely distinct and separate; and it
is to the confusion between the two that we owe the appearance
of Mrs Grundy, that amusing old lady who represents the only
original form of humour that the middle classes of this country
have been able to produce." . . . (pp. 138-39)

Mrs. Grundy was the Victorian comic personification of ul-
trarespectability. In *The Importance of Being Earnest,* the critics of *Dorian Gray* are humorously satirized in the person of
the mentally short-sighted Miss Prism, who is really Wilde's
version of Mrs. Grundy. When we first meet her, Prism is a

stiff-necked and morally upright person convinced of Cecily's
great need to study German grammar as a means of "improving" herself. Amusingly, Prism connects the study of German,
geology, and political economy with ethical improvement—
presumably because of the dry, ascetic nature of these subjects.
She speaks in a stilted manner and utters only moral platitudes,
but these are constantly undercut by Cecily. In the four-act
version, Cecily makes a flippant observation at one point, and
Miss Prism wonders where Cecily is getting such ideas from,
since they are "certainly not to be found in any of the improving
books that I have procured for you."

It soon turns out that Prism has written a three-volume novel:

MISS PRISM. Do not speak slightingly of the
three-volume novel, Cecily. I wrote one myself
in earlier days.

CECILY. Did you really, Miss Prism? How
wonderfully clever you are! I hope it did not
end happily? I don't like novels that end happily. They depress me so much.

MISS PRISM. The good ended happily, and the
bad unhappily. That is what Fiction means. . . .

Miss Prism subscribes to the view that the function of art is
to preach morality. As soon as Dr. Chasuble appears on the
scene, however, she abandons the task of "improving" Cecily
and begins to pursue the rector. All her moral platitudes and
the preachings of her three-volume novel are dropped as she
surrenders to her sexual drive. She tries to maintain a façade
of respectability, but this façade is hilariously shattered when
she obliquely tries to suggest to Chasuble that she is the best
woman for him:

MISS PRISM. No married man is ever attractive
except to his wife.

CHASUBLE. And often, I've been told, not even
to her.

MISS PRISM. That depends on the intellectual
sympathies of the woman. Maturity can always
be depended on. Ripeness can be trusted. Young
women are green. (*Dr. Chasuble starts*) I spoke
horticulturally. My metaphor was drawn from
fruits. . . .

Prism attempts to turn a sexual relationship into one of "intellectual sympathies," but her metaphor betrays her real intentions.

Toward the end of the play, the subject of Miss Prism's novel
crops up again and Lady Bracknell passes judgment on it,
calling it "a three-volume novel of more than usually revolting
sentimentality." . . . This is the final word on Prism's moral
work of fiction; the final word on Prism herself comes when
Dr. Chasuble embraces her and she cries out enthusiastically,
"At last!" The critics of *Dorian Gray* and their moral airs
were, after all, so much hypocritical nonsense.

A good deal of the fun in *The Importance of Being Earnest* is
directed against *Salome.* A huge Negro executioner brought
Iokanaan's head to Salome on a silver shield, and she lustfully
proceeded to feast upon it. This gruesome event is parodied
when Lane brings Algernon some cucumber sandwiches on a
salver, and he gluttonously devours them all and remains hungry. Algy's action is not quite proper, as the sandwiches were
intended for Lady Bracknell. Far from being crushed between

huge salvers, moreover, Algy lives to dine again, first at Willis's, then on muffins at Jack's country home. (pp. 139-41)

So Salome's insatiable, hellish sexual appetite is reduced in *Earnest* to the level of mild gluttony. Whereas Salome meets death for yielding to her uncontrollable appetite, Jack and Algy both escape punishment in *Earnest.* Wilde dismisses Salome with a peal of laughter, declaring that her hunger was, after all, nonsense. She would have done better to order some cucumber sandwiches—or to have gone, perhaps, to Willis's or even the Savoy!

Iokanaan is also parodied in the play. He makes a charming reappearance in the figure of the Reverend Frederick Chasuble, doctor of divinity. Like Iokanaan, Dr. Chasuble is continually baptizing people:

> JACK. Ah! that reminds me, you mentioned christenings I think, Dr. Chasuble? I suppose you know how to christen all right? (*Dr. Chasuble looks astounded*) I mean, of course, you are continually christening, aren't you?
>
> MISS PRISM. It is, I regret to say, one of the Rector's most constant duties in this parish. I have often spoken to the poorer classes on the subject. But they don't seem to know what thrift is. . . .

The chief similarity between Iokanaan and Dr. Chasuble, however, is that they are both celibates whose slips of the tongue betray deep sexual longings. Miss Prism, who is in full pursuit of Chasuble throughout the play, calls him a "womanthrope," and he replies, in a stilted, scholarly manner: "Believe me, I do not deserve so neologistic a phrase. The precept as well as the practice of the Primitive Church was distinctly against matrimony." . . . Chasuble remains celibate by virtue of repressing his longing for Miss Prism, but his words continually betray him and reveal his true nature. For instance:

> CHASUBLE. I hope, Cecily, you are not inattentive.
>
> CECILY. Oh, I am afraid I am.
>
> CHASUBLE. That is strange. Were I fortunate enough to be Miss Prism's pupil, I would hang upon her lips. (*Miss Prism glares*) I spoke metaphorically.—My metaphor was drawn from bees. Ahem! . . .

> (pp. 141-42)

The canon's slips of the tongue are always amusing, as for instance when Lady Bracknell begins to question him about Prism:

> LADY BRACKNELL. Is this Miss Prism a female of repellent aspect, remotely connected with education?
>
> CHASUBLE. (*Somewhat indignantly*) She is the most cultivated of ladies, and the very picture of respectability.
>
> LADY BRACKNELL. It is obviously the same person. May I ask what position she holds in your household?
>
> CHASUBLE. (*Severely*) I am a celibate, madam.
>
> JACK. (*Interposing*) Miss Prism, Lady Bracknell, has been for the last three years Miss Car-

dew's esteemed governess and valued companion.

> LADY BRACKNELL. In spite of what I hear of her, I must see her at once. Let her be sent for.
>
> CHASUBLE. (*Looking off*) She approaches; she is nigh. (*Enter Miss Prism hurriedly*) . . .

In this scene Chasuble automatically misconstrues Lady Bracknell's question and leaps to the defense of his chastity. Jack, by interposing, undercuts the canon's reply and makes his slip seem even more ridiculous. Then Chasuble proceeds to announce the coming of Prism as though she were a divinity. Chasuble is very much like Iokanaan, but whereas Iokanaan was shrouded in an atmosphere of horror and evil, Chasuble is a comic figure with a ridiculous lust for the middle-aged, unattractive Prism. He is a reductio ad absurdum of Iokanaan. Unlike the prophet, he does not have to die to possess his lover. He merely lowers his defenses and embraces the delighted Prism. All ends harmlessly and happily for him.

A Woman of No Importance is ridiculed in a brief episode toward the end of act 3. Jack mistakenly falls under the impression that Prism is his mother and suddenly becomes ridiculously sentimental:

> JACK. (*In a pathetic voice*) Miss Prism, more is restored to you than this hand-bag. I was the baby you placed in it.
>
> MISS PRISM. (*Amazed*) You?
>
> JACK. (*Embracing her*) Yes . . . mother!
>
> MISS PRISM. (*Recoiling in indignant astonishment*) Mr. Worthing! I am unmarried!
>
> JACK. Unmarried! I do not deny that is a serious blow. But after all, who has the right to cast a stone against one who has suffered? Cannot repentance wipe out an act of folly? Why should there be one law for men, and another for women? Mother, I forgive you. (*Tries to embrace her again*) . . .

The blind sentimentalism of *A Woman of No Importance* is uproariously made fun of here. Behind the barrage of sentimentality in the former play had lurked the hideous leprosy of incest. This is ridiculed when Jack embraces Prism, for the embrace has clear and amusing sexual overtones. Miss Prism knows—and we immediately learn—that she is not Jack's mother. She recoils from his embrace, but he stupidly persists in trying to put his arms around his "mother."

Finally, in *An Ideal Husband,* Mrs. Cheveley lost a snake-bracelet and Lord Goring found it. When she tried to reclaim the bracelet, she was trapped, exposed as a thief, threatened with the police, and defeated. Similarly, Jack loses a cigarette-case and Algernon finds it. When Jack moves to reclaim his case, Algy discovers that Jack is "one of the most advanced Bunburyists" he knows. In one of the funniest episodes in *The Importance of Being Earnest,* Jack is trapped and exposed; but the result is that he gets his cigarette-case back and deepens his friendship with a fellow-Bunburyist. What had proved lethal for Mrs. Cheveley proves advantageous for Jack. Indeed, everything can be counted on to prove harmless in this never-never land of farce, Wilde's funniest and most delightful play. (pp. 143-45)

Christopher S. Nassaar, in his Into the Demon Universe: A Literary Exploration of Oscar Wilde, *Yale University Press, 1974, 191 p.*

DENNIS J. SPININGER (essay date 1976)

[*In the following excerpt, Spininger discusses* Earnest *as an absurdist drama in which Wilde used parody to both present and undercut his meaning.*]

What Richard Ellmann has initiated and accomplished for Wilde's criticism [see *TCLC*, Vol. 8] needs to be done for his work generally. Indeed, through the suggestion that Wilde balanced, without seeking to reconcile, opposing views of art's incrimination with and disengagement from life, an established ethical posture for art coexisting with its own cancellation, Ellmann posits the point of departure for such an effort. The starkly aesthetic treatment of the social concerns, the cancellation of those serious issues raised only to be dissipated, makes of *The Importance of Being Earnest* a play which is also an anti-play, a drama that is a parody of its own conventions and terms of existence. It is evident that parody is one of the tools of comedy within the play, since it is consistently directed at the nature and gestures of the society represented there. Much of the early dialogue devastates through mockery the standard notions of marriage, which, despite Algernon's manservant's claim that he believes "it *is* a very pleasant state, sir," is characterized as "demoralizing," unromantic, "business" as opposed to pleasure, and "not a very interesting subject." None of this prevents the play from ending with three marriages, a reconstituted society that is one of the conventions of domestic comedy, as Northrop Frye describes it, "a society ushered in with a happy rustle of bridal gowns and banknotes." It is typical of the operations of this play that the things the characters say are discontinuous with the actions they perform. Nor is it that the caustic language applied to marriage has somehow been disproved in the course of the play. Quite the contrary—by the time the trio of marriages is to take place, its benefits have been effectively undermined and the exaggeratedly negative commentary on marriage has been thoroughly reinforced: it *is* unromantic, a business (the overriding importance of the rustling banknotes), and demoralizing.

That it is also "not a very interesting subject" is a comment from within the play on the play itself, self-directed parody of at least the play's apparent subject. In fact the deployment of one of the major conventions of comedy, the crystallization of a new society around the married couple(s), becomes a way of pushing comedy past its own limits. The conventionally happy endings of comedy are, according to Frye, "not true so much as desirable," and there is audience agreement that this should be a social rather than moral judgment. Wilde uses the most typical example of the happy ending, the marriage, to deflate the very possibility of lasting happiness or any happiness at all. As the society in this play has moved toward a new reality, the illusions (disguise, hypocrisy, unknown parentage—all, again, standard conventions of the comic mode) are only partially dispelled. The revelations which dissipate the absurd obstacles to marriage and make possible the ending we witness also show how absurd that ending itself really is and expose the fact that deception and illusion are the very fabric of this society, old and new. The ending, in other words, is not desirable so much as true. In Ellmann's words, "the ceremonial unmasking at the play's end . . . leaves everyone barefaced for a new puppet show, that of matrimony." . . . (pp. 49-51)

Wilde parodies the conventions of comedy even as he uses them, a process which pushes his play beyond the confines of "play" and thrusts his comic mode into a demonstration or evocation of its opposite. And he does this by juxtaposing, without reconciling, a thing with its own cancellation—a procedure I would characterize not as a failure to move toward some third term of synthesis, which might accomplish the reconciliation, but a deliberate (Wilde would have said "studied") unwillingness to embrace a theory of reconciliation.

Despite all of the high-gear hilarity of the play, there is a half-conscious realization for the alert reader that the world of the play, the virtual society it portrays, and of actual life, the real Victorian society it captures in its mirror, is standing on the edge of an abyss partially illustrated by the bankruptcy of social, economic, and moral values exposed within the play. Something like anarchy emerges from beneath the madness and the frivolity. A sense of futility pervades not only the restored society at the end, which is as absurd as anything that has preceded it, but the very structural elements of comedy itself and, therefore, the component parts of absurdity, which ceases to be strictly comic.

Comedy is on the whole more social than tragedy. The latter tends to isolate its protagonist from social norms, while comedy tends to incorporate its central characters into a reintegrated society. In *The Importance of Being Earnest,* however, the social procedures of comedy are employed in the most conventional way for very unconventional results. The successful reintegration of society does depend on reducing the obstacles to illusions, but the wonderful series of strange coincidences and contrivances, which manages to accomplish this, does so only because the values of this society are illusory. Lady Bracknell takes note, in the midst of the revelations that comprise the "discovery" and propel the change of fortune, that "in families of high position strange coincidences are not supposed to occur. They are hardly considered the thing." They are, however, precisely the thing of which comic *anagnorisis* ["recognition"] is made and without them this play could not conclude with its promised marriage ceremonies. But the pivotal twists of plot are twisted in a very special way, for it is by revealing the illusory nature of the obstacles that the marriages can take place in a society that promotes and depends on illusions. When all of the deceptions and manipulations of the protagonists are uncovered, they become eligible for a place in a society in which deception is the prevailing way of life, where it is fostered and required by those who pretend to abjure it. The most important quality in this society is not being earnest.

Gwendolyn says of Jack Worthing, "Ernest has a strong upright nature. He is the very soul of truth and honour. Disloyalty would be as impossible to him as deception." . . . If that were true, as she also admits, his (personal) "history would be quite unreadable." . . . The exposure of his secretive deceptions, she goes on to acknowledge, makes him grow "more interesting hourly." If "the action of comedy . . . moves towards the incorporation of the hero into the society that he naturally fits," Jack Worthing achieves this, not by being earnest, but by being Ernest (first by artifice, then by nature—nature imitating art, à la Wilde, in this respect), that is, by being or becoming the illusion he had manufactured for deceptive purposes. Then, and only then, does he naturally fit into a society that depends on artificial surfaces as much as this one.

It turns out that Jack is really named Ernest, but this is peripheral to the conclusion of the play. Observation of formality, not truth, is what is required, as the general consent to the baptisms, which would rename both Jack and Algernon as Ernest, amply shows. "In matters of grave importance, style, not sincerity is the vital thing." . . . The "insuperable barrier" is the Christian names of the heroes. Both Gwendolyn and Cecily have loved the name before and even more than the person and are willing to accept a ceremonial change. It is not the puncturing of deception that clears the way for the reconstituted society, but the general willingness to mount illusions which are in accord with the operative deceptions of the existing society. Everything's in a name, if the scaffold is supported by a bank account. Appearance is all that is required: "He has nothing, but he looks everything. What more can one desire?" . . . (pp. 51-3)

The subtitle of Wilde's play is *A Trivial Comedy for Serious People* and he once identified the play's "philosophy" in the following words: "that we should treat all the trivial things of life seriously, and all the serious things of life with sincere and studied triviality." That is the kind of paradox typical of Wilde in his most flippant moods, but there is some element of genuine application to his play. At one level this reversal of the serious and the trivial is the unconscious credo of his cast of characters. At another level it is his own operating credo of opposites placed in unreconciled tension. Of course, Wilde, as creative dramatist, ultimately controls both levels.

The characters really believe that "there are principles at stake that one cannot surrender" . . . ; if they did not, humor would dissipate into a sense of them as villainous. But situation after situation reduces the claims of serious principle to absurdities. While she is scarcely capable of applying the statement to herself, Lady Bracknell raises this idea: "The two weak points in our age are its want of principle and its want of profile." . . . The confusion of the trivial and the serious is part of the caricature of Victorian society; it is exaggerated for satirical effect. Reality is overblown so that the Victorian Caliban might see its own face in the glass without going into a rage. But the play goes well beyond satire; indeed satire is only a minor by-product of the play.

Wilde's wit, insofar as it stations the trivial and the serious in a position of equal status, has other objectives. He exalts the trivial to prevent us from taking life too seriously. He deflates the serious to show how, not simply Victorian reality, but reality itself is empty and hollow. He postulates a level of equivalence (principles and profiles), but does so in a way that reveals the tendency of high comedy to expose forces more traditionally associated with tragedy. The juxtaposition of incongruous elements is a feature shared by both comedy and tragedy, and Wilde knew how to use it for comic effect, while sustaining its threatening potential as a tragic dimension. This possibility of comedy is carefully documented in Walter Sorell's *Facets of Comedy:* ". . . the safest measure of the comic is its sensitivity to its tragic reflection. I imagine it as an iceberg, the greater part of which is submerged. We think we laugh about what we see on the surface, but, while laughing, we are consciously or unconsciously aware of the tremendous and tragic power lying in the submerged part of its threatening potentialities."

The special tragic potential in Wilde is of a complex sort and depends on a prior procedure which has two subsidiary movements. First he uses the instruments of the satirist and the caricaturist without seeking to cure the follies he castigates. Ridicule is not prompted by moral intent in the sense we associate with Bernard Shaw's social comedies. Nor is it, as

those who look for social meaning in every drawing-room comedy would have us believe, that Wilde lacked the higher purpose of the satirist. His own purpose is very much higher than the sugar-coating of a curative pill. He is not set on reconstituting the world in an ethical image of his own making (that is the intent and the greatest folly of some of his characters); the reconstituted society that emerges at the end of this play is changed merely in its surface configurations, which is entirely in accord with the observation that the only Christian (and ethical) concern its members register is a concern for Christian names. For very different and not superficial reasons, Wilde, too, dismisses ethics from the purpose of his satirical mode.

The second movement displaces the battery of comic devices from the position of means toward an end, that is, service on behalf of the conventions of social satire to puncture the veneer of priggishly moral codes as the first step toward correction, to an end in themselves. As illustrated by the verbal brilliance of Wilde's epigrams, the inverted clichés on which so many of these depend (e.g., "Divorces are made in heaven"), the whimsical nonsense that all of his characters are led to speak, the puns, and the frequent *non sequitur*, wit is detached from its potential service for social reform. The highly sophisticated wit in Oscar Wilde's drama becomes through this second movement its own *raison d'être*.

In the earlier plays the sparkling verbal wit often outstripped its latent or even explicit social commentary, but was nevertheless more closely tied to it through the serious nature of certain characters or the more serious quality of the plot. Even George Woodcock, who emphasizes the social criticism of Wilde's work more than any other commentator [see Additional Bibliography], admits that *The Importance of Being Earnest* stands alone among Wilde's plays in having no explicit social theme." Henry Popkin is more direct when he describes the attack on society as based on aesthetic grounds: "To invert these respectable, conventional clichés is to subvert respectability and conventionality themselves, and that is just what Wilde intended. He is saying that respectability is tiresome, repetitious, unoriginal; in short, he is applying an aesthetic judgment by bringing in the contrasting brightness and inventiveness of his witty characters." (pp. 53-6)

But it was W. H. Auden [see *TCLC*, Vol. 1] who made the imaginative leap to the very essence of Wilde's masterpiece, which he called "the only pure verbal opera in English," where Wilde managed "to subordinate every other dramatic element to dialogue for its own sake and create a verbal universe in which the characters are determined by the kinds of things they say, and the plot is nothing but a succession of opportunities to say them." If Auden is right, as I believe he is, it is through the two movements I have delineated that Wilde reduces or eliminates the moral impact of his satirical mode and frees wit to constitute its own universe, a *verbal universe*, which translates life into an aesthetic phenomenon. It is in this sense only that those critics are correct who, either complainingly or admiringly, have noted that the verbal display is inconsequential. The brilliantly turned lines the characters utter, the highly polished *bon mots* they deliver in scene after scene, do not really affect the issues of the plot and do not contribute to the development of character, for neither of these elements matters in the least in Wilde's play. Like the designs of corrective satire, they are subordinated or dismissed: style, not sincerity, is the vital thing. In a universe coordinated by aesthetics, profiles are linked to principles by alliteration, and that is justification enough.

Through this wonderful release of style from sincerity and even from meaning, however, Wilde created a world which is at once hilariously dizzy and more than a little terrifying. By detaching dramatic language from its conventional anchors in plotting and character development, by freeing language from the mandates of sense and logic, he liberates a world that is, to use his own word from *The Critic as Artist,* sterile. The effect is both exhilarating and frightening and, coupled with the procedure of aesthetic detachment, projects a special kind of absurd atmosphere onto two worlds, the virtual one of the play and the actual one in which we live.

The verbal acrobatics, dancing along capricious patterns, retain some slight satirical thrust, but because they typically make as much sense turned upside down as right side up, they have a cumulatively bewildering effect on the audience more than on the characters. Two of the exchanges, both from Act 1, illustrate this bewildering quality:

> ALGERNON. All women become like their mothers. That is their tragedy. No man does. That's his.
>
> JACK. Is that clever?
>
> ALGERNON. It is perfectly phrased! And quite as true as any observation in civilised life should be.
>
> JACK. I am sick to death of cleverness. Everybody is clever nowadays. You can't go anywhere without meeting clever people. The thing has become an absolute public nuisance. I wish to goodness we had a few fools left.
>
> ALGERNON. We have.
>
> JACK. I should extremely like to meet them. What do they talk about?
>
> ALGERNON. The fools? Oh! about the clever people of course.
>
> JACK. What fools. . . .

And again:

> ALGERNON. . . . Do you know it is nearly seven?
>
> JACK. (*Irritably*) Oh! it always is nearly seven.
>
> ALGERNON. Well, I'm hungry.
>
> JACK. I never knew you when you weren't. . . .
>
> ALGERNON. What shall we do after dinner? Go to a theatre?
>
> JACK. Oh, no! I loathe listening.
>
> ALGERNON. Well, let us go to the Club?
>
> JACK. Oh, no! I hate talking.
>
> ALGERNON. Well, we might trot round to the Empire at ten?
>
> JACK. Oh, no! I can't bear looking at things. It is so silly.
>
> ALGERNON. Well, what shall we do?
>
> JACK. Nothing!

> ALGERNON. It is awfully hard work doing nothing. However, I don't mind hard work where there is no definite object of any kind. . . .

The first example is but a verbal pirouette away from Beckett, and the second takes a whimsical stag leap into what we now call the Theatre of the Absurd. In fact the second passage is used by Walter Sorell [in his *The Facets of Comedy*] in close comparison to one from Pinter's *A Birthday Party* to demonstrate his point that "the recognition of the absurdity in man's existence is not peculiar to our era only." He describes it as an example of the "no-exit feeling of the *fin de siècle,*" and the way it reduces the various possibilities of (an evening's) experience to utter nothing is a paradigm of what this play does to human experience as such. Finding sense in nonsense through absurd logic, Wilde brings the Cheshire cat into the drawing room, where it fades in the same way it did before Alice's astounded eyes, leaving its glittering smile to the last, and then: nothing. Like most nonsense literature it achieves its "liberating effect by expanding the limits of sense and opening up vistas of freedom from logic and cramping convention." Also like most nonsense literature it tends to leave us stranded in that new expanse without a map.

As readers or audience, we take the trivial seriously and we witness the serious reduced to studied triviality in a way the characters cannot. If there is sense in nonsense, the reverse of this is also true, and one serious aspect of all this mad whimsy is that, perhaps, nonsense governs life. Again, Wilde refuses to reconcile the opposites he juxtaposes so maddeningly and provides no justification other than the aesthetic one. As Algernon says of his epigram: "It is perfectly phrased! and quite as true as any observation in civilized life should be." And again the impact is different for the characters within the play and the audience without. The characters are not disturbed, beyond Jack's occasional aggravation, and certainly not shattered by the nonsense in their lives. They are, as Auden noted, determined by what they say. As characters, the very substance of their existence is words; the elegant phrasing defines them and confines them. They are never stranded, because they are never liberated. They do not react to the *reductio ad absurdum* because they are its constituent parts as well as its mouthpieces.

A continuous reduction to the absurd nonetheless takes place, though not in precisely the way it would in logic (proving a proposition by showing its opposite to be foolish or impossible, or disproving a proposition by showing its consequences to be absurd or impossible when carried to a logical conclusion). In Wilde's play, the reductive process occurs most typically through the juxtaposition of opposites (a serious proposition and a trivial one) in a manner that gives them equal status and thus cancels or inverts the expected distinction. The title and the very slight plot which derives from it are based on a pun. To be Ernest or not to be earnest—that is the question. At the level of sound, there is no difference; at the level of meaning, there could be a difference, but it is eradicated in a world where meaning capitulates to paranomasia, and reason falls to rhyme. (pp. 56-9)

There is indeed no serious motif in the play which does not have its trivial counterpart to reduce it by equation. The double life not only is reduced to the camouflage of Bunburying, but is also connected to the convention of mixed identities appropriate to comedy. It provides an opportunity to play with the notions of the serious and the trivial:

> JACK. This ghastly state of things is what you call Bunburying, I suppose?

ALGERNON. Yes, and a perfectly wonderful Bunbury it is. The most wonderful Bunbury I have ever had in my life.

JACK. Well, you've no right whatsoever to Bunbury here.

ALGERNON. That is absurd. One has a right to Bunbury anywhere one chooses. Every serious Bunburyist knows that.

JACK. Serious Bunburyist! Good heavens!

ALGERNON. Well, one must be serious about something, if one wants to have any amusements in life. I happen to be serious about Bunburying. What on earth you are serious about I haven't got the remotest idea. About everything, I should fancy. You have such an absolutely trivial nature. . . .

Even the moral ambiguities of a double life are brought in for burlesque treatment. When Algernon first assumes the identity of Ernest, he decides, as a tactic, to deflate the wicked reputation Jack has nourished, expecting this will improve his access to Cecily. But Cecily, raised in the country by Miss Prism on morality, political economy, and German grammar (another set of absurd equivalents), is bored by her moral education and finds wickedness appealing. (pp. 60-1)

The moral dimension is constantly called forth in this play only to be canceled. To do so establishes a kind of virtual immorality for the characters, but amorality for the play. Near the end, one character invokes the Christian formula of expiation: "Cannot repentance wipe out an act of folly?" . . . But, as Ellmann has noted, the notion of expiation is parodied, reduced by equation to the level of eating muffins. Expiation *is* an act of folly, since no syllogisms are false in a world where logic does not operate. . . . The muffins, in the course of a rather short scene, serve as the source of discussion for standards of propriety, consolation, selfishness, greed, hospitality, and then repentance. The connections are verbal ones, but these are wholly adequate, indeed supreme, in a world where style surpasses sincerity and where, following the dictate of *The Critic as Artist*, "language is the parent, and not the child of thought." . . . (pp. 61-2)

In this world, error consists of poor phrasing, a sin committed by only one character, Jack, when early in his courtship of Gwendolyn, he blurts out a nervous and poorly constructed compliment. Otherwise the victory of style over sincerity is uninterrupted. Even the Reverend Chasuble has sermons that can be adjusted to any occasion, and offers to use one of them to register notice of brother Ernest's death. "My sermon on the meaning of the manna in the wilderness can be adapted to almost any occasion, joyful, or, as in the present case, distressing. (All sigh.) I have preached it at harvest celebrations, christenings, confirmations, on days of humiliation and festal days." . . . The very adaptability of his sermon diminishes its theological value; and, expectably, his pride in it is aesthetic, not religious (the Bishop, who heard it once, he boasts, was much struck by some of the analogies). Its potential equivalence for the joyful or the distressing gives it the double status that everything in this play possesses. The "double life" is both a motif and a procedure: Wilde creates and sustains a dialectic without synthesis.

Rites and ceremonies consistently cater to changes in the surface configurations; nor, considering the inverted scale of val-

ues, would it be proper for them to do more. Baptism, which should signify regeneration to a more serious, authentic, or earnest life is entertained casually . . . and for the sole purpose of changing one's name. Since the two women make the name of Ernest the insuperable barrier, both men announce their plans to be christened, an act on their behalf which the women inflate as "this terrible thing," "this fearful ordeal." There is a sense in which the traditional lover's test of going through fire and water (another kind of rite) is also recalled, though reduced to a ritual sprinkling. When Jack withdraws from the possibility of full immersion, Dr. Chasuble assures him: "Sprinkling is all that is necessary, or indeed I think advisable. Our weather is so changeable." . . . Lady Bracknell adds the final touch to the incongruous perspective, when she learns of the impending baptisms: "The idea is grotesque and irreligious! . . . I will not hear of such excesses." . . . (pp. 62-3)

Reform, the social parallel to religious rebirth, is a concomitant motif, and appears with the same casual prompting, and is deflated in the same way, through parody. It is a game one might play on an afternoon, if one has the time. . . . Miss Prism delivers the fatal blow to the notion of reform: "I am not in favour of this modern mania for turning bad people into good people at a moment's notice" . . . , and, a few lines later, "The good end happily, and the bad unhappily. That is what fiction means."

Death and its concomitant ritual are similarly reduced by parody. Two deaths occur, but they are both of imaginary creatures, Ernest and Bunbury. When Jack, dressed in deepest mourning, announces his brother's death, Miss Prism takes an educator's stance toward the event: "What a lesson for him! I trust he will profit by it." . . . When, in Act 3, it is Bunbury's turn to die, there is no question of mourning:

ALGERNON. . . . The doctors found out that Bunbury could not live . . . so Bunbury died.

LADY BRACKNELL. He seems to have had great confidence in the opinion of his physicians. I am glad, however, that he made up his mind at last to some definite course of action, and acted with proper medical advice. . . .

(pp. 63-4)

Imaginary events propel the movement of this play and language carries it along in a way that is suitable only if one appreciates that it is governed by aesthetic criteria. The serious and the trivial are equal, or are distinct only in terms of expression. Language is substituted for reality. The ultimate deflating equation, disclosed only obliquely and in retrospect, is that between a three-volume manuscript and a baby. Miss Prism's "work of fiction," put in the bassinette "in a moment of abstraction," replaced or displaced the baby put in her charge. This equivalence contributes another set of balanced opposites that confuses (rather than fuses) the serious and the trivial.

The elegant phrasing and polished style set in counterpoint to the absurd activities complement and absorb the similar contrast between smooth, confident appearance and inner emptiness. There are either no villains in this play (Ernest is imaginary), or both leading men are villains (Algernon turns out to be Jack's brother and Jack turns out to be named Ernest). The play is what Northrop Frye calls "an ironic comedy directed at the melodramatic spirit itself." It is also a satire directed at the conventional objectives of satire. Both of the young men are variants of the impostor character of comedy, the *alazon*, who traditionally delays the comic action. Indeed, with respect to one another's intentions, each man does impede progress. In the first act, Algernon threatens to withhold his consent to Jack's marriage with Gwendolyn. In the last act Jack reverses this position and claims to disapprove of Algernon's moral character: "I suspect him of being untruthful." ... Jack's moral stance is, of course, his playing card in the game of moral blackmail. He will grant his permission, when Lady Bracknell withdraws her objection to his own marriage with Gwendolyn.

This impasse persists until nature imitates art and everyone turns out to prefer Ernest to earnestness. Both of the young men are also variants of the rogue or picaro, usually the counterpart to the *alazon,* but here represented by the same characters, a serviceable double life of comic types. They are most likeable when unprincipled or tricky or, as they almost always are, verbally clever. The latter rescues them even from moral posing, for "though of all poses a moral pose is the most offensive, still to have a pose at all is something," as Wilde says in **The Critic as Artist.** ... Since the standard virtues of morality, sincerity, and charity are adopted or dismissed as personal convenience dictates, the revelations, which rearrange identities and relationships and permit the multiple marriages at the end, do not dispel all the deceptive illusions that have been created; rather they give them the status of provisional truths. If nature imitates art—"I always told you ... my name was Ernest, didn't I? Well, it is Ernest after all. I mean it naturally is Ernest" ...—then truth can imitate deception. ... (pp. 64-5)

Wilde's identification of triviality as the play's philosophy is correct in a very disconcerting and devastating way. The state of utter playfulness, in which Wilde's own creative or critical spirit takes the role of the "vice," the spirit governed by whimsy, insouciance, and mischief, is manipulated so as to suggest its tragic reversal. If sense and nonsense are brothers by design and by nature and may go by the same name, and if names themselves can be altered as easily as fashionable sides of a street, the world, even this perfectly ordered verbal world, is absurd. Facsimiles of the natural are as acceptable or as unavoidable in our lives, the ultimate three-volume novel, as in this play. Cecily writes out the details of her romance with Ernest before she meets him (another instance of art preceding nature), and Gwendolyn admits she also loved the name before the person. Algernon's hair "curls naturally," "with a little help from others," and Cecily's appearance, "almost as nature might have left it," can, Lady Bracknell assures her, be changed.

The inquiries of "a really affectionate mother" establish a question and answer sequence between Lady Bracknell and Jack that is sheer verbal, if not intellectual, slapstick, one of the great farcical scenes of the play. The question of highest priority is whether or not he smokes; his affirmative answer is received with gladness, for "a man should always have an occupation of some kind." Since she believes "that a man who desires to get married should know either everything or nothing," she asks which he knows, and his reply, "I know nothing," is again received with pleasure. After several queries about income, property, and politics, she reverts to "minor matters," namely his parents.

It is delightful high camp, as audience and readers attest, but its underside becomes distinctly visible. Everything or nothing and minor or major are two more abstracted opposites juxtaposed as equivalents and reduced by parallels that turn them upside down. The one natural thing that Lady Bracknell supports is "natural ignorance" ... and so she commends Jack for knowing nothing, an ironic admission that recalls Socrates's similar statement in style, not substance. (pp. 65-6)

The everything-nothing motif—one must say motif rather than theme because thematic recurrence has too heavy a tread for a play whose verbal patterns resemble music—recurs several times and thus generates both a binding power and a cumulative force. Jack knows nothing and chooses, from the set of possibilities for an evening's pleasure proffered by Algernon, to do nothing. He approaches Dr. Chasuble with his desire to be christened, "if you have nothing better to do." And he could negate everything through verbal denial ("I could deny anything if I liked" ...). If Jack represents *action* reduced to nothing (but words), Algernon is *being* reduced to nothing (but words). As he notes with mock solemnity, "it isn't easy to be anything nowadays." ... According to Lady Bracknell, Algernon has nothing, but looks everything. It would be truer to say that he verbalizes everything, for he shares with Lady Bracknell herself a position as *arbiter nugarum* ["representative of nonsense"] of the play. He is as overeducated as he is overdressed. He is perfectly phrased and quite as true as anyone can be in this civilized verbal universe. "In life there is really no great or small thing. All things are of equal value and of equal size" [**De Profundis**].

This state of things, in which the difference between everything and nothing is two syllables, is appropriate to the capricious manner of Wilde's "verbal saturnalia." Yet it also contributes to the cumulative sense of "nothing" as a nihilistic force, the partially exposed underside of the universe turned upside down. Wilde's first play, **Vera, or the Nihilists** ..., was a melodrama about nihilism, scarcely redeemed by occasional flashes of wit. His last play, in which melodrama is a target of the wit and wit itself is the play's essence, evokes a nihilistic spirit that places Wilde closer to Beckett than to Shaw. The play is a kind of Bunburying of the genres whereby the comic spirit, set free in a purely aesthetic domain, releases a tragicomic perspective (one thinks of the phrase Wilde used in **De Profundis:** "we are the zanies of sorrow"). The exchange is all at the level of masks and mirrors, but there is no other level. James M. Ware has analyzed the disorientation produced by Wilde's most typical comic strategy, the inverted platitude, in terms of mirror play [see Additional Bibliography]: "In Algernon's inverted cliché, 'I hate people who are not serious about meals. It is so shallow of them,' we have almost a compendium of the ambiguity of **Earnest.** He puts 'shallow' and 'serious,' the earnest man's touchstones, in a hall of mirrors." By way of this strategy writ large, Wilde's most frivolous play is also his most serious.

It is not surprising that this comedy depends on incongruous contraries, since that is part of the essential nature of comedy. What is unique is the perfectly sustained dependence on opposites which do not fuse together. There is no *tertium quid* ["compromise"], for even art and reality are stationed in the hall of mirrors. If life can be justified only as an aesthetic phenomenon, ... it cannot be justified at all, or at least not in any final or ultimate way. Wilde displaces the conventional morality of life by elevating form and style to a position higher than virtue and truth, by reversing the distinction between the serious and the trivial. On the other hand, he displaces the conventions of comedy by maintaining them, but for a situation in which they become forms of parody. Manipulation and contrivance are acceptable in comedy if they are instrumental in delivering its humorous society from absurdity. In this case, the absurdity is described in an oxymoron as "a passionate celibacy," which is "all that any of us can look forward to" . . ., if the obstacles to the projected marriages are not bypassed. They are, of course, bypassed in grand style, when the comic *cognitio* ["recognition of identity"] takes place. . . . As Jack rushes off to get Miss Prism's handbag, the object which will initiate the final stage of the *cognitio,* he asks Gwendolyn to wait and she responds with, "If you are not too long, I will wait here for you all my life," and then, while the noises of his offstage rummaging fill the theater, she comments, "This suspense is terrible. I hope it will last." . . . Her mother's comment, already quoted, pronounces that "strange coincidences are not supposed to occur." These lines are the transitional absurdities, and mark the line of development from the absurd obstacle to the absurd fulfillment, from passionate celibacy to dispassionate marriage, from the impossible to the improbable. The improbable (and that marriage is conducive to pleasure, much less happiness, is very improbable in this play) is the keystone of Wilde's wit and the key to the ambivalent nature of the play.

Algernon's request, when in the first act Jack is about to explain the inscription on his cigarette case, is: "Now produce your explanation, and pray make it improbable." . . . The explanations that manipulate the happy ending are more improbable, and the projected happy future most improbable. But just as the overt attention paid to the ongoing nonsense diminishes from act to act, an inverse relation to the increase of nonsense, so the vocabulary of cognition concerning the ridiculous, the incongruous, and the improbable (phrases like "that's absurd") decreases in the same way. Wilde uses the word "absurd" to signify "out of harmony with propriety, reason, or available evidence." At no particular point does it have the darker meanings that the twentieth century has given it, but there is nevertheless a sense in which the play as a whole pushes toward this darker meaning. For cognition of nonsense and of the incongruous does not release the characters from participating in these, any more than the comic *cognitio* frees them from absurdity, since it manages to secure another form of the absurd situation, the "new puppet show," as Ellmann phrases it, of the act we never see. (pp. 67-70)

The breaching of conventions through parodied usage contributes to the intuition of the absurd that the play provokes. Like the variety of epigram (the inverted cliché) most associated with Wilde, this parody of the conventions recalls the very thing it punctures and sustains the opposites in a state of unresolved tension. One of Wilde's most explicit statements about tragicomedy was made as an accusation against modernity: "I remember I used to say that I thought I could bear a real tragedy if it came to me with purple pall and a mask of noble sorrow, but that the dreadful thing about modernity was that it put Tragedy into the raiment of Comedy, so that the great realities seemed commonplace or grotesque or lacking in style. It is quite true about modernity. It has probably always been true about actual life" [*De Profundis*]. In the solemnity of this pronouncement, Wilde failed to recognize the real paradox, that his own most modern play caught the truth of this double life of the genres precisely because it evokes tragedy through the comic absurd. To translate everything into aesthetic terms and then to acknowledge the sterility of the new order was Wilde's anticipation of a modern dilemma. . . . Beyond the frontiers of reason he found irrepressible whim and its earnest brother, absurdity: "nothing that one can imagine is worth doing, and . . . one can imagine everything" [*Critic as Artist*]. . . . Chiseled aesthetic order is the answer to life's blunt

chaos, but the answer is ineffectual, sterile, beautiful but futile. . . . (p. 71)

Life is a failure "from this artistic point of view," but so is art, though not for the same reasons. "For life is terribly deficient in form. Its catastrophes happen in the wrong way and to the wrong people. There is a grotesque horror about its comedies, and its tragedies seem to culminate in farce" [*Critic as Artist*]. . . . Art resolves the formal deficiency but does not correct the incongruities; rather, it subjects them to a heightening effect. And in *The Importance of Being Earnest* this heightened sense of incongruity manifests itself as a "fanciful, absurd, comedy."

Jorge Luis Borges thought it would be difficult "to imagine the universe without Wilde's epigrams" [see *TCLC,* Vol. 1]. It is just as difficult to imagine a universe composed almost entirely of them, yet that verbal universe exists in this play, the "delicate bubble of fancy," "exquisitely trivial," as Oscar Wilde himself described it, which is also, through the devices of wild paradox, his most serious step toward the twentieth century. (p. 72)

> *Dennis J. Spininger, "Profiles and Principles: The Sense of the Absurd in 'The Importance of Being Earnest'," in* Papers on Language & Literature, *Vol. 12, No. 1, Winter, 1976, pp. 49-72.*

KATHARINE WORTH   (essay date 1983)

[*Worth is an English educator and critic. In the following excerpt, she surveys the stylistic and structural elements of* Earnest *and examines its influence as an existential drama.*]

In *The Importance of Being Earnest* the pleasure principle at last enjoys complete triumph. Some critics disapprove of this, notably Mary McCarthy [see Additional Bibliography] who censures the dandies' determination to live a life of pleasure as "selfishness." Perhaps it is, but we are not being required to examine their moral behaviour in humane Chekhovian terms. This is a philosophical farce, an existential farce, to use the modern term which modern criticism is beginning to see as appropriate for this witty exploration of identities. "Pleasure," a word which recurs much, is a shorthand for the idea Wilde expounded in **"The Soul of Man under Socialism"**:

> Pleasure is Nature's test, her sign of approval. When man is happy, he is in harmony with himself and his environment. The new Individualism, for whose service Socialism, whether it wills it or not, is working, will be perfect harmony.

Only in Utopia can this harmony be achieved; in theatrical terms that meant farce, the form that refused the agonies of melodrama. . . . In this extravagant genre, which no one took seriously, the dionysiac spirit could be fully released, to overturn respectable reality, and through paradox, fantasy and contradiction establish a logic of its own, defying the censorious super-ego. . . . It is a play of mirror images in which ordinary, everyday life can still be glimpsed through the comic distortions imposed upon it. Everything is double, from the double life of Algernon and Jack to the sets of doubles at the end, when the girls form themselves into opposition to the male image which has so conspicuously failed to be "Ernest." (pp. 153-54)

"Everything matters in art except the subject," said Wilde. In *The Importance of Being Earnest* the subject certainly cannot

be distinguished from the style, yet the fact that the play succeeded . . . even when the actors were playing it wrongly shows
what a steely construction it has. It must have given Wilde the
craftsman much pleasure to take the familiar melodrama mechanism (mistaken identities, incriminating inscriptions, secrets
of the past) and exploit its inherent absurdity instead of trying
to restrain it. The closeness of farce to melodrama is one of
his strong cards, in fact, allowing all kinds of oblique references
to the oppressive moral laws which had malign consequences
in the earlier plays—and, as Wilde thought, in English society.
As well as being an existential farce, *The Importance of Being
Earnest* is his supreme demolition of late nineteenth-century
social and moral attitudes, the triumphal conclusion to his career as revolutionary moralist. (p. 155)

Farce should have the speed of a pistol shot, said Wilde, and
speed is, indeed, a distinctive and curious feature of *The Importance of Being Earnest*; curious, because it co-exists with
extreme slowness and stateliness in the dialogue. No one is
ever so agitated that he cannot take time to round a sentence,
find the right metaphor—or finish off the last muffin. Yet all
the time sensational changes are occurring at the speed of light.
Proposals of marriage are found to have been received even
before they were uttered, relations lost and found before one
can say "hand-bag." Time, like everything else, goes double
and through the "gaps" Wilde insinuates the notion that the
action is really all happening somewhere else, in the mental
dimension where ruling fantasies are conceived, which is not
to say of course that there is no connection with reality: "Life
imitates Art far more than Art imitates life." The outlines of
reality are easily discernible; Lane offering deadpan excuses
for the absence of cucumber sandwiches, Dr. Chasuble fitting
in the absurd christening to his perfectly normal programme:
"In fact I have two similar ceremonies to perform at that time.
A case of twins that occurred recently in one of the outlying
cottages on your own estate. Poor Jenkins the carter, a most
hard-working man." What is wrong with this society, so the
farce implies, is its fatal inability to distinguish between the
trivial and the serious. Sense and nonsense, reason and fantasy,
facts and truth, are juggled with, forcing new perspectives,
offering release from the cramp of habit and logic. . . . (p. 156)

It is an urbane Utopia we see when the curtain goes up on the
first act. Algernon's rooms in Half Moon Street (a more relaxed
environment than the grand locales of earlier plays) are "lux-
uriously and artistically furnished"; music is heard from the
off-stage piano (perhaps a dubious pleasure, as Algernon saves
his science for life and relies on sentiment in his piano playing).
The elegant sallies between Algernon and his "ideal butler,"
Lane, are another feature of Wilde's Utopia; servants are more
than equal to masters. With the entrance of Jack, the "pleasure" motif rings out loud and clear:

> ALGERNON. How are you, my dear Ernest? What
> brings you up to town?
>
> JACK. Oh pleasure, pleasure! What else should
> bring one anywhere . . .

Tom Stoppard lifted this debonair entrance to serve as a "time
stop" in *Travesties*, a sticking place in the mind to which the
action obsessively returns. He assigns Jack's lines to Tristan
Tzara, the Dadaist, making a connection between the pleasure
philosophy, revolution and nihilism. Jack and Algernon are
not exactly revolutionaries, but they do bring into the play from
time to time a rather modern emphasis on the idea of nothingness. . . . [Malaise] is kept at bay most of the time by the

complications of the double life. Wilde amusingly recalls the
impassioned detective sequences of *An Ideal Husband* in the
inquisition conducted by Algernon into Jack's secrets. A precious mislaid object, the inscribed cigarette case, provides a
crucial clue (parallelling the bracelet/brooch of the other play);
Algernon presses his questions as unremittingly as Lady Chiltern ("But why does she call you little Cecily, if she is your
aunt and lives at Tunbridge Wells?") and like Robert Chiltern,
Jack fights off discovery with inventive lies. "Earnest" was
the word for the Chiltern double life and "Earnest" is the word
for Jack's too, in the double sense perceived by Algernon the
moment Jack reveals his "real" name:

> ALGERNON. . . . Besides, your name isn't Jack
> at all; it is Ernest.
>
> JACK. It isn't Ernest; it's Jack.
>
> ALGERNON. You have always told me it was
> Ernest. I have introduced you to everyone as
> Ernest. You answer to the name of Ernest. You
> look as if your name is Ernest. You are the
> most earnest-looking person I ever saw in my
> life.

The brilliant pun is the corner-stone of a structure dedicated
to dualities of all kinds. Jack is "Ernest in town and Jack in
the country": he becomes "Ernest" in fact when he wants to
escape from being "earnest"; the pun perfectly encapsulates
the split in the personality. Neatness, taken to the point of
surrealist absurdity, makes the same sort of suggestion throughout. Algernon's situation is a mirror image of Jack's. When
he sums up the situation, he falls into a rhythm which is the
quintessential rhythm of the play; a balancing of opposites, the
"masks," which as the play goes on are to be juggled with
increasingly manic ingenuity:

> You have invented a very useful younger brother
> called Ernest in order that you may be able to
> come up to town as often as you like. I have
> invented an invaluable permanent invalid called
> Bunbury, in order that I may be able to go down
> into the country whenever I choose.

Critics in Wilde's time did not grasp the subtlety of the structure. Even Max Beerbohm [see excerpt dated 1902], an admirer, thought the play triumphed despite its farcical "scheme"
which he summarised as: "the story of a young man coming
up to London 'on the spree,' and of another young man going
down conversely to the country, and of the complications that
ensue." This comes nowhere near expressing the mysterious
sense of what "town" and "country" represent for Jack and
Algernon. "On the spree" is a phrase for the French *boulevard*
farce and its "naughty" behaviour, which English audiences
could enjoy in suitably watered down adaptations, with a feeling of moral superiority. Wilde slyly draws attention to this
characteristic hypocrisy when Algernon gives Jack some very
French advice:

> ALGERNON. A man who marries without know-
> ing Bunbury has a very tedious time of it.
>
> JACK. That is nonsense. If I marry a charming
> girl like Gwendolen, and she is the only girl I
> ever saw in my life that I would marry, I cer-
> tainly won't want to know Bunbury.
>
> ALGERNON. Then your wife will. You don't
> seem to realise, that in married life three is
> company and two is none.

JACK. (*Sententiously*) That, my dear young friend, is the theory that the corrupt French Drama has been propounding for the last fifty years.

ALGERNON. Yes; and that the happy English home has proved in half the time.

There is little sense in the play of orgiastic goings on. "Eating" is the chief symbol of sensual activity. The dandies' will to eat is part of the larger will which drives them and the girls (and indeed everyone in the play). Shaw might have called it the Life Force. Wilde uses a favourite metaphor: health. As Jack explains to Algernon, he needs Ernest because as Uncle Jack he is expected to maintain a high moral tone, and a high moral tone can hardly be said to conduce to one's health or happiness. We might wonder why the insouciant Algernon needs an escape route. But we find out when Lady Bracknell appears on the scene, ringing the bell in "Wagnerian manner" and greeting her nephew in a most remarkable variant of common usage: "I hope you are behaving very well?" He fights back with "I'm feeling very well, Aunt Augusta," only to be overridden with magisterial finality: "That is not quite the same thing. In fact the two rarely go together." (pp. 157-61)

Lady Bracknell herself is dedicated to health; a supreme irony. As she tells Algernon when he produces Bunbury's illness yet again, as an excuse for avoiding her dinner party:

I think it is high time that Mr. Bunbury made up his mind whether he was going to live or to die. This shilly-shallying with the question is absurd. Nor do I in any way approve of the modern sympathy with invalids. I consider it morbid. Illness of any kind is hardly a thing to be encouraged in others. Health is the primary duty of life . . .

We can well see why Lord Bracknell had to become an invalid: she has taken all the health for herself. It is a measure of Wilde's ability to stand back from his own passionately held beliefs that the most completely realised personality in the play should be such a monster; as Jack says, "a monster without being a myth, which is rather unfair."

There is no doubt in this play that "women rule society." Lady Bracknell has a more central position in the dramatic action than the dowagers of earlier plays. The marriages are in her control, and it is she who (unwittingly) holds the key to Jack's identity. She comes on with Gwendolen in tow, in the manner of the Duchess of Berwick and Lady Agatha, and though Gwendolen is no Agatha, she is just as much in thrall to her mother when husbands are in question. On one of its levels the farce is certainly conducting the old campaign against the tyrannies that afflict women. There is an extra layer of irony indeed; we see how the system will perpetuate itself as the victims prepare to become tyrants in their turn, for Gwendolen is clearly her mother's daughter. It is not just a joke when Jack anxiously enquires: "You don't think there is any chance of Gwendolen becoming like her mother in about a hundred and fifty years, do you, Algy?" The proposal scene certainly gives him warning, with its focus on Gwendolen's will and the intensity of the inner life which surfaces (in appropriately "absurd" form) in her curious obsession:

My ideal has always been to love someone of the name of Ernest. There is something in that name that inspires absolute confidence. The

moment Algernon first mentioned to me that he had a friend called Ernest, I knew I was destined to love you.

There is obviously a dig here at the troublesome idealists of earlier plays: the whole ideal-oriented ethos is reduced to absurdity. (pp. 161-62)

The "limitations of real life" are soon imposed on the idyll when Lady Bracknell sweeps in, to surprise Jack on his knees: "Rise, sir, from this semi-recumbent posture. It is most indecorous." Her marriage questionnaire carries, in its absurd way, the whole weight of the commercially-minded society she epitomises:

LADY BRACKNELL. . . . What is your income?

JACK. Between seven and eight thousand a year.

LADY BRACKNELL. (*Makes a note in her book*) In land, or in investments?

JACK. In investments, chiefly.

LADY BRACKNELL. That is satisfactory. What between the duties expected of one during one's lifetime, and the duties exacted from one after one's death, land has ceased to be either a profit or a pleasure. It gives one position, and prevents one from keeping it up. That's all that can be said about land.

Anyone who can talk as well as this is bound to charm—still she cannot be thought totally charming. Real life is hovering there in the background, making us feel just a little mean at laughing when she holds forth on the nature of society from the height of her conservative hauteur. Her power is political as well as social; Wilde's point is that the two are one. Liberal Unionists are acceptable, she concedes, when Jack admits to being one: "they count as Tories. They dine with us. Or come in the evenings, at any rate." The fine shades of her condescension are droll, but a telling reminder of a real-life Byzantine grading system which ensures that politics are controlled by the right people.

It does not really matter what Jack admits to in the way of taste: there is no way of kowtowing to Lady Bracknell, for, as Mary McCarthy says, she has the unpredictability of a thorough *grande dame*. . . . It makes him understandably wary when she declares that "a man who desires to get married should know either everything or nothing," and asks "which" he knows. It is only "after some hesitation" that he commits himself: "I know nothing, Lady Bracknell." A fitting remark for an existential hero. She, of course, takes it in a social sense, as she does everything, and approves; a rich irony, for Jack's devotion to "nothing" goes along with his mercurial changeability, something she would deeply disapprove of. "Knowing nothing" for her means "ignorance," a very desirable quality in the lower classes:

The whole theory of modern education is radically unsound. Fortunately in England, at any rate, education produces no effect whatsoever. If it did, it would prove a serious danger to the upper classes, and probably lead to acts of violence in Grosvenor Square.

Great fun, in the context, yet are we meant to quite shut out reverberations from history—the Nihilists, the Irish, all the social ferment which troubled Wilde's conscience and is reflected in his other plays? It seems not, for the revolution theme comes up again in an explicit historical reference when Jack reveals the peculiar circumstances of his birth. Even Lady Bracknell cannot assimilate that anarchical phenomenon:

> . . . I don't actually know who I am by birth. I was . . . well, I was found . . . In a hand-bag—a somewhat large, black, leather hand-bag, with handles to it . . .

All her worst nightmares crowd—majestically—into the scene:

> To be born, or at any rate bred, in a hand-bag, whether it had handles or not, seems to me to display a contempt for the ordinary decencies of family life that reminds one of the worst excesses of the French Revolution. And I presume you know what that unfortunate movement led to?

This is no casual reference. The French Revolution figures in **"The Soul of Man under Socialism"** as illustration of the inevitability of change: "The systems that fail are those that rely on the permanency of human nature, and not on its growth and development. The error of Louis XIV was that he thought that human nature would always be the same. The result of his error was the French Revolution. It was an admirable result." By analogy, Lady Bracknell is necessary to the process she is resisting; Wilde provides us with a moral justification for the fact that we cannot help liking the monster!

There is also a little germ of existential anxiety in the great joke: "being" in an empty hand-bag; being in a void. Like a Vladimir or a Winnie in Beckett's empty spaces, Jack has to construct himself from virtually nothing. (pp. 163-66)

At the fall of the curtain on the first act the metaphysical dimension is thickening. Jack is in a tortuous relationship with the mythic self which he needs both to destroy ("I am going to kill my brother") and at the same time possess more completely (by having himself christened, a comical psychic ordeal). And Algernon, with the address of "excessively pretty Cecily" surreptitiously registered on his shirt-cuff, is gleefully preparing to get into his Bunbury clothes and take over the adaptable "Ernest" identity for himself. The juggling with personae is becoming more and more "absurd" in the modern sense.

The second act opens in a garden, a utopian setting such as Wilde had never quite allowed himself in earlier plays where the furthest we got into nature was a lawn under a terrace. . . . This is not very wild nature, of course: still, there is emphasis on luxuriance (an old-fashioned abundance of roses) and various hints that this is the scene where growth and change are to be achieved. . . . In the four-act version a gardener appeared, an unexpected addition to the usual cast of butlers and valets. Here Cecily (significantly seen at the back of the stage, deep in the garden) is doing the gardener's work, a fact Miss Prism observes with distaste:

> MISS PRISM. (*Calling*) Cecily, Cecily! Surely such a utilitarian occupation as the watering of flowers is rather Moulton's duty than yours? Especially at a moment when intellectual pleasures await you. Your German grammar is on the table. Pray open it at page fifteen. We will repeat yesterday's lesson.

> CECILY. (*Coming over very slowly*) But I don't like German. It isn't at all a becoming language. I know perfectly well that I look quite plain after my German lesson.

The reference to German as the bone of contention is no accident. Like the "pessimist" joke at the close of Act one (Algernon accuses Lane of being a pessimist and is told "I always endeavour to give satisfaction, sir"), it is one of those oblique allusions to German philosophy which slyly suggest that the characters are enacting a Schopenhauer style struggle to realise the "will" and engage with the concept of "nothing." Jack always lays particular stress on the importance of Cecily's German when he goes off to town (to become his alter ego). So Miss Prism observes, while Cecily notes the strain involved: "Dear Uncle Jack is so very serious! Sometimes he is so serious that I think he cannot be quite well." She draws attention to the existential confusion which surely overtakes the audience by now. Who really is Jack/Ernest? Is he acting when he is serious Uncle Jack and is Ernest his true identity (as Gwendolen asserts)? Or is he really Jack struggling to manage the wicked brother, Ernest? He is often half way between the two, as the fluctuations in his style indicate. The man who entered the play on so airy a note ("Oh, pleasure, pleasure!") can talk very sententiously, and look the part too, as Algernon had observed.

Cecily has no such complications. Yet she is also in her way an existentialist, using her diary as the young men use Ernest to act out her "will." Wilde strikes very modern notes in the discussion sparked off by the diary about the difficulty of distinguishing between memory and fiction, both seen here as part of the self-creating process:

> CECILY. I keep a diary in order to enter the wonderful secrets of my life. If I didn't write them down, I should probably forget all about them.

> MISS PRISM. Memory, my dear Cecily, is the diary that we all carry about with us.

> CECILY. Yes, but it usually chronicles the things that have never happened, and couldn't possibly have happened. I believe that Memory is responsible for nearly all the three-volume novels that Mudie sends us.

Miss Prism's confession that she once wrote a three-volume novel . . . contributes to the Beckettian shades in the comedy. But she, like her other half, Canon Chasuble, is really essence of nineteenth century. Through their delicious absurdities we discern, like shadows, characteristics that had to be taken more grimly in earlier plays: pomposity, self-importance, cruelty even (Miss Prism is much given to pronouncing "As a man sows, so also shall he reap"). But rigid morality loses its power when the absurdly serious pair represent it. They have a foot in the utopian world.

Miss Prism too pursues a dream: "You are too much alone, dear Dr. Chasuble. You should get married. A misanthrope I can understand—a womanthrope never!" His scholarly shudder at the "neologistic" phrase reminds us, like his reference to Egeria which Miss Prism fails to understand ("My name is Laetitia, Doctor"), that there is a social gulf between them. She is hardly a highly-educated governess; we learn later that she started life as a nursemaid. Wilde is extending the satire on Victorian moral attitudes to take in the middle to lower classes, an interesting development which makes one more than ever sad at what may have been lost when catastrophe brought his playwriting to an end.

Cecily soon clears the stage for her own freedom. In her manipulation of the wobbling celibates . . . she displays the masterfulness which makes her, like Gwendolen, more than a match for the men. Like a modern girl, she cuts Algernon down to size when he makes his appearance as Ernest on a somewhat arch note:

> ALGERNON. You are my little cousin, Cecily, I'm sure.
>
> CECILY. You are under some strange mistake. I am not little. In fact, I believe I am more than usually tall for my age.

Algernon, says the stage direction, is "rather taken aback." Well he might be: it is the end of his Bunburying days when Cecily takes charge, leading him into the house to start the process of "reforming" him.

It is an exquisite stroke of comic timing that at the very moment when brother Ernest has materialised for the first time, Jack should enter, in mourning for his death in Paris of a chill. Pictures of George Alexander in the part show him the very spirit of lugubriousness, in funereal black, with the "crepe hatband and black gloves" which Dr. Chasuble calls his "garb of woe." It is a great visual joke, demonstrating, as C. E. Montague said [in *Dramatic Values*], the scenic imagination which distinguishes playwrights from other writers: "To an audience, knowing what it knows, the mere first sight of those black clothes is convulsingly funny; it is a visible stroke of humour, a witticism not heard but seen." Wilde did not make much of the stage directions for *The Importance of Being Earnest*: they are less detailed than in earlier plays. . . . Yet Montague was right to stress the value of the scenic element. We do not need to know the colour of the characters' hair—what colour would Ernest's be?—but, as in all the plays, a delicate visual symbolism operates in *The Importance of Being Earnest,* crystallising underlying meanings. The spectacle of the "man in black" making those absurd arrangements to be christened ("Ah, that reminds me, you mentioned christenings, I think, Dr. Chasuble?") is surely, for us now, an existential joke.

Of course none of this shows to the stage audience. Jack's rather disturbing fluidity of character is highlighted by the rigidity of Miss Prism and Canon Chasuble: they move on the narrowest of lines and appeal to our sense of humour by having none themselves. It is one of Wilde's most dionysiac moments of glee when Jack, acting solemnity, draws forth the real solemnity of the celibate pair:

> CHASUBLE. Was the cause of death mentioned?
>
> JACK. A severe chill, it seems.
>
> MISS PRISM. As a man sows, so shall he reap.
>
> CHASUBLE. (*Raising his hand*) Charity, dear Miss Prism, charity! None of us are perfect. I myself am peculiarly susceptible to draughts. Will the interment take place here?
>
> JACK. No. He seems to have expressed a desire to be buried in Paris.
>
> CHASUBLE. In Paris! (*Shakes his head*) I fear that hardly points to any very serious state of mind at the last.

This is the sort of caricature which is more lifelike than life itself. The consistent pair are in their way an anchor to a solid world where we expect people to be much the same from one day to another. In the other dimension, where there seems no limit to the characters' ability to change themselves, the action is becoming manic:

> My brother is in the dining-room? I don't know what it all means. I think it is perfectly absurd.

It is "absurd" in Pinteresque vein when Jack, in mourning for Ernest, is impudently advised to "change."

> Why on earth don't you go up and change? It is perfectly childish to be in deep mourning for a man who is actually staying for a whole week with you in your house as a guest. I call it grotesque.

The alter ego is out of hand. Even the imperturbable Algernon is taken aback, in his second scene with Cecily, to realise how firmly she has defined his role in her "girlish dream." It was "on the 14th of February last that worn out by your entire ignorance of my existence, I determined to end the matter one way or the other, and after a long struggle with myself I accepted you under this dear old tree here." A very determined piece of dreaming, this,—a comical version of Schopenhauer's "world as idea"—held together, like Gwendolen's scenario, by the "ideal" Ernest.

Repetition and increasingly heavy stylisation from now on build up the impression that some psychic process is being acted out—in the absurd form appropriate to events in the unconscious. Algernon and Cecily must go through the same performance as Jack and Gwendolen; he must react in the same way as Jack to the realisation that "Ernest" is no longer a voluntary role by rushing off to be christened. And Gwendolen must appear, for a quarrel scene with Cecily which is in a way closer to the norm of nineteenth century comedy (Gilbert's *Engaged* was mentioned by contemporary critics), but acquires strangeness from the dream-like gap Wilde contrives between the solid, decorous surface (Merriman totally absorbed in supervising the tea-table rites) and the increasingly uninhibited argument about someone who doesn't exist. As the lines become ever more crossed—"Oh, but it is not Mr. Ernest Worthing who is my guardian. It is his brother—his elder brother"—the audience has almost certainly lost its own grip on who is who, a confusion Wilde surely intends.

He evidently intends also the exaggerated stylisation which begins to push the farce away from even minimal realism when Jack and Algernon are brought face to face with Gwendolen and Cecily. Like automata, the girls ask the same questions and use the same movements, each in turn demanding of "her" Ernest, "May I ask if you are engaged to be married to this young lady?", and on receiving the desired assurance, proceeding to prick the bubble of the other's dream with a mannered precision which has drawn from modern critics terms like "courtship dance" to describe the manoeuvrings of the quartet:

> The gentleman whose arm is at present round your waist is my guardian, Mr. John Worthing.
>
> The gentleman who is now embracing you is my cousin, Mr. Algernon Moncrieff.

The breaking up and re-forming of pairs, the neat oppositions, the stilted repetitions, the speaking for each other . . . all create

a curious impression, of personality flowing unstoppably between two poles. Everything surprises us by being its own
opposite ("A truth in Art is that whose contradictory is also
true"). Things taken with deadly seriousness in the "modern
life" plays are stood on their head, as in Jack's parodic confession:

> Gwendolen—Cecily—it is very painful for me
> to be forced to speak the truth. It is the first
> time in my life I have ever been reduced to
> such a painful position, and I am really quite
> inexperienced in doing anything of the kind.
> However I will tell you quite frankly that I have
> no brother Ernest. . . .

A subtle joke; for by the end we know that his brilliant invention
was the truth; it was the facts that were untrustworthy ("Life
imitates art far more than art imitates life").

Before we arrive at that revelation, the doubles have to reor-
ganise themselves. The female pair retire into the house "with
scornful looks" and the male pair are left to pick up the pieces
of the shattered personality. (pp. 167-74)

In the final act we move back into the house; the garden idyll
(the "beautiful" act, Wilde called it) is over, the "truth" is
out and time is flowing back towards daylight. Gwendolen and
Cecily are seen looking out of the windows at the young men,
as if no time at all has elapsed, or just enough for them to say,
in the past tense, "they have been eating muffins." Stylisation
reaches its peak when the young men join them and both pairs
address each other in choral unison, Gwendolen beating time
"with uplifted finger." . . . It is an altogether musical scene:
the men come on whistling "some dreadful popular air from
a British opera" (not identified, but could Wilde wickedly have
intended *Patience*?). In earlier drafts the stylisation was even
more extreme and balletic. Jack and Algernon were to "move
together like Siamese twins in every movement" when they
make their announcement that they are to be christened:

> First to front of sofa, then fold hands together,
> then raise eyes to ceiling, then sit on sofa, un-
> fold hands, lean back, tilting up legs with both
> feet off the ground, then twitch trousers above
> knee à la dude . . .

It is almost surrealist farce now; Jarry's painted puppets are
over the horizon, and Ionesco's automata chorusing "The future is in eggs." Directors, alas, seldom pick up Wilde's hints
for a modern style; they tend to keep a uniform tone, ignoring
the upsurge of stylisation that makes the characters speak in
tune, whistle, chant in chorus until, symmetrical to the last,
the pairs are reconciled and fall into each other's arms, exclaiming "Darling!"

Only if this fantastic, balletic/musical effect is achieved . . .
can there be the right contrast of tone when Lady Bracknell
sweeps in to drag them back to the real world. Despite the
fun, that is what is happening when she sets about demolishing
one unsuitable engagement and investigating the other with the
suspicion induced by the previous day's revelations. "Until
yesterday I had no idea that there were any families or persons
whose origin was a Terminus." The wit warms us to her but
cannot quite disguise the glacial nature of the snub. The whole
tone is harder in this scene, perhaps because she is ruder (she
makes Jack "perfectly furious" and "very irritable"); perhaps
because repetition slightly reduces the comicality of her rou-
tines, making their social unpleasantness more apparent. When

she asks "as a matter of form" if Cecily has any fortune and
on learning that she has a hundred and thirty thousand pounds
in the Funds, finds her "a most attractive young lady," we
laugh, of course, but remembering the similar business with
Jack, probably feel the edge in the joke more. There is something increasingly alarming as well as droll about her unself-
consciousness: can she really be so unaware or impervious,
we wonder, or is she amusing herself with conscious irony
when she reflects on Cecily's "really solid qualities" and how
they will "last and improve with time," and with supreme
effrontery presents herself as the opponent of mercenary marriages:

> Dear child, of course you know that Algernon
> has nothing but his debts to depend on. But I
> do not approve of mercenary marriages. When
> I married Lord Bracknell I had no fortune of
> any kind. But I never dreamed for a moment
> of allowing that to stand in my way.

There is no way of penetrating that formidable façade, to find
out what goes on behind it (Peter Hall [director of the National
Theatre's 1982 revival of **Earnest**] saw the whole action as
determined by the will to conceal very strong and real feelings).
Wilde planted a time bomb in this character, seemingly set for
our time, when there would be a better chance of audiences
picking up the serious points the jokes are making—about the
"woman question" and marriage. The revelation that Cecily
remains a ward till she is thirty-five, for instance, yields much
fun, culminating in Lady Bracknell's dry comment that her
reluctance to wait till then to be married shows "a somewhat
impatient nature." Yet there are sour realities at the back of
it, which Wilde does not mean to go unnoticed: we are laughing
at (laughing down?) the idea of women being always someone's
property, always pawns in the marriage business. Lady Bracknell has made it grotesquely clear that "business" is the word,
and she controls society. It is total impasse—the only way out
in the other dimension, where Ernest has his equivocal being.

That unpredictable force makes its way back when Canon Chasuble appears, unctuously announcing that he is ready to perform the christenings. It is a wonderful clash of the two worlds.
"Algernon, I forbid you to be baptised," booms Lady Bracknell. "Lord Bracknell would be highly displeased if he learned
that that was the way in which you wasted your time and
money." But the materialist money values, so comically invoked, must give way before the strange inner drive that dictated the christenings; now it brings on Miss Prism, in anxious
pursuit of the Canon ("I was told you expected me in the
vestry, dear Canon") to be confronted with Lady Bracknell's
stony glare and the terrible question: "Prism! Where is that
baby?" The absurd tale of the three-volume novel left in the
perambulator and the baby left in the hand-bag closely parodies
attitudes taken in Wilde's other plays. Miss Prism "bows her
head in shame," the young men "pretend" to protect the girls
from hearing "the details of a terrible public scandal," Jack
becomes ever more portentous, requiring Miss Prism to examine *his* hand-bag carefully to see if it is also hers: "The
happiness of more than one life depends on your answer." The
third act was "abominably clever," Wilde said. Nothing is
cleverer than the way he uses the individualism of his characters
to undermine the old attitudes, overturn them, indeed, by being
irresistibly themselves. Miss Prism cannot keep her head down
for long: one sight of the hand-bag, and she is away in her
own world where other things, like damage to the lining, are
far more important than a sense of shame:

... here is the injury it received through the upsetting of a Gower Street omnibus in younger and happier days. Here is the stain on the lining caused by the explosion of a temperance beverage, an incident that occurred at Leamington. . . . The bag is undoubtedly mine. I am delighted to have it so unexpectedly restored to me. It has been a great inconvenience being without it all these years.

No melodrama morality could survive the absurdity of this. Wilde rolls the whole drama of the "woman with a past," the seduced victim, the illegitimate child (one critic would include the idea of incest), into the tiny hilarious episode when Jack tries to embrace Miss Prism, taking her for his mother. (pp. 174-78)

Laughing at himself, as well as at the mores of his time, Wilde in this scene breaks quite free of his century and becomes the "modern" playwright he wished to be. It is a modern moment for an audience brought up on Pirandello and Beckett when Jack, turning from one character to another in search of the truth about himself, is directed by Miss Prism to Lady Bracknell—"There is the lady who can tell you who you really are"—and asks her the question that has been causing existential tremors throughout the play: ". . . Would you kindly inform me who I am?" The answer may be something we have seen coming but still it causes a shock and it is not purely comic; it is bound to be a little disturbing to find that his wild and seemingly casual invention was no more than the truth: he is the brother of Algernon and his name is Ernest.

The existential hero receives the news "quite calmly"—"I always said I had a brother! Cecily,—how could you have ever doubted that I had a brother?; I always told you, Gwendolen, my name was Ernest . . ." But it is surely the calm of one emerging from an experience that has been growing steadily more manic and disorientating. The crisis of identity is over. Each pair of the quartet fall into each other's arms with the usual symmetry, and Lady Bracknell and Jack share the curtain lines:

> LADY BRACKNELL. My nephew, you seem to be displaying signs of triviality.
>
> JACK. On the contrary, Aunt Augusta, I've now realised for the first time in my life the vital Importance of Being Earnest.

It is the recall to Lady Bracknell's world where "trivial" and "earnest" reverse the values the farce has been asserting. She has won, in a way: the nameless foundling whose very existence was subversive has been assimilated into the Establishment. His father a General, his aunt a Lady: the "decencies of family life" are safe from the revolutionary horrors conjured up by the notion of being "born, or at any rate, bred, in a hand-bag." Yet we cannot be sure. The pun retains its teasing irony to the end. Jack speaks as an actor, looking out to the audience, slyly (never openly) sharing with them the joke closed from Lady Bracknell, that if there is a moral it is only the title for a farce. And the title reminds us that the farce is about being an actor, playing a part, being Ernest by "realising" him, as actors and playwrights realise for their audiences the creations of their fantasy and everybody, in the long run, has to realise his own identity.

With *The Importance of Being Earnest* Wilde anticipated a major development in the twentieth century, the use of farce

to make fundamentally serious (not earnest!) explorations into the realm of the irrational. The play has been immensely influential, serving as model for writers as diverse as T. S. Eliot, who gave a religious turn to the foundling motif in *The Confidential Clerk* (1953), and Charles Wood, in his bleakly funny play about the Second World War, *Dingo* (1969), which has British soldiers performing *The Importance of Being Earnest* in a German prison camp. Wilde's devotees, Joe Orton and Tom Stoppard, have paid especially full tribute to his genius. Orton, whose life had features in common with Wilde's, (homosexuality, traumatic experience of prison), said that his aim was to write a play as good as *The Importance of Being Earnest*. He came very near to doing this in *What the Butler Saw* (1969), a more manic version, in the vulgar postcard, sexy style proclaimed by its title, of Wilde's farce of identity: characters split into two, commandeer each other's identities, discover that they really are what they thought they were only pretending to be, in a way which continually acknowledges the Wildean source. (pp. 178-80)

[Wilde] would have approved W. H. Auden's comment that *The Importance of Being Earnest* was "the only pure verbal opera in English" [see *TCLC*, Vol. 1]. In none of his plays, not even *Salomé,* is the musical treatment more pronounced. Verbal music is heightened by a host of musical devices and allusions; as in opera the curtain rises to the sound of music (Algernon's piano playing); Lady Bracknell contributes a Wagnerian peal and pays idiosyncratic tribute to the power of music by banning French songs from Algernon's concert programme; the spoken word moves irresistibly nearer the condition of music till the lovers are keeping the beat dictated by Gwendolen's uplifted forefinger, practically singing and dancing. Perhaps it is not surprising that actors have had difficulty in capturing this intricate stylisation. (p. 181)

In the post-Orton world we might hope for performances of *The Importance of Being Earnest* that would . . . realise the "heartlessness" so troublesome to Shaw in bold, modern terms, bringing out the subversive and surreal elements. Such a production would have to end on a different note however, from the anarchic stupefaction of *What the Butler Saw*. Wilde does indeed, like Orton, show the world as tending to cruelty and heartlessness, life as an absurd performance, personality as a fluid thing, endlessly forming and reforming itself with the aid of masks (an emphasis on impermanence that alarmed even Yeats, the master of masks). But Wilde's optimistic, benevolent nature required a more harmonious ending for his farce than anything Orton, or perhaps any modern existentialist, would be likely to envisage. *The Importance of Being Earnest* ends with all the dissonances resolved and harmony achieved. It can only happen in Utopia, which means "nowhere"—but as Wilde said, "A map of the world that does not include Utopia is not worth even glancing at, for it leaves out the one country at which Humanity is always landing." (p. 182)

Katharine Worth, in her Oscar Wilde, *1983. Reprint by Grove Press, Inc., 1984, 199 p.*

ADDITIONAL BIBLIOGRAPHY

Barnes, Clive. "Theater: An All-Male *As You Like It*." *The New York Times* (6 July 1968): 9.

    An unfavorable review of Robert Chetwyn's 1968 production of *Earnest* at London's Theater Royal. According to Barnes: "Everyone is supposed to murmur respectfully how brilliant Oscar Wilde's comedies still are, but personally they seem to me horribly dated; camp art carried beyond the boundaries of triviality into oblivion. The once daring paradoxes now sound more like journalism than playwrighting, and time has made Wilde's cleverness a little pitiable because it now seems so cheap.''

Beaurline, L. A. "The Director, the Script, and Author's Revisions: A Critical Problem." In *Papers in Dramatic Theory and Criticism,* edited by David M. Knauf, pp. 78-91. Iowa City: University of Iowa, 1969.

> Compares and contrasts manuscript and typescript versions of *The Importance of Being Earnest.*

Bird, Alan. *"The Importance of Being Earnest."* In his *The Plays of Oscar Wilde,* pp. 160-83. New York: Barnes & Noble, 1977.

> An introductory essay supplying historical and biographical information, plot summary, and general criticism. According to Bird: "*Earnest* is Wilde's masterpiece in which his wit, his invention, his sense of social reality, his deep-seated and radical love of justice and the fundamental benevolence of his character are most perfectly mingled."

Bose, Tirthankar. "Oscar Wilde's Game of Being Earnest." In *Modern Drama* XXI, No. 1 (March 1978): 81-6.

> Discusses courtship rituals and parallel set structure in *The Importance of Being Earnest.*

Cohen, Philip K. "Fortunes of the Christian Hero: The Later Plays and Scenarios." In his *The Moral Vision of Oscar Wilde,* pp. 181-234. Rutherford, N.J.: Fairleigh Dickinson University Press, 1978.

> Includes an introductory analysis of *Earnest,* the play in which, according to Cohen, "Wilde trivializes not only specific sources of anxiety in his personal life, but also his own literary embodiments of his moral preoccupations. He exploits the license of farce for loose, episodic construction in order to produce encapsulated parodies of scenes, themes, and even passages in his other works."

Dickson, Sarah Augusta. Introduction to *The Importance of Being Earnest: A Trivial Comedy for Serious People* by Oscar Wilde, pp. ix-xxviii. New York: The New York Public Library, 1956.

> Historical account of the development of *The Importance of Being Earnest,* which catalogs and compares known versions of the play.

Ellmann, Richard. "The Critic as Artist as Wilde." In *The Artist as Critic: Critical Writings of Oscar Wilde,* edited by Richard Ellmann, pp. ix-xxviii. London: W. H. Allen, 1970.

> Brief examination of Wilde's trivialization in *The Importance of Being Earnest* of conventionally serious dramatic subjects. According to Ellmann: "[Wilde] could dissolve by the critical intellect all notions of sin and guilt. . . . In *The Importance of Being Earnest* sins which are presented as accursed in *Salomé* and unnameable in *Dorian Gray* are translated into a different key, and appear as Algernon's inordinate and selfish craving for—cucumber sandwiches. The substitution of mild gluttony for fearsome lechery renders all vice harmless."

Fido, Martin. "Years of Triumph." In his *Oscar Wilde,* pp. 86-103. New York: Peter Bedrick Books, 1973.

> Biography which includes brief critical passages. According to Fido: "*Earnest* is a farce of perfect charm, utterly removed from the sphere of real moral problems, which had been handled so melodramatically in Wilde's earlier comedies. To Shaw and Shaw alone has this ever seemed a weakness."

Ganz, Arthur. "The Divided Self in the Society Comedies of Oscar Wilde." *Modern Drama* III, No. 1 (May 1960): 16-23.

> Examines the opposition of the Philistine and the Dandy in Wilde's *Lady Windermere's Fan, A Woman of No Importance,* and *An Ideal Husband,* concluding that "only in *The Importance of Being Earnest* did Wilde overcome this pattern and produce a work of pure dandyism and a masterpiece."

Green, William. "Oscar Wilde and the Bunburys." *Modern Drama* XXI, No. 1 (March 1978): 67-80.

> Proposes Henry Shirley Bunbury of Waterford, Ireland, and Sir Edward Herbert Bunbury of Suffolk, England, as two possible models for Wilde's character of the same name, whom Green calls "one of the most memorable non-appearing characters in drama."

Leverson, Ada. "The Last First Night." *The New Criterion* IV, No. 1 (January 1926): 148-53.

> Reminiscence of the opening night of *Earnest* at the St. James's Theatre in February 1895. According to Leverson: "Whoever still lives who was present that night will remember the continual ripple of laughter from the very first moment—the excitement, the strange almost hysterical joy with which was accepted this 'Trivial Comedy for Serious People.'"

McCarthy, Mary. "The Unimportance of Being Oscar." In her *Sights and Spectacles: 1937-1956,* pp. 106-10. New York: Farrar, Straus and Cudahy, 1956.

> An unfavorable appraisal of *The Importance of Being Earnest.* According to McCarthy: "In spite of the exhausting triviality of the second act, *The Importance of Being Earnest* is Wilde's most original play. It has the character of a ferocious idyl."

McCollom, William G. "The Area of Comedy." In his *The Divine Average: A View of Comedy,* pp. 31-51. Cleveland: The Press of Case Western Reserve University, 1971.

> Illustrates Wilde's use of irony in *Earnest* through an examination of the first proposal scene between Gwendolyn Fairfax and Jack Worthing.

Miller, Robert Keith. "Exploring the Absurd: *The Importance of Being Earnest.*" In his *Oscar Wilde,* pp. 72-89. New York: Ungar, 1982.

> Introductory essay focusing on the modern view of *Earnest* as a drama of the absurd.

Nethercot, Arthur H. "Prunes and Miss Prism." *Modern Drama* VI, No. 2 (September 1963): 112-16.

> Examines Wilde's choice of the name Laetitia Prism for Cecily's tutor in *The Importance of Being Earnest* and cites the name's allusions to classical mythology and the works of Charles Dickens.

Paul, Charles B. and Pepper, Robert D. "The Importance of Reading Alfred: Oscar Wilde's Debt to Alfred de Musset." *Bulletin of the New York Public Library* 75, No. 10 (December 1971): 506-42.

> Analyzes Wilde's debt to the French dramatist for his *Il ne faut jurer de rien* (1836), noting similarities of plot, setting, characterization, and dialogue between Musset's play and Wilde's *The Importance of Being Earnest.*

Poague, L. A. *"The Importance of Being Earnest:* The Texture of Wilde's Irony." In *Modern Drama* XVI, Nos. 3 & 4 (December 1973): 251-57.

> An analysis of Wilde's ironic techniques in the text of *The Importance of Being Earnest.*

Sammells, Neil. "Earning Liberties: *Travesties* and *The Importance of Being Earnest.*" *Modern Drama* XXIX, No. 3 (September 1986): 376-87.

> Explores the "critical engagement" between Tom Stoppard's *Travesties* (1974) and its model, *The Importance of Being Earnest.* According to Sammells: "Stoppard's critical strategies are both interpretive and transformational. He exploits the host-play by pinpointing a recurrent element and elevating it to a position of ostentatious prominence."

Shaw, Bernard. "My Memories of Oscar Wilde." In *Oscar Wilde* by Frank Harris, pp. 329-43. East Lansing: Michigan State University Press, 1959.

> Contends that in Wilde's earlier comedies "the chivalry of the eighteenth century Irishman and the romance of the disciple of Theophile Gautier . . . not only gave a certain kindness and gallantry to the serious passages and to the handling of women, but provided that proximity of emotion without which laughter, however irresistible, is destructive and sinister. In *The Importance of Being Earnest* this had vanished; and the play, though extremely funny, was essentially hateful. I had no idea that Oscar was going

to the dogs, and that this represented a real degeneracy produced
by his debaucheries.''

Styan, J. L. ''Dramatic Dialogue is More than Conversation'' and
''Tempo and Meaning.'' In his *The Elements of Drama*, pp. 11-26,
141-62. Cambridge: University Press, 1960.

> Illustrates precepts of dramatic theory citing dialogue and tempo
> in the meeting of Cecily Cardew and Gwendolyn Fairfax in Act
> Two of *The Importance of Being Earnest*. Styan notes: ''For
> purposes of satire, Wilde gives us two-dimensional people who
> speak, not as people do speak, but as some would speak if their
> habits of thought were distorted by simplification. Two-dimen-
> sional speech precludes interest in complexity of motive, in order
> both to stress some kinds of basic and typical behavior and to
> keep an audience detachedly critical of it.''

Wadleigh, Paul C. ''*Earnest* at St. James's Theatre.'' *The Quarterly
Journal of Speech* LII, No. 1 (February 1966): 58-62.

> Historical and biographical data, excerpted reviews, and personal
> accounts of *Earnest*'s eighty-six performance run in London be-
> tween February and May 1895.

Ware, James M. ''Algernon's Appetite: Oscar Wilde's Hero as Restoration Dandy.'' *English Literature in Transition* 13, No. 1 (1970):
17-26.

> Proposes that ''Algernon's hunger is reminiscent of appetite-sat-
> isfaction motifs found in several Restoration comedies of manners,
> and that Wilde returned in [*The Importance of Being Earnest*] to
> the *tone* of the purest—that is, Etheregean—comedy of manners.''

Woodcock, George. *The Paradox of Oscar Wilde*. London: T. V.
Boardman & Co., 1949, 239 p.

> Critical biography containing several references to *Earnest*, the
> play which according to Woodcock, represents ''the peak of Wilde's
> dramatic achievement, and the one piece of writing in which he
> came nearest to artistic perfection.''

Appendix

The following is a listing of all sources used in Volume 23 of *Twentieth-Century Literary Criticism*. Included in this list are all copyright and reprint rights and acknowledgments for those essays for which permission was obtained. Every effort has been made to trace copyright, but if omissions have been made, please let us know.

THE EXCERPTS IN TCLC, VOLUME 23, WERE REPRINTED FROM THE FOLLOWING PERIODICALS:

The Academy, v. LIV, July 30, 1898.

American Literature, v. XLII, November, 1970. Copyright © 1970 Duke University Press, Durham, NC. Reprinted by permission of the publisher.

The American Magazine, Vol. 106, September, 1928.

Ariel, v. 1, July, 1970. Copyright © 1970 The Board of Governors, The University of Calgary. Reprinted by permission of the publisher.

Arts in Society, v. 6, Summer-Fall, 1969. Copyright, 1969, by the Regents of The University of Wisconsin. Reprinted by permission of the publisher.

The Bookman, New York, v. II, January, 1896; v. XXXII, January, 1911; v. XLIII, April, 1916; v. L, October, 1919; v. LXVIII, January, 1929.

Books Abroad, v. 28, Autumn, 1954.

Boston Evening Transcript, p. 4, November 29, 1933.

Bucknell Review, v. IX, May, 1960. Reprinted by permission of the publisher.

Bulletin of Hispanic Studies, v. LI, January, 1974. © copyright 1974 Liverpool University Press. Reprinted by permission of the publisher.

The Cambridge Journal, v. IV, October, 1950-September, 1951.

The Catholic World, v. CLXXV, June, 1952.

Aaron, Daniel. From ''Sinclair Lewis, 'Main Street','' in *The American Novel: From James Fenimore Cooper to William Faulkner*. Edited by Wallace Stegner. Basic Books, 1965. Copyright © 1965 by Basic Books, Inc., Publishers. Reprinted by permission of the publisher.

Annan, Noel Gilroy. From *Leslie Stephen: His Thought and Character in Relation to His Time*. MacGibbon & Kee, 1951.

Améry, Jean. From *Radical Humanism: Selected Essays*. Edited and translated by Sidney Rosenfeld and Stella P. Rosenfeld. Indiana University Press, 1984. Copyright © 1984 by Maria Améry née Eschenauer. All rights reserved. Reprinted by permission of the publisher.

Bechhofer, C. E. From *The Literary Renaissance in America*. William Heinemann Ltd., 1923.

Bresky, Dushan. From *Cathedral or Symphony: Essays on ''Jean-Christophe.''* Lang, 1973. © Herbert Lang & Co. Ltd., Bern (Switzerland) Peter Lang Ltd., Frankfurt/M. (West-Germany) 1973. All rights reserved. Reprinted by permission of the publisher.

Brostrom, Kenneth Norman. From *The Novels of Boris Pil'njak as Allegory*. A dissertation submitted to The University of Michigan, 1973. Reprinted by permission of the author.

Browning, Gary. From *Boris Pilniak: Scythian at a Typewriter*. Ardis, 1985. © 1985 by Ardis Publishers. All rights reserved. Reprinted by permission of the publisher.

Burrell, Sidney A. From ''Sir Leslie Stephen (1832-1904),'' in *Some Modern Historians of Britain: Essays in Honor of R. L. Schuyler*. Herman Ausubel, J. Bartlet Brebner, and Erling M. Hunt, eds. The Dryden Press, 1951.

Clark, Barrett H. From ''Romain Rolland and the People's Theater,'' in *The Fourteenth of July and Danton: Two Plays of the French Revolution*. By Roman Rolland, translated by Barrett H. Clark. Henry Holt and Company, 1918.

Colum, Padraic. From *The Road Round Ireland*. Macmillan, 1926. Copyright 1926 by Macmillan Publishing Company. Renewed 1954 by Padraic Colum. Reprinted with permission of Macmillan Publishing Company.

Connolly, Joseph. From *Jerome K Jerome: A Critical Biography*. Orbis Publishing, 1982. © 1982 by Joseph Connolly. All rights reserved. Reprinted by permission of the author.

Courtney, Janet E. From *Freethinkers of the Nineteenth Century*. E. P. Dutton & Company, 1920.

Curtayne, Alice. From *Francis Ledwidge: A Life of the Poet (1887-1917)*. Martin Brian & O'Keeffe, 1972. © Alice Curtayne 1972. Reprinted by permission of the publisher.

De Vries, Peter. From an introduction to *Three Men in a Boat: To Say Nothing of the Dog*. By Jerome K. Jerome. Time-Life Books, 1964. Time Reading Program Special Edition © 1964 Time-Life Books Inc. All rights reserved. Reprinted by permission of the publisher.

Devkota, Laxmiprasad. From *Nepali Visions, Nepali Dreams: The Poetry of Laxmiprasad Devkota*. Edited and translated by David Rubin. Columbia University Press, 1980. Copyright © 1980 Columbia University Press. All rights reserved. Reprinted by permission of the publisher.

Dolmetsch, Carl Richard. From ''The Writer in America: The Strange Case of 'S. S. Van Dine','' in *Literatur und Sprache der Vereinigten Staaten: Aufsätze zu Ehren von Hans Galinsky*. Hans Helmcke, Klaus Lubbers, Renate Schmidt-v. Bardeleben, eds. Winter, 1969. © 1969, Carl Winter Universitätsverlag, Heidelberg. Reprinted by permission of the author.

Drake, William A. From *Contemporary European Writers*. The John Day Company, 1928.

Drinkwater, John. From *The Muse in Council: Being Essays on Poets and Poetry*. Houghton Mifflin Company, 1925. Copyright 1925 by John Drinkwater. Renewed 1952 by Daisy Kennedy Drinkwater. Reprinted by permission of the Literary Estate of John Drinkwater.

Dunsany, Lord. From an introduction to *Songs of the Fields*. By Francis Ledwidge. Herbert Jenkins Limited, 1916.

Edwards, Thomas R. *Imagination and Power: A Study of Poetry on Public Themes*. Oxford University Press, 1971, Chatto & Windus, 1971. © Thomas Edwards 1971. All rights reserved. Reprinted by permission of Oxford University Press, Inc. In Canada by the author and Chatto & Windus.

457

Jennings, Elizabeth. From *Every Changing Shape*. Andre Deutsch, 1961. Copyright © 1961 by Elizabeth Jennings. Reprinted by permission of the author.

Jerome, Jerome K. From *My Life and Times*. Harper & Brothers Publishers, 1926. Copyright, 1926, by Jerome K. Jerome. Renewed 1953 by Rowena Jerome. Reprinted by permission of A. P. Watt Ltd. on behalf of The Society of Authors.

Kallir, Jane. From *Alfred Kubin: Visions from the Other Side*. Galerie St. Etienne, 1983. Copyright © 1983 by Galerie St. Etienne, New York. All rights reserved. Reprinted by permission of the publisher.

Kazin, Alfred. From ''The Gift,'' in *The Inmost Leaf: A Selection of Essays*. Harcourt Brace Jovanovich, 1955. Copyright 1952, 1980 by Alfred Kazin. Reprinted by permission of Harcourt Brace Jovanovich, Inc.

Lalou, René. From *Contemporary French Literature*. Translated by William Aspenwall Bradley. Knopf, 1924. Copyright 1924 and renewed 1952 by Alfred A. Knopf, Inc. Reprinted by permission of the publisher.

Lawrence, D. H. from a preface to *The Mother*. By Grazia Deledda, translated by M. G. Steegmann. Jonathan Cape, 1928.

Lee, C. Nicholas. From *The Novels of Mark Aleksandrovič Aldanov*. Mouton, 1969. © copyright 1969 Mouton & Co., Publishers. Reprinted by permission of the author.

Lewis, Jay. From *Other Men's Minds: The Critical Writings of Jay Lewis*. Edited by Phyllis Hanson. G. P. Putnam's Sons, 1948.

Lowe, Elizabeth. From *The City in Brazilian Literature*. Fairleigh Dickinson University Press, 1982. © 1982 by Associated University Presses, Inc. Reprinted by permission of the publisher.

Lundquist, James. From *Sinclair Lewis*. Frederick Ungar Publishing Co., 1973. Copyright © 1973 by The Ungar Publishing Company. Reprinted by permission of the publisher.

Machwe, Prabhakar. From ''Introduction B,'' in *Mahakavi Laxmi Prasad Deokota*. By Paras Mani Pradhan. Bhagya Laxmi Prakashan, 1978. All rights reserved. Reprinted by permission of the publisher.

MacLeod, Sheila. From an introduction to *After the Divorce*. By Grazia Deledda, translated by Susan Ashe. Quartet Books, 1985. Introduction copyright © 1985 by Sheila MacLeod. Reprinted by permission of the publisher.

Maguire, Robert A. From *Red Virgin Soil: Soviet Literature in the 1920's*. Princeton University Press, 1968, Cornell University Press, 1987. Copyright © 1987 by Cornell University. Used by permission of the publisher, Cornell University Press.

March, Harold. From *Romain Rolland*. Twayne, 1971. Copyright 1971 by Twayne Publishers. All rights reserved. Reprinted with the permission of Twayne Publishers, a division of G. K. Hall & Co., Boston.

MacCarthy, Desmond. From *Leslie Stephen*. Cambridge at the University Press, 1937.

McFarlane, James Walter. From *Ibsen and the Temper of Norwegian Literature*. Oxford University Press, Oxford, 1960. © Oxford University Press 1960. Reprinted by permission of the publisher.

Milosz, Czeslaw. From *Emperor of the Earth: Modes of Eccentric Vision*. University of California Press, 1977. Copyright © 1977 by The Regents of the University of California. Reprinted by permission of the publisher.

Mirsky, Prince D. S. From *Contemporary Russian Literature: 1881-1925*. Alfred A. Knopf, 1926.

Moore, T. Sturge. From *Some Soldier Poets*. Grant Richards Ltd., 1919.

Nassaar, Christopher S. From *Into the Demon Universe: A Literary Exploration of Oscar Wilde*. Yale University Press, 1974. Copyright © 1974 by Yale University. All rights reserved. Reprinted by permission of the publisher.

Nayir, Yaşar Nabi. From ''Remembering Sait Faik,'' translated by Talat Sait Halman, in *A Dot on the Map: Selected Stories and Poems*. By Sait Faik, edited by Talat Sait Halman. Indiana University Turkish Studies, 1983. Copyright © 1983 by Indiana University Turkish Studies. All rights reserved. Reprinted by permission of the publisher.

Norseng, Mary K. From *Sigbjørn Obstfelder*. Twayne, 1982. Copyright 1982 by Twayne Publishers. Reprinted with the permission of Twayne Publishers, a division of G. K. Hall & Co., Boston.

Nunes, Maria Luisa. From *Lima Barreto: Bibliography and Translations*. Hall & Co., 1979. Copyright 1979 by G. K. Hall & Co. Reprinted with the permission of G. K. Hall & Co., Boston.

Nunes, Maria Luisa. From "Lima Barreto's Theory of Literature," in *From Linguistics to Literature: Romance Studies Offered to Francis M. Rogers*. Edited by Bernard H. Bichakjian. Benjamins, 1981. © copyright 1981—John Benjamins B. V. Reprinted by permission of the publisher.

Olinto, Antonio. From "A Brazilian Don Quixote," in *The Patriot*. By Lima Barreto, translated by Robert Scott-Buccleuch. Rex Collings, 1978. © Robert Scott-Buccleuch 1978. Reprinted by permission of the publisher.

Orel, Harold. From *Victorian Literary Critics: George Henry Lewes, Walter Bagehot, Richard Holt Hutton, Leslie Stephen, Andrew Lang, George Saintsbury and Edmund Gosse*. St. Martin's Press, 1984, Macmillan, 1984. © Harold Orel 1984. All rights reserved. Reprinted by permission of St. Martin's Press, Inc. In Canada by Macmillan, London and Basingstoke.

Pacifici, Sergio. From *The Modern Italian Novel: From Capuana to Tozzi*. Southern Illinois University Press, 1973. Copyright © 1973 by Southern Illinois University Press. All rights reserved. Reprinted by permission of the publisher.

Perrin, J. M. From "Her Message," in *Simone Weil: As We Knew Her*. By J. M. Perrin and G. Thibon, translated by Emma Craufurd. G. Routledge & Kegan Paul, 1953.

Pritchett, V. S. From *The Living Novel & Later Appreciations*. Revised edition. Random House, 1964. Copyright © 1975 by V. S. Pritchett. All rights reserved. Reprinted by permission of Literistic, Ltd.

Rees, Richard. From *Brave Men: A Study of D. H. Lawrence and Simone Weil*. Victor Gollancz Ltd., 1958. © Richard Rees, 1958. Reprinted by permission of the publisher.

Reilly, Alayne P. From *America in Contemporary Soviet Literature*. New York University Press, 1971. Copyright © 1971 by New York University. Reprinted by permission of the publisher.

Riley, Helene Kastinger. From "The Quest for Reason: Stefan Zweig's and Romain Rolland's Struggle for Pan-European Unity," in *Stefan Zweig: The World of Yesterday's Humanist Today*. Edited by Marion Sonnenfeld. State University of New York Press, 1983. © 1983 State University of New York. All rights reserved. Reprinted by permission of the publisher.

Roditi, Edouard. From *Oscar Wilde*. New Directions, 1947. Copyright 1947 by New Directions Publishing Corporation. Renewed 1975 by Edouard Roditi. Reprinted by permission of the publisher.

Rolland, Romain. From "Introduction to Tolstoy's Letter of October 4, 1887," in *Earth: A History*. Edited by Joseph Niver, Sr., translated by William T. Starr. KTO Press, 1977. © 1977. KTO Press. All rights reserved. Reprinted by permission of the publisher.

Roulston, Robert. From *James Norman Hall*. Twayne, 1978. Copyright 1978 by Twayne Publishers. All rights reserved. Reprinted with the permission of Twayne Publishers, a division of G. K. Hall & Co., Boston.

Rubin, David. From "Introduction: Laxmiprasad Devkota, His Life and Work and His Place in Nepali Literature," in *Nepali Visions, Nepali Dreams: The Poetry of Laxmiprasad Devkota*. By Laxmiprasad Devkota, edited and translated by David Rubin. Columbia University Press, 1980. Copyright © 1980 by Columbia University Press. All rights reserved. Reprinted by permission of the publisher.

Ruehlmann, William. From *Saint with a Gun: The Unlawful American Private Eye*. New York University Press, 1974. Copyright © 1974 by New York University. Reprinted by permission of the publisher.

Samazeuilh, Gustave. From "Romain Rolland and Music," in *Richard Strauss & Romain Rolland: Correspondence*. Edited and translated by Rollo Myers. University of California Press, 1968. Copyright © 1968 by Calder and Boyars. Reprinted by permission of the University of California Press.

Schmied, Wieland. From *Alfred Kubin*. Translated by Jean Steinberg. Pall Mall Press, 1969. Originally published as *Der Zeichner Alfred Kubin*. Residenz, 1967. Copyright 1967 by Residenz Verlag Salzburg, Austria. Reprinted by permission of Residenz Verlag.

Schorer, Mark. From an afterword to *Main Street*. By Sinclair Lewis, New American Library, 1961. Afterword copyright © 1961 by New American Library. All rights reserved. Reprinted by arrangement with New American Library, New York, N.Y.

Schuetz, Verna. From *The Bizarre Literature of Hanns Heinz Ewers, Alfred Kubin, Gustav, Meyrink, and Karl Hans Strobl*. The University of Wisconsin, 1974. Reprinted by permission of the author.

Sedgwick, Ellery. From a foreword to *Mutiny on the Bounty*. By Charles Nordhoff and James Norman Hall. Little, Brown, 1932. Copyright 1932, renewed 1960, by Little, Brown and Company. Reprinted by permission of Little, Brown and Company.

Sherman, Stuart P. From *The Significance of Sinclair Lewis*. Harcourt Brace Jovanovich, 1922.

Slonim, Marc. From *Modern Russian Literature: From Chekhov to the Present*. Oxford University Press, 1953. Copyright 1953 by Oxford University Press, Inc. Renewed 1981 by Tatiana Slonim. Reprinted by permission of the publisher.

Soloveytchik, George. From a preface to *The Naked Year*. By Boris Pilnyak, translated by Alec Brown. Payson & Clarke Ltd., 1928.

Spindler, Michael. From *American Literature and Social Change: William Dean Howells to Arthur Miller*. Indiana University Press, 1983. Copyright © 1983 by Michael Spindler. All rights reserved. Reprinted by permission of the publisher.

Stang, Richard. From *The Theory of the Novel in England: 1850-1870*. Columbia University Press, 1959.

Thibon, Gustave. From an introduction to *Gravity and Grace*. By Simone Weil, translated by Arthur Wills. Putnam's 1952. Copyright, 1952, renewed 1980, by G. P. Putnam's Sons. All rights reserved. Reprinted by permission of The Putnam Publishing Group.

Thomson, H. Douglas. From *Masters of Mystery: A Study of the Detective Story*. Wm. Collins Sons & Co. Ltd., 1931.

Trotsky, Leon. From *Literature and Revolution*. Translated by Rose Strunsky. International Publishers, 1925, University of Michigan Press, 1960. Reprinted by permission of The University of Michigan Press.

Ullmann, S. O. A. From an introduction to *Men, Books, and Mountains: Essays*. By Leslie Stephen, edited by S. O. A. Ullmann. The Hogarth Press, 1956.

Vittorini, Domenico. From *The Modern Italian Novel*. University of Pennsylvania Press, 1930.

Watkins, Floyd C. From *In Time and Place: Some Origins of American Fiction*. University of Georgia Press, 1977. Copyright © 1977 by the University of Georgia Press. All rights reserved. Reprinted by permission of the publisher.

Wellek, René. From *A History of Modern Criticism, 1750-1950: The Later Nineteenth Century*. Yale University Press, 1965. Copyright © 1965 by Yale University. All rights reserved. Reprinted by permission of the publisher.

Weygandt, Cornelius. From *The Time of Yeats: English Poetry of To-Day Against an American Background*. Appleton-Century, 1937. Copyright, 1937 by D. Appleton-Century Company, Inc. Renewed 1964 by Cornelius N. Weygandt. Reprinted by permission of the Literary Estate of Cornelius Weygandt.

Williams, Ben Ames. From "Kenneth Roberts," in *Kenneth Roberts: An American Novelist*. By Ben Ames Williams and Others. Doubleday, Doran & Company, Inc., 1938. Copyright 1938, renewed 1965, by Doubleday & Company, Inc. Reprinted by permission of the publisher.

Worth, Katharine. From *Oscar Wilde*. Macmillan, 1983, Grove Press, 1984. Copyright © 1983 by Katharine Worth. All rights reserved. Reprinted by permission of Grove Press, Inc.

Zink, David D. From *Leslie Stephen*. Twayne, 1972. Copyright 1972 by Twayne Publishers. All rights reserved. Reprinted with the permission of Twayne Publishers, a division of G. K. Hall & Co., Boston.

Cumulative Index to Authors

This index lists all author entries in the Gale Literary Criticism Series and includes cross-references to other Gale sources. For the convenience of the reader, references to the *Yearbook* in the *Contemporary Literary Criticism* series include the page number (in parentheses) after the volume number. References in the index are identified as follows:

Aiken, Conrad (Potter)
    1889-1973............CLC 1, 3, 5, 10
    See also CANR 4
    See also CA 5-8R
    See also obituary CA 45-48
    See also SATA 3, 30
    See also DLB 9, 45

Aiken, Joan (Delano) 1924- ....CLC 35
    See also CLR 1
    See also CANR 4
    See also CA 9-12R
    See also SAAS 1
    See also SATA 2, 30

Ainsworth, William Harrison
    1805-1882.................. NCLC 13
    See also SATA 24
    See also DLB 21

Ajar, Emile 1914-1980
    See Gary, Romain

Akhmatova, Anna
    1888-1966............... CLC 11, 25
    See also CAP 1
    See also CA 19-20
    See also obituary CA 25-28R

Aksakov, Sergei Timofeyvich
    1791-1859................... NCLC 2

Aksenov, Vassily (Pavlovich) 1932-
    See Aksyonor, Vasily (Pavlovich)

Aksyonov, Vasily (Pavlovich)
    1932-................... CLC 22, 37
    See also CANR 12
    See also CA 53-56

Akutagawa Ryūnosuke
    1892-1927................. TCLC 16

Alain-Fournier 1886-1914 .... TCLC 6
    See also Fournier, Henri Alban

Alarcón, Pedro Antonio de
    1833-1891................... NCLC 1

Albee, Edward (Franklin III)
    1928-..... CLC 1, 2, 3, 5, 9, 11, 13, 25
    See also CANR 8
    See also CA 5-8R
    See also DLB 7
    See also AITN 1

Alberti, Rafael 1902-..............CLC 7
    See also CA 85-88

Alcott, Amos Bronson
    1799-1888................... NCLC 1
    See also DLB 1

Alcott, Louisa May 1832-1888..... NCLC 6
    See also CLR 1
    See also YABC 1
    See also DLB 1, 42

Aldanov, Mark 1887-1957 .... TCLC 23
    See also CA 118

Aldiss, Brian W(ilson)
    1925-..................CLC 5, 14, 40
    See also CAAS 2
    See also CANR 5
    See also CA 5-8R
    See also SATA 34
    See also DLB 14

Aleichem, Sholom 1859-1916...... TCLC 1
    See also Rabinovitch, Sholem

Aleixandre, Vicente
    1898-1984................... CLC 9, 36
    See also CA 85-88
    See also obituary CA 114

Alepoudelis, Odysseus 1911-
    See Elytis, Odysseus

Alexander, Lloyd (Chudley)
    1924-.......................CLC 35
    See also CLR 1, 5
    See also CANR 1
    See also CA 1-4R
    See also SATA 3

Alger, Horatio, Jr. 1832-1899..... NCLC 8
    See also SATA 16
    See also DLB 42

Algren, Nelson
    1909-1981.............. CLC 4, 10, 33
    See also CA 13-16R
    See also obituary CA 103
    See also DLB 9
    See also DLB-Y 81, 82

Allen, Heywood 1935-
    See Allen, Woody
    See also CA 33-36R

Allen, Roland 1939-
    See Ayckbourn, Alan

Allen, Woody 1935-..............CLC 16
    See also Allen, Heywood
    See also DLB 44

Allende, Isabel 1942-........ CLC 39 (27)

Allingham, Margery (Louise)
    1904-1966...................CLC 19
    See also CANR 4
    See also CA 5-8R
    See also obituary CA 25-28R

Allston, Washington
    1779-1843.................. NCLC 2
    See also DLB 1

Almedingen, E. M. 1898-1971......CLC 12
    See also Almedingen, Martha Edith von
    See also SATA 3

Almedingen, Martha Edith von 1898-1971
    See Almedingen, E. M.
    See also CANR 1
    See also CA 1-4R

Alonso, Dámaso 1898-.............CLC 14
    See also CA 110

Alta 1942-.......................CLC 19
    See also CA 57-60

Alter, Robert B(ernard)
    1935-.................. CLC 34 (515)
    See also CANR 1
    See also CA 49-52

Alther, Lisa 1944-............. CLC 7, 41
    See also CANR 12
    See also CA 65-68

Altman, Robert 1925-.............CLC 16
    See also CA 73-76

Alvarez, A(lfred) 1929-......... CLC 5, 13
    See also CANR 3
    See also CA 1-4R
    See also DLB 14, 40

Amado, Jorge 1912- .... CLC 13, 40
    See also CA 77-80

Ambler, Eric 1909-........... CLC 4, 6, 9
    See also CANR 7
    See also CA 9-12R

Amichai, Yehuda 1924- .... CLC 9, 22
    See also CA 85-88

Amiel, Henri Frédéric
    1821-1881................... NCLC 4

Amis, Kingsley (William)
    1922-........CLC 1, 2, 3, 5, 8, 13, 40
    See also CANR 8
    See also CA 9-12R
    See also DLB 15, 27
    See also AITN 2

Amis, Martin 1949-.......... CLC 4, 9, 38
    See also CANR 8
    See also CA 65-68
    See also DLB 14

Ammons, A(rchie) R(andolph)
    1926-............ CLC 2, 3, 5, 8, 9, 25
    See also CANR 6
    See also CA 9-12R
    See also DLB 5
    See also AITN 1

Anand, Mulk Raj 1905-............CLC 23
    See also CA 65-68

Anaya, Rudolfo A(lfonso)
    1937-......................CLC 23
    See also CAAS 4
    See also CANR 1
    See also CA 45-48

Andersen, Hans Christian
    1805-1875.................. NCLC 7
    See also CLR 6
    See also YABC 1

Anderson, Jessica (Margaret Queale)
    19??-.......................CLC 37
    See also CANR 4
    See also CA 9-12R

Anderson, Jon (Victor) 1940- ......CLC 9
    See also CA 25-28R

Anderson, Lindsay 1923- ....CLC 20

Anderson, Maxwell 1888-1959 .... TCLC 2
    See also CA 105
    See also DLB 7

Anderson, Poul (William)
    1926-......................CLC 15
    See also CAAS 2
    See also CANR 2, 15
    See also CA 1-4R
    See also SATA 39
    See also DLB 8

Anderson, Robert (Woodruff)
    1917-......................CLC 23
    See also CA 21-24R
    See also DLB 7
    See also AITN 1

Anderson, Roberta Joan 1943-
    See Mitchell, Joni

Anderson, Sherwood
    1876-1941............... TCLC 1, 10
    See also CA 104
    See also DLB 4, 9
    See also DLB-DS 1

Andrade, Carlos Drummond de
    1902-......................CLC 18

Andrewes, Lancelot 1555-1626 .... LC 5

Andrews, Cicily Fairfield 1892-1983
    See West, Rebecca

Andreyev, Leonid (Nikolaevich)
    1871-1919.................. TCLC 3
    See also CA 104

Author Index

Author Index

Author Index

Author Index

De Vries, Peter
    1910-.......... CLC 1, 2, 3, 7, 10, 28
    See also CA 17-20R
    See also DLB 6
    See also DLB-Y 82

Dexter, Pete 1943-.......... CLC 34 (43)

Diamond, Neil (Leslie) 1941-.......CLC 30
    See also CA 108

Dick, Philip K(indred)
    1928-1982............... CLC 10, 30
    See also CANR 2, 16
    See also CA 49-52
    See also obituary CA 106
    See also DLB 8

Dickens, Charles 1812-1870..... NCLC 3, 8
    See also SATA 15
    See also DLB 21

Dickey, James (Lafayette)
    1923-.......... CLC 1, 2, 4, 7, 10, 15
    See also CANR 10
    See also CA 9-12R
    See also DLB 5
    See also DLB-Y 82
    See also AITN 1, 2

Dickey, William 1928-.......... CLC 3, 28
    See also CA 9-12R
    See also DLB 5

Dickinson, Peter (Malcolm de Brissac)
    1927-.................... CLC 12, 35
    See also CA 41-44R
    See also SATA 5

Didion, Joan 1934- .... CLC 1, 3, 8, 14, 32
    See also CANR 14
    See also CA 5-8R
    See also DLB 2
    See also DLB-Y 81
    See also AITN 1

Dillard, Annie 1945-...............CLC 9
    See also CANR 3
    See also CA 49-52
    See also SATA 10
    See also DLB-Y 80

Dillard, R(ichard) H(enry) W(ilde)
    1937-........................CLC 5
    See also CANR 10
    See also CA 21-24R
    See also DLB 5

Dillon, Eilís 1920- ....CLC 17
    See also CAAS 3
    See also CANR 4
    See also CA 9-12R
    See also SATA 2

Dinesen, Isak 1885-1962...... CLC 10, 29
    See also Blixen, Karen (Christentze
        Dinesen)

Disch, Thomas M(ichael)
    1940-.................... CLC 7, 36
    See also CAAS 4
    See also CANR 17
    See also CA 21-24R
    See also DLB 8

Disraeli, Benjamin 1804-1881 ..... NCLC 2
    See also DLB 21

Dixon, Paige 1911-
    See Corcoran, Barbara

Döblin, Alfred 1878-1957........ TCLC 13
    See also Doeblin, Alfred

Dobrolyubov, Nikolai Alexandrovich
    1836-1861................... NCLC 5

Dobyns, Stephen 1941-............CLC 37
    See also CANR 2, 18
    See also CA 45-48

Doctorow, E(dgar) L(aurence)
    1931-.......... CLC 6, 11, 15, 18, 37
    See also CANR 2
    See also CA 45-48
    See also DLB 2, 28
    See also DLB-Y 80
    See also AITN 2

Dodgson, Charles Lutwidge 1832-1898
    See Carroll, Lewis
    See also YABC 2

Doeblin, Alfred 1878-1957
    See also CA 110

Doerr, Harriet 1914?-....... CLC 34 (151)

Donleavy, J(ames) P(atrick)
    1926-.................CLC 1, 4, 6, 10
    See also CA 9-12R
    See also DLB 6
    See also AITN 2

Donnadieu, Marguerite 1914-
    See Duras, Marguerite

Donnell, David 1939?-....... CLC 34 (155)

Donoso, José 1924- ....CLC 4, 8, 11, 32
    See also CA 81-84

Donovan, John 1928- ....CLC 35
    See also CLR 3
    See also CA 97-100
    See also SATA 29

Doolittle, Hilda 1886-1961
    See H(ilda) D(oolittle)
    See also CA 97-100
    See also DLB 4, 45

Dorn, Ed(ward Merton)
    1929-.................... CLC 10, 18
    See also CA 93-96
    See also DLB 5

Dos Passos, John (Roderigo)
    1896-1970..... CLC 1, 4, 8, 11, 15, 25,
                            34 (419)
    See also CANR 3
    See also CA 1-4R
    See also obituary CA 29-32R
    See also DLB 4, 9
    See also DLB-DS 1

Dostoevski, Fedor Mikhailovich
    1821-1881................. NCLC 2, 7

Douglass, Frederick
    1817-1895................... NCLC 7
    See also SATA 29
    See also DLB 1, 43, 50

Dourado, (Waldomiro Freitas) Autran
    1926-........................CLC 23
    See also CA 25-28R

Dowson, Ernest (Christopher)
    1867-1900................... TCLC 4
    See also CA 105
    See also DLB 19

Doyle, (Sir) Arthur Conan
    1859-1930................... TCLC 7
    See also CA 104
    See also SATA 24
    See also DLB 18

Dr. A 1933-
    See Silverstein, Alvin and Virginia
        B(arbara Opshelor) Silverstein

Drabble, Margaret
    1939-.......... CLC 2, 3, 5, 8, 10, 22
    See also CANR 18
    See also CA 13-16R
    See also DLB 14

Dreiser, Theodore (Herman Albert)
    1871-1945............... TCLC 10, 18
    See also CA 106
    See also DLB 9, 12
    See also DLB-DS 1

Drexler, Rosalyn 1926-.......... CLC 2, 6
    See also CA 81-84

Dreyer, Carl Theodor
    1889-1968....................CLC 16
    See also obituary CA 116

Drieu La Rochelle, Pierre
    1893-1945................. TCLC 21
    See also CA 117

Droste-Hülshoff, Annette Freiin von
    1797-1848................... NCLC 3

Drummond de Andrade, Carlos 1902-
    See Andrade, Carlos Drummond de

Drury, Allen (Stuart) 1918-........CLC 37
    See also CANR 18
    See also CA 57-60

Dryden, John 1631-1700 .... LC 3

Duberman, Martin 1930-...........CLC 8
    See also CANR 2
    See also CA 1-4R

Dubie, Norman (Evans, Jr.)
    1945-........................CLC 36
    See also CANR 12
    See also CA 69-72

Du Bois, W(illiam) E(dward) B(urghardt)
    1868-1963............... CLC 1, 2, 13
    See also CA 85-88
    See also SATA 42
    See also DLB 47, 50

Dubus, André 1936- .... CLC 13, 36
    See also CANR 17
    See also CA 21-24R

Ducasse, Isidore Lucien 1846-1870
    See Lautréamont, Comte de

Duclos, Charles Pinot 1704-1772 ..... LC 1

Dudek, Louis 1918-........... CLC 11, 19
    See also CANR 1
    See also CA 45-48

Dudevant, Amandine Aurore Lucile Dupin
    1804-1876
    See Sand, George

Duerrenmatt, Friedrich 1921-
    See also CA 17-20R

Duffy, Maureen 1933-.............CLC 37
    See also CA 25-28R
    See also DLB 14

Dugan, Alan 1923-.............. CLC 2, 6
    See also CA 81-84
    See also DLB 5

Duhamel, Georges 1884-1966 ....CLC 8
    See also CA 81-84
    See also obituary CA 25-28R

Dujardin, Édouard (Émile Louis)
1861-1949 . . . . TCLC 13
See also CA 109

Duke, Raoul 1939-
See Thompson, Hunter S(tockton)

Dumas, Alexandre (*père*)
1802-1870 . . . . NCLC 11
See also SATA 18

Dumas, Alexandre (*fils*)
1824-1895 . . . . NCLC 9

Dumas, Henry (L.) 1934-1968 . . . . . . CLC 6
See also CA 85-88
See also DLB 41

Du Maurier, Daphne 1907- . . . . . CLC 6, 11
See also CANR 6
See also CA 5-8R
See also SATA 27

Dunbar, Paul Laurence
1872-1906 . . . . TCLC 2, 12
See also CA 104
See also SATA 34
See also DLB 50

Duncan (Steinmetz Arquette), Lois
1934- . . . . CLC 26
See also Arquette, Lois S(teinmetz)
See also CANR 2
See also CA 1-4R
See also SAAS 2
See also SATA 1, 36

Duncan, Robert (Edward)
1919- . . . . CLC 1, 2, 4, 7, 15, 41
See also CA 9-12R
See also DLB 5, 16

Dunlap, William 1766-1839 . . . . NCLC 2
See also DLB 30, 37

Dunn, Douglas (Eaglesham)
1942- . . . . CLC 6, 40
See also CANR 2
See also CA 45-48
See also DLB 40

Dunn, Stephen 1939- . . . . CLC 36
See also CANR 12
See also CA 33-36R

Dunne, John Gregory 1932- . . . . CLC 28
See also CANR 14
See also CA 25-28R
See also DLB-Y 80

**Dunsany, Lord (Edward John Moreton Drax
   Plunkett)** 1878-1957 . . . . TCLC 2
See also CA 104
See also DLB 10

Durang, Christopher (Ferdinand)
1949- . . . . CLC 27, 38
See also CA 105

Duras, Marguerite
1914- . . . . . . CLC 3, 6, 11, 20, 34 (161),
                                                            40
See also CA 25-28R

Durban, Pam 1947- . . . . CLC 39 (44)

Durrell, Lawrence (George)
1912- . . . . CLC 1, 4, 6, 8, 13, 27, 41
See also CA 9-12R
See also DLB 15, 27

Dürrenmatt, Friedrich
1921- . . . . CLC 1, 4, 8, 11, 15
See also Duerrenmatt, Friedrich

Dwight, Timothy 1752-1817 . . . . . . NCLC 13
See also DLB 37

Dylan, Bob 1941- . . . . CLC 3, 4, 6, 12
See also CA 41-44R
See also DLB 16

East, Michael 1916-
See West, Morris L.

Eastlake, William (Derry) 1917- . . . . . CLC 8
See also CAAS 1
See also CANR 5
See also CA 5-8R
See also DLB 6

Eberhart, Richard 1904- . . . . CLC 3, 11, 19
See also CANR 2
See also CA 1-4R
See also DLB 48

Eberstadt, Fernanda
1960- . . . . CLC 39 (48)

**Echegaray (y Eizaguirre), José (María
   Waldo)** 1832-1916 . . . . TCLC 4
See also CA 104

Eckert, Allan W. 1931- . . . . CLC 17
See also CANR 14
See also CA 13-16R
See also SATA 27, 29

Eco, Umberto 1932- . . . . CLC 28
See also CANR 12
See also CA 77-80

Eddison, E(ric) R(ucker)
1882-1945 . . . . TCLC 15
See also CA 109

Edel, Leon (Joseph)
1907- . . . . CLC 29, 34 (534)
See also CANR 1
See also CA 1-4R

Eden, Emily 1797-1869 . . . . NCLC 10

Edgar, David 1948- . . . . CLC 42
See also CANR 12
See also CA 57-60
See also DLB 13

Edgerton, Clyde 1944- . . . . CLC 39 (52)
See also CA 118

Edgeworth, Maria 1767-1849 . . . . . NCLC 1
See also SATA 21

Edmonds, Helen (Woods) 1904-1968
See Kavan, Anna
See also CA 5-8R
See also obituary CA 25-28R

Edmonds, Walter D(umaux)
1903- . . . . CLC 35
See also CANR 2
See also CA 5-8R
See also SATA 1, 27
See also DLB 9

Edson, Russell 1905- . . . . CLC 13
See also CA 33-36R

Edwards, G(erald) B(asil)
1899-1976 . . . . CLC 25
See also obituary CA 110

Ehle, John (Marsden, Jr.)
1925- . . . . CLC 27
See also CA 9-12R

Ehrenbourg, Ilya (Grigoryevich) 1891-1967
See Ehrenburg, Ilya (Grigoryevich)

Ehrenburg, Ilya (Grigoryevich)
1891-1967 . . . . CLC 18, 34 (433)
See also CA 102
See also obituary CA 25-28R

Eich, Guenter 1907-1971
See also CA 111
See also obituary CA 93-96

Eich, Günter 1907-1971 . . . . CLC 15
See also Eich, Guenter

Eichendorff, Joseph Freiherr von
1788-1857 . . . . NCLC 8

Eigner, Larry 1927- . . . . CLC 9
See also Eigner, Laurence (Joel)
See also DLB 5

Eigner, Laurence (Joel) 1927-
See Eigner, Larry
See also CANR 6
See also CA 9-12R

Eiseley, Loren (Corey)
1907-1977 . . . . CLC 7
See also CANR 6
See also CA 1-4R
See also obituary CA 73-76

Ekeloef, Gunnar (Bengt) 1907-1968
See Ekelöf, Gunnar (Bengt)
See also obituary CA 25-28R

Ekelöf, Gunnar (Bengt)
1907-1968 . . . . CLC 27
See also Ekeloef, Gunnar (Bengt)

Ekwensi, Cyprian (Odiatu Duaka)
1921- . . . . CLC 4
See also CANR 18
See also CA 29-32R

Eliade, Mircea 1907- . . . . CLC 19
See also CA 65-68

Eliot, George 1819-1880 . . . . NCLC 4, 13
See also DLB 21, 35

Eliot, John 1604-1690 . . . . LC 5
See also DLB 24

Eliot, T(homas) S(tearns)
1888-1965 . . . . CLC 1, 2, 3, 6, 9, 10,
                                    13, 15, 24, 34 (387; 523), 41
See also CA 5-8R
See also obituary CA 25-28R
See also DLB 7, 10, 45

Elkin, Stanley (Lawrence)
1930- . . . . CLC 4, 6, 9, 14, 27
See also CANR 8
See also CA 9-12R
See also DLB 2, 28
See also DLB-Y 80

Elledge, Scott 19??- . . . . CLC 34 (425)

Elliott, George P(aul)
1918-1980 . . . . CLC 2
See also CANR 2
See also CA 1-4R
See also obituary CA 97-100

Elliott, Sumner Locke 1917- . . . . CLC 38
See also CANR 2
See also CA 5-8R

Ellis, A. E. 19??- . . . . CLC 7

Ellis, Alice Thomas 19??- . . . . CLC 40

Ellis, Bret Easton 1964- . . . . . . CLC 39 (55)
See also CA 118

Garrett, George (Palmer)
1929-.....................CLC 3, 11
See also CANR 1
See also CA 1-4R
See also DLB 2, 5
See also DLB-Y 83

Garrigue, Jean 1914-1972 .... CLC 2, 8
See also CA 5-8R
See also obituary CA 37-40R

Gary, Romain 1914-1980..........CLC 25
See also Kacew, Romain

Gascar, Pierre 1916-..............CLC 11
See also Fournier, Pierre

Gaskell, Elizabeth Cleghorn
1810-1865...................NCLC 5
See also DLB 21

Gass, William H(oward)
1924-.....CLC 1, 2, 8, 11, 15, 39 (477)
See also CA 17-20R
See also DLB 2

Gautier, Théophile 1811-1872..... NCLC 1

Gaye, Marvin (Pentz)
1939-1984...................CLC 26
See also obituary CA 112

Gébler, Carlo (Ernest)
1954-.................... CLC 39 (60)

Gee, Maurice (Gough) 1931-.......CLC 29
See also CA 97-100

Gelbart, Larry (Simon) 1923-......CLC 21
See also CA 73-76

Gelber, Jack 1932- .... CLC 1, 6, 14
See also CANR 2
See also CA 1-4R
See also DLB 7

Gellhorn, Martha (Ellis) 1908- .....CLC 14
See also CA 77-80
See also DLB-Y 82

Genet, Jean 1910- ..... CLC 1, 2, 5, 10, 14
See also CA 13-16R

Gent, Peter 1942-..................CLC 29
See also CA 89-92
See also DLB-Y 82
See also AITN 1

George, Jean Craighead 1919- .....CLC 35
See also CLR 1
See also CA 5-8R
See also SATA 2

George, Stefan (Anton)
1868-1933............... TCLC 2, 14
See also CA 104

Gerhardi, William (Alexander) 1895-1977
See Gerhardie, William (Alexander)

Gerhardie, William (Alexander)
1895-1977...................CLC 5
See also CANR 18
See also CA 25-28R
See also obituary CA 73-76
See also DLB 36

Gertler, T(rudy) 1946?- ...... CLC 34 (49)
See also CA 116

Gessner, Friedrike Victoria 1910-1980
See Adamson, Joy(-Friederike Victoria)

Ghelderode, Michel de
1898-1962................ CLC 6, 11
See also CA 85-88

Ghiselin, Brewster 1903- ....CLC 23
See also CANR 13
See also CA 13-16R

Ghose, Zulfikar 1935-.............CLC 42
See also CA 65-68

Giacosa, Giuseppe 1847-1906 ..... TCLC 7
See also CA 104

Gibbon, Lewis Grassic
1901-1935................... TCLC 4
See also Mitchell, James Leslie

Gibran, (Gibran) Kahlil
1883-1931................ TCLC 1, 9
See also CA 104

Gibson, William 1914- ....CLC 23
See also CANR 9
See also CA 9-12R
See also DLB 7

Gibson, William 1948- ...... CLC 39 (139)

Gide, André (Paul Guillaume)
1869-1951..............TCLC 5, 12
See also CA 104

Gifford, Barry (Colby)
1946-.................. CLC 34 (457)
See also CANR 9
See also CA 65-68

Gilbert, (Sir) W(illiam) S(chwenck)
1836-1911................... TCLC 3
See also CA 104
See also SATA 36

Gilbreth, Ernestine 1908-
See Carey, Ernestine Gilbreth

Gilbreth, Frank B(unker), Jr. 1911-
See Gilbreth, Frank B(unker), Jr. and
Carey, Ernestine Gilbreth
See also CA 9-12R
See also SATA 2

Gilbreth, Frank B(unker), Jr. 1911- and
Carey, Ernestine Gilbreth
1908-.......................CLC 17

Gilchrist, Ellen 1935- .... CLC 34 (164)
See also CA 113, 116

Giles, Molly 1942- .... CLC 39 (64)

Gilliam, Terry (Vance) 1940-
See Monty Python
See also CA 108, 113

Gilliatt, Penelope (Ann Douglass)
1932-.................. CLC 2, 10, 13
See also CA 13-16R
See also DLB 14
See also AITN 2

Gilman, Charlotte (Anna) Perkins (Stetson)
1860-1935.................. TCLC 9
See also CA 106

Gilmour, David 1944-
See Pink Floyd

Gilroy, Frank D(aniel) 1925-........CLC 2
See also CA 81-84
See also DLB 7

Ginsberg, Allen
1926-.........CLC 1, 2, 3, 4, 6, 13, 36
See also CANR 2
See also CA 1-4R
See also DLB 5, 16
See also AITN 1

Ginzburg, Natalia 1916-........ CLC 5, 11
See also CA 85-88

Ghiselin, Brewster — (header col 3)

Giono, Jean 1895-1970......... CLC 4, 11
See also CANR 2
See also CA 45-48
See also obituary CA 29-32R

Giovanni, Nikki 1943-........ CLC 2, 4, 19
See also CLR 6
See also CANR 18
See also CA 29-32R
See also SATA 24
See also DLB 5
See also AITN 1

Giovene, Andrea 1904-.............CLC 7
See also CA 85-88

Gippius, Zinaida (Nikolayevna) 1869-1945
See also Hippius, Zinaida
See also CA 106

Giraudoux, (Hippolyte) Jean
1882-1944................. TCLC 2, 7
See also CA 104

Gironella, José María 1917-........CLC 11
See also CA 101

Gissing, George (Robert)
1857-1903................... TCLC 3
See also CA 105
See also DLB 18

Glanville, Brian (Lester) 1931- ......CLC 6
See also CANR 3
See also CA 5-8R
See also DLB 15
See also SATA 42

Glasgow, Ellen (Anderson Gholson)
1873?-1945............... TCLC 2, 7
See also CA 104
See also DLB 9, 12

Glassco, John 1909-1981 ....CLC 9
See also CANR 15
See also CA 13-16R
See also obituary CA 102

Glasser, Ronald J. 1940?- ....CLC 37

Glissant, Édouard 1928-...........CLC 10

Gloag, Julian 1930-...............CLC 40
See also CANR 10
See also CA 65-68
See also AITN 1

Glück, Louise 1943- .... CLC 7, 22
See also CA 33-36R
See also DLB 5

Godard, Jean-Luc 1930-...........CLC 20
See also CA 93-96

Godwin, Gail 1937-.......CLC 5, 8, 22, 31
See also CANR 15
See also CA 29-32R
See also DLB 6

Godwin, William 1756-1836 ..... NCLC 14
See also DLB 39

Goethe, Johann Wolfgang von
1749-1832.................. NCLC 4

Gogarty, Oliver St. John
1878-1957................. TCLC 15
See also CA 109
See also DLB 15, 19

Gogol, Nikolai (Vasilyevich)
1809-1852.................. NCLC 5

Gökçeli, Yasar Kemal 1923-
See Kemal, Yashar

Greene, Graham (Henry)
1904-....... CLC **1, 3, 6, 9, 14, 18, 27,**
37
See also CA 13-16R
See also SATA 20
See also DLB 13, 15
See also DLB-Y 85
See also AITN 2

Gregor, Arthur 1923-..............CLC **9**
See also CANR 11
See also CA 25-28R
See also SATA 36

Gregory, Lady (Isabella Augusta Persse)
1852-1932.................. TCLC **1**
See also CA 104
See also DLB 10

Grendon, Stephen 1909-1971
See Derleth, August (William)

Greve, Felix Paul Berthold Friedrich
1879-1948

Grey, (Pearl) Zane
1872?-1939................. TCLC **6**
See also CA 104
See also DLB 9

Grieg, (Johan) Nordahl (Brun)
1902-1943................. TCLC **10**
See also CA 107

Grieve, C(hristopher) M(urray) 1892-1978
See MacDiarmid, Hugh
See also CA 5-8R
See also obituary CA 85-88

Griffin, Gerald 1803-1840 .... NCLC **7**

Griffin, Peter 1942-......... CLC **39** (398)

Griffiths, Trevor 1935-............CLC **13**
See also CA 97-100
See also DLB 13

Grigson, Geoffrey (Edward Harvey)
1905-1985........... CLC **7, 39** (330)
See also CA 25-28R
See also obituary CA 118
See also DLB 27

Grillparzer, Franz 1791-1872 ..... NCLC **1**

Grimm, Jakob (Ludwig) Karl 1785-1863
See Grimm, Jakob (Ludwig) Karl and
Grimm, Wilhelm Karl

Grimm, Jakob (Ludwig) Karl 1785-1863
and **Grimm, Wilhelm Karl**
1786-1859.................. NCLC **3**
See also SATA 22

Grimm, Wilhelm Karl 1786-1859
See Grimm, Jakob (Ludwig) Karl and
Grimm, Wilhelm Karl

Grimm, Wilhelm Karl 1786-1859 and
Grimm, Jakob (Ludwig) Karl
1785-1863
See Grimm, Jakob (Ludwig) Karl and
Grimm, Wilhelm Karl

Grindel, Eugene 1895-1952
See also CA 104

Grossman, Vasily (Semënovich)
1905-1964....................CLC **41**

Grove, Frederick Philip
1879-1948................. TCLC **4**
See also Greve, Felix Paul Berthold
Friedrich

Grumbach, Doris (Isaac)
1918-.................... CLC **13, 22**
See also CAAS 2
See also CANR 9
See also CA 5-8R

Grundtvig, Nicolai Frederik Severin
1783-1872.................. NCLC **1**

Guare, John 1938-......... CLC **8, 14, 29**
See also CA 73-76
See also DLB 7

Gudjonsson, Halldór Kiljan 1902-
See Laxness, Halldór (Kiljan)
See also CA 103

Guest, Barbara 1920- .... CLC **34** (441)
See also CANR 11
See also CA 25-28R
See also DLB 5

Guest, Judith (Ann) 1936-...... CLC **8, 30**
See also CANR 15
See also CA 77-80

Guild, Nicholas M. 1944-.........CLC **33**
See also CA 93-96

Guillén, Jorge 1893-1984.........CLC **11**
See also CA 89-92
See also obituary CA 112

Guillevic, (Eugène) 1907-.........CLC **33**
See also CA 93-96

Gunn, Bill 1934- ....CLC **5**
See also Gunn, William Harrison
See also DLB 38

Gunn, Thom(son William)
1929-...................CLC **3, 6, 18, 32**
See also CANR 9
See also CA 17-20R
See also DLB 27

Gunn, William Harrison 1934-
See Gunn, Bill
See also CANR 12
See also CA 13-16R
See also AITN 1

Gurney, A(lbert) R(amsdell), Jr.
1930-.......................CLC **32**
See also CA 77-80

Gustafson, Ralph (Barker)
1909-.......................CLC **36**
See also CANR 8
See also CA 21-24R

Guthrie, A(lfred) B(ertram), Jr.
1901-.......................CLC **23**
See also CA 57-60
See also DLB 6

Guthrie, Woodrow Wilson 1912-1967
See Guthrie, Woody
See also CA 113
See also obituary CA 93-96

Guthrie, Woody 1912-1967 ....CLC **35**
See also Guthrie, Woodrow Wilson

Guy, Rosa (Cuthbert) 1928-........CLC **26**
See also CANR 14
See also CA 17-20R
See also SATA 14
See also DLB 33

Haavikko, Paavo (Juhani)
1931-............. CLC **18, 34** (167)
See also CA 106

Hacker, Marilyn 1942-....... CLC **5, 9, 23**
See also CA 77-80

Haggard, (Sir) H(enry) Rider
1856-1925................. TCLC **11**
See also CA 108
See also SATA 16

Haig-Brown, Roderick L(angmere)
1908-1976....................CLC **21**
See also CANR 4
See also CA 5-8R
See also obituary CA 69-72
See also SATA 12

Hailey, Arthur 1920-................CLC **5**
See also CANR 2
See also CA 1-4R
See also DLB-Y 82
See also AITN 2

Hailey, Elizabeth Forsythe
1938-......................CLC **40**
See also CAAS 1
See also CANR 15
See also CA 93-96

Haley, Alex (Palmer) 1921- ..... CLC **8, 12**
See also CA 77-80
See also DLB 38

Hall, Donald (Andrew, Jr.)
1928-.................. CLC **1, 13, 37**
See also CANR 2
See also CA 5-8R
See also SATA 23
See also DLB 5

Hall, James Norman
1887-1951................. TCLC **23**
See also SATA 21

Hall, (Marguerite) Radclyffe
1886-1943................. TCLC **12**
See also CA 110

Halpern, Daniel 1945-.............CLC **14**
See also CA 33-36R

Hamburger, Michael (Peter Leopold)
1924-..................... CLC **5, 14**
See also CAAS 4
See also CANR 2
See also CA 5-8R
See also DLB 27

Hamill, Pete 1935-................CLC **10**
See also CANR 18
See also CA 25-28R

Hamilton, Edmond 1904-1977.......CLC **1**
See also CANR 3
See also CA 1-4R
See also DLB 8

Hamilton, Gail 1911-
See Corcoran, Barbara

Hamilton, Mollie 1909?-
See Kaye, M(ary) M(argaret)

Hamilton, Virginia (Esther)
1936-......................CLC **26**
See also CLR 1, 11
See also CA 25-28R
See also SATA 4
See also DLB 33

Hammett, (Samuel) Dashiell
1894-1961...........CLC **3, 5, 10, 19**
See also CA 81-84
See also AITN 1

Hammon, Jupiter
1711?-1800?................. NCLC **5**
See also DLB 31, 50

Author Index

Author Index

McCaffrey, Anne 1926- ....CLC 17
  See also CANR 15
  See also CA 25-28R
  See also SATA 8
  See also DLB 8
  See also AITN 2

McCarthy, Cormac 1933-..........CLC 4
  See also CANR 10
  See also CA 13-16R
  See also DLB 6

McCarthy, Mary (Therese)
  1912-.....CLC 1, 3, 5, 14, 24, 39 (484)
  See also CANR 16
  See also CA 5-8R
  See also DLB 2
  See also DLB-Y 81

McCartney, (James) Paul
  1942-.......................CLC 35
  See also Lennon, John (Ono) and
    McCartney, Paul

McClure, Michael 1932-........ CLC 6, 10
  See also CANR 17
  See also CA 21-24R
  See also DLB 16

McCourt, James 1941-.............CLC 5
  See also CA 57-60

McCrae, John 1872-1918........ TCLC 12
  See also CA 109

McCullers, (Lula) Carson
  1917-1967...........CLC 1, 4, 10, 12
  See also CANR 18
  See also CA 5-8R
  See also obituary CA 25-28R
  See also SATA 27
  See also DLB 2, 7

McCullough, Colleen 1938?- ....CLC 27
  See also CANR 17
  See also CA 81-84

McElroy, Joseph 1930-.............CLC 5
  See also CA 17-20R

McEwan, Ian 1948-...............CLC 13
  See also CA 61-64
  See also DLB 14

McGahern, John 1935-.......... CLC 5, 9
  See also CA 17-20R
  See also DLB 14

McGinley, Patrick 1937-..........CLC 41

McGinley, Phyllis 1905-1978......CLC 14
  See also CA 9-12R
  See also obituary CA 77-80
  See also SATA 2, 44
  See also obituary SATA 24
  See also DLB 11

McGinniss, Joe 1942- ....CLC 32
  See also CA 25-28R
  See also AITN 2

McGivern, Maureen Daly 1921-
  See Daly, Maureen
  See also CA 9-12R

McGrath, Thomas 1916- ....CLC 28
  See also CANR 6
  See also CA 9-12R
  See also SATA 41

McGuane, Thomas (Francis III)
  1939-................... CLC 3, 7, 18
  See also CANR 5
  See also CA 49-52
  See also DLB 2
  See also DLB-Y 80
  See also AITN 2

McHale, Tom 1941-1982 .... CLC 3, 5
  See also CA 77-80
  See also obituary CA 106
  See also AITN 1

McIlvanney, William 1936- ....CLC 42
  See also CA 25-28R
  See also DLB 14

McIlwraith, Maureen Mollie Hunter 1922-
  See Hunter, Mollie
  See also CA 29-32R
  See also SATA 2

McInerney, Jay 1955-........ CLC 34 (81)
  See also CA 116

McIntyre, Vonda N(eel) 1948-......CLC 18
  See also CA 81-84

McKay, Claude 1890-1948........ TCLC 7
  See also CA 104
  See also DLB 4, 45

McKuen, Rod 1933- .... CLC 1, 3
  See also CA 41-44R
  See also AITN 1

McLuhan, (Herbert) Marshall
  1911-1980...................CLC 37
  See also CANR 12
  See also CA 9-12R
  See also obituary CA 102

McManus, Declan Patrick 1955-
  See Costello, Elvis

McMurtry, Larry (Jeff)
  1936-............. CLC 2, 3, 7, 11, 27
  See also CA 5-8R
  See also DLB 2
  See also DLB-Y 80
  See also AITN 2

McNally, Terrence 1939- ..... CLC 4, 7, 41
  See also CANR 2
  See also CA 45-48
  See also DLB 7

McPhee, John 1931- ....CLC 36
  See also CA 65-68

McPherson, James Alan 1943- .....CLC 19
  See also CA 25-28R
  See also DLB 38

McPherson, William
  1939-................. CLC 34 (85)
  See also CA 57-60

McSweeney, Kerry 19??- .... CLC 34 (579)

Mead, Margaret 1901-1978........CLC 37
  See also CANR 4
  See also CA 1-4R
  See also obituary CA 81-84
  See also SATA 20
  See also AITN 1

Meaker, M. J. 1927-
  See Kerr, M. E.
  See Meaker, Marijane

Meaker, Marijane 1927-
  See Kerr, M. E.
  See also CA 107
  See also SATA 20

Medoff, Mark (Howard)
  1940-..................... CLC 6, 23
  See also CANR 5
  See also CA 53-56
  See also DLB 7
  See also AITN 1

Megged, Aharon 1920-.............CLC 9
  See also CANR 1
  See also CA 49-52

Mehta, Ved (Parkash) 1934- ....CLC 37
  See also CANR 2
  See also CA 1-4R

Mellor, John 1953?-
  See The Clash

Meltzer, Milton 1915-.............CLC 26
  See also CA 13-16R
  See also SAAS 1
  See also SATA 1

Melville, Herman
  1819-1891................ NCLC 3, 12
  See also DLB 3

Mencken, H(enry) L(ouis)
  1880-1956.................. TCLC 13
  See also CA 105
  See also DLB 11, 29

Mercer, David 1928-1980...........CLC 5
  See also CA 9-12R
  See also obituary CA 102
  See also DLB 13

Meredith, George 1828-1909..... TCLC 17
  See also DLB 18, 35

Meredith, William (Morris)
  1919-.................. CLC 4, 13, 22
  See also CANR 6
  See also CA 9-12R
  See also DLB 5

Mérimée, Prosper 1803-1870...... NCLC 6

Merrill, James (Ingram)
  1926-.......... CLC 2, 3, 6, 8, 13, 18,
                    34 (225)
  See also CANR 10
  See also CA 13-16R
  See also DLB 5
  See also DLB-Y 85

Merton, Thomas (James)
  1915-1968.... CLC 1, 3, 11, 34 (460)
  See also CA 5-8R
  See also obituary CA 25-28R
  See also DLB 48
  See also DLB-Y 81

Merwin, W(illiam) S(tanley)
  1927-.........CLC 1, 2, 3, 5, 8, 13, 18
  See also CANR 15
  See also CA 13-16R
  See also DLB 5

Metcalf, John 1938-...............CLC 37
  See also CA 113

Mew, Charlotte (Mary)
  1870-1928................... TCLC 8
  See also CA 105
  See also DLB 19

Mewshaw, Michael 1943-..........CLC 9
  See also CANR 7
  See also CA 53-56
  See also DLB-Y 80

Meyer-Meyrink, Gustav 1868-1932
  See Meyrink, Gustav
  See also CA 117

Neufeld, John (Arthur) 1938- ......CLC 17
  See also CANR 11
  See also CA 25-28R
  See also SATA 6

Neville, Emily Cheney 1919- ....CLC 12
  See also CANR 3
  See also CA 5-8R
  See also SAAS 2
  See also SATA 1

Newbound, Bernard Slade 1930-
  See Slade, Bernard
  See also CA 81-84

Newby, P(ercy) H(oward)
  1918- .... CLC 2, 13
  See also CA 5-8R
  See also DLB 15

Newlove, Donald 1928-.............CLC 6
  See also CA 29-32R

Newlove, John (Herbert) 1938- .....CLC 14
  See also CANR 9
  See also CA 21-24R

Newman, Charles 1938- .... CLC 2, 8
  See also CA 21-24R

Newman, Edwin (Harold)
  1919- ....CLC 14
  See also CANR 5
  See also CA 69-72
  See also AITN 1

Newton, Suzanne 1936-............CLC 35
  See also CANR 14
  See also CA 41-44R
  See also SATA 5

Ngugi, James (Thiong'o)
  1938- ....CLC 3, 7, 13, 36
  See also Ngugi wa Thiong'o
  See also Wa Thiong'o, Ngugi
  See also CA 81-84

Ngugi wa Thiong'o
  1938- ....CLC 3, 7, 13, 36
  See also Ngugi, James (Thiong'o)
  See also Wa Thiong'o, Ngugi

Nichol, B(arrie) P(hillip) 1944- .....CLC 18
  See also CA 53-56
  See also DLB 53

Nichols, John (Treadwell)
  1940-........................CLC 38
  See also CANR 6
  See also CA 9-12R
  See also DLB-Y 82

Nichols, Peter (Richard)
  1927-...................... CLC 5, 36
  See also CA 104
  See also DLB 13

Nicolas, F.R.E. 1927-
  See Freeling, Nicolas

Niedecker, Lorine
  1903-1970............... CLC 10, 42
  See also CAP 2
  See also CA 25-28
  See also DLB 48

Nietzsche, Friedrich (Wilhelm)
  1844-1900.............. TCLC 10, 18
  See also CA 107

Nightingale, Anne Redmon 1943-
  See Redmon (Nightingale), Anne
  See also CA 103

Nin, Anaïs
  1903-1977......... CLC 1, 4, 8, 11, 14
  See also CA 13-16R
  See also obituary CA 69-72
  See also DLB 2, 4
  See also AITN 2

Nissenson, Hugh 1933- .... CLC 4, 9
  See also CA 17-20R
  See also DLB 28

Niven, Larry 1938-...............CLC 8
  See also Niven, Laurence Van Cott
  See also DLB 8

Niven, Laurence Van Cott 1938-
  See Niven, Larry
  See also CANR 14
  See also CA 21-24R

Nixon, Agnes Eckhardt 1927- ......CLC 21
  See also CA 110

Nordhoff, Charles 1887-1947..... TCLC 23
  See also CA 108
  See also SATA 23
  See also DLB 9

Norman, Marsha 1947-............CLC 28
  See also CA 105
  See also DLB-Y 84

Norris, Leslie 1921-..............CLC 14
  See also CANR 14
  See also CAP 1
  See also CA 11-12
  See also DLB 27

North, Andrew 1912-
  See Norton, Andre

North, Christopher 1785-1854
  See Wilson, John

Norton, Alice Mary 1912-
  See Norton, Andre
  See also CANR 2
  See also CA 1-4R
  See also SATA 1, 43

Norton, Andre 1912-..............CLC 12
  See also Norton, Mary Alice
  See also DLB 8

Norway, Nevil Shute 1899-1960
  See Shute (Norway), Nevil
  See also CA 102
  See also obituary CA 93-96

Nossack, Hans Erich 1901-1978 .....CLC 6
  See also CA 93-96
  See also obituary CA 85-88

Nova, Craig 1945-............. CLC 7, 31
  See also CANR 2
  See also CA 45-48

Novalis 1772-1801 .... NCLC 13

Nowlan, Alden (Albert) 1933-......CLC 15
  See also CANR 5
  See also CA 9-12R
  See also DLB 53

Noyes, Alfred 1880-1958 .... TCLC 7
  See also CA 104
  See also DLB 20

Nunn, Kem 19??-............ CLC 34 (94)

Nye, Robert 1939-............ CLC 13, 42
  See also CA 33-36R
  See also SATA 6
  See also DLB 14

Nyro, Laura 1947-...............CLC 17

Oates, Joyce Carol
  1938-.....CLC 1, 2, 3, 6, 9, 11, 15, 19,
                                      33
  See also CA 5-8R
  See also DLB 2, 5
  See also DLB-Y 81
  See also AITN 1

O'Brien, Darcy 1939-.............CLC 11
  See also CANR 8
  See also CA 21-24R

O'Brien, Edna
  1932-............. CLC 3, 5, 8, 13, 36
  See also CANR 6
  See also CA 1-4R
  See also DLB 14

O'Brien, Flann
  1911-1966......... CLC 1, 4, 5, 7, 10
  See also O Nuallain, Brian

O'Brien, Richard 19??-............CLC 17

O'Brien, (William) Tim(othy)
  1946-................. CLC 7, 19, 40
  See also CA 85-88
  See also DLB-Y 80

Obstfelder, Sigbjørn
  1866-1900................. TCLC 23

O'Casey, Sean
  1880-1964......... CLC 1, 5, 9, 11, 15
  See also CA 89-92
  See also DLB 10

Ochs, Phil 1940-1976 ....CLC 17
  See also obituary CA 65-68

O'Connor, Edwin (Greene)
  1918-1968....................CLC 14
  See also CA 93-96
  See also obituary CA 25-28R

O'Connor, (Mary) Flannery
  1925-1964...... CLC 1, 2, 3, 6, 10, 13,
                                   15, 21
  See also CANR 3
  See also CA 1-4R
  See also DLB 2
  See also DLB-Y 80

O'Connor, Frank
  1903-1966............... CLC 14, 23
  See also O'Donovan, Michael (John)

O'Dell, Scott 1903- ....CLC 30
  See also CLR 1
  See also CANR 12
  See also CA 61-64
  See also SATA 12

Odets, Clifford 1906-1963 ...... CLC 2, 28
  See also CA 85-88
  See also DLB 7, 26

O'Donovan, Michael (John) 1903-1966
  See O'Connor, Frank
  See also CA 93-96

Ōe, Kenzaburō 1935- .... CLC 10, 36
  See also CA 97-100

O'Faolain, Julia 1932- .... CLC 6, 19
  See also CAAS 2
  See also CANR 12
  See also CA 81-84
  See also DLB 14

O'Faoláin, Seán
  1900-................CLC 1, 7, 14, 32
  See also CANR 12
  See also CA 61-64
  See also DLB 15

Quasimodo, Salvatore
  1901-1968....................CLC 10
  See also CAP 1
  See also CA 15-16
  See also obituary CA 25-28R

Queen, Ellery 1905-1982 .... CLC 3, 11
  See also Dannay, Frederic
  See also Lee, Manfred B(ennington)

Queneau, Raymond
  1903-1976...........CLC 2, 5, 10, 42
  See also CA 77-80
  See also obituary CA 69-72

Quin, Ann (Marie) 1936-1973.......CLC 6
  See also CA 9-12R
  See also obituary CA 45-48
  See also DLB 14

Quinn, Simon 1942-
  See Smith, Martin Cruz

Quiroga, Horatio (Sylvestre)
  1878-1937................. TCLC 20
  See also CA 117

Quoirez, Françoise 1935-
  See Sagan, Françoise
  See also CANR 6
  See also CA 49-52

Rabelais, François 1494?-1553 .... LC 5

Rabe, David (William)
  1940-...................CLC 4, 8, 33
  See also CA 85-88
  See also DLB 7

Rabinovitch, Sholem 1859-1916
  See Aleichem, Sholom
  See also CA 104

Radcliffe, Ann (Ward)
  1764-1823................... NCLC 6
  See also DLB 39

Radnóti, Miklós 1909-1944 ...... TCLC 16
  See also CA 118

Rado, James 1939-
  See Ragni, Gerome and
    Rado, James
  See also CA 105

Radomski, James 1932-
  See Rado, James

Radvanyi, Netty Reiling 1900-1983
  See Seghers, Anna
  See also CA 85-88
  See also obituary CA 110

Raeburn, John 1941-........ CLC 34 (477)
  See also CA 57-60

Ragni, Gerome 1942-
  See Ragni, Gerome and Rado, James
  See also CA 105

Ragni, Gerome 1942- and
    Rado, James 1939-...........CLC 17

Rahv, Philip 1908-1973 ....CLC 24
  See also Greenberg, Ivan

Raine, Craig 1944- ....CLC 32
  See also CA 108
  See also DLB 40

Raine, Kathleen (Jessie) 1908-.......CLC 7
  See also CA 85-88
  See also DLB 20

Rand, Ayn 1905-1982......... CLC 3, 30
  See also CA 13-16R
  See also obituary CA 105

Randall, Dudley (Felker) 1914-......CLC 1
  See also CA 25-28R
  See also DLB 41

Ransom, John Crowe
  1888-1974......... CLC 2, 4, 5, 11, 24
  See also CANR 6
  See also CA 5-8R
  See also obituary CA 49-52
  See also DLB 45

Rao, Raja 1909-..................CLC 25
  See also CA 73-76

Raphael, Frederic (Michael)
  1931-.................... CLC 2, 14
  See also CANR 1
  See also CA 1-4R
  See also DLB 14

Rathbone, Julian 1935-...........CLC 41
  See also CA 101

Rattigan, Terence (Mervyn)
  1911-1977...................CLC 7
  See also CA 85-88
  See also obituary CA 73-76
  See also DLB 13

Raven, Simon (Arthur Noel)
  1927-....................CLC 14
  See also CA 81-84

Rawlings, Marjorie Kinnan
  1896-1953................. TCLC 4
  See also CA 104
  See also YABC 1
  See also DLB 9, 22

Ray, Satyajit 1921- ....CLC 16

Read, Herbert (Edward)
  1893-1968....................CLC 4
  See also CA 85-88
  See also obituary CA 25-28R
  See also DLB 20

Read, Piers Paul 1941-...... CLC 4, 10, 25
  See also CA 21-24R
  See also SATA 21
  See also DLB 14

Reade, Charles 1814-1884 .... NCLC 2
  See also DLB 21

Reade, Hamish 1936-
  See Gray, Simon (James Holliday)

Reaney, James 1926-.............CLC 13
  See also CA 41-44R
  See also SATA 43

Rechy, John (Francisco)
  1934-................CLC 1, 7, 14, 18
  See also CAAS 4
  See also CANR 6
  See also CA 5-8R
  See also DLB-Y 82

Redgrove, Peter (William)
  1932-.................... CLC 6, 41
  See also CANR 3
  See also CA 1-4R
  See also DLB 40

Redmon (Nightingale), Anne
  1943-....................CLC 22
  See also Nightingale, Anne Redmon

Reed, Ishmael
  1938-.......... CLC 2, 3, 5, 6, 13, 32
  See also CA 21-24R
  See also DLB 2, 5, 33

Reed, John (Silas) 1887-1920...... TCLC 9
  See also CA 106

Reed, Lou 1944-..................CLC 21

Reid, Christopher 1949-...........CLC 33
  See also DLB 40

Reid Banks, Lynne 1929-
  See Banks, Lynne Reid
  See also CANR 6
  See also CA 1-4R
  See also SATA 22

Reiner, Max 1900-
  See Caldwell, (Janet Miriam) Taylor
    (Holland)

Remark, Erich Paul 1898-1970
  See Remarque, Erich Maria

Remarque, Erich Maria
  1898-1970....................CLC 21
  See also CA 77-80
  See also obituary CA 29-32R

Renard, Jules 1864-1910 .... TCLC 17

Renault, Mary
  1905-1983.............. CLC 3, 11, 17
  See also Challans, Mary
  See also DLB-Y 83

Rendell, Ruth 1930- ....CLC 28
  See also CA 109

Renoir, Jean 1894-1979 ....CLC 20
  See also obituary CA 85-88

Resnais, Alain 1922- ....CLC 16

Rexroth, Kenneth
  1905-1982....... CLC 1, 2, 6, 11, 22
  See also CA 5-8R
  See also obituary CA 107
  See also DLB 16, 48
  See also DLB-Y 82

Reyes y Basoalto, Ricardo Eliecer Neftali
  1904-1973
  See Neruda, Pablo

Reymont, Wladyslaw Stanislaw
  1867-1925................... TCLC 5
  See also CA 104

Reynolds, Jonathan 1942?- ..... CLC 6, 38
  See also CA 65-68

Reznikoff, Charles 1894-1976.......CLC 9
  See also CAP 2
  See also CA 33-36
  See also obituary CA 61-64
  See also DLB 28, 45

Rezzori, Gregor von 1914-.........CLC 25

Rhys, Jean
  1894-1979........ CLC 2, 4, 6, 14, 19
  See also CA 25-28R
  See also obituary CA 85-88
  See also DLB 36

Ribeiro, Darcy 1922-........ CLC 34 (102)
  See also CA 33-36R

Ribeiro, João Ubaldo (Osorio Pimentel)
  1941-.......................CLC 10
  See also CA 81-84

Ribman, Ronald (Burt) 1932- ....CLC 7
  See also CA 21-24R

Rice, Anne 1941-..................CLC 41
  See also CANR 12
  See also CA 65-68

Rice, Elmer 1892-1967 . . . . CLC 7
See also CAP 2
See also CA 21-22
See also obituary CA 25-28R
See also DLB 4, 7

Rice, Tim 1944-
See Rice, Tim and Webber, Andrew Lloyd
See also CA 103

Rice, Tim 1944- and
Webber, Andrew Lloyd
1948- . . . . CLC 21

Rich, Adrienne (Cecile)
1929- . . . . CLC 3, 6, 7, 11, 18, 36
See also CA 9-12R
See also DLB 5

Richard, Keith 1943-
See Jagger, Mick and Richard, Keith

Richards, I(vor) A(rmstrong)
1893-1979 . . . . CLC 14, 24
See also CA 41-44R
See also obituary CA 89-92
See also DLB 27

Richards, Keith 1943-
See Richard, Keith
See also CA 107

Richardson, Dorothy (Miller)
1873-1957 . . . . TCLC 3
See also CA 104
See also DLB 36

Richardson, Ethel 1870-1946
See Richardson, Henry Handel
See also CA 105

Richardson, Henry Handel
1870-1946 . . . . TCLC 4
See also Richardson, Ethel

Richardson, Samuel 1689-1761 . . . . LC 1
See also DLB 39

Richler, Mordecai
1931- . . . . CLC 3, 5, 9, 13, 18
See also CA 65-68
See also SATA 27
See also DLB 53
See also AITN 1

Richter, Conrad (Michael)
1890-1968 . . . . CLC 30
See also CA 5-8R
See also obituary CA 25-28R
See also SATA 3
See also DLB 9

Richter, Johann Paul Friedrich 1763-1825
See Jean Paul

Riding, Laura 1901- . . . . CLC 3, 7
See also Jackson, Laura (Riding)

Riefenstahl, Berta Helene Amalia 1902-
See Riefenstahl, Leni
See also CA 108

Riefenstahl, Leni 1902- . . . . CLC 16
See also Riefenstahl, Berta Helene Amalia

Rilke, Rainer Maria
1875-1926 . . . . TCLC 1, 6, 19
See also CA 104

Rimbaud, (Jean Nicolas) Arthur
1854-1891 . . . . NCLC 4

Ritsos, Yannis 1909- . . . . CLC 6, 13, 31
See also CA 77-80

Rivers, Conrad Kent 1933-1968 . . . . . CLC 1
See also CA 85-88
See also DLB 41

Robbe-Grillet, Alain
1922- . . . . CLC 1, 2, 4, 6, 8, 10, 14
See also CA 9-12R

Robbins, Harold 1916- . . . . CLC 5
See also CA 73-76

Robbins, Thomas Eugene 1936-
See Robbins, Tom
See also CA 81-84

Robbins, Tom 1936- . . . . CLC 9, 32
See also Robbins, Thomas Eugene
See also DLB-Y 80

Robbins, Trina 1938- . . . . CLC 21

Roberts, (Sir) Charles G(eorge) D(ouglas)
1860-1943 . . . . TCLC 8
See also CA 105
See also SATA 29

Roberts, Kate 1891-1985 . . . . CLC 15
See also CA 107
See also obituary CA 116

Roberts, Keith (John Kingston)
1935- . . . . CLC 14
See also CA 25-28R

Roberts, Kenneth 1885-1957 . . . . . TCLC 23
See also CA 109
See also DLB 9

Robinson, Edwin Arlington
1869-1935 . . . . TCLC 5
See also CA 104

Robinson, Jill 1936- . . . . CLC 10
See also CA 102

Robinson, Kim Stanley
19??- . . . . CLC 34 (105)

Robinson, Marilynne 1944- . . . . CLC 25
See also CA 116

Robinson, Smokey 1940- . . . . CLC 21

Robinson, William 1940-
See Robinson, Smokey
See also CA 116

Robison, Mary 1949- . . . . CLC 42
See also CA 113, 116

Roddenberry, Gene 1921- . . . . CLC 17

Rodgers, Mary 1931- . . . . CLC 12
See also CANR 8
See also CA 49-52
See also SATA 8

Rodgers, W(illiam) R(obert)
1909-1969 . . . . CLC 7
See also CA 85-88
See also DLB 20

Rodríguez, Claudio 1934- . . . . CLC 10

Roethke, Theodore (Huebner)
1908-1963 . . . . CLC 1, 3, 8, 11, 19
See also CA 81-84
See also DLB 5

Rogers, Sam 1943-
See Shepard, Sam

Rogers, Will(iam Penn Adair)
1879-1935 . . . . TCLC 8
See also CA 105
See also DLB 11

Rogin, Gilbert 1929- . . . . CLC 18
See also CANR 15
See also CA 65-68

Rohan, Kōda 1867-1947 . . . . TCLC 22

Rohmer, Eric 1920- . . . . CLC 16
See also Scherer, Jean-Marie Maurice

Roiphe, Anne (Richardson)
1935- . . . . CLC 3, 9
See also CA 89-92
See also DLB-Y 80

**Rolfe, Frederick (William Serafino Austin
Lewis Mary)** 1860-1913 . . . . . TCLC 12
See also CA 107
See also DLB 34

Rolland, Romain 1866-1944 . . . . . . TCLC 23
See also CA 118

Rölvaag, O(le) E(dvart)
1876-1931 . . . . TCLC 17
See also DLB 9

Romains, Jules 1885-1972 . . . . CLC 7
See also CA 85-88

Romero, José Rubén
1890-1952 . . . . TCLC 14
See also CA 114

Rooke, Leon 1934- . . . . . . CLC 25, 34 (250)
See also CA 25-28R

Rosa, João Guimarães
1908-1967 . . . . CLC 23
See also obituary CA 89-92

Rosen, Richard (Dean)
1949- . . . . CLC 39 (194)

Rosenberg, Isaac 1890-1918 . . . . . . TCLC 12
See also CA 107
See also DLB 20

Rosenblatt, Joe 1933- . . . . CLC 15
See also Rosenblatt, Joseph
See also AITN 2

Rosenblatt, Joseph 1933-
See Rosenblatt, Joe
See also CA 89-92

Rosenthal, M(acha) L(ouis)
1917- . . . . CLC 28
See also CANR 4
See also CA 1-4R
See also DLB 5

Ross, (James) Sinclair 1908- . . . . CLC 13
See also CA 73-76

Rossetti, Christina Georgina
1830-1894 . . . . NCLC 2
See also SATA 20
See also DLB 35

Rossetti, Dante Gabriel
1828-1882 . . . . NCLC 4
See also DLB 35

Rossetti, Gabriel Charles Dante 1828-1882
See Rossetti, Dante Gabriel

Rossner, Judith (Perelman)
1935- . . . . CLC 6, 9, 29
See also CANR 18
See also CA 17-20R
See also DLB 6
See also AITN 2

Rostand, Edmond (Eugène Alexis)
1868-1918 . . . . TCLC 6
See also CA 104

Author Index

Storm, Hyemeyohsts 1935-.........CLC 3
 See also CA 81-84

Storm, (Hans) Theodor (Woldsen)
 1817-1888.................NCLC 1

Storni, Alfonsina 1892-1938......TCLC 5
 See also CA 104

Stout, Rex (Todhunter)
 1886-1975....................CLC 3
 See also CA 61-64
 See also AITN 2

Stow, (Julian) Randolph 1935- .....CLC 23
 See also CA 13-16R

Stowe, Harriet (Elizabeth) Beecher
 1811-1896.................NCLC 3
 See also YABC 1
 See also DLB 1, 12, 42

Strachey, (Giles) Lytton
 1880-1932.................TCLC 12
 See also CA 110

Strand, Mark 1934-.........CLC 6, 18, 41
 See also CA 21-24R
 See also SATA 41
 See also DLB 5

Straub, Peter (Francis) 1943- ......CLC 28
 See also CA 85-88
 See also DLB-Y 84

Strauss, Botho 1944-.................CLC 22

Straussler, Tomas 1937-
 See Stoppard, Tom

Streatfeild, Noel 1897- ....CLC 21
 See also CA 81-84
 See also SATA 20

Stribling, T(homas) S(igismund)
 1881-1965....................CLC 23
 See also obituary CA 107
 See also DLB 9

Strindberg, (Johan) August
 1849-1912.............TCLC 1, 8, 21
 See also CA 104

Strugatskii, Arkadii (Natanovich) 1925-
 See Strugatskii, Arkadii (Natanovich) and
  Strugatskii, Boris (Natanovich)
 See also CA 106

Strugatskii, Arkadii (Natanovich) 1925-
 and **Strugatskii, Boris**
 (Natanovich) 1933- ....CLC 27

Strugatskii, Boris (Natanovich) 1933-
 See Strugatskii, Arkadii (Natanovich) and
  Strugatskii, Boris (Natanovich)
 See also CA 106

Strugatskii, Boris (Natanovich) 1933- and
 Strugatskii, Arkadii (Natanovich) 1925-
 See Strugatskii, Arkadii (Natanovich) and
  Strugatskii, Boris (Natanovich)

Strummer, Joe 1953?-
 See The Clash

Stuart, (Hilton) Jesse
 1906-1984..........CLC 1, 8, 11, 14,
          34 (372)
 See also CA 5-8R
 See also obituary CA 112
 See also SATA 2
 See also obituary SATA 36
 See also DLB 9, 48
 See also DLB-Y 84

Sturgeon, Theodore (Hamilton)
 1918-1985.......... CLC 22, 39 (360)
 See also CA 81-84
 See also obituary CA 116
 See also DLB 8
 See also DLB-Y 85

Styron, William
 1925-............ CLC 1, 3, 5, 11, 15
 See also CANR 6
 See also CA 5-8R
 See also DLB 2
 See also DLB-Y 80

Sudermann, Hermann
 1857-1928................. TCLC 15
 See also CA 107

Sue, Eugène 1804-1857........... NCLC 1

Sukenick, Ronald 1932- .... CLC 3, 4, 6
 See also CA 25-28R
 See also DLB-Y 81

Suknaski, Andrew 1942-..........CLC 19
 See also CA 101
 See also DLB 53

Summers, Andrew James 1942-
 See The Police

Summers, Andy 1942-
 See The Police

Summers, Hollis (Spurgeon, Jr.)
 1916-........................CLC 10
 See also CANR 3
 See also CA 5-8R
 See also DLB 6

Summers, (Alphonsus Joseph-Mary Augustus)
 Montague 1880-1948 .... TCLC 16

Sumner, Gordon Matthew 1951-
 See The Police

Surtees, Robert Smith
 1805-1864................. NCLC 14
 See also DLB 21

Susann, Jacqueline 1921-1974.......CLC 3
 See also CA 65-68
 See also obituary CA 53-56
 See also AITN 1

Sutcliff, Rosemary 1920- ....CLC 26
 See also CLR 1
 See also CA 5-8R
 See also SATA 6, 44

Sutro, Alfred 1863-1933......... TCLC 6
 See also CA 105
 See also DLB 10

Sutton, Henry 1935-
 See Slavitt, David (R.)

Svevo, Italo 1861-1928 .... TCLC 2
 See also Schmitz, Ettore

Swados, Elizabeth 1951-..........CLC 12
 See also CA 97-100

Swados, Harvey 1920-1972 ....CLC 5
 See also CANR 6
 See also CA 5-8R
 See also obituary CA 37-40R
 See also DLB 2

Swarthout, Glendon (Fred)
 1918-......................CLC 35
 See also CANR 1
 See also CA 1-4R
 See also SATA 26

Swenson, May 1919-...........CLC 4, 14
 See also CA 5-8R
 See also SATA 15
 See also DLB 5

Swift, Graham 1949-............CLC 41
 See also CA 117

Swift, Jonathan 1667-1745.......... LC 1
 See also SATA 19
 See also DLB 39

Swinburne, Algernon Charles
 1837-1909.................. TCLC 8
 See also CA 105
 See also DLB 35

Swinfen, Ann 19??-......... CLC 34 (576)

Swinnerton, Frank (Arthur)
 1884-1982...................CLC 31
 See also obituary CA 108
 See also DLB 34

Symons, Arthur (William)
 1865-1945................. TCLC 11
 See also CA 107
 See also DLB 19

Symons, Julian (Gustave)
 1912-.................CLC 2, 14, 32
 See also CAAS 3
 See also CANR 3
 See also CA 49-52

Synge, (Edmund) John Millington
 1871-1909.................. TCLC 6
 See also CA 104
 See also DLB 10, 19

Syruc, J. 1911-
 See Miłosz, Czesław

Tabori, George 1914- ....CLC 19
 See also CANR 4
 See also CA 49-52

Tagore, (Sir) Rabindranath
 1861-1941................. TCLC 3
 See also Thakura, Ravindranatha

Talese, Gaetano 1932-
 See Talese, Gay

Talese, Gay 1932- ....CLC 37
 See also CANR 9
 See also CA 1-4R
 See also AITN 1

Tally, Ted 1952-..................CLC 42

Tamayo y Baus, Manuel
 1829-1898................. NCLC 1

Tanizaki, Jun'ichirō
 1886-1965............ CLC 8, 14, 28
 See also CA 93-96
 See also obituary CA 25-28R

Tarkington, (Newton) Booth
 1869-1946................. TCLC 9
 See also CA 110
 See also SATA 17
 See also DLB 9

Tasso, Torquato 1544-1595 .... LC 5

Tate, (John Orley) Allen
 1899-1979...... CLC 2, 4, 6, 9, 11, 14,
           24
 See also CA 5-8R
 See also obituary CA 85-88
 See also DLB 4, 45

Tate, James 1943-............CLC 2, 6, 25
 See also CA 21-24R
 See also DLB 5

Author Index

Author Index

Cumulative Index to Nationalities

AMERICAN

Adams, Henry **4**
Agee, James **1, 19**
Anderson, Maxwell **2**
Anderson, Sherwood **1, 10**
Atherton, Gertrude **2**
Barry, Philip **11**
Baum, L. Frank **7**
Beard, Charles A. **15**
Belasco, David **3**
Benchley, Robert **1**
Benét, Stephen Vincent **7**
Bierce, Ambrose **1, 7**
Bourne, Randolph S. **16**
Bromfield, Louis **11**
Burroughs, Edgar Rice **2**
Cabell, James Branch **6**
Cable, George Washington **4**
Cather, Willa **1, 11**
Chandler, Raymond **1, 7**
Chapman, John Jay **7**
Chesnutt, Charles Waddell **5**
Chopin, Kate **5, 14**
Comstock, Anthony **13**
Crane, Hart **2, 5**
Crane, Stephen **11, 17**
Crawford, F. Marion **10**
Crothers, Rachel **19**
Cullen, Countee **4**
Davis, Rebecca Harding **6**
Dreiser, Theodore **10, 18**
Dunbar, Paul Laurence **2, 12**
Fisher, Rudolph **11**
Fitzgerald, F. Scott **1, 6, 14**
Forten, Charlotte L. **16**
Freeman, Douglas Southall **11**
Freeman, Mary Wilkins **9**
Futrelle, Jacques **19**
Gale, Zona **7**

Garland, Hamlin **3**
Gilman, Charlotte Perkins **9**
Glasgow, Ellen **2, 7**
Goldman, Emma **13**
Grey, Zane **6**
Hall, James Norman **23**
Harper, Frances Ellen
  Watkins **14**
Harris, Joel Chandler **2**
Harte, Bret **1**
Hearn, Lafcadio **9**
Hergesheimer, Joseph **11**
Howard, Robert E. **8**
Howe, Julia Ward **21**
Howells, William Dean **7, 17**
James, Henry **2, 11**
James, William **15**
Jewett, Sarah Orne **1, 22**
Johnson, James Weldon **3, 19**
Kornbluth, C. M. **8**
Kuttner, Henry **10**
Lardner, Ring **2, 14**
Lewis, Sinclair **4, 13, 23**
Lewisohn, Ludwig **19**
Lindsay, Vachel **17**
London, Jack **9, 15**
Lovecraft, H. P. **4, 22**
Lowell, Amy **1, 8**
Marquis, Don **7**
Masters, Edgar Lee **2**
McKay, Claude **7**
Mencken, H. L. **13**
Millay, Edna St. Vincent **4**
Mitchell, Margaret **11**
Monroe, Harriet **12**
Nathan, George Jean **18**
Nordhoff, Charles **23**
O'Neill, Eugene **1, 6**

Porter, Gene Stratton **21**
Rawlings, Majorie Kinnan **4**
Reed, John **9**
Roberts, Kenneth **23**
Robinson, Edwin Arlington **5**
Rogers, Will **8**
Rölvaag, O. E. **17**
Rourke, Constance **12**
Runyon, Damon **10**
Saltus, Edgar **8**
Sherwood, Robert E. **3**
Slesinger, Tess **10**
Steffens, Lincoln **20**
Stein, Gertrude **1, 6**
Sterling, George **20**
Stevens, Wallace **3, 12**
Tarkington, Booth **9**
Teasdale, Sara **4**
Thurman, Wallace **6**
Twain, Mark **6, 12, 19**
Van Dine, S. S. **23**
Van Doren, Carl **18**
Washington, Booker T. **10**
West, Nathanael **1, 14**
Wharton, Edith **3, 9**
White, Walter **15**
Wister, Owen **21**
Wolfe, Thomas **4, 13**
Woollcott, Alexander **5**
Wylie, Elinor **8**

ARGENTINIAN

Lugones, Leopoldo **15**
Storni, Alfonsina **5**

AUSTRALIAN

Brennan, Christopher John **17**
Franklin, Miles **7**
Richardson, Henry Handel **4**

AUSTRIAN

Broch, Hermann **20**
Hofmannsthal, Hugo von **11**
Kafka, Franz **2, 6, 13**
Kraus, Karl **5**
Kubin, Alfred **23**
Meyrink, Gustav **21**
Musil, Robert **12**
Schnitzler, Arthur **4**
Steiner, Rudolf **13**
Trakl, Georg **5**
Werfel, Franz **8**
Zweig, Stefan **17**

BELGIAN

Bosschère, Jean de **19**
Lemonnier, Camille **22**
Maeterlinck, Maurice **3**
Verhaeren, Émile **12**

BRAZILIAN

Lima Barreto **23**
Machado de Assis, Joaquim
  Maria **10**

CANADIAN

Campbell, Wilfred **9**
Carman, Bliss **7**
Garneau, Hector Saint-
  Denys **13**
Grove, Frederick Philip **4**
Leacock, Stephen **2**
McCrae, John **12**
Nelligan, Emile **14**
Pickthall, Marjorie **21**
Roberts, Charles G. D. **8**
Scott, Duncan Campbell **6**
Service, Robert W. **15**

Witkiewicz, Stanislaw
    Ignacy **8**

RUSSIAN
Aldanov, Mark **23**
Andreyev, Leonid **3**
Annensky, Innokenty **14**
Babel, Isaak **2, 13**
Balmont, Konstantin
    Dmitriyevich **11**
Bely, Andrey **7**
Blok, Aleksandr **5**
Bryusov, Valery **10**
Bulgakov, Mikhail **2, 16**
Bunin, Ivan **6**
Chekhov, Anton **3, 10**
Esenin, Sergei **4**
Gorky, Maxim **8**
Hippius, Zinaida **9**
Ilf, Ilya **21**
Khlebnikov, Velimir **20**
Khodasevich, Vladislav **15**
Korolenko, Vladimir **22**
Kuprin, Aleksandr **5**
Mandelstam, Osip **2, 6**

Mayakovsky, Vladimir **4, 18**
Petrov, Evgeny **21**
Pilnyak, Boris **23**
Platonov, Andrei **14**
Sologub, Fyodor **9**
Tolstoy, Alexey
    Nikolayevich **18**
Tolstoy, Leo **4, 11, 17**
Trotsky, Leon **22**
Tsvetaeva, Marina **7**
Zamyatin, Yevgeny
    Ivanovich **8**
Zhdanov, Andrei **18**
Zoshchenko, Mikhail **15**

SCOTTISH
Barrie, J. M. **2**
Bridie, James **3**
Gibbon, Lewis Grassic **4**
Graham, R. B.
    Cunninghame **19**
Lang, Andrew **16**
MacDonald, George **9**
Muir, Edwin **2**
Tey, Josephine **14**

SOUTH AFRICAN
Campbell, Roy **5**
Schreiner, Olive **9**

SPANISH
Barea, Arturo **14**
Baroja, Pío **8**
Benavente, Jacinto **3**
Blasco Ibáñez, Vicente **12**
Echegaray, José **4**
García Lorca, Federico **1, 7**
Jiménez, Juan Ramón **4**
Machado, Antonio **3**
Martínez Sierra, Gregorio **6**
Miró, Gabriel **5**
Ortega y Gasset, José **9**
Pereda, José María de **16**
Salinas, Pedro **17**
Unamuno, Miguel de **2, 9**
Valera, Juan **10**
Valle-Inclán, Ramón del **5**

SWEDISH
Dagerman, Stig **17**
Heidenstam, Verner von **5**

Lagerlöf, Selma **4**
Strindberg, August **1, 8, 21**

SWISS
Spitteler, Carl **12**
Walser, Robert **18**

TURKISH
Sait Faik **23**

URUGUAYAN
Quiroga, Horacio **20**

WELSH
Davies, W. H. **5**
Lewis, Alun **3**
Machen, Arthur **4**
Thomas, Dylan **1, 8**

YIDDISH
Aleichem, Sholom **1**
Asch, Sholem **3**
Peretz, Isaac Leib **16**

Nationality Index

Cumulative Index to Critics

Alexandrova, Vera
  Sergei Esenin **4**:113
  Alexey Nikolayevich Tolstoy **18**:370

Alford, Norman
  Lionel Johnson **19**:253

Allen, Clifford
  Radclyffe Hall **12**:190

Allen, M. D.
  T. E. Lawrence **18**:180

Allen, Mary
  Jack London **15**:273

Allen, Paul
  Hanns Heinz Ewers **12**:135

Allen, Paul Marshall
  Rudolf Steiner **13**:447, 448
  Jakob Wassermann **6**:520

Allen, Priscilla
  Kate Chopin **14**:70

Allen, Walter
  Arnold Bennett **5**:40
  W. W. Jacobs **22**:113
  Wyndham Lewis **2**:394
  Dorothy Richardson **3**:358

Allison, J. E.
  Heinrich Mann **9**:331

Alpers, Antony
  Katherine Mansfield **8**:291

Alpert, Hollis
  O. Henry **1**:350

Alsen, Eberhard
  Hamlin Garland **3**:200

Alter, Robert
  Hermann Broch **20**:65

Altrocchi, Rudolph
  Gabriele D'Annunzio **6**:135

Al'tshuler, Anatoly
  Mikhail Bulgakov **16**:80

Alvarez, A.
  Hart Crane **2**:118
  Thomas Hardy **10**:221
  D. H. Lawrence **2**:364
  Wallace Stevens **3**:454
  William Butler Yeats **1**:564

Alworth, E. Paul
  Will Rogers **8**:336

Amann, Clarence A.
  James Weldon Johnson **3**:247

Améry, Jean
  Simone Weil **23**:402

Amis, Kingsley
  G. K. Chesterton **1**:185
  C. M. Kornbluth **8**:213
  David Lindsay **15**:218
  Jules Verne **6**:493

Ammons, Elizabeth
  Edith Wharton **9**:552

Amoia, Alba della Fazia
  Edmond Rostand **6**:381

Amon, Frank
  D. H. Lawrence **9**:220

Anders, Gunther
  Franz Kafka **2**:302

Anderson, C. G.
  James Joyce **16**:208

Anderson, David D.
  Sherwood Anderson **1**:52
  Louis Bromfield **11**:85, 87
  Sinclair Lewis **13**:351

Anderson, Frederick
  Mark Twain **12**:445

Anderson, Isaac
  Raymond Chandler **7**:167
  Rudolph Fisher **11**:204

Anderson, Margaret C.
  Anthony Comstock **13**:90
  Emma Goldman **13**:210

Anderson, Maxwell
  Sherwood Anderson **10**:31
  Vicente Blasco Ibáñez **12**:32
  Joseph Hergesheimer **11**:261
  Edna St. Vincent Millay **4**:306

Anderson, Quentin
  Willa Cather **1**:163

Anderson, Rachel
  Sheila Kaye-Smith **20**:117

Anderson, Sherwood
  Sherwood Anderson **10**:31
  Stephen Crane **11**:133
  Theodore Dreiser **10**:169
  Ring Lardner **14**:291
  Sinclair Lewis **13**:333
  Vachel Lindsay **17**:233
  Gertrude Stein **6**:407
  Mark Twain **6**:459

Andreas, Osborn
  Henry James **11**:330

Andrews, William L.
  Charles Waddel Chesnutt **5**:136

Angenot, Marc
  Jules Verne **6**:501

Angoff, Charles
  Havelock Ellis **14**:116
  George Jean Nathan **18**:318

Angus, Douglas
  Franz Kafka **13**:264

Annan, Gabriele
  Colette **16**:135

Annan, Noel Gilroy
  Leslie Stephen **23**:317

Annenkov, P. V.
  Leo Tolstoy **4**:444

Annensky, Innokenty
  Innokenty Annensky **14**:16

Anninsky, L.
  Andrei Platonov **14**:403

Anouilh, Jean
  Jean Giraudoux **7**:320

Anthony, Edward
  Don Marquis **7**:443

Anthony, G. F. Penn
  Pierre Teilhard de Chardin **9**:501

Antoine, Jacques C.
  Jacques Roumain **19**:333

Antoninus, Brother
  Hart Crane **2**:119

Anwar, Chairil
  Chairil Anwar **22**:16

Appignanesi, Lisa
  Robert Musil **12**:257

Apter, T. E.
  Thomas Mann **14**:359; **21**:203
  Virginia Woolf **20**:424

Aptheker, Herbert
  Booker T. Washington **10**:530

Aquilar, Helene J.F. de
  Federico García Lorca **7**:302

Aragon, Louis
  Paul Eluard **7**:249

Aratari, Anthony
  Federico García Lorca **1**:316

Arce de Vazquez, Margot
  Gabriela Mistral **2**:477

Archard, Marcel
  Georges Feydeau **22**:78

Archer, William
  Bliss Carman **7**:135
  W. S. Gilbert **3**:207
  A. E. Housman **10**:239
  Laurence Housman **7**:352
  Henrik Ibsen **2**:224
  Selma Lagerlöf **4**:229
  Alice Meynell **6**:294
  Duncan Campbell Scott **6**:385
  Bernard Shaw **21**:306
  Arthur Symons **11**:428
  Francis Thompson **4**:434
  Mark Twain **12**:427
  Oscar Wilde **23**:409
  William Butler Yeats **11**:510

Archer, William Kay
  Sadeq Hedayat **21**:70

Arden, Eugene
  Paul Laurence Dunbar **12**:113

Arendt, Hannah
  Bertolt Brecht **1**:114
  Franz Kafka **2**:301
  Stefan Zweig **17**:429

Arms, George
  Kate Chopin **5**:149

Armstrong, Martin
  Katherine Mansfield **2**:446

Arner, Robert D.
  Kate Chopin **5**:155; **14**:63, 65

Arnold, G. L.
  Simone Weil **23**:370

Arnold, Matthew
  Leo Tolstoy **11**:458

Aron, Albert W.
  Jakob Wassermann **6**:509

Arrowsmith, William
  Cesare Pavese **3**:334
  Dylan Thomas **1**:468

Arvin, Newton
  Henry Adams **4**:12

Ashbery, John
  Raymond Roussel **20**:238
  Gertrude Stein **1**:442

Ashworth, Arthur
  Miles Franklin **7**:264

Asimov, Isaac
  George Orwell **15**:314

Asselineau, Roger
  Theodore Dreiser **18**:51

Aswell, Edward C.
  Thomas Wolfe **4**:515

Atheling, William Jr.
  See also **Blish, James**
  Henry Kuttner **10**:266

Atherton, Gertrude
  Ambrose Bierce **7**:88
  May Sinclair **3**:434

Atherton, Stanley S.
  Robert W. Service **15**:406

Atkins, Elizabeth
  Edna St. Vincent Millay **4**:311

Atkins, John
  Walter de la Mare **4**:75; **15**:352
  George Orwell **6**:341; **15**:352

Atkinson, Brooks
  Rudolph Fisher **11**:204
  Ring Lardner **14**:293

Atlas, James
  Gertrude Stein **1**:442
  Thomas Wolfe **4**:538

Atlas, Marilyn Judith
  Sherwood Anderson **10**:54

Attebery, Brian
  L. Frank Baum **7**:25

Atterbury, Rev. Anson P.
  Annie Besant **9**:13

Auchincloss, Louis
  Paul Bourget **12**:72
  Willa Cather **1**:164
  Ellen Glasgow **2**:188
  Henry James **2**:275
  Sarah Orne Jewett **1**:367
  Edith Wharton **3**:570

Auden, W. H.
  James Agee **19**:19
  Max Beerbohm **1**:72
  Hilaire Belloc **7**:41
  C. P. Cavafy **2**:90
  Raymond Chandler **7**:168
  G. K. Chesterton **1**:184, 186
  Walter de la Mare **4**:81
  Hugo von Hofmannsthal **11**:310
  A. E. Housman **1**:358
  Rudyard Kipling **8**:189
  George MacDonald **9**:295
  George Orwell **2**:512
  Rainer Maria Rilke **6**:359
  Frederick Rolfe **12**:268
  Bernard Shaw **3**:389
  Paul Valéry **4**:499
  Denton Welch **22**:435
  Nathanael West **1**:480
  Oscar Wilde **1**:504, 507
  Charles Williams **1**:516
  Virginia Woolf **1**:546
  William Butler Yeats **1**:562; **18**:443

Auernheimer, Raoul
  Stefan Zweig **17**:431

Austin, Henry
  Charlotte Gilman **9**:96

Austin, James C.
  Rebecca Harding Davis **6**:151

Avery, George C.
  Robert Walser **18**:420, 426

Avery, P. W.
Sadeq Hedayat **21**:70

Avins, Carol
Mikhail Bulgakov **16**:107

Avseenko, V. G.
Leo Tolstoy **4**:446

Ayer, A. J.
William James **15**:186

Azorín
Ramón del Valle-Inclán **5**:479

Bab, Julius
Alfred Döblin **13**:158

Babbitt, Irving
H. L. Mencken **13**:371

Babel, Isaac
Isaac Babel **13**:17

Bacigalupo, Mario Ford
José María de Pereda **16**:382

Bacon, Leonard
Alexander Woollcott **5**:522

Baguley, David
Emile Zola **21**:442

Bailey, Joseph W.
Arthur Schnitzler **4**:391

Bailey, Mabel Driscoll
Maxwell Anderson **2**:7

Baird, James
Wallace Stevens **3**:471

Baker, Carlos
Sherwood Anderson **1**:64
Edwin Muir **2**:483
Kenneth Roberts **23**:236

Baker, George P.
Philip Barry **11**:45

Baker, Houston A., Jr.
Countee Cullen **4**:52
Paul Laurence Dunbar **12**:128
James Weldon Johnson **19**:214
Booker T. Washington **10**:533

Baker, I. L.
E. C. Bentley **12**:16

Baker, Joseph E.
O. E. Rölvaag **17**:330

Baker, Stuart E.
Georges Feydeau **22**:87

Bakewell, Charles M.
William James **15**:148

Balakian, Anna
Guillaume Apollinaire **8**:19
Paul Claudel **10**:131
Paul Eluard **7**:257

Baldanza, Frank
Mark Twain **19**:373

Baldwin, Charles C.
Louis Bromfield **11**:71
Booth Tarkington **9**:458

Baldwin, James Mark
William James **15**:137

Baldwin, Richard E.
Charles Waddell Chesnutt **5**:135

Baldwin, Roger N.
Emma Goldman **13**:216

Ball, Clive
Benjamin Péret **20**:203

Ball, Robert Hamilton
David Belasco **3**:88

Balmforth, Ramsden
Laurence Housman **7**:355

Balogh, Eva S.
Emma Goldman **13**:223

Baltrušaitis, Jurgis
Emile Verhaeren **12**:467

Bander, Elaine
Dorothy L. Sayers **2**:537

Bandyopadhyay, Manik
Saratchandra Chatterji **13**:83

Bangerter, Lowell A.
Hugo von Hofmannsthal **11**:311

Banks, Nancy Huston
Charles Waddell Chesnutt **5**:130

Bannister, Winifred
James Bridie **3**:134

Baranov, Vadim
Alexey Nikolayevich Tolstoy **18**:377

Barbour, Ian G.
Pierre Teilhard de Chardin **9**:488

Barbusse, Henri
Henri Barbusse **5**:14

Barclay, Glen St John
H. Rider Haggard **11**:252
H. P. Lovecraft **4**:273
Bram Stoker **8**:399

Barea, Arturo
Miguel de Unamuno **2**:559

Barea, Ilsa
Miguel de Unamuno **2**:559

Bareham, Terence
Malcolm Lowry **6**:251

Barfield, Owen
Rudolf Steiner **13**:453

Baring, Maurice
Maurice Baring **8**:32
Hilaire Belloc **7**:32
Anton Chekhov **3**:145
Anatole France **9**:40
W. S. Gilbert **3**:211
Saki **3**:363
Leo Tolstoy **11**:459

Barker, Dudley
G. K. Chesterton **6**:101

Barker, Frank Granville
Joseph Conrad **1**:219

Barker, John
H. G. Wells **12**:515

Barker, Murl G.
Fyodor Sologub **9**:445

Barkham, John
James Hilton **21**:99

Barksdale, Richard K.
Charlotte L. Forten **16**:148
Claude McKay **7**:466

Barltrop, Robert
Jack London **15**:260

Barnard, Ellsworth
Edwin Arlington Robinson **5**:411

Barnard, Marjorie
Miles Franklin **7**:270

Barnes, Clive
August Strindberg **8**:420

Barnsley, John H.
George Orwell **15**:324

Barnstone, Willis
C. P. Cavafy **7**:163
Edgar Lee Masters **2**:472

Barooshian, Vahan D.
Velimir Khlebnikov **20**:137

Barrett, Francis X.
Wallace Thurman **6**:450

Barrett, William
F. Scott Fitzgerald **1**:246
William James **15**:182
Friedrich Nietzsche **10**:378

Barrow, Leo L.
Pío Baroja **8**:57
Machado de Assis **10**:293

Barrows, Susanna
Emile Zola **21**:452

Barson, Alfred T.
James Agee **19**:31

Barthes, Roland
Bertolt Brecht **1**:102
Pierre Loti **11**:363
Jules Verne **6**:491

Bartkovich, Jeffrey
Maxim Gorky **8**:89

Baruch, Elaine Hoffmann
George Orwell **15**:344

Barzun, Jacques
E. C. Bentley **12**:20
Raymond Chandler **7**:171, 176
John Jay Chapman **7**:195
William James **15**:188
Malcolm Lowry **6**:236
Friedrich Nietzsche **10**:371
Bernard Shaw **3**:398

Basdekis, Demetrios
Miguel de Unamuno **2**:566

Baskervill, William Malone
George Washington Cable **4**:24
Joel Chandler Harris **2**:209

Baskett, Sam S.
Jack London **9**:267

Basney, Lionel
Dorothy L. Sayers **15**:382

Basso, Hamilton
Denton Welch **22**:439

Bate, Walter Jackson
T. E. Hulme **21**:131

Bateman, May
Grazia Deledda **23**:31

Bates, Ernest Sutherland
Ludwig Lewisohn **19**:271

Bates, H. E.
A. E. Coppard **5**:179
Radclyffe Hall **12**:188
Thomas Hardy **4**:161
Katherine Mansfield **8**:278

Bates, Scott
Guillaume Apollinaire **3**:37

Battiscombe, Georgina
Stella Benson **17**:24

Baudouin, Charles
Carl Spitteler **12**:335
Emile Verhaeren **12**:472

Baugh, Edward
Arthur Symons **11**:445

Bauland, Peter
Bertolt Brecht **13**:58
Gerhart Hauptmann **4**:209

Baum, L. Frank
L. Frank Baum **7**:12, 15

Baxandall, Lee
Bertolt Brecht **1**:119

Bayerschmidt, Carl F.
Sigrid Undset **3**:525

Bayley, John
Thomas Hardy **4**:177
Bruno Schulz **5**:427
Virginia Woolf **1**:550

Beach, Joseph Warren
Joseph Conrad **1**:199
Theodore Dreiser **10**:175
Thomas Hardy **4**:154; **18**:92
James Joyce **3**:257
D. H. Lawrence **2**:350
Ludwig Lewisohn **19**:264
George Meredith **17**:266
Hugh Walpole **5**:498
Edith Wharton **3**:562
Emile Zola **1**:588

Beadle, Gordon
George Orwell **15**:354

Beals, Carleton
Mariano Azuela **3**:74

Beard, Charles A.
Charles A. Beard **15**:19
Beatrice Webb **22**:402
Sidney Webb **22**:402

Beard, Michael
Sadeq Hedayat **21**:76, 88

Beard, William
Charles A. Beard **15**:33

Beards, Richard D.
D. H. Lawrence **16**:317

Beauchamp, Gorman
George Orwell **15**:361

Beaumont, E. M.
Paul Claudel **10**:132

Beaumont, Keith S.
Alfred Jarry **14**:278

Bechhofer, C. E.
Randolph S. Bourne **16**:48
Sinclair Lewis **23**:129

Beckelman, June
Paul Claudel **2**:104

Becker, Carl
Charles A. Beard **15**:20

Becker, George J.
D. H. Lawrence **16**:320

Becker, May Lamberton
Marie Belloc Lowndes **12**:203

Critic Index

Critic Index

Critic Index

Critic Index

Critic Index

CUMULATIVE INDEX TO CRITICS — *TWENTIETH-CENTURY LITERARY CRITICISM, Vol. 23*

Engle, Paul
Stephen Vincent Benét 7:75

Englekirk, John Eugene
Mariano Azuela 3:75, 79
Leopoldo Lugones 15:284
Amado Nervo 11:394
Horacio Quiroga 20:209

Enright, D. J.
Bertolt Brecht 1:121
Hermann Broch 20:58
Rupert Brooke 7:129
Aleister Crowley 7:207
Stefan George 14:200
Knut Hamsun 2:208
D. H. Lawrence 2:371
Thomas Mann 2:427
Georg Trakl 5:461

Ensor, R. C. K.
Detlev von Liliencron 18:205

Eoff, Sherman H.
Pío Baroja 8:54
Vicente Blasco Ibáñez 12:44
José María de Pereda 16:373, 375
José Rubén Romero 14:436
Juan Valera 10:504

Epstein, Perle S.
Malcolm Lowry 6:242

Erickson, John D.
Joris-Karl Huysmans 7:414

Ericson, Edward E., Jr.
Mikhail Bulgakov 2:69

Erlich, Victor
Innokenty Annensky 14:29
Aleksandr Blok 5:94
Valery Bryusov 10:88
Velimir Khlebnikov 20:129
Vladimir Mayakovsky 18:246
Boris Pilnyak 23:213

Erskine, John
Lafcadio Hearn 9:123
Marcel Schwob 20:323
Mark Twain 19:355

Ervine, St. John G.
A. E. 10:15
G. K. Chesterton 1:178
John Galsworthy 1:293
Bernard Shaw 3:385
William Butler Yeats 1:552

Erwin, John F., Jr.
Paul Claudel 2:108

Eshleman, Clayton
César Vallejo 3:527

Eskin, Stanley G.
Giuseppi Tomasi di Lampedusa 13:293

Esslin, Martin
Antonin Artaud 3:59
Bertolt Brecht 1:102, 117
Henrik Ibsen 2:237
Alfred Jarry 2:285
George Orwell 15:349
Luigi Pirandello 4:352
Arthur Schnitzler 4:401
Boris Vian 9:530
Frank Wedekind 7:588
Stanisław Ignacy Witkiewicz 8:511

Esteban, Manuel A.
Georges Feydeau 22:89

Etkind, Efim
Mikhail Bulgakov 16:99

Etō, Jun
Sōseki Natsume 2:492

Etulain, Richard W.
Zane Grey 6:182
George MacDonald 9:281
Owen Wister 21:398

Evans, Calvin
Maurice Maeterlinck 3:330

Evans, Elizabeth
Ring Lardner 14:311

Evans, I. O.
Jules Verne 6:494

Evans, Ifor
George MacDonald 9:300

Evans, Robert O.
Joseph Conrad 13:110

Evans, Walter
O. Henry 19:197

Ewart, Gavin
E. C. Bentley 12:24

Ewen, Frederic
Bertolt Brecht 13:52

Ewers, John K.
Miles Franklin 7:267

Fabrizi, Benedetto
Valéry Larbaud 9:201

Fackler, Herbert V.
A. E. 3:12

Fadiman, Clifton P.
Mark Aldanov 23:17
Ambrose Bierce 1:87
Louis Bromfield 11:76
Willa Cather 11:94
Oliver St. John Gogarty 15:105
Knut Hamsun 14:228
Joseph Hergesheimer 11:276
James Hilton 21:97
Ricarda Huch 13:242
Ring Lardner 2:328
T. E. Lawrence 18:138
Marie Belloc Lowndes 12:204
T. F. Powys 9:360
O. E. Rölvaag 17:323
Dorothy L. Sayers 15:374
May Sinclair 11:412
Leo Tolstoy 4:466; 11:466
Mark Twain 19:362
Carl Van Doren 18:399
Thomas Wolfe 4:513

Fagin, N. Bryllion
Anton Chekhov 3:151

Faguet, Émile
Andrew Lang 16:254

Fain, John Tyree
Joseph Hergesheimer 11:278

Faiq, Salah
Benjamin Péret 20:203

Fairchild, Hoxie Neale
Charlotte Mew 8:299
Alice Meynell 6:302
Charles Williams 1:521

Fairlie, Henry
Randolph S. Bourne 16:65

Falen, James E.
Isaak Babel 2:32

Falk, Doris V.
Eugene O'Neill 6:332

Fallis, Richard
Standish O'Grady 5:357

Fanger, Donald
Mikhail Bulgakov 2:64

Fant, Åke
Rudolf Steiner 13:455

Farber, Manny
James Agee 1:6

Fargue, Léon-Paul
Léon-Paul Fargue 11:199

Farkas, Zoltan L.
Attila József 22:155

Farnsworth, Robert M.
Charles Waddell Chesnutt 5:134

Farrar, John
Robert Benchley 1:77

Farrell, James T.
Sherwood Anderson 1:45
Anton Chekhov 10:104
Theodore Dreiser 10:180
James Joyce 16:205
Ring Lardner 14:297
Jack London 9:262
H. L. Mencken 13:384
Leo Tolstoy 4:461

Farren, Robert
John Millington Synge 6:435

Farrison, W. Edward
Booker T. Washington 10:524

Farrow, Anthony
George Moore 7:498

Farson, Daniel
Bram Stoker 8:394

Farwell, Marilyn R.
Virginia Woolf 1:549

Fast, Howard
Franz Kafka 13:262

Faulhaber, Uwe Karl
Lion Feuchtwanger 3:184

Faulkner, William
Sherwood Anderson 1:45; 10:35
Mark Twain 6:471
Thomas Wolfe 4:521

Faurot, Ruth Marie
Jerome K. Jerome 23:85

Fauset, Jessie
Countee Cullen 4:40

Featherstone, Joseph
Randolph S. Bourne 16:63

Feder, Lillian
Joseph Conrad 13:106
William Butler Yeats 1:583

Fedin, Konstantin
Alexey Nikolayevich Tolstoy 18:364

Feger, Lois
Willa Cather 11:105

Feibleman, James
Will Rogers 8:332

Fein, Richard J.
Isaac Leib Peretz 16:403

Feld, Rose
James Hilton 21:97

Feld, Ross
Guillaume Apollinaire 8:27

Feldman, A. Bronson
Lionel Johnson 19:244

Fen, Elisaveta
Mikhail Zoshchenko 15:494

Fender, Stephen
Eugene O'Neill 6:337

Fennimore, Keith J.
Booth Tarkington 9:473

Ferenczi, László
Endre Ady 11:24

Fergusson, Francis
Anton Chekhov 3:158
Federica García Lorca 1:315
James Joyce 3:262
D. H. Lawrence 2:351
Robert E. Sherwood 3:413
Paul Valéry 4:496

Ferlinghetti, Lawrence
John Reed 9:388

Festa-McCormick, Diana
Andrey Bely 7:65
Rainer Maria Rilke 19:316
Emile Zola 21:446

Feuchtwanger, Lion
Lion Feuchtwanger 3:178, 180
Frank Wedekind 7:578

Feuerlight, Ignace
Thomas Mann 8:260

Fickert, Kurt J.
Wolfgang Borchert 5:110

Ficowski, Jerzy
Bruno Schulz 5:425

Fiedler, Leslie A.
James Agee 1:1
Ronald Firbank 1:228
F. Scott Fitzgerald 1:249, 263
Jaroslav Hasek 4:181
Nikos Kazantzakis 5:260
Ludwig Lewisohn 19:281
Margaret Mitchell 11:385
Cesare Pavese 3:335
Isaac Leib Peretz 16:394
Olaf Stapledon 22:332
Mark Twain 6:467; 12:439
Simone Weil 23:272
Nathanael West 1:485
Owen Wister 21:392

Field, Andrew
Fyodor Sologub 9:437, 438

Field, Frank
Henri Barbusse 5:17

Field, Leslie
Thomas Wolfe 13:495

Field, Louise Maunsell
Algernon Blackwood 5:71
Vicente Blasco Ibáñez 12:36
F. Scott Fitzgerald 1:235
Sheila Kaye-Smith 20:99
Montague Summers 16:425, 426

Critic Index

Critic Index

Critic Index

Hind, Charles Lewis
G. K. Chesterton **1**:177
Laurence Housman **7**:353

Hinde, Thomas
Thomas Hardy **18**:114

Hinden, Michael
Friedrich Nietzsche **10**:396

Hindus, Milton
F. Scott Fitzgerald **1**:243
Marcel Proust **13**:415
Israel Zangwill **16**:448

Hines, Thomas M.
Pierre Drieu La Rochelle **21**:32

Hingley, Ronald
Anton Chekhov **3**:165
Andrei A. Zhdanov **18**:480

Hinton, Norman D.
Hart Crane **5**:194

Hirsch, Edward
Robert W. Service **15**:408

Hirsch, Jerrold
Ludwig Lewisohn **19**:289

Hirschbach, Frank Donald
Thomas Mann **14**:333

Hirschman, Jack
Gustav Meyrink **21**:218

Hitchman, Janet
Dorothy L. Sayers **15**:380

Hively, Evelyn T. Helmick
Elinor Wylie **8**:531

Hobbs, Gloria L.
Marcel Schwob **20**:327

Hobman, D. L.
Olive Schreiner **9**:397

Hobson, J. A.
Olive Schreiner **9**:394

Hochfield, George
Henry Adams **4**:16

Hochman, Stanley
Jules Renard **17**:313

Hockey, Lawrence
W. H. Davies **5**:208

Hodson, W. L.
Marcel Proust **7**:538

Hofacker, Erich P.
Christian Morgenstern **8**:309

Hoffman, Charles G.
Joyce Cary **1**:143

Hoffman, Daniel
Edwin Muir **2**:488

Hoffman, Frederick J.
Sherwood Anderson **1**:48, 53
Willa Cather **1**:159, 161
Hart Crane **2**:117
F. Scott Fitzgerald **1**:255, 256;
14:152
James Joyce **3**:263
Franz Kafka **2**:293
D. H. Lawrence **2**:354
Thomas Mann **2**:420
Gertrude Stein **1**:432

Hofmannsthal, Hugo von
Hugo von Hofmannsthal **11**:290
Eugene O'Neill **6**:325
Arthur Schnitzler **4**:392

Hofstadter, Richard
Charles A. Beard **15**:34

Hogan, Robert
Bernard Shaw **9**:422

Hoggart, Richard
George Orwell **2**:506

Holbrook, David
Dylan Thomas **8**:452

Holden, Inez
Ada Leverson **18**:187

Holdheim, William W.
André Gide **5**:230

Holl, Karl
Gerhart Hauptmann **4**:196

Hollingdale, R. J.
Thomas Mann **8**:266; **14**:353
Friedrich Nietzsche **10**:387

Hollinghurst, Alan
Denton Welch **22**:459

Hollis, Christopher
George Orwell **2**:502

Holloway, John
Wyndham Lewis **2**:393

Holman, C. Hugh
Ellen Glasgow **7**:348
Sinclair Lewis **13**:346
Thomas Wolfe **4**:526, 528;
13:489

Holmes, H. H.
C. M. Kornbluth **8**:212

Holmes, James S
Chairil Anwar **22**:16

Holmes, John Haynes
Kahlil Gibran **9**:82

Holoch, Donald
Liu E **15**:251

Holroyd, Michael
Lytton Strachey **12**:413

Holroyd, Stuart
Rainer Maria Rilke **1**:416
Dylan Thomas **1**:470
William Butler Yeats **1**:564

Honig, Edwin
Federico García Lorca **1**:318

Hood, Stuart
Alfred Kubin **23**:98

Hook, Sidney
Charles A. Beard **15**:25

Hooker, Brian
George Sterling **20**:371

Hooker, Jeremy
Edward Thomas **10**:460

Hope, A. D.
Henry Handel Richardson **4**:376

Hope, John
Booker T. Washington **10**:515

Hopkins, Kenneth
Walter de la Mare **4**:81

Hopkins, Mary Alden
Anthony Comstock **13**:90

Hopper, Vincent F.
Oscar Wilde **23**:420

Horgan, Paul
Maurice Baring **8**:40

Hough, Graham
T. E. Hulme **21**:136
Wallace Stevens **3**:457

Houston, John Porter
Emile Zola **21**:437

Houston, Ralph
Alun Lewis **3**:287

Hovey, Richard B.
John Jay Chapman **7**:196, 200

Howard, Richard
Marcel Proust **13**:423
Jules Renard **17**:309

Howard, Robert E.
Robert E. Howard **8**:128

Howard, Thomas
Dorothy L. Sayers **15**:378

Howarth, Herbert
A. E. **3**:8
Ford Madox Ford **1**:291
James Joyce **3**:270

Howe, Irving
Sholom Aleichem **1**:23, 26
Sherwood Anderson **1**:43
Isaac Babel **13**:19
Arturo Barea **14**:46
Mikhail Bulgakov **16**:79
Stig Dagerman **17**:87
Theodore Dreiser **10**:187
George Gissing **3**:235
Thomas Hardy **18**:102
Sarah Orne Jewett **1**:364
Rudyard Kipling **8**:207
Sinclair Lewis **4**:256
H. L. Mencken **13**:385
George Orwell **2**:512; **15**:337
Isaac Leib Peretz **16**:401
Boris Pilnyak **23**:202
Luigi Pirandello **4**:341
Isaac Rosenberg **12**:306
Wallace Stevens **3**:464
Leo Tolstoy **4**:472
Leon Trotsky **22**:386
Edith Wharton **3**:574
Emile Zola **1**:595

Howe, Julia Ward
Julia Ward Howe **21**:108

Howe, M. A. DeWolfe
John Jay Chapman **7**:189

Howe, Marguerite
José Ortega y Gasset **9**:350

Howe, P. P.
John Millington Synge **6**:428

Howell, Elmo
George Washington Cable **4**:34

Howells, Bernard
Paul Claudel **2**:106

Howells, William Dean
Arnold Bennett **20**:17
Bjørnsterne Bjørnson **7**:105
Vicente Blasco Ibáñez **12**:33
George Washington Cable **4**:25
Charles Waddell Chesnutt
5:130
Stephen Crane **11**:126
Paul Laurence Dunbar **2**:127;
12:103
Mary Wilkins Freeman **9**:60
Hamlin Garland **3**:190

Charlotte Gilman **9**:101
Thomas Hardy **4**:150
William Dean Howells **7**:368
Henrik Ibsen **2**:218; **16**:155
Henry James **11**:319
Sarah Orne Jewett **22**:116
Sinclair Lewis **13**:325
Vachel Lindsay **17**:222
Booth Tarkington **9**:452
Leo Tolstoy **4**:450
Mark Twain **6**:456; **12**:424
Juan Valera **10**:497
Giovanni Verga **3**:538
Booker T. Washington **10**:516
Edith Wharton **9**:54
Owen Wister **21**:373
Emile Zola **1**:586

Hsia, T. A.
Lu Hsün **3**:296

Hsueh-Feng, Feng
Lu Hsün **3**:295

Hubbard, Elbert
Edgar Saltus **8**:344

Hubben, William
Franz Kafka **2**:296

Hudson, Lynton
Ferenc Molnár **20**:170

Hueffer, Ford Madox
See **Ford, Ford Madox**

Hueffer, Oliver Madox
Jack London **9**:256

Huffman, Claire Licari
Vitaliano Brancati **12**:86

Huggins, Nathan Irvin
Claude McKay **7**:465

Hughes, Glenn
David Belasco **3**:88

Hughes, Helen Sard
May Sinclair **3**:440

Hughes, Langston
Jacques Roumain **19**:331
Wallace Thurman **6**:447
Mark Twain **6**:474

Hughes, Merritt Y.
Luigi Pirandello **4**:329

Hughes, Randolph
Christopher John Brennan
17:36

Hughes, Riley
F. Scott Fitzgerald **1**:247

Hughes, Robert P.
Vladislav Khodasevich **15**:208

Hughes, Ted
Wilfred Owen **5**:370

Hulbert, Ann
W. H. Davies **5**:210

Hull, Keith N.
T. E. Lawrence **18**:159

Hume, Robert A.
Henry Adams **4**:10

Humphries, Rolfe
Federico García Lorca **1**:309
Lady Gregory **1**:334

Critic Index

Critic Index

Critic Index

Moorman, Charles
Charles Williams **1**:519

Mora, José Ferrater
Miguel de Unamuno **2**:560

Moran, Carlos Alberto
Raymond Chandler **1**:174

Moran, John C.
F. Marion Crawford **10**:157
Montague Summers **16**:435

More, Paul Elmer
James Branch Cabell **6**:66
Lafcadio Hearn **9**:119
William James **15**:156
Sarah Orne Jewett **22**:122
Lionel Johnson **19**:231
Friedrich Nietzsche **10**:361
José Ortega y Gasset **9**:335
Arthur Symons **11**:430

Moreau, Geneviève
James Agee **19**:39

Moreau, John Adam
Randolph S. Bourne **16**:56

Moreland, David Allison
Jack London **9**:282

Moreno, Janice Sanders
Leopoldo Lugones **15**:289

Morgan, A. E.
Harley Granville-Barker **2**:194

Morgan, Bayard Quincy
Christian Morgenstern **8**:304
Arthur Schnitzler **4**:386

Morgan, Charles
Mikhail Bulgakov **16**:75
George Moore **7**:481

Morgan, Edwin
Edwin Muir **2**:489

Morgan, Florence A. H.
Charles Waddell Chesnutt
5:129

Morgan, H. Wayne
Hart Crane **2**:122
Hamlin Garland **3**:198

Morgan, John H.
Pierre Teilhard de Chardin
9:504

Morita, James R.
Tōson Shimazaki **5**:438

Morley, Christopher
Arthur Conan Doyle **7**:219
Havelock Ellis **14**:108
Don Marquis **7**:434, 439
Saki **3**:365

Morley, S. Griswold
Rubén Darío **4**:57

Morris, C. B.
Pedro Salinas **17**:361

Morris, Irene
Georg Trakl **5**:456

Morris, Ivan
Akutagawa Ryūnosuke **16**:19

Morris, Lawrence S.
Mark Aldanov **23**:16

Morris, Lloyd
Sherwood Anderson **1**:42
Willa Cather **1**:12
F. Scott Fitzgerald **1**:244
Emma Goldman **13**:219
O. Henry **1**:349
Eugene O'Neill **1**:391
Marjorie Kinnan Rawlings
4:361
Edwin Arlington Robinson
5:405
Alexey Nikolayevich Tolstoy
18:357
Franz Werfel **8**:466

Morris, Virginia B.
Dorothy L. Sayers **15**:390

Morris, Wright
F. Scott Fitzgerald **1**:251
Ring Lardner **14**:310
Thomas Wolfe **13**:480

Morrow, Carolyn
Antonio Machado **3**:306

Morrow, Felix
Montague Summers **16**:429

Morrow, Patrick D.
O. E. Rölvaag **17**:340

Morsberger, Robert E.
Edgar Rice Burroughs **2**:85

Morse, A. Reynolds
M. P. Shiel **8**:360

Morse, J. Mitchell
James Joyce **3**:272

Morse, Samuel French
Wallace Stevens **3**:477

Morshead, E.D.A.
Andrew Lang **16**:250

Mortensen, Brita M. E.
August Strindberg **8**:408

Mortimer, Raymond
Marie Belloc Lowndes **12**:204
Lytton Strachey **12**:392

Morton, Frederic
Arturo Barea **14**:47
Anne Frank **17**:108

Morton, J. B.
Hilaire Belloc **7**:37

Moseley, Edwin M.
F. Scott Fitzgerald **1**:264

Moser, Thomas
Joseph Conrad **1**:208; **13**:113

Moses, Edwin
F. Scott Fitzgerald **14**:170

Moses, Montrose J.
Philip Barry **11**:54
David Belasco **3**:85

Mosig, Dirk W.
H. P. Lovecraft **4**:272; **22**:210

Moskowitz, Sam
Arthur Conan Doyle **7**:224
William Hope Hodgson **13**:234
Henry Kuttner **10**:266
M. P. Shiel **8**:361

Moss, Howard
Anton Chekhov **3**:175
Carl Van Doren **18**:409

Moss, Robert F.
Rudyard Kipling **17**:209

Mostafavi, Rahmat
Sadeq Hedayat **21**:67

Motion, Andrew
Edward Thomas **10**:464

Motofugi, Frank T.
Mori Ōgai **14**:370

Mott, Frank Luther
Zane Grey **6**:180

Moynahan, Julian
D. H. Lawrence **16**:301

Mphahlele, Ezeke
Thomas Mofolo **22**:246

Muchnic, Helen
Andrey Bely **7**:61
Aleksandr Blok **5**:93
Mikhail Bulgakov **2**:65
Maxim Gorky **8**:78
Vladimir Mayakovsky **4**:296
Yevgeny Ivanovich Zamyatin
8:551

Muddiman, Bernard
Duncan Campbell Scott **6**:396

Mudrick, Marvin
Joseph Conrad **13**:119
D. H. Lawrence **2**:366
Wyndham Lewis **2**:386
Frederick Rolfe **12**:271
Bernard Shaw **3**:402

Mueller, Dennis
Lion Feuchtwanger **3**:185

Mueller, Gustave
Carl Spitteler **12**:343

Mueller, Janel M.
Henrik Ibsen **16**:175

Muggeridge, Malcolm
Havelock Ellis **14**:128

Muir, Edwin
Hermann Broch **20**:46
Joseph Conrad **1**:198
Knut Hamsun **14**:225
Thomas Hardy **4**:173
Hugo von Hofmannsthal **11**:295
Franz Kafka **6**:219
Marie Belloc Lowndes **12**:203
Lytton Strachey **12**:396
Virginia Woolf **1**:527; **5**:507
William Butler Yeats **18**:451

Muirhead, James F.
Carl Spitteler **12**:340

Mukoyama, Yoshihiko
Akutagawa Ryūnosuke **16**:28

Mulhern, Chieko Irie
Kōda Rohan **22**:294

Muller, Herbert
Thomas Mann **21**:167

Muller, Herbert J.
Thomas Wolfe **4**:519

Mumford, Lewis
Charles A. Beard **15**:28
Randolph S. Bourne **16**:48
Heinrich Mann **9**:318

Munblit, Georgy
Ilya Ilf and Evgeny Petrov
21:152

Munk, Erika
George Orwell **15**:340

Munro, Ian S.
Lewis Grassic Gibbon **4**:126

Munro, John M.
Arthur Symons **11**:450

Munson, Gorham B.
Hart Crane **2**:111
Edgar Saltus **8**:347
Wallace Stevens **3**:445
Emile Zola **1**:590

Murch, A. E.
E. C. Bentley **12**:17
Cesare Pavese **3**:340
Dorothy L. Sayers **2**:531

Murfin, Ross C.
Algernon Charles Swinburne
8:445

Murray, Edward
F. Scott Fitzgerald **1**:272

Murray, Les
Isaac Rosenberg **12**:312

Murry, John Middleton
See also **Henry King**
Arnold Bennett **20**:24
Ivan Bunin **6**:43
Anton Chekhov **3**:150
Paul Claudel **10**:121
Anatole France **9**:45
George Gissing **3**:233
Aleksandr Kuprin **5**:296
D. H. Lawrence **2**:346; **9**:214,
215; **16**:283
Katherine Mansfield **2**:451;
8:281
Wilfred Owen **5**:359
Marcel Proust **13**:401
Edward Thomas **10**:451
Hugh Walpole **5**:493

Muzzey, Annie L.
Charlotte Gilman **9**:99

Myers, David
Carl Sternheim **8**:377

Myers, Doris T.
Charles Williams **11**:496

Nabokov, Vladimir
See also **Sirin, Vladimir**
Andrey Bely **7**:55
James Joyce **8**:158
Franz Kafka **6**:230
Vladislav Khodasevich **15**:200
Marcel Proust **7**:552

Nadeau, Maurice
Alfred Jarry **14**:271

Nadel, Ira Bruce
Lytton Strachey **12**:420

Naess, Harald S.
Nordahl Grieg **10**:208
Knut Hamsun **14**:239

Naff, William E.
Tōson Shimazaki **5**:441

Nagel, James
Stephen Crane **11**:166

Nagy, Moses M.
Paul Claudel **2**:109

Naimy, Mikhail
Kahlil Gibran **9**:82

Critic Index

Critic Index

Critic Index

Critic Index

Critic Index

Whay, R. A.
Jacques Futrelle **19**:89

Wheatley, Dennis
William Hope Hodgson **13**:237

Wheatley, Elizabeth D.
Arnold Bennett **5**:36

Wheelwright, John
Federico García Lorca **1**:307

Whipple, T. K.
Sherwood Anderson **1**:39
Willa Cather **1**:151
Zane Grey **6**:178
Sinclair Lewis **4**:248
Eugene O'Neill **1**:384

Whitaker, Paul K.
Hermann Sudermann **15**:432, 434

White, Antonia
Arturo Barea **14**:44
Anne Frank **17**:101

White, D. Fedotoff
Alexey Nikolayevich Tolstoy **18**:361

White, David
José Ortega y Gasset **9**:342

White, E. B.
Louis Bromfield **11**:79
Don Marquis **7**:441

White, Edmund
James Agee **19**:47

White, G. Edward
Owen Wister **21**:389

White, George Leroy, Jr.
O. E. Rölvaag **17**:325

White, Gertrude M.
Hilaire Belloc **7**:42

White, Greenough
Bliss Carman **7**:134
Francis Thompson **4**:434

White, Ray Lewis
Sherwood Anderson **1**:58

White, Walter F.
James Weldon Johnson **19**:205

Whitford, Robert C.
W. W. Jacobs **22**:100

Whitman, Walt
John Ruskin **20**:258

Whitney, Blair
Vachel Lindsay **17**:244

Whittemore, Reed
Joseph Conrad **1**:212
Ford Madox Ford **15**:82
Bernard Shaw **3**:401

Whittier, John Greenleaf
Julia Ward Howe **21**:105

Whittock, Trevor
Bernard Shaw **9**:423

Widdows, P. F.
Emile Nelligan **14**:392

Widmer, Kingsley
Nathanael West **14**:490

Wiehr, Joseph
Knut Hamsun **14**:222

Wiener, Leo
Isaac Leib Peretz **16**:388

Wiesel, Elie
Isaac Leib Peretz **16**:402

Wiggins, Robert A.
Ambrose Bierce **1**:90

Wilbur, Richard
A. E. Housman **10**:256

Wilcox, Earl
Jack London **9**:271

Wilde, Oscar
William Ernest Henley **8**:96
Rudyard Kipling **8**:175
Algernon Charles Swinburne **8**:427
Oscar Wilde **8**:488
William Butler Yeats **11**:507

Wilden, Anthony
Italo Svevo **2**:550

Wildiers, N. M.
Pierre Teilhard de Chardin **9**:493

Wilenski, R. H.
John Ruskin **20**:282

Wiley, Paul L.
Ford Madox Ford **15**:87

Wilkes, G. A.
Christopher John Brennan **17**:38

Wilkins, Eithne
Robert Musil **12**:232

Wilkins, Ernest Hatch
Gabriele D'Annunzio **6**:136

Wilkinson, Louis U.
T. F. Powys **9**:359

Wilkinson, Marguerite
Charlotte Mew **8**:295

Wilks, Ronald
Maxim Gorky **8**:83

Will, Frederic
Nikos Kazantzakis **5**:264
Kostes Palamas **5**:381-82

Willard, Nancy
Rainer Maria Rilke **1**:421

Williams, Ben Ames
Kenneth Roberts **23**:232

Williams, C. E.
Robert Musil **12**:258
Stefan Zweig **17**:444

Williams, Charles
Hilaire Belloc **18**:26
E. C. Bentley **12**:14
Ford Madox Ford **15**:75
Rudyard Kipling **17**:195
John Middleton Murry **16**:340
Dorothy L. Sayers **15**:374

Williams, Cratis D.
Sherwood Anderson **1**:55

Williams, Ellen
Harriet Monroe **12**:223

Williams, Harold
W. H. Davies **5**:200
Harley Granville-Barker **2**:193
Laurence Housman **7**:353
Katharine Tynan **3**:504

Williams, I. M.
George Meredith **17**:279

Williams, John Stuart
Alun Lewis **3**:288

Williams, Kenny J.
Paul Laurence Dunbar **12**:119
Frances Ellen Watkins Harper **14**:258

Williams, Orlo
Luigi Pirandello **4**:327

Williams, Raymond
Bertolt Brecht **1**:105; **13**:66
George Orwell **6**:348
August Strindberg **1**:457; **8**:411
Ernst Toller **10**:484

Williams, Rhys W.
Carl Sternheim **8**:379

Williams, T. Harry
Douglas Southall Freeman **11**:227

Williams, William Carlos
Ford Madox Ford **15**:81
Federico García Lorca **7**:290
Wallace Stevens **3**:451
Nathanael West **14**:468

Williams-Ellis, A.
Charlotte Mew **8**:296

Williamson, Audrey
James Bridie **3**:133

Williamson, Edward
Dino Campana **20**:85

Williamson, Hugh Ross
Alfred Sutro **6**:423

Williamson, Karina
Roger Mais **8**:240, 250

Willibrand, William Anthony
Ernst Toller **10**:480

Willoughby, L. A.
Christian Morgenstern **8**:304

Wills, Garry
Hilaire Belloc **18**:32

Willson, A. Leslie
Wolfgang Borchert **5**:110

Wilmer, Clive
Miklós Radnóti **16**:413

Wilshire, Bruce
William James **15**:178

Wilson, A. N.
Hilaire Belloc **18**:43, 45

Wilson, Angus
Arnold Bennett **5**:43
Samuel Butler **1**:137
Rudyard Kipling **8**:205
Bernard Shaw **3**:398
Emile Zola **1**:591

Wilson, Anne Elizabeth
Marjorie Pickthall **21**:242

Wilson, Christopher P.
Lincoln Steffens **20**:364

Wilson, Clotilde
Machado de Assis **10**:281

Wilson, Colin
Henri Barbusse **5**:14
Arthur Conan Doyle **7**:233
F. Scott Fitzgerald **1**:251
M. R. James **6**:210
Nikos Kazantzakis **2**:317
T. E. Lawrence **18**:152
David Lindsay **15**:225, 230
H. P. Lovecraft **4**:270
Rainer Maria Rilke **1**:417
Bernard Shaw **3**:400; **9**:425
August Strindberg **8**:411

Wilson, Daniel J.
Zane Grey **6**:186

Wilson, Donald
André Gide **5**:240

Wilson, Edmund
Henry Adams **4**:13
Maxwell Anderson **2**:3
Sherwood Anderson **1**:35, 50
Maurice Baring **8**:43
Philip Barry **11**:46, 51
Charles A. Beard **15**:22
Max Beerbohm **1**:68, 73
Robert Benchley **1**:76
Ambrose Bierce **1**:89
Louis Bromfield **11**:80
Samuel Butler **1**:134
James Branch Cabell **6**:70
George Washington Cable **4**:29
Willa Cather **1**:152
John Jay Chapman **7**:187, 190
Anton Chekhov **3**:159
Kate Chopin **5**:148
Hart Crane **5**:185
Arthur Conan Doyle **7**:222
Theodore Dreiser **10**:178
Ronald Firbank **1**:226, 228
F. Scott Fitzgerald **1**:233; **6**:159; **14**:147
Anatole France **9**:48
A. E. Housman **10**:252
Julia Ward Howe **21**:113
James Weldon Johnson **3**:240
James Joyce **3**:256, 260
Franz Kafka **2**:294
Rudyard Kipling **8**:187
Giuseppe Tomasi di Lampedusa **13**:301
Ring Lardner **2**:325
D. H. Lawrence **2**:345
H. P. Lovecraft **4**:268
H. L. Mencken **13**:363
Edna St. Vincent Millay **4**:317
Ferenc Molnár **20**:172
George Jean Nathan **18**:310
Emile Nelligan **14**:392
Marcel Proust **7**:524
Jacques Roumain **19**:332
Dorothy L. Sayers **2**:530
Bernard Shaw **3**:391, 396
Gertrude Stein **1**:426; **6**:404
Wallace Stevens **3**:444
Lytton Strachey **12**:398
Algernon Charles Swinburne **8**:443
Leo Tolstoy **4**:480
Paul Valéry **4**:487; **15**:442
Denton Welch **22**:436
H. G. Wells **12**:500
Nathanael West **14**:470

Critic Index